Contemporary Authors®

NEW REVISION SERIES

ISSN 0275-7176

Contemporary Authors®

**A Bio-Bibliographical Guide to
Current Writers in Fiction, General Nonfiction,
Poetry, Journalism, Drama, Motion Pictures,
Television, and Other Fields**

JAMES G. LESNIAK
Editor

NEW REVISION SERIES
volume 30

Gale Research Inc. · DETROIT · NEW YORK · LONDON

STAFF

James G. Lesniak, *Editor, New Revision Series*

Marilyn K. Basel, Kevin S. Hile, Sharon Malinowski, Michael E. Mueller, Kenneth R. Shepherd,
Diane Telgen, and Thomas Wiloch, *Associate Editors*

Marian Gonsior, Margaret Mazurkiewicz, Jani Prescott,
and Michaela Swart Wilson, *Assistant Editors*

Ronald Brashear, Jean W. Ross, Walter W. Ross, and Michael D. Senecal, *Interviewers*

David Stephen Colonne, Cheryl Gottler, Anne Janette Johnson, and Susan Salter, *Contributing Editors*

Hal May, *Senior Editor, Contemporary Authors*

Mary Rose Bonk, *Research Supervisor*

Jane Cousins-Clegg, Andrew Guy Malonis, and Norma Sawaya, *Editorial Associates*

Reginald A. Carlton, Shirley Gates, Clare Kinsman, Sharon McGilvray,
and Tracey Head Turbett, *Editorial Assistants*

Library of Congress Catalog Card Number 81-640179
ISBN 0-8103-1984-5
ISSN 0275-7176

Printed in the United States of America.

Published simultaneously in the United Kingdom
by Gale Research International Limited
(An affiliated company of Gale Research Inc.)

Contents

Indexing note: All *Contemporary Authors New Revision Series* entries are indexed in the *Contemporary Authors* cumulative index, which is published separately and distributed with even-numbered *Contemporary Authors* original volumes.

Authors and Media People
Featured in This Volume

David Attenborough (British naturalist, television producer, and host)—Perhaps best known to American audiences through his appearances on public television, Attenborough examines the complexities of the natural world in programs and books such as *Life on Earth, The Living Planet,* and *The First Eden.*

Ray Bradbury (American science fiction and fantasy writer)—Bradbury's oeuvre includes the well-known *Martian Chronicles, Fahrenheit 451, Dandelion Wine,* and *Something Wicked This Way Comes.* Widely acclaimed for his colorful style, he has received the World Fantasy Award for life achievement and the Gandalf Award. (Entry contains interview.)

Leo Buscaglia (American educator and author)—Internationally recognized as a lecturer and educator, Buscaglia proclaims in his best-selling books and numerous public television appearances a philosophy founded upon self-acceptance and personal growth nourished by love in its many manifestations. The celebrated hug that has become his trademark has earned him the title "Dr. Hug." (Entry contains interview.)

Lin Carter (American fantasist who died in 1988)—Carter was known for his devotion to, and erudite knowledge of, fantastic literature. With L. Sprague De Camp, he brought the character "Conan the Barbarian" to public attention in the late 1960s, and in the early 1970s edited a paperback-reprint series of important works of fantastic literature.

Mircea Eliade (Romanian-American novelist and historian of religion who died in 1986)—Eliade's novels and scholarly works concentrate on the religious experiences of man and the power of myth. His development of a methodology for the study of religion legitimized religious studies as an academic discipline in American universities.

Jules Feiffer (American cartoonist, screenwriter, and playwright)—Although probably best known for the political and social commentary in his Pulitzer Prize-winning syndicated cartoon "Feiffer" (originally entitled "Sick, Sick, Sick"), Feiffer is also an accomplished playwright and screenwriter. His screen credits include "Carnal Knowledge" and "Popeye." (Entry contains interview.)

Michael Frayn (British novelist and playwright)—Family conflicts play a major role in Frayn's work, a motif that has led critics to compare him to Anton Chekhov. Frayn's adaptation of Chekhov's "Wild Honey" was a critical and popular success in 1984, but he is also known for his wild Broadway farce "Noises Off."

Christopher Fry (British verse playwright, scriptwriter, and translator)—After more than a decade of intense popularity followed by many years of critical neglect, Fry is beginning to attract attention again. His elegant dialogue stands out from the "man-on-the-street" speech frequently found in modern drama, and he is sometimes likened to Shakespeare. His credits include the blank-verse play "The Lady's Not for Burning" and the screenplay "Ben-Hur."

William H. Gass (American fiction writer and essayist)—Gass, a philosopher by training and a spokesman for the self-referential integrity of literary texts, is considered one of the most accomplished stylists of his generation. He has won international acclaim for his fiction, including *Omensetter's Luck* and *In the Heart of the Heart of the Country.*

Edward Gorey (American author and illustrator)—In works such as *The Doubtful Guest, The Gashlycrumb Tinies,* and the *Amphigorey* anthologies, Gorey combines deceptively "traditional" pen and ink drawings of Victorian people and situations with stories of mishap, misadventure, misfortune, and sometimes murder. The result is hard to classify, but his works appeal to a variety of readers ranging from children (who are frequently the victims of his macabre humor) to adults. (Entry contains interview.)

Chester Gould (American cartoonist who died in 1985)—Gould's "Dick Tracy" comic strip is one of the classics of the genre. The detective hero's adventures were carried in one thousand newspapers and have been adapted for television and motion pictures.

Stephen King (American fiction writer and essayist)—Credited with revivifying the macabre in both fiction and film, King has become synonymous with the genre itself. A publishing marvel with nearly one hundred million copies of his work in print worldwide, he ranks among twenty individuals selected by *People* magazine who defined the decade of the eighties. An entry for his wife, Tabitha King, also appears in this volume.

Fritz Lang (German-born filmmaker who died in 1976)—Lang is considered one of the finest directors in film history. His work, which includes the classics "Metropolis" and "M," has influenced many directors and shaped the conventions of many suspense and adventure films.

George Lucas (American screenwriter, producer, and director)—Lucas has been associated with some of the highest-grossing films in history, including "American Graffiti," the "Star Wars" trilogy, and the "Indiana Jones" films. Many of his productions are fantasies and reveal his profound belief in the importance of myth as a means of conveying basic ideals and morality.

Steve Martin (American film actor, comedian and screenwriter)—A stand-up comic in the mid-1970s, Martin has since become a popular film actor and screenwriter. His appearances in such movies as "The Jerk," "All of Me," "Roxanne," "Planes, Trains, and Automobiles," and "Parenthood" have made him one of the most sought-after stars in Hollywood.

Arthur Miller (American playwright)—Best known for his Pulitzer Prize-winning play *Death of a Salesman*, Miller is one of the most important playwrights in contemporary American theatre. His dramas, which explore the social and moral imperatives of ordinary men and women, have been staples of the American stage for four decades and have won him the John F. Kennedy Award for Lifetime Achievement.

Eugenio Montale (Italian poet and critic who died in 1981)—Winner of the 1975 Nobel Prize, Montale was a prominent figure in Italian poetry and leader of the hermetic school. His critical essays, some of which are collected in *The Second Life of Art: Selected Essays of Eugenio Montale*, have also been influential.

Allan Nevins (American historian who died in 1971)—The Pulitzer Prize-winning biographer of Grover Cleveland and Hamilton Fish, Nevins also wrote several noteworthy histories of the Civil War, including *The Ordeal of the Union, The Emergence of Lincoln*, and *The War for the Union*. Critics found his work solidly researched yet high in romance and drama.

Scott O'Dell (American children's writer who died in 1989)—O'Dell's novels for children are often set in the American Southwest and deal with conflicts between races. His *Island of the Blue Dolphins* won the Newbery Medal and a Hans Christian Andersen Award, while *The King's Fifth, The Black Pearl*, and *Sing Down the Moon* were Newbery Honor Books.

Jerry Pournelle (American science fiction writer and editor)—Pournelle's "hard" science fiction, dealing with the high technology of the future, has earned him a John W. Campbell Award. His novel *Lucifer's Hammer*, written in collaboration with fellow science fiction author Larry Niven, has sold over three million copies.

Hans Richter (German artist and filmmaker who died in 1976)—A founding member of the Dada avant-garde art movement, Richter went on to pioneer the field of abstract films and animation. His films include "Dreams That Money Can Buy," "Ghosts before Breakfast," and "Rhythm 21." *Dada: Art and Anti-art* is his memoir of his early years as an artist.

Howard Sackler (American playwright and screenwriter who died in 1982)—Best known for his play "The Great White Hope," which won a Pulitzer Prize, a New York Drama Critics Circle Award, and a Tony Award, Sackler also founded Caedmon Records, a company which has recorded hundreds of contemporary plays.

William Saroyan (Armenian-American story writer, play-wright, and novelist who died in 1981)—Saroyan's early stories, set in the 1930s, portray the simple pleasures of family life and community. His plays, particularly the Pulitzer Prize- and New York Drama Critics Circle Award-winning "The Time of Your Life," contain what David Stephen Colonne called a "rambunctious energy."

Dorothy Simpson (British mystery novelist)—Simpson is the creator of the Inspector Thanet series of detective novels, featuring a mild-mannered policeman who solves murder mysteries in small British towns. Often compared to Agatha Christie and Margery Allingham, Simpson won a Silver Dagger Award in 1985 for *Last Seen Alive*. (Entry contains interview.)

Jane Smiley (American novelist and story writer)—Smiley's award-winning fiction always focuses on family life, though her work has ranged from a contemporary mystery novel to a historical novel set in fourteenth-century Greenland. Jane Yolen, writing in the *Washington Post*, calls Smiley "a true storyteller." (Entry contains interview.)

Gary Snyder (American poet and essayist)—A member of the Beat generation of writers, Snyder writes poetry that seeks to re-establish the elemental bonds between man and nature. Drawing on Zen Buddhism and the myth and ritual of primitive cultures, his work proposes new cultural possibilities for modern society. Snyder's collection *Turtle Island* won a Pulitzer Prize in 1975.

R. S. Thomas (Welsh poet and Anglican priest)—One of the leading poets of modern Wales, Thomas writes about the harsh landscape of his native land, the lives of rural farmers, and his own strong religious convictions. W. J. Keith in the *Dictionary of Literary Biography* calls him "a prominent voice in British poetry of the second half of the twentieth century."

P. L. Travers (British children's author)—The creator of Mary Poppins, one of the most-loved characters in children's literature, Travers has been chronicling the magical nanny's adventures since the 1930s. Her books include *Mary Poppins, Mary Poppins Comes Back, Mary Poppins Opens the Door*, and *Mary Poppins in Cherry Tree Lane*.

Preface

The *Contemporary Authors New Revision Series* provides completely updated information on authors listed in earlier volumes of *Contemporary Authors (CA)*. Entries for active individual authors from *any* volume of *CA* may be included in a volume of the *New Revision Series*. The sketches appearing in *New Revision Series* Volume 30, for example, were selected from more than twenty previously published *CA* volumes.

As always, the most recent *Contemporary Authors* cumulative index continues to be the user's guide to the location of an individual author's listing.

Compilation Methods

The editors make every effort to secure information directly from the authors. Copies of all sketches in selected *CA* volumes published several years ago are routinely sent to the listees at their last-known addresses. Authors mark material to be deleted or changed and insert any new personal data, new affiliations, new writings, new work in progress, new sidelights, and new biographical/critical sources. All returns are assessed, more comprehensive research is done, if necessary, and those sketches requiring significant change are completely updated and published in the *New Revision Series*.

If, however, authors fail to reply or are now deceased, biographical dictionaries are checked for new information (a task made easier through the use of Gale's *Biography and Genealogy Master Index* and other Gale biographical indexes), as are bibliographical sources such as *Cumulative Book Index* and *The National Union Catalog*. Using data from such sources, revision editors select and revise nonrespondents' entries that need substantial updating. Sketches not personally reviewed by the biographees are marked with an asterisk (*) to indicate that these listings have been revised from secondary sources believed to be reliable, but they have not been personally reviewed for this edition by the authors sketched.

In addition, reviews and articles in major periodicals, lists of prestigious awards, and, particularly, requests from *CA* users are monitored so that writers on whom new information is in demand can be identified and revised listings prepared promptly.

Format

CA entries provide biographical and bibliographical information in an easy-to-use format. For example, individual paragraphs featuring such rubrics as "Addresses," "Career," and "Awards, Honors" ensure that a reader seeking specific information can quickly focus on the pertinent portion of an entry. In sketch sections headed "Writings," the title of each book, play, and other published or unpublished work appears on a separate line, clearly distinguishing one title from another. This same convenient bibliographical presentation is also featured in the "Biographical/Critical Sources" sections of sketches where individual book and periodical titles are listed on separate lines. *CA* readers can therefore quickly scan these often-lengthy bibliographies to find the titles they need.

Comprehensive Revision

All listings in this volume have been revised and/or augmented in various ways, though the amount and type of change vary with the author. In many instances, sketches are totally rewritten, and the resulting *New Revision Series* entries are often considerably longer than the authors' previous listings. Revised entries include additions of or changes in such information as degrees, mailing addresses, literary agents, career items, career-related and civic activities, memberships, awards, work in progress, and biographical/critical sources. They may also include extensive bibliographical additions and informative new sidelights.

Writers of Special Interest

CA's editors make every effort to include in each *New Revision Series* volume a substantial number of revised entries on active authors and media people of special interest to *CA*'s readers. Since the *New Revision Series* also includes sketches on noteworthy deceased writers, a significant amount of work on the part of *CA*'s editors goes into the revision of entries on important deceased authors. Some of the prominent writers, both living and deceased, whose sketches are contained in this volume are noted in the list on pages vii-viii headed Authors and Media People Featured in This Volume.

Exclusive Interviews

CA provides exclusive, primary information on certain authors in the form of interviews. Prepared specifically for *CA,* the never-before-published conversations presented in the section of the sketch headed "*CA* Interview" give users the opportunity to learn the authors' thoughts, in depth, about their craft. Subjects chosen for interviews are, the editors feel, authors who hold special interest for *CA*'s readers.

Authors and journalists in this volume whose sketches contain exclusive interviews are Ray Bradbury, Leo Buscaglia, Jules Feiffer, Timothy Ferris, Dorothy Gilman, Edward Gorey, Richard Rosen, Harrison E. Salisbury, Dorothy Simpson, and Jane Smiley.

Contemporary Authors Autobiography Series

Designed to complement the information in *CA* original and revision volumes, the *Contemporary Authors Autobiography Series* provides autobiographical essays written by important current authors. Each volume contains from twenty to thirty specially commissioned autobiographies and is illustrated with numerous personal photographs supplied by the authors. Common topics of discussion for these authors include their motivations for writing, the people and experiences that shaped their careers, the rewards they derive from their work, and their impressions of the current literary scene.

Autobiographies included in the series can be located through both the *CA* cumulative index and the *Contemporary Authors Autobiography Series* cumulative index, which lists not only personal names but also titles of works, geographical names, subjects, and schools of writing.

Contemporary Authors Bibliographical Series

The *Contemporary Authors Bibliographical Series* is a comprehensive survey of writings by and about the most important authors since World War II in the United States and abroad. Each volume concentrates on a specific genre and nationality and features approximately ten major writers. Series entries, which complement the information in other *CA* volumes, consist of three parts: a primary bibliography that lists works written by the author, a secondary bibliography that lists works about the author, and a bibliographical essay that thoroughly analyzes the merits and deficiencies of major critical and scholarly works.

These bibliographies can be located through both the *CA* cumulative index and the *Contemporary Authors Bibliographical Series* cumulative author index. A cumulative critic index, citing critics discussed in the bibliographical essays, also appears in each *Bibliographical Series* volume.

CA Numbering System

Occasionally questions arise about the *CA* numbering system. Despite numbers like "97-100" and "129," the entire *CA* series consists of only 100 physical volumes with the publication of *CA New Revision Series* Volume 30. The following information notes changes in the numbering system, as well as in cover design, to help users better understand the organization of the entire *CA* series.

***CA* First Revisions**	• 1-4R through 41-44R (11 books) *Cover:* Brown with black and gold trim. There will be no further *First Revisions* because revised entries are now being handled exclusively through the more efficient *New Revision Series* mentioned below.
***CA* Original Volumes**	• 45-48 through 97-100 (14 books) *Cover:* Brown with black and gold trim. • 101 through 129 (29 books) *Cover:* Blue and black with orange bands. The same as previous *CA* original volumes but with a new, simplified numbering system and new cover design.
***CA* New Revision Series**	• *CANR*-1 through *CANR*-30 (30 books) *Cover:* Blue and black with green bands. Includes only sketches requiring extensive change; **sketches are taken from any previously published *CA* volume.**

***CA* Permanent Series**	• *CAP*-1 and *CAP*-2 (2 books) *Cover:* Brown with red and gold trim. There will be no further *Permanent Series* volumes because revised entries are now being handled exclusively through the more efficient *New Revision Series* mentioned above.
***CA* Autobiography Series**	• *CAAS*-1 through *CAAS*-11 (11 books) *Cover:* Blue and black with pink and purple bands. Presents specially commissioned autobiographies by leading contemporary writers to complement the information in *CA* original and revision volumes.
***CA* Bibliographical Series**	• *CABS*-1 through *CABS*-3 (3 books) *Cover:* Blue and black with blue bands. Provides comprehensive bibliographical information on published works by and about major modern authors.

Retaining *CA* Volumes

As new volumes in the series are published, users often ask which *CA* volumes, if any, can be discarded. The Volume Update Chart on page xiii is designed to assist users in keeping their collections as complete as possible. All volumes in the left column of the chart should be retained to have the most complete, up-to-date coverage possible; volumes in the right column can be discarded if the appropriate replacements are held.

Cumulative Index Should Always Be Consulted

The key to locating an individual author's listing is the *CA* cumulative index, which is published separately and distributed with even-numbered original volumes. Since the *CA* cumulative index provides access to *all* entries in the *CA* series, the latest cumulative index should always be consulted to find the specific volume containing a listee's original or most recently revised sketch.

Those authors whose entries appear in the *New Revision Series* are listed in the *CA* cumulative index with the designation **CANR-** in front of the specific volume number. For the convenience of those who do not have *New Revision Series* volumes, the cumulative index also notes the specific earlier volumes of *CA* in which the sketch appeared. Below is a sample index citation for an author whose revised entry appears in a *New Revision Series* volume.

> Clavell, James (duMaresq) 1925- CANR-26
>   Earlier sketch in CA 25-28R
>   See also CLC 6, 25

For the most recent *CA* information on Clavell, users should refer to Volume 26 of the *New Revision Series,* as designated by "CANR-26"; if that volume is unavailable, refer to *CA* 25-28 First Revision, as indicated by "Earlier sketch in CA 25-28R," for his 1977 listing. (And if *CA* 25-28 First Revision is unavailable, refer to *CA* 25-28, published in 1971, for Clavell's original listing.)

Sketches not eligible for inclusion in a *New Revision Series* volume because the biographee or a revision editor has verified that no significant change is required will, of course, be available in previously published *CA* volumes. Users should always consult the most recent *CA* cumulative index to determine the location of these authors' entries.

For the convenience of *CA* users, the *CA* cumulative index also includes references to all entries in these related Gale literary series: *Authors and Artists for Young Adults, Authors in the News, Bestsellers, Black Writers, Children's Literature Review, Concise Dictionary of American Literary Biography, Contemporary Literary Criticism, Dictionary of Literary Biography, Short Story Criticism, Something About the Author, Something About the Author Autobiography Series, Twentieth-Century Literary Criticism,* and *Yesterday's Authors of Books For Children.*

Acknowledgments

The editors wish to thank Judith S. Baughman for her assistance with copyediting.

Suggestions Are Welcome

The editors welcome comments and suggestions from users on any aspect of the *CA* series. If readers would like to suggest authors whose *CA* entries should appear in future volumes of the *New Revision Series,* they are cordially invited to write: The Editors, *Contemporary Authors New Revision Series,* 835 Penobscot Bldg., Detroit, MI 48226-4094; or, call toll-free at 1-800-347-GALE.

Volume Update Chart

IF YOU HAVE:	YOU MAY DISCARD:
1-4 First Revision (1967)	1 (1962) 2 (1963) 3 (1963) 4 (1963)
5-8 First Revision (1969)	5-6 (1963) 7-8 (1963)
Both 9-12 First Revision (1974) AND *Contemporary Authors Permanent Series*, Volume 1 (1975)	9-10 (1964) 11-12 (1965)
Both 13-16 First Revision (1975) AND *Contemporary Authors Permanent Series*, Volumes 1 and 2 (1975, 1978)	13-14 (1965) 15-16 (1966)
Both 17-20 First Revision (1976) AND *Contemporary Authors Permanent Series*, Volumes 1 and 2 (1975, 1978)	17-18 (1967) 19-20 (1968)
Both 21-24 First Revision (1977) AND *Contemporary Authors Permanent Series*, Volumes 1 and 2 (1975, 1978)	21-22 (1969) 23-24 (1970)
Both 25-28 First Revision (1977) AND *Contemporary Authors Permanent Series*, Volume 2 (1978)	25-28 (1971)
Both 29-32 First Revision (1978) AND *Contemporary Authors Permanent Series*, Volume 2 (1978)	29-32 (1972)
Both 33-36 First Revision (1978) AND *Contemporary Authors Permanent Series*, Volume 2 (1978)	33-36 (1973)
37-40 First Revision (1979)	37-40 (1973)
41-44 First Revision (1979)	41-44 (1974)
45-48 (1974) 49-52 (1975) ↓ ↓ 129 (1990)	NONE: These volumes will not be superseded by corresponding revised volumes. Individual entries from these and all other volumes appearing in the left column of this chart will be revised and included in the *New Revision Series*.
Volumes in the *Contemporary Authors New Revision Series*	NONE: The *New Revision Series* does not replace any single volume of *CA*. All volumes appearing in the left column of this chart must be retained to have information on all authors in the series.

Contemporary Authors

NEW REVISION SERIES

* Indicates that a listing has been revised from secondary sources believed to be reliable but has not been personally reviewed for this edition by the author sketched.

AHL, Frederick Michael 1941-

PERSONAL: Born September 5, 1941, in Barrow-in-Furness, Lancashire, England; immigrated to the United States, 1962; son of Edwin Sidney (an engineer) and Catherine (Cain) Ahl; married Mary McAninch, August 30, 1969; children: Katherine Isabel, Eamonn Sidney. *Education:* Cambridge University, B.A., 1962, M.A., 1966; University of Texas, Ph.D., 1966.

ADDRESSES: Home—5 Knoll Tree Rd., Ithaca, N.Y. 14850. *Office*—Department of Classics, 121 Goldwin Smith Hall, Cornell University, Ithaca, N.Y. 14853.

CAREER: University of Utah, Salt Lake City, assistant professor of classics, 1966-68; University of Texas, Austin, assistant professor of classics, 1968-71; Cornell University, Ithaca, N.Y., assistant professor, 1971-74, associate professor, 1974-77, professor of classics, 1978—, chairman of department, 1974-77.

MEMBER: American Philological Association.

WRITINGS:

(Co-author) *To Read Greek,* University of Texas Press, 1969.
Lucan: An Introduction, Cornell University Press, 1976.
Metaformations: Soundplay and Wordplay in Ovid and Other Classical Poets, Cornell University Press, 1985.
(Translator and author of introduction) Seneca, *The Trojan Women* (also see below), Cornell University Press, 1986.
(Translator and author of introduction) Seneca, *Phaedra* (also see below), Cornell University Press, 1986.
(Translator and author of introduction) Seneca, *Medea* (also see below), Cornell University Press, 1986.
(Translator and author of introduction) *Seneca: Three Tragedies* (includes *The Trojan Women, Phaedra,* and *Medea*), Cornell University Press, 1986.

Contributor to language journals.

WORK IN PROGRESS: A study of Sophocles; translating the *Thebaid,* by Statius.

SIDELIGHTS: One of Frederick Ahl's secondary interests is theatre. He reports that he has directed several plays and acted in repertory performances, both dramatic and operatic.

BIOGRAPHICAL/CRITICAL SOURCES:

PERIODICALS

Modern Language Journal, March, 1977.

*　　*　　*

**AINSLEY, Alix
See STEINER, Barbara A(nnette)**

*　　*　　*

**ALBERT, Marvin H(ubert) 1924-
(Mike Barone, Al Conroy, Albert Conroy, Ian MacAlister, Nick Quarry, Anthony Rome)**

PERSONAL: Born in 1924, in Philadelphia, Pa.; divorced.

ADDRESSES: Home—Paris, France. *Office*—c/o Fawcett Books, 201 East 50th St., New York, N.Y. 10022.

CAREER: Author and editor. Has worked at various jobs, including positions as copyperson for *Philadelphia Record,* magazine editor, researcher for *Look* magazine, and television and motion picture scriptwriter. *Military service:* Chief Radio Officer on Liberty ships during World War II.

WRITINGS:

NOVELS

Lie down with Lions, Gold Medal Books, 1955.
The Law and Jake Wade, Fawcett, 1956.
Apache Rising (also see below), Gold Medal Books, 1957, reprinted, 1987 (published in England as *Duel at Diablo,* Coronet, 1966).
The Bounty Killer (also see below), Gold Medal Books, 1958.
Renegade Posse (also see below), Gold Medal Books, 1958.
That Jane from Maine, Gold Medal Books, 1959.
Pillow Talk (screenplay novelization), Gold Medal Books, 1959.
Rider from Wind River, Gold Medal Books, 1959, reprinted, 1988.
The Reformed Gun, Gold Medal Books, 1959, reprinted, 1989.
All the Young Men (screenplay novelization), Pocket Books, 1960.
Come September, Dell, 1961.
Lover Come Back (screenplay novelization), Fawcett, 1962.
The VIP's (also see below), Dell, 1963.

Move over, Darling (screenplay novelization), Dell, 1963.
Palm Springs Weekend, Dell, 1963.
Under the Yum-Yum Tree (screenplay novelization), Dell, 1963.
The Outrage (screenplay novelization), Pocket Books, 1964.
Honeymoon Hotel, Dell, 1964.
Posse at High Pass, Fawcett, 1964.
What's New, Pussycat? (screenplay novelization), Dell, 1965.
Strange Bedfellows (screenplay novelization), Pyramid, 1965.
Do Not Disturb, Dell, 1965.
The Great Race, Dell, 1965.
A Very Special Favor (screenplay novelization), Dell, 1965.
The Corsican, Hestia, 1980.
The Stone Angel, Gold Medal Books, 1986.
Get off at Babylon, Gold Medal Books, 1987.
Long Teeth, Gold Medal Books, 1987.

CRIME NOVELS

Party Girl (screenplay novelization), Gold Medal Books, 1958.
(Under pseudonym Anthony Rome) *Miami Mayhem* (also see below), R. Hale, 1961, published under name Marvin H. Albert as *Tony Rome,* Dell, 1967.
(Under pseudonym Anthony Rome) *My Kind of Game,* Dell, 1962.
(Under pseudonym Anthony Rome) *The Lady in Cement* (also see below), R. Hale, 1962.
Goodbye Charlie (screenplay novelization), Dell, 1964.
The Pink Panther (screenplay novelization), Bantam, 1964.
(Under pseudonym Ian MacAlister) *Driscoll's Diamonds,* Fawcett, 1973.
(Under pseudonym Ian MacAlister) *Skylark Mission,* Fawcett, 1973.
(Under pseudonym Ian MacAlister) *Strike Force 7,* Fawcett, 1974.
(Under pseudonym Mike Barone) *Crazy Joe* (screenplay novelization), Bantam, 1974.
(Under pseudonym Ian MacAlister) *Valley of the Assassins,* Fawcett, 1975.
The Gargoyle Conspiracy, Doubleday, 1975.
The Dark Goddess, Doubleday, 1978.
The Medusa Complex, Arbor House, 1981.
Hidden Lives, Delacorte, 1981.
Operation Lila, Arbor House, 1983.

NOVELS UNDER PSEUDONYM AL CONROY

Clayburn, Dell, 1961.
Last Train to Bannock, Dell, 1963.
Three Ride North, Dell, 1964.
The Man in Black (also see below), Dell, 1965.
Death Grip! (crime novel), Lancer, 1972.
Soldato! (crime novel), Lancer, 1972.
Blood Run (crime novel), Lancer, 1973.
Murder Mission! (crime novel), Lancer, 1973.
Strangle Hold! (crime novel), Lancer, 1973.

CRIME NOVELS UNDER PSEUDONYM ALBERT CONROY

The Road's End, Fawcett, 1952.
The Chiselers, Fawcett, 1953.
Nice Guys Finish Dead, Fawcett, 1957.
Murder in Room 13, Fawcett, 1958.
The Mob Says Murder, Fawcett, 1958.
Mr. Lucky (novelization of TV series), Dell, 1960.
Devil in Dungarees, Crest Books, 1960.
The Looters, Crest Books, 1961.

CRIME NOVELS UNDER PSEUDONYM NICK QUARRY

Trail of a Tramp, Fawcett, 1958.
The Hoods Come Calling, Fawcett, 1958.
The Girl with No Place to Hide, Fawcett, 1959.
No Chance in Hell, Fawcett, 1960.
Till It Hurts, Fawcett, 1960.
Some Die Hard, Fawcett, 1961.
The Don Is Dead (also see below), Fawcett, 1972.
The Vendetta, Fawcett, 1972.

SCREENPLAYS

"The VIP's" (based on his novel), Metro-Goldwyn-Mayer, 1963.
"Bullet for a Badman" (based on his novel *Renegade Posse*), Universal, 1964.
(With Michel M. Grilikhes) "Duel at Diablo" (based on his novel *Apache Rising*), United Artists, 1966.
(With Sydney Boehm) "Rough Night in Jericho" (based on his novel *The Man in Black*), Universal, 1967.
(Under pseudonym Anthony Rome) "Tony Rome" (based on his novel *Miami Mayhem*), Twentieth Century-Fox, 1967.
(With Jack Guss, under pseudonym Anthony Rome) "Lady in Cement" (based on his novel), Twentieth Century-Fox, 1968.
"A Twist of Sand" (based on the novel by G. Jenkins), United Artists, 1968.
"The Ugly Ones" (based on his novel *The Bounty Killer*), United Artists, 1968.
"The Don Is Dead" (based on his novel), Universal, 1974.

OTHER

Broadsides and Boarders (history), Appleton-Century, 1957.
The Long White Road: Sir Ernest Shackleton's Adventures (juvenile nonfiction), illustrations by Patricia Windrow, MacKay, 1957.
(With Theodore R. Seidman) *Becoming a Mother,* Premier Books, 1958, 3rd revised edition, Fawcett, 1978.
The Divorce: A Re-Examination of the Great Tudor Controversy, Simon & Schuster, 1965.
The Golden Circle, edited by Linda L. Stringer, Beach Books, 1985.
The Last Smile, Fawcett, 1988.

Also author of *The Warmakers,* 1985, and *Back in the Real World,* 1986.

SIDELIGHTS: While Marvin H. Albert spent much of his early writing career creating traditional hard-boiled detective stories, both in novel and screenplay form, his recent novels are "marked by a multiple point of view, a complex plot, [and] a global arena of conflict," asserts Shelly Lowenkopf in *Twentieth-Century Crime and Mystery Writers.* Lowenkopf notes that while Albert is a "journeyman" who makes intermittent mistakes of plot or characterization, she admits that he "can see drama, conflict, and tension in any gathering of two or more characters, and, at his best, moves forth with fluid ease." 1983's *Operation Lila* is typical of the author's latest work, as *New York Times Book Review* contributor Peter Andrews remarks: "Balanced against such occasional lapses [of plot] is some first-class adventure-story writing. The plot rips along in good style and makes all of the mandatory stops." The critic concludes that *Operation Lila* is "a sturdy piece of work that provides spirited entertainment."

BIOGRAPHICAL/CRITICAL SOURCES:

BOOKS

Twentieth-Century Crime and Mystery Writers, St. James/St. Martin's Press, 1985.

PERIODICALS

New York Times Book Review, August 10, 1975, January 29, 1978, May 22, 1983.*

*   *   *

ALBERTYN, Dorothy
   See BLACK, Dorothy

*   *   *

ALIKI
   See BRANDENBERG, Aliki Liacouras

*   *   *

ALLARDT, Erik   1925-

PERSONAL: Born August 9, 1925, in Helsinki, Finland; son of Arvid (a registrar) and Marita (a teacher; maiden name, Heikel) Allardt; married Sagi Nylander, September 7, 1947; children: Jorn, Monica, Barbro. *Education:* University of Helsinki, M.S.S., 1947, Ph.D., 1952; postdoctoral study at Columbia University, 1953-54.

ADDRESSES: Office—Academy of Finland, P.O. Box 78, Helsinki, 00551 Finland.

CAREER: University of Helsinki, Helsinki, Finland, instructor in sociology, 1948-53; School of Social Sciences, Helsinki, research director, 1955-57; University of Helsinki, professor of sociology, 1958—; Academy of Finland, Helsinki, research professor of sociology at University of Helsinki, 1971-80. Visiting professor, University of California, Berkeley, 1962-63, University of Illinois, 1966-67, University of Wisconsin—Madison, 1970, and Universitaet Mannheim. Fellow at Woodrow Wilson International Center, Washington, D.C., 1978-79.

MEMBER: Amnesty International (chairman of Finnish section, 1977-79), International Sociological Association, Finnish Academy of Sciences, Finnish Sociological Association (chairman, 1961-66), Finnish Political Science Association (chairman, 1972-75), Norwegian Academy of Science and Letters, American Sociological Association.

AWARDS, HONORS: Rockefeller Fellowship, 1953-54; honorary doctorate degrees, University of Stockholm and Abo Academy, both 1978, and University of Uppsala, 1984.

WRITINGS:

Syntyperaeae ja sosiaalista kohoamista koskevat arvostukset (title means "Value Orientations as Regards Social Origin and Social Mobility"), Karisto, 1956.
Social struktur och politisk aktivitet: En studie av vaeljaraktiviteten vid riksdagsvalen i Finland, 1945-1954 (title means "Social Structure and Political Activity: A Study of Electoral Participation at the Parliamentary Elections in Finland, 1945-1954"), Soederstroems, 1956.
(With Pentti Jartti, Faina Jyrkilae, and Yrjoe Littunen) *Tyoelaeisnuorison harrastustoiminta* (title means "The Social Activities of Working Class Youth"), Tammi, 1956.
Nuorison harrastukset ja yhteisoen rakenne (title means "The Leisure Use of Youth and Social Structure"), Soederstroem Osakeyhtoe, 1958.

(With Littunen) *Sosiologia* (title means "Sociology"), Soederstroem Osakeyhtoe, 1958, 4th revised edition, 1972, abridged edition published as *Sociologian perusteet* (title means "Introductory Sociology"), 3rd edition, 1972.
Yhteiskunnan rakenne ja sosiaalinen paine (title means "Social Structure and Social Pressures"), Soederstroem Osakeyhtoe, 1964.
(Editor with Littunen) *Cleavages, Ideologies, and Party Systems: Contributions to Comparative Political Sociology*, Academic Bookstore for Westermarck Society, 1964.
Foerankringar (title means "Solidarities"), Soederstroems, 1970.
(With Klaus Waris and Osmo A. Wiio) *Valinnan yhteiskunta* (title means "A Society of Options"), Weilin & Goeoes, 1970.
(Contributor and editor with Stein Rokkan) *Mass Politics: Studies in Political Sociology*, Free Press, 1970.
Att ha, att aelska, att vara: Om vaelfaerd i Norden (title means "To Have, to Love, to Be: On Well-Being in Nordic Countries"), Argos, 1975.
Hyvinvoinnin ulottuvuuksia (title means "About Dimensions of Welfare"), Soederstroem Osakeyhtoe, 1976.
Implications of the Ethnic Revival in Industrialized Society, Finnish Society of Sciences and Letters, 1979.
(With Christian Starck) *Sprakgraenser och social struktur* (title means "Language Borders and Social Structure"), AWE/Gebers, 1981.
(Editor with others) *Nordic Democracy*, Munksgaard, 1981.
Sociologi: symbolmiljo, samhallsstrucktiv, och institutioner (title means "Sociology: Culture, Structure, and Institutions"), AWE/Gebers, 1985.
(Contributor) R. Rose and R. Shiratori, editors, *The Welfare State, East and West*, Oxford University Press, 1986.
(Contributor) S. R. Granbard, editor, *Norden—The Passion for Equality*, Norwegian University Press, 1986.
(With Sverre Lysgaard and Aage Sorensen) *Sociologin i Sverige veteushap, miljo, och organisation* (title means "Sociology in Sweden as Science, Milieu, and Organisation"), Swedish Science Press, 1988.

Contributor to numerous books on sociology and political science. Contributor of articles to sociology journals in the United States and Europe. Chief editor of *Acta Sociologica*, 1967-70, and *Scandanavian Political Studies*, 1973-76; member of editorial board of several journals.

WORK IN PROGRESS: Studies in sudden shifts in opinions and attitudes, and comparative studies of science policy.

*   *   *

ALLEN, Charlotte Vale   1941-
   (Claire Vincent)

PERSONAL: Born January 19, 1941, in Toronto, Ontario, Canada; came to the United States in 1966; Canadian citizen; married Walter Bateman Allen, Jr. (an insurance broker), July 21, 1970 (divorced, 1976); married Barrie Baldaro (an actor and writer), January 23, 1980 (divorced, 1982); children: (first marriage) Kimberly Jordan Allen (daughter). *Education:* Attended drama school in Toronto, Ontario. *Politics:* No affiliation. *Religion:* No affiliation.

ADDRESSES: Home—144 Rowayton Woods Dr., Norwalk, Conn. 06854. *Agent*—Harold Ober Associates, 40 East 49th St., New York, N.Y. 10017.

CAREER: Actress and singer, 1959-63; revue performer and singer, 1963-71; insurance broker, 1971-74; writer, 1975—. Lecturer on the sexual abuse of children, 1980—.

WRITINGS:

Love Life (novel), Delacorte, 1976.
Hidden Meanings (novel), Warner Books, 1976.
Sweeter Music (novel), Warner Books, 1976.
Gentle Stranger (novel), Warner Books, 1977.
Another Kind of Magic (novel), Warner Books, 1977.
Mixed Emotions (novel), Warner Books, 1977.
Running Away (novel), New American Library, 1977.
Becoming (novel), Warner Books, 1977.
Julia's Sister (novel), Warner Books, 1978.
(Under pseudonym Claire Vincent) *Believing in Giants* (novel), New American Library, 1978.
Acts of Kindness (novel), New American Library, 1979.
Moments of Meaning (novel), New American Library, 1979.
Promises (novel), Dutton, 1979.
Times of Triumph (novel), New American Library, 1980.
Gifts of Love (novel), Dutton, 1980.
Daddy's Girl (nonfiction), Wyndham Books, 1980.
The Marmalade Man (novel), Dutton, 1981.
Perfect Fools (novel), New English Library, 1981.
Intimate Friends (novel), Dutton, 1982.
Meet Me in Time (novel), Berkley Publishing, 1983.
Pieces of Dreams (novel), Berkley Publishing, 1985.
Matters of the Heart (novel), Berkley Publishing, 1986.
Time/Steps (novel), Atheneum, 1986.
Illusions (novel), Atheneum, 1987.
Dream Train (novel), Atheneum, 1988.
Night Magic (novel), Atheneum, 1989.

SIDELIGHTS: Charlotte Vale Allen told *CA* that although her books are about women, they are not just *for* women but "for everyone. I like to include issues of both social and emotional significance." Having written a number of successful novels in this vein, she published *Daddy's Girl,* an autobiographical work in which she comes to grips with a childhood made almost intolerable by her sexually abusive father. It is, writes Marilyn Murray Willison in the *Los Angeles Times Book Review,* "the harrowing tale of a childhood spent amidst a bitter, exploited mother and a manipulative and selfish father. Charlotte and her two older brothers were victims trapped by circumstance, but Charlotte bore the added indignity of being forced to suffer through her father's incestuous demands." *Library Journal* reviewer Janet Husband says that this is "altogether a powerful story, told with the considerable skill and restraint necessary to keep the facts from seeming sensational or maudlin." And Eleanor Wachtel, in a *Books in Canada* article, states that Allen "writes effectively. . . . She has written a genuinely troubling book, annoying, uncomfortable, and compelling."

Intertwined with the childhood recollections in *Daddy's Girl* are what Willison calls "verbal snapshots" of the author's struggle to free herself from her past. She had been conditioned to think of herself as ugly and unloveable, and thus "learning to love herself (much less a man) became a full-time assignment" during her adulthood. Writes Willison: "One finishes the book thinking that if it weren't for the kind and understanding attention of a high-school teacher (as well as the earlier ministrations of an aunt and uncle) the author would surely not be with us today." In addition to these early positive influences, Allen was aided by two friends, Norman and Lola, who helped her to face her distasteful childhood and rebuild her life. As a result, she is able to write about her past with complete candor. As she says in

Daddy's Girl, "It's impossible to forget what happened. I can't use Liquid Paper on 10 years of my life [from the ages of seven to seventeen] and put a nice, thick white coat over it the way I do typing errors."

At one time in her life, Allen did try to forget by changing her name when she began to pursue a new life away from her family. Since then, she has turned her painful past into positive social action. She travels throughout North America "lecturing to professionals about how to deal with sexually abused children," reports Sybil Steinberg in *Publishers Weekly.* Mary Lassance Parthun remarks in the Toronto *Globe and Mail,* "A significant aspect of public education is the dissemination of information about social, psychological and medical problems through popular novels favored by women. Charlotte Vale Allen is a notable practitioner of this important social function. Her work is approved by human service professionals because she takes on the tough problems (incest, for example) and handles them in a tasteful and nonexploitative manner." In *Pieces of Dreams,* for instance, a woman who was once abandoned by her mother later meets the challenge of facial disfigurement prolonged by an inept surgeon. The victim of a sexual kidnapping ordeal gives her perspective on the experience in the novel *Illusions.* "I think I'm uniquely qualified to write about certain areas of female experience," Allen told Steinberg. "When you get into abusive situations, you have to find a way to explain what happened. So I've narrated this whole entrapment scenario, and then I tell what happens afterwards. And believe me, when you read the ending of this book the hair all over your body will stand on end. In fact, it's the only time I couldn't wait to finish writing a book, it upset me so much."

Not all of Allen's novels are as "upsetting." Reviewers call *Dream Train* a romance because the major challenge to heroine Joanna James is to choose between two suitors who are equally sincere and attractive. Particularly well-written, says *Times Literary Supplement* reviewer Roz Kaveney, is the scene in which Joanna "is given good advice by an older woman, one of her companions on the train to Venice," a scene which stresses "the theme of female friendships: as important to women's lives as any relationships, sexual or other, with men."

BIOGRAPHICAL/CRITICAL SOURCES:

BOOKS

Allen, Charlotte Vale, *Daddy's Girl,* Wyndham Books, 1980.

PERIODICALS

Books in Canada, January, 1981.
Globe and Mail (Toronto), May 26, 1984, April 30, 1988.
Library Journal, December 1, 1980.
Los Angeles Times Book Review, September 18, 1980.
Publishers Weekly, July 4, 1986.
Times Literary Supplement, June 3, 1988.
Washington Post, July 28, 1986.

*   *   *

ALLINGTON, Richard L(loyd) 1947-

PERSONAL: Born May 13, 1947, in Grand Rapids, Mich.; son of George C. (a farmer) and Eldona (a copy editor; maiden name, Weller) Allington; married Susan Gordon, April 6, 1968 (divorced May 5, 1978); married Anne McGill (a legislative analyst), January 11, 1980; children: Heidi Jo, Tinker Marie, Margaret Anne, Richard Bo, Michael McGill. *Education:* Western

Michigan University, B.A., 1968, M.A., 1969; Michigan State University, Ph.D., 1973.

ADDRESSES: Home—246 Van Wie Point Rd., Glenmont, N.Y. 12077. *Office*—Department of Reading, State University of New York at Albany, Albany, N.Y. 12222.

CAREER: Elementary school teacher in Rockford, Mich., and Kent City, Mich., 1968-69; Belding Area Schools, Belding, Mich., Title I director, 1969-71; Michigan State University, East Lansing, graduate assistant and lecturer, 1971-73; State University of New York at Albany, assistant professor, 1973-78, associate professor, 1978-83, professor, 1983—, chairman of department of reading, 1982-88. Visiting professor at the University of Minnesota, 1976, and Eastern Montana College, 1981. Consultant to National Assessment of Educational Progress, 1976-78, Institute for Research on Teaching, Michigan State University, 1977-80, New York State Insurance Department, 1982-83, U.S. Department of Education, 1987-89, and Center for the Study of Reading, 1988-89.

MEMBER: International Reading Association (chairman of advisory group for analysis of reading programs data, 1976-77; chairman of studies and research committee, 1987—), American Educational Research Association (Division C assistant program chairman, 1986-87), National Reading Conference (member of board of directors, 1988—), National Conference of Research in English (fellow), New York State Reading Association (director of preconference institute, 1982; chairman of studies and research committee, 1985-88).

AWARDS, HONORS: Grants from State University of New York Research Foundation, 1976-79, National Institute of Education, 1977-78, National Institutes of Health, 1977-79, International Reading Association, 1983-84, Office of Educational Research and Improvement, 1985-86, and Office of Special Education Programs, 1987-88.

WRITINGS:

(With Gerald G. Duffy, George S. Sherman, Michael McElwee, and Laura R. Roehler) *How to Teach Reading Systematically,* Harper, 1973.

(Contributor) Robert C. Calfee and Priscilla A. Drum, editors, *Teaching Reading in Compensatory Classes,* International Reading Association, 1979.

(With Michael Strange) *Learning through Reading: An Introduction for Content Area Teachers,* Heath, 1980.

(Contributor) Lance M. Gentile, editor, *Reading Research Revisited,* C. E. Merrill, 1983.

(Editor) *Reading in Classrooms: New Ways of Looking,* Institute for School Development, 1983.

(Contributor) P. David Pearson, editor, *Handbook of Research in Reading,* Longman, 1984.

(Contributor) James V. Hoffman, editor, *The Effective Teacher of Reading: From Research to Practice,* International Reading Association, 1986.

(Contributor) Dorothy Lipsky and Alan Gartner, editors, *Beyond Separate Education,* Paul Brookes, 1989.

INTERACTIONAL MATERIALS FOR CHILDREN

The Reading Fact (remedial reading program), Macdonald-Raintree, 1979.

Focus: Reading for Success (basal reading program), Scott, Foresman, 1984.

Scott, Foresman Reading: An American Tradition (basal reading program), Scott, Foresman, 1987.

Collections (a literary anthology), Scott, Foresman, 1989.

"BEGINNING TO LEARN ABOUT" SERIES; PUBLISHED BY MACDONALD-RAINTREE

Beginning to Learn About Colors, illustrations by Noel Spangler, 1979.

. . . *Numbers,* illustrated by Tom Garcia, 1979.

. . . *Opposites,* illustrated by Eulala Connor, 1979.

. . . *Shapes,* illustrated by Lois Ehlert, 1979.

(With Kathleen Cowles, pseudonym of Kathleen Krull) . . . *Feelings,* illustrated by Brian Cody, 1980.

(With Cowles) . . . *Hearing,* illustrated by Wayne Dober, 1980.

(With Cowles) . . . *Looking,* illustrated by Bill Bober, 1980.

(With Cowles) . . . *Smelling,* illustrated by Rick Thrun, 1980.

(With Cowles) . . . *Tasting,* illustrated by Spangler, 1980.

(With Cowles) . . . *Touching,* illustrated by Yoshi Miyake, 1980.

(With Kathleen Krull) . . . *Reading,* illustrated by Joel Naprstek, 1980.

(With Krull) . . . *Talking,* illustrated by Thrun, 1980.

(With Krull) . . . *Thinking,* illustrated by Garcia, 1980.

(With Krull) . . . *Writing,* illustrated by Miyake, 1980.

(With Krull) . . . *Autumn,* illustrated by Bruce Bond, 1981.

(With Krull) . . . *Spring,* illustrated by Dee Rahn, 1981.

(With Krull) . . . *Summer,* illustrated by Dennis Hockerman, 1981.

(With Krull) . . . *Winter,* illustrated by John Wallner, 1981.

(With Krull) . . . *Measuring,* illustrated by Spangler, 1983.

(With Krull) . . . *Science,* illustrated by James Teason, 1983.

(With Krull) . . . *Stories,* illustrated by Helen Cogancherry, 1983.

(With Krull) . . . *Time,* illustrated by Miyake, 1983.

(With Krull) . . . *Words,* illustrated by Ray Cruz, 1983.

. . . *Letters,* illustrated by Garcia, 1983.

OTHER

Contributor of over 100 articles and reviews to education and reading journals, including *Journal of Educational Psychology, Journal of Reading Behavior,* and *Reading Research Quarterly.* Co-editor, *Journal of Reading Behavior,* 1978-83; member of editorial advisory boards of *Elementary School Journal* and *Remedial and Special Education.*

WORK IN PROGRESS: Children Who Find Learning to Read Difficult.

SIDELIGHTS: Richard L. Allington once told *CA:* "I grew up in Cedar Springs, Michigan, the eldest of six children. I was raised on a dairy farm and attended a one-room country school. I now work as a university professor and live in an old Victorian summer home on the Hudson River south of Albany, New York. I have five children, all of whom think it is nice to be able to go to the library and check out a book written by their father."

About his work in progress, *Children Who Find Learning to Read Difficult,* Allington later added: "[This book] discusses the problems that current practices, such as retention in grade, special education placement, ability grouping, tracking, and remedial services, present for children. It attempts to explain why these practices rarely work in the best interests of children and offers workable models for eliminating school failure generally and reading failure particularly."

*   *   *

ALTHER, Lisa 1944-

PERSONAL: Born July 23, 1944, in Tennessee; daughter of John Shelton (a surgeon) and Alice Margaret (Greene) Reed; married

Richard Philip Alther (a painter), August 26, 1966; children: Sara Halsey. *Education:* Wellesley College, B.A., 1966. *Politics:* None. *Religion:* None.

ADDRESSES: c/o Alfred A. Knopf, Inc., 201 East 50th St., New York, N.Y. 10022.

CAREER: Atheneum Publishers, New York, N.Y., secretary and editorial assistant, 1967; free-lance writer, 1967—. Writer for Garden Way, Inc., Charlotte, Vt., 1970-71. Member of board of directors of Planned Parenthood of Champlain Valley, 1972.

MEMBER: PEN, National Writers Union, Authors Guild, Authors League of America.

WRITINGS:

Kinflicks (novel), Knopf, 1976.
(Author of introduction) Flannery O'Connor, *A Good Man Is Hard to Find,* Women's Press, 1980.
Original Sins (novel), Knopf, 1981.
Other Women (novel), Knopf, 1984.

Also contributor of a short story, "Termites," to *Homewords,* edited by Douglas Paschell and Alice Swanson. Contributor of articles and stories to national magazines, including *Vogue, Cosmopolitan, Natural History, New Society, Yankee, Vermont Freeman, New Englander, New York Times Magazine,* and *New York Times Book Review.*

WORK IN PROGRESS: A novel.

SIDELIGHTS: Lisa Alther's *Kinflicks* made publishing news. Instead of a small press run, the novel boasted an initial printing of 30,000 hardback copies; it quickly ascended to the bestseller lists and was widely and favorably reviewed. In fact, Alther's satiric portrayal of a young woman's coming of age in the sixties so captivated the critics that it was immediately elevated to the company of J. D. Salinger's classic apprenticeship novel, *Catcher in the Rye.*

This comparison stems largely from the similarity between the novels' protagonists. In her search for a meaningful existence, Ginny Babcock emerges as a female Holden Caulfield. Like him, she is a survivor, and while the story of how adolescents survive is now a familiar one, Alther's graphic depiction of Ginny's Tennessee teens, her flight north, and subsequent return south to her mother's deathbed rescues the novel from predictability. As a *New Yorker* critic puts it: "A number of other excellent writers have covered various parts of the turf covered here," but "no other writer has yet synthesized this material as well as Miss Alther has. In fact, it would not be an exaggeration to say that her cynical, clear-eyed, well-heeled, disaster-prone heroine, Ginny Babcock, can easily take her place alongside Holden Caulfield as a symbol of everything that is right and wrong about a generation." Furthermore, notes Valentine Cunningham in the *New Statesman,* "her account is often to be caught uproariously in the rye."

In her second novel, *Original Sins,* Alther covers much the same territory she did in her first, only this time there are five protagonists. "*Kinflicks* followed a single heroine from her Tennessee upbringing through a series of wacky encounters up North with the countercultures of the '60s," Paul Gray explains in *Time.* "*Original Sins* quintuples its predecessor, offering five main characters, all Southerners, who try to grow up in a region and a country that are changing even faster than they are."

Alther chronicles the relocation of three of the five to the North while painting a broad social history of the sixties and seventies. Women's liberation, Vietnam, black power, civil rights, and the counterculture movement are among her subjects, and the portrait that emerges is unsatisfactory to some. Several critics charge that in her attempt to cover so much ground, Alther has sacrificed her characters' individuality. "The reader is haunted by the thought that the central characters, with the exception, perhaps, of the obstinately individualistic Emily, exist chiefly in order to illustrate differently developing states of political consciousness, as their progress from childhood to maturity is traced in often absorbing but sometimes oppressive detail," a *Times Literary Supplement* reviewer notes.

Whereas her first novel is a burlesque satire bordering on farce, *Original Sins* "is a protest novel of a conventional sort, a compound of outrage and doctrine," according to Mark Schechner. "It is an all-out assault on the South for its rigidly maintained double standards on matters of race, sex, and class and for its failures to live up to its deficiencies," he continues in his *New Republic* review.

Critics find fault in Alther's use of dialect and in what some refer to as a didactic tone. "The essential problem with those nearly 600 pages," Susan Wood writes in the *Washington Post Book World,* "is that they present every cliche you've ever heard about the South or about the political movements of the last two decades as though they are really, truly true: that is, with no sense of the complexities of individual lives, with no sympathy for the characters." Wood adds that such characters, like stick figures, are difficult to perceive as real people. Gray suggests, "Alther takes risks that sometimes fail. She is willing to sacrifice plausibility for comic effect, to put her characters through paces that occasionally seem dictated rather than inevitable. But such lapses are more than offset by the novel's page-turning verve and intelligence." Alther "gives generously, both to her readers and to the children of her imagination," Gray concludes. Cyra McFadden maintains that Alther's "excesses are those of overflowing talent and high spirits," and in her *Chicago Tribune Book World* review, proclaims *Original Sins* "a thoroughly endearing book."

Other Women examines how women relate to each other in various roles, as friends, lovers, and patient-to-therapist. Heroine Caroline Kelley is a doctor's ex-wife who gives up on men for women, and after a disappointing affair with a female friend, seeks aid in psychotherapy. Suspense builds around the question of what her sexual preference will be after analysis. Caroline and therapist Hannah Burke are "believable characters with real problems and realistic attitudes," notes Merle Rubin in a *Los Angeles Times* review. According to critics, elements in the novel identified as problematic are balanced against its positive features. Isabel Raphael of the London *Times,* for example, takes particular delight in Alther's portrait of Caroline's parents, two self-sacrificing people who give so much of themselves to others that they have little left to offer their own children. In addition, says Raphael, *Other Women* has "some sharp insights and a disarmingly fluent style."

BIOGRAPHICAL/CRITICAL SOURCES:

BOOKS

Contemporary Literary Criticism, Gale, Volume 7, 1977, Volume 41, 1987.

PERIODICALS

Chicago Tribune Book World, June 14, 1981, December 9, 1984.
Harper's, May, 1976.
Los Angeles Times, June 4, 1981, December 20, 1984.
Ms., May, 1981.

Nation, April 25, 1981.
New Republic, June 13, 1981.
New Statesman, August 27, 1976, May 29, 1981.
New Yorker, March 29, 1976, May 4, 1981.
New York Review of Books, April 1, 1976.
New York Times, March 16, 1976, December 10, 1984.
New York Times Book Review, March 14, 1976, May 3, 1981, November 11, 1984.
Time, March 22, 1976, April 27, 1981.
Times (London), February 28, 1985.
Times Literary Supplement, June 26, 1981.
Village Voice, March 8, 1976, December 18, 1984.
Washington Post Book World, March 28, 1976, May 31, 1981.

* * *

ALTMAN, Linda Jacobs 1943-
(Linda Jacobs; pseudonym: Claire Blackburn)

PERSONAL: Born January 22, 1943, in Winston-Salem, N.C.; daughter of Lloyd Daniel and Elizabeth (Parker) Blackburn; married Thomas D. Austin (a psychiatric technician), September 16, 1965 (divorced, 1970); married Joseph D. Jacobs (a former social worker), October 9, 1972 (divorced); married Richard Altman (a musician), April 16, 1981; children: (first marriage) Brian Vincent. *Education:* Attended Ventura College, Los Angeles Valley College, and University of California, Santa Barbara.

ADDRESSES: Home—Clearlake, Calif. *Office*—c/o Carolrhoda Books, Inc., 241 First Ave. N., Minneapolis, Minn. 55401.

CAREER: Writer.

MEMBER: Society of Children's Book Writers.

WRITINGS:

UNDER NAME LINDA JACOBS; "WOMEN WHO WIN" SERIES; YOUNG ADULT BIOGRAPHY

Janet Lynn: Sunshine on Ice, EMC Corp. (St. Paul, Minn.), 1974.
Olga Korbut: Tears and Triumph, EMC Corp., 1974.
Shane Gould: Olympic Swimmer, EMC Corp., 1974.
Chris Evert: Tennis Pro, EMC Corp., 1974.
Laura Baugh: Golf's Golden Girl, EMC Corp., 1975.
Wilma Rudolph: Run for Glory, EMC Corp., 1975.
Evonne Goolagong: Smiles and Smashes, EMC Corp., 1975.
Cathy Rigby: On the Beam, EMC Corp., 1975.
Mary Decker: Speed Records and Spaghetti, EMC Corp., 1975.
Joan Moore Rice: The Olympic Dream, EMC Corp., 1975.
Annemarie Proell: Queen of the Mountain, EMC Corp., 1975.
Rosemary Casals: The Rebel Rosebud, EMC Corp., 1975.
Cindy Nelson: North Country Skier, EMC Corp., 1976.
Robyn Smith: In Silks, EMC Corp., 1976.
Martina Navratilova: Tennis Fury, EMC Corp., 1976.
Robin Campbell: Joy in the Morning, EMC Corp., 1976.
Barbara Jordan: Keeping Faith, EMC Corp., 1978.
Jane Pauley: A Heartland Style, EMC Corp., 1978.

UNDER NAME LINDA JACOBS; "WINNERS ALL" SERIES; YOUNG ADULT FICTION

Ellen the Expert, EMC Corp., 1974.
In Tennis, Love Means Nothing, EMC Corp., 1974.
For One—Or for All, Go for Six, EMC Corp., 1974.

UNDER NAME LINDA JACOBS; "REALLY ME" SERIES; YOUNG ADULT FICTION

A Candle, a Feather, a Wooden Spoon, EMC Corp., 1974.

Will the Real Jeannie Murphy Please Stand Up?, EMC Corp., 1974.
Everyone's Watching Tammy, EMC Corp., 1974.
Checkmate, EMC Corp., 1974.
Julie, EMC Corp., 1974.
God, Why Is She the Way She Is?, Concordia, 1979.

UNDER NAME LINDA JACOBS; "WOMEN BEHIND THE BRIGHT LIGHTS" SERIES; YOUNG ADULT BIOGRAPHY

Olivia Newton-John: Sunshine Supergirl, EMC Corp., 1975.
Valerie Harper: The Unforgettable Snowflake, EMC Corp., 1975.
Roberta Flack: Sound of Velvet Melting, EMC Corp., 1975.
Cher: Simply Cher, EMC Corp., 1975.
Natalie Cole: Star Child, EMC Corp., 1977.
Lindsay Wagner: Her Own Way, EMC Corp., 1977.

UNDER NAME LINDA JACOBS; "MEN BEHIND THE BRIGHT LIGHTS" SERIES; YOUNG ADULT BIOGRAPHY

Stevie Wonder: Sunshine in the Shadow, EMC Corp., 1975.
John Denver: A Natural High, EMC Corp., 1975.
Elton John: Reginald Dwight and Company, EMC Corp., 1975.
Jim Croce: The Feeling Lives On, EMC Corp., 1975.
Jimmy Walker: Funny Is Where It's At, EMC Corp., 1977.
John Travolta: Making an Impact, EMC Corp., 1977.
Henry Winkler: Born Actor, EMC Corp., 1978.
Gabe Kaplan: A Spirit of Laughter, EMC Corp., 1978.

UNDER NAME LINDA JACOBS; "BLACK AMERICAN ATHLETES" SERIES; YOUNG ADULT BIOGRAPHY

Madeline Manning Jackson: Running on Faith, EMC Corp., 1976.
Julius Erving: Dr. J. and Julius W., EMC Corp., 1976.
Lee Elder: The Daring Dream, EMC Corp., 1976.
Arthur Ashe: Alone in the Crowd, EMC Corp., 1976.

UNDER NAME LINDA JACOBS

Nobody Wants Annie, New Readers, 1984.
The King Who Wore No Crown, Random House, 1985.
The Witch's Spell Book, Random House, 1985.
Letting Off Steam: The Story of Geothermal Energy, Carolrhoda Books, 1986.

UNDER PSEUDONYM CLAIRE BLACKBURN

Return Engagement, Bouregy, 1970.
A Teacher for My Heart, Bouregy, 1972.
Rainbow for Clairi, Bouregy, 1973.
Heart on Ice, Bouregy, 1976.

WORK IN PROGRESS: Wellspring, a young adult fantasy based upon her short story, "The Land of Living Waters."

SIDELIGHTS: Linda Jacobs Altman once told *CA:* "I believe that balance is important to me as a writer and as a human being. When I first started writing, I simply wanted to make a decent living doing what I like most. Now I find my goals are expanding and the projects buzzing in my head are increasingly aimed at exploring and sharing my own 'interior landscape.'"

* * *

ANDERSON, Edgar 1920-
(Edgars Andersons)

PERSONAL: Born June 17, 1920, in Tukums, Latvia; naturalized United States citizen; son of Voldemar (a civil servant) and Emilija Alma (Kaneps) Anderson; married Velta Peterson, 1950 (divorced, 1958); married Ligita Apinis (an actress), June 19,

1958; children: (first marriage) Raymond Edgar; (second marriage) Philip Rudolf. *Education:* University of Riga, M.A., 1944; graduate study at University of Wuerzburg, 1945-49, University of Leiden, 1948, and University of Pennsylvania, 1950-53; University of Chicago, Ph.D., 1956. *Religion:* Lutheran.

ADDRESSES: Home—2571 Booksin Ave., San Jose, Calif. 95125. *Office*—Department of History, School of Social Sciences, San Jose State University, San Jose, Calif. 95114.

CAREER: University of Wuerzburg, extension division, Wuerzburg, Germany, instructor in history, 1945-49; Lake Forest College, Lake Forest, Ill., instructor in history, 1953-57; San Jose State University, San Jose, Calif., assistant professor, 1957-59, associate professor, 1959-63, professor of history, 1963—. Regular broadcaster for Voice of America, 1970—. Distinguished professor of history, Livingston University, 1969; visiting professor and lecturer in North America, West Indies, Australia, New Zealand, U.S.S.R., and Europe. Leader of historical and archaeological expedition to Trinidad and Tobago, 1960. General chairman, second International Conference on East European and Slavic Studies, 1974; division chairman for many conferences on Baltic studies in the United States, Canada, Sweden, France, and the U.S.S.R.

MEMBER: Academy of Political Science, American Association for the Advancement of Slavic Studies, American Historical Association, Association for the Advancement of Baltic Studies (vice president, 1969-70; president, 1972-73), Society for the Advancement of Scandinavian Study, Conference on British Studies, Institute of Caribbean Studies, Baltisches Forschungsinstitut, Baltische Historische Kommission, Naval Records Club.

AWARDS, HONORS: American Council of Learned Societies fellow, 1956-57; Outstanding Educator of America, 1972; named Outstanding Professor, 1973, and President's Scholar, 1981, by San Jose State University; research grants from American Philosophical Society, Baltiska Humanistiska Institutet, American Council of Learned Societies, American Social Science Council, Hoover Institution on War, Revolution and Peace, International Research and Exchanges Board, U.S. Endowment for Humanities, and Academy of Sciences of Latvia.

WRITINGS:

Western World, Castle of Light (Hanau, West Germany), 1949.
Western Horizon, Castle of Light, 1949.
(Editor) *Cross-Road Country, Latvia,* Latvju Gramata (Waverly, Iowa), 1953.
Tobago, Harro von Hirschheydt Verlag (Hanover), 1962.
(Editor) Adolfs Kaktins, *Dzives Opera,* Daugava Foerlag (Stockholm), 1965.
History of Latvia: Foreign Policy, 1914-1920, Daugava Foerlag, 1967.
Die Militaerische Situation der baltischen Staaten, Institutum Balticum, 1969.
The Ancient Couronians in Africa, Gramatu Draugs (New York), 1970.
The Ancient Couronians in America and the Colonization of Tobago, Daugava Foerlag, 1970.
The United States and the Soviet Union in the 1980s, San Jose State University, 1981.
History of Latvia, 1920-1940: Foreign Affairs, Daugava Foerlag, Volume 1, 1982, Volume 2, 1984.
Armed Forces of Latvia and Their Historical Background, Amber Publishing, 1983.
History of Northern Europe: Scandinavian and Baltic States, San Jose State University, 1986.

CONTRIBUTOR

The American Historical Association Guide to Historical Literature, Macmillan, 1961.
Janis Silins, editor, *Rakstu Krajums,* Volume 2, Latvian Association for Humanities and Arts, 1963.
Jueri G. Poska, editor, *Pro Baltica: Melanges dedies a Kaarel R. Pusta,* Publications du comite des amis de K. R. Pusta, 1965.
Hans von Rimscha, Arved F. von Taube, and Juergen von Hehn, editors, *Beitraege zur Geschichte der Losloesung der baltischen Provinzen von Russland und zur Entstehung der baltischen Staaten,* Johann Gottfried Herder-Institut, Volume 1, 1971, Volume 2, 1977.
Handbook for Graduate Students in East Central European Studies, Institute on East Central Europe, Columbia University, 1971.
Witold S. Sworakowski, editor, *World Communism: A Handbook, 1918-1965,* Hoover Institution, 1971.
Arvids Ziedonis, Mardi Valgemae, and William L. Winter, editors, *Baltic History,* Ohio State University Press, 1974.
Daniel H. Thomas and Lynn Case, editors, *The Guide to the Diplomatic Archives of Western Europe,* University of Pennsylvania Press, 1975.
V. Stanley Vardys and Romuald J. Misiunas, editors, *The Baltic States in Peace and War, 1917-1945,* Pennsylvania State University Press, 1978.
Stephen Thernstrom, editor, *Harvard Encyclopedia of American Ethnic Groups,* Harvard University Press, 1980.
Czaba Janos Kenez and von Hehn, editors, *Reval und die baltischen Laender,* Johann Gottfried Herder-Institut, 1980.
The International Countermeasures Handbook, 1918-1982, EW Communications, 1981-82.
The New Encyclopedia Britannica-Macropaedia, University of Chicago Press, 1983.
National Movements in the Baltic Countries during the 19th Century, Studia Baltica Stockholmiensis, 1985.
Labor Migration Project Universitut Bremen, Universitut Bremen, 1986.
The Ethnic Press in the United States, Greenwood Press, 1987.
The Immigrant Labor Press in North America, 1840s-1970s, Volume 2, Greenwood Press, 1987.
Gli inizi del Christianesimo in Livonia e Lettonia, Atti e Documenti, Libreria editrice Vaticana, 1987.
Echos lointains de la revolution francaise, Universite de Paris, 1988.
The Baltic in International Relations between the Two World Wars, Studia Baltic Stockholmiensis, University of Stockholm, 1988.

OTHER

Latvian Encyclopedia, editor in chief, 1962—, and editor of six supplementary volumes; editor and contributor to volumes of proceedings of Conference on Baltic Studies, 1969, 1971. Contributor of more than 150 articles, essays, and reviews to magazines and journals, including *Baltic Review, East European Quarterly, Journal of Central European Studies, American Historical Review, Scholar, Choice,* and *History.*

WORK IN PROGRESS: A three-volume work, *The Baltic Area in World Affairs, 1914-1920, 1920-1940,* and *1940-1945; The Crimean War in Northern Europe; The Third Front; Overseas Activities of the Duchy of Courland and Semigallia during the 17th Century.*

ANDERSONS, Edgars
   See ANDERSON, Edgar

*   *   *

ANDREISSEN, David
   See POYER, David

*   *   *

APOSTOLOS-CAPPADONA, Diane   1948-

PERSONAL: Born May 10, 1948, in Trenton, N.J.; daughter of Vasilios D. (a restaurateur) and Stacia (Pappayliou) Apostolos; married Joseph B. Cappadona (in restaurant management), April 24, 1971. *Education:* George Washington University, B.A., 1970, M.A. (religion and art history), 1973, Ph.D., 1988; Catholic University of America, M.A. (religion and culture), 1979.

ADDRESSES: Office—Georgetown University/SSCE, ICC #306, Washington, D.C. 20057.

CAREER: George Washington University, Washington, D.C., editorial assistant, 1970-73; Bellarmine College, Louisville, Ky., assistant to director of development, 1974-75; Georgetown University, Washington, D.C., lecturer in religion and art, 1978—. Visiting lecturer at various universities, including Mount Vernon College, 1980-85, George Washington University, 1981-86, and Pacific School of Religion, 1985—; public speaker; coordinator of workshops. Resident fellow at Alden B. Dow Creativity Center, Northwood Institute, 1982, and Edward F. Albee Foundation at William Flanagan Memorial Creative Persons Center, 1983; teaching fellow, Graduate Theological Foundation, 1989. Member of board of directors, Mimesis Institute, 1980-82; member of board of advisors, Jane and John Dillenberger Endowment for the Visual Arts, Graduate Theological Union, Berkeley, Calif., 1982—; core consultant and member of board of advisors, "Dance and Religion Project," WNET/Thirteen Television, 1988-92.

MEMBER: American Academy of Religion, American Association of University Women, American Studies Association, Associates for Religion and Intellectual Life, College Art Association of America, Society for Art, Religion and Contemporary Culture (member of board of directors, 1986-89), College Theology Society, Sacred Dance Guild.

AWARDS, HONORS: Grant-in-aid-of-research, American Council of Learned Societies, 1989.

WRITINGS:

The Sacred Play of Children, Seabury, 1983.
(Contributor) Jane Kopas, editor, *Interpreting the Tradition,* Scholars Press, 1984.
(Editor and contributor) *Art, Creativity, and the Sacred: An Anthology in Religion and Art,* Crossroad Publishing, 1984.
(Translator with Alf Hiltebeitel) Mircea Eliade, *The History of Religious Ideas,* Volume III: *From Mahomet to the Reformers,* University of Chicago Press, 1985.
(Editor) Eliade, *Symbolism, the Sacred and the Arts,* Crossroad Publishing, 1985.
(Editor with Doug Adams, and contributor) *Art as Religious Studies,* Crossroad Publishing, 1987.
(Editor with Adams, and contributor) *Dance as Religious Studies,* Crossroad Publishing, 1990.
(Editor) Jane Dillenberger, *The Image and Spirit: Essays in Sacred and Secular Art,* Crossroad Publishing, 1990.

Art editor, *Encyclopedia of World Spirituality,* twenty-five volumes. Contributor of articles and reviews to magazines, including *Horizons, Art International, Cross Currents, Liturgy,* and *Living Light.*

WORK IN PROGRESS: Editing taped conversations and published essays of Isamu Noguchi; *Sojourn of Communion with Stone: An Interpretation of the Art and Philosophy of Isamu Noguchi;* editing three volumes of the *Encyclopedia of Religious Art;* editing, with Doug Adams and Margaret R. Miles, *The Human Body in Sacred and Secular Art: Essays in Honor of Jane Dillenberger;* contributing to John R. May's *Religious Dimensions of American Film Classics;* research on Grunewald's influence on Picasso; research on 19th-century ministers as patrons and collectors; research on the history of the history of Christian art; research on the relationship between art and myth in the works of the abstract expressionists, especially Jackson Pollack and Mark Rothko; research on iconography of the women of the Bible.

SIDELIGHTS: Diane Apostolos-Cappadona told *CA:* "As an undergraduate at George Washington University, I became dissatisfied with my international affairs major and took my adviser's advice to look into the humanities. A history of religions course pulled everything together for me—art, literature, history, politics. The course focused on symbols and myths and how changes in symbolism throughout the centuries represented changes in theology and culture—and how these mirrored what was going on in people's lives. Finally, I was linked into what really interested me.

"My continuing interest in connections between religion and the arts led me, recently, to the work of Isamu Noguchi, the Japanese-American sculptor whose work is characterized by simplicity, naturalness, incongruity, asymmetry, functionality, austerity, and sensuousness. His work defies categorization into any aspect of traditional religion, but somehow his work is spiritual in the largest sense. It is mythic in the best sense of the word, in terms of the universal experiences of human beings that transcend time and space.

"I am pleased with my progress on the Noguchi study, which is somewhat nontraditional. Doing a traditional study is much easier, because it's safer to deal with traditional religion. It has boundaries and definition and borders. In fact, however, it is the nontraditional or the nondefinable parts of religion—what might be called folk tradition, or common human experience—that perhaps affect people more."

Apostolos-Cappadona added: "Many people feel that art has worked its way out of religion because it represents a threat to religion. Now there is a theory that in the twentieth century art has replaced religion and become a religion itself, and that museums are the cathedrals of this century."

BIOGRAPHICAL/CRITICAL SOURCES:

PERIODICALS

George Washington Times, winter, 1984.

*   *   *

ARNOLD, Joseph H.
   See HAYES, Joseph

ARRINGTON, Leonard J(ames) 1917-

PERSONAL: Born July 2, 1917, in Twin Falls, Idaho; son of Noah Wesley (a farmer) and Edna (Corn) Arrington; married Grace Fort, April 24, 1943 (died March 10, 1982); married Harriet Ann Horne, November 19, 1983; children: (first marriage) James Wesley, Carl Wayne, Susan Grace (Mrs. Dean Madsen). *Education:* University of Idaho, B.S., 1939; Latter-day Saints Institute of Religion, Moscow, Idaho, graduate, 1939; University of North Carolina at Chapel Hill, Ph.D., 1952. *Politics:* Independent. *Religion:* Church of Jesus Christ of Latter-day Saints.

ADDRESSES: Home—2236 South, 2200 East, Salt Lake City, Utah 84109. *Office*—Department of History, Brigham Young University, Provo, Utah 84601.

CAREER: University of North Carolina at Chapel Hill, Kenan Teaching Fellow, 1939-40, teaching assistant in economics, 1940-41; North Carolina State College (now North Carolina State University at Raleigh), instructor in economics, 1941-42; economic analyst, North Carolina Office of Price Administration, 1942-43; North Carolina State College, assistant professor of economics, 1946; Utah State University, Logan, assistant professor, 1946-52, associate professor, 1952-58, professor of economic history, 1958-72; Brigham Young University, Provo, Utah, Lemuel H. Redd Professor of Western History, 1972-87, director of Charles Redd Center for Western History, 1972-80. Professor of economics and history, Brigham Young University, 1956, 1958, and 1966; Fulbright professor of American economics, University of Genoa and other Italian universities, 1958-59; lecturer in American civilization, University of Texas radio program, 1963; visiting professor of history, University of California, Los Angeles, 1966-67; instructor, Latter-day Saints Institute of Religion, Logan, Utah, 1969-70. Historian, Church of Jesus Christ of Latter-day Saints, 1972-80. Coordinator of social and economic planning, State of Utah, 1964-66. *Military service:* U.S. Army, 1943-46; allied representative, Central Institute of Statistics, Rome, Italy, 1944-45, and Committee for Price Control in Northern Italy, Milan, 1945; also served in Morocco, Tunisia, and Algeria.

MEMBER: American Historical Association (member of council, Pacific Coast Branch, 1963-66, president, 1981-82), Organization of American Historians, Economic History Association (chairman of Western Section, 1957-59), Agricultural History Society (president, 1969-70), Mormon History Association (president, 1965-66), Western Economic Association, Western History Association (president, 1968-69), Utah Historical Association (fellow), Utah Academy of Sciences, Arts, and Letters (member of council, 1960-63; member of board of fellows, 1973—; vice-president, 1974-75, president, 1975-76), Phi Beta Kappa, Rotary International, Sons of Utah Pioneers.

AWARDS, HONORS: Koontz Award, Pacific Coast Branch of American Historical Association, 1956, for best article published in *Pacific Historical Review;* Huntington Library fellow, 1957-58; awards of merit, American Association for State and Local History, and Pacific Coast Branch of American Historical Association, both 1959, both for *Great Basin Kingdom: An Economic History of the Latter-day Saints, 1830-1900;* Charles Redd Humanities Award, Utah Academy of Sciences, Arts, and Letters, 1966; research grants from American Philosophical Society, 1966, American Council of Learned Societies, 1966-68, Roland Rich Woolley Foundation, 1970-75, and Nora Eccles Treadwell Foundation, 1970-72; David O. McKay Humanities Award, Brigham Young University, 1969; named Alumnus of the Year, Utah State University, 1975; D.H.L., University of Idaho, 1977; D.Hum., Utah State University, 1982; *Brigham Young: Ameri-*

can Moses was nominated by National Book Critics Circle for autobiography/biography division, 1986.

WRITINGS:

Great Basin Kingdom: An Economic History of the Latter-day Saints, 1830-1900, Harvard University Press, 1958.
Introduzione alla storia economica degli Stati Uniti, Libraria Mario Bozzi (Genoa), 1959.
The Changing Economic Structure of the Mountain West, 1850-1950 (monograph), Utah State University Press, 1963.
(With Gary B. Hansen) *The Richest Hole on Earth: A History of the Bingham Copper Mine,* Utah State University Press, 1963.
(With George Jensen) *The Defense Industry of Utah,* Utah State University Press, 1965.
Beet Sugar in the West: A History of the Utah-Idaho Sugar Company, 1891-1966, University of Washington Press, 1966.
(With Jensen) *Impact of Defense Spending on the Economy of Utah,* Utah State University Press, 1967.
(With Anthony T. Cluff) *Federally Financed Industrial Plants Constructed in Utah during World War II,* Utah State University Press, 1969.
(With William L. Roper) *William Spry: Man of Firmness, Governor of Utah,* Utah State University Press, 1971.
Charles C. Rich: Mormon General and Western Frontiersman, Brigham Young University Press, 1974.
David Eccles: Pioneer Western Industrialist, Utah State University Press, 1975.
From Quaker to Latter-day Saint: Bishop Edwin D. Woolley, Deseret, 1976.
(With Feramorz Y. Fox and Dean L. May) *Building the City of God: Community and Cooperation among the Mormons,* Deseret, 1976.
(With Davis Bitton) *The Mormon Experience: A History of the Latter-day Saints,* Knopf, 1979.
The Mormons in Nevada, Las Vegas Sun, 1979.
(With Bitton) *Saints without Halos: The Human Side of Mormon History,* Signature Books, 1981.
(With daughter, Susan Madsen) *Sunbonnet Sisters,* Bookcraft, 1984.
Tracy Collins Bank and Trust Company: A Record of Responsibility, 1884-1984, Eden Hill, 1984.
Brigham Young: American Moses (biography), Knopf, 1985.
(With Madsen) *Mothers of the Prophets,* Deseret, 1987.

Contributor to periodicals. Member of editorial board, *Pacific Historical Review,* 1959-62, *Dialogue: Journal of Mormon Thought,* 1966-69, and *Arizona and the West,* 1973-86; editor, *Western Historical Quarterly,* 1969-72; contributing editor, *Improvement Era,* 1969-70, and *Ensign,* 1971-76.

SIDELIGHTS: Brigham Young: American Moses, Leonard J. Arrington's biographical account of the man who was the spiritual, political, and economic leader of the Mormons in the nineteenth century, was nominated by the National Book Critics Circle in 1986 for the autobiography/biography category. Despite this fact, the book met with mixed critical reception. According to reviewers, Arrington's emphasis is chiefly on Brigham Young's years in Salt Lake City, Utah, as President of the Church of Jesus Christ of Latter-day Saints. On the one hand, *New York Times Book Review* contributor R. Laurence Moore expresses the opinion that Arrington's volume "replaces older, badly flawed biographies and gives readers as good a picture as they are likely to get of the man who assumed leadership of the major part of the church when Smith was assassinated in 1844." On the other hand, Moore suspects that "Arrington . . . has placed too much faith in documents that are consistently read in a way that puts the best face on Young's actions . . . . One result of relying so heavily on manuscripts dictated by Young is that Mr. Arrington fails to give a lively sense of why many people despised him." In terms of the latter argument, a *Chicago Tribune Book World* critic similarly claims that although the book is thorough it is "flawed by an insularity that has been a Mormon hallmark." According to this critic, Arrington might have fared better had he provided more of an outsider's perspective. As for *New York Times* reviewer Michiko Kakutani, he feels Arrington's text presents Young too "gingerly": "[Arrington's] willful reluctance to interpret events or situate them within any larger context results in a baggy, plodding narrative that slurs over important issues. . . . If . . . Arrington's impulse in treating Young so gingerly was to create a sympathetic yet balanced portrait of a controversial figure, he's somehow gone astray." Finally, even though Laura Kalpakian for the *Los Angeles Times Book Review* speaks positively of this "ordered, well-documented, well-written and balanced" book, her ultimate analysis is that "Arrington seems to shake his head at the enormity of his task. Perhaps Brigham Young cannot be contained in the pages of any book; perhaps he needs a mural the size of Zion National Park and a brush dipped in nothing less than God's Great Plan."

BIOGRAPHICAL/CRITICAL SOURCES:

PERIODICALS

Chicago Tribune Book World, June 9, 1985.
Los Angeles Times Book Review, July 14, 1985.
New York Times, April 17, 1985.
New York Times Book Review, July 21, 1985.
Washington Post Book World, June 30, 1985.

*   *   *

ASHLEY, Michael (Raymond Donald) 1948-

PERSONAL: Born October 1, 1948, in Southall, Middlesex, England; son of Albert Cecil (a laboratory technician) and Ada (Locke) Ashley; married Susan Mary Ogilvie (a social worker), July 6, 1972. *Education:* Maidstone College of Further Education, ONC in Public Administration, 1970.

ADDRESSES: Home—4 Thistlebank, Walderslade, Chatham, Kent ME5 8AD, England.

CAREER: Writer, researcher, bibliographer. Kent County Highway Department, Kent, England, local government official, 1967-74; Kent County Treasurer's Department, local government official, 1974-79, auditor, 1979.

WRITINGS:

The History of the Science Fiction Magazine, Part 1, New English Library, 1974, Regnery, 1976, Part 2, New English Library, 1975, Regnery, 1976, Part 3, New English Library, 1976, Part 4, New English Library, 1978.
The Seven Wonders of the World, Fontana, 1979.

EDITOR

Weird Legacies, Star, 1977.
Souls in Metal, St. Martin's, 1977.
SF Choice 77, Quartet, 1977.
The Best of British SF, two volumes, Futura, 1977.
Mrs. Gaskell's Tales of Mystery and Horror, Gollancz, 1978.
Jewels of Wonder, William Kimber, 1981.
Algernon Blackwood: Tales of the Supernatural, Boydell & Brewer, 1983.

The Mammoth Book of Short Horror Novels, Carroll & Graf, 1988.
Robert E. Howard's World of Heroes, Robinson Books, 1989.
The Magic Mirror: Lost Supernatural and Mystery Stories by Algernon Blackwood, Kimber/Equation, 1989.
The Pendragon Chronicles, Robinson Books, 1989.

COMPILER

Who's Who in Horror and Fantasy Fiction, Elm Tree Books, 1977, Taplinger, 1978.
Fantasy Readers Guide to Ramsey Campbell, Cosmos, 1980.
The Complete Index to Astounding/Analog, Robert Weinberg Publications, 1981.
The Writings of Barrington J. Hayley, Beccon, 1981.
The Illustrated Book of Science Fiction Lists, Virgin Books, 1982, revised edition, Cornerstone Library, 1983.
(With Frank Parnell) *Monthly Terrors: An Index to the Weird Fantasy Magazines,* Greenwood Press, 1985.
(With Marshall B. Tymn) *Science Fiction, Fantasy, and Weird Fiction Magazines,* Greenwood Press, 1985.
Algernon Blackwood: A Bio-Bibliography, Greenwood Press, 1987.

CONTRIBUTOR

Brian Ash, editor, *The Visual Encyclopedia of Science Fiction,* Trewin Copplestone, 1977.
Robert Holdstock, editor, *Encyclopedia of Science Fiction,* Octopus Books, 1978.
Tymn, editor, *Horror Literature,* Bowker, 1981.
Holdstock, editor, *The Encyclopedia of Horror,* Octopus Books, 1981.
Brian W. Aldiss, compiler, *Science Fiction Quiz,* Weidenfeld & Nicolson, 1983.
Frank N. Magill, editor, *Survey of Modern Fantasy Literature,* Salem Press, 1983.
James Gunn, editor, *The New Encyclopedia of Science Fiction,* Viking, 1988.
Robert Weinberg, compiler, *A Biographical Dictionary of Science Fiction and Fantasy Artists,* Greenwood Press, 1988.
Neil Barron, editor, *Anatomy of Fear,* Bowker, 1989.

OTHER

Author of unpublished fifth part of *The History of the Science Fiction Magazine.* Contributor to periodicals, including *Science Fiction Monthly, Dark Horizons, Rod Serling's "The Twilight Zone" Magazine, Fantasy Commentator, Fantasy Macabre, Short Stories Magazine, Book and Magazine Collector, Etchings & Odysseys,* and *Horrorstruck.* Contributing editor to *Fantasy Review, Gothic,* and *Crypt of Cthulhu.*

WORK IN PROGRESS: (With Robert A. W. Lowndes) *Hugo Gernsback: Evangelist of Science,* for Starmont House; *The Starlight Man: the Biography of Algernon Blackwood;* compiling *The Supernatural Index: An Index to Horror and Fantasy Anthologies,* for Greenwood Press.

SIDELIGHTS: Michael Ashley once told *CA:* "There are always so many things that I want to do but for which time does not allow. Having a full-time day job, I still devote almost all of my spare time to writing and research, but, as all of my recent projects have been large, I have had to limit my delvings considerably. I am still appalled by the amount of slip-shod research that goes on in the fields of science fiction, fantasy, and horror, much of it as a result [of the need] to meet the growing demands of academia and their interest in the genre."

Ashley later added that he is concentrating on four subjects: "Firstly, I am concentrating primarily on original source publications such as magazines and anthologies, and thereby concentrating mostly on short fiction. This is chiefly in the fields of fantasy, horror, and science fiction, but since I am broadening to cover all magazine sources this brings in imaginative fiction published in the general magazines. One consequential long-term project is the evolution of fantasy and horror fiction in the general/popular periodicals, primarily in Britain. Secondly, I am interested in the pioneers of particular fields, hence my current project on Hugo Gernsback. I intend to do a series of bibliographies, profiles, and studies on many pioneer writers in science fiction, fantasy, and horror. Thirdly, I am interested in the history of pulp fiction and generally both in the United States and Britain, and particularly in the interface between them as exemplified by the twin development of popular authors on both sides of the Atlantic. British pulp fiction has been sorely neglected as has its relationship to its American counterparts. Finally, I shall continue to produce anthologies or author compilations as and when opportunities arise. There is a wealth of untapped material in old books and magazines just awaiting changes in public tastes for a revival of interest."

*   *   *

ASHTON, Dore 1928-

PERSONAL: Born May 21, 1928, in Newark, N.J.; daughter of Ralph Neil (a physician) and Sylvia Smith (Ashton) Shapiro; married Adja Yunkers (an artist), July 8, 1953 (died, 1983); married Matti Megged, March 5, 1985; children: (first marriage) Alexandra Louise, Marina Svietlana. *Education:* University of Wisconsin, B.A., 1949; Harvard University, M.A., 1950. *Politics:* "Ranging from liberal to radical."

ADDRESSES: Home—217 East 11th St., New York, N.Y. 10003. *Office*—Cooper Union, New York, N.Y. 10003.

CAREER: Art Digest, New York City, associate editor, 1951-54; *New York Times,* New York City, associate art critic, 1955-60; Pratt Institute, Brooklyn, N.Y., lecturer, 1962-63; School of Visual Arts, New York City, lecturer in philosophy of art, head of department of humanities, 1965-68; Cooper Union, New York City, professor of art history, 1969—. Writer, teacher, and lecturer, 1960—; curator of exhibitions for the Museum of Modern Art, the American Federation of Artists, and individual museums in the United States and abroad. Instructor, City University of New York, 1973, Columbia University, 1975, and New School for Social Research, 1986—. Member of advisory boards, John Simon Guggenheim Foundation and Swann Foundation.

MEMBER: International Association of Art Critics (vice-president), International Arts Critics Association, PEN (member of executive board), College Art Association (member of board of directors, 1974-77), New York University Society of Fellows, Phi Beta Kappa.

AWARDS, HONORS: Ford Foundation fellowship, 1960; F. J. Mather Award for art criticism, College Art Association, 1963; Graham Foundation Grant, 1963; Guggenheim fellowship, 1964; honorary doctorates from Moore College of Art, 1975, and Hamline University, 1982; National Endowment for the Humanities grant, 1980; Asian Cultural Council grant, 1989.

WRITINGS:

Abstract Art before Columbus, A. Emmerich, 1957.
Poets and the Past, A. Emmerich, 1959.
Philip Guston (monograph), Grove, 1960.

(Co-editor) *Redon, Moreau, Bresdin,* Museum of Modern Art, 1961.
The Unknown Shore, Atlantic/Little, Brown, 1962.
(Author of commentary) Robert Rauschenberg, *Rauschenberg's Dante,* Abrams, 1964.
(Contributor) Gregory Battock, editor, *The New Art: A Critical Anthology,* Dutton, 1966.
Modern American Sculpture, Abrams, 1968.
A Reading of Modern Art, Harper, 1969.
Richard Lindner: A Full-Length Study, Abrams, 1970.
The Sculpture of Pol Bury, Maeght, 1970.
The Life and Times of the New York School, Adams & Dart, 1972, published as *The New York School: A Cultural Reckoning,* Viking, 1973.
Drawings by New York Artists (exhibition catalogue), Utah Museum of Fine Arts, 1972.
(With others) *New York: Cultural Capital of the World, 1940-1965,* edited by Leonard Wallock, photographs by Mario Carrieri, Holt, 1972, reprinted, Rizzoli International, 1988.
(Editor) Pablo Picasso, *Picasso on Art: A Selection of Views,* Viking, 1972, reprinted, Da Capo, 1988.
A Joseph Cornell Album, Viking, 1974.
Yes, but . . .: A Critical Study of Philip Guston, Viking, 1976.
(With Suzanne Delehanty) *Eight Abstract Painters,* University of Pennsylvania, Institute of Contemporary Art, 1978.
(With Peter Howard Selz) *Zwei Jahrzehnte amerikanischer Malerei, 1920-1940,* [Duesseldorf], 1979.
A Fable of Modern Art, Thames & Hudson, 1980.
(With Denise Brown Hare) *Rosa Bonheur: A Life and a Legend,* Viking, 1981.
American Art since 1945, Oxford University Press, 1982.
(With Jack Flam) *Robert Motherwell,* Abrams, 1982.
(With Joan M. Marter) *Jose de Rivera Constructions,* Abner Schram, 1983.
About Rothko, Oxford University Press, 1983.
Jacobo Borges, [Caracas, Venezuela], 1983.
Deborah Remington: A 20-Year Survey, Newport Harbor Art Museum, 1983.
Multiplicity in Clay, Metal, Fiber: Skidmore College Craft Invitational, The College (Saratoga Springs, N.Y.), 1984.
Jean Cocteau and the French Scene, edited by Arthur Peters, Abbeville Press, 1984.
(Editor) *20th-Century Artists on Art,* Pantheon, 1985.
(Editor) *Antonio Sant'Elia,* A. Mondadori (Milan, Italy), 1986.
Out of the Whirlwind: Three Decades of Arts Commentary, edited by Donald Kuspit, UMI Research Press, 1987.
Fragonard in the Universe of Painting, Smithsonian Institution Press, 1988.

Contributor to the "Vision and Value" series, edited by Gyorgy Kepes, Braziller, 1966, and to *On Art,* edited by Rudolf Baranik. Contributor of articles to over 70 journals, including *XXieme Siecle, Cimaise* and *Aujourd'hui.* New York contributing editor for *XXieme Siecle, Cimaise,* 1955-70, *Studio International,* 1961-74, *Opus International,* 1968-74, and *Art International,* 1987—; associate editor and columnist, *Arts,* 1974—.

SIDELIGHTS: Art critic and educator Dore Ashton specializes in the study of 20th-century art. She is well known for her books concerning the New York School of modern art and New York artists like Mark Rothko and Joseph Cornell. Ashton speaks fluent French, as well as Italian and Spanish, and can understand some Russian, German, and Portuguese.

AVOCATIONAL INTERESTS: Preservation of world peace.

BIOGRAPHICAL/CRITICAL SOURCES:

PERIODICALS

Los Angeles Times Book Review, June 22, 1980, April 26, 1981, January 29, 1984.

New York Review of Books, August 21, 1969, June 14, 1973.

New York Times, April 24, 1980, November 7, 1983.

New York Times Book Review, December 6, 1970, December 2, 1973, December 29, 1974, July 4, 1976, May 24, 1981, January 1, 1984.

Spectator, May 29, 1982, September 8, 1984.

Times Literary Supplement, February 11, 1965, November 9, 1973, December 5, 1980, October 16, 1981, March 19, 1982.

Village Voice, May 29, 1984, March 15, 1988.

Washington Post Book World, July 6, 1980, April 12, 1981, February 19, 1984.

*   *   *

ATTENBOROUGH, David (Frederick) 1926-

PERSONAL: Born May 8, 1926, in London, England; son of Frederick Levi and Mary (Clegg) Attenborough; married Jane Elizabeth Oriel, 1950; children: Robert, Susan. *Education:* Clare College, Cambridge, M.A., 1947.

ADDRESSES: Home—5 Park Rd., Richmond, Surrey TW10 6NS, England.

CAREER: Editorial assistant in British publishing house, 1949-52; British Broadcasting Corp., Television Service, London, England, producer, 1952-62; controller of programs for BBC-2 television, 1965-68, director of programs and member of board of management, 1969-72; independent producer and television series host, 1972—, shows include "Life on Earth," 1979, "The Living Planet," 1984, and "The First Eden: The Mediterranean World and Man," 1987. Member of Nature Conservancy Council, 1973—; trustee of British Museum, 1980—, World Wildlife Fund, 1981—, and Science Museum, 1984—. Has undertaken numerous zoological, geological, and ethnographic filming expeditions, including Sierra Leone, 1954, New Guinea, 1957, Zambesi, 1964, Borneo, 1973, Solomon Islands, 1975, and the Mediterranean region, 1986. *Military service:* Royal Navy, 1947-49; became lieutenant.

MEMBER: Society of Film and Television Arts (fellow, 1980—).

AWARDS, HONORS: Society of Film and Television Arts special award, 1961; silver medals from Zoological Society of London and Royal Television Society, both 1966; Desmond Davis Award, 1970; Cherry Kearton Award from Royal Geographical Society, 1972; Commander of the Order of the British Empire, 1974; Kalinga Prize from UNESCO and medal from Academy of Natural Sciences, Philadelphia, both 1982. Honorary degrees include D.Litt., University of Leicester, 1970, City University (London), 1972, and Birmingham University; D.Sc., University of Liverpool, 1974, Heriot-Watt University, 1978, University of Ulster, Sussex University, University of Bath, Durham University, and Keele University; honorary fellow, Manchester Polytechnic, 1976; LL.D., University of Bristol and University of Glasgow, both 1977; D.Univ., Open University, 1980.

WRITINGS:

Zoo Quest to Guiana (also see below), Lutterworth, 1956, Crowell, 1957, abridged edition, University of London Press, 1962.

Zoo Quest for a Dragon (also see below), Lutterworth, 1957.

Zoo Quest in Paraguay (also see below), Lutterworth, 1959.

Quest in Paradise, Lutterworth, 1960.

People of Paradise, Harper, 1961.

Zoo Quest to Madagascar, Lutterworth, 1961, published as *Bridge to the Past: Animals and People of Madagascar,* Harper, 1962.

Quest under Capricorn, Lutterworth, 1963.

(Editor) *My Favorite Stories of Exploration,* Lutterworth, 1964.

(With Molly Cox) *David Attenborough's Fabulous Animals,* BBC Publications, 1975.

The Tribal Eye, Norton, 1976.

Life on Earth: A Natural History, BBC Publications, 1979, Little, Brown, 1980.

Journeys to the Past: Travels in New Guinea, Madagascar, and the Northern Territory of Australia, Lutterworth, 1981.

Discovering Life on Earth: A Natural History (juvenile), Little, Brown, 1981.

The Zoo Quest Expeditions: Travels in Guyana, Indonesia, and Paraguay (contains *Zoo Quest to Guiana, Zoo Quest for a Dragon,* and *Zoo Quest in Paraguay*), Penguin, 1982.

(With Michael MacIntyre) *The Spirit of Asia,* Salem House, 1983.

The Living Planet: A Portrait of the Earth, Little, Brown, 1984.

(Author of introduction) *Wildlife through the Camera,* Parkwest Publications, 1985.

(Author of foreword) Andrew Langley, *The Making of "The Living Planet,"* Little, Brown, 1985.

The First Eden: The Mediterranean World and Man, Little, Brown, 1987.

WORK IN PROGRESS: A television series on fossils and another on animal behavior.

SIDELIGHTS: David Attenborough has spent most of his career explaining the wonders of the natural world to public television audiences. As producer and host of such popular series as "Zoo Quest," "Life on Earth," "The Living Planet," and "The First Eden: The Mediterranean World and Man," Attenborough has travelled around the world, and—striding through marshes or cuddling baby mountain gorillas—has communicated his personal enthusiasm for natural phenomena. Attenborough has two aims in his award-winning work: to entertain and to inform. His productions find a balance between the "believe-it-or-not" approach of some animal shows and the complex theoretical approach associated with strict schooling. *Newsweek* contributor Harry F. Waters writes: "Attenborough, schooled in geology, zoology and biology, possesses a remarkably eclectic scientific range as well as the sensibilities of a poet." According to Timothy S. Green in *Smithsonian,* the naturalist "has a rare talent for describing with great simplicity the complexities of evolution," while he "never underrates the intelligence of his audience." In addition to his television series, Attenborough has authored lavishly-illustrated companion volumes that cover the same topics as his films. *New York Times Book Review* correspondent Clifford D. May notes that these books add up to "an outstanding introduction to natural history and a sobering reminder that the works of man don't amount to a hill of bat guano beside the miracles of nature."

Attenborough was born and raised in London, the son of scholar Frederick Levi Attenborough and the younger brother of actor-director Richard Attenborough. The spirit of intellectual curiosity was paramount in the Attenborough household, and young David was encouraged to pursue his interest in fossils and in the live animals he extracted from the ponds near his home. He told the *Chicago Tribune* that his father's academic colleagues "were my gods. Subconsciously I absorbed their standards. The attitude in our household was that the greatest success you could have in life was to acquire knowledge. That's what made you admirable, what made adults important." Attenborough has also praised his father for the educational role he played. He told *Smithsonian:* "My father . . . believed that the way you teach children is to allow them to discover for themselves. . . . I'd find a fossil and show it to my father and he'd say, 'Good, good, tell me all about it.' So I responded and became my own expert." Not surprisingly, Attenborough went on to Clare College, Cambridge, where he majored in geology and zoology. He earned a master's degree in 1947. After completing his military service in the Royal Navy, he became an editorial assistant at an educational publishing house. In 1952 he joined the British Broadcasting Corporation, where he was trained to produce television programs.

At first Attenborough produced BBC shows on a variety of topics, from politics to ballet. In 1954 he and Jack Lester, a curator of the London Zoo, proposed an animal collecting expedition. Attenborough would film what happened for the BBC and Lester would bring back animals for the London Zoo. The resulting series of programs was called "Zoo Quest." Attenborough told *Smithsonian* that his idea was to "combine the benefits" of an up-close studio look at an animal and a field trip to its natural environment. He thought it would be interesting to see an animal in the wild and then show it live in the studio. The first trip, to Sierra Leone in West Africa, resulted in the capture of a great variety of animals, the most famous of whom was the bald-headed rock crow (*Picathartes gymnocephalus*). Thereafter Attenborough went to British Guiana, Indonesia, New Guinea, Paraguay, Madagascar, and northern Australia, always in search of largely-unknown species of wild animals. Lester was stricken with a fatal illness in 1955, and Attenborough took over as show host as well as producer. Green describes Attenborough's unexpected success in front of the cameras: "Clad in shorts and hiking boots, he . . . trekked through jungles and waded across swamps in search of orangutans, birds of paradise, or a spectacular [Indonesian] lizard known as the Komodo dragon. His infectious enthusiasm . . . for every kind of animal he found appealed to armchair travelers who felt that here was a real explorer taking them along and sharing wildlife secrets, gamely brushing discomfort aside." Attenborough's adventures were collected in a series of "Zoo Quest" books, reprinted together in two volumes as *The Zoo Quest Expeditions* (1980) and *Journeys to the Past* (1981).

In 1965 Attenborough was named controller of a second BBC channel that became the first in Europe to offer color programming. The station was established to provide a planned alternative to the BBC's first channel, but Attenborough set out to capture most if not all of Great Britain's nightly audience. He was soon attracting five million viewers with dramatic series such as "Henry the Eighth" and "The Forsyte Saga," and he earned critical acclaim by commissioning Jacob Bronowski's "The Ascent of Man" and Kenneth Clark's "Civilization." Attenborough told *Smithsonian* that his idea for the latter series was to use color television to show "all the loveliest things of this civilization over the last 2,000 years," and do it in a historical sequence. On the strength of his programming capabilities, Attenborough was promoted to director of programs for both BBC channels in 1968. He held the position for four years, then resigned in order to return to the creative work of producing and directing shows. He wanted to do an epic series on natural history in the same style as Clark's "Civilization," but first he produced and hosted a series on art in primitive societies. His seven-part work, "The Tribal Eye," aired in 1975 and drew four million viewers.

The series "Life on Earth" began as a six-page outline tracing life from its origins in the sea to the advent of the human race. Attenborough wanted to produce "not just a natural history but a history of nature," he told *CA.* He did so by exploring the fossil record and by showing footage of living species of animals and plants. The series required a team of more than fifty wildlife photographers, more than a million miles of travel to thirty countries, and the cooperation of major zoos, museums, and universities worldwide. First broadcast in England in 1979, "Life on Earth" quickly became the most popular science series ever put on the air, with twelve million regular viewers each week. It was received with equal enthusiasm when it ran in America early in 1982. *Washington Post* contributor Bruce Brown has called the work "a tour de force: fresh and vivid with incredible variety married to the clear exposition of the mechanisms of evolution." Waters offers a similar opinion in *Newsweek:* "By coupling lyrical rhythms and evocative images, ['Life on Earth'] achieves the emotional power of a cinematic poem." Attenborough also wrote a companion book, *Life on Earth: A Natural History,* that has likewise drawn praise from reviewers. In the *Washington Post Book World,* Joseph Kastner writes that the volume "is the best kind of spin-off—literate, witty, full of earthly marvels presented without any of the orotund self-consciousness of some cosmic TV guides." Elisabeth Whipp elaborates in *Spectator:* "With a pleasant enthusiasm [Attenborough] effortlessly encompasses 3000 million years in 300 pages, from the very start of life to its most bizarre and intricate manifestations. Using the historical framework of the gradually evolving species, he juxtaposes fossil evidence and comparative anatomy to give a vivid picture of our present understanding of how life came about."

If "Life on Earth" examined the overall history of evolution, "The Living Planet," first broadcast in America in 1984, showed how plants and animals adapt to extreme environments. Once again Attenborough travelled the length and breadth of the globe, filming sequences from the rim of an active volcano, in a mangrove swamp, and in the sweltering heat of Death Valley, among others. Brown writes of the series: "Natural adaptations are compared and contrasted until—almost by surprise—the reader has acquired a pretty good idea of how life is shaped on the [global] anvil." Another illustrated companion volume, *The Living Planet: Portrait of the Earth,* appeared at the same time the series aired. In his *Newsweek* review, Jim Miller contends that the reader first notices "the arresting images: a hairy sloth hanging upside down, an ocean of brightly tasseled foxtail grass, two albatrosses courting, a beach blanketed with breeding sea turtles, an uncanny ghost crab looking quite like its name. The text almost seems an afterthought—until you begin to read it. Like Attenborough's on-air scripts, it has the lilt and texture of the spoken word and something of the offhand appeal of a face-to-face conversation. The real pleasure of the book, though, lies in Attenborough's old-fashioned skill as a prose stylist."

Attenborough's next series, "The First Eden: The Mediterranean World and Man," focused on the Mediterranean region from the Ice Age to the present. Aired in 1987, the series showed how various sophisticated human cultures developed around the inland sea, some holding nature in reverence and others exploiting it until forests turned into deserts. *Earth Science* contributor Louise J. Fisher notes that the point of "The First Eden" is that nature "has never failed to support people, but people have failed to support nature." The short series and its book of the same title helped to counter a complaint formerly leveled at Attenborough; namely, that he has tended to underplay the devastation humankind is wreaking on the global environment. Attenborough himself told *Earth Science:* "My television programs are just for the wonder of it all. I don't start with a message or preach to people, but try to enrich their lives by showing them our fascinating and delightful planet." He did state, however: "I hope my work has helped people become more aware of nature and the Earth. Understanding the geosciences gives us a sense of time and evolution. . . . I have always thought an education in the natural sciences illuminates your life forever. You can't be a natural scientist without acquiring a profound reverence for nature." Everyone starts with that reverence, he said, "it's just that some of us lose sight of it. We can't let that happen. We would be deprived of so much." Attenborough told *People* magazine that his unusual career has been a source of constant pleasure for him, no matter what conditions he confronted in his travels. "I'm the luckiest man," he said. "I go to the most marvelous places in the world, and I'm paid for it."

AVOCATIONAL INTERESTS: Music, tribal art.

BIOGRAPHICAL/CRITICAL SOURCES:

BOOKS

Langley, Andrew, *The Making of "The Living Planet,"* Little, Brown, 1985.

PERIODICALS

Chicago Tribune, January 19, 1982.
Earth Science, fall, 1987.
Los Angeles Times Book Review, April 13, 1986.
Newsweek, February 4, 1985, February 11, 1985.
New York, November 2, 1987.
New Yorker, November 19, 1984.
New York Times Book Review, January 3, 1982, December 4, 1983.
People, February 8, 1982.
Smithsonian, November, 1981.
Spectator, March 31, 1979.
Times Literary Supplement, September 28, 1984.
Washington Post, January 12, 1982, January 19, 1985.
Washington Post Book World, November 8, 1981, December 8, 1985.

—*Sketch by Anne Janette Johnson*

B

BACHMAN, Richard
See KING, Stephen (Edwin)

* * *

BAECHLER, Jean 1937-

PERSONAL: Born March 28, 1937, in Thionville, France; son of Maurice (a merchant) and Marie (Hoss) Baechler; married Fabienne Scheffler, December 24, 1959; children: Anne, Beatrice, Sabine, Laurent. *Education:* University of Strasbourg, Licence d'Histoire, 1959; University of Paris, Agregation d'Histoire, 1962, Doctorat es Lettres, 1975. *Politics:* "Liberal, in the European sense of the word." *Religion:* "Tolerant agnostic."

ADDRESSES: Home—4, avenue de Rocroy, 91380 Chilly-Mazarin, France. *Office*—Maison des Sciences de l'Homme, 54, boulevard Raspail, 75270 Paris, France.

CAREER: Taught history and geography in a secondary school in Le Mans, France, 1962-66; Centre National de la Recherche Scientifique, Paris, France, director of research, 1966-88; Ecole des Hautes Etudes en Sciences Sociales, Paris, associate professor, 1975-86; University of Paris-Sorbonne, Paris, professor of philosophy, 1988—. *Military service:* French Army, 1962-64.

AWARDS, HONORS: Prize from Fondation de la Paix, 1974, for *Les Phenomenes revolutionnaires;* prize from *Spectacle du Monde,* 1976, for *Les Suicides.*

WRITINGS:

Politique de Trotsky (title means "The Politics of Trotsky"), Armand Colin (Paris), 1968.
Les Phenomenes revolutionnaires, Presses Universitaires de France, 1970, translation by Joan Vickers published as *Revolution,* Harper, 1975.
Les Origines de capitalisme, Gallimard, 1971, translation by Barry Cooper published as *The Origins of Capitalism,* Basil Blackwell, 1975.
Les Suicides, Calmann-Levy (Paris), 1975, 2nd edition, 1981, translation by Cooper published as *Suicides,* Basic Books, 1979.
Qu'est-ce que l'ideologie? (title means "What Is Ideology?"), Gallimard, 1976.
Le Pouvoir pur, Calmann-Levy, 1978.
Democraties, Calmann-Levy, 1985.

La Solution indienne: Essai sur les origines du regime des castes, Presses Universitaires de France, 1988.

Contributor of articles to professional journals. Member of editorial committee, *European Journal of Sociology, Commentaire,* and *L'Annee Sociologique.*

WORK IN PROGRESS: "Working on two books in parallel, one aiming at a general theory of history, and the other at a general history of mankind as such, of its principal steps reached and accomplished by particular cultures, in a non-evolutionist way. Completion not anticipated before the late 1990s."

SIDELIGHTS: In a letter to *CA,* Jean Baechler says that despite the wide range of topics he has addressed in his writings, he is nevertheless "fascinated and obsessed by a single question: why does something happen rather than nothing, be it a matter of a revolution, a suicide, capitalism, or the Neolithic age? In other words, why is there history rather than indefinite repetition of the same thing? It so happens that, by temperament and by inclination, I apply the question to human affairs. If I had been different, I would have just as easily been able to devote myself to the history of life or that of the universe. (All the same, I make every effort to keep up with, as best I can, current developments in the theories of evolution and cosmogony.) Limited by my background to the study of the history of mankind, it seemed to me that politics was the best possible observation post, because everything that happens in human societies has political consequences, and vice versa. Which explains all these years devoted to the comparative study of political regimes. It is not a question, for me, of being a political scientist in the ordinary sense of the term, but, in placing my steps in those of Aristotle, Hobbes, Montesquieu, and Hegel, of succeeding at isolating and explaining the ultimate motives of human history.

"My mind is made is such a fashion that I perceive everything in terms of problems likely to meet with rational responses. Consequently, if someone asked me why I am involved in the social sciences, I would respond: because I can't help being involved with them. To the question, why do you write?, I would answer: because I discover things, not only while searching for them, but while writing about them. For years I have hesitated responding to the question, why publish? Money has no part in it, because my books exhibit an austerity that precludes best-seller status. Vanity must have its part, for it is nice to meet with the approval of people one holds in high esteem. But they are so few in number

16

that there is an excessive disproportion between the goal and the means used to attain it. Finally, age has made me understand that, from the moment one writes, one must also publish—preferably little—because one cannot exclude the possibility that others might be, not interested, but prompted and encouraged to think for themselves. If a god proposed that I make a wish and promised me to fulfill it, I would choose the following: that for as long as there are men, each year one hundred men from all over the world would have, while reading me, the feeling of having become a little more intelligent and of having approached a little closer to the truth. When all is said and done, one writes for oneself, and one publishes in the same way that one throws a bottle into the sea—without hope of return, but in making the perhaps stupid bet that it will be recovered by someone and that its message will be transmitted even farther in another bottle thrown into the sea by someone else, and so on until the end of the human adventure, tomorrow or in some thousands of millions of years."

BIOGRAPHICAL/CRITICAL SOURCES:

PERIODICALS

New Republic, December 8, 1979.
New York Times Book Review, September 23, 1979.
Spectator, February 16, 1980.

*   *   *

BAKLANOFF, Eric N. 1925-

PERSONAL: Born December 9, 1925, in Graz, Austria; son of Nicholas W. and Lucile (King) Baklanoff; married H. Christina Janes (an art professor), May 1, 1956 (divorced June, 1972); children: Nicholas, Tanya. *Education:* Attended Antioch College, 1943-44; Ohio State University, B.A., 1949, M.A., 1950, Ph.D., 1958. *Politics:* Republican. *Religion:* Eastern Orthodox.

ADDRESSES: Home—1913 Eighth St., Tuscaloosa, Ala. 35401. *Office*—Economics Department, University of Alabama, Box J, University, Ala. 35486.

CAREER: Chase National Bank, New York, N.Y., member of International Division in Puerto Rico, 1950-54; Louisana State University, Baton Rouge, assistant professor of economics, 1958-61; Vanderbilt University, Nashville, Tenn., associate professor of economics and director of Graduate Center for Latin American Studies, 1962-65; Louisiana State University, professor of economics and director of Latin American Studies Institute, 1965-68; University of Alabama, University, professor of economics and dean of International Studies and Programs, 1969-73, Board of Visitors Research Professor of Economics, 1974—. *Military service:* U.S. Navy, 1944-46.

MEMBER: Latin American Studies Association, Southeastern Council on Latin American Studies (president, 1963-64), Southern Economic Association, Western Economics Association, Omicron Delta Epsilon, Sigma Delta Pi, Beta Gamma Sigma.

AWARDS, HONORS: Fulbright fellowship, University of Chile, 1957; Vanderbilt University fellowship to Brazil, summer, 1963; Center for Advanced Studies in the Behavioral Sciences fellowship, 1964-65; Louisiana State University grants, University of the Americas, summer, 1966, Spain, summer, 1968; Wenner-Gren Foundation grant, 1966; U.S. State Department travel grant to Spain, 1974; University of Alabama Research Grants Committee summer fellowships, 1975-76, 1978, 1980, 1982, 1984; Outstanding Scholar Award, University of Alabama, 1980-81; Sturgis Leavitt Prize, Southeastern Council on Latin

American Studies, 1981, for best published article; Capstone International Program Center grant, July, 1985; U.S. Department of Education grant, fall, 1986; Andrew W. Mellon Foundation research fellowship, July, 1986.

WRITINGS:

(Editor and contributor) *New Perspectives of Brazil,* Vanderbilt University Press, 1966.
(Editor and contributor) *The Shaping of Modern Brazil,* Louisiana State University Press, 1969.
(Contributor) Carmelo Mesa-Lago, editor, *Revolutionary Change in Cuba,* University of Pittsburgh Press, 1971.
(Contributor) John Saunders, editor, *Modern Brazil: New Patterns and Development,* University of Florida Press, 1971.
(Contributor) Robert B. Williamson, William P. Glade, Jr., and Karl M. Schmitt, editors, *Latin American-U.S. Economic Interactions,* American Enterprise Institute for Public Policy Research, 1974.
Expropriation of U.S. Investments in Cuba, Mexico, and Chile, Praeger, 1975.
(Editor and contributor) *Mediterranean Europe and the Common Market,* University of Alabama Press, 1976.
The Economic Transformation of Spain and Portugal, Praeger, 1978.
(Contributor) Robert Freeman Smith, editor, *Background to Revolution: The Development of Modern Cuba,* Robert E. Krieger, 1979.
La transformacion de Espana y Portugal: La economia del Franquismo y del Salazarismo, Espasa-Calpe, 1980.
(Contributor) Edward Moseley and Edward Terry, editors, *Yucatan: A World Apart,* University of Alabama Press, 1980.
(Contributor) T. Noel Osborn, editor, *El dilema de dos naciones: Relaciones economicas entre Mexico y Estados Unidos,* Editorial Trillas, 1981.
(Contributor) Gilbert M. Joseph and Allen Wells, editors, *Yucatan y la International Harvester,* Maldonado Editores, 1986.
(Contributor) Howard J. Wiarda, editor, *The Iberian-Latin American Connection: Implications for U.S. Foreign Policy,* Westview Press, 1986.
(Contributor) Glade, editor, *State Shrinking: A Comparative Inquiry into Privatization,* University of Texas at Austin, Institute of Latin American Studies, 1986.
(With Jeffery Brannon) *Agrarian Reform and Public Enterprise in Mexico: The Political Economy of Yucatan's Henequen Industry,* University of Alabama Press, 1987.
(Contributor) Kenneth Maxwell, editor, *Portugal: Ancient Country, Young Democracy,* Woodrow Wilson International Center for Scholars, 1989.

*   *   *

BALES, Jack
See BALES, James E(dward)

*   *   *

BALES, James E(dward) 1951-
(Jack Bales)

PERSONAL: Born November 1, 1951, in Milwaukee, Wis.; son of James Edward (a teacher) and Phyllis (a teacher; maiden name, Steinkamp) Bales. *Education:* Illinois College, B.A., 1973; University of Illinois, M.S., 1974.

ADDRESSES: Home—Fredericksburg, Va. *Office*—Mary Washington College Library, Fredericksburg, Va. 22401-5358.

CAREER: Eureka College, Eureka, Ill., assistant librarian, 1974-76; Illinois College, Jacksonville, public service librarian, 1976-80; Mary Washington College, Fredericksburg, Va., reference librarian, 1980—. Member, Kenneth Roberts Centennial Commission.

MEMBER: Horatio Alger Society, American Library Association, Virginia Library Association, Fredericksburg-Rappahannock Rotary Club.

AWARDS, HONORS: President's award, Horatio Alger Society, 1981, for *Horatio Alger, Jr.;* recipient of various other literary awards, "newsletter of the year" awards from Rotary district, and awards of merit from Horatio Alger Society.

WRITINGS:

UNDER NAME JACK BALES

(Author of foreword) Herbert R. Mayes, *Alger: A Biography without a Hero,* Gilbert K. Westgard II, 1978.
(With Gary Scharnhorst) *Horatio Alger, Jr.: An Annotated Bibliography of Comment and Criticism,* Scarecrow, 1981.
(With Scharnhorst) *The Lost Life of Horatio Alger, Jr.,* Indiana University Press, 1985.
Kenneth Roberts: The Man and His Works, Scarecrow, 1989.

Contributor to magazines, including *Journal of Popular Culture.* Editor, *Newsboy,* 1974-86.

SIDELIGHTS: "I became fascinated with the books of Horatio Alger, Jr., at the age of fifteen, after coming across one in my father's bookcase," Jack Bales told *CA.* "This interest culminated in two books on the legendary 'rags to riches' author that Gary Scharnhorst and I published, including a thoroughly documented biography." In scores of books published during the late nineteenth century's Gilded Age, Alger advanced the premise that through much hard work and a little luck, one can succeed at anything. Alger's work sold respectably during his own lifetime, but his reputation soared posthumously, notes Patrick Renshaw in the *Times Literary Supplement.* Alger became a legend with the establishment of the Horatio Alger Awards in the late 1940s for those who have "pulled themselves up by their own bootstraps in the American tradition," continues Renshaw. Among the recepients of the Horatio Alger Award have been such individuals as Dwight D. Eisenhower and Ronald Reagan.

In the late 1920s, the plans of journalist Herbert R. Mayes to write a biography of Alger disintegrated when he discovered that all biographical data had been destroyed by the author's family in an attempt to keep veiled his pederastic tendencies. So, in the spirit of parody, Mayes then concocted a biography based upon nonexistent letters and diaries. The fabrication was published as "a deliberate hoax, intended as its author subsequently acknowledged to be a 'delightful spoof' of the Alger mythology," writes Jonathan Yardley in the *Washington Post Book World.* "Instead it was received quite soberly as the definitive word, and remained the principal source of information—or, more accurately, misinformation—about Alger."

Decades later, suspicion began to mount; and by the 1970s, says Renshaw, Mayes desired to rectify his prank and set the record straight. With the encouragement of Mayes, Bales and Scharnhorst sought out the surviving letters and records of Alger to produce *The Lost Life of Horatio Alger, Jr.,* which, in Yardley's estimation, represents "a nice piece of scholarship, done against considerable odds and done very well." Calling it a "fascinating book," Renshaw adds that "it uncovers a remarkable story—what might be called the myth within the Alger myth." The legendary Alger, who served to propagandize "American capital-ism, which enabled those with 'the right stuff' to rise from the bottom of society to the very top," as Renshaw points out, actually was "often very critical of the American system and the way it produced and distributed wealth." In Renshaw's opinion, this biography "can be regarded as definitive."

Bales also told *CA:* "I've always enjoyed the works of American historical novelist Kenneth Roberts (1885-1957), and in 1986 I began work on an annotated bibliography of criticism on Roberts. With such meticulously researched books as *Arundel, Rabble in Arms, Oliver Wiswell,* and the enormously popular *Northwest Passage,* Roberts established and maintained a reputation throughout his literary career as an author whose books were not only enjoyable to read but were models of historical writing and accuracy. When I realized that no biography of Roberts existed, I decided to incorporate a lengthy biographical essay in the volume, largely based on letters, interviews, and other primary resource material. To complete this task I traveled to New England to research in several major Roberts collections in libraries.

"One of the favorite aspects of my literary and historical research is the opportunity to meet so many fascinating people in libraries around the country. Since most of the librarians whom I met knew of me through countless letters I had written previous to my visit, they literally let me have free reign throughout the book stacks; thus, I was able to happily immerse myself in rare books, manuscripts, and letters. Of course, living so close to the Library of Congress was another big help. Even now, with the book completed, I still keep up the correspondence with most of these librarians and scholars, and have donated Roberts items to all of their respective institutions. Librarians may have an 'image problem,' but the ones I've dealt with are tops as far as I'm concerned."

AVOCATIONAL INTERESTS: Literary and historical research; reading; letter writing.

BIOGRAPHICAL/CRITICAL SOURCES:

BOOKS

Doering, Henry, editor, *The World Almanac Book of Buffs, Masters, Mavens, and Uncommon Experts,* Prentice-Hall, 1980.

PERIODICALS

Times Literary Supplement, October 18, 1985.
Washington Post Book World, June 5, 1985.

*   *   *

BALKEY, Rita 1922-
(Rita Balkey Oleyar)

PERSONAL: Born October 26, 1922, in Glenshaw, Pa.; daughter of Frank and Katherine (Sponsel) Balkey; married Edward Oleyar, 1946 (marriage ended, 1968); children: Rebecca Oleyar Wiemer, Jane Oleyar Fadden, Marjorie Oleyar Jackson, Heidi Oleyar McGeorge. *Education:* Seton Hall College, A.B., 1945; California State College at Fullerton (now California State University, Fullerton), M.A., 1965; University of California, Irvine, Ph.D., 1968.

ADDRESSES: Home and office—2614 Rutherford Dr., Los Angeles, Calif. 90068. *Agent*—Florence Feiler Literary Agency, 1524 Sunset Plaza Dr., Los Angeles, Calif. 90069.

CAREER: California State University, Fullerton, professor of English, 1962-80; writer, 1975—.

MEMBER: International PEN, Romance Writers of America.

WRITINGS:

(Under name Rita Balkey Oleyar) *The Bible as Literature* (nonfiction), privately printed, 1975.

(Under name Rita Balkey Oleyar) *The Jesus Myth* (nonfiction), Harper, 1975.

(Under name Rita Balkey Oleyar) *Myths of Creation and Fall* (nonfiction), Harper, 1975.

Prince of Passion (romance novel), Pinnacle Books, 1980.

Tears of Glory (romance novel), Pinnacle Books, 1981.

Silk and Steel (romance novel), Zebra Books, 1986.

Glorious Conquest (romance novel), Zebra Books, 1987.

Passion's Disguise (romance novel), Zebra Books, 1988.

Passion's Fury (romance novel), Zebra Books, 1989.

Also author, under name Rita Balkey Oleyar, of *The Job Story* (nonfiction), 1975. Contributor to magazines and newspapers.

WORK IN PROGRESS: Orphans in America: An Oral History.

*   *   *

BALLARD, Edward Goodwin 1910-

PERSONAL: Born January 3, 1910, in Fairfax, Va.; son of James W. (a lawyer) and Margaret Lewis (Goodwin) Ballard; married Lucy McIver Watson, November 22, 1938 (deceased, 1983); children: Susanne (Mrs. M. Dowouis), Lucy (Mrs. David Armentrout-Ma), Edward Marshall. *Education:* College of William and Mary, A.B., 1931; Harvard University, additional study, 1931-32; University of Montpelier, France, diploma, 1932; University of Virginia, M.A., 1934, Ph.D., 1946; University of Sorbonne, postgraduate study, 1951. *Religion:* Anglican Catholic.

ADDRESSES: Home—The Tamalpais, #1008, 501 Via Casitas, Greenbrae, Calif. 94904.

CAREER: Virginia Military Institute, Lexington, instructor in English, 1939-41; University of Virginia, Charlottesville, assistant in philosophy, 1941-42; Tulane University, New Orleans, La., assistant professor, 1946-53, associate professor, 1953-58, professor of philosophy, 1958-77, W. R. Irby Professor of Philosophy, 1977-80, emeritus professor, 1980—. Visiting professor at Yale University, 1963-64, Louisiana State University at Baton Rouge, 1969, and University of Missouri—Columbia, 1981; Brown Foundation Visiting Professor, University of the South, 1981-82. Member of selection committee, Woodrow Wilson Fellowship, 1966-69; member of selection panel, National Endowment for the Humanities, 1970-74; member of board of directors, Center for Advanced Research in Phenomenology, 1979—. *Military service:* U.S. Naval Reserve, 1942-70; active duty, 1942-46; became commander; received three battle stars for service in Pacific theater.

MEMBER: Society for Phenomenology and Existential Philosophy, American Philosophical Association, Metaphysical Society of America, Southern Society for Philosophy and Psychology (president, 1967), Husserl Circle (chairman, 1970), Heidegger Circle.

WRITINGS:

Art and Analysis, Nijhoff, 1957, reprinted, American Biographical Service, 1985.

(Translator and author of introduction) *The Philosophy of Jules Lachelier,* Nijhoff, 1960.

Socratic Ignorance: An Essay on Platonic Self-Knowledge, Nijhoff, 1965.

(Translator with Lester E. Embree) *Husserl: An Analysis of His Phenomenology,* Northwestern University Press, 1967.

Philosophy at the Crossroads, Louisiana State University Press, 1971.

(Editor with Charles E. Scott and contributor) *Martin Heidegger: In Europe and America,* Nijhoff, 1973.

Man and Technology: Toward the Measurement of a Culture, Duquesne University Press, 1978.

Principles of Interpretation, Ohio University Press, 1983.

Philosophy and the Liberal Arts, Kluwer Academic, 1989.

Responses, Deaver's Alley Publishing (Lexington, Va.), 1989.

CONTRIBUTOR

George A. Schrader, Jr., editor, *Existential Philosophers,* McGraw, 1967.

John Sallis, editor, *Heidegger and the Path of Thinking,* Duquesne University Press, 1970.

F. J. Smith, editor, *Phenomenology in Perspective,* Nijhoff, 1970.

Embree, editor, *Life-World and Consciousness: Essays for Aaron Gurwitsch,* Northwestern University Press, 1972.

P. J. Bossert, editor, *Phenomenological Perspectives: Historical and Systematic Essays in Honor of Herbert Spiegelberg,* Nijhoff, 1973.

C. Bigger and D. Cornay, editors, *Eros and Nihilism,* Kendall/Hunt, 1976.

D. Lovekin and D. P. Verene, editors, *Essays in Humanity and Technology,* Sauk Valley College, 1978.

Michael J. Hyde, editor, *Communication Philosophy: The Human Condition in a Technological Age,* University of Alabama Press, 1981.

Stephen Skousgaard, editor, *Phenomenology and the Understanding of Human Destiny,* University Press of America, 1981.

Embree, editor, *Essays in Memory of Aaron Gurwitsch,* University Press of America, 1983.

OTHER

Contributor to *American Encyclopedia of Philosophy* and *Dictionary of the History of Ideas.* Contributor of more than fifty articles, three critical reviews, and about twenty-five short reviews to professional journals. Member of editorial boards for *Southern Journal of Philosophy,* 1963-78, *Research in Phenomenology,* 1979—, and *Tulane Studies in Philosophy,* 1970-80. Member of editorial board of "Continental Thought" series, University of Ohio Press, 1979—, and "Current Continental Research" series, University Press of America, 1980—.

WORK IN PROGRESS: A volume of essays; co-editing a volume of writings on the liberal arts; a novel: *Broken Images.*

SIDELIGHTS: New Republic contributor Marjorie Grene notes on Edward Goodwin Ballard's work *Man and Technology: Toward the Measurement of a Culture:* "Ballard's essay records the effort of an honest and serious thinker to wrestle systematically with a fundamental problem. It is short, clearly and soberly written, without frills, presenting a sustained inquiry that holds the reader's unflagging attention whether in assent or—as was often the case with this reviewer—in respectful disagreement. . . . *Man and Technology* is that rare entity, a philosophical page-turner. One can scarcely put it down."

Ballard once told *CA:* "I write for the satisfaction of expressing what I have to say as well as I can at the time (believing that such linguistic satisfactions are not the least which life has to offer), with the desire that what I have said may somehow be of use to someone, and with the wistful hope that I may add a slight bit to the collective effort to compensate for the ravages of time, forgetfulness, and human foolishness."

AVOCATIONAL INTERESTS: Gardening, boating, judo, travel.

BIOGRAPHICAL/CRITICAL SOURCES:

PERIODICALS

New Republic, October 14, 1978.

*   *   *

BALLIETT, Whitney 1926-

PERSONAL: Born April 17, 1926, in New York, N.Y.; son of Fargo and Dorothy (Lyon) Balliett; married Elizabeth Hurley King, July 21, 1951; married second wife, Nancy Kraemer, June 4, 1965; children: (first marriage) Julia Lyon, Elizabeth Erving, Will King; (second marriage) Whitney Lyon, Jr., James Fargo. *Education:* Attended Phillips Exeter Academy; Cornell University, B.A., 1951. *Politics:* Democrat.

ADDRESSES: Office—New Yorker, 25 West 43rd St., New York, N.Y. 10036. *Agent*—Harold Ober Associates, Inc., 40 East 49th St., New York, N.Y. 10017.

CAREER: New Yorker, New York, N.Y., collator, proofreader, then reporter, 1951-57, staff writer, 1957—, doing column on jazz, movie and drama reviews, occasional short essays, book reviews, profiles, and other reporting. Originator of Columbia Broadcasting System television show "Sound of Jazz," 1957; writer and broadcaster of two segments of National Educational Television series "Trio," 1962. *Military service:* U.S. Army Air Corps, 1946-47; became sergeant.

MEMBER: Delta Phi.

WRITINGS:

The Sound of Surprise: Forty-six Pieces on Jazz, Dutton, 1959.
Dinosaurs in the Morning: Forty-one Pieces on Jazz, Lippincott, 1962.
Such Sweet Thunder: Forty-nine Pieces on Jazz, Bobbs-Merrill, 1966.
Super-Drummer: A Profile of Buddy Rich, Bobbs-Merrill, 1968.
Ecstasy at the Onion: Thirty-one Pieces on Jazz, Bobbs-Merrill, 1971.
Alec Wilder and His Friends, Houghton, 1974.
New York Notes: A Journal of Jazz, 1972-74, Houghton, 1975.
Improvising: Sixteen Jazz Musicians and Their Art, Oxford University Press, 1977.
Night Creature: A Journal of Jazz, 1974-1980, Oxford University Press, 1981.
Jelly Roll, Jabbo, and Fats: Nineteen Portraits in Jazz, Oxford University Press, 1983.
American Musicians: Fifty-six Portraits in Jazz, Oxford University Press, 1986.
American Singers: Twenty-seven Portraits in Song, Oxford University Press, 1988.
Barney, Bradley, and Max: Fifteen Portraits in Jazz, Oxford University Press, 1989.

Contributor of articles and reviews to *Atlantic, New Republic, Reporter;* contributor of poetry to *Saturday Review, Atlantic,* and *New Yorker.*

SIDELIGHTS: "Whitney Balliett has covered jazz for the *New Yorker* since 1957; he has done so with taste, knowledge, consistency and splendid skill as a writer," claims Don Gold in the *New York Times Book Review.* Gold goes on to comment that "it is not easy to communicate what jazz sounds like to people who weren't there. Balliett masters it better than anyone else writing about jazz today." Considered informed about his subject and gifted in his presentation by most reviewers, Balliett writes both substantive studies of jazz artists and short, impressionistic articles likened to diary entries by several critics. According to Joseph McLellan in the *Washington Post,* "Balliett's job is to be entertaining as well as illuminative and not to take too long about it. . . . [He] does it superbly. . . . [His] musicology is largely impressionistic, descriptive, and focused on such points as the textures and rhythms of the sound, looseness or tightness of structures, and above all on what the music is saying." Echoing American critics' praise for Balliett's treatment of an American genre, Bill Luckin concludes in the *Times Literary Supplement* that "Balliett is among the most stylish and perceptive of living jazz writers."

American Musicians: Fifty-six Portraits in Jazz is a compilation of biographical profiles that Balliett had written for the *New Yorker* from the early 1960s to 1985. In the *New York Times Book Review,* John Litweiler remarks that "of Mr. Balliett's 11 previous books—mostly shorter collections—'American Musicians' makes at least three entire volumes plus hunks of several others obsolete. His biographical articles are his best, so this is his most valuable book." According to Litweiler, Balliett had interviewed all but fifteen of his subjects and "the quality of his portraits depends on his subjects and his patience. He says he generally chose his subjects because they were 'irresistible.' " In his *Washington Post Book World* assessment, David Nicholson likewise comments about the book's interview format: "When the musicians were alive to be interviewed, Balliett—for the most part—allowed them to speak for themselves. Thus we get a sense of each person, as well as insights into the personal connections between musicians and the evolving of musical eras and styles. . . . There are also telling (and sometimes amusing) details of the rigors of musicians' lives." With respect to overall style, Nicholson maintains that Balliett "writes with grace, style and insight. While reading, one wishes for a complete record collection so that one could listen to samples of each musician's work: Balliett is unmatched at describing how a particular musician sounds."

The chief flaw that critics detect in this work is Balliett's omission of many of the more contemporary artists in the field of jazz; "He leaves unexplored so many mansions in the house of jazz," states Nicholson. "Apart from anecdotes included in other essays, Dizzy Gillespie and Charlie Parker, the co-founders of bebop, go unacknowledged, as do Miles Davis and, more important, John Coltrane, for many *the* greatest jazz musician of all time." Francis Davis for the *Times Literary Supplement* detects this same flaw when he notes that Balliett presents studies of only two contemporary jazz artists under fifty years of age, which he feels is "in no way indicative of current directions within the genre." Nevertheless, Davis concludes that "the musicians on whom Balliett lavishes his attentions emerge as unique, and that, one suspects, is what has drawn him to them, regardless of their musical style. One is drawn to Whitney Balliett for much the same reason. Say what one will about his profiles, there is no mistaking them for the work of anyone else."

BIOGRAPHICAL/CRITICAL SOURCES:

PERIODICALS

American Scholar, spring, 1982.
Los Angeles Times, June 12, 1981.
Los Angeles Times Book Review, April 24, 1983.
New Republic, May 5, 1979.
New York Review of Books, February 12, 1987.

New York Times Book Review, September 12, 1976, April 1, 1979, July 19, 1981, December 21, 1986.
Time, March 19, 1979.
Times Literary Supplement, February 24, 1978, May 4, 1984, April 1-7, 1988.
Washington Post, June 4, 1981, July 19, 1983.
Washington Post Book World, December 21, 1986.

* * *

BARKAS, J. L.
See YAGER, Jan

* * *

BARKAS, Janet
See YAGER, Jan

* * *

BARLOW, Frank 1911-

PERSONAL: Born April 19, 1911, in Stoke-on-Trent, England; son of Percy Hawthorn (a schoolmaster) and Margaret Julia (Wilkinson) Barlow; married Moira Stella Brigid Garvey, July 1, 1936; children: John Francis, Michael Edward. *Education:* St. John's College, Oxford, B.A., 1933, M.A., D.Phil., 1937.

ADDRESSES: Home—Middle Court Hall, Kenton, Exeter, Devon, England.

CAREER: University of London, University College, London, England, assistant lecturer, 1936-40; University College of the South-West, Exeter, Devon, England, lecturer, 1946-49, reader, 1949-53; University of Exeter, Exeter, professor of history, 1953-76, emeritus professor, 1976—, dean of faculty of arts, 1955-59, deputy vice-chancellor, 1961-63, public orator, 1974-76. *Military service:* British Army, 1941-46; became major.

MEMBER: British Academy (fellow), Royal Society of Literature (fellow), Royal Historical Society (fellow; member of council, 1960-63).

AWARDS, HONORS: D.Litt., University of Exeter, 1981; commander, Order of the British Empire, 1989, for "services to the study of English medieval history."

WRITINGS:

(Editor) *The Letters of Arnulf of Lisieux,* Royal Historical Society, 1939.
(Editor) *Durham Annals and Documents of the Thirteenth Century,* Surtees Society, 1945.
Durham Jurisdictional Peculiars, Oxford University Press, 1950.
The Feudal Kingdom of England, 1042-1216, Longmans, Green, 1955, 4th edition, 1988.
(Editor, translator, and author of introduction and notes) *The Life of King Edward, Who Rests at Westminster,* Oxford University Press, 1962.
The English Church, 1000-1066: A Constitutional History, Shoe String, 1963, 2nd edition, Longman, 1979.
William I and the Norman Conquest, English Universities Press, 1965, Collier, 1967.
(With Dorothy Whitelock, David C. Douglas, and Charles H. Lemmon) *The Norman Conquest: Its Setting and Impact,* Eyre & Spottiswoode, 1966.
Edward the Confessor and the Norman Conquest, Historical Association, 1966.
(Editor) *Exeter and Its Region,* University of Exeter, 1969.

Edward the Confessor, University of California Press, 1970, 2nd edition, Eyre Methuen, 1979.
(With Martin Biddle, Olof von Feilitzen, and D. J. Keene) *Winchester in the Early Middle Ages: An Edition and Discussion of the Winton Domesday,* Oxford University Press, 1976.
The English Church, 1066-1154, Longman, 1979.
(Contributor) Timothy Reuter, editor, *The Greatest Englishman: Essays on St. Boniface and the Church at Creditor,* Paternoster Press, 1980.
The Norman Conquest and Beyond (selected papers), Hambledon Press, 1983.
William Rufus, Eyre Methuen, 1983.
Thomas Becket, Weidenfeld & Nicolson, 1986.

SIDELIGHTS: "Frank Barlow," declares Christopher Brooke in the *Times Literary Supplement,* "has long been one of the most distinguished exponents of new-style biography, and narrative history, among our senior medievalists." "His *Edward the Confessor* (1970) and *William Rufus* (1983)," Brooke continues, "are classics of biography in this sense: they are essentially detailed studies of political history, shot through with precise and intelligent summaries of the wider context of their heroes, from time to time lit up by vivid touches of insight and humour."

It is his ability to put his subjects in the context of their times that distinguishes Barlow's work from other biographies. Writing about *William Rufus* in the *Times Literary Supplement,* fellow medieval historian R. H. C. Davis asserts: "The truth is that Barlow's book is a great deal more than a Life. One of its delights is the way in which the narrative frequently becomes discursive, so that (for example) the chapter on William's 'Background and Youth' turns into a general discussion of the upbringing of noble and royal youths in this period."

Similarly, R. W. Southern, another medieval historian, writes in *History Today* about *Thomas Becket:* "It may be said at once that what [Professor Barlow] has produced is by far the best biography of Thomas Becket that we have, or are likely to have for a long time." "The questions whether Becket was an actor or a saint, whether his character or only his role changed when he became archbishop, fade into insignificance in the recognition of his greatness of mind in pursuing to the end whatever ideal it was that gripped him. . . . It must suffice," Southern concludes, "to congratulate the author on his brilliant success in filling a central gap in the literature on a great subject."

AVOCATIONAL INTERESTS: Gardening.

BIOGRAPHICAL/CRITICAL SOURCES:

PERIODICALS

Globe and Mail (Toronto), May 9, 1987.
History Today, December, 1986.
Times Literary Supplement, January 13, 1984, April 13, 1984, October 17, 1986.

* * *

BARNEY, Harry
See LOTTMAN, Eileen

* * *

BARONE, Mike
See ALBERT, Marvin H(ubert)

BARR, Pat(ricia Miriam) 1934-

PERSONAL: Born April 25, 1934, in Norwich, Norfolk, England; daughter of Spencer and Miriam Copping; married John Marshall Barr (a journalist), June 22, 1956 (deceased). *Education:* University of Birmingham, B.A. (with honors), 1956; University College, London, M.A. (with honors in English), 1964. *Politics:* Liberal. *Religion:* None.

ADDRESSES: Home—6 Mount Pleasant, Norwich, Norfolk NR2 20G, England. *Agent*—Carol Smith Literary Agency, 25 Hornton Ct., Kensington High St., London W8 7RT, England.

CAREER: Yokohama International School, Yokohama, Japan, teacher of English, 1959-61; teacher of English with University of Maryland Overseas Program in Japan, 1961-62; National Old People's Welfare Council, London, England, assistant secretary, 1965-66; full-time writer, 1966—.

AWARDS, HONORS: Winston Churchill fellowship, 1971, for nonfiction writing.

WRITINGS:

The Coming of the Barbarians: The Opening of Japan to the West, 1853-1870, Dutton, 1967.
The Deer Cry Pavilion: A Story of Westerners in Japan, 1868-1905, Macmillan, 1968.
A Curious Life for a Lady: The Story of Isabella Bird, a Remarkable Victorian Traveller, Doubleday, 1970.
To China with Love: The Lives and Times of Protestant Missionaries in China, 1860-1900, Doubleday, 1972.
The Memsahibs, Secker & Warburg, 1976.
Taming the Jungle, Secker & Warburg, 1977.
Framing the Female, Kestrel, 1978.
(With Ray Desmond) *Simla: A Hill Station in British India*, Scribner, 1978.
Japan, David & Charles, 1980.
Chinese Alice, Secker & Warburg, 1981.
Jade: A Novel of China, St. Martin's, 1982.
Kenjiro, Warner Books, 1985.
Coromandel, Hamish Hamilton, 1988.
Dust in the Balance, Hamish Hamilton, 1989.

Contributor to periodicals, including *Homes & Gardens, Times Educational Supplement*, and *Guardian*.

WORK IN PROGRESS: British Women in India 1905-45.

SIDELIGHTS: Many of Pat Barr's books are historical studies of Japan and China. After living in the Orient for several years, Barr combined her fascination with the culture and history of this area with her talent for writing historical nonfiction. As a result, "[Pat] Barr has won a place for herself as a writer who can present, in a style both popular and elegant, the fruits of accurate research," remarks a reviewer for the *Times Literary Supplement.*

In a review of *The Deer Cry Pavilion: A Story of Westerners in Japan, 1868-1905*, Kenneth Lamott states in *Book World* that "Barr's lively and informative account . . . is really quite an extraordinary story involving some extraordinary characters. . . . Barr is an accomplished writer, and her story, witty and graceful as it is, cuts deeply below the brilliant surface description of life in emerging Japan. [This] is an admirable book." A writer for *Times Literary Supplement* observes that in *The Coming of the Barbarians: The Opening of Japan to the West, 1853-1870*, Barr "makes no pretense to Japanese scholarship or to a novel interpretation of the facts. . . . Barr earns high marks for the attractive and intelligent presentation of her tale."

According to a writer for *Choice,* Barr's book *To China with Love* is "a lively description of the life styles and personalities of British Protestant missionaries in China during the pioneering decades before the Boxer holocaust of 1900." As a critic for the *Times Literary Supplement* notes, "Barr's judgment of these people is warmed by a sympathy that is clear-headed in its charity."

In 1982 Barr published her first novel, *Jade: A Novel of China.* Set in nineteenth-century China, *Jade* follows the life of the daughter of English missionary parents. Orville Schell states in the *Los Angeles Times Book Review* that "Barr has put her Chinese historical backdrop to good purpose. . . . One must say that Barr has used history effectively to illustrate not only the . . . nature of [her heroine's experiences], but of China's anguished efforts to preserve cultural balance at a time when foreign encroachment compelled it to borrow science and technology from abroad." Reid Beddow remarks in the *Washington Post Book World* that "at its best, *Jade* carries the reader along effortlessly. One certainly gets a sense of the sweep and variety of the old China. . . . Author Barr has woven what is evidently a lot of scholarly reading into her text."

In correspondence with *CA,* Barr explains how she happened to write her first novel: "After publishing several works of nonfiction I decided to try my hand at historical fiction. . . . I was encouraged in this by my agent, Carol Smith, and my publishers, Secker & Warburg, and I had a considerable amount of unused or half-used background material to draw upon. I've now had sufficient success with my first novel . . . to give me confidence, and I'm quite fascinated by the fictional challenge. The writing of a novel spills over into one's whole life, and the limitations are one's own instead of being imposed by the available material as with nonfiction. Consequently there's always the hope of further development, of doing a little better next time. I am lucky in that I now thoroughly 'relish my habitual pursuit' and am earning sufficient money from it at long last to give me time to find out how far I can go."

BIOGRAPHICAL/CRITICAL SOURCES:

PERIODICALS

Book World, June 1, 1969.
Choice, December, 1973.
Los Angeles Times Book Review, September 19, 1982.
Times Literary Supplement, September 28, 1967, February 6, 1969, January 5, 1974, October 30, 1981.
Washington Post Book World, September 17, 1982, September 4, 1983.

*   *   *

BARROW, Geoffrey W(allis) S(teuart) 1924-

PERSONAL: Born November 28, 1924, in Headingley, Leeds, England; son of Charles Embleton (an architect) and Marjorie (Steuart) Barrow; married Heather Elizabeth A. Lownie, July 6, 1951; children: Julia Steuart, Andrew Charles Steuart. *Education:* University of St. Andrews, M.A. (with honors), 1948; Pembroke College, Oxford, B.Litt., 1950. *Religion:* Christian.

ADDRESSES: Office—Department of Scottish History, William Robertson Building, George Square, University of Edinburgh, Edinburgh EH8 9JY, Scotland.

CAREER: University of London, University College, London, England, lecturer in history, 1950-61; University of Newcastle upon Tyne, Newcastle upon Tyne, England, professor of medieval history, 1961-74; University of St. Andrews, St. Andrews,

Scotland, professor of Scottish history, 1974-79; University of Edinburgh, Edinburgh, Scotland, Sir William Fraser Professor of Scottish History, 1979—. Ford's lecturer, Oxford University, 1977; Rhind lecturer, Society of Antiquaries of Scotland, 1985. Member, Royal Commission on Historical Manuscripts, 1984—. *Military service:* Royal Navy, 1943-46.

MEMBER: British Academy, Royal Historical Society, Scottish Historical Society (former chairman; president, 1972-75), Society of Antiquaries of Scotland, Royal Society of Edinburgh (fellow, 1977).

AWARDS, HONORS: Alexander Prize, Royal Historical Society, 1952, for essay; Joint Senior Hume Brown Prize, 1961, for *Acts of Malcolm IV, King of Scots, 1153-1165;* Agnes Mure MacKenzie Award, Saltire Society, 1965, for *Robert Bruce and the Community of the Realm of Scotland;* D.Litt., University of St. Andrews, 1971; Hon. D.Litt., University of Glasgow, 1988.

WRITINGS:

Feudal Britain: The Completion of the Medieval Kingdoms, 1066-1314, St. Martin's, 1956.
Acts of Malcolm IV, King of Scots, 1153-1165, University of Edinburgh Press, 1960.
Robert Bruce and the Community of the Realm of Scotland, University of California Press, 1965, 3rd edition, University of Edinburgh Press, 1988.
Acts of William I, King of Scots, 1165-1214, University of Edinburgh Press, 1971.
The Kingdom of the Scots: Government, Church and Society from the Eleventh to the Fourteenth Century, Edward Arnold, 1973.
(Editor) *The Scottish Tradition: Essays in Honour of R. G. Cant,* Scottish Academic Press, 1974.
The Anglo-Norman Era in Scottish History, Oxford University Press, 1980.
Kingship and Unity: Scotland, 1000-1306, Edward Arnold, 1981.
Robert the Bruce and the Scottish Identity, Saltire, 1984.

Contributor to historical journals, including *Scottish Historical Review, Northern History, Annales de Normandie,* and *The Stewarts.*

SIDELIGHTS: Geoffrey W. S. Barrow's "stature amongst British and indeed European medievalists," reports the *Times Literary Supplement,* "needs hardly to be stressed." For example, the significance of *Robert Bruce and the Community of the Realm of Scotland,* his biography of Robert Bruce, who reestablished an independent Scottish throne by defeating the English king Edward II at Bannockburn, "lies in his meticulously critical use of sources to show the conditions in which Scotland developed toward nationhood," declares C. V. Wedgwood in the *New York Times Book Review.* A reviewer for the *Times Literary Supplement* asserts, "Robert Bruce here stands authentically in the forefront of his own Scotland—a man who, for all his faults, may justly be described as of abiding importance—a great ruler of a small kingdom." "This authoritative book," Wedgwood concludes, "will long remain the standard work on Bruce and his time."

AVOCATIONAL INTERESTS: Hill walking; visiting old graveyards.

BIOGRAPHICAL/CRITICAL SOURCES:

PERIODICALS

New York Times Book Review, April 11, 1965.

Times Literary Supplement, February 11, 1965, November 30, 1973, November 20, 1981.

* * *

BASU, Romen 1923-

PERSONAL: Born October 1, 1923, in Calcutta, India; came to the United States in 1948; married wife, Rasil (a lawyer); children: Amrita, Rekha.

ADDRESSES: Home—345 East 69th St., New York, N.Y. 10021.

CAREER: Writer, 1968—; economist. Affiliated with the United Nations, 1948—, acted as deputy director of office of technical co-operation, Asia and Pacific branch, and on assignments in Egypt, Libya, and Thailand.

WRITINGS:

A House Full of People, Navana, 1968.
Canvas and the Brush (short stories), Firma K. L. Mikhupadhaya, 1970.
Your Life to Live, Firma K. L. Mikhupadhaya, 1972.
A Gift of Love, Writers Workshop (Calcutta), 1974.
The Tamarind Tree, Writers Workshop, 1976.
Candles and Roses, Sterling Publishers (New Delhi), 1977.
Portrait on the Roof, Sterling Publishers, 1980.
Rustling of Many Winds, Sterling Publishers, 1982.
Sands of Time, Facet Books International, 1985.
Outcast, Facet Books International, 1986.
Hours before Dawn, Facet Books International, 1988.
Wings at a Distance (poems), Facet Books International, 1988.

* * *

BATTIN, B(rinton) W(arner) 1941-
(Buck Battin, Warner Lee)

CAREER: Born November 15, 1941, in Ridgewood, N.J.; son of Harold Taylor (an engineer) and Dorothy (Warner) Battin; married Leslie Sue Curb, August 27, 1966 (divorced, 1974); married Sandra McCraw (a journalist), February 14, 1976. *Education:* University of New Mexico, B.A., 1969. *Religion:* None.

ADDRESSES: Home and office—711 North Mesa Rd., Belen, N.M. 87002. *Agent*—Dominick Abel Literary Agency, Inc., 146 West 82nd St., New York, N.Y. 10024.

CAREER: KOAT-TV, Albuquerque, N.M., reporter, 1969, 1971-75; KTBS-TV, Shreveport, La., assistant news director, 1975-76; KEVN-TV, Rapid City, S.D., news director, 1976; KDAL-TV, Duluth, Minn., news director, 1976-77; free-lance writer, 1977—. *Military service:* U.S. Coast Guard, in damage control, 1959-63.

AWARDS, HONORS: Awards from Albuquerque Press Club, 1973, for documentary "When the Dream Becomes a Nightmare" and feature story about an outlaw motorcycle gang, and 1974, for news story on housing contractor fraud.

WRITINGS:

NOVELS

Angel of the Night, Fawcett, 1983.
The Boogeyman, Fawcett, 1984.
Mary, Mary, Pocket Books, 1984.
Satan's Servant, Paper Jacks, 1984.
Programmed for Terror, Fawcett, 1985.
The Attraction, Fawcett, 1986.

The Creep, Fawcett, 1986.
Smithereens, Fawcett, 1987.
Demented, Fawcett, 1988.
(Under pseudonym Warner Lee) *Into the Pit,* Pocket Books, 1988.
(Under pseudonym Warner Lee) *It's Loose,* Pocket Books, in press.
Distorted Image, Berkley, in press.
The Murder Club, Berkley, in press.

WORK IN PROGRESS: A novel, *Nightsounds,* under pseudonym Warner Lee.

SIDELIGHTS: B. W. Battin told *CA:* "I gave up on television a few years ago, unable to contend with the backstabbing and the general rat race. My wife handed me a copy of a horror novel and, after reading it, I thought I could do as well. Since my wife was working and I wouldn't starve, I started writing. After I'd sold five novels, we decided to leave Minnesota, where we'd lived for eight years, and return to New Mexico to be near our families.

"I enjoy writing, the manipulation of words as well as trying to make my characters come to life. I take special care with the women I write about in my suspense stories. I like them to be self-sufficient, level-headed, and not the sort who go to pieces when terrible things begin to happen in their lives. They're not screamers like so many women in the movies. My women characters don't want for some man to come and rescue them; they take care of themselves—in ingenious ways, I hope. But if they happen to fall in love along the way, well, more power to them.

"Recently I began writing horror novels again—under the pseudonym Warner Lee. The first one was *Into the Pit,* a ghost story of a sort—in which the ghost is as absolutely mad in death as she was in life. Horror novels are fun because you can do anything, go anywhere you want, the only limitation being how creative your imagination is.

"Now I'm experimenting with combining horror and science fiction. That just adds another element to the traditional formula. Yes, it is a ghost you're seeing, but it's the time—ghost of someone who hasn't been born yet. That sort of thing. Science is responsible for some pretty scary notions, after all."

*   *   *

BATTIN, Buck
    See BATTIN, B(rinton) W(arner)

*   *   *

BEHRMAN, Jack N(ewton) 1922-

PERSONAL: Born March 5, 1922, in Waco, Tex.; son of Mayes and Marguerite (Newton) Behrman; married Louise Sims, September 6, 1945; children: Douglas, Gayle, Andrea. *Education:* Davidson College, B.S. (cum laude), 1943; University of North Carolina, M.A., 1945; Princeton University, M.A., 1950, Ph.D., 1952. *Politics:* Democratic. *Religion:* Presbyterian.

ADDRESSES: Home—1702 Audubon Rd., Chapel Hill, N.C. 27514. *Office*—Graduate School of Business Administration, University of North Carolina, Chapel Hill, N.C. 27599.

CAREER: International Labor Office, Montreal, Quebec, research assistant, 1945-46; Davidson College, Davidson, N.C., assistant professor of economics, 1946-48; Princeton University, Princeton, N.J., instructor, 1949-50, research assistant, 1950-52;

Washington and Lee University, Lexington, Va., associate professor of economics and political science, 1952-57; University of Delaware, Newark, professor of economics and business administration, 1957-61; U.S. Department of Commerce, Washington, D.C., deputy assistant secretary for international affairs, 1961, assistant secretary for international affairs, 1961-62, assistant secretary for domestic and international business, 1962-64; University of North Carolina at Chapel Hill, professor of international business, 1964-77, Drexel research professor, 1970-71, Luther Hodges Distinguished Professor, 1977—. Harvard Business School, visiting professor, 1967, chairman of M.B.A. program, 1971-77, associate dean of academic programs, 1983-87; lecturer at seminars and conferences. Director of businesses and financial institutions; member of numerous boards and panels on international economics and technology. Consultant to national and international organizations and private businesses, including Committee for Economic Development, National Planning Association, Pan American Union, United Nations, and U.S. Department of State.

MEMBER: Academy of International Business (fellow), Association for Education in International Business (secretary, 1959-60; president, 1966-68), Council on Foreign Relations, Regional Export Expansion Council (vice chairman, 1971-73), North Carolina World Trade Association (director), Sigma Phi Epsilon, Pi Gamma Mu, Alpha Phi Omega, Beta Gamma Sigma.

AWARDS, HONORS: LL.D., Davidson College, 1979.

WRITINGS:

(With Gardner Patterson) *Survey of United States International Finance,* Princeton University Press, 1951, annual editions, 1952, and (with John M. Gunn and others) 1953.
(With Wilson E. Schmidt) *International Economics,* Rinehart, 1957.
(With Raymond F. Mikesell) *Financing of Free-World Trade with the Sino-Soviet Bloc,* Princeton Studies in International Finance, 1958.
(Contributor) Mikesell, editor, *U.S. Private and Government Investment Abroad,* University of Oregon Press, 1962.
(With Roy Blough) *Regional Integration and the Trade of Latin America,* Committee for Economic Development, 1968.
(Contributor) Walter Krause and F. J. Mathis, editors, *International Economics and Business: Selected Readings,* Houghton, 1968.
Some Patterns in the Rise of the Multinational Enterprise (monograph), Graduate School of Business Administration, University of North Carolina, 1969.
National Interests and the Multinational Enterprise, Prentice-Hall, 1970.
U.S. International Business and Governments, McGraw, 1971.
The Role of International Companies in Latin American Integration: Autos and Petrochemicals, Committee for Economic Development, 1972.
(With J. J. Boddewyn and A. Kapoor) *International Business-Government Communications,* Lexington Books, 1975.
(Contributor) Susan S. Holland, editor, *Codes of Conduct for the Transfer of Technology,* Council of the Americas, 1976.
(With H. Wallender) *Transfer of Manufacturing Technology within Multinational Enterprises,* Ballinger, 1976.
Industry Ties with Science and Technology Policies in Developing Countries, Oelgeschlager, 1980.
(With Mikesell) *The Impact of U.S. Foreign Direct Investment on U.S. Export Competitiveness in Third World Markets,* University Press of America, 1980.

(With William A. Fischer) *Overseas Research and Development Activities of Transnational Companies,* Oelgeschlager, 1980.

(With Fischer) *Science and Technology for Development: Corporate and Government Policies and Practices,* Oelgeschlager, 1980.

(Contributor) Otto Hieronymi, editor, *The New Economic Nationalism,* Macmillan (London), 1980.

Tropical Diseases: Responses of Pharmaceutical Companies, American Enterprise Institute for Public Policy Research, 1980.

Discourses on Ethics and Business, Oelgeschlager, 1981.

(Editor with Robert E. Driscoll) *National Industrial Policies,* Oelgeschlager, 1984.

Industrial Policies: International Restructuring and Transnationals, Lexington Books, 1984.

The Rise of the Phoenix: The United States in a Restructured World Economy, Westview, 1987.

Essays on Ethics in Business and the Professions, Prentice-Hall, 1988.

Author of monographs for National Foreign Trade Council and Committee for Economic Development, and of research studies for Pan American Union and Economic Council of Canada. Contributor to *American People's Encyclopedia* and to professional journals and business magazines. Member of editorial board, *Journal of International Business Studies,* 1976-82.

WORK IN PROGRESS: Research on technology transfers and international research and development activities, on international industrial integration, and on foreign investment problems.

SIDELIGHTS: Jack N. Behrman has traveled widely in Latin America, Canada, Europe, and the Far East as a government delegate, consultant, speaker, and researcher.

*   *   *

BENDERLY, Beryl Lieff 1943-

PERSONAL: Born December 25, 1943, in Chicago, Ill.; daughter of Morris (a chemist) and Pearl (a sociologist; maiden name, Jacobs) Lieff; married Jordan Benderly (a government official), May 22, 1964; children: Daniel Ethan, Alicia Nadine. *Education:* Attended Universidad de los Andes, Bogota, Colombia, 1964; University of Pennsylvania, B.A., 1964, M.A., 1966; graduate study at Washington University, 1966.

ADDRESSES: Home—Washington, D.C. *Agent*—Virginia Barber Literary Agency, Inc., 353 West 21st St., New York, N.Y. 10011.

CAREER: Fisk University, Nashville, Tenn., instructor, 1966-67; University of Puerto Rico, Rio Piedras, instructor in sociology and anthropology, 1967-69; American University, Washington, D.C., research scientist and social-cultural specialist, 1969-76; free-lance writer, 1976—. Member of judging committee, MacDougal Creative Writing Prize, 1979-82.

MEMBER: National Book Critics Circle, American Society of Journalists and Authors (member of national board, 1985-87; chairperson of Washington, D.C., chapter, 1987—), National Association of Science Writers, Authors Guild, Authors League of America, Washington Independent Writers (member of board of directors, 1978-79, 1980-81; vice-president, 1979-80), Phi Beta Kappa.

AWARDS, HONORS: Woodrow Wilson fellowship, 1964; university fellowships from Washington University and University of Pennsylvania, both 1965; national finalist in White House Fellows competition, 1974; National Media Award, American Psychological Foundation, 1981, for article "The Great Ape Debate"; honorable mention in national features category, Odyssey Institute, 1981, for article "Dialogue of the Deaf"; Exceptional Achievement Award, Council for the Advancement and Support of Education, 1984; Gallaudet Journalism Prize, 1984; American Society of Journalists and Authors Book Award, 1989.

WRITINGS:

(With Richard F. Nyrop and others) *The Area Handbook,* 18 volumes, U.S. Government Printing Office, 1971-77.

(With Mary F. Gallagher and John Young) *Discovering Culture: An Introduction to Anthropology* (textbook), Van Nostrand, 1977.

Dancing without Music: Deafness in America, Anchor/Doubleday, 1980.

Thinking about Abortion, Dial/Doubleday, 1984.

High Schools and the Changing Workplace, National Academy of Science, 1984.

The Myth of Two Minds: What Gender Means and Doesn't Mean, Doubleday, 1987.

Also author of accompanying print material for Public Broadcasting Service series "The Hurt That Does Not Show," first broadcast by KOCE-TV, 1983, and of numerous news reports. Contributor of articles to magazines, including *Change, Ms., Health, Moment, Redbook, Self, Science, Smithsonian, Working Mother,* and *Woman's Day.* Contributor of book reviews to *Present Tense, The World and I, Washington Post Book World* and *Smithsonian.* Contributing editor, *Psychology Today.*

SIDELIGHTS: Beryl Lieff Benderly once told *CA:* "My writing centers on the social, or human, effects of the ideas we hold—on how what we think governs the way we act. I explore this theme mainly at the intersection of society and technology, where what is possible runs up against the way we would like the world to be." She later added that "this theme comes out particularly strongly in [*The Myth of Two Minds: What Gender Means and Doesn't Mean*], a critique of current thinking on gender differences." In a *Washington Post Book World* review of this book, critic Susan Dooley calls Benderly's work "a fascinating exploration of what science actually knows about the differences between men and women."

Similar praise was given to the author's earlier book about the deaf, *Dancing without Music: Deafness in America,* about which *Washington Post Book World* contributor Evelyn Wilde Mayerson notes: "[Benderly offers] both lay readers and interested professionals in the health sciences a comprehensive layout, as rich as an illustrated story board, of the deaf experience." Benderly once depicted her book to *CA* as "the first general trade book on this subject to appear in almost forty years. It describes the social, educational, and psychological situation of the deaf community and outlines the historic development that produced the world that today's deaf people inhabit. Communication mode largely determines a deaf child's social future. I examine the various communications options available to deaf people in terms of their social and human outcomes."

More recently, Benderly addresses the delicate subject of abortion in *Thinking about Abortion.* Fitzhugh Mullan comments in *Washington Post Book World* that "Benderly deals straightforwardly with the subject" of abortion in her book. "Her text is thoughtful, informative and, ultimately, pro-choice," Mullan concludes. "She dutifully reviews the theological and polemical arguments against abortion as well as those made in its favor."

BIOGRAPHICAL/CRITICAL SOURCES:

PERIODICALS

Smithsonian, November, 1980.
Teaching English to the Deaf, fall, 1981.
Washington Post Book World, October 5, 1980, August 25, 1984, November 13, 1987.

*   *   *

BENFIELD, Derek 1926-

PERSONAL: Born March 11, 1926, in Bradford, Yorkshire, England; son of William Thomas (a journalist) and Pansy (Raymond) Benfield; married Susan Lyall Grant (an actress), July 17, 1953; children: Kate, Jamie. *Education:* Attended Royal Academy of Dramatic Art, 1947-49. *Religion:* Church of England.

ADDRESSES: Home—4 Berkeley Rd., Barnes, London SW13 9LZ, England.

CAREER: Playwright and actor. Began professional acting career in English repertory theaters; first played in London in "The Young Elizabeth"; starred in British Broadcasting Corp. series "The Brothers"; has worked extensively in theater, films, and television. *Military service:* British Army, Infantry, 1943-46; Forces Broadcasting Service, 1947.

MEMBER: League of Dramatists, British Actors' Equity.

WRITINGS:

PLAYS

The Young in Heart, H. F. W. Deane, 1953.
Champagne for Breakfast, H. F. W. Deane, 1954.
The Way the Wind Blows, H. F. W. Deane, 1954.
Wild Goose Chase (farce), Samuel French, 1954, acting edition, 1983.
Running Riot (farce), Samuel French, 1958.
Out of Thin Air (comedy), H. F. W. Deane, 1961.
Fish Out of Water (comedy), acting edition, Samuel French, 1963, revised edition, 1986.
Down to Brass Tacks (comedy), H. F. W. Deane, 1964.
Third Party Risk (one-act), Samuel French, 1964.
The Party (one-act), Samuel French, 1964.
Post Horn Gallop (sequel to *Wild Goose Chase*), Samuel French, 1965, acting edition, 1982.
Murder for the Asking (thriller), Samuel French, 1967.
Off the Hook (farce), Samuel French, 1969.
A Bird in the Hand (comedy), Samuel French, 1973.
Panic Stations (farce), acting edition, Samuel French, 1975.
Caught on the Hop (comedy), acting edition, Samuel French, 1976.
Beyond a Joke (comedy), acting edition, Samuel French, 1980.
In for the Kill (thriller), acting edition, Samuel French, 1981.
Touch and Go (comedy; produced in Germany, Austria, and Switzerland as "Love-Jogging," 1983-88), acting edition, Samuel French, 1984.
Look Who's Talking (comedy), acting edition, Samuel French, 1984.
Flying Feathers: A Farce, acting edition, Samuel French, 1987.
"Bedside Manners," first produced in German translation as "Zwei Links—Zwei Rechts," in Bonn, West Germany, 1987.

WORK IN PROGRESS: "Mixed Company," for Samuel French.

SIDELIGHTS: Derek Benfield once told *CA:* "My family are delighted with my success as a playwright as it helps to prop up my tottering career as an actor." The playwright's works have been performed in many parts of the world, in English and in translation. Benfield later told *CA* that "Touch and Go," "was a runaway success in Germany, Austria and Switzerland. It has also been produced in Holland and Belgium, and is due to open in Denmark in the 1988/89 season." He added that "Bedside Manners" "looks like repeating the success of 'Touch and Go' with productions in 1988 in Hannover, Aachen, Berlin and Vienna."

*   *   *

BERENDT, Joachim Ernst 1922-

PERSONAL: Born July 20, 1922, in Berlin, Germany; son of Ernst (a minister) and Maria (Hammerschmidt) Berendt; children: Christian.

ADDRESSES: Home—Auf der Alm 11, D-7570 Baden-Baden 22, West Germany. *Office*—Sudwestfunk, Baden-Baden, West Germany.

CAREER: Sudwestfunk (southwestern German radio and television network), Baden-Baden, West Germany, co-founder and broadcaster, 1945—; ARD (German TV), Baden-Baden, host and writer of "Jazz—Heard and Seen" series, 1954-72. Producer of over 250 jazz albums, including "Jazz Meets the World" series, 1969—; lecturer. Founder, American Folk Blues Festival, 1962, and Berlin Jazz Days, 1964; director, Olympic Games Jazz Festival, Munich, 1972. *Military service:* German Army; served in a Panzer Division in World War II.

AWARDS, HONORS: Preis der Deutschen Fernsehkritik, 1957, for best musical television production of the year; Deutsch Bundesfilmpreis in Gold, 1962, for best film music of the year; Polish Cultural Award, 1978.

WRITINGS:

Der Jazz, Deutsche Verlagsanstalt (Stuttgart), 1950.
Das Jazzbuch, S. Fischer Verlag, 1953.
Jazz Optisch, Nymphenburger Verlagshandlung, 1956.
Variationen uber Jazz, Nymphenburger Verlagshandlung, 1957.
Blues, Nymphenburger Verlagshandlung, 1957.
Prisma der Gegenwartigen Musik, Furche, 1959.
Das Neue Jazzbuch: Entwicklung und Bedeutung der Jazzmusik, S. Fischer Verlag, 1959, translation by Dan Morganstern published as *The New Jazz Book: A History and Guide,* Hill & Wang, 1962.
(With Ed van der Elsken) *Foto-Jazz,* Nymphenburger Verlagshandlung, 1959.
Jazzlife, Burda Druck und Verlag, 1961.
Blues, English-Deutsch, Nymphenburger Verlagshandlung, 1962.
Blues, Gerig, 1970.
Das Jazzbuch: von Rag bis Rock, Fischer-Taschenbuch Verlag, 1975.
Ein Fenster aus Jazz, S. Fischer Verlag, 1977.
Photo Story des Jazz, Krueger Verlag, 1980, translation published as *Jazz: A Photo History,* Macmillan, 1981.
Mein Lesebuch, S. Fischer Verlag, 1981.
Das Grobe Jazzbuch, Fischer-Taschenbuch Verlag, 1982, translation published as *The Jazz Book: From Ragtime to Fusion and Beyond,* Lawrence Hill & Co., 1982.
Nada Brahma: Die Welt ist Klang, Rororo, 1985, translation published as *Nada Brahma: The World Is Sound,* Destiny Books, 1987.

Das Dritte Ohr: Vom Hoeren der Welt, Rororo, 1988, translation published as *The Third Ear: On Listening to the World* (with foreword by Yehudi Menuhin), Great Tradition, 1988.

SIDELIGHTS: *CA* asked Joachim Ernst Berendt what relationships he sees between European and American jazz. He responded: "There is a strong influence of folk blues and archaic blues on today's scene. Contemporary jazz forms like soul and funk are unthinkable without the jazz tradition. Jazz as a whole is unthinkable without its tradition—not only in blues, but also in spirituals and gospel, and, of course, all the way back to West Africa (especially Yoruba and Dahomey cultures). The central figures of jazz are Louis Armstrong, Duke Ellington, Charlie Parker, John Coltrane, Miles Davis, Cecil Taylor, and Ornette Coleman.

"Jazz in Europe is considered much more as an art form than in America (where it is still part of the huge entertainment industry). European jazz from the twenties to the early sixties was not much more than an imitation of American jazz. But during the sixties, there was an emancipation process, and now, there are musicians in Europe who play their own kind of jazz, without looking much to America. For instance: German trombone player Albert Mangelsdorff, British saxophonist John Surman, Polish violinist Zbiggniew Seifert, etc. These musicians are using part of their own European tradition—in a way similar to American musicians using their tradition."

Berendt first became interested in jazz in 1935 when he was thirteen years old. "I was quite a radio fan," he told Hollie I. West in a *Washington Post* interview. "I got hooked listening to Benny Carter playing with the Ramblers." As jazz fell into disrepute in Nazi Germany, gradually the government stifled the music. Berendt was drafted into the German Army and sent to the Russian front, where he was injured and subsequently returned to Germany. Berendt then made his way into Allied territory near the end of the war. Following the war, he resumed his musical activities and interests, helping to found the Sudwestfunk radio and television network as well as broadcasting his popular "Jazz—Heard and Seen" TV series.

The author has visited the United States about thirty times, including 1976 when he joined in a Bicentennial conference sponsored by the Smithsonian Institution which featured international scholars discussing U.S. contributions to the world. Berendt explained his views to West: "Several of us said jazz was the most important American contribution. . . . Not film, comic strips, the atom bomb, politics. Many American scholars took issue with us. Americans have a very special relationship to jazz. In one sense, they know it. But they take it for granted. In Europe it's so much of an art form that it's special. It's a music of freedom and tolerance."

Berendt adds: "My newer books are about the art and the mystery of the human ear and of listening. We live in a very visual culture. 18% of our perception goes through our eyes. So the balance of our perception is destroyed. In most other great traditions and cultures, not the eye but the ear is the most important and holy of the human organs. Every student of physiology knows 'the eye estimates, but the ear measures.' In the crises of our time we cannot afford any longer to use only a fraction of our perception possibilities. We have to regain the possibilities of our ear and of listening. The eye leads us into the world, but the ear leads the world into us. The eye is the organ of aggression; the ear is female and receptive. Every hour of watching TV feeds and programs our aggressivity. Every hour of listening feeds and programs our receptivity and sensibility. Not by accident, the most common reproach in modern relations is, 'You

don't ever listen to me!' We can change the world in better listening to our human brothers and sisters—and to our own heart and soul!"

BIOGRAPHICAL/CRITICAL SOURCES:

PERIODICALS

Washington Post, February 5, 1980.

*   *   *

BERGER, Bruce 1938-

PERSONAL: Born August 21, 1938, in Evanston, Ill.; son of Robert O. (an accountant) and Nancy (a commercial artist; maiden name, Lander) Berger. *Education:* Yale University, B.A., 1961; graduate study at University of California, Berkeley, 1961.

ADDRESSES: Home—P.O. Box 482, Aspen, Colo. 81611.

CAREER: Writer, 1961—. Professional pianist in Spain, 1965-67, and Aspen, Colo., 1968-74; Aspen Recycling Center, Aspen, operator, 1976-78. Member of advisory board, Southern Utah Wilderness Alliance.

MEMBER: Sierra Club (life member), Friends of the Earth, Wilderness Society, Nature Conservancy.

AWARDS, HONORS: Ralph Kreiser Nonfiction Award, *Amelia* magazine, 1986, for "The Mysterious Brotherhood"; co-recipient, *Sierra* Nature Writing Contest award, 1988, for "Among My Souvenirs"; Nathan Haskell Dole Award, *Lyric* magazine, for poem "Moon and Back."

WRITINGS:

There Was a River (nonfiction), Northland Press, 1979.
Hangin' On (nonfiction), Northland Press, 1980.
Notes of a Half-Aspenite, edited by Susan Michael, Ashley & Associates, 1987.
The Telling Distance: Conversations with the American Desert (essay collection), Breitenbush, 1989.
A Dazzle of Hummingbirds, Blake Publishing, 1989.

Work represented in anthologies, including *Aspen Anthology.* Contributor of articles and poems to magazines and newspapers, including *Americana, Poetry, Yale Review, Westways, Commonweal, Western Humanities Review, Rocky Mountain, Barron's, Negative Capability, New York Times,* and *Carolina Quarterly.*

WORK IN PROGRESS: Two poetry collections, *Facing the Music* and *Bedrock; Connoisseur of Thirst,* a collection of desert fables.

SIDELIGHTS: Bruce Berger once told *CA:* "In my essays I try to explore the impact of the Southwestern desert landscape on human psychology and the arts. Recent poetry is less about place, more about changes in people that I am increasingly aware of. I am very tired of the flat, conversational tone of contemporary poetry, and I would like to see the medium reclaim the compression that is forced upon it by formal elements."

*   *   *

BERKOWITZ, Marvin 1938-

PERSONAL: Born October 8, 1938, in Perth Amboy, N.J.; son of Harry and Ruth (Rosenberg) Berkowitz; children: Nathalia, Melisanda, Gregor, Ameena. *Education:* Rutgers·University, B.S., B.A., 1961; University of East Africa, diploma in education, 1962; Columbia University, M.S., 1966, Ph.D., 1973; Fordham University, M.S.W., 1989.

ADDRESSES: Home—780 West End Ave., New York, N.Y. 10025. *Office*—Fordham Tremont Community Mental Health Center, 2250 Ryer Ave., Bronx, N.Y. 10458.

CAREER: New York City Planning Commission, New York City, principal quantitative analyst, 1968-71; Hofstra University, Hempstead, N.Y., assistant professor of management, 1968-71; New York University, Graduate School of Public Administration, New York City, adjunct professor, 1970-72; New York City Police, New York City, special assistant to police commissioner, 1971-75; American Foundation for the Blind, New York City, associate director, 1975-80; Cy Charkin Research Group, Danbury, Conn., director of research, 1981-86; Fairfield University, Fairfield, Conn., associate professor of management, 1981-88; Fifth Avenue Center for Counseling and Psychotherapy, New York City, psychotherapist, 1987-88; Fordham Tremont Community Mental Health Center, Bronx, N.Y., clinician, 1988-89.

WRITINGS:

The Conversion of Military-Oriented Research and Development to Civilian Uses, Praeger, 1970.
The Social Costs of Human Underdevelopment, Praeger, 1974.
Reading with Print Limitations, Volumes 1-5, American Foundation for the Blind, 1979.

Contributor to numerous books and to various journals.

WORK IN PROGRESS: Empirical studies on public administration, social services, and mental health.

*   *   *

BERNARDO, Stephanie
See JOHNS, Stephanie Bernardo

*   *   *

BERNIER, Olivier 1941-

PERSONAL: Born August 12, 1941, in Hartford, Conn.; son of Georges and Jessie (Bernheim) Bernier; divorced. *Education:* Lycee Henri IV, Paris, France, baccalaureate, 1958; Harvard University, B.A., 1962; New York University, M.A., 1966.

ADDRESSES: Home and office—157 East 72nd St., New York, N.Y. 10021. *Agent*—Paul R. Reynolds & Co., 12 East 41st St., New York, N.Y. 10017.

CAREER: Martha Jackson Gallery, New York City, director of exhibitions, 1966-68; private art dealer in New York City, 1968-78; writer, 1978—.

WRITINGS:

Pleasure and Privilege: Life in France, Naples, and America, 1770-1790, foreword by Louis Auchincloss, Doubleday, 1981.
Art and Craft (novel), Seaview, 1981.
The Eighteenth-Century Woman, Doubleday, 1982.
Lafayette, Hero of Two Worlds, Dutton, 1983.
Louis the Beloved: The Life of Louis XV, Doubleday, 1984.
Venice II, photographs by Fulvio Roiter, Rizzoli International, 1985.
(Editor and translator) *Secrets of Marie Antoinette: A Collection of Letters,* Doubleday, 1985.
Louis XIV: A Royal Life, Doubleday, 1987.
Words of Fire, Deeds of Blood, Little, Brown, 1989.

Contributor of articles to periodicals, including *House and Garden, Vogue, Town and Country,* and *New York Times.*

WORK IN PROGRESS: Liberty, Equality, Fraternity: A History of the French Revolution, for Little, Brown.

SIDELIGHTS: "In a history filled with detail and rich in nuance Olivier Bernier presents a delightful picture of life in the civilized western world of the late eighteenth century," observes Dennis Linehan of *Best Sellers* in his review of *Pleasure and Privilege: Life in France, Naples, and America, 1770-1790.* A social history of pre-revolutionary France, the book describes life in the country's major cities, such as Paris and Versailles, and discusses the tourist centers in Naples, Italy and the New World from a French perspective. Bernier, an American born of French parents, writes on a variety of topics, including food, fashion, art, literature, and medicine, illustrating the pageantry as well as the poverty of the era. As the *New York Times*'s Anatole Broyard notes: "Just as French nobility found it refreshing to read about America and its homey differences, so Americans in their unadorned affluence ought to find it entertaining and instructive to look through the other end of the opera glasses." The critic concludes that "for a learned and witty excursion through savoir vivre, one could hardly ask for a better companion than Mr. Bernier."

Bernier has also written biographies of two French kings of the eighteenth century, Louis XIV and Louis XV, as well as the famed French hero of the American Revolution, the Marquis de Lafayette. While Lafayette's exploits in the war are familiar to many Americans, his life afterwards remains obscured. In detailing Lafayette's later years, "Bernier gives us the remarkable answer in a well-written biography, *Lafayette: Hero of Two Worlds,*" states *Washington Post Book World* contributor James T. Yenkel. As Donald Morrison remarks in *Time,* while the Marquis's service to America helped establish good relations between the two countries, "[as Bernier] points out in this stirring biography, the French did not always have special affection for Lafayette," who never fulfilled his early promise as a political leader.

Bernier also illuminates the human character of famous individuals in his other biographies; *Louis the Beloved: The Life of Louis XV,* for example, is "a graceful, entertaining portrait of France's penultimate monarch before the Revolution," comments Wendy Smith in the *New York Times Book Review.* Bernier "paints an appealing picture of Louis XV as a human being—affectionate, loyal, considerate and kind, a far cry from the dissolute roue of legend." *Quill & Quire* writer Paul Stuewe likewise calls *Louis the Beloved* "a fascinating panorama," although he believes Bernier tries too hard to counter the traditionally negative assessment of the king's reign. Nevertheless, the critic admits that the study is "a lucid and well-organized presentation of a surprisingly interesting story." Similarly, according to *New York Times Book Review* contributor A. S. Byatt, *Louis XIV: A Royal Life* "deals excellently with both man and icon, shrewd politician and semi-divine Sun King." Byatt concludes that Bernier "has the advantage of liking and admiring his subject, unlike some modern iconoclastic biographers, but he is neither rhapsodic nor overintimate. . . . His account of Louis's deliberate construction of [his] artificial world . . . is wholly fascinating."

Bernier told *CA:* "I am interested in literature, history, and travel. I speak French and Italian and am familiar with Europe and North Africa. I am also willing and able to give lectures on a variety of subjects."

BIOGRAPHICAL/CRITICAL SOURCES:

PERIODICALS

Best Sellers, June, 1981.
Los Angeles Times, November 25, 1983.
New York Times, April 11, 1981.
New York Times Book Review, June 7, 1981, January 20, 1985, January 31, 1988.
Quill & Quire, July, 1981, December, 1984.
Time, January 2, 1984.
Times Literary Supplement, February 22, 1985.
Washington Post Book World, November 13, 1983.

*　　*　　*

BERTRAND, Alvin L(ee) 1918-

PERSONAL: Born July 6, 1918, in Elton, La.; son of Jacob William and Ludy (Treme) Bertrand; married Mary Nic Ellis, August 29, 1941; children: William Ellis, Mary Lynne. *Education:* Louisiana State University, B.S., 1940, Ph.D., 1948; University of Kentucky, M.S., 1941. *Politics:* Democrat. *Religion:* Baptist.

ADDRESSES: Home—1046 West Lakeview Dr., Baton Rouge, La. 70810.

CAREER: Louisiana State University, Baton Rouge, assistant professor, 1948-51, associate professor, 1951-55, professor of sociology and rural sociology, 1955-74, Boyd Professor, 1974-78, Boyd Professor Emeritus, 1978—. Visiting professor and University International Chair, Virginia Polytechnic Institute and State University, 1978-79; adjunct professor of sociology, Tulane University, 1979-80. Founder, president, Socio-Technological Consultants, Inc., 1980—. U.S. Department of Agriculture, section head in Economics Division, Agricultural Marketing Service, 1957-58, consultant to Farm Population and Rural Life Branch, 1958-62. Member of board of directors, Association of Southern Agricultural Workers, 1959-60; chairman of International Committee for Cooperation in Rural Sociology, 1968-72; member of national advisory committee, National Park Service, 1970-74; member of scientific and statistical committee, Gulf of Mexico Fisheries Council, 1977-79; leader of integrated community development project in Haiti, Agency for International Development, 1978. *Military service:* U.S. Army Air Forces, 1942-46; became lieutenant.

MEMBER: International Rural Sociological Association, American Sociological Association (fellow), Rural Sociological Society (member of executive committee, 1959-60; president, 1967-68), Population Association of America, American Country Life Association, American Association of University Professors, National Parks and Conservation Association, European Congress for Rural Sociology, Asociacion Latino-Americana de Sociologia Rural, Southern Sociological Society (secretary-treasurer, 1955-57; vice-president, 1960-61; president, 1962-63), Southern Association of Agricultural Scientists, Southwestern Sociological Society (secretary-treasurer, 1954-55; vice-president, 1960-61; president, 1961-62), Southwestern Social Science Association, Mid-South Sociological Association (president, 1977-78), Community Development Society, Louisiana Academy of Sciences, Louisiana Historical Association, Phi Kappa Phi, Alpha Kappa Delta, Alpha Zeta, Gamma Sigma Delta, Alpha Sigma Lambda, Alpha Gamma Rho, Alpha Delta.

AWARDS, HONORS: Distinguished service award, Rural Sociological Society; distinguished service award for rural sociology, Sociological Association of Agricultural Scientists; merit teaching and research award, Gamma Sigma Delta.

WRITINGS:

Social Life in the United States: An Introductory Volume for Foreign Students, Division of Latin American Relations, Louisiana State University, 1953, revised edition, 1958.
(Editor and senior author) *Rural Sociology: An Analysis of Contemporary Rural Life,* McGraw, 1958.
(With Lee M. Brooks) *History of the Southern Sociological Society,* University of Alabama Press, 1962.
(Editor with Floyd L. Corty) *Rural Land Tenure in the United States: A Socioeconomic Approach to Problems, Programs and Trends,* Louisiana State University Press, 1962.
Basic Sociology, Appleton, 1967, 2nd edition, 1973.
(Compiler) Frederick L. Bates, *Collected Works of Frederick L. Bates on the Theory of Social Structure,* Louisiana State University, 1969.
(With Zbigniew T. Wierzbicki) *Socjologia wsi w Stanach Zjednoczonych* (title means "Development and Trends in American Rural Sociology"), Ossolineum (Warsaw), 1970.
Social Organization: A General Systems and Role Theory Perspective, F. A. Davis, 1972.

CONTRIBUTOR

Thomas Hansbrough, editor, *Southern Forests and Southern People,* Louisiana State University Press, 1963.
James Copp, editor, *Projection Papers: Orientations for Rural Sociological Research and Action,* Rural Sociological Society, 1964.
Daniel E. Alleger, editor, *Social Change and Aging in the Twentieth Century,* University of Florida Press, 1964.
Corty, editor, *Local Government Problems in Urbanizing Rural Areas,* Southern Land Economics and Agribusiness, Louisiana State University, 1964.
Thomas D. Horn, editor, *Reading for the Disadvantaged,* Harcourt, 1970.
Carle C. Zimmerman and Richard E. Duwors, editors, *Sociology of Underdevelopment,* Copp, 1970.

OTHER

Author or co-author of about fifty bulletins and monographs published by Louisiana Agricultural Experiment Station, Southwest Educational Development Laboratory, U.S. Department of Agriculture, and others. Contributor to *American Peoples Encyclopedia,* and *American Educator Encyclopedia;* contributor of over 100 articles to professional journals. Chairman of publication committee, Rural Sociological Society, 1962-64.

SIDELIGHTS: Alvin L. Bertrand once told *CA:* "As I contemplate my career I can always detect a fierce determination to help improve the lot of rural people in the U.S. and elsewhere. Having been brought up on a small struggling family farm I became aware of the discrepancy in the opportunity structure faced by young persons (and old) in such circumstances. This, no doubt, accounts for my attraction to rural sociology. I feel greatly appreciative for the opportunity I have had to study and chronicle the changing rural scene in the U.S. over the past . . . years, and especially in the South where I have more clearly understood the impact of 'sudden' technology and an emerging mass society."

Several of Bertrand's works have been translated in other countries; he more recently told *CA* that his research has "been used as a basis for the formulation of program or policy decisions at local, state, national, and international levels." The author also added that his theories and analytical concepts in sociology, "such as the stress-strain element in social systems, the social process of confrontation, and the use of the structural dimensions of roles for delineating types of social organization, have

been widely accepted and used in the development of conceptual frameworks for major research projects."

*   *   *

BEURDELEY, Michel 1911-

PERSONAL: Born January 17, 1911, in Paris, France; son of Jean (a mayor) and Marcelle (Elluin) Beurdeley; married Cecile Cyprien-Fabre (a writer on art), March 10, 1941; children: Gladys (Mrs. Hubert Cyprien-Fabre), Jean-Michel. *Education:* Lycee Janson-de-Sailly a Paris, diploma, 1929.

CAREER: Expert in Oriental art, 1947—; official expert for court of appeals, arbitrator for commercial court, and appraiser for estate administration. Former president of Chambre Syndicale des Experts.

WRITINGS:

Porcelaine de la compagnie des Indes, Office du Livre (Fribourg, Switzerland), 1962, translation by Diana Imber published as *Chinese Trade Porcelain,* Tuttle, 1962, 2nd edition, 1963 (published in England as *Porcelain of the East India Companies,* Barrie & Rockliff, 1962).

L'Amateur chinois des Han au vingtieme siecle, Office du Livre, 1966, translation by Imber published as *The Chinese Collector through the Centuries: From the Han to the Twentieth Century,* Tuttle, 1966.

(With others) *Jeux des nuages et de la pluie,* Bibliotheque des Arts, 1969, translation by Imber published as *Chinese Erotic Art,* Tuttle, 1969 (published in England as *The Clouds and the Rain: The Art of Love in China,* Hammond, 1969).

(With wife, Cecile Beurdeley) *Castiglione, peintre jesuite a la cour de Chine,* Biblioteque des Arts, 1971, translation by Michael Bullock published as *Giuseppe Castiglione: A Jesuit Painter at the Court of the Chinese Emperors,* Tuttle, 1972.

Chant de l'Oreiller, Bibliotheque des Arts, 1972.

(With C. Beurdeley) *Guide de la ceramique chinoise,* Office du Livre, 1974, translation by Kathleen Watson published as *A Connoisseur's Guide to Chinese Ceramics,* Harper, 1974 (published in England as *Chinese Ceramics,* Thames & Hudson, 1974).

(With Jean Boisselier) *The Heritage of Thai Sculpture,* John Weatherhill, 1975.

(With C. Beurdeley) *Le Mobilier chinois: Le guide du connaisseur,* Office du Livre, 1979, translation by Watson published as *Chinese Furniture,* Kodansha International/ Harper, 1979.

(Collaborator) *The Edward T. Chow Collection,* Part One: *Catalogue of Ming and Qing Porcelain,* Part Two: *Catalogue of Early Chinese Ceramics and Ancient Bronzes,* Southeby Park Bernet, 1980.

La France a l'encan, 1789-1799: Exode des objets d'art sous la Revolution, Office du Livre, 1981.

L'eunuque aux trois joyaux: Collectionneurs et esthetes chinois, Office du Livre, 1984.

(With Guy Raindre) *Qing Porcelain: Famille Rose, Famille Verte, 1644-1912,* Rizzoli International, 1987.

Also author, with others, of *Erotic Art of Japan: The Pillow Poem,* Leon Amiel.*

*   *   *

BIEBUYCK, Daniel P. 1925-

PERSONAL: Born October 1, 1925, in Deinze, Belgium; son of Marcel G. and Bertha (Van Laere) Biebuyck; married Laure-Marie de Rycke, November 21, 1950; children: Brunhilde, Anne-Marie, Edwin, Hans, Jean-Christophe, Jean-Marie, Beatrice. *Education:* University of Ghent, B.A. (classics), 1946, B.A. (law), 1947, Licencie es Philosophie et Lettres, 1948, Ph.D., 1954; University of London, graduate study, 1948-49.

ADDRESSES: Home—271 West Main St., Newark, Del. 19711. *Office*—Department of Anthropology, University of Delaware, Newark, Del. 19716.

CAREER: Institut pour la Recherche Scientifique en Afrique Centrale, Kinshasa, Belgian Congo (now Zaire Republic), research fellow, 1949-57; Lovanium University of Kinshasa (now Universite Nationale du Zaire), Kinshasa, Zaire Republic, 1957-61, began as associate professor, became professor; University of Delaware, Newark, visiting professor, 1961-64; University of California, Los Angeles, professor of anthropology and curator of African collection, 1964-66; University of Delaware, H. Rodney Sharp Professor of Anthropology, 1966-74, H. Rodney Sharp Professor of Anthropology and Humanities, 1974—, chairman of anthropology department, 1969-72 and 1974-75, interim director of black studies program. Visiting lecturer in anthropology, University of Liege, 1956-58; visiting professor of anthropology, University of London, 1960; visiting lecturer in anthropology and art history, Yale University, 1970-71 and 1976-77; adjunct professor of anthropology, New York University, 1971-72. Conducted field work on expeditions throughout Zaire, 1949-61, with intensive research among the Zoba, Bembe, Lega, and Nyanga. *Military service:* Belgian Army, 1954-56; became sergeant.

MEMBER: Academie Royale des Sciences d'Outre-Mer (Brussels), Institut des Civilisations Differentes (Brussels), Phi Beta Kappa, Phi Kappa Phi.

AWARDS, HONORS: Annual prize, Academie Royale des Sciences d'Outre-Mer, 1956, for *De Hond bij de Nyanga: Rituel en sociologie;* grants from numerous institutions, including African Studies Center of University of California, Los Angeles, 1965-67, Social Science Council, 1967-68, University of Delaware, 1968 and 1969-70, and National Endowment for the Humanities, 1971-74 and 1985-87; Rockefeller Foundation fellowship, 1979-80; Guggenheim Memorial fellowship, 1980-81.

WRITINGS:

De Hond bij de Nyanga: Rituel en sociologie, Academie Royale des Sciences d'Outre-Mer (Brussels), 1956.

(With M. Douglas) *Congo Tribes and Parties,* Royal Anthropological Institute (London), 1961.

Les Mitamba: Systeme de mariages enchaines chez les Babembe, Academie Royale des Sciences d'Outre-Mer, 1962.

(Editor) *African Agrarian Systems,* Oxford University Press, 1963.

Rights in Land and Its Resources among the Nyanga, Academie Royale des Sciences d'Outre-Mer, 1966.

(Editor and translator with Kahombo C. Mateene) *The Mwindo Epic from the Banyanga,* University of California Press, 1969.

(Editor) *Tradition and Creativity in Tribal Art,* University of California Press, 1969.

(With Mateene) *Anthologie de la litterature orale Nyanga,* Academie Royale des Sciences d'Outre-Mer, 1970.

Lega Culture: Art, Initiation, and Moral Philosophy among a Central African People, University of California Press, 1973.

Symbolism of the Lega Stool, ISHI Publications, 1977.

Hero and Chief: Epic Literature from the Banyanga (Zaire Republic), University of California Press, 1978.

Statuary from the Pre-Bembe Hunters, Musee Royale de l'Afrique Centrale (Belgium), 1981.

(With Nelly Van Den Abbeele) *Power of Headdresses: A Cross-Cultural Study of Forms and Functions,* Snoeck-Ducaju en Zoon (Belgium), 1984.

Southwestern Zaire, University of California Press, 1985.

Eastern Zaire: The Ritual and Artistic Context of Voluntary Associations, University of California Press, 1986.

Arts of Central Africa: An Annotated Bibliography, G. K. Hall, 1987.

(With daughter, Brunhilde Biebuyck) *"We Test Those Whom We Marry": An Analysis of Thirty-Six Nyanga Tales,* African Research Program, Lorand Eoetvoes University (Budapest), 1987.

CONTRIBUTOR

W. H. Whiteley, editor, *A Selection of African Prose,* Volume I, Clarendon Press, 1964.

Joseph Okpaku, editor, *New African Literature and the Arts,* Crowell, 1967.

Contributions to the Colloquium on the Function and Significance of Negro-African Art in the Life of the People and for the People, Presence Africaine (Paris), 1971.

D. Fraser and H. Cole, editors, *African Art and Leadership,* University of Wisconsin Press, 1972.

N. Graburn, *Ethnic and Tourist Arts: Cultural Expressions from the Fourth World,* University of California Press, 1976.

Peter Ucko, editor, *Form in Indigenous Art: Schematisation in the Art of Aboriginal Australia and Prehistoric Europe,* Australian Institute of Aboriginal Studies (Canberra), 1977.

Felix J. Oinas, editor, *Heroic Epic and Saga: An Introduction to the World's Great Folk Epics,* Indiana University Press, 1978.

G. Buccellati and C. Speroni, editors, *The Shape of the Past: Studies in Honor of Franklin D. Murphy,* University of California Press, 1981.

M. H. Burssens, editor, *Liber Memorialis for Professor Vandenhoutte,* University of Ghent (Belgium), 1982.

Mircea Eliade, editor-in-chief, *Encyclopedia of Religion,* Volume IV, Macmillan, 1985.

Festschrift for Dr. Renee Boser-Sarivaxevanis, Museum fuer Voelkerkunde (Basel), 1987.

James L. Connelly and others, editors, *Art Museums of the World,* Greenwood Press, 1987.

John Miles Foley, editor, *Comparative Research on Oral Tradition: Memorial for Milman Parry,* Slavica, 1987.

OTHER

Contributor to numerous periodicals, including *African Arts, Man, Journal of American Folklore, American Anthropologist, Cultures et Developpement, African Studies Review,* and *American Ethnologist.*

WORK IN PROGRESS: The memoirs of Mr. Burinda Muriro Sherungu, a Nyanga hunter, musician, bard, and healer.

SIDELIGHTS: Daniel P. Biebuyck speaks and reads Dutch, French, and German; he also reads Greek, Latin, and Portuguese. While conducting field research in Zaire, he has used Swahili and three other Bantu languages. He traveled widely while engaged in field work in Africa, 1949-61, and he has also traveled extensively in Europe and North America.

BLACK, Clinton V(ane De Brosse) 1918-

PERSONAL: Born August 26, 1918, in Kingston, Jamaica; son of Thomas Henry and Violet (Bogle) Black; married Anna Mellor, February 6, 1951. *Education:* Attended Kingston College and University of London. *Religion:* Anglican.

ADDRESSES: Home—5 Avesbury Ave., Kingston 6, Jamaica.

CAREER: Archivist and author; first government archivist of Jamaica. Associated with West India Reference Library, Jamaica, 1945-48; Jamaica Archives, Spanish Town, archivist, 1949-89. Jamaican representative at various archivist conferences around the world. Member of numerous committees, commissions, and boards concerned with archives, libraries, monuments, and history. Archival consultant, generally under auspices of UNESCO, and development planner for a number of Caribbean countries, in addition to Belize and Guyana. Honorary archivist, Jamaica Defence Force. Justice of the peace; game warden.

MEMBER: International Council on Archives (honorary member of General Assembly and of Caribbean branch), Jamaica Historical Society (honorary member), Jamaica Library Association, National Council on Libraries, Archives, and Documentation Services, Jamaica Archaeological Society (honorary member), Jamaica National Heritage Trust (member of board of directors), Indo-Jamaican Cultural Society, Indian Historical Records Commission, Society of Antiquaries of London (fellow), Society of Archivists of Great Britain (honorary member), British Records Association, Moravian Archives Committee, Gosse Bird Club.

AWARDS, HONORS: H. M. Queen Elizabeth II's Coronation Medal, 1953; Commander, Order of Distinction (C.D.), Jamaica, 1975; Centenary Medal, Institute of Jamaica, 1979; Gold Musgrave Medal, Institute of Jamaica, 1982; anniversary medal, Jamaica Historical Society, 1983; outstanding achievement award, Royal Bank Foundation, 1983.

WRITINGS:

Living Names in Jamaica's History, Jamaica Welfare (Kingston), 1946.

Tales of Old Jamaica, Pioneer Press (Kingston), 1952, new edition, Longman, 1988.

History of Jamaica, Collins, 1958, new edition, Longman, 1988.

Spanish Town: The Old Capital, Parish Council of St. Catherine, 1960.

Port Royal: A History and Guide, Bolivar Press, 1970, new edition, Institute of Jamaica, 1988.

Jamaica Guide, Collins, 1973.

The Pirates of the West Indies, Cambridge University Press, 1989.

Also co-author of *Historic Port Royal,* 1952; also author of *Our Archives,* 1962, and *History of Montego Bay,* 1984; also editor of *Jamaica's Banana Industry,* 1984. Contributor to *Encyclopaedia Britannica* and to anthologies. Author of column on "words" in *Daily Gleaner* (Kingston). Contributor to periodicals in Jamaica and abroad.

AVOCATIONAL INTERESTS: Words, birds.

BLACK, Dorothy 1914-
(Dorothy Albertyn, Kitty Black)

PERSONAL: Born April 30, 1914, in Johannesburg, South Africa; daughter of Francis (a quantity surveyor) and Elizabeth Johanna (Albertyn) Black. *Education:* Educated in South Africa.

ADDRESSES: Home—16 Brunswick Gardens, London W8, England. *Agent*—Curtis Brown Ltd., 162-168 Regent St., London W1R 5TA, England.

CAREER: H. M. Tennent Ltd., London, England, secretary, 1937-53; Curtis Brown Ltd., London, agent, 1953-59; Granada Television, London, producer in London and Manchester, 1961-63; Associated-Rediffusion, London, in drama department, 1963-66; MacOwan Theatre, London, house manager, 1976-86; playwright and translator.

MEMBER: PEN, Society of Authors, Apollo Society for Words and Music (secretary, 1975-86).

WRITINGS:

(Translator, under name Dorothy Albertyn) Felicite de Choiseul-Meuse, *Julie* (novel), Odyssey Press, 1970.
Upper Circle, a Theatrical Chronicle, Methuen, 1984.

PLAYS; UNDER PSEUDONYM KITTY BLACK

"The Prince of Bohemia" (for radio; adapted from the story by Robert Louis Stevenson, "The Suicide Club"), first broadcast by British Broadcasting Corp. (BBC), 1942.
(With David Peel) "Landslide" (three-act), first produced in Cambridge, England; produced on West End at Westminster Theatre, 1943.
(With Beverley Cross) "The Singing Dolphin" (two-act), first produced in London at Hampstead Theatre Club, 1963.

TRANSLATIONS; UNDER PSEUDONYM KITTY BLACK

Jean-Paul Sartre, *Three Plays* (contains "Crime Passionnel" [also see below], "Men without Shadows," and "The Respectable Prostitute"), Hamish Hamilton, 1949.
Sartre, *Lucifer and the Lord* (play), Hamish Hamilton, 1952.
Sartre, *Kean; or, Disorder and Genius* (play), Hamish Hamilton, 1954.
(With Michael Flanders) C. F. Ramuz, *The Soldier's Tale* (libretto), J. & W. Chester, 1955.
Freddy and Jean Carlier, *Flying Mannequin* (biography), Hurst & Blackett, 1958.
Fritz Hochwaelder, *The Public Prosecutor* (play), Samuel French, 1958.
(With Pamela Hansford Johnson) Jean Anouilh, *The Rehearsal* (play), Samuel French, 1961.
Sartre, *Crime Passionnel* (play), Methuen, 1961.
Jacques de Launay, *De Gaulle and His France* (nonfiction), Julian Press, 1968.
Evelyne Coquet, *Riding to Jerusalem* (nonfiction), Murray, 1978.

Also translator of plays: Anouilh, "The Untamed," 1951; Georges Simenon, "The Snow Was Black," 1953; (with Mike Iveria) Anton Chekhov, "Three Sisters," 1955; Fritz Hochwaelder, "Donadie," 1956; Alexandre Rivemale, "Wings of the Wind," 1957; Hochwaelder, "The Innocent Man," 1958; Louis Decreux, "Love from Italy," 1960; Felicien Marceau, "Bonne Soupe," 1961; Jacques Deval, "Isabelle," 1964; Marcel Ayme, "Maxibules," 1964; Albert Camus, "The Misunderstanding," 1965; Tauno Yliruusi, "Murder for Fun," 1967; Hochwaelder, "Sword of Vengeance," 1975; "A Place Called Armageddon,"

with Michael Moynihan, 1978; and, Gilbert Leautier, "I'll Never Be Seven," for radio, 1982.

SIDELIGHTS: Dorothy Black once told *CA:* "I count myself lucky in that having become stagestruck at an early age I have been able to work in the theatre all my life—not as an actress, but in the undercover areas of management, production, and translation. What began as a hobby has become a profession, and having retired from office work, translations can still offer an income and an interest. My approach to translation has always been an absolute fidelity to the author's spirit and intention—adaptations are for other people."

*   *   *

BLACK, Kitty
See BLACK, Dorothy

*   *   *

BLACKBURN, Claire
See ALTMAN, Linda Jacobs

*   *   *

BLUMBERG, Rhoda L(ois Goldstein) 1926-
(Rhoda L. Goldstein)

PERSONAL: Born February 3, 1926, in Brooklyn, N.Y.; divorced; children: Leah, Meyer Harold, Helena Jo. *Education:* Brooklyn College (now of the City University of New York), B.A., 1946; New School for Social Research, M.A., 1948; University of Chicago, Ph.D., 1954.

ADDRESSES: Home—New York, N.Y. *Office*—Department of Sociology, Lucy Stone Hall, Rutgers University, New Brunswick, N.J. 08903.

CAREER: Part-time teacher and consultant in Brooklyn, N.Y., 1947-48, and Chicago, Ill., 1948-56; Rutgers University, Douglass College, New Brunswick, N.J., part-time instructor, 1957-61, lecturer, 1962-68, assistant professor, 1968-71, associate professor, 1971-80, professor of sociology, 1980—. Visiting scholar, Stanford University, fall, 1986. Member of executive board, Committee to End Discrimination in Chicago Medical Institutions, 1953-55, Central Jersey Civil Rights Council, 1960-62, Parents' League for Educational Advancement, 1963-65, Highland Park Fair Housing Committee, 1965-66, Special Emergency Legal Force, 1970-72, and Greater New Brunswick Urban League, 1972-74; chairman, Franklin Township Civil Rights Commission, 1961-62. Organizer and first president, Pine Grove Manor Cooperative Nursery School, 1957-59. Consultant, Heritage Foundation.

MEMBER: American Sociological Association, Society for the Study of Social Problems (former member of board of directors), Sociologists for Women in Society, Eastern Sociological Association (former member of executive committee).

AWARDS, HONORS: Fulbright-Hays scholarship, 1966-67; New Jersey Teachers of English award, for *Life and Culture of Black People in the United States.*

WRITINGS:

UNDER NAME RHODA L. GOLDSTEIN

(Contributor) Clifton O. Dummett, editor, *The Growth and Development of the Negro in Dentistry in the United States,* National Dental Association, 1952.

(Contributor) Arthur B. Shostak, editor, *Sociology in Action*, Dorsey, 1966.

(With Bernard Goldstein) *Doctors and Nurses in Industry: Social Aspects of In-Plant Medical Programs* (monograph), Institute of Management and Labor Relations, Rutgers University, 1967.

(Contributor) F. Baker, P. J. M. McEwan, and A. Sheldon, editors, *Industrial Organizations and Health: Selected Readings*, Tavistock Publications, 1969.

(Editor and author of introduction) *Life and Culture of Black People in the United States*, Crowell, 1971.

Indian Women in Transition: A Bangalore Case Study, Scarecrow, 1972.

(With June T. Albert) *Black Studies Programs at American Colleges and Universities: A Preliminary Report* (pamphlet), Rutgers University, 1973.

(Contributor) J. V. Gordon and J. M. Rosser, editors, *The Black Studies Debate*, University Press of Kansas, 1974.

(Contributor) Dhirendra Narain, editor, *Explorations in the Family and Other Essays: Professor K. M. Kapadia Commemoration Volume*, Thacker & Co., 1975.

OTHER

(Co-editor) *Interracial Bonds*, General Hall, 1979.

(With Leela Dwaraki) *India's Educated Women: Options and Constraints*, Hindustan Publishing Corp., 1980.

Civil Rights: The 1960s Freedom Struggle, G. K. Hall, 1984, 2nd edition, in press.

Organizations in Contemporary Society, Prentice-Hall, 1987.

(Editor with Guida West) *Women and Social Protest*, Oxford University Press, in press.

Contributor of more than twenty articles and reviews to sociology journals. Book review editor, *Journal of Asian and African Studies*, 1969-71.

*   *   *

BLUTIG, Eduard
    See GOREY, Edward (St. John)

*   *   *

BOK, Bart J(an)   1906-1983

PERSONAL: Born April 28, 1906, in Hoorn, Netherlands; died August 5, 1983, of an apparent heart attack, in Tucson, Ariz.; immigrated to United States, 1929; naturalized citizen, 1938; son of Jan (a Dutch soldier) and Gesina Annetta (van der Lee) Bok; married Priscilla Fairfield (a college professor and writer), September 9, 1929 (died November 19, 1975); children: John Fairfield, Joyce Annetta Bok Ambruster. *Education:* University of Leiden, candidaat, 1926; University of Groningen, Ph.D., 1932. *Politics:* Democrat.

ADDRESSES: Home—200 Sierra Vista Dr., Tucson, Ariz. 85719.

CAREER: University of Groningen, Kapteyn Observatory, Groningen, Netherlands, assistant in astronomy, 1927-29; Harvard University, Cambridge, Mass., Robert Wheeler Willson Fellow in Astronomy, 1929-33, 1947-57, assistant professor, 1933-39, associate professor of astronomy, 1939-46, associate director of observatory, 1946-52; Australian National University, Canberra, professor of astronomy and director of Mount Stromlo Observatory, 1957-66; University of Arizona, Tucson, professor of astronomy, 1966-74, professor emeritus, 1974-83, head of de-

partment and director of Steward Observatory, 1966-70. Trustee-at-large, Associated Universities, Inc., 1969-71; chairman, Gould Fund, 1969-75.

MEMBER: International Astronomical Union (vice president, 1970-74), National Academy of Sciences, American Astronomical Society (vice president, 1970-71; president, 1972-74), American Association for the Advancement of Science, American Academy of Arts and Sciences, Royal Astronomical Society (fellow), Institute of Physics (Australia), Royal Astronomical Society of Canada (honorary member), Royal Astronomical Society of New Zealand (honorary member), Astronomical Society of Australia (honorary member; corresponding member), Royal Netherlands Academy of Arts and Sciences (honorary member), Royal Australian Academy of Sciences (corresponding member), Astronomical Society of the Pacific (former director), Sigma Xi.

AWARDS, HONORS: Dorothy Klumpke Roberts Prize, Astronomische Gesellschaft, 1934; Oranje-Nassau Medal, Netherlands, 1959; Adion Medal, France, 1971; Catharine De Wolf Bruce gold medal, Astronomical Society of the Pacific, 1977; D.Sc., Arizona State University, 1978; D.Sc., University of Nevada at Las Vegas, 1979; Klumpke-Roberts Award, Astronomical Society of the Pacific, 1982; Henry Norris Russell Lectureship, American Astronomical Society, 1982; fellow, Australian College of Education.

WRITINGS:

The Distribution of the Stars in Space, University of Chicago Press, 1937.

(With wife, Priscilla F. Bok) *The Milky Way*, Blakiston, 1941, 5th edition, Harvard University Press, 1981.

Navigation in Emergencies, U.S. Coast Guard, 1942.

(With F. W. Wright) *Basic Marine Navigation*, Houghton, 1944.

The Astronomer's Universe, Melbourne University Press, 1958.

(With Lawrence E. Jerome) *Objections to Astrology*, Prometheus Books, 1975.

CONTRIBUTOR

W. Becker and G. Contoupolos, editors, *The Spiral Structure of Our Galaxy*, D. Reidel, 1970.

Hong-Yee Chiu and Amador Muriel, editors, *Galactic Astronomy*, Volume 1, Gordon & Breach, 1970.

B. T. Lynds, editor, *Dark Nebulae, Globules, and Protostars*, University of Arizona Press, 1971.

C. de Jager, editor, *Highlights of Astronomy*, D. Reidel, 1971.

M. A. Gordon and L. E. Snyder, editors, *Molecules in the Galactic Environment*, Wiley, 1973.

H. Messel and S. T. Butler, editors, *Focus on the Stars*, Shakespeare Head Press, 1974.

David W. Corson, editor, *Man's Place in the Universe: Changing Concepts*, University of Arizona, 1977.

OTHER

Contributor to *Encyclopedia Americana*. Contributor of more than two hundred articles and reviews to scientific journals, including *Astronomical Journal, Sky and Telescope, American Scientist, Scientific American, American Scholar,* and *Publications of the Astronomical Society of the Pacific*.

WORK IN PROGRESS: Star Birth and Evolution; Structure and Kinematics of Our Galaxy; Star Clouds of Magellan.

SIDELIGHTS: A highly-respected authority on the Milky Way galaxy, Bart J. Bok was the director of two major observatories, Steward Observatory at the University of Arizona and Mount

Stromlo Observatory at the Australian National University, and was a professor at several universities, including Harvard. Among his contributions to the science of astronomy, Bok was the first to calculate the age of the universe to be twenty billion years, rather than the previous estimate of ten million million years. His book, *The Milky Way,* which he wrote with his wife Priscilla, has gone into five editions and is still "considered a classic work on the Earth's home galaxy," according to a *Chicago Tribune* obituary. For his work Bok received many awards, including the Henry Norris Russell Lectureship in 1982 from the American Astronomical Society, which is the equivalent of the Nobel Prize among astronomers; and a small group of dark nebulae in the Milky Way were named "Bok globules" in his honor. Bok was also an inspirational teacher, according to several sources. "An ebullient and humorous speaker, Dr. Bok wooed generations of students into astronomy and particularly into his passion for the Milky Way," wrote Walter Sullivan in the *New York Times.*

Bok once told *CA:* "I take great pride in the semi-popular Harvard Book on Astronomy, entitled *The Milky Way,* which my wife Priscilla . . . and I wrote in the late 1930s. . . . Priscilla and I were among the dwindling group of astronomers who consider themselves true Nightwatchmen of the Heavens. As a boy scout at the age of twelve (in Holland) I became curious about the Milky Way. Trying to satisfy this curiosity has stayed with me throughout my professional career, and in retirement, giving me much pleasure. . . ." About *The Milky Way,* Bok also added: "Priscilla and I wanted to write a book aimed specially at beginning university students and at bright boys and girls of high school age. Our grandchildren were fine test objects when judging what to include and how to approach each subject. The age group 13 to 20 was the one for which we liked to write. Quite a few distinguished astronomers of today became at an early age first acquainted with the Milky Way through the reading of our book."

OBITUARIES:

PERIODICALS

Chicago Tribune, August 7, 1983.
Los Angeles Times, August 9, 1983.
Newsweek, August 22, 1983.
New York Times, August 11, 1983.
Washington Post, August 7, 1989.*

*   *   *

BOLD, Alan Norman 1943-

PERSONAL: Born April 20, 1943, in Edinburgh, Scotland; son of William (a clerk of works) and Marjory (Wilson) Bold; married Alice Howell (an art teacher), June 29, 1963; children: Valentina. *Education:* Attended University of Edinburgh, 1961-65.

ADDRESSES: Home—Balbirnie Burns East Cottage, Glenrothes, Fife KY7 6NE, Scotland.

CAREER: Free-lance writer, poet, and graphic artist. *Times Educational Supplement,* Edinburgh, Scotland, member of staff, 1965-66.

WRITINGS:

POETRY

Society Inebrious, introduction by Hugh MacDiarmid, Mowat-Hamilton, 1965.

To Find the New, Chatto & Windus, 1967, Wesleyan University Press, 1968.
A Perpetual Motion Machine, Wesleyan University Press, 1969.
(With Edwin Morgan and Edward Brathwaite) *Penguin Modern Poets 15,* Penguin, 1969.
The State of the Nation, Wesleyan University Press, 1969.
The Auld Symie, Akros Publications, 1971.
(And illustrator) *He Will Be Greatly Missed: A Poem,* Turret Books, 1971.
A Century of People, Academy Editions, 1971.
A Pint of Bitter, Chatto & Windus, 1971.
Scotland, Yes: World Cup Football Poems, Beekman Publications, 1978.
This Fine Day, Borderline, 1979.
(With John Bellany) *A Celtic Quintet,* Balbirnie Editions, 1983.
In This Corner: Selected Poems, 1963-83, M. Macdonald, 1983.
(With Bellany) *Haven,* Balbirnie Editions, 1984.
(With Bellany) *Homage to MacDiarmid,* Balbirnie Editions, 1985.
Summoned by Knox: Poems in Scots, Dufour, 1985.
(With Gareth Owen and Julie O'Callaghan) *Bright Lights Blaze Out,* Oxford University Press, 1986.

NONFICTION

(Translator) Charles-Pierre Baudelaire, *The Voyage,* M. Macdonald, 1966.
Thom Gunn and Ted Hughes (criticism), Oliver & Boyd, 1976.
George Mackay Brown (criticism), Barnes & Noble, 1978.
The Ballad (criticism), Methuen, 1979.
The Sensual Scot, cartoons by Weef, Harris Publishing, 1982.
Modern Scottish Literature (criticism), Longman, 1983.
MacDiarmid: The Terrible Crystal (criticism), Routledge & Kegan Paul, 1983.
(Author of introduction) Hugh MacDiarmid, *Annals of the Five Senses: The First Collected Work by Hugh MacDiarmid,* Polygon, 1983.
Modern Scottish Literature, Longman, 1983.
(With Robert Giddings) *True Characters: Real People in Fiction,* Longman, 1984.
(With Giddings) *The Book of Rotters,* Mainstream Publishing, 1985, State Mutual Book, 1986.
Muriel Spark, Methuen, 1986.
(With Giddings) *Who Was Really Who in Fiction,* Longman, 1987.
MacDiarmid: A Critical Biography, J. Murray, 1988.
Scotland: A Literary Guide, Routledge & Kegan Paul, 1989.

EDITOR

The Penguin Book of Socialist Verse, Penguin, 1970.
(And author of introduction and notes) *The Martial Muse: Seven Centuries of War Poetry,* Wheaton & Co., 1976.
The Cambridge Book of English Verse, 1939-75, Cambridge University Press, 1976.
(And author of introduction) *Making Love: The Picador Book of Erotic Verse,* Pan Books, 1978.
The Bawdy Beautiful: The Sphere Book of Improper Verse, Sphere Books, 1979.
Mounts of Venus: The Picador Book of Erotic Prose, Pan Books, 1980.
Drink to Me Only: The Prose (and Cons) of Drinking, Clark, 1982.
Smollet: Author of the First Distinction, Barnes & Noble, 1982.
A Scottish Poetry Book, illustrated by Bob Dewar, Iain McIntosh, and Rodger McPhail, Oxford University Press, 1983.

The Poetry of Motion: The Junction Book of Sporting Verse, Junction, 1983, reprinted as *The Poetry of Motion: An Anthology of Sporting Verse,* Mainstream Publishing, 1984.
Hugh MacDiarmid, *Aesthetics in Scotland,* Vision Press, 1984, Barnes & Noble, 1985.
Muriel Spark: An Odd Capacity for Vision, Barnes & Noble, 1984.
Harold Pinter: You Never Heard Such Silence, Barnes & Noble, 1984.
The Thistle Rises: A MacDiarmid Miscellany, Hamish Hamilton, 1984.
The Letters of Hugh MacDiarmid, University of Georgia Press, 1984.
The Longman Dictionary of Poets: Lives & Works of 1001 Poets in the English Language, Longman, 1985.
W. H. Auden: The Far Interior, Barnes & Noble, 1985.
A Second Scottish Book of Poetry, Oxford University Press, 1985.
Scottish Quotations, Mercat Press, 1985.
The Quest for Le Carre, Barnes & Noble, 1988.

OTHER

(With David Morrison) *Hammer and Thistle* (short stories), Caithness Books, 1973.
Mary, Queen of Scots, Wayland, 1977.
The Edge of the Wood (short stories), State Mutual Book, 1984.

Translator of French poetry into English. Contributor to national newspapers and periodicals. Editor, *Gambit,* 1963, 1965; founding editor, *Rocket,* 1965-66.

SIDELIGHTS: Alan Bold told *CA:* "Poetry is not made by the subject itself but by the amount of imaginative pressure brought to bear on it. Some time before Eliot made poems out of the 'burnt-out smoky days' there was a realization that poetry could only survive by making itself more accessible and dropping some aristocratic affectations. . . ." He later continued: "My own approach to poetry is to encourage a state of mind that accepts the special verbal qualities of verse yet also appreciates that the poet has the same emotional aspirations as everyone else. The poet is not different; he is everyman possessed by an artistic power. In making my poems I always recall Ezra Pound's remark that technique is the test of sincerity and I hope to exhibit sound craftsmanship and formal control. Stylistically I have been greatly influenced by two other modern poets who are similar to Pound in stature. Hugh MacDiarmid, whose work I have written about and edited, shows that the Scot need not be a spirit-sodden caricature but can rise (as does MacDiarmid's immortal Drunk Man [in 'A Drunk Man Looks at the Thistle']) to a soaring spirituality. While I admire MacDiarmid's intellectual elitism I also respond to the populism of Pablo Neruda who insisted that the function of poetry is to make a direct appeal to the people. Aware of these diverse influences I have tried to express myself, not in any antisocial or solipsistic way, but with enough passion to earn the attention of those who agree with me that art exists to enhance life.'

BIOGRAPHICAL/CRITICAL SOURCES:

BOOKS

Royle, Trevor, *Companion to Scottish Literature,* Macmillan, 1983.

PERIODICALS

Books, February, 1970.
Books and Bookmen, June, 1969, April, 1971.
Glasgow Herald, August 8, 1983.
New Statesman, December 1, 1967.

Poetry, July, 1969.
Sunday Times (London), February 8, 1970.
Times Literary Supplement, November 9, 1967, April 16, 1971, April 7, 1978, February 22, 1980, December 19, 1980, April 22, 1983, June 3, 1983, August 26, 1983, October 5, 1984, January 4, 1985, August 30, 1985, June 13, 1986, October 28, 1988.

*　　*　　*

BOUCOLON, Maryse 1937-
(Maryse Conde)

PERSONAL: Born February 11, 1937, in Guadeloupe, West Indies; daughter of Auguste and Jeanne (Quidal) Boucolon; married Mamadou Conde, 1958 (divorced, 1981); married Richard Philcox (a translator), 1982; children: (first marriage) Leila, Sylvie, Aicha. *Education:* Sorbonne, University of Paris, Ph.D., 1976.

ADDRESSES: *Home*—Montebello, 97170 Petit Bourg, Guadeloupe, French West Indies. *Agent*—Rosalie Siegel, Act III Productions, 711 Fifth St., New York, N.Y. 10022.

CAREER: Ecole Normale Superieure, Conakry, Guinea, instructor, 1960-64; Ghana Institute of Languages, Accra, Ghana, 1964-66; Lycee Charles de Gaulle, Saint Louis, Senegal, instructor, 1966-68; French Services of the BBC, London, England, program producer, 1968-70; University of Paris, Paris, France, assistant at Jussieu, 1970-72, lecturer at Nanterre, 1973-80, charge de cours at Sorbonne, 1980-85; program producer, Radio France Internationale, France Culture, 1980—. Bellagio Writer in Residence, Rockefeller Foundation, 1986; lecturer in the United States, Africa, and the West Indies. Presenter of a literary program for Africa on Radio-France.

AWARDS, HONORS: Fulbright Scholar, 1985-86; Prix litteraire de la Femme, Prix Alain Boucheron, 1986, for *Moi, Tituba, sorciere Noire de Salem;* Guggenheim fellow, 1987-88.

WRITINGS:

UNDER NAME MARYSE CONDE

(Editor) *Anthologie de la litterature africaine d'expression francaise,* Ghana Institute of Languages, 1966.
Dieu nous l'a donne (four-act play; title means "God Given"; first produced in Martinique, West Indies, at Fort de France, 1973), Oswald, 1972.
Mort d'Oluwemi d'Ajumako (four-act play; title means "Death of a King"; first produced in Haiti at Theatre d'Alliance Francaise, 1975), Oswald, 1973.
Heremakhonon (novel), Union Generale d'Editions, 1976, translation by husband, Richard Philcox, published under same title, Three Continents Press, 1982.
(Translator into French with Philcox) Eric Williams, *From Columbus to Castro: The History of the Caribbean,* Presence Africaine, 1977.
(Editor) *La Poesie antillaise* (also see below), Nathan (Paris), 1977.
(Editor) *Le Roman antillais* (also see below), Nathan, 1977.
La Civilisation du bossale (criticism), Harmattan (Paris), 1978.
Le profil d'une oeuvre: Cahier d'un retour au pays natal (criticism), Hatier (Paris), 1978.
La Parole des femmes (criticism), Harmattan, 1979.
Tim tim? Bois sec! Bloemlezing uit de Franstalige Caribsche Literatuur (contains revised and translated editions of *Le*

Roman antillais and *La Poesie antillaise*), edited by Andries van der Wal, In de Knipscheer, 1980.

Une Saison a Rihata (novel), Robert Laffont (Paris), 1981, translation by Philcox published as *A Season in Rihata,* Heinemann, 1988.

Segou: Les murailles de terre, (novel), Robert Laffont, 1984, translation by Barbara Bray published as *Segu,* Viking, 1987.

Segou II: La terre en miettes (novel), Robert Laffont, 1985, translation by Linda Coverdale published as *The Children of Segu,* Viking, 1989.

Pays Mele (short stories), Hatier, 1985.

Moi, Tituba, sorciere noire de Salem (novel), Mercure de France (Paris), 1986.

La Vie scelerate (novel), Seghers, 1987.

Haiti Cherie (juvenile), Bayard Presse, 1987.

Pension les Alizes (play), Mercure de France, 1988.

Victor et les barricades (juvenile), Bayard Presse, 1989.

Traversee de la mangrove (novel), Mercure de France, 1990.

Also author of recordings for Record CLEF and Radio France Internationale. Contributor to anthologies; contributor to journals, including *Presence Africaine* and *Recherche Pedagogique.*

SIDELIGHTS: West Indian author Maryse Boucolon, who writes under the name Maryse Conde, "deals with characters in domestic situations and employs fictitious narratives as a means of elaborating large-scale activities," assert *World Literature Today* writers Charlotte and David Bruner. Drawing on her experiences in Paris, West Africa, and her native Guadeloupe, Conde has created several novels which "attempt to make credible on an increasingly larger scale the personal human complexities involved in holy wars, national rivalries, and migrations of peoples," the Bruners state. *Heremakhonon,* for example, relates the journey of Veronica, an Antillean student searching for her roots in a newly liberated West African country. During her stay Veronica becomes involved with both a powerful government official and a young school director opposed to the new regime; "to her dismay," David Bruner summarizes, "she is unable to stay out of the political struggle, and yet she is aware that she does not know enough to understand what is happening."

The result of Veronica's exploration, which is told with an "insinuating prose [that] has a surreal, airless quality," as Carole Bovoso relates in the *Voice Literary Supplement,* is that "there were times I longed to rush in and break the spell, to shout at this black woman and shake her. But no one can rescue Veronica," the critic continues, "least of all herself; Conde conveys the seriousness of her plight by means of a tone of relentless irony and reproach." "Justly or not," write the Bruners, "one gains a comprehension of what a revolution is like, what new African nations are like, yet one is aware that this comprehension is nothing more than a feeling. The wise reader will go home as Veronica does," the critics conclude, "to continue more calmly to reflect, and to observe."

Conde expands her scope in *Segu,* "a wondrous novel about a period of African history few other writers have addressed," notes *New York Times Book Review* contributor Charles R. Larson. In tracing three generations of a West African family during the early and mid-1800s, "Conde has chosen for her subject . . . [a] chaotic stage, when the animism (which she calls fetishism) native to the region began to yield to Islam," the critic describes. "The result is the most significant historical novel about black Africa published in many a year." Beginning with Dousika, a Bambara nobleman caught up in court intrigue, *Segu* trails the exploits of his family, from one son's conversion to

Islam to another's enslavement to a third's successful career in commerce, connected with stories of their wives and concubines and servants. In addition, Conde's "knowledge of African history is prodigious, and she is equally versed in the continent's folklore," remarks Larson. "The unseen world haunts her characters and vibrates with the spirits of the dead."

Some critics, however, fault the author for an excess of detail; *Washington Post* contributor Harold Courlander, for example, comments that "the plethora of happenings in the book does not always make for easy reading." The critic explains that "the reader is sometimes uncertain whether history and culture are being used to illuminate the fiction or the novel exists to tell us about the culture and its history." While Howard Kaplan concurs with this assessment, he adds in the *Los Angeles Times Book Review* that *Segu* "glitters with nuggets of cultural fascination. . . . For those willing to make their way through this dense saga, genuine rewards will be reaped." "With such an overwhelming mass of data and with so extensive a literary objective, the risks of . . . producing a heavy, didactic treatise are, of course, great," the Bruners maintain. "The main reason that Conde has done neither is, perhaps, because she has written here essentially as she did in her two earlier novels: she has followed the lives of the fictional characters as individuals dominated by interests and concerns which are very personal and often selfish and petty, even when those characters are perceived by other characters as powerful leaders in significant national or religious movements." Because of this, the critics conclude, *Segu* is "a truly remarkable book. . . . To know [the subjects of her work] better, as well as to know Maryse Conde even better, would be a good thing."

BIOGRAPHICAL/CRITICAL SOURCES:

PERIODICALS

Los Angeles Times Book Review, March 8, 1987.
New York Times Book Review, May 31, 1987.
Voice Literary Supplement, November, 1982.
Washington Post, March 3, 1987, December 8, 1989.
World Literature Today, winter, 1982, winter, 1985, spring, 1985, summer, 1986, spring, 1987, summer, 1988.

*   *   *

BOUDON, Raymond 1934-

PERSONAL: Born January 27, 1934, in Paris, France; son of Raymond and Helene (Millet) Boudon; married Rosemarie Riessner, April 22, 1962; children: Stephane. *Education:* Attended Ecole Normale Superieure and Sorbonne, both University of Paris, receiving Ph.D., 1967.

ADDRESSES: Home—51, avenue Trudaine 75009, Paris, France. *Office*—Maison des Sciences de l'Homme 54, boulevard Raspail 75006, Paris, France.

CAREER: University of Bordeaux, Bordeaux, France, associate professor of sociology, 1964-67; University of Paris—Sorbonne, Paris, France, professor of sociology, 1967—, director of Centre d'Etudes Sociologiques, 1968-71. Ford Foundation fellow at Columbia University, 1961-62; fellow at Center for Advanced Study in the Behavioral Sciences, Stanford University, 1972-73. Visiting professor at Harvard University, 1974-75. *Military service:* French Navy, 1960-61.

MEMBER: International Academy of Education, American Academy of Arts and Sciences (honorary member), Academia Europaea.

AWARDS, HONORS: Chevalier de l'ordre national du Merite.

WRITINGS:

(With Paul Lazarsfeld) *Vocabulaire des sciences sociales: Concepts et indices,* Humanities, 1965.

L'Analyse mathematique des faits sociaux (title means "The Mathematical Analysis of Social Facts"), Plon, 1967, 2nd edition, 1970.

A quoi sert la notion de structure?: Essai sur la signification dans les sciences humaines, Gallimard, 1968, translation by Michalina Vaughan published as *The Uses of Structuralism,* Heinemann, 1971.

L'analyse empirique de la casualite, Mouton, 1969, 3rd edition, 1976.

Les Methodes en sociologie, Presses Universitaires de France, 1969, 3rd edition, 1973.

Les Mathematiques en sociologie, Presses Universitaires de France, 1971, translation by Tom Burns published as *The Logic of Sociological Explanation,* Penguin Books, 1974.

La Crise de la sociologie: Questions d'epistemologie sociologique, Droz, 1971, translation by Howard Davis published as *The Crisis in Sociology: Problems of Sociological Epistemology,* Columbia University Press, 1980.

Mathematical Structures of Social Mobility, Elsevier Publishing, 1973.

Inegalite des chances, Colin, 1973, translation by Boudon published as *Education, Opportunity, and Social Inequality: Changing Prospects in Western Society,* Wiley, 1974.

Effets pervers et ordre social, Presses Univeritaires de France, 1977.

La logique du social: Introduction a l'analyse sociologique, Hachette, 1979, translation by David Silverman published as *The Logic of Social Action: An Introduction to Sociological Analysis,* Routledge & Kegan Paul, 1981.

(With F. Bourricaud and A. Girard) *Science et theorie de l'opinion publique,* Retz, 1981.

The Unintended Consequences of Social Action, St. Martin's, 1982.

Dictionnaire critique de la sociologie, Presses universitaires de France, 1982.

La place du desordre, Presses universitaires de France, 1985, translation published as *Theories of social change,* University of California Press, 1986.

L'ideologie, ou, L'origine des idees recues, Fayard, 1986.

The Analysis of Ideology, University of Chicago Press, in press.

Contributor to *Social Sciences Information, Quality and Quantity, American Sociological Review, European Journal of Sociology,* and other journals in his field.

WORK IN PROGRESS: Research on the sociology of knowledge.

* * *

BRADBURY, Ray (Douglas) 1920-
(Douglas Spaulding, Leonard Spaulding)

PERSONAL: Born August 22, 1920, in Waukegan, Ill.; son of Leonard Spaulding and Esther (Moberg) Bradbury; married Marguerite Susan McClure, September 27, 1947; children: Susan, Ramona, Bettina, Alexandra. *Education:* Attended schools in Waukegan, Ill., and Los Angeles, Calif. *Politics:* Independent. *Religion:* Unitarian Universalist.

ADDRESSES: Home—10265 Cheviot Drive, Los Angeles, Calif. 90064. *Agent*—Don Congdon, 156 Fifth Ave., #625, New York, N.Y. 10010.

CAREER: Newsboy in Los Angeles, Calif., 1940-43; full-time writer, primarily of fantasy and science fiction, 1943—.

MEMBER: Writers Guild of America, Science Fantasy Writers of America.

AWARDS, HONORS: O. Henry Prize, 1947, and 1948; Benjamin Franklin Award for best story of 1953-54 in an American magazine, for "Sun and Shadow" in *The Reporter;* Commonwealth Club of California gold medal, 1954, for *Fahrenheit 451;* award from National Institute of Arts and Letters, 1954, for contribution to American literature; Boys' Clubs of America Junior Book Award, 1956, for *Switch on the Night;* Golden Eagle Award, 1957, for screenwriting; Academy Award nomination for short film, 1963, for "Icarus Montgolfier Wright"; Mrs. Ann Radcliffe Award, Count Dracula Society, 1965, 1971; Writers Guild Award, 1974; World Fantasy Award, 1977, for life achievement; D.Litt., Whittier College, 1979; Balrog Award, 1979, for best poet; Aviation and Space Writers Award, 1979, for television documentary; Gandalf Award, 1980; Body of Work Award, PEN, 1985; the play version of "The Martian Chronicles" won five Los Angeles Drama Critics Circle Awards.

WRITINGS:

NOVELS

The Martian Chronicles (also see below), Doubleday, 1950, revised edition published in England as *The Silver Locusts,* Hart-Davis, 1951.

Dandelion Wine (also see below), Doubleday, 1957, reprinted, Knopf, 1975.

Something Wicked This Way Comes (also see below), Simon & Schuster, 1962.

Death Is a Lonely Business, Knopf, 1985.

A Graveyard for Lunatics, Knopf, 1990.

STORY COLLECTIONS

Dark Carnival, Arkham, 1947, revised edition, Hamish Hamilton, 1948.

The Illustrated Man, Doubleday, 1951, reprinted, Bantam, 1967, revised edition, Hart-Davis, 1952.

Fahrenheit 451 (contains "Fahrenheit 451" [also see below], "The Playground," and "And the Rock Cried Out"), Ballantine, 1953, reprinted, G. K. Hall, 1988.

The Golden Apples of the Sun (also see below), Doubleday, 1953, reprinted, Greenwood Press, 1971, revised edition, Hart-Davis, 1953.

Fahrenheit 451 (previously published as part of short story collection), Hart-Davis, 1954.

The October Country, Ballantine, 1955, reprinted, Knopf, 1970.

A Medicine for Melancholy (also see below), Doubleday, 1959, revised edition published in England as *The Day It Rained Forever* (also see below), Hart-Davis, 1959.

The Ghoul Keepers, Pyramid Books, 1961.

The Small Assassin, Ace Books, 1962.

The Machineries of Joy, Simon & Schuster, 1964.

The Vintage Bradbury, Vintage Books, 1965.

The Autumn People, Ballantine, 1965.

Tomorrow Midnight, Ballantine, 1966.

Twice Twenty-Two (contains *The Golden Apples of the Sun* and *A Medicine for Melancholy*), Doubleday, 1966.

I Sing the Body Electric!, Knopf, 1969.

(With Robert Bloch) *Bloch and Bradbury: Ten Masterpieces of Science Fiction,* Tower, 1969 (published in England as *Fever Dreams and Other Fantasies,* Sphere, 1970).

(With Bloch) *Whispers from Beyond,* Peacock Press, 1972.

(Selected Stories), Harrap, 1975.

Long after Midnight, Knopf, 1976.
The Best of Bradbury, Bantam, 1976.
To Sing Strange Songs, Wheaton, 1979.
The Stories of Ray Bradbury, Knopf, 1980.
Dinosaur Tales, Bantam, 1983.
A Memory of Murder, Dell, 1984.
The Toynbee Convector, Random House, 1988.

JUVENILES

Switch on the Night, Pantheon, 1955.
R Is for Rocket (story collection), Doubleday, 1962.
S Is for Space (story collection), Doubleday, 1966.
The Halloween Tree, Knopf, 1972.
The April Witch, Creative Education, Inc., 1987.
The Other Foot, Creative Education, Inc., 1987.
The Foghorn (also see below), Creative Education, Inc., 1987.
The Veldt (also see below), Creative Education, Inc., 1987.
Fever Dream, St. Martin's, 1987.

PLAYS

"The Meadow," first produced in Hollywood at the Huntington Hartford Theatre, March, 1960.
"Way in the Middle of the Air," first produced in Hollywood at the Desilu Gower Studios, August, 1962.
The Anthem Sprinters, and Other Antics (includes "The Anthem Sprinters," first produced in Beverly Hills at the Beverly Hills Playhouse, October, 1967), Dial, 1963.
"The World of Ray Bradbury." (three one-acts), first produced in Los Angeles at the Coronet Theater, October, 1964, produced Off-Broadway at Orpheum Theatre, October 8, 1965.
"Leviathan 99" (radio play), British Broadcasting Corp., 1966, first produced in Hollywood at the Stage 9 Theater, November, 1972.
The Day It Rained Forever (one-act), Samuel French, 1966.
The Pedestrian (one-act), Samuel French, 1966.
"Dandelion Wine" (based on his novel of same title; music composed by Billy Goldenberg), first produced at Lincoln Center's Forum Theatre, 1967.
"Christus Apollo" (music composed by Jerry Goldsmith), first produced in Los Angeles at Royce Hall, University of California, December, 1969.
The Wonderful Ice-Cream Suit and Other Plays (contains "The Wonderful Ice-Cream Suit," first produced in Los Angeles at the Coronet Theater, February, 1965, "The Veldt" [based on his story of same title], first produced in London, 1980, and "To the Chicago Abyss"), Bantam, 1972 (published in England as *The Wonderful Ice-Cream Suit and Other Plays for Today, Tomorrow, and Beyond Tomorrow,* Hart-Davis, 1973).
Madrigals for the Space Age (for mixed chorus and narrator, with piano accompaniment; music composed by Lalo Schifrin; first performed in Los Angeles at the Dorothy Chandler Pavilion, January, 1976), Associated Music Publishers, 1972.
Pillar of Fire and Other Plays for Today, Tomorrow, and Beyond Tomorrow (contains "Pillar of Fire," [first produced in Fullerton at the Little Theatre, California State College, December, 1973], "Kaleidoscope," and "The Foghorn" [based on his story of same title], first produced in New York, 1977), Bantam, 1975.
That Ghost, That Bride of Time: Excerpts from a Play-in-Progress, Squires, 1976.
"The Martian Chronicles" (based on his novel of same title), first produced at the Colony Theater in Los Angeles, 1977.
"Fahrenheit 451" (based on his story of same title; musical), first produced at the Colony Theater in Los Angeles, 1979.

A Device Out of Time, Dramatic Publishing, 1986.
"Falling Upward," first produced in Los Angeles at the Melrose Theatre, March, 1988.

FILMS

"It Came from Outer Space," Universal Pictures, 1953.
"The Beast from 20,000 Fathoms" (based on his story, "The Foghorn"), Warner Bros., 1953.
"Moby Dick," Warner Bros., 1956.
(With George C. Johnson) "Icarus Montgolfier Wright," Format Films, 1962.
(Author of narration and creative consultant) "An American Journey," U.S. Government for United States Pavilion at New York World's Fair, 1964.
(Under pseudonym Douglas Spaulding with Ed Weinberger) "Picasso Summer," Warner Bros./Seven Arts, 1972.
"Something Wicked This Way Comes" (based on his novel of same title), Walt Disney, 1983.

Also author of television scripts for "Alfred Hitchcock Presents," "Jane Wyman's Fireside Theatre," "Steve Canyon," "Trouble Shooters," "Twilight Zone," "Alcoa Premiere," and "Curiosity Shop" series. Author of 42 television scripts for "Ray Bradbury Television Theatre," USA Cable Network, 1985-90.

POEMS

Old Ahab's Friend, and Friend to Noah, Speaks His Piece: A Celebration, Roy A. Squires Press, 1971.
When Elephants Last in the Dooryard Bloomed: Celebrations for Almost Any Day in the Year (also see below), Knopf, 1973.
That Son of Richard III: A Birth Announcement, Roy A. Squires Press, 1974.
Where Robot Mice and Robot Men Run Round in Robot Towns (also see below), Knopf, 1977.
Twin Hieroglyphs That Swim the River Dust, Lord John, 1978.
The Bike Repairman, Lord John, 1978.
The Author Considers His Resources, Lord John, 1979.
The Aqueduct, Roy A. Squires Press, 1979.
This Attic Where the Meadow Greens, Lord John, 1979.
The Last Circus, Lord John, 1980.
The Ghosts of Forever (five poems, a story, and an essay), Rizzoli, 1980.
The Haunted Computer and the Android Pope (also see below), Knopf, 1981.
The Complete Poems of Ray Bradbury (contains *Where Robot Mice and Robot Men Run Round in Robot Towns, The Haunted Computer and the Android Pope,* and *When Elephants Last in the Dooryard Bloomed*), Ballantine, 1982.
The Love Affair (a short story and two poems), Lord John, 1983.
Forever and the Earth, limited edition, Croissant & Co., 1984.
Death Has Lost Its Charm for Me, Lord John, 1987.

OTHER

(Editor and contributor) *Timeless Stories for Today and Tomorrow,* Bantam, 1952.
(Editor and contributor) *The Circus of Dr. Lao and Other Improbable Stories,* Bantam, 1956.
(With Lewy Olfson) *Teacher's Guide: Science Fiction,* Bantam, 1968.
Zen and the Art of Writing, Capra Press, 1973.
(With Bruce Murray, Arthur C. Clarke, Walter Sullivan, and Carl Sagan) *Mars and the Mind of Man,* Harper, 1973.
The Mummies of Guanajuato, Abrams, 1978.
Beyond 1984: Remembrance of Things Future, Targ, 1979.
(Author of text) *Los Angeles,* Skyline Press, 1984.
(Author of text) *Orange County,* Skyline Press, 1985.

(Author of text) *The Art of "Playboy,"* Alfred Van der Marck, 1985.

Work is represented in over seven hundred anthologies. Contributor of short stories and articles, sometimes under pseudonyms, to *Playboy, Saturday Review, Weird Tales, Magazine of Fantasy and Science Fiction, Omni, Life,* and other publications.

SIDELIGHTS: Ray Bradbury's science fiction, unlike that of many of his colleagues, de-emphasizes the Buck Rogers-Flash Gordon variety of space hardware and gadgetry in favor of an exploration of the impact of scientific development on human lives. In general, he warns man against becoming too dependent on science and technology at the expense of moral and aesthetic concerns, contending that his stories "are intended as much to instruct how to prevent dooms, as to predict them." Writing in the *Dictionary of Literary Biography,* George Edgar Slusser notes that "to Bradbury, science is the forbidden fruit, destroyer of Eden. . . . In like manner, Bradbury is a fantasist whose fantasies are oddly circumscribed: he writes less about strange things happening to people than about strange imaginings of the human mind. Corresponding, then, to an outer labyrinth of modern technological society is this inner one—fallen beings feeding in isolation on their hopeless dreams."

"If you're too good a scientist, you're not a good writer," Ray Bradbury once told an interviewer. This quote summarizes his unorthodox approach to writing science fiction, an approach which has led some critics to insist that calling him "the world's greatest living science fiction writer" (a phrase which appears on the covers of the paperback editions of his books) does an injustice to the scope of his talent. As Damon Knight observes in his *In Search of Wonder: Critical Essays on Science Fiction:* "The purists are right in saying that [Bradbury] does not write science fiction, and never has." Donald A. Wollheim agrees with Knight's assessment. Writing in *The Universe Makers,* Wollheim states: "Only a very small percentage of Bradbury's works can be classified as science fiction. Although his most 'science-fictional' book, *The Martian Chronicles,* is a classic, its s-f plausibility is slight. . . . It has the form of science fiction but in content there is no effort to implement the factual backgrounds. His Mars bears no relation to the astronomical planet. His stories are stories of people—real and honest and true in their understanding of human nature—but for his purposes the trappings of science fiction are sufficient—mere stage settings. . . . He is outside the field [of science fiction]—a mainstream fantasist of great brilliance, . . . but certainly not 'the world's greatest living science fiction writer.' "

Knight credits Bradbury with a greater range than the science fiction label implies: "His imagery is luminous and penetrating, continually lighting up familiar corners with unexpected words. He never lets an idea go until he has squeezed it dry, and never wastes one. As his talent expands, some of his stories become pointed social commentary; some are surprisingly effective religious tracts, disguised as science fiction; others still are nostalgic vignettes; but under it all is still Bradbury the poet of 20th-century neurosis. Bradbury the isolated spark of consciousness, awake and alone at midnight; Bradbury the grown-up child who still remembers, still believes."

Over the past five decades, Bradbury has managed to create a tremendous amount of work in several genres, including short stories, plays, novels, film scripts, poems, children's books, and nonfiction. He attributes this prolific production to a steady writing routine. "Every single day for 50 years," he tells Aljean Harmetz in the *New York Times,* "if I can get to my typewriter by 9 o'clock, by 10:30 I'm protected against the world." An in-credible memory also helps. Bradbury claims total recall of every book he has read and of every film he has seen. This enables him to "cross-pollinate metaphors," as he tells *CA,* from hundreds of sources for his own fiction. He also utilizes a spontaneous writing technique similar to the automatic writing of the surrealists. William F. Touponce in *Extrapolation* quotes Bradbury explaining: "In my early twenties I floundered into a word-association process in which I simply got out of bed each morning, walked to my desk, and put down any word or series of words that happened along in my head." As Touponce relates, Bradbury "advises the aspiring writer to relax and concentrate on the unconscious message. This way of writing shorts out the mind's critical and categorizing activities, allowing the subconscious to speak."

The Martian Chronicles, a lyrical and basically optimistic account of man's colonization of Mars, is widely regarded as Bradbury's most outstanding work. It blends many of his major themes and metaphors, including the conflict between individual and social concerns (that is, freedom versus confinement and conformity) and the idea of space as a frontier wilderness, a place where man sets out on a quasi-religious quest of self-discovery and spiritual renewal. In addition, *The Martian Chronicles* provides the author with an opportunity to explore what he perceives to be the often deadly attraction of the past as opposed to the future and of balance and stability versus change. As in many other Bradbury stories, this idea is expressed in *The Martian Chronicles* via the metaphor of the small, old-fashioned midwestern town ("Green Town, Ill.") which represents peaceful childhood memories of a world that man hesitates to abandon to the passage of time. In his contribution to *Voices for the Future: Essays on Major Science Fiction Writers,* A. James Stupple writes: "Bradbury's point [in *The Martian Chronicles*] is clear: [The Earthmen] met their deaths because of their inability to forget, or at least resist, the past. Thus, the story of this Third Expedition acts as a metaphor for the book as a whole. Again and again the Earthmen make the fatal mistake of trying to recreate an Earth-like past rather than accept the fact that this is Mars—a different, unique new land in which they must be ready to make personal adjustments."

Russell Kirk feels that the greatest strength of *The Martian Chronicles* is its ability to make us look closely at ourselves. In *Enemies of the Permanent Things: Observations of Abnormality in Literature and Politics,* Kirk states: "What gives [*The Martian Chronicles*] their cunning is . . . their portrayal of human nature, in all its baseness and all its promise, against an exquisite stageset. We are shown normality, the permanent things in human nature, by the light of another world; and what we forget about ourselves in the ordinariness of our routine of existence suddenly bursts upon us as a fresh revelation. . . . Bradbury's stories are not an escape from reality; they are windows looking upon enduring reality."

In his essay for *Voices for the Future,* Willis E. McNelly concludes that Bradbury's works, especially *The Martian Chronicles* and the highly-acclaimed *Fahrenheit 451,* prove that "quality writing is possible in [a] much-maligned genre. Bradbury is obviously a careful craftsman, an ardent wordsmith whose attention to the niceties of language and its poetic cadences would have marked him as significant even if he had never written a word about Mars." In short, McNelly continues, Bradbury's "themes . . . place him squarely in the middle of the mainstream of American life and tradition. His eyes are set firmly on the horizon-frontier where dream fathers mission and action mirrors illusion. And if Bradbury's eyes lift from the horizon to the stars, the act is merely an extension of the vision all Americans share.

His voice is that of the poet raised against the mechanization of mankind."

In an interview with *Future* magazine, Bradbury admits that poetry does play an important role in his writing. In fact, he notes, "I've found inspiration for many of my short stories in other people's poetry. . . . There have been many times when I've taken a single line of poetry and turned it into a short story. Poetry is an old love of mine, one which is central to my life." Though he is most often called a science fiction writer, Bradbury considers himself to be an "idea writer" instead. "Everything of mine is permeated with my love of ideas—both big and small. It doesn't matter what it is as long as it grabs me and holds me, fascinates me. And then I'll run out and do something about it." Furthermore, he explains, "I write for fun. You can't get too serious. I don't pontificate in my work. I have fun with ideas. I play with them. I approach my craft with enthusiasm and respect. If my work sparks serious thought, fine. But I don't write with that in mind. I'm not a serious person, and I don't like serious people. I don't see myself as a philosopher. That's awfully boring. I want to shun that role. My goal is to entertain myself and others. Hopefully, that will prevent me from taking myself too seriously."

MEDIA ADAPTATIONS: Fahrenheit 451 was filmed by Universal in 1966, and it was adapted as an opera by Georgia Holof and David Mettere and first produced at the Indiana Civic Theater, Fort Wayne, Ind., in November, 1988; *The Illustrated Man* was filmed by Warner Bros. in 1969; the story "The Screaming Woman" was filmed for television in 1972; the story "Murderer" was filmed for television by WGBH-TV in Boston in 1976; *The Martian Chronicles* was filmed as a television mini-series in 1980. Many of Bradbury's works have also been adapted as sound recordings.

AVOCATIONAL INTERESTS: Painting in oil and water colors, collecting Mexican artifacts.

CA INTERVIEW

CA interviewed Ray Bradbury by telephone on June 7, 1989, at his home in Los Angeles, California.

CA: Your special brand of imagination first became evident to large numbers of readers with the publication of The Martian Chronicles *in 1950. How much do you think that imagination owes to the free-ranging education you gave yourself?*

BRADBURY: I think that's where it came from—from not going to college, because college so often constricts people. If you're lucky, you get a teacher here and there, I suppose, as we do in high school, who is open and has no bad opinions of certain kinds of literature. What we need is teachers who are willing to accept the sort of thing we need as beginners, when we're eight, nine, ten. As long as we're reading, that's the important thing; we can just take off and fly. Then, along the way, you move from Edgar Rice Burroughs to Jules Verne and H. G. Wells and finally to Shakespeare and George Bernard Shaw; they're all great loves to me. The important thing is not to tell people to give up on their loves, but to accept all of them. I can get just as much a bang out of looking at my old "Prince Valiant" Sunday strips, which I began to collect when I was seventeen, as I do from reading Alexander Pope. It's the ability to accept that's important.

CA: You saw a lot of movies, too, when you were a kid.

BRADBURY: I saw all the important movies of our time up until about ten years ago, when they started making movies I hated

because they were too violent and too ridiculously sexual. But when I walk through the Academy of Motion Picture Arts and Sciences and look at the posters, which date back to 1920 or so, I realize that every single important film on the wall is something I've seen not only once but perhaps six or seven times.

CA: When you started writing stories, did you go through the usual process of imitating authors whose work you admired?

BRADBURY: Sure. I wrote sequels to Edgar Rice Burroughs's Martian novels. The very first thing I did, when I was twelve, was to write a sequel to an Edgar Rice Burroughs novel because I couldn't afford to buy it. Burroughs was a very sly character. He wrote one of his Martian novels and left his heroine trapped in the Sun Prison, and you had to buy the next book to find out how she got out. I had no money, so I wrote the sequel and got her out.

CA: You've always said that you avoid working slowly and carefully, that it's important not to analyze what you're doing as you do it.

BRADBURY: Right; you must never do that. Get it done. And it's true of everything in life. If you're a painter, paint a picture; don't think about it. If you're an actor, get on the stage and act. If you're an athlete, go out and throw one thousand baseballs or two thousand basketballs, but don't think about it. Get it done, and after the action, when you have finished a thing or you've worked on it for a number of hours or days, then is where your intellect comes into play. People believe thinking is supposed to precede an action, but it shouldn't. It should come after an action. It's there to correct, to help you, but if you think in the midst of an action, you cripple yourself. Movement, action, repetition—from that comes learning, and from the learning you can intellectualize and say, "I've accomplished *this;* what do I do *next?*" Then you burst into passionate action again.

CA: You're saying in all of this that you have to trust your unconscious mind.

BRADBURY: If you don't, you're sunk. The intellect can't do the work for you; it's got to be bursts of activity that let all your intuition come to the surface. Intellect drives away intuition because it doubts it.

CA: How does that philosophy apply to the creation of your landscapes such as your Mars of The Martian Chronicles *and later stories? How much do you have in your head before you begin to write?*

BRADBURY: It's all there. You make your own forms. You learn from the photographs from the Lowell Observatory which were made earlier in the century. You've picked up information from your favorite writer, Edgar Rice Burroughs. Carl Sagan and Arthur Clarke and I all admit a debt to Burroughs as an influence when we were ten years old. We wouldn't have become the writers we are if he hadn't started us on our way. A part of the atmosphere of *The Martian Chronicles* is the influence of Burroughs.

CA: You recreate so well the Midwestern towns of your boyhood. That's going back in memory. Does it work in the same sort of way?

BRADBURY: Even more so. I was born in Waukegan, Illinois, and lived there until I was almost fourteen, so all that stuff is put away. You must remind every writer, every painter, every dancer, every you-name-it, that we remember *everything*. Everything's in your head, though we don't believe it's there. Through word association you summon these things out, and the more you summon them out, the more follows. I like to use the metaphor of the magician who comes on the stage with an empty hat—that's your head; everyone thinks that they've got an empty head, they don't remember anything. The magician reaches into his hat and pulls out a red handkerchief. My God, where'd that come from! Then he reaches in and pulls out two handkerchiefs, a blue one and a yellow one. He shows you the hat, and it's empty. Then he pulls out more, of different colors. At the end of his act he pulls out twenty-two handkerchiefs, all different colors. All this from an empty hat!

That's what word association can do for you. You begin with the simple association of the feeling of grass the first night of summer when you run barefoot. What do you find in the grass? Old bits of the fourth of July left over from the year before, little pieces of junk or firecrackers that didn't go off or a piece of a rocket stick. Then you remember the ferns, which were like green fountains sprinkling up around the porch. And then all of your relatives seated on the porch, which ones were there and how they were dressed and who did what. And you wanted to listen to the mysterious talk of these wise people who knew everything, so, at the age of three or four or five, you crept around behind all the rocking chairs and the swing and put your head down on the porch floor and listened to your grandfather's voice thundering down through the rocking chair into the floorboards and into your ear, and you've got a xylophone there being played by the voices. The more of this you do, the more comes out. Five minutes before, you didn't know any of this; it wasn't there. These are the handkerchiefs that you're pulling out of your head. As the days and months and years go by, you pull out more and it becomes a novel.

CA: There have always been humanistic concerns behind or in your stories, and perhaps the most familiar example is Fahrenheit 451, *published as a book in 1954. How does that story feel to you today?*

BRADBURY: It feels great. But, though the end result in that book may be humanistic, the cause was my love of the library. I've written more books and stories and essays and plays and poetry about libraries than any other living author. All of the women in my life, going way back to when I was ten or so, have been English teachers, librarians, or booksellers. I met my wife at Fowler Brothers forty-three years ago; she was a book clerk who waited on me. My tenth-grade English teacher, Jennet Johnson, I took with me into life and she remained my friend and instructor until she died a few years ago at the age of ninety-two. The library and books are *it* for me; all of life is in there. If that is humanistic, then it's the result of my knowing that the library was to be my college, my university.

CA: Do you think books are in danger now?

BRADBURY: No, not a bit of it. After all, a computer is a book and a long-playing record is a book—they just have different shapes. It doesn't matter where you get your knowledge, as long as you get it. You can get it from a wonderful motion picture, you can get it from a book of poetry, and you can get it from all the great audio discs and tapes that are being made. Those are all books, and people shouldn't mistake the shape.

CA: Books do seem to be particularly under attack now, though, from fundamentalist groups.

BRADBURY: That's just not true. There have been no book-burnings in this country, and very few authors have been hurt in any way. It's all minor; it all blows away in a few months. There is no danger. You must just stand firm against anyone who attacks books.

CA: The uses and abuses of technology have also been a concern in your writing. How would you evaluate our space program now?

BRADBURY: We've let seventeen years go by since we were on the moon, and that's ridiculous. We've got to go back there; we've got to go back to Mars. We've got to be dynamic about this. What I'd like to do in the immediate future is write a program for Cape Canaveral and build bleachers down there around the gantries and every night at sunset put on a light-and-sound show so that the millions of people who come through as tourists will see the history of rocket flight and the Apollo missions and be reinvigorated about our past. If we teach it to people as they come through Canaveral and Cape Kennedy, they will go away excited and write their congressmen and we'll get the funding for future space programs. But NASA doesn't know what it's doing, and there are no programs at Canaveral that are worth a damn.

CA: What goes on at NASA seems to be tied to politics.

BRADBURY: It always has been. We would never have gone to the moon in the first place if we hadn't had a competition with Russia. I just wish we'd get back into a competition again. Out of war or the warfare of commerce comes all the good that ever has existed. It's one of those terrible ironies, but it's true.

CA: You've been able to write science fiction without being ignored by general readers and reviewers. Do you have any thoughts on how science fiction and its writers have been critically received?

BRADBURY: The critics have always been wrong about this. Science fiction is the most important literature in the history of the world, because it's the history of ideas, the history of our civilization birthing itself. Gutenberg was a science fiction dreamer; he dreamt of the printing press and then he invented it. At the moment at which it became a reality, science fictional dreaming became science fact. The history of all our machines, all our technologies, had to be in the head first. That's what science fiction is: it's the space between the left and the right ear where our dreams turn upon themselves and get ready to come forth out of our fingertips as blueprints to be built. Science fiction is central to everything we've ever done, and people who make fun of science fiction writers don't know what they're talking about.

CA: Do you think science fiction writers are becoming more accepted now?

BRADBURY: Oh, God, yes. It's happened in the last twenty years, since we landed on the moon. When we did that, all of a sudden people said, "Gee, whiz! They were right!"

CA: You told Aljean Harmetz for the New York Times, *"My idea of hell is having to watch NBC's mini-series of 'The Martian Chronicles.'" Would you comment on the pros and cons of television and movies as vehicles for science fiction?*

BRADBURY: They're fine, but some people misuse them. The main problem with the movie version of "The Martian Chronicles" wasn't that it was bad; it was simply boring. I don't know which is worse. If you're bad enough, at least you can be funny—you can get a Golden Turkey Award. With "Martian Chronicles" I wanted to buy a bull whip and give it to the director and have him crack it at the actors and say, "Move your buns!" The scenes were all too long and languid; I just couldn't believe it. It was a two six-pack of beer movie for me. I've got tapes here, and I've never looked at them. I tried. I had a short version sent to me which was put out for theaters in Europe, and I thought, Surely I can stand ninety minutes of this. After the first five minutes, I shut it off.

But I've had better luck on television: I'm very proud of my own series. When you get Peter O'Toole playing John Huston for you and doing it brilliantly, then you have something to be proud of. I'm doing all the things I want to do on television now, and I have control. If I don't like a thing, I have it changed. Not many writers have that privilege.

CA: Do you think the space-opera movie spectaculars have in any way dulled the impact of written science fiction?

BRADBURY: No, they've increased it. This week we've got "Star Trek V: The Final Frontier" out. All my daughters and my sons-in-law are going to the theater this weekend to see it. Millions and millions of people will see it in the next week. "Indiana Jones" is out, and that's a variety of science fiction and fantasy. All the important films of our time that have made the most amounts of money have been science fiction films. That shows our hunger for science fiction ideas, and our civilization still hasn't learned it. The good teachers, the ones that are really smart, have learned it; they use s-f in their classes as a tool. Boys are always the lousy readers and they need motivation. The girls are brighter. Boys get bright later, if they're going to get bright at all, and catch up. But you've got to motivate a boy who's six or seven or eight or nine, and then you can save him. If you don't reach him in those years, you lose him.

CA: You've written a lot of poetry over the years and had a big collection published in 1982. How does writing poetry fit into the overall pattern of your work, and how do you feel it helps in doing the fiction?

BRADBURY: It all intermixes. If you can write good haiku or a decent poem of any kind, you are on your way to starting to know how to write a screenplay. The writing of poetry is very similar to the writing of screenplays, and I feel I'm a good screenwriter because I grew up on poetry and have stuffed myself constantly with the works of Shakespeare, Pope, Robert Frost, Emily Dickinson, all the important poets of the last two or three hundred years. Poets shove metaphors in your head, and they hide there waiting to be ransacked along with your knowledge of archaeology and astronomy and Renaissance art. When you stuff your head with images from every field of activity in the world, you have a rich supply, a real banking system of metaphors.

CA: Your fiction is so often poetry, really.

BRADBURY: That's true. I met Aldous Huxley for the first time back in 1951; Christopher Isherwood introduced us. We sat at tea one afternoon and Mr. Huxley said to me, "You know what you are?" I said, "No. Tell me." He said, "You're a poet." He had read *The Martian Chronicles.* I was so proud to have my hero, Aldous Huxley, telling me this. I had read everything of his by the time I was thirty-one.

CA: In the past you've spoken of painting as a hobby. Are you still painting?

BRADBURY: No. I used to do a lot of it. But when my daughters were growing up, I was painting with them and they were making unfair comparisons. There was no use telling them that Daddy was better simply because he was older, so I stopped painting and just helped them, and I haven't gotten back to it. But one of the paintings I did thirty years ago, a huge painting called "The Halloween Tree," turned into a novel. I did the painting as metaphor and took it to my friend Chuck Jones, the animator-cartoonist who helped create "Bugs Bunny" and "The Road Runner." He looked at it and said, "My God, that's the history of Halloween. Let's do it as an animated film." So I wrote the screenplay for him, at which point M.G.M shut down its animation unit and threw everyone out on the street and we were all unemployed. Almost all the animation units went out of business that year. Then I said the hell with it and wrote the screenplay into a novel.

CA: You've done something new recently, the 1985 detective novel Death Is a Lonely Business. *What prompted that foray into the mystery genre, and a return to the novel after twenty-three years?*

BRADBURY: That's mysterious. My intuitive self lives its life and I live mine; we live in this body together inside my head. Who knows? But I started as a mystery writer. Back when I was in my twenties, I did twenty-five or thirty short stories for *Dime Detective, Dime Mystery,* and *Detective Tales.* They weren't very good. I was too young. Detective writing is much more difficult than science fiction or fantasy, because it does have to have some kind of logic to it or else people are going to catch you in terrible fits of fraudulence.

I started making notes on this murder mystery thirty years ago, and I wrote the first chapter and some other material and put it away in a file and looked at it again and again hoping that someday I would be old enough and wise enough and intuitive enough to finish it. About six years ago the novel came to me one day and said, "Hey! I'm ready." So I stood aside and it birthed itself in about three months.

The whole process of writing is very mysterious. Most of my creative work occurs, as it did this morning, lying in bed and waking up. Little dialogues go through my head. I call it "The Theater of Morning," this little theater inside my head in which my characters talk and act out parts. When they get to a certain point, it's time to write. This happened just forty-five minutes ago: I got up and went to my typewriter and wrote two thousand words of my new murder mystery, which I'm now finishing. Everything happens either in bed waking in the morning, so that you're not asleep and you're not awake—you're in-between and your brain is floating loose like an embryo inside your head; or in the shower, when you're totally relaxed and the water is beating on the back of your neck or the top of your head; or taking afternoon naps. I've tried to teach all of my friends, regardless of whether they're in computerology or whatever, to take more naps, to watch themselves early in the morning when they're waking up, to let things drift into their heads in the shower. Those are the creative moments. Then you can trap some of these things that are let free of the intellect so they can become themselves.

CA: You write in such a way as to make everything seem new, as if you were seeing it for the first time and through innocent eyes. Not downplaying your art and craft, I think it must spring first of all from the child in you, and that seems related to what you've been saying through this interview.

BRADBURY: Also, when you're a certain age you go to the library and get out books on the senses. There are wonderful books on the sense of hearing that will teach you what hearing is. There are books on seeing, on the gift of sight, on colors. There are books about the gift of smelling scents and the history of the perfume industry, books on tasting. There is a book on the olfactory senses that I bought thirty-five years ago; I still have it in my library. It names all the different kinds of scents there are in the world and categorizes them so that you can learn the difference between the various odors. You stash all that stuff in you finally, and then you are able to use it to attack the senses of your readers. If I can convince you that you are where you are, then you'll believe anything, because you're in the middle of it. I can put you in there.

CA: In the New York Times *article I quoted earlier, you also said, "Every single day for 50 years, if I can get to my typewriter by 9 o'clock, by 10:30 I'm protected against the world." Would you like to think you've given your readers something to protect them against the world?*

BRADBURY: A lot of people talk about getting through the night. I want to get readers through the day. Nightmares are plenty bad, but we've got to help save one another from day-mares too. I can't completely protect others; nobody can. There is no final protection. Look what's been going on in China the last week. Good God, all we can do is sit in front of the TV set and cry. We don't know these people, do we? And yet, suddenly we do. They're up close, talking to us. Their friends have been shot right in front of them. How can I help with that? Well, I suppose I can help by writing a poem or a story so that I can re-call that moment to you and help purge you of the memory. But beyond a certain point, you have to do your own weeping.

CA: You seem to be having as good a time now with everything you're doing as you've always had in the past.

BRADBURY: Everything's play. If you work at it, it turns into rocks and dust. Everything must be approached happily, for hav-ing a lot of fun—even the most serious thing. *Fahrenheit 451* was a joy to write; all my most serious novels were. What fun I had writing my murder mystery! But it had some serious moments, terribly sad moments. My new murder mystery is even better; I'm having even more fun with it.

Why should people work at things? Why should they do things they hate? When I lecture, I try to get people to quit their jobs and do something they really want to do. I was on a jet flight five days ago from Tulsa to Salt Lake City, and there was a delightful young man of about twenty-five sitting with me. He's a lawyer for a computer firm, and from the way he talked I knew he was on the verge of some change in his life; he was becoming restive. I suggested a few things to him that he should do to free his mind. I said, "How much poetry do you read? There's a lot of wonderful poetry out there. What about essays? There are in-credible books of essays and ideas waiting out there." I got a let-ter from him yesterday saying he went right to the bookstore—a real smart kid—and bought a book on ideas and a book on Charles Darwin. He was writing to thank me for helping change his life. That's what we must do to help one another so that we bring out the joy and help save people from the ennui of work they hate. If they can't leave their job—if it's totally impossi-ble—then they've got to find time each day at the library or the bookstore, or in some hobby late at night, to revitalize them-selves.

BIOGRAPHICAL/CRITICAL SOURCES:

BOOKS

Authors in the News, Gale, Volume 1, 1976, Volume 2, 1976.

Breit, Harvey, *The Writer Observed,* World Publishing, 1956.
Clareson, Thomas D., editor, *Voices for the Future: Essays on Major Science Fiction Writers,* Volume 1, Bowling Green State University Press, 1976.
Contemporary Literary Criticism, Gale, Volume 1, 1973, Volume 3, 1975, Volume 10, 1979, Volume 15, 1980, Volume 42, 1987.
Dictionary of Literary Biography, Gale, Volume 2: *American Novelists since World War II,* 1978, Volume 8: *Twentieth Century American Science Fiction Writers,* 1981.
Greenberg, Martin H. and Joseph D. Olander, editors, *Ray Bradbury,* Taplinger, 1980.
Johnson, Wayne L., *Ray Bradbury,* Ungar, 1980.
Kirk, Russell, *Enemies of the Permanent Things: Observations of Abnormality in Literature and Politics,* Arlington House, 1969.
Knight, Damon, *In Search of Wonder: Critical Essays on Science Fiction,* 2nd edition, Advent, 1967.
Nolan, William F., *The Ray Bradbury Companion,* Gale, 1974.
Platt, Charles, *Dream Makers: Science Fiction and Fantasy Writ-ers at Work,* Ungar, 1987.
Slusser, George Edgar, *The Bradbury Chronicles,* Borgo, 1977.
Touponce, William F., *Ray Bradbury and the Poetics of Reverie: Fantasy, Science Fiction and the Reader,* UMI Research Press, 1984.
Wollheim, Donald, *The Universe Makers,* Harper, 1971.

PERIODICALS

Extrapolation, fall, 1984.
Future, October, 1978.
National Review, April 4, 1967.
New York Times, April 24, 1983.
New York Times Book Review, August 8, 1951, December 28, 1969, October 29, 1972, October 26, 1980.
Reader's Digest, September, 1986.
Time, March 24, 1975, October 13, 1980.
Washington Post, July 7, 1989.
Writer's Digest, December, 1974, February, 1976.

—*Sketch by Thomas Wiloch*

—*Interview by Jean W. Ross*

*   *   *

BRANDENBERG, Aliki Liacouras 1929-
(Aliki)

PERSONAL: Born September 3, 1929, in Wildwood Crest, N.J.; daughter of James Peter (a grocer) and Stella (a homemaker; maiden name, Lagakos) Liacouras; married Franz Brandenberg (an author), March 15, 1957; children: Jason, Alexa Demetria. *Education:* Museum College of Art, Philadelphia, Pa., graduate, 1951.

ADDRESSES: Home—17, Regent's Park Terrace, London NW1 7ED, England.

CAREER: Muralist and commercial artist in Philadelphia, Pa., and New York City, 1951-56, and Zurich, Switzerland, 1957-60; commercial artist, writer, and illustrator of children's books in New York City, 1960-77, and London, England, 1977—.

AWARDS, HONORS: Boys' Clubs of America Junior Book Award, 1968, for *Three Gold Pieces: A Greek Folk Tale; At Mary Bloom's* was chosen by the American Institute of Graphic Arts for the Children's Book Show, 1976, and by the Children's Book Council for the Children's Book Showcase, 1977; New York

Academy of Sciences Children's Science Book Award, 1977, for *Corn Is Maise: The Gift of the Indians;* Dutch Children's Book Council Silver Slate Pencil award, and Garden State (New Jersey) Children's Book Award, both 1981, for *Mummies Made in Egypt;* Prix du Livre pour Enfants (Geneva), 1987, for *Feelings.*

WRITINGS:

SELF-ILLUSTRATED; UNDER NAME ALIKI

The Story of William Tell, Faber & Faber, 1960, A. S. Barnes, 1961.
My Five Senses, Crowell, 1962.
My Hands, Crowell, 1962.
The Wish Workers, Dial, 1962.
The Story of Johnny Appleseed (Junior Literary Guild selection), Prentice-Hall, 1963.
George and the Cherry Tree, Dial, 1964.
The Story of William Penn (Junior Literary Guild selection), Prentice-Hall, 1964.
A Weed Is a Flower: The Life of George Washington Carver, Prentice-Hall, 1965, reprinted, Simon & Schuster, 1988.
Keep Your Mouth Closed, Dear, Dial, 1966.
Three Gold Pieces: A Greek Folk Tale, Pantheon, 1967.
New Year's Day, Crowell, 1967.
(Editor) *Hush Little Baby: A Folk Lullaby,* Prentice-Hall, 1968.
My Visit to the Dinosaurs, Crowell, 1969, reprinted, 1985.
The Eggs: A Great Folk Tale, Pantheon, 1969.
Diogenes: The Story of the Greek Philosopher, Prentice-Hall, 1969.
Fossils Tell of Long Ago, Crowell, 1972.
June 7, Macmillan, 1972.
The Long Lost Coelacanth and Other Living Fossils, Crowell, 1973.
Green Grass and White Milk, Crowell, 1974.
Go Tell Aunt Rhody, Macmillan, 1974.
At Mary Bloom's (Junior Literary Guild selection), Greenwillow, 1976.
Corn Is Maise: The Gift of the Indians, Crowell, 1976.
The Many Lives of Benjamin Franklin, Prentice-Hall, 1977.
Wild and Woolly Mammoths, Crowell, 1977.
The Twelve Months, Greenwillow, 1978.
Mummies Made in Egypt, Crowell, 1979.
The Two of Them, Greenwillow, 1979.
Digging Up Dinosaurs, Crowell, 1981.
We Are Best Friends, Greenwillow, 1982.
Use Your Head, Dear, Greenwillow, 1983.
A Medieval Feast, Harper, 1983.
Feelings, Greenwillow, 1984.
Dinosaurs Are Different, Crowell, 1985.
How a Book Is Made, Crowell, 1986.
Jack and Jake, Greenwillow, 1986.
Overnight at Mary Bloom's, Greenwillow, 1987.
Welcome Little Baby, Greenwillow, 1987.
Dinosaur Bones, Crowell, 1988.
The King's Day: Louis XIV of France, Crowell, 1989.

ILLUSTRATOR; UNDER NAME ALIKI

Pat Witte and Eve Witte, *Who Lives Here?,* Golden Press, 1961.
Joan M. Lexau, *Cathy Is Company,* Dial, 1961.
Paul Showers, *Listening Walk,* Crowell, 1961.
Margaret Hodges, *What's for Lunch, Charley?,* Dial, 1961.
Mickey Marks, *What Can I Buy?,* Dial, 1962.
Dorothy Les Tina, *A Book to Begin On: Alaska,* Holt, 1962.
James Holding, *The Lazy Little Zulu,* Morrow, 1962.
Joan K. Heilbroner, *This Is the House Where Jack Lives,* Harper, 1962.

Vivian L. Thompson, *The Horse That Liked Sandwiches,* Putnam, 1962.
Arthur Jonas, *Archimedes and His Wonderful Discoveries,* Prentice-Hall, 1962.
Bernice Kohn, *Computers at Your Service,* Prentice-Hall, 1962.
Jonas, *New Ways in Math,* Prentice-Hall, 1962.
Eugene David, *Television and How It Works,* Prentice-Hall, 1962.
David, *Electricity in Your Life,* Prentice-Hall, 1963.
Holding, *Mister Moonlight and Omar,* Morrow, 1963.
Lexau, *That's Good, That's Bad,* Dial, 1963.
Judy Hawes, *Bees and Beelines,* Crowell, 1964.
Jonas, *More New Ways in Math,* Prentice-Hall, 1964.
Holding, *Sherlock on the Trail,* Morrow, 1964.
Kohn, *Everything Has a Size* (also see below), Prentice-Hall, 1964.
Kohn, *Everything Has a Shape* (also see below), Prentice-Hall, 1964.
Kohn, *One Day It Rained Cats and Dogs,* Coward, 1965.
Helen Clare, *Five Dolls in a House,* Prentice-Hall, 1965.
Rebecca Kalusky, *Is It Blue as a Butterfly?,* Prentice-Hall, 1965.
Mary K. Phelan, *Mother's Day,* Crowell, 1965.
Betty Ren Wright, *I Want to Read!,* A. Whitman, 1965.
Sean Morrison, *Is That a Happy Hippopotamus?,* Crowell, 1966.
Kohn, *Everything Has a Shape and Everything Has a Size,* Prentice-Hall, 1966.
Clare, *Five Dolls in the Snow,* Prentice-Hall, 1967.
Clare, *Five Dolls and the Monkey,* Prentice-Hall, 1967.
Clare, *Five Dolls and Their Friends,* Prentice-Hall, 1968.
Clare, *Five Dolls and the Duke,* Prentice-Hall, 1968.
Wilma Yeo, *Mrs. Neverbody's Recipes,* Lippincott, 1968.
Esther R. Hautzig, *At Home: A Visit in Four Languages,* Macmillan, 1968.
Polly Greenberg, *Oh Lord, I Wish I Was a Buzzard,* Macmillan, 1968.
Roma Gans, *Birds at Night,* Crowell, 1968.
Jane Jonas Srivastava, *Weighing and Balancing,* Crowell, 1970.
Joanne Oppenheim, *On the Other Side of the River,* Watts, 1972.
Philip M. Sherlock and Hilary Sherlock, *Ears and Tails and Common Sense: More Stories from the Carribbean,* Crowell, 1974.
Srivastava, *Averages,* Crowell, 1975.

ILLUSTRATOR OF BOOKS BY HUSBAND, FRANZ BRANDENBERG; UNDER NAME ALIKI

I Once Knew a Man, Macmillan, 1970.
Fresh Cider and Pie, Macmillan, 1973.
No School Today!, Macmillan, 1975.
A Secret for Grandmother's Birthday, Greenwillow, 1975.
A Robber! A Robber!, Greenwillow, 1976.
I Wish I Was Sick, Too!, Greenwillow, 1976 (published in England as *I Don't Feel Well,* Hamish Hamilton, 1977).
What Can You Make of It?, Greenwillow, 1977.
Nice New Neighbors (Junior Literary Guild selection), Greenwillow, 1977.
A Picnic, Hurrah!, Greenwillow, 1978.
Six New Students, Greenwillow, 1978.
Everyone Ready? (Junior Literary Guild selection), Greenwillow, 1979.
It's Not My Fault! (Junior Literary Guild selection), Greenwillow, 1980.
Leo and Emily, Greenwillow, 1981.
Leo and Emily's Big Ideas, Greenwillow, 1982.
Aunt Nina and Her Nephews and Nieces, Greenwillow, 1983.
Aunt Nina's Visit, Greenwillow, 1984.

Leo and Emily and the Dragon, Greenwillow, 1984.
The Hit of the Party, Greenwillow, 1985.
Cock-A-Doodle-Doo, Greenwillow, 1986.
What's Wrong with a Van?, Greenwillow, 1987.
Aunt Nina Good Night!, Greenwillow, 1989.

WORK IN PROGRESS: "Eight books, currently in one form or another."

SIDELIGHTS: Aliki Brandenberg told *CA:* "I write 'fiction' (feeling) books because I need to express an experience. I write nonfiction because I'm curious about a subject. I do a great deal of research for the latter books, both for the writing and for the illustrations. I write only about subjects I am interested in, and am delighted to see (having visited schools) children are interested in my subjects, too. Words, pictures, and expressing myself are vital to my survival, and I'm lucky to be spending my life doing something I love."

AVOCATIONAL INTERESTS: Working with various mediums: paper, fabric, clay, metal; macrame; weaving; music; baking; traveling; reading; gardening.

MEDIA ADAPTATIONS: Filmstrip adaptations of *Hush Little Baby* and *The Two of Them* were produced by Weston Woods in 1976 and 1981, respectively.

BIOGRAPHICAL/CRITICAL SOURCES:

BOOKS

The Children's Bookshelf, Child Study Association of America, Bantam, 1965.
Kingman, Lee, and others, compilers, *Illustrators of Children's Books,* Horn Book, *1957-1966,* 1968, *1967-1976,* 1978.

PERIODICALS

New York Times Book Review, November 18, 1979, March 8, 1981, October 16, 1983.
Publishers Weekly, July 22, 1983.
Times Literary Supplement, March 28, 1980.
Washington Post Book World, May 9, 1982.

*　　*　　*

BRANDENBERG, Franz 1932-

PERSONAL: Born February 10, 1932, in Zug, Switzerland; son of Franz and Marie (Sigrist) Brandenberg; married Aliki Liacouras (an author and illustrator under name Aliki), March 15, 1957; children: Jason, Alexa Demetria. *Education:* Attended boarding school in Einsiedeln, Switzerland.

ADDRESSES: Home—17, Regent's Park Terrace, London NW1 7ED, England.

CAREER: Began apprenticeship with publisher and bookseller in Lucerne, Switzerland, 1949; continued in book trade, 1952-60, working in bookshops or publishing houses in London, Paris, and Florence; literary agent in New York, N.Y., 1960-72; writer for children, 1970—.

WRITINGS:

ILLUSTRATED BY WIFE, ALIKI

I Once Knew a Man, Macmillan, 1970.
Fresh Cider and Pie, Macmillan, 1973.
No School Today!, Macmillan, 1975.
A Secret for Grandmother's Birthday, Greenwillow, 1975.
A Robber! A Robber!, Greenwillow, 1976.
I Wish I Was Sick, Too!, Greenwillow, 1976 (published in England as *I Don't Feel Well,* Hamish Hamilton, 1977).

What Can You Make of It?, Greenwillow, 1977.
Nice New Neighbors (Junior Literary Guild selection), Greenwillow, 1977.
A Picnic, Hurrah!, Greenwillow, 1978.
Six New Students, Greenwillow, 1978.
Everyone Ready? (Junior Literary Guild selection), Greenwillow, 1979.
It's Not My Fault! (Junior Literary Guild selection), Greenwillow, 1980.
Leo and Emily, Greenwillow, 1981.
Leo and Emily's Big Ideas, Greenwillow, 1982.
Aunt Nina and Her Nephews and Nieces, Greenwillow, 1983.
Aunt Nina's Visit, Greenwillow, 1984.
Leo and Emily and the Dragon, Greenwillow, 1984.
The Hit of the Party, Greenwillow, 1985.
Cock-A-Doodle-Doo, Greenwillow, 1986.
What's Wrong with a Van?, Greenwillow, 1987.
Aunt Nina Good Night!, Greenwillow, 1989.

OTHER

Otto Is Different, illustrated by James Stevenson, Greenwillow, 1985.
Leo and Emily's Zoo, illustrated by Yossi Abolafia, Greenwillow, 1988.

WORK IN PROGRESS: "I am superstitious about talking about projects before they are finished."

SIDELIGHTS: Franz Brandenberg, whose books have been translated into several languages, including Japanese, Chinese, Hebrew, French, German, Dutch, Danish, Swedish, and Catalan, told *CA:* "Writing for children is my way of perpetuating my own childhood, which was very happy. Grandparents, aunts, and uncles played an important role in my family. We went to visit them; they came to visit us. One spinster aunt in particular, Aunt Nina, had a great influence on me. She took me on trips, introduced me to the circus and the theatre, and always brought me books. My latest series of picture books is about her. Neighbors, too, were important. We constantly climbed over each other's garden fences. The 'Leo and Emily' books are a result of these memories. Also, our own children were a good source for stories. The 'Edward and Elizabeth' books were inspired by them. I am very lucky to have my wife illustrate my books, as she, naturally, understands me better than anyone else. I enjoy sharing my experiences with children, and I hope children enjoy reading about them."

BIOGRAPHICAL/CRITICAL SOURCES:

PERIODICALS

New York, December 17, 1973.

*　　*　　*

BRANDON, Sheila
See RAYNER, Claire (Berenice)

*　　*　　*

BREHM, Sharon S(tephens) 1945-

PERSONAL: Born April 18, 1945, in Roanoke, Va.; daughter of John Wallis and Jane (Phenix) Stephens; divorced. *Education:* Duke University, B.A. (magna cum laude), 1967, Ph.D., 1973; Harvard University, M.A., 1968.

ADDRESSES: Home—2401 Massachusetts, Lawrence, Kan. 66046. *Office*—Department of Psychology, University of Kansas, Lawrence, Kan. 66045.

CAREER: Northeast Nassau Psychiatric Hospital, Kings Park, N.Y., staff psychologist for adolescent unit, 1968-69; University of Washington, Seattle, clinical psychology intern at Medical Center, 1973-74; Virginia Polytechnic Institute and State University, Blacksburg, assistant professor of psychology, 1974-75; University of Kansas, Lawrence, assistant professor, 1975-78, associate professor, 1978-83, professor of psychology, 1983—, associate dean of college of liberal arts and sciences, and director of college honors program, 1987—. Reviewer for several research grant foundations.

MEMBER: American Psychological Association, National Council of Family Relations, Society of Experimental Social Psychology, Phi Beta Kappa.

AWARDS, HONORS: Fulbright research scholar, Paris, France, 1981-82.

WRITINGS:

The Application of Social Psychology to Clinical Practice, Hemisphere Publishing, 1976.
Help for Your Child: A Parent's Guide to Mental Health Services, Prentice-Hall, 1978.
(With Saul Kassin and Frederick X. Gibbons) *Developmental Social Psychology: Theory and Research,* Oxford University Press, 1981.
(With Jack W. Brehm) *Psychological Reactance: A Theory of Freedom and Control,* Academic Press, 1981.
Intimate Relationships, Random House, 1985.
Seeing Female, Greenwood Press, 1988.
(With Kassin) *Social Psychology,* Houghton, in press.

CONTRIBUTOR

S. Moscovici, editor, *Psychologie sociale,* Presses Universitaires de France, 1984, 2nd edition, 1988.
S. L. Garfield and A. E. Bergin, editors, *Handbook of Psychotherapy and Behavior Change,* Wiley, 3rd edition, 1986.
R. Snyder and C. Ford, editors, *Coping with Negative Life Events,* Plenum, 1987.
J. E. Maddux, C. D. Stoltenberg, and R. Rosenwein, editors, *Social Processes in Clinical and Counseling Psychology,* Springer-Verlag, 1987.
R. J. Sternberg and M. L. Barnes, editors, *The Psychology of Love,* Yale University Press, 1988.

Contributor to numerous other scholarly collections.

OTHER

Contributor to various psychology journals, including *Contemporary Psychology, Journal of Personality and Social Psychology, Journal of Social and Clinical Psychology,* and *Sex Roles.* Member of various editorial boards, including *Journal of Personality, Journal of Social and Clinical Psychology,* and *Series on Social Psychological Applications to Social Issues.*

WORK IN PROGRESS: Second edition of *Intimate Relationships* for McGraw.

*   *   *

BRITTAIN, Bill
    See BRITTAIN, William (E.)

BRITTAIN, William (E.)   1930-
    (Bill Brittain; James Knox, a pseudonym)

PERSONAL: Born December 16, 1930, in Rochester, N.Y.; son of Knox (a medical doctor) and Dorothy (a nurse; maiden name, Sunderlin) Brittain; married Virginia Ann Connorton (a teacher), February 6, 1954; children: James, Susan. *Education:* Attended Colgate University, 1948-50; State Teachers College at Brockport (now New York State University at Brockport), B.S., 1952; Hofstra University, M.S., 1958.

ADDRESSES: Home—17 Wisteria Dr., Asheville, N.C. 28804.

CAREER: Writer. English teacher in LeRoy, N.Y., 1952-54; elementary teacher in Lawrence, N.Y., 1954-60; Lawrence Junior High School, Lawrence, remedial reading teacher, 1960-86.

MEMBER: Mystery Writers of America, Society of Children's Book Writers.

AWARDS, HONORS: Children's Choice citation, International Reading Association/Children's Book Council, 1980, and Charlie May Simon award, 1982, for *All the Money in the World;* Notable Children's Book citation, American Library Association, 1981, for *Devil's Donkey;* Newbery Award honor book citation, 1984, for *The Wish Giver: Three Tales of Coven Tree.*

WRITINGS:

Survival Outdoors, Monarch, 1977.

UNDER NAME BILL BRITTAIN

All the Money in the World, illustrations by Charles Robinson, Harper, 1979.
Devil's Donkey, illustrations by Andrew Glass, Harper, 1981.
The Wish Giver: Three Tales of Coven Tree, illustrations by Glass, Harper, 1983.
Who Knew There'd Be Ghosts?, Harper, 1985.
Dr. Dredd's Wagon of Wonders, Harper, 1987.
The Fantastic Freshman, Harper, 1988.
My Buddy, the King, Harper, 1989.

OTHER

Contributor of stories to *Ellery Queen's Mystery Magazine* and *Alfred Hitchcock's Mystery Magazine,* sometimes under pseudonym James Knox.

WORK IN PROGRESS: Professor Popkin's Prodigious Polish for Harper.

SIDELIGHTS: William Brittain told *CA:* "Retirement, after thirty-six years of teaching, has provided a lot more time for my writing. I still, however, regard this writing as a hobby which I enjoy very much. Any 'teaching' in my stories is purely in the eye of the beholder. I'm quite content to produce a tale that's interesting and exciting, both to me and to the boys and girls who read my books. I'm extremely grateful to all the established authors who were so helpful when, as a teacher, I was doing my best to make it as a part-time writer. Chief among those offering assistance was Frederic Dannay, editor of *Ellery Queen's Mystery Magazine,* whose help and encouragement were invaluable. I'm also blessed with a wife who has the patience of Job, coupled with razor-sharp critical faculties. Without her, it's doubtful that any of my books would have been completed."

*   *   *

BROUGHTON, James (Richard)   1913-

PERSONAL: Born November 10, 1913, in Modesto, Calif.; son of Irwin (a banker) and Olga (Jungbluth) Broughton; married

Suzanna Hart (an artist), December 6, 1962 (divorced, 1978); children: Serena, Orion. *Education:* Stanford University, B.A., 1936; advanced study, New School for Social Research, 1943-45.

ADDRESSES: Office—P.O. Box 1330, Port Townsend, Wash. 98368.

CAREER: Poet, playwright, filmmaker. Was involved with Art in Cinema experimental film group at the San Francisco Museum in late 1940s, and with San Francisco Renaissance poetry movement in late 1950s and early 1960s; resident playwright with Playhouse Repertory Theatre in San Francisco, 1958-64; lecturer in creative arts, San Francisco State University, 1964-76, and instructor in film, San Francisco Art Institute, 1968-82. Has given public readings of his poetry. Member of board of directors, Farallone Films, 1948—, and Anthology Film Archives, 1969—.

AWARDS, HONORS: Alden Award, 1945, for play "Summer Fury"; James D. Phelan Award in Literature, 1948, for play "The Playground," and 1987, for creative cinema; Avon Foundation grant-in-aid, 1968; Eugene O'Neill Theatre Foundation playwright fellow, 1969; Guggenheim fellowships, 1970-71 and 1973-74; National Endowment for the Arts grants, 1976 and 1982; Citation of Honor, City of San Francisco, 1983, for contributions to the arts; Doctor of Fine Arts degree, San Francisco Art Institute, 1984; Edinburgh Film Festival Award of Merit, 1953; Cannes Film Festival Prix du fantaisie poetique, 1954, for "The Pleasure Garden"; Oberhausen Film Festival Hauptpreis der Kurzfilmtage, 1968, for "The Bed"; Bellevue Film Festival grand prize, 1970, for "The Golden Positions"; Twelfth Independent Film Award from *Film Culture* magazine, 1975, for "outstanding work of thirty years" as "grand classic master of independent cinema"; Maya Deren award, American Film Institute, 1989, for lifetime achievement.

WRITINGS:

POETRY

Songs for Certain Children, Adrian Wilson, 1947.
The Playground (also see below), Centaur Press, 1949.
The Ballad of Mad Jenny, Centaur Press, 1949.
Musical Chairs: A Songbook for Anxious Children, Centaur Press, 1950.
An Almanac for Amorists, Collection Merlin (Paris), 1954, Grove Press, 1954.
True and False Unicorn, Grove Press, 1957.
The Water Circle: A Poem of Celebration, Pterodactyl Press, 1965.
Tidings, Pterodactyl Press, 1966.
Look In, Look Out, Toad Press, 1968.
High Kukus (also see below), Jargon Society, 1968.
A Long Undressing: Collected Poems, 1949-1969, Jargon Society, 1971.
Going through Customs, Arion Press, 1976.
Erogeny (also see below), ManRoot Press, 1976.
Odes for Odd Occasions, ManRoot Press, 1977.
Song of the Godbody (also see below), ManRoot Press, 1979.
Hymns to Hermes, ManRoot Press, 1979.
Shaman Psalm (also see below), Syzygy Press, 1981.
Graffiti for the Johns of Heaven, Syzygy Press, 1982.
Ecstasies, Syzygy Press, 1983.
Atteindre l'inevitable, Nadir Press (France), 1985.
A to Z, Syzygy Press, 1986.
Vrai et Fausse Licorne, Editions Aeolian (France), 1987.
Hooplas, Pennywhistle Press, 1988.
75 Life Lines, Jargon Society, 1988.

PLAYS

"A Love for Lionel," first produced in New York, N.Y. at Actors Stage, 1944.
"Summer Fury"(one-act; first produced in Palo Alto, Calif., at Stanford University, 1945), published in *Best One Act Plays of 1945,* edited by Margaret Mayorga, Dodd, 1946, reprinted as *Best Short Plays,* 1957.
The Playground (first produced in Oakland, Calif., at Mills College, 1948), Centaur Press, 1949, reprinted, Baker's Plays, 1965.
"Burning Questions" (four-act), first produced in San Francisco, Calif., at Playhouse Repertory Theatre, 1958.
The Last Word (one-act; first produced in San Francisco at Playhouse Repertory Theatre, 1958; also see below), Baker, 1958.
Where Helen Lies (first produced in New York at American Theatre Wing, 1959), University of Colorado Press, 1961.
"The Rites of Women" (two-act), first produced in San Francisco at Playhouse Repertory Theatre, 1959.
"How Pleasant It Is to Have Money," first produced in San Francisco at Playhouse Repertory Theatre, 1964.
"Bedlam; or, America the Beautiful Mother" (one-act), first produced at San Francisco State College, 1967; produced in Waterford, Conn., by Eugene O'Neill Theatre Foundation, 1969.

Also author of "Eggs of the Ostrich," adapted from the French of Andre Roussin, 1956.

FILMS

(With Sydney Peterson) "The Potted Psalm," Farallone Films, 1946.
"Mother's Day," Farallone Films, 1950.
"Adventures of Jimmy," Farallone Films, 1951.
"Four in the Afternoon," Farallone Films, 1951.
"Loony Tom and Happy Lover," Farallone Films, 1951.
"The Pleasure Garden," Flights of Fancy Committee for Farallone Films, 1953.
"The Bed," Farallone Films, 1968.
"Nuptiae," Farallone Films, 1969.
"The Golden Positions," Farallone Films, 1970.
"This Is It," Farallone Films, 1971.
"Dreamwood," Farallone Films, 1972.
"High Kukus" (with poems from *High Kukus*) Farallone Films, 1973.
"Testament," Farallone Films, 1974.
"The Water Circle," Farallone Films, 1975.
"Erogeny," Farallone Films, 1976.
(With Joel Singer) "Together," Farallone Films, 1976.
(With Singer) "Windowmobile," Farallone Films, 1977.
(With Singer) "Song of the Godbody"(with poems from *Song of the Godbody*), Farallone Films, 1978.
"Hermes Bird," Farallone Films, 1979.
(With Singer) "The Gardener of Eden," Farallone Films, 1981.
(With Singer) "Shaman Psalm" (with poems from *Shaman Psalm*), Farallone Films, 1982.
(With Singer) "Devotion," Farallone Films, 1983.
(With Singer) "Scattered Remains," Farallone Films, 1988.

OTHER

The Right Playmate, Farrar, Straus, 1952, revised edition, Pterodactyl Press, 1964.
San Francisco Poets (sound recording), Evergreen Records, 1958.
The Bard & the Harper (sound recording), MEA Records, 1965.

Something Just for You, Pisani Press, 1966.
The Androgyne Journal (autobiographical), Scrimshaw Press, 1977.
Seeing the Light, City Lights Books, 1977.
(Editor) *Whitman's Wild Children* (anthology), Lapis Press, 1988.
(Editor) *Gay and Lesbian Poetry in Our Time* (anthology), St. Martin's Press, 1988.

Films and poems also recorded on video and audio cassettes. Contributor to more than a dozen anthologies, including *Sparks of Fire,* edited by James Bogan, 1982, and *Practicing Angels,* 1986. Contributor of articles to *Theatre Arts, Sight and Sound* (London), *Film Culture, Film Quarterly,* and *Filmagazine;* frequent contributor to *Canyon Cinemanews.* Broughton's manuscripts, papers and memorabilia are housed in the special collections section of the Kent State University Library, Kent, Ohio.

SIDELIGHTS: Since 1948, James Broughton has made his international reputation as a poet, playwright, and " 'guru' of the independent film subculture in the United States," notes Janis Crystal Lipzin in the *Antioch Review. Dictionary of Literary Biography* contributor Idris McElveen relates that Broughton describes himself as "a visionary and a parodist" who is "happy among the Transcendentalists." His poetry expresses Zen philosophy and celebrates the ecstasies of life, particularly eroticism. In both poetry and film, he uses the possibilities of the art forms to their full extent, often extending the recognized boundaries of technique. In both genres, "he insists . . . that both the original impulse and the product of his work be natural, spontaneous leaps of his own imagination, without artifice, without novelty for the sake of novelty, and without masks," reports McElveen. Nudity—emotional and physical—characterizes his works. Thus he fulfills his role as a poet, which to him means "being obstreperous, outlandish and obscene. [The poet's] business is to ignite a revolution of insight in the soul," he says in *Seeing the Light.*

The Modesto-born, third-generation Californian says in "Testament" that he received a vision of his destiny early in life: "When I was three years old I was wakened in the night by a glittering stranger, who told me I was a poet and never to fear being alone or being laughed at. That was my first meeting with my angel, who is the most interesting poet I have ever met." Sent to military school at age ten, he developed a love for language and soon began to write imitations of the poems in the *Oxford Book of English Verse.* After earning a B.A. from Stanford in 1936, Broughton joined the merchant marine and visited the Near East. He returned to New York and two years of study at the New School for Social Research, then home to San Francisco, where he learned poetry reading from Robert Duncan and Madeline Gleason. His initiation to filmmaking came in 1946 when Sydney Peterson suggested they abandon the play they were writing together to make a film instead. The result was "The Potted Psalm," "a rather crazy thing" exploring camera techniques on location in an abandoned graveyard, Broughton stated to interviewer Clark McKowen (interview collected in Broughton issue of *Film Culture*). The film, which he later referred to as "an energetic surrealist lark," was completed in time to be part of the Art in Cinema movement in San Francisco, which helped its makers to become known as pioneers in the art world.

The originality of his works, in which he expresses an essentially comic and erotic vision of life, verifies his often-stated independence from social and aesthetic norms. His first independent offering, "Mother's Day," "was not meant to please anyone but myself," he says in *Seeing the Light.* "It was done out of absolute necessity, to discover what my inner haunting looked like. I accepted it as my first and last chance, a one and only shot: I risked everything. All work should be approached that way. Still today every film I make is my 'last.' " To critics who see in "Mother's Day" the influence of earlier avant garde films, Broughton says, "That sort of thing is only a critic's means of putting one in one's place (or someplace where he can file you away) so that originality can be discounted." Because "it linked a specifically American way of seeing to the French avant-garde tradition," Broughton reports in *Film Culture,* "Mother's Day" has been the subject of detailed study in France and has had an important shaping influence on the American avant garde.

Broughton's next major work was *The Pleasure Garden,* made in London at the request of the director of the British Film Institute. "That film was a bit ahead of its time, being maybe the first Love-In in a public park," Broughton told McKowen. He added that at first, it was most popular among Europeans, who viewed it as "a satire on the English." It won the Edinburgh Festival award in 1953 and the Cannes Festival award the following year. The making of the film plunged him deeply into debt, and when he returned to San Francisco he rejoined the flourishing poetry scene, not intending to make another film. Eventually, however, he was to produce another prize-winner, "The Bed," a tribute to the piece of furniture so closely linked to birth, death, and all the major events of human life. He explains in *Seeing the Light,* "I had not made a film for 13 years and I was prodded into making 'just one more' by Jaques Ledoux of the Belgian Film Archive for his international experimental powwow of 1968. All I did was express how life felt to me in my 50s. . . . I wanted to show as directly as possible my vision of the flowing river of existence and I thought of it as a private communication to an old friend in Brussels. The public success of the film astounded me." His enthusiasm for making films thus renewed, he continued making films, including "The Golden Positions," which won the Bellevue Film Festival grand prize in 1970.

Broughton has shared his enthusiasm with students at the San Francisco Playhouse, San Francisco State College Poetry Center, San Francisco State University, and the San Francisco Art Institute. He has also worked at film institutes in Denmark and England. His lifetime achievement was recognized in 1975, when he received the 12th annual Independent Film Award from *Film Culture* magazine for thirty years of "outstanding work" as "the grand classic master of independent cinema." About success, he advises in a *Film Culture* essay, "One asks merely for a little magic. If the magician's act turns out to be Great Art, that part of it will not be his concern." Broughton told *CA:* "In whatever I do—writing, filming, lecturing—I am first and always a poet, trying to live poetically. Because that is the only way I can feel well. And a poet is in the service of something greater than his published works or his public reputation. Poetry is an act of love, it asks no rewards. Therefore all my work is celebrational and passionate, my hobby is the care and feeding of ecstasy, and my goal in life is to attain my own inevitability."

BIOGRAPHICAL/CRITICAL SOURCES:

BOOKS

Broughton, James, *A Long Undressing: Collected Poems, 1949-1969,* Jargon Society, 1971.
Broughton, James, *Seeing the Light,* City Lights Books, 1977.
Broughton, James, *The Androgyne Journal* (autobiographical), Scrimshaw Press, 1977.
Curtis, David, *Experimental Cinema,* Universe Books, 1971.
Dictionary of Literary Biography, Volume 5: *American Poets since World War II,* Gale, 1980.

Sitney, P. Adams, *Visionary Film,* Oxford University Press, 1974.

PERIODICALS

Antioch Review, summer, 1978.
Cahiers du Cinema (Paris), Number 10, 1952.
Canyon Cinemanews, September/October, 1974, January/February, 1975, July/August, 1975, November/December, 1975, September/October, 1976, November/December, 1976.
Cinema News, November/December, 1977, September/October, 1978, Number 3, 1980, Number 6, 1980-81.
Credences, March, 1978.
Ekran, Volume 8, number 5/6, 1983.
Evergreen Review, Volume 1, number 2, 1957.
Film and Filmmakers, November, 1954.
Film Comment, summer, 1964.
Film Culture, summer, 1963, Number 61, 1975-76.
Film Quarterly, spring, 1960, summer, 1968, Volume 29, number 4, 1976, summer, 1978.
Lamp, Volume 74, 1984.
Los Angeles Free Press, March 15, 1968.
Millenium, winter, 1977/78.
New Leader, December 13, 1971.
Poetry, March, 1951, December, 1967.
Saturday Review, October 13, 1951.
Sight and Sound (London), January/March, 1952, January/March, 1954.
Small Press Review, August, 1980.
Spiral, October, 1986.
Take One (Montreal), July, 1972.
Theatre Arts, August, 1946.
University Film Studies, Volume 8, number 1, 1977.
Village Voice, July 9, 1979.

OTHER

"Testament" (film autobiography), Farallone Films, 1974.

—*Sketch by Marilyn K. Basel*

* * *

BUNNELL, Peter C(urtis) 1937-

PERSONAL: Born October 25, 1937, in Poughkeepsie, N.Y.; son of Harold C. (an engineer) and Ruth (Buckhout) Bunnell. *Education:* Rochester Institute of Technology, B.F.A., 1959; Ohio University, M.F.A., 1961; Yale University, M.A., 1965.

ADDRESSES: Home—40 McCosh Circle, Princeton, N.J. 08540. *Office*—Department of Art and Archaeology, Princeton University, Princeton, N.J. 08544.

CAREER: Museum of Modern Art, New York City, curator of photography, 1966-72; Princeton University, Princeton, N.J., visiting lecturer in department of art and archaeology, 1970-72, McAlpin Professor of the History of Photography and Modern Art, 1972—, faculty curator of photography, 1972—, director of an art museum, 1973-78; writer. Visiting lecturer at Institute of Film and Television, New York University, 1968-70, department of art, Dartmouth College, 1968, and college seminar program, Yale University, 1973. Television host of special seventy-five-minute program, "Time, Light and Vision: The Art of Photography," for WNET-TV, New York City.

MEMBER: Society for Photographic Education (member of board of directors, 1968—; secretary, 1970-73; chairman, 1973-77), College Art Association (member of board of direc-

tors, 1975-79), Friends of Photography (member of board of trustees, 1974—; vice president, 1977; president, 1978-87; chairman, 1987—), American Federation of Arts (member of exhibitions committee, 1976-79), Photographic Historical Society of America.

AWARDS, HONORS: Robert Chapman Bates fellow, Yale University, 1963-65; fellowship for studies in the history of photography, Polaroid Corp., 1965-66; Guggenheim fellowship, 1979; Asian Cultural Council fellowship, 1984.

WRITINGS:

(Assistant to Egbert Haverkamp-Begeman, senior editor) *Color in Prints: European and American Color Prints, 1500 to the Present,* Art Gallery, Yale University, 1962.
(Contributor of bibliographies and chronologies) *Paul Caponigro,* Grossman, 1967, 2nd edition, Aperture, 1972.
(Contributor of bibliographies and chronologies) *Mirrors Messages Manifestations,* Aperture, 1969, 2nd edition, 1982.
(Contributor of bibliographies and chronologies) *W. Eugene Smith,* Aperture, 1969.
(With Russell Edson) *Jerry N. Uelsmann,* Aperture, 1970, revised and enlarged edition, 1973.
Eight Photographs/Edward Weston, Doubleday, 1971.
(Editor with Alan Trachtenberg and Peter Neill) *The City: American Experience,* Oxford University Press, 1971.
(Contributor of bibliographies and chronologies) *Paul Strand: A Retrospective Monograph,* Aperture, 1971.
(Author of introduction) Max Waldman, *Waldman on Theater,* Doubleday, 1971.
Barbara Morgan, Morgan & Morgan, 1972.
(Author of introduction) Dianne Vanderlip, editor, *Photographic Portraits,* Moore College of Art, 1972.
(Editor with Robert Sobieszek) *The Literature of Photography,* sixty-two volumes, Arno, 1973.
(Author of introduction) *A Portfolio of Ten Photographs by Elliott Erwitt,* Witkin-Berley, 1974.
Jerry N. Uelsmann: Silver Meditations, Morgan & Morgan, 1975.
(Author of introduction) *Helen Gee and the Limelight,* Carlton Gallery, 1977.
(Contributor) *Conversations with Wright Morris: Critical Views and Responses,* University of Nebraska Press, 1977.
(Editor with Sobieszek) *The Sources of Modern Photography,* Arno, 1978.
(Author of introduction) *Aaron Siskind: 75th Anniversary Portfolio,* Light Gallery, 1979.
Lynton Wells: Paintings 1971-1978, Art Museum, Princeton University, 1979.
(Editor) *A Photographic Vision: Pictorial Photography 1889-1923,* Peregrine Smith, 1980.
Altered Landscapes: The Photographs of John Pfahl, Friends of Photography, 1981.
(Author of introduction) *Paul Caponigro: Photography 25 Years,* Photograph Gallery, 1981.
(Editor) *Edward Weston on Photography,* Gibbs M. Smith, 1983.
Emmet Gowin, Corcoran Gallery of Art, 1983.
The Robert O. Dougan Collection of Historical Photographs and Photographic Literature, Art Museum, Princeton University, 1983.
(Editor and author of introduction) *EW:100/Centennial Essays in Honor of Edward Weston,* Friends of Photography, 1986.
Clarence H. White: The Reverence for Beauty, Ohio University Gallery of Fine Art, 1987.
Nina Alexander Photographs, Yellowstone Art Center, 1987.
Minor White/The Eye That Shapes, Art Museum, Princeton University, 1989.

Also author of *Non-silver Printing Processes: Four Selections, 1886-1927,* Arno, and of bibliographies, exhibition brochures, and checklists. Editor with Nathan Lyons of *Photography 63* and *Photography 64,* George Eastman House. Contributor of articles and reviews to periodicals, including *Aperture, Arts in Virginia, Artscanada, Camera, Art in America, Afterimage, Creative Camera, Print Collector's Newsletter, Choice,* and *New York Times Book Review.*

WORK IN PROGRESS: A critical history of twentieth-century photography; monographs on photographers Alfred Stieglitz and Minor White; an anthology of writings on photography, 1917-1945; a collection of essays and reviews.

SIDELIGHTS: Peter C. Bunnell is the first McAlpin Professor of the History of Photography at Princeton University. He wrote *CA:* "The principal motivation in my writing is to expand the understanding of photography as a creative medium. In this endeavor I hope to speak both to the viewer of photographs and to the photographer. In each case the challenge is to broaden the conceptual and intellectual orientation through which photographs are usually made and interpreted." He has travelled throughout England, France, Belgium, Holland, Germany, Austria, Japan, Switzerland, and Italy.

BIOGRAPHICAL/CRITICAL SOURCES:

PERIODICALS

Newsweek, October 21, 1974.
New York Times, June 6, 1971, April 18, 1972.
Time, April 13, 1970.
Village Voice, July 19, 1976.

*   *   *

BURROS, Marian (Fox)

PERSONAL: Born in Waterbury, Conn.; daughter of Myron and Dorothy (Derby) Fox; married Donald Burros (president of White Conveyor), 1959; children: Michael, Ann. *Education:* Wellesley College, B.A., 1954.

ADDRESSES: Home—7215 Helmsdale Rd., Bethesda, Md. 20817. *Office*—*New York Times,* 229 West 43rd St., New York, N.Y. 10036.

CAREER: Teacher of cooking, 1961-64; *Maryland News* (weekly), Montgomery County, food columnist, 1962-63; *Maryland Monitor* (weekly), Montgomery County, food columnist, 1963-64; *Washington Daily News,* Washington, D.C., food editor, 1964-68; *Washington Evening Star,* Washington, D.C., food editor, 1968-74; *Washington Post,* Washington, D.C., food editor, 1974-81; *New York Times,* New York, N. Y., food columnist, 1981-83, restaurant critic, 1983-84, food columnist specializing in consumer and nutritional information, 1984—. Consumer affairs reporter for WRC-TV, 1973-81; radio columnist for WQXR, 1985—.

MEMBER: Washington Press Club, Les Dames d'Escoffier.

AWARDS, HONORS: Emmy Award, National Academy of Television Arts and Sciences, 1974, for consumer affairs reporting; JC Penney-Missouri award, 1988, for health and nutrition; won Vesta award three times, for best newspaper food pages; Association of Federal Investigators award for consumer reporting; won American Association of University Women Mass Media award twice, for consumer reporting and nutrition education; Tastemaker awards, for *The Summertime Cookbook* and *Pure and Simple.*

WRITINGS:

COOKBOOKS

(With Lois Levine) *Elegant but Easy: A Cookbook for Hostesses,* Collier Books, 1962, reprinted, Macmillan, 1984.
(With Levine) *Freeze with Ease,* Macmillan, 1965, reprinted, 1984.
(With Levine) *The Elegant but Easy Cookbook,* Macmillan, 1967, reprinted, 1984.
(With Levine) *Come for Cocktails, Stay for Supper,* Macmillan, 1970.
(With Levine) *The Summertime Cookbook: Elegant but Easy Dining In-Doors and Out,* Macmillan, 1972.
Pure and Simple: Delicious Recipes for Additive-Free Cooking, Morrow, 1978.
Keep It Simple, Morrow, 1981.
You've Got It Made, Morrow, 1984.
The Best of De Gustibus, Simon & Schuster, 1988.
20-Minute Menus, Simon & Schuster, 1989.

SIDELIGHTS: Within recent years, food columnist Marian Burros has become known for her quick recipes geared for small families on the go, and for her attacks on the use of harmful substances in food. According to Nan Robertson in the *New York Times Book Review,* "Mrs. Burros, like Mr. [Ralph] Nader, is a giant-killer. In recent years, she has tackled junk food, fake 'natural' food and other nutritional ringers. . . . [However,] unlike the fierce and somewhat humorless Mr. Nader, Mrs. Burros projects a witty, affable but tough-minded image in her conversation, in her writing and on the air." *Baltimore Sun* contributor Rob Kasper calls Burros "a lively, peppery woman who gets straight to the point. In food terms her style is to skip the garnishes and get right down to the entree."

Pure and Simple: Delicious Recipes For Additive-Free Cooking and *Keep It Simple* are cookbooks featuring recipes for entire meals that take only thirty minutes to prepare; both books made the *New York Times* best seller list. In her introduction to *Pure and Simple,* Burros writes: "I have just one simple rule of thumb determining the naturalness of a product. If I can't make it in my kitchen, it doesn't fit my idea of natural." The two books were departures from her earlier cookbooks, which used packaged foods to make cooking easier. According to *Chicago Tribune* contributor Joanne Will, "because of her current stands against chemicals and additives in food and her present cooking philosophy that embraces whole foods, Burros is 'a little embarrassed' about the use of convenience foods in her early books. 'But times have changed,' she said. 'All of us thought convenience foods were a terrific boon. I actually think some of the convenience foods tasted better then.' New technologies have brought ingredient changes and substitutes and have reduced the quality of the early convenience foods, Burros believes."

Will states that "the recipes [in *Pure and Simple*] as a whole have an appealing simplicity and style that will help today's consumers get food on the table in a hurry—and additive-free." And *Washington Post Book World* contributor S. Schoenbaum comments on *Keep It Simple:* "The prose is efficient journalese, notable for Burros' no-nonsense candor. . . . Her book will not transform the novice into a gourmet cook, but will help wean anyone away from the expensive degradation of junk-food takeaways and convenience meals which sometimes look as though they have already been eaten. *Keep It Simple* is good for both the pocketbook and the gastronomic cause."

In *20-Minute Menus,* Burros has further simplified recipes and presents meal ideas that "get away from the time-worn idea of a dinner plate that holds a separate meat, vegetable and starch," *Oregonian* contributor Yvonne Rothert explains. "Instead, the recipes combine two in one dish—sometimes all three." She also states, however, that while the book "has an excellent introduction filled with time-saving tips," the reader should know that "use of the recipes does require some familiarity with the kitchen and cooking methods, as well as a fair amount of organization."

BIOGRAPHICAL/CRITICAL SOURCES:

BOOKS

Burros, Marian, *Pure and Simple: Delicious Recipes for Additive-Free Cooking,* Morrow, 1978.

PERIODICALS

Baltimore Sun, February 28, 1988.
Chicago Tribune, October 11, 1979.
New York Times Book Review, November 1, 1981.
Oregonian, April 25, 1989.
Washington Post Book World, June 14, 1981.

*   *   *

BURROW, John W(yon) 1935-

PERSONAL: Born June 4, 1935, in Southsea, England; son of Charles Wyon (a salesman) and Alice (Vosper) Burrow; married Diane Dunnington, October 27, 1958; children: Laurence, Francesca. *Education:* Christ's College, Cambridge, B.A., 1957, M.A., 1960, Ph.D., 1961.

ADDRESSES: Office—Arts Building, University of Sussex, Brighton, England.

CAREER: Cambridge University, Downing College, Cambridge, England, fellow, 1962-65; University of East Anglia, School of European Studies, Norwich, England, lecturer in history, 1965-69; University of Sussex, Brighton, England, reader, 1969-82, professor of history, 1982—. Visiting professor, University of California, Berkeley, 1981.

AWARDS, HONORS: Wolfson Literary Prize for History, 1981.

WRITINGS:

Evolution and Society: A Study in Victorian Social Theory, Cambridge University Press, 1966.
(Editor and author of introduction) Charles R. Darwin, *The Origin of the Species by Means of Natural Selection,* Penguin, 1968.
(Editor and author of introduction) Wilhelm Humboldt, *The Limits of State Action: History and Theory of Political Science,* Cambridge University Press, 1969.
A Liberal Descent: Victorian Historians and the English Past, Cambridge University Press, 1981.
Gibbon (study of Edward Gibbon), Oxford University Press, 1985.
Whigs and Liberals, Oxford University Press, 1988.

SIDELIGHTS: In *A Liberal Descent: Victorian Historians and the English Past,* John W. Burrow, says J. P. Kenyon in the *Times Literary Supplement,* "demonstrates the strength, the flexibility and the omniutility of the Whig tradition as it survived in the work of five nineteenth-century historians of very disparate types [Edward August Freeman, J. A. Froude, John Richard Green, William Stubbs, and Thomas B. Macaulay]; and particularly in their interpretation of three key events in English history, the Norman Conquest, the Reformation and the Revolution of 1688." According to John Clive in the *New York Review of*

Books, "No summary can possibly do justice to the richness, subtlety, and originality of this book, to my mind one of the finest volumes on modern English intellectual history to have appeared since his own *Evolution and Society.*" Clive adds that Burrow's "deep knowledge of the Victorian age has stood him in good stead in [this] book, which he intends not so much as a study of technical historiography as, in the words of Burckhart, a record of what one age finds of interest in another." Calling *A Liberal Descent* "a magnificent piece of historical archaeology," Kenyon adds that "Burrow's [writing] style, subtly inquisitive and highly literary, has . . . reached full maturity. . . . It is a condensed style, sucking idea upon idea, meaning upon meaning, implication upon implication, down into an intellectual black hole; whence they are funnelled out the other end into a new world of lucidity."

BIOGRAPHICAL/CRITICAL SOURCES:

PERIODICALS

New York Review of Books, June 24, 1982.
Times (London), November 19, 1981.
Times Literary Supplement, December 4, 1981.

*   *   *

BUSCAGLIA, (Felice) Leo(nardo) 1924-
(Leo F. Buscaglia)

PERSONAL: Professionally known as Leo F. Buscaglia; surname is pronounced Boo-*skal*-ya; born March 31, 1924, in East Los Angeles, Calif.; son of Tulio Bartolomeo (a restaurant owner) and Rosa (Cagna) Buscaglia. *Education:* University of Southern California, B.A., 1950, M.A., 1954, General Administrative Credential, 1960, Ph.D., 1963.

ADDRESSES: Home—Los Angeles, Calif. *Office*—P.O. Box 599, Glenbrook, Nev. 89413.

CAREER: Educator and author. Pasadena City School System, Pasadena, Calif., teacher and speech therapist, 1951-60, special education supervisor, 1960-65; University of Southern California, Los Angeles, Calif., assistant professor, 1965-68, associate professor, 1968-75, professor of education, 1975—; currently on extended leave of absence. Frequent lecturer on television and throughout the United States; has recorded more than a dozen speeches for Public Broadcasting Service (PBS-TV). President and chairman of the board, Felice Foundation, South Pasadena, Calif., 1984—. *Military service:* U.S. Navy, 1941-44; became medical corpsman second class.

AWARDS, HONORS: California Governor's award, 1965; elected professor of the year, 1970 and 1972, and received Teaching Excellence Award, 1978, University of Southern California; special recognition awards, American Academy of Dentistry for the Handicapped, 1972, and Royal Thai Navy, 1973; Meritorious Service Award, International School (Bangkok), 1973; Outstanding Services award, U.S. Air Force (Misawa, Japan), 1976; certification of appreciation, 5th Air Force (Japan), 1976; Appreciation Award, Public Broadcasting Service, 1981; received keys to several cities, including Charlotte, N.C., 1981, Carbondale, Pa., 1983, Scranton, Pa., 1983, and Wilkes-Barre, Pa., 1983; Leo F. Buscaglia Day declared, Dunmore, Pa., 1983.

WRITINGS: Because I Am Human!, photographs by Bruce Ferguson, Charles B. Slack (Thorofare, N.J.), 1972.

UNDER NAME LEO F. BUSCAGLIA

Love (lectures), Charles B. Slack, 1972.

The Way of the Bull: A Voyage, illustrations by Roberta Ludlow, Charles B. Slack, 1974.

(Editor) *The Disabled and Their Parents: A Counseling Challenge,* Charles B. Slack, 1975, revised edition, Slack, Inc./Holt, 1983.

Personhood: The Art of Being Fully Human (lectures), Charles B. Slack, 1978.

(Editor with Eddie H. Williams) *Human Advocacy and PL94-142: The Educator's Roles,* Charles B. Slack, 1979.

Living, Loving, and Learning (lectures), edited by Steven Short, introduction by Betty Lou Kratoville, Charles B. Slack/Holt, 1982.

The Fall of Freddie the Leaf: A Story of Life for All Ages (juvenile fiction), Charles B. Slack/Holt, 1982.

Loving Each Other: The Challenge of Human Relationships, Charles B. Slack/Holt, 1984.

(Contributor) *Belief in Action,* Center for the Study of Contemporary Belief, 1984.

Bus 9 to Paradise: A Loving Voyage (syndicated column selections), edited by Daniel Kimber, Slack, Inc./Morrow, 1986.

(Contributor) Barry and Joyce Vissell, *Models of Love: The Parent-Child Journey,* illustrations by Rami and Mira Vissell, foreword by Eileen Caddy, Ramira, 1986.

Seven Stories of Christmas Love, Slack, Inc./Morrow, 1987.

A Memory for Tino (juvenile fiction), illustrations by Carol Newsom, Slack, Inc./Morrow, 1988.

Papa, My Father: A Celebration of Dads (Book-of-the-Month Club alternate selection), Slack, Inc./Morrow, 1989.

Sounds of Love, Nightingale-Conant, 1989.

Also author of New York Times Syndicate column "Living and Loving," 1984—. Contributor of fiction and articles to magazines, including *Woman's Day, Reader's Digest, Modern Bride,* and *Seventeen.*

WORK IN PROGRESS: Research and writing for the New York Times Syndicate.

SIDELIGHTS: "Columnist, lecturer and TV social philosopher Leo [F.] Buscaglia is a man you love to love," remarks Roselle M. Lewis in the *Los Angeles Times.* Buscaglia, or "Dr. Hug" as he is affectionately known, ebulliently proclaims a philosophy founded upon self-acceptance and growth, and nourished by love in its many manifestations, which he personally demonstrates by the celebrated hug that has become his trademark. Calling him a "one-man encounter group," Bernie Zilbergeld adds in a *Psychology Today* profile of Buscaglia that he represents "a good illustration of emotional expressiveness, nonconformity, and touching." Internationally recognized, Buscaglia has lectured throughout the world and has appeared on numerous public television broadcasts. He has also established a reputation as a publishing phenomenon, with four titles once appearing simultaneously on bestseller lists. While the collections of his popular lectures are probably the most widely read of his books, he has also published personal memoirs of family experiences, fiction for children, and, most recently, has penned a paean to his father, to whom he attributes many of his own conceptions of life, love, and self.

Buscaglia (or Leo, as he prefers to be addressed) grew up in a large, closely knit Italian immigrant family—"an enviable family," remarks a *Publishers Weekly* contributor in a review of *Papa, My Father: A Celebration of Dads.* In his memoir, Buscaglia describes his father's various roles, including that of the gardener and ecologist, the winemaker, and especially the undereducated teacher who insisted his children bring to the dinner table for discussion one fact learned during that day. According

to Pauline Mayer in the *Los Angeles Times Book Review,* Buscaglia's dad was a "hands-on-father"; and although this "sometimes meant corporal punishment," he was "a passionately involved parent and constant dispenser of hugs and homilies." Mayer suggests that the elder Buscaglia exemplified a forerunner of contemporary fatherhood: "Dad as nurturer and caretaker, Dad as—well, let's face it—Mom."

Specializing in the problems of disadvantaged children, Buscaglia served as a teacher in Pasadena's public school system for several years, becoming supervisor of special education before leaving that position during the middle 1960s to travel. He journeyed to Asia, where he encountered various Eastern religions, including Zen Buddhism and Hinduism. Examining these faiths and comparing them with other religions, Buscaglia focused upon their inherent similarities for the philosophy he embraces and outlines in his 1974 *The Way of the Bull: A Voyage.* Calling the book "the finest writing I've done, though no one ever reads it," Buscaglia adds in a *Time* profile: "All [religions] agree on the same principles for humanity. There is no religion that disagrees on the basic tenet being love. You can be a follower of Muhammad or Jesus or Buddha or whomever. Always they said that the most essential factor is to love your neighbor. And to love you." The image of the bull in the title, explains Buscaglia in the introduction to the book, comes from the Chinese Zen master Kakuan, for whom the bull represented life energy, truth, and action; and the "way" refers to the path the author followed toward self-awareness. However, Buscaglia stresses in the epilogue that his path toward self-awareness is relevant only to him, and he encourages people to look within themselves for their own way: "*Your* WAY can be equally exciting as it will lead you back to you, the only place where you can ever *become.*"

John Leo suggests in *Time* that "Buscaglia took that sense of self-celebration, which helped fuel the narcissism of the Me decade, and grafted it onto the traditional message of love thy neighbor." When he returned to the University of Southern California and after one of his students committed suicide, he persuaded the dean of the school of education to let him conduct a noncredit course on love. The course proved enormously popular and earned Buscaglia the campus title of "Dr. Love." *Love, Personhood,* and *Living, Loving and Learning* are collections of his lectures. In *Love,* Buscaglia examines the topics of love as a learned phenomenon, self-love as a prerequisite to loving others, and the strength and responsibilities that love entails. *Personhood* discusses human fulfillment, what it means at different stages of life and as seen from various religious perspectives, and how to attain it. And *Living, Loving, and Learning* iterates the ideas and attitudes advanced in *Love* and *Personhood.*

"Buscaglia writes very much as he talks: with passion," comments Joseph M. Hamernick in *Best Sellers.* "Not unbridled passion, but with a warmth and fire tempered by a mind that seeks to explain what is ultimately inexpressible." At the core of his messages, both in his writings and in his lectures, is the premise of universal love of neighbor and of self. Popular with readers, Buscaglia's books are appreciated for their "wisdom, common sense and directness," writes Margaret Mironowicz in the Toronto *Globe and Mail.* "The main reason for Leo's appeal, I suspect," explains Zilbergeld, "is that his messages are few and easy to comprehend. We are lonely, anxious, and unhappy not because of the human condition, our genetic makeup, or because of anything we have done, but because society oppresses us. We have been twisted and forced to conform by others, and it is up to us as individuals to find a way out. Leo says we can find a better way because all of us, even the most despairing and least talented, are special and beautiful."

Although John Leo points out that "most of Buscaglia's prose is beyond criticism, simply recommending full-time kindness," Buscaglia is not without his critics. Zilbergeld, for instance, proposes that his message has little to offer "beyond momentary inspiration" essentially because "this great lover of love, families, and children has never been married, and has no children," and only "seems" to share our world. However, as Buscaglia explains to Walter W. Ross in an interview for *CA:* "I think we have to make choices in life, and the choice for me was to embrace all personkind rather than concentrate on one single individual. . . . The universal is what I've selected." Mironowicz remarks that "no matter what cynics have called him over the years, [Buscaglia] has cut a unique and endearing figure in our society." Likening him to "something like the Pavarotti of positive thinking," Martin Smith Holmes adds in a *People* interview that "Buscaglia is quick to say he is no guru." As the author explains to Holmes: "I have too much respect for people to try to control them. But they are estranged from love, afraid to reach out and touch one another. We're afraid to appear sentimental or speak in platitudes because people will say, 'What a jerk!' It takes courage in our culture to be a lover."

Buscaglia once told *CA:* "Over the entirety of my lifetime I have attempted to develop a clearer vision of the world. I have learned that love is a common language throughout the world. This knowledge has released me from the internal and external religious and cultural obstacles that artificially separate people. I have always, even as a child, felt a deep responsibility to develop all that I am, not for myself alone, but so I could be more for everyone in my life. This deep desire led me to my chosen profession. There was never any doubt that I was to become a teacher. In a far less restrictive sense, I believe that we are all teachers. We teach with every act we perform; we are models of our professed beliefs. It is, therefore, the responsibility of each of us to create the environment in which we choose to live. If we select caring, responsibility, commitment, and loving, then we must manifest this in daily action. I am certain that the major forces which will lead us from our present confusion to greater insight and more personal alternatives for life are the basic values of concern, commitment, joy, responsibility, courage, hope, and, of course, love."

AVOCATIONAL INTERESTS: Opera, eating, cooking, good wines, traveling, meeting people.

CA INTERVIEW

CA interviewed Leo Buscaglia by telephone on February 7, 1989, at his office in Pasadena, California.

CA: I heard you speak in Lexington, Kentucky, twenty years ago at a time when young people were idealistic and adventurous. Today many young people seem to be interested in making money and acquiring material things. Do you note this change in values?

BUSCAGLIA: Your perception is correct, and as far as I'm concerned, it's heartbreaking. The time for real celebration, exploration, and risk is when you're young. One of the most dramatic things I've noticed is that I was challenged in my classrooms at USC at least three times as much during that time as I am twenty years later. People are now reticent to argue; they're more determined to complete the course and get out as fast as possible and make as much money as they can. And all of the excitement and the questioning and the wondering—they can't tell me that didn't lead to something very, very important in people's lives. I'm not likely to forget those beautiful people that I spent time

with and the sharing that we had. Granted that the big movement may have fallen on its face, but the people who experienced it can't erase what they had. I wish that we could bring some of that back to our youth.

CA: What do you think about Alan Bloom's assessment of today's youth in his best-selling book The Closing of the American Mind?

BUSCAGLIA: His approach was rather strange, as far as I'm concerned. He wants to go back to a classical education, and I think that's all very interesting. Certainly if we read the classics and understood them, they wouldn't hurt us. (And, by the way, the number of classics he mentioned in his book was very limited, as far as I was concerned, and pretty tunnel-visioned.) The classics have all of the same anxieties, the same fears, the same questions that we're dealing with today. So does all literature, from the beginning of time. But I would tend to feel that that could be an addition to an education more toward broader concepts than what Alan Bloom was dealing with.

CA: Your parents obviously had a tremendous influence on you. You refer to them often in your writings and lectures, and now you've written the new book Papa, My Father, *scheduled for publication this spring. Did you realize at a young age that you were very fortunate to have such a special mama and papa?*

BUSCAGLIA: That book gave me more insight into my own self than anything I have ever done. I always thought that my parents were crazy. I thought that in a very real sense they were freaks, because they were so different from everybody else's parents. And of course they were different in the fact that they were Italian immigrants. They spoke with very different accents, they ate different foods, they believed different things, they dealt with the family in different ways, and I wished while I was growing up that I could be more like the other children. Why do we have to be so unique, I thought, and why do I have to have a mother who is so different and a father who is so crazy? I must admit I had some difficulty with that, and I talk about it in the book. But now I realize—I realized, of course, years ago, but not during childhood—that what they gave me was something so wonderfully rich that I would not be me without it.

There was another thing that I realized, which I mentioned in the book sort of casually because I didn't want it to be a heavy thing. My father was in my life for all of my life; he was always there, and he only died several years ago. But I realized after he died, and I wanted people to recognize this, that as close as I was to him and as much as I loved him, he really died a stranger to me. It's a very shocking thing to think that someone you can love so much, you know so little about. The question I asked myself as a result of this book was, Did I only ask my father the questions that pertained to me, the answers of which pertained to me? Should I have considered asking him more of the questions that really pertained to him? Then he might not have died a comparative stranger. That for me was the great lesson of writing this book: I must now ask people questions that don't pertain to me, that haven't got some significance for me but are more directed toward understanding them and who they really are.

CA: That's very interesting. We're always searching for our identity with our parents and friends and relatives, and in doing so we may forget about them.

BUSCAGLIA: Exactly, that's the whole thing. And here I am, supposed to be fairly sophisticated in the field of human relations, only recognizing this at my age. That's a frightening thing, and as I was writing this book I kept wondering, What about Papa's dreams? What about his fantasies? Was it enough for him that he raised a big family and that we all did pretty well, or did he also want to go to a mountaintop in Machu Picchu? What were the things that he gave up in order to give us the things that he did? I never asked him those questions. So in a real sense I missed him, though I think I experienced him much as most individuals experience their parents, perhaps more so.

CA: In working on that book, did you go back to Italy and talk with relatives there?

BUSCAGLIA: No, because most of our relatives who were in Italy are now no longer there. But I spent a lot of time with my father's younger brother, who died just this year. That was a magical time. I spent time with his elder brother's wife, who also died this year. We had long conversations about Papa. Of course they gave me other insights; they gave me a different view of the man. There was another thing, something that happened many, many years ago, but I also wrote about it in the book because it was a stunning realization for me. My elder brother was much older than I. I was a love baby years and years after all the rest of the family was grown. My brother was getting married when I was just a two- or three-year-old, and life was very different for my family then. My father was always looking for work, and, being an immigrant and not speaking English, he had a hard time. I dedicated the first book I wrote about love and about my parents to them, and I said it was because they didn't teach me about love, they showed me, they demonstrated it. In the book I recalled a lot of ways in which they did so. When my brother read this book, he said to me, "Who's this man you're talking about as our father? I don't even know who he is." Well, my first response to that was real indignation. I mean, how dare he imply that my perception of my father was not the real one? Then I recognized, of course, that we never give our families, especially our parents, the prerogative to grow and to change. Of course Papa wasn't the same man with my brother. He was struggling to keep alive. By the time I came along and interacted with him, he already had a secure job. He knew that he wasn't going to starve and that he could support his family, he could relax, he had hobbies, he was a different man. That was another very insightful thing that my brother gave me.

CA: Although you refer to your parents a lot in your books I've noticed that there's very little reference to your brothers and sisters.

BUSCAGLIA: I talk about them a little bit more in the last book that I did, *Seven Stories of Christmas Love,* because they were involved in the same Christmas experiences that I was involved in. I have mentioned them along the line, but you're right that I haven't mentioned them as much as perhaps I should. Except for my brother, they're still living, and I always hesitate to walk into their space. I feel that it's fine for me to reveal myself and my feelings, but I cannot do anything that would endanger their privacy. So I've been very careful about that. In fact, after I finished *Papa, My Father,* I gave it to both my sisters and I said, "You read it, and anything that offends you, you scratch out. I don't care what you do. You can remove pages and chapters." Well, my older sister took out one word, and my younger sister took out nothing. I was very pleased that they were able to handle that. Both of them cried over the book, but so did I, so it was okay for all of us.

CA: In the 1970s you wrote a book with the intriguing title The Way of the Bull, *which was about your trip to such faraway places*

as Saigon and Bangkok. What made you decide to go to the Orient?

BUSCAGLIA: There were two considerations. Five years before I left, I had been promoted and made a director of special education. This was supposed to be a very prestigious position, to be taken out of the classroom and made the director of a program, especially at my young age. But once I got into that, I realized that I was never meant to be a director of anything; it's just not my personality. I could not tell people what to do, I could not fire people, I could not be negative about other people's responses—it was very difficult for me. So I had five very unhappy years, and I wondered at that point, What am I doing here? People convinced me that if I left that job for good, I would never find one equal to it again as long as I lived, but I was sure that I would rather be a hash-slinger at some restaurant and be happy than be miserable every day and not enjoy what I was doing. So I thought, I'm going to quit, and I thought this would be a perfect time to just give up everything and take off, because I'd be between this job and whatever I was going to do next. Also, I had always wondered about the two-thirds of the world about which I knew nothing, especially Asia. Here I'd had a university education—at that point I'd gotten a master's degree—and I knew nothing about Cambodia or Vietnam, very little about Japan, almost nothing about China. I thought, I really must go and find out what this other part of the world is. Those were the two major incentives. I spent several years. I went where the wind blew. If I was on a train and someone said, "You must go to this village because they have beautiful flowers," I would go to smell the flowers or climb a mountain. The big thing was that I wasn't really as interested in the history as I was in the culture and the people.

CA: The first chapter of that book was particularly interesting to me, about your brief stay at the Zen monastery. I think most of us in the West are so preoccupied with things that it would be nearly impossible for us to sit alone in a relatively bare room as you did at the monastery.

BUSCAGLIA: I spent some time with Thai peasants. I lived with Indians in India. I had an opportunity to learn that while there is hate and envy and greed in every culture, there's also love and gentleness and kindness, that people are universally people, regardless of whether they wear a dhoti or a sari or a business suit.

CA: Much of your writing is inspired by your love for mankind. Do you have specific religious beliefs? I don't believe you belong to any particular sect or church.

BUSCAGLIA: I was raised a Catholic, and I guess once a Catholic, always a Catholic. But I'm not in the strict sense a practicing Catholic. I certainly have a concept of God, and that's a very strong concept. I do know that there is a God; in that sense I have a religious belief. But in terms of any kind of institutionalized form of worship, no, I don't have that.

CA: Were your parents strongly religious?

BUSCAGLIA: Oh, yes, my goodness, especially my mother. She had statues of Jesus and the Virgin Mary and everything else all over the house and kept flowers underneath them, and votive candles. She was a very religious woman. But she was religious in a very Italian way. The Italians have a very loose form of religion, a very human kind of religion. It's hard to describe. It's religious and it's real, but it's also warm and understanding and forgiving. It isn't a *mea culpa* kind of thing, a guilt trip. It's a realization that we're all human and therefore we will not be perfect.

CA: You've written two children's books, The Fall of Freddie the Leaf *and* A Memory for Tino.

BUSCAGLIA: Actually, *The Fall of Freddie the Leaf* was not particularly for children, though I did write it originally for children. I wrote it when I was teaching second grade, because all these little kids were having experiences with death and somehow adults were not satisfying their needs in terms of explanation. I thought it would be good to write something to read to them and share with them and discuss with them that would help them to not fear death but to recognize that death was part of the process of living. So I used the metaphor of the trees and the leaves, which have always been important to me, and I found that they were able to handle this and understand it. But when I wrote it as a book, I really intended it to be for all ages. I wrote *A Memory for Tino* in the hope that I could write a series for children based on different values, the importance of things like caring and sharing and loving and accumulating memories. I don't think that there is enough in the literature. I don't want to preach to children, but I would like to use stories and metaphors to help them to understand that the good life is waiting for them, and that kindness and goodness do exist. If you look at literature and the arts—and at television, which they watch all the time—there's so much negativity and violence. I thought, Wouldn't it be good if I could expose them in an interesting way to the real values? There were two things I wanted to show in *A Memory for Tino:* the value of sharing and giving, and the fact that when you give you receive far more than what you give. That's why I wrote the book.

The story was based on a true story that was sent in for a contest sponsored by the company that makes Care Bears and by *Woman's Day,* a magazine I write for often. They invited kids from all over the country, or their parents, to write in their stories about things they had done out of the goodness of their hearts, not with any kind of hope of getting anything back. One mother wrote in about her son, who had given his television to a lonely elderly woman. That really struck me. That's a real gift for a kid nowadays, to put a television on a wagon and take it to an elderly woman he had met. So I created my story based upon that.

CA: It was a very touching story. Do you plan to write more children's books? Will you go ahead with the series you envisioned?

BUSCAGLIA: I have in mind now another one that will deal more directly with love. It's taking much more time than I thought it would, but I think I will definitely complete it. Yes, I would like to make this a series on human values—not call it that, but just have a series of books dealing with sharing and caring and loving.

CA: In your talks you often allude to and quote from writers as diverse as Martin Buber and the author of The Little Prince, *Antoine de Saint-Exupery. Are there any writers who have been particular inspirations to you?*

BUSCAGLIA: There are so many. One of the big frustrations in my life, and I think it's true for all of us, is that I'm overloaded with wonderful things to read and new things that are coming out all the time. I try to read a couple of books a week. I read the *New York Times,* the *Los Angeles Times.* Magazines accumulate, you know; we're all having an overload. But there are certain things that I really read for my own edification and have read and reread. Thomas Merton is one of the writers whose books I often pick up and read.

CA: With all the demands upon you from so many people, do you find you need to get away by yourself for brief periods of time during the year?

BUSCAGLIA: I do that very, very often. In fact, I don't wait to get away each year. I have a private time every day, and that I insist upon. There's a private time here in my office when I simply tell my secretary that for all intents and purposes I've disappeared, and I take a half-hour or an hour and read something very calmly, or I close my eyes and rest, or I meditate. I do that all the time. I also have places I like to go where I am replenished, where I can become a part of everything that's there, and everything that's there is beautiful. Places like the Hawaiian Islands. In fact, I just got back from Kona, where I spent a week. It was one of those marvelous places where I could walk along the beach and look at all the beautiful flowers, or swim in the warm sea and have fishes swim around me. I also get an enormous vibration when I'm in the Lake Tahoe region, and I spend time up there whenever I can. I have my little places of refuge. It's taken me a long time to get there, but I want to say that I am wise enough now to know that I can't be to anybody else what I can't be to myself. Unless I can be centered, I can't be centered with anybody. So I owe myself the getting away. And I think too often those of us who really care about people dedicate ourselves so completely to them that we can't really be there because we're so exhausted and beat up that we're no longer listening or caring or really being involved. It's a good thing for people to learn that all of us need to get away and to refill and reorient ourselves so that we can come back and be fully there.

CA: You must be flooded with mail. Can you possibly respond to all the mail you get?

BUSCAGLIA: We respond to everything that arrives in this office. Nobody that writes to me is ignored. Of course I can't do it all myself, but I do answer all of those letters that are of a personal nature. Letters that are asking, for instance, if I'm available for a lecture in 1989 or 1990, my secretary and I work out. And then we have someone else who answers the letters that say, "Will you be in the Chicago area in 1989?" and "When will you be here?" and "What new programs are you going to do?" and "Are you writing any new books?" Information questions people can help me with, but personal letters I answer myself.

CA: Are you still teaching?

BUSCAGLIA: No, I'm on an extended leave of absence. I'm still on the faculty roster at USC, but I'm not actively teaching. The wonderful thing is that they've left it open for me; they've said, "If you want to come back at any time, you can teach a seminar, you can teach a weekend workshop, you can teach a course, you can teach a full load." So that's still there as an alternative, but right now I'm out trying things I've never done before.

CA: If you did go back and teach, do you think you'd teach your class on love?

BUSCAGLIA: Definitely. What I miss probably more than any other single thing is the interaction with the students. I don't miss all the garbage that goes with it, like the evaluating and the faculty meetings and all of that. I realize that they're essential, but I don't miss those things. What I really do miss is the challenge of being with young people and seeing what they're doing and hearing what they're thinking. I try to visit a lot. Just the other day I went into a pre-school and sat down with pre-school kids and had a wonderful, wonderful day. I try to keep in touch in that way, but it's not the same.

CA: You certainly are an inspiration for a lot of people. When I first heard you speak, I had never heard anybody speak in such a way before. I remember that several people in the audience went running up on the stage after you had finished and threw their arms around you. One of them hugged you so hard he dislocated your shoulder!

BUSCAGLIA: I remember that; it caused some pain for a little while. But that's okay. If there's a show of spontaneity, if I can awaken in somebody a spark of the excitement of being alive, then I'll suffer the dislocated shoulder.

CA: In a brief interview in People *back in July, 1982, you said that you were a bachelor because no woman could ever get used to your life-style. But you must have had many temptations to get married.*

BUSCAGLIA: Not as many temptations as you might think. I've really been on the move much of my life; I'm constantly going places and doing things and meeting people. I think we have to make choices in life, and the choice for me was to embrace all personkind rather than concentrate on one single individual. I do believe that it's an enormous responsibility and a real challenge to select someone out of all the people in the world and to say to that person, Of everyone, I'm most willing to grow with you. That's the supreme compliment. But I agree with Erich Fromm, who addresses this issue. He says we can come to love in both ways, either by concentrating on an individual and a family or by accepting the responsibility for a universal kind of love. The universal is what I've selected.

BIOGRAPHICAL/CRITICAL SOURCES:

BOOKS

Buscaglia, Leo F., *Love,* Charles B. Slack, 1972.
Buscaglia, Leo F., *The Way of the Bull: A Voyage,* Charles B. Slack, 1974.
Buscaglia, Leo F., *Personhood: The Art of Being Fully Human,* Charles B. Slack, 1978.

PERIODICALS

Best Sellers, November, 1984.
Current Health, December, 1981.
Globe and Mail (Toronto), March 1, 1986.
Los Angeles Times, May 5, 1982, February 16, 1983, November 26, 1987.
Los Angeles Times Book Review, June 18, 1989.
Newsweek, May 9, 1983.
New York Times Book Review, May 16, 1982.
People, July 5, 1982.
Psychology Today, November, 1983.
Publishers Weekly, May 5, 1989.
Seventeen, February, 1983, November, 1983.
Time, November 15, 1982.

—*Sketch by Sharon Malinowski*

—*Interview by Walter W. Ross*

*   *   *

BUSCAGLIA, Leo F.
   See BUSCAGLIA, (Felice) Leo(nardo)

*   *   *

BUTTERS, Dorothy Gilman
   See GILMAN, Dorothy

C

CALDECOTT, Moyra 1927-

PERSONAL: Born June 1, 1927, in Pretoria, South Africa; naturalized British citizen; daughter of Frederick Stanley (a receiver of revenue) and Jessy Florence (Harris) Brown; married Oliver Zerffi Stratford Caldecott (a publisher and artist), April 5, 1951; children: Stratford Stanley, Julian Oliver, Rachel Lester. *Education:* University of Natal, B.A. (honors), 1949, M.A., 1950. *Politics:* "No political affiliation." *Religion:* "Religious, but no particular affiliation."

ADDRESSES: Home—Bath, England. *Office*—52 Southdown Rd., Southdown, Bath BA2 1JQ, England.

CAREER: University of Cape Town, Cape Town, South Africa, junior lecturer in English, 1950; teacher at a high school in London, England, 1951; Central Board for Conscientious Objectors, London, art gallery assistant and clerk, 1951-52; writer, 1953—. Has given poetry readings.

WRITINGS:

"The Runaway" (play), British Broadcasting Corp., Overseas Service, 1960.
"The Wanting Bird" (play for children), first produced in London at Rosendale Junior School, 1963.
The Weapons of the Wolfhound (juvenile novel), Rex Collings, 1976.
The Sacred Stones (trilogy of novels), Volume 1: *The Tall Stones,* Rex Collings, 1977, Hill & Wang, 1978, Volume 2: *The Temple of the Sun,* Rex Collings, 1977, Hill & Wang, 1978, Volume 3: *Shadow on the Stones,* Rex Collings, 1978, Hill & Wang, 1979.
Adventures by Leaf Light (juvenile), Green Tiger, 1978.
"The Forty-Nine Days" (three act play), first produced in California, 1978.
The Lily and the Bull (novel), Rex Collings, 1979.
Child of the Dark Star (science fiction), Corgi, 1980.
The King of Shadows: A Glastonbury Story, Bran's Head Books, 1981.
The Twins of the Tylwyth Teg, Bran's Head Books, 1983.
Taliesin and Avagddu, Bran's Head Books, 1983.
Bran, Son of Llyr, Bran's Head Books, 1985.
The Tower and the Emerald, Arrow, 1985.
Guardians of the Tall Stones, Arrow, 1986, Celestial Arts, 1987.
The Son of the Sun, Allison & Busby, 1986.
The Silver Vortex, Arrow, 1987.

Etheldreda, Arkana, 1987.
Women in Celtic Myth, Arrow, 1988.
Daughter of Amun, Arrow, 1989.
The Green Lady and the King of Shadows, Gothic Image Publications, 1989.
The Sow of the Sun, revised edition, Arrow, 1989.
The Crystal Legends, Aquarian Press, 1990.

Also author of novel, *The Eye of Callanish.* Contributor to anthologies, including *Gallery,* Methuen, and *Rhyme and Rhythm* and *Reading Aloud,* Macmillan. Contributor of poems and articles to magazines, including *Outposts, New Celtic Review, Freeway, Brief, British Wheel of Yoga,* and *Caerdroia.*

WORK IN PROGRESS: The Daughter of the Sun, "a novel about the wife of Tutankhamun."

AVOCATIONAL INTERESTS: Gardening, pottery and batik making, painting, legends, myths.

*   *   *

CAMPBELL, Angus
See CHETWYND-HAYES, R(onald Henry Glynn)

*   *   *

CAMPBELL, Donald 1940-

PERSONAL: Born February 25, 1940, in Wick, Caithness, Scotland; son of William Henry (a plumber) and Mary Elizabeth (a cook; maiden name, Mackenzie) Campbell; married Jean Elliot Fairgrieve (a teacher), October 15, 1966; children: Gavin Douglas. *Education:* Attended schools in Edinburgh, Scotland. *Politics:* Socialist. *Religion:* Agnostic.

ADDRESSES: Home and office—85 Spottiswoode St., Edinburgh EH9 1BZ, Scotland. *Agent*—Joanna Marston, Rosica Colin Ltd., One Clareville Grove Mews, London SW7 5AH, England.

CAREER: Writer. Writer in residence, Lothian Region of Scotland, 1971—, Edinburgh Education Department, 1974-77, and Royal Lyceum Theatre, 1981-82; creative writing coach in Scottish schools; involved in community arts programs. Fellow in creative writing, University of Dundee, 1987-89.

MEMBER: Saltire Society, Edinburgh Sir Walter Scott Club.

AWARDS, HONORS: Bursary Award, Scottish Arts Council, 1973; playwright award, Arts in Fife, 1975; "Fringe First" Award, Edinburgh International Festival, 1979, for "The Widows of Clyth," and 1985, for "Howard's Revenge."

WRITINGS:

Poems, Akros Publications, 1971.
Rhymes 'n Reasons, Gordon Wright, 1972.
Murals: Poems in Scots, Lothlorien, 1975.
The Jesuit: A Play, Paul Harris, 1976.
Somerville the Soldier: A Play, Paul Harris, 1978.
The Widows of Clyth: A Play, Paul Harris, 1979.
Blether: A Collection of Poems, Akros Publications, 1979.
(Author of introduction) Ian Macpherson, *Wild Harbour,* Paul Harris, 1981.
A Brighter Sunshine: A Hundred Years of the Edinburgh Royal Lyceum Theatre, Polygon Books, 1983.

Also author of plays "Blackfriars Wynd," "Till All the Seas Run Dry," "Sun Circle," "Howard's Revenge," "Victorian Values," and "Strikers"; author of teleplays "The End of an Auld Sang" and "The Old Master." Author of over forty radio plays and stage adaptations/translations of Henrik Ibsen's "Ghosts," Sir Walter Scott's *The Heart of Midlothian* and *St. Ronan's Well,* and Robert Louis Stevenson's *Dr. Jekyll and Mr. Hyde.*

WORK IN PROGRESS: "The New Waverley Dramas," a long cycle of plays based on the novels of Sir Walter Scott, including *The Heart of Midlothian, St. Ronan's Well, The Bride of Lammermoor, The Fair Maid of Perth,* and *Guy Mannering.*

SIDELIGHTS: Donald Campbell told *CA:* "All my writing arises out of a fascination with Scottish life, literature and history. I am excited by the fact that many of the developments which have taken place in other literatures have, so far, left Scotland untouched, thereby creating many opportunities for the consciously Scottish artist. On the other hand, I believe that there are some fields—particularly poetry—in which a Scottish cultural consciousness can make a fresh and invigorating contribution to World Literature. All my work is pursued with the aim of promoting these ends."

BIOGRAPHICAL/CRITICAL SOURCES:

BOOKS

Mason, Leonard, *Two Younger Poets: Duncan Glen and Donald Campbell,* Akros Publications, 1976.

*   *   *

CANNON, Garland (Hampton) 1924-

PERSONAL: Born December 5, 1924, in Fort Worth, Tex.; son of Garland Hampton and Myrtle (Goss) Cannon; married Patricia Richardson, February 14, 1947; children: Margaret, India, Jennifer, William. *Education:* University of Texas, B.A., 1947, Ph.D., 1954; Stanford University, M.A., 1952. *Religion:* Methodist.

ADDRESSES: Home—805 Hawthorn, College Station, Tex. 77840. *Office*—Department of English, Texas A & M University, College Station, Tex. 77843.

CAREER: University of Hawaii, Honolulu, instructor, 1949-52; University of Texas, Main University (now University of Texas at Austin), instructor, 1952-54; University of Michigan, Ann Arbor, instructor, 1954-55; University of California, Berkeley, assistant professor of speech, 1955-56; American University Language Center, Bangkok, Thailand, academic director,

1956-57; University of Florida, Gainesville, assistant professor, 1957-58; University of Puerto Rico, Rio Piedras, visiting professor of linguistics, 1958-59; Columbia University, Teachers College, New York, N.Y., and Kabul, Afghanistan, assistant professor, 1959-62, director of English Language Program in Afghanistan, 1960-62; Northeastern Illinois State College (now Northeastern Illinois University), Chicago, associate professor, 1962-63; Queens College of the City University of New York, Flushing, N.Y., associate professor of English, 1963-66; Texas A & M University, College Station, associate professor, 1966-68, professor of English, 1968—; founder and director of linguistics program, 1970—. Visiting professor at University of Michigan, 1970-71, Kuwait University, 1979-81, and Institut Teknologi Mara, Kuala Lumpur, Malaysia, 1987-88; visiting summer professor at Massachusetts Institute of Technology, 1969, Oxford University, 1974, and Cambridge University, 1980. Has conducted field work in many countries, including Pakistan, India, and the U.S.S.R. Public lecturer at Columbia University, Cornell University, Princeton University, and other institutions. Consultant. *Military service:* U.S. Marine Corps, 1943-46.

MEMBER: Dictionary Society of North America, American Dialect Society (member of executive committee, 1982-85 and 1990, member of executive council, 1989-92), Linguistic Society of America, Modern Language Association of America (member of delegate assembly, 1985-88), South Asian Literary Association (president, 1979-85).

AWARDS, HONORS: American Philosophical Society grants, 1964, 1966, 1974; *Sunday London Telegraph* Book of the Year Award, 1971, for *The Letters of Sir William Jones;* faculty distinguished achievement award in research, Texas A & M University, 1972; visiting fellow, University of Oxford, 1974; Hospitality Grant, Indian Council for Cultural Relations, 1984; grants from Indian government, 1984, and from American Council of Learned Societies and Linguistic Society of America, 1984.

WRITINGS:

Sir William Jones, Orientalist: A Bibliography, University of Hawaii Press, 1952, reprinted, 1972.
Oriental Jones: A Biography, Asia Publishing House, 1964.
(Contributor) John Newman, editor, *Meanings of Language,* Queens College, 1964.
(Editor) *The Letters of Sir William Jones,* two volumes, Clarendon Press, 1970.
A History of the English Language, Harcourt, 1972.
Teacher's Manual to a History of the English Language, Harcourt, 1972.
An Integrated Transformational Grammar of the English Language, Rodopi, 1978.
Sir William Jones: A Bibliography of Primary and Secondary Sources, John Benjamins, 1979.
(Editor with Helmut Esau and others, and contributor) *Language and Communication,* Hornbeam Press (Columbia, S.C.), 1980.
Historical Change and English Word Formation: Recent Vocabulary, Peter Lang, 1987.
Hans Aarsleff and others, editors, *Papers in the History of Linguistics,* John Benjamins, 1987.

Contributor to *Biographical Dictionary of the Phonetic Sciences,* 1977, *Comparative Criticism: A Year Book,* 1981, *Oxford Companion to the English Language, Oxford International Encyclopedia of Linguistics,* and *Dictionary of Literary Biography.* Contributor to about forty linguistics and Asian studies journals, and other journals, including *American Anthropologist, Asian Affairs, College English,* and *Semiotica.*

WORK IN PROGRESS: *The Life and Mind of Oriental Jones; Arabic Influences on the English Language;* and *German Linguistic Contribution to English through the Centuries,* with Pfeffer.

BIOGRAPHICAL/CRITICAL SOURCES:

PERIODICALS

Acta Orientalia, 1983.
Language, December, 1971.

*　　*　　*

CAPRIO, Betsy
See CAPRIO, Elizabeth Blair

*　　*　　*

CAPRIO, Elizabeth Blair 1933-
(Betsy Caprio)

PERSONAL: Surname is accented on first syllable; born June 1, 1933, in New York, N.Y.; daughter of Arthur Bryan (a civil servant) and Jane (Blair) Whitworth; married Alphonse E. Caprio, April 16, 1955; children: Sarah Caprio Masiero, Mark, Mary, Cecelia Caprio Kirts, Andrew, Lucy Caprio Benson, Michael, Julia. *Education:* Attended Cedar Crest College, 1950-52; Hunter College (now Hunter College of the City University of New York), B.A., 1954; Beacon College, M.A., 1976; Loyola Marymount University, M.A. (art therapy), 1989.

ADDRESSES: *Home*—Box 643, Gateway Station, 9942 Culver Blvd., Culver City, Calif. 90232.

CAREER: Independent consultant in education and spiritual direction in Massachusetts and California, 1969—; Center for Sacred Psychology, Culver City, Calif., director, 1984—. Parish minister at American Martyrs Roman Catholic Church, 1981-86.

MEMBER: Association for Humanistic Psychology, Association for Transpersonal Psychology, Religious Education Association.

AWARDS, HONORS: Nomination for Catholic Press Association Award, 1973, for *Experiments in Prayer.*

WRITINGS:

UNDER NAME BETSY CAPRIO

Experiments in Prayer, Ave Maria Press, 1973.
Experiments in Growth, Ave Maria Press, 1976.
(Contributor) Ronald Gross, editor, *The Lifelong Learner,* Simon & Schuster, 1977.
Star Trek: Good News in Modern Images, Andrews & McMeel, 1978.
The Woman Sealed in the Tower: A Psychological Approach to Feminine Spirituality, Paulist Press, 1983.
(With Thomas M. Hedberg) *Coming Home: A Handbook for Exploring the Sanctuary Within,* with manual for spiritual direction, Paulist Press, 1986.
(With Hedberg) *At a Dream Workshop,* Paulist Press, 1987.

WORK IN PROGRESS: *At a Fairy Tale Workshop* and *First Steps: The Legends of Mary's Girlhood.*

SIDELIGHTS: Betsy Caprio told *CA:* "My work has come from my own interior searchings, first as a religion teacher of young people, and more recently as a spiritual guide for adults. My books are the ones I wished I could find for my work.

"Inner exploring is the base of my psychospiritual growth, and the more exploring I do, the more material there is for my books. My mentors are Morton Kelsey and John Sanford, Anglican priest-psychologists who have broken new ground to bring the thought of C. G. Jung into the Christian tradition. I write about this blend for the average reader ('Mary Smith'), rather than the specialized student, and consider myself a translator of 'Jungian growth knowledge' to make it accessible to the layperson.

"The two *Experiments in . . .* books are collections of classroom exercises for religion teachers. They aim at helping students (and teachers) experience that which is religious and holy rather than just learn about it. *Star Trek* is a pop-culture study; it aims to show how that TV classic is a modern-day parable, a carrier of spiritual insight. *The Woman Sealed in the Tower* is an adaptation of the medieval legend of Saint Barbara, martyr of the early Christian era, whose father sealed her in a tower. The story became secularized as 'Rapunzel,' and, I believe, is a rich carrier of meaning for women today. In a way, all these books tell my story too.

"In my work at the Center for Sacred Psychology, where both spiritual direction and psychotherapy are offered for those seeking a religious/Jungian mix, I do both spiritual direction and art therapy. Our focus is on using visual means to help people explore their 'soul-scapes'—pictures, sacred art and iconography, the sand tray, etc.—since this is the language of the psyche or soul. It is always a privilege to see the inner life of a person emerge."

BIOGRAPHICAL/CRITICAL SOURCES:

PERIODICALS

Chicago Studies, fall, 1985.
National Catholic Reporter, October 7, 1983.
Pecos Benedictine (New Mexico), June, 1983.

*　　*　　*

CARDEW, Michael (Ambrose) 1901-1983

PERSONAL: Surname accented on second syllable; born May 26, 1901, in London, England; died February 11, 1983, in Truro, Cornwall, England; son of Arthur (a civil servant) and Alexandra Rhonda (Kitchin) Cardew; married Mariel Baron Russell, December 24, 1933; children: Seth Christopher Mason, Brian Cornelius McDonough, Ennis Tuel. *Education:* Exeter College, Oxford, B.A., 1923.

ADDRESSES: *Home*—Wenford Bridge Pottery, St. Breward, Bodmin, Cornwall, England.

CAREER: Leach Pottery, St. Ives, Cornwall, England, apprentice, 1923-26; Winchcombe Pottery, Winchcombe, Gloucestershire, England, founder and owner, 1926-39; Wenford Bridge Pottery, St. Breward, Bodmin, Cornwall, founder and owner, 1939-42, 1948-50; West African Institute of Arts, Industries and Social Sciences, Achimota College, Accra, Ghana, ceramist, 1942-45; Volta Pottery, Vume Dugame, Accra, founder, owner, and partner, 1945-48; Ministry of Trade and Industry, Nigeria, senior pottery officer, 1950-65; Wenford Bridge Pottery, owner, 1965-83. Founder and developer, Pottery Training Centre, Abuja, Nigeria, during 1950s. Visiting pottery instructor to aborigines, Northern Territory, Australia, 1968. Gave workshops and lectures in New Zealand, United States, Canada, Nigeria, and Ghana during 1960s and 1970s.

MEMBER: International Academy of Ceramics, World Crafts Council, Craftsmen Potters Association of Great Britain, British Ceramic Society.

AWARDS, HONORS: Member of Order of the British Empire, 1964; Commander of the British Empire, 1981; honorary doctorate, 1982.

WRITINGS:

(Contributor) Hassan and Na'ibi, editors, *A Chronicle of Abuja,* African Universities Press, 1962.
Pioneer Pottery, Longmans, 1969, St. Martin's, 1971.
(With Sylvia Leith Ross) *Nigerian Pottery,* Ibadan University Press, 1971.
(Contributor) *Michael Cardew: A Collection of Essays,* introduction by Bernard Leach, Watson-Guptill, 1976.
(Contributor) Garth Clark, editor, *Ceramic Art: Comment and Review, 1882-1977,* Dutton, 1978.
Michael Cardew and Pupils, York City Art Gallery, 1983.
A Pioneer Potter: An Autobiography, Collins, 1988.

Contributor to *Pottery Quarterly, Nigeria, Studio Potter, Craft Horizons, Ceramic Review,* and *Ceramics Monthly.*

WORK IN PROGRESS: Notes for memoirs on life as a potter, *Don't Trouble the World* (tentative title).

OBITUARIES:

PERIODICALS

Times (London), February 16, 1983.*

*   *   *

CARNES, Mark C(hristopher)   1950-

PERSONAL: Born November 17, 1950, in Pocatello, Idaho; son of Jack C. (a merchant) and Jennie Claire (Comstock) Carnes; married Mary Elin Korchinsky (a teacher), June 26, 1976; children: Stephanie Lauren. *Education:* Harvard University, B.A., 1974; Columbia University, M.A., 1978, Ph.D., 1982.

ADDRESSES: Home—Seven Central Ave., Newburgh, N.Y. 12550. *Office*—Department of History, Barnard College, 606 West 120th St., New York, N.Y. 10027.

CAREER: Columbia University, New York City, instructor in history, 1979-81; Vassar College, Poughkeepsie, N.Y., visiting assistant professor of history, 1981-82; Barnard College, New York City, assistant professor of history, 1982—.

MEMBER: American Historical Association, Organization of American Historians.

WRITINGS:

(Editor) Guy Emerson Bowerman, Jr., *The Compensations of War: The Diary of an Ambulance Driver during the Great War,* University of Texas Press, 1983.
(Editor with John A. Garraty) *Dictionary of American Biography, Supplement VIII (1966-1970),* Scribner, 1988.
Secret Ritual and Manhood in Victorian America, Yale University Press, 1989.
(Editor with Clyde Griffen) *Meanings for Manhood: Constructions of Masculinity in Victorian America,* University of Chicago Press, 1990.
(Assistant general editor) *American National Biography,* Oxford University Press, 1990.

WORK IN PROGRESS: Atlas of American History, with John A. Garraty, for publication by Doubleday in 1992.

CARPENTER, Mimi Gregoire   1947-

PERSONAL: Born June 29, 1947, in Waterville, Maine; daughter of Henry Oliver and Emilia (Fontesse) Gregoire; married James Ronald Carpenter (a special education teacher), August 17, 1968; children: Fontessa R. G. *Education:* University of Southern Maine, B.S., 1969. *Politics:* Independent Democrat. *Religion:* Episcopalian.

ADDRESSES: Home—Box 500, Belgrade Rd., Oakland, Maine 04963.

CAREER: Elementary school art teacher in York, Maine, 1969-70; elementary school classroom teacher in Belgrade, Maine, 1970-73; junior and senior high school art teacher in Oakland, Maine, 1973-75; touring artist, 1976-82; artist in residence, Maine State Department of Arts and Humanities, and affiliate of Touring Artist Program, 1983—.

MEMBER: Society of Children's Book Writers, Maine Illustrators.

WRITINGS:

(Self-illustrated) *What the Sea Left Behind* (juvenile), Down East, 1981.
(Self-illustrated) *Mermaid in a Tidal Pool* (juvenile), Beachcomber Press, 1985.
(Self-illustrated) *The Cross-Eyed Cat* (juvenile), Beachcomber Press, 1985.
(Self-illustrated) *Shorah the Merwitch* (juvenile), Windswept House, 1990.

WORK IN PROGRESS: Writing and illustrating *A Castle Fantasy;* illustrating *Summerweek.*

SIDELIGHTS: Mimi Gregoire Carpenter told *CA:* "My children's stories radiate from the artwork I produce. *What the Sea Left Behind* contains a collection of paintings consisting of those broken, scarred, or blemished objects left by the sea and most commonly overlooked by all but the most fervent beachcomber. I prefer to work within this more intimate scope, to alert the viewer to the sensitivity of finding beauty in objects not otherwise thought to have aesthetic value. This philosophy is reflected in my writing. In each book I ask that you become involved beyond the surface." The author added that *Shorah the Merwitch* "comes from the characters and method of writing and illustrating I've been using as I travel around the state of Maine in the Touring Artist program. The characters are ugly on the outside, but kind and gentle on the inside."

*   *   *

CARRIGAN, Richard A(lfred), Jr.   1932-

PERSONAL: Born February 17, 1932, in Miami, Fla.; son of Richard Alfred Carrigan; married in 1954; children: two. *Education:* Attended University of Florida, 1949-51; University of Illinois, B.S., 1953, M.S., 1956, Ph.D., 1962; attended New Mexico State University, 1954-55.

ADDRESSES: Home—2S 526 Williams Rd., Warrenville, Ill. 60555. *Office*—Fermi National Acceleration Laboratory, P.O. Box 500, Batavia, Ill. 60510.

CAREER: Junior physicist for Firestone Tire & Rubber Co., 1953; Carnegie Institute of Technology (now Carnegie-Mellon University), Pittsburgh, Pa., research physicist, 1961-64, assistant professor of physics, 1964-68; Fermi National Acceleration Laboratory (Fermilab), Batavia, Ill., physicist, 1968—, director of Personnel Service, 1972-76, assistant head of Research Division, 1977-84, head of Office of Research and Technology Applications, 1984—. Guest research associate at Brookhaven National Laboratory, 1962-63, guest assistant physicist, 1963-67; consultant to American Institute of Research. *Military service:* U.S. Army, Ordnance, 1953-55.

MEMBER: National Association of Science Writers, American Association for the Advancement of Science, American Physical Society, Signa Xi, Phi Gamma Delta.

AWARDS, HONORS: Senior Fulbright fellow at Deutsches Elektron-Synchrotron, West Germany, 1967-68.

WRITINGS:

(With Nancy Carrigan) *The Siren Stars,* Pyramid Publications, 1970.
(With W. R. Huson and M. Month) *Proceedings of the Fermilab Summer School on Accelerators,* two volumes, American Institute of Physics, 1982.
(With W. Peter Trower) *Magnetic Monopoles,* Plenum, 1983.
(With James A. Ellison) *Relativistic Channeling,* Plenum, 1987.
(With Trower) *Particle Physics in the Cosmos,* Freeman, 1989.
(With Trower) *Particles and Forces: At the Heart of Matter,* Freeman, in press.

Contributor to scientific journals and popular magazines, including *Analog* and *Scientific American.*

WORK IN PROGRESS: Super Year; research on decimal time and the metric system.

*   *   *

CARTER, Lin(wood Vrooman)   1930-1988

PERSONAL: Born June 9, 1930, in St. Petersburg, Fla.; died of cardiac arrest brought on by chronic emphysema, in Montclair, N.J., February 7, 1988; son of Raymond Linwood and Lucy (Vrooman) Carter; married Judith Ellen Hershkowitz, 1958 (divorced, 1959); married Noel Vreeland, August 19, 1964 (divorced, 1975). *Education:* Attended Columbia University, 1953-54. *Religion:* "None, but anti-all."

ADDRESSES: Agent—Henry Morrison, P.O. Box 235, Bedford Hills, N.Y. 10507.

CAREER: Copywriter for advertising agencies and book publishers, including Prentice-Hall, and Albert Frank-Guenther Law Agency, 1957-69; full-time free-lance writer of science fiction and heroic fantasy, 1969-88. Editorial consultant, Ballantine Books, Inc. Originator and funder of Gandalf Award for Grand Master of Fantasy, World Science Fiction Convention, 1976. *Military service:* U.S. Army, infantry, 1951-53; served in Korea.

MEMBER: Swordsmen and Sorcerers' Guild of America (SAGA; founding member), Sons of the Desert, Sax Rohmer Society, Trap Door Spiders, James Branch Cabell Society, Dark Brotherhood.

WRITINGS:

The Star Magicians (bound with *The Off-Worlders* by Howard Hunt), Ace Books, 1966.
The Flame of Iridar (bound with *Peril of the Starmen* by Kris Neville), Belmont, 1967.
(With David Grinnell) *Destination: Saturn* (bound with *Invader on My Back* by Philip E. High), Ace Books, 1967.
The Thief of Thoth (bound with *And Others Shall Be Born* by Frank Belknap Long), Belmont, 1968.
Tower at the Edge of Time, Belmont, 1968.
Giant of World's End, Belmont, 1969.

The Purloined Planet (bound with *The Evil That Men Do* by John Brunner), Belmont, 1969.
Lost World of Time, New American Library, 1969.
Tower of the Medusa, Ace Books, 1969.
The Quest of Kadji, Belmont, 1972.
The Black Star, Dell, 1973.
The Man Who Loved Mars, Fawcett, 1973.
The Valley Where Time Stood Still, Doubleday, 1974.
Time War, Dell, 1974.
The City outside the World, Berkley, 1977.
The Wizard of Zao, DAW Books, 1978.
Journey to the Underground World, DAW Books, 1979.
Tara of the Twilight, Zebra, 1979.
Zanthodon (sequel to *Journey to the Underground World*), DAW Books, 1980.
Darya of the Bronze Age, DAW Books, 1981.
Hurok of the Stone Age, DAW Books, 1981.
Eric of Zanthodon, DAW Books, 1982.
Kesrick, DAW Books, 1982.
Kellory the Warlock, Doubleday, 1984.
Dragonrouge: Further Adventures in Terra Magica (sequel to *Kesrick*), DAW Books, 1984.
Down to a Sunless Sea, DAW Books, 1984.
Found Wanting, DAW Books, 1985.
Horror Wears Blue, Doubleday, 1987.
Mandricardo: New Adventures in Terra Magica, DAW Books, 1987.

"CALLISTO" SERIES; SCIENCE FICTION NOVELS

Black Legion of Callisto, Dell, 1972.
Jandar of Callisto, Dell, 1972.
Sky Pirates of Callisto, Dell, 1973.
Mad Empress of Callisto, Dell, 1975.
Mind Wizards of Callisto, Dell, 1975.
Lankar of Callisto, Dell, 1975.
Ylana of Callisto, Dell, 1977.
Renegade of Callisto, Dell, 1978.

"CONAN" SERIES; SWORDS AND SORCERY

(With Robert E. Howard and L. Sprague de Camp) *Conan,* Ace Books, 1967.
(With Howard and de Camp) *Conan the Wanderer,* Lancer, 1968.
(With de Camp) *Conan of the Isles,* Lancer, 1968, reprinted, Ace Books, 1986.
(With Howard and de Camp) *Conan of Cimmeria,* Lancer, 1969.
(With de Camp) *Conan the Buccaneer,* Lancer, 1971, reprinted, Ace Books, 1986.
(With de Camp) *Conan of Aquilonia,* Lancer, 1971.
(With L. Sprague de Camp, Catherine Crook de Camp, and Bjorn Nyberg) *Conan the Swordsman,* Bantam, 1978.
(With L. Sprague de Camp and Catherine Crook de Camp) *Conan the Liberator,* Bantam, 1979.
(With L. Sprague de Camp and Catherine Crook de Camp) *Conan the Barbarian* (screenplay novelization), Bantam, 1982.

"GREAT IMPERIUM" SERIES; SCIENCE FICTION NOVELS

The Man without a Planet (bound with *Time to Live* by John Rackham), Ace Books, 1966.
Star Rogue, Lancer, 1970.
Outworlder, Lancer, 1971.

"GREEN STAR SAGA" SERIES; SCIENCE FICTION NOVELS

Under the Green Star, DAW Books, 1972, reprinted, Starmont House, 1987.
When the Green Star Calls, DAW Books, 1973.
By the Light of the Green Star, DAW Books, 1974.
As the Green Star Rises, DAW Books, 1975.
In the Green Star's Glow, DAW Books, 1976.

"GONDWANE EPIC" SERIES; SCIENCE FICTION NOVELS

The Warrior of World's End, DAW Books, 1974.
The Enchantress of World's End, DAW Books, 1975.
The Immortal of World's End, DAW Books, 1976.
The Barbarian of World's End, DAW Books, 1977.
The Pirate of World's End, DAW Books, 1978.

"LEMURIAN BOOKS" SERIES; FANTASY NOVELS

The Wizard of Lemuria, Ace Books, 1965, revised edition published as *Thongor and the Wizard of Lemuria,* Berkley, 1969.
Thongor of Lemuria, Ace Books, 1966, revised edition published as *Thongor and the Dragon City,* Berkley, 1970.
Thongor against the Gods, Paperback Library, 1967.
Thongor at the End of Time, Paperback Library, 1968.
Thongor in the City of Magicians, Paperback Library, 1968.
Thongor Fights the Pirates of Tarakus, Berkley, 1970 (published in England as *Thongor and the Pirates of Tarakus,* Tandem, 1971).

"ZARKON, LORD OF THE UNKNOWN" SERIES; SCIENCE FICTION NOVELS

The Nemesis of Evil, Doubleday, 1975.
Invisible Death, Doubleday, 1975.
The Volcano Ogre, Doubleday, 1976.
The Earth Shaker, Doubleday, 1982.

EDITOR

Dragons, Elves, and Heroes, Ballantine, 1969.
The Young Magicians, Ballantine, 1969.
Golden Cities, Far, Ballantine, 1970.
The Magic of Atlantis, Lancer, 1970.
New Worlds for Old, Ballantine, 1971.
The Spawn of Cthulhu, Ballantine, 1971.
Discoveries in Fantasy, Ballantine, 1972.
Great Short Novels of Adult Fantasy #1, Ballantine, 1972.
Great Short Novels of Adult Fantasy #2, Ballantine, 1973.
(And contributor) *Kingdoms of Sorcery,* Doubleday, 1975.
Realms of Wizardry, Doubleday, 1976.
Warriors and Wizards, Dell, 1976.
Barbarians and Black Magicians, Doubleday, 1977.

OTHER

Sandalwood and Jade (verse), Sign of the Centaur, 1951.
(With Howard) *King Kull* (short stories), Lancer, 1967.
Tolkien: A Look behind "The Lord of the Rings" (criticism; excerpts published in *Xero,* 1961-67), Ballantine, 1969.
Beyond the Gates of Dream (short stories), Belmont, 1969.
(Contributor) August Derleth, editor, *Dark Things,* Arkham House, 1971.
Lovecraft: A Look behind the "Cthulhu Mythos" (criticism), Ballantine, 1972.
Imaginary Worlds: The Art of Fantasy, Ballantine, 1973.
Dreams from R'lyeh (verse; originally published in *Amra*), introduction by L. Sprague de Camp, Arkham House, 1975.
(Contributor) Gerald W. Page, editor, *Nameless Places,* Arkham House, 1975.

(Contributor) Edward P. Berglund, editor, *The Disciples of Cthulhu,* DAW Books, 1976.
(Contributor) Donald A. Wollheim, editor, *The DAW Science Fiction Reader,* DAW Books, 1976.
(Author of text) David Wenzel, *Middle-Earth: The World of Tolkien Illustrated,* Centaur, 1977.
Lost Worlds (anthology), DAW Books, 1980.

Editor and occasional author of introductions for "Ballantine Adult Fantasy Series," Ballantine Books, 1969-73; editor and occasional contributor to *Flashing Swords!* anthology series, five volumes, Doubleday-Dell, 1973-81; editor and occasional contributor to *The Year's Best Fantasy Stories* series, six volumes, DAW Books, 1975-80; editor and contributor to *Weird Tales* anthology series, four volumes, Zebra Books, 1981-83; editor of "Lin Carter Fantasy Selections," for Zebra Books. Contributor of short stories, poems, and criticism to periodicals, including *Amra, Canadian Fandom, Fantastic, Inside, Magazine of Fantasy and Science Fiction,* and *Xero.* Editor and publisher of fan magazines, including *Spaceteer, The Saturday Evening Toad,* and *Spectrum.*

WORK IN PROGRESS: Khymyrium: The City of a Hundred Kings, from the Coming of Aviathar to the Passing of Spheridon the Doomed, an epic fantasy planned for a length of 500,000 words; *The Book of Eibon,* a posthumous collaboration with Clark Ashton Smith, drawing on Smith's unpublished notes and manuscripts; a compilation of the complete text of the imaginary *Necronomicon* of Abdul Alhazred, to be made up of the quotations from the text found in the works of H. P. Lovecraft, August Derleth, Clark Ashton Smith, Frank Belknap Long, Robert E. Howard, Brian Lumley, Ramsey Campbell, and others.

SIDELIGHTS: Lin Carter's name, declared Bill Crider in the *Dictionary of Literary Biography Yearbook 1981,* was "one of the most prominent . . . in the field of fantasy." Besides editing the significant "Ballantine Adult Fantasy Series" that reintroduced works of fantasy by major authors, Carter produced major works of criticism on the genre, wrote stories in the style of 1930s pulp magazines, and helped spark the revolution in fantasy publishing of the 1960s and 1970s. Also, for over twenty years, wrote Catherine Crook and L. Sprague de Camp in *Locus,* Carter "was an active producer of heroic fantasy and sword-and-planet tales," authoring more than one hundred science fantasy and fantasy stories.

Fantasy was Carter's great passion. An early devotee of L. Frank Baum's Oz books, Robert E. Howard's stories of Conan the Barbarian, and Edgar Rice Burroughs' Martian tales and stories of Tarzan, Carter began publishing stories, articles and reviews in fan magazines while he was still in high school. Some of his articles later formed the basis for his important critical study of J. R. R. Tolkien, *Tolkien: A Look Behind "The Lord of the Rings."* It was on the basis of his Tolkien study that he was asked to edit Ballantine Books' adult fantasy series. In his capacity as general editor Carter performed some of his most influential work, stated Crider, reprinting relatively unknown books by authors such as Evangeline Walton, Poul Anderson, William Morris, Lord Dunsany, H. Rider Haggard, and George MacDonald, anthologizing "fantastic episodes from varied sources of world literature ranging from *The Kalevala* and *The Volsung Saga* to the poetry of Browning and Tennyson," and publishing works by new authors such as Katherine Kurtz and Joy Chant.

Carter also expressed his tastes in fantasy in his own fiction. "Much of Lin's work," said the de Camps, "tended to be derivative, leaning heavily on Burroughs, Howard, and Tolkien." His first book, *The Wizard of Lemuria,* wrote John Boardmen in *Sci-*

ence Fiction Review, read like "the result of a head-on collision between Burroughs and Howard"—"a description," Carter later commented in *Imaginary Worlds,* "that rather pleased me, as that is exactly what the story was supposed to be." Carter's enthusiasm for Howard's work led L. Sprague de Camp, who was working on a series of stories about Conan the Barbarian for Howard's estate, to invite Carter to collaborate with him on the stories. Carter and de Camp completed several Conan stories that Howard had left unfinished and then wrote a number of original Conan tales at the behest of the Howard heirs. "Although opinions differ as to the success of these collaborations," the de Camps explained, ". . . the readers thus introduced to Conan clamored for more, until there were twelve volumes of stories about the Great Barbarian."

"It's been said of Lin Carter," announced Mark Willard in *Science Fiction Review,* "that his tremendous enjoyment of and enthusiasm for the sword-and-sorcery and fantasy fields go a long way to atone for whatever his works may lack in technical polish and absolute first-line quality." Some reviewers, however, found Carter's style unappealing; William M. Schuyler, Jr., wrote in *Fantasy Review* of *Down to a Sunless Sea,* "Even on pain of death do not read this book," and in the same periodical Paul M. Lloyd exclaimed about *Kellory the Warlock,* "Alas, my heart was grieved within me when I thought of how many innocent trees gave their lives that this tome might live." But others recognised the value of his fiction: "One should not overlook the entertainment value of Carter's work," warned Crider, and added, "It might also be pointed out that the theme of much Sword & Sorcery literature, including Carter's, that of Order versus Chaos, is not an ignoble one."

Carter attempted to define his own fascination with fantasy in *Imaginary Worlds,* his history of fantastic literature. "Why do we who love fantasy read it with such delight and gusto, returning to it again and again over the years as to a source of entertainment that is inexhaustible?" he asked. "We read fantasy because we love it; we love it because we find it a source of the marvel and mystery and wonder and joy that we can find nowhere else. . . . Why do I read fantasy? I really don't know; I really don't care. All I know is that something within me wakes and thrills and responds to phrases like 'the splendid city of Celephais, in the Valley of Ooth-Nargai, beyond the Tanarian Hills,' where galleys 'sail up the river Oukranos past the gilded spires of Thran,' and 'elephant caravans tramp through perfumed jungles in Kled,' where 'forgotten palaces with veined ivory columns sleep lovely and unbroken under the moon.' Such phrases, such sequences of gorgeous imagery, touch something that is within most of us, really. I believe that a hunger of the fabulous is common to the human condition. . . . But whatever it is that sings within me to such imagery," he concluded, "I am happy that it is there."

Throughout his long and industrious career, stated Crider, Lin Carter "established himself as a figure of the first importance in the field of fantasy. He [had] the ability to entertain and the ability to inform, and he . . . preserved and caused to be published volumes of importance to any scholar interested in the fantastic in literature." Carter himself was something of a fantasy figure: "Despite his many virtues," reported the de Camps, ". . . Lin was a living embodiment of Peter Pan. His view of the world and his relation to it was totally unrealistic." His heavy smoking, and his refusal to seek medical attention for the mouth cancer that developed because of it, led to a disfiguring operation in 1985 and to his death about three years later. Perhaps the fullest revelation of Carter's commitment to the genre, however, is revealed in the dedication to his *Imaginary Worlds;* he inscribed the volume "to

the fantasy writers of tomorrow, to those men and women not yet born, whom I shall never know, whose books I shall not live to read, but whose dreams I have shared and whose visions would not be strange or alien to me."

MEDIA ADAPTATIONS: A folk-rock musical, *Thongor in the City of Magicians,* loosely based on Carter's book of the same title, was produced in London in the late 1960s.

BIOGRAPHICAL/CRITICAL SOURCES:

BOOKS

Carter, Lin, *Imaginary Worlds: The Art of Fantasy,* Ballantine, 1973.
Dictionary of Literary Biography Yearbook: 1981, Gale, 1982.
Schweitzer, Darrell, *Science Fiction Voices #5,* Borgo Press, 1981.
Searles, Baird, Martin Last, Beth Meacham, and Michael Franklin, *A Reader's Guide to Science Fiction,* Avon, 1979.
Searles, Baird, Beth Meacham, and Michael Franklin, *A Reader's Guide to Fantasy,* Avon, 1982.

PERIODICALS

Fantasy Review, September, 1984, October, 1984, January, 1985, March, 1987.
Locus, March, 1988.
Los Angeles Times Book Review, February 6, 1983.
Magazine of Fantasy and Science Fiction, March, 1976.
Science Fiction and Fantasy Book Review, October, 1982.
Science Fiction Chronicle, May, 1985.
Science Fiction Review, February, 1983, February, 1985.
Valhalla, number 1, 1979.
Washington Post Book World, January 25, 1981.

OBITUARIES:

PERIODICALS

Locus, March, 1988.

—*Sketch by Kenneth R. Shepherd*

[Sketch reviewed by L. Sprague and Catherine Crook de Camp]

*   *   *

CARTER, Nick
See CRIDER, (Allen) Bill(y)

*   *   *

CEBULASH, Mel 1937-
(Ben Farrell, Glen Harlan, Jared Jansen, Jeanette Mara)

PERSONAL: Surname is pronounced *Seb*-yu-lash; born August 24, 1937, in Jersey City, N.J.; son of Jack (a mailman) and Jeanette (Duthie) Cebulash; married Deanna Penn, August 19, 1962 (divorced); married Dolly Hasinbiller, June 19, 1977; children: (first marriage) Glen Harlan, Benjamin Farrell, Jeanette Mara. *Education:* Jersey City State College, B.A., 1962, M.A., 1964; University of South Carolina, graduate study, 1964-65. *Religion:* Jewish.

ADDRESSES: Home—232 Stockbridge Ave., Alhambra, Calif. 91801.

CAREER: Junior high school teacher of reading in Teaneck, N.J., 1962-64; Fairleigh Dickinson University, Rutherford, N.J., instructor in reading clinic, 1965-67; Scholastic Magazines, Inc., New York, N.Y., editor for language arts, 1966-76; Bowmar/Noble Publishing Co., Los Angeles, Calif., editor in chief, 1976-80; Pitman Learning, Belmont, Calif., publisher, 1982-85; currently publisher, Cebulash Associates, Inc., Pasadena, Calif. *Military service:* U.S. Army, 1955-58.

MEMBER: Authors Guild, Authors League of America, Mystery Writers of America (regional vice-president, 1982-83).

AWARDS, HONORS: Author Award, New Jersey Association of Teachers of English, 1969, for *Through Basic Training with Walter Young;* Children's Choice Award, International Reading Association (IRA), 1975, for *Football Players Do Amazing Things,* and 1976, for *Basketball Players Do Amazing Things;* IRA Young Adult Choice Award, 1987, for *Ruth Marini, World Series Star.*

WRITINGS:

Monkeys, Go Home (screenplay novelization), Scholastic Book Services, 1967.

Through Basic Training with Walter Young, Scholastic Book Services, 1968.

The Love Bug (screenplay novelization), Scholastic Book Services, 1969.

Man in a Green Beret and Other Medal of Honor Winners, Scholastic Book Services, 1969.

The Boatniks (screenplay novelization), Scholastic Book Services, 1970.

The Ball That Wouldn't Bounce, Scholastic Book Services, 1972.

(Under pseudonym Glen Harlan) *Petey the Pup,* Scholastic Book Services, 1972.

(Under pseudonym Jared Jansen) *Penny the Poodle,* Scholastic Book Services, 1972.

Baseball Players Do Amazing Things, Random House, 1973.

Herbie Rides Again (screenplay adaptation), Scholastic Book Services, 1974.

Dic-tion-ar-y Skilz, Scholastic Book Services, 1974.

The Strongest Man in the World (screenplay adaptation), Scholastic Book Services, 1975.

Football Players Do Amazing Things, Random House, 1975.

Basketball Players Do Amazing Things, Random House, 1976.

The Grossest Book of World Records, Pocket Books, 1978.

Math Zingo, Bowmar/Noble, 1978.

Reading Zingo, Bowmar/Noble, 1978.

Big League Baseball Reading Kit, Bowmar/Noble, 1979.

Spanish Math Zingo, Bowmar/Noble, 1979.

Crosswinds Reading Program, Bowmar/Noble, 1979.

The Champion's Jacket, Creative Education, 1979.

Blackouts, Scholastic Book Services, 1979.

The 1,000 Point Pro Sports Quiz Book: Football, Random House, 1979.

The 1,000 Point Pro Sports Quiz Book: Basketball, Random House, 1979.

The 1,000 Point Pro Sports Quiz Book: Baseball, Random House, 1980.

A Horse to Remember, Bowmar/Noble, 1980.

I'm an Expert: Motivating Independent Study Projects for Grades 4-6, Scott, Foresman, 1982.

The Spring Street Boys Team Up, Scholastic, Inc., 1982.

The Spring Street Boys Settle a Score, Scholastic, Inc., 1982.

The Spring Street Boys Hit the Road, Scholastic, Inc., 1982.

The Spring Street Boys Go for Broke, Scholastic, Inc., 1982.

Ruth Marini of the Dodgers, Lerner Publications, 1983.

Ruth Marini—Dodger Ace, Lerner Publications, 1983.

Ruth Marini—World Series Star, Lerner Publications, 1985.

Hot like the Sun: A Terry Tyndale Mystery, Lerner Publications, 1986.

Carly & Co. Series, Ballantine, in press.

Editor, "ACTION Reading Kit" series, Scholastic Book Services, 1970. Contributor, sometimes under pseudonyms Ben Farrell and Jeanette Mara, of short stories to university literary journals. Contributing editor, *Scholastic Scope.*

WORK IN PROGRESS: A novel.

SIDELIGHTS: Mel Cebulash told *CA:* "The idea of writing entered my mind when I was a senior in college. The first short story I tried was published, and although the stories that followed didn't meet with the same approval, my small measure of success was enough to sustain a continuing effort.

"Just before my first child was born, I left teaching and moved into writing and editing as a full-time activity. My parents and friends looked upon the move as the foolish pursuit of a far-fetched dream. Fortunately, years of reading had led me to believe in the possibility of dreams. My writing has ranged from picture book stories for children to books for adults. I have been especially interested in stories and books for young people who have difficulty in reading, and I suppose these efforts have been most rewarding to me.

"Most of my fiction stems either directly or indirectly from experience. I use experience for ideas, but I allow the writing to shape the experience into something new—something that hasn't happened to me or anyone else.

"I've been gratified by the sales of my books, but my real joy has been the realization that my writing continues to improve with each effort."

AVOCATIONAL INTERESTS: Teaching, trying to handicap race horses.

*   *   *

CELESTE, Sister Marie

PERSONAL: Born in Altoona, Pa.; daughter of Frank (an electrical engineer) and Mary Ann (Dente) Cuzzolina. *Education:* Attended Seton Hill College, 1939, Western Reserve University (now Case Western Reserve University), 1940, 1943; University of Pittsburgh, B.A., 1947; Laval University, M.A. (magna cum laude), 1957, Ph.D. (cum laude), 1959; Sorbonne, University of Paris, certificate (magna cum laude), 1962; University of Madrid, certificate, 1969; University of Perugia, certificate, 1969.

ADDRESSES: Home—6301 North Sheridan Rd., Chicago, Ill. 60660. *Office*—Department of Modern Languages, Loyola University, Chicago, Ill. 60611.

CAREER: Member of Roman Catholic women's religious community, the Sisters of Charity; high school French teacher in Pittsburgh, Pa., 1943-51; Seton Hill College, Greensburg, Pa., assistant professor of French, 1951-57; Laval University, Faculty of Letters, Quebec City, Quebec, teacher in School of English, summers, 1959-64; Loyola University, Chicago, Ill., associate professor of modern languages, 1963-67; Wisconsin State University at Eau Claire (now University of Wisconsin—Eau Claire), Eau Claire, associate professor in department of foreign languages, 1969-70; Office of the Superintendent of Public Instruction, Springfield, Ill., director of foreign languages, 1971-73; Loyola University, Chicago, associate professor, 1973-77, professor of modern languages, 1977—. Visiting professor at University of Ottawa, 1962-63. Member of board of advisors for American Institute for Foreign Studies, 1965-71.

MEMBER: American Association of Teachers of French, American Association of University Professors, Illinois Modern Language Association, La Societe des Amis de Georges Bernanos.

AWARDS, HONORS: Raymond Casgrain Prize from Laval University, 1962, for *Le sens de l'agonie dans l'oeuvre de Georges Bernanos;* Chevalier dans l'Order des Palmes Academiques from French Ministry of Education, 1965; Moderator's Award from National French Honor Society, 1976; Arthur Schmitt Foundation Award, 1979; Illinois Foreign Language Teachers Association, first service award, 1985, and distinguished service award, 1988.

WRITINGS:

Le sens de l'agonie dans l'oeuvre de Georges Bernanos (title means "The Meaning of Suffering in the Works of Georges Bernanos"), Lethielleux, 1962.
A Challenge to the Church, Newman, 1965.
Etudes bernanosiennes: Bernanos et Graham Greene (title means "Bernanos Studies: Bernanos and Graham Greene"), Minard, 1965.
Georges Bernanos et son optique de la vie chretienne (title means "Georges Bernanos and His Vision of the Christian Life"), Nizet, 1967.
(Contributor) *Basic Catechetical Perspectives,* Paulist-Newman, 1970.
A Survey on Foreign Education in Illinois: A Statewide Report, Office of the Superintendent of Public Instruction, State of Illinois, 1971.
A New Rationale for the Teaching of Foreign Languages: A Humanistic View, Office of the Superintendent of Public Instruction, State of Illinois, 1972.
New Guidelines for Foreign Language Education in the Seventies: French, German, Latin, Spanish, Russian, Office of the Superintendent of Public Instruction, State of Illinois, 1973.
(Translator) Jean Ladame, *The Church and Love,* Franciscan Publishers, 1973.
Elizabeth Ann Seton-A Self-Portrait: A Study of Her Spirituality, Prow Books, 1986.

Also author of script "A Citizen of the World," broadcast on the Eternal Word Television Network. Editor of *Illinois Foreign Languages Directory,* 1972. Contributor to *Revue Dominicaine, Revue de l'Universite Laval, Culture,* and *Lectures.*

*   *   *

CHACE, James (Clarke) 1931-

PERSONAL: Born October 16, 1931, in Fall River, Mass.; son of Hollister Remington and Harriet Mildred (Clarke) Chace; married Jean Valentine, 1957 (divorced, 1968); married Susan Denvir, 1975; children: (first marriage) Sarah, Rebecca; (second marriage) Zoe. *Education:* Harvard University, A.B., 1953; graduate study at University of Paris, Institut d'Etudes Politiques, 1954. *Religion:* Episcopalian.

ADDRESSES: Office—School of International and Public Affairs, Columbia University, 420 West 118th St., New York, N.Y. 10027.

CAREER: Esquire, New York City, assistant editor, 1957-58; *East Europe,* New York City, managing editor, 1958-64; *Interplay,* New York City, managing editor, 1964-69; *Foreign Affairs,* New York City, managing editor, 1970-83; *New York Times*

Book Review, New York City, member of editorial board, 1983-87; Carnegie Endowment for International Peace, Washington, D.C., senior associate, 1987-88; Columbia University, School of International and Public Affairs, New York City, director of Program on International Affairs and the Media, 1988—. Visiting lecturer at Yale University, 1973, 1974, 1976, 1978, 1979, Georgetown University School of Foreign Service, 1974-77, and Columbia University, 1980. Fellow, Jonathan Edward College, Yale University. Member of committees on fellows and programs, Lehrman Institute, 1972-86; member of board of directors, French-American Foundation, 1975—. *Military service:* U.S. Army, 1954-56.

MEMBER: International Institute of Strategic Studies, Council of Foreign Relations, PEN, German-American Council, Phi Beta Kappa, Century Association.

AWARDS, HONORS: Rotary International fellow, 1954; Guggenheim fellow, 1985; decorated Chevalier des Arts et Lettres, government of France, 1986.

WRITINGS:

The Rules of the Game (novel), Doubleday, 1960.
(Editor) *Conflict in the Middle East,* H. W. Wilson, 1969.
A World Elsewhere: The New American Foreign Policy, Scribner, 1973.
(Editor with Earl C. Ravenal) *Atlantis Lost: U.S.-European Relations after the Cold War,* New York University Press, 1976.
Solvency: The Price of Survival, Random House, 1980.
Endless War: How We Got Involved in Central America and What Can Be Done, Vintage Trade, 1984.
(With Caleb Carr) *America Invulnerable: The Quest for Absolute Security from 1812 to Star Wars,* Summit Books, 1988.

Contributor to *New Republic, Esquire, Harper's, New York Review of Books,* and *New York Times Magazine.*

WORK IN PROGRESS: A book on foreign policy; a biography of Dean Acheson.

SIDELIGHTS: In *Solvency: The Price of Survival,* veteran foreign affairs scholar James Chace has created "a brief, intelligent exposition of the connection between our economy and our foreign policy," states a *New Yorker* critic. Describing it as a balance of a nation's military commitments with its available resources and power, Chace takes his definition of political "solvency" from Walter Lippman's classic work *U.S. Foreign Policy: Shield of the Republic.* Although Lippman's work is over forty years old, Chace "reminds us in his important new work [that] Lippman's concept still provides the key to an understanding of America's world position which we ignore at our own peril," describes David Fromkin in the *New Republic.* Chace expands on the earlier theory, however, by suggesting that the U.S. "must continue to meet this enormous [foreign policy] commitment," adds Fromkin, "and that we have to do so while meeting enormous but equally necessary social, economic, and political commitments within the United States. Like Lippmann, Chace tells us that the problem is that we don't have the means to make good on our pledges. Unlike Lippmann, Chace believes that we have to go out and create those means by ourselves." The author traces the nation's insolvency to wasteful defense spending; he is "clear . . . [and] persistent on the relationship between Vietnam and inflation," asserts John Leonard of the *New York Times.* "We have to learn to pay for what we want to do instead of just printing money that our allies will cease to hold in reserve—there went the dollar."

Although *Commentary* contributor Peter W. Rodman believes that Chace's description of the nation's economic situation is basically sound, he calls *Solvency* "a sermon on foreign policy, not on economics. The dismal economic diagnosis serves to soften up the reader for the true message: that overextension and overcommitment abroad have weakened our foreign policy and have even been a main cause of our economic woes." The critic also considers Chace's prescriptions incorrect, claiming that "[American] weakness [has been] underscored if not created by four years of policies following precisely the precepts he now urges upon us." Paul C. Warnke, however, finds Chace's analysis and solutions suitable: writing in the *Washington Post Book World,* the critic observes that "Chace in no way ignores the reality of Soviet military strength and the threat it presents. But he contends that the threat cannot be met by policies that erode our economic power, that frighten our allies and that yield increased tensions between the United States and the Soviet Union." In addition, Warnke characterizes Chace's presentation as written "with felicitous style and clarity." And while Fromkin notes that some of Chace's suggestions are politically unsuitable, he remarks that "Chace's illuminating and eloquent essay makes it clear that political leaders must start fighting for programs regarded as politically impossible if they are serious about meeting our problems." In *Solvency,* Chace "has written a short (107-page) essay," comments William J. Miller in the *Los Angeles Times Book Review;* "its importance is in inverse proportion to its length."

Chace, along with Caleb Carr, once again explores U.S. foreign affairs in *America Invulnerable: The Quest for Absolute Security from 1812 to Star Wars,* this time from the standpoint of national security. "*America Invulnerable* is a feast of historical perspective," notes *Washington Post Book World* contributor Richard Rhodes, "tracing the American obsession with absolute security from Star Wars all the way back to the burning of Washington in 1814." The authors follow the progress of the American empire, including movements such as manifest destiny and expansionism, proposing that "absolute security" has been the justification for this empire. Jefferson Morley elaborates in the *Los Angeles Times Book Review:* "[Chace and Carr] say that the American empire was built as a buffer from all manner of territorial and ideological threats. They make their case through a series of witty and illuminating historical essays," and note that the idea that had its beginnings with the sacking of Washington, D.C., during the War of 1812.

While he finds the authors' analysis of current U.S. policy reasonable, *New York Times Book Review* contributor Gaddis Smith remarks that in their historical analysis, "the authors seldom clarify the difference between necessary responses to real threats to national security and violent, irrational responses to imaginary enemies. Leaders in the history of American foreign policy are depicted, with few exceptions, as obsessed devotees of unilateralism, violence, and absolute security." Smith also faults Chace and Carr for overarguing "their case by selecting episodes illustrative of unilateralism . . . while ignoring or misinterpreting contrary examples of reliance on diplomacy." Some critics have also remarked on a number of historical errors; George Russell, for example, calls *America Invulnerable* an "arresting, quirky, quite flawed, and sometimes misleading work," adding in his *Commentary* review that the book "is marked throughout by misleading assertions . . . and occasional inaccuracy." But Rhodes believes that in *America Invulnerable* "much of the story is examined with penetration and is powerfully told. Even the obscure James Polk comes alive." The critic concludes that "*America Invulnerable* discovers one important reason, rooted

in our national character, why he have found [nuclear compromise] hard to learn." While the authors are less successful in their attempts to influence current national policy, says Morley, "In '*America Invulnerable,*' Chace and Carr succeed in their primary aim: to provide an enlightening history of U.S. imperial ambitions."

AVOCATIONAL INTERESTS: Sailing.

BIOGRAPHICAL/CRITICAL SOURCES:

PERIODICALS

Commentary, June, 1981, August, 1988.
Los Angeles Times Book Review, August 23, 1981, March 13, 1988.
New Republic, June 6, 1981.
New Yorker, June 1, 1981.
New York Times, May 21, 1981.
New York Times Book Review, October 7, 1984, April 10, 1988.
Washington Post Book World, May 31, 1981, March 27, 1988.

—*Sketch by Diane Telgen*

*   *   *

CHARLES, Henry
   See HARRIS, Marion Rose (Young)

*   *   *

CHARLES, Maggi
   See KOEHLER, Margaret (Hudson)

*   *   *

CHEETHAM, Erika   1939-

PERSONAL: Born July 7, 1939, in London, England; daughter of Eric Arthur (under secretary to the Admiralty and company director of E.M.I.) and Helen Lilian McMahon (Calnan) Turner; married James Nicholas Milne Cheetham (a money broker), August 4, 1961 (divorced, 1981); children: Alexander Nicholas Milne. *Education:* St. Anne's College, Oxford, M.A., 1961, Ph.D., 1962. *Politics:* "Humanist."

ADDRESSES: Home—164 rue du Faubourg, Saint Honore, 75008 Paris, France. *Agent*—Wylie, Aitken & Stone, Inc., 250 West 52nd St., Suite 2108, New York, N.Y. 10019.

CAREER: Harcourt Tutors, London, England, owner, 1962-68; writer, 1968—. Past member of editorial staff of London's Daily Mail Newspaper Group.

MEMBER: British Museum, Warburg Institute, London Library, Guards and Cavalry Club, Les Ambassadeurs, Press Club, Grouchos.

WRITINGS:

(Editor, translator, and author of introduction) Michel de Notredame, *The Prophecies of Nostradamus,* Neville Spearman, 1973, Putnam, 1974, revised edition, Putnam/Transworld, 1981.
(Editor, translator, and author of introduction) Michel de Notredame, *The Further Prophecies of Nostradamus: 1985 and Beyond,* Putnam, 1985.
(Editor) Michel de Notredame, *The Final Prophecies of Nostradamus,* Putnam, 1989.

Also author of screenplays of two films on Nostradamus, "The Man Who Saw Tomorrow" (with Orson Welles), 1982, and

"Nostradamus," 1987, and an as yet unproduced full-length black comedy for women tentatively titled "Cheque Mate." Contributor to periodicals, including *Vogue, Cosmopolitan, Nova, Reader's Digest,* and *Over 21.* Contributor to encyclopedias.

SIDELIGHTS: Erika Cheetham wrote to *CA:* "I was prompted to write a definitive book on Nostradamus because he wrote mainly in Ancien Provencal (he lived there). Ancien Provencal was the subject of my M.A. degree at Oxford. I came across Nostradamus's work by accident when researching another book in the Taylorian Library at Oxford. Two or three years after the birth of my son I decided to go back and research Nostradamus further.

"I am basically lazy, trying to meet deadlines, however long, by hours, if not minutes, and my main source of relaxation is good detective fiction. I also collect boxes—mainly eighteenth-century porcelain boxes—and sixteenth-century books, particularly those relating to Nostradamus and Catherine de Medici. When you can get me out-of-doors, I love gardening. My great fault is that I find organizing easy, but I prefer someone else to do the donkey work."

* * *

CHETWYND, Berry
See RAYNER, Claire (Berenice)

* * *

CHETWYND-HAYES, R(onald Henry Glynn) 1919-
(Angus Campbell)

PERSONAL: Born May 30, 1919, in Middlesex, England; son of Henry (a movie theatre manager) and Rose May (Cooper) Chetwynd-Hayes. *Education:* Educated in England. *Politics:* Liberal. *Religion:* Church of England.

ADDRESSES: Home and office—4 Edward Rd., Hampton Hill, Middlesex, TW12 1LD England. *Agent*—London Management, 235/241 Regent St., London W1A 2JT, England; and Cherry Weiner Literary Agency, 28 Kipling Way, Manalapan, New Jersey, 07726; and Thomas Schluck, Hinter der Worth 12, 3008 Garbsen 9, West Germany.

CAREER: Writer and editor, 1973—. Salesman in London, England, for Harrods Ltd., Army and Navy Stores, and Bourne & Hollingsworth Ltd.; showroom and exhibition manager for Peerless Build-In Furniture Ltd. *Military service:* British Army, 1939-46.

MEMBER: Society of Authors.

WRITINGS:

FICTION

The Man from the Bomb, John Spencer, 1959.
The Dark Man, Sidgwick & Jackson, 1964, published as *And Love Survived,* Zebra Books, 1979.
The Unbidden, Tandem Books, 1971, Pyramid Press, 1975.
Cold Terror, Tandem Books, 1973, Pyramid Press, 1975.
The Elemental, Fontana Books, 1974.
The Night Ghouls, Fontana Books, 1975.
The Monster Club, New English Library, 1975.
Terror by Night, Pyramid Press, 1976.
Tales of Fear and Fantasy, Fontana Books, 1977.
The Cradle Demon and Other Stories of Fantasy and Terror, Kimber, 1978.
(Author of novelization) *Dominique,* Star Books, 1978.

The Brats (science fiction), Kimber, 1979.
The Partaker, Kimber, 1980.
Kamtellar, Kimber, 1980.
(Author of novelization) *The Awakening,* Magnum Books, 1980.
Tales of Darkness, Kimber, 1981.
Tales from Beyond, Kimber, 1982.
Tales from the Other Side, Kimber, 1983, published as *The Other Side,* TOR Books, 1988.
The King's Ghost, Kimber, 1985, published as *The Grange,* TOR Books, 1988.
The Haunted Grange, Kimber, 1987.
The Curse of the Snake God, Kimber, 1989.

EDITOR AND CONTRIBUTOR

Cornish Tales of Terror, Fontana Books, 1971.
(Under pseudonym Angus Campbell) *Scottish Tales of Terror,* 1972.
Welsh Tales of Terror, Fontana Books, 1973.
Ninth Fontana Book of Great Ghost Stories, Fontana Books, 1973.
Tenth Fontana Book of Great Ghost Stories, Fontana Books, 1974.
First Armada Monster Book, Armada Books, 1975.
Eleventh Fontana Book of Great Ghost Stories, Fontana, 1975.
Terror Tales from Outer Space, Fontana Books, 1975.
Second Armada Monster Book, Armada Books, 1976.
Gaslight Tales of Terror, Fontana Books, 1976.
Twelfth Fontana Book of Great Ghost Stories, Fontana Books, 1976.
Third Armada Monster Book, Armada Books, 1977.
Thirteenth Fontana Book of Great Ghost Stories, Fontana Books, 1977.
Doomed to the Night, Kimber, 1978.
Fourth Armada Monster Book, Armada Books, 1978.
Fourteenth Fontana Book of Great Ghost Stories, Fontana, 1978.
Fifth Armada Monster Book, Armada Books, 1979.
Fifteenth Fontana Book of Great Ghost Stories, Fontana, 1979.
Sixth Armada Monster Book, Armada Books, 1981.
Sixteenth Fontana Book of Great Ghost Stories, Fontana Books, 1982.
Seventeenth Fontana Book of Great Ghost Stories, Fontana Books, 1983.
Eighteenth Fontana Book of Great Ghost Stories, Fontana Books, 1984.
A Quiver of Ghosts, Kimber, 1984.
Tales from the Dark Lands, Kimber, 1984.
Ghosts from the Mist of Time, Kimber, 1985.
Nineteenth Fontana Book of Great Ghost Stories, Fontana Books, 1985.
Twentieth Fontana Book of Great Ghost Stories, Fontana Books, 1986.
Tales from the Shadows, Kimber, 1986.
Tales from the Haunted House, Kimber, 1986.
Dracula's Children, Kimber, 1987.
The House of Dracula, Kimber, 1987.
Tales from the Hidden World, Kimber, 1988.
Shivers and Shudders, Kimber, 1989.

OTHER

Contributor to periodicals, including *Reveille.*

WORK IN PROGRESS: Eighteenth Fontana Book of Great Ghost Stories; "Yesterday's Phantoms," a thirteen-part television series.

MEDIA ADAPTATIONS: "From Beyond the Grave," a film based on four stories by R. Chetwynd-Hayes, was made by Anicus Films for Warner Brothers in 1974; "Something in the Woodwork," a television adaptation of his story "Household," was shown on the program "Night Gallery,"; *The Monster Club* was made into a film in 1980.

SIDELIGHTS: R. Chetwynd-Hayes told *CA* that his works contain "the three following ingredients: Humor, Pathos," and "Chilling situations." He believes that "the current obsession with stomach-turning horror will pass, but the ghost story or horror-send-up is eternal. Having said all that," he wrote, "*The Curse of the Snake God* is very grim, whereas *The Haunted Grange* has been described as charming fantasy."

He added, "If one hundred years from now an editor who is five thousand words short when compiling an anthology should slip in one of my stories because it is the right length and—most important—it is free, then twenty-odd years of writing will not have been in vain."

Many of R. Chetwynd-Hayes' books have been translated into German.

* * *

CHURCHILL, E(lmer) Richard 1937-

PERSONAL: Born May 25, 1937, in Greeley, Colo.; son of Emery Roy and Olive (Whitteker) Churchill; married Linda Ruler (a junior high school teacher), August 18, 1961; children: Eric Richard, Robert Sean. *Education:* Colorado State College (now University of Northern Colorado), A.B., 1959, M.A., 1962.

ADDRESSES: Home—25890 WCR 53, Kersey, Colo. 80644.

CAREER: Public Library employee in Greeley, Colo., for ten years; Park Elementary School, Greeley, fifth grade teacher, 1959-74; Maplewood Middle School, Greeley, librarian, 1974—. Co-owner of Timberline Books, beginning 1971. *Military service:* Colorado Air National Guard, 1961-67.

WRITINGS:

(With E. H. Blair) *Games and Puzzles for Family Leisure,* Abingdon, 1965.
Everybody Came to Leadville, Timberline, 1971.
The McCartys: They Rode with Butch Cassidy, Timberline, 1972.
Colorado Quiz Bag, Timberline, 1973.
Doc Holliday, Bat Masterson, and Wyatt Earp: Their Colorado Careers, Timberline, 1974.
Math Duplicator Masters for Basic Math, J. Weston Walch, 1974.
One Hundred and One Shaggy Dog Stories, Scholastic Book Services, 1975.
(Compiler) *The Six-Million Dollar Cucumber: Riddles and Fun for Children,* F. Watts, 1976.
(With sons, Eric Churchill and Sean Churchill) *Holiday Hullabaloo!: Facts, Jokes, and Riddles,* F. Watts, 1977.
The Timberline Books, eight volumes, Pruett, 1981.
New Puzzles, Scholastic Book Services, 1981.
Bet I Can, Sterling, 1982.
Devilish Bets to Fool Your Friends, Sterling, 1985.
Instant Paper Toys to Pop, Spin, Whirl and Fly, Sterling, 1986.
(Editor) *Sneaky Tricks to Fool Your Friends,* Sterling, 1986.
Quick and Easy Paper Toys, Sterling, 1988.
Instant Paper Airplanes, Sterling, 1988.
Optical Illusion Tricks and Puzzles, Sterling, 1989.
Paper Toys That Fly, Soar, Zoom and Whistle, Sterling, 1989.

WITH WIFE, LINDA R. CHURCHILL

(And with E. H. Blair) *Fun with American History,* Abingdon, 1966.
(And with E. H. Blair and K. K. Blair) *Fun with American Literature,* Abingdon, 1968.
Short Lessons in World History, J. Weston Walch, 1971.
Puzzle It Out, Scholastic Book Services, 1971.
How Our Nation Became Great, J. Weston Walch, 1971.
Community Civics Case Book, J. Weston Walch, 1973.
Enriched Social Studies Teaching through the Use of Games and Activities, Fearon, 1973.
Puzzles and Quizzes, Scholastic Book Services, 1973.
American History Activity Reader, J. Weston Walch, 1974.
Puzzles and Games for Concepts and Inquiry, Allyn & Bacon, 1974.
World History Activity Reader, J. Weston Walch, 1975.
Casebook on Marriage and the Family, J. Weston Walch, 1975.
Family Health Casebook, J. Weston Walch, 1975.
Hidden Word Puzzles, Scholastic Book Services, 1975.
You and the Law, J. Weston Walch, 1976.
Twentieth-Century Europe Activity Reader, J. Weston Walch, 1976.
Middle Ages Activity Reader, J. Weston Walch, 1977.
Hidden Word Puzzles 2, Scholastic Book Services, 1977.
Bionic Banana, F. Watts, 1979.

OTHER

Also author of more than one hundred other books, activity readers, and duplicator packages for J. Weston Walch, including *Understanding Our Economy, Supernatural Reader, Musicians Activity Reader, Artists Activity Reader, World Geography Puzzles, Vocabulary Boosters, State Puzzles, Spanish Puzzles,* and *Latin American Map Studies.*

* * *

COGAN, Mike
See LOTTMAN, Eileen

* * *

COHEN, Jerome Alan 1930-

PERSONAL: Born July 1, 1930, in Elizabeth, N.J.; son of Philip and Beatrice (Kaufman) Cohen; married Joan F. Lebold (a writer and photographer), June 30, 1954; children: Peter Lebold, Seth Aloe, Ethan Randolph. *Education:* Yale University, B.A., 1951, LL.B., 1955; graduate study at University of Lyon, 1951-52.

ADDRESSES: Home—50 East 89th St., New York, N.Y. 10128. *Office*—Paul, Weiss, Rifkind, Wharton & Garrison, 2008 Two Exchange Square, 8 Connaught Place, Central, Hong Kong.

CAREER: Admitted to Connecticut Bar, 1955, District of Columbia Bar, 1957, and New York Bar, 1982; law secretary for U.S. Supreme Court, under Chief Justice Earl Warren, 1955-56, and Justice Felix Frankfurter, 1956-57; Covington & Burling (law firm), Washington, D.C., associate, 1957-58; U.S. Department of Justice, Washington, D.C., assistant U.S. attorney, 1958-59; University of California, Berkeley, associate professor, 1959-61, professor of law, 1961-64; Harvard University, Law School, Cambridge, Mass., professor, 1964-80, Jeremiah Smith, Jr., Professor of Law, 1980-81, lecturer, beginning 1981, former director of East Asian legal studies and associate dean; Paul, Weiss, Rifkind, Wharton & Garrison, New York, N.Y., Washington, D.C., Paris, France, Tokyo, Japan, and Hong Kong, partner, 1981—. Consultant to U.S. Senate Committee on Foreign Relations, 1959; visiting professor at Doshisha University, Kyoto, 1971-72. Chairman of subcommittee on Chinese law of Joint Committee on Contemporary China, American Council of Learned Societies—Social Science Research Council, 1965-71.

MEMBER: Asia Society (New York; trustee, 1983—), American Society of International Law (chairman of China and world order study group, 1967-72), Association for Asian Studies, Phi Beta Kappa, Order of the Coif.

AWARDS, HONORS: Fulbright scholar, 1951-52; Rockefeller Foundation grant, 1960-64; Guggenheim fellow, 1971-72; award from American Society of International Law, 1975, for best documentary study.

WRITINGS:

The Criminal Process in the People's Republic of China, 1949-1963: An Introduction, Harvard University Press, 1968.
(Editor with others) *Contemporary Chinese Law: Research Problems and Perspectives,* Harvard University Press, 1970.
(Editor) George Ginsburgs and others, *The Dynamics of China's Foreign Relations,* East Asian Research Center, Harvard University, 1970.
(With Robert F. Dernberger and John R. Garson) *China Trade Prospects and U.S. Policy,* Praeger for National Committee on United States-China Relations, 1971.
(Contributor) John Wilson Lewis, editor, *The City in Communist China,* Stanford University Press, 1971.
(With others) *Taiwan and American Policy: The Dilemma in U.S.-China Relations,* Praeger, 1971.
China and Intervention: Theory and Practice, Harvard Law School, 1973.
Law and Cooperation in American-Northeast Asian Relations, Harvard Law School, 1973.
(Editor) *China's Practice of International Law: Some Case Studies,* Harvard University Press, 1973.
(With Hungdah Chiu) *People's China and International Law: A Documentary Study,* two volumes, Princeton University Press, 1974.
(With wife, Joan Lebold Cohen) *China Today and Her Ancient Treasures* (Book-of-the-Month Club alternate selection), Abrams, 1974, 3rd edition, 1986.
(Editor with R. Randle Edwards and Fu-mei Chang Chen) *Essays on China's Legal Tradition,* Princeton University Press, 1980.
(Translator from the Chinese with others) *The Criminal Law and the Criminal Procedure Law of China,* China Books, 1984.
Contract Laws of the People's Republic of China, Longman, 1988.

Author or co-author of a number of papers published in legal journals and reprinted separately as monographs in Harvard University Law School's "Studies in Chinese Law" series; also author of cassette recording, "China's Legal System." Contributor to popular magazines and to newspapers in the United States and Japan. Member of editorial board, *American Journal of International Law,* 1972—.

WORK IN PROGRESS: A book, *Legal Problems of Doing Business with China.*

*   *   *

COHEN, Joan Lebold 1932-

PERSONAL: Born August 19, 1932, in Highland Park, Ill.; daughter of Samuel N. Lebold (a businessman) and Patricia

(Aloe) Lebold Tucker; married Jerome Alan Cohen (a lawyer and professor), June 30, 1954; children: Peter Lebold, Seth Aloe, Ethan Randolph. *Education:* Smith College, B.A., 1954. *Politics:* Democrat.

ADDRESSES: Home and office—50 East 89th St., New York, N.Y. 10128; and 22A Century Tower, One Tregunter Path, Hong Kong. *Agent*—Photo Researchers, 60 East 56th St., New York, N.Y. 10022.

CAREER: Corcoran Gallery of Art, Washington, D.C., registrar, 1955-56; professional and volunteer worker for Democratic Party in Virginia, California, and District of Columbia, 1956-60; volunteer teacher of English at youth clubs in Hong Kong, 1963-64; Museum of Fine Arts, Boston, Mass., lecturer and member of department of public education staff, 1965-73, Tufts Lecturer in art history at School of the Museum of Fine Arts, 1968—. Research associate at John King Fairbank Center for East Asian Research, Harvard University, 1981—; associate of modern China seminar, Columbia University, 1982—; guest curator at Smith College Museum of Art, 1982, and at Sarah Lawrence College Art Gallery, 1987. Lecturer on American and Asian art and film at various universities and museums in the United States and Asia. Has exhibited photographs at numerous museums and galleries.

WRITINGS:

Buddha (juvenile), Seymour Lawrence, 1969.
(With husband, Jerome Alan Cohen) *China Today and Her Ancient Treasures* (Book-of-the-Month Club alternate selection), Abrams, 1974, 3rd edition, 1986.
Angkor: The Monuments of the God-Kings, Abrams, 1975.
Painting the Chinese Dream (exhibition catalogue), Smith College Museum of Art, 1982.
(With Ralph Croizier and Roger Connant) *"Chinese Art after Mao"* (slides/video), University of Pittsburgh Press, 1983.
The New Chinese Painting, 1949-1986, Abrams, 1987.
Artists from China: New Expressions (exhibition catalogue), Sarah Lawrence Art Gallery, 1987.
The Yunnan School, a Renaissance in Chinese Painting, Fingerhut, 1988.

Author of television scripts, including "An American Romance: 19th Century Landscape," 1965, "The Journey of the Buddha," 1965, "A Survey of American Art" (six shows), "Images" (series), and three segments for "Highlights of Japanese Art." Also author of film strips, "Ancient Art" and "Art Today in the People's Republic of China," Mass Communications, Inc., 1977. Contributor of articles, photographs, and reviews to museum and other publications, including *Art News, Asian Wall Street Journal, Book Digest, Harvard Magazine, Time, Newsweek, New York Times,* and *Saturday Review.*

SIDELIGHTS: Joan Lebold Cohen told *CA:* "Writing about and photographing contemporary Chinese film, art, and culture have become the primary focus of my work in the last ten years. I continue to teach part-time at the School of the Museum of Fine Arts in Boston about Asian film, art, and culture. I have been lecturing in the U.S. and abroad, as well. I spend about one half of each year in Asia."

BIOGRAPHICAL/CRITICAL SOURCES:

PERIODICALS

Los Angeles Times Book Review, August 21, 1988.

COLE, Annette
  See STEINER, Barbara A(nnette)

*   *   *

COLLEY, Ann C(heetham) 1940-

PERSONAL: Born January 9, 1940, in Bury, England; came to the United States in 1953, naturalized citizen, 1962; daughter of Henry Harris (a Unitarian minister) and Constance Meta (Edwards) Cheetham; married John Scott Colley, 1964 (divorced, c.1980); children: Gwen Hilary. *Education:* College of William and Mary, A.B., 1962; University of Virginia, M.A., 1964; University of Chicago, Ph.D. (with honors), 1983. *Religion:* Unitarian-Universalist.

ADDRESSES: Home—332 Ashland Ave., Buffalo, N.Y. 14222. *Office*—Department of English, State University College at Buffalo, 1300 Elmwood Ave., Buffalo, N.Y. 14222.

CAREER: University of Chicago, Chicago, Ill., curator of manuscripts at library, 1965-67; Fisk University, Nashville, Tenn., assistant professor of English, 1969-82; Daemen College, Amherst, N.Y., associate professor of English, 1982-85; State University College at Buffalo, Buffalo, N.Y., associate professor of English, 1985—.

MEMBER: Modern Language Association of America, Tennyson Society, Northeastern Victorian Studies Association.

WRITINGS:

(With Judy K. Moore) *Starting with Poetry,* Harcourt, 1973.
Tennyson and Madness, University of Georgia Press, 1983.
The Search for Synthesis in Literature and Art: The Paradox of Space, University of Georgia Press, 1990.

Contributor to poetry and Victorian studies journals. Associate editor of *Journal of Pre-Raphaelite Studies,* 1983-86.

WORK IN PROGRESS: A study of the experience of nostalgia in the Victorian Period.

SIDELIGHTS: Ann C. Colley told *CA:* "*Tennyson and Madness* is about Alfred Lord Tennyson's painful experiences with madness and morbidity and the ways in which this nineteenth-century poet transposed these experiences and his knowledge of insanity into his poetry. The book opens with a survey of nineteenth-century attitudes towards madness and a discussion of the uses of madness in literature. The book then offers a biographical study of madness in the Tennyson family and goes on to explore Tennyson's fears concerning his own instability. Because Tennyson faced the threat of madness, it was inevitable that he would use these experiences to approach his poetry. Much of his poetry's imagery, subject matter, preoccupations, and style are affected by his fear of madness. A majority of the poems take their shape from a creative force that is fighting to remain sane and to moderate its 'wilder' impulses. To begin to understand how Tennyson's experiences helped form his poetic posture, it is necessary to think of Tennyson as an observer of madness and not, as some might claim, its victim. He chose to stand outside himself and to analyze experience. He adopted an almost clinical view of his subject matter.

"*The Search for Synthesis in Literature and Art: The Paradox of Space* dwells upon various artists' and writers' search for synthesis, whether that be a wish to fuse images and words or a desire to merge in friendship or love. The range of artistic and literary figures in this study is wider than usual: Edward Lear, Alfred Lord Tennyson, Claude Monet, Gustave Flaubert, Gerard Manley Hopkins, Ovid, Dante, and Paul Klee."

AVOCATIONAL INTERESTS: Music, travel, painting.

*   *   *

COLLINGS, Michael R(obert) 1947-

PERSONAL: Born October 29, 1947, in Rupert, Idaho; son of Ralph Willard (a land appraiser) and Thella (Hurd) Collings; married Judith Lynn Reeve (a career counselor and skin care consultant), December 21, 1973; children: Michael-Brent, Erika Marie, Ethan Hunt, Kendra Elayne. *Education:* Attended Chapman College, 1965; Bakersfield College, A.A., 1967; Whittier College, B.A., 1969; University of California, Riverside, M.A., 1973, Ph.D., 1977.

ADDRESSES: Home—1089 Sheffield Pl., Thousand Oaks, Calif. 91360. *Office*—Humanities Division, Pepperdine University, Malibu, Calif. 90265.

CAREER: University of California, Riverside, associate in English, 1973-78; University of California, Los Angeles, instructor in English, 1978-79; Pepperdine University, Malibu, Calif., assistant professor, 1979-81, associate professor of English, 1981—. Instructor, San Bernardino Community College, 1976-78; consultant to Rockefeller Foundation.

MEMBER: Science Fiction Research Association, Science Fiction Poetry Association.

WRITINGS:

A Season of Calm Weather (poetry), Hawkes, 1974.
(With wife, Judith Collings) *Whole Wheat Harvest* (cookbook), Hawkes, 1980.
A Reader's Guide to Piers Anthony (criticism), edited by Roger C. Schlobin, Starmont House, 1983.
The Many Facets of Stephen King (criticism), Starmont House, 1985.
(With David A. Engebretson) *The Shorter Works of Stephen King* (criticism), Starmont House, 1985.
Stephen King as Richard Bachman (criticism), Starmont House, 1985.
Naked to the Sun: Dark Visions of Apocalypse (poetry), Starmont House, 1985.
The Annotated Guide to Stephen King: A Primary and Secondary Bibliography of the Works of America's Premier Horror Writer (bibliography), Starmont House, 1986.
(Editor) *Reflections on the Fantastic: Selected Essays from the First International Conference on the Fantastic in Literature and Film,* Greenwood Press, 1986.
Brian W. Aldiss: A Reader's Guide (criticism), Starmont House, 1986.
The Films of Stephen King (criticism), Starmont House, 1987.
Card Catalogue: The Science Fiction and Fantasy of Orson Scott Card (bibliography), Hypatia, 1987.
The Stephen King Phenomenon (criticism), Starmont House, 1987.

CONTRIBUTOR

Luk de Vos, editor, *Just the Other Day: Science Fiction and the Construction of Reality,* Restant, 1984.
Carl B. Yoke and Donald M. Hassler, editors, *Death and the Serpent,* Greenwood Press, 1984.
Robert Collins and Howard Pearce, editors, *The Scope of the Fantastic—Theory, Technique, Major Authors,* Greenwood Press, 1985.

George Slusser and Eric S. Rabkin, editors, *Hard Science Fiction,* Southern Illinois University Press, 1985.

Darrell Schweitzer, editor, *Discovering Stephen King,* Starmont House, 1985.

William Coyle, editor, *Aspects of Fantasy,* Greenwood Press, 1986.

Jan Hokenson and Pearce, editors, *Forms of the Fantastic,* Greenwood Press, 1986.

Yoke, editor, *Phoenix from the Ashes: The Literature of the Remade World,* Greenwood Press, 1987.

Slusser and Rabkin, editors, *Intersections: Fantasy and Science Fiction,* Southern Illinois University Press, 1987.

Donald Palumbo, editor, *Spectrum of the Fantastic,* Greenwood Press, 1988.

Bill Munster, editor, *Sudden Fear: The Horror and Dark Suspense Fiction of Dean R. Koontz,* Starmont House, 1988.

Slusser and Rabkin, editors, *Mindscapes,* Southern Illinois University Press, 1989.

OTHER

Also author of the unpublished novels *The House Beyond the Hill, Images, Singer of Lies,* and *Wordsmith;* author of 12 poetry chapbooks written in 1988, including *Fields of Starflowers and Other Poems: Science Fiction, Fantasy, and Horror, In Memoriam: A Father . . . and a Friend, Apprenticeship in Love, and Other Christmas Meditations, The Joys of Quiet Wanderings: Selected Poems, 1984-1988,* and *A Nephite Christmas.* Contributor to anthologies, including *LDSF: Science Fiction by and for Mormons,* edited by Scott Smith and Vickie Smith, Millennium House, 1982; *Aliens and Lovers,* edited by Millea Kenin, Unique Graphics, 1983; *LDSF-2: Latter-Day Saint Science Fiction,* edited by Benjamin Urutia, Parable, 1985; and *LDSF-3,* edited by Urutia, Parable, 1987. Contributor to numerous periodicals, including *California State Poetry Quarterly, Cuyahoga Review, Extrapolation, Science Fiction and Fantasy Book Review, West Coast Review of Books,* and *International Association for the Fantastic in the Arts Newsletter.* Editor, *The Lamp Post of the Southern California C. S. Lewis Society,* 1981-83; poetry editor, *Dialogue: A Journal of Mormon Thought,* 1984.

WORK IN PROGRESS: The Image of God: Theme, Character, and Landscape in the Fiction of Orson Scott Card, criticism, for Greenwood Press; *Beyond Deep Heaven: Genre, Structure and Christian Meaning in C. S. Lewis's Ransom Novels,* criticism; *The Works of Orson Scott Card: An Annotated Bibliography and Guide,* for Borgo; *The Works of David Gerrold: An Annotated Bibliography and Guide,* for Borgo; two novels, *Fast Foods* and *The Staling Stones;* (with Terry Benedict) "Wrathwind," a screenplay.

SIDELIGHTS: Michael R. Collings once told *CA:* "My critical and scholarly studies nearly all relate to uses of language in creating science fiction and fantasy. I am intrigued by the methods writers use to suggest alternate realities, particularly since their basic tools—words—are conventionally seen as reflections of *this* reality. For the past few years, I have been exploring the possibilities of language, from matters as specific as typographic variations and word choice to areas as generalized as communication theories, and I have been trying to identify particular techniques that seem especially effective. . . .

"In addition, and perhaps most important, I am working on a blending of speculative, futuristic fictions and poetry and on my own background in Mormonism. One of the difficulties I have encountered is that both science fiction and Mormonism deal heavily with the future (or possibilities for the future) and at the same time in effect invalidate each other—science fiction and re-

ligion both claim to have answers to the same questions. In what ways can those answers be integrated into a single vision?"

Collings more recently added: "My work with Stephen King, Dean R. Koontz, Brian W. Aldiss, and Orson Scott Card stems from a conviction that contemporary science fiction, fantasy, and horror are among the most vital and important genres today—and these writers are doing more to define what it is to be part of late twentieth-century technological culture than perhaps any others. At the same time, I attempt to bridge the gap between academicians (for most of whom such genres are at best frivolous, at worst anathema) and fans (who in turn see no redeeming social value in literary criticism). Through my critical studies, which are admittedly and designedly less scholarly than most, I try to suggest ways in which these literary forms help give meaning to readers, and at the same time how readers might gain more from the literature by applying some of the standards of traditional criticism."

*　　*　　*

COLOMBO, Furio　1931-

PERSONAL: Born January 1, 1931, in Chatillon, Italy; immigrated to the United States, 1977; son of Giuseppe (a publishing executive) and Ottavia (Scala) Colombo; married Alice Oxman, 1969; children: Daria. *Education:* University of Torino, D.Law, 1954.

ADDRESSES: Home—New York, N.Y. *Office*—375 Park Ave., New York, N.Y. 10022.

CAREER: Writer for Italian television, 1955-57; business executive with Olivetti (a business machine manufacturer) in the United States, c. 1957; worked in cultural relations in Italy and the United States, 1957-64; free-lance writer, 1961-66; filmmaker and director of cultural programs for Italian television, 1966-72; special correspondent for *La Stampa,* 1972, became U.S. correspondent, currently columnist; University of Bologna, Bologna, Italy, associated with philosophy department and Institute of Communication, 1970-77; Barnard College, New York City, professor of Italian studies, 1977; Columbia University, New York City, lecturer in political science, 1980; writer. Visiting professor at several universities, including Yale University and New York University. Member of Center for American Studies, Rome, Italy, and Center for Italian Studies at Columbia University. Member of executive committee of International Scholarly Exchange Center at Columbia University.

MEMBER: Century Association, Instituto Affari Internazionali.

AWARDS, HONORS: Premio Tevere for literature, 1987, for *Cosa Faro' da Grande;* Premio Amalfi for television, 1988; Premio Capri for journalism, 1988.

WRITINGS:

IN ENGLISH

The Chinese, Viking, 1972.
In Italy: Postwar Political Life, Richard Karz, 1981.
Il Dio d'America, Mondadori, 1983, translation by Kristin Jarrat published as *God in America: Religion and Politics in the United States,* Columbia University Press, 1984.

IN ITALIAN

Nuovo teatro americano (title means "New American Theatre"), Bompiani, 1963.
L'America di Kennedy (title means "Kennedy's America"), Feltrinelli, 1964.

Le donne matte (novel; title means "The Crazy Women"), Feltrinelli, 1965.

Le condizioni del conflitto (title means "The Rule of the Conflict"), Bompiani, 1967.

Invece della violenza (title means "On Violence"), Bompiani, 1969.

Arte e violenza (title means "Art and Violence"), Bompiani, 1970.

(With Umberto Eco) *Il nuovo medioevo* (title means "The New Middle Ages"), Bompiani, 1972.

Da Kennedy a Watergate (title means "From Kennedy to Watergate"), Sei, 1974.

I prossimi americani (title means "The Next American Generation"), Garzanti, 1975.

Agenti segreti (stories; title means "Secret Agents"), Garzanti, 1976.

Passaggio a Occidente (title means "Passage to the West"), Rizzoli, 1980.

Cosa Faro' da Grande (title means "What Will I Do When I Grow Up?"), Mondadori, 1987.

Mille Americhe (title means "A Thousand Americas"), La Stampa, 1988.

Occhio Testimone (text for photographic essay; title means "Eyewitness"), Bompiani, 1988.

Intervista sulla Televisione (title means "Interview on Television"), Pironti, 1988.

WORK IN PROGRESS: "Giovanni Verga," an essay to be included in the *European Writers* collection for Scribner; a collection of essays whose title means "The Unexpected Future," for Mondadori.

SIDELIGHTS: Furio Colombo once told *CA:* "I am considered an expert on American affairs in Italy and quoted as such quite frequently in the Italian, French, and German press. My interests, although frequently pointed toward the political process, were never strictly political. Rather, they organized around the effort to offer a comprehensive portrait of society. That is why social behavior so frequently appears in my published work on the theatre, popular music, books, movies, and trends.

"Communication, in its process, instruments, organization, and social impact, is another focal point. There are parallel aspects in my professional/public life and one may say each aspect verifies and supports the other. I have written extensively about American culture and I have been living and working extensively in the United States, sometimes associating with cultural institutions and sometimes having a nine-to-five job—that is, living the American experience and writing about it and working on a specific field and then opening up to a larger perspective.

"I want to mention, as a further example, my television connection. For almost ten years I have been a documentary filmmaker and concurrently I have been teaching communications and writing about it. I moved to the United States in 1977 to broaden the activity around the basic interest on which I have been writing, teaching, and filming: the American life in all its implications, seen with the direct approach of the journalist and commented upon using documents and materials, books, theatre, authors, and the visual arts. At the same time, through my academic commitment and the Center for Italian Studies, my effort is to present a credible and realistic image of the contemporary Italian culture using the same approach employed to present the American reality to my country."

BIOGRAPHICAL/CRITICAL SOURCES:

PERIODICALS

Art World, February, 1984.
Il Corriere della sera, October 15, 1976, December 12, 1976.
La Republica, June 7, 1982, February 16, 1983.
L'Espresso, May 20, 1973.
New York Times, October 15, 1983.

* * *

CONDE, Maryse
See BOUCOLON, Maryse

* * *

CONNELLY, Marc(us Cook) 1890-1980

PERSONAL: Born December 13, 1890, in McKeesport, Pa., died December 21, 1980, in New York, N.Y.; son of Patrick Joseph (an actor and hotel owner) and Mabel Louise (an actress; maiden name, Cook) Connelly; married Madeline Hurlock, 1930 (divorced, 1935). *Education:* Attended Trinity Hall, Washington, Pa., 1902-07.

ADDRESSES: Home—25 Central Park West, New York, N.Y. 10023.

CAREER: Playwright, actor, director and producer. *Pittsburgh Press* and *Gazette Times,* Pittsburgh, Pa., reporter, 1908-16; *New York Morning Telegraph,* New York, N.Y., reporter, 1916-21; Yale University, New Haven, Conn., professor of playwriting, 1946-50. Lecturer and teacher at several colleges and universities throughout the United States. Actor in plays, including "Our Town," New York City Center, 1944, in films "The Spirit of St. Louis," 1957, and "Tall Story," 1959, and in the television series "The Defenders," 1963. Director of Broadway plays, including many of his own, beginning with "The Wisdom Tooth," 1926; co-director of film version of his play *The Green Pastures: A Fable Suggested by Roark Bradford's Southern Sketches "Ol' Man Adam an' His Chillun,"* 1936.

MEMBER: American Federation of TV & Radio Artists, Authors League of America (past president), National Institute of Arts and Letters (president, 1953-56), Actors Equity Association, Dramatists Guild (founding member), Screen Actors Guild, Players Club (New York), Dutch Treat Club (New York), Savage Club (London).

AWARDS, HONORS: O. Henry Short Story Prize, 1930, for "Coroner's Inquest"; Pulitzer Prize for Drama, 1930, for *The Green Pastures; Little David: An Unproduced Scene from "The Green Pastures"* appeared in *The Best One-Act Plays of 1937;* honorary degree from Bowdoin College, 1952, and Baldwin-Wallace College, 1962; received a certificate of appreciation at New York's City Hall on the occasion of his 90th birthday, 1980.

WRITINGS:

A Souvenir from Qam (novel), Holt, 1965.
Voices Off-Stage: A Book of Memories, Holt, 1968.

PLAYS

"2.50" (one-act), first produced in Pittsburgh, 1914.
(Author of lyrics) "The Amber Express," produced in New York at Globe Theatre, September 19, 1916.
"Erminie" (a revision of the operetta by Henry Paulton), first produced in New York at Park Theatre, January 3, 1921.

(With George S. Kaufman) *Dulcy* (three-act; first produced in New York at Frazee Theatre, August 13, 1921), Putnam, 1921.

(With Kaufman) *To the Ladies!* (three-act; first produced in New York at Liberty Theatre, February 20, 1922), Samuel French, 1923.

(With Kaufman) "The '49ers" (a revue), first produced in New York at Punch and Judy Theatre, November 7, 1922.

(With Kaufman) *Merton of the Movies* (four-act; first produced on Broadway at Cort Theatre, November 13, 1922), Samuel French, 1925.

(With Kaufman) "Helen of Troy, New York" (musical comedy), first produced in New York at Selwyn Theatre, June 19, 1923.

(With Kaufman) "The Deep Tangled Wildwood" (comedy), first produced in New York at Frazee Theatre, November 5, 1923.

(With Kaufman) *Beggar on Horseback* (comedy; first produced on Broadway at Broadhurst Theatre, February 12, 1924), Liveright.

(With Kaufman) "Be Yourself" (musical comedy), first produced in New York at Harris Theatre, September 3, 1924.

The Wisdom Tooth: A Fantastic Comedy (three-act; first produced on Broadway at Little Theatre, February 15, 1926), Samuel French, 1927.

(With Herman J. Mankiewicz) "The Wild Man of Borneo" (comedy), first produced in New York at Bijou Theatre, September 13, 1927.

"How's the King?" (musical comedy), first produced in New York, 1927.

The Green Pastures: A Fable Suggested by Roark Bradford's Southern Sketches "Ol' Man Adam an' His Chillun" (first produced in New York at Mansfield Theatre, February 26, 1930), Farrar & Rinehart, 1929, reprinted, Holt, 1959.

"The Survey" (a skit), published in *New Yorker*, 1934.

(With Frank B. Elser) "The Farmer Takes a Wife" (comedy; an adaptation of the novel *Rome Haul* by Walter Edmonds), first produced on Broadway at Forty-sixth Street Theatre, October 30, 1934, abridged edition contained in *Best Plays of 1934-35*, edited by Burns Mantle, Dodd, 1935.

Little David: An Unproduced Scene from "The Green Pastures" (one-act), Dramatists Play Service, 1937.

(With Arnold Sundgaard) "Everywhere I Roam," first produced in New York at National Theatre, December 29, 1938.

The Traveler (one-act), Dramatists Play Service, 1939.

"The Flowers of Virtue" (comedy), first produced on Broadway at Royale Theatre, February 5, 1942.

"Story for Strangers" (comedy), first produced on Broadway at Royale Theatre, September 21, 1948.

"Hunter's Moon," first produced in London at the Winter Garden Theatre, February 26, 1958.

"The Portable Yenberry," produced at Purdue University Workshop, May 24, 1961.

SCREENPLAYS

"Whispers," 1920.

"Exit Smiling," Metro-Goldwyn-Mayer, 1926.

"The Bridegroom," "The Suitor," and "The Uncle" (film shorts), 1929.

"The Unemployed Ghost" (film short), 1931.

"The Cradle Song," Paramount, 1933.

"The Little Duchess" (film short), 1934.

(With others) "Captains Courageous," Metro-Goldwyn-Mayer, 1934.

"I Married a Witch," Paramount, 1936.

"Crowded Paradise," Tudor, 1956.

OTHER

Author of radio plays "The Mole on Lincoln's Cheek," 1941; author of lyrics for "The Lady of Luzon," 1914, and "Follow the Girl," 1915. With others, author of *Webster's Poker Book,* 1925. Contributor to magazines, including *New Yorker, Collier's, Life, Saturday Review,* and *Reader's Digest.*

SIDELIGHTS: In a *Dictionary of Literary Biography* article, Marc Connelly was described as "a central but not pivotal figure of twentieth-century American theatre: a man of enormous popularity but little lasting influence." As the article writer Ward W. Briggs, Jr., goes on to say, Connelly was a man "of considerable instinctive talent but scant genius, of grand ideas but slight thought." Because he wrote and directed plays primarily in the 1920s and 1930s, and because most of those works were too idiosyncratic of their time to become classics, Connelly was perhaps best known for just one stage work: a Pulitzer Prize-winning musical with the lengthy title of *The Green Pastures: A Fable Suggested by Roark Bradford's Southern Sketches "Ol' Man Adam an' His Chillun."* In this piece Connelly presented a rarity of its time, a mainstream entertainment concerning a black interpretation of the Gospels, and starring an all-black cast.

The Green Pastures is "structured in two parts," according to Briggs. "The theme throughout is that man eternally sins and is either punished or renounced by God. The play turns on the recognition by the protagonist, De Lawd, that man not only sins but also suffers and is ennobled by that suffering, for that is how he learns." In the study *Marc Connelly* author Peter T. Nolan remarked that what distinguishes the play "is its scope. . . . Even by current standards of criticism, [*The Green Pastures*] holds a position as one of the important plays in American drama; but it is the only one of Connelly's plays that does."

As a dramatist Connelly worked steadily and gained respect from his peers. But in his offstage life, the writer was as well known for his involvement in the Algonquin Round Table, a now-legendary daily gathering of great New York-based wits and thinkers, founded in the 1920s. Among his Round Table cronies, Connelly counted as friends editor Harold Ross, critic Alexander Woollcott, satirist Dorothy Parker, and playwright George S. Kaufman. It was with Kaufman that Connelly enhanced his own career, collaborating with the better-known playwright on a number of comedies and musicals that characterized the carefree attitudes of pre-Depression America.

On the occasion of Connelly's death at age 90, just weeks after receiving a certificate of appreciation from New York City, playwright/director Garson Kanin delivered a eulogy reprinted in the *Dictionary of Literary Biography Yearbook: 1980.* "Marc simply *loved* playwriting and plays—particularly his own. Everything he wrote astonished and surprised him. He was delighted at what ran down his sleeve every day and he wanted to share that joy." Kanin concluded that Connelly, "playwright, journalist, humorist, memoirist, director, actor, screenwriter, wit, gentleman, and all-around jolly good fellow, . . . will never be replaced because he is irreplaceable."

MEDIA ADAPTATIONS: A film adaptation of Connelly's play *The Green Pastures* was produced by Warner Bros. in 1936.

BIOGRAPHICAL/CRITICAL SOURCES:

BOOKS

Connelly, Marc, *Voices Off-Stage: A Book of Memoirs,* Holt, 1968.

Contemporary Literary Criticism, Volume 7, Gale, 1977.
Dictionary of Literary Biography, Gale, Volume 7: *Twentieth-Century American Dramatists,* 1981.
Dictionary of Literary Biography Yearbook: 1980, Gale, 1981.
Nolan, Peter T., *Marc Connelly,* Twayne, 1969.

PERIODICALS

American Heritage, February, 1970.
Nation, November 14, 1934.
New York Times, October 3, 1968.
Saturday Review, April 7, 1951.

OBITUARIES:

PERIODICALS

Newsweek, January 5, 1981.
New York Times, December 22, 1980.
Time, January 12, 1981.
Times (London), December 23, 1980.
Washington Post, December 23, 1980.*

* * *

CONROY, Al
See ALBERT, Marvin H(ubert)

* * *

CONROY, Albert
See ALBERT, Marvin H(ubert)

* * *

COOKSON, William 1939-

PERSONAL: Born May 8, 1939, in London, England; son of George H. F. (an inspector of schools and editor) and Rachel (Pelham Burn) Cookson; married Vera Lungu (a poet), December 19, 1973 (divorced, 1976); married Margaret Craddock, July 20, 1985; children: (second marriage) Emma Alice. *Education:* New College, Oxford, B.A., 1962. *Politics:* Green Party.

ADDRESSES: *Office*—Agenda Editions, 5 Cranbourne Ct., Albert Bridge Rd., London SW11 4PE, England.

CAREER: *Agenda* (poetry magazine), London, England, editor and founder, 1959—.

WRITINGS:

(Editor) Ezra Pound, *Selected Prose, 1909-1965,* New Directions, 1973.
Dream Traces: A Sequence, Hippopotamus, 1975.
A Guide to the Cantos of Ezra Pound, Persea Books, 1985.
Spell: A Sequence, Agenda Editions, 1986.
Vestiges (poems), Big Little Poem Books, 1987.

* * *

COOPER, Jilly 1937-

PERSONAL: Born February 21, 1937, in Hornchurch, England; daughter of W. B. (an engineer and brigadier) and Elaine Mary (Whincup) Sallitt; married Leo Cooper (a publisher), October 7, 1961; children: Matthew Felix, Emily Maud Lavinia. *Education:* Attended a private girls' school in Salisbury, England. *Religion:* Church of England.

ADDRESSES: *Office*—Mail on Sunday, Carmelite House, Carmelite St., London EC4Y 0JA, England. *Agent*—Desmond Elliott, 15-17 King St., St. James's, London SW1Y 6QU, England.

CAREER: *Middlesex Independent,* Brentford, England, reporter, 1957-59; worked at various jobs in advertising and publishing, 1958-69; *Sunday Times,* London, England, author of column, 1969-82; *Mail on Sunday,* London, writer, 1982—.

WRITINGS:

NEWSPAPER COLUMN COLLECTIONS

Jolly Super, Methuen, 1971.
Jolly Super Too, Methuen, 1973.
Jolly Superlative, Methuen, 1976.
Super Jilly, Methuen, 1978.
Supercooper, Methuen, 1980.
Jolly Marsupial, Methuen, 1982.
Turn Right at the Spotted Dog, Methuen, 1987.

NONFICTION

How to Stay Married, illustrations by Timothy Jacques, Methuen, 1969, Taplinger, 1970.
How to Survive from Nine to Five, illustrations by Jacques, Methuen, 1970, new edition published as *Work and Wedlock,* Magnum, 1978.
Men and Super Men (also see below), illustrations by Jacques, Methuen, 1972.
Women and Super Women (also see below), illustrations by Jacques, Methuen, 1974.
Super Men and Super Women (includes new editions of *Men and Super Men* and *Women and Super Women*), Methuen, 1976.
The British in Love: An Amorously Autobiographical Anthology, Arlington, 1979.
Class: A View from Middle England, illustrations by Jacques, Methuen, 1979, Knopf, 1981.
(Editor with Tom Hartman) *Violets and Vinegar: An Anthology of Women's Writings and Sayings,* Allen & Unwin, 1980, Stein & Day, 1981.
(Editor) *Love and Other Heartaches,* Arlington, 1981, new edition published as *Lisa & Co.,* Corgi, 1982.
Intelligent and Loyal: A Celebration of the Mongrel, Methuen, 1981.
(With Imperial War Museum) *Animals in War,* Heinemann, 1983.
The Common Years, illustrations by Paul Cox, Methuen, 1984.
(With husband, Leo Cooper) *On Rugby,* Bell & Hyman, 1984.
(With L. Cooper) *On Cricket,* Bell & Hyman, 1985.
Hotfoot to Zabriskie Point, photographs by Patrick Lichfield, Constable, 1985.
(With L. Cooper) *Horse Mania!,* Bell & Hyman, 1986.
How to Survive Christmas, illustrations by Jacques, Methuen, 1986.

OTHER

Emily (novel), Arlington, 1975.
Bella (novel), Arlington, 1976.
Harriet (novel), Arlington, 1976.
Octavia (novel), Arlington, 1977.
Imogen (novel), Arlington, 1978.
Prudence (novel), Arlington, 1978.
Little Mabel (juvenile), Granada, 1980.
Little Mabel's Great Escape (juvenile), illustrations by Jacques, Granada, 1981.
Little Mabel Wins (juvenile), Granada, 1982.
Little Mabel Saves the Day (juvenile), Granada, 1985.
Riders (novel), Arlington, 1985, Ballantine, 1986.
Rivals (novel), Bantam Press, 1988, published as *Players,* Ballantine, 1989.

WORK IN PROGRESS: A sequel to *Class,* "but seen from a country rather than an urban angle"; a novel about polo, as yet untitled.

SIDELIGHTS: In *Class: A View from Middle England,* Jilly Cooper "assures us," social reforms to the contrary, "that the class system continues to thrive in England," as Ann Geneva describes in *Saturday Review.* Because the author "is not satisfied with the simple you-either-are-or-you-aren't [upper class]" method of classification, she "breaks everybody down—and her readers, not at all inadvertently, up," states *Washington Post Book World* contributor Carolyn Banks. A columnist noted for her amusing and satirical work, Cooper uses a number of generic upper, middle, and lower class representatives (such as "Harry Stow-Crat" and "Mr. and Mrs. Nouveau-Richards") to lampoon class differences in Britain. An *Economist* reviewer comments that *Class* is a "highly entertaining, acerbic and wickedly observant book," explaining that "Cooper observes her friends across the social divide with hawk-like eye . . . and the book is packed with quotable, frequently unladylike but shrewd comments." While Robin Coleridge faults the author for failing to take her observations outside the limits of class boundaries, the critic admits in the *Times Literary Supplement* that "nevertheless she hits some nails shrewdly, [and] is excellent fun." "*Class* is obviously fun stuff," concludes Banks. "I can't think of any book I've read recently which I wanted to read *to* people: And it took some doing."

Cooper told *CA:* "My aim as a writer is to cheer people up and occasionally, amid the laughs, to make a serious point. I think I started off a very flip, brittle writer because I was frightened of sentimentality. But gradually, I think, I'm putting more heart into my writing."

AVOCATIONAL INTERESTS: Wildflowers, music, mongrels, reading, astronomy.

BIOGRAPHICAL/CRITICAL SOURCES:

PERIODICALS

Economist, November 10, 1979.
Saturday Review, June, 1981.
Times (London), March 7, 1981.
Times Literary Supplement, January 11, 1980.
Washington Post Book World, July 12, 1981, July 6, 1986.

*   *   *

COOPER, John C(harles) 1933-

PERSONAL: Born April 3, 1933, in Charleston, S.C.; son of Chauncey Miller (in U.S. Navy) and Margarete Anna (Gerard) Cooper; married Clelia Ann Johnston, June 6, 1954 (divorced, 1986); married Deborah Karen Bjornson, December 30, 1986 (divorced, 1988); married Victoria Ann Davis, 1988; children: (first marriage) Martin Christopher, Catherine Marie, Cynthia Ann, Paul Conrad; (second marriage) John Kenneth Bruce; stepchildren: Sean Christopher. *Education:* University of South Carolina, B.A. (cum laude), 1955; Lutheran Theological Southern Seminary, M.Div. (cum laude), 1958; Lutheran School of Foreign Missions, certificate, 1959; Chicago Lutheran Theological Seminary, S.T.M., 1960; University of Chicago, M.A., 1964, Ph.D., 1966.

ADDRESSES: Home—2441 Botton Rd., Harrodsburg, Ky. 40330. *Office*—Transylvania University, Lexington, Ky. 40508.

CAREER: Ordained minister of the Lutheran Church in America, 1958; Thiel College, Greenville, Pa., lecturer in English and Bible, 1959-60; pastor in Tampa, Fla., 1960-61; Newberry College, Newberry, S.C., assistant professor of Bible and philosophy, 1961-63, associate professor, 1965-66, professor of philosophy, 1968, head of department, 1966-68; Eastern Kentucky University, Richmond, professor of philosophy and chairman of department, 1968-71; Winebrenner Theological Seminary, Findlay, Ohio, professor of systematic theology and dean of academic affairs, 1971-82; Susquehanna University, Selinsgrove, Pa., professor of religion, 1982-89, chairman of department of philosophy and religion, 1985-89. Visiting professor of philosophy, Transylvania University, 1989—. Member of Commission on Youth Activities, The Lutheran Church in America, 1967-72; supply pastor, St. John's Lutheran Church, McComb, Ohio, 1971-82. Trustee, Wittenberg University, 1976-80. *Military service:* U.S. Marine Corps, 1950-52; served in Korea and Japan; became sergeant; retired due to combat injuries; received Presidential Unit Citation.

MEMBER: American Academy of Religion, American Philosophical Association, MENSA, Society of Ancient Historians, American Legion, Marine Corps Association, Marine Corps Historical Foundation, Phi Beta Kappa.

AWARDS, HONORS: Pennsylvania Council on the Humanities grant, 1987.

WRITINGS:

The Roots of the Radical Theology, Westminster Press, 1967, reprinted, University Press of America, 1988.
(Editor with Charles Sauer) *Wine in Separate Cups,* Commission on Youth Activities, Lutheran Church, 1967.
The Christian and Politics (pupil's book and teacher's book), Lutheran Church Press, 1968.
Radical Christianity and Its Sources, Westminster Press, 1970.
(Editor with Carl Skrade) *Celluloid and Symbols,* Fortress, 1970.
Religion in the Age of Aquarius, Westminster Press, 1971.
Paul for Today, Lutheran Church Press, 1971.
A New Kind of Man, Westminster Press, 1972.
Getting It Together, Lutheran Church Press, 1972.
The Recovery of America, Westminster Press, 1973.
Religion after Forty, Pilgrim Press, 1973.
Finding a Simpler Life, Pilgrim Press, 1974.
Fantasy and the Humane Spirit, Seabury, 1975.
Your Exciting Middle Years, Word, Inc., 1976.
Amos, Prophet of Justice, Lutheran Church Press, 1976.
Living, Loving, and Letting Go, Word, Inc., 1977.
Why We Hurt and Who Can Heal, Word, Inc., 1978.
(With Una McManus) *Not for a Million Dollars,* Impact Books, 1980.
The Joy of the Plain Life, Impact Books, 1981.
Religious Pied Pipers, Judson, 1981.
(Contributor) J. R. Royce and L. P. Mos, editors, *Humanistic Psychology,* Plenum, 1981.
Dealing with Destructive Cults, Zondervan, 1982.
(Contributor) M. M. Gentz, editor, *Writing to Inspire,* Writer's Digest, 1982.
Coping with Rejection, Prentice-Hall, 1983.
Throwing the Sticks: Occult Self-Therapy—The Arts of Self-Transcendence in Post-Freudian Modes of Thought, Wyndham Hall, 1985.
(Contributor) William H. Gentz, editor, *Dictionary of Bible and Religion,* Abingdon, 1986.
(Contributor) *First Quartet,* Time of Singing Press, 1988.
This Fast I Choose: A Day Book for Lent, Friendship Press, 1990.

Contributor of poetry, reviews, and more than two hundred articles to periodicals.

WORK IN PROGRESS: All the Flora of the Bible; Holy Ground; Handbook of Liberation Theology; Cast a Single Shadow, a novel; *Homemade Sin,* a book about the rise of satanism among American youths; *The Devil Made Me Do It,* a book about the Matamoros cult murders; *The Black Flag,* another work concerning Satanism in America.

AVOCATIONAL INTERESTS: Travel (has been to Europe, North Africa, the Middle East, the Far East, and to islands in the Caribbean and the Pacific), wilderness camping, hiking, exploring, rafting, swimming.

*   *   *

CORREY, Lee
   See STINE, G(eorge) Harry

*   *   *

COWART, David (Guyland) 1947-

PERSONAL: Born December 22, 1947, in Tuscaloosa, Ala.; son of Eugene Guyland (in engineering management) and Margaret (a publisher; maiden name, Matthews) Cowart; married Georgia Ann Jackson (divorced, January, 1986); children: Rachel Victoria. *Education:* University of Alabama, B.A., 1969; Indiana University, M.A., 1971; Rutgers University, Ph.D., 1977.

ADDRESSES: Home—236 South Gregg St., Columbia, S.C. 29205. *Office*—Department of English, University of South Carolina, Columbia, S.C. 29208.

CAREER: U.S. Peace Corps, Washington, D.C., volunteer teacher of English in Ethiopia, 1969-70; University of South Carolina, Columbia, instructor, 1977-79, assistant professor, 1979-83, associate professor, 1983-88, professor of English, 1988—. *Military service:* U.S. Army, radio and television broadcaster, 1971-73; served in Panama.

MEMBER: Modern Language Association of America, South Atlantic Modern Language Association, Philological Association of the Carolinas.

AWARDS, HONORS: Omicron Delta Kappa award, 1969; research grants from University of South Carolina, 1978, 1982, 1985, 1987, 1988, 1989; *Thomas Pynchon: The Art of Allusion* was named to *Choice*'s 1980 Outstanding Academic Books list; Amoco Teaching Award, 1987.

WRITINGS:

(Contributor) *Dictionary of Literary Biography,* Gale, Volume 2: *American Novelists since World War II,* 1978, Volume 4: *American Writers in Paris, 1920-1939,* 1980, Volume 5: *American Poets since World War II,* 1980.
Thomas Pynchon: The Art of Allusion, Southern Illinois University Press, 1980.
(Contributor) Robert Morace and Katherine Vanspanckeren, editors, *Critical Perspectives on John Gardner,* Southern Illinois University Press, 1981.
(Editor with Thomas L. Wymer) *Twentieth-Century American Science Fiction Writers, Dictionary of Literary Biography,* Volume 8: Gale, 1981.
Arches and Light: The Fiction of John Gardner, Southern Illinois University Press, 1983.
History and the Contemporary Novel, Southern Illinois University Press, 1989.

Contributor of numerous articles and reviews to periodicals, including *Critique, Twentieth Century Literature, Journal of Nar-* rative Technique, Novel, American Literature, James Joyce Quarterly, Journal of English and German Philology,* and *Studies in American Fiction.* Consulting editor, *Critique;* advisory editor, *Studies in Short Fiction.*

WORK IN PROGRESS: Literary Symbiosis, "a book-length study of the increasingly common practice of basing a new literary work on a pre-existent work."

SIDELIGHTS: David Cowart once told *CA:* "I try to write criticism that is interpretive and pedagogical. . . . My literary interests are catholic but with special interest in fiction and the modern period. . . . As a teacher, I become less and less willing to con students with courses in film, science fiction, and other popular culture subjects. Such courses allow students to dodge the classics, which they desperately need to read. They are sadly lacking in a sense of the cultural continuity of Western civilization—a continuity that ephemeral popular culture can hardly supply."

AVOCATIONAL INTERESTS: Classical music, travel, movies.

BIOGRAPHICAL/CRITICAL SOURCES:

PERIODICALS

Los Angeles Times Book Review, February 12, 1984.
Washington Post Book World, November 29, 1981.

*   *   *

COX, Richard 1931-

PERSONAL: Born March 8, 1931, in Winchester, England; son of Hubert Eustace (an engineer) and Joan (Thornton) Cox; married Caroline Jennings, October, 1963; children: Lorna Katherine, Ralph Pelham, Jeremy Philip. *Education:* St. Catherine's College, Oxford, second class honors in English language and literature, 1955. *Politics:* Conservative. *Religion:* Church of England.

ADDRESSES: Office—P.O. Box 88, Alderney, Channel Islands, Great Britain. *Agent*—Curtis Brown Ltd., 162-168 Regent St., London W.1, England.

CAREER: Writer. Colman, Prentis & Varley (advertising agency), London, England, advertising executive, 1957-1959; *Sunday Times,* London, staff foreign correspondent, 1961-64, with foreign office, 1964-66; *Daily Telegraph,* London, correspondent, 1966-73; Thornton Cox Ltd., and Brassey's Publishers, London, managing director, 1974-78. Radio and television commentator on African and British Commonwealth affairs; temporary African correspondent, Westinghouse Broadcasting Corp. Private pilot. Chelsea borough councillor, 1962-65. *Military service:* British Army, Royal Artillery, 1949-51; became reserve major. Member of 44th Parachute Brigade, 1967-78.

MEMBER: Army and Navy Club, Freemen, Guild of Air Pilots and Navigators.

WRITINGS:

Pan-Africanism in Practice, Oxford University Press, 1964.
Kenyatta's Country, Hutchinson, 1965, Praeger, 1966.
(Editor) *Institute of Directors Guide to Europe,* Thornton Cox, 1968, 2nd edition, 1970.
Operation Sea Lion, Thornton Cox, 1975.
Sam 7, Hutchinson, 1976, Reader's Digest Press, 1977.
The Botticelli Madonna, McGraw, 1978.
The KGB Directive, Viking, 1981.
The Ice Raid, Hutchinson, 1983, Berkeley, 1988.
Ground Zero, Stein & Day, 1985.

The Columbus Option, Secker & Warburg, 1986, Berkeley, 1988. *An Agent of Influence,* Secker & Warburg, 1988.

Also editor of "Thornton Cox Traveller's Guides." Contributor to periodicals, including *Writer.*

SIDELIGHTS: Richard Cox's thriller-detective novels, including *Sam 7, The Botticelli Madonna,* and *The KGB Directive,* are noted for their meticulous attention to detail, according to reviewers. Newgate Callendar comments in the *New York Times Book Review:* "It is not the story alone, good as it is, that is the main interest of *The Botticelli Madonna.* Without slowing down the plot, Mr. Cox goes into great detail about what happens when a great painting surfaces: the legalities of the situation, the way a strapped art concern goes about financing the painting, the way a good art historian thinks, the wheeling and dealing between seller and buyer, the problem of authentication, the dealings with an auction house, the hesitation and deficiencies of a so-called 'expert' and the search for the provenance of the painting."

Hubert Saal, referring to *The KGB Directive* in the *New York Times Book Review,* describes Cox's "grasp of the book's diverse background" as "formidable," adding: "He seems to know the Soviet spy apparatus in London and is able to trace it all the way back to Moscow, and his portrayal of the K.G.B. is convincing. He knows his unions too, right down to the musicians union, which has one member at Western Aircraft to handle the single piece of piano wire used in manufacturing the 207. Moreover, he is most persuasive in describing the way the 207 is manufactured, as well as where and how it is sabotaged." Saal further admires Cox's protagonists, observing that "Norris is a first-class villain, clever and ruthless. Donaldson, plodding and indefatigable, is the very symbol of British perseverance. These characters and the exciting context invest this book with the climate of frightening reality."

Other critics, however, find Cox's extensive use of detail sometimes tedious. In a *Library Journal* review of *Sam 7,* a critic labels the book "a rather long disaster-terrorist thriller, padded out by a great deal of corroborative detail which could have been cut in half." Yet, the reviewer concludes "in spite of all the relentlessly meticulous detail, this one is still exciting."

AVOCATIONAL INTERESTS: Flying, studying art and architecture, traveling.

BIOGRAPHICAL/CRITICAL SOURCES:

PERIODICALS

Library Journal, April 1, 1977.
New York Times Book Review, June 24, 1979, January 24, 1982.
Times (London), January 22, 1987.

* * *

CRAWFORD, John W(illiam) 1914-

PERSONAL: Born September 16, 1914, in Chicago, Ill.; son of William A. and Frances (Eller) Crawford; married Margaret Stephens, 1942; children: John Stephens, Paul, James. *Education:* Northwestern University, B.A., 1935; Michigan State University, M.A., 1958.

ADDRESSES: Home—2044 Eastwood Lane, Eugene, Ore. 97401. *Office*—School of Journalism, University of Oregon, Eugene, Ore. 97403.

CAREER: Toronto Daily Star, Toronto, Ontario, copywriter, 1935-37; J. Walter Thompson Co., Chicago, Ill., copywriter,

1937-38; Allis-Chalmers Manufacturing Co., Milwaukee, Wis., copywriter, 1938; Leo Burnett Co., Inc., Chicago, 1938-55, began as copywriter, became manager of copy department; Kenyon & Eckhardt, Inc., Chicago, vice-president, 1955-56; Michigan State University, East Lansing, 1956-69, began as lecturer, became professor of advertising, chairman of department, and chairman of division of mass communications; University of Oregon, Eugene, professor of journalism, 1969-80, professor emeritus, 1980—, dean of School of Journalism, 1969-75. *Military service:* U.S. Naval Reserve, 1943-46; became lieutenant.

MEMBER: Association for Education in Journalism, American Academy of Advertising (fellow; president, 1967-68), Phi Beta Kappa, Phi Eta Sigma, Alpha Delta Sigma.

AWARDS, HONORS: Silver Medal, Advertising Federation of America/Advertising Association of the West/Printers' Ink, 1965.

WRITINGS:

(Editor) *Report of the Committee on the Future of the University,* Michigan State University, 1959.
Advertising: Communications for Management, Allyn & Bacon, 1960, 2nd edition published as *Advertising,* 1965.
(With Vergil Reed) *Teaching of Advertising at the Graduate Level* (monograph), Columbia University Graduate School of Business, 1963.
Impact of Advertising on Society and Culture (monograph in Japanese), Advertising Conference Board of Japan (Tokyo), 1972.

Also author of *The Classic Ads for the Classic Cars.* Contributor to professional journals. *Advertising* has been translated into Spanish.

WORK IN PROGRESS: Oh, Upright Judge!, a historical novel.

* * *

CRIDER, (Allen) Bill(y) 1941-
(Jack MacLane; Nick Carter, a house pseudonym)

PERSONAL: Born July 28, 1941, in Maxia, Tex.; son of Billy (a freight agent) and Frances (Brodnax) Crider; married Judy Stutts, June 4, 1965; children: Angela, Allen. *Education:* University of Texas at Austin, B.A., 1963, Ph.D., 1971; North Texas State University, M.A., 1966.

ADDRESSES: Home—1606 South Hill St., Alvin, Tex. 77511. *Office*—Department of English, Alvin Community College, Alvin, Tex. 77511.

CAREER: High school English teacher in Corsicana, Tex., 1963-65; Howard Payne University, Brownwood, Tex., associate professor, 1971-74, professor of English, 1974-85, chairman of department, 1977-83; Alvin Community College, Alvin, Tex., professor of English and chairman of department, 1984—.

MEMBER: Mystery Writers of America, Private Eye Writers of America.

WRITINGS:

(With Jack N. Davis, under house pseudonym Nick Carter) *The Coyote Connection* (espionage novel), Charter Books, 1981.
Too Late to Die (mystery), Walker & Co., 1986.
Shotgun Saturday Night (mystery), Walker & Co., 1987.
Cursed to Death (mystery), Walker & Co., 1988.
One Dead Dean (mystery), Walker & Co., 1988.
Ryan Rides Back (western), M. Evans, 1988.
Galveston (western), M. Evans, 1988.

(Under pseudonym Jack MacLane) *Keepers of the Beast* (horror), Zebra, 1988.

Death on the Move (mystery), Walker & Co., 1989.

Dying Voices (mystery), St. Martin's, 1989.

A Time for Hanging (western), M. Evans, 1989.

(Under pseudonym Jack MacLane) *Goodnight Moom* (horror), Zebra, 1989.

(Under pseudonym Jack MacLane) *Blood Dreams* (horror), Zebra, 1989.

OTHER

(Contributor) *Dimensions of Detective Fiction*, Popular Press, 1976.

(Contributor) John M. Reilly, editor, *Twentieth-Century Crime and Mystery Writers*, St. Martin's, 1980.

(Contributor) James Vinson and D. L. Kirkpatrick, editors, *Twentieth-Century Western Writers*, Gale, 1982.

(Editor) *Mass Market American Publishing*, G. K. Hall, 1982.

Also contributor to *Dictionary of Literary Biography*, Gale. Contributing editor of *Paperback Quarterly*.

SIDELIGHTS: Educator and author Bill Crider, who has penned several mysteries, westerns, and horror novels, once told *CA:* "My 1982 book, *Mass Market American Publishing*, is a history of paperback publishing in America from 1939 until the late 1970s. All the major houses and many of the minor ones are treated in separate articles. This book grew out of my interest in collecting and preserving old paperback books, both for their intrinsic and historical value."

*   *   *

CROOKALL, Robert   1890-1981

PERSONAL: Born July 31, 1890, in Lancaster, England; died January, 1981; son of Robert (a clerk of works) and Margaret (Hastings) Crookall; married Gladys Kate Stoneham, April 10, 1928 (died, 1969); children: John Roland. *Education:* Westminster College, Diploma in Education, 1911; Bristol University, B.Sc. (first class honors), 1922, Ph.D., 1926, D.Sc., 1930.

ADDRESSES: Home—9 Lansdown Road Mansions, Bath BA1 5ST, England.

CAREER: University of Aberdeen, Aberdeen, Scotland, lecturer in botany, 1925-26; Her Majesty's Geological Survey, Institute of Geological Studies, London, England, geologist, 1926-52. Scientist with National Coal Board, London.

WRITINGS:

ON GEOLOGICAL TOPICS

Coal Measure Plants, Edward Arnold, 1929.

(With Francis B. A. Welch) *British Regional Geology: Bristol and Gloucester District*, H.M.S.O., 1935, 2nd edition, edited by G. A. Kellaway and Welch, 1948.

The Kidston Collection of Fossil Plants, with an Account of the Life and Work of Robert Kidston, H.M.S.O., 1938.

(Contributor) George Hoole Mitchell, *The Geology of the Warwickshire Coalfield*, Geological Survey & Museum, 1942.

(Contributor) Mitchell, *The Geology of the Northern Part of the South Staffordshire Coalfield, Cannock Chase Region*, Geological Survey & Museum, 1945.

(Contributor) Benjamin Hilton Barrett and W. E. Graham, *Economic Geology of Canonbie Coalfield, Dumfriesshire and Cumberland*, Geological Survey & Museum, 1945.

Fossil Plants of the Carboniferous Rocks of Great Britain (monograph), H.M.S.O., Part 1, 1955, Part 2, 1959, Part 3, 1964, Part 4, 1966, Part 5, 1958, Part 6, 1969, Part 7, 1977.

Contributor of articles to *Geological Magazine, Naturalist*, and other scientific periodicals. Contributor to *Memoirs* of Geological Survey of Great Britain.

ON ASTRAL PROJECTION

The Study and Practice of Astral Projection, Wehman, 1961 (published in England as *The Study and Practice of Astral Projection: Analyses of Case Histories*, Aquarian Press, 1961).

The Supreme Adventure: Analyses of Psychic Communications, Fernhill, 1961, 2nd edition, James Clarke, 1975.

The Techniques of Astral Projection: Denouement after Fifty Years, Wehman, 1964.

More Astral Projections: Analyses of Case Histories, Wehman, 1964.

During Sleep: The Possibility of "Co-operation," Theosophical Publishing, 1964.

Intimations of Immortality: "Seeing" That Led to "Believing," James Clarke, 1965.

The Next World—and the Next: Ghostly Garments, Theosophical Publishing, 1966.

The Mechanism of Astral Projection, Darshana International, 1968.

The Interpretation of Cosmic and Mystical Experiences, James Clarke, 1969.

Out-of-the-Body Experiences: A Fourth Analysis, University Books, 1970.

The Jung-Jaffe View of Out-of-the Body Experiences, World Fellowship Press, 1970.

(Contributor) *Case Book of Astral Projection*, University Books, 1972.

Life, "A Cheat" or "A Sacred Burden"?, Darshana International, 1976.

What Happens When You Die, Smythe, 1978.

Psychic Breathing: Cosmic Vitality from the Air, Newcastle, 1985.

Also author of *Events on the Threshold of the After Life*, 1969, *Ecstasy: The Release of the Soul from the Body*, 1973, and *"Dreams" of High Significance*, 1974. Contributor to *Light*.

SIDELIGHTS: After a long career as a geologist, Robert Crookall became an authority on astral projection, the phenomenon ascribed by theosophists to the existence within individuals of a second, "astral" body, sometimes able to carry the spirit away from the material body during sleep, and surviving it in death. Contained in the folklore and literature of several ancient cultures, "out-of-body" experiences have been typically viewed by contemporary scientists and psychologists as subjective feats of human imagination. Crookall, however, belonged to the school of parapsychologists which considers these experiences based on semi- or super-physical non-reality. Crookall documented and classified thousands of cases of astral projection in *The Jung-Jaffe View of Out-of-the-Body Experiences*, which Laura Bartlett in *Books and Bookmen* called a "deeply argued, fascinating" account of an intriguing phenomenon that reinforces "the old Christian idea of survival after death."

Crookall, who considered himself "a deeply religious man," once commented that he believed "concepts of the soul are not unscientific," and that he hoped to "reconcile religious faith and scientific integrity in matters relating to the human soul." He wrote: "Out-of-the-body experiences are taking the foremost place in the study of survival, the earlier, mediumistic, phenomena having failed to clinch the question. The present result, though not absolute 'proof,' is practical certainty."

BIOGRAPHICAL/CRITICAL SOURCES:

BOOKS

Barden, Dennis, *Mysterious World,* W. H. Allen, 1970.

PERIODICALS

Books and Bookmen, August, 1970.*

* * *

CUNDIFF, Margaret Joan   1932-

PERSONAL: Born March 23, 1932, in Minehead, England; daughter of Charles Herbert John and Ethel (Davey) Smith; married Peter Neville Cundiff (a sales consultant), June 11, 1960; children: Julian Peter, Alison Margaret. *Education:* St. Michael's House Theological College, Inter-Diocesan Certificate (with merit), 1953; Manchester College of Science and Technology, Diploma in Management Studies, 1960.

ADDRESSES: Home and office—37 Oaklands, Camblesforth, Selby, North Yorkshire YO8 8HH, England.

CAREER: Church of England parish worker in Wolverhampton, England, 1953-54, youth leader in Nottingham, England, 1954-56, personnel officer in Manchester, England, 1956-62; St. James's Church, Selby, England, deaconess and parish worker, 1973-87. Member of General Synod of the Church of England; Anglican adviser to Yorkshire Television Ltd., 1979—; broadcasting officer for Church of England Diocese of York, 1975—.

WRITINGS:

Called to Be Me, S.P.C.K., 1982.
Following On, S.P.C.K., 1983.
I'd Like You to Meet . . . , S.P.C.K., 1984.
Living by the Book, S.P.C.K., 1985.
The Church around the Corner, Herheimsund, 1986.

The Cost of Living, S.P.C.K., 1987.
Good Morning, It's Margaret, S.P.C.K., 1988.
My Kind of Day, S.P.C.K., 1990.

Also contributor to *My Pathway of Prayer,* 1984. Author of "Margaret Cundiff's Thought for the Week," a weekly column in *Selby Times.* Regular contributor to local and national programs broadcast on British Broadcasting Radio and British Forces Broadcasting Service Radio. Contributor to religious magazines and newspapers.

SIDELIGHTS: Margaret Joan Cundiff told *CA:* "My writing has risen out of my life as a Christian and my work as a minister. I feel that humor is sadly lacking in the church, so my writings have a large degree of humor. I feel that I should never take myself too seriously, but I take the gospel of Christ very seriously. Humor *is* very important to me. It enables me to relax, it takes the 'agro' out of situations, and allows me to get alongside all sorts of people. I believe laughter is part of the healing ministry.

"I suppose one of the issues that comes out in my books is that there is a place for women in the ministry of the Church of England. I tell it as it is—there are problems and frustrations but many joys. I wouldn't change my life—but do hope and pray that one day I may have my vocation as a priest tested. Whatever happens, though, I would not defy the values of the Church of England—I love the Church too much to do that, but I do hope to see changes in my lifetime.

"The style of my writings is very much a broadcasting style— talking in print! I was a broadcaster before I was a writer, but I am finding more and more a satisfaction in writing; for books remain—the spoken word goes into air."

* * *

CURTIS, Wade
See POURNELLE, Jerry (Eugene)

D

DAGAN, Avigdor 1912-
(Viktor Fischl)

PERSONAL: Original name, Viktor Fischl; born June 30, 1912, in Hradek Kralove, Czechoslovakia; emigrated to Israel, 1949; son of Moritz (a merchant) and Frieda (Ehrenstein) Fischl; married Stella Berger, April 10, 1938; children: Daniel, Gabriel. *Education:* University of Prague, D.rer.pol., 1938. *Religion:* Jewish.

ADDRESSES: Home—14, Sderot Hameiri, Jerusalem, Israel.

CAREER: Zidovske Zpravy (Zionist weekly), Prague, Czechoslovakia, editor, 1935-39; Czechoslovakian Parliament, Prague, parliamentary secretary of Jewish Party, 1936-39; Israel Ministry of Foreign Affairs, Jerusalem, diplomat, 1950—, serving as counsellor in Tokyo, 1955-59, and Rangoon, 1959-60, director of East European Division, Jerusalem, 1960-61, ambassador to Poland, 1961-64, ambassador to Yugoslavia, 1965-67, ambassador to Norway and Iceland, 1969-72, ambassador to Austria, 1974—. Lecturer on Soviet and Eastern European affairs at Columbia University and Harvard University.

AWARDS, HONORS: Melantrich Prize (Czechoslovakia), 1937, for *Hebrejske melodie;* Euorpean Literary Club Prize (Prague), 1948, for *Pisen o litosti* (first published as *Shir Harakhamim*).

WRITINGS:

Moscow and Jerusalem: Twenty Years of Relations between Israel and the Soviet Union, foreword by Abba Eban, Abelard, 1970.

Binat hasehvi (title means "Wisdom of a Rooster"), Am Oved, 1978.

Leitzanei Hachatzer, Sifriat Poalim, 1982, translation published as *The Court Jesters,* Jewish Pubn. Soc., 1989.

Sipurim Jerushalmiim (title means "Jerusalem Stories"), Dvir, 1983.

Die Stoerche im Regenbogen (title means "The Storks in the Rainbow"), Edition Roetzer, 1983.

Rehov ushmo Mamila (title means "A Street Called Mamilla"), Sifriat Poalim, 1984.

(With brother, Gabriel Dagan) *Hashaan mesimtat hamazalot* (title means "The Watchmaker from Zodiac Street"), Am Oved, 1984.

Hakarusela hakhulah (title means "The Blue Merry-Go-Round"), Am Oved, 1985.

Misipurei Ovadia hasabal (title means "From the Stories of the Porter Ovadia"), Keter, 1985.

Ktav ishum (title means "The Indictment"), Sifriat Poalim, 1987.

Hatunat hazahav shel Figaro (title means "Figaro's Golden Wedding"), Dvir, 1988.

UNDER NAME VIKTOR FISCHL

Jaro (title means "The Spring"; poems), F. J. Mueller, 1933.

Kniha Noci (title means "Book of Nights"; poems), Druzstevni Prace, 1936.

Hebrejske melodie (title means "Hebrew Melodies"; poems), Melantrich, 1936.

Evropske zalmy (title means "European Psalms"; poems), Czechoslovak (London), 1941.

Mrtva ves (title means "Dead Village"; poems), Edice Mladeho Ceskoslovakia (London), 1943, 2nd edition, Pax, 1946, translation by Laurie Lee published as *The Dead Village,* Young Czechoslovakia (London), 1943.

Anglicke sonety (title means "English Sonnets"; poems), Melantrich, 1946.

Lyricky zapisnik (title means "Lyrical Notebook"; poems), Vaclav Petr, 1946.

Shir Harakhamim (title means "Song of Pity"; novel), Hebrew translation by Gideon Pollak, Am Oved, 1951, published in Czech as *Pisen o litosti,* Sixty-Eight Publishers (Toronto), 1982.

Hovory s Janem Masarykem (title means "Conversations with Jan Masaryk"), Izraelske Listy, 1952, Kruh Pratel Ceskoslovenske Knihy (Chicago), 1953.

Kuropeni (title means "The Song of a Rooster"), Konfrontace (Zurich), 1975.

Dum u tri jousli (title means "The House of the Three Violins"; poems), Reva (Munich), 1981.

Hraci hadiny, Polygon Zuerich, 1982.

Jeruzalemske povidky (title means "Stories from Jerusalem"), Index (Koeln), 1985.

Vsichni moji stryckore (title means "All My Uncles"), Polygon (Zurich), 1987.

Figarova zlata svatbe (title means "Figaro's Golden Wedding"), Index, 1987.

WORK IN PROGRESS: Fifth Quarter, a novel; *Kafka in Jerusalem,* a book of short stories; *Uncle Bosco,* a book for children.

SIDELIGHTS: Although *Pisen o litosti* received the European Literary Club Prize in Prague in 1948, the novel was not published until three years later in Israel; publication in Czechoslovakia was forbidden after the Communist coup there. It was published in Czech only in 1982. Several of Avigdor Dagan's books have also appeared in Hebrew and German.

AVOCATIONAL INTERESTS: Painting.

BIOGRAPHICAL/CRITICAL SOURCES:

PERIODICALS

New Leader, May 3, 1971.
Saturday Review, February 6, 1971.

* * *

DAHL, Robert A(lan) 1915-

PERSONAL: Born December 17, 1915, in Inwood, Iowa; son of Peter Ivor and Vera (Lewis) Dahl; married Mary Louise Bartlett, June 20, 1940 (died June, 1970); married Ann Sale Barber, May 26, 1973; children: (first marriage) Ellen Kirsten, Peter Bartlett (deceased), Eric Lewis, Christopher Robert. *Education:* University of Washington, Seattle, A.B., 1936; Yale University, Ph.D., 1940.

ADDRESSES: Home—17 Cooper Rd., North Haven, Conn. 06473. *Office*—Department of Political Science, Yale University, New Haven, Conn. 06473.

CAREER: Office of the Secretary, U.S. Department of Agriculture, Washington, D.C., management analyst, 1940; economist in Office of Production Management, 1941, and on War Production Board, 1942; Yale University, New Haven, Conn., instructor, 1946-47, assistant professor, 1948-52, associate professor, 1953-57, Ford Research Professor, 1957, Eugene Meyer Professor of Political Science, 1957-63, Sterling Professor of Political Science, 1963—, chairman of department, 1957-62. Walgreen lecturer at University of Chicago, 1954; lecturer in Chile, 1967. Fellow, Center for the Advanced Study of the Behavioral Science, 1955-56, 1967. Member of board of directors, Yale University Press. Consultant to U.S. Department of State and State Government Reorganization Commission. *Military service:* U.S. Army, 1943-45; became first lieutenant; received Bronze Star Medal with oak leaf cluster.

MEMBER: American Civil Liberties Union, American Academy of Arts and Sciences (fellow; councilor, 1989—), American Philosophical Society (fellow), National Academy of Sciences (fellow), American Political Science Association (president, 1966-67), British Academy of Arts and Sciences (corresponding member), Southern Political Science Association, New England Political Science Association (president, 1951), Phi Beta Kappa.

AWARDS, HONORS: Guggenheim fellowship, 1950-51, 1978; Woodrow Wilson Prize from American Political Science Association, 1961; Talcott Parsons Prize for Social Science from the American Academy of Arts and Sciences, 1977; James Madison Prize, 1978; Gladys M. Kammerer Award, 1983; Lippincott Award, 1989; Cavaliere of the Republic of Italy, 1989.

WRITINGS:

Congress and Foreign Policy, Harcourt, 1950, reprinted, Greenwood Press, 1983.
(Editor) *The Impact of Atomic Energy,* American Academy of Political and Social Science, 1953.
(With Charles E. Lindblom) *Politics, Economics, and Welfare: Planning and Politico-Economic Systems Resolved into Basic*

Social Processes, Harper, 1953, published with new preface by the authors, University of Chicago Press, 1976.
A Preface to Democratic Theory, University of Chicago Press, 1956.
A Critique of the Ruling Elite Model, Bobbs-Merrill, 1958.
(With Mason Haire and Paul F. Lazarsfeld) *Social Science Research on Business: Product and Potential,* Columbia University Press, 1959.
(Contributor) William V. D'Antonio and Howard J. Ehrlich, editors, *Power and Democracy in America,* University of Notre Dame Press, 1961, reprinted, Greenwood Press, 1980.
Who Governs?: Democracy and Power in an American City, Yale University Press, 1961.
Modern Political Analysis, Prentice-Hall, 1963, 4th edition, 1984.
(Editor) *Political Oppositions in Western Democracies,* Yale University Press, 1966.
Pluralist Democracy in the United States: Conflict and Consent, Rand McNally, 1967, 2nd edition published as *Democracy in the United States: Promise and Performance,* 1972, 4th edition, Houghton, 1981.
(Compiler with Deane E. Neubauer) *Readings in Modern Political Analysis,* Prentice-Hall, 1968.
After the Revolution?: Authority in a Good Society, Yale University Press, 1970.
New Haven: Community Study of New Haven Voters in Regard to Local Politics, 1959, Dartmouth College, 1970, revised edition, with William Flanigan, published as *The New Haven Community Study,* Inter-University Consortium for Political Research, 1971.
Polyarchy: Participation and Opposition, Rand McNally, 1971.
(Editor) *Regimes and Opposition,* Rand McNally, 1971.
(With Edward R. Tufte) *Size and Democracy,* Stanford University Press, 1973.
Dilemmas of Pluralistic Democracy: Autonomy vs. Control, Yale University Press, 1982.
Controlling Nuclear Weapons: Democracy Versus Guardianship, Syracuse University Press, 1985.
A Preface to Economic Democracy, University of California Press, 1985.
Democracy, Liberty, and Equality, Oxford University Press, 1986.
Democracy and Its Critics, Yale University Press, 1989.

Also author, with Ralph S. Brown, Jr., of pamphlet *Domestic Control of Atomic Energy,* Social Science Research Council, 1951.

WORK IN PROGRESS: Research on essential conditions, characteristics, and consequences of democratic political orders.

BIOGRAPHICAL/CRITICAL SOURCES:

BOOKS

Contemporary Issues Criticism, Volume 1, Gale, 1982.

* * *

DAKERS, Elaine Kidner 1905-1978
(Jane Lane)

PERSONAL: Born 1905, in Rorslip, England; died January 6, 1978; daughter of Mason and Enid Kidner; married Andrew Dakers, 1937; children: Stewart. *Education:* Attended schools in Middlesex, England.

ADDRESSES: Home—Kingsbury, 97 Rea Rd., Angmering-on-Sea, Sussex, England.

CAREER: Writer, 1933-78.

WRITINGS:

NOVELS; UNDER PSEUDONYM JANE LANE

King's Critic, Rich & Cowan, 1935.

Be Valiant Still, Rich & Cowan, 1935, reprinted, Sphere, 1971.

Prelude to Kingship, Rich & Cowan, 1936, reprinted, International Publications Service, 1969.

Sir Devil-May-Care, Methuen, 1937, reprinted, Muller, 1971.

He Stooped to Conquer, Dakers, 1943, reprinted, International Publications Service, 1968.

England for Sale, Dakers, 1943.

Gin and Bitters, Dakers, 1945, reprinted, Muller, 1966, published as *Madame Geneva,* Rinehart, 1946.

His Fight Is Ours, Dakers, 1946, new edition, Muller, 1970.

London Goes to Heaven, Dakers, 1947.

Parcel of Rogues, Rinehart, 1948, new edition, Muller, 1967.

Fortress in the Forth, Dakers, 1950, reprinted, Muller, 1967, revised edition, Sphere, 1971.

Dark Conspiracy, R. Hale, 1952.

The Sealed Knot, R. Hale, 1952, revised edition, Sphere, 1971.

The Lady of the House, R. Hale, 1953.

Thunder on St. Paul's Day, Newman Press, 1954, reprinted, P. Davies, 1974.

The Phoenix and the Laurel, P. Davies, 1954, reprinted, 1974.

Conies in the Hay, R. Hale, 1957, reprinted, P. Davies, 1973, published as *Rabbits in the Hay,* Newman Press, 1958.

Command Performance, R. Hale, 1957.

Queen of the Castle, R. Hale, 1958, reprinted, P. Davies, 1974.

Cat among the Pigeons, R. Hale, 1959.

Sow the Tempest, Muller, 1960.

The Crown for a Lie, Muller, 1962.

A State of Mind, Muller, 1964.

A Wind through the Heather: A Novel of the Highland Clearances, International Publications Service, 1965, published as *Wind in the Heather,* Sphere, 1970.

From the Snare of the Hunters, International Publications Service, 1968.

The Young and Lonely King, Muller, 1969.

The Questing Beast, International Publications Service, 1970.

A Call of Trumpets, International Publications Service, 1971.

The Countess at War, Sphere, 1971.

The Severed Crown, P. Davies, 1972, Simon & Schuster, 1973.

Bridge of Sighs, P. Davies, 1973, John Day, 1975.

Heirs of Squire Harry, P. Davies, 1974.

A Summer Storm, P. Davies, 1976.

A Secret Chronicle, P. Davies, 1977.

Also author of *Undaunted,* 1934, *Come to the March,* 1937, and *You Can't Run Away,* 1940.

NONFICTION; UNDER PSEUDONYM JANE LANE

King James the Last, Dakers, 1942.

Titus Oates, Dakers, 1949.

Puritan, Rake, and Squire, Richard West, 1950.

The Reign of King Covenant, R. Hale, 1956.

Ember in the Ashes, Muller, 1960, P. Davies, 1976.

Farewell to the White Cockade, 1961, Sphere, 1970.

FOR CHILDREN; UNDER PSEUDONYM JANE LANE

Escape of the King, illustrations by Jack Mathew, Evans Brothers, 1950, reprinted, White Lion, 1975.

The Escape of the Prince, illustrations by Douglas Relf, Evans Brothers, 1951.

Desperate Battle, illustrations by Relf, Evans Brothers, 1953.

The Escape of the Queen, illustrations by Relf, Evans Brothers, 1957.

The Escape of the Duke, Evans Brothers, 1960.

The Escape of the Princess, illustrations by Relf, Evans Brothers, 1962.

The Trial of the King, illustrations by Relf, Evans Brothers, 1963.

The Return of the King, illustrations by Relf, Evans Brothers, 1964.

The March of the Prince, illustrations by Relf, Evans Brothers, 1965.

The Champion of the King, illustrations by Martin Bronkhurst, Evans Brothers, 1966.

SIDELIGHTS: Historical novelist Elaine Kidner Dakers, who wrote under the pseudonym Jane Lane, centered *Madame Geneva* on a fictional young agent for the Stuarts in eighteenth-century London. A *Times Literary Supplement* reviewer believed Kidner "paints a vivid picture of the City and the citizens of London; and her bankers, brewers and apprentices, her ladies of easy virtue and the poor gin-sodden victims . . . are all of them lively and well drawn." *Parcel of Rogues,* Kidner's novelization of Mary Queen of Scots' ascension to the throne and subsequent difficulties, is "a book which is fascinatingly skilful in detail and so realistic in atmosphere that it seems told by a woman of the period," wrote a *Times Literary Supplement* contributor. S. H. Hay in *Saturday Review of Literature* also enjoyed the tale and stated that Kidner had "written a rousing good crime story, full of suspense and excitement, and the more gripping because it is true."

Elaine Kidner Dakers' son, Stewart Dakers, once wrote *CA:* "Jane Lane believed strongly that a writer was no different from any other worker; that in effect, background, personal status, and any other sociological data were irrelevant and intrusive. As a person she was a private individual, known to her friends; as a writer she was known to her readers. To confuse the two was, to her, anathema."

BIOGRAPHICAL/CRITICAL SOURCES:

PERIODICALS

Saturday Review of Literature, August 28, 1948.

Times Literary Supplement, September 1, 1945, August 28, 1948.*

*   *   *

DALY, Mary 1928-

PERSONAL: Born October 16, 1928, in Schenectady, N.Y.; daughter of Frank X. (a salesman) and Anna Catherine (Morse) Daly. *Education:* College of St. Rose, B.A., 1950; Catholic University of America, M.A., 1952; St. Mary's College, Notre Dame, Ind., Ph.D., 1954; University of Fribourg, S.T.D., 1963, Ph.D., 1965.

ADDRESSES: Home—55A Norwood Ave., Newton Centre, Mass. 02159. *Office*—Department of Theology, Boston College, Chestnut Hill, Mass. 02167. *Agent*—Charlotte Raymond, 23 Waldron Ct., Marblehead, Mass. 01945.

CAREER: Cardinal Cushing College, Brookline, Mass., teacher of philosophy and theology, 1954-59; Junior Year Abroad programs, Fribourg, Switzerland, teacher of philosophy and theology, 1959-66; Boston College, Chestnut Hill, Mass., assistant professor, 1966-69, associate professor of theology, 1969—. Visiting lecturer in English, St. Mary's College, 1952-54.

MEMBER: American Catholic Philosophical Association, American Academy of Religion, American Academy of Political and Social Science, American Association of University Professors, National Organization for Women, Society for the Scientific Study of Religion.

WRITINGS:

Natural Knowledge of God in the Philosophy of Jacques Maritain, Catholic Book Agency (Rome), 1966.

The Church and the Second Sex, Harper, 1968, with a new Feminist Postchristian introduction by the author, 1975, revised edition, Beacon Press, 1985.

(Contributor) William Jerry Boney and Lawrence E. Molumby, editors, *The New Catholic Day: Catholic Theologians of the Renewal,* John Knox, 1968.

(Contributor) William J. Wilson, editor, *Demands for Christian Renewal,* Maryknoll Publications, 1968.

Beyond God the Father: Toward a Philosophy of Women's Liberation, Beacon Press, 1973, 2nd revised edition, 1985.

Gyn/Ecology: The Metaethics of Radical Feminism, Beacon Press, 1978.

Pure Lust: Elemental Feminist Philosophy, Beacon Press, 1984.

(With Jane Caputi) *Websters' First New Intergalactic Wickedary of the English Language,* Beacon Press, 1987.

Contributor to numerous anthologies, including *Sisterhood Is Powerful,* edited by Robin Morgan, Random House, 1970, and *Voices of the New Feminism,* edited by Mary Lou Thompson, Beacon Press, 1970. Contributor to *Dictionary of the History of Ideas;* contributor of articles and reviews to *Commonweal, National Catholic Reporter, Quest, Social Policy,* and other journals.

SIDELIGHTS: Theologian Mary Daly's work has evolved from criticism of the anti-feminist stance of the Catholic Church—in *The Church and the Second Sex*—to later books of more universal scope, centering on the misogynistic tendencies of society and how to deal with them. Religion is a cornerstone of society, however, and remains the starting point for Daly's theories. She maintains that all religions are patriarchal and thus explains the patriarchal attitudes of the modern world. "All [religions] . . . ," she writes in *Gyn/Ecology: The Metaethics of Radical Feminism,* "are erected as parts of the male's shelter against anomie. And the symbolic message of all the sects of the religion which is patriarchy is this: Women are the dreaded anomie. Consequently, women are the objects of male terror, the projected personifications of 'The Enemy.' "

As the scope of Daly's books widened from a religious to a societal focus so did her interest in what *New York Times Book Review* contributor Demaris Wehr describes as "the role of language in the transformation of consciousness," a theme which Wehr finds throughout Daly's work. In Wehr's review of *Pure Lust: Elemental Feminist Philosphy* the critic notes that, while in *The Church and the Second Sex* Daly focuses on "antifeminism in language" and in *Beyond God the Father* suggests that new non-sexist words need to be created, in *Gyn/Ecology* and *Pure Lust* Daly offers the reader a new feminist vocabulary. In both of the later books Daly takes derogatory terms for women, such as shrew, hag, or crone, and uses them as words of praise, capitalizing them to emphasize the importance of the women to which they refer. Her *Websters' First New Intergalactic Wickedary of the English Language,* a collaborative effort with Jane Caputi, is a glossary of these old words with new definitions as well as the many new words created by Daly. Commenting on the feminist's vocabulary, Wehr notes, "Whether it is invigorating or arduous to read [these new words] (they are all Very Big) depends on varying factors, such as how alert the reader is at the time. But the point is, new words challenge us to think different thoughts in different ways. This is exciting."

In his *Spectator* review of *Pure Lust* David Sexton elaborates more fully on Daly's unique use of language to express her beliefs. "Daly herself," he observes, "attempts to write a language that is free of unwanted associations—a form of alliterative thought chant, decorated with typographical freaks. Words are given arbitrary new histories—('we are not surprised to hear that *dream* is said to be etymologically related to the Latvian word (dunduris) meaning gadfly, wasp. For Metamorphosing women sting and provoke each other to Change'). . . . Daly's prose is in fact thrillingly horrid; it reads like Carlyle under the influence of *Finnegans Wake.*" In Sara Maitland's *New Statesman* review of the same volume, the critic expresses similar doubts about Daly's style but also praises her work, "Daly is probably the most important Radical Feminist thinker around; she is also a writer of flamboyant brilliance—despite the fact that her addiction to alliteration is wearing, she has an unmatched depth of passion, imagination and pure verbal wit."

Other critics suggest that Daly's use of language may obscure her message, thus diluting her substantial contribution to feminist theory. In a *Ms.* essay devoted to Daly's work, noted feminist Lindsy Van Gelder complains about the difficulty of reading *Gyn/Ecology.* Van Gelder comments: "The first Passage, some 100 pages long, abounds with lengthy quotations from Merriam-Webster, forays into Greek and Latin derivations, invented words . . ., and endless puns. . . . The section may seem tiresome to women who have already thought through the limitations of patriarchal language and tiring to those who have not." Helen McNeil also finds fault with the same volume: "Throughout *Gyn/Ecology,* words are punned upon, slashed apart and stitched together, and broken down into polemic etymologies. . . . Unfortunately Daly's verbal play often obfuscates her argument, forcing even what she would call a Revolting Hag Searcher, like this reviewer, to struggle just to make basic sense of passages which as often as not are about the most gross and hideous persecutions of women. Having suffered these outrages, must we now kill ourselves *reading* about them too?" But, while Van Gelder sees little in the work to praise, McNeil calls it "an important book for its fierceness as much as for its facts."

Summarizing her views for *CA,* Daly once wrote: "My fundamental interest is the women's revolution, which I see as the radical source of possibility for other forms of liberation from oppressive structures. I am interested precisely in the spiritual dimension of women's liberation, in its transforming potential in relation to religious consciousness and the forms in which this consciousness expresses itself. This is not 'one area' of theology; rather, it challenges the whole patriarchal religion."

BIOGRAPHICAL/CRITICAL SOURCES:

BOOKS

Contemporary Issues Criticism, Volume 1, Gale, 1982.
Daly, Mary, *Gyn/Ecology: The Metaethics of Radical Feminism,* Beacon Press, 1978.

PERIODICALS

Ms., February, 1979.
New Statesman, April 4, 1980, January 18, 1985.
New York Times Book Review, July 22, 1984.
Spectator, February 23, 1985.

*   *   *

D'ANDREA, Kate
    See STEINER, Barbara A(nnette)

DANGERFIELD, Harlan
See PADGETT, Ron

*   *   *

DANIEL, Anne
See STEINER, Barbara A(nnette)

*   *   *

DANIEL, Glyn (Edmund)   1914-1986
(Dilwyn Rees)

PERSONAL: Born April 23, 1914, in Lampeter Velfrey, Pembrokeshire, England; died December 13, 1986; son of John (a schoolmaster) and Mary Jane (Edmunds) Daniel; married Ruth Langhorne, 1946. *Education:* Attended University College, University of Wales, 1931-32; St. John's College, Cambridge, B.A. (with first class honors), 1935; Cambridge University, Ph.D., 1938, M.A., 1939.

ADDRESSES: Home—The Flying Stag, 70 Bridge St., Cambridge, England; and La Marniere, Zouafques-par-Tournehem, 62890 France. *Office*—St. John's College, Cambridge University, Cambridge, England.

CAREER: Archaeologist, educator, broadcaster, author, and editor; Cambridge University, Cambridge, England, fellow of St. John's College, 1938-45, faculty assistant lecturer, 1945-48, university lecturer in archaeology, 1948-74, Disney Professor of Archaeology, 1974-81, professor emeritus, 1981-86. Steward of St. John's College, 1946-55. Munro Lecturer, University of Edinburgh, 1954; Rhys Lecturer, British Academy, 1954; O'Donnell Lecturer, University of Edinburgh, 1956; Josiah Mason Lecturer, University of Birmingham, 1956; Gregynog Lecturer, University College, Cardiff, 1968; Ballard-Matthews Lecturer, University College of North Wales, 1968; visiting professor, University of Aarhus, 1968; Ferrens Professor, University of Hull, 1969; George Grant MacCurdy Lecturer, Harvard University, 1971. Director of Anglia Television Ltd. and Antiquity Publications Ltd.; director and trustee of Cambridge Arts Theatre. *Military service:* Royal Air Force, intelligence officer, 1940-45; became wing commander.

MEMBER: Society of Antiquaries (fellow), Instituto Italiano di Preistoria e Protostoria (honorary member), British Academy (fellow), German Archaeological Institute (corresponding fellow), Jutland Archaeological Society (corresponding member), South Eastern Union of Scientific Societies (president, 1955), Bristol and Gloucestershire Archaeological Society (president, 1962-63), United Oxford and Cambridge University Club.

AWARDS, HONORS: Knight (first class) of the Dannebrog, 1961; Litt.D., Cambridge University, 1962.

WRITINGS:

The Three Ages: An Essay on Archaeological Method, Cambridge University Press, 1943.
(Under pseudonym Dilwyn Rees) *The Cambridge Murders* (novel), Gollancz, 1945.
A Hundred Years of Archaeology, Duckworth, 1950, revised edition published as *A Hundred and Fifty Years of Archaeology,* 1975.
The Prehistoric Chamber Tombs of England and Wales, Cambridge University Press, 1950.
(With Stuart Piggott) *A Picture Book of Ancient British Art,* Cambridge University Press, 1951.
(Under pseudonym Dilwyn Rees) *Welcome Death* (novel), Gollancz, 1954, Dodd, 1955, reprinted, Hamilton, 1972.

Who Are the Welsh?, British Academy, 1954.
Lascaux and Carnac, Lutterworth, 1955, revised and enlarged edition published as *The Hungry Archaeologist in France: A Travelling Guide to Caves, Graves, and Good Living in the Dordogne and Brittany,* Faber, 1963.
(With others) *Myth or Legend?* (broadcasts), Macmillan, 1955, Capricorn Books, 1968.
(With Thomas George Eyre Powell) *Barclodiad y Gawres: The Excavation of a Megalithic Chamber Tomb in Anglesey, 1952-53,* Liverpool University Press, 1956.
The Megalith Builders of Western Europe, Hutchinson, 1958, Praeger, 1959.
(Editor of translation) Raymond Block, *Die Etrusker,* M. DuMont Schauberg, 1960.
The Prehistoric Chamber Tombs of France: A Geographical, Morphological, and Chronological Survey, Thames & Hudson, 1960.
The Idea of Prehistory, C. A. Watts, 1962, World Publishing, 1963.
The Pen of My Aunt, Merry Boys (Cambridge), 1962.
(With Sean P. O'Riordain) *New Grange and the Bend of the Boyne,* Praeger, 1964.
(Editor with Idris Llewelyn Foster) *Prehistoric and Early Wales,* Routledge & Kegan Paul, 1965.
Oxford Chicken Pie, Merry Boys, 1966.
Man Discovers His Past, Duckworth, 1966, Crowell, 1968.
The Origins and Growth of Archaeology, Penguin, 1967, Crowell, 1968.
(With J. D. Evans) *The Western Mediterranean,* Cambridge University Press, 1967.
The First Civilizations: The Archaeology of Their Origins, Crowell, 1968.
Archaeology and the History of Art, University of Hull Press, 1970.
Megaliths in History, Thames & Hudson, 1972.
(Editor with R. F. Paget) *Central Italy: An Archaeological Guide,* Noyes Data, 1973.
(Editor) Margaret Guido, *Southern Italy: An Archaeological Guide,* Noyes Data, 1973.
La France de la prehistoire, Tallandier, 1973.
(With Piggott and Charles McBurney) *France before the Romans,* Thames & Hudson, 1974.
Cambridge and the Back-Looking Curiosity: An Inaugural Lecture, Cambridge University Press, 1976.
(Editor) *The Illustrated Encyclopedia of Archaeology,* Macmillan, 1978.
(Editor) *Towards a History of Archaeology,* Thames & Hudson, 1981.
A Short History of Archaeology, Thames & Hudson, 1981.
Some Small Harvest (autobiography), Thames & Hudson, 1986.

General editor of "Ancient Peoples and Places" series, Thames & Hudson, beginning 1958. Contributor to *Nation, Natural History,* and archaeological journals. Editor, *Antiquity,* beginning 1958.

SIDELIGHTS: Glyn Daniel was an internationally-known archaeologist who devoted his energies to popularizing the field, as well as to conducting disciplined research in it, his specialty being the study of megalithic chamber tombs. In the first sense, Daniel was particularly admired for his role, along with Mortimer Wheeler, in establishing the British Broadcasting Corporation's television program "Animal, Vegetable, Mineral?" In a London *Times* review of Daniel's autobiography, *Some Small Harvest,* Peter Ackroyd explains: "Relentlessly middlebrow it may have been, but *Animal, Vegetable, Mineral?* was nevertheless responsible for a whole generation of young children who wanted to be nothing other than archaeologists." Daniel further popularized the field through his numerous books, lectures, and radio and television broadcasts. In the more scholarly sense, Daniel taught archaeology at Cambridge University; he joined the faculty of St. John's College, Cambridge, in 1938, acted as Disney Professor of Archaeology there from 1974 to 1981, and later became professor emeritus. Colin Renfrew elaborates in his *Times* obituary for Daniel that the archaeologist "was an innovator in at least two ways. He was the first systematic historian of archaeology, at any rate in the English language. His pioneering *The Three Ages* laid the foundation for the first coherent account of the history of the subject, *A Hundred Years of Archaeology* [later revised as *A Hundred and Fifty Years of Archaeology*]. . . . This body of work gave several generations of students and scholars their first appreciation that archaeology and prehistory are about ideas, not simply about things, and that ideas are produced by people who are themselves the products of their time." Apart from archaeology, Daniel penned two detective novels, *The Cambridge Murders* and *Welcome Death*, under the pseudonym Dilwyn Rees.

AVOCATIONAL INTERESTS: Travel, walking, swimming, food, wine, writing detective novels.

BIOGRAPHICAL/CRITICAL SOURCES:

BOOKS

Cunliffe, Barry, John D. Evans, and Colin Renfrew, editors, *Antiquity and Man: Essays in Honor of Glyn Daniel,* Thames & Hudson, 1981.
Daniel, Glyn, *Some Small Harvest* (autobiography), Thames & Hudson, 1986.

PERIODICALS

Booklist, September 15, 1979.
Natural History, November, 1968.
Spectator, June 9, 1950.
Times (London), September 25, 1986.
Times Literary Supplement, June 9, 1950, May 2, 1968, April 9, 1982, November 21, 1986.

OBITUARIES:

PERIODICALS

Times (London), December 15, 1986, December 20, 1986.

[Sketch reviewed by wife, Ruth Daniel]

*   *   *

DANN, Jack 1945-

PERSONAL: Born February 15, 1945, in Johnson City, N.Y.; son of Murray I. (an attorney) and Edith (Nash) Dann; married Jeanne Van Buren, January 1, 1983; children: (stepson) Jody Scobie. *Education:* State University of New York at Binghamton, B.A., 1968, graduate study, 1971—; attended St. John's Law School, 1969-70.

ADDRESSES: Home and office—825 Front St., Binghamton, N.Y. 13905. *Agent*—Patrick Delahunt, John Schaffner Associates, 114 East 28th St., New York, N.Y. 10016.

CAREER: Writer. Instructor in writing and science fiction, Broome Community College, Binghamton, N.Y., 1972; assistant professor, Cornell University, summer, 1973. Lecturer for Science Fiction Writers Speakers Bureau, 1971—; has appeared on television and radio.

MEMBER: World Future Society, Science Fiction Writers of America.

AWARDS, HONORS: Nebula Award nominations, Science Fiction Writers of America, 1973, for novella "Junction," 1975, for novelette "The Dybbuk Dolls," 1978, for short story "A Quiet Revolution for Death," 1979, for novelette "Camps," 1981, for novella "Amnesia," and for short story "Going Under," 1982, for short story "High Steel," 1983, for novelette "Blind Shemmy," 1984, for novelette "Bad Medicine," and for novel *The Man Who Melted,* and 1985, for novelette "The Gods of Mars"; British Science Fiction Association Award finalist, 1979, for novelette "Camps"; World Fantasy Award finalist, 1981, for short story "Fairy Tale," 1984, for novelette "Bad Medicine," and 1987, for anthology *In the Field of Fire;* Gilgamesh Award, 1986, for short story "Down among the Dead Men."

WRITINGS:

(Editor) *Wandering Stars: An Anthology of Jewish Fantasy and Science Fiction,* Harper, 1974.
(Editor with George Zebrowski) *Faster Than Light: An Original Anthology about Interstellar Travel,* Harper, 1976.
(Editor with Gardner Dozois) *Future Power: A Science Fiction Anthology,* Random House, 1976.
Starhiker (novel), Harper, 1977.
Christs and Other Poems (chapbook), Bellevue Press, 1978.
(Editor) *Immortal: Short Novels of the Transhuman Future,* Harper, 1978.
Timetipping (short stories), introduction by Roger Zelazny, Doubleday, 1980.
(Editor with Dozois) *Aliens!,* Pocket Books, 1980.
Junction (novel), Dell, 1981.
(Editor and contributor) *More Wandering Stars: Outstanding Stories of Jewish Fantasy and Science Fiction,* Doubleday, 1981.
(Editor with Dozois) *Unicorns!,* Ace Books, 1982.
The Man Who Melted (novel), Bluejay Books, 1984.
(Editor and contributor with Dozois) *Magicats!,* Ace Books, 1984.
(Editor with Dozois) *Bestiary!,* Ace Books, 1985.
(Editor with Dozois) *Mermaids!,* Ace Books, 1986.
(Editor with Dozois) *Sorcerers!,* Ace Books, 1986.
(Editor with Dozois) *Demons!,* Ace Books, 1987.
(Editor with wife, Jeanne Van Buren Dann) *In the Field of Fire,* Tor Books, 1987.
(Editor with Dozois) *Dogtails!,* Ace Books, 1988.
(Editor with Dozois) *SeaSerpents!,* Ace Books, in press.
(Editor with Dozois) *Dinosaurs!,* Ace Books, in press.

Contributor of stories and poetry to numerous science fiction and horror anthologies; contributor to magazines, including *Omni, Fantasy and Science Fiction, Amazing,* and *Fantastic.* Managing editor, *SFWA Bulletin,* 1970-75.

WORK IN PROGRESS: Counting Coup, a mainstream novel; *The Path of Remembrance,* a mainstream novel about Leonardo da Vinci, for Doubleday; *Distances,* a novel, for Doubleday; *The Black Horn,* a chapbook, for Amber Beetle Press; an untitled novella and a novel, *High Steel,* both with Jack C. Haldeman II, both for TOR Books; editing *Slow Dancing in Time,* a collection of stories co-authored by Gardner Dozois, for Ursus Imprints; editing *Littlepeople!,* with Dozois, for Ace Books.

SIDELIGHTS: In his science fiction, Jack Dann "often ignores the loftier spiritual aspirations of humanity to descend again and again into the nightmare terrain of the subconscious," summarizes Michael Bishop in his *Washington Post Book World* review of *Timetipping*. The collection, which includes four Nebula-nominated stories, "actually deliver[s] the goods," Bishop adds, "albeit with a staccato, knife-edged prose and a purposely disorienting passion that corroborate [one writer's] avowal that Dann is a genuine original." As Gregory Feeley relates in *Twentieth-Century Science Fiction Writers*, Dann's work is grounded in a central theme, developing "a recognizable figure in the solitary, obsessive young man whose disaffection with the stratified society he belongs to leads to a dramatic encounter with a larger strangeness that resonates in the telling with a powerful and sometimes disturbing resonance."

One such work is the Nebula finalist *The Man Who Melted*, which "is in a way the culmination of the themes he had the unparalleled courage to tackle in [the novel] *Junction* and *Timetipping*," John Shirley claims in *Science Fiction Review*. "But stylistically and in terms of sheer authorial control, this is his best book, and one that may well be influential, not only in the science fiction field, but in the realms of metaphysics, psychology and in mainstream literature." *The Man Who Melted* takes place in a post-apocalypse twenty-first century where "Screamers" wreak havoc in the streets, sweeping up onlookers in a great psychic riot. Raymond Mantle is searching for both his wife and his memory, for while his wife may have joined the Screamers, he is unsure whether she is dead or alive. While the surface of the story deals with Mantle's quest to find his wife, "what the book is ultimately about is the Apocalypse—what is unveiled are things that should be," observes Howard Waldrop in the *Washington Post Book World*. The critic explains: "The novel chronicles the loss of self in myriad ways—loss of loved ones, of individuality in a group, of memory, of selfhood."

While Shirley concurs that *The Man Who Melted* deals more with Mantle's search of his own nature than the actual physical search, he notes that unlike some psychological, "literary" fiction, the novel "is gripping, harrowing, a fascinating journey through the world as it is becoming," adding that "the onionskin peeling of psychological reality and sociological conspiracy becomes increasingly intriguing as the book goes on." Craig Shaw Gardner similarly observes in the *Cleveland Plain Dealer* that Dann's portrayal of the protagonists adds to the authenticity of the story; the novel is "one in which we feel intimate with the characters and involved with the seeming reality of their situation." In contrast, *Fantasy Review* contributor Steve Carper believes that at times the book sacrifices characterization for literary effects; nevertheless, the critic states that the book is "well-written, with powerful scenes, a truly frightening central concept, and masses of imaginative imagery." "This is a deeply felt, intense, finally cathartic book," concludes Waldrop. "It is Dann's best so far. . . . If other people don't know how good this is, I'll be mighty surprised."

Dann commented to *CA:* "I remember being asked why I write sf—that was about [fifteen] years ago when I first began to publish. I answered by saying that science fiction gave me the most room to investigate/work out my ideas. I feel differently about that today. Indeed, I feel that science fiction can be very restricting. One can easily get lost in all the small details that have to be invented and lose the main thrust of the work, which might be why so many science fiction novels are still populated by cardboard characters. It's not that the authors don't care about characterization, but that they are overwhelmed by the details of their creation.

"Perhaps why I write science fiction can be inferred by how I write it. I first begin with a mood, a feeling, an idea or vision that I feel must be put to paper, lest it be lost forever. . . . For me,

a novel is a series of such tiny explosions. The initial idea is a joy; anything is possible, and one can drop into that special place where daydreams and inventions and stories are made and play God. There are no limits in sight, but as we extrapolate the idea's possibilities, we come upon other ideas and must choose one course out of many. As one chooses, other possibilities are closed. As the idea takes form, attaches itself to other ideas and patterns as grows, the initial joy must give way to critical thought. The mostly unconscious, intuitive processes must give way to the hard work of analysis."

The author added that this intuitive aspect "will only carry you so far—far enough to get you to the initial ideas, but as soon as you have the sense that you are about to find the pattern for the whole, everything falls apart, and you find yourself criticizing all your assumptions. Although this is a most frustrating time, it is when the work is initially forged into workable fiction rather than the daydream it had been. This critical time is agonizing for me, especially as it comes right on the heels of such growth and percolation. It's like waking up sober in the drunk-tank. I feel totally blocked, but I begin to ask questions. . . ."

Dann further observed that "sometimes, as on [*The Man Who Melted*], I know the end, although it didn't become really clear until I had written some three hundred pages. The novel is my working to read that end; that's the way I think of it, anyway. . . . In *Junction* I discovered the ending late in the process and had to rewrite previous portions as a consequence.

"As I see it, one way is as good as the other. I don't think the writer has any choice, anyway! Each idea, story, or novel must be dealt with in or on its own terms."

BIOGRAPHICAL/CRITICAL SOURCES:

BOOKS

Elliot, Jeffrey N., *The Work of Jack Dann: An Annotated Bibliography and Guide,* Borgo, in press.
Twentieth-Century Science Fiction Writers, St. James Press, 1986.

PERIODICALS

Analog Science Fiction/Science Fact, April, 1985.
Cleveland Plain Dealer, March 29, 1985.
Delap's Fantasy & Science Fiction Review, July, 1977.
Fantasy Review, March, 1985.
Magazine of Fantasy and Science Fiction, September, 1981.
New York Times Book Review, July 24, 1977.
Science Fiction Review, summer, 1986.
Washington Post Book World, March 23, 1980, April 26, 1981, October 28, 1984.

* * *

DAVID, Jack 1946-

PERSONAL: Born October 27, 1946, in Regina, Saskatchewan, Canada; son of Louis (in sales) and Madge (Demels) David; married Sharon Lee Goldstein (a veterinarian), May 22, 1971. *Education:* University of Western Ontario, B.A., 1967; University of Windsor, M.A., 1973.

ADDRESSES: Home—48 Maclean Ave., Toronto, Ontario, Canada M4E 3A1. *Office*—ECW Press, 307 Coxwell Ave., Toronto, Ontario, Canada M4L 3B5.

CAREER: Addiction Research Foundation, Toronto, Ontario, drug counselor, 1970-71; Catholic Children's Aid Society, Toronto, child care worker, 1971-73; ECW Press, Toronto, publisher and editor, 1974—. English master at Centennial College, 1976—.

AWARDS, HONORS: Grant from Ontario Arts Council, 1977.

WRITINGS:

EDITOR

(With Michael Park) *Playback: Canadian Selections,* McClelland & Stewart, 1978.
(With Caroline Bayard) *Out-Posts/Avant-Postes,* Porcepic, 1978.
Brave New Wave, Black Moss, 1979.
(With Robert Lecker) *The Annotated Bibliography of Canada's Major Authors,* ECW Press, Volume I, 1979, Volume II, 1980, Volume III, 1981, Volume IV, 1983, Volumes V-VIII, 1984-89.
(And author of introduction) *As Elected: Selected Writing of bp Nichol,* Talon Books, 1980.
(With Park) *Replay: A Canadian College Reader,* Methuen, 1981.
(With Jon Redfern) *Short Short Stories,* Holt, 1981.
(With Lecker) *Introduction to Poetry: British, American, Canadian,* Holt, 1981.
(With Lecker) *Introduction to Fiction,* Holt, 1982.
(With Lecker) *Canadian Poetry,* two volumes, General Publishing (Toronto), 1982.
(With Lecker and Ellen Quigley) *Canadian Writers and Their Works,* Volumes I-XX, ECW Press, 1983-88.
(With Lecker) *The New Canadian Anthology,* Nelson, 1988.
(With Redfern and Susan Ianucci) *The Prose Workout,* Copp, 1988.

OTHER

Contributor to periodicals, including *Waves, Canadian Notes and Queries, Antigonish Review,* and *Alive.* Founder and co-editor, *Essays on Canadian Writing,* 1974—.

SIDELIGHTS: Jack David told *CA:* "My career as an editor began, officially, in 1973 when I started the journal *Essays on Canadian Writing.* This was more serendipitous than planned, but once underway I felt certain that my skills and energy would at last be fully utilized. About 1978 or so I virtually stopped writing criticism, poetry, and fiction; editing and publishing and teaching had come to dominate my life. Along with my partner Robert Lecker, I have promoted a vision of Canadian literature that takes quality for granted and proceeds from that point. We have not redefined the corpus, but we have prodded the critical field in two ways: First, we reevaluated the literary canon; and second, we promoted a nonthematic approach to the literature. We have affirmed the value of quality for its own sake—in writing, editing, and production. We have set our standards high and have had to accept the consequences within a close-knit literary community."

*   *   *

DAVIN, D(aniel) M(arcus)   1913-
(Dan Davin)

PERSONAL: Born September 1, 1913, in Invercargill, New Zealand; son of Patrick (a railway worker) and Mary (Sullivan) Davin; married Winifred Kathleen Gonley (an editor), July 22, 1939; children: Anna, Delia Davin Morgan, Brigid Sanford-Smith. *Education:* Attended Sacred Heart College, Auckland, New Zealand; Otago University, M.A., 1934, Dip.M.A., 1935; Balliol College, Oxford, B.A., 1939, M.A., 1945.

ADDRESSES: Home—103 Southmoor Rd., Oxford OX2 6RE, England. *Agent*—David Higham Associates, Ltd., 5-8 Lower John St., Golden Square, London W1R 4HA, England.

CAREER: Writer. Affiliated with Clarendon Press, Oxford, England, 1945-78. Oxford University Press, Oxford, assistant secretary to the delegates, 1948-70, deputy secretary to the delegates, 1970-78.

MEMBER: PEN, Authors Society, Royal Society of Arts (fellow).

AWARDS, HONORS: Balliol College fellow, 1920-78, emeritus fellow, 1978—; D.Litt., Otago University, 1984; Commander of the Order of the British Empire, 1987.

WRITINGS:

FICTION

Cliffs of Fall, Nicholson & Watson, 1945.
For the Rest of Our Lives, Nicholson & Watson, 1947, reprinted, M. Joseph, 1965.
The Gorse Blooms Pale (short stories), M. Joseph, 1947.
Roads from Home, M. Joseph, 1949, new edition, Oxford University Press, 1977.
The Sullen Bell, M. Joseph, 1956.
No Remittance, M. Joseph, 1959.
Not Here, Not Now, R. Hale, 1970.
Brides of Price, R. Hale, 1972, Coward, 1973.
Breathing Spaces (short stories), R. Hale, 1975.
(Under name Dan Davin) *Selected Stories,* R. Hale, 1981.
(Under name Dan Davin) *The Salamander and the Fire: Collected War Stories,* Oxford University Press, 1986.

NONFICTION

(With John Mulgan) *Introduction to English Literature,* Clarendon Press, 1947.
Crete (official history), War History Branch, Department of Internal Affairs (Wellington, New Zealand), 1953.
(With wife, W. K. Davin) *Writing in New Zealand: The New Zealand Novel,* Parts 1 and 2, School Publications Branch, Department of Education (Wellington), 1956.
Katherine Mansfield in Her Letters, School Publications Branch, Department of Education, 1959.
(Under name Dan Davin) *Closing Times* (literary memoirs), Oxford University Press, 1975.

EDITOR

(And author of introduction) *New Zealand Short Stories; First Series,* Oxford University Press, 1953, new edition, 1982.
English Short Stories of Today; Second Series, Oxford University Press, 1958, reprinted under name Dan Davin as *The Killing Bottle: Classic English Short Stories,* Oxford University Press, 1988.
(And author of introduction; under name Dan Davin) Katherine Mansfield, *Selected Stories,* Oxford University Press, 1963, reprinted, 1981.
(Under name Dan Davin) *Short Stories from the Second World War,* Oxford University Press, 1982.
(With Victor Selwyn, Eric de Mauny, and Ian Fletcher; under name Dan Davin) *From Oasis into Italy: War Poems and Diaries from Africa and Italy, 1940-1946,* Shepheard-Walwyn, 1983.

AVOCATIONAL INTERESTS: Reading, writing, talking.

BIOGRAPHICAL/CRITICAL SOURCES:

PERIODICALS

Globe and Mail (Toronto), May 24, 1986.
Times Literary Supplement, June 12, 1981, November 12, 1982,
   July 6, 1984, May 13, 1988.

* * *

DAVIN, Dan
   See DAVIN, D(aniel) M(arcus)

* * *

DAVIS, Adelle   1904-1974
   (Jane Dunlap)

PERSONAL: Name was originally Daisie Adelle Davis; born
February 25, 1904, in Lizton, Ind.; died May 31, 1974, of bone
cancer; daughter of Charles Eugene (a farmer) and Harriette
(McBroom) Davis; married George Edward Leisey (an engineer), October, 1943 (divorced, 1953); married Frank Vernon
Sieglinger (an accountant), April 23, 1960; children: (first marriage) George Davis Leisey, Barbara Adelle Leisey Frodahl. *Education:* Attended Purdue University, 1923-25; University of California, Berkeley, B.A., 1927; received dietetics training at Bellevue Hospital and Fordham Hospital, New York, N.Y., 1927-28;
University of Southern California, M.S., 1939; postgraduate
work at Columbia University and University of California, Los
Angeles. *Religion:* Protestant.

ADDRESSES: Home—Palos Verdes Estates, Calif.

CAREER: Yonkers Public Schools, Yonkers, N.Y., supervisor
of nutrition, 1928-30; consulting nutritionist to physicians and
in a health clinic in Oakland, Calif., 1931-33, Los Angeles, Calif.,
1934-38, and Palos Verdes, Calif., 1948-74. Lecturer on nutrition
to numerous organizations, including women's clubs, dental and
medical seminars, and colleges and universities.

MEMBER: International College of Applied Nutrition (honorary fellow).

AWARDS, HONORS: Brazilian Award of Merit, 1971; D.Sc.,
Plano University, 1972; Raymond A. Dart Human Potential
Award, 1972.

WRITINGS:

Optimum Health, privately printed, 1935.
You Can Stay Well, privately printed, 1939, condensed version,
   Graphic Arts Research Foundation, 1957.
Vitality through Planned Nutrition, Macmillan, 1942, revised
   edition, 1949.
Let's Cook It Right, Harcourt, 1947, 3rd edition, New American
   Library, 1970.
Let's Have Healthy Children, Harcourt, 1951, revised edition,
   New American Library, 1981.
Let's Eat Right to Keep Fit, Harcourt, 1954, revised edition,
   1970.
(Under pseudonym Jane Dunlap) *Exploring Inner Space: Per-
   sonal Experiences Under LSD-25,* Harcourt, 1961.
Let's Get Well, Harcourt, 1965.
Let's Stay Healthy: A Guide to Lifelong Nutrition, edited by Ann
   Gildroy, forward by Leonard Lustgarten, Harcourt, 1981.

Contributor of numerous articles on health and nutrition to periodicals.

SIDELIGHTS: "Mass advertising of refined foods has exploited
health for money to the extent that it amounts to mass murder,"

Adelle Davis said in *Let's Get Well.* Most of Davis's statements
on nutrition were based on the assumption that the majority of
Americans are badly nourished. A veteran nutritionist of almost
forty years who planned special diets for over 20,000 persons suffering from practically every known disease, Davis knew her
subject. She was trained in nutrition through dietetics courses at
New York City hospitals in the late 1920s, received a master's
degree in biochemistry in 1938, and acted as consulting nutritionist in various clinics in New York and California beginning
in the early 1930s. Initially ignored by publishers, by the early
1970s, she was called the "high priestess" or the "guru" of popular nutrition by talk show hosts and "earth mother to the food-
ists" by *Life* magazine. At the time of her death, reports the
Washington Post, her four books on nutrition and health (*Let's
Cook It Right, Let's Have Healthy Children, Let's Eat Right to
keep Fit,* and *Let's Get Well*) had sold close to ten million copies.
An early *Survey* article called *Optimum Health* "fascinating material new to most laymen and to many physicians," and reported that much of it was "taken from the Journal of the American Medical Association . . . and translated into popular
terms." A *New York Times* review by Lois Palmer said of *Let's
Cook It Right:* "Guidance toward the best in cooking is given
through friendly, firm, often amusing advice."

Davis's books detail the horrors of overprocessed commercial
foods, empty calories, chemical additives, and imitation flavor-
ings and dyes (for example, she claimed that much of the brown
bread on the market is only overrefined white bread dyed brown
to fool the consumer). She blamed many of America's ills, including most diseases, crime, drug abuse, mental instability, and
depression at least partially on malnutrition. Some of Davis's
ideas were called dangerous by the medical community, however. A *Time* article found unhealthy elements in Davis's diet:
"Her emphasis on raw milk, eggs and cheese could be an invitation to overweight and heart trouble. She does insist, to be sure,
that proper nutrition is no substitute for medical care. But her
grand design of diet could induce the medically naive to ignore
symptoms of serious diseases while waiting for vitamins and
wheat germ to work their wonders."

AVOCATIONAL INTERESTS: Tennis, swimming, bridge, sewing, reading, painting.

BIOGRAPHICAL/CRITICAL SOURCES:

BOOKS

Davis, Adelle, *Let's Get Well,* Harcourt, 1965.

PERIODICALS

Look, December 15, 1970.
New York Times, May 25, 1947, June 1, 1974.
Publishers Weekly, June 21, 1971, June 17, 1974.
Survey, January, 1936.
Time, December 18, 1972.*

* * *

DAVIS, Kenneth S(idney)   1912-

PERSONAL: Born September 29, 1912, in Salina, Kan.; son of
Charles DeForest (a college professor) and Lydia (Ericson)
Davis; married Florence Marie Olenhouse (an artist and gift
shop owner), February 19, 1938 (died March 4, 1988). *Education:* Kansas State University of Agriculture and Applied Science (now Kansas State University), B.S., 1934; University of
Wisconsin, M.S., 1935.

ADDRESSES: Home—907 East Virginia Ter., Santa Paula, Calif. 93060. Agent—Paul R. Reynolds, Inc., 71 West 23rd St., Suite 1600, New York, N.Y. 10010.

CAREER: Topeka Daily Capital, Topeka, Kan., reporter, 1934; U.S. Soil Conservation Service, information specialist in La Crosse, Wis., Des Moines, Iowa, and Milwaukee, Wis., 1936-42; New York University, New York, N.Y., instructor in journalism, 1945-47; U.S. Commission for UNESCO, public relations assistant to chairman Milton S. Eisenhower, 1947-49; Kansas State University of Agriculture and Applied Science (now Kansas State University), Manhattan, part-time editor, 1949-51, visiting professor of history, 1975, 1977; full-time writer, 1951—. Adjunct professor of English, Clark University, 1977-80. Member of Adlai Stevenson's personal staff, 1955-56; consultant, Worcester Public Library, 1963—. Wartime service: War correspondent for Doubleday & Co., attached to Supreme Headquarters Allied Expeditionary Forces (SHAEF) in London and Normandy, 1945.

MEMBER: Society of American Historians (fellow), Century Club (New York).

AWARDS, HONORS: Friends of American Writers award, 1943, for In the Forests of the Night; honorable mention, Thormod Monsen Award, Society of Midland Authors, 1960, for The Hero: Charles A. Lindbergh and the American Dream; Centennial Award for distinguished service, Kansas State University, 1963; doctor of letters, Assumption College, 1968; Francis Parkman Prize, Society of American Historians, 1973, for FDR: The Beckoning of Destiny, 1882-1928; Guggenheim fellow, 1974, 1976; Achievement award, Kansas Authors Club, 1977.

WRITINGS:

In the Forests of the Night (novel), Houghton, 1942.
Soldier of Democracy: A Biography of Dwight Eisenhower (also see below), Doubleday, 1945, new edition, 1952.
The Years of the Pilgrimage (novel), Doubleday, 1948.
General Eisenhower, Soldier of Democracy: From Boyhood to Supreme Commander (juvenile; based on Soldier of Democracy), Doubleday, 1949.
Morning in Kansas (novel), Doubleday, 1952.
River on the Rampage (nonfiction), Doubleday, 1953.
A Prophet in His Own Country: The Triumphs and Defeats of Adlai E. Stevenson, Doubleday, 1957, expanded and updated edition published as The Politics of Honor: A Biography of Adlai Stevenson, Putnam, 1967.
The Hero: Charles A. Lindbergh and the American Dream, Doubleday, 1959, (published in England as The Hero: Charles A. Lindbergh, the Man and the Legend, Longmans, Green, 1960).
Flight to Glory: The Story of Charles A. Lindbergh and the Spirit of St. Louis (juvenile), Garden City Books, 1960.
(With John A. Day) Water: The Mirror of Science, Anchor Books, 1961.
Experience of War: The United States in World War II, Doubleday, 1965, (published in England as The American Experience of War, 1939-1945, Secker & Warburg, 1967).
The Cautionary Scientists: Priestly, Lavoisier, and the Founding of Modern Chemistry, Putnam, 1966.
(With Luna Bergere Leopold and others) Water, Time-Life Books, 1966, revised edition, 1980.
Eisenhower: American Hero, American Heritage Press, 1969, reprinted, 1984.
(Editor) The Paradox of Poverty in America, H. W. Wilson, 1969.
(Editor) Arms, Industry, and America, H. W. Wilson, 1971.

FDR, Volume 1: The Beckoning of Destiny, 1882-1928, Putnam, 1972, Volume 2: The New York Years, 1928-1933, Random House, 1985, Volume 3: The New Deal Years, 1933-1937, Random House, 1986.
(Author of text) The Eisenhower College Collection: The Paintings of Dwight D. Eisenhower, Nash Publishing, 1973.
Invincible Summer: An Intimate Portrait of the Roosevelts, Atheneum, 1974.
Kansas: A Bicentennial History, Norton, 1976.
(Contributor) A Sense of History: The Best Writing from the Pages of American Heritage, American Heritage/ Houghton, 1985.

Editor, Newberry Library Bulletin, 1955-59.

SIDELIGHTS: Kenneth S. Davis's multivolume history FDR "seems likely to rival, at least, the histories of the New Deal by Arthur M. Schlesinger, Jr., Frank Freidel and James MacGregor Burns," declares New York Times Book Review contributor Irving Howe. In three volumes published over a period of fourteen years, Davis presents a picture of Franklin Delano Roosevelt as "warm kind, zestful, incredibly even-tempered under stress, eager for new experience, interested in everything," states Walter Goodman in the New York Times; but, Goodman adds, "he does not gloss over the great man's weaknesses." "One might presume," remarks Sidney Blumenthal in the Washington Post Book World, "that after the writings of the master historians on FDR—Schlesinger, Freidel, Burns, and Leuchtenberg—the subject would be exhausted. Yet, after all their work, Davis' book is a valuable contribution to the literature." "If not as fluent a writer as Mr. Schlesinger or acute a political theorist as Mr. Burns," Howe concludes, "Mr. Davis surpasses both in the meticulous density of his socioeconomic material."

AVOCATIONAL INTERESTS: Gardening, hiking.

BIOGRAPHICAL/CRITICAL SOURCES:

PERIODICALS

New Republic, March 17, 1986.
New Yorker, December 23, 1985.
New York Review of Books, November 21, 1985.
New York Times, December 13, 1985, September 23, 1986.
New York Times Book Review, January 19, 1986, September 28, 1986.
Washington Post Book World, January 19, 1986, October 26, 1986.

*   *   *

DELANEY, Shelagh 1939-

PERSONAL: First name is pronounced She-la; born November 25, 1939, in Salford, Lancashire, England; daughter of Joseph (a bus inspector) and Elsie Delaney; children: one daughter. Education: Attended Broughton Secondary School.

ADDRESSES: Home— London, England. Agent—Tessa Sayle, 11 Jubilee Place, London, SW3 3TE, England.

CAREER: Writer. Has worked as a salesperson, milk depot clerk, and usherette; former photography assistant, Metro-Vickers, London, England.

AWARDS, HONORS: Charles Henry Foyle New Play Award, 1958, New York Drama Critics Award, 1961, and Arts Council bursary, all for A Taste of Honey; British Film Academy Award, 1961, Robert Flaherty Award, both for screenplay of "A Taste of Honey"; Encyclopedia Britannica award, 1963; Writers Guild

Award for best screenplay, 1968, for "Charlie Bubbles"; Prix Film Jeuness-Etranger, 1985, for "Dance with a Stranger"; Fellow of the Royal Society of Literature, 1985.

WRITINGS:

A Taste of Honey (play; first produced in Stratford, England, at Theatre Royal, May 27, 1958; produced on Broadway at Lyceum Theatre, October 4, 1960; screenplay adaptation, with Tony Richardson, produced by Continental Film Corp., 1962.), Grove, 1959.

The Lion in Love (play; first produced in Coventry, England, at the Belgrade Theatre, September 5, 1960; produced in New York City at One Sheridan Square, April 25, 1963), Grove, 1961.

Sweetly Sings the Donkey (short stories), Putnam, 1963.

"Charlie Bubbles" (screenplay), Memorial Enterprises/Universal Films, 1968.

"Did Your Nanny Come from Bergen?" (television play), British Broadcasting Corp. (BBC-TV), 1970.

"The Raging Moon" (screenplay), Associated British Films, 1970.

"St. Martin's Summer" (television play), London Weekend Television, 1974.

The House That Jack Built (play; first produced as a television series by BBC-TV, 1977; produced Off-Off-Broadway at the Cubiculo Theater, 1979), Duckworth, 1977.

"Find Me First" (television play), BBC-TV, 1979.

"So Does the Nightingale" (radio play), BBC Radio, 1980.

"Don't Worry about Matilda" (radio play), BBC Radio, 1981.

"Rape" (television play), Granada Television, 1981.

Writing Woman, Schocken, 1984.

"Dance with a Stranger" (screenplay), Samuel Goldwyn Co., 1985.

Also author of screenplay, "The White Bus," 1966. Contributor of articles to *New York Times Magazine, Saturday Evening Post, Cosmopolitan,* and *Evergreen Review.*

SIDELIGHTS: In 1958, 18-year-old Shelagh Delaney made her successful debut as a playwright with a work she had written in only two weeks, "A Taste of Honey." Winning the New York Drama Critics Award and, in its film version, a British Film Academy Award, "A Taste of Honey" portrays the seamy side of life in an industrial northern England town. With its realistic setting and characters, use of slang, and inclusion of black and homosexual characters, the play initially caused Delaney to be grouped with other playwrights of the 1950s, like John Osborne, who were known collectively as the "Angry Young Men." Her involvement in anti-nuclear demonstrations with the Committee of 100, which led to her and Osborne's arrest in London's Trafalgar Square on September 17, 1961, reinforced the social protester label. However, as Susan Whitehead points out in a *Dictionary of Literary Biography* entry, Delaney is different from writers like Osborne "because she knew what to be angry about. But anger of any kind is not an emotion which underlies her writing. Instead, Delaney has created characters . . . , who, while struggling against each other, ultimately accept their lives."

The playwright wrote "A Taste of Honey" partly as a reaction to plays like Terence Rattigan's "Variation on a Theme," and partly because she wanted to "write as people talk. . . . I had strong ideas about what I wanted to see in the theater," Delaney says in the *Dictionary of Literary Biography.* The play concerns a mother and daughter who cannot relate to each other, a typical avant guarde theme of alienation. The daughter has an affair with a black sailor and is helped through pregnancy by a young homosexual. "These are people living hand-to-mouth and mak-

ing a bad meal of it," describes Walter Kerr in the *New York Herald Tribune.* But despite the bleak situation, "it is a gutsy play, full of rowdy impertinence and genuinely comic indignation," claims *New York* magazine contributor John Simon. Unlike other plays of the time, the character of Jo in "A Taste of Honey" does not "rail savagely and ineffectually against the others—authority, the Establishment, fate," remarks John Russell Taylor in his book *The Angry Theatre: New British Drama.* Instead, as *Encounter* reviewer Colin MacInnes says, the play "gives a final overwhelming impression of good health—of a feeling for life that is positive, sensible, and generous." Simon concludes that "A Taste of Honey" is "honest rather than stagy, forthright rather than would-be-symbolic—in short, pungently, poignantly, unself-consciously human."

Delaney's next play, "The Lion in Love," was neither commercially nor critically successful. Therefore, remarks Taylor, "a number of commentators were quite ready to write ['A Taste of Honey'] off as a freak success." Whitehead maintains that although "The Lion in Love" is not as strong a play as its predecessor, it "bears witness to Delaney's development as a writer, being more dramatically complex than *A Taste of Honey.*" The story involves an English working class couple named Frank and Kit, who are trapped in an unhappy marriage. Despite being an unhappy story, Edith Oliver comments in the *New Yorker* that "there is more ebullience in it . . . than in many comedies I can think of." Taylor is also encouraged by the increase in scope in "The Lion in Love," remarking that "it has more characters, a more diffuse action, and the central character is now a mature woman, instead of a girl just emerging from childhood," as in "A Taste of Honey."

After her initial success in writing for the stage, Delaney did not write for the theater again until 1979, when she adapted her script for the 1977 BBC television series "The House That Jack Built" for an Off-Off-Broadway production. Her writing during this interim was mostly directed toward television and radio, except for her short story collection *Sweetly Sings the Donkey.* But after she had written several more plays for radio and television, film producer Roger Randall-Cutler asked her in 1985 to write a film script about the real-life story of Ruth Ellis, the last woman in England to be convicted and executed for murder.

Delaney had some misgivings about the project, though. "It wasn't my style," she reflects in an article she wrote for the *New York Times.* "It was too difficult. And it was dangerous. After all, Ruth Ellis was real and hitherto I had only dealt, professionally, at least, with fragments of my imagination." In a review of "Dance with a Stranger," *Washington Post*'s Paul Attanasio notes that the author's reservations about the dangers of this subject were not unfounded. Since the conclusion of the film is inevitable, says Attanasio, "it's not exactly the kind of movie that will have you grabbing onto your armrests." Nevertheless, *New York Times* critic Vincent Canby believes that " 'Dance With a Stranger' is a startling and involving melodrama about the sort of banal crime that obsessed [French filmmaker Francois] Truffaut." And in a later *New York Times* article, Canby explains that "the film is fascinating not because it works in sentimental ways to lead us into some sort of identification with Ruth Ellis," but because the film "successfully locate[s] the humanity of this woman."

It is Delaney's ability to portray the humanity of her characters that adds an important dimension to her realistic approach. "Delaney seems to write from an urge to communicate direct experience rather than from any sociopathic standpoint," comments Whitehead. In the stories in *Sweetly Sings the Donkey,* for example, *Best Sellers* contributor Sister M. Gregory feels that the author's pessimistic viewpoint and realistic style are "mitigated by her respect for the dignity of the human personality, her uncompromising honesty and her wry humor." The author also has a "natural sense of theatre" which Gregory perceives even in the playwright's short stories. Oliver similarly calls Shelagh Delaney "a natural playwright if ever there was one. She is able to give the audience . . . not only a sense of the diversity of the life she depicts but a feeling of being part of it."

BIOGRAPHICAL/CRITICAL SOURCES:

BOOKS

Armstrong, W. A., editor, *Experimental Drama,* G. Bell, 1963.
Contemporary Literary Criticism, Volume 29, Gale, 1984.
Dictionary of Literary Biography, Volume 13: *British Dramatists since World War II,* Gale, 1982.
Taylor, John Russell, *The Angry Theater: New British Drama,* Hill & Wang, 1969.
Welwarth, George, *Theater of Protest and Paradox,* New York University Press, 1964.

PERIODICALS

Best Sellers, September 1, 1963.
Encounter, April, 1959.
New York, May 11, 1981.
New Yorker, May 4, 1963.
New York Herald Tribune, October 10, 1960.
New York Times, August 4, 1985, August 9, 1985, August 18, 1985.
Times (London), September 13, 1960.
Washington Post, August 21, 1985.*

* * *

de la ROCHE, Mazo   1879-1961

PERSONAL: Surname is pronounced day-lah-*rosh;* adopted de la Roche as surname as a child; born January 15, 1879, in Newmarket, Ontario, Canada; died July 12, 1961, in Toronto, Ontario, Canada; daughter of William Richmond (a salesman and a farmer) and Alberta (a carpenter; maiden name, Lundy) Roche; children: (adopted) Rene (son), Esme (Mrs. David Rees). *Education:* Attended University of Toronto and School of Art, Toronto.

ADDRESSES: Home—Windrush Hill, York Mills, Ontario, Canada.

CAREER: Writer.

AWARDS, HONORS: Two Daughters of the British Empire prizes, 1925, for plays; *Atlantic Monthly* prize, 1927, for *Jalna;* Lorne Pierce Medal, Royal Society of Canada, 1938, for distinguished contributions to Canadian literature; University of Alberta National Award in Letters, 1951.

WRITINGS:

"WHITEOAK CHRONICLES" SERIES; NOVELS

Jalna, Little, Brown, 1927.
Whiteoaks of Jalna (also see below), Little, Brown, 1929, published as *Whiteoaks,* Macmillan, 1929, reprinted, Fawcett, 1977.
Finch's Fortune, Little, Brown, 1931.
The Master of Jalna, Little, Brown, 1933, reprinted, Fawcett, 1975.
Young Renny, Little, Brown, 1935.
Whiteoak Harvest, Little, Brown, 1936.

Whiteoak Heritage, Little, Brown, 1940, reprinted, Fawcett, 1974.
Wakefield's Course, Little, Brown, 1941.
The Building of Jalna, Little, Brown, 1944.
Return to Jalna, Little, Brown, 1946, reprinted, Fawcett, 1977.
Mary Wakefield, Little, Brown, 1949, reprinted, 1977.
Renny's Daughter, Little, Brown, 1951, reprinted, Fawcett, 1975.
Whiteoak Brothers: Jalna 1923, Little, Brown, 1953.
Variable Winds at Jalna, Little, Brown, 1954, reprinted, Fawcett, 1975.
Centenary at Jalna, Little, Brown, 1958.
Morning at Jalna, Little, Brown, 1960.

OTHER

Explorers of the Dawn (collection of previously published sketches), Knopf, 1922.
Possession (novel), Macmillan, 1923, reprinted, C. Chivers, 1973.
Low Life: A Comedy in One Act (play; first produced as "Low Life" in Toronto, Ontario, at Trinity Memorial Hall, May 14, 1925; also see below), Macmillan, 1925.
Delight (novel), Macmillan, 1926, reprinted with introduction by Desmond Pacey, McClelland & Stewart, 1961.
Come True (play; first produced in Toronto at Trinity Memorial Hall, May 16, 1927; also see below), Macmillan, 1927.
"The Return of the Emigrant" (play; also see below), first produced in Toronto at Trinity Memorial Hall, March 12, 1928.
Low Life and Other Plays (contains "Low Life," "Come True," and "The Return of the Emigrant"), Little, Brown, 1929.
Portrait of a Dog (novel), Little, Brown, 1930.
Lark Ascending (novel), Little, Brown, 1932.
The Thunder of the New Wings, Little, Brown, 1932.
Beside a Norman Tower, Little, Brown, 1934.
(With Nancy Price) *Whiteoaks: A Play* (adapted from *Whiteoaks of Jalna;* first produced in London, England, at Little Theatre in the Adelphi, April 13, 1936; produced on Broadway, 1938), Macmillan, 1936.
The Very Little House (novel), Little, Brown, 1937.
Growth of a Man (novel), Little, Brown, 1938.
The Sacred Bullock and Other Stories of Animals, Little, Brown, 1939, reprinted, Books for Libraries Press, 1969.
The Two Saplings (novel), Macmillan, 1942.
Quebec: Historic Seaport (nonfiction), Doubleday, 1944.
"Mistress of Jalna," first produced in Bromley, Kent, England, at New Theatre, November 12, 1951.
A Boy in the House, and Other Stories, Little, Brown, 1952.
The Song of Lambert (juvenile), Macmillan, 1955, Little, Brown, 1956.
Ringing the Changes: An Autobiography, Little, Brown, 1957.
Bill and Coo (juvenile), Macmillan, 1958, Little, Brown, 1959.
(Author of introduction) George F. Nelson, editor, *Northern Lights: A New Collection of Distinguished Writing by Canadian Authors,* Doubleday, 1960.
Selected Stories of Mazo de la Roche, edited and introduced by Douglas Daymond, University of Ottawa Press, 1979.

Contributor of short stories to U.S. and Canadian magazines.

SIDELIGHTS: Mazo de la Roche wrote a variety of novels, short stories, and plays, but her masterwork is the "Whiteoak Chronicles" series which during her lifetime sold more than eleven million copies in one hundred ninety-three English and ninety-two foreign editions. The series follows several generations of the Whiteoak family and evolves around a lakeside Ontario estate named "Jalna." The household is comprised of Adeline Whiteoak, Adeline's son, the pragmatic children from his first marriage who manage Jalna, and the artistic and temperamental children from his second marriage. Adeline's husband, an officer in the English-Indian Army, rarely appears in the narrative. The matriarch of the Whiteoak family lives to celebrate her one hundredth birthday, and, following her death, is succeeded by her equally spirited grandson, Renny.

The popular series was praised for its exceptional characterizations and, at the same time, criticized for focusing on what George Hendrick referred to in *Mazo de la Roche* as a "hermetically sealed world," far removed from reality. Noting the appeal of de la Roche's work to thousands of loyal readers, Hendrick observed that despite such criticism de la Roche's "audience was one that admired ornate style. Her readers were obviously entertained by [*Jalna*'s] appeal to snobbery, its romanticism, its erotic scenes, and its titillating incidents. All of these help to explain the popularity of *Jalna* and the novels which followed it."

Other critics, including Jo-Ann Fellows and Douglas M. Daymond, saw de la Roche's work as a significant part of Canadian culture and literature. In the *Dalhousie Review,* for example, Fellows commented: "The Jalna novels describe obliquely some very basic ideas of the Canadian national identity, at least of the English-speaking identity. Leaving aside consideration of the novels as literature, they provide a most interesting source for the student of social and intellectual history." *Dictionary of Literary Biography* contributor Daymond concluded: "Although Mazo de la Roche's work does not rank among the most important Canadian fiction, her achievement and her contribution to Canadian literature are considerable. At a time when Canadian writing was dominated by historical fiction and sentimental stories of village and rural life, she challenged prevailing fashions with novels such as *Possession* and *Delight,* and despite the many romantic elements in her work she added to the development of realism in the Canadian novel."

BIOGRAPHICAL/CRITICAL SOURCES:

BOOKS

de la Roche, Mazo, *Ringing the Changes: An Autobiography,* Little, Brown, 1957.
Dictionary of Literary Biography, Volume 68: *Canadian Writers, 1920-1959, First Series,* 1988.
Hendrick, George, *Mazo de la Roche,* Twayne, 1970.

PERIODICALS

Dalhousie Review, summer, 1976.

OBITUARIES:

PERIODICALS

Newsweek, July 24, 1961.
New York Times, July 13, 1961.
Publishers Weekly, July 24, 1961.
Time, July 21, 1961.
Times (London), July 13, 1961.*

* * *

DELINSKY, Barbara (Ruth Greenberg) 1945-
(Billie Douglass, Bonnie Drake)

PERSONAL: Born August 9, 1945, in Boston, Mass.; daughter of David H. (a lawyer) and Edith (Finn) Greenberg; married Stephen R. Delinsky (a lawyer), August 20, 1967; children: Eric,

Andrew and Jeremy (twins). *Education:* Tufts University, B.A., 1967; Boston College, M.A., 1969.

ADDRESSES: Home—Needham, Mass.

CAREER: Children's Protective Services, Boston, Mass., sociological researcher, 1968-69; Dover-Sherborn School System, Dover, Mass., instructor in photography, 1978-82; writer. Member of board of directors, Beth Israel Hospital Women's Auxiliary, 1976-82, and Friends of the Massachusetts General Hospital Cancer Center, 1986—.

MEMBER: Authors Guild, Authors League of America, Romance Writers of America.

AWARDS, HONORS: Best Contemporary Romance of 1984, *Romantic Times,* for *Finger Prints;* Best-Selling Harlequin Temptation of 1984, Waldenbooks, for *A Special Something;* Golden Leaf Award, New Jersey Chapter of Romance Writers of America, and Golden Medallion, Romance Writers of America, both 1987, both for *Twilight Whispers;* Reviewer's Choice Award, *Romantic Times,* 1987, for *Cardinal Rules;* Special Achievement Award for Best Contemporary Novel, *Romantic Times,* 1988, for *Commitments.*

WRITINGS:

"TEMPTATION" ROMANCE NOVELS

A Special Something, Harlequin, 1984.
Bronze Mystique, Harlequin, 1984.
The Forever Instinct, Harlequin, 1985.
Secret of the Stone, Harlequin, 1985.
Chances Are, Harlequin, 1985.
First Things First, Harlequin, 1985.
Straight from the Heart, Harlequin, 1986.
First, Best and Only, Harlequin, 1986.
Jasmine Sorcery, Harlequin, 1986.
The Real Thing, Harlequin, 1986.
Twelve Across, Harlequin, 1987.
A Single Rose, Harlequin, 1987.
Cardinal Rules, Harlequin, 1987.
Heat Wave, Harlequin, 1987.
TLC, Harlequin, 1988.
Fulfillment, Harlequin, 1988.
Through My Eyes, Harlequin, 1989.
Montana Man, Harlequin, 1989.
Having Faith, Harlequin, 1990.
Cross My Heart, Harlequin, 1990.

"CANDLELIGHT ECSTASY" ROMANCE NOVELS; UNDER PSEUDONYM BONNIE DRAKE

The Passionate Touch, Dell, 1981.
Surrender by Moonlight, Dell, 1981.
Sweet Ember, Dell, 1981.
Sensuous Burgundy, Dell, 1981.
The Ardent Protector, Dell, 1982.
Whispered Promise, Dell, 1982.
Lilac Awakening, Dell, 1982.
Amber Enchantment, Dell, 1982.
Lover from the Sea, Dell, 1983.
The Silver Fox, Dell, 1983.
Passion and Illusion, Dell, 1983.
Gemstone, Dell, 1983.
Moment to Moment, Dell, 1984.

"SPECIAL EDITION" ROMANCE NOVELS; UNDER PSEUDONYM BILLIE DOUGLASS

Search for a New Dawn, Silhouette, 1982.

A Time to Love, Silhouette, 1982.
Knightly Love, Silhouette, 1982.
Fast Courting, Silhouette, 1983.
An Irresistible Impulse, Silhouette, 1983.
The Carpenter's Lady, Silhouette, 1983.

OTHER

(Contributor) Sylvia K. Burack, editor, *Writing and Selling the Romance Novel,* The Writer, 1983.
(Contributor) Kathryn Falk, editor, *How to Write a Romance and Get It Published: With Intimate Advice from the World's Most Popular Romance Writers,* Crown, 1983.
(Under pseudonym Billie Douglass) *Sweet Serenity,* Silhouette, 1983.
(Under pseudonym Billie Douglass) *Flip Side of Yesterday,* Silhouette, 1983.
(Under pseudonym Billie Douglass) *Beyond Fantasy,* Silhouette, 1983.
Finger Prints, Worldwide Library, 1984.
(Under pseudonym Billie Douglass) *Variation on a Theme,* Silhouette, 1985.
Within Reach, Worldwide Library, 1986.
Threats and Promises ("Intrigue" romance novel), Harlequin, 1986.
Twilight Whispers, Warner Books, 1987.
Commitments, Warner Books, 1988.
Heart of the Night, Warner Books, 1989.

SIDELIGHTS: Barbara Delinsky told *CA:* "Above and beyond the ability to put words to paper, the writing of romance requires a love of romance. When I first discovered the romantic novel I felt as if I'd come home, as though there were indeed others in the world who loved love and beauty and idealism as I did. I try to express these sentiments in my books and in doing so I find myself inextricably involved with my plot, my setting, and, most critically, my characters. Writing has come to me to be a form of self-expression, a digging into roots, a sharing of and elaboration on so many of the wonderful experiences in life I've been privileged to have. I believe that a writer, of whatever genre, cannot possibly be successful without this kind of intense personal involvement.

"During the past few years, as the genre of romance has come out of the closet, there are many who have eyed the writers of romance as people who 'churn out' books for the sake of the dollar bill alone. Impossible! Such writers never make it out of the slush pile, for their works inevitably reflect their baser motivations. Those of us who have been fortunate enough to find a place in the genre *work hard.* We don't 'churn out' books; rather, we discipline ourselves to work every day, pushing our minds to their limits, finding creative niches within that we never dreamed we possessed. We agonize over the dilemmas of our characters, and struggle to put into words emotions that, far too often in an age of computerization, are either taken for granted or simply ignored. In turn, we are rewarded with feelings of accomplishment and self-satisfaction. Never, never can a price tag be put on such feelings."

BIOGRAPHICAL/CRITICAL SOURCES:

BOOKS

Falk, Kathryn, editor, *Love's Leading Ladies,* Pinnacle Books, 1982.

de MILLE, Agnes
See PRUDE, Agnes George de Mille

*   *   *

DENGLER, Sandy 1939-

PERSONAL: Born June 8, 1939, in Newark, Ohio; daughter of Walter Stecker and Alyce (Kabrhel) Hance; married William F. Dengler (a National Park Service ranger), January 11, 1963; children: Alyce Ann, Mary Margaret. *Education:* Bowling Green State University, B.S., 1961; Arizona State University, M.S., 1967. *Religion:* "Non-sectarian Christian."

ADDRESSES: *Home*—Ashford, Wash. *Office*—Tahoma Woods, Star Route, Ashford, Wash. 98304.

CAREER: Writer, 1972—. Volunteer worker at Death Valley, Grand Canyon, Saguaro National Monument, Acadia National Park, Joshua Tree National Monument, Yosemite National Park, and Mount Rainier National Park, 1965—; in charge of horses at children's summer camp, 1975-80; first aid instructor for American Red Cross.

WRITINGS:

Getting Into the Bible, Moody, 1979.
Beasts of the Field (puzzle book), Moody, 1979.
Birds of the Air (puzzle book), Moody, 1979.
Summer of the Wild Pig (juvenile novel), Moody, 1979.
Yosemite's Marvelous Creatures, Flying Spur Press, 1980.
The Horse Who Loved Picnics (juvenile novel), Moody, 1980.
Melon Hound (juvenile novel), Moody, 1980.
Arizona Longhorn Adventure (juvenile novel), Moody, 1980.
Rescue in the Desert (juvenile novel), Moody, 1981.
Man and Beast Together (puzzle book), Moody, 1982.
Mystery at McGeehan Ranch (juvenile novel), Moody, 1982.
Socorro Island Treasure (juvenile novel), Moody, 1983.
Chain Five Mystery (juvenile novel), Moody, 1984.
Song of the Nereids (romance novel), Zondervan, 1984.
Summer Snow (romance novel), Zondervan, 1984.
Fanny Crosby (fictional biography), Moody, 1985.
Winterspring (romance novel), Zondervan, 1985.
John Bunyan (fictional biography), Moody, 1986.
Opal Fire (romance novel), Zondervan, 1986.
This Rolling Land (romance novel), Zondervan, 1986.
To Die in the Queen of Cities (historical novel), Thomas Nelson, 1986.
D. L. Moody (fictional biography), Moody, 1987.
Susanna Wesley (fictional biography), Moody, 1987.
Jungle Gold (adventure), Zondervan, 1987.
Florence Nightingale (fictional biography), Moody, 1988.
Code of Honor (historical novel), Bethany House, 1988.
Power of Pinjarra (historical novel), Bethany House, 1989.

WORK IN PROGRESS: Nonfiction on symbolism; a series of historical sagas set in Australia.

SIDELIGHTS: Sandy Dengler told *CA:* "The apostle Paul adjured his assistant, Timothy, to preach the word in season. Christian mainstream books (how-to books, exegesis, inspirational works, and so on) preach in season. Christian romances and historical romances preach out of season, in a new direction. They are for readers who want good reading but would never crack open a 'religious' book. 'Light reading' shapes the reader's attitude just as surely as does 'heavy reading,' and I feel as great a responsibility for excellence in romance novels as I feel for weighty tomes on creationism and evolution.

"The contemporary scene changes from moment to moment; a historical setting is frozen in place. Perhaps that's why I enjoy writing historical fiction (my children's novels and romance novels are all historical). Once I research a pretty good vision of a particular frozen moment, the moment itself suggests plot and situations. It shapes the characters. It seems more colorful and exciting than today's world (a curious thing, for the good old days weren't good in most respects). If it is presented well, that distant moment sharpens our perceptions of the present and shows us flaws in our attitudes—and some strong points as well.

"It is always easiest to write about a setting you know intimately. That makes the National Park Service a wonderful place to be, for I move every few years. If I haven't been somewhere I have friends who have, and friends' libraries are a trove of research information."

* * *

DENVER, Rod
See EDSON, J(ohn) T(homas)

* * *

DENZIN, Norman K(ent) 1941-

PERSONAL: Born March 24, 1941, in Iowa City, Iowa; son of Kenneth F. (a foreman) and Betty (Townsley) Denzin; married second wife, Katherine Ryan; children: Johanna, Rachel, Nathan Stevens. *Education:* University of Iowa, A.B., 1963, Ph.D., 1966.

ADDRESSES: Home—607 South New St., Champaign, Ill. 61820. *Office*—Department of Sociology, University of Illinois, Urbana, Ill. 61801.

CAREER: University of Illinois at Urbana-Champaign, assistant professor of sociology, 1966-69; University of California, Berkeley, assistant professor of sociology, 1969-71; University of Illinois at Urbana-Champaign, associate professor, 1971-73, professor of sociology, 1973-80, professor of criticism, interpretive theory, communication, and sociology, 1981—. Consulting sociologist, Federal Offenders Rehabilitation Project, Seattle, Wash., 1967-68. Referee on grant applications, National Foundation on the Arts and Humanities, 1970.

MEMBER: International Sociological Association (secretary-treasurer of social psychology section, 1978-80), American Anthropological Association, American Psychological Association, American Association for Public Opinion Research, Society for the Study of Symbolic Interaction (vice president, 1975-76), Society for the Sociological Study of Social Problems, Society for the Psychological Study of Social Issues, Society for the Study of Applied Anthropology, Pacific Sociological Society, Midwest Sociological Society (president, 1988-89).

WRITINGS:

(Editor and contributor with Stephen P. Spitzer) *The Mental Patient: Studies in the Sociology of Deviance,* McGraw, 1968.
The Research Act: A Theoretical Introduction to Sociological Methods, Aldine, 1970, 3rd edition, Prentice-Hall, 1989.
(Contributor) Eliot Freidson and Janet Lobeser, editors, *Medical Men and Their Work,* Atherton, 1970.
(Contributor) Anthony L. Guenther, editor, *Criminal Behavior and Social Systems: Contributions of American Society,* Rand McNally, 1970.
(Editor and contributor) *Sociological Methods: A Sourcebook,* Aldine, 1970, 2nd edition, McGraw, 1977.

(Editor and contributor) *The Values of Social Science,* Aldine, 1970, 2nd edition, Dutton, 1973.
(With others) *Social Relationships,* Aldine, 1970.
(Contributor) Gregory P. Stone and Harvey A. Farberman, editors, *Social Psychology through Symbolic Interaction,* Ginn-Blaisdell, 1970.
(Contributor) Jack D. Douglas, editor, *Understanding Everyday Life,* Aldine, 1970.
(Contributor) Douglas, editor, *Situations and Structures: Introduction to Sociology,* Free Press, 1970.
(Editor) *Children and Their Caretakers,* Dutton, 1973.
(With Alfred R. Lindesmith and A. R. Strauss) *Social Psychology,* 4th edition (Denzin was not associated with previous editions), Dryden, 1975, 6th edition, Prentice-Hall, 1988.
(With Lindesmith and Strauss) *Readings in Social Psychology,* 2nd edition (Denzin was not associated with previous edition), Holt, 1975.
Childhood Socialization, Jossey-Bass, 1977.
(Editor) *Studies in Symbolic Interaction: A Research Annual,* eleven volumes, Jai Press, 1978-89.
On Understanding Emotion, Jossey-Bass, 1984.
The Alcoholic Self, Sage, 1987.
The Recovering Alcoholic, Sage, 1987.
Treating Alcoholism, Sage, 1987.
Interpretive Interactionism, Sage, 1989.
Doing Biography, Sage, 1989.

Contributor to numerous journals, including *Social Forces, Journal of Health and Social Behavior, Mental Hygiene, Sociological Quarterly, Social Problems, American Sociological Review, American Sociologist, American Journal of Sociology, Word, Quest,* and *Slavic Review.* Special issue editor, *Trans-action,* June-July, 1971; associate editor of *Sociological Quarterly,* 1972-82, *Urban Life,* 1972—, and *Contemporary Sociology,* 1978-81; editorial referee, *American Journal of Sociology.*

WORK IN PROGRESS: Postmodern Social Theory; Symbolic Interactionism; Film and the American Alcoholic; developing the conceptual and empirical foundations of a critical, interpretive point of view in the human disciplines.

SIDELIGHTS: Norman K. Denzin told *CA:* "[My] basic position is that human conduct can only be understood by grasping the historical perspectives, languages and points of view of those we study. Instrumental works have been by G. H. Mead, C. H. Cooley, H. Blumer, C. Peirce, W. James, J. Dewey, A. Smith, E. Husserl, M. Scheler, S. Freud, Karl Marx, Martin Heidegger, Jean-Paul Sartre, and Merlea-Ponty. [The] basic question guiding my work is 'How is meaning constructed and lived in the lives of ordinary people and how may we, as interpretive scholars, ground our understandings in the spoken prose of the people we study?' "

* * *

DiGIACOMO, James J(oseph) 1924-

PERSONAL: Born November 22, 1924, in Brooklyn, N.Y.; son of Philip (a construction foreman) and Catherine Margaret (in insurance sales; maiden name, Gargiula) DiGiacomo. *Education:* Woodstock College, Woodstock, Md., Ph.L., 1950, M.A., 1952, S.T.L., 1957; International School of Religious Formation, Brussels, Belgium, Diplome de Lumen Vitae, 1965.

ADDRESSES: Home—America House, 106 West 56th St., New York, N.Y. 10019. *Office*—Regis High School, 55 East 84th St., New York, N.Y. 10028.

CAREER: Entered Society of Jesus (Jesuits), 1943, ordained Roman Catholic priest, 1956; teacher of Latin, Greek, English, and religion at Roman Catholic high schools in Washington, D.C., 1950-53; teacher of religious studies at Roman Catholic preparatory schools in New York City, 1958-77, department chairman, 1970-77; Regis High School, New York City, teacher of theology, 1977—. Fordham University, member of board of trustees, 1981—, assistant adjunct professor. Member of faculty at University of St. Thomas, Houston, Tex.; summer lecturer at University of Notre Dame, Boston College, Loyola University, and University of Detroit. Lecturer in Australia, New Zealand, Germany, and Canada. Member of Commission on Religious Education.

MEMBER: Religious Education Association, Jesuit Secondary Education Association (member of commission of religious education, 1970-88).

WRITINGS:

Conscience and Authority, Holt, 1969.
Violence, Holt, 1969.
Race, Holt, 1969.
Church Involvement, Holt, 1969.
Faith, Holt, 1969.
Sexuality, Holt, 1969.
See You in Church, Holt, 1970.
Meaning, Holt, 1970.
(With Edward Wakin) *We Were Never Their Age,* Holt, 1971.
Would You Believe . . . ?, Holt, 1971.
Jesus Who?, Winston Press, 1973.
(With John Walsh) *The Longest Step: Searching for God,* Winston Press, 1977.
(With Walsh) *Meet the Lord: Encounters With Jesus,* Winston Press, 1977.
(With Walsh) *Going Together: The Church of Christ,* Winston Press, 1978.
(With Thomas Shannon) *An Introduction to Bioethics,* Paulist Press, 1979.
When Your Teenager Stops Going to Church, Abbey Press, 1980.
(With Wakin) *Understanding Teenagers,* Argus Communications, 1983.
(With Walsh) *So You Want to Do Ministry,* Sheed & Ward, 1986.
Facing the Hard Questions, Franciscan Communication, in press.

TAPE RECORDINGS AND VIDEO CASSETTES

"The Bible and the Real Teenage World," Argus Communications, 1966.
"The Christian Understanding of Man," Argus Communications, 1968.
"The Child's World," Argus Communications, 1968.
"Whaddayameangoodnews?," Ave Maria Press, 1971.
"The Value Revolution," Creative Sights and Sounds, 1971.
"Teaching Jesus," Creative Sights and Sounds, 1972.
"The Art of Being," NCR Cassettes, 1973.
"Person in Process," NCR Cassettes, 1973.
"Dialogue on Becoming a Person," NCR Cassettes, 1973.
"How Solid Is Solid Doctrine?," Creative Sights and Sounds, 1973.
"Civil Religion: The American Idolatry," NCR Cassettes, 1974.
"What Comes Before Education," NCR Cassettes, 1976.
"Problems of Liberty and Justice for Youth," NCR Cassettes, 1976.
"It's Only Good News If They Hear It," NCR Cassettes, 1978.
(With Walsh) "Coming to Faith: Dynamics of Evangelization," NCR Cassettes, 1978.

"Just Follow Your Conscience," Time Associates, 1979.
"God Is Not a Blue Elephant," St. Paul Catholic Education Center, 1979.
"Assisting Growth in Faith," NCR Cassettes, 1980.
"Role of Youth in the Family," NCR Cassettes, 1980.
"Junior High Catechesis," San Francisco Archdiocesan Cassettes, 1981.
"Back to Real Basics," San Francisco Archdiocesan Cassettes, 1981.
"Turning Out the Next New Breed," NCEA Cassettes, 1981.
"Moral Maturity and Growth in Faith," NCEA Cassettes, 1981.
"Understanding Teenagers: A Video Experience for Parents," Argus Communications, 1983.
"The Faith of the Next Generation," National Pastoral Life Committee, 1987.
"The Detrivialization of Sex," NCEA Cassettes, 1988. ·
"Teaching Religion in Catholic High School," NCEA Cassettes, 1989.

OTHER

Contributor of over fifty articles to numerous magazines, including *Youth Update, Modern Liturgy, America, Marriage and Family Living, New Catholic World,* and *Family Digest.*

SIDELIGHTS: James J. DiGiacomo wrote *CA:* "My main audiences are those concerned with the religious and moral development of adolescents—youth ministers, parents, teachers, and young people themselves. For almost thirty years I have been in day-to-day contact with teenagers. Keeping up with the changing scene is a challenge. I started teaching high schoolers when Truman was president. I worked with youngsters in the quiet fifties, the explosive sixties, the laid-back seventies, and the mellow eighties.

"In some ways kids are always the same, but they are also different in significant, often dramatic ways. They are always trying to find themselves in the search for identity that is youth's main task. But the search takes different forms in different eras, as they grow up in times of comparative stability or upheaval. Their attitudes toward authority may be predominantly submissive or rebellious; they may identify with adult values or reject them; they may reject religious institutions and concerns or be open to the mystery at the heart of human life. To keep up with them, to help them, and to provide guidance and encouragement for the adults who love them has become my life's work.

"In young people today, a remarkable receptivity to religion and religious experience is combined with apathy and even alienation from institutional religion. Their yearning for ideals is mocked by a pervasive relativism that leaves them morally adrift, vulnerable to the ideological quick-fix offered by cults and fundamentalist groups. Most will probably settle for consumerism in the plastic paradise, but many yearn for something more to do with their lives than devote them to earning and owning and conspicuously consuming.

"Authentic Christianity holds out the highest ideals, the fulfillment of their noblest aspirations, but the churches are uncertain trumpets that play weak tunes or false notes. In my writings, as in my teaching, I try not to lay out the paths they should take, but to challenge them with the Christian vision of a meaningful life and invite them to make that vision their own. As a Roman Catholic priest, I speak from within a church that is often perceived as repressive and authoritarian, the enemy of freedom and self-determination. I believe that at our best we are better than that, and I invite the young to help us realize our best collective self—a people faithful to a rich tradition, attentive to authority properly exercised, respectful of the rights of individual conscience, and obedient to the larger truth that makes claims on us all.

"It is not just the young who need to hear such a call. Their parents, ministers, and teachers need help to live up to the sublime vocation of guides on the way to the kingdom of God. I try to explain young people to them to help them hear, under their growing children's noise and even more threatening silence, the cry for a fuller life. I believe that God holds out such a life in the person of Jesus Christ, and whether I write of God or church or youth or freedom or sex or faith or war or peace or many other concerns, my aim is to help both young and old hear and respond to that call."

*   *   *

DOGAN, Mattei   1920-

PERSONAL: Born October 16, 1920, in Rumania; son of Ian and Giselle Dogan. *Education:* Sorbonne, University of Paris, 1946-50, Docteur es Lettres, Diplome de l'Institut d'Etudes Politiques, Diplome d'Etudes Superieures de Philosophie, Diplome d'Etudes Superieures d'Histoire.

ADDRESSES: Home—72 Blvd. Arago, Paris 13, France. *Office*—Centre National de la Recherche Scientifique, Paris, France.

CAREER: French sociologist and political scientist. Centre National de la Recherche Scientifique, Paris, France, research associate, 1952-55, master of research, 1955-63, deputy director of research, 1963-64, director of research, 1969—. Director, Bureau d'Analyses Sociologiques Europeenes, Paris, 1970-78; adjunct professor of political science, University of California, Los Angeles, 1973—. Member of committee for social and economic development, Delegation Generale a la Recherche Scientifique et Technique, 1966-69. Visiting professor at University of Trento, Italy, 1967, Indiana University, 1971, Yale University, 1972, Institute of Statistical Mathematics, Tokyo, 1975, and University of Florence, 1987; organizer of several international scientific conferences.

MEMBER: International Sociological Association (president of social ecology committee, 1970-1986, president, comparative sociology committee, 1986—), International Political Science Association (chairman of committee on political elites, 1971—), International Social Science Council (member of standing committee on social science data archives, 1966—), French Sociological Association, French Political Science Association (member of executive council, 1970-78), French National Committee of Scientific Research, Centre d'Etudes Sociologiques (member of executive board, 1964-68).

AWARDS, HONORS: Silver Medal of National Center of Scientific Research, 1966; award of Academie des Sciences Morales et Politiques.

WRITINGS:

(With Jacques Narbonne) *Les Francaises face a la politique,* Colin (Paris), 1956.
(Contributor) Institut de Sociologie Solvay, *La Condition sociale de la femme,* Bruxelles, 1956.
Partiti Politici e Strutture Sociali in Italia, Editore Communita (Milan), 1968.
(With S. Rokkan) *Quantitative Ecological Analyses in the Social Sciences,* MIT Press, 1969, published as *Social Ecology,* 1974.
(With R. Rose) *European Politics,* Little, Brown, 1971.

The Mandarins of Western Europe, Halsted, 1975.
(Co-author) *Report on German Universities,* International Council on the Future of the University, 1977.
La comparaison internationale en sociologie politique, Litec (Paris), 1980.
Sociologie politique comparative, Economica (Paris), 1981.
(Contributor) *Science et theorie de l'opinion publique,* Retz (Paris), 1981.
(Contributor) *Liber amicorum leo moulin,* Lemaire (Brussels), 1982.
(With D. Pelassy) *How to Compare Nations,* Chatham House, 1983.
(Contributor) Myron Weiner and Ergun Ozbudun, editors, *Competitive Elections in Developing Countries,* American Enterprise Institute, 1983.
(Contributor) Ali Kazancigl and Ozbudun, editors, *Ataturk, Fondateur d'un etat moderne,* Masson, 1983.
Le Moloch en Europe: Etatisation et Corporatisation, Economica, 1987.
(With D. Kasarda) *A World of Giant Cities,* Sage, 1988.
Mega-Cities, Sage, 1988.
Comparing Pluralist Democracies: Strains on Legitimacy, Westview Press, 1988.
Pathways to Power: Selecting Rulers in Plurarlist Democracies, Westview Press, 1988.
Le Mandarinat politique dans les democraties avancees, Economica, 1988.

Contributor to more than twenty books on comparative political science in Europe. Contributor of more than sixty essays and articles published in French, English, Italian, Spanish, Chinese, Japanese, German, and Arabic academic journals. Member of editorial review board of *Revue Francaise de Sociologie,* 1965-71, *Affari Sociali Internazionali,* 1973-78, *Comparative Political Studies,* 1971—, *Journal of European Integration,* 1980-86, and *Studies in Comparative International Development,* 1988—.

WORK IN PROGRESS: Democracies in Western Europe; Political Leadership.

SIDELIGHTS: In addition to writing, political scientist Mattei Dogan told *CA* he enjoys "the gift of ubiquity and the capacity of commuting between Paris and Los Angeles every year." *Sociologie politique comparative* was translated into Japanese.

*   *   *

DOGYEAR, Drew
See GOREY, Edward (St. John)

*   *   *

DORST, Tankred   1925-

PERSONAL: Born December 19, 1925, in Sonneberg, Germany (now East Germany); son of Max (an engineer) and Elisabeth (Lettermann) Dorst. *Education:* Studied drama and history at University of Munich, 1952-56.

ADDRESSES: Home—Schleissheimerstrasse 218, D-8000 Munich 40, West Germany.

CAREER: Author, playwright, and director. Lecturer in United States, 1970, and other countries.

MEMBER: German PEN Centre, Deutsche Akademie fuer Sprache und Dichtung, Deutsche Akademie der darstellenden Kuenste, Bayerische Akademie der schoenen Kuenste, Akademie der Wissenschaften und der Kuenste (Mainz), Akademie der schoenen Kuenste (Munich).

AWARDS, HONORS: Prize of National Theater of Mannheim, 1960; State of Munich Prize, 1964; Gerhart Hauptmann Prize, 1964 (Berlin); Literaturpreis der bayerischen Akademie der schoenen Kuenste (Munich).

WRITINGS:

Das Geheimnis der Marionette (title means "Secret of the Marionettes"), foreword by Marcel Marceau, H. Rinn, 1957.
Die Kurve (play; also see below; first produced in Germany, 1960), Kiepenheuer & Witsch, 1960, translation published as *Curve* in *New Theatre of Europe*, Volume 3, edited by Robert W. Corrigan, Dell, 1968.
Grosse Schmaehrede an der Stadtmauer: mit einem Essay des Autors (play; also see below; first produced in Luebeck, West Germany, 1962), Kiepenheuer & Witsch, 1962, reprinted, Philipp Reclam, 1981.
Grosse Schmaehrede an der Stadtmauer [and] *Freiheit fuer Clemens* [and] *Die Kurve* (three plays), Kiepenheuer & Witsch, 1962.
(Adapter) Ludwig Tiek, *Der gestiefelte Kater; oder, wie man das Spiel spielt* (play; also see below; title means "The Cat in Boots; or, How One Plays the Game"; first produced in Hamburg, 1963), Kiepenheuer & Witsch, 1963.
(Translator and adaptor) Denis Diderot, *Rameaus Neffe* (play; also see below; title means "Rameaus Nephew"; first produced in Nuernberg, 1968), Kiepenheuer & Witsch, 1963.
"Die Mohrin" (play; also see below), first produced in Frankfurt, West Germany, 1964.
Yolimba (libretto of musical farce; first produced in Wiesbaden, West Germany, 1965), music by Wilhelm Killmayer, Schott Music Corp., 1965.
(Editor) *Die Muenchner Raeterepublik: Zeugnisse und Kommentar* (history; title means "The Munich Republic: Reports and Commentary"), Suhrkamp, 1966.
Die mehreren Zauberer (juvenile stories; title means "Several Magicians"), Kiepenheuer & Witsch, 1966.
(Translator) Jean-Baptiste Moliere, "Der Geizige" (title means "The Miser"; translation of *L'Avare*), first produced in Stuttgart, West Germany, 1967.
Toller (play; also see below; first produced in Stuttgart, West Germany), Suhrkamp, 1968.
(And director with Peter Zadek) "Rotmord; oder, I was a German" (television screenplay adaptation of Dort's *Toller*), produced in West Germany, 1968.
"Piggies" (television screenplay), produced in Germany, 1969.
(Translator) Moliere, "Der eingebildete Kranke" (translation of *Le Malade imaginaire*), frist produced in Kassel, West Germany, 1969.
Sand (television screenplay), Kiepenheuer & Witsch, 1971.
(Adapter) *Kleiner Mann, was nun?* (play; title means "Little Man, What Now?"; adapted from the novel by H. Fellada; first produced in Bochum, West Germany, 1972), Suhrkamp, 1972.
Eiszeit (play; title means "Ice Age"; first produced in Bochun and Hamburg, 1973), Suhrkamp, 1973.
(With Ursula Ehler) *Auf dem Chimborazo: eine Komoedie* (play; also see below; first produced in Berlin, 1975, translation produced as "On Mount Chimborazo" in New York City at the Brooklyn Academy of Music, 1979), Suhrkamp, 1975.
(With Ehler) *Dorothea Merz* (also see below), Suhrkamp, 1976.
Stuecke (title means "Plays"), two volumes, Suhrkamp, 1978.

(With Ehler) *Klaras Mutter* (title means "Klara's Mother"; also see below), Suhrkamp, 1978.
(With Ehler) *Die Villa* (title means "The Villa"; also see below), Suhrkamp, 1979.
Mosch: ein Film (title means "Mosch: A Film"; also see below), Suhrkamp, 1980.
(With Ehler) *Merlin; oder, das wueste Land* (title means "Merlin; or, the Wasteland"), Suhrkamp, 1981.
(With Ehler) *Eisenhans: Ein Szenarium,* Prometh (Cologne), 1982.
(With Ehler) "Aureley, der Bieber und der Koenig auf dem Dach" (juvenile play), first produced in Vienna, Austria, at the Burgtheater, 1982.
(With Ehler) *Der verbotene Garten: Fragmente ueber "d'Annunzio,"* (title means "The Forbidden Garden: Fragments about 'd'Annunzio' "), Hauser (Munich), 1983.
(With Ehler) *Die Reise nach Stettin* (novel; title means "The Trip to Stettin"), Suhrkamp, 1984.
(With Ehler) *Der nackte Mann* (title means "The Naked Man"), Suhrkamp, 1985.
(With Ehler) *Deutsche Stuecke* (title means "German Plays"; contains *Dorothea Merz, Klaras Mutter, Heinrich; oder, die Schmerzen der Phantasie, die Villa, Mosch: ein Film,* and *Auf dem Chimborazo: eine Komoedie*), Suhrkamp, 1985.
Fruehe Stuecke (title means "Early Plays"; contains *Der Kater; oder, wie man das Spiel spielt, Gesellschaft im Herbst, Die Kurve, Grosse Schmachrede an der Stadtmauer, Rameaus Neffe, Die Mohrin,* and *Der Richter von London*), Suhrkamp, 1986.
(With Ehler) *Ich, Feuerbach* (title means "I, Feuerbach"), Suhrkamp, 1986.
(With Ehler), *Korbes: Ein Drama,* illustrated by Johannes Gruetzke, Insel Verlag, 1988.

Also author of play "George Daudin," first produced in Bad Hersfeld, West Germany.*

* * *

DOTTS, Maryann J. 1933-

PERSONAL: Born November 11, 1933, in Pittsburgh, Pa.; daughter of Charles A. and Mary J. (Dryer) Dreese; married M. Franklin Dotts (an editor), August 9, 1958 (divorced, 1982); children: Ruthann C. *Education:* National College, Kansas City, Mo., A.B., 1956; Scarritt College for Christian Workers, M.A., 1974; George Peabody College for Teachers (now of Vanderbilt University), M.L.S., 1975. *Religion:* United Methodist.

ADDRESSES: Home—4118 Coronado Pkwy., Cape Coral, Fla. 33904.

CAREER: Director of Christian education at United Methodist churches in Erie, Pa., 1956-58, and Arlington Heights, Ill., 1958-61; Riverside Church, New York, N.Y., teacher and supervisor, 1965-67; Upper Room Library and Museum, Board of Discipleship, Nashville, Tenn., librarian and cataloguer, 1975; Belle Meade United Methodist Church, Nashville, director of Christian education, 1976-79; Andrew Price Memorial United Methodist Church, Nashville, director of Christian education, 1980-84; Mulberry Street United Methodist Church, Macon, Ga., director of Christian education, 1984-85; First United Methodist Church, Cape Coral, Fla., director of Christian education, 1985—.

MEMBER: Church and Synagogue Library Association (member of board of directors, 1976-77; president, 1978-79), Christian Educators Fellowship, Florida Conference Christian Educators Fellowship.

WRITINGS:

I Am Happy (juvenile), Abingdon, 1971.
(With M. Franklin Dotts) *Clues to Creativity: Providing Learning Experiences for Children,* three volumes, Friendship Press, 1974-76.
The Church Resource Library, Abingdon, 1975.
When Jesus Was Born (juvenile), Abingdon, 1979.
You Can Have a Church Library, Abingdon, 1988.

Author of curriculum material for United Methodist Church, 1963—.

WORK IN PROGRESS: Librarian's Guide to Displays; a book of chorale readings from the Bible for children; *Cooking with Young Children;* a handbook for volunteer librarians; a book on the relationships of colors, sizes, and shapes; programs for older adults from 70– to 100–plus–year–olds.

AVOCATIONAL INTERESTS: Chinese cooking, needlepoint, travel, reading.

* * *

DOUGLAS, Roy (Ian) 1924-

PERSONAL: Born December 28, 1924, in London, England; son of Percy Oswald (a company secretary) and Lilian (Bowley) Douglas; married Jean Rosemary Roberts, January, 1955; children: Alison, Michael, Bruce, Nigel. *Education:* University of London, B.Sc., 1946; University of Edinburgh, Ph.D., 1952. *Politics:* "Liberal (nineteenth-century type!)"

ADDRESSES: Home—26 Downs Rd., Coulsdon, Surrey CR3 1AA, England. *Office*—University of Surrey, Guildford, Surrey GU2 5XH, England.

CAREER: Barrister-at-law; called to the Bar in 1956. Has taught biology, history, and law at tertiary level, beginning 1946; University of Surrey, Guildford, Surrey, England, lecturer, 1955-76, senior lecturer, beginning 1976, reader, beginning 1983. Liberal Parliamentary candidate, 1950, 1951, 1955, 1959, 1964.

WRITINGS:

Law for Technologists, Gee & Co., 1964.
Fortunes of Free Trade in Britain, Land & Liberty Press, 1968.
The History of the Liberal Party, 1895-1970, foreword by Jeremy Thorpe, Sidgwick & Jackson, 1971.
(Contributor) K. D. Brown, editor, *Essays in Anti-Labour History,* Macmillan, 1974.
(Contributor) A. J. A. Morris, editor, *Edwardian Radicalism,* Routledge & Kegan Paul, 1974.
Land, People, and Politics: A History of the Land Question in the United Kingdom, 1878-1952, St. Martins, 1976.
In the Year of Munich, Macmillan, 1977.
The Advent of War, 1939-1940, Macmillan, 1978.
(Contributor) Robert V. Andelson, editor, *Critics of Henry George,* Fairleigh Dickinson University Press, 1979.
From War to Cold War 1942-1948, Macmillan, 1981.
New Alliances 1940-1941, Macmillan, 1982.
(Editor) *1939: A Retrospect Forty Years After; Proceedings of a Conference Held at the University of Surrey, 27 October, 1979,* Macmillan, 1983.
(Contributor) Wolfgang J. Mommsen and Lothar Kettenacker, editors, *The Fascist Challenge and the Policy of Appeasement,* Allen & Unwin, 1983.
World Crisis and British Decline, 1929-1956, Macmillan, 1986.

Contributor to learned journals.

WORK IN PROGRESS: Two books of international cartoons with explanatory text, one of the Second World War and one of the inter-war period; history of the University of Surrey and its predecessors, 1891—.

SIDELIGHTS: Roy Douglas told *CA:* "I began by producing a text book for my students. I rather enjoyed the process and started on the task of writing a book about the history of the Liberal Party because it seemed to me that people were so frequently wrong on simple facts that somebody ought to try to set the record straight. Again, I enjoyed the process and soon started on a book about the land question because that was a connecting thread running through British history that has often been ignored. I then started to write a book about the Munich crisis of 1938. When I looked at the original documents, I soon came to the conclusion that I had been as wrong in my judgements as everybody else. People seemed to be repeating what appeared a perfectly reasonable, but no longer tenable, interpretation of events at the time. That job I also enjoyed, and so I wrote several more books about the period around the Second World War. I don't know whether anybody else has learnt anything from my writings, but I have learnt a lot from doing it.

"I have recently got onto two different tracts. One is a history of my employer, the University of Surrey, and its predecessors, who go back for almost a century. This is teaching me quite a lot about education, how it fits in with society as a whole, and about the administrative problems. The other job is, I think, more original. I have always found that cartoons throw a lot of light on events and attitudes. So I decided to tell the story of the Second World War using cartoons as my principal source, and padding them out with just enough text to make the story meaningful. I have drawn on cartoons not only from Britain and the United States, but also from Germany, the Soviet Union, France, and other countries. I think this will be useful to help show why people in different countries thought and acted as they did. While I am waiting for it to be published, I am getting on with another book of cartoons, this time telling the story of the inter-war period."

BIOGRAPHICAL/CRITICAL SOURCES:

PERIODICALS

Times Literary Supplement, December 31, 1982.

* * *

DOUGLASS, Billie
See DELINSKY, Barbara (Ruth Greenberg)

* * *

DOWDY, Mrs. Regera
See GOREY, Edward (St. John)

* * *

DRAKE, Bonnie
See DELINSKY, Barbara (Ruth Greenberg)

* * *

DRANSFIELD, Michael (John Pender) 1948-1973
(Edward Tate)

PERSONAL: Born September 12, 1948, in Sydney, New South Wales, Australia; died 1973, as the result of a 1972 motorcycle accident; son of John Francis (a company director) and Elspeth (Pender) Dransfield. *Education:* "Dropped out" of University of New South Wales, 1966, and University of Sydney, 1967. *Religion:* "I am of the race that sings under torture."

CAREER: Worked as journalist, cleaner, postman, taxation assessor with the Federal Treasury in Australia, farmed own land, and did on-camera work in television; full-time writer.

AWARDS, HONORS: Commonwealth Literary Award of Australian Broadcasting Commission, 1963-64; Harri Jones Memorial Prize for poetry, University of Newcastle upon Tyne, 1970; Commonwealth Literary Fund Fellowship, 1973.

WRITINGS:

Streets of the Long Voyage (poems), University of Queensland Press, 1970.
The Inspector of Tides (poems; section originally published in *Poetry Australia* under pseudonym Edward Tate), University of Queensland Press, 1972.
Drug Poems, Macmillan, 1972.
Memoirs of a Velvet Urinal (poems), Maximus Books, 1975.
Voyage into Solitude (poems; 1969-71), collated and edited by Rodney Hall, Queensland University Press, 1978.
The Second Month of Spring (poems; 1972-73), collated and edited by Hall, University of Queensland Press, 1980.
Michael Dransfield: Collected Poems, University of Queensland Press, 1988.

Assistant editor of *More Verse by Young Australians,* Ribgy, 1971. Contributor to underground magazines, newspapers, and journals.

WORK IN PROGRESS: Research for several prose works, "ranging from fiction to art monograph to early Australian history."

SIDELIGHTS: Michael Dransfield once told *CA* that he was born scion of an ancient baronial line, but soon escaped society and defected to the counter-culture. He continued: "The world poisons itself, ours is a sick age but the victims are the poor, the minorities. Cities exemplify the worst of man's nature." Dransfield's lifestyle involved "living on my farm without the 'benefits' of western civilization."

AVOCATIONAL INTERESTS: "Getting into conservation, forest living, wandering, music, gold prospecting."*

*　　　*　　　*

DRIVER, C(harles) J(onathan) 1939-

PERSONAL: Born August 19, 1939, in Cape Town, South Africa; son of Kingsley Ernest (an Anglican priest) and Phyllis (a university warden; maiden name, Gould) Driver; married Ann Elizabeth Hoogewerf (an occupational therapist), June 8, 1967; children: Dominic, Thackwray, Tamlyn. *Education:* University of Cape Town, B.A., 1960, B.A. (honors), 1961, B.Ed., 1962; Trinity College, Oxford, M.Phil., 1967. *Politics:* Liberal Conservative. *Religion:* Anglican.

ADDRESSES: Office—Wellington College, Crowthorne, Berkshire RG11 7PU, England. *Agent*—John Johnson, 45-47 Clerkenwell Green, London EC1R 0HT, England.

CAREER: President, National Union of South African Students, 1963-64; left South Africa in 1964 after being detained in solitary confinement under 90 Day Detention Law; Sevenoaks School, Sevenoaks, Kent, England, teacher of English, 1964-73, housemaster of International Sixth Form Centre, 1968-73; Matthew

Humberstone Comprehensive School, Cleethorpes, Humberside, England, director of sixth form studies, 1973-78; Island School, Hong Kong, principal, 1978-83; Berkhamsted School, Berkhamsted, Hertfordshire, England, headmaster, 1983-89; Wellington College, Crowthorne, Berkshire, England, Master, 1989—. Research fellow, University of York, 1976; Commonwealth Linking Trust fellow, North India, 1987. Member of governing bodies, Benenden School, the Beacon School, Thorpe House School, Eagle House School; trustee, Lomans Trust, Alexandria Schools Trust.

MEMBER: Arts Council of Great Britain (member of literature panel, 1975-77), Royal Society of Arts (fellow), Headmasters' Conference, Board of Architectural Education.

WRITINGS:

Elegy for a Revolutionary (novel), Faber, 1969, Morrow, 1970.
(Contributor) *Penguin Book of South African Verse,* Penguin, 1969.
(Contributor) *Seven South African Poets,* Heinemann, 1969.
Send War in Our Time, O Lord (novel), Faber, 1970.
(Contributor) *Penguin Modern Stories,* Number 8, Penguin, 1971.
Death of Fathers (novel), Faber, 1972.
A Messiah of the Last Days (novel), Faber, 1974.
(Editor with H. B. Joicey) *Landscape and Light: Photographs and Poems of Lincolnshire and Humberside,* Lincolnshire and Humberside Arts, 1978.
I Live Here Now (poetry), Lincolnshire and Humberside Arts, 1979.
(With Jack Cope) *Jack Cope/C. J. Driver* (poetry), Philip, 1979.
Patrick Duncan, South African and Pan-African (biography), Heinemann, 1980.

Also author of poetry volume, *Hong Kong Portraits,* 1986. Contributor to *Contrast, New Review,* and other periodicals.

WORK IN PROGRESS: Two novels, *In a Green Tree* and *Love and Death.*

SIDELIGHTS: "A recurring theme in C. J. Driver's novels has been that of people obliged, in certain crucial circumstances, to take cognisance of grave issues almost against their will," a *Times Literary Supplement* contributor describes, explaining that "the nice, the sensitive, the unexceptional and the untypical suddenly find themselves having to answer large questions about society." *Elegy for a Revolutionary,* for example, relates the dilemma of six young, white South Africans who are arrested for planning sabotage as a form of protest against apartheid. While the novel's topic is political, it is the author's portrayal of his characters which stands out, as another *Times Literary Supplement* reviewer comments: "It is a tribute to [Driver's] skill that both the people and the setting in [this novel] emerge with immense vividness, that the clash of motives and temperaments among his six anti-apartheid saboteurs seems fresh, real, subtle and touching." A third *Times Literary Supplement* writer concludes that *Elegy for a Revolutionary* is "a first novel of remarkable power and promise: an understated yet immensely telling study of political activists restricted by their own conflicts."

Driver's later novels also present individuals in conflict with both their consciences and society; *Send War in Our Time, O Lord* explores a South African widow's examination of her own attitudes and ethics with "a beautifully simple and lucid prose [which] conceals a considerable unobtrusive sophistication in . . . plot and character," the same *Times Literary Supplement* critic observes. In *A Messiah of the Last Days,* Driver "has transferred all the skill he showed in describing the South African political situation to his intelligent—and uncomfortable—analysis of English life today," notes the first *Times Literary Supplement* commentator. The novel follows the enchantment of a middle-aged lawyer with a group of young, idealistic anarchists; "the most ambitious of the four novels, *The Messiah of the Last Days* contrasts a number of different life styles, and presents a complex image of contemporary Britain," states Ursula Edmands in *Contemporary Novelists,* concluding that the novel exemplifies what she calls "Driver's most persistent theme: the need society has for a 'leader' with a compelling vision, and its equal need to destroy him."

AVOCATIONAL INTERESTS: Long-distance running, rugby, reading, writing.

BIOGRAPHICAL/CRITICAL SOURCES:

BOOKS

Contemporary Novelists, St. James Press/St. Martin's, 1986.

PERIODICALS

New Statesman, September 5, 1969, September 18, 1970, February 25, 1972.
Times Literary Supplement, September 18, 1969, September 2, 1970, October 2, 1970, March 10, 1972, October 4, 1974, October 16, 1980.

* * *

DUBNICK, Mel(vin Jay) 1946-

PERSONAL: Born July 21, 1946, in Brooklyn, N.Y.; son of Herman and Rose (Aptaker) Dubnick; married Randa K. Zagon (a college teacher, administrator, and author), June 9, 1968; children: Heather, Philip. *Education:* Southern Colorado State College (now University of Southern Colorado), B.S. (with honors), 1968; University of Colorado, M.A., 1969, Ph.D., 1974.

ADDRESSES: Office—Department of Public Administration, Bernard M. Baruch College of the City University of New York, 17 Lexington Ave., New York, N.Y. 10010.

CAREER: Southern Colorado State College (now University of Southern Colorado), Pueblo, instructor in political science, 1969; University of Northern Colorado, Greeley, instructor in political science, 1971-72; Emporia State University, Emporia, Kan., assistant professor of political science, 1974-76; Loyola University, Chicago, Ill., assistant professor of political science, 1976-80, coordinator of Institute of Political Philosophy and Policy Analysis, 1978-79, director of public affairs and administration program, 1978-80; University of Kansas, Lawrence, associate professor of political science, 1980-88, director of Edwin O. Stene Graduate Program in Public Administration, 1982-83; Bernard M. Baruch College of the City University of New York, professor of public administration and chairperson of department, 1988—. Policy analyst for U.S. Department of Commerce, Office of Regulatory Economics and Policy, 1979-80. Conference organizer; testified before U.S. Senate; consultant to Advisory Commission on Intergovernmental Relations, Illinois State Comptroller's Office, and Western Interstate Commission on Higher Education.

MEMBER: American Political Science Association, American Society for Public Administration (vice-president of Kansas chapter, 1982-83), National Association of Schools of Public Affairs and Administration (chairman of undergraduate task force on curriculum materials development, 1976-77; member of executive committee of undergraduate section, 1979-80), Policy Studies Organization, Midwest Political Science Association, Southern Political Science Association, Western Political Science Association, Western Social Science Association, Southwestern Political Science Association, Kansas Political Science Association, Pi Sigma Alpha.

AWARDS, HONORS: Fellow of National Association of Schools of Public Affairs and Administration, 1979-80; Mosher Award from American Society for Public Administration, 1987.

WRITINGS:

Three Approaches to Health Care, test edition with instructor's manual, American Political Science Association, 1978.
(Contributor) Nicholas Henry, editor, *Doing Public Administration,* Allyn & Bacon, 1978, 2nd edition, 1982.
(Contributor) James R. Scarritt, editor, *Analyzing African Political Change,* Westview, 1980.
(Contributor) Stuart Nagel, editor, *Improving Policy Analysis,* Sage Publications, 1980.
(Contributor) Jerome J. Hanus, editor, *The Nationalization of State Government,* Lexington Books, 1981.
(Contributor) Don F. Hadwiger and Ross B. Talbott, editors, *Food Policy and Farm Programs,* Academy of Political Science, 1982.
(With Barbara A. Bardes) *Thinking about Public Policy: A Problem Solving Approach,* Wiley, 1983.
(With A. Gitelson and R. Dudley) *American Government,* Houghton, 1987.
Expectations, Macmillan, 1991.
(Editor with James E. Anderson and Alan R. Gitelson) *Public Policy and Economic Institutions,* JAI Press, in press.
American Business and Public Policy: An Introduction to Business-Government Relations, St. Martin's, in press.

Contributor of articles and reviews to political science and administration journals. *Policy Studies Journal,* member of editorial board, 1979, literature review editor, 1982-85, co-editor in chief, 1985—. Member of editorial board and literature review editor of *Policy Studies Review,* 1981-85.

SIDELIGHTS: Mel Dubnick wrote *CA:* "If there is a purpose or theme throughout my work, it is the need to have my readers—whether they be students or colleagues—break loose from current patterns of thought about specific topics. I have the greatest admiration for those who challenge the conventional wisdom, not through rhetoric but through *re*thinking what they or others know. That is the purpose of my textbooks, and it underlies all my 'research.' This has, of course, left me open to the charge of being a 'synthesizer' rather than a true empirical researcher. However, if we were to rely only on empirical researchers for our understanding of politics and public policy, we would in fact 'understand' very little, in spite of having a great deal of accumulated 'knowledge.'

"To understand is to think, and to think one must deal with intellectual constructs as well as empirical observations. The least desirable approach is a myopic emphasis on either side of that equation; the most desirable is a joining of theory to data in a way that improves our understanding."

* * *

DUFFY, Francis R(amon) 1915-

PERSONAL: Born March 26, 1915, in Philadelphia, Pa.; son of John J. (a police inspector) and Anna C. (Rodgers) Duffy. *Education:* Attended Holy Ghost College, 1933-35; St. Mary's College, Norwalk, Conn., B.A., 1938, B.D. (in association with Yale

University), 1942; Catholic University of America, M.A., 1944; University of Pittsburg, Ph.D., 1955; Duquesne University, post-doctoral study, 1955-68.

ADDRESSES: Home—St. Joseph's House, 8101 Cresco Ave., Philadelphia, Pa. 19136. *Office*—8538 Frankford Ave., Philadelphia, Pa. 19136. *Agent*—Edward Dunn, Bradley Printing and Publishing, Philadelphia, Pa.

CAREER: Entered Order of Fathers of the Holy Ghost (C.S.Sp.), 1933; ordained Roman Catholic Priest, 1941. Duquesne University, Pittsburgh, Pa., began as assistant professor, 1943, professor of sociology and criminology, 1960-68, chairman of department, 1943-66, assistant to vice-president, 1966; St. Joseph's House, Philadelphia, Pa., director, 1968—. Visiting professor of psychology and social work at St. Joseph's Hospital School of Nursing, 1952-60, and St. Joseph's College, Philadelphia, 1969-72; visiting lecturer at St. Vincent's College, Seton Hall College, University of Pittsburgh, University of Lagos, Steubenville College, Loyola University of Los Angeles, Wheeling College, and Marion College; in-service training instructor to Pennsylvania Board of Parole, 1949-55; instructor, Pittsburgh Police Department, 1950-60; instructor in behavioral sciences, Philadelphia Prison Training Academy, 1972—. Chaplain and counselor at Pittsburgh Police Academy, 1945-68, and Juvenile Court in Pittsburgh, 1947-67. Producer of radio series, "Exploring the Child's World," for 75 colleges, 1962-68. Chairman of religious affairs for High Commissioner of Germany, 1950-51, and Adoption Board, Stuttgart, 1951. Consultant to Children's Home, Allegheny County Behavior Clinic, medical department of Gulf Oil Corp, and the Pennsylvania governor's Justice Commission; consultant, psychiatry department, Nazareth Hospital; smoking intervention specialist, research division, Lankenau Hospital, Philadelphia. *Military service:* U.S. Army, chaplain, 1950-52; instructor in Army Chaplain School, 1965-74; received Legion of Merit and General Stewart Award; became colonel.

MEMBER: International Society of Hypnosis, Royal Anthropological Institute (England and Ireland; fellow), Royal College of Psychiatrists (corresponding associate), American Society of Clinical Hypnosis (fellow), American Sociological Society, American Association of University Professors, Pennsylvania Sociological Society, Pennsylvania Police Chiefs Association, Philadelphia Society of Clinical Hypnosis, Knights of Columbus, Knights of Equity, Pi Gamma Mu, Bala Club, Serra Club (Heidelberg, West Germany), Commodore Club.

WRITINGS:

Title System in Nigeria, Catholic University of America Press, 1942.
Follow-Up Study of Delinquents, University of Pittsburgh Press, 1955.
Exploring the Child's World, Bradley Brothers, 1968.
Social Psychology of Growing Up, Bradley Brothers, 1968.
Juvenile Delinquency, St. Joseph's House, 1969.
Personality and Adjustment, St. Joseph's House, 1969.
Accommodations for Teen-Agers, St. Joseph's House, 1970.
Hypnosis, St. Joseph's House, 1974.

Also author of *Social Monuments, Social Monuments Revisited, Social Growth and Development, Conformity and Deviation in Society, Results of Some New Methods in Orphanage Administration, Counseling, Relax!,* and *Minute Thoughts.* Author of book reviews for periodicals.

WORK IN PROGRESS: Follow-Up Study of Smoking Intervention with Hypnosis, to be published by Bradley Brothers.

AVOCATIONAL INTERESTS: Painting, target shooting, photography, travel, stamp collecting, motorcycling, playing the saxophone and organ.

*   *   *

DUNLAP, Jane
  See DAVIS, Adelle

E

EARLE, William
See JOHNS, William Earle

*   *   *

EARLY, Jon
See JOHNS, William Earle

*   *   *

EDGY, Wardore
See GOREY, Edward (St. John)

*   *   *

EDMONDS, I(vy) G(ordon) 1917-
(Gary Gordon)

PERSONAL: Born February 15, 1917, in Frost, Tex.; son of Ivy Gordon (an oil field worker) and Delia (Shumate) Edmonds; married Reiko Mimura, July 12, 1956; children: Annette. *Education:* Attended high school in Hillsboro, Tex.

ADDRESSES: Agent—Scott Meredith Literary Agency, Inc., 845 Third Ave., New York, N.Y. 10022.

CAREER: U.S. Air Force, aerial photography and public relations assignments, 1940-63, spent half of service in overseas posts and retired as chief master sergeant; Federal Civil Service, public relations work in Los Angeles, Calif., 1963-68; Northrup Corp., Hawthorne, Calif., industrial editor, 1968-72, division public relations in Anaheim, Calif., 1972-79, industrial editor, Aircraft division, 1979—. Writer, mainly for young people.

MEMBER: Authors Guild, Authors League of America.

AWARDS, HONORS: Military—Distinguished Flying Cross, Air Medal, and Bronze Star Medal.

WRITINGS:

Solomon in Kimono (folklore), Pacific Stars and Stripes, 1956.
Ooka: More Tales of Solomon in Kimono, Pacific Stars and Stripes, 1957.
Ooka the Wise (folklore), Bobbs-Merrill, 1961, published as The Case of the Marble Monster, Scholastic Book Services, 1966.
The Bounty's Boy, Bobbs-Merrill, 1962.
Hollywood RIP, Regency, 1963.

Isometric and Isotonic Exercises, Monarch, 1964.
Joel of the Hanging Gardens, Lippincott, 1966.
Trickster Tales (folklore), Lippincott, 1966.
Our Heroes' Heroes, Criterion, 1966.
Lassie and the Wild Mountain Trail, Whitman Publishing, 1966.
(With John J. Gribbons) Young Sportsmen's Guide to Gymnastics and Tumbling, Thomas Nelson, 1966, published as Gymnastics and Tumbling, Cornerstone Library, 1971.
Rat Patrol: Iron Monster Raid, Whitman Publishing, 1967.
Revolts and Revolutions, Hawthorn, 1969.
Khmers of Cambodia: The Story of a Mysterious People, Bobbs-Merrill, 1970.
Hot Rodding for Beginners, Macrae Smith, 1970.
The Possible Impossibles of Ikkyu the Wise (folklore), Macrae Smith, 1971.
Taiwan: The Other China, Bobbs-Merrill, 1971.
Motorcycling for Beginners, Macrae Smith, 1972.
The Magic Man (biography), Thomas Nelson, 1972.
Thailand: The Golden Land, Bobbs-Merrill, 1972.
Drag Racing for Beginners, Bobbs-Merrill, 1972.
Minibikes and Minicycles for Beginners, Macrae Smith, 1973, published as Minibikes and Minicycles, Archway, 1975.
Mao's Long March, Macrae Smith, 1973.
China's Red Rebel: The Story of Mao Tse-Tung, Macrae Smith, 1973.
The New Malaysia, Bobbs-Merrill, 1973.
Rocket and Jet Engines: How They Work, Putnam, 1973.
Automotive Tune-Ups for Beginners, Macrae Smith, 1974.
Micronesia, Bobbs-Merrill, 1974.
Pakistan, Holt, 1975.
Ethiopia: Land of the Conquering Lion of Judah, Holt, 1975.
The Shah of Iran, Holt, 1976.
The Magic Makers, Thomas Nelson, 1976.
Motorcycle Racing for Beginners, Holt, 1977.
Allah's Oil: Mideast Petroleum, Thomas Nelson, 1977.
Second Sight: People Who Saw the Future, Thomas Nelson, 1977.
The Mysteries of Troy, Thomas Nelson, 1977.
Big U: Universal in the Silent Days, Barnes, 1977.
Islam: A First Book, Watts, 1977.
D. D. Home: The Man Who Talked to Ghosts, Thomas Nelson, 1978.
Buddhism: A First Book, Watts, 1978.
The Girls Who Talked to Ghosts, Holt, 1979.
BMX: Bicycle Motocross for Beginners, Holt, 1979.

The Magic Brothers, Thomas Nelson, 1979.
Hinduism: A First Book, Watts, 1979.
Other Lives, McGraw-Hill, 1979.
Roller Skating: A Beginner's Guide, Archway, 1979.
(With William H. Gebhardt) *Broadcasting for Beginners,* Holt, 1980.
The Oscar Directors, Barnes, 1980.
Mysteries of Homer's Greeks, Thomas Nelson, 1981.
The Magic Dog, Lodestar, 1982.

UNDER PSEUDONYM GARY GORDON

Rise and Fall of the Japanese Empire, Monarch, 1962.
Robert F. Kennedy, Assistant President, Monarch, 1962.
Sins in Our Cities, Monarch, 1962.
Sex in Business, Monarch, 1964.
The Anatomy of Adultery, Monarch, 1964.
Law and the Marriage Bed, Monarch, 1965.

IN OTHER LANGUAGES

Junglens Musketerer, Winters Foerlag, Kobenhaun, 1966.
DJEVELSK OPPDRAG, Magasinet fur Alle, 1966.
Moerder sind meine Beute, Verlag Friedrich W. Loh (Hamburg), 1969.

OTHER

Also author of more than forty additional novels under five undisclosed pseudonyms.

SIDELIGHTS: I. G. Edmonds's interest in folklore began when he was serving in the South Pacific during World War II. Impressed by a native chief's story of how his atoll in the Ellice Islands was created, Edmonds started collecting folk tales in the countries he visited.

*   *   *

EDSON, J(ohn) T(homas)   1928-
(Rod Denver, Chuck Nolan, house pseudonyms)

PERSONAL: Born February 17, 1928, in Worksop, Nottinghamshire, England; son of Thomas John (a coal miner) and Eliza Charlotte (Gill) Edson; married Dorothy Mary Thompson, December 14, 1957 (divorced, 1974); children: Leslie Brian, Raymond, Steven, Peter John, Samantha Diane, Mark William James. *Education:* Attended schools in Nottinghamshire, England. *Politics:* None ("against all organised political groups"). *Religion:* Church of England ("nominally").

ADDRESSES: Home—One Cottesmore Ave., Melton Mowbray, Leicestershire LE13 0HY, England. *Agent*—Rosica Colin Ltd., One Clareville Grove Mews, London SW7 5AH, England.

CAREER: Haulage hand at a stone quarry in Steetley, England, 1943-46; British Army, Royal Army Veterinary Corps, dog trainer, 1946-58, serving as sergeant in Germany, Malaya, Hong Kong, and North Africa, with combat duty in Kenya and Cyprus; owner of a fish and chip shop in Melton Mowbray, England, 1958-62; Petfoods Industries, Mowbray, production hand, 1962-65; postman in Mowbray, 1965-68; writer of western novels.

MEMBER: Western Writers of America, Royal Army Veterinary Corps Old Comrades Association, Northampton Lower Forty Club (honorary member).

AWARDS, HONORS: Second prize, western section, Brown, Watson Literary Contest, for *Trail Boss.*

WRITINGS:

WESTERN NOVELS

Trail Boss, Brown, Watson, 1961, reprinted, Ace Books, 1987.
The Hard Riders, Brown, Watson, 1962, reprinted, Corgi Books, 1981.
Rio Guns, Brown, Watson, 1962, reprinted, R. Hale, 1980.
Sagebrush Sleuth, Brown, Watson, 1962, reprinted, Ulverscroft, 1986.
(Under house pseudonym Chuck Nolan) *Quiet Town,* Brown, Watson, 1962, published under name J. T. Edson, R. Hale, 1968.
Waco's Debt, Brown, Watson, 1962, reprinted, Berkley Publishing, 1986.
The Rio Hondo Kid, Brown, Watson, 1963, reprinted, R. Hale, 1980.
Apache Rampage, Brown, Watson, 1963, reprinted, Berkley Publishing, 1987.
The Fastest Gun in Texas, Brown, Watson, 1963, reprinted, R. Hale, 1982.
The Drifter, Brown, Watson, 1963, reprinted, Berkley Publishing, 1989.
The Half Breed, Brown, Watson, 1963, reprinted, Ace Books, 1988.
Gun Wizard, Brown, Watson, 1963, reprinted, Corgi Books, 1981.
Gunsmoke Thunder, Brown, Watson, 1963, reprinted, Ulverscroft, 1979.
Wagons to Backsight, Brown, Watson, 1964, reprinted, R. Hale, 1984.
Waco Rides In, Brown, Watson, 1964, reprinted, R. Hale, 1981.
The Rushers, Brown, Watson, 1964.
The Rio Hondo War, Brown, Watson, 1964.
Trigger Fast, Brown, Watson, 1964.
The Wildcats, Brown, Watson, 1965, reprinted, Berkley Publishing, 1989.
The Peacemakers, Brown, Watson, 1965, reprinted, R. Hale, 1984.
Troubled Range, Brown, Watson, 1965.
The Fortune Hunters, Brown, Watson, 1965, reprinted, Corgi Books, 1981, revised edition, R. Hale, 1978.
Slaughter's Way, Brown, Watson, 1965, Bantam, 1969, reprinted, Ulverscroft, 1983.
The Man from Texas, Brown, Watson, 1965.
The Trouble Busters, Brown, Watson, 1965.
Trouble Trail, Brown, Watson, 1965.
The Cow Thieves, Brown, Watson, 1965, reprinted, Ulverscroft, 1985.
The Bullwhip Breed, Brown, Watson, 1965, Bantam, 1969.
Guns in the Night, Brown, Watson, 1966, reprinted, R. Hale, 1984.
A Town Called Yellowdog, Brown, Watson, 1966.
The Devil Gun, Brown, Watson, 1966, Bantam, 1969, reprinted, Berkley Publishing, 1987.
The Colt and the Sabre, Brown, Watson, 1966, reprinted, Berkley Publishing, 1986.
The Law of the Gun, Brown, Watson, 1966, reprinted, R. Hale, 1984.
Return to Backsight, Brown, Watson, 1966, reprinted, Berkley Publishing, 1986.
The Fast Gun, Brown, Watson, 1967.
The Big Hunt, Brown, Watson, 1967, reprinted, R. Hale, 1984.
Terror Valley, Brown, Watson, 1967, reprinted, Berkley Publishing, 1987.

Comanche, Brown, Watson, 1967, reprinted, Berkley Publishing, 1988.

Hound Dog Man, Brown, Watson, 1967.

Sidewinder, Brown, Watson, 1967.

The Hooded Riders, Corgi Books, 1968.

Where Is Evie Alton?, Corgi Books, 1968.

Rangeland Hercules, Corgi Books, 1968.

McGraw's Inheritance, Corgi Books, 1968, reprinted, R. Hale, 1984.

The Making of a Lawman, Corgi Books, 1968, Bantam, 1971.

The Professional Killers, Corgi Books, 1968.

The Bloody Border, Corgi Books, 1969.

The Small Texan, Corgi Books, 1969.

The Quarter-Second Draw, Corgi Books, 1969.

Cuchilo, Corgi Books, 1969.

The Deputies, Corgi Books, 1969, reprinted, Severn House, 1988.

Goodnight's Dream, Corgi Books, 1969.

From Hide and Horn, Corgi Books, 1969, Bantam, 1974.

.44 Caliber Man, Corgi Books, 1969.

Back to the Bloody Border, Corgi Books, 1970.

White Stallion, Red Mare, Corgi Books, 1970.

Point of Contact, Corgi Books, 1970.

The Owlhoot, Corgi Books, 1970.

Hell in the Palo Duro, Corgi Books, 1971, reprinted, Berkley Publishing, 1987.

Slip Gun, Corgi Books, 1971.

Run for the Border, Corgi Books, 1971.

Bad Hombre, Corgi Books, 1971.

Go Back to Hell, Corgi Books, 1972, reprinted, Berkley Publishing, 1987.

The South Will Rise Again, Corgi Books, 1972.

To Arms! To Arms, in Dixie!, Corgi Books, 1972.

Two Miles to the Border, Corgi Books, 1972.

The Best of J. T. Edson (omnibus), R. Hale, 1973.

The Big Gun, Corgi Books, 1973.

Set Texas Back on Her Feet, Corgi Books, 1973.

(With Peter Clawson) *Blonde Genius,* Corgi Books, 1973.

The Quest for Bowie's Blade, Corgi Books, 1974.

Sixteen Dollar Shooter, Corgi Books, 1974.

J. T. Edson Omnibus, R. Hale, Volume 2, 1975, Volume 3, 1983, Volume 4, 1984, Volume 5, 1985.

Sacrifice for the Quagga God, Corgi Books, 1975.

Get Urrea, Corgi Books, 1975.

Doc Leroy, M.D., Corgi Books, 1977.

Texas Ranger, Corgi Books, 1977.

Set A-Foot, Corgi Books, 1977.

Beguinage, Corgi Books, 1978.

Beguinage Is Dead, Corgi Books, 1978.

The Remittance Kid, Corgi Books, 1978.

J. T.'s Hundredth, Corgi Books, 1979.

The Gentle Giant, Corgi Books, 1979.

J. T.'s Ladies, Corgi Books, 1980.

The Justice of Company 'Z,' Corgi Books, 1980.

Master of Triggernometry, Corgi Books, 1981.

Old Moccasins on the Trail, Corgi Books, 1981.

The Sheriff of Rockabye County, Corgi Books, 1981.

The Lawmen of Rockabye County, Corgi Books, 1982.

Waco's Badge, Corgi Books, 1982.

A Matter of Honour, Corgi Books, 1982.

White Indians, Corgi Books, 1982.

Cut One, They All Bleed, Corgi Books, 1983.

The Hide and Horn Saloon, Corgi Books, 1983.

Wanted! Belle Starr, Corgi Books, 1983.

Buffalo Are Coming!, Corgi Books, 1984.

Is-a-Man, Corgi Books, 1984.

No Finger on the Trigger, Corgi Books, 1985.

Diamonds, Emeralds, Cards and Colts, Corgi Books, 1986, published as *Cards and Colts,* Berkley Publishing, 1988.

The Texas Assassin, Berkley Publishing, 1986.

Trigger Master, Berkley Publishing, 1986.

More J. T.'s Ladies, Corgi Books, 1987.

Rebel Vengeance, Berkley Publishing, 1987.

J. T.'s Ladies Ride Again, Corgi Books, 1988.

Mark Counter's Kin, Corgi Books, 1989.

"ALVIN DUSTINE 'CAP' FOG" SERIES

Kill Dusty Fog, Corgi Books, 1970, reprinted, Berkley Publishing, 1987.

You're in Command Now, Mr. Fog, Corgi Books, 1973.

'Cap' Fog, Texas Ranger, Meet Mr. J. G. Reeder, Corgi Books, 1977.

You're a Texas Ranger, Alvin Fog, Corgi Books, 1979.

Rapido Clint, Corgi Books, 1980.

The Return of Rapido Clint and Mr. J. G. Reeder, Corgi Books, 1984.

Decision for Dusty Fog, Corgi Books, 1986.

The Code of Dusty Fog, Corgi Books, 1988.

Rapido Clint Strikes Back, Corgi Books, 1989.

"CALAMITY JANE" SERIES

Calamity Spells Trouble, Corgi Books, 1968, reprinted, R. Hale, 1983.

Cold Deck, Hot Lead, Corgi Books, 1969.

The Whip and the War Lance, Corgi Books, 1979.

Calamity, Mark and Belle, Corgi Books, 1980.

"FLOATING OUTFIT" SERIES

The Texan, Brown, Watson, 1962, reprinted, Berkley Publishing, 1989.

The Ysabel Kid, Brown, Watson, 1962, reprinted, Berkley Publishing, 1985.

(Under house pseudonym Rod Denver) *Arizona Ranger,* Brown, Watson, 1962, published under name J. T. Edson, Wright & Brown, 1964, reprinted, Ace Books, 1988.

The Floating Outfit, Corgi Books, 1967.

The Bad Bunch, Corgi Books, 1968, reprinted, Berkley Publishing, 1987.

The Town Tamers, Corgi Books, 1969, Bantam, 1973.

A Horse Called Mogollon, Corgi Books, 1971.

The Hide and Tallow Men, Corgi Books, 1974.

Young Ole Devil, Corgi Books, 1975.

Ole Devil and the Caplocks, Corgi Books, 1976.

Ole Devil and the Mule Train, Corgi Books, 1976.

Ole Devil at San Jacinto, Corgi Books, 1977.

Ole Devil's Hands and Feet: They Were Called His Floating Outfit, Corgi Books, 1983.

OTHER

The Rebel Spy ("Civil War" series), Corgi Books, 1968, reprinted, Berkley Publishing, 1987.

Under the Stars and Bars ("Civil War" series), Corgi Books, 1970, reprinted, Berkley Publishing, 1987.

Bunduki ("Bunduki" series), Corgi Books, 1975.

Bunduki and Dawn ("Bunduki" series), Corgi Books, 1976.

Fearless Master of the Jungle ("Bunduki" series), Corgi Books, 1978.

Writer of serials, series, short stories, and nonfiction for *Rover, Hotspur,* and *Victor.*

WORK IN PROGRESS: The Amazons of Zillikian; More Justice from Company 'Z'; Waco and Doc Leroy.

SIDELIGHTS: J. T. Edson, "England's answer to Zane Grey," told *CA* that his writing "is of action, adventure, escapist variety, written purely for the enjoyment of people who like that kind of a story," and added that he has "become hooked on the fictionist genealogy style of writing perfected by Philip Jose Farmer. This allows me to tie in various of my Western characters with the protagonists of the 'Bunduki' series of books. . . . All my work is action-escapism-adventure motivated and I try to steer clear of the 'message' style of writing." The honorary Texas Navy admiral went on to say: "I refuse to accept the frequently made statement that the traditional type of Western novel is not wanted by the reading public and my sales figures seem to prove me correct. One thing I will not do is produce books featuring the 'liberal' anti-hero. My pet hate is journalists who label me a 'postman-turned-author,' or pretend to think I need to dress in 'cowboy' clothes to write. To me this is merely an extension of their middle class 'liberal' snobbery. I was a moderately, if not financially successful writer before I became a postman. If they have to use a label, I would prefer to be called an ex-regular soldier turned author, which is correct."

Edson was also made an honorary commodore in the Powder River Navy, Wyoming, and an honorary deputy sheriff of Travis County, Texas, and Thurston County, Washington. His books have been translated into Danish, Dutch, Serbo-Croatian, Swedish, Norwegian, German, and Afrikaans.

AVOCATIONAL INTERESTS: Fishing, golf, collecting police concealment holsters, "adding to my collection of Japanese replica-nonfiring firearms," telling the "world's worst jokes," and building up his reference library.

*   *   *

ELEGANT, Robert (Sampson) 1928-

PERSONAL: Born March 7, 1928, in New York, N.Y.; son of Louis and Lillie Rebecca (Sampson) Elegant; married Moira Clarissa Brady, April 16, 1956; children: Victoria Ann, Simon David Brady. *Education:* University of Pennsylvania, A.B., 1946; Yale University, Certificate in Chinese, 1948; Columbia University, M.A., 1950, M.S., 1951.

ADDRESSES: Home—Manor House, Middle Green near Langley, Berks SL3 6BS, England. *Agent*—Ed Victor Ltd., 162 Wardour St., London W1V 4AT, England.

CAREER: Overseas News Agency, correspondent in Far East, 1951-52; International News Service, correspondent in Japan and Korea, 1953; Ford Foundation fellow in Southeast Asia, 1954-56, and part-time correspondent for Columbia Broadcasting System, North American Newspaper Alliance, and McGraw-Hill News Service; *Newsweek,* New York, N.Y., South Asian correspondent stationed in India, 1956-57, and in Hong Kong, 1958-61, chief of bureau, Central Europe, with headquarters in Bonn, West Germany, 1962-65; *Los Angeles Times,* Los Angeles, Calif., chief of Hong Kong Bureau, 1965-69; foreign affairs columnist operating from Munich, West Germany, 1970-72, and Hong Kong, 1973-75; free-lance writer, 1977—. Lecturer, 1964—; visiting professor, University of South Carolina, 1976. *Military service:* U.S. Army, Infantry, 1946-48; became sergeant; studied and taught Japanese at Army Language School.

MEMBER: International Institute of Strategic Studies, Authors League of America, Society of Authors (London), Asia Society, Hong Kong Foreign Correspondent Club (president, 1960), Lansdowne Club (London), Royal Hong Kong Yacht Club, Phi Beta Kappa.

AWARDS, HONORS: Pulitzer Prize traveling fellow, 1951; Ford Foundation fellow, 1954-55; Overseas Press Club citation for best magazine reporting from abroad, 1961, and annual awards for best interpretation of news from abroad, 1967, 1969, 1972; Edgar Allan Poe Award runner-up, Mystery Writers of America, 1967, for *A Kind of Treason;* Sigma Delta Chi award for foreign correspondence, 1967; Columbia University Alumni Award, 1970; research fellow, American Enterprise Institute for Public Policy Research, 1977-79.

WRITINGS:

China's Red Masters, Twayne, 1951, reprinted, Greenwood Press, 1971 (published in England as *China's Red Leaders,* Bodley Head, 1951).
The Dragon's Seed, St. Martin's, 1959.
The Center of the World, Doubleday, 1964, revised edition, Funk & Wagnalls, 1968.
(Contributor) *Journalists in Action,* Cresset, 1964.
A Kind of Treason (novel), Holt, 1966.
The Seeking (novel), Funk & Wagnalls, 1969.
Mao's Great Revolution, World Publishing, 1971.
Mao vs. Chiang: The Battle for China, Grosset, 1972.
Dynasty (novel), McGraw, 1976.
The Great Cities: Hong Kong, Time-Life Books, 1977.
Manchu, McGraw, 1979, new edition, Fawcett, 1982.
Mandarin (novel), Simon & Schuster, 1983.
White Sun, Red Star (novel), Hamish Hamilton, 1986, published as *From a Far Land,* Random House, 1987.
Pacific Destiny (nonfiction), Crown, 1990.

Contributor to periodicals, including *Reporter, New Leader, Reader's Digest, Foreign Affairs, Look, Business World, Nation, National Review, Pacific Community, China Quarterly, Business Management, L'Espresso,* and *Travel and Leisure.* Most of Elegant's novels have been translated into French, German, Italian, Dutch, Swedish, Indonesian, Japanese, and Hebrew.

SIDELIGHTS: As a former journalist who now writes novels, Robert Elegant comments on the advantages of having spent many years reporting news and writing nonfiction in a *Publishers Weekly* interview with Robert Dahlin: "[Journalists] have been trained to observe not only unconsciously, but also consciously. If you're a journalist, you make judgments in your mind, assessing people and events. And, it is a trained faculty, this communication. Reporters aren't rewarded for obscurity." Elegant believes that writing fiction does allow the writer certain freedoms not available to writers of nonfiction. "We all know things about people, things that would be unfair to use in nonfiction because we can't prove them," he tells Dahlin. "And there are other issues. I know that at one time we led the Chinese to believe we were willing to commit ourselves to their defense against Russia, if anything should happen. But there's nothing I would be able to use in nonfiction to prove it."

In the same interview, Elegant discusses his novel *Dynasty,* which is set in China. "What I hope I've been able to convey . . . is an atmosphere," the author reveals. "And to show that the people themselves are not simply the inscrutable East. They have real and personal problems just like everyone else. Making that observation journalistically can be bloodless. In a novel, you can develop character. You can find your own length." Although in a *New York Times* review of *Dynasty,* Robert Lask calls it an "uneven, sprawling novel [which] recapitulates the violent history of the Orient since 1900," he also writes that the book is filled with "highly colored incidents and characters." Particularly impressed with the novel's setting, Lask adds that Elegant's career as a newspaper correspondent in Hong Kong enabled him to include "those small details, customs, ceremonies and touches of folklore that make the time and place more vivid than the characters he has created. And history fascinates him. . . . You can read *Dynasty* as a short course in Chinese history since 1900. Anything additional is pure dividend."

Since *Dynasty,* Elegant has returned to the subject of China in three other novels. *Manchu* is set in the seventeenth century, the time when the Ming Dynasty collapsed before the Manchus. In order not to alienate his readers from the events in the novel, Elegant tells his story from the viewpoint of Francis Arrowsmith, a Catholic missionary, who gets involved in the intrigue and politics of the times. Comparing the book to *Dynasty, Washington Post Book World* contributor Jay Mathews remarks that "Elegant enlivens this rather minor tale by putting Arrowsmith in contact with as many of the giants of the era as he can." The reviewer later concludes that "those who liked *Dynasty* should find much to enjoy here." However, Ross Terrill comments in the *Chicago Tribune Book World* that although the author "keeps the pages alive with sharp dialog, and offers vivid descriptions of Macao and sometimes of China," he also "has an obsessive fascination with gore." Another flaw, Terrill avers, is that there is "very little human drama in its 560 pages." Similar criticism of *Mandarin* is offered by *Los Angeles Times* critic Pat Hilton, who notes that "the author presents history with competence but is less sure in creating compelling human drama." Nevertheless, according to John Jay Osborne, Jr., in the *New York Times Book Review, Mandarin,* the story of two families in the silk business during the nineteenth-century Taiping Rebellion, is "historically accurate, a good read." And although Osborne has some problems with characterization in the novel, he maintains: "It is classic material, and Mr. Elegant handles it very well indeed."

More recently, Elegant's *From a Far Land* takes his readers to the Shanghai of the 1920s through 1940s, a time of turmoil in China as the Communist Party built power for its overthrow of Chiang Kai-shek's government. Characterization is again the novel's shortcoming, according to some reviewers. In a *New York Times Book Review* article, for example, Jonathan Fast asserts that "to be satisfying, popular fiction should be moral fiction too. Yet the characters who inhabit this novel don't seem to care much about the implications of anything they do." But on this point *Washington Times* writer William J. Coughlin warns: "Do not be put off by what seems to be a shallow beginning; just as the characters mature, so has their creator, becoming over the course of his four fictional works on China not merely one of our best historical novelists but one of our best novelists." "Elegant possesses an asset that many of his rival blockbuster builders do not," adds Harrison E. Salisbury in Chicago *Tribune Books.* "He knows the territory—he knows China, has lived there, worked there as a correspondent and devoted time to its study. It shows in his work, and 'From a Far Land' is no exception."

Elegant told *CA:* "I believe that I have in the four novels of the 'China and the West' series given Western readers a view of China's recent history, encounters with the West, and the characters of Chinese . . . they would obtain nowhere else." About *Pacific Destiny* the author says that he "attempts in nonfiction prose to describe East Asia in its Renaissance for the general reader."

BIOGRAPHICAL/CRITICAL SOURCES:

PERIODICALS

Chicago Tribune Book World, November 16, 1980.
Los Angeles Times, December 5, 1980, December 15, 1983, October 26, 1987.
National Review, May 18, 1971.
New York Times, April 1, 1971, September 22, 1977, October 22, 1983.
New York Times Book Review, September 4, 1977, October 23, 1983, September 20, 1987.
Publishers Weekly, October 10, 1977.
Saturday Review, May 29, 1971.
Tribune Books (Chicago), August 16, 1987.
Washington Post Book World, October 26, 1980.
Washington Times, October 26, 1987.

*   *   *

ELIADE, Mircea   1907-1986

PERSONAL: Born March 9, 1907, in Bucharest, Romania; came to United States, 1956; died April 22, 1986, in Chicago, Ill.; son of Gheorghe and Ioana (Stonescu) Eliade; married Nina Mares, 1935 (some sources say 1933; died in Portugal during World War II); married Georgette Christinel Cottescu, January 9, 1950; children: Adalgiza Tattaresco, a stepdaughter. *Education:* University of Bucharest, M.A., 1928, Ph.D., 1933; graduate study at University of Calcutta, 1928-32.

ADDRESSES: Office—Swift Hall, University of Chicago, 1025-35 East 58th St., Chicago, Ill. 60637.

CAREER: University of Bucharest, Bucharest, Romania, assistant professor of philosophy, 1933-39; Romanian legation, cultural attache in London, England, 1940-41, cultural adviser in Lisbon, Portugal, 1941-45; University of Paris, Sorbonne, Paris, France, visiting professor of history of religion, 1946-48; lecturer at universities in Rome, Lund, Marburg, Munich, Frankfurt, Uppsala, Strasbourg, and Padua, 1948-56; University of Chicago, Chicago, Ill., Haskell Lecturer, 1956, professor of history of religions, 1957-62, Sewell L. Avery Distinguished Service Professor, beginning in 1962, professor emeritus until 1985.

MEMBER: American Academy of Arts and Sciences, American Society for the Study of Religion (president, 1963-67), British Academy, Centre Roumain de Recherches (Paris; president, 1950-55), Societe Asiatique, Romanian Writers Society (secretary, 1939), Frobenius Institut, Acadmemie Royale de Belgique, Osterreichische Akademie der Wissenschaften.

AWARDS, HONORS: Honorary doctorates from Yale University, 1966, Universidad Nacional de la Plata, 1969, Universidad del Salvador, 1969, Ripon College, 1969, Loyola University, 1970, Boston College, 1971, La Salle College, 1972, Oberlin College, 1972, University of Lancaster, 1975, and Sorbonne, University of Paris, 1976.

WRITINGS:

IN ENGLISH

Metallurgy, Magic, and Alchemy, Geunther, 1938.
Traite d'histoire des religions, Payot, 1948, translation by Rosemary Sheed published as *Patterns in Comparative Religion,* Sheed, 1958, new French edition, Payot, 1964, reprinted, 1974.
Le Mythe de l'eternel retour; Archetypes et repetition, Gallimard, 1949, translation by Willard R. Trask published as *The*

Myth of the Eternal Return; or, Cosmos and History, Pantheon, 1954, published as *Cosmos and History,* Pantheon, 1955, published as *Cosmos and History: The Myth of the Eternal Return,* Harper, 1959, reprinted version edited by Robin W. Winks, Garland Publishing, 1985, original Trask edition reprinted, Princeton University Press, 1987.

Le Chamanisme et les techniques archaiques de l'extase, Payot, '1951, translation by Trask published as *Shamanism: Archaic Techniques of Ecstasy,* Pantheon, 1964, 2nd French edition, Payot, 1968, 2nd English edition, Princeton University Press, 1970.

Images et symboles: Essais sur le symbolisme magicoreligieux, Gallimard, 1952, translation by Philip Mairet published as *Images and Symbols: Studies in Religious Symbolism,* Harvill Press, 1961.

Le Yoga: Immortalitie et liberte, Payot, 1954, translation by Trask published as *Yoga: Immortality and Freedom,* Pantheon, 1958, 2nd edition with corrections and notes, Princeton University Press, 1969.

Forgerons et alchemistes, Flammarion, 1956, translation by Stephen Corrin published as *The Forge and the Crucible,* Harper, 1962, 2nd edition, University of Chicago Press, 1978.

Das Heilige und das profane: Vom Wesen des religiosen, Rowohlt, 1957, translation by Trask published as *The Sacred and the Profane: The Nature of Religion,* Harcourt, 1959, reprinted, 1968.

Mythes, reves, et mysteres, Gallimard, 1957, reprinted in two volumes, 1972, translation by Mairet published as *Myths, Dreams, and Mysteries: The Encounter between Contemporary Faiths and Archaic Realities,* Harvill Press, 1960, reprinted, Harper, 1987.

Birth and Rebirth: The Religious Meaning of Initiation in Human Culture, translated by Trask, Harper, 1958, published as *Rites and Symbols of Initiation: The Mysteries of Birth and Rebirth,* 1965.

(Editor with Joseph M. Kitagawa) *The History of Religions: Essays in Methodology,* University of Chicago Press, 1959, reprinted, 1973.

Patanjali et le yoga, Editions du Seuil, 1962, translation by Charles Lam Markmann published as *Patanjali and Yoga,* Funk, 1969, Schocken, 1975.

Mephistopheles et l'androgyne, Gallimard, 1962, translation by J. M. Cohen published as *Mephistopheles and the Androgyne: Studies in Religious Myth and Symbol,* Sheed, 1965, published in England as *The Two and the One,* Harvill Press, 1965, reprinted, University of Chicago Press, 1979.

Myth and Reality, translated by Trask, Harper, 1963.

Aminitiri: I. Mansarda (title means "An Autobiography: I. The Attic"), Editura Destin, 1966, translation from the Rumanian by MacLinscott Ricketts published as *Autobiography,* Volume 1: *Journey East, Journey West: 1907–1937,* Harper, 1981, Volume 2: *1937–1960, Exile's Odyssey,* University of Chicago Press, 1988.

(Editor) *From Primitives to Zen: A Thematic Sourcebook of the History of Religions,* Collins, 1967, reprinted in four parts, Part 1: *Gods, Goddesses, and Myths of Creation,* Part 2: *Man and the Sacred,* Part 3: *Death, Afterlife, and Eschatology,* Part 4: *From Medicine Man to Muhammad,* Harper, 1974.

(Editor with Kitagawa and Charles H. Long, and contributor) *The History of Religions: Essays on the Problem of Understanding,* University of Chicago Press, 1967.

Pe Strada Mantuleasa (title means "On Mantuleasa Street"), Caitele Inorugului, 1968, translation by Stevenson published as *The Old Man and the Bureaucrats,* University of Notre Dame Press, 1979.

The Quest: History and Meaning in Religion, University of Chicago Press, 1969, reprinted, 1984.

(With Mihai Niculescu) *Fantastic Tales,* translated and edited by Eric Tappe, Dillon's University Bookstore, 1969.

De Zalmoxis a Gengis Khan: Etudes comparatives sur les religions et le folklore de la Dacie et de l'Europe orientale, Payot, 1970, translation by Trask published as *Zalmoxis, the Vanishing God: Comparative Studies in the Religions and Folklore of Dacia and Eastern Europe,* University of Chicago Press, 1972, reprinted, 1986.

Two Tales of the Occult, translation from the Rumanian by William Ames Coates, Herder & Herder, 1970, published as *Two Strange Tales,* Shambhala Publications, 1986.

Religions australiennes (two volumes; translation of lectures originally given in English), translation by L. Jospin, Payot, 1972, published as *Australian Religions: An Introduction,* Cornell University Press, 1973.

Fragments d'un journal, translation from the Rumanian by Luc Badesco, Gallimard, 1973, translation by Fred H. Johnson, Jr., published as *No Souvenirs: Journal, 1957-1969,* Harper, 1977.

Myths, Rites and Symbols: A Mircea Eliade Reader, edited by Wendell C. Beane and William G. Doty, Harper, 1976.

Occultism, Witchcraft, and Cultural Fashions: Essays in Comparative Religions, University of Chicago Press, 1976.

Histoire des croyances et des idees religieuses, Payot, Volume 1: *De l'age de la Pierre aux mysteres d'Eleusis,* 1976, Volume 2: *De Gautama Bouddha au triomphe du christianisme,* 1978, Volume 3: *De Mahomet a l'age des reformes,* 1983, published as *A History of Religious Ideas,* University of Chicago Press, Volume 1: *From the Stone Age to the Eleusinian Mysteries,* translation from French by Trask, 1979, Volume 2: *From Gautama Buddha to the Triumph of Christianity,* translation from French by Trask, 1982, Volume 3: *From Muhammed to the Age of Reforms,* translation by Alf Hiltebeiten and Diane Apostolos-Cappadona, 1985.

La foret interdite (novel; title means "The Forbidden Forest"), translation by Ricketts amd Mary P. Stevenson, University of Notre Dame Press, 1978.

L'Epreuve du labyrinthe: Entretien avec Claude-Henri Rocquet, Belfond (Paris), 1978, translation from the French by Derek Coltman published as *Ordeal by Labyrinth: Conversations with Claude-Henri Rocquet, with an Essay on Brancusi and Mythology,* University of Chicago Press, 1982.

(Editor with David Tracy) *What Is Religion?: An Inquiry for Christian Theology,* T. & T. Clarke, 1980.

Tales of the Sacred and the Supernatural, Westminster Press, 1981.

Imagination and Meaning, Seabury Press, 1982.

The Quest: History and Meaning in Religion, University of Chicago Press, 1984.

Symbolism, the Sacred, and the Arts, edited by Apostolos-Cappadona, Crossroad Publishing, 1985.

(Editor) *Encyclopedia of Religion,* sixteen volumes, Macmillan, 1986.

Youth without Youth and Other Novellas, edited by Matei Calinescu, translated by Ricketts, Ohio State University Press, 1988.

OTHER

Isabel si Apele Diavolului (novel; title means "Isabel and the Devil's Waters"), Editura Nationala-Ciornei (Bucharest), 1930.

Intr'o Manastire din Hamalaya (title means "In a Himalayan Monastery"), Editura Cartea Romaneasca, 1932.

Soliliquii (aphorisms; title means "Soliloquies"), Editura Cartea ce Semne, 1932.

Maitreyi (novel), Editura Nationala-Ciornei, 1933.

India (autobiographical novel), Editura Cugetarea, 1934.

Lumina ce se stinge (title means "The Light that Fails"), Editura Cartea Romaneasca, 1934.

Alchimia Asiatica (title means "Asiatic Alchemy"), Editura Cultura Porporului, 1934.

Oceanographie (essays), Editura Cultura Porporului, 1934.

(Translator) T. E. Lawrence, *Revolt in the Desert,* two volumes, Editura Fundatia Regala pentru Literatura si Arta, 1934.

Intoarcerea din Rai (novel; also see below; first part of trilogy; title means "The Return from Paradise"), Editura Nationala-Ciornei, 1934-54.

Huliganii (novels; two-volume sequel to *Intoarcerea din Rai;* title means "The Hooligans"), Editura Nationala-Ciornei, 1935.

Santier (autobiographical novel; title means "Work in Progress"), Editura Cugetarea, 1935.

Yoga: Essai sur les origines de la mystique indienne (title means "Yoga: Essays on the Origins of Indian Mystic Techniques"), Librairie Orientaliste Geunther (Paris), 1936.

(Editor) Nae Ionescu, *Roza Vanturilor,* Cultura Nationala, 1936.

Domnisoara Christina (novel; title means "Mademoiselle Christina"), Editura Cultura Nationala, 1936.

Sarpele (novel; title means "The Serpent"), Editura Nationala-Ciornei, 1937.

(Editor) *Scrieri Literare, Morlae si Politice de B. P. Hasdeu,* two volumes, Editura Fundatia Regala pentru Literatura si Arta, 1937.

Cosmologie si Alchimie Babiloniana (title means "Babylonian Cosmology and Alchemy"), Editura Vremea, 1937.

Nunta in Cer (novel; title means "Marriage in Heaven"), Editura Cugetarea, 1938.

Mitul Reintegrarii (title means "The Myth of Reintegration"), Editura Vremea, 1938.

Fragmentarium (essays), Editura Vremea, 1939.

(Translator) Pearl S. Buck, *Fighting Angel,* Editura Fundatia Regala pentru Literatura si Arta, 1939.

Secretul Doctoru lui Honigberger (title means "The Secret of Dr. Honigberger"; also see below), Editura Socec, 1940.

Salaza si Revolutia in Portugalia (title means "Salazar and the Revolution in Portugal"), Editura Gorjan, 1942.

Commentarii la Legenda Mesterlui Manole (title means "Commentaries on the Legend of Master Manole"), Editura Publicom, 1943.

Insula lui Euthanasius (title means "The Island of Euthanasius"), Editura Fundatia Regala pentru Literatura si Arta, 1943.

Os Romenos, Latinos do Oriente (title means "The Romanians, Latins of the East"), Livraria Classica Editora, 1943.

Techniques du Yoga (title means "Techniques of Yoga"), Gallimard, 1948, new edition in three volumes, 1975.

Iphigenia (a play), Editura Cartea Pribegiei, 1951.

Minuit a Serampore [suivi de] *Le Secret du Docteur Honigberger* (title means "Midnight at Seramapore" and "The Secret of Dr. Honigberger"), translated from the Rumanian by Albert Marie Schmidt, Stock, 1956.

Nuvele (novellas; includes "La Tiganci," "O fotografie veche de 14 ani," "Ghicitor in pietre," "Un om mare," "Feta capitanului," and "Douasprezece mil de capete de vite"), Editura Destin, 1963.

Aspects du mythe, Gallimard, 1963.

(With others) *Temoignages sur Brancusi,* Arted (Paris), 1967.

La Tiganci si Alte Povestiri, cu un Studiu Introductiv de Sorin Alexandrescu (title means "At the Gypsies and Other Short Stories"), Editura pentru Literatura (Bucharest), 1969.

Die Pelerine (title means "The Cape"), Suhrkamp (Frankfurt), 1970.

In Curte la Dionis, Caitele Inorogului, 1977.

La Colonne sans fin, translation by Florence M. Hetzler, University Press of America, 1984.

Briser le toit de la maison: La Creativite et ses symbols, Gallimard, 1986.

Also author of some twenty volumes published in Rumanian, 1933-45. Contributor to many books about religions and religious history, including Joseph Campbell's *Man and Time,* Pantheon, 1957, and *Man and Transformation,* Pantheon, 1964. Founder and editor, *Zalmoxis* (an international journal for history of religions), 1938-42; founder and senior editor, *History of Religions,* 1961-1986. Contributor to journals in his field.

SIDELIGHTS: Romanian novelist and religious historian Mircea Eliade sought a place among the intellectuals of his homeland "who thought of themselves as provincial outposts on the confines of European culture," encyclopedists who "often found a kind of over-compensation in . . . a thirst for universalism, in prodigies of (disorderly) knowledge, and in resorting to an aesthetic management of their material," reports *Times Literary Supplement* contributor Virgil Nemoianu. The reviewer adds that a survey of Eliade's numerous works in a variety of languages reveals "how the mixture of encyclopedic and aesthetic impulses . . . shaped his entire career."

Eliade was a voracious reader and a life-long student. At first fascinated with natural science, he collected rocks, plants and insects and set up a small chemistry lab in his family's home, filling notebooks with his observations. More than one hundred articles he wrote were published before he turned twenty. By the time he entered the University of Bucharest, his interests turned to the study of metaphysics and mystical experience. His enthusiasm for the study of primitive and Eastern religions led him to Rome, Geneva, and eventually India, where he became the avid student of Surendranath Dasgupta, a religious historian from whom he learned Yoga. The influence of this religious discipline on his understanding of religious experience appears throughout his writings. Of *Images and Symbols: Studies in Religious Symbolism,* for example, *Hibbert Journal* contributor S. G. F. Brandon remarked that it is "characterized by his . . . implied conviction that the praxis of Yoga is the way par excellence to a proper apprehension of reality."

Writing in the *New York Times Book Review,* Gerald Sykes recognized Eliade as "a scientist-artist who [wrote] not only works of scholarship but novels of admirable intensity." The novels reflect his understanding of world cultures, and their themes parallel his findings "as a historian of religions," George Uscatescu wrote in *Myths and Symbols: Studies in Honor of Mircea Eliade,* edited by Joseph M. Kitagawa and Charles H. Long. Spiritual crisis is the "central problem" in Eliade's "great novel *Foret Interdite,*" a seven-hundred-page work that shows its author "at the fullest unfolding of his epic faculties and establishes for the reader a problematical situation of great literary authenticity and verisimilitude," Uscatescu remarked. Critics praised the novelist for his craftsmanship as much as for his subject matter, Uscatescu noted: "The first long novels, *Isabel si Apele Diavolului* (1930) and *Maitreyi* (1933), draw their inspiration from Indian themes of a strong erotic character and reveal in the hands of a new author both a solid technique and understanding which assures significant success to the works."

Eliade is best known in the United States for his critical and philosophical works on Indian religions, Asiatic alchemy, and mythical thought. However, he felt that his well-received novels—in particular, *La foret interdite (The Forbidden Forest)*—more competently conveyed the experience of the power of myth. He continued writing in both forms because he believed that history, philosophy, and fiction are complementary as instruments of expression. Both his fiction and non-fiction are united by their focus on problems which obsessed him from his youth, including the history of religions, the structure of myths, and religious symbolism.

Eliade identified two stances toward reality: the religious stance, in which man and the world are perceived as sacred, inhabited by powers and meanings beyond the mundane; and the profane, in which man denies the existence of the sacred. Eliade cited Rudolph Otto's book *Das Heilige* (title means "The Sacred") for his definition of the sacred as "something 'wholly other'. . . . Confronted with it, man senses his profound nothingness, feels that he is only a creature." This statement in *The Sacred and the Profane: The Nature of Religion* precedes Eliade's observation that man knows the sacred exists only after something from beyond nature reveals itself to man. The history of religions, therefore, can be seen as a series of "manifestations of sacred realities," encounters with "something of a wholly different order, a reality that does not belong to our world, in objects that are an integral part of our natural 'profane' world," he wrote.

The difference between religious and nonreligious man, Eliade observed in *The Sacred and the Profane,* is that "the nonreligious man refuses transcendence. . . . In other words, he accepts no model for humanity outside the human condition," and "desacralizes himself and the world." Yet beyond that, the tragedy of modern nonreligious man is that his "camouflaged myths and degenerate rituals" show that he can never completely desacralize himself and should not try: "Do what he will he is an inheritor. He cannot utterly abolish his past, since he is himself the product of his past. . . . He continues to be haunted by the realities that he has refused and denied. To acquire a world of his own, he has desacralized the world in which his ancestors lived; but to do so he has been obliged to adopt the opposite of an earlier type of behavior, and that behavior is still emotionally present to him, in one form or another, ready to be reactualized in his deepest being."

Eliade contended it is worthwhile to examine the nature of religious experience because it occurs in every culture. To understand religious man, "to understand his spiritual universe, is, in sum, to advance our general knowledge of man," he claimed in *The Sacred and the Profane.* Eliade criticized early ethnologists and philologists for taking an outsider's approach to religious experience. Eliade insisted the historian of religions needs to empathize, if not to participate, with those who claim to encounter the sacred. In *The Sacred and the Profane,* Eliade stated, "There is no other way of understanding a foreign mental universe than to place oneself *inside* it, at its very center, in order to progress from there to all the values that it possesses." Furthermore, for the historian of religions, scientific study means dealing with religious facts, man's experiences of time and space.

Central to the patterns of Eliade's thought on the history of religions are sacred time and space, problems to which he has returned frequently and about which he has contributed much significant research. As he explained in *The Myth of the Eternal Return; or, Cosmos and History,* some cultures view time as history, as a one-way progression from the irretrievable past into the unknown future. Others view time as cosmos, an infinitely repeat-able cycle reactivated by ceremonies preserved in myths. Men who perceive time as cyclical periodically abolish history by reenacting the conquering of chaos and the creation of the world; actions in the present acquire meaning from their similarity to "first things," encounters with the sacred at the beginning of time. Man trapped in history, however, lives in terror, unable to extract himself from meaningless events. In Christian man, Eliade saw components of both views: "Christianity translates the periodic regeneration of the world into a regeneration of the human individual. But for him who shares in this eternal *nunc* of the reign of God, history ceases as totally as it does for the man of the archaic cultures, who abolishes it periodically."

Substantial sections of *The Myth of the Eternal Return, The Sacred and the Profane,* and *Patterns in Comparative Religion* discuss religious man's concepts of sacred space. Any place where "*something* that does not belong to this world has manifested itself " becomes a symbolic foundation of the world, "a fixed point . . . in the chaos," a central point from which religious man draws his orientation to time and space, Eliade wrote in *The Sacred and the Profane.* Thus certain landmarks and buildings become, for religious man, gateways to continued communication with the sacred. These three books, particularly *The Myth of the Eternal Return,* provide a wealth of supporting examples from cultures in all nations and time periods.

Critics were consistently impressed by Eliade's encyclopedic mode, but were not uncritical of the role that his personal beliefs played in his studies. "Too great a respect for the intimations of Indian thought (great though its achievement is) can be misleading," Brandon stated. Eliade's "apparent assumption of social evolution" was "a hindrance to acceptance by non-religious scholars," reported Dorothy Libby in *American Anthropology.* T. J. J. Altizer, writing in the *Journal of Religion,* commented that generally speaking, "One expects from Eliade an argument that is clear, precise, comprehensive, and fully documented." However, he added, when Eliade equates religious man with primitive man, this "romantic" view makes it difficult for him to discuss modern-day religious experience. Apart from this, Altizer called Eliade a master of the art of describing religions without proposing questionable explanations or claims about their origins.

Eliade's studies of religious experience gave him a permanent place in the history of religious thought. "On the plane of international academic life, Eliade became a kind of prophet of the trans-historical," or timeless common ground shared by members of many cultures, explained Ivan Strenski in the *Los Angeles Times Book Review.* Before he entered the American academic community as a professor at the University of Chicago, the study of religions consisted of pitting belief systems against each other—a process which fell outside the parameters set by the law of separation of church and state in the United States. Eliade saw in the history of religious man a desire for contact with the sacred that transcended cultural boundaries. This new approach helped to establish the study of religion as an academic discipline in American schools. "A true cultural revolutionary to the end, Eliade challenged the whole secular bourgeois world's comforting belief in the adequacy of its own works of science, politics, and economics," Strenski related. Robert S. Ellwood, Jr. remarked in the *New York Times Book Review,* "Only a few in his often arcane discipline have equaled his broad impact on his age. With C. G. Jung and Joseph Campbell, Mircea Eliade helped create the midcentury vogue for myth and ritual popularized by critics, dramatists and assorted spiritual seekers."

All but Eliade's earliest works are still in print, and many have been translated into more than a dozen languages. Reviewers repeatedly call for more English translations of the Romanian scholar's works. Considering these facts and Eliade's impact on the American academic community, Sykes concluded, "The work of this important scholar gains yearly in effect."

BIOGRAPHICAL/CRITICAL SOURCES:

BOOKS

Allen, Douglas, *Structure and Creativity in Religion: Hermeneutics in Mircea Eliade's Phenomenology and New Directions,* Mouton, 1978.
Allen, Douglas and Dennis Doeing, *Mircea Eliade: An Annotated Bibliography,* Garland Press, 1980.
Altizer, Thomas J. J., *Mircea Eliade and the Dialectic of the Sacred,* Westminster Press, 1963.
Apostolos-Cappadona, Diane, editor, *Symbolism, the Sacred, and the Arts,* Crossroad Publishing, 1985.
Carrasco, David and Jane Swanberg, editors, *Waiting for the Dawn: Mircea Eliade in Perspective,* Westview Press, 1985.
Contemporary Literary Criticism, Volume 19, Gale, 1981.
Dudley, G., *Religion on Trial: Mircea Eliade and His Critics,* Temple University Press, 1977.
Eliade, Mircea, *The Sacred and the Profane: The Nature of Religion,* Harper, 1961.
Eliade, Mircea, *Two Tales of the Occult,* Herder, 1970.
Eliade, Mircea, *The Myth of the Eternal Return; or, Cosmos and History,* Princeton University Press, 1974.
Eliade, Mircea, *Autobiography,* Volume 1: *1907-1937, Journey East, Journey West,* Harper, 1981, Volume 2: *1937-1960, Exile's Odyssey,* University of Chicago Press, 1989.
Encyclopedia of Occultism and Parapsychology, 2nd edition, Gale, 1985.
Girardot, Norman and MacLinscott Ricketts, editors, *Imagination and Meaning: The Scholarly and Literary Worlds of Mircea Eliade,* Seabury, 1982.
Kitagawa, Joseph M. and Charles H. Long, editors, *Myths and Symbols: Studies in Honor of Mircea Eliade,* University of Chicago Press, 1969.
Silabu, John A., *"Homo Religiosus" in Mircea Eliade: An Anthropological Evaluation,* Brill, 1976.

PERIODICALS

America, March 10, 1979.
American Anthropologist, August, 1959.
Books Abroad, Volume 49, number 1, 1975.
Encounter, March, 1980.
Hibbert Journal, October, 1961.
Journal of Asian Studies, Volume 30, number 3, 1971.
Journal of Bible and Religion, July, 1965.
Journal of Religion, April, 1960, January 1, 1961, April, 1972, October, 1986.
Listener, January 19, 1978.
Los Angeles Times Book Review, December 22, 1985, January 22, 1989.
New Statesman, December 17, 1960, October 16, 1964.
Newsweek, July 15, 1985.
New York Review of Books, October 20, 1966.
New York Times Book Review, July 12, 1964, August 11, 1974, April 15, 1979, November 22, 1981.
Religion in Life, spring, 1967.
Religion: Journal of Religion and Religions, spring, 1973.
Religious Studies, 1972, 1974.
Time, February 11, 1966, October 26, 1981.

Times Literary Supplement, November 11, 1960, October 13, 1978, April 2, 1982, September 26, 1986.
Tribune Books (Chicago), October 9, 1988.
Union Seminary Quarterly Review, winter, 1970, summer, 1970.
World Literature Today, Volume 51, number 3, 1977, Volume 52, number 4, 1978, Volume 54, number 1, 1980.

OBITUARIES:

BOOKS

Encyclopedia of Occultism and Parapsychology, 2nd edition, Gale, 1984.

PERIODICALS

Chicago Tribune, April 24, 1986.
Los Angeles Times, April 26, 1986.
National Review, June 6, 1986.
New York Times, April 23, 1986.
Time, May 5, 1986.
Times (London), April 29, 1986.*

—*Sketch by Marilyn K. Basel*

* * *

ELKIN, H. V.
    See HINKLE, Vernon

* * *

ELKINS, Dov Peretz   1937-

PERSONAL: Born December 7, 1937, in Philadelphia, Pa.; married Elaine Rash, June 12, 1960; married Maxine G. Stadlin, November 16, 1986; children: (first marriage) Hillel Michael, Jonathan Saul, Shira Bataya. *Education:* Gratz College, Teacher's Diploma, 1958; Temple University, B.A., 1959; Jewish Theological Seminary of America, M.H.L., 1962, Rabbi, 1964; Hebrew University of Jerusalem, additional study, 1962-63; Colgate Rochester Divinity School, D.Min., 1976.

ADDRESSES: Office—Growth Associates, Box 18429, Rochester, N.Y. 14618-0429.

CAREER: Rabbi at Har Zion Temple, Philadelphia, Pa., and Radnor, Pa., 1966-70, in Jacksonville, Fla., 1970-72, at Temple Beth El, Rochester, N.Y., 1972-76, and at the Park Synagogue, Cleveland, Ohio, 1987—; Growth Associates (human relations consulting firm), Rochester, president, 1976—. Jewish chaplain, Haverford State Hospital, 1967-70; faculty member of department of theology, Villanova University, 1969-70. Member of commission on Jewish chaplaincy, National Jewish Welfare Board, 1967-70; member of board, Philadelphia Zionist Organization, 1968-70. Consultant in couple and family therapy and in individual and group counseling; consultant for educational and industrial organizations. *Military service:* U.S. Army, chaplain, 1964-66.

AWARDS, HONORS: Isaac Siegel Memorial Award, National Jewish Welfare Board, Jewish Book Council of America, 1964, for *Worlds Lost and Found: Discoveries in Biblical Archaeology.*

WRITINGS:

(With Azriel Eisenberg) *Worlds Lost and Found: Discoveries in Biblical Archaeology* (juvenile), Abelard, 1964.
So Young to Be a Rabbi (essays), Yoseloff, 1969.
(With Eisenberg) *Treasures from the Dust,* Abelard, 1972.
Rejoice with Jerusalem, Media Judaica, 1972.
A Tradition Reborn: Sermons and Essays on Liberal Judaism, A. S. Barnes, 1973.

God's Warriors: Heroic Stories of Jewish Military Chaplains, Jonathan David, 1974.

Proud to Be Me: Raising Self-Esteem in Individuals, Families, Schools and Minority Groups, Growth Associates, 1975, revised edition published as *Glad to Be Me: Raising Self-Esteem in Yourself and Others,* Prentice-Hall, 1976, revised and expanded edition, Growth Associates, 1989.

Shepherd of Jerusalem: A Biography of Chief Rabbi Abraham Isaac Kook, Shengold, 1976.

Humanizing Jewish Life: Judaism and the Human Potential Movement, A. S. Barnes, 1976.

Teaching People to Love Themselves: A Leader's Handbook of Theory and Technique for Self-Esteem and Affirmation Training, Growth Associates, 1977.

Clarifying Jewish Values, Growth Associates, 1977.

Jewish Consciousness Raising, Growth Associates, 1977.

Experiential Programs, Growth Associates, 1978.

Self-Concept Sourcebook, Growth Associates, 1979.

Twelve Pathways to Feeling Better about Yourself, Growth Associates, 1980.

My Seventy-Two Friends: Encounters with Refuseniks in the U.S.S.R., Growth Associates, 1989.

Sermons included in *Best Jewish Sermons,* Jonathan David, 1966 and 1968, in *Sermons and Jewish Holidays and Festivals,* National Jewish Welfare Board, 1966, and in *Sermons for Special Occasions,* Jonathan David, 1967. Columnist for Seven Arts Feature Syndicate. Contributor of articles to numerous periodicals. Editor, *Benineinu;* contributing editor, *Judaica Book Guide.* Book review editor, *Torch;* regular reviewer, *The Jewish Exponent* and *The Jewish Advocate.*

WORK IN PROGRESS: Meeting Your Jewish Self: Personal Growth for Jews; Exercises in Creativity.

SIDELIGHTS: Dov Peretz Elkins is a certified instructor for Parent Effectiveness Training (P.E.T.) and Teacher Effectiveness Training (T.E.T.). Elkins told *CA* his "specialty is integrating religion, education, and behavioral sciences." His latest focus is promoting holistic health, wellness lifestyles, and spirituality.

*   *   *

ELPHINSTONE, Francis
   See POWELL-SMITH, Vincent (Walter Francis)

*   *   *

ELTON, G(eoffrey) R(udolph) 1921-

PERSONAL: Original surname, Ehrenberg; born August 17, 1921, in Tuebingen, Germany (now West Germany); son of Victor L. (a classical scholar) and Eva (Sommer) Ehrenberg; married Sheila Lambert (a historian), August 30, 1952. *Education:* Attended Rydal School, Colwyn Bay, Wales, 1939-40; University of London, B.A., Ph.D.; Cambridge University, M.A., Litt.D.

ADDRESSES: Office—Clare College, Cambridge University, Cambridge CB2 1TL, England.

CAREER: University of Glasgow, Glasgow, Scotland, assistant in history, 1948-49; Cambridge University, Cambridge, England, 1949—, began as assistant lecturer, lecturer in history, 1949-63, reader in Tudor studies, 1963-67, professor of English constitutional history, 1967-83, Regius professor of modern history, 1983-88, fellow of Clare College, 1954—, syndic, Cambridge University Press, 1960-73. *Military service:* British Army, Infantry and Intelligence, during World War II; became sergeant.

MEMBER: British Academy (fellow), Royal Historical Society (fellow; president, 1973-77), American Academy of Arts and Sciences (foreign member), Seldeon Society (president, 1983-85).

AWARDS, HONORS: Knighted, 1986.

WRITINGS:

The Tudor Revolution in Government: Administrative Changes in the Reign of Henry VIII, Cambridge University Press, 1953.

England under the Tudors, Putnam, 1955, 2nd edition, Chapman & Hall, 1974.

Star Chamber Stories, Methuen, 1958.

Henry VIII: An Essay in Revision, Routledge & Kegan Paul, 1962.

(With George Kitson Clark) *Guide to Research Facilities in History in the Universities of Great Britain and Ireland,* Cambridge University Press, 1963, 2nd edition, 1965.

Reformation Europe, 1517-1559, Collins, 1963, Meridian Books, 1964.

The Practice of History, Sydney University Press, 1967, Crowell, 1968, new edition, Fontana Press, 1987.

The Future of the Past: An Inaugural Lecture, Cambridge University Press, 1968.

Reform by Statute: Thomas Starkey's "Dialogue" and Thomas Cromwell's Policy, Longwood, 1968.

The Body of the Whole Realm: Parliament and Representation in Medieval and Tudor England, University Press of Virginia, 1969.

England, 1200-1640, Cornell University Press, 1969.

Political History: Principles and Practice, Basic Books, 1970, reprinted, Garland Publishing, 1985.

Modern Historians on British History, 1485-1945: A Critical Bibliography, 1945-1969, Methuen, 1970, Cornell University Press, 1971.

Twenty-Five Years of Modern British History: A Bibliographical Survey, 1945-1969, British Book Centre, 1971.

Policy and Police: The Enforcement of the Reformation in the Age of Thomas Cromwell, Cambridge University Press, 1972.

Reform and Renewal: Thomas Cromwell and the Commonweal, Cambridge University Press, 1973.

Studies in Tudor and Stuart Politics and Government, Cambridge University Press, Volumes 1-2: *Papers and Reviews, 1946-1972,* 1974, Volume 3: *Papers and Reviews, 1973-1981,* 1982.

Reform and Reformation: England, 1509-1558, Harvard University Press (London), 1977.

England in the Sixteenth Century: Reform in an Age of Change, Selden Society, 1980.

(With Robert William Fogel) *Which Road to the Past?: Two Views of History,* Yale University Press, 1983.

The History of England: An Inaugural Lecture, Cambridge University Press, 1984.

F. W. Maitland, Yale University Press, 1985.

The Parliament of England, 1559-1581, Cambridge University Press, 1986.

EDITOR

New Cambridge Modern History, Volume 2: *The Reformation, 1520-1559,* Cambridge University Press, 1958.

The Tudor Constitution: Documents and Commentary, Cambridge University Press, 1960, 2nd edition, 1982.

Ideas and Institutions: Renaissance and Reformation, 1300-1648, Volume 3, Macmillan, 1963, 3rd edition, 1976.

Albert Frederick Pollard, *Wolsey,* Collins, 1965.
The Royal Historical Society Annual Bibliography of British and Irish History, ten volumes, St. Martin, 1976-85.

SIDELIGHTS: G. R. Elton is a respected conservative historian who specializes in the English Renaissance and Reformation periods. "Elton's creed is very simple," remarks Geoffrey Barraclough in the *New York Review of Books.* "We should return to the paths marked out by our forefathers. 'The documents remain paramount'; 'the written record dominates.' It is a plea which is particularly attractive to medievalists, because their basic problem is the paucity of their sources." In *Which Road to the Past?: Two Views of History,* Elton's traditionalist views are contrasted with a leading cliometrician, Robert William Fogel. Cliometrics is the approach to history which relies completely upon statistics. Debating this method in *Which Road to the Past?,* Elton writes that "Cliometrics can effectively operate by suppressing the individual—by reducing its subject-matter to a collectivity of human data in which the facts of humanity have real difficulty in surviving. . . . Cliometrics therefore serves the history of mankind quite admirably when that history is seen as one of concepts and structures, but it is markedly less useful when that history turns to the story of people."

BIOGRAPHICAL/CRITICAL SOURCES:

BOOKS

Elton, G. R. and Robert W. Fogel, *Which Road to the Past?: Two Views of History,* Yale University Press, 1983.

PERIODICALS

Books and Bookmen, June, 1969.
Listener, January 11, 1968.
New Statesman, September 18, 1970.
New York Review of Books, June 4, 1970, March 22, 1973, February 13, 1986.
New York Times, August 13, 1966, July 30, 1984.
New York Times Book Review, March 12, 1978, May 20, 1979.
Observer, November 16, 1969.
South Atlantic Quarterly, summer, 1968.
Spectator, September 27, 1969, June 22, 1985.
Times Literary Supplement, January 11, 1968, October 16, 1970, March 17, 1972, April 20, 1973, December 6, 1974, June 16, 1978, April 15, 1983, February 28, 1986, June 5, 1987.
Washington Post Book World, February 12, 1984.

*   *   *

EMPEY, LaMar T(aylor) 1923-

PERSONAL: Born April 9, 1923, in Price, Utah; son of Claudius M. (a banker) and Mabel (Taylor) Empey; married Betty Mitchell, August 25, 1949; children: John, Kathleen, Martha, James. *Education:* Brigham Young University, B.A., 1950, M.A., 1951; Washington State University, Ph.D., 1955. *Politics:* Democrat. *Religion:* None.

ADDRESSES: Office—Department of Sociology, University of Southern California, University Park, Los Angeles, Calif. 90007.

CAREER: Brigham Young University, Provo, Utah, assistant professor, 1955-57, associate professor of sociology, 1958-62; University of Southern California, Los Angeles, associate professor, 1962-67, professor of sociology, 1967—, chairman of department, 1967-71, senior research associate, 1963-64, and director, 1964-67, of Youth Studies Center, associate research director of Gerontology Center, 1971-74. Member, research advisory committee, California Department of Mental Hygiene; consultant to

various state and federal departments and commissions, including the U.S. Department of Labor. *Military service:* U.S. Army, infantry, 1943-46; became first lieutenant. U.S. Army Reserves, 1946-52; became captain.

MEMBER: American Sociological Association, American Society of Criminology, Society for the Study of Social Problems, Pacific Sociological Association (vice-president, 1967-68, 1970-71), Phi Beta Kappa, Phi Kappa Phi.

AWARDS, HONORS: Research grants from Ford Foundation, Rosenberg Foundation, Office of Juvenile Delinquency, National Science Foundation, and National Institute of Mental Health, 1959-1977.

WRITINGS:

Alternatives to Incarceration, U.S. Government Printing Office, 1967.
(With Anthony J. Manocchio and Jimmy Dunn) *The Time Game: Two Views of a Prison,* Sage Publications, 1970.
(With Steven G. Lubeck) *The Silverlake Experiment: Testing Delinquency Theory and Community Intervention,* Aldine, 1971.
(With Lubeck) *Explaining Delinquency,* Heath, 1971.
(With Maynard L. Erickson) *The Provo Experiment: Impact and Death of an Innovation,* Lexington Books, 1972.
American Delinquency: Its Meaning and Construction, Dorsey, 1978, revised edition, 1982.
(Editor) *Juvenile Justice: The Progressive Legacy and Current Reforms,* University Press of Virginia, 1979.
(Editor and contributor) *The Future of Childhood and Juvenile Justice,* University Press of Virginia, 1980.

Contributor to professional journals, including *American Sociological Review.* Associate editor, *American Sociological Review* and *Sociology and Social Research.*

SIDELIGHTS: LaMar T. Empey once told *CA* that he has been "interested primarily in youth and their problems. Like many of my contemporaries, I have concentrated on the scientific study of delinquency and juvenile justice. My recent work, however, convinces me that we have often been off target because of our failure to grasp the significance of broad historical and cultural changes. Our current preoccupation with childhood in Western Civilization is a product of the last two or three centuries. Furthermore, that preoccupation is now undergoing radical change. As a result, the status of youth will be altered and, with it, will come sharp changes in our perceptions of, and reactions to, them."*

*   *   *

EPSTEIN, June

PERSONAL: Born in Perth, Australia; daughter of Simon (a businessman) and Annie (Walters) Epstein; married Julius Guest (a lecturer in mathematics), March 7, 1949; children: Katharine-Anne (Mrs. William Garland), John Carey, Philip Ross (deceased). *Education:* Trinity College of Music, London, licentiate; Royal Academy of Music, licentiate; Royal School of Church Music, licentiate.

ADDRESSES: Office—Institute of Early Childhood Studies, School of Education, University of Melbourne, 4 Madden Grove, Kew, Victoria, Australia.

CAREER: Australian Broadcasting Commission, Melbourne, Australia, broadcaster and scriptwriter, 1933—; director of music at Melbourne Church of England Girls' Grammar School,

1946-49; Melbourne College of Advanced Education, Institute of Early Childhood Development, Kew, Australia, senior lecturer, 1972-78; University of Melbourne, School of Education, currently affiliated with Institute of Early Childhood Studies.

MEMBER: Australian Society of Authors, Fellowship of Australian Writers, Society of Women Writers, Kew Cottages' Parents' Association (foundation president, 1957).

AWARDS, HONORS: Overseas scholar at Trinity College of Music, 1936-39; silver medal from Worshipful Company of Musicians, 1938; Literature Board of the Australia Council grant, 1973 and 1982; Best Children's Book Award, Royal Zoological Society of New South Wales, 1981, for *The Friends of Burramys;* Rigby Literary Award, 1982, for *Scarecrow and Company;* Order of Australia Medal for services to the arts and to people with disabilities.

WRITINGS:

The Nine Muses, Robertson & Mullens, 1951.
Mermaid on Wheels: The Story of Margaret Lester, Ure Smith, 1967, Taplinger, 1968.
Image of the King: A Parent's Story of Mentally Handicapped Children, Ure Smith, 1970.
Enjoying Music with Young Children, Allans, 1972, 2nd edition, 1984.
"A Paltry Affair," first produced in Victoria, Austria, November, 1976.
Mr. Nightingale, Allans, 1978.
Boy on Sticks, National Press, 1979.
No Music by Request: A Portrait of the Gorman Family, Collins, 1980.
A Golden String: The Story of Dorothy J. Ross, Greenhouse, 1981.
The Friends of Burramys, Oxford University Press, 1981.
A Swag of Songs (with cassette), Oxford University Press, 1984.
Scarecrow and Company, Rigby, 1984.
The Icecream Kids, Jacaranda-Wiley, 1984.
The Emperor's Tally, Jacaranda-Wiley, 1984.
Concert Pitch: The Story of the National Music Camp Association and the Australian Youth Orchestra, Hyland House, 1984.
A Second Swag of Songs (with cassette), Oxford University Press, 1986.
Woman with Two Hats, Hyland House, 1988.
Turn a Deaf Ear: The Story of the Bionic Ear, Hyland House, 1989.

"BIG DIPPER" SERIES; WITH CASSETTES

Big Dipper, Oxford University Press, 1981.
. . . Rides Again, Oxford University Press, 1982.
. . . Returns, Oxford University Press, 1985.
. . . Songs, Oxford University Press, 1985.

OTHER

Also author of educational recordings for children and composer of music. Music critic, *Australian Journal of Music Education.*

SIDELIGHTS: June Epstein told *CA:* "I've always combined the two professional careers of music and writing. In music I began in childhood as a concert pianist, studied on an overseas scholarship, returned to tour Australia as a concert pianist for the Australian Broadcasting Commission, and later became involved in music education.

"In writing I have been influenced by my great interest and involvement with handicapped people and have written three full-length biographies of people with different handicaps, as well as a number of other books concerning disabilities. I also write many books for children of different ages."

* * *

EVANS, Alice Frazer 1939-

PERSONAL: Born June 19, 1939, in Mobile, Ala.; daughter of Emmett Baxter (a surgeon) and Mary Jane (Knight) Frazer; married Robert Allen Evans (a minister and executive), June 9, 1961; children: Mellinda, Judith, Allen. *Education:* Attended University of Edinburgh, 1959-60, University of Wisconsin—Madison, 1961-62, and Goethe Institute, Berlin, Germany; Agnes Scott College, B.A., 1961. *Religion:* Presbyterian.

ADDRESSES: Office—Plowshares Institute, P.O. Box 243, Simsbury, Conn. 06070.

CAREER: High school English teacher in Woodbridge, Conn., 1962-63; free-lance writer, 1963-77; Lakeview Spanish Center, Chicago, Ill., teacher of English as a second language, 1972-74; Hartford Seminary, Hartford, Conn., adjunct faculty member in lay theology, 1977-81; Plowshares Institute, Simsbury, Conn., director of research and writing, 1982—. Fellow and member of faculty at Case Study Institute in Cambridge, Mass., Pasadena, Calif., Wake Forest, Ill., Evanston, Ill., and Toronto, Ont., 1977-89; G. W. Thatcher Lecturer at United Theological College, Sydney, Australia, 1978; visiting lecturer at other universities in Australia and elsewhere around the globe. Member of Connecticut Christian Conference of Churches Council on Social Concerns; church elder; chair, Permanent Judicial Commission, and member of Presbytery Council, Southern New England Presbytery. Scuba diver and lecturer at Shedd Aquarium.

MEMBER: Association for Case Teaching (co-executive director), American Academy of Religion.

AWARDS, HONORS: Danforth Foundation grant, 1980; Walsh-Price fellowship from Maryknoll Society, 1980-82; Lilly Endowment grant, 1981.

WRITINGS:

(With husband, Robert Allen Evans, Louis Weeks, and Carolyn Weeks) *Casebook for Christian Living,* John Knox, 1977.
(With R. A. Evans) *Introduction to Christianity: A Case Method Approach,* John Knox, 1980.
(With R. A. Evans and D. H. Gregg) *Case Studies in Higher Education Ministries,* National Institute for Campus Ministries, 1980.
(With R. A. Evans) *Human Rights: A Dialogue between the First and Third Worlds,* Orbis, 1983.
(With R. A. Evans, Paolo Freire, and William B. Kennedy) *Pedagogies for the Non-Poor,* Orbis, 1987.
(With Robert Stivers, Christine Gudorf, and R. A. Evans) *Christian Ethics: A Case Method Approach,* Orbis, 1989.

CONTRIBUTOR

R. A. Evans and T. D. Parker, editors, *Christian Theology: A Case Method Approach,* Harper, 1976.
O. F. Williams and J. W. Houck, editors, *Full Value: Cases in Christian Business Ethics,* Harper, 1978.
P. H. Hill and others, editors, *Making Decisions: A Multidisciplinary Introduction,* Addison-Wesley, 1979.
R. A. Evans, M. H. Davis, and G. D. Lewis, editors, *Dynamics of Faith,* Alban Institute, 1981.
Lewis, editor, *Resolving Church Conflicts,* Harper, 1981.
Carl Dudley, editor, *Building Effective Ministry,* Harper, 1983.
Zelle W. Andrews, editor, *War in Slow Motion,* Pilgrim, 1985.

H. S. Wilson, editor, *Indian Theological Case Studies,* Tamil Nadu, 1986.

Wilson, editor, *Human Rights Issues and the Pastoral Ministry,* Board of Theological Education, 1989.

OTHER

Contributor to magazines. Editor of newsletter of Association for Case Teaching.

WORK IN PROGRESS: Rhythms in Marital Bonding, with James Reed.

SIDELIGHTS: Alice Frazer Evans wrote: "My world view has been most significantly affected by living for extended periods in the Third and Fourth Worlds (East Africa and Fiji), and by having opportunities to teach in India and Asia. My teaching and writing emphasize the need for the First World to move from a myopic perspective to a realization of interdependence with the rest of the world. This involves acknowledgement of the First World's responsibility for many of the world's problems and an awareness and appreciation of the many gifts the Third World offers.

"I am convinced of the need to bridge the gap between the theoretical and practical in theological education. I have invested heavily in the development and promotion of the case study approach toward this goal. This is a dialogical teaching method which values the insights and experiences of the participants."

*   *   *

EVANS, Jessica
  See LOTTMAN, Eileen

F

FABER, Doris (Greenberg) 1924-

PERSONAL: Born January 29, 1924, in New York, N.Y.; daughter of Harry and Florence (Greenwald) Greenberg; married Harold Faber (a writer for *New York Times*), June 21, 1951; children: Alice, Marjorie. *Education:* Attended Goucher College, 1940-42; New York University, B.A., 1943.

ADDRESSES: Home—R.D. 1, Ancram, N.Y. 12502.

CAREER: New York Times, New York, N.Y., reporter, 1943-51; writer.

WRITINGS:

JUVENILES

Elaine Stinson: Campus Reporter, Knopf, 1955.
The Wonderful Tumble of Timothy Smith, Knopf, 1958.
Printer's Devil to Publisher: Adolph S. Ochs of the New York Times (Junior Literary Guild selection), Messner, 1963.
Luther Burbank: Partner of Nature, Garrard, 1963.
The Life of Pocahontas, Prentice-Hall, 1963.
Behind the Headlines: The Story of Newspapers, Pantheon, 1963.
The Miracle of Vitamins, Putnam, 1964.
Horace Greeley: The People's Editor, Prentice-Hall, 1964.
Robert Frost: America's Poet (Junior Literary Guild selection), Prentice-Hall, 1964.
Clarence Darrow: Defender of the People, illustrations by Paul Frame, Prentice-Hall, 1965.
Captive Rivers: The Story of Big Dams, Putnam, 1966.
Enrico Fermi: Atomic Pioneer, Prentice-Hall, 1966.
John Jay, Putnam, 1966.
Rose Greenhow: Spy for the Confederacy, Putnam, 1967.
Petticoat Politics: How American Women Won the Right to Vote, Lothrop, 1967.
(With husband, Harold Faber) *American Heroes of the 20th Century,* Random House, 1967.
Anne Hutchinson, Garrard, 1970.
I Will Be Heard: The Life of William Lloyd Garrison, Lothrop, 1970.
Lucretia Mott, Garrard, 1971.
Enough! The Revolt of the American Consumer, Farrar, Straus, 1972.
Harry Truman, Abelard, 1972.
Oh, Lizzie! The Life of Elizabeth Cady Stanton, Lothrop, 1972.
Nationalism, Harper, 1973.

The Perfect Life: The Shakers in America (young adult), Farrar, Straus, 1974.
Franklin Roosevelt, Abelard, 1975.
Wall Street: A Story of Fortunes and Finance, Harper, 1979.
Love and Rivalry: Three Exceptional Pairs of Sisters (young adult), Viking, 1983.
Eleanor Roosevelt: First Lady of the World (Junior Literary Guild selection), Viking, 1985.
Margaret Thatcher: Britain's "Iron Lady," Viking, 1985.
(With H. Faber) *Martin Luther King, Jr.* (young adult), Messner, 1986.
(With H. Faber) *Mahatma Gandhi* (juvenile), Messner, 1986.
(With H. Faber) *We the People,* Scribner, 1987.
(With H. Faber) *Great Lives: American Government* (juvenile), Scribner, 1988.
(With H. Faber) *The Birth of a Nation: The First Years of the United States,* Scribner, 1989.

ADULT NONFICTION

The Mothers of American Presidents, New American Library, 1968.
The Presidents' Mothers, St. Martin's, 1978.
(With H. Faber) *The Assassination of Martin Luther King, Jr.,* F. Watts, 1978.
The Life of Lorena Hickok: E. R.'s Friend (Book-of-the-Month Club alternate selection), Morrow, 1980.

OTHER

Contributor of feature stories to newspapers, 1951—.

WORK IN PROGRESS: Several biographical and historical books.

SIDELIGHTS: Doris Faber was doing routine research for a commissioned book on the life of Eleanor Roosevelt when she made a startling discovery. A bundle of letters, previously unavailable to scholars, suggested that the first lady may have been, as *Los Angeles Times Book Review* critic Carolyn See suggests, "'in love,' perhaps even in a physical sense" with Lorena Hickok, one of the foremost women journalists of the time. Faber's first reaction, reports Kenneth S. Lynn of the *Times Literary Supplement,* was "to have the Hickok papers sealed up again until at least the year 2,000. When this proved impossible, she decided that she simply could not walk away from a biographical discovery of such magnitude. She would turn the papers into a book." Abandoning her original project, Faber instead produced *The Life of Lorena Hickok: E. R.'s Friend.*

Though critics speculate that Hickok's biography would never have been written were it not for her friendship with Eleanor Roosevelt, they find her an interesting woman in her own right. "She reminds one of those brave young women in a Dreiser novel who, in shirtwaist and long skirt, struggled determinedly in the early years of this century to escape the dreariness of small-town life in the Middle West and seek their fortunes in the great city," Arthur Schlesinger, Jr., writes in the *New York Times Book Review.* Born to a poverty-stricken family, Hickok was abused by her father and neglected by her mother, who died when Lorena was only thirteen. After her mother's death, Hickok became a domestic servant in a boarding house. Eventually, she worked her way through college and got a job at the *Battle Creek Journal.* "Fifteen years later," Schlesinger says, "she was a top reporter for the Associated Press in New York, chain-smoking and hard-drinking, covering events such as the sinking of the Vestris and the Lindberg kidnapping and reputed to be the first woman whose byline appeared above a page-one story in the *New York Times.*"

It was as a journalist that Hickok first came in contact with Eleanor Roosevelt in 1932. Lynn writes: "While waiting to learn whether the Democratic convention in Chicago had nominated her husband for president, Eleanor Roosevelt invited two reporters from the Associated Press to have breakfast with her in the Executive Mansion in Albany. As they left the mansion a short time later, one of the reporters turned to the other and said, 'That woman is unhappy about something.' The speaker was Lorena Hickok who knew something of unhappiness herself."

Sylvia Jukes Morris writes in the *Washington Post Book World* that Hickok was "immediately attracted to Eleanor Roosevelt's patrician qualities. She also felt a special empathy with her plainness, ungainly height and poor dress sense. For her part, Eleanor Roosevelt was drawn to Hickok's directness, humor, quick intelligence and imagination. She envied women of achievement and longed to be one of them." Though she had already spent twenty-three years in the public eye by the time her husband had become president, Eleanor Roosevelt felt inadequate to assume the role of first lady. She feared she would be unfavorably compared with her Uncle Theodore's wife, Edith, whom, Faber reports, she considered "one of the most successful and admired hostesses the White House had ever had." She had also learned of her husband's affair with his secretary, Lucy Mercer, and felt despondent that she "had not been able to hold the attention of a man she loved," Lynn says.

Soon after Roosevelt was inaugurated president, Hickok quit her Associated Press job and went to work for Harry Hopkin's Federal Emergency Relief Administration. There, as a chief field investigator, she filed reports of bureaucratic bungling and deception, which *Los Angeles Times Book Review* writer Walter Wells calls "among the most vivid records we have of that time of not-so-quiet depression." Her work sometimes took her out of Washington, D.C., for months at a time; nevertheless, she and Eleanor wrote to one another daily. Critics say the intimate tone of their correspondence suggests that the two women were deeply in love. "Hick darling," Eleanor Roosevelt wrote in a letter dated March 7, 1933, "All day long I've thought of you & another birthday I *will* be with you. . . . Oh! I want to put my arms around you. I ache to hold you close. Your ring is a great comfort. I look at it & I think she does love me or I wouldn't be wearing it." Over a year later, on September 1, 1934, Eleanor Roose-

velt wrote, "I wish I could lie down beside you tonight & take you in my arms."

Though evidence indicates that Eleanor Roosevelt's infatuation with Lorena Hickok diminished as her self-confidence increased, her friend's ardor never cooled. Elizabeth Cleland notes in the *Washington Star* that after election night Hickok "all but ceased being a reporter. She was Mrs. Roosevelt's confidant; her love for Eleanor Roosevelt was the most important thing in her life, then and for the next thirty years."

The correspondence that the women exchanged during this time was entrusted to Hickok. Though she destroyed those letters she deemed too private to be seen by others, over 3000 still remain. In noting what she calls the "sensational tinge" of this writing, Faber arouses her readers' curiosity. "What we want to know—to put it less decorously than Mrs. Faber ever does: Were Hick and Mrs. Roosevelt actually lovers?" writes Christopher Lehmann-Haupt of the *New York Times.*

According to Elizabeth Ollen of the *Cincinnati Enquirer,* that question can never be answered. "The exact nature of Hickok's friendship with Eleanor Roosevelt," she writes, "will never be known for sure." The uncertainty persists, not because of any flaw in Faber's "carefully written and thoroughly researched" biography, but rather because it is difficult to interpret the evidence correctly. "The language of their correspondence is warm and intense," explains Ollen, "but since the general public was far less informed and far less paranoid about homosexuality, and colloquial English permitted more effusiveness some forty years ago, it was permissible then for women to walk arm in arm and to use terms of endearment that would raise eyebrows today." But Morris argues that it may be misleading to see the content of these letters in "some innocent historic context." Regardless of the general public's awareness, Morris believes Hickok and Roosevelt were too "well-read and well-traveled" to be so naive. Florence Mouckley, on the other hand, believes that Faber has "threaded her way carefully through fact and inference insofar as it was possible." She suggests that to read the book for sensationalism is to miss the point. "The book is serious biography, not pulp disclosure," she writes in her *Christian Science Monitor* review.

If Faber's intention was to downplay the sensational, why, wonder several reviewers, does she invest the issue with so much significance? Lehmann-Haupt thinks the omnipresence of the question "throws a glaring spotlight on the middle chapters of the book—those covering the period when the two protagonists were closest to each other—and makes everything that comes before and after seem as relatively unimportant as a prologue and an afterword." Schlesinger suggests that what Faber should have explored is "the light Hickok's life cast on the times—the problems of a female reporter in a male-dominated profession, for instance, or the significance of Hickok's work for Hopkins." And Kenneth S. Lynn of the *Times Literary Supplement* thinks Faber could have explored more fully the "significant implications of her subject," but tempers this criticism by applauding her responsible presentation of evidence. "Thanks to her," he says, "future historians will be able to write vastly more believable appraisals of Eleanor Roosevelt than those we now have." Elizabeth Cleland of the *Washington Star* also praises the careful job of reporting that Faber has done: "She assumed nothing. She checked and rechecked every date, every event. She sought out, with difficulty, people who knew Hickok, or knew about her and her friendship with Mrs. Roosevelt. The copious notes at the back of the book justify every statement. If the story 'had to come out,' Doris Faber was the one to tell it."

BIOGRAPHICAL/CRITICAL SOURCES:

PERIODICALS

Christian Science Monitor, April 9, 1980.
Cincinnati Enquirer, March 16, 1980.
Los Angeles Times Book Review, February 10, 1980.
Newsday, February 10, 1980.
New York Times, February 5, 1980.
New York Times Book Review, February 17, 1980.
Times Literary Supplement, July 11, 1980.
Washington Post Book World, February 17, 1980.

*　　*　　*

FARBER, Donald C.

PERSONAL: Born in Columbus, Neb.; son of Charles and Sarah (Epstein) Farber; married Ann Eis (a mathematics professor), December 28, 1947; children: Seth, Patricia. *Education:* University of Nebraska, B.S., 1948, J.D. (with honors), 1950. *Politics:* Independent. *Religion:* Jewish.

ADDRESSES: Home—14 East 75th St., New York, N.Y. 10021. *Office*—Tanner, Propp, Fersko & Sterner, 99 Park Ave., New York, N.Y. 10016.

CAREER: Formerly counsel to firm of Conboy, Hewitt, O'Brien & Boardman, New York City; currently partner and head of theatrical department of Tanner, Propp, Fersko & Sterner, New York City. Professor of law at Hofstra University, Hempstead, N.Y., 1974-75; currently teaching courses in theatre law at New School for Social Research, New York City. Visiting professor, York University, Toronto, Ontario, 1970-73; chairman of Practicing Law Institute seminar in theatre law, 1972; guest lecturer or speaker at Brooklyn College of the City University of New York, New York University, Iowa Arts Council Seminar, and Hofstra Institute for the Arts and National Theatre Conference. Founder of and participant in Commercial Theatre Institute, sponsored by Foundation for the Extension and Development of the American Professional Theatre. *Military service:* U.S. Army, Infantry, World War II; became sergeant.

MEMBER: Order of the Coif.

WRITINGS:

From Option to Opening (also see below), DBS Publications, 1968, 4th edition, 1988.
Producing on Broadway: A Comprehensive Guide (also see below), DBS Publications, 1969.
Actor's Guide: What You Should Know about the Contracts You Sign, DBS Publications, 1971.
(With Paul Baumgarten) *Producing, Financing and Distributing Film,* DBS Publications, 1973.
Producing Theatre: A Comprehensive Legal and Business Guide (contains *From Option to Opening* and *Producing on Broadway: A Comprehensive Guide*), DBS Publications, 1981, 3rd edition, 1987.
(Author of Volume 3 on theatre, and editor) *Entertainment Industry Contracts: Negotiating and Drafting Guide,* Matthew Bender, 1986, annual supplements, 1987, 1988, 1989.

Contributor to *New York Law Journal.*

*　　*　　*

FARRELL, Ben
　　See CEBULASH, Mel

FEIFFER, Jules (Ralph) 1929-

PERSONAL: Born January 26, 1929, in Bronx, N.Y.; son of David (held a variety of positions, including dental technician and salesman) and Rhoda (a fashion designer; maiden name, Davis) Feiffer; married Judith Sheftel (a production executive with Warner Bros.), September 17, 1961 (divorced); married Jennifer Allen (a journalist); children: (first marriage) Kate; (second marriage) one daughter. *Education:* Attended Art Students League, New York, N.Y., 1946, and Pratt Institute, 1947-48 and 1949-51.

ADDRESSES: Home—325 West End Ave., New York, N.Y. 10023. *Office*—c/o Universal Press Syndicate, 4400 Johnson Dr., Fairway, Kan. 66205.

CAREER: Assistant to cartoonist Will Eisner, 1946-51, and ghostwriter for Eisner's comic book "The Spirit," 1949-51; author of syndicated cartoon strip, "Clifford," 1949-51; held a variety of positions in the art field, 1953-56, including producer of slide films, writer for Columbia Broadcasting System, Inc.'s "Terry Toons," and designer of booklets for an art firm; author of cartoon strip (originally entitled "Sick, Sick, Sick," later changed to "Feiffer"), published in *Village Voice,* 1956—, published weekly in London *Observer,* 1958-66, and 1972-82, and regularly in *Playboy,* 1959—; syndicated cartoonist, 1959—. Faculty member, Yale Drama School, 1973-74. *Military service:* U.S. Army, Signal Corps, 1951-53; worked in cartoon animation unit.

MEMBER: Authors League of America, Dramatists Guild (member of council), PEN, Writers Guild of America, East.

AWARDS, HONORS: Special George Polk Memorial Award, 1962; named most promising playwright of 1966-67 season by New York drama critics, London Theatre Critics Award, 1967, Outer Circle Critics Award, 1969, and Obie Award of *Village Voice,* 1969, all for "Little Murders"; Outer Circle Critics Award, 1970, for "The White House Murder Case"; Pulitzer Prize, 1986, for editorial cartooning.

WRITINGS:

CARTOON BOOKS

Sick, Sick, Sick, McGraw, 1958, published with introduction by Kenneth Tynan, Collins, 1959.
Passionella, and Other Stories (also see below), McGraw, 1959.
Boy, Girl, Boy, Girl, Random House, 1961.
Feiffer's Album, Random House, 1963.
The Penguin Feiffer, Penguin, 1966.
Feiffer's Marriage Manual, Random House, 1967.
Feiffer on Civil Rights, Anti-Defamation League of B'nai B'rith, 1967.
Pictures at a Prosecution: Drawings and Text from the Chicago Conspiracy Trial, Grove, 1971.
Feiffer on Nixon: The Cartoon Presidency, Random House, 1974.
(With Israel Horovitz) *VD Blues,* Avon, 1974.
Tantrum: A Novel in Cartoons, Knopf, 1979.
Jules Feiffer's America: From Eisenhower to Reagan, edited by Steve Heller, Knopf, 1982.
Marriage Is an Invasion of Privacy and Other Dangerous Views, Andrews & McMeel, 1984.
Feiffer's Children, Andrews & McMeel, 1986.
Ronald Reagan in Movie America: A Jules Feiffer Production, Andrews & McMeel, 1988.

PUBLISHED PLAYS

The Explainers (satirical review; produced in Chicago, Ill., at Playwright's Cabaret Theatre, May 9, 1961), McGraw, 1960.

Crawling Arnold (one-act; first produced in Spoleto, Italy, at Festival of Two Worlds, June 28, 1961; first produced in United States in Cambridge, Mass., at Poets' Theatre, 1961), Dramatists Play Service, 1963.

Hold Me! (first produced Off-Broadway at American Place Theatre, January, 1977), Random House, 1963.

The Unexpurgated Memoirs of Bernard Mergendeiler (one-act; first produced in Los Angeles, Calif., at Mark Taper Forum, October 9, 1967), Random House, 1965.

Little Murders (two-act comedy; first produced on Broadway at Broadhurst Theatre, April 25, 1967; first American play produced on the West End by Royal Shakespeare Co. at Aldwych Theatre, 1967; also see below), Random House, 1968, reprinted, Penguin, 1983.

(Contributor) "Dick and Jane" (one-act; produced in New York City at Eden Theatre as part of "Oh! Calcutta!," devised by Tynan, June 17, 1969; also see below), published in *Oh! Calcutta!,* edited by Tynan, Grove, 1969.

Feiffer's People: Sketches and Observations (produced as "Feiffer's People" in Edinburgh, Scotland, at International Festival of Music and Drama, August, 1968), Dramatists Play Service, 1969.

The White House Murder Case: A Play in Two Acts [and] *Dick and Jane: A One-Act Play* ("The White House Murder Case" first produced Off-Broadway at Circle in the Square Downtown, February 18, 1970), Grove, 1970.

Knock Knock (first produced Off-Off-Broadway at Circle Repertory Theatre, January 18, 1976), Hill & Wang, 1976.

Elliot Loves (first produced on Broadway, 1989), Grove, 1989.

UNPUBLISHED PLAYS

"The World of Jules Feiffer," produced in New Jersey at Hunterdon Hills Playhouse, 1962.

"God Bless," first produced in New Haven, Conn., at Yale School of Drama, October 10, 1968; produced on the West End by Royal Shakespeare Co. at Aldwych Theatre, 1968.

"Munro" (adapted by Feiffer from story in *Passionella, and Other Stories*), first produced in Brooklyn, N.Y., in Prospect Park, August 15, 1971.

(With others) "Watergate Classics," first produced at Yale School of Drama, November 16, 1973.

"Grownups," first produced in Cambridge, Mass., at Loeb Drama Center, June, 1981; produced on Broadway at Lyceum Theater, December, 1981.

"A Think Piece," first produced Off-Off-Broadway at Circle Repertory Theatre, 1982.

"Carnal Knowledge" (revised version of play of same title originally written c. 1970; also see below), first produced in Houston, Tex., at Stages Repertory Theater, spring, 1988.

Also author of "Interview" and "You Should Have Caught Me at the White House," both c. 1962.

SCREENPLAYS

"Munro" (animated cartoon; adapted by Feiffer from story in *Passionella, and Other Stories*), Rembrandt Films, 1961.

"Carnal Knowledge" (adapted from Feiffer's unpublished, unproduced play of same title written c. 1970), Avco Embassy, 1971.

"Little Murders" (adapted by author from play of same title), Twentieth Century-Fox, 1971.

"Popeye," Paramount/Walt Disney Productions, 1980.

Also author of unproduced screenplays, "Little Brucie," "Bernard and Huey," and "I Want to Go Home."

OTHER

(Illustrator) Robert Mines, *My Mind Went All to Pieces,* Dial, 1959.

(Illustrator) Norton Juster, *The Phantom Tollbooth,* Random House, 1961.

Harry, the Rat with Women (novel), McGraw, 1963.

(Editor and annotator) *The Great Comic Book Heroes,* Dial, 1965.

"Silverlips" (teleplay), Public Broadcasting Service, 1972.

(With Herb Gardner, Peter Stone, and Neil Simon) "Happy Endings" (teleplay), American Broadcasting Companies, 1975.

Ackroyd (novel), Simon & Schuster, 1977.

(Author of introduction) Rick Marshall, editor, *The Complete E. C. Segar Popeye,* Fantagraphics (Stamford, Conn.), 1984.

WORK IN PROGRESS: Feiffer's screenplay, "I Want to Go Home," is being made into a film directed by Alain Resnais.

SIDELIGHTS: On learning that *Hudson Review* contributor John Simon describes Jules Feiffer's play "Little Murders" as "bloody-minded," and makes reference to its "grotesque horror" and "hideous reality," those who only know Feiffer as a cartoonist and not as a playwright might be more than a little surprised. Such brutal words are unexpected when used to characterize the work of a cartoonist—whom we might imagine would only want to make us laugh—but, then, Feiffer comes to his work as a playwright from the perspective of someone, as Clive Barnes points out in the *New York Times,* who despite his profession "never makes jokes." Instead of looking for a laugh, Barnes observes, Feiffer "muses on urban man, the cesspool of urban man's mind, the beauty of his neurosis, and the inevitability of his wilting disappointment." The laughter Feiffer seeks centers on our willingness to find humor in some of life's darkest moments.

Feiffer reveals the origins of his somewhat black humor in a *Washington Post* interview with Henry Allen: "Back then [in the fifties], comedy was still working in a tradition that came out of World War I. . . . Comedy was mired in insults and gags. It was Bob Hope and Bing Cosby, Burns and Allen, Ozzie and Harriet. There was no such thing as comedy about relationships, nothing about the newly urban and collegiate Americans. What I was interested in was using humor as a reflection of one's own confusion, ambivalence and dilemma, dealing with sexual life as one knew it to be." The *Chicago Tribune*'s Connie Lauerman notes that because his cartoons dealt with the social reality of the day, Feiffer became "the original satirist-spokesman for the urban, middle-class, newly educated, going-through-analysis, post World War II generation." His cartoons presented a mixture of social commentary and political satire previously reserved for—and seen there only in fleeting glimpses—the editorial page of the newspaper.

From the very beginning of his career Feiffer avoided the silliness expected of a non-political cartoonist and created what Barnes calls "the magically peculiar and peculiarly magical world of Feiffer: a world full of the perils of rejection, the dangers of acceptance, the wild and perpetual struggles of ego for id, the dire discomfort of parenthood, [and] the unceasing wars between men and women." His characters include people who are odd enough to be humorous but who at the same time can elicit a painful, empathetic response from his readers: Passionella, who achieves movie stardom because she has the world's largest breasts; Bernard Mergeneiler, known for his romantic failures; and an inventor who creates a "Lonely Machine" that makes light conversation and delivers sympathetic remarks whenever necessary.

Feiffer's concerns as a cartoonist have followed him to the stage, as the *New York Times*'s Michiko Kakutani observes: "Clearly those cartoons . . . share with 'Grown Ups' and his earlier plays certain recognizable themes and preoccupations. The interest in adult responsibilities and the difficulty of 'growing up,' for instance, first surfaced in Mr. Feiffer's early cartoons about Munro, a 4-year-old boy who finds himself drafted into the Army; and it was developed further in such works as 'Tantrum,' the story of a husband and father who reverts to being a 2-year old." In the *Chicago Tribune,* Richard Christiansen notes that "Hold Me!" is filled with "humorous Jules Feiffer sketches that deal with the . . . cartoonist's constant themes of anxiety, depression, rejection, disappointment, and other light matters."

Some critics fault Feiffer's plays for being too dependent on his cartoons for inspiration. In the *Village Voice* Carll Tucker, for example, comments: "Feiffer's genius as a cartoonist is for dramatic moments—establishing and comically concluding a situation in eight still frames. His characters have personality only for the purpose of making a point: They do not have, as breathing dramatic characters must, the freedom to develop, to grow away from their status as idea-bearers." A similar criticism is leveled by the *New York Times*'s Frank Rich, who writes: "As yet more cartoonist than dramatist, Mr. Feiffer presents his most inspired riffs as set pieces, often monologues."

Other critics voice their approval for what they see as the influence of Feiffer's cartoons on his work for the theater. In Alan Rich's *New York* review of Feiffer's play, "Knock Knock," for example, the critic notes: "What gives ['Knock Knock'] its humor—and a great deal of it is screamingly funny—is the incredible accuracy of [Feiffer's] language, and his use of it to paint the urban neurosis in exact colors. This we know from his cartoons, and we learn it anew from this endearing, congenial theater piece." Other commentators on New York's theatrical scene, such as *Dictionary of Literary Biography* contributor Thomas Edward Ruddick, are able to separate Feiffer's dramatic work from his other creative efforts. "Feiffer's plays show considerable complexity of plot, character, and idea, and command attention," Ruddock asserts, "not dependent upon Feiffer's other achievements. His plays, independently, constitute a noteworthy body of work."

Feiffer, undaunted by negative criticism, continues to write plays, as well as novels, screenplays, and cartoons. "It bothers him not," observes Jay Sharbutt in the *Los Angles Times,* "that his plays tend to demand a lot from an audience." As Feiffer remarked to Sharbutt: "I found that when a play didn't ask of me anything but to love it, I almost never loved it. But when a play attacked me, confused me, made me wonder about myself and my attitudes, I found that, in the end, most entertaining and most edifying. . . . And that was the kind of theater I was hoping that I could learn to write."

MEDIA ADAPTATIONS: "The Feiffer Film," based on Feiffer's cartoons, was released in 1965; *Harry, the Rat with Women* was made into a play and produced at Detroit Institute of Arts, 1966; *Passionella, and Other Stories* was adapted by Jerry Bock and Seldon Harnick into "Passionella," a one-act musical produced on Broadway as part of "The Apple Tree," 1967; *Jules Feiffer's America: From Eisenhower to Reagan* was adapted by Russell Vandenbroucke into a play entitled "Feiffer's America"; "What

Are We Saying?," a parody on Feiffer's cartoons, was produced in Rome.

CA INTERVIEW

CA interviewed Jules Feiffer by telephone on March 22, 1988, at his home in New York, New York.

CA: You've managed an admirable set of careers as cartoonist, playwright, screenwriter, and novelist, doing innovative things in all of those categories and refusing to be pigeonholed in any of them. How easily do they mesh?

FEIFFER: I don't know that they mesh at all other than in my imagination. Each has a different set of rules, a different set of circumstances, different limitations, and that's what I enjoy. One of the things I've always enjoyed as both writer and cartoonist is understanding, acknowledging, respecting, and then ignoring the limitations of the different mediums I'm working in.

CA: Does much the same kind of energy go into each activity?

FEIFFER: I don't think so. The cartoon is the short shot and the plays and screenplays are long shots. A cartoon has to be thought of in short bursts. It's six or eight panels, and the sort of energy you bring to it is in terms of a flash—it's here and it's gone. The pleasure that comes from it is that you can comment immediately on something that grabs your interest, whether it's political or social or sexual or whatever. You've done it, there it appears in print, and it's all in a matter of days.

With a play you're going into much more complex relationships and details, and dealing in dialogue and action with things that are or should be more subtle. It's a whole different frame of thought. A screenplay is somewhere between the two. The scenes are shorter. What you can say, because of the commercial movie medium, is by necessity less complex. You can't have long speeches, because people won't stand for it in a movie theater. But you have the freedom of action that you don't have in the theater.

CA: One of the familiar figures in your cartoons, and sometimes on stage, is the dancer in the black leotard. You've also done a portrait of yourself as a dancer, which has been photographed for at least one magazine. What do the dancers mean to you?

FEIFFER: I've been doing a dancer since the beginning of the cartoon. It's hard to remember what I meant in the beginning, but I know what I mean now. She's a figure who is constantly examining and reexamining and rationalizing her life. Whatever the problems and disasters, and however often hope is dashed, she rises up and dances again. She'll never be defeated by the realities. She insists on retaining a spirit of optimism.

CA: And what about the portrait of yourself as a dancer?

FEIFFER: I don't recognize that. There used to be a character in the cartoon called Bernard, who more or less reflected the dismal aspects of my sexual life when I was a single man, back in the fifties. The more married I got, the more infrequent his appearances became. I don't think there's a character who truly represents me except for political commentators in the cartoon from time to time, and I occasionally actually use myself now and again in the cartoon—a bearded figure leaning over the drawing board—but that's only been the last couple of years. There isn't anyone who truly represents me. I've just brought

Bernard back in a screenplay called "Bernard and Huey," which I hope will be made soon.

CA: Recognition for your cartoons began with their publication in the Village Voice *back in 1956, when the magazine was just getting started. Would you like to comment on your long association with the* Voice?

FEIFFER: It began as an association with deep bonds of affection. It was the only paper that would publish me. The paper existed primarily in the fifties to give space to writers on the scene who couldn't get their work published elsewhere. Or if they did, it was not on a subject of their own choosing; magazine assignments generally would be written from the point of view of the magazine and not from the point of view of the writer. The *Voice,* for the first time, would give writers and artists a chance to write and draw from their own personal sense of self rather than from an editor's. This sounds crazy, but it had never been done before. It hasn't been done since, and the *Voice* is no longer that kind of paper. My continued association with the *Voice* is also realistic: the sort of political comment I make is not much more appreciated today in the mass-market, certainly in New York, than it was back in the fifties. If I left the *Voice,* it would be to retire. I'd have no other place to go.

CA: It's hard to imagine anything more ego-threatening than writing plays and having them produced, yet you seem to thrive on it, through the boos and the raves. What got you addicted?

FEIFFER: It was a reluctant addiction. As a lifelong theatergoer I realized, because of the plays that I liked and how frequently I saw them close and because of the plays I didn't like and how frequently I saw them as hits, that if I wrote a play I really liked, it would probably close in a week. I was making little enough money out of the cartoon to believe that theater was a viable alternative or extension. I didn't want, in my thirties, to move into an area where I was going to do just as poorly financially as I was in cartooning.

So I started work on a novel, which I called *Little Murders.* After about two and a half years it was getting nowhere, and really out of desperation, because I thought the material was important to deal with and no one else seemed to be dealing with it, I tried dramatizing it. It wasn't anything that I truly had an ambition to do; I just felt that, having been committed to these ideas for so long, I had to find some way—even theater, least of all theater—to express them. When I started writing *Little Murders* as a play, suddenly it took off and I realized that I was a playwright and that my fate was sealed and I was finished. Whatever happened to these plays, success or failure, was no longer the deciding factor. That was beside the point; this was something that I loved doing, and I've loved doing it since. And since I'm never wrong about these things, "Little Murders" opened in April of 1967 and closed in a week.

CA: But the plays do badly in one place and well another, on Broadway or Off-Broadway, or they're unpopular one year and well received another without any obvious explanation.

FEIFFER: I work very hard to make sure they stay around, and sooner or later the critics, who are not really stupid but just slow-witted, reevaluate and either comment on the remarkable rewriting job I've done to improve the play or for other reasons will like the production better and start liking the play better.

CA: In a New York Times Magazine *article, Robin Brantley commented on the optimism of "Knock Knock" and said it*

marked a turning point for you, reflecting an interest in coming to terms with yourself and with the despair society creates. Was the play so consciously motivated?

FEIFFER: I remember wincing when I read that. The need to label is so strong. I was entering middle age, and we know what happens to middle-aged writers: they sell out. Several years later I wrote "Grownups," which was the blackest play I've ever written. At the time I wrote "Knock Knock," the private aspects of my life were quite dismal, and therefore I wanted to write a play in which I simply had a good time. I wanted to enjoy myself. I didn't care whether it had an idea behind it or not.

"Knock Knock" was the first play I wrote—and it was a breakthrough in the regard—that didn't have an essay point to make. With "Little Murders" I decided what it had to be about before I figured out the characters. In my second play, "God Bless," I did the same, and I did the same in "Carnal Knowledge," which was my third play. With all those plays I first had an idea and then I invented a story and characters to illustrate the idea. I was tired of doing that, and I thought my characters could take on more life and reality if I didn't.

So I just fooled around and doodled with some characters until I had Cohn and Abe, and figured out where they would live, and then let them write the play. Within a day or two I had a story. It evolved by itself, and I loved the way that happened. It did turn out to be about something after all, but I didn't figure out what I was about two or three weeks into the play.

CA: In the case of the plays based on your cartoon characters, which include "The Explainers," "Crawling Arnold," "The World of Jules Feiffer," "Feiffer's People," "Hold Me!," and others, how difficult has it been to transform the characters from the cartoon form to the live one?

FEIFFER: An odd thing happens too often when the cartoons are adapted to the stage. There will be producers or directors who'll tell me that these cartoons are really little plays all in themselves; that they're not really cartoons, they're real life. Then they'll stage them to be more cartoony than they were on paper. No reality, just overstatement. So over the years I've had strong negative feelings about putting the cartoons on stage, especially after I had become a playwright myself. I didn't want to draw comparisons, and I didn't like what I had seen of the staged cartoons.

Then the American Place Theatre in New York asked me to do an adaptation of the work, and I thought I would take one last shot at it and take control of how it was done for the first time. I worked with a talented director, Caymichael Patten, and we came up with an approach which dealt with the characters as if they were real. We ignored them as cartoons, didn't show the actors the cartoons at all, just regular script. We integrated the material so that there would be no blackouts, no punch lines; everybody was on stage all the time and one piece led into another piece so we didn't worry about getting a laugh or a big response on the last line of a cartoon. It just blended.

It worked beautifully. The laughs were there, but the reality was there more or less like a real play as opposed to a series of skits. I'm trying that again at this very moment in Chicago with a show called "Feiffer's America" at the North Light.

CA: "Oh! Calcutta!," for which you wrote "Dick and Jane," made the news for its nudity and sexual content at a time when there was a great deal of ferment in theater. It's interesting that in this very conservative present time, it still seems always to be playing somewhere. What do you think the theatrical experimentation of the late sixties and early seventies left as its legacy?

FEIFFER: For me, the only interest in "Oh! Calcutta!" was using the material I wrote in "Dick and Jane" as a dry run to see if I could write "Carnal Knowledge." I wanted to do a piece on narcissistic men and the way they use women. "Dick and Jane" is a kind of outlandish satire on that, but it really was designed to see if I could expand the material into what later became "Carnal Knowledge," and I did. But by no means was "Oh! Calcutta!" experimental other than in its use of nudity. It mostly didn't use actors, but bodies, so that "Dick and Jane" was done deplorably. I've never seen it put on well, and it's a piece that I used to like a lot. I don't know what I think now because I haven't read it in years.

As far as sixties experimentation goes, while that flourish is over, it still exists. There are a lot of odd and wonderful and sometimes not so wonderful happenings going around in the guise of traditional theater. There's a delightful play in New York at the moment called "Tony and Tina's Wedding," put on by a group called Artificial Intelligence, that clearly draws inspiration from these happenings.

CA: How did "Carnal Knowledge" go from play to movie?

FEIFFER: By sending it to Mike Nichols, who read it, loved it, and said, "Let's do it as a movie." I said, "What about the language?" That sort of language had never appeared on the screen. He said, "No problem," and there wasn't. He said we wouldn't have to do very much rewriting for the screenplay, and he turned out to be lying. But he was also the best editor I've ever worked with in any form, and it was absolutely a riveting and wonderful experience, certainly one of the best collaborative experiences I've ever had. We're about to try it again on a new play, which goes on next year. He's an old friend. I've known him forever, and I love working with him.

CA: Would you like to talk about working with Robert Altman on "Popeye"?

FEIFFER: It was up and down. Altman is also an old friend, and I knew long before we worked together of his cavalier attitude toward scripts, so I hardly went into "Popeye" as an innocent. I decided that Altman is brilliant and I've always been a fan and on those grounds it was worth doing, even though I expected the results to be less than ideal. The results *are* less than ideal, but, I must say, better than expected. I got more of my script on the screen than I anticipated—about fifty percent, maybe a record for Altman.

There are certain things I regret—for example, Wimpy has a much more major role in my script than in Altman's movie. Altman insists on sticking in these little backstage characters that he invents at the moment, who have nothing to do with anything other than the fact that he likes them; the characters have no lines but somehow dominate the foreground. Nonetheless, I think the look of the film is fanciful and wonderful, the casting was brilliant, and much of the film, say, the first three quarters, works wonderfully well. I still get many positive comments on it. I was speaking at a college in New Jersey last night, and a number of people told me how much they love "Popeye." I hear that all the time.

CA: How many speaking engagements do you do?

FEIFFER: More and more. I do about fifteen dates a year, mostly at colleges. It keeps me in touch and it supplements the income very nicely. I try not to do more than that because I've got a three-year-old and I don't like to be away from home more than a night at a time.

CA: A recurring character in your work is the adult-child; the stage and animated film character Munro, a four-year-old drafted into the army by mistake; thirty-five-year-old Arnold Enterprises, who reverts to infant behavior in the early one-act "Crawling Arnold"; Leo and finally his wife Carol in the book Tantrum, *a novel in cartoons. Will the baby return?*

FEIFFER: I don't know. I some ways I'm appalled by how I can't ever get away from this theme. "Munro" was the very first piece of satire I ever wrote. *Tantrum* was thirty years later, and I'm still at it. Then I do plays with titles like "Grownups." I guess if I haven't expunged this from my psyche in thirty years, the chances of somehow managing to get rid of it in the next ten years seem rather slim.

CA: Your baby is such a sympathetic figure, I think, because most of us from time to time would like to revert to babyhood and be taken care of.

FEIFFER: There's another thing. I'm fifty-nine now, and I think my parents' generation must have been about the last generation who saw themselves as adults, in a class different from their children. As we all know, what's happened, certainly in the sixties and even before, is that there's been a muddying of the lines so that grownups don't feel like grownups anymore; they don't feel like authority figures; they don't feel as if they're in charge. In the past, despite all the doubts they had, there was a pose parents felt they had to project that was rather effective publicly. By and large, that pose no longer exists.

CA: Tantrum worked beautifully as a novel in cartoons. Is that a form you'll likely do again?

FEIFFER: I always wanted to do a cartoon novel. The one shortcoming in doing the weekly strip is that it's still a distance from what I grew up loving most in comics: a continuity strip. As a kid I used to read the daily four-panel strips in the newspapers and couldn't get enough of them. I wanted to do my version, and finally got a chance, of sorts, in *Tantrum*. *Tantrum* also gave me a chance for the first time to combine all the different fields I work in. I used what I know from theater and a lot of what I know from screenplays. It was a terrific experience, and I thought after I had done one that I would do many more, but I simply have not had an idea that fits the form since.

CA: What's your general working schedule for the cartoons? Do you do several at a stretch?

FEIFFER: They go out in syndication two at a time, so that's the way I write them and draw them. Every other week, toward the weekend, I start fiddling round with ideas. I give a day or two to that and another day and a half to drawing the two of them, and then they go out to Kansas City, and from there they're syndicated.

CA: Do ideas occur to you while you're away from the drawing table and get jotted down for future use?

FEIFFER: Not very often. I think it used to happen more, but now I'm much more dependent on the professional writer's adrenaline panic: On my God, I'll never think of another one and it's due tomorrow! Then you sit down and something happens.

CA: How much revision do you normally do in the drawing and the writing?

FEIFFER: Generally I will write a first draft and revise, revise, revise, revise. I sort of go into a trance, and I'm sometimes amazed when I see these dozens of sheets of paper where I've re-written the same lines over and over again. I'm not even aware that I'm doing it. I'll get it refined to the way I like it, or I may find that I've overly refined it and go back to an earlier draft. I really like, if I can, to have a day between the writing and the drawing, because I find that my judgment may be quite different on the second day than it was on the first in terms of what works and what doesn't.

The drawing has changed. I drew *Tantrum* freehand without any preliminary sketches, and I fell in love with the immediacy of that, the fun of drawing without preparation, like a little boy again as opposed to a more traditional, professional approach where a tedious pencil outline is followed by a tedious ink out-line. Then clean it up. That was never as much fun as the way I drew as a kid. So I went back to just doing it, doing these draw-ings in pen on scraps of paper. And the ones that work go in and the ones that don't work get thrown away.

Often I'll do two or three times as much work as I used to. And it will take longer. But I'm having a good time drawing again. I'm not bored as I was for a very long time indeed. And some-times I'll just hit it right the first time out and do six rough draw-ings which will be just what I want and I'm through in twenty minutes. The earlier I begin in the morning, the better the work goes, the more facility my hand has.

CA: Your work cuts across class boundaries and even across cul-tures, since it's published in many languages. What countries out-side the United States do you get a particularly strong response from?

FEIFFER: I have never known about response to my work ex-cept by accident. I'm told that I'm popular in the Scandinavian countries. I'm virtually unknown in Paris, which galls me. I used to be popular there, but I haven't been published there in some years. The English love me, and the Italians. I remember the first time I met Fellini, what a big fuss he made and what a thrill that was. I'm also popular in the Latin countries—in Cuba, of all places. They pirate the cartoons and run them. A great thrill a few years ago was to run into a black South African poet who told me how much pleasure he and his friends got from reading my cartoons in a Capetown weekly.

CA: Ackroyd seems quite different from anything else you've done, a very clever mystery with a reference to the Agatha Christie character Roger Ackroyd. What prompted it?

FEIFFER: What prompted the book was that I couldn't get "Knock Knock" on. I loved the play and nobody would do it; I had gone through five producers in three years. As I talk about this, I can still feel that feeling in my stomach where it all turned into chopped liver—rage, anger, frustration. I realized that it was going to drive me crazy to go on obsessed with getting this play on when I had no control over when it would go on or when it wouldn't. It was not going to be my decision, but somebody else's. I would either get lucky or I wouldn't, but there was noth-ing I could do about it and I'd better get on to some other work.

But I was so angry at the theater I couldn't get on to another the-ater piece—I wasn't going to write another play when nobody would put on *this* play, which I thought to be a damn good play. This left me nothing to do but a novel, and I'd written one novel, *Harry, the Rat with Women,* which was a joyless experience and very hard work, and I realized at the end of it that I wasn't a nov-

elist. I loved the form and given my druthers that's probably what I would have been over anything else. But I don't really know how to write prose. I don't see *verbally,* that is I don't know how to describe what anything looks like. Anything at all. So I decided to try to write a novel as if it were all in dialogue: create a character, give him a voice, and have everything seen through his persona. What followed was *Ackroyd.* I thought it would be amusing and interesting to do a young man who's ob-sessed with private detective fiction and becomes a private eye only to get involved in the neurotic hangups and details of his client's life, where there is no murder case but only an investiga-tion into why his famous client has been dropped from the A party list.

Ackroyd kept me pure. Nobody bought it. My wife won't even read it. One nice thing came of it. The French are perverse in re-gard to American culture. About a year and a half ago I was ap-proached by Alain Resnais, who asked me if I wanted to write a movie because he was a fan of *Ackroyd* and *that* book, not my plays or movies or cartoons, had made him want to work with me. That movie, which is called "I Want to Go Home," goes into production in September.

CA: You've always said that too much success would be an indica-tion that you're doing something wrong. How do you measure suc-cess for yourself? What makes you happy with your work?

FEIFFER: A long time ago I decided that the first aspect of any-thing I did was to have a good time, to love the work itself and to enjoy the process. That doesn't mean that it should be easy—often just the opposite; it's hard but it's fascinating. But that meant that, to the extent that I could afford to, I would stay away from any work that didn't excite me, that I would not do hack work. Now, with a bigger family and living in a city where in order to live decently you must be rich, I've reached a point where I have to start looking seriously for the sort of work I would have scorned twenty years ago. But I'll try and have a good time doing that too if I can. Stay tuned for a Feiffer sitcom.

BIOGRAPHICAL/CRITICAL SOURCES:

BOOKS

Contemporary Literary Criticism, Gale, Volume 2, 1974, Volume 8, 1978.
Dictionary of Literary Biography, Gale, Volume 7: *Twentieth-Century American Dramatists,* 1981, Volume 44: *American Screenwriters, Second Series,* 1986.

PERIODICALS

Chicago Tribune, June 29, 1979, November 2, 1982.
Hudson Review, summer, 1967.
Los Angeles Times, November 13, 1988.
New York, February 2, 1976.
New York Times, January 21, 1977, December 15, 1981, May 7, 1987.
New York Times Magazine, May 16, 1976.
Village Voice, February 2, 1976.
Washington Post, August 17, 1979.*

—*Sidelights by Marian Gonsior*

—*Interview by Jean W. Ross*

*   *   *

FEINGOLD, S. Norman 1914-

PERSONAL: Born February 2, 1914, in Worcester, Mass.; son of William and Aida (Salit) Feingold; married Marie Goodman (a rehabilitation counselor), March 24, 1947; children: Elizabeth Anne, Margaret Ellen, Deborah Carol, Marilyn Nancy. *Education:* Indiana University, A.B., 1937; Clark University, M.A., 1940; Boston University, Ed.D., 1948. *Religion:* Jewish.

ADDRESSES: Home—9707 Singleton Dr., Bethesda, Md. 20817.

CAREER: Licensed psychologist, District of Columbia. Associated Jewish Philanthropies, Boston, Mass., director of Jewish Vocational Service of Greater Boston, executive director, 1946-58, executive director of Work Adjustment Center, 1956-58; B'nai B'rith Career and Counseling Services (formerly B'nai B'rith Vocational Service), Washington, D.C., national director, 1958-80; president, National Career and Counseling Services, 1980—. Part-time instructor and special lecturer, Boston University, 1953-58; professorial lecturer in psychology, American University; guest lecturer at more than twenty universities. Member of Massachusetts Committee on Employment of Aging, 1953-57, of President's Committee on Employment of the Handicapped, and of executive committee of National Association for Industry-Education Cooperation; former chairman of subcommittee on human relations, Graduate School, U.S. Department of Agriculture. Former member of accrediting commission of the National Home Study Council; former trustee, Edward Waters College. Former member of professional advisory board, Epilepsy Foundation of America. Vocational consultant to Social Security Administration. *Military service:* U.S. Army, 1943-46; served in Asiatic-Pacific and European theaters; became first lieutenant.

MEMBER: International Council of Psychologists; American Board on Counseling Services (former vice-president), American Association of Marriage and Family Counselors (clinical member), American Association of Counseling and Development, American Psychological Association (fellow), American Association for the Advancement of Science, National Vocational Guidance Association (trustee, former president), National Rehabilitation Association, Maryland Psychological Association, Massachusetts Psychological Association, Washington, D.C., Psychological Association.

AWARDS, HONORS: Citations from B'nai B'rith, B'nai B'rith Career and Counseling Services, Commonwealth of Massachusetts Division of the Blind, American Academy of Medical Administrators, Milwaukee Jewish Vocational Service, and Scholarship Foundation of Building Laborers' Local No. 74; eminent career award, National Capital Personnel and Guidance Association; honorary Doctor of Laws from Saints College and Edward Waters College.

WRITINGS:

Scholarships, Fellowships and Loans, eight volumes, Bellman Publishing, 1949-1982.
(With Harold List) *Opportunities in Unusual Occupations,* Science Research Associates, 1952.
How to Choose That Career: Civilian and Military; A Guide for Parents, Teachers, and Students, Bellman Publishing, 1954.
(With List) *How to Get That Part-time Job: A Handbook of Job Opportunities Available Now,* Arco, 1958.
(With Alfred Jospe) *College Guide for Jewish Youth,* B'nai B'rith Vocational Service, 1963, revised edition, 1969.
(Editor) *The College and Career Plans of Jewish High School Youth,* B'nai B'rith Vocational Service, 1964.
A Career Conference for Your Community, B'nai B'rith Vocational Service, 1964.

(Editor) *Prep School Guide for Jewish Youth: A Comprehensive Guide to Selecting a Prep School for Counselors, Teachers, Parents, and Students,* B'nai B'rith Career and Counseling Services, 1966.
(With Sol Swerdloff) *Occupations and Careers,* Webster, 1969.
(Editor) *The Vocational Expert in the Social Security Disability Program: A Guide for the Practitioner,* C. C Thomas, 1969.
(Editor) Daniel Sinick, *Part-time, Summer and Volunteer Jobs for Jewish and Other Minority Group Youth,* B'nai B'rith Vocational Service, 1969.
(With List) *Finding Part-time Jobs,* Science Research Associates, 1971.
A Counselor's Handbook: Readings in Counseling, Student Aid and Rehabilitation, Carroll Press, 1972.
(With Dora R. Evers) *Your Future in Exotic Occupations,* Richards Rosen, 1972, revised edition, 1980.
Explorations, two volumes, B'nai B'rith Career and Counseling Services, revised edition, 1975.
(Editor with William B. Silverman) *Kivie Kaplan: A Legend in His Own Time,* Union of American Hebrew Congregations, 1976.
(With Alice Fins) *Your Future in More Exotic Careers,* Richards Rosen, 1978.
Counseling for Careers in the 1980s, Garrett Park Press, 1979.
(With Shirley Levin) *What to Do until the Counselor Comes: A Handbook for Educational, Vocational and Career Planning,* Richards Rosen Press, 1980.
(With Norma R. Miller) *Your Future: A Guide for the Handicapped Teenager,* Richards Rosen Press, 1981.
(With Leonard G. Perlman) *Making It on Your Own,* Acropolis Books, 1981, revised edition, 1988.
Whither Guidance: Future Directions, Garrett Park Press, 1981.
(With Glenda Hansard-Winkler) *Nine-Hundred Thousand Plus Jobs Annually: Published Sources of Employment Listings,* Garrett Park Press, 1982, revised edition, 1989.
(With Miller) *Emerging Careers: New Occupations for the Year Two Thousand and Beyond,* Garrett Park Press, 1983.
(With Avis Nicholson) *The Professional and Trade Association Job Finder,* Garrett Park Press, 1983.
(With Nicholson) *Getting Ahead: A Woman's Guide to Career Success,* Acropolis Books, 1983.
(With Maxine Atwater) *New Emerging Careers Today, Tomorrow, and in the 21st Century,* Garrett Park Press, 1988.
Futuristic Exercises: A Workbook for Emerging Lifestyles and Careers in the 21st Century and Beyond, Garrett Park Press, 1989.

Contributor of more than one hundred articles to professional journals, including *Performance, Cerebral Palsy Review,* and *Occupational Outlook Quarterly.* Editor, *Counselor's Information Service,* 1958-79; consulting editor, *Scholarships, Fellowships, and Loans News Service* and *Counselors Information Services,* 1980—.

AVOCATIONAL INTERESTS: Photography, travel.

BIOGRAPHICAL/CRITICAL SOURCES:

PERIODICALS

Washington Post Book World, April 25, 1982.

*   *   *

FERGUSON, M(ilton) Carr, Jr. 1931-

PERSONAL: Born February 10, 1931, in Washington, D.C.; son of Milton Carr (a federal judge) and Gladys (Emery) Ferguson;

married Marian Evelyn Nelson (a speech therapist), August 21, 1954; children: Laura, Sharon, Marcia, Sandra. *Education:* Cornell University, B.A., 1952, LL.B., 1954; New York University, LL.M., 1960.

ADDRESSES: Home—32 Washington Square W., New York, N.Y. 10011. *Office*—Davis, Polk & Wardell, One Chase Manhattan Plaza, New York, N.Y. 10005.

CAREER: Admitted to Bar of New York State, 1954; U.S. Department of Justice, Tax Division, Washington, D.C., trial attorney, 1954-60, assistant to Attorney General, 1977-81; University of Iowa, College of Law, Iowa City, assistant professor of law, 1960-62; New York University, School of Law, New York City, associate professor, 1962-65, professor of law, 1965-77; Wachtell, Lipton, Rosen & Katz, New York City, attorney, 1969-76; Davis, Polk & Wardell, New York City, attorney, 1981—. Special consultant, Treasury Department, Puerto Rico, 1967, 1974; visiting professor, Stanford University, 1972-73.

MEMBER: American Bar Association, New York State Bar Association, Society of Illustrators.

AWARDS, HONORS: Ford Foundation fellowship, 1959-60.

WRITINGS:

(With others) *Federal Income Taxation Legislation of 1962-64 in Perspective,* American Law Institute, 1965.
(With J. M. J. Freeland and R. B. Stevens) *Federal Income Taxation of Estates and Beneficiaries,* Little, Brown, 1970.
Income Taxation of Estates and Trusts, Practising Law Institute, 1973, . . . *Workshop,* 1973, . . . *1974,* 1974, . . . *1976,* 1976.
(With Freeland and Stevens) *Federal Income Taxation of Estates and Beneficiaries: 1976 Supplement,* Little, Brown, 1976, . . . *1977 Supplement,* 1977, . . . *1984 Supplement,* 1984.
Income in Respect of Decedent: Liquidation or Sale of Business Interest, American College of Probate Counsel, 1976.
(With Victor Zonana) *The Tax Reform Act of 1976,* Practicing Law Institute, 1976.
(With Harvey P. Dale) *The Economic Recovery Tax Act of 1981,* Practising Law Institute, 1981.
Research and Development Limited Partnerships: Structuring, Financing, and Marketing, Practising Law Institute, 1985.

Also author of monographs. Contributor to *Iowa Law Review* and *Tax Law Review.**

*   *   *

FERRACUTI, Franco 1927-

PERSONAL: Born April 1, 1927, in Montottone, Italy; son of Vasco and Antonietta (Berdini) Ferracuti; married Mirella Garutti, January 26, 1955; children: Stefano, Daniele (sons). *Education:* University of Rome, M.D. (cum laude), 1951, Diploma in Forensic Medicine, 1955, Diploma in Criminal Anthropology, 1960.

ADDRESSES: Home—Via G. Marchi 3, Rome 00161, Italy.

CAREER: Licensed to practice medicine, 1952. University of Rome Hospitals, Rome, Italy, intern, 1951; University of Rome, Rome, assistant in Institute of Psychology, 1951-56, 1966-73, instructor in Postgraduate Training School in Penal Law, 1952-66, assistant in Institute of Criminal Anthropology, 1957-66, professor of criminal anthropology in School of Law, 1966-73, professor of criminological medicine and forensic psychiatry in Medical School, 1973—; Carabinieri Officers Training School, Rome, instructor, 1955-62, 1966-81.

Research associate in Psychiatric Institute, University of Wisconsin, 1954; University of Puerto Rico, visiting professor of psychology, 1956-57, research professor and later director of research and training program in criminology of Social Science Research Center, 1959-67; professor of criminal anthropology, University of Modena School of Law, 1961-63; instructor in juvenile delinquency, New York University School of Law, 1963-64. Psychologist, Istituto Nazionale di Osservazione, Rome, 1952-74; social affairs officer, United Nations, 1963-64; member of criminological scientific council, Council of Europe, 1965-68. Consultant to United Nations Social Defence Research Institute, Rome, 1968-73 and 1980-81, and to Italian Ministry of the Interior, 1978-81.

MEMBER: International Society for Criminology (member of scientific council, 1967-69), Societa Italiana di Psicologia, Societa Romana di Medicina Legale a della Assicurazioni, Society for Projective Techniques, American Psychological Association (fellow in Division 18), American Psychiatric Association (corresponding fellow).

AWARDS, HONORS: Italian League for the Control of Tumors scholarships to study psychological aspects of terminal cancer cases, 1952, 1953; Rotary Club scholarship to study penal institutions and psychiatric clinics for criminals in Sweden, 1952; Fulbright travel grant to study at University of Wisconsin, 1954; National Institute of Mental Health research grant, 1963; American Society for Criminology Award, 1974; de Greef Award, International Society for Criminology, 1983.

WRITINGS:

Appunti di psicologia giudiziaria (text in forensic psychology), Tipografia Ufficiali Carabinieri, 1959.
(With M. E. Wolfgang) *Il comportamento violento: Moderno studio criminologico,* Giuffre, 1966, translation published as *The Subculture of Violence,* Tavistock Publications, 1967.
(With others) *Delinquents and Nondelinquents in the Puerto Rican Slum Culture,* Ohio State University Press, 1975.
(With S. Dinitz and A. Piperno) *Deterioramento mentale da detenzione,* Italian Ministry of Justice, 1976, translation published as *Mental Deterioration in Prison,* Center for the Study of Crime and Delinquency, Ohio State University, 1976.
(With M. L. Solivetti) *La pornografia nei mezzi di comunicazione di massa con particolare riguardo alla televisione* (title means "Pornography in Mass-Media, with Particular Reference to Television"), RAI (Rome), 1977.
Trendo de la cultura economica, 2nd edition, Sage Publications, 1982.
(With F. Bruno) *Terapia andogenirda dell'enerium-dipendense* (title means "Andogonid Therapy of Heroin Dependency"), [Tunis], 1982.
(Editor with Wolfgang) *Criminological Diagnosis: An International Perspective,* two volumes, Lexington Books, 1983.

CONTRIBUTOR

E. S. Schneidman and N. C. Farberow, editors, *Corso per analisti di mercato,* Giuffre, 1955.
Clues to Suicide, Blakiston Co., 1957.
Il Corso di perfezionamento per Uditori Giudiziari, Giuffre, 1959.
Principi di criminologia clinica e psichiatria forense, Istituto di Medicina Sociale, 1960.
G. Mueller, editor, *Essays in Criminal Science,* Sweet & Maxwell, 1961.
B. Di Tullio, *Principi di criminologia clinica,* Istituto di Medicina Sociale, 1963.

Daniel Glaser, editor, *Handbook for Criminology,* Random House, 1975.

L. Martin and Motta, editors, *Androgens and Anti-Androgens,* Raven Press, 1977.

I. L. Barek-Glantz and C. R. Huff, editors, *The Used, the Bad, the Different,* Lexington Books, 1981.

A. P. Goldstein and M. H. Segall, *Aggression in Global Perspective,* Pergamon, 1983.

BIBLIOGRAPHIES

(With S. P. Fragola and F. Gioggi) *Bibliografia criminologica italiana, 1955-1964,* Giuffre, 1965.

Intelligenza e criminalita, Giuffre, 1966.

(With A. Hess and G. Keh Fang Hess) *Il delinquente giovane adulto,* Giuffre, 1967.

(With M. Fontanesi, I. Melup, and G. Minervini) *Bibliografia sui delinquenti anormali psichici,* Mantellate, 1967.

TRANSLATOR INTO ITALIAN

Lean Radzinowicz, *In Search of Criminology,* Giuffre, 1964.

(With G. Tartaglione) Eleanor Glueck and Sheldon Glueck, *Physique and Delinquency,* Editrice Universitaria (Florence), 1965.

(With wife, Mirella Ferracuti) B. B. Burgemeister, *Psychological Techniques in Neurological Diagnosis,* O. S. (Florence), 1967.

OTHER

Also editor, with others, of a 17-volume textbook in criminology and forensic psychiatry; also co-author of report, "Replication of 'Unraveling Juvenile Delinquency' in Puerto Rico," Harvard University, 1966; also translator of several psychology texts and their manuals published by O. S. Contributor of over three hundred articles and reviews on psychology and criminology to professional journals. Editorial consultant, *Journal of Criminal Law and Criminology,* 1965—; member of advisory board, *British Journal of Criminology,* 1965—.

*   *   *

FERRELL, Mallory Hope   1935-

PERSONAL: Born November 23, 1935, in Portsmouth, Va.; son of Mallory Hope (a contractor) and Laura Evelyn (Bunn) Ferrell; married Gloria Timm, March 8, 1975; children: Susan Constance, Mallory Hope III, Kimberly Lynn, Eric Bradford. *Education:* Attended Virginia Polytechnic Institute, 1954-55; University of Miami, Coral Gables, Fla., A.B., 1958, graduate study in architecture, 1958-59; Air University, Command and Staff College, Associate in Military Science, 1963. *Politics:* Independent. *Religion:* Baptist.

ADDRESSES: Home—103 St. Andrews Sq., Peachtree City, Ga. 30269. *Office*—Chief Pilot's Office, Delta Airlines, Atlanta, Ga. 30320.

CAREER: U.S. Air Force, pilot and instructor pilot, 1960-65, flew more than 165 jet fighter combat missions and left service as captain, retired as Lt. Col. from the Air National Guard; self-employed architectural engineer, Norfolk, Va., 1965-67; Western Airlines International, Salt Lake City, Utah, commercial pilot, 1967-86; Delta Airlines, Atlanta, Ga., captain, 1986—. Free-lance photographer. Member of board of directors, Colorado Railroad Museum.

MEMBER: Air Line Pilots Association, U.S. Junior Chamber of Commerce, Rocky Mountain Railroad Club, New Mexico Railroad Club, Sigma Delta Chi, Kappa Alpha Mu.

AWARDS, HONORS: Named photographer of the year by *Life-Encyclopaedia Britannica,* 1959; Golden Spur Award, Western Writers of America, 1975. Received Air Medal twelve times.

WRITINGS:

Rails, Sagebrush and Pine, Golden West, 1967.
The Gilpin Gold Tram, Pruett, 1970.
The 1871 Grant Locomotive, Pruett, 1971.
Silver San Juan, Pruett, 1972.
Tweetsie Country, Pruett, 1976.
West Side, PFM Books, 1977.
Utah & Northern, Colorado Railroad Museum, 1982.
Colorado & Southern Narrow Gauge, Pruett, 1982.
Southern Pacific Narrow Gauge, PFM Books, 1983.
El Dorado Narrow Gauge, PFM Books, 1989.
ARGENT: Last of the Swamp Rats, PFM Books, 1989.

Contributor of photographic essays to *Photography Annual, Life, Look, This Week, Sports Illustrated, Trains, Fortune, Friends,* and other periodicals.

WORK IN PROGRESS: A two-volume study, *Denver & Rio Grande; Louisiana Plantation Railroads; Nevada Central; Rio Grande Southern: A Silver San Juan Pictorial;* preparing his work for a photographic exhibit, "My American West."

SIDELIGHTS: Over the years Mallory Hope Ferrell has gathered together about 90,000 old West railroad scenes, from which he obtains many of the illustrations for his books on narrow gauge and short line railroads. In addition to flying Boeings commercially, he piloted F-84, F-100, F105, and A-7 fighter aircraft on weekends with the Air National Guard, and "collects material associated with WWI flying," now housed in a museum.

Ferrell once told *CA:* "Much of my research comes directly from flying over parts of the West that are the subjects of my books. As a captain for Delta Airlines (Boeing 727s and 737s), I frequently have a bird's eye view of historic sites, old railroad grades and abandoned ghost towns that is not available otherwise. On-sight inspections have turned up a number of heretofore forgotten sites. For example, one can gain a feeling of what the Owens' Valley of California must have looked like to Fremont's party, or the interrelationships of mountain passes, rivers and lofty peaks in Colorado's San Juan mountains. All these play a part in getting the 'feel' of an area about which I am writing and help me and my readers to understand how the West developed the way it has. Looking down from 35,000 feet can give you an understanding of why the Oregon Trail took the path it did, and also an appreciation for those early trailblazers, settlers, townspeople, railroaders and cattlemen. The West is vast." Ferrell more recently added that he has returned to his native southland where he and his wife Gloria have completed a "Savannah House." Says Ferrell: "Between flights as captain of Boeing 757s and 767s, I have found that 'pockets of gentleness' can still be found there—old mills, covered bridges and, of course, a steam train or two. Future books will include some of this."

BIOGRAPHICAL/CRITICAL SOURCES:

PERIODICALS

Denver Post, August 24, 1969, September 21, 1969, December 19, 1971.
Flight Times, November, 1975.
Railroad Magazine, January, 1974.

FERRIS, Timothy 1944-

PERSONAL: Born August 29, 1944, in Miami, Fla.; son of Thomas A. (a publicist) and Jean (a literary critic; maiden name, Baird) Ferris. *Education:* Northwestern University, B.A., 1966, graduate study, 1966-67.

ADDRESSES: Home—2120 Washington St., San Francisco, Calif. 94109. *Office*—Graduate School of Journalism, University of California, Berkeley, Calif. 94720. *Agent*—Owen Laster, William Morris Agency, 1350 Avenue of the Americas, New York, N.Y. 10019.

CAREER: United Press International, New York City, reporter, 1967-69; *New York Post,* New York City, reporter, 1969-71; *Rolling Stone,* New York City, associate editor, 1971-73, contributing editor, 1973-80; Brooklyn College of the City University of New York, professor of English, 1974-82; University of Southern California, Los Angeles, professor of journalism, 1982-85; University of California, Berkeley, professor of journalism, 1986—. Notable assignments include the Democratic and Republican national conventions in 1972 and the Viking landing on Mars in 1976.

AWARDS, HONORS: American Institute of Physics Prize, 1978, for *The Red Limit: The Search for the Edge of the Universe,* 1989, for *Coming of Age in the Milky Way;* American Book Award in science nomination, 1981, for *Galaxies;* American Association for the Advancement of Science award, 1983, for "Beyond Newton and Einstein," 1986, for "The Creation of the Universe"; Guggenheim fellowship, 1986-87; Emmy nomination, 1986, for "The Creation of the Universe"; Pulitzer Prize nomination, 1989, for *Coming of Age in the Milky Way;* Astronomical Society of the Pacific prize for lifetime achievement.

WRITINGS:

The Red Limit: The Search for the Edge of the Universe, Morrow, 1977, revised edition, 1983.
Galaxies, Sierra Club Books, 1980.
Space Shots: The Beauty of Nature Beyond Earth, Pantheon Books, 1984.
"The Creation of the Universe" (television special), Public Broadcasting Service, 1985.
(With Bruce Porter) *The Practice of Journalism: A Guide to Reporting and Writing the News,* Prentice-Hall, 1988.
Coming of Age in the Milky Way, Morrow, 1988.

Contributor to periodicals, including *Harper's, Playboy, Esquire, New Republic,* and *New York Times Magazine.*

WORK IN PROGRESS: A book of essays; editing an anthology.

SIDELIGHTS: Originally a journalist for the *New York Post* and United Press International, and a former editor for *Rolling Stone,* Timothy Ferris has turned his life-long fascination with astronomy into several successful books that explain this complex science in layman's terms. "A lot of what I do consists of pointing out that there is more to the world than *this* world, and more to this world than we know," Ferris told *CA.* "This idea got hold of me years ago, and never let go. It is *my* author."

In his 1980 book, *Galaxies,* Ferris takes the reader on an imaginary starship that travels from Earth to the edge of the universe. "When Timothy Ferris extends an invitation to join him on a guided tour of the universe, you would be wise to accept," notes George Alexander in the *Los Angeles Times Book Review.* The book is "at once a linear, visual, historical, futurist, cultural and philosophical journey to forever, as good books on astronomy ought to be," says contributing *New York Times* book reviewer

Richard Severo. "It is easy to read because the author insists on being as incisive as he is imaginative. He gives us the data we need to appreciate the premise, but we are not inundated by numbers that would be, at the least, intimidating, and frequently speculative."

In his review of *Galaxies* for *Saturday Review,* Isaac Asimov deems the lavishly illustrated text "a very good candidate for the most beautiful book in the world. . . . In outsize opulence, it spreads its photographs over a square foot and more. . . . The captions are concise and clear," Asimov continues, "and Ferris's running commentary could stand on its own as an essay designed to give the reader a dramatic overview of the universe." "One wades into it not knowing quite what to expect and leery of romantics, and is enthralled," attests *Village Voice's* Eliot Fremont-Smith.

Ferris's more recent astronomy book, *Coming of Age in the Milky Way,* has also earned him high praise from critics, as well as a Pulitzer Prize nomination. In this work, Ferris covers three thousand years of the history of astronomy in less than five hundred pages. Much of *Coming of Age* is filled with enlightening stories about the various personalities who contributed to science, such as Plato, Aristotle, Copernicus, Ptolemy, Galileo, Kepler, Newton, Darwin, and Einstein. "This is not to say that Mr. Ferris presents us with a book of anecdotes," notes *New York Times Book Review* contributor Marcia Bartusiak. "To the contrary, he allows us to view humanity's growing cosmic awareness—the result of either plodding effort or serendipity—as the consummate human adventure, in which intellectual genius is fed by both jealousy and friendship, and scientific progress is measured as much by failure as by triumphs."

Although Bartusiak feels that Ferris rushes through the more recent history of astronomy, and "tends to use [too] much of the technical jargon of the modern-day specialties," she concludes that "the richness and texture of Mr. Ferris's overall presentation . . . far outweigh the book's feverish denouement." Other critics offer more positive remarks about *Coming of Age.* For example, Peter Gorner says in the *Chicago Tribune* that Ferris's work "is the best book about the cosmos since Carl Sagan's 'Cosmos.'" And *Los Angeles Times* reviewer Lee Dembart asserts that the author's recounting of this much-discussed subject "contains details and insights that give it new life."

In an interview with Bob Sipchen of the *Los Angeles Times* after the publication of *Coming of Age,* Ferris discusses the significance of astronomy and the other sciences in our world today: "I think more and more people are coming to realize that science is to us what painting was to the Italian Renaissance, what music was to Baroque Germany with Bach. . . . It is the hottest art form around, and not to know something about it is to ignore the foremost endeavor of our time."

CA INTERVIEW

CA interviewed Timothy Ferris by telephone on May 11, 1989, at his home in San Francisco, California.

CA: First, congratulations on your 1988 book, Coming of Age in the Milky Way, *which was, you said in your introduction, a twelve-year labor of love. Does the book continue to attract new readers?*

FERRIS: It seems to have found an audience. Sales are currently somewhere between ninety and a hundred thousand. Inasmuch as it is not the sort of book that people read instantly, it had a slow but steady acceptance. It comes out next month in London from the Bodley Head, and it's being published this year in Spain, Holland, Germany, Japan, Argentina, and Italy.

CA: You have the distinction of being an award-winning writer on science, specializing in astronomy, without having had an academic background primarily in science.

FERRIS: I only took one science course in university, and that was an astronomy course. I don't think I even did very well in it.

CA: Is the amateur approach, in the real sense of that word amateur, *more an advantage than a disadvantage in your work?*

FERRIS: I'm not sure. The word *amateur* comes from *love,* and it's certainly an advantage for a writer to feel love for his or her subject, but one can feel that emotion and also have trained in the subject; there are plenty of astronomers who are in love with astronomy. I think the important thing is to have affection for your subject. When I decided to try my hand at writing a book, I wanted to be assured that the subject would not exhaust itself for me, so I chose my childhood interest. I've continued with it ever since. It's opened out into everything else, and I've never felt confined by this so-called specialization.

CA: What was the terrific appeal of astronomy for you, and when did it begin?

FERRIS: My initial interest had to do with the idea that this world had had an origin. This was revealed to me by a book that I read when I was about five years old. I was astonished by the idea that the earth under our feet had been put together at some finite point in the past. In retrospect I think it introduced me to the idea that naive reality is an illusion, that there's something deeper hidden beneath things. I started to read astronomy books and got a little telescope and learned the constellations. The sheer beauty of it—the beauty of the stars—attracted me in a way that rocks do some people, or insects or birds do others.

It's interesting how many myths of national or tribal origins invoke the stars. I was just reading last night that in Bali, the myth of the country's formation is that the seven stars of the Pleiades were maidens who had come down to earth to bathe, and one of them was captured by a human and made to stay for a while. Their union marked the origin of the Balinese people. That's a very pretty image. There are a lot of myths like that. We have a high regard for the stars, without knowing why.

CA: How did you happen to approach science through journalism rather than the other way around?

FERRIS: My father was a writer, and I've always thought of myself as a writer. I was sixteen when I first attempted to write a book, and I had written a lot of fiction by that time. It really never occurred to me to be a scientist, and I don't think I would have been particularly good at it. It was natural for me to be a writer.

When I went off to school, I set aside astronomy and did more allegedly practical things. I even went to law school, but I disliked law school and simply walked out one day—it was just too nice a day to stay in class—and I never went back. I went to New York and got a job as a newspaper reporter, and as I got to writing longer articles, I began to return to my original interest. I had to catch up quite a lot—at that point I hadn't read any astron-

omy for something over five years—and also to get more serious about it. The great thing about writing is that you have to somehow figure out what it is you're trying to say. But I've always thought of myself simply as a writer who has a subject at hand. I get called upon to stand up on my hind legs and pontificate on this subject on occasion, which I do because I think it would be prissy to refuse to do it. But I'm uncomfortable at the idea of being some sort of expert at it, and I wouldn't want to take that very far. I'm really not an expert; I'm just a writer.

CA: Did you find it hard to get a foot in the door as a science journalist, to get whatever recognition and approval such a writer needs from the scientific community?

FERRIS: No. I've been treated quite hospitably by the scientists. For one thing, the scientific community is a dream for a reporter to cover, because it is the opposite of secretive; it operates on maximum free exchange of information. One of the real perversions in the increasingly ugly "cold fusion" story that's going on right now is the insistence on the part of these two chemists on keeping aspects of their work secret, apparently because they hope to profit by it. I doubt that they'll profit by it—because I doubt that the work is sound—but their secrecy offends the spirit of science. Generally in science the assumption is that everyone will try to make as clear to you as possible what they're doing and why. I've had the experience of walking down the hall of a major laboratory and pretty much sticking my head in the door without even an introduction, and by and large people will look up and say hi and immediately try to explain to you what they're doing. It's the opposite of a military installation. This openness makes science a pleasant beat for a reporter. One is less often in the business—as in, say, political reporting—of trying to dig out information that others are trying to keep hidden.

CA: Having acquired your knowledge of astronomy and physics without having spent a lot of time in the classroom, how would you advise people who are interested in pursuing such a study without going to school?

FERRIS: The quality of books and materials available to study science has improved considerably. It is possible now to learn about science in a variety of ways, from reading books (which is still the best way) to interactive computer and video disc sessions. But, that said, I have to add that my heart really isn't in it, because I myself have never been any good at learning something from motives that are purely self-improvement. I would know much less astronomy today were I not writing about it. The wonderful thing about writing a subject is that you agree to write an article or a book, and you are then put in a position in which you must either find something sensible to say and really know what you are talking about, or fail. To be a writer is to mandate your own continuing education. That, I think, is the best thing about writing. It's also one of the things that makes it so hard. In terms of my own education, it's been a matter of brute force, of doggedly insisting on figuring things out and not quitting until I have.

Interestingly, though, I find that clarity of speech and of writing is often an index to whether people do know what they are talking about. I'm a sort of literary critic of scientists, and I tend to be more attracted to those who can speak and write in a comprehensible manner. And I have found that those who can make themselves understood tend to be the better scientists. When a scientist starts saying that an ordinary layman cannot understand what he's talking about, what he's really saying, often, is that he himself does not understand it. The British physicist Ernest Rutherford said to his students, in the more sexist language of an earlier generation, that if you can't explain your theory to a barmaid, it's probably not a very good theory.

CA: There seems to be quite a lively lay audience now for science journalism, non-technical books about the sciences, and such television programs as your award-winning 1985 PBS special, "Creation of the Universe." What do you think accounts for the general interest?

FERRIS: Science is the foremost intellectual adventure of our time. It is to our time what painting and sculpture were to the Renaissance; it's what philosophy was in the age of Kant; it's *the* game in town. I have the impression that, in increasing numbers, people are becoming aware of this and are exerting themselves to understand more of what's going on.

CA: Do you find metaphors for human behavior in astronomy and physics?

FERRIS: Yes, but one has to be very cautious about that, I think. Some metaphors are planted by scientists as an aid in their own comprehension, so you want to be discriminating about how you take them back out. For instance, a physicist may say that an electron "feels" an electromagnetic field. That's a way of expressing it, and it obviously doesn't mean that the electron is a sensate object. There's a lot of that sort of anthropormophic talk that goes on in science. It's useful. Then, more subtly, there's a lot of projection of ourselves into nature.

These dangers aside, science *does* proffer deeply personal human images. I think, for instance, that it's very important for us to understand that we evolved on a planet through some working of natural processes. That's a miraculous fact, and it fundamentally alters the way we think of ourselves and our planet. That realization may not yet have got out very widely, and a lot of people are actively engaged in combatting it, but I think it's a healthy one.

CA: Do you feel there are religious implications in recent developments in astronomy and physics?

FERRIS: There are implications of *every* kind—religious, philosophical, aesthetic, tragical, comical an infinite number of implications. I do *not* think that the implications are obvious or immediate, or that they can be readily laid hands upon without a great deal of thought. What I do find repugnant is the easy assumption in some quarters of religion that one or another scientific finding has simply confirmed what they always knew. A few years ago there was a conference of theologians and cosmologists. It was quite well put together, and first-rate scientists were there—and, for all I know, first-rate theologians as well; I'm not familiar enough with theologians to be able to tell. I wasn't able to attend the conference, but I saw a report on it on one of the religious broadcasting networks. Several scientists and a couple of philosophers and theologians were shown talking in a film clip of the conference, and they all seemed to be reasonable, intelligent, caring people. After the clip the camera came back to the studio, where there were several religious TV people sitting around, and they turned to each other with smug smiles and said, "Well, it just goes to show that the man of science laboriously climbs the mountain and gets to the top and finds that the man of religion has been there all the time." Well, that's a load of crap. They really do not know what they're talking about. There is a great distinction between hard-working people and lazy people in the world, and I'd much rather talk to someone who is earnest and

hard-working and whose good-faith opinion is diametrically opposed to my own, than to someone who shares my opinions, but does so in a lazy and careless fashion.

CA: You were a semifinalist in the NASA Journalist-in-Space Program in 1986. What's the status of that program now?

FERRIS: NASA has put the Journalist-in-Space Program on hold, indefinitely. It's possible that the program will be reactivated, someday, but I have no way of assessing the chances.

CA: How would you grade our space program now?

FERRIS: I think it's lost—lost not in space, but here on earth. The space program has been one among many examples of a kind of indulgence in this country, an arrogant mode of behavior that seems to assume that we're so blessed we can be almost infinitely careless about things and it'll all work out fine. It *hasn't* worked out fine, and its woes serve as a reminder that we Americans are not God's chosen people, that we're subject to the same rules of conduct that attend to everyone else. When the shuttle program was being planned, many people in the scientific community were quite clear about the dangers it posed. They trooped down to Congress and said, "You're putting all your eggs in one basket; it's not a pretty basket, and if you drop that basket you're not going to have any space program. That's all come true, to no one's satisfaction, and yet no lesson seems to 'have been learned. The space program continues to blunder ahead with the same lack of purpose and the same kind of mid-brain thinking that got it into this situation in the first place. NASA currently seems to be preoccupied with building a space station, even though no one knows what it's for—which is just how they got into over-emphasizing the shuttle. It's clear that NASA should never have tied so much of the space program to the fortunes of the shuttle.

CA: At Berkeley you teach not only an astronomy course but also science writing, I believe.

FERRIS: Yes. I'm actually a professor of journalism in the graduate school of journalism there at Berkeley, and they loan me to the astronomy department every so often.

CA: What are the main points you stress to your students who are or would like to be science writers?

FERRIS: Pretty much the same things you'd stress to anyone covering any other beat in journalism—the need for accuracy, and clarity, and economy of phrase, and all those sorts of things. Some science writers feel one should avoid becoming co-opted by science, becoming kind of an advocate of science. They feel science writers should look coldly on their subject, just as a political or business reporter would. Others, of whom I'm one, think of ourselves more as advocates of science and we're not terribly embarrassed by it. I'm enthusiastic; I don't try to pretend to a cold objectivity.

I do think there is one lesson to be learned from the science writers who are enthusiastic about science that might be useful for journalists more widely, and that is that you don't necessarily have to be hostile towards your subject in order to do a credible job as a reporter. Hostility works for some journalists, but I do think that some damage has been done by the assumption that a journalist is not tough or hard-working or clearheaded unless he actively dislikes the people he is writing about. If you're going to cover, say, the Exxon Valdez oil spill, one way you can do it is to say, "I hate the oil company, and here's another example of this evil they've done." But that doesn't strike me as the only way, or even necessarily the best way, to cover the story. You can also cover it from the standpoint of someone who understands the oil companies very well and has some sympathy for them and recognizes that if Exxon were dismantled tomorrow, something else much like it would soon spring up in its place. In my view, both the hostile and the sympathetic approaches are legitimate. Certainly you see them both working within science writing. I don't think one is right and the other wrong.

CA: Among the reader's pleasures in your writing is that you manage to convey that sense of enthusiasm that you were just talking about. What sustains it?

FERRIS: Nature itself. There is this great thing happening—the toiling of the vast universe—and somehow we get to learn a little about it. We've learned something about it from the observations of the poets and artists, and something further from the scientists. We still know only an infinitesimal amount, but that's already enough to enchant us. Who it's enchanting I don't know. It's easy to say that it's because we're part of it, but you can be part of the Rotary Club and not necessarily be enchanted by it. There's something going on between that part of nature that is inside the skull and the rest of it that is engrossing and appealing to us, even though we don't know why.

CA: What's ahead for you? Anything in the works or the plans that you'd like to talk about?

FERRIS: I'm writing a book of essays, so first I have to learn how to write essays. I'm also editing an anthology of other people's science writing. And I'm going to do some traveling: I'm going away to Bali for a couple of months, and I'm going to go back to New York—just move around for a while and get out of this office where I've finished a couple of books and have begun to feel a little cooped up. I'm mostly trying to concentrate on doing a few things well. You get offered a lot of things, of course, and it's a mistake that people make—I've seen my friends make it, and I've made it often enough myself—to start thinking that you're so clever that you can do them all.

The dynamic of a writer's life is that the time when you enjoy the maximum attention is just when you're leading the least typical part of your life. Typically you're locked away writing for long periods of time, and it's a quiet and not terribly interesting sort of life—I'd much rather watch a blacksmith at work than a writer. Then you publish a book and there's this brief flurry during which you're not writing. You're out promoting the book, or just enjoying the fact that you're not writing; you're showing up on TV, speechifying. It's during this period that you get lots of offers, and the great danger is that you'll start saying yes. You think you can do all these wonderful things. You've forgotten how hard it was just to do this one little thing you did.

BIOGRAPHICAL/CRITICAL SOURCES:

PERIODICALS

Chicago Tribune, August 10, 1988.
Los Angeles Times, July 15, 1988, September 2, 1988.
Los Angeles Times Book Review, December 14, 1980.
New York Times, March 12, 1979, August 26, 1982.
New York Times Book Review, July 15, 1979, January 25, 1981, July 11, 1982, March 3, 1985, July 17, 1988.
Saturday Review, December, 1980.
Village Voice, December 3, 1980.
Washington Post Book World, August 21, 1988.

—*Interview by Jean W. Ross, with Ronald Brashear and Michael D. Senecal*

*   *   *

FINE, Seymour H(oward) 1925-

PERSONAL: Born April 21, 1925, in New York, N.Y.; son of Max (a merchant) and Sylvia (Topol) Fine; married Adell P. Gross (a social worker), 1948; children: Michael David, Paul Robert. *Education:* City University of New York, B.B.A., 1952; Fairleigh Dickinson University, M.S. (magna cum laude), 1968; Columbia University, Ph.D., 1978.

ADDRESSES: Home—138 Gaynor Pl., Glen Rock, N.J. 07452. *Office*—Graduate School of Business, New York University, New York, N.Y. 10003.

CAREER: Fine Marketing Associates, Inc. (wholesale consumer products company), Glen Rock, N.J., founder and president, 1948-74; Rutgers University, Newark, N.J., professor of business, 1977—; Fine Associates (consultants in marketing research and strategic planning), Glen Rock, president, 1979—; New York University, Graduate School of Business, New York, N.Y., professor of marketing, 1988—. Public speaker. Consultant to U.S. Department of Energy, Robert Wood Johnson Foundation, Ingersoll-Rand Co., Onkyo USA Corp., U.S. Treasury Department, Rockefeller Foundation, and United Nations World Health Organization.

MEMBER: Association for Consumer Research, American Academy of Advertising (fellow), American Marketing Association, American Institute for Decision Sciences.

AWARDS, HONORS: Manuscript award from Association for Consumer Research, 1979, for article "Toward a Theory of Segmentation by Objectives in Social Marketing."

WRITINGS:

The Marketing of Ideas and Social Issues, Praeger, 1981.
(Contributor) Philip Kotler and other editors, *Readings and Cases in Marketing for Nonprofit Organizations,* Prentice-Hall, 1983.
(With Raymond Dreyfach) *Customers: How to Get, Serve, and Keep Them,* Dartnell Corp., 1983.
Social Marketing: Promoting the Causes of Public and Nonprofit Agencies, Allyn & Bacon, 1989.

Contributor to *Encyclopedia of Management.* Contributor to business, education, health care, and management journals.

SIDELIGHTS: Reviewing for the *Library Quarterly,* Andrea C. Dragon of Rutgers University states that Seymour H. Fine's *Marketing of Ideas and Social Issues* "is important because it provides librarians with a clear description of the ways in which marketing is used to produce and promote ideas and social issues. . . . Libraries are entering a new world of marketing where competition for readers and information seekers is apt to be fierce. In order to be successful, an understanding of the rules is required. Seymour Fine's book is an excellent place to start learning the game."

Fine told *CA:* "If there is one point emphasized in my writings, teachings and consulting it is this: Marketing is not just product design, advertising, selling, pricing, delivery, or research. It is all of these things and more. Most would-be marketers commit the error of spending the entire hard-earned budget on advertising, before an overall marketing plan is drawn up. That is like trying to build a house without a blueprint."

BIOGRAPHICAL/CRITICAL SOURCES:

PERIODICALS

Library Quarterly, October, 1982.

*   *   *

FISCHL, Viktor
See DAGAN, Avigdor

*   *   *

FISHER, Barbara   1940-
(Barbara Fisher Perry)

PERSONAL: Born December 10, 1940, in New York, N.Y.; daughter of David (an attorney) and Regina (Mandel) Fisher; married Ernest Perry, September 23, 1967 (divorced, 1980); married Richard Alan Spiegel, June 21, 1983; children: (first marriage) Athelantis. *Education:* Hunter College of the City University of New York, B.A., 1962.

ADDRESSES: Home and office—393 St. Pauls Ave., Staten Island, N.Y. 10304. *Agent*—Philip G. Spitzer Literary Agency, 1465 Third Ave., New York, N.Y. 10028.

CAREER: Dauntless Books, Inc., New York City, editorial assistant, 1962-63; Academic Press, Inc., New York City, writer in promotion department, 1963-64; Chelsea Theater Center, New York City, director of research and development, 1966-68; Ten Penny Players, New York City, co-director and editor of publications, 1967—. Manager and fiscal director of 799 Greenwich Street Tenants Corp., New York City, 1972-89; fundraiser for Institutes for the Achievement of Human Potential, 1974-76; fiscal director of New York Book Fair, 1978-87; co-director of Waterways Project, 1978—. Consultant to New York State Narcotics Control Commission, 1971-73. Instructor at library workshops and at New York Board of Education Alternative High School and Program Sites.

MEMBER: Authors Guild, Dramatists Guild, Authors League of America, National Writers Union, United Federation of Teachers.

AWARDS, HONORS: Grants from New York State Council on the Arts, 1970, 1987, 1988, 1989, Rockefeller Brothers Fund, 1970, International Business Machines Corp., 1971, Con Edison, 1986, 1987, 1988, New York City Department of Cultural Affairs, 1987, 1988, National Endowment for the Arts, and J. M. Kaplan Fund; Coordinating Council for Literary Magazines grant for the Waterways Project.

WRITINGS:

JUVENILE

(And illustrator) *Big Harold and Tiny Enid,* Ten Penny Players, 1975.
(And illustrator) *Jud: A Play for Two Voices,* Ten Penny Players, 1976.
(And illustrator) *Philpin's Tree,* Ten Penny Players, 1976.
Nutrition Awareness Program, U.S. Department of Agriculture, 1976.
(And illustrator) *Car Boy,* Ten Penny Players, 1977.
(And illustrator) *Linkups,* Ten Penny Players, 1977.
(And illustrator) *Jolly Molly Molar,* Ten Penny Players, 1979.
(And illustrator) *Harmony Hurricane Muldoon,* Ten Penny Players, 1979.
(And illustrator) *Max St. Peter McBride and Theodora,* Ten Penny Players, 1981.

(And illustrator) *Dan,* Ten Penny Players, 1981.
Davy, Davy Dumpling, SZ Press, 1985.

EDITOR; JUVENILE; WITH HUSBAND, RICHARD ALAN SPIEGEL

Poetry Hunter, No. 1, Ten Penny Players, 1981.
More Poetry Hunter, Ten Penny Players, 1981.
Still More Poetry Hunter, Ten Penny Players, 1981.
Subway Slams, Ten Penny Players, 1981.
In Search of Song, Ten Penny Players, Volume 1: *PS-114,* Volume 2: *PS-276,* 1981, Volume 3: *Jefferson Market Library,* 1982, Volume 4, by Adrienne Day, 1983, Volume 5, by New York Book Fair, 1983, Volume 6, by Roxanne Mennella, 1984, Volume 7, by Sarah Wilkins, 1984, Volume 8: *Inner Clockwork,* 1985.
Greenwich Village Lore and Chinatown Tales, Ten Penny Players, 1983.
Menella and Wilkins, *Dolls,* Ten Penny Players, 1984.
Yearning to Breathe Free, Ten Penny Players, 1984.
Fairies, Elves, and Gnomes, Ten Penny Players, 1985.
Streams I, New York City Board of Education, 1987.
Streams II, New York City Board of Education, 1988.
Streams III, New York City Board of Education, 1989.
Streams IV, New York City Board of Education, 1990.

OTHER

(Under name Barbara Fisher Perry) *Care without Care,* Avon, 1970.
"Noisy City Sam" (one-act juvenile play), first produced in New York City at Clinton Park, July, 1970.
(Adapter and director) "Goblin Market" (juvenile play), first produced in New York City at Jefferson Market Library, April 7, 1984.

Also author of juvenile plays "A Museum Project," "Mother Mandelbaum: Queen of the Fences," "Jud and Honoria," and "Jud and the Oil Slick." Contributor to periodicals. Contributor to the anthology *More Than a Gathering of Dreamers,* Coordinating Council of Literary Magazines, 1980. Co-editor, with Spiegel, and designer, *Waterways: Poetry in the Mainstream,* 1979—; editor, *Design* and *Young Adult,* both for Waterways Project, 1980—; co-editor with Spiegel, *Forward Face,* Cranio-Facial Unit of New York University Hospital, and *Newsletter* of the Active New York City Committee on the Handicapped Parent.

WORK IN PROGRESS: Adah Isaacs Menken; a revised edition of *Care without Care,* with supplement on educational advocacy; a resource book for parents and professionals.

SIDELIGHTS: For more information, see entry in this volume on author's husband, Richard Alan Spiegel.

*   *   *

FISHER, Benjamin Franklin IV   1940-

PERSONAL: Born July 21, 1940, in Orwigsburg, Pa.; son of B. Frank and Mary E. (Kantner) Fisher. *Education:* Ursinus College, B.A. (with honors), 1962; Duke University, M.A., 1963, Ph.D., 1969. *Religion:* United Church of Christ.

ADDRESSES: Home—P.O. Box 941, Oxford, Miss. 38655. *Office*—Department of English, University of Mississippi, University, Miss. 38677.

CAREER: University of Pennsylvania, Philadelphia, instructor, 1967-69, assistant professor of English, 1969-73; Hahnemann

Medical College, Philadelphia, assistant professor, 1973-75, associate professor of humanities, 1975-79, chairman of department, 1977-79; University of Mississippi, University, associate professor of English, 1979—.

MEMBER: Poe Studies Association (vice-president, 1973-79; president, 1979-83), Edgar Allan Poe Society, Housman Society (bibliographer, 1972—; American vice-president, 1986—), Phi Beta Kappa.

WRITINGS:

(Editor and contributor) *Nineteenth-Century Literary Perspectives,* Duke University Press, 1973.
The Very Spirit of Cordiality: The Literary Uses of Alcohol and Alcoholism in the Fiction of Edgar Allan Poe, Edgar Allan Poe Society, 1978.
(Editor) *Poe at Work: Seven Textual Studies,* Edgar Allan Poe Society, 1978.
(Contributor) M. B. Tymn, editor, *Horror Literature,* Bowker, 1982.
(Contributor) G. R. Thompson and V. K. Lokke, editors, *A Ruined Eden of the Present,* Purdue University Press, 1983.
(Editor) *Poe and Our Times,* Edgar Allan Poe Society, 1986.
(Contributor) Edward E. Chielens, editor, *American Literary Magazines: The Eighteenth and Nineteenth Centuries,* Greenwood Press, 1986.
(Contributor) David E. E. Sloane, editor, *American Humor Magazines and Comic Periodicals,* Greenwood Press, 1987.
Frederick Irving Anderson (1877-1947): A Biobibliography, Brownstone Books, 1987.
(Contributor) Steven H. Gale, editor, *Encyclopedia of American Humorists,* Garland Publishing, 1988.
(Contributor) Sally Mitchell, editor, *Victorian Britain: An Encyclopedia,* Garland Publishing, 1988.
The Gothic's Gothic: Study Aids to the Tradition of the Tale of Terror, Garland Publishing, 1988.
(Editor) *Poe and His Times,* Edgar Allen Poe Society, 1989.
Handbook to Poe's Tales, G. K. Hall, in press.

Contributor to *American Literature.* Member of editorial board of *English Literature in Transition, Poe Studies,* and *Victorian Poetry.* Editor of *University of Mississippi Studies in English,* 1979—.

SIDELIGHTS: Benjamin Franklin Fisher IV told *CA:* "My interest in Poe stems from studies of American-Renaissance literature and from reading detective fiction. I also enjoy Wilkie Collins, Frederick Irving Anderson, J. D. Carr, and Charles Dickens. Recently, I have turned again to interests from long ago: Tennyson, the Pre-Raphaelites, American women in the local color mode, and Edith Wharton."

*   *   *

FLUTE, Molly
  See LOTTMAN, Eileen

*   *   *

FLYNN, Don
  See FLYNN, Donald R(obert)

*   *   *

FLYNN, Donald R(obert) 1928-
  (Don Flynn; Kate Williams, a house pseudonym)

PERSONAL: Born November 18, 1928, in St. Louis, Mo.; son of George Joseph and Mary (Foley) Flynn; married Charlotte J.

Bayton (a free-lance writer), October 26, 1957; children: Kevin, Christopher, Colin. *Education:* University of Missouri, B.A., 1952.

ADDRESSES: Office—*New York Daily News,* 220 East 42nd St., New York, N.Y. 10017. *Agent*—International Creative Management, 40 West 57th St., New York, N.Y. 10019.

CAREER: Newspaper reporter, *St. Joseph Gazette,* St. Joseph, Mo., 1953-54, *Topeka State-Journal,* Topeka, Kan., 1955-56, *Kansas City Star,* Kansas City, Mo., 1956, *Chicago Daily News,* Chicago, Ill., 1957-58, *New York Journal-American,* New York City, 1959-65, and *New York Herald Tribune,* 1966, New York City; *New York Daily News,* New York City, reporter and writer, 1967—. Creator of one-hour action/adventure television series with Sonny Grosso, "Night Heat," CBS-TV, 1984—.

MEMBER: Mystery Writers of America, Dramatists Guild, Writers Guild of America, East.

WRITINGS:

UNDER NAME DON FLYNN; NOVELS

Murder Isn't Enough, Walker & Co., 1982.
Murder on the Hudson, Walker & Co., 1984.
Ordinary Murder, Walker & Co., 1987.
Murder in A-Flat, Walker & Co., 1988.
A Suitcase in Berlin, Walker & Co., 1989.

PLAYS

"Now It Makes Sense" (three-act comedy), first produced in Bellport, L.I., at Gateway Playhouse, August 26, 1969.
"Pull the Covers over My Head" (three-act drama), first produced Off-Off-Broadway at The Actor's Place, fall, 1969.
"A Money-Back Guarantee" (one-act comedy), first produced Off-Off-Broadway at American Theatre, fall, 1969.
"The Petition" (one-act comedy), first produced in Waterford, Conn., at Eugene O'Neill Memorial Theatre Center, summer, 1970.
"The Man Who Raped Kansas" (two-act comedy), first produced at Gilford Playhouse, August 3, 1970, produced as "Keep Krap out of Kansas" in Long Island at Arena Players Repertory Theater, 1982.
"Something That Matters" (two-act comedy), first produced Off-Off-Broadway at American Theatre, 1973.
"A Meaningful Relationship," first produced in New York at the Shandol Theatre, 1974.
"The Pilgrims Landed Just down the Road" (three-act comedy), first produced in Long Island at Arena Players Repertory Theater, 1982.
"Around the Corner from the White House" (two-act comedy), first produced in New York at No Smoking Playhouse, 1983.

WITH WIFE, CHARLOTTE J. BAYTON FLYNN, UNDER HOUSE PSEUDONYM KATE WILLIAMS; "SWEET VALLEY HIGH" SERIES

Power Play, Bantam, 1983.
Double Love, Bantam, 1983.
Dear Sister, Bantam, 1984.
Too Easy, Bantam, 1984.

OTHER

Also author under name Don Flynn of two episodes of "One of the Boys," starring Mickey Rooney, for NBC-TV, 1981, and of comedy series "Room Nine," optioned by Columbia Pictures; creator and writer, with Sonny Grosso, of one-hour action/

adventure series, "Night Heat," for CBS-TV, 1984—. Some of Flynn's novels have been published in French by Editions Gallimard.

BIOGRAPHICAL/CRITICAL SOURCES:

PERIODICALS

New York Times Book Review, November 13, 1983.

* * *

FORD, Phyllis M(arjorie) 1928-

PERSONAL: Born March 18, 1928, in Ludlow, Mass.; daughter of Wendell Bradford (a management consultant) and Phyllis (Symonds) Ford. *Education:* University of Massachusetts, B.S., 1949; Arizona State University, M.A., 1954; Indiana University, Re.D., 1962.

ADDRESSES: Office—Department of Park and Recreation Resources, Michigan State University, East Lansing, Mich. 48824.

CAREER: University of Massachusetts—Amherst, research technician, 1949-50; Young Women's Christian Association (Y.W.C.A.), Orange, N.J., teenage program director, 1950-51; Florence Union High School, Florence, Ariz., teacher, 1951-54; Hammond Technical Vocational High School, Hammond, Ind., teacher of physical education, 1954-58; Schools of the City of Hammond, supervisor of girls physical education, 1958-59; University of Oregon, Eugene, assistant professor, 1961-66, associate professor of recreation and park management, 1966-69; University of Iowa, Iowa City, associate professor of recreation and chairman of the department, 1969-71; University of Oregon, associate professor, 1971-75, professor of recreation and park management, 1975-84, head of department, 1972-75, 1980-84, graduate coordinator, 1975-80; Washington State University, Pullman, professor of recreation and chair of department of physical education, sport, and leisure studies, 1984-87; Michigan State University, East Lansing, professor and chair of department of park and recreation resources, 1987—. Visiting lecturer, Indiana University, 1959-61. Assistant professor at Portland State College (now Portland State University), summers, 1963, 1964, and Oregon State University, summer, 1965. Member of board of directors, Western Rivers Girl Scouts. Consultant in outdoor education to various school systems.

MEMBER: American Camping Association (president of Oregon section, 1966-68; national secretary, 1969-73; vice president, 1972-73; national leadership chairman, 1976), National Recreation and Park Association, American Alliance for Health, Physical Education, Recreation, and Dance, Society of Professional Recreation Educators, Nature Conservancy, Oregon Association for Health, Physical Education and Recreation (vice president for recreation, 1963-64), Oregon Recreation Society (member of board of directors, 1972-73), Pi Lambda Theta, Phi Delta Kappa.

AWARDS, HONORS: Hedley S. Dimock Award, American Camping Association, 1973; Garrett Eppley Alumni Award, Indiana University Department of Recreation and Park Administration, 1976; Distinguished Service Award, Oregon Parks and Recreation Society, 1982; Distinguished Citizen in Environmental Education, Environmental Education Association of Oregon, 1983; Golden Ice Axe Award for outdoor recreation, Oregon Parks and Recreation Society, 1984; Loredo Taft Award, Northern Illinois University, 1987; Julian Smith Award for outdoor education, American Alliance for Health, Physical Education, Recreation, and Dance, 1989.

WRITINGS:

(Editor) *GAA Songbook,* Indiana League of High School Girls Athletic Associations, 1957.

Leisure and the Senior Citizens (monograph), Department of Recreation, Indiana University, 1962.

(Editor) *Professional Preparation Standards in Recreation,* Northwest Council on Teacher Education Standards for Health, Physical Education and Recreation, 1965.

The Handicapped Camper and the Regular Camp, American Camping Association, 1966.

A Guide for Leaders of Informal Recreation Activities, University of Iowa Press, 1970, published as *Informal Recreation Activities: A Leader's Guide,* American Camping Association, 1977.

(Editor) Janet Tobitt, *A Counselor's Guide to Camp Singing,* revised edition, American Camping Association, 1971.

(With Lynn S. Rodney) *Camp Administration,* Ronald, 1971.

(With Effie L. Fairchild) *Kool Summer Fun* (summer playground cards), National Recreation and Parks Association, 1972.

(With A. R. Dreher and K. C. Crandall) *Survey of Outdoor Education Sites,* University of Oregon Press, 1974.

Principles and Practices of Outdoor/Environmental Education, Wiley, 1980.

(With C. Edginton) *Leadership of Recreation and Leisure Services Organization,* Wiley, 1984.

(With J. Blanchard) *Leadership and Administration of Outdoor Pursuits,* Venture, 1984.

Also author of surveys on recreation for government agencies. Contributor of numerous articles to various periodicals, including *Health Bulletin* (Indiana State Board of Health), *Journal of Health, Physical Education and Recreation, Journal of Outdoor Education, Journal of Environmental Education, Bradford Papers, Camping,* and *Outing Guide.*

AVOCATIONAL INTERESTS: Hiking, camping, nature study.

* * *

FOSBURGH, Liza 1930-

PERSONAL: Born July 6, 1930, in Moultrie, Ga.; daughter of Henry T. (a physician) and Elizabeth (a writer; maiden name, Camp) Edmondson; married Pieter Whitney Fosburgh (a conservationist and writer), April 13, 1957 (deceased); children: Pieter Whitney, Jr., James H. E. *Education:* Holyoke College, B.A., 1951. *Politics:* Democrat. *Religion:* Episcopalian.

ADDRESSES: Home—Mattison Hollow Rd., Cherry Plain, N.Y. 12040. *Agent*—Jean V. Naggar Literary Agency, 336 East 73rd St., Suite A, New York, N.Y. 10021.

CAREER: Town and Country, New York, N.Y., copy editor, 1952-57; *Albany-Times-Union,* Albany, N.Y., editor of woman's page, 1957-58; free-lance writer, 1958—; Pine Cobble School, Williamstown, Mass., librarian, 1973-78.

MEMBER: Authors Guild, Authors League of America, Lenox Garden Club, New Haven Lawn Club.

WRITINGS:

With Friends Like These . . . (novel), Pocket Books, 1983.
Bella Arabella (juvenile), Macmillan, 1985.
Mrs. Abercorn and the Bunce Boys, Macmillan, 1986.
Summer Lion (young adult), Morrow, 1987.
Cruise Control (young adult), Bantam, 1988.
Afternoon Magic (young adult), Macmillan, 1989.
The Wrong Way Home (young adult), Bantam, 1990.

Contributor to *Berkshire Eagle, Vermont Sportsman,* magazines, and cookbooks.

WORK IN PROGRESS: The Pilgrim Soul and *Parable of the Last Wife,* both novels.

SIDELIGHTS: Liza Fosburgh told *CA:* "I believe a writer can be as diversified as he or she wishes, writing for adults and children, for the supermarket crowd and the 'serious' reader. For me, a writer has two main purposes: to put on paper the words, ideas, and emotions that are bursting from within; and to produce material people want to read. Sometimes these are not compatible. I hope, in my case, they will be. My late great-aunt, Leslie Ford, a mystery writer of the 1940s and 1950s, believed a writer should write what readers want. As is evident, she was a strong influence on me."

AVOCATIONAL INTERESTS: Gardening, entertaining, cooking, travel.

*   *   *

FRAYN, Michael   1933-

PERSONAL: Born September 8, 1933, in London, England; son of Thomas Allen (a manufacturer's representative) and Violet Alice (Lawson) Frayn; married Gillian Palmer (a social worker), February 18, 1960 (divorced, 1989); children: three daughters. *Education:* Emmanuel College, Cambridge University, B.A., 1957.

ADDRESSES: Agent—Elaine Green Ltd., 31 Newington Green, London N16, England.

CAREER: Novelist and playwright. *Guardian,* Manchester, England, general-assignment reporter, 1957-59, "Miscellany" columnist, 1959-62; *Observer,* London, England, columnist, 1962-68. Contributor to weekly comedy series, "Beyond a Joke," British Broadcasting Corp., 1972; has made regular appearances on Granada Television's "What the Papers Say." *Military service:* British Army, 1952-54.

MEMBER: Royal Society of Literature.

AWARDS, HONORS: Somerset Maugham Award, 1966, for *The Tin Men;* Hawthornden Prize, 1967, for *The Russian Interpreter;* National Press Club Award for distinguished reporting, International Publishing Corporation, 1970, for series of *Observer* articles on Cuba; Best Comedy of the Year award, *Evening Standard,* 1975, for "Alphabetical Order," 1982, for "Noises Off," and 1984, for "Benefactors"; Society of West End Theatre Award for best comedy of the year, 1976, for "Donkeys' Years," 1982, for "Noises Off," and 1984, for "Benefactors"; American Theatre Wing's Antoinette Perry ("Tony") Award nomination for best play, 1984, Laurence Olivier Award for best play, 1984, *Plays and Players* award for best new play, 1986, and New York Drama Critics Circle award for best new foreign play, 1986, all for "Benefactors."

WRITINGS:

The Day of the Dog (selections from his *Guardian* column), illustrations by Timothy Birdsall, Collins, 1962, Doubleday, 1963.

(Editor) John Bingham Morton, *The Best of Beachcomber,* Heinemann, 1963.

(Contributor) Michael Sissons and Philip French, *Age of Austerity,* Hodder & Stoughton, 1963.

The Book of the Fub (selections from his *Guardian* column), Collins, 1963, published as *Never Put off to Gomorrah,* Pantheon, 1964.

(Editor with Bamber Gascoigne) *Timothy: The Drawings and Cartoons of Timothy Birdsall,* M. Joseph, 1964.

On the Outskirts, Collins, 1964.

At Bay in Gear Street (selections from his *Observer* column), Fontana, 1967.

Constructions (philosophy), Wildwood House, 1974.

The Original Michael Frayn: Satirical Essays, Salamander Press (Edinburgh), 1983.

NOVELS

The Tin Men, Collins, 1965, Little, Brown, 1966.

The Russian Interpreter, Viking, 1966.

Towards the End of the Morning, Collins, 1967, reprinted, 1985, published as *Against Entropy,* Viking, 1967.

A Very Private Life, Viking, 1968.

Sweet Dreams, Collins, 1973, Viking, 1974.

The Trick of It, Viking, 1989.

PLAYS

(With John Edwards) "Zounds!" (musical comedy), first produced in Cambridge, England, May, 1957.

The Two of Us: Four One-Act Plays for Two Players (contains "Black and Silver," "The New Quixote," "Mr. Foot," and "Chinamen"; first produced on West End at Garrick Theatre, July 30, 1970), Fontana, 1970.

The Sandboy (first produced in London at Greenwich Theatre, September 16, 1971), Fontana, 1971.

"Alphabetical Order" (also see below), first produced in London at Hampstead Theatre Club, March 11, 1975; transferred to May Fair Theatre on West End, April 8, 1975; produced in New Haven, Conn., at Long Wharf Theatre, October 14, 1976.

Donkeys' Years: A Play (first produced on West End at Globe Theatre, July 15, 1976; produced Off-Off-Broadway at New Theatre of Brooklyn, March, 1987; also see below), French, 1977.

Clouds (first produced in London at Hampstead Theatre Club, August 16, 1976; produced on West End at Duke of York's Theatre, November 1, 1978; also see below), French, 1977.

Alphabetical Order [and] *Donkeys' Years,* Methuen, 1977.

Liberty Hall (first produced in London at Greenwich Theatre, January 24, 1980), Methuen, 1977.

Make and Break (first produced in Hammersmith, England, at Lyric Theatre, March 18, 1980; transferred to Haymarket Theatre Royal on West End, April 24, 1980; produced in Washington, D.C., at John F. Kennedy Center for the Performing Arts, 1982; also see below), Methuen, 1980.

Noises Off: A Play in Three Acts (first produced in Hammersmith at Lyric Theatre, February 11, 1982; transferred to Savoy Theatre on West End, March 31, 1982; produced in Washington, D.C., at Eisenhower Theater, November, 1983; produced on Broadway at Brooks Atkinson Theatre, December, 1983; also see below), Methuen, 1982, acting edition, French, 1982.

Benefactors: A Play in Two Acts (first produced on West End at Vaudeville Theatre, April, 1984; produced on Broadway at Brooks Atkinson Theatre, December 22, 1985), Methuen, 1984.

Plays: One (contains "Alphabetical Order," "Donkeys' Years," "Clouds," "Make and Break," and "Noises Off "), Methuen, 1985.

Balmoral: Methuen Modern Play, Routledge Chapman & Hall, 1988.

TRANSLATOR FROM THE RUSSIAN, AND ADAPTER

(And author of introduction) Anton Chekhov, *The Cherry Orchard: A Comedy in Four Acts* (first produced on West End at National Theatre, 1978), Methuen, 1978.

(And author of introduction) Leo Tolstoy *The Fruits of Enlightenment: A Comedy in Four Acts* (first produced on West End at National Theatre, 1979), Methuen, 1979.

(And author of introduction) *Three Sisters: A Drama in Four Acts* (first produced in Manchester, England, at Royal Exchange Theatre, 1985), Methuen, 1983.

Chekhov, *Wild Honey: The Untitled Play* (unofficially known as "Platonov"; first produced on West End at National Theatre, 1984; produced in New York at Virginia Theatre, December 18, 1986), Methuen, 1984.

(And author of introduction) Chekhov, *The Seagull* (first produced in Hammersmith at the Lyric Theatre, 1986), Methuen, 1986.

Chekhov, *Uncle Vanya,* Methuen, 1987.

Chekhov, "The Sneeze" (short stories and sketches), first produced on West End at Aldwych Theatre, November, 1988.

OTHER

"Jamie, On a Flying Visit" (teleplay), British Broadcasting Corp. (BBC-TV), January, 1968.

"One Pair of Eyes" (documentary film), BBC-TV, 1968.

"Birthday" (teleplay), BBC-TV, 1969.

"Laurence Stern Lived Here" (documentary film), BBC-TV, 1973.

"Making Faces" (comedy broadcast in six parts), BBC-TV, September 25-October 30, 1975.

"Imagine a City Called Berlin" (documentary film), BBC-TV, 1975.

"Vienna: The Mask of Gold" (documentary film), BBC-TV, 1977.

"Three Streets in the Country" (documentary film), BBC-TV, 1979.

"The Long Straight," BBC-TV, 1980.

(With others) *Great Railway Journeys of the World* (based on film broadcast by BBC-TV; contains Frayn's segment on Australia), BBC, 1981, Dutton, 1982.

Clockwise: A Screenplay (produced and released by Universal, 1986), Methuen, 1986.

Also contributor to periodicals, including the *New York Times Book Review.*

SIDELIGHTS: Though best known in the United States as the playwright behind the hit stage farce "Noises Off," Briton Michael Frayn has actually produced a wide variety of writing. His beginnings as a columnist and critic for two newspapers, the Manchester *Guardian* and the London *Observer,* led to a number of published collections. Frayn's novels, including *The Tin Men* and *The Russian Interpreter,* have garnered praise for both their humor and their insights into complicated modern times. Among his other plays, Frayn's translations of Anton Chekhov's classics draw particular attention. And more recently, the writer has ventured into cinema, with a produced screenplay, "Clockwise."

A native Londoner, "Frayn believes his sense of humor began to develop during his years at Kingston Grammar School where, to the delight of his classmates, he practiced the 'techniques of mockery' on his teachers," reports Mark Fritz in the *Dictionary of Literary Biography.* "Referring to this early practice of making jokes at the expense of others, Frayn says, 'I sometimes wonder if this isn't an embarrassingly exact paradigm of much that I've done since.' " Frayn established himself as a keen social satirist on two newspapers, the *Guardian* and *Observer.* For the former, as Frayn saw it, "his job with [the column] Miscellany was to write cool, witty interviews with significant film directors passing through, but there were never enough film directors so he started making up humorous paragraphs to fill," as Terry Coleman writes in the *Guardian.* Malcolm Page explains in the *Dictionary of Literary Biography* that Frayn "invented for the column the Don't Know Party and such characters as the trendy Bishop of [Twicester]; Rollo Swavely, a public relations consultant; and the ambitious suburban couple, [Christopher and Lavinia Crumble]."

Comparing Frayn's "wit, sophistication, and imagination" to "that of American humorist S. J. Perelman," Fritz declares that Frayne's "satire is sharper." That sense of satire, along with an emerging seriousness, carried the author to his first novel, *The Tin Men.* The story, about the suitability of computers to take over the burden of human dullness, won the Somerset Maugham Award for fiction in 1963. A year later, Frayn produced *The Russian Interpreter,* "a spy story which deals more with the deceit between individuals than between nations," according to Fritz. That novel took the Hawthornden Prize.

Two more Frayn novels earned critical admiration. *A Very Private Life,* written in the future tense, "explains how life has grown more private, first through physical privacy, then through the development of drugs to cope with anger and uncertainty," writes Page. To *Spectator* reviewer Maurice Capitanchik, "Frayn, in his parable of the horrific future, does not escape the impress which [George] Orwell and [Aldous] Huxley have made upon the genre, nor does he really go beyond the area of authoritarian oppression so brilliantly illumined by [Franz] Kafka, but he does something else both valuable and unique: he shows that his 'Brave New World' is really our cowardly old world, if we did but, shudderingly, know it, in a prose which is often beautiful and, almost, poetry." And in *Sweet Dreams,* the novel Frayn considers his best to date, a young architect dies and goes to a distinctly familiar sort of English heaven, "a terribly decent place, really, where one's pleasantest dreams come true and one's most honest longings are fulfilled," as *Washington Post Book World* critic L. J. Davis describes. Caught in a permanent fantasy world, Howard, the architect, "immediately joins the small, intimate, and brilliantly unorthodox architectural firm he'd always yearned for," Davis continues. After redesigning the Matterhorn, engaging in a dramatic love affair, and realizing other superlative encounters, Howard "sells out to the movies, purges himself with a spell of rustic simplicity, rallies the best minds of his generation by means of letters to The Times, meets God . . . and eventually winds up, crinkle-eyed and aging, as prime minister. It is all rather poignant," says Davis.

Frayn's dramatic work began with a number of television plays. His prior theatrical background included a sojourn with the Cambridge Footlights revue, and a walk-on in a production of Nikolai Gogol's "The Inspector General"—a disaster that prefigured the backstage slapstick of "Noises Off." "I pulled instead of pushed at the door, it jammed in the frame, and there was no other way off," the writer tells Benedict Nightingale for a *New York Times Magazine* profile. "So I waited for what seemed like many, many hours while stagehands fought with crowbars on the other side and the audience started to slow-handclap. I've never been on the stage since."

Frayn has, however, brought to the stage many critically acclaimed productions. Among his stage plays, "Alphabetical Order" and "Donkeys' Years" earned plaudits, profits, and some measure of reputation for their author. In "Alphabetical Order," the happy disarray of a newspaper's research department—the "morgue"—is changed forever when a hyperefficient young woman joins the staff. "By the second act she has transformed [the morgue] into a model of order and efficiency. But somehow the humanness is gone," notes Fritz. "The young woman then proceeds to reorganize the personal lives of the other characters as well. She is not a total villain, however. In a way, the newspaper staff needs her: without a strong-willed person to manipulate them, weak-willed people often stagnate. At the heart of the play is the question: which is better, order or chaos?" The successful "Donkeys' Years" focuses upon a group of university graduates reunited twenty years later, only to revert to their adolescent roles and conflicts. Voted the best comedy of 1982 by London's West End Theatre Society, the play was dubbed by Stephen Holden in the *New York Times,* a "well-made farce that roundly twits English propriety."

Frayn's 1980 production "Make and Break," a comedy-drama about a salesman whose aggressive talent for business overshadows his humanity, played to capacity audiences in London, but premiered in the United States to mixed reviews. Finding the play "wretchedly constructed," *Drama* critic Harold Hobson, for instance, was also disappointed in its "old-fashioned . . . views of women." But more favorable notices came from other reviewers, including *Observer* contributor Michael Ratcliffe, who considered the production Frayn's "best play to date." Describing it as "an excessively neat, neoclassical sort of piece which draws on only a fraction of his imaginative range," the critic pointed out that the only "real problem with the play is simply that the men remain shadows and only the women come to life."

Although many renowned comedies and dramas have used the play-within-a-play format in the past—it is a device that predates Shakespeare—perhaps no self-referential play has been so widely received in this generation as "Noises Off," a no-holds-barred slapstick farce. Using the kind of manic entrances and mistaken identities reminiscent of the French master Georges Feydeau, "Noises Off" invites the audience to witness the turmoil behind a touring company of has-beens and never-weres as they attempt to perform a typically English sex farce called "Nothing On." Referring to the production as "a show that gave ineptitude a good name," *Insight* writer Sheryl Flatow indicates that "Noises Off" was criticized by some as nothing more than a relentless, if effective, laugh-getting machine. The charge of being too funny, however, is not the sort of criticism that repels audiences, and "Noises Off" enjoyed a long run on the West End and Broadway.

"The fun begins even before the curtain goes up," Frank Rich reports in his *New York Times* review of Frayn's comedy. "In the Playbill, we find a program-within-the-program. . . . Among other things, we learn that the author of 'Nothing On' is a former 'unsuccessful gents hosiery wholesaler' whose previous farce 'Socks before Marriage' ran for nine years." When the curtain does rise, Rich continues, "it reveals a hideous set . . . that could well serve all those sex farces . . . that do run for nine years." As the story opens, the "Nothing On" cast and crew are blundering through their final rehearsal; importantly, everyone establishes his onstage and offstage identities. Remarks Rich: "As the run-through is mostly devoted to setting up what follows, it's also the only sporadically mirthless stretch of Mr. Frayn's play: We're asked to study every ridiculous line and awful performance in 'Nothing On' to appreciate the varied replays yet to come. Still, the lags are justified by the payoff: Having painstakingly built his house of cards in Act I, the author

brings it crashing down with exponentially accelerating hilarity in Acts II and III."

While the backstage romances simmer, the troupe systematically skewers whatever appeal the cheesy "Nothing On" should have provided. Even the props get involved: by Act II, a plate of sardines is as important an element to the play as any of the actors. By this time, "Frayn's true inspiration strikes," in the words of *Washington Post* reviewer David Richards. "The company is a month into its tour and the set has been turned around, so that we are viewing 'Nothing On' from backstage. The innocent little romances in Act I have turned lethal and, while the actors are still vaguely mindful of their cues, they are more mindful of wreaking vengeance upon one another. . . . An ax is wielded murderously, a skirt is torn off, toes are stomped on, shoelaces are tied together, bone-crunching tumbles are taken, bouquets are shredded, a cactus is sat upon and, of course, the ingenue's damned [contact] lens pops out again!" Although Richards remarks that the play "lost" him "about the time 'Nothing On' orbited into outer space," he adds, that "up to the last quarter hour, Frayn maintains contact with reality, however exaggerated, but finally the connection just snaps and what has been incisively silly turns just plain silly. Elsewhere, though, there is such an abundance of invention and such an astute knotting of misunderstanding and mishap that it would be ungrateful to carp."

"Noises Off" established Frayn in America as a farceur, on the order of Feydeau and Ben Travers. To that end, the author tells *Los Angeles Times* reporter Barbara Isenberg that farce is serious business. Its most important element, he says, is "the losing of power for coherent thought under the pressure of events. What characters in farce do traditionally is try to recover some disaster that occurred, by a course of behavior that is so ill-judged that it makes it worse. In traditional farce, people are caught in a compromising situation, try to explain it with a lie and, when they get caught, have then to explain both the original situation *and* the lie. And, when they're caught in that lie, they have to have another one."

Frayn's first produced screenplay, "Clockwise," closely resembles "Noises Off" in its wild construction. Like the play, the film takes a simple premise and lets circumstances run amok. In "Clockwise," protagonist Brian Stimpson, a small-town headmaster and a man obsessed with punctuality, wins Headmaster of the Year honors and must travel by train to a distant city to deliver his acceptance speech. Inevitably, Brian catches the wrong train, and the thought that he may arrive late drives him to desperate means. By the film's end, he has stolen a car, invaded a monastery, robbed a man of his suit, and set two squadrons of police on his trail. "It isn't the film's idea of taking a prim, controlled character and letting him become increasingly unhinged that makes 'Clockwise' so enjoyable; it's the expertise with which Mr. Frayn's screenplay sets the wheels in motion and keeps them going," according to Janet Maslin's *New York Times* critique. Noting that "Clockwise" is "far from perfect—it has long sleepy stretches and some pretty obvious farce situations," *Washington Post* critic Paul Attanasio nonetheless adds, "but at its best, here is a comedy unusual in its layered complexity, in the way Frayn has worked everything out. 'Gonna take a bit o' sortin' out, this one,' says one of the pursuing bobbies. The joke, of course, is in the understatement. And rarely has the 'sortin' out' been so much fun."

Departing from farce, Frayn has written the stage work "Benefactors" as an acerbic look at a 1960s couple wrestling with their ideals as they try to cope with their troubled neighbors, a couple caught in a failing marriage. Frank Rich, who so enjoyed "Noises Off," saw a production of "Benefactors" and told the *New York Times,* "It's hard to fathom that these two works were written by the same man. Like 'Noises Off,' 'Benefactors' is ingeniously constructed and has been directed with split-second precision . . . but there all similarities end. Mr. Frayn's new play is a bleak, icy, microcosmic exploration of such serious matters as the nature of good and evil, the price of political and psychological change and the relationship of individuals to the social state. Though 'Benefactors' evokes Chekhov, 'Othello' and 'The Master Builder' along its way, it is an original, not to mention demanding, achievement that is well beyond the ambitions of most contemporary dramatists." Likewise, Mel Gussow of the same newspaper finds strong ties between Chekhov and Frayn: "Thematically, . . . the work remains [close] to Chekhov; through a closely observed, often comic family situation we see the self-defeating aspects of misguided social action."

Fluent in Russian, Frayn served with the British Army in 1952 and was sent to Cambridge, where he trained as an interpreter and used the opportunity to hone his "passion that started in late adolescence for things Soviet," as *New York Times Magazine* writer Benedict Nightingale puts it. From his early days, Frayn has emulated the Russian writer Anton Chekhov; and references to Chekhov are more than apt to describe Frayn also. After working on English versions of Chekhov's classics "The Cherry Orchard," "Three Sisters" and "The Seagull," Frayn embarked on a more unusual project—reworking for the stage "an unwieldy, six-hour play discovered in 1920 with its title page missing," writes Flatow. "The work is usually called 'Platonov,' after its leading character, a roguish teacher who is the object of affection of every woman in town." Flatow finds Frayn's version, "Wild Honey," to be "very much a collaboration," and offers the author's own remarks about the difficulty separating his own work from Chekhov's: "It's hard to say how much is mine and how much is his. As I wrote in the introduction to the play, I thought the only thing to do was treat it as if it were a rough draft of one of my own plays and proceed from there. If that meant giving one character's speech to another or rewriting dialogue or adding my own speeches, fine—anything to make a better second draft."

Scholars have noted that the original manuscript was left largely to the archives because when he was thought to have written the work—in his late teens or early twenties—Chekhov had hardly made his reputation as a creative artist. According to Rich in his *New York Times* column, " 'Wild Honey' isn't the only distillation of ['Platonov'], but it may be the most economical and witty. Even Mr. Frayn, a master of theatrical construction . . . and Chekhovian nuance . . . , cannot turn a journeyman's work into the masterpiece it sometimes prefigures ('The Cherry Orchard'). Yet the adapter has achieved his goal, as stated in his published introduction, of making 'a text for production' rather than 'an academic contribution or a pious tribute.' " As Rich goes on, "Let academics have fun detailing, applauding or deploring the transpositions, telescopings, elisions and outright alterations Mr. Frayn has made in the original work. What's fascinating about 'Wild Honey' is how elegantly the embryonic Chekhovian cartography pops into relief."

"Although one cannot say that Michael Frayn's plays revolutionized the British stage during [our era], they certainly helped to enliven it," concludes Fritz. "Frayn contributed a string of lively, witty comedies with some serious philosophical questions lurking beneath the surfaces. Like many other playwrights of [the 1970s and 1980s,] Frayn experimented with dramatic structures borrowed from film and television—perhaps an attempt to find new methods of expression." And in Malcolm Page's opinion, the playwright "has such gifts for humor that his reputation is for comedy; however, he may be disappointed that the more solemn implications have yet to be perceived. His future may be in less comic theatre, as he continues to focus mainly on people of his age, class, and education."

BIOGRAPHICAL/CRITICAL SOURCES:

BOOKS

Contemporary Literary Criticism, Gale, Volume 3, 1975, Volume 7, 1977, Volume 31, 1985, Volume 47, 1988.
Dictionary of Literary Biography, Gale, Volume 13: *British Dramatists since World War II,* 1982, Volume 14: *British Novelists since 1960,* 1983.

PERIODICALS

Chicago Tribune, November, 1988.
Drama, summer, 1975, July, 1980.
Guardian (Manchester, England), October 1, 1968, March 11, 1975.
Horizon, January/February, 1986.
Insight, February 3, 1986.
Listener, January 21, 1965, January 15, 1966, March 20, 1975.
Los Angeles Times, October 30, 1984, February 3, 1985, February 12, 1985, October 10, 1986, July 20, 1987.
New Statesman, October 4, 1968, November 1, 1974.
Newsweek, February 18, 1974, January 20, 1986.
New York Times, September 11, 1970, June 13, 1971, June 3, 1979, December 12, 1983, July 23, 1984, January 28, 1985, December 23, 1985, January 5, 1986, March 19, 1986, September 4, 1986, October 10, 1986, December 14, 1986, December 19, 1986, March 12, 1987.
New York Times Book Review, September 15, 1968.
New York Times Magazine, December 8, 1985.
Observer (London), June 11, 1967, July 18, 1976, April 27, 1980, April 4, 1984.
Plays and Players, September, 1970, March, 1982, December, 1984.
Saturday Review, January 15, 1966.
Spectator, November 23, 1962, October 4, 1968, December 10, 1983.
Sunday Times (London), January 27, 1980.
Time, September 27, 1968, July 12, 1982.
Times (London), February 25, 1982, February 15, 1983, April 6, 1984, March 14, 1986, November 10, 1986.
Times Literary Supplement, February 1, 1980, March 5, 1982, September 22-28, 1989.
Washington Post, October 16, 1983, October 27, 1983, December 24, 1985, October 25, 1986.
Washington Post Book World, January 10, 1974.

—*Sketch by Susan Salter*

*   *   *

FRIEDRICH, Carl Joachim   1901-1984

PERSONAL: Born June 5, 1901, in Leipzig, Germany (now East Germany); came to the United States in 1922, naturalized citizen, 1938; died after a long illness, September 19, 1984, in Lexington, Mass.; son of Paul Leopold and Charlotte (Baroness von Buelow) Friedrich; married Lenore Pelham, October 6, 1924; children: Paul William, Otto Alva, Elizabeth Charlotte (deceased), Matilda Cornwall, Dorothea Amanda. *Education:* Attended University of Marburg, University of Frankfurt, and

University of Vienna; University of Heidelberg, Ph.D., 1925. *Religion:* Episcopalian.

CAREER: Harvard University, Cambridge, Mass., lecturer, 1926-27, assistant professor, 1927-31, associate professor, 1931-37, Eaton Professor of Science of Government, 1955-71, professor emeritus, beginning 1971, director of School of Overseas Administration, 1943-46; writer, beginning 1971. Professor, University of Heidelberg, 1956-66, professor emeritus, beginning 1966; visiting professor, Sorbonne, University of Paris, winter, 1955, spring, 1971; Culver Lecturer at Brown University; Avalon Lecturer at Colby College. Governmental affairs advisor to the American Military Governor (General Lucius D. Clay) in Germany, 1946-49.

MEMBER: International Political Science Association (president, 1967-70), International Institute of Political Philosophy (president, 1969), American Political Science Association (president, 1962), American Historical Association, American Academy of Arts and Sciences, American Society of Political and Legal Philosophy (president, 1958), Phi Beta Kappa, Athenaeum Club, Harvard Club (New York City).

AWARDS, HONORS: Guggenheim fellowship; first prize in Greater Boston Contest; knight commander's cross with star, German Order of Merit, 1967; officier de l'Ordre de Leopold (Belgium), 1970; A.V. Humboldt Gold Medal. A.M., Harvard University, 1941; U.J.D., University of Heidelberg, 1951; LL.D. from Grinnell College, 1952, Duke University, 1963, and Washington University, St. Louis, Mo., 1968; Dr.rer.pol. from University of Cologne, 1954, and University of Padua, 1964; L.H.D. from Colby College, 1963.

WRITINGS:

(With Taylor Cole) *Responsible Bureaucracy: A Study of the Swiss Civil Service, Studies in Systematic Political Science and Comparative Government,* Harvard University Press, 1932, Russell & Russell, 1967.

Constitutional Government and Politics: Nature and Development, Harper, 1937, revised edition published as *Constitutional Government and Democracy: Theory and Practice in Europe and America,* Little, Brown, 1941, 4th edition, Blaisdell, 1968.

Foreign Policy in the Making: The Search for a New Balance of Power, Norton, 1938.

Controlling Broadcasting in Wartime: A Tentative Public Policy, Littauer Center, Harvard University, 1940, Arno Press and the New York Times, 1971.

(With Jeanette Sayre Smith) *The Development of the Control of Advertising on the Air,* Littauer Center, Harvard University, 1940, Arno Press and the New York Times, 1971.

The Poison in Our System, Council for Democracy, 1941.

The New Belief in the Common Man, Little, Brown, 1942, revised edition published as *The New Image of the Common Man,* Beacon Press, 1950, reprinted, 1984.

(With Smith) *Radio Broadcasting and Higher Education,* Littauer Center, Harvard University, 1942, Arno Press and the New York Times, 1971.

War, the Causes, Effects, and Control of International Violence, National Council for the Social Studies and National Association of Secondary-School Principals, 1943.

(With Evelyn Sternberg) *Congress and the Control of Radio Broadcasting,* Littauer Center, Harvard University, 1944.

American Policy toward Palestine, Public Affairs Press, 1944, Greenwood Press, 1971.

Inevitable Peace, Harvard University Press, 1948, Greenwood Press, 1969.

(Editor) *The Philosophy of Kant,* Modern Library, 1949.

The Age of the Baroque, 1610-1660, Harper, 1952, Greenwood Press, 1983.

(Editor and author of introduction) *The Philosophy of Hegel,* Modern Library, 1953.

(Editor with Robert Richardson Bowie) *Studies in Federalism,* Little, Brown, 1954.

(With Bowie) *Probleme einer europaeischen Staatengemein schaft,* Institut fuer Europaeische Politik und Wirtschaft, 1954.

(Editor) *Totalitarianism,* Harvard University Press, 1954, Grosset, 1964.

(Editor with Robert G. McCloskey) *From the Declaration of Independence to the Constitution: The Roots of American Constitutionalism,* Liberal Arts Press, 1954.

Die Philosophie des Rechts in historischer Perspective, Springer-Verlag, 1955, translation published as *The Philosophy of Law in Historical Perspective,* University of Chicago Press, 1958, 2nd edition, 1963.

(Editor) *The Soviet Zone of Germany,* Human Relations Area File Press, 1956.

(With Zbigniew K. Brzezinski) *Totalitarian Dictatorship and Autocracy,* Harvard University Press, 1956, 3rd edition, 1967.

Cours d'histoire des idees politiques: Evolution de la liberte constitutionelle en Angleterre a travers les deux revolutions, Cours de droit, 1956.

Constitutional Reason of State: The Survival of the Constitutional Order, Brown University Press, 1957.

(With Charles Blitzer) *The Age of Power* (juvenile), Cornell University Press, 1957, Greenwood Press, 1982.

(Editor) *Authority,* Harvard University Press, 1958, Greenwood Press, 1981.

(Editor with Seymour E. Harris) *Problems of Defense,* Graduate School of Public Administration, Harvard University, 1958.

Puerto Rico: Middle Road to Freedom, Holt, 1959, Arno Press, 1975.

Demokratie als Herrschafts-und Lebensform (originally appeared as part of *The New Belief in the Common Man*), Quelle & Meyer, 1959.

(Editor) *Community,* Liberal Arts Press, 1959.

(Editor) *Responsibility,* Liberal Arts Press, 1960.

Die politische Wissenschaft, K. Alber, 1961.

(Editor) *The Public Interest,* Atherton Press, 1962.

(Editor) *Liberty,* Atherton Press, 1962.

(Editor) *Justice,* Atherton Press, 1963.

(With Geleitwort von Dolf Sternberger) *Zur theorie und Politik der Verfassungsordnung: Augewaehlte Aufsaetze,* Quelle & Meyer, 1963.

Man and His Government: An Empirical Theory of Politics, McGraw, 1963.

(Editor) *Rational Decision,* Atherton Press, 1964.

Report on the Commission on Presidential Campaign Debates, American Political Science Association, 1964.

Transcendent Justice: The Religious Dimension of Constitutionalism, Duke University Press, 1964.

(Editor) *Revolution: Yearbook,* Atherton Press, 1966.

An Introduction to Political Theory: Twelve Lectures at Harvard, Harper, 1967.

The Impact of American Constitutionalism Abroad, Boston University Press, 1967.

Prolegomena der Politik: Politische Erfahrung und ihre theorie, (originally appeared in *Man and His Government*), Duncker & Humblot, 1967.

Trends of Federalism in Theory and Practice, Praeger, 1968.

Europe: An Emergent Nation?, Harper, 1969.

(Translator) Alfred Weber, *Theory of the Location of Industries,* Russell & Russell, 1971.

The Pathology of Politics: Violence, Betrayal, Corruption, Secrecy, and Propaganda, Harper, 1972.

Tradition and Authority, Praeger, 1972.

Ich zeichne Menschen, Starczewski, 1973.

Limited Government: A Comparison, Prentice-Hall, 1974.

Johannes Althusius und sein Werk in Rahmen der Enthwicklung der Theorie von der Politik, Duncker & Humblot, 1975.

Also editor of *American Experiences in Military Government in World War II,* 1947; author of *Philosophy of History,* published by Peter Smith. Contributor to magazines, including *Atlantic Monthly.* Editor of *Public Policy,* 1940-53, and *Nomas Yearbook* of the American Society of Political and Legal Philosophy, 1958-66.

OBITUARIES:

PERIODICALS

New York Times, September 22, 1984.

Time, October 1, 1984.*

*   *   *

FRY, Christopher   1907-

PERSONAL: Name originally Christopher Fry Harris; born December 18, 1907, in Bristol, England; son of Charles John (a builder and later a church reader) and Emma Marguerite Fry (Hammond) Harris; married Phyllis Marjorie Hart, December 3, 1936; children: one son. *Education:* Attended Bedford Modern School, Bedford, England, 1918-26. *Religion:* Church of England.

ADDRESSES: Home—The Toft, East Dean, near Chichester, West Sussex PO18 0JA, England. *Agent*—ACTAC Ltd., 16 Cadogan Ln., London S.W.1, England.

CAREER: Bedford Froebel Kindergarten, Bedford, England, teacher, 1926-27; Citizen House, Bath, England, actor and office worker, 1927; Hazelwood Preparatory School, Limpsfield, Surrey, England, schoolmaster, 1928-31; secretary to H. Rodney Bennett, 1931-32; Tunbridge Wells Repertory Players, founding director, 1932-35, 1940, 1944-46; Dr. Barnardo's Homes, lecturer and editor of schools magazine, 1934-39; Oxford Playhouse, director, 1940; Arts Theatre Club, London, England, director, 1945, staff dramatist, 1947. Visiting director, Oxford Playhouse, 1945-46, Arts Theatre Club, 1947. Composer. *Military service:* Pioneer Corps, 1940-44.

MEMBER: Dramatists Guild, Garrick Club.

AWARDS, HONORS: Shaw Prize Fund award, 1948, for *The Lady's Not for Burning;* William Foyle Poetry Prize, 1951, for *Venus Observed;* New York Drama Critics Circle Award, 1951, for *The Lady's Not for Burning,* 1952, for *Venus Observed,* and 1956, for *Tiger at the Gates;* Queen's Gold Medal for Poetry, 1962; Heinemann Award, Royal Society of Literature, 1962, for *Curtmantle;* D.A., 1966, and Honorary Fellow, 1988, Manchester Polytechnic; Writers Guild Best British Television Dramatization award nomination, 1971, for "The Tenant of Wildfell Hall"; Doctor of Letters, Lambeth and Oxford University, 1988; Royal Society of Literature Fellow.

WRITINGS:

PLAYS

(With Monte Crick and F. Eyton) "She Shall Have Music," first produced in London, England, 1934.

"Open Door," first produced in London, England, 1936.

The Boy with a Cart: Cuthman, Saint of Sussex (also see below; first produced in Coleman's Hatch, Sussex, England, 1938; produced on the West End at Lyric Theatre, January 16, 1950), Oxford University Press, 1939, 2nd edition, Muller, 1956.

(Author of libretto) "Robert of Sicily: Opera for Children," first produced in 1938.

"The Tower" (pageant), first produced at Tewkesbury Festival, Tewkesbury, England, July 18, 1939.

Thursday's Child: A Pageant (first produced in London, 1939), Girl's Friendly Press (London), 1939.

(Author of libretto) "Seven at a Stroke: A Play for Children," first produced in 1939.

A Phoenix Too Frequent (comedy; also see below; first produced in London at Mercury Theatre, April 25, 1946; produced on Broadway with "Freight," 1950), Hollis & Carter, 1946, Oxford University Press, 1949.

The Firstborn (also see below; tragedy; broadcast on radio, 1947; first produced at Gateway Theatre, Edinburgh, Scotland, September 6, 1948), Cambridge University Press, 1946, 3rd edition, Oxford University Press, 1958.

The Lady's Not for Burning (also see below; comedy; first produced in London at Arts Theatre, March 10, 1948; produced on the West End, May 11, 1949; produced on Broadway at Royale Theatre, November 8, 1950), Oxford University Press, 1949, revised edition, 1973.

Thor, with Angels (also see below; first produced at Chapter House, Canterbury, England, June, 1948; produced on the West End at Lyric Theatre, September 27, 1951), H. J. Goulden, 1948, Oxford University Press, 1949.

Venus Observed (also see below; first produced in London at St. James Theatre, January 18, 1950; produced on Broadway at Century Theatre, February 13, 1952), Oxford University Press, 1950.

A Sleep of Prisoners (also see below; first produced in Oxford, England, at University Church, April 23, 1951; produced in London at St. Thomas's Church, May 15, 1951), Oxford University Press, 1951, 2nd edition, 1965.

The Dark Is Light Enough: A Winter Comedy (also see below; first produced on the West End at Aldwych Theatre, April, 30, 1954; produced on Broadway at ANTA Theatre, February 23, 1955) Oxford University Press, 1954.

Curtmantle: A Play (also see below; first produced in Dutch in Tilburg, Netherlands, at Stadsschouwburg, March 1, 1961; produced on the West End at Aldwych Theatre, October 6, 1962), Oxford University Press, 1961.

A Yard of Sun: A Summer Comedy (first produced at Nottingham Playhouse, Nottingham, England, July 11, 1970; produced on the West End at Old Vic Theatre, August 10, 1970), Oxford University Press, 1970.

One Thing More, or Caedmon Construed (first produced at Chelmsford Cathedral, England, 1986; broadcast on radio, 1986), Oxford University Press, 1985, Dramatists Play Service, 1987.

Also author of "Youth of the Peregrines," produced at Tunbridge Wells with premiere production of George Bernard Shaw's "Village Wooing." Author of radio plays for "Children's Hour" series, 1939-40, and of "Rhineland Journey," 1948.

SCREENPLAYS AND TELEPLAYS

"The Canary," British Broadcasting Corp. (BBC-TV), 1950.
"The Queen Is Crowned" (documentary), Universal, 1953.
(With Denis Cannan) "The Beggar's Opera," British Lion, 1953.
"Ben Hur," Metro-Goldwyn-Mayer, 1959.
"Barabbas," Columbia, 1961.
(With Jonathan Griffin, Ivo Perilli, and Vittorio Bonicelli) "The Bible: In the Beginning" (also see below), Twentieth Century-Fox, 1966.
"The Tenant of Wildfell Hall," BBC-TV, 1968.
"The Brontes of Haworth" (also see below; four teleplays), BBC-TV, 1973.
"The Best of Enemies," BBC-TV, 1976.
"Sister Dora," BBC-TV, 1977.
"Star Over Bethlehem," BBC-TV, 1981.

TRANSLATOR

(And adaptor from *L'Invitation au Chateau* by Jean Anouilh), *Ring Round the Moon: A Charade with Music* (first produced on the West End at Globe Theatre, January 26, 1950), Oxford University Press, 1950.
(And adaptor) Jean Giraudoux, *Tiger at the Gates* (also see below; first produced on the West End at Apollo Theatre, October 3, 1955), Methuen, 1955, 2nd edition, 1961, Oxford University Press, 1956, produced as *The Trojan War Will Not Take Place* (London, 1983), Methuen, 1983.
(And adaptor) Anouilh, *The Lark* (first produced on the West End at Lyric Theatre, May 11, 1955; produced on Broadway at Longacre Theatre, November 17, 1955), Methuen, 1955, Oxford University Press, 1956.
(And adaptor from *Pour Lucrece* by Giraudoux), *Duel of Angels* (also see below; first produced on the West End at Apollo Theatre, April 22, 1958; produced on Broadway at Helen Hayes Theatre, April 19, 1960), Methuen, 1958, Oxford University Press, 1959.
(And adaptor) Giraudoux, *Judith* (also see below; first produced on the West End at Her Majesty's Theatre, June 20, 1962), Methuen, 1962.
Sidonie Gabrielle Colette, *The Boy and the Magic,* Dobson, 1964, Putnam, 1965.
(And adaptor) Henrik Ibsen, *Peer Gynt* (first produced at Chichester Festival Theatre, Chichester, England, May 13, 1970), Oxford University Press, 1970, revised edition, 1989.
(And adaptor) Edmond Rostand, *Cyrano de Bergerac* (first produced at Chichester Festival Theatre, May 14, 1975), Oxford University Press, 1975.

OMNIBUS VOLUMES

Three Plays: The Firstborn; Thor, with Angels; A Sleep of Prisoners, Oxford University Press, 1960.
(Translator) Giraudoux, *Plays* (contains *Judith, Tiger at the Gates,* and *Duel of Angels*), Methuen, 1963.
Plays (contains *Thor, with Angels* and *The Lady's Not for Burning*), Oxford University Press, 1969.
Plays (contains *The Boy with a Cart: Cuthman, Saint of Sussex, The Firstborn,* and *Venus Observed*), Oxford University Press, 1970.
Plays (contains *A Sleep of Prisoners, The Dark Is Light Enough,* and *Curtmantle*), Oxford University Press, 1971.
Selected Plays (contains *The Boy with a Cart: Cuthman, Saint of Sussex, A Phoenix Too Frequent, The Lady's Not for Burning, A Sleep of Prisoners, Curtmantle*), Oxford University Press, 1985.
(Translator with Timberlake Wertebaker) *Jean Anouilh: Five Plays,* Heinemann, 1986.

OTHER

(Contributor) Kaye Webb, editor, *An Experience of Critics and the Approach to Dramatic Criticism,* Perpetua, 1952, Oxford University Press, 1953.
(Author of libretto) "Crown of the Year" (cantata), first produced in 1958.
(Contributor) Robert W. Corrigan, editor, *The Modern Theatre,* Macmillan, 1964.
The Boat That Mooed (juvenile fiction), Macmillan, 1965.
(Contributor) H. F. Rubinstein, editor, *The Drama Bedside Book,* Atheneum, 1966.
(With Jonathan Griffin) *The Bible: Original Screenplay,* Pocket Books, 1966.
The Brontes of Haworth, published in two volumes, Davis-Poynter, 1975.
Can You Find Me: A Family History, Oxford University Press, 1978.
(Adaptor) *Paradise Lost* (first produced in Chicago, 1978), Schott, 1978.
Death Is a Kind of Love (lecture; drawings by Charles E. Wadsworth), Tidal Press, 1979.
Charlie Hammond's Sketch Book, Oxford University Press, 1980.
Genius, Talent and Failure (lecture), King's College, 1987.

Also contributor to anthology, *Representative Modern Plays: Ibsen to Tennessee Williams,* edited by Robert Warnock, Scott, Foresman, 1964. Contributor to *Theatre Arts* and *Plays and Players.*

SIDELIGHTS: British playwright, screenwriter, translator, and critic Christopher Fry is best known for his elegant verse plays, which emerged in the 1940s and 1950s as a sharp contrast to the naturalism and realism popular since the late nineteenth century. When Fry's blank-verse comedy "The Lady's Not for Burning" first appeared on stage in London during the 1950s, it became an immediate sensation. According to Harold Hobson in *Drama:* "It is difficult to exaggerate the sense of freshness and excitement that swept through the theatrical world when *The Lady's Not for Burning,* with the extraordinary brilliance of the fancies, the conceits, and the imagination of its dialogue, the originality of its verse-form, and the joyous mediaeval paradox of its story seemed to shatter the by then somnolent reign of naturalism on the British stage." Derek Stanford recalls in *Christopher Fry:* "Without the creaking machinery of any cranked-up manifesto, the plays of Fry appeared on the stage, receiving a progressive succession of applause. For the first time for several centuries, we were made to realise that here was a poet addressing the audience from the boards with that immediacy of effect which had seemed to have deserted the muse as far as its dramatic office was concerned. . . . Like a man who is conscious of no impediment, and does not anticipate embarrassing rebuffs, Fry spoke out with a power natural to him. He was heard—with surprise, with pleasure, and relief."

Fry's style attracted as many detractors as devotees; some complained that his rapidly moving, glittering language masked nonexistent plots and shallow characterizations. In a *Times Literary Supplement* review of *The Lady's Not for Burning,* a critic finds the play "without the comparatively pedestrian power of developing character and situation," and adds: "It is surprising how rich a play may be in fine speeches and yet be a bad play because the speeches alter nothing." But Stanford determines that "so readily magniloquent and rich, in fact, is Fry that in an age of verbal paucity his own Elizabethan munificence of diction appears to our 'austerity' reviewers as suspect. None of these critics, it is true, has been able to deny the impact of his language, but have rather tended to minimise its import by treating it as the playwright's sole talent."

"The Lady's Not for Burning," directed by and starring John Gielgud, was the first installment of a series of four comedies, each corresponding to a different season. The series continued with "Venus Observed" (autumn), "The Dark Is Light Enough" (winter), and concluded, twenty-two years after its commencement, with "A Yard of Sun" (summer). While the other plays, especially "Venus Observed," received critical acclaim, none surpassed "The Lady's Not for Burning" in popularity. "The Lady's Not for Burning" is set in a somewhat fantastic medieval world, and primarily concerns two characters: Thomas, an embittered ex-soldier who wishes to die, and Jennet, a wealthy young orphan who loves life, but has been sentenced to burn on a trumped-up witchcraft charge so that the town may inherit her property. The play intertwines irony and comedy, with a dense mayor, his practical wife, and their two quarrelling sons all playing clownish roles. In *Dictionary of Literary Biography,* Audrey Williamson describes the play as "a lyric of spring: it has an April shimmer, like the dust of pollination shot by sunlight." Williamson continues: "There is a kind of golden haze about it that is penetrated by the occasional bawdiness of the humor: for Fry has combined the robustness of the Elizabethans with touches of the cheerful blasphemy that mingled with piety in the medieval morality play. But the sense of the abundance, mystery, and poetry of life is unimpaired."

"Venus Observed" involves an emotionally remote and aging duke who intends to choose a wife from his many ex-lovers. But in the process he becomes infatuated with the young woman his son also loves. The role of the elderly stargazer was played by Laurence Olivier in London and Rex Harrison in New York; *Theatre Arts* contributor L. N. Roditte writes of the character: "The Duke is a hero of considerable magnitude; his story, though mild and witty, has an element of tragedy. . . . [Fry] has created an extraordinary part that other great actors will want to play." Although "Venus Observed" was well received by the public and critics, Fry's style again received criticism. According to *Saturday Review* contributor John Mason Brown: "Mr. Fry is blessed with one of the most delightful talents now contributing to the theatre. He has a wit, nimble and original; an agile and unpredictable mind, as playful as it is probing; and a love of language which can only be described as a lust." But Brown continues that Fry "is an anachronism, if you will; a fellow who has wandered from one Elizabethan age into another," and concludes: "Mr. Fry concentrates on all the sensuous splendors of the flesh, ignoring the skeleton of sustained ideas or dramatic structure." Harold Clurman in the *New Republic,* however, strongly objects to this view: "Let no one say that Fry's work consists of playful, euphonious words and no more. The meaning is clear to anyone who will pay attention. . . . And the meaning . . . is historically or (socially) revealing. Fry's plays are poems of resignation in which tragic substance is flattened into lovely ornament."

The Dark is Light Enough delves into the past, this time using the background of revolutions on the Hungarian border in 1848. The heroine, Countess Rosmarin, is an elderly lady who attempts to rescue her ex-son-in-law, an army deserter, from execution. While the play ends in death, "the viewer senses a summer radiance on which winter has set its feathered touch, light and cold as the snowflakes descending outside the window," explains Williamson. In *Ariel,* Stanley Wiersma also sees the conclusion as a positive one: "The Countess . . . finds warmth enough in the winter of our discontent, goodness enough in a

wicked world, life enough in death." *Chicago Sunday Tribune* contributor F. E. Faverty sees a conflict between the plot and dialogue, however. "In spite of the heavy themes, the dialogue is light and sparkling," he writes. "There is a quotable epigram on every page. Nonetheless, one's final impression is that there is too much talk and too little action." But Williamson admires the interplay: "Fry adapts his verse to his theme, conveying wisdom and a new verbal austerity," she continues. "It makes for a play of dramatic tension and fascination."

Fry's abhorrence of violence is an important part of *The Dark Is Light Enough.* Wiersma identifies the play's themes as "violence as self-assertion, violence as loyalty to the state, violence as loyalty to God, and, finally, violence to be endured but not to be inflicted," and explains that the playwright sees such violence as "an infection with its own irrational necessities. The violence in the situation and within the people is moving toward a duel; who fights it or against whom is beside the point." Fry's answer to violence is love: love that endures pain but refuses to inflict it. Emil Roy, in his monograph on Fry, finds this treatment unique: "Unlike most of his contemporaries, Fry has not given man's meanness, animality, and evil a central position in his work. If men are selfish, egoistic, and blind to love, it belongs to his more enlightened, self-controlled, and discerning characters to bring their understanding and tolerance to bear upon the pain and anguish that results."

A Yard of Sun ends the quartet; it deals with the return of two absent members of an Italian family: the black sheep and a betrayed friend. A *Times Literary Supplement* reviewer calls the characters and situation "stereotyped" and claims they "receive a thick coating of Fry's Christmas-tree versification which serves to convert cliches into fanciful imagery and camouflage the fact that no issue is being squarely faced." But according to Williamson, the play contains "a concentrated glow of language, pared to a new, more austere structure. The Italianate characterization is vivid and varied, and the story line taut and gripping." And a *Newsweek* reviewer finds that *A Yard of Sun* "shimmers with poetry and affirms Fry's belief in a basically mystical Christian benevolence."

All of the plays in the quartet are described as comedies, although the "fall" and "winter" episodes are darker than their counterparts. In *Literary Half-Yearly,* J. A. Collins connects the playwright's view of these works with his religious beliefs: "Christopher Fry has defined comedy as 'an escape, not from truth but from despair: a narrow escape into faith.'" Collins finds this view of faith innovative in that it suggests ways of reacting to the universe and does not concern itself with solutions to paradoxes: "The attitude of faith is always love—romantic love, brotherly love, love of God and the universe; but even in love (the acceptance of faith) spirit and flesh refuse to harmonize and the old battle continues."

Overall, Stanford sees Fry as a joyous free-thinker in a narrow world: "In a universe often viewed as mechanic, he has posited the principle of mystery; in an age of necessitarian ethics, he has stood unequivocally for ideas of free-will. In theatre technique, he has gaily ignored the sacrosanct conventions of naturalistic drama; and in terms of speech he has brought back poetry onto the stage with undoctored abandon." Roy states: "Fry has occasionally seemed wordy, sentimental, and lacking in conventional kinds of conflict, but he has more than compensated with vital and compassionate characters, the courage to deal with contemporary human conflicts and issues, and some of the most vital language in the theater today." And Williamson concludes: "In Fry's hands the English theater turned, for an elegantly creative period, away from prosaic reality and explored both the poetry and the mystery of life."

Fry's plays have been translated into French, German, Spanish, Dutch, Norwegian, Finnish, Italian, Swedish, Danish, Greek, Serbo-Croat, Hungarian, Tamil, Portuguese, Flemish, Czech, Polish, and Albanian. A manuscript collection is held by Harvard University Theatre Collection. [For more information, see sketch in *Contemporary Authors New Revision Series,* Volume 9.]

BIOGRAPHICAL/CRITICAL SOURCES:

BOOKS

Contemporary Literary Criticism, Gale, Volume 2, 1974, Volume 10, 1979, Volume 14, 1980.
Dictionary of Literary Biography, Volume 13: *British Dramatists since World War II,* Gale, 1982.
Kirkpatrick, D. L., editor, *Contemporary Dramatists,* 4th edition, St. James Press, 1988.
Leeming, Glenda, *Poetic Drama,* Macmillan, 1989.
Roy, Emil, *Christopher Fry,* Southern Illinois University Press, 1968.
Stanford, Derek, *Christopher Fry: An Appreciation,* Peter Nevill, 1951.
Wiersma, Stanley, *More Than the Ear Discovers: God in the Plays of Christopher Fry,* Loyola University Press, 1983.

PERIODICALS

Ariel, October, 1975.
Chicago Sunday Tribune, September 12, 1954.
Drama, spring, 1979.
Literary Half-Yearly, July, 1971.
New Republic, August 20, 1951, March 3, 1952, December 2, 1978.
Newsweek, July 27, 1970.
New York Times Book Review, January 21, 1979.
New York Times Magazine, March 12, 1950.
Plays and Players, December, 1987.
Saturday Review, March 1, 1952, March 21, 1953.
Theatre Arts, L. N. Roditte, September, 1950.
Times Literary Supplement, April 2, 1949, August 21, 1970, October 20, 1978.

—*Sketch by Jani Prescott*

*   *   *

FUCHS, Lucy   1935-

PERSONAL: Born April 13, 1935, in Ohio; daughter of Frank X. (a machinist) and Mary (Honigford) Weber; married Frank J. Fuchs (a teacher), August 14, 1971. *Education:* University of Dayton, B.S., 1961; Ohio State University, M.A., 1967; Florida State University, M.S., 1973; University of South Florida, Ph.D., 1984. *Politics:* Democrat. *Religion:* Roman Catholic.

ADDRESSES: Home and office—505 South Oakwood Ave., Brandon, Fla. 33511.

CAREER: High school French teacher in Cincinnati, Ohio, 1966-69; Florida State University, Tallahassee, counselor, 1969-71; social worker in Tampa, Fla., 1971-73; Hillsborough County Elementary School, Hillsborough, Fla., teacher, beginning 1974; St. Leo College, St. Leo, Fla., professor, 1980—. Instructor in sociology and French at Hillsborough Community College, 1972—.

MEMBER: International Reading Association.

WRITINGS:

Wild Winds of Mayaland, Bouregy, 1978.
Dangerous Splendor, Bouregy, 1978.
Shadow of the Walls, Bouregy, 1980.
Pictures of Fear, Bouregy, 1981.
Serving Adolescents' Reading Interests through Young Adult Literature, Phi Delta Kappa Education Foundation, 1987.
Teaching Reading in the Secondary School, Phi Delta Kappa Education Foundation, 1987.
Ways with Words: Classroom-Tested Word Activities, Instructor Press, 1988.
(Contributor) James J. Horgan and Joseph A. Cernik, editors, *The Reagan Years,* St. Leo College Press, 1988.

Also author of three school workbooks. Contributor of numerous articles and children's stories to education and religion periodicals and children's magazines, including *Highlights for Children, Primary Treasure,* and *Our Little Friend.*

WORK IN PROGRESS: A novel; a nonfiction book.

SIDELIGHTS: Lucy Fuchs told *CA:* "I write because I am not happy when I am not writing. I have learned very much from other writers, both through personal conversations and from publications of writers, such as the magazines for writers. I am interested in just about everything, especially people as they relate to each other."

She adds: "Writing has enriched my life enormously. Everything I learn in my work, everywhere I travel, everything that happens to me, all are experienced two-fold: first in actuality and secondly in writing. Or perhaps it is in the writing that it becomes real."

AVOCATIONAL INTERESTS: Travel, religion, reading, crafts, gardening, cooking.

*   *   *

FURMAN, Laura (J.)   1945-

PERSONAL: Born November 19, 1945, in Brooklyn, N.Y.; married Joel Warren Barna (a journalist and editor), 1981. *Education:* Bennington College, B.A., 1968.

ADDRESSES: Office—English Department, University of Texas, Austin, Tex. 78712-1164.

CAREER: Writer. Menil Foundation, Houston, Tex., editor, 1973-78; *Houston City Magazine,* Houston, senior editor, 1978-79; Southern Methodist University, Dallas, Tex., lecturer, 1981-82; University of Texas, Austin, 1983—, currently associate professor of English. Writer in residence, Wilkes College, 1977. Visiting assistant professor, University of Houston, 1980.

AWARDS, HONORS: Residence grants, Yaddo, 1972-78, 1984; Creative Artists Public Service Award in fiction, New York State Council on the Arts, 1976; short story award, Texas Institute of Letters, 1980, for "Eldorado"; Jesse Jones Award for best book of fiction, Texas Institute of Letters, 1981, for *The Glass House: A Novella and Stories;* Dobie Paisano fellowship, Texas Institute of Letters and University of Texas, 1981; Guggenheim fellowship, 1982-83.

WRITINGS:

(Contributor) Robin Morgan, editor, *Sisterhood Is Powerful,* Random House, 1970.
The Glass House: A Novella and Stories, Viking, 1980.
The Shadow Line (novel), Viking, 1982.
Watch Time Fly: Stories, Viking, 1983.

Tuxedo Park (novel), Summit Books, 1986.

Contributor of stories and essays to *New Yorker, Redbook, Fiction, Texas Humanist, Mademoiselle,* and *House and Garden.* Editor, *Texas Architect.*

WORK IN PROGRESS: The Stars at Night, a novel set in Texas; *The Natural Memory,* a short story collection; a memoir.

SIDELIGHTS: Since her first published stories in the *New Yorker* during the 1970s, Laura Furman's writing has received a steady wave of critical praise. In his assessment of Furman's story collection *Watch Time Fly,* Eliot Fremont-Smith for the *Washington Post Book World* calls her a "precisionist. As with her first collection, *The Glass House,* and her . . . novel . . . *The Shadow Line,* there is never the slightest doubt as to who is in control: her observation is as acute as her sense of timing, her language that exact. Her art, so calculated, is the art of comedy, though with an eerie edge." On the whole, Furman has confined herself to a few themes. For one, she emphasizes that as individuals we are and will always remain separate and distinct despite our many attempts at uniting with others, and for another she underscores the importance of developing coping abilities in a world that offers no guarantees but often hardships.

Furman's first book-length work, *The Glass House: A Novella and Stories,* received positive critical attention primarily because of its subtlety, precision, and exacting prose, although there was some criticism regarding characterization. An *Antioch Review* critic is careful to stress that Furman's stories in *The Glass House* are not about " 'big' subjects" but that they, nevertheless, provide the reader with "a sustained, somehow spell-binding experience." In addition, reviewer Lynne Sharon Schwartz for the *New York Times Book Review* calls Furman's style "lean and strictly functional, quite unlike the elaborately baroque dwellings she invents. But in the novella of the title she allows herself space, and the still understated language becomes streamlined and obliquely beautiful. 'The Glass House' is a jewel of a piece. . . . Furman plays out her glass-house metaphor with delicate composure." Furman's recurring theme in this collection involves coming to terms with the adult world of instability and insecurity, which is made complete by letting go of past mistakes, hurts, and disappointments. The characters who "emerge most admirably" in the stories, remarks *Washington Post Book World* contributor Stephen Goodwin, "are the stoical, sensible young women who lose husbands, lovers, or parents and yet manage to stay upright on their own two feet and to walk forward on them." Goodwin feels Furman's characters in *The Glass House* "aren't quite large enough to fill the space Furman allots them," but he later expresses confidence in the author's future undertakings: "She is a resourceful, discriminating writer, and her glass house may prove to be only a miniature, a model for the more substantial edifice that she will construct in books to come."

Furman's two works to follow, *The Shadow Line* and *Watch Time Fly,* address issues similar to those found in *The Glass House,* and with a style that is equally clear and precise. In the mystery novel *The Shadow Line,* for instance, New Yorker Liz Gold moves to Houston as a means of uprooting herself from a troubled past. Life in her new environment, however, is every bit as troubled. As a journalist who is assigned to solve a twenty-year-old murder mystery, her life becomes endangered; as a widow whose guerrilla activist husband either committed suicide or was killed, painful memories restrict her from promising herself to David, her new lover. In *Dictionary of Literary Biography Yearbook,* William J. Scheick maintains that for Liz, "the shadow line she must cross [is] between a childish hope for something stable and a mature acceptance of the impermanence of everything, including life itself. . . . Ideally Liz must accept the reality of isolation of self in a world where 'people expect security out of the very thing that's the most insecure' and at the same time the reality of the self 's need for others, who nonetheless remain separate, strange entities capable of betraying the closest of friends."

In a favorable *Washington Post Book World* review of *The Shadow Line,* Suzanne Freeman maintains that "Furman has constructed her story just as painstakingly as her shorter fiction and with the same strong results. But if those earlier [stories] were like small, well-made buildings, this book must be a kind of Houston high-rise, tall and solid and wrapped in clouds. . . . Furman has given her novel a solid structure—a real plot with a mystery to be solved. . . . The real point here is that in sorting it all out, Furman's heroine, Liz Gold, has to sort out a tangle of other issues involving family and friends and money and love, all of the things that Laura Furman has written about so well before."

In line with what Furman has written previously, her well-received novel *Tuxedo Park* centers on the theme of our ultimate separateness from other humans. According to Scheick, "of all of Furman's women characters, the one who most resists the fact of [the] fundamental solitariness of the self is Sadie Ash, the protagonist of *Tuxedo Park.* Orphaned at the age of twelve, Sadie felt from that event as if time had stopped. . . . She seeks human connections, attachments which would (she thinks) contribute to the firming up and stabilization of her sense of identity." Thus, in 1945 and at age nineteen, Sadie meets and immediately falls in love with Willard Weaver, a failed painter whom Frances Taliaferro in the *New York Times Book Review* says "might as well be of another species. He is handsome, clever and rich. He is a chilly voluptuary." Sadie and Willard get married after Sadie becomes pregnant and, for Sadie, this is where her life starts once again, for she believes marriage is a fated, forever thing. Several years and two daughters later, Willard moves his family to the ancestral home in Tuxedo Park which he inherited when his father died: "Tuxedo Park is a declining bastion for the very rich," explains *New Republic* reviewer Laura E. Obolensky; "but to Sadie, who has sensed with some alarm Willard's growing restiveness, the Weavers' 'brick Italianate mansion' . . . looms as a haven. Here on his ancestral ground, the tug of genetic memory will assist her in convincing Willard that he's 'bound to her by fate,' that family is life's only sanctuary." Soon after the move, however, Willard demands a divorce from Sadie, but Sadie objects, which sends Willard fleeing with his mistress Cherry Wilde, a rootless, failed painter like himself. Additionally, Sadie's objection to the divorce subjects her and her two daughters to poverty because Willard will provide only a subsistence fee unless Sadie agrees to terminate their marriage. In the opinion of Elaine Kendall for the *Los Angeles Times,* when Sadie denies Willard a divorce, she "unconsciously recreates the limbo in which she spent her adolescence, waiting now for her real life to resume as she once waited for it to begin." Sadie remains on at Tuxedo Park, all of the time thinking Willard's desertion is temporary and never revealing the truth of her separation to her growing daughters. Several years later when the eldest daughter, Louise, chances upon some of her father's letters to Sadie and discovers her mother's hidden truths, she attempts suicide. This final, climactic event shocks Sadie into finally accepting the disintegration of her marriage. Scheick surmises that "Sadie can no more live inside her childish dream of a safe haven for her self than she can maintain her mistaken hope in merging identities with Willard. . . . After the shock of Louise's attempted suicide makes her realize how she has even failed to know her daughter, she recognizes that her life has not been as fated as she had thought, she ceases her 'stubborn waiting for a miracle,' she gives up her dream as if it were 'one of the last beautiful days of summer,' and she faces the reality of life's insecurity (most evident in death) and of the irremediable loneliness of each self."

Most critics of *Tuxedo Park* cite this work as Furman's most ambitious to date. *Washington Post* writer Jonathan Yardley, for one, describes it as an "intelligent, affecting, agreeably old-fashioned novel. Its only serious flaw is that Willard is a spineless, characterless man; that Sadie should fall so madly in love with him is an utter mystery, one . . . Furman never manages to solve." Nevertheless, in his conclusion Yardley states that " 'Tuxedo Park' is something we see too little of these days: genuinely adult fiction." In the opinion of Obolensky, "Furman proves once again that she is a writer of enormous grace and sensitivity who possesses a keen if unsettling genius for stripping the psyche of its deceptions . . . in order to reveal the subliminal conceits that at their most insidious make human compatibility such a formidable challenge." In his conclusion, Scheick elaborates that "although the verdict on Furman's standing among great American writers is still undecided, she is certainly a novelist worthy of attention. It will be interesting to see whether she will eventually range philosophically, structurally, and aesthetically beyond the narrow region she has so far mapped out as her own, especially the region of the lonely heart and separate self. She evinces a wealth of talent that might take some artistically surprising and rewarding excursions in her future work."

BIOGRAPHICAL/CRITICAL SOURCES:

BOOKS

Dictionary of Literary Biography Yearbook: 1986, Gale, 1987.
Furman, Laura, *The Shadow Line,* Viking, 1982.
Furman, Laura, *Tuxedo Park,* Summit Books, 1986.
Gardner, John, *The Art of Fiction: Notes on Craft for Young Writers,* Vintage Book, 1985.

PERIODICALS

Antioch Review, spring, 1981.
Library Journal, June 15, 1982.
Los Angeles Times, September 13, 1982, October 10, 1986.
New Republic, January 5, 1987, January 12, 1987.
New York Times Book Review, November 9, 1980, October 9, 1983, September 28, 1986.
Tribune Books (Chicago), January 11, 1987.
Voice Literary Supplement, November, 1982.
Washington Post, August 20, 1986.
Washington Post Book World, October 19, 1980, September 19, 1982, October 16, 1983.

G

GADDIS, John Lewis 1941-

PERSONAL: Born April 2, 1941, in Cotulla, Tex.; son of Harry P. and Isabel M. Gaddis; married Barbara Sue Jackson, September 4, 1965; children: John Michael, David Matthew. *Education:* University of Texas at Austin, B.A., 1963, M.A., 1965, Ph.D., 1968.

ADDRESSES: Home—1 Orchard Lane, Athens, Ohio 45701. *Office*—Department of History, Ohio University, Athens, Ohio 45701.

CAREER: Indiana University Southeast, Jeffersonville, assistant professor, 1968-69; Ohio University, Athens, assistant professor, 1969-71, associate professor, 1971-76, professor, 1976-83, distinguished professor of history, 1983—. Visiting professor of strategy, U.S. Naval War College, 1975-77; Bicentennial professor of American history, University of Helsinki, 1980-81; visiting professor of politics, Princeton University, 1987.

MEMBER: American Historical Association, Organization of American Historians, Society for Historians of American Foreign Relations, American Committee for History of Second World War.

AWARDS, HONORS: Bancroft Prize, Columbia University, and Stuart L. Bernath Prize, Society for Historians of American Foreign Relations, both 1973, both for *The United States and the Origins of the Cold War: 1941-47;* National Historical Society prize, 1973.

WRITINGS:

The United States and the Origins of the Cold War: 1941-47, Columbia University Press, 1972.
Russia, the Soviet Union, and the United States: An Interpretative History, Wiley, 1978.
(Editor with Thomas Etzold) *Containment: Documents on American Policy and Strategy, 1945-50,* Columbia University Press, 1978.
Strategies of Containment: A Critical Appraisal of Postwar American National Security Policy, Oxford University Press, 1982.
(Editor with Terry L. Diebel) *Containment: Concept and Policy,* Volume 2, U.S. Government Printing Office, 1986.
The Long Peace: Inquiries into the History of the Cold War, Oxford University Press, 1987.

SIDELIGHTS: "In the spectrum of historians writing about the cold war, John Lewis Gaddis belongs in the category of post-revisionists," claims *Commentary* contributor Donald Kagan. The critic explains that while early analyses of superpower relations first focused on Soviet and then American responsibility for perpetuating the cold war, Gaddis, "one of the first post-revisionists . . . [and] one of the ablest and most influential," is part of "a newly emerging consensus that seems to take an impartial position." Fareed Zakaria observes in the *New Republic* that Gaddis has "quickly garnered a reputation for thoroughness, writing with more balance and nuance than most of his predecessors." "Constantly in the midst of the international community of scholars writing on the last half century's history," comments Robert L. Beisner in the *Washington Post Book World,* the author "is not only *au courant* but always eager to tackle the toughest questions of all. Gaddis' very first book, published just when both America's diplomatic and historiographic consensus had crumbled, provided nothing less than a definitive account of Moscow's and Washington's roles in setting off the Cold War—*The United States and the Origins of the Cold War: 1941-47.*" As Zara Steiner asserts in the *Times Literary Supplement,* "Gaddis is the respected dean of American Cold War studies. His reputation, in a field noted for its rapid changes, rests on his willingness to take into account new material based on repeated returns to the documentary evidence."

In *Strategies of Containment: A Critical Appraisal of Postwar American National Security Policy,* for example, "Gaddis picks his way with precision, good judgment, and wit, to produce the most balanced and clear-eyed account to date of the Cold War," maintains R. W. Winks in *Library Journal.* The analysis, according to *Washington Post Book World* contributor Carl Kaysen, "offers us a neatly schematic view of U.S. foreign policy since the end of the Second World War. . . . [Gaddis sees] the Soviet Union's drive to expand its power and influence as the central problem for American foreign policy," explains the critic. "Analysis of our responses and their fluctuations over time form the substance of his study." The author theorizes that the United States has always followed a policy of "containment," but in two different fashions: symmetrical, where Soviet political moves are matched at all points; and asymmetrical, where different situations are assigned importance and then dealt with selectively. "What is important, says Mr. Gaddis, is that the oscillations in the United States' policy toward the Soviet Union have had their origins in our domestic politics more often than in changes in Soviet behavior," summarizes Joseph S. Nye in the *New York Times Book Review*. The author concludes, as Nye describes it, "that wavering between types of containment will not serve our interests in coping with a stronger Soviet Union."

While he finds *Strategies of Containment* "coherent, clearly written, and carefully argued," Kaysen believes that "the great shortcoming is that the book is not what it claims to be." The critic elaborates: "It is actually an analytical history of doctrines, not of strategies: what presidents, secretaries of state and other officials said, rather than what the country did, is the focus of Gaddis's efforts." *New Republic* contributor Barry Rubin, however, remarks that Gaddis's work "provides a good starting point for [debate over current crises]. It presents a judicious and balanced view of the ways in which U.S. security policy . . . developed." Like the author's previous studies, comments the critic, "this new volume is a superb synthesis of the latest scholarship and documentary evidence."

The Long Peace: Inquiries into the History of the Cold War collects many of Gaddis's writings on the subject of modern U.S. foreign relations. "Without ever drawing attention to himself with any of the fireworks of a 'stylist,' " states Beisner, "Gaddis writes superbly well, no mean task when mixing narrative, analysis, personal reflection and advocacy. Though an energetic and imaginative researcher undaunted by days in dusty archives," continues the critic, "Gaddis' powers of synthesis are, as ever, most impressive of all." Because of the availability of evidence, the author "focuses on American foreign policy-making," writes Zakaria. "The essays dealing with the origins of the cold war are the best ones in the book. Each begins with a puzzle posed by traditional explanations and solves it by taking the reader on a journey inside the American policy-making process." *New York Times Book Review* contributor Charles S. Maier, who calls Gaddis "an intelligent historian . . . [who] combines theoretical reflection with a deep knowledge of the massive American archives," similarly observes that "Mr. Gaddis' most striking pieces explore often overlooked policy debates to reveal how the varying claims were adjudicated and how moderation came to prevail." Maier also suggests that while the essays in *The Long Peace* were written separately, "they constitute a unified history of the cold war, not as a mobilization of political ideologies, but as a strategic competition."

Kagan, however, while he also finds Gaddis "a sober and hardworking professional," faults the author's treatment of his subject, which focuses on each side equally without looking at their differences. "The problem with this approach," claims the critic, "as with the 'evenhanded' analysis of the cold war, is that it treats all players as fundamentally the same and thereby loses touch with reality." But Zakaria believes that rigorous judgments of both sides are not part of Gaddis's purpose: "He attempts to explain events as they took place, when they took place, through the participants' eyes. He tries to free himself from 'the tyranny of knowing what came next,' exploring the very real alternatives that policy-makers chose among. Most of all," adds the critic, "he resists judging the past from the perspective of the present." "Gaddis does not offer simplicities in print," asserts Beisner, "so it would be better for readers to discover for themselves not only his answers but how he has arrived at them. They will discover at work a restless mind and a historian shrewder than most in using the work of his cousins in political science." In addition, concludes Beisner, readers "will find a sober and skeptical view of human nature."

BIOGRAPHICAL/CRITICAL SOURCES:

PERIODICALS

Commentary, January, 1988.
Library Journal, January 1, 1982.
New Republic, August 2, 1982, May 30, 1988.
New York Times Book Review, September 10, 1972, January 17, 1982, November 15, 1987.
Times Literary Supplement, March 5, 1982, April 1, 1988.
Washington Post Book World, February 21, 1982, November 8, 1987.

—*Sketch by Diane Telgen*

*   *   *

GALLAHUE, David L(ee)   1943-

PERSONAL: Born February 15, 1943, in Niagara Falls, N.Y.; son of Douglas (a printer) and Loretta (a file clerk) Gallahue; married Elnora Bredenberg; children: David Lee, Jr., Jennifer. *Education:* Indiana University, B.S., 1964; Purdue University, M.S., 1967; Temple University, Ed.D., 1970. *Religion:* Christian.

ADDRESSES: Home—Blackberry Ridge Farm, 8010 North St. Rd. 37, Bloomington, Ind. 47401. *Office*—Department of Physical Education, Indiana University, Bloomington, Ind. 47405.

CAREER: Indiana University at Bloomington, assistant professor, 1970-74, associate professor, 1974-83, professor of physical education, 1983—, assistant dean for research and development, 1977-87, assistant chairman, department of physical education, 1982-83, acting dean of graduate studies, 1984-85. Visiting professor at various universities, including State University of New York at Buffalo, 1975, 1977, University of Kuwait, 1979, and University of Alaska at Fairbanks and Anchorage, 1989. Guest lecturer at universities, including Purdue University, Temple University, and University of British Columbia. Pubic lecturer and director of workshops on a national and international level. Chairman, Council on Physical Education for Children, 1987. Owner and director, Challengers Day Camp, 1973-88.

AWARDS, HONORS: Leadership-Recognition Award, Indiana Alliance for Health, Physical Education, Recreation and Dance, 1979; State of Indiana Recognition award, Governor's Task Force for the Year of the Child, 1980; Midwest Alliance Scholar Award, Midwest/American Alliance for Health, Physical Education, Recreation and Dance, 1987; distinguished scholar at University of Delaware, 1987, Ball State University, 1988, Anderson University, 1988, and Long Beach State University, 1989.

MEMBER: International Playground Association, North American Society for Psychology of Sport and Physical Activity, American Camping Association, American Alliance for Health, Physical Education, Recreation, and Dance (life member), National Association for Sport and Physical Education (president of Motor Development Academy 1988; president, 1989; life member), American Association for Leisure and Recreation, Educational Press Association, Indiana Association for Health, Physical Education, Recreation, and Dance, Phi Delta Kappa, Phi Epsilon Kappa (life member).

WRITINGS:

(With Peter H. Werner and George C. Luedke) *A Conceptual Approach to Moving and Learning,* Wiley, 1971, 2nd edition, 1975.
(With Maryhelen Vannier and Mildred Foster) *Physical Education for Elementary School Children,* Saunders (Philadel-

phia, Penn.), 5th edition, 1973, 6th edition (with Vannier), 1978.

Individualized Movement Experiences for Young Children, Phi Delta Kappa (Bloomington, Ind.), 1974.

(With W. Meadors) *Let's Move: A Physical Education Program for Elementary Classroom Teachers,* Kendall/Hunt, 1974, 2nd edition, 1979.

Individualized Movement Experiences for Young Children, Phi Delta Kappa, 1974.

"Yes I Can!: Movement and the Developing Self" (film strip), Phi Delta Kappa, 1975.

Developmental Play Equipment for Home and School, illustrations and instructional development by Rogers Glenn, Wiley, 1975.

Motor Development and Movement Experiences for Young Children, Wiley, 1976.

(With Bruce A. McClenaghan) *Fundamental Movement: A Developmental and Remedial Approach,* Saunders, 1978.

(With McClenaghan) *Fundamental Movement: An Observational Assessment Instrument,* Saunders, 1978.

(With M. Botha) "The Progressive Development of Fundamental Movement Abilities" (film strip), Indiana University, 1982.

Understanding Motor Development: Infants, Children, Adolescents, Benchmark Press (Indianapolis, Ind.), 1982, 2nd edition, 1989.

Developmental Movement Experiences for Children, Wiley, 1982.

Developmental Physical Education for Today's Elementary School Children, Macmillan, 1987.

Your Growing Child, Time-Life Books, 1987.

Developing Your Child's Potential, Time-Life Books, 1987.

Contributor to numerous journals, including *Research Quarterly for Exercise and Sport, Physical Educator, Studies in Educational Evaluation,* and *Perceptual and Motor Skills.* Editor-in-chief of *Physical Educator,* 1973-83.

WORK IN PROGRESS: "Developmentally Appropriate Movement Activities for Young Children"; "Movement Literacy and the Young Child."

SIDELIGHTS: David L. Gallahue once told *CA:* "Writing must be a labor of love. The financial rewards are too uncertain and often too meager in the textbook market for it to be anything else. For the most part, writing is hard work. It is time-consuming, demanding of one's complete attention and long-range commitment. It is, however, a tremendous thrill to see a completed manuscript in print and to be able to express your views to people all over the world."

AVOCATIONAL INTERESTS: Horseback trail riding, running, swimming, camping.

*   *   *

GALLOWAY, Patricia Kay 1945-

PERSONAL: Born September 7, 1945, in Bloomington, Ind.; daughter of Samuel B. (in U.S. Air Force) and Mary Kay (Miller) Galloway. *Education:* Millsaps College, B.A. (with honors), 1966; University of North Carolina, M.A., 1968, Ph.D., 1973; attended Goodman School of Drama, 1968-69.

ADDRESSES: Home—Jackson, Miss. *Office*—Mississippi Department of Archives and History, P.O. Box 571, Jackson, Miss. 39205.

CAREER: University of North Carolina at Chapel Hill, instructor in French and German, 1969-71; University of North Caro-

lina at Wilmington, instructor in French and German, 1971-72; Winchester Research Unit, Winchester, England, medieval archaeologist, 1973-74; Rheinisches Landesmuseum, Bonn, West Germany, medieval archaeologist, 1974-75; Department of the Environment, London, England, medieval archaeologist, 1976; University of London, Westfield College, London, humanities programming adviser in computer unit, 1977-79; Mississippi Department of Archives and History, Jackson, editor of Mississippi Provincial Archives French Dominion Project, 1979-80, administrative assistant to director of Information and Education Division, 1980-83, special projects officer, 1983—. Medieval archaeologist with Norwich Survey Project, 1973, 1974, and Riksantikvarens Arkeologiske Undersoekelser, Trondheim, Norway, 1974, 1975, 1976. Member of Mississippi Choctaw Heritage Council. Member of staff of Hope Arts Centre, Belfast, Northern Ireland, 1973.

MEMBER: American Society for Ethnohistory (member of executive council, 1987-90), Association for Literary and Linguistic Computing, Association for Computational Linguistics, Association for Computing Machinery, Association for Computers and the Humanities (member of executive council, 1982-85), Classification Society, Society for Medieval Archaeology, French Colonial Historical Society, Royal Archaeological Institute, Mississippi Archaeological Association, Mississippi Historical Society.

AWARDS, HONORS: Woodrow Wilson fellowship, 1966-67; Chinard Prize, 1984; National Endowment for the Humanities research grant, 1988-89.

WRITINGS:

La Salle and His Legacy, University Press of Mississippi, 1982.
Mississippi Provincial Archives: French Dominion, Volumes 4-5, Louisiana State University Press, 1983.
(Contributor) Carolyn Reeves, editor, *The Choctaw before Removal,* University Press of Mississippi, 1985.
(With Robert Weddle and Mary Christine Morkovsky) *La Salle, the Mississippi, and the Gulf of Mexico,* Texas A & M University Press, 1987.
(Contributor) Winthrop Jordan and Sheila Skemp, editors, *Race and Family in the Colonial South,* University Press of Mississippi, 1987.
(Editor) *Southeastern Ceremonial Complex: Artifacts and Analysis,* University of Nebraska Press, 1989.
(Contributor) Peter Wood, Gregory Waselkov, and Thomas Hatley, editors, *Powhatan's Mantle,* University of Nebraska Press, 1989.
(Contributor) Hester Davis, editor, *Arkansas before the Americans,* University of Arkansas Press, in press.

Editor of series "Archaeological Reports," Mississippi Department of Archives and History. Contributor to archaeology and history journals. Editor of *Mississippi Archaeology.*

WORK IN PROGRESS: Editing *The Choctaw Revolt,* written in 1753 by Edmond Atkin; translating Antoine Simon Le Page du Pratz's *History of Louisiana;* completing *Choctaws and Chiefdoms,* the first of two volumes on the ethnohistory of the Choctaw Indians.

SIDELIGHTS: Patricia Kay Galloway told *CA:* "I spent a great deal of my childhood and early youth planning to be a professor of literature so that I would have an excuse to read all the time. That determination got me through undergraduate school and my master's degree before extracurricular participation in dramatics as an actress convinced me that if I didn't try my hand at it I would be sorry.

"So, in 1968 and 1969 I was an acting student at what was then the Goodman School of Drama in Chicago. After that I decided, not that I was not talented enough, but that I would prefer not to starve while awaiting discovery. In this spirit of tough-minded practicality, I returned to school to complete my doctorate in comparative literature and medieval studies. I completed the degree just in time to have my career shot out of the water by the nationwide collapse of foreign language programs, so I went to Europe to sulk and perhaps to attempt a career in the theatre again.

"I had been granted an audition at the Lyric Theatre in Belfast (the competition was not exactly heavy for employment there at the time) when a sudden and serious illness in the family called me back to the United States. In the meantime, following up a curiosity about the material side of the medieval culture I had studied so diligently, I had begun working on archaeological excavations of medieval sites, and it was to this I returned when the family crisis was over. I spent summer seasons in excavation and winter ones in artifact analysis for some four years in several northern European countries.

"In the course of this peripatetic existence, I learned to use computers for artifact and site analysis. This interest led eventually to employment in the computer center of one of the colleges of the University of London. This was one of only three jobs of its kind in the United Kingdom at that time—the other two were at Oxford and Cambridge. After two years of this, and with the impetus of Maggie Thatcher's intention to get foreigners out of government jobs, I decided that I had better go home before I forgot what a hamburger tasted like.

"I had a choice of two jobs: writing user documentation for Data General Corp.'s computers in North Carolina or editing translations of historical documents relating to the Louisiana colony in Mississippi. I chose the latter, and working for the Mississippi Department of Archives and History has enabled me to combine all the skills picked up along the way. I perform historical research and do historical editing and writing; I planned and implemented a computer system consisting of multiple minicomputer systems that is used for archival, administrative, archaeological, and publishing activities, on most of which I consult and design applications and even sometimes purify my soul by programming; and I edit and write for house and state archaeological publications. From time to time, I even serve as an expert witness (historical) on cases involving the state attorney general's office, which I find a very interesting application of dramatic art.

"In the course of my historical research on the colonial period of what used to be called the Old Southwest, I developed a strong interest in the ethnohistory of the Indians who then lived in the area of the state of Mississippi, and I am concentrating my research particularly on the protohistoric period (between De Soto and La Salle), for which the evidence must be a combination of early documents and archaeology."

*   *   *

GARDEN, Nancy 1938-

PERSONAL: Born May 15, 1938, in Boston, Mass. *Education:* Columbia University, B.F.A., 1961, M.A., 1962.

ADDRESSES: Home—Carlisle, Mass. *Agent*—Dorothy Markinko, Markinko, McIntosh & Otis, Inc., 475 Fifth Ave., New York, N.Y. 10017.

CAREER: Junior Scholastic, New York City, contributing editor, 1969-70; *American Observer,* Washington, D.C., contribut-

ing editor, 1970-72; Houghton Mifflin Co., New York City, associate editor, 1972, assistant editor, 1973, editor, 1974-76; teacher and free-lance writer, 1976—. Has also worked in the theatre as an actress and lighting designer, taught at various levels, and done free-lance editorial work for various publishers. Lecturer at schools and libraries to children on writing.

AWARDS, HONORS: Annie on My Mind was selected to the 1982 *Booklist* Reviewer's Choice, the 1982 American Library Association (ALA) Best Books, and the 1970-83 ALA Best of the Best lists; *Fours Crossing* was selected to the 1983-84 William Allen White Award Master List.

WRITINGS:

FOR YOUNG PEOPLE

What Happened in Marston, Four Winds, 1971.
Berlin: City Split in Two, Putnam, 1971.
The Loners (novel), Viking, 1972.
Vampires, Lippincott, 1973.
Werewolves, Lippincott, 1973.
Witches, Lippincott, 1975.
Demons and Devils, Lippincott, 1976.
Fun with Forecasting Weather, Houghton, 1977.
Fours Crossing (first novel in "Fours Crossing" fantasy series), Farrar, Straus, 1981.
The Kids' Code and Cipher Book, Holt, 1981.
Maria's Mountain, Houghton, 1981.
Annie on My Mind (novel), Farrar, Straus, 1982.
(Adaptor) *Favorite Tales from Grimm,* Four Winds, 1982.
Watersmeet (second novel in "Fours Crossing" fantasy series), Farrar, Straus, 1983.
Prisoner of Vampires (novel), Farrar, Straus, 1984.
Peace, O River (novel), Farrar, Straus, 1986.
The Door Between (third novel in "Fours Crossing" fantasy series), Farrar, Straus, 1987.
Mystery of the Night Raiders (The "Monster Hunters" series, Case 1), Farrar, Straus, 1987.
Mystery of the Midnight Menace (The "Monster Hunters" series, Case 2), Farrar, Straus, 1988.
Mystery of the Secret Marks (The "Monster Hunters" series, Case 3), Farrar, Straus, 1989.

WORK IN PROGRESS: Two young adult novels, one contemporary, one historical.

SIDELIGHTS: Nancy Garden told *CA:* "I write for young people because I like them, and because I think they are important. Children's books can be mind-stretchers and imagination-ticklers and builders of good taste in a way that adult books cannot, because young people usually come to books with more open minds. It's exciting to be able to contribute to that in a small way."

Garden divides her time between Massachusetts and Maine, and, though she lived in New York City for fifteen years, she said she "cannot imagine living in the city again. It's fun to go back once in a while," the author added, "but after about two days, I long for woods and sea, fresh air and quiet."

AVOCATIONAL INTERESTS: Gardening, weaving, hiking, running, cross-country skiing, traveling.

*   *   *

GARDNER, Joseph L(awrence) 1933-

PERSONAL: Born January 26, 1933, in Willmar, Minn.; son of Elmer Joseph (a railroad executive) and Margaret Eleanor (Archer) Gardner; married Sadako Miyasaka, February 25, 1967; children: Miya Elise, Justin Lawrence. *Education:* Attended University of Portland, 1951-52; University of Oregon, B.A. (with honors), 1955; University of Wisconsin, M.A., 1956.

ADDRESSES: Home—17 Cohawney Rd., Scarsdale, N.Y. 10583. *Office*—Reader's Digest, 260 Madison Ave., New York, N.Y. 10016.

CAREER: American Heritage Publishing Co., Inc., New York City, editor of Book Division, 1959-65, editor of American Heritage Juvenile Library and Horizon Caravel Books, 1965-68; Newsweek, Inc., Newsweek Books division, New York City, managing editor, 1968-70, editor, 1971-76; Reader's Digest General Books, New York City, senior staff editor, 1976-81, group editor of general reference, 1982-84; Reader's Digest Association, Inc., New York City, director of international book publications, 1984—. Friends of Scarsdale Library, member of board of directors, 1976-81, vice-president, 1979-81; Scarsdale Adult School, trustee, 1978-84, treasurer, 1981-83; trustee, Scarsdale Public Library, 1983-84, 1986—. *Military service:* U.S. Army, 1956-58.

MEMBER: PEN, Phi Beta Kappa, Sigma Delta Chi, Phi Kappa Psi, Coffee House (New York).

WRITINGS:

(Managing editor) *American Heritage History of World War I,* American Heritage Press, 1964.
(Editor) S. L. A. Marshall, *Swift Sword,* American Heritage Press, 1967.
Labor on the March, American Heritage Press, 1969.
Departing Glory: Theodore Roosevelt as Ex-President, Scribner, 1973.
(Editor and author of introduction) *Thomas Jefferson: A Biography in His Own Words,* Newsweek, 1976.
(Editor) *The World's Last Mysteries,* Reader's Digest Association, 1978.
(Editor) *Reader's Digest Wide World Atlas,* Reader's Digest Association, 1979.
(Editor) *Reader's Digest Atlas of the Bible,* Reader's Digest Association, 1981.
(Editor) *Eat Better, Live Better,* Reader's Digest Association, 1982.
(Editor) *Mysteries of the Ancient Americas,* Reader's Digest Association, 1986.
(Editor) *Reader's Digest Atlas of the World,* Reader's Digest Association, 1987.

Editor of "Wonders of Man," "Milestones of History," "Founding Fathers," and "World of Culture" series, Newsweek, 1971-76.

WORK IN PROGRESS: A biography of Gilbert Stuart.*

*　　*　　*

GASS, William H(oward) 1924-

PERSONAL: Born July 30, 1924, in Fargo, N.D.; son of William Bernard and Claire (Sorensen) Gass; married Mary Patricia O'Kelly, June 17, 1952; married Mary Alice Henderson, September 13, 1969; children: (first marriage) Richard G., Robert W., Susan H.; (second marriage) Elizabeth, Catherine. *Education:* Kenyon College, A.B., 1947; Cornell University, Ph.D., 1954.

ADDRESSES: Home—6304 Westminster Pl., St. Louis, Mo. 63130. *Office*—Department of Philosophy, Washington Univer-

sity, St. Louis, Mo. 63130. *Agent*—Lynn Nesbit, International Creative Management, 40 West 57th St., New York, N.Y. 10019.

CAREER: College of Wooster, Wooster, Ohio, instructor in philosophy, 1950-54; Purdue University, Lafayette, Ind., assistant professor, 1954-60, associate professor, 1960-66, professor of philosophy, 1966-69; Washington University, St. Louis, Mo., professor of philosophy, 1969-79, David May Distinguished University Professor in the Humanities, 1979—. Visiting lecturer in English and philosophy, University of Illinois, 1958-59. Member of Rockefeller Commission on the Humanities, 1978-80; member of literature panel, National Endowment for the Arts, 1979-82. *Military service:* U.S. Navy, 1943-46; served in China and Japan; became ensign.

MEMBER: PEN, American Philosophical Association, American Academy and Institute of Arts and Letters, National Academy of Arts and Sciences.

AWARDS, HONORS: Longview Foundation Award in fiction, 1959, for "The Triumph of Israbestis Tott"; Rockefeller Foundation grant for fiction, 1965-66; Standard Oil Teaching Award, Purdue University, 1967; Sigma Delta Chi Best Teacher Award, Purdue University, 1967 and 1968; *Chicago Tribune* award for Big-Ten teachers, 1967; Guggenheim fellowship, 1969-70; Alumni Teaching Award, Washington University, 1974; National Institute of Arts and Letters prize for literature, 1975; National Medal of Merit for fiction, 1979; National Book Critics Circle award for criticism, 1986, for *The Habitations of the Word.* Honorary degrees include D.Litt., Kenyon College, 1974; D.Litt., George Washington University, 1982; D.Litt., Purdue University, 1985.

WRITINGS:

FICTION

Omensetter's Luck (novel), New American Library, 1966.
In the Heart of the Heart of the Country (short stories), Harper, 1968, revised edition, David R. Godine, 1981.
Willie Masters' Lonesome Wife (novella; first published in *TriQuarterly* magazine, 1968), Knopf, 1971 .

NONFICTION

Fiction and the Figures of Life, Knopf, 1970.
(Author of introduction) *The Geographical History of America,* Random House, 1973.
On Being Blue, David R. Godine, 1975.
The World within the Word, Knopf, 1978.
The Habitations of the Word: Essays, Simon & Schuster, 1984.

OTHER

Contributor to numerous periodicals, including *New York Review of Books, New York Times Book Review, New Republic, Nation, TriQuarterly, Salmagundi,* and to philosophical journals. William Gass's manuscripts have been collected in the Washington University Library.

WORK IN PROGRESS: The Tunnel (novel); *The Master of Secret Revenges and Other Stories; The Surface of No City* (photographs); essays on architecture.

SIDELIGHTS: "Both as an essayist and as a writer of fiction, William Gass has earned the reputation of being one of the most accomplished stylists of his generation," writes Arthur M. Saltzman in *Contemporary Literature.* Gass, who is the David May Distinguished Professor in the Humanities at Washington University, is a principal advocate of the primacy of language in literature and of the self-referential integrity of literary texts. *Times*

Literary Supplement reviewer Robert Boyers contends that Gass's fictions—represented by novels, novellas, and short stories—"give heart to the structuralist enterprise," while his essays "may be said to promote the attack on realist aesthetics." Viewed as a whole, Boyers concludes, Gass's work constitutes "the most vigorous anti-realist literary 'programme' we have had in our time." A philosopher by training, Gass "maintains an art-for-art's-sake 'ethic' of infinite aesthetic value, in a structure of the sublime grotesque, as his principle of creativity," to quote *Criticism* contributor Reed B. Merrill. Merrill adds: "His interest lies in the pleasures of the imagination, in model making, and in aesthetic projections composed in the face of an all-pervasive determinism." Whatever his views, Gass remains one of the most respected creative literary minds in modern American letters. In the *New York Times Book Review,* Robert Kiely notes that the author "has written some of the freshest and most finely disciplined fictional prose to have appeared in America since World War II. . . . The unlikely combination of criticism, philosophy and metaphorical inventiveness has resulted in a kind of poetry."

As a collegian Gass studied philosophy, specializing in the philosophy of language. This training manifests itself in his later work principally in a sense of the musical and intellectual nature of words, sentences, and paragraphs. *Los Angeles Times Book Review* correspondent Jonathan Kirsch observes that Gass "does not merely celebrate language; quite the contrary, he is gifted with the nagging intellectual curiosity that prompts a precocious child to take apart a pocket watch to see what makes it tick." In the *Saturday Review,* Brom Weber comments on the fusion of fiction and philosophy in Gass's view. "Gass holds that philosophy and fiction are alike in that both are fictional constructions, systems based on concepts expressed linguistically, worlds created by minds whose choice of language specifies the entities and conditions comprising those worlds," Weber explains. "The reality of these fictional worlds does not depend upon correspondence with or reflection of other worlds, such as the sociophysical one customarily regarded as the 'real' world. Consequently, such concepts as cause and effect—designed to explain the 'real' world—are not necessarily relevant to a fictional world if its creator's language does not encompass causality." Kiely puts it more succinctly when he suggests Gass holds that "philosophy and fiction are both 'divine games,' that they do not so much interpret reality as contribute to it."

To call Gass's opinion on fiction a "theory" is perhaps to overstep the bounds of his intentions. He told the *Southwest Review* that especially in his own fiction, he is "not interested in trying to write according to some doctrine." He continued: "When I'm writing fiction, it's very intuitive, so that what happens, or what I do, or how it gets organized, is pretty much a process of discovery, not a process of using some doctrine that you can somehow fit everything into." Gass merely feels that fictions should constitute their own worlds of words and not necessarily attempt to represent some external reality. Weber notes that the author "is dissatisfied with 'character,' 'plot,' 'realism,' and similar conceptual terms that relate fiction to more than itself, and dislikes explication and paraphrase as analytic methods that superimpose 'meaning' upon fiction." Boyers elaborates: "We all know what Gass is writing against, including the tiresome use of novels for purposes of unitary moral uplift and penetrating 'world-view.' What he detests is the goody sweepstakes, in which works of art are judged not by their formal complexity or nuances of verbal texture but by their ability to satisfy easy moral imperatives." The critic declares that, as essayist and fiction writer, Gass "has had some hand in discrediting the kind of righteous moralism that so corrupts ordinary apprehension of the literary arts."

"The esthetic aim of any fiction is the creation of a verbal world, or a significant part of such world, alive through every order of its Being," Gass writes in *Fiction and the Figures of Life.* "The artist's task is therefore twofold. He must show or exhibit his world, and to do this he must actually make something, not merely describe something that might be made." Obviously, Gass is calling for a literature that makes demands of both its creator and its readers; reaching beyond reportage, it is its own reality unfolding on the page. In *Critique: Studies in Modern Fiction,* Richard J. Schneider claims that Gass "suggests that any philosophic separation of spirit from body, reason from emotion, experience from innocence, and words from deeds is destructive of life. He reminds us (and we need reminding) that fiction, like poetry, should not merely mean but, above all, be." *New York Times Book Review* contributor Frederic Morton addresses the ways in which Gass's fictions reflect this concept. Gass, notes Morton, "chooses the small gray lulls in life: rural twilights, small-town still-lifes, shadowed backyards. From them he draws dolor and music and a resonance touching us all. Gass is, in fact, a virtuoso with homely textures. They are the perfect foil for the nightmare leaps of his language. You are about to relax in those hick locales, even to feel comfortably bored, when the ambush of metaphors starts together with the shock of jagged elisions. . . . It's a tension that keeps the reader revealingly off-balance. . . . In brief, Gass engenders brand-new abrupt vulnerabilities. We read about the becalmed Midwest, about farmers mired in their dailiness, and realize too late that we've been exposed to a deadly poetry."

Omensetter's Luck, Gass's first novel, was "immediately recognized as a stunning achievement," according to Larry McCaffery in the *Dictionary of Literary Biography.* Published in 1966 after numerous rejections, the book established the unique verbal qualities that would come to be associated with all of Gass's work. The novel resists summarization; set in an Ohio river town, it explores the relationship between Brackett Omensetter, a happily unselfconscious "prelapsarian Adam," to quote McCaffery, and two conscious and thoughtful men, Henry Pimber and Jethro Furber. A *Newsweek* correspondent calls the book "a masterpiece of definition, a complex and intricate creation of level within level, where the theme of Omensetter's luck becomes an intense debate on the nature of life, love, good and evil, and finally, of death. . . . [It] is a story of life and death in the little countries of men's hearts." Richard Gilman offers a different interpretation in *The Confusion of Realms.* The novel, writes Gilman, "*is* Gass's prose, his style, which is not committed to something beyond itself, not an instrument of an idea. In language of amazing range and resiliency, full of the most exact wit, learning and contemporary emblems, yet also full of lyric urgency and sensuous body, making the most extraordinary juxtapositions, inventing, coining, relaxing at the right moments and charging again when they are over, never settling for the rounded achievement or the finished product, he fashions his tale of the mind, which is the tale of his writing a novel."

Given the difficulty Gass endured trying to find a publisher for *Omensetter's Luck,* he must have been immensely gratified by the critical reception the work received once it found its way into print. Gilman has called it "the most important work of fiction by an American in this literary generation . . . marvelously original, a whole Olympic broad jump beyond what almost any other American has been writing, the first full replenishment of language we have had for a very long time, the first convincing fusion of speculative thought and hard, accurate sensuality that we have had, it is tempting to say, since [Herman] Melville." *Nation* reviewer Shaun O'Connell describes *Omensetter's Luck* as "a difficult, dazzling first novel, important in its stylistic achievement and haunting in its dramatic evocation of the most essential human questions." Not every assessment has been entirely favorable, however. In his *Bright Book of Life: American Novelists & Storytellers from Hemingway to Mailer,* Alfred Kazin writes: "Everything was there in *Omensetter's Luck* to persuade the knowing reader of fiction that here was a great step forward: the verve, the bursting sense of possibility, the gravely significant atmosphere of contradiction, complexity of issue at every step. But it was all in the head, another hypothesis to dazzle the laity with. Gass had a way of dazzling himself under the storm of his style." Conversely, *Harper's* reviewer Earl Shorris praises Gass's stylistic achievement. *Omensetter's Luck,* Shorris declares, is, "page after page, one of the most exciting, energetic, and beautiful novels we can ever hope to read. It is a rich fever, a parade of secrets, a novel as American as [Mark Twain's] *Huckleberry Finn* and as torturously comic as [James Joyce's] *Ulysses.*"

Gass followed *Omensetter's Luck* with *In the Heart of the Heart of the Country,* a short story collection "whose highly original form exactly suits its metafictional impulses," to quote McCaffery. McCaffery describes the book as a development of the related themes of isolation and the difficulties of love through the use of experimental literary forms. The characters "control their lives only to the extent that they can organize their thoughts and descriptions into meaningful patterns. Not surprisingly, then, we come to know them mainly as linguistic rather than psychological selves, with their actions usually less significant to our understanding of them than the way they project their inner selves through language." Again critics have praised the volume as a significant contribution to American letters. *Hudson Review* correspondent Robert Martin Adams notes that Gass's techniques, "which are various and imaginative, are always in the service of vision and feeling. Mr. Gass's stories are strict and beautiful pieces of writing without waste or falsity or indulgence." In the *New Republic,* Richard Howard writes: "This is a volume of fictions which tell the truth, and speak even beyond the truth they tell; it is in that outspokenness, the risk of leaving something standing in his mind, that the authority of William Gass persists." *Nation* contributor Philip Stevick concludes that *In the Heart of the Heart of the Country* "finally amounts to an eccentric and ingratiating book, like no other before it, full of grace and wit, displaying a mind in love with language, the human body, and the look of the world."

No Gass work reveals "a mind in love with language" more clearly than *Willie Masters' Lonesome Wife,* the author's 1971 novella. Merrill feels that the piece "stands, along with his fascinating, impressionistic literary criticism, as perhaps [Gass's] best work to date. . . . Structurally, it is clear from the beginning that the subject of this book is the act of creation, and that [the narrator] Babs is William Gass's 'experimental structure' composed of language and imagination. The book *is* literally Babs. The book is a woman from beginning to end. The covers are the extrinsic flesh, the pages are the intrinsic contents of Bab's consciousness—her interior world. It would be difficult to find a better example of the use of structural principles than in Gass's stylistic combination of form and content in his book." In a *Critique* essay, McCaffery calls the novella "a remarkably pure example of metafiction" and adds: "As we watch 'imagination imagining itself imagine,' . . . we are witnessing a work self-consciously create itself out of the materials at hand—words. As the best metafiction does, *Willie Masters' Lonesome Wife* forces us to examine the nature of fiction-making from new perspectives. If Babs (and Gass) have succeeded, our attention has been focused on the act of reading words in a way we probably have not experienced before. The steady concern with the *stuff* of fiction, words, makes Gass's work unique among metafictions which have appeared thus far." *New York Review of Books* contributor Michael Wood observes that the work reveals "a real urgency, a powerful vision of the loneliness inherent in writing . . . and of writing as a useful and articulate image for loneliness of other kinds."

Whatever the subject at hand, Gass's essays are invariably artistic creations in and of themselves. *Village Voice* reviewer Sam Tanenhaus notes that each piece "is a performance or foray: [Gass] announces a topic, then descants with impressive erudition and unbuttoned ardor for the surprising phrase. The results often dazzle, and they're unfailingly original, in the root sense of the word—they work back toward some point of origin, generally a point where literature departs from the external world to invent a world of its own." Gass may serve as a spokesman for technical experimentation in fiction and for the value of innovative form, but his nonfiction also "asks us to yield ourselves in loving attentiveness to the being of language, poetic word, and concept, as it unfolds and speaks through us," according to Jeffrey Maitland in *Modern Fiction Studies.* V. S. Pritchett offers a similar view in the *New Yorker.* Writes Pritchett, "Gass is a true essayist, who certainly prefers traveling to arriving, who treats wisdom as a game in which no one wins. . . . His personality, his wit and affectations are part of the game." Kiely, on the other hand, finds a common core in Gass's meditations. The critic contends that in a variety of ways "—by means of startling metaphor and philosophical cajolery—he does the same thing in each essay: he calls our attention to art." The "art" to which attention is called is one that resists ease and proves imagination—beginning and ending with itself. "Gass is not 'ordering experience,' sending us on to higher morality;" explains Shorris, "he is not documenting anything. The work is there, and the work is beautiful. The experience of it is a significant and exciting ordeal from which we cannot emerge unchanged."

The cumulative impression left by Gass's essays is, to quote Kiely, "that of a man thinking." Gass calls his whole imagination into play and then develops his obsessions stylistically with complicated flights of prose. *New Republic* essayist Robert Alter calls Gass "clearly a writer willing to take chances" with a "freewheeling inventiveness." Alter suggests, however, that the "casting aside of inhibitions also means that unconscious materials are constantly popping through the surface of the writing, often in ways that subvert its effectiveness." *New York Times Book Review* correspondent Denis Donoghue also admits a certain discomfort with some of Gass's assertions. Still, Donoghue claims, "his sentences, true or false, are pleasures. Reading them, I find myself caring about their truth or error to begin with, but ending up not caring as much as I suppose I ought, and taking them like delicacies of the palate." Boyers remarks: "Gass's books are wonderful books because they raise all of the important aesthetic issues in the starkest and most inventive way. The writing is informed by a moral passion and a love of beautiful things that are never compromised by the author's compulsive addiction to aestheticizing formulations." Wood puts it another way: "The writer speaks tenderly to his paper, and, by caring for his words, constructs a world for his readers."

As Candyce Dostert notes in the *Wilson Library Bulletin,* to read William Gass "is to accompany an extraordinary mind on a quest for perfection, an invigorating voyage for the strong of heart." Gass is acclaimed equally for his ground-breaking fiction and for the essays that defend the fiction's aesthetics. In the *Dictionary of Literary Biography,* McCaffery states: "Certainly no other writer in America has been able to combine his critical intelligence with a background as a student of both the literary and philosophical aspects of language and to make this synthesis vital." Edmund White arrives at a similar conclusion in the *Washington Post Book World.* Gass's "discursive prose always reminds us that he is an imaginative writer of the highest order," White contends. "Indeed, among contemporary American writers of fiction, he is matched as a stylist only by a very select group." Another *Washington Post Book World* contributor, Paul West, observes that Gass's world "*is* words, *his* way of being. . . . Gass sings the flux, under this or that commercial pretext, and in the end renders what he calls 'the interplay of genres . . . skids of tone and decorum' into cantatas of appreciative excess. A rare gift that yields startling art."

Gass has given numerous interviews on his art to scholarly periodicals. In one for the *Chicago Review,* he said of his fiction: "What you want to do is create a work that can be read non-referentially. There is nothing esoteric or mysterious about this. It simply means that you want the work to be self-contained. A reader can do with a work what he or she wants. You can't force interpretations and you can't prevent them." He added: "I'm interested in how the mind works—though not always well—by sliding off into sneakily connected pathways, parking the car at another level of discourse, arriving by parachute."

BIOGRAPHICAL/CRITICAL SOURCES:

BOOKS

Bellamy, Joe David, editor, *The New Fiction: Interviews with Innovative American Writers,* University of Illinois Press, 1974.

Contemporary Fiction in America and England, 1950-1970, Gale, 1976.

Contemporary Literary Criticism, Gale, Volume 1, 1973, Volume 2, 1974, Volume 8, 1978, Volume 11, 1979, Volume 15, 1980, Volume 39, 1986.

Dictionary of Literary Biography, Volume 2: *American Novelists since World War II,* Gale, 1978.

Gass, William H., *Fiction and the Figures of Life,* Knopf, 1970.

Gilman, Richard, *The Confusion of Realms,* Random House, 1969.

Kazin, Alfred, *Bright Book of Life: American Novelists & Storytellers from Hemingway to Mailer,* Little, Brown, 1973.

McCaffery, Lawrence, *Metafictional Muse,* Pittsburgh University Press, 1982.

Vidal, Gore, *Matters of Fact and of Fiction: Essays 1973-1976,* Random House, 1977.

PERIODICALS

Book World, November 21, 1971.
Bulletin of Bibliography, July-September, 1974.
Chicago Daily News, February 1, 1969.
Chicago Review, autumn, 1978.
Contemporary Literature, summer, 1984.
Criticism, fall, 1976.
Critique: Studies in Modern Fiction, December, 1972, summer, 1976.
Delaware Literary Review, Volume 1, 1972.
Falcon, winter, 1972.
Harper's, May, 1972, October, 1978.
Harvard Advocate, winter, 1973.
Hudson Review, spring, 1968.
Iowa Review, winter, 1976.
Los Angeles Times Book Review, March 24, 1985, January 26, 1986.

Modern Fiction Studies, autumn, 1973, winter, 1977-78, winter, 1983.
Nation, May 9, 1966, April 29, 1968, March 22, 1971, January 29, 1977.
New Republic, May 7, 1966, May 18, 1968, March 20, 1971, October 9, 1976, May 20, 1978, March 11, 1985.
Newsweek, April 18, 1966, February 15, 1971, March 25, 1985.
New Yorker, January 10, 1977.
New York Review of Books, June 23, 1966, April 11, 1968, December 14, 1972, July 15, 1974, April 17, 1975, May 1, 1975, May 15, 1975, August 5, 1976, October 14, 1976.
New York Times, October 4, 1976, February 14, 1985.
New York Times Book Review, April 17, 1966, April 21, 1968, February 21, 1971, November 14, 1971, November 7, 1976, July 9, 1978, June 3, 1979, March 10, 1985.
Pacific Coast Philology, Volume 9, 1974.
Partisan Review, summer, 1966.
Salmagundi, fall, 1973.
Saturday Review, March 2, 1968, September 21, 1968, May 29, 1971.
Shenandoah, winter, 1976.
Southern Review, spring, 1967.
Southwest Review, spring, 1979, autumn, 1985.
Time, November 15, 1976.
Times Literary Supplement, May 18, 1967, August 14, 1969, April 22, 1977, November 3, 1978.
Twentieth Century Literature, May, 1976.
Village Voice, June 4, 1985.
Washington Post Book World, July 9, 1978, March 3, 1985.
Western Humanities Review, winter, 1978.
Wilson Library Bulletin, May, 1985.
World Literature Today, spring, 1979, winter, 1987.

—*Sketch by Anne Janette Johnson*

*   *   *

GELB, Norman 1929-

PERSONAL: Born November 9, 1929, in New York, N.Y.; son of Samuel and Minnie (Friedman) Gelb; married Barbara Judith Levine, June 5, 1960; children: Mallary, Amos. *Education:* Attended Brooklyn College (now of the City University of New York), Columbia University, and University of Vienna, 1947-51.

ADDRESSES: Home—London, England. *Office*—c/o Foreign Press Association, 11 Carleton House Terrace, London SW1, England.

CAREER: WOR-Radio, New York, N.Y., news editor, 1957-60; Mutual Broadcasting System, Washington, D.C., correspondent in Berlin, Germany, and London, England, 1960-73; Voice of America London correspondent, 1973-78; *New Leader,* London, correspondent, 1978—. *Military service:* U.S. Army, 1952-54.

MEMBER: Foreign Press Association.

WRITINGS:

NONFICTION

Enemy in the Shadows, Luscombe, 1976.
The Irresistible Impulse, Paddington Press, 1979.
The British, Everest House, 1982.
Less than Glory, Putnam, 1984.
Scramble: A Narrative History of the Battle of Britain, Harcourt, 1986.
The Berlin Wall: Kennedy, Khrushchev and a Showdown in the Heart of Europe, Times Books, 1987.

Dunkirk: The Complete Story of the First Step in the Defeat of Hitler, Morrow, 1989.

SIDELIGHTS: Norman Gelb wrote to *CA:* "I became a journalist because the U.S. Army had me writing news broadcasts for the American Forces Network in Frankfurt, Germany, when I was a GI. Upon discharge, I realized that the Army had taught me my trade. The most exciting moment of my journalism career was covering the building of the Berlin Wall and the circumstances surrounding it. Most journalistic work gets to be mechanical and predictable. Book writing, or any writing, is no pleasure unless it is absorbing, exciting, and surprising to the writer as well as the reader."

BIOGRAPHICAL/CRITICAL SOURCES:

PERIODICALS

New York Times Book Review, July 15, 1984, February 8, 1987, October 8, 1989.
Times Literary Supplement, February 27, 1987.

*   *   *

GETZELS, Jacob Warren   1912-

PERSONAL: Born February 7, 1912, in Bialystok, Poland; immigrated to United States, 1921; naturalized United States citizen, 1933; son of Hirsch and Frieda (Solon) Getzels; married Judith Nelson (a city planner), December 24, 1949; children: Katherine, Peter, Julia. *Education:* Brooklyn College (now Brooklyn College of the City University of New York), B.A., 1936; Columbia University, M.A., 1939; Harvard University, Ph.D., 1951.

ADDRESSES: Home—5704 South Dorchester Ave., Chicago, Ill. 60637. *Office*—Department of Education, University of Chicago, 5835 South Kimbark Ave., Chicago, Ill. 60637.

CAREER: University of Chicago, Chicago, Ill., instructor, 1951, assistant professor, 1952-54, associate professor, 1955-57, professor of education and behavioral science, 1957-68, R. Wendell Harrison Distinguished Service Professor, 1968—. Visiting professor, Stanford University, 1963, and University of Puerto Rico. U.S. Office of Education, member of mission to Russia, 1960, member of research advisory council, 1964-70; member of council of scholars, Library of Congress, 1980-84. Member of board of directors, Morgan Park Academy, 1965-68, and Spencer Foundation, 1970—. *Wartime service:* Office of Strategic Services, 1942-46.

MEMBER: National Academy of Education (first vice-president, 1972-76), National Society for the Study of Education (director, 1975-77), American Educational Research Association (member of executive board), American Academy of Arts and Sciences (fellow), American Sociological Association, American Psychological Association.

AWARDS, HONORS: Research award, American Personnel and Guidance Association, 1959; Center for the Advanced Study in the Behavioral Sciences fellow, 1960-61; Center for Policy Study fellow, University of Chicago, 1967-75; Teachers College medal, 1977; Nicholas Murray Butler Medal for theory and philosophy of education, Columbia University, 1978; distinguished alumnus award, Brooklyn College of the City University of New York, 1984; L.H.D., Hofstra University, 1984.

WRITINGS:

(With Arthur P. Coladarci) *The Use of Theory in Educational Administration,* Stanford University Press, 1955.
(With P. W. Jackson) *Creativity and Intelligence: Explorations with Gifted Students,* Wiley, 1962.

(With J. M. Lipham and R. F. Campbell) *Educational Administration as a Social Process: Theory, Research, Practice,* Harper, 1968.
(With Irving A. Taylor) *Perspectives in Creativity,* Aldine, 1975.
(With Mihaly Csikszentmihalyi) *The Creative Vision: A Longitudinal Study of Problem Finding in Art,* Wiley, 1976.
(With others) *The Role of the School in the Acquisition of Values* (sound recording), Center for the Study of Democratic Institutions (Santa Barbara, Calif.), 1976.

Contributor to scholarly journals.*

*   *   *

GEWE, Raddory
See GOREY, Edward (St. John)

*   *   *

GHEORGHIU, (Constantin) Virgil   1916-

PERSONAL: Born September 15, 1916, in Razbeoni-Neamtz, Moldavie, Rumania; son of Constantin (a priest of the Rumanian Orthodox Church) and Maria (Scobay) Gheorghiu; married Ecaterina Burbea (a lawyer), July 29, 1939. *Education:* Attended University of Bucharest, Royal Military College, Kishiniev, Rumania, and University of Heidelberg. *Politics:* "No party politics."

ADDRESSES: Home—16 Rue de Siam, Paris 16, France.

CAREER: Rumanian novelist, living in exile in France since 1948; priest of the Paris Colony Rumanian Orthodox Church, 1963—. *Military service:* Rumanian Army.

AWARDS, HONORS: Royal Poetry Prize (Rumania), 1940, for *Caligrafie pe zapada.*

WRITINGS:

IN RUMANIAN

Viata de toate zilele a poetului (poems; title means "The Daily Life of a Poet"), Cartea Romanesca, 1938.
Armand Calinescu (poems), Socec, 1940.
Caligrafie pe zapada (poems; title means "Calligraphy on the Snow"), Fundatiilor Regale, 1940.
Ard Malurile Nistrului (documentary; title means "The Flaming Banks of the Dniester"), Nationala, 1941.
Am luptat in Crimeea (documentary; title means "I Fought in the Crimea"), Nationala, 1942.
Cu submarinul la asediul Sevastopolului (documentary; title means "In Submarine at the Siege of Sebastopol"), Nationala, 1942.
Ultima ora (novel; title means "The Last Hour"), Nationala, 1942.
Ceasul de rugaciune (poems; title means "The Hour of Prayer"), Nationala, 1942.

IN FRENCH

La vingt-cinquieme heure (autobiographical novel), translated from the Rumanian by Monique Saint-Come, Plon, 1949, English translation by Rita Eldon published as *The Twenty-Fifth Hour,* Knopf, 1950, Regnery, 1966.
La seconde chance (autobiographical novel; also see below), translated from the Rumanian by Livia Lamoure, Plon, 1952.
L'homme qui voyagea seul (novel), translation by Lamoure, Plon, 1954.
Le peuple des immortels (stories), translation by Lamoure, Plon, 1955.

Vertu a forte dose (novel), translation by Lamoure, Plon, c. 1956, published as *Les sacrifies du Danube,* c. 1957.

Saint Jean Bouche d'Or (fictionalized biography), Plon, 1957.

Les mendiants de miracles (novel; also see below), translation by Lamoure, Plon, 1958.

(And author of postface) *La cravache* (novel), translation by Lamoure, Plon, 1960.

Perahim (novel), translation by Lamoure, Plon, 1961.

La maison de Petrodava (novel), translation by Lamoure, Plon, 1961.

La vie de Mahomet (biography), translation by Lamoure, Plon, 1962.

Les immortels d'Agapia (novel), French translation by Lamoure, Plon, 1964, English translation by Milton Stansbury published as *The Immortals of the Mountain,* Regnery, 1969.

De la vingt-cinquieme heure a l'heure eternelle (memoir of father, Constantin Gheorghiu), translation by Lamoure, Plon, 1965.

La jeunesse du docteur Luther (novel), translation by Lamoure, Plon, 1965.

Le meurtre de Kyralessa (novel), French translation by Lamoure, Plon, 1966, English translation by Marika Mihalyi published as *The Death of Kyralessa,* Regnery, 1968.

La condottiera (novel), Plon, 1967.

La tunique de peau (novel), Plon, 1967.

Pourquoi m'a-t-on appele Virgil? (novel), Plon, 1968.

La vie du Patriarch Athenagoras (biography), Plon, 1969.

L'espionne (novel), Plon, 1971.

La seconde chance [and] *Les mendiants de miracles,* Plon, 1971.

L'oeil Americain (novel), Plon, 1972.

Dieu ne recoit que le dimanche (novel), Plon, 1975.

Les inconnus de Heidelberg (novel), Plon, 1977.

Le grand exterminateur (novel), Plon, 1978.

Les Amazones du Danube (novel), Plon, 1978.

Christ au Liban: De moise aux Palestiniens, Plon, 1979.

Dieu a Paris (novel), Plon, 1980.

Poezii: 1928-1977 (poems), Eminescu, 1986.

Memoires: Le temoin de la vingt-cinquieme heure, Plon, 1986.

OTHER

Rumaenische Maerchen (fairy tales), Aehren-Verlag (Heidelberg), 1948.

De Verdenking (novel), Van Hoeve (The Hague), 1962.

Contrata de Heroes (novel), Editorial Luis de Caralt (Barcelona), c. 1963.

Also author of *Alibi pour Limitroff,* 1962, and *Ambrosius de Milan.*

SIDELIGHTS: Marilyn Gaddis Rose writes about Virgil Gheorghiu in *Books Abroad:* "A visitor [to Gheorghiu's home in Paris] finds it hard to realize that this kind, genial host with a soft Rumanian accent and a whimsical sense of humor has written such violence-filled novels, or could, as he admits in the epilogue of [*La cravache*] often have provoked deliberately the controversy that has followed his career as an *emigre* novelist." Gheorghiu's cultural background is both Eastern and Western, his church is a blend of Greek Orthodoxy and Roman Catholicism, and his native country has undergone considerable changes in policy in recent years. These forces all contribute to the urgency in his writing, and what Rose calls "his search for a spiritual no man's land." Rose describes the author as "the oldest child of very young parents. Steadfast piety made existence bearable for these folk who considered oppression normal."

Before he was called into the Rumanian Army, Gheorghiu wrote and published poetry. While in the army, he penned pro-

government books when Marshal Ion Antonescu, a German ally and leader of Rumania's militaristic movement, was in power. The author was a member of the Rumanian diplomatic corps in Yugoslavia when Antonescu was overthrown with the aid of the Soviets in 1944. Because of his loyalty to Antonescu, Gheorghiu was imprisoned in Czechoslovakia; but he was freed again when the Americans arrived in 1945. Still under the suspicion of the Rumanian government, Gheorghiu decided to leave the country. He traveled for three years before settling down in France. His experiences during these years are recorded in his autobiographies, *La seconde chance* and *The Twenty-Fifth Hour,* the latter of which he composed while living in two concentration camps; it remains his most successful and widely translated book.

About *The Twenty-Fifth Hour,* Rose remarks: "Father Gheorghiu says that . . . the characters are composites of people he knew, and that he himself protested his imprisonment by means of Swiftian petitions." During this time he increased his familiarity with Anglo-American literature. "Walt Whitman, he says," according to Rose, "had been a revelation of his adolescence. He gained facility reading the guards' pocketbooks. He went on to T. S. Eliot and W. H. Auden, whom he quotes in *The Twenty-Fifth Hour,* and Ezra Pound."

Relating his childhood and wartime experiences, and his life since that time, Rose comments: "With such conflicting loyalties in his past, Father Gheorghiu is bound to have an apocalyptic, but clouded, world view . . . [his] experiences made his partial, but spiritualizing, perspective necessary. To him death has to be martyrdom; suffering has to be penance. He may suggest unwittingly that oppression requires both a group willing to oppress and a group willing to be oppressed. From his point of view this impasse is never-ending, making necessary a spiritual mid-world. Today, a successful Western novelist for fifteen years [whose work has been translated into 34 languages], Father Gheorghiu has to keep creating this mid-world, for he says it is clearer than ever that we live in the twenty-fifth hour."

MEDIA ADAPTATIONS: The Twenty-Fifth Hour was made into a movie in 1966, starring Anthony Quinn and directed by Carlo Ponti and Henri Verneuil.

BIOGRAPHICAL/CRITICAL SOURCES:

PERIODICALS

Best Sellers, May 15, 1968.
Books Abroad, summer, 1950, spring, 1967, autumn, 1968.
Hudson Review, spring, 1967.
Le Figaro Litteraire, June 30, 1966.
Le Monde, May 9, 1970.
New York Times Book Review, November 13, 1966, February 8, 1970.
Time, October 24, 1969.
Village Voice, May 9, 1970.*

*   *   *

GIFFORD, Barry (Colby) 1946-

PERSONAL: Born October 18, 1946, in Chicago, Ill.; son of Adolph Edward (a pharmacist) and Dorothy (a model; maiden name, Colby) Gifford; married Mary Lou Nelson, 1970; children: Phoebe Lou, Asa Colby. *Education:* Attended University of Missouri, 1964, and Cambridge University, 1966.

ADDRESSES: Home—1213 Peralta Ave., Berkeley, Calif. 94706.

CAREER: Poet, novelist, memoirist, essayist, biographer; visiting lecturer at State University of New York at Buffalo, 1974.

Has worked as a merchant seaman, musician, journalist, and truck driver.

AWARDS, HONORS: Silverthorne Award for poetry from Silverthorne Press, 1967, for *The Blood of the Parade;* American Library Association Notable Book Award, 1978, for *Jack's Book: An Oral Biography of Jack Kerouac;* National Endowment for the Arts fellowship, 1982; Maxwell Perkins Editor's Award from PEN, 1983; PEN Syndicated Fiction Award, 1985.

WRITINGS:

The Blood of the Parade (poems), Silverthorne Press, 1967.
A Boy's Novel (short stories), Christopher's Books, 1973.
Kerouac's Town on the Second Anniversary of His Death (essay), photographs by Marshall Clements, Capra, 1973.
Coyote Tantras (poems), Christopher's Books, 1973.
My Mother's People, Creative Arts Book Co., 1976.
Persimmons: Poems for Paintings, Shaman Drum Press, 1976.
The Boy You Have Always Loved (poems), Talon Books, 1976.
(Translator) Francis Jammes, *Selected Poems of Francis Jammes,* Utah State University Press, 1976.
(Editor) *The Portable Curtis: Selected Writings of Edward S. Curtis,* Creative Arts Book Co., 1976.
Living in Advance (lyrics and music), Open Reading Books, 1976.
A Quinzaine in Return for a Portrait of Mary Sun (poems), Workingmans Press, 1977.
(Editor and author of introduction) *As Ever: The Collected Correspondence of Allen Ginsberg and Neal Cassady,* foreword by Carolyn Cassady, afterword by Ginsberg, Creative Arts Book Co., 1977.
Horse Hauling Timber out of Hokkaido Forest (poems), Christopher's Books, 1978.
(With Lawrence Lee) *Jack's Book: An Oral Biography of Jack Kerouac,* St. Martin's, 1978.
Lives of the French Impressionist Painters (poems), Donald S. Ellis, 1978.
Landscape with Traveler: The Pillow Book of Francis Reeves (novel), Dutton, 1980.
Port Tropique (novel), Black Lizard Books, 1980.
The Neighborhood of Baseball: A Personal History of the Chicago Cubs (memoir), Dutton, 1981.
Francis Goes to the Seashore (novella and short stories), St. Martin's, 1982.
(With Lee) *Saroyan: A Biography,* Harper, 1984.
An Unfortunate Woman (novel), Creative Arts Book Co., 1984.
Giotto's Circle (poems), St. Andrews Press, 1987.
The Devil Thumbs a Ride (essay), Grove, 1988.
A Day at the Races, Atlantic Monthly Press, 1988.
A Good Man to Know (memoir), Tombouctou Books, 1988.
Ghosts No Horse Can Carry: Collected Poems, 1967-1987, Creative Arts Book Co., 1989.

Contributor of stories, poems, articles, and reviews to numerous periodicals, including *New York Times, Rolling Stone, Beloit Poetry Journal, Esquire, San Francisco Examiner,* and *Punch* (London).

SIDELIGHTS: Barry Gifford wrote to *CA:* "I grew up in Chicago where my father's friends were racketeers. He ran an all-night drugstore on the corner of Chicago and Rush, and I would stay up late listening to their talk and dunking doughnuts with the organ grinder's monkey. Afternoons I spent watching showgirls rehearse at the Club Alabam next door.

"I was always interested in language; always listened. After my father died (I was twelve) there was no money, so my mother and I went to work. I began to read everything: influences were Jack London, Jack Kerouac, B. Traven; later Pound, Emily Dickinson, Jean Rhys, Proust, and Flaubert."

AVOCATIONAL INTERESTS: Travel in Europe, South and Central America, Japan, and North Africa.

BIOGRAPHICAL/CRITICAL SOURCES:

PERIODICALS

Chicago Tribune Book World, June 14, 1981.
Los Angeles Times Book Review, October 24, 1982.
New York Times Book Review, January 18, 1981.
Saturday Review, August, 1978.
Washington Post Book World, October 22, 1978, June 29, 1980, December 26, 1980, May 2, 1982.

*   *   *

GILMAN, Dorothy   1923-
(Dorothy Gilman Butters)

PERSONAL: Born June 25, 1923, in New Brunswick, N.J.; daughter of James Bruce (a minister) and Essa (Starkweather) Gilman; married Edgar A. Butters, Jr. (a teacher), September 15, 1945 (divorced, 1965); children: Christopher Butters, Jonathan Butters. *Education:* Attended Pennsylvania Academy of Fine Arts, 1940-45, University of Pennsylvania and Art Students' League, 1963-64. *Politics:* Democrat. *Religion:* Unitarian Universalist.

ADDRESSES: Home—Portland, Me. *Agent*—Howard Morhaim Literary Agency, 175 Fifth Ave., New York, N.Y. 10010.

CAREER: Samuel Fleischer Art Memorial, Philadelphia, Pa., instructor in drawing in adult evening school, two years; switchboard operator, New Jersey Bell Telephone Co., one year; Cherry Lawn School, Darien, Conn., instructor in creative writing, 1969-70.

MEMBER: Authors Guild.

AWARDS, HONORS: Catholic Book Award for *A Nun in the Closet.*

WRITINGS:

JUVENILE BOOKS; ALL UNDER NAME DOROTHY GILMAN BUTTERS

Enchanted Caravan, illustrations by Janet Smalley, Macrae, 1949.
Carnival Gypsy, Macrae, 1950.
Ragamuffin Alley, Macrae, 1951.
The Calico Year, Macrae, 1953.
Four-Party Line, Macrae, 1954.
Papa Dolphin's Table, Knopf, 1955.
Girl in Buckskin (Junior Literary Guild selection), Macrae, 1956.
Heartbreak Street (Junior Literary Guild selection), Macrae, 1958.
Witch's Silver (Junior Literary Guild selection), Macrae, 1959.
Masquerade, Macrae, 1961.
Ten Leagues to Boston Town (Junior Literary Guild selection), Macrae, 1962.
The Bells of Freedom (Weekly Reader Book Club selection), illustrations by Carol Wilde, Macrae, 1963, reprinted, Peter Smith, 1984.
(Under name Dorothy Gilman) *The Maze in the Heart of the Castle,* Doubleday, 1983.

ADULT NOVELS

The Unexpected Mrs. Pollifax (*Reader's Digest* Book Club selection) Doubleday, 1966, reprinted, Fawcett, 1985 (published in England as *Mrs. Pollifax, Spy,* Tandem, 1971).

Uncertain Voyage, Doubleday, 1967, reprinted, Fawcett, 1989.

The Amazing Mrs. Pollifax (*Reader's Digest* Book Club selection), Doubleday, 1970, Fawcett, 1986.

The Elusive Mrs. Pollifax, Doubleday, 1971.

A Palm for Mrs. Pollifax (*Reader's Digest* Book Club selection), Doubleday, 1973.

A Nun in the Closet, Doubleday, 1975 (published in England as *A Nun in the Cupboard,* R. Hale, 1976).

The Clairvoyant Countess, Doubleday, 1975.

Mrs. Pollifax on Safari (*Reader's Digest* Book Club selection), Doubleday, 1977.

The Tightrope Walker (*Reader's Digest* Book Club selection), Doubleday, 1979.

Mrs. Pollifax on the China Station (*Reader's Digest* Book Club selection), Doubleday, 1983.

Mrs. Pollifax and the Hong Kong Buddha (*Reader's Digest* Book Club selection), Doubleday, 1985.

Mrs. Pollifax and the Golden Triangle (*Reader's Digest* Book Club selection), Doubleday, 1988.

Incident at Badamya (Literary Guild alternate selection), Doubleday, 1989.

Mrs. Pollifax and the Whirling Dervish, Doubleday, 1990.

OTHER

(Contributor) *On Creative Writing,* edited by Paul Engle, Dutton, 1964.

A New Kind of Country (nonfiction), Doubleday, 1978.

Contributor to *Good Housekeeping, Jack and Jill, Redbook, Ladies' Home Journal, Cosmopolitan, Writer,* and other magazines; contributor of short stories, under name Dorothy Gilman Butters, to *Redbook.*

SIDELIGHTS: Popular suspense writer Dorothy Gilman "creates appealing characters whose 'ordinary' lives are changed by their encounters with danger," writes Mary Helen Becker in *Twentieth-Century Crime and Mystery Writers.* "Naive and innocent to begin with, apparently handicapped by age, poverty, or emotional problems, they pit their courage, perseverance, and resourcefulness (fortified by inner strength discovered in time of need), against the organized powers of evil." Gilman's most popular creation is Mrs. Emily Pollifax, a bored and lonely New Jersey widow in her sixties who applies to the CIA for a job and is chosen for special assignments. Looking more like a tourist than a spy, "Mrs. Pollifax is (at least, on the surface) the archetypal little old lady," writes *New York Times Book Review* contributor Allen J. Hubin. *New York Times* reviewer Thomas Lask calls Mrs. Pollifax "the picture of the innocent abroad." The Pollifax novels chronicle their intrepid heroine's adventures in exotic locales, where her kindly and sympathetic nature often leads her to involve herself with a variety of unusual people. As Becker explains: "Warmhearted and open minded, Mrs. Pollifax is without prejudice and is always sympathetic to those in trouble." This sympathy for strangers, however, frequently involves her in adventures unforeseen by her CIA employers. But the resourceful Pollifax always extracts herself from real trouble. "Disarmingly self-mocking, whenever she is in a tight spot, Mrs. Pollifax imagines what would happen in the movies and acts accordingly, all the while regretting her own cliches," Becker states.

Lask, however, sees the spy as sometimes too inactive: "Mrs. Pollifax is like an obstacle around whom the rough waters churn and boil. Things happen to her rather than the other way around, and her chancy approach to events are so open-eyed that it's a wonder she survives at all." Commenting on *Mrs. Pollifax and the Golden Triangle,* Elaine S. Povich in the *Chicago Tribune* notes a similar failing: "The book keeps readers wondering what is coming next, but it fails to portray Emily Pollifax as much more than a victim of events she cannot control." Other reviewers, however, willingly accept the elderly lady as an alternative to the James Bond stereotype. Hubin concludes: "Mrs. Pollifax is an enchantress—long may she terrorize spydom!"

CA INTERVIEW

CA interviewed Dorothy Gilman by telephone on December 16, 1988, at her former home in New York State.

CA: You're best known for the Mrs. Pollifax series of spy novels. How did you happen to create the elderly, kind, and very wise Emily Pollifax for your star rather than a James Bond type or a glamorous female spy?

GILMAN: I'd say there were two influences. One was that I grew up the daughter of a minister—he was nearly fifty when I was born—and my parents' friends in the church were these slightly eccentric, charming ladies who were sort of surrogate mothers to me at times. Their characters made an imprint on me. The second influence is that when I wrote the first Mrs. Pollifax book—I had written a dozen young adult books by that time—it was a very difficult year for me—my marriage was breaking up—and I thought I would simply escape by writing a book about a woman who had all the things happen to her that I would like to have happen to me. I had made up stories when I was a child about being a spy and that sort of thing. (In those days the CIA was very glamorous. I'm a little embarrassed at times now that Mrs. Pollifax works for the CIA; I call it the Department these days.) And I had always wanted to travel. I grew up with maps hanging on my walls, and I read travel books. This was a hunger in me, so Mrs. Pollifax was not only a spy, but she was sent off to foreign countries to have adventures. I just had a good time writing and escaping my own reality. My life had been very uneventful until then, and I had this very plucky heroine do a lot of things that pleased me.

CA: If Emily Pollifax was a case of writer's wish-fulfillment, did she then actually change your life in some ways?

GILMAN: She was certainly therapy. And at the end of the year I had left my husband and taken the two kids, and we had embarked on quite an adventurous life. It was delightful. There wasn't that much money, and I was making this great move with two children, nine and thirteen at the time. There were a lot of changes after that year. And Emily Pollifax surprised me; I think perhaps my own intense escapism met some needs in other people. On the day of publication, I was called and told that Rosalind Russell wanted to do the movie. It looked as if we were going to make it, the three of us, and that was very rewarding and a lovely surprise.

CA: Early on you studied art seriously, though you always seem to have been writing. How did writing happen to win out as a career choice?

GILMAN: It had always won out. I started writing when I was nine, and when I was eleven—it was one of the biggest moments of my life—I entered a short-story contest in the local newspaper for children ten to sixteen and won first prize of three dollars. I guess my parents didn't know what to do with me. I wanted, like most writers, to go out and get a job and experience life when I got out of high school, but I was only sixteen. We sat down one day and went through the list of places I could go (they had sent my sister off to college, and I had equal rights with my sister) and picked out an art school in Philadelphia. My art teacher had said I had some talent, but it was never a consuming thing. The writing was. I did end up winning a traveling scholarship at the Academy of Fine Arts, and at that time I thought maybe I could write and illustrate children's books. But I was never that good at art, really; I was competent, but not great. I wrote all through art school.

CA: Uncertain Voyage, published in 1968, came between the first and second Pollifax books. Were you unsure at that point about doing a series?

GILMAN: I never dreamed it would be a series. Fawcett, by the way, has just reissued *Uncertain Voyage.* The only book of mine that's out of print is a nonfiction, rather slender one that came out in 1978, *A New Kind of Country.* They're reissuing that in April 1989. After I wrote *Uncertain Voyage* I realized that I might alternate, because there was considerable pressure for me to do another Pollifax book. And when I did the second one, it was hard getting back to where I had been, because I was happy.

CA: Does writing the Pollifax books require quite a different frame of mind from doing the non-Pollifax books?

GILMAN: Yes, completely. A certain pattern was established early—off-beat countries, for instance, and certain political situations in those countries to ground the plots. I feel that I *build* the Pollifax books, whereas in the non-Pollifax books, like this April's *Incident at Badamya,* the words just flow. It brings a very different approach, the Pollifax adventures.

CA: Mrs. Pollifax's adventures take her to all sorts of interesting and potentially dangerous countries. Have you seen all your settings firsthand now?

GILMAN: Almost all. I was too poor to travel for the first one, which is why Mrs. Pollifax ended up in Albania, where no Americans could go. That was very sneaky of me. I went to Bulgaria for *The Elusive Mrs. Pollifax.* Yes, after the first one I traveled, which fed into my longing for travel very nicely. I have been to China. My book coming out in April is set in Burma, which I loved—but that's not a Pollifax. Then there's Thailand. I've been fortunate to go and look things up myself, to get the feel and impressions.

CA: The settings always sound quite authentic; I thought you must have seen your locations.

GILMAN: I started doing *Mrs. Pollifax on Safari* without going to Zambia. I was in touch with their bureau of travel and their embassy, which are combined in New York City. But there came a time when I realized that I was going to have to go, because even they couldn't tell me the color of the policemen's uniforms, and other little things like that.

CA: By the time you go to visit a country, do you know what kind of information you need? Is the book already started?

GILMAN: Usually I go without much research and just experience the country. Then I go home to write. Having done a non-Pollifax book, I'm back working on a Pollifax book, this one set in Morocco. I knew very little about Morocco when I went. It was when I got back that I found out all kinds of horrible things about Morocco, which I'm trying to weave into the plot without insulting them too much.

CA: Are your books read in all the countries in which they're set?

GILMAN: I don't think so. They've been translated into about a dozen languages, including Japanese. But I don't think they're in Arabic. I don't think Thailand has them. Bulgaria, I'm sure, wouldn't have them. Mostly they're in the European countries, South America, and Japan.

CA: You're very daring with your plots, but, as several reviewers have noted, they're such fun that the reader should willingly suspend disbelief. How carefully do you plan the action before you write a book?

GILMAN: Well, Mrs. Pollifax grows harder and harder, frankly. She was sixty-three in 1966, and I suppose she's sixty-five now. There are limitations with her. So when I can do a non-Pollifax, I feel much freer. The plots do seem a bit improbable, because it's awfully difficult to find one where she won't have to walk a hundred miles over mountains and do things that would be even more unlikely.

CA: When you're finishing one book, is the next already hatching in your mind?

GILMAN: Sometimes, and sometimes not. And when it's not, I go through a painful several months.

CA: In A New Kind of Country, *which you mentioned earlier, you wrote about your life in a village in Nova Scotia and how that became a good setting for exploring your own place in the environment. How do you look back on that experience and on the book from the perspective of ten more years?*

GILMAN: That book was probably the closest to an autobiography that I'll ever write. It's mostly a feminist book, I'd say: how women can do things they've wanted to do, philosophy, and that sort of thing. It is about a single woman living in a fishing village by herself in Nova Scotia. It went out of print very quickly; my agent at the time raged about that and said they hadn't given it a chance. I got more mail about that book than I've gotten about any book. Most of my mail since has been from people wanting to know how to get a copy; they've tried book detectives and haven't found it. I have a new agent who's really pushed to get it out again, who sent copies to Leona Nevler at Fawcett, and she said she felt that it had a lot of staying power. She was very enthusiastic about reissuing it. It was kind of my orphan book.

Personally, I think that was one of the freest and happiest times of my life. I had never lived alone before, which I hadn't realized; I'd either lived with parents, husband, or children. I had hoped to have an adventure all mine as soon as my younger son went off to college. I dropped him at college in Worcester, Massachusetts, and just kept going, right on up to Nova Scotia, with my immigration papers. In Nova Scotia I had ten acres and an old house and barn. I raised my own vegetables and chopped wood—I had wood stoves. There was one severe storm and I was ready for it. I learned what I call problem-solving. It was tremendously creative. It's unfortunate that we change. After all, I wrote about change in *A New Kind of Country,* but I was there ten years, and it grew increasingly isolated. I realized that I had been supplying my own stimulation in many ways, and it was running thin; books and ideas weren't as accessible. I had to leave, and it was very painful.

CA: Your adult writing as well as the work for children reflects a distinct sympathy and respect for young people. Would you comment on your feelings about them and your concerns for them?

GILMAN: I think so many of us grow up wounded from our childhood. One of my books was *The Tightrope Walker,* which I enjoyed writing very much. The heroine in that was twenty-two. She'd had a very troubled childhood, and in the book she finds herself. I like writing about finding one's self—this sounds like the lost-and-found department! In a way I think that in writing Mrs. Pollifax, I'm still writing children's books, just more sophisticated, more polished. I think I'm sympathetic to the child in everyone.

CA: There's sometimes a rather arbitrary dividing line between children's and young adult books anyway.

GILMAN: That's true. I'm just looking now at a spin-off of *The Tightrope Walker—The Maze in the Heart of the Castle,* which was published by Doubleday in 1983 as a young-adult novel; they didn't know which to make it. I've had two letters in the last month from adult women who are asking now where they can get copies of that. I've only had one letter from a child. Most of the mail on that book has been from adults.

CA: Has there been talk of doing more of the books as movies or television plays?

GILMAN: Yes. It tends to come and go. But there's talk of a Pollifax miniseries, and it's gotten farther than usual. CBS has a script-writer developing it, and it will depend entirely on the script. It would be great fun to see one of these options happen.

CA: Does writing continue to be a great pleasure for you, as it would seem from the sense of fun you put into your books?

GILMAN: Well, lately I've been reading a number of biographies of writers, and I think that the people who say we write to stay sane are probably not too far off the track. I think Hemingway said it, Fitzgerald, Capote. I'm at a point now where I'm re-examining my life and trying to figure out where to settle for the rest of it, where to put down roots for my last years, so to speak, and write the couple of books I want very much to write. You don't write them dashing around too much. Some books are a great pleasure, and there are others that you feel you must write. Those are not as pleasurable; then it's craft. With those, I have to take pleasure in doing the best I can with craft. Then there are the books that really consume me, and the ideas don't arrive every day. I deliver my life to them and live inside of them. Then it's great; it's wonderful. It still happens. The book that's coming out in April, *Incident at Badamya,* is like that. That was wonderful fun to do.

CA: Beyond that book and the Pollifax you're working on, are there plans or ideas?

GILMAN: Nothing is concrete. I'm hoping that I will suddenly be struck by lightning one day—not literally but figuratively—with an idea that has to be developed.

MEDIA ADAPTATIONS: The Unexpected Mrs. Pollifax was filmed by United Artists in 1970 as "Mrs. Pollifax—Spy," starring Rosalind Russell.

BIOGRAPHICAL/CRITICAL SOURCES:

BOOKS

Reilly, John M., editor, *Twentieth-Century Crime and Mystery Writers,* second edition, St. James/St. Martin's, 1985.

PERIODICALS

Chicago Tribune, February 25, 1988.
New York Times, January 1, 1972.
New York Times Book Review, March 20, 1966, October 15, 1967, March 8, 1970.
Times Literary Supplement, February 23, 1967.

—*Interview by Jean W. Ross*

*   *   *

GIROUX, Henry A(rmand) 1943-

PERSONAL: Born September 18, 1943, in Providence, R.I.; son of Armand and Alice (Waldron) Giroux; married Jeanne Brady, January 6, 1979; children: Jack, Chris, Brett. *Education:* University of Maine, B.S., 1977; Appalachian State University, M.A., 1978; Carnegie-Mellon University, D.Arts, 1977.

ADDRESSES: Home—216 West High St., Oxford, Ohio 45056. *Office*—School of Education, Miami University, Oxford, Ohio 45056.

CAREER: High school history teacher in Barrington, R.I., 1968-75; Boston University, Boston, Mass., professor of education, 1977-83; Miami University, Oxford, Ohio, 1983—, began as associate professor, became professor of education and renown scholar in residence.

WRITINGS:

Ideology, Culture, and the Process of Schooling, Temple University Press, 1981.
(Editor with Anthony Penna and William Pinar) *Curriculum and Instruction: Alternatives in Education,* McCutchan, 1981.
Theory and Resistance in Education: A Pedagogy for the Opposition, J. F. Bergin, 1983.
Pedagogia radical: Subsidios (title means "Radical Pedagogy: A Beginning"), Editora Autores Associados, 1983.
(Editor with David Purpel) *The Hidden Curriculum and Moral Education,* McCutchan, 1983.
(With Michael Ryan) *Education Under Siege,* Bergin & Garvey, 1985.
School and the Struggle for Public Life, University of Minnesota Press, 1988.
Teachers as Intellectuals, Bergin and Garvey, 1988.
(Editor with Peter McLaren) *Critical Pedagogy, the State, and the Struggle for Culture,* State University of New York Press, 1989.
(Editor with Roger Simon) *Schooling, Popular Culture, and Everyday Life,* Bergin & Garvey, 1989.

Contributor to education and social theory journals.

SIDELIGHTS: Henry A. Giroux told *CA:* "My work has always been informed by the notion that it is imperative to make hope practical and despair unconvincing. My focus is primarily on schools and the roles they play in promoting both success and failure among different classes and groups of students. I am particularly interested in the way in which schools mediate—through both the overt and hidden curricula—those messages and values that serve to privilege some groups at the expense of others. By viewing schools as political and cultural sites as well as instructional institutions, I have tried in my writings to provide educators with the categories and forms of analyses that will help them to become more critical in their pedagogies and more visionary in their purposes. Schools are immensely important sites for constituting subjectivities, and I have and will continue to argue that we need to make them into models of critical learning, civic courage, and active citizenship."

*   *   *

GLOVER, Denis (James Matthews) 1912-1980
(Peter Kettle)

PERSONAL: Born December 10, 1912, in Dunedin, New Zealand; died August 8, 1980, in Wellington, New Zealand; son of Henry Lawrence (a dental surgeon) and Lyla (a writer; maiden name, Matthews) Glover; married Mary Granville, 1936; married Lyn Cameron, 1972; married third wife, Gladys Evelyn; children: (first marriage) Rupert. *Education:* Attended Christ's College, Cambridge; University of Canterbury, B.A., 1934. *Politics:* Socialist. *Religion:* Church of England.

CAREER: Author, poet, and typographer. *The Press,* Christchurch, New Zealand, reporter, 1932-34; Caxton Press, Christchurch, founder and managing director, 1934-51; University of Canterbury, Christchurch, instructor in English, 1936-38; Technical Correspondence Institute, Wellington, New Zealand, instructor in typography, 1960-68. Worked for Pegasus Press, Christchurch, 1953, and Wingfield Press, Wellington, 1955. Founder of literary journal, *Landfall,* 1947. Member, New Zealand State Literary Fund Committee. *Military service:* Served in the Royal Navy during World War II; commanded a landing craft during the D-Day invasion; became lieutenant commander; received Distinguished Service Cross.

MEMBER: International PEN (former president of New Zealand Center), Friends of Turnbull Library (former president), Wellington Poetry Society (patron), Canterbury University Council.

AWARDS, HONORS: Jesse Mackay Award for poetry, International PEN, 1960; Queen Elizabeth II grant, 1975; D.Litt., Victoria University of Wellington.

WRITINGS:

POEMS

Short Reflection on the Present State of Literature in This Country, Caxton Club (Christchurch, New Zealand), 1935.
(With Allen Curnow and Arthur Rex Dugard Fairburn) *Another Argo,* Caxton Club, 1935.
Thistledown, Caxton Club, 1935.
Six Easy Ways of Dodging Debt Collectors, Caxton Press, 1936.
(With others) *A Caxton Miscellany,* Caxton Press, 1937.
The Arraignments of Paris, Caxton Press, 1937.
Thirteen Poems, Caxton Press, 1939.
Cold Tongue, Caxton Press, 1939.
(With others) *Recent Poems,* Caxton Press, 1941.
The Wind and the Sand: Poems, 1934-44, Caxton Press, 1945.
Summer Flowers, Caxton Press, 1946.
Sings Harry, and Other Poems, Caxton Press, 1951.
Arowata Bill: A Sequence of Poems, Pegasus Press (Christchurch, New Zealand), 1953.
Since Then, Mermaid Press, 1957.
(With A. R. D. Fairburn) *Poetry Harbinger,* Pilgrim Press (Aukland), 1958.

Enter without Knocking: Selected Poems, Pegasus Press, 1964, augmented edition, 1972.
Sharp Edge Up: Verses and Satires, Blackwood and Janet Paul, 1968.
Myself When Young, Nag's Head Press, 1970.
To a Particular Woman, Nag's Head Press, 1970.
Diary to a Woman, Catspaw, 1971.
Dancing to My Tune, edited by Laurie Edmond, Catspaw, 1974.
Wellington Harbor, photography by Chris Black, Catspaw, 1974.
For Whom the Cock Crows, J. McIndoe, 1976.
Or Hawk of Basilisk, Catspaw, 1977.
Come High Water, Dunmore Press, 1977.
Clutha River, J. McIndoe, 1978.
To Friends in Russia, Nag's Head Press, 1979.
Towards Bands Peninsula: A Sequence, Pegasus Press, 1979.
Selected Poems, Penguin, 1981.

OTHER

(Editor with Ian Milner) *New Poems,* Caxton Club, 1934.
3 Short Stories, Caxton Press, 1936.
Till the Star Speak (short stories), Caxton Press, 1939.
D Day, Caxton Press, 1944.
(Editor) A. R. D. Fairburn, *The Disadvantages of Being Dead and Other Sharp Verses,* Mermaid Press, 1958.
A Clutch of Authors and a Clot, Wingfield Press, 1960.
(Editor) Merrill Moore, *Cross Currents,* Pegasus Press, 1961.
Hot Water Sailor (autobiography; also see below), A. H. and A. W. Reed, 1962.
Denis Glover's Bedside Book, by Himself (prose and poetry), A. H. and A. W. Reed, 1963.
(Editor) A. R. D. Fairburn, *Collected Poems,* Pegasus Press, 1966.
(Editor with Geoffrey Fairburn) A. R. D. Fairburn, *The Woman Problem and Other Prose,* Blackwood and Janet Paul, 1967.
The Men of God (prose), Dunmore, 1978.
Hot Water Sailor and Landlubber Ho, International Specialized Book Services, 1982.

Also author of screenplays "The Coaster," 1951, and (with John Lang) "Mick Stimson," 1972; author of radio play "They Sometimes Float at Sea," 1970. Contributor, sometimes under pseudonym Peter Kettle, to periodicals, including *Tomorrow, New Zealand Listener, Islands, Dominion, English New Writing,* and *Tribune.*

SIDELIGHTS: A devoted printer for whom writing was only an avocation, Denis Glover "could not abide what he called the 'pap' of fixed ideologies," according to his London *Times* obituary. Because of this belief, Glover founded his own publishing company and wrote his own prose and poetry in order to provide readers with an alternative to books that he considered commercialistic. Although his poetry was not progressive or modernistic, the *Times* writer noted that "no other New Zealand poet has caught with such compact and deft imagery and musicality the primary aspects of the country's land, mountain and seascape, and the way in which these work upon the mind and heart of the people."

AVOCATIONAL INTERESTS: Sailing.

OBITUARIES:

PERIODICALS

Times (London), September 12, 1980.*

GOLDBECK, David M. 1942-

PERSONAL: Born September 23, 1942, in New York, N.Y.; son of Kurt J. and Ilse (Weinberger) Goldbeck; married Nikki Schulman (a writer), December 14, 1969. *Education:* Queens College of the City University of New York, B.A., 1964; Brooklyn Law School, L.L.B., 1967. *Politics:* "The Bill of Rights and the Golden Rule."

ADDRESSES: Home—P.O. Box 87, Woodstock, N.Y. 12498. *Office*—Ceres Press, Box 87, Woodstock, N.Y. 12498.

CAREER: Elementary school teacher in New York, N.Y., 1967-70; admitted to the Bar of New York State, 1968; South Brooklyn Legal Services, Brooklyn, N.Y., assistant attorney in charge, 1969-71; Ceres Press, Woodstock, N.Y., co-founder, editor, and publisher, 1977—; founder, publisher, and editor, *True Food* newsletter, 1988—; free-lance writer.

WRITINGS:

WITH WIFE, NIKKI GOLDBECK

The Supermarket Handbook: Access to Whole Foods, Harper, 1973, expanded edition, New American Library, 1976.
The Good Breakfast Book, Links Books, 1975.
The Dieter's Companion: A Guide to Nutritional Self-Sufficiency, McGraw, 1975.
Nikki and David Goldbeck's American Wholefoods Cuisine: Over 1300 Meatless Wholesome Recipes from Short Order to Gourmet, New American Library, 1983.
The Goldbecks' Guide to Good Food, New American Library, 1987.
The Goldbecks' Short Order Cookbook, New American Library, 1988.

OTHER

Designing the Smart Kitchen, Ceres Press, 1989.

Contributor to *American Health, Practical Homeowner, Journal of Gastronomy, Vegetarian Times, Mother Earth News,* and *Garbage: The Journal of the Enviroment.*

SIDELIGHTS: David M. Goldbeck commented to *CA:* "We must preserve our ecology of foods just as we preserve our natural ecology." Goldbeck and his wife and co-author Nikki consider themselves "food ecologists," as he explained to Sally A. Lodge in *Publishers Weekly:* "Our study of nutrition has taught us that it's necessary to eat lots of different foods, since they all provide different nutrients in various combinations. And we're very concerned about the fact that our food supply is becoming so narrow. The philosophy behind our work, and specifically behind [*Nikki and David Goldbeck's American Wholefoods Cuisine: Over 1300 Meatless Wholesome Recipes from Short Order to Gourmet*], is to give people a style of cooking that is appealing and contemporary and that at the same time is good for them and good for the environment," the author continued. "This way we will be able to maintain the ecology of our food supply."

For more information, see entry for Nikki Goldbeck, also in this volume.

AVOCATIONAL INTERESTS: Refinishing old furniture, rebuilding his house and garden, running his four acres "like a homestead."

BIOGRAPHICAL/CRITICAL SOURCES:

PERIODICALS

Publishers Weekly, April 22, 1983.

GOLDBECK, Nikki 1947-

PERSONAL: Born March 16, 1947, in New York, N.Y.; daughter of Irwin and Florence (Fischer) Schulman; married David M. Goldbeck (a writer), December 14, 1969. *Education:* Cornell University, B.S., 1968; New School for Social Research, graduate study, 1968-69.

ADDRESSES: Home—P.O. Box 87, Woodstock, N.Y. 12498. *Office*—Ceres Press, Box 87, Woodstock, N.Y. 12498.

CAREER: Creative Food Services, Inc., New York City, free-lance worker in product development, 1967; D'Arcy Advertising Co., New York City, administrative assistant to account executive, 1968-69; Dudley-Anderson-Yutzy, New York City, public relations worker, 1969-71; Ceres Press, Woodstock, N.Y., co-founder, 1977—; food editor, *True Food* newsletter, 1988—; free-lance writer.

MEMBER: Omicron Nu.

WRITINGS:

WITH HUSBAND, DAVID M. GOLDBECK

The Supermarket Handbook: Access to Whole Foods, Harper, 1973, expanded edition, New American Library, 1976.
The Good Breakfast Book, Links Books, 1975.
The Dieter's Companion: A Guide to Nutritional Self-Sufficiency, McGraw, 1975.
Nikki and David Goldbeck's American Wholefoods Cuisine: Over 1300 Meatless Wholesome Recipes from Short Order to Gourmet, New American Library, 1983.
The Goldbecks' Guide to Good Food, New American Library, 1987.
The Goldbecks' Short Order Cookbook, New American Library, 1988.

OTHER

Cooking What Comes Naturally, Doubleday, 1972, revised edition, Ceres Press, 1981.
As You Eat, So Your Baby Grows: A Guide to Nutrition in Pregnancy, Ceres Press, 1977.

Contributor to *American Health, True Food, Mother Earth News,* and *Vegetarian Times.*

SIDELIGHTS: Nikki Goldbeck, who with husband and co-author David has sold over a million cookbooks, explained her long-time interest in the culinary arts to *Publishers Weekly*'s Sally A. Lodge: "I recognized that through cooking I could influence others and make a contribution to society." After receiving a degree in nutrition, Goldbeck at first "worked for a public relations firm that handled mostly food accounts," she related to Lodge. "As I began developing recipes and new products, I realized that most Americans get their knowledge about food from the food industry, from those who have a product to sell. And I thought that as an independent person I could do the same thing for foods that I believed have merit for other reasons than that they were going to benefit someone else's pocketbook." The result has been a series of books that emphasize nutrition and the prudent use of food supplies, including one volume that took ten years to develop, *Nikki and David Goldbeck's American Wholefoods Cuisine: Over 1300 Meatless Wholesome Recipes from Short Order to Gourmet.*

For more information, see entry for David M. Goldbeck, also in this volume.

BIOGRAPHICAL/CRITICAL SOURCES:

PERIODICALS

Publishers Weekly, April 22, 1983.

*   *   *

GOLDSTEIN, Rhoda L.
See BLUMBERG, Rhoda L(ois Goldstein)

*   *   *

GOLDSTEIN, Stephen R(obert) 1938-

PERSONAL: Born July 12, 1938, in Philadelphia, Pa.; immigrated to Israel, August 11, 1976; married; children: two. *Education:* University of Pennsylvania, A.B. (with highest honors), 1959, LL.B. (summa cum laude), 1962.

ADDRESSES: Home—School of Law, Hebrew University of Jerusalem, Mount Scopus, Jerusalem 91905, Israel.

CAREER: Wolf, Block, Schorr, and Solis-Cohen (law firm), Philadelphia, Pa., practicing attorney, 1962-64, 1965; law clerk to U.S. Supreme Court Justice Goldberg, 1964-65; University of Pennsylvania, Philadelphia, assistant professor, 1966-69, associate professor, 1969-72, professor of law, 1972-76; Hebrew University of Jerusalem, Jerusalem, Israel, Edward S. Silver Professor of Civil Procedure, 1976—, dean of faculty of law, 1987—. Visiting professor at University of California, Berkeley, 1970-71; visiting member of law faculty, Cambridge University, 1984; visiting fellow commoner, Trinity College. Director of Harry Sacher Institute for Legislative Research and Comparative Law. Member of advisory committee to the Minister of Justice on Civil Procedure.

MEMBER: International Association on Procedural Law, American Association of University Professors (general counsel, 1972-74), American Bar Association, American Law Institute, Institute of Judicial Administration, Juvenile Justice Standards Project.

WRITINGS:

(With Louis B. Schwartz) *Police Guidance Manuals: A Philadelphia Model,* Office of Law Enforcement Assistance, University of Pennsylvania, 1968.

Materials on School Law, School of Law, University of Pennsylvania, 1969.

(Contributor) Earl Phillips, editor, *Proceedings of the National Conference on the Teaching of Anti-Poverty Law,* Association of American Law Schools, 1969.

(With Schwartz) *Law Enforcement Handbook for Police,* West Publishing, 1970, 2nd edition, 1980.

Cases and Materials on Education Law, School of Law, University of Pennsylvania, 1972, revised edition, 1973.

Law and Public Education: Cases and Materials, Bobbs-Merrill, 1974, 2nd edition (with G. E. Gee), 1980.

(Compiler) *Impeachment: Miscellaneous Documents,* U.S. Government Printing Office, 1974.

(With William G. Buss) *Standards Relating to Schools and Education,* Ballinger, 1977.

(Editor) *Israeli Reports to the Tenth International Congress of Comparative Law,* Harry Sacher Institute for Legislative Research and Comparative Law, Hebrew University of Jerusalem, 1978.

(Editor) *Law and Equality in Education,* Jerusalem Van Leer Foundation, 1980.

(Editor) *Israeli Reports to the Eleventh International Congress of Comparative Law,* Harry Sacher Institute for Legislative

Research and Comparative Law, Hebrew University of Jerusalem, 1982.

(Editor) *Israeli Reports to the Twelfth International Congress of Comparative Law,* Harry Sacher Institute for Legislative Research and Comparative Law, Hebrew University of Jerusalem, 1986.

The Right to Education, Israeli Association for Civil Rights, 1989.

Contributor to *American Jewish Yearbook, Yearbook of School Law,* and to law journals. Former research editor of *University of Pennsylvania Law Review.*

WORK IN PROGRESS: Studies in comparative civil procedure, including preliminary relief, expedition of the litigation process, protection of diffused and collective interests, and enforcement of court orders.

*   *   *

GOPALAKRISHNAN, Chennat 1936-

PERSONAL: Born October 9, 1936, in Elankunnapuzha, Kerala, India; immigrated to the United States, 1963, naturalized citizen, 1976; son of Palliyil Narayana Menon (a banker) and Chennat Sarada Amma Gopalakrishnan; married wife, Malini (a university junior specialist), September 15, 1962; children: Shalini (daughter). *Education:* University of Kerala, B.S., 1955, M.S., 1957; Montana State University, Ph.D., 1967.

ADDRESSES: Home—2333 Kapiolani Blvd., Apt. 1101, Honolulu, Hawaii 96826. *Office*—Department of Agricultural and Resource Economics, University of Hawaii at Manoa, 3050 Maile Way, Gilmore 115, Honolulu, Hawaii 96822.

CAREER: National Council of Applied Economic Research, New Delhi, India, researcher, 1958-61; *Economic Times,* Bombay, India, senior researcher, 1961-63; Montana State University, Bozeman, assistant professor of agricultural and resource economics, 1967-69; University of Hawaii at Manoa, Honolulu, associate professor, 1969-74, professor of agricultural and resource economics, 1974—, professor of social sciences at Law of the Sea Institute, 1978. Visiting professor at University of Southern California, 1976-77, and University of Wyoming, 1982-83. Chairman of organizing committee of International Conference on Ocean Resource Development in the Pacific, 1981; consultant to Gas Research Institute of Chicago, Oceanic Institute of Honolulu, and Argonne National Laboratory.

MEMBER: International Association of Energy Economics, International Agricultural Economics Association, American Agricultural Economics Association, Association of Environmental and Resource Economists, American Water Resources Association, Policy Studies Organization, Marine Technology Society, Western Agricultural Economics Association.

AWARDS, HONORS: Senior fellowship at Honolulu's East-West Food Institute, 1974; outstanding researcher award for research and writings in energy and marine economics, Gamma Sigma Delta, 1980; Marine Technology Society award, 1981; national fellowship, University of Wisconsin—Madison, 1988; International Award for Distinguished Service to Agriculture, 1989.

WRITINGS:

(Contributor) William Lockeretz, editor, *Energy and Agriculture,* Academic Press, 1977.

Natural Resources and Energy: Theory and Policy, Ann Arbor Science Publishers, 1980.

(With Neal Patrick and Marilyn Altobello) *Energy in Western Agriculture,* Hawaii Institute of Tropical Agriculture and Human Resources, University of Hawaii, 1981.

(Editor) *The Emerging Marine Economy of the Pacific,* Butterworths, 1984.

(Contributor) Norman Whittlesey, editor, *Energy and Water Management in Western Irrigated Agriculture,* Westview Press, 1986.

(With John Sisson) *Economic Impact of Ocean Research Funding on the State of Hawaii,* Sea Grant College Study on Marine Economics, University of Hawaii, 1987.

(With R. Bowen and K. Samples) *A Review and Critique of the Socioeconomic Impact Assessment for the Kahe Point OTEC Facility,* Argonne National Laboratory, 1988.

(Contributor) Manas Chatterji, editor, *Technology Transfer in the Developing Countries,* Macmillan, 1989.

Contributor of about sixty articles and reviews to energy, agricultural, and economic journals in the United States and India. Member of editorial board, Hawaii Institute of Tropical Agriculture and Human Resources, 1980-82.

WORK IN PROGRESS: Natural Resources, Economic Growth, and Quality of Life; Studies in Energy Economics and Policy.

SIDELIGHTS: Chennat Gopalakrishnan told *CA:* "The role of natural resources and energy in the context of economic growth, both at the micro and macro levels, has recently begun to engage the serious attention of scholars, policymakers, planners, and even laymen. This resurgence of interest in a vital, although heretofore somewhat neglected, area is largely the result of increasingly critical energy shortages and natural resources scarcities, which pose a serious threat to continued economic growth. One of the more important spin-offs of the scholarly concern with natural resources and energy is the identification and delineation of specific issues and problems for in-depth critical scrutiny—something that had not been attempted until recently in any sustained fashion, except for random studies by an occasional interested scholar.

"*Natural Resources and Energy: Theory and Policy* was a modest attempt to fill this gap. The nine chapters in the book represent a synthesis of theoretical insights and empirical research on some frontier issues in the natural resources and energy field. The problems examined are wide-ranging in scope and diversity. In spite of the importance and relevance of these problems, very few attempts have been made in the past to explore the topics discussed in this book in terms of theory as well as practice. In that sense, my book is an original contribution to a rapidly-growing field of increasing importance.

"*The Emerging Marine Economy of the Pacific* brings together a multidisciplinary team of marine scientists, resource planners, and policy analysts to examine the key issues involved in tapping the ocean economic potential of the Pacific Basin. There are currently few books on the market which attempt to do this. The book explores in depth a diversity of issues such as fuel from ocean thermal conversion; economics, technology, and policy of manganese nodule mining; impact of the exploitation of new ocean resources on the developing countries of the Pacific; economic potential of marine recreation; radio-active waste disposal in the Pacific Basin; ocean and the quality of life; and possible marine resource development scenarios for Micronesia and Polynesia. Local, national, and international contexts of the Pacific Basin's marine resource development and management are examined. Institutional and cultural dimensions of resource development are studied in detail. Theoretical discussions are sup-

ported by empirical research findings and illustrated by case studies.

"While researching and writing the two books cited above I became acutely aware of the fact that the key role of culture in economic development and quality of life has received comparatively little attention in theoretical and/or empirical investigations by economists. The preoccupation of economists with quantification, measurement, and the ascribing of monetary values to output (e.g., per capita income or per capita GNP) has often prompted them to exclude from their studies a careful consideration of such crucial components of culture as institutions, values, and laws in the complex dynamics of economic development. The omission or exclusion of these important unpriced cultural variables had led to a 'culturally-deprived' theory of economic development, lacking both in realism and relevance. My growing discontent with such an approach has spurred the search for alternate analytical paradigms where these unpriced variables would be accorded due importance. The two books I am currently working on—*Natural Resources, Economic Growth, and Quality of Life* and *Studies in Energy Economics and Policy*—attempt to explore the dominant and decisive role of culture in the context of economic development, economic well-being, and quality of life.

"As an economist and a writer, I firmly believe that the notion of an 'economic man' is a figment of one's imagination and is not grounded in reality. The mindless pursuit of economic efficiency at the expense of economic well-being could easily lead to one's losing the forest for the trees. Perhaps my philosophy is best summarized by a statement by political economist Rexford Guy Tugwell to the effect that 'an economist who's simply an economist is a poor, pretty fish!' "

*   *   *

GORDON, Gary
   See EDMONDS, I(vy) G(ordon)

*   *   *

GOREY, Edward (St. John) 1925-
   (Eduard Blutig, Drew Dogyear, Mrs. Regera Dowdy, Wardore Edgy, Raddory Gewe, Roy Grewdead, Redway Grode, O. Mude, Edward Pig, E. D. Ward, Ogdred Weary, Dreary Wodge, Dogear Wryde)

PERSONAL: Born February 22, 1925, in Chicago, Ill.; son of Edward Leo (a newspaperman) and Helen (Garvey) Gorey. *Education:* Harvard University, A.B., 1950; attended Art Institute of Chicago.

ADDRESSES: Home—Box 146, Yarmouth Port, Mass. 02675.

CAREER: Writer, illustrator, and designer. Employed in art department of Doubleday & Co., Inc., New York City, 1953-60. Gorey's illustrations have been shown in museums and galleries, including Graham Gallery, New York City, and Yale University Library, both 1974. *Military service:* U.S. Army, 1943-46.

AWARDS, HONORS: Best Illustrated Book of the Year award, *New York Times,* 1969, for illustrations of Edward Lear's *Dong with the Luminous Nose,* and 1971, for illustrations of Florence Parry Heide's *The Shrinking of Treehorn; The Shrinking of Treehorn* was named best picture book at Bologna Children's Book Fair, 1977; Antoinette Perry ("Tony") Award, 1978, for costume design of the Broadway revival "Dracula."

WRITINGS:

SELF ILLUSTRATED

The Unstrung Harp; or, Mr. Earbrass Writes a Novel (also see below), Duell, Sloan & Pearce/Little, Brown, 1953.

The Listing Attic (also see below), Duell, Sloan & Pearce/Little, Brown, 1954.

The Doubtful Guest (also see below), Doubleday, 1957, reprinted, Dodd, 1978.

The Object-Lesson (also see below), Doubleday, 1958.

(Compiler) *The Haunted Looking Glass: Ghost Stories,* Looking Glass Library, 1959, reprinted as *Edward Gorey's Haunted Looking Glass: Ghost Stories,* Crown, 1984.

The Bug Book (also see below), Epstein & Carroll, 1960, reprinted, Adama Books, 1987.

The Fatal Lozenge (also see below), Obolensky, 1960 (published in England as *The Gorey Alphabet,* Constable, 1960).

The Hapless Child (also see below), Obolensky, 1961, reprinted, Dodd, 1980.

(Under pseudonym Ogdred Weary) *The Curious Sofa* (also see below), Obolensky, 1961, reprinted, Dodd, 1980.

(Under pseudonym Ogdred Weary) *The Beastly Baby,* Fantod Press, 1962.

The Willowdale Handcar; or, The Return of the Black Doll (also see below), Bobbs-Merrill, 1962, reprinted, Dodd, 1979.

The Gashlycrumb Tinies (also see below), Simon & Schuster, 1962, reprinted, Beaufort Books (New York), 1986.

The Vinegar Works (includes *The Gashlycrumb Tinies, The Insect God,* and *The West Wing;* also see below), Simon & Schuster, 1963.

The Wuggly Ump (also see below), Lippincott, 1963, reprinted, Adama Books, 1986.

15 Two: or, The Nursery Frieze, Fantod Press, 1964.

The Sinking Spell (also see below), Obolensky, 1964.

The Remembered Visit: A Story Taken from Life (also see below), Simon & Schuster, 1965.

The Inanimate Tragedy, Fantod Press, 1966.

The Gilded Bat, Simon & Schuster, 1966.

(Under pseudonym Eduard Blutig) *The Evil Garden,* Fantod Press, 1966.

(Under pseudonym Mrs. Regera Dowdy) *The Pious Infant,* Fantod Press, 1966.

The Utter Zoo Alphabet, Dutton, 1967.

(With Victoria Chess) *Fletcher and Zenobia,* Meredith Corp., 1967.

The Other Statue, Simon & Schuster, 1968.

The Blue Aspic, Meredith Corp., 1968.

The Epiplectic Bicycle, Dodd, 1968.

The Secrets, Simon & Schuster, 1968.

The Deranged Cousins: or, Whatever, Fantod Press, 1969.

The Iron Tonic: or, A Winter Afternoon in Lonely Valley, Albondonaci Press, 1969.

(Under pseudonym Raddory Gewe) *The Eleventh Episode,* Fantod Press, 1969.

(With Peter F. Neumeyer) *Donald and the . . .,* Young Scott Books, 1969, reprinted, Borgo, 1988.

(With Neumeyer) *Donald Has a Difficulty,* Fantod Press, 1970.

(With Neumeyer) *Why We Have Day and Night,* Young Scott Books, 1970, reprinted, Borgo, 1989.

The Osbick Bird, Fantod Press, 1970.

The Chinese Obelisks: Fourth Alphabet, Fantod Press, 1970.

The Sopping Thursday, Gotham Book Mart, 1970, reprinted, Borgo Press, 1988.

(With Chess) *Fletcher and Zenobia Save the Circus,* Dodd, 1971.

The Disrespectful Summons, Fantod Press, 1971.

(Translator) Alphonse Allais, *Story for Sara: What Happened to a Little Girl,* Albondocani Press, 1971.

(Under pseudonym Edward Pig) *The Untitled Book,* Fantod Press, 1971.

The Awdrey-Gore Legacy, Dodd, 1972, reprinted, Beaufort Books (New York), 1988.

Leaves from a Mislaid Album, Gotham Book Mart, 1972.

The Abandoned Sock, Fantod Press, 1972.

Amphigorey (includes *The Unstrung Harp, The Listing Attic, The Doubtful Guest, The Object-Lesson, The Bug Book, The Fatal Lozenge, The Hapless Child, The Curious Sofa, The Willowdale Handcar, The Gashlycrumb Tinies, The Insect God, The West Wing, The Wuggly Ump, The Sinking Spell,* and *The Remembered Visit*), Putnam, 1972.

The Lavender Leotard: or, Going a Lot to the New York City Ballet, Gotham Book Mart, 1973.

A Limerick, Salt-Works Press, 1973.

Category: Fifty Drawings, Gotham Book Mart, 1973, reprinted as *Cat E Gory,* Adama Books, 1986.

The Lost Lions, Fantod Press, 1973.

The Glorious Nosebleed: Fifth Alphabet, Dodd, 1974.

The Listing Attic [and] *The Unstrung Harp,* Abelard Schumann, 1975.

Amphigorey Too (anthology), Putnam, 1975.

L'Heure bleue, Fantod Press, 1975.

The Broken Spoke, Dodd, 1976.

Gorey x 3: Drawings by Edward Gorey, Addison-Wesley, 1976.

The Loathsome Couple, Dodd, 1977.

The Fantod Words, ten volumes, Diogenes (Zurich), 1978.

Gorey Endings: A Calendar for 1978, Workman, 1978.

The Green Beads, Albondocani Press, 1978.

(With Larry Evans) *Gorey Games,* Troubadour Printing, 1979.

Dracula: A Toy Theatre, Scribner, 1979.

Gorey Posters, Abrams, 1979.

Dancing Cats and Neglected Murderesses, Workman, 1980.

Le Melange, Gotham Book Mart, 1981.

Melange Funeste, Gotham Book Mart, 1981.

The Dwindling Party, Random House, 1982.

The Water Flowers, Congdon & Weed, 1982.

Gorey Cats: Paper Dolls, Troubadour Press, 1982.

(With Howard Moss) *Instant Lives,* Avon, 1982.

The Prune People, Albondocani Press, 1983.

(Under pseudonym E. D. Ward) *A Mercurial Bear,* Gotham Book Mart, 1983.

The Eclectic Abecedarium, Bromer, 1983.

Amphigorey Also (anthology), Congdon & Weed, 1983.

The Tunnel Calamity, Putnam, 1984.

Les Echanges Malandreux, Metacom, 1985.

The Insect God, Beaufort Books (New York), 1986.

The Raging Tide: or, The Black Doll's Imbroglio, Beaufort Books (New York), 1987.

Also author of *The Fantod Pack of Edward Gorey,* Owl Press.

OTHER

The Black Doll (filmscript), Gotham Book Mart, 1973.

"Tinned Lettuce, or The New Musical" (musical revue), music by David Aldrich, first produced in New York by New York University's Tisch School of the Arts, April, 1985.

Illustrator of numerous books, including Edward Lear's *The Jumblies,* Young Scott Books, 1968, Lear's *The Dong with the Luminous Nose,* Young Scott Books, 1969, Florence Parry Heide's *The Shrinking of Treehorn,* Holiday House, 1971, and T. S. Eliot's *Old Possum's Book of Practical Cats,* Harcourt, 1982; also illustrator of title sequence animation for PBS's "Mystery" television series, and of numerous book jackets, posters, and magazines. Designer of sets for productions of "Les Ballets Trockadero de Monte Carlo," 1977, and of sets and costumes for the musical "Dracula," and adaptation "Gorey's Stories," both 1978. Contributor of cartoons to periodicals, including *New York Times, Sports Illustrated,* and *Esquire.*

SIDELIGHTS: "Stepping into the bizarre world of Edward Gorey is a deceptive and dangerous experience: one is lured by the surface coziness of overstuffed Victorian rooms and staid Edwardian figures, only to be swept off-balance by a sinister tug of the rug," asserts *Newsweek*'s David Ansen. "It's a spectral milieu delicately poised between decorum and decadence." Works such as *The Doubtful Guest, The Hapless Child, The Beastly Baby,* and *The Loathsome Couple* combine detailed illustrations with "tales of unlucky adventure, disaster and betrayal," as Elizabeth Janeway describes them in the *New York Times Book Review.* While his work has been called macabre or eccentric, "it's hopeless to write about Gorey in terms of what his work seems to be about," the critic claims, "hopeless to stick labels on. Black comedy? The term is at once too broad and too narrow. Parody? But he's parodying more than the apparent butt of the joke. And to say that he's so funny that aficionados fall about laughing when re-reading him for the 20th time is true, but not a description."

Indeed, Gorey's work has defied critics' classifications for over thirty years; *Detroit Free Press* contributor Colin Covert terms the author's work "spooky little editions that are not children's books, comic books, nor fine art, but something in a league all its own." In the typical Gorey tale, "prose or verse [are] accompanied by exquisitely fine-lined pen and inks," Susan Stark relates in the *Detroit News,* creating "a world where, invariably, the worst happens. His people, all with small eyes and prominent noses, all Victorians by their dress and attitude, inflict or suffer grievous pain." The result "gives off an emanation of horror, a suggestion of the unnatural, a whiff of rot," notes *New Republic* contributor Gerald Weales. "This is not to be taken seriously, of course, but the *frisson* is supposed to be there, just under the laugh." Martin Gottfried presents a similar assessment in the *Saturday Review:* "Gorey more or less bases his humor on the contrast between perfect manners (the *style* of behavior) and immorality, sexual perversion, and sadism (a somewhat extreme *content* of behavior)."

While the author has claimed in *People* that many of his books are "intended for children primarily," children very frequently find themselves the targets of Gorey's unique sense of humor. D. Keith Mano remarks in *People* that Gorey "would make W. C. Fields sound like Father of the Year," explaining that children "are swallowed by huge cats or carried off by large bugs. In his work the infant mortality rate is higher than it was in 1556." *The Hapless Child,* for example, recounts the trials of Charlotte Sophia, who is orphaned, sold to a drunken brute, forced to make paper flowers until she goes blind, and is eventually run over by a carriage containing her lost father. And *The Gashlycrumb Tinies* offers this alphabetical catalog of infanticide: "A is for Amy who fell down the stairs/ B is for Basil assaulted by bears. . . . U is for Una who slipped down a drain/ V is for Victor squashed under a train." The author explained to *Publishers Weekly* interviewer Sally A. Lodge that young victims lend themselves to his brand of humor: "I tend to use children in my books, not symbolically really, but it's much easier to do all this overdone pathos business with children."

Although Gorey has intended some of his work for children, he has gathered a remarkable cult following among adults; first editions of his work—which he avoids reprinting except in his "Amphigorey" anthologies—have become valuable collectors' items. Nevertheless, the author continues to write independently, without specific readers in mind, as he told Lodge: "What does [a cult following] mean to me? I'd say very, very little. On the other hand it means that people think of me as their private discovery, which I guess is sort of nice. It's kind of flattering but I don't think it has much to do with anything. It certainly doesn't mean anything to me in terms of how I work," Gorey explained; "I don't really have any sense of audience. I really try not to think of my work except insofar as I'm doing it." As a result of "working quite perversely to please himself," as *New Yorker* critic Edmund Wilson maintains, Gorey "has created a whole little personal world, equally amusing and sombre, nostalgic at the same time as claustrophobic, at the same time poetic and poisoned."

Other critics agree that Gorey's work is highly inventive, due to its frequent twisting of visual and literary conventions. *Commentary* contributor John Hollander, for instance, states that Gorey, whom he calls "a major graphic artist," is "no mere pasticheur, and yet most of his work is trivially or deeply parodic. His pseudo-Victorian fictions and verses provide materials to illustrate in pseudo-Victorian ways," the critic elaborates, "and yet his originality is profound." Gorey has admitted the influence of various art forms; in *Conversations with Writers* he commented to Robert Dahlin that "sometimes I will take about equally from life, or from other artwork, or another book. . . . Sometimes it's dance; sometimes it's movies; sometimes it's other books; sometimes it's pictures. It may be verbal; it may be visual." The author added that while "I tend to be very imitative . . . no matter how hard you try to [imitate something], of course, eventually you wander off on something completely different." These differences, "because they are conscious, designed comments on life made by a subtle and powerful mind," observes Janeway, " . . . transmute mere representation into art; minor art, perhaps, but authentic and totally individual."

Janeway proposes that these subtle alterations of convention or expectation heighten the unsettling effect of the author's work: "Gorey's messages to the readers, then, are conveyed by his style, by his content of text and not-always-consonant content of drawings," the critic writes, "but most of all by the tension with which these elements attract and repel each other." Gorey himself, however, believes that it is his attempts to approach the conventional that make his work interesting, as he noted to Lodge: "Obviously I'm somewhat eccentric as an artist, but I think you should try to be as middle-of-the-road as you can be. If you see yourself going off the rails you should try to pull yourself back to a kind of norm, which I do try to do. . . . I think that where people consciously try to pull themselves off the track, it doesn't work," he explained. "The tension comes from spinning off and then trying to get yourself back."

"Edward Gorey, the craftsman of numerous little books for the child and childlike, is a unique figure in contemporary literature," comments Douglas Street in a *Dictionary of Literary Biography* essay. Although "his drawings easily rank him with the most respected children's illustrators, [his] little books show that he also deserves recognition as this century's heir-apparent to the great tradition of Heinrich Hoffmann and Edward Lear—two of the nineteenth century's most esteemed practitioners of nonsense literature for children." The critic concludes that similar to the best books of these artists, with Gorey's work "it is often hard to discern between the children's tale and the adult's. The most whimsical of Gorey's children's tales seem quite adult; while many of his adult pieces exude the devilish merriment only allowable in the fantastical confines of childhood." Gorey, however, doesn't believe he should be considered an author of fantastic or macabre literature. As he told *Newsweek:* "What I'm really interested in is everyday life. It's dreadfully hazardous. I never could understand why people always feel they have to climb Mount Everest when you know it's quite dangerous getting out of bed."

MEDIA ADAPTATIONS: Eighteen of Gorey's works were adapted as a musical revue and produced in New York as "Gorey's Stories" in 1978; *The Vinegar Works,* comprised of *The Gashlycrumb Tinies, The Insect God,* and *The West Wing,* was adapted for the theatre and produced in London in 1989.

AVOCATIONAL INTERESTS: Cats, movies, opera, concerts, country cooking, ballet, book collecting.

CA INTERVIEW

CA interviewed Edward Gorey by telephone on November 4, 1988, at his home in Yarmouth Port, Massachusetts.

CA: You told D. Keith Mano for People *that you taught yourself to read when you were three-and-a-half years old. Can you remember when you started to write, and what kinds of things you wrote first?*

GOREY: Oh God, no. Probably I started in high school. I wasn't writing seriously, exactly, but I have a vague recollection of writing things apart from school assignments. I don't remember what they were.

CA: I'm curious about how your drawing and writing became linked. Were you drawing from an early age?

GOREY: Yes. I think every child does. A couple of years ago, after my mother died, I was going through batches of stuff that she had saved. There were lots of drawings I had done as a child, and they showed no talent whatever. I saved a few pieces that didn't seem too bad. The first drawings I have that were dated were done when I was two-and-a-half. But children are encouraged to draw. I don't think I became more serious about it than anybody else until I got into high school.

CA: So the drawing became more serious about the time the writing did.

GOREY: Yeah, though *serious* is not the word I would apply. I just did these drawings, and I suppose somewhere along the line I separated myself from the other people who were drawing; I became serious in the sense that I kept doing it when other people my age had stopped doing it very much.

CA: You didn't have any formal training, then, before you went to the Art Institute of Chicago?

GOREY: No, and I only went to the Art Institute very briefly. I think of myself as largely self-taught. Whenever I did take any courses, I didn't absorb very much from them.

CA: Did you sit down with engravings in books, or other models, and try to do something similar?

GOREY: I was very much fascinated by nineteenth-century book illustrations, the black-and-white engravings and things of that sort. I suppose in a way I tried to imitate them, but I've never been very good at imitating anything, so it came out different.

CA: In the People *article I quoted earlier, Mano referred to your "obsession with the boater-hatted past." Is that as accurate as your books would indicate?*

GOREY: Oh, no. The more I did it, the more it became self-perpetuating. And the drawings themselves are not really that style. They're quite inaccurate by those standards, and a terrible hodgepodge of this thing and that. I just take from whatever strikes me.

CA: Generally, I understand, it has been your practice to finish writing a book before you begin the illustrations for it.

GOREY: Yeah. A couple of times I got carried away and started doing the drawings before the book was finished. Total catastrophe ensued. I find it very difficult to work any other way than to have the finished book first. I think of myself primarily as a writer anyway, and the writing is what's holding the whole thing up. I can't somehow think of doing the drawings for a book and then writing the text to go with them—though I might try it sometime just to see what happens.

CA: Does a drawing or set of drawings often give you the idea for a story?

GOREY: About half my books start from visual ideas, and half from words. The very little thing that starts me off might be a sketch I do, but I would then push it away and start thinking in terms of words.

CA: How do you feel about illustrating other people's writing as compared to illustrating your own?

GOREY: I usually feel very annoyed. Unfortunately, the things that I've been most successful with have been other people's, like "Dracula" and T. S. Eliot's *Old Possum's Book of Practical Cats,* neither one of which am I any great admirer of. For one thing, I don't think that book is Mr. Eliot's best work. And it was difficult to illustrate because sometimes, within the same verse, he would treat the cats anthropomorphically and also just as cats. So I felt I was walking a tightrope as to which to make them, trying to combine in my drawings cats as cats and cats as people. That was a technical problem.

CA: Speaking of cats, I know how they love to sit on whatever their people are working on. Since you always have cats around, does that create a problem for you?

GOREY: Oh God, yes. They tend to get up on the drawing board and then I have to clear a little space. They're also great for knocking over the ink bottle, which has sometimes resulted in their wrecking almost-finished drawings. A slash of the tail, and over goes the ink bottle.

CA: Probably deliberate, too.

GOREY: Probably. Cats are capable of anything.

CA: The names of your characters are marvelously bizarre, and somehow just right. Do they come to you out of the blue, or are they the result of a lot of work?

GOREY: Sometimes they just come to me. I tend to pick up a lot of names by coming across something that isn't really a name but will work as a name, and I jot them down. I tend to keep lots of notebooks—which I almost never refer to, of course. That's one of those things. I can't bear not to write anything down, but I almost never make use of it. Sometimes I will go combing through everything looking for an idea I jotted down years earlier. It's all very messy.

CA: Has the experience of publishing some of your own books made it harder in any way for you to work with publishers?

GOREY: No. In a way I've been very lucky with publishers. I just have one editor now, though he's been with various publishing houses over the last twenty or twenty-five years. I published with a lot of different publishers in the beginning. Everybody thought they'd gotten on to somebody who was going to make a lot of money but then that didn't happen and they'd decide, Oh, forget it. But, except for one period of about two years very early on, I've never been without a publisher. And I suppose that now, if something happened to the publishers I have, I'd probably find a publisher for anything I did if I scrounged around enough. But nobody has ever had the temerity to try and edit me, fortunately. It's always been a sort of lukewarm relationship. They'll publish the book and they won't promote it very much, but on the other hand they won't try to tell me what to do. In that respect I think it's been fine. I don't really believe in editing or anything like that.

CA: Your relationship with the Gotham Book Mart has obviously been very important in your career.

GOREY: Oh, yes. I'd be somewhere else completely if it weren't for them.

CA: You've said you don't spend as much time in New York City now as you used to.

GOREY: That's true. As a matter of fact, I had a rent-controlled apartment in New York, which I still have until the end of the month. About fifteen years ago the landlord tried to get it away from me and I managed to keep possession of it. But they started up again about six months ago, and they were going to haul me to court. I realized that I was going to New York less and less. The days are over when I was going to every performance of the New York City Ballet and their schedule determined when I was going to be in New York and when I was going to be up here. After George Balanchine died, I gave up the New York City Ballet. So I don't get to New York much anymore, and I decided I would let them have their little nasty, falling-apart apartment back.

I'm not going to have a base in New York now, so I'll probably never get down there again. I find it more and more spooky every time I go down there, and there are fewer things I want to do. I was just down last week arranging to move my stuff out. There are more people lying around in the street, more people talking to themselves. I still don't worry about where I'm going there or what I'm doing, as far as danger is concerned. I've really been lucky; only once did anybody ever try to break into my apartment and succeed. But practically everybody I know has been mugged a couple of times. And I never really liked New York all that much; I liked what you could do there. I actually only lived there for about ten years. The last twenty-five, I've spent more than half the year up here on the Cape, and I always felt the Cape was where I was living rather than New York.

CA: Back to the ballet for a moment, I've read that you didn't fall in love with it until you were thirty. What was the magic it held for you?

GOREY: I'd been going to ballet as such since I was about twelve. I had seen a few Balanchine ballets, but I hadn't liked them very much because I'd grown up on entirely other things. But all my friends were great devotees of the New York City Ballet, and when I first moved to New York, in the winter of 1953, I got dragged off to see the performances. I got hooked fairly quickly and I began going to every performance, since that was

easier than trying to decide which nine out of ten I was going to. It really wasn't so much ballet; it was George Balanchine. I felt he was the ballet equivalent of Mozart, at least, and I couldn't get enough of him and his company. When he died, though I heard for a while afterward that they were still dancing as well as before, somehow the whole meaning began dropping out of it for me, and now the company doesn't interest me that much anymore. I've hardly been this last couple of years.

CA: In the past you've made various comments on your feelings about children, in response to questions triggered by the awful things that happen to them in some of your books—some of your funniest books, I might add. How do you really feel about children?

GOREY: I don't really feel about children much at all. I don't know any children as children; I never have. It's obviously more awful for something to happen to a tiny little figure than to somebody full-grown. Nothing serious should be deduced about my attitude towards children from what I put them through. But I don't tend to think of my work as being as strange as everybody else does. Every now and then somebody completely baffles me by telling me that *The Curious Sofa* is their seven-year-old child's favorite story, and I think, What? Obviously children have no idea what it's about, but that doesn't bother them. Of course it never bothered me that I never understood a great many things. A lot of my favorite stuff, I don't really know what it's about.

CA: You've said previously that you were reading Victor Hugo at the age of eight and that you admire Jane Austen and Anthony Trollope. Are there current writers whose work you enjoy reading?

GOREY: Let me see: who is still alive that I like? The last few months I've been reading through all the "Dr. Who" books. I've read something over a hundred now, and I have about thirty to go. I love Dr. Who. But I don't think there's anybody writing now who's as congenial to me as Jane Austen or Trollope.

CA: Many people know your work from the lead-in to Public Television's "Mystery" series. Are you doing any other work for television now, or contemplating doing any?

GOREY: I would like to if somebody ever gave me the opportunity. Now that we have cable on the Cape, I'm planted in front of the television more hours than I care to tell you.

CA: From time to time your art work is shown at galleries. Do you have any bad feelings about parting with drawings when they're sold?

GOREY: I had two exhibitions years ago which I actually did work for, and I do etchings and things like that occasionally. But I have hung on to all of the drawings for my books. They have been exhibited a lot, but I don't really like to exhibit them; I think they were drubbed up for books and not to be put on walls. So I have hung on to all of them hoping to sell them to some college or museum for a sum to get me through my old age. That's sort of in the works now; Gotham is seriously trying to get a buyer for them. I have sold very little of my stuff, just the things I did for exhibitions, and I didn't really mind that because I knew that's what I was doing them for.

CA: Are you drawing now for anything besides books?

GOREY: A friend of mine is doing a ballet of *The Gilded Bat,* to be done by Ballet West in Salt Lake, which I'm designing. And

I'm rewriting the text to make it work for ballet. A couple of years ago, with a girl who lives over in Woods Hole, I did a musical revue from some of my unpublished stuff. She's now in New York and we're hoping to get that or the equivalent of it going Off-Broadway. If that takes place, I'll be redesigning it.

CA: How do you feel about designing sets as compared to doing small drawings?

GOREY: I think I've said before that, had my life been different, I probably would have ended up in the theater or movies. But nobody ever encouraged me in that line, so I ended up doing what I do. In a way, though, I'm not really temperamentally suited to the theater or movies because of the collaborative work involved and the endless sitting around. Actually, I had fun two years ago when we were doing this revue I mentioned. I used to go to Woods Hole every night, and I saw all the rehearsals. The sets and costumes were very minimal, but I was there to say what looked right and what didn't. With most of the things I've done, I've had very little opportunity to do that. I did see "Dracula," but I've done four or five other things that I never even saw, so I have no idea whether they looked right finally.

CA: I guess there's often the feeling that they aren't yours anymore.

GOREY: They aren't mine anymore, and it gets frustrating. When I was working on "Dracula," for instance—of course I had no experience—I used to go back and forth between New York and the Cape. I'd go down to the costume people and give them sketches, and they would show me fabrics. Several times I said, "I don't think that's right for this," and they would say, "It'll be perfectly all right; wait until you see it under the lights." Well, when I saw it under the lights, it wasn't what I had in mind. But since everybody was treating me as an inspired nincompoop, as it were, I never argued. That's probably unfair; they were professional people. But I realized that, as far as I was concerned, my eye was better than theirs—though, on the whole, they did an extraordinary job of executing "Dracula."

In a way I don't understand how people do theater all the time. There are so many intangibles in any production, you wonder how anything ever comes out at all. Ideally, when I've done a theater project, I would love to have been there twenty-four hours a day and flung myself into it, but it was never possible. I was always completely dependent on other people's ideas for execution. What I have seen, I've felt was dandy. This one we did two years ago was about the fifth adaptation of my work to the stage. The adaptations started with "Gorey's Stories" back in 1978. It originated with a young man at the University of Kentucky and he took it to New York to peddle around. There was an Off-Broadway production, and I wasn't even going to go, but everybody persuaded me that I should see what it was like. I went with extreme reluctance, and I laughed about five minutes when I was appalled with my words coming out of people's mouths, but I loved it. When people talk about story theater, I cringe. But, at least as far as I was concerned, I thought my stuff worked very well on the stage, and practically anything could be turned into a revue. That first one was from published books, but I've now done three others that were from unpublished stuff. I had great fun working on them. They are kind of fun to see on the stage, if you like that sort of thing. I've never really liked my work once I've got done with it, but I discovered this was a way of being able to enjoy it later.

CA: As I've read your books through the years, I've had the feeling that drawing and writing were great fun for you. Is that true?

GOREY: I guess. Though I have a couple of projects, one a children's book that I've been illustrating for about five years now, that I can't seem to get done, and I don't know why. It's partly because I'm always trying to do too many things at once, and I'm terribly lazy. If a thing hangs over me long enough, I usually get it done, though. Most of it is structuring anyway. Drawing repetitive wallpaper is annoying rather than soothing after a while. But, on the whole, I guess I've been very lucky. I have more or less supported myself by doing what I want to do, which doesn't seem to be the case for many people.

BIOGRAPHICAL/CRITICAL SOURCES:

BOOKS

Conversations with Writers, Volume 1, Gale, 1977.
Dictionary of Literary Biography, Volume 61: *American Writers for Children since 1960: Poets, Illustrators, and Nonfiction Authors,* Gale, 1987.
Gorey, Edward, *The Gashlycrumb Tinies,* Simon & Schuster, 1962.

PERIODICALS

Commentary, January, 1973.
Detroit Free Press, October 29, 1982.
Detroit News, November 15, 1983.
Esquire, June, 1974.
Horizon, November, 1977.
New Republic, November 26, 1966.
Newsweek, August 26, 1963, October 30, 1972, October 31, 1977.
New Yorker, December 26, 1959.
New York Times, May 1, 1985.
New York Times Book Review, October 29, 1972, November 6, 1983.
People, July 3, 1978.
Publishers Weekly, November 26, 1982.
Saturday Review, January 6, 1979.

—*Sketch by Diane Telgen*

—*Interview by Jean W. Ross*

* * *

GORYAN, Sirak
See SAROYAN, William

* * *

GOSLING, Paula 1939-
(Ainslie Skinner)

PERSONAL: Born October 12, 1939, in Detroit, Mich.; daughter of Paul (a design engineer and inventor) and Sylvie (Van Slembrouck) Osius; married Christopher Gosling, July, 1968 (divorced, 1978); married John A. Hare (bike shop owner), September 17, 1981; children: (first marriage) Abigail Judith, Emily Elizabeth. *Education:* Wayne State University, B.A., 1962.

ADDRESSES: Home—22 Shelley Rd., Beechen Cliff, Bath, Avon BA2 4RJ, England. *Agent*—Elaine Greene Ltd., 31 Newington Green, Islington, London N16 9PU, England.

CAREER: Campbell-Ewald Co. (advertising agency), Detroit, Mich., copywriter trainee, 1962-64; C. Mitchell & Co., London, England, copywriter, 1964-67, copy consultant, 1969-70; copywriter at advertising agencies in London, 1967-69; ATA Advertising, Bristol, England, copy consultant, 1976-79; full-time writer, 1979—.

MEMBER: Mystery Writers of America, Crime Writers' Association (chairman, 1988-89), Mensa.

AWARDS, HONORS: John Creasey Memorial Award, 1978, for *A Running Duck;* Gold Dagger Award, 1986, for *Monkey Puzzle.*

WRITINGS:

CRIME THRILLERS

A Running Duck, Macmillan (London), 1978, published as *Fair Game,* Coward, 1979.

Zero Trap, Macmillan, 1979, Coward, 1980.

Loser's Blues, Macmillan, 1980, published as *Solo Blues,* Coward, 1981.

(Under pseudonym Ainslie Skinner) *Mind's Eye,* Secker & Warburg, 1980, published as *The Harrowing,* Rawson, Wade, 1981.

The Woman in Red, Macmillan, 1983, Doubleday, 1984.

Monkey Puzzle, Macmillan, 1985, Doubleday, 1986.

The Wychford Murders, Macmillan, 1986, Doubleday, 1987.

Hoodwink, Doubleday, 1987.

Backlash, Doubleday, 1989.

OTHER

Also author of magazine serials such as "The Man in the Bicycle Shop," published in *Woman,* 1981.

WORK IN PROGRESS: "I never discuss my work in progress. I can only say that I am deep in research for my next thriller."

MEDIA ADAPTATIONS: A Running Duck has been filmed by Warner Bros. as "Cobra," starring Sylvester Stallone.

SIDELIGHTS: Paul Gosling wrote to *CA:* "Many people consider crime fiction to be a confining form, but I find in it a great challenge—and that is, to stick to the rule of playing fair with the reader, while bending and even breaking some of the other rules of form and content. Crime fiction allows me to show characters under the most intense pressure. Murder is the ultimate crime, and the ripples and vibrations it produces enable me not only to demonstrate each character's public personality, but also to gradually reveal the secret persona that hides behind it. It is that secret persona which drives someone to kill. Murder is an act of ego, and the killer's most primal motivation is simply this: 'you must die so I can live.' Crime writers today are encouraged to explore and experiment because their readers are knowledgeable and demanding—they want not only a challenging puzzle, but also a good, strong, well-written novel containing imaginative description, lively dialogue, and powerful characterization. That's why, in comparison to writing crime fiction, writing 'straight' novels seems like child's play to us—and these days often reads like it!"

*   *   *

GOUGH, Barry Morton   1938-

PERSONAL: Born September 17, 1938, in Victoria, British Columbia, Canada; son of John (an educator and historian) and Dorothy (a pianist; maiden name, Mouncy) Gough; married second wife Marilyn Joy Morris, December 11, 1981; children: (first marriage) Melinda, Jason; (second marriage) Spencer, Zachary. *Education:* University of British Columbia, B.Ed., 1962; University of Montana, M.A., 1966; Kings College, London, Ph.D., 1969. *Religion:* United Church of Canada.

ADDRESSES: Home—37 Ahrens St. W., Kitchener, Ontario, Canada N2H 4B6. *Office*—Department of History, Wilfrid Laurier University, Waterloo, Ontario, Canada N2L 3C5.

CAREER: Western Washington University, Bellingham, lecturer, 1968-69, assistant professor, 1969-71, associate professor

of history, 1972, founder of Canadian Studies Program, 1970; Wilfrid Laurier University, Waterloo, Ontario, associate professor, 1972-78, professor of history, 1978—, founder of Canadian Studies Program, 1974. Adjunct professor at University of Waterloo, 1973-78; visiting professor at University of Victoria, 1972, Duke University, 1974, University of Maine, 1978, 1979, Simon Fraser University, 1980-81, University of British Columbia, 1981, and Otago University, Dunedin, New Zealand, 1982; visiting fellow, Clare Hall, Cambridge University, 1984-85. Has lectured in the United States on Canadian-American relations. *Military service:* Royal Canadian Air Force Reserve.

MEMBER: North American Society for Oceanic History (president), Conference on British Studies, American Historical Association, Canadian Institute for International Affairs (past president), Canadian Historical Association, Champlain Society (vice-president), Canadian Nautical Research Society (president).

AWARDS, HONORS: Social Science Council-Canada Council publishing award, 1971, for *The Royal Navy and the Northwest Coast of North America, 1810-1914: A Study of British Maritime Ascendancy;* Leon and Thea Koerner research grant, 1974; Canada Council leave fellowship, 1977-78; John Lyman Award for Oceanic History, 1980, 1985; Royal Historical Society fellowship, 1980; European Community visiting fellowship, 1981; NATO visiting fellowship, 1985.

WRITINGS:

The Royal Navy and the Northwest Coast of North America, 1810-1914: A Study of British Maritime Ascendancy, University of British Columbia Press, 1971.

To the Pacific and Arctic with Beechey, Cambridge University Press, 1973.

Canada, Prentice-Hall, 1975.

(Editor) *Search for the Visible Past,* Wilfrid Laurier University Press, 1975.

Distant Dominion: Britain and the Northwest Coast of North America, 1579-1809, University of British Columbia Press, 1980.

(Contributor) *The Discoverers,* McGraw, 1980.

Gold Rush, Grolier, 1983.

Gunboat Frontier: British Maritime Authority and Northwest Coast Indians, 1846-1890, University of British Columbia Press, 1984.

(Editor) *The Journal of Alexander Henry the Younger, 1799-1814,* Volume I: *Red River and the Missouri,* Champlain Society, 1988.

Also contributor to *The Dictionary of Canadian Biography,* University of Toronto Press/Laval University Press. Contributor to journals. Corresponding editor, *British Studies Intelligencer,* 1971—; *Albion,* associate editor, 1968-69, managing editor, 1969-72, editor, 1972—.

WORK IN PROGRESS: Research on the Royal Navy and Eastern Canada, 1815-1914; research on the rise and fall of the *Pax Britannica* in the nineteenth and twentieth centuries; ongoing studies in the history of British Columbia including native studies, missionary endeavors, and economic developments; writing in various interrelated subjects on naval, maritime, and imperial history and historiography directed towards a new theory of imperialism.

SIDELIGHTS: Barry Morton Gough told *CA:* "I write on the themes of Canada and the sea. Living hard by the pervasive power of the United States, Canadians have scarcely given much attention to the oceans over which they travelled to get to their new homeland. To my way of thinking, Canada owes its existence to the interplay of land and sea. I started with the least known aspect of Canadian maritime history—British Columbia—and I hope to complete the whole continental cycle from the Pacific to the Arctic to the Atlantic and to the Great Lakes. But my work transcends national and continental boundaries, and I am seeking to understand how the seas join human societies and how control of the seas determines human history.

"My fellow historians can write about the miseries of the human condition, or they can press forward with recondite and largely illiterate econometric studies. These are important themes. But I still prefer to think of history as literature in which narrative coupled with analysis still has a place. History ought to be a good read, and it ought to make the reader think about the meaning and purpose of life."

AVOCATIONAL INTERESTS: Travel (has travelled widely in Canada, the United States, New Zealand, and Europe), fly fishing, the flute.

*   *   *

GOULD, Chester 1900-1985

PERSONAL: Born November 20, 1900, in Pawnee, Okla.; died May 11, 1985, in Woodstock, Ill., of congested heart failure; son of Gilbert R. (a newspaper publisher) and Alice (Miller) Gould; married Edna Gauger, November 6, 1926; children: Jean (Mrs. Richard O'Connell). *Education:* Attended Oklahoma A & M College (now Oklahoma State University), 1919-21; Northwestern University, diploma, 1923; also attended Chicago Art Institute.

CAREER: Tulsa Democrat, Tulsa, Okla., editorial cartoonist, 1918; *Daily Oklahoman,* Oklahoma City, Okla., sports cartoonist, 1919-21; worked for several Chicago newspapers during early 1920s; *Chicago American,* Chicago, Ill., cartoonist for syndicated comic strips "Fillum Fables" and "Radio Cats," 1924-29; *Chicago Daily News,* Chicago, ad illustrator, 1929-31; Chicago Tribune-New York Daily News Syndicate (now Tribune Media Services Syndicate), Chicago, cartoonist for "Dick Tracy" comic strip, 1931-77.

MEMBER: National Cartoonists Society, Woodstock Country Club, Lambda Chi Alpha.

AWARDS, HONORS: American Institute of Men's and Boys' Wear special plaque, 1957; Reuben Award, National Cartoonists Society, 1959; Special Edgar Award, Mystery Writers of America, 1979, for "Dick Tracy" comic strip; also received numerous awards from law enforcement agencies and police departments, including the Police Athletic League Award, 1949, and the Associated Police Communications Officers Award, 1953.

WRITINGS:

Dick Tracy and Dick Tracy, Jr., and How They Captured "Stooge" Viller, Cupples & Leon, 1933.
How Dick Tracy and Dick Tracy, Jr., Caught the Racketeers, Cupples & Leon, 1934.
Dick Tracy, Ace Detective, Whitman Publishing, 1943.
Dick Tracy Meets the Night Crawler, Whitman Publishing, 1945.
Dick Tracy and the Woo Woo Sisters, Dell, 1947.
The Celebrated Cases of Dick Tracy, 1931-1951, with an introduction by Ellery Queen, edited by Herb Galewitz, Chelsea House, 1970.
Prune Face, Fawcett, 1975.
Snowflake and Shaky, Fawcett, 1975.

Dick Tracy, the Thirties: Tommy Guns and Hard Times, edited by Galewitz, Chelsea House, 1978.
Dick Tracy and the Kidnapped Princess, T. Raiola, 1983.
Dick Tracy: America's Most Famous Detective, edited by Bill Crouch, Jr., Lyle Stuart, 1987.

SIDELIGHTS: Chester Gould was the creator of the comic strip character Dick Tracy, one of America's most popular fictional detectives. From 1931 until his retirement in 1977, Gould chronicled the square-jawed, hawk-nosed Tracy's heroic battles against a steady stream of wildly surreal underworld villains, always being sure to have his hero strictly follow actual police procedures. By the late 1940s, Tracy was so well known that he was the second-most recognized figure in America, just behind Bing Crosby and ahead of then-president Harry S. Truman. At the peak of the strip's popularity in the late 1950s, "Dick Tracy" was carried in well over one thousand newspapers around the world, and the character was featured in movies, serials, and on television and radio shows. A host of Dick Tracy products, ranging from cap pistols to toy dolls, have been successfully marketed, while many of Gould's "Dick Tracy" comic strips have been gathered into book-length collections.

Gould's career as a cartoonist began when he was still a young man in Oklahoma. After spending $20 on a mail-order cartooning course, he began working for a local newspaper while still attending high school. Gould later worked for another newspaper while majoring in commerce and marketing at Northwestern University. (His father, wary of his son becoming an artist, insisted he take business courses.) Gould's first big break came in 1924 when he landed a job as cartoonist on the syndicated comic strip "Fillum Fables," a parody of the silent films of the day. "Radio Cats," a similar strip poking fun at radio, soon followed. Gould later claimed that both strips were "stinkeroo."

In an effort to secure his own comic strip, Gould spent ten years bombarding Captain Joseph Patterson of the Chicago Tribune-New York Daily News Syndicate with strip ideas. He offered everything from romances to westerns to comedy without success. But in 1931 the effort paid off when Patterson thought Gould's idea for a strip called "Plainclothes Tracy" showed some promise, and the young artist was called in for a meeting. As the two men discussed the idea, Patterson decided that the detective hero's first name was too long. He suggested that the name "Dick," a then-popular slang term for police detectives, be used instead, and he gave Gould an idea for the strip's first adventure. Gould took the advice and the comic strip "Dick Tracy" was born.

The new comic strip debuted in the now-defunct *Detroit Daily Mirror* on October 4, 1931, was picked up by the *New York Daily News* a week later, and was quickly syndicated nationwide. The strip's first adventure introduced young detective Dick Tracy and his fiancee, Tess Trueheart. Tess's father, a grocer, is murdered during a hold-up at his store, and Tracy is assigned to track down the killers. Gould broke new ground with the story, which depicted the first murder in comic strip history. He also "invented a hero who was not intended to be humorous," as Albin Krebs noted in the *New York Times*. "Tracy dealt grimly with murderers and racketeers. . . . Gould's 'Dick Tracy' was the first uncomic comic strip."

Early newspaper editors sometimes objected to Gould's realistic depiction of bloodshed. Wes Smith and Kenan Heise reported in the *Chicago Tribune* that "Dick Tracy" was the first to "graphically portray bullets spurting from brains and blood gushing from wounds." As Gould recounted in *Comics and Their Creators: Life Stories of American Cartoonists,* "Back in

1931 no cartoon had ever shown a detective character fighting it out face to face with crooks via the hot lead route." But the comic strip's violence only reflected the violence of Prohibition. Gould lived in gangster-ridden Chicago where street shootings, underworld battles, and murders were common. He claimed in *Dick Tracy, the Thirties: Tommy Guns and Hard Times* that "it was this era that planted the idea of Dick Tracy in my head. The revelations of fixed juries, crooked judges, bribery of public officials and cops who looked the other way showed the crying need for a strong representative of law and order who would take an eye for an eye and a tooth for a tooth. Tracy was the man." In an affectionate parody of Gould, fellow cartoonist Al Capp of "Li'l Abner" fame introduced the detective character Fearless Fosdick in his own comic strip. Fosdick, a square-jawed, steely-eyed copy of Tracy, confronted his criminal adversaries in wild shooting sprees that left villains and bystanders alike riddled with bullets.

To keep Dick Tracy's crime-fighting realistic, Gould took classes in forensics, fingerprinting, and ballistics at Northwestern University. Story ideas were gleaned from actual crimes reported in the newspapers, and a police officer friend reviewed each panel for accuracy before publication. An added feature, the Crimestoppers Textbook, appeared in the upper right-hand corner of each Sunday "Dick Tracy" strip and gave readers useful advice on detecting and deterring crime in their neighborhoods. Writing in his introduction to *The Celebrated Cases of Dick Tracy, 1931-1951,* Ellery Queen noted Tracy's use of strictly scientific method. Tracy, Queen wrote, was "the world's first procedural detective of fiction, in the modern sense."

Because he kept abreast of the latest breakthroughs in crime-fighting technology, sometimes Gould would stray from realism into science fiction. Over the years "Dick Tracy" readers were the first to see such futuristic gadgets as two-way wrist radios (later updated to wrist TVs), closed-circuit television surveillance, and space shuttles. Tracy's eccentric industrialist friend Diet Smith was often the source of such advanced crime-fighting equipment. Many of these devices were later adapted for use by the police, although in somewhat different form than Gould imagined. Tracy's wrist radios, for example, became the police walkie-talkies of today. In 1963 one of Gould's characters even performed a human heart transplant, four years before that operation was performed in the real world.

When it came to depicting his villains, Gould could stray from realism into surrealism. All of his villains were colorful, grotesque figures with pronounced physical abnormalities and matching nicknames. Flattop, for example, had a head as flat as the deck of an aircraft carrier. Pruneface was hideously wrinkled; the Mole resembled his animal namesake; and the Brow had deep fissures in his forehead. "I wanted my villains to stand out definitely so that there would be no mistake who the villain was. . . .," Gould explained in *The Celebrated Cases of Dick Tracy, 1931-1951.* "I never looked at them as being ugly. . . . I think the ugliest thing in the world is the face of a man who has killed seven nurses—or who has kidnapped a child. His face to me is ugly."

Justice always prevailed in "Dick Tracy," albeit a sometimes bloody justice. Gould's villains were rarely brought before a court of law; they usually received their due punishment in spectacular and bizarre ways while attempting to flee the police. One was impaled on a flag pole; another was scalded to death in a Turkish bath; and, according to Kelbs, "the nefarious B. B. Eyes met a most timely demise by being smothered under the cargo of a garbage scow."

Tracy, too, was often the victim of violence. In the strip's first 24 years he was shot some 27 times. In the course of his career he was beaten, stabbed, run over by cars, dragged from a speeding car, buried alive, tortured, burned, and gassed. Tess Trueheart, Tracy's fiancee and, beginning in 1949, his wife, was also a frequent target of underworld threats and mischief. But the couple managed to come through all such encounters with no lasting damage, and Tracy always got his man.

With at least one of his villains Gould dropped his usually grim approach and chose to be humorous, creating "the seedy, bewhiskered and odiforous farmer, B. O. Plenty," as Krebs remarked. After marrying the equally malodorous Gravel Gertie, Plenty became a solid citizen, a close friend to Tracy, and the father of Sparkle Plenty, a little girl born with long golden curls. B. O. became one of the most popular of the strip's characters, and Gould was obliged to bring the genial rustic back time and again. Sparkle also proved popular with Tracy fans; in the first year they were on the market, Sparkle Plenty dolls enjoyed over $3 million in sales.

Gould's drawing style gave "Dick Tracy" a distinctive look quite different from that of other comic strips. Tracy himself is a square-jawed, hawk-nosed figure who wears a porkpie hat and trench coat; Gould usually drew him in profile to accentuate his facial features. He revealed in *Comics and Their Creators* that he conceived of Tracy as "a modern Sherlock Holmes, if Holmes were a young man living today, dressed as a modern G-man and bearing the traditional characteristics." Speaking of Gould's artwork, Jerry Belcher of the *Los Angeles Times* said that "the strong-lined drawings were impressionistic rather than realistic," while a writer for the London *Times* claimed that the strip featured "brutally simple, almost crude graphics." Yet in 1982, when the Graham Gallery of New York held an exhibition of Gould's "Dick Tracy" artwork, the *New York Times* critic John Russell called Gould "a workman of a very high order in a craft that is much harder than it looks. The images survive well as exhibition material, and as tokens of a time when issues were clearcut, when law was law, order was order and the best man won out in the end."

Gould modestly described himself as a kind of newsboy. "The sole purpose of a comic strip," he wrote in *Cartoonist Profile,* "is to sell newspapers; that makes me a newsboy. The American comic strip is responsible for and has sold more newspapers since its creation than any other feature in American journalism, and I'm proud to be part of it." According to Krebs, Gould once spoke of audience reaction to Tracy in these words: "I just want them to say, 'I wonder what that damned fool Gould did today.' " And for over forty-five years, some 100 million fans wondered just that every time they opened their newspapers to read the latest "Dick Tracy" episode.

After Gould retired in 1977, the strip was taken over by Richard Fletcher. Since Fletcher's death in 1983, Dick Locher and Max Collins have continued Dick Tracy's adventures. Speaking to Smith and Heise, Collins explained that Gould "virtually invented the adventure cartoon strip and he popularized the tough, two-fisted American detective." Mark Evenier said in the *Los Angeles Times* that "Gould was a legend" and "Dick Tracy was the greatest detective strip ever."

Writing in *Comics and Their Creators,* Gould allowed that Dick Tracy's "mission in life is entertainment. His motto is 'Crime Does Not Pay.' And his author's sincere hope and prayer is that he will continue to do those things the readers like and wish to see him do."

MEDIA ADAPTATIONS: The "Dick Tracy" radio series was produced by the Mutual Broadcasting System, 1935-37, by the National Broadcasting Company (NBC), 1937-39, by the NBC Blue Network, 1943-44, and by the American Broadcasting Company (ABC), 1944-48; a number of multi-part serials were produced by Republic, including "Dick Tracy," 1936, "Dick Tracy Returns," 1938, "Dick Tracy's G-Men," 1939, and "Dick Tracy versus Crime, Inc.,'" 1941, later released as "Dick Tracy versus the Phantom Empire," 1952; a series of films was produced by RKO, including "Dick Tracy, Detective," 1945, "Dick Tracy versus Cueball," 1946, "Dick Tracy Meets Gruesome," 1947, and "Dick Tracy's Dilemma," 1947; the "Dick Tracy" television series was produced by ABC-TV, 1950-51; the "Dick Tracy Show," an animated cartoon series, was produced by United Productions of America, 1961.

BIOGRAPHICAL/CRITICAL SOURCES:

BOOKS

Gould, Chester, *The Celebrated Cases of Dick Tracy, 1931-1951,* edited by Herb Galewitz, Chelsea House, 1970.
Gould, Chester, *Dick Tracy, the Thirties: Tommy Guns and Hard Times,* edited by Galewitz, Chelsea House, 1978.
Sheridan, Martin, *Comics and Their Creators: Life Stories of American Cartoonists,* Hyperion Press, revised edition, 1977.

PERIODICALS

Cartoonist Profile, March, 1973.
Coronet, June, 1966.
Holiday, June, 1958.
Newsweek, October 16, 1961, January 14, 1963.
New York Daily News, May 19, 1985.
New York Sunday News, December 18, 1955, April 4, 1971.
New York Times, December 11, 1970.
Saturday Evening Post, December 17, 1949.
Washington Post, January 15, 1971.

OBITUARIES:

PERIODICALS

Chicago Tribune, May 12, 1985, May 13, 1985.
Los Angeles Times, May 12, 1985.
Newsweek, May 20, 1985.
New York Times, May 12, 1985.
Time, May 20, 1985.
Times (London), May 14, 1985.*

—*Sketch by Thomas Wiloch*

*   *   *

GOURLAY, Elizabeth 1917-

PERSONAL: Born March 10, 1917, in Toronto, Ontario, Canada; daughter of Oscar William (a businessman) and Rose (Wastfield) Dunham; married Robert H. Gourlay (a surgeon), September 5, 1942; children: Rob, Mary. *Education:* McGill University, B.A., 1938, B.L.S., 1939; University of British Columbia, M.A., 1969. *Politics:* "I vote for whoever is on the side of peace, ecology, and true democracy." *Religion:* Anglican.

ADDRESSES: Home—6224 Carnarvon St., Vancouver, British Columbia, Canada V6N 1K3.

CAREER: Royal Victorian Hospital, Montreal, Quebec, librarian, 1940-42; writer. Worked part time as librarian at Redpath Library, 1946-48.

MEMBER: Association of Canadian Television and Radio Artists, League of Canadian Poets, Playwrights Canada, Friends of the Garden of the University of British Columbia Botanical Gardens (member of art committee).

AWARDS, HONORS: Alumnae Award, University of British Columbia, 1967, for "The Transport Survey," and 1968, for "One for Fission"; award from New Play Centre, 1975, for "The One Eyed Jack"; nomination for award from Association of Canadian Television and Radio Artists, 1981, and from Smile Company, 1982, both for "The Glass Bottle."

WRITINGS:

"Narrow Is the Margin" (one-act radio play), first broadcast by Canadian Broadcasting Corp. (CBC-Radio), 1958.
"When Stars Were Bright" (one-act radio play), first broadcast by CBC-Radio, 1959.
"The Transport Survey" (one-act play), first performed in Vancouver, British Columbia, at Freddy Wood Theatre, 1967.
Motions, Dreams, and Aberrations (poems), Morris & Company, 1969.
"One for Fission" (one-act play), first produced in Vancouver at Freddy Wood Theatre, 1969.
"Andrea del Sarto" (two-act play), first produced in Vancouver, September 6, 1973, adapted for radio and broadcast by CBC-Radio, 1973.
Isabel (three-act play; first produced in Seattle, Washington, at Discovery Theatre, January, 1977), Playwrights Canada, 1979.
Songs and Dances (poems), Caitlin Press, 1981.
M Poems, Fiddlehead, 1983.
The Glass Bottle (one-act radio play; first broadcast by CBC-Radio, 1980), Prism International, 1983.
"The Cut Off" (one-act play), first produced in Vancouver at Langara College, April, 1983.
"No Recourse" (one-act play), first produced in Vancouver at Waterfront Theatre, April, 1984.
The Celluloid Barrette (short stories), Caitlin Press, 1987.
"Hair of the Dog" (one-act play) first produced in Ottawa, Ontario, at Atelier Theatre, National Arts Center, October, 1989.

Also author of play "The One-Eyed Jack," 1975. Poetry represented in anthologies, including *Woman's Eye,* Air, 1974, *Whale Sound,* Douglas, 1976, and *Poetry by Canadian Women,* edited by Rosemary Sullivan, Oxford University Press (Toronto), 1989. Contributor of poems and stories to periodicals, including *Atlantic Advocate, Canadian Forum, Canadian Literature, Fiddlehead, Cross Canada Quarterly,* and *Malahat Review.*

WORK IN PROGRESS: A play, "Livvy and Edward"; "The Roses of Malmaison," a story; another play, as yet untitled.

SIDELIGHTS: Elizabeth Gourlay told *CA:* "I write for a number of reasons: to communicate, to praise or blame, to ferret out meanings and reasons. Poems choose me it seems—I mean the writing of them—but I write plays for two reasons: from an interest in character, or as a polemic, as in 'No Recourse,' a one-act play concerning the nuclear dilemma."

*   *   *

GRACIA, Jorge J(esus) E(miliano) 1942-

PERSONAL: Born July 18, 1942, in Camaguey, Cuba; naturalized Canadian citizen, 1971; permanent U.S. resident, 1975; son of Ignacio Jesus Loreto (a pharmacist and landowner) and Leonila (a poet; maiden name, Otero) Gracia; married Norma

Elida Silva (a treasurer); children: Leticia Isabel, Clarisa Raquel. *Education:* Wheaton College, B.A., 1965; University of Chicago, M.A., 1966; Pontifical Institute of Mediaeval Studies, M.S.L., 1970; University of Toronto, Ph.D., 1971.

ADDRESSES: Home—420 Berryman Dr., Amherst, N.Y. 14226. *Office*—Department of Philosophy, Baldy Hall, State University of New York at Buffalo, Buffalo, N.Y. 14260.

CAREER: State University of New York at Buffalo, assistant professor, 1971-76, associate professor, 1976-80, professor of philosophy, 1980—, chairman of department, 1980-86. Visiting professor at University of Puerto Rico, 1972-73. Member of New York Council for the Humanities, 1987.

MEMBER: Societe Internationale pour l'Etude de la Philosophie Medievale, International Federation of Latin American and Caribbean Studies (president, 1987-79), American Philosophical Association, Metaphysical Society of America, Mediaeval Academy of America, Society for Medieval and Renaissance Philosophy (member of executive committee, 1986—), Society for Iberian and Latin American Thought (vice-president, 1985-86; president, 1986-88), Sociedad Filosofica Ibero-Americana (member of executive council, 1985—).

AWARDS, HONORS: Grant from National Endowment for the Humanities, 1981-82.

WRITINGS:

El hombre y los valores en la filosofia latinoamericana del siglo veintavo (title means "Man and Values in Twentieth-Century Latin American Philosophy"), Fondo de Cultura Economica, 1975, 2nd edition, 1981.
Com usar be de beure e menjar (title means "How to Drink and Eat Well"), Curial, 1977.
Man and His Conduct, University of Puerto Rico Press, 1980.
Suarez on Individuation, Marquette University Press, 1982.
Filosofia e indentidad cultural (title means "Philosophy and Cultural Identity"), Monte Avila, 1983.
Introduction to the Problem of Individuation in the Early Middle Ages, Philosophia Verlag, 1984, 2nd revised edition, 1988.
Philosophical Analysis in Latin America, Reidel, 1984.
Ensayos filosoficas de Risieri Frondizi, Fondo de Cultura Economica, 1986.
Latin American Philosophy in the Twentieth Century, Prometheus Books, 1986.
Individuality: An Essay on the Foundations of Metaphysics, State University of New York Press, 1988.
The Metaphysics of Good and Evil According to Suarez, Philosophia Verlag, 1988.
Directory of Latin American Philosophers, Society for Iberian and Latin American Thought, 1988.
Philosophy and Literature in Latin America, State University of New York, in press.
Individuation in Scholasticism: The Later Middle Ages and the Counter-Reformation, Philosophia Verlag, in press.

Contributor of more than fifty articles to periodicals, including *Review of Metaphysics, Journal of the History of Philosophy,* and *New Scholasticism.*

WORK IN PROGRESS: The Metaphysics of Good and Evil; Philosophy and Its History; La filosofia latinoamericana de hoy.

SIDELIGHTS: Jorge J. E. Gracia told *CA:* "My research and writing has centered on three subject areas: the Middle Ages, Latin America, and metaphysics. I was trained as a medievalist in Toronto and therefore a great part of my work is concerned with the history of medieval thought. Most of this is technical and deals with such questions as the views of individuality developed during the period. In my book on the problem of individuation I argue, for example, that the basic problems related to individuality, its causes and its nature, are raised for the first time in an explicit way in the early middle ages. The book on Francis Suarez, which contains a translation of his treatise on this topic as well as an extensive glossary of technical terms, argues that Suarez's views on individuality are the most sophisticated and developed to come out of the middle ages and that Suarez provides one of the most clear and systematic treatments of the topic to date.

"More recently I have been working on the theories of good and evil in late scholasticism and particularly on the views of Suarez. In my book on evil I present the key texts on this topic by Suarez, and I argue that he gives a credible defense of the traditional scholastic interpretation of evil as privation by introducing the concept of evil as a kind of disagreeability. Likewise, I find much merit in the view of good as a kind of agreeability, which I explore in my other book in preparation. But I also argue that neither theory goes far enough, since neither of them develops sufficiently the relational character of value.

"After coming to Buffalo and visiting Puerto Rico for a year, I became interested in the thought and philosophy of Latin America both because I was asked to teach a course on the subject and because I have never forgotten my background. Given the scarcity of sources available I decided, with the help of my good friend, and late Risieri Frondizi, to put together a collection of readings from Latin American philosophers centered around the themes of man and values. These themes are the areas where Latin American philosophy has made its most important contributions in the first half of this century. This anthology-study was published in Spanish, but an English version is in preparation. *Man and His Conduct,* on the other hand, is in fact a *Festschrift* in Frondizi's honor. It contains twenty-six essays written especially for the volume by noted American, European, and Latin American philosophers. In addition it contains a complete bibliography of Frondizi's works and a brief biography.

"Another area of my research has been concerned with the impact that philosophical analysis, as practiced in the Anglo-American tradition, has had on Latin America. I have also been working on the crisis of philosophical identity which Latin America is undergoing. One of the most discussed issues in Latin America for the past thirty years has been the question of whether there is such a thing as a Latin American philosophy that may be idiosyncratically unique and authentic. In my book on the subject, I point out that the source of the question is a misunderstanding about the very nature of philosophy and philosophical method and that once a proper understanding of these is achieved, the problem dissolves.

"Finally, in the area of metaphysics, my main concern has been with the so-called problem of universals and individuals—the ontological categorization of two of our most basic notions. In the book on individuals, I present my view that individuality has to do primarily with non-instantiability, while universality has to do with instantiability. I argue, moreover, that much of the concern with individuals and universals in the course of the history of philosophy is a result of a lack of understanding this fact as well as a lack of understanding and distinguishing the various issues involved in the notions of individuality and universality. These are the faults that flaw the work of most philosophers concerned with these issues, from Plato to Strawson."

GRAEBNER, William Sievers 1943-

PERSONAL: Born September 16, 1943, in Chicago, Ill.; son of Elmer Robert and Dorothy (Zilisch) Graebner; married Dianne Bennett (an attorney), August 27, 1966; children: Bennett Sievers, Riley James Bennett. *Education:* Stanford University, B.A., 1965; University of Illinois, M.A., 1966, Ph.D., 1970. *Politics:* "Radical." *Religion:* None.

ADDRESSES: Home—185 Chapin Parkway, Buffalo, N.Y. 14209. *Office*—Department of History, State University of New York College at Fredonia, Fredonia, N.Y. 14063.

CAREER: State University of New York College at Fredonia, assistant professor, 1971-76, associate professor, 1976-80, professor of history, 1980—, Kasling Lecturer, 1981. Curator, "Coming of Age in Buffalo" exhibit, Buffalo and Erie County Historical Society, 1986.

MEMBER: Organization of American Historians, Labor Historians.

AWARDS, HONORS: Frederick Jackson Turner Prize, Organization of American Historians, 1975, for *Coal-Mining Safety in the Progressive Period: The Political Economy of Reform;* fellow, American Council of Learned Societies, 1977-78.

WRITINGS:

Coal-Mining Safety in the Progressive Period: The Political Economy of Reform, University Press of Kentucky, 1976.
A History of Retirement: The Meaning and Function of an American Institution, 1885-1978, Yale University Press, 1980.
(Editor with Leonard Richards) *The American Record: Images of the Nation's Past,* two volumes, Knopf, 1981, 2nd edition, 1987.
The Engineering of Consent: Democracy and Authority in Twentieth-Century America, University of Wisconsin Press, 1987.
Coming of Age in Buffalo: Teenage Culture in the Postwar Era, Temple University Press, 1989.

Contributor to *Journal of Social Issues.*

WORK IN PROGRESS: An intellectual and cultural history of the 1940s, for G. K. Hall.

SIDELIGHTS: William Sievers Graebner once told *CA:* "I became a historian because the alternative was military service; only later did I learn to love it. I benefited enormously from the superior library at the University of Illinois and from association with Marilee Sargent and Jerry Clore in the late 1960s. I was radicalized sometime in 1968 and remain so. Running through my work (increasingly so) is a strong anti-authoritarian streak. We need to know much more about how authority is organized and exercised, especially in 'democratic' environments and systems. Subtle mechanisms of control and coercion exist both in institutions and processes that are represented as non-coercive and democratic, such as our child-rearing processes, the clubs and social organizations created for juveniles and the aged, and non-directive, 'progressive' education."

Graebner later added, "[*The Engineering of Consent: Democracy and Authority in Twentieth-Century America*] is, I'm sure, my best and most original work. But the more original I get—the further away from mainstream history—the harder it is to get published. I am astonished at the conservatism of many publishing houses.

"I spent the last six months of 1989 living in Bologna, Italy. The experience has caused me to reevaluate the role of the United States in world affairs. Americans think the United States is at the center of world events. In contrast, Europeans think of us as a failed and increasingly irrelevant people."

AVOCATIONAL INTERESTS: Camping, skiing, hiking, soccer, collecting modernist furniture and other objects.

BIOGRAPHICAL/CRITICAL SOURCES:

PERIODICALS

Los Angeles Times Book Review, November 16, 1980.
Times Literary Supplement, February 6, 1981.*

*   *   *

GRANSDEN, Antonia 1928-

PERSONAL: Born October 7, 1928, in Somerset, England; daughter of Stephen Coleby and Hilda Lucy (Street) Morland; married Michael David Nightingale, 1953; married second husband, Karl Watts Gransden, 1958; married third husband, Jonathan Harrison, 1978; children: (second marriage) Katherine, Deborah. *Education:* Somerville College, Oxford, B.A. (first class honors), 1951; University of London, Ph.D., 1957.

ADDRESSES: Home—10 Halifax Rd., Cambridge CB4 3PX, England.

CAREER: British Museum, London, England, assistant keeper of manuscripts, 1952-60, superintendent of students' room, 1960-62; Buckland Hall, Berkshire, England, tutor in medieval history, 1963-65; University of Nottingham, Nottingham, England, assistant lecturer, 1965-66, lecturer, 1966-73, reader in medieval history, 1973-88.

MEMBER: Royal Historical Society (fellow), Society of Antiquaries (fellow).

AWARDS, HONORS: D.Litt., Oxford University, 1984.

WRITINGS:

The Letter-Book of William of Hoo, Sacrist of Bury St. Edmunds, 1280-1294, Suffolk Records Society, 1963.
The Customary of the Benedictine Abbey of Eynsham in Oxfordshire, Corpus Consuetudinem Monasticarum, 1963.
The Chronicle of Bury St. Edmunds, 1212-1301, Thomas Nelson, 1964.
The Customary of Bury St. Edmunds, Henry Bradshaw Society, 1973.
Historical Writing in England, Cornell University Press, Volume 1: *c. 550 to c. 1307,* 1974, Volume 2: *c. 1307 to the Early Sixteenth Century,* 1982.

Contributor of articles and reviews to history journals. Editor, "Nottingham Medieval Studies," 1977-88.

WORK IN PROGRESS: A history of the abbey of Bury St. Edmunds for Cambridge University Press.

SIDELIGHTS: Antonia Gransden's survey of medieval historiography, *Historical Writing in England,* states R. B. Dobson in the *Times Literary Supplement,* is a "massive work of synthesis . . . which should do more than any other recent work to ensure not so much perhaps the rehabilitation of the chronicles as the likelihood that they will now be approached with greater understanding and enthusiasm than in the past." Beginning with the earliest chroniclers writing of the collapse of Roman Britain, Gransden examines changes in the way history in England was written to the Renaissance. "Anyone interested in the narrative sources for the history of medieval England," declares Bernard S. Bachrach in the *American Historical Review,* "now has a reliable guide, and at least a generation of scholars will be in her debt."

BIOGRAPHICAL/CRITICAL SOURCES:

PERIODICALS

American Historical Review, December, 1983.
Times Literary Supplement, March 18, 1983.

*   *   *

GRAY, Malcolm
See STUART, Ian

*   *   *

GREEN, Janet   1939-

PERSONAL: Born October 30, 1939, in Burnley, Lancashire, England; daughter of Frances May (a hotel employee; maiden name, Dyson) Henderson; married John Green (an economist and training consultant), August 8, 1964 (divorced, 1983). *Education:* University of Durham, B.A., 1961; Oxford University, Diploma in Education, 1962. *Politics:* Socialist. *Religion:* Christian.

ADDRESSES: Home—25 Yeomeads, Long Ashton, Bristol BS18 9BE, England. *Office*—Greenway School, Southmead, Bristol, England.

CAREER: Teacher at comprehensive school in Kidsgrove, Staffordshire, England, 1962-64; teacher of religious education and English at high school in Nyanza Province, Kenya, 1964-67; tutor in Maseno, Kenya, 1967-69; Greenway School, Southmead, England, teacher, assistant head of lower school, and head of drama and religious education departments, 1970—. Chairman of Religious Education Panel for Certificate of Secondary Education, 1979-82; chief examiner in religious education for Southwestern Examinations Board, 1982—; member of Schools Broadcasting Council, 1983—. Lecturer at conferences; guest speaker on radio programs.

WRITINGS:

The Six (young adult novel), Bodley Head, 1976, published in the United States as *Us: Inside a Teenage Gang,* Hastings House, 1982.
Getting By (young adult novel), Longman, 1978.
Turning Points (young adult novel), Longman, 1978.
The Jesus Puzzle (young adult short stories), Oxford University Press, 1978.
Love at a Bus Stop (young adult short stories), Longman, 1979.
Harlequinade (puzzles and resources for teachers), Church Information Office, 1982.
(Editor) *Home-Made Prayers* (anthology), Lion, 1983,
God's Rules O.K. (projects by teenagers), Lion, 1984.
(Editor) *Best Bible Bits* (Bible readings), Church Information Office, 1984.

TELEVISION SCRIPTS

"Anatomy of a Gang," first broadcast by British Broadcasting Company, (BBC-TV), June 2, 1977.
"Funny People," first broadcast by BBC-TV, December 3, 1981.
"Where Are They Now?," first broadcast by BBC-TV, November 10, 1983.
"What Are You Afraid Of?," first broadcast by BBC-TV, 1984.

OTHER

"Man Out of Time" (musical to celebrate 150 years of Great Western Railway), performed in Bristol, England, 1985.

"Messages from the Memory Banks" (video with workbooks *Considering Origins* and *Considering Meaning*), Bible Society, 1989.

Script consultant and compiler of teacher's notes for BBC-TV's programs "Scene," 1977—, and "Why? Because . . . ," 1985. Contributor to "Words into Action," produced by BBC-TV. Creator of card game "Logikon," for Christian Education Movement, 1978. Contributor of material on religious studies to BBC radio programs. Contributor of articles and reviews to theology and education journals.

WORK IN PROGRESS: The Black Prince; Murder at Mataranka; "Mr. Popjoy," a musical about Beau Nash; a BBC radio documentary about a slave ship with additional material about John Paul Jones; a religious studies quiz television game show.

SIDELIGHTS: Janet Green commented to *CA:* "I write with groups of children—usually teenagers from my school. They do research, provide material, and try out manuscripts. They also work on and act in television documentaries. The aim is to interest teenagers in topics that occur in religious education lessons. We're not didactic, however. We try to explore, rather than to explain.

"In 1972 a class of fourteen-year-old boys asked me to tell them a story. I asked them to tell me one. They replied that 'nothing ever happens to us.' 'What happened last night?,' I asked them. Two lads launched into an account of a night at the entertainment center. That account fired my imagination. On one level it was a simple boy-meets-girl story, but I sensed that though they didn't know it they were telling me a tale about the first seeds that would grow into the eventual breakup of their teenage gang.

"I wrote it up as a short story. I read it back to them. They thought it was ace but they made criticisms, such as 'the guy on the door, he didn't look like that. He had a shirt like frilly knickers.' I rewrote the story line-by-line with their help.

"At their request we added more stories until we had six. Each story stands alone, yet the collection makes a novel. Other teachers began to borrow the stories. A representative of Longman heard one read, unaware that there was a full book. He managed to trace me eventually, and the book came into print.

"I have continued to work with groups of teenagers. The work now includes television material. The producer of the BBC television series 'Scene' wanted to make a documentary, 'Anatomy of a Gang,' so he came to consult me. Having met our writing team, he decided to make the film about gangs in our area of Bristol.

"At University I studied theology and my main teaching subject is religious education. Inevitably some of the projects my groups take on are intended to fill gaps in resources for use in religious education. The card game, 'Logikon,' is for teaching about the various criteria for believing things to be true. *The Jesus Puzzle* is the life of Jesus seen through the eyes of four teenagers as they might have seen him if they lived in those days. As with all our books, the team included teenagers of all different faiths and life stances because, for us, religious education is more about exploring than about explaining.

"When we learned that our school would close in 1984, we threw ourselves into a number of varied projects. We sensed we were living through a unique experience in cooperation and communication. *Home-Made Prayers* was unusual in that the boys took the photographs that illustrate the text. *Harlequinade* contained word puzzles because we had discovered an easy way for teachers to mark them. *Best Bible Bits* is a collection of replies from famous people to letters written by the children. I find that I am becoming an editor rather than a writer. The children themselves have found that they have things to say and that their ordinary everyday language can express them."

BIOGRAPHICAL/CRITICAL SOURCES:

PERIODICALS

Buzz, January, 1983.
Guardian, December 22, 1982.
Together, June, 1976, July-August, 1978, June, 1983.

* * *

GREENFIELD, Darby
  See WARD, Philip

* * *

GREENSPOON, Leonard J(ay)   1945-

PERSONAL: Born December 5, 1945, in Richmond, Va.; son of Alvin Louis (in wine sales) and Rose (a State of Virginia employee; maiden name, Levy) Greenspoon; married Eliska Morsel (a commercial and creative artist), August 25, 1968; children: Gallit, Talya. *Education:* University of Richmond, B.A., 1967, M.A., 1970; Harvard University, Ph.D., 1977; postdoctoral study at University of California, Santa Barbara, 1978-79.

ADDRESSES: Home—300 Hunting Hill Circle, Greer, S.C. 29650. *Office*—Department of Philosophy and Religion, Clemson University, Clemson, S.C. 29634-1508.

CAREER: Social studies teacher at public school in Charles County, Va., 1968-70; Clemson University, Clemson, S.C., instructor, 1975-77, assistant professor, 1977-83, associate professor of history, 1983-87, professor of religion, 1987—.

MEMBER: International Organization for Septuagint and Cognate Studies (executive secretary and treasurer), American Schools of Oriental Research, Association for Jewish Studies, B'nai B'rith (state president and local president), B'nai B'rith Academic Associates, Catholic Biblical Association, Society for Values in Higher Education, South Carolina Academy of Religion (president), Congregation Beth Israel (president of Greenville, S.C., branch).

AWARDS, HONORS: Fulbright fellow at University of Rome, 1967-68; Clemson University grants, 1976, 1978, 1981, 1982, 1984, 1985, 1986, 1988; National Endowment for the Humanities grants, 1978-79, 1981, 1986, 1987; American Council of Learned Societies grant, 1984; American Jewish Archives grant, 1985; American School of Oriental Research grant, 1986; fellow at Annenberg Research Institute, 1988.

WRITINGS:

(Assistant editor) *Ezekiel,* Fortress, Volume I, 1979, Volume II, 1983.
(Contributor) Baruch Halpern and Jon Levenson, editors, *Traditions in Transformation: Turning Points in Biblical Faith,* Eisenbrauns, 1981.
Textual Studies in the Book of Joshua (monograph), Scholars Press (Chico, Calif.), 1983.
(Contributor) Peter Merkl and Ninian Smart, editors, *Religion and Politics in the Modern World,* New York University Press, 1983.
(Contributor) Charles H. Lippy, editor, *Religious Periodicals of the United States,* Greenwood Press, 1986.

Max Leopold Margolis: A Scholar's Scholar, Scholars Press, 1987.
(Contributor) Frank N. Magill, editor, *Great Lives from History: Ancient and Modern Series,* Salem Press, 1988.

Contributor to *Dictionary of Biblical Tradition in English Literature, Dictionary of Biblical Interpretation, Anchor Bible Dictionary,* and *Reform Judaism in America.* Contributor of about one hundred articles and reviews to biblical, religious, and Jewish studies journals.

WORK IN PROGRESS: Two monographs to contain important unpublished works by Max Leopold Margolis; several scholarly and semi-popular articles on various aspects of Bible translation; a book on translating the Bible.

SIDELIGHTS: Leonard J. Greenspoon told *CA:* "A few years ago, when I was asked to compose my first 'Sidelights' [section], I placed emphasis on my desire to produce solid scholarship for specialists and equally solid scholarship aimed at a general audience. During the intervening years, I have emphasized the former in my publications, but I have increasingly emphasized the latter in a growing number of lectures and talks. I am especially interested in the long process of Bible translating from the earliest attempts (that produced the Septuagint of Greek translation of the first five books of the Hebrew Bible) to the most recent efforts at paraphrase. I center my attention on two areas that have been relatively neglected: (1) the ways in which translations of the Bible are 'products of their time' (taken for granted with any other type of literature); (2) the need to study the backgrounds and personalities of the translators themselves. So much of the previous work on Bible versions has dealt only with the translations as finished products; little, if any account was taken of the religious, social, or political environment in which these texts were produced. Through my efforts I hope to breathe some life into these inherently lively and relevant topics. And to do so in a responsible (in accordance with the best results of scholarly research), impartial (without any theological or other axe to grind), and entertaining manner."

* * *

GREENWOOD, Edward Alister   1930-
  (Ted Greenwood)

PERSONAL: Born December 4, 1930, in Melbourne, Victoria, Australia; son of George Frederick (an architect) and Ilma (McDonald) Greenwood; married Florence Lorraine Peart (a kindergarten director), January 15, 1954; children: Catherine, Meredith, Alister, Emma. *Education:* Melbourne Teachers' College, Primary Teaching Qualification, 1949; Royal Melbourne Institute of Technology, Diploma of Art, 1959. *Politics:* Uncommitted. *Religion:* "Personal."

ADDRESSES: Home and office—50 Hilton Rd., Ferny Creek, Victoria 3786, Australia.

CAREER: Education Department of Victoria, Melbourne, Australia, primary teacher, 1948-56; Melbourne Teachers' College, Melbourne, lecturer in art education, 1956-60; Toorak Teachers' College, Toorak, Melbourne, lecturer in art education, 1961-68; currently writer and illustrator. Deputy-chairman of Community Arts Board, Australia Arts Council, 1978-83.

AWARDS, HONORS: Children's Book Council of Australia Picture Book of the Year Award, 1968, for illustrations in *Sly Old Wardrobe,* and commendation, 1969, for *Obstreperous; Joseph and Lulu and the Prindiville House Pigeons* received a high commendation from Children's Book Council of Australia and was named to the Hans Christian Anderson Honours List, both 1974; Visual Arts award for illustration from Australian Council for the Arts and commendation from the Children's Book Council of Australia, 1976, both for *Terry's Brrrmmm GT;* commendation from the Children's Book Council of Australia for *The Pochetto Coat.*

WRITINGS:

ALL UNDER NAME TED GREENWOOD

(Self-illustrated) *Obstreperous,* Angus & Robertson, 1970.
(Self-illustrated) *Aelfred,* Angus & Robertson, 1970.
(Self-illustrated) *V.I.P.,* Angus & Robertson, 1971.
(Self-illustrated) *Joseph and Lulu and the Prindiville House Pigeons,* Angus & Robertson, 1972.
(Self-illustrated) *Terry's Brrrmmm GT,* Angus & Robertson, 1975.
(Self-illustrated) *Curious Eddie,* Angus & Robertson, 1977.
The Pochetto Coat, Hutchinson, 1978.
(Self-illustrated) *Ginnie,* Kestrel, 1979.
The Boy Who Saw God, Hutchinson, 1980.
(Self-illustrated) *Everlasting Circle,* Hutchinson, 1981.
Flora's Treasures, Hutchinson, 1982.
(Self-illustrated) *Marley and Friends,* Angus & Robertson, 1983.
(Self-illustrated) *Ship Rock,* Hutchinson, 1985.
(With Shane Fennessy) *Warts and All,* Hutchinson, 1985.
(With Fennessy) *I Don't Want to Know,* Hutchinson, 1986.
Windows, McPhee Gribble, 1988.

ILLUSTRATOR

Ivan Southall, *Sly Old Wardrobe,* Cheshire, 1968, St. Martin's, 1970.
Children Everywhere (Australian section; text by Southall), Field Enterprises Educational Corp., 1970.

WORK IN PROGRESS: 2 by 2 But Why Save You, "a book in various verse forms which concerns ten creatures who are asked by Noah's sons to put up a convincing case for their acceptance into the Ark. The creatures are ones generally regarded by many humans as rather nasty for one reason or another."

SIDELIGHTS: Edward Alister Greenwood is particularly interested in cultivating the senses of children "in an age where so many experiences come to them in a vicarious form." He adds, "Although the illustrated book is such a form, I hope my books will act as catalysts for activity by those who read and look at them."

*   *   *

GREENWOOD, Ted
See GREENWOOD, Edward Alister

*   *   *

GREWDEAD, Roy
See GOREY, Edward (St. John)

*   *   *

GRODE, Redway
See GOREY, Edward (St. John)

GRUNEAU, Richard S(teven) 1948-

PERSONAL: Born March 29, 1948, in Toronto, Ontario, Canada; son of Victor Cornelius (a market researcher) and Veronica Donita (Kaiser) Gruneau; married Shelley Bentley (a lawyer), July 11, 1981; children: Danielle Elizabeth Bentley. *Education:* University of Guelph, B.A. (with honors), 1970; University of Calgary, M.A., 1972; University of Massachusetts, Ph.D., 1981.

ADDRESSES: Home—6374 Argyle Ave., Horseshoe Bay, West Vancouver, British Columbia, Canada. *Office*—Department of Communication, Simon Fraser University, Burnaby, British Columbia, Canada U5A 1S6.

CAREER: Massachusetts State College, Worcester, instructor in economics and sociology, 1972; University of Massachusetts, Amherst, lecturer in urban education, 1973; University of Waterloo, Waterloo, Ontario, visiting lecturer in human kinetics and leisure studies, 1974; Queen's University, Kingston, Ontario, lecturer, 1974-75, assistant professor, 1975-80, associate professor of sociology, 1980-83, co-founder of Centre for Sport and Leisure Studies, 1978-83; University of British Columbia, Vancouver, associate professor of leisure studies, 1983-87; Simon Fraser University, Burnaby, British Columbia, member of faculty in department of communication, 1987—. Organizes workshops and conferences.

MEMBER: Canadian Communication Association, Society for Socialist Studies.

AWARDS, HONORS: Canada Council doctoral fellow, 1971-74; Social Sciences and Humanities Research Council fellowship, 1981.

WRITINGS:

(Editor with John Albinson, and contributor) *Canadian Sport: Sociological Perspectives,* Addison-Wesley, 1976.
(Editor with Hart Cantelon, and contributor) *Sport, Culture, and the Modern State,* University of Toronto Press, 1982.
Class, Sports, and Social Development, University of Massachusetts Press, 1983.
(Editor and contributor) *Popular Cultures and Political Practices,* Garamond Press (Toronto), 1988.

CONTRIBUTOR

Donald Ball and J.W. Loy, editors, *Sport and Social Order: Contributions to the Sociology of Sport,* Addison-Wesley, 1975.
R.J. Ossenberg, editor, *Power and Change in Canada,* McClelland & Stewart, 1980.
Loy and Gerald Kenyon, editors, *Sport, Culture, and Society,* 2nd edition, Lea & Febiger, 1981.
Marie Hart and Susan Birrell, editors, *Sport in the Sociocultural Process,* W.C. Brown, 1981.
Alan Tomlinson and Gary Whannel, editors, *Five Ring Circus,* Pluto Press, 1984.
Jean Harvey and Cantelon, editors, *Not Just a Game,* University of Ottawa Press, 1988.
Roger Jackson, editor, *The Olympic Movement and the Mass Media,* University of Calgary Press, 1988.

OTHER

Also contributor to J. Seagrave, editor, *The Olympic Games in Transition.* Editor, *Working Papers in the Sociological Study of Sports and Leisure,* Centre for Sport and Leisure Studies, Queen's University, 1978-82. Contributor of articles and reviews to numerous periodicals.

WORK IN PROGRESS: Research on cultural studies theory, television, and popular culture.

SIDELIGHTS: Richard S. Gruneau told *CA:* "My early interest in the sociological study of play, games, and sports developed out of my own involvement in athletics in high school and university. Sport has touched the lives of millions of people, yet few academics have taken it seriously as an element of culture.

"My first books were designed to show the ways in which sports *are* important cultural forms that have been ignored, romanticized, and layered with considerable ideological rhetoric. More recently I have tried to show that sports are not 'natural' features of the human condition but are socially and culturally produced in a way that bears the mark of broader forms of social organization, conflicts, and cultural struggles between, for example, dominant and subordinate or classes or men and women.

"Indeed, I have tried to reveal how the very social definition of sport is itself an object of such struggles. At stake is the monopolistic capacity to impose the legitimate definition of sporting practice and the legitimate use of the body. The study of the social production of particular sport forms and their various meanings tells us a great deal about the complex relationships between culture and ideology in modern societies."

He adds, "In more recent work I have extended my interest in sport to include other areas of popular culture and am currently teaching and conducting research on media and a broad range of popular cultural practices."

AVOCATIONAL INTERESTS: Skiing, sailboarding, politics, blues, jazz, backyard barbecues.

H

HALE, Allean Lemmon 1914-

PERSONAL: Given name pronounced Al-lean; born July 13, 1914, in Bethany, Neb.; daughter of Clarence Eugene (a clergyman and writer) and Constance (Harlan) Lemmon; married Mark Pendleton Hale, December 31, 1936 (died November 4, 1977); children: Susanna (Mrs. Robert Day), Mark Pendleton, Jr. *Education:* Christian College (now Columbia College), Columbia, Mo., A.A., 1933; University of Missouri, B.A., 1935; University of Iowa, M.A., 1963. *Politics:* Democrat. *Religion:* Disciples of Christ.

ADDRESSES: Home—22 G. H. Baker Dr., Urbana, Ill. 61801.

CAREER: Free-lance writer. Chicago Theological Seminary, Chicago, Ill., production assistant in drama, 1941; Christian College (now Columbia College), Columbia, Mo., alumnae director and editor of college magazine, 1951-56; University of Iowa, Iowa City, instructor in communication skills, 1960-62; Committee to Restore the Jane Addams Hull-House, Chicago, Ill., research assistant to Mark Hale, 1964; instructor in fiction writing in adult education program, Urbana, Ill., 1965; editorial assistant to Oscar Lewis, writer/anthropologist, Urbana, 1966-69; Ministry of Health Library, Paris, France, research assistant to Mark Hale, 1975; Parkland College, Champaign, Ill., instructor in creative writing, 1979-80. Member of board of directors, Lenoir Memorial Home, Columbia, 1972-77. Panelist and chairperson for literary workshops and seminars.

MEMBER: University of Illinois Women's Club, Champaign-Urbana Social Science Club, Columbia College Alumni Association (member of board of directors, 1968-75), Illinois Writers, Inc., Phi Beta Kappa.

AWARDS, HONORS: First prize, Zeta Phi Eta National Playwriting Contest, 1933, for *The Hero,* 1935, for *Last Flight Over;* first place, University of Missouri Dramatic Arts Contest, and Samuel French Award, both 1933, both for *The Hero;* first prize in Midwestern Intercollegiate Folk Playwriting Contest, 1935, for *Last Flight Over;* first prize, University of Missouri short story contest, 1935, for "The Red Bastard of Genesis"; four awards from National Federation of Press Women, 1953; Phi Beta Kappa 25th Year Honoree, University of Missouri, 1960; Distinguished Alumna Award, Christian College, 1964.

WRITINGS:

Petticoat Pioneer: The Christian College Story, 1851-1951, (history/higher education for women), Christian College, 1957, revised edition, 1968.

(Editor) Oscar Lewis, *A Death in the Sanchez Family,* Random House, 1969.

PLAYS

"The Hero" (first produced at the University of Missouri, Columbia, May, 1933), published in *Christian College Prize Plays,* Christian College, 1934.

Last Flight Over (first produced Southeast Missouri State College, Cape Girardeau, Mo., May, 1935), Row, Peterson, 1935, reprinted, Harper, 1962.

"The Hundred Years," first produced in Columbia, Mo., by the Disciples of Christ Church, 1937.

"Feed My Lambs," first produced in Jefferson City, Mo., at the Little Theater, 1937.

"The Imp and the Editor," first produced in Indianapolis by the Disciples of Christ Church, 1938.

"They Walk in Darkness," first produced at the University of Missouri, Columbia, 1949.

"White Collar Follies," first produced at the University of Missouri, Columbia, 1949.

"Red Is the Color of Apple Polish," first produced at the University of Missouri, Columbia, Fortnightly Club, 1949.

"Under the Ivy," first produced at Christian College, June, 1951.

Remind Me to Live: A One-Act Play, Friendship, 1960.

Two in a Trap: A One-Act Play, Friendship, 1966.

A Whole New Life, Friendship, 1969.

The Second Coming of Mrs. C., Friendship, 1971.

"The Battle at Liberty Courthouse," published in *Witness Against Odds,* Friendship, 1975.

OTHER

Contributor of verses to *Saturday Evening Post* and *Parents' Magazine;* contributor of fiction and articles to *World Call, Tennessee Williams Literary Journal, Missouri Review, New Theatre Quarterly, Missouri Alumnus,* and other periodicals, and to newspapers. Member of editorial board, *Tennessee Williams Literary Journal,* 1989.

WORK IN PROGRESS: Beyond the Moon: The Late Plays of Tennessee Williams.

AVOCATIONAL INTERESTS: Languages, art, history.

BIOGRAPHICAL/CRITICAL SOURCES:

PERIODICALS

Champaign News Gazette, January 4, 1969, June 27, 1982.
Christian College Magazine, February, 1969.
Spectator, September, 1971.

*   *   *

HAMILTON, Michael (Pollock) 1927-

PERSONAL: Born January 28, 1927, in Belfast, Northern Ireland; came to the United States, 1948; naturalized citizen, 1956; son of Hugh Pollock and Blanche (Webb) Hamilton; married Sarah Glidden Clippinger, November 23, 1956; married Eleanore McGroarty Raven, June 13, 1981; children: (first marriage) Patrick, Katrina. *Education:* University of Toronto, B.A., 1951; Protestant Episcopal Theological Seminary in Virginia, B.D., 1955.

ADDRESSES: Home—3509 Woodley Rd. N.W., Washington, D.C. 20016. *Office*—Washington Cathedral, Mount St. Alban, Washington, D.C. 20016.

CAREER: Ordained Episcopal priest, 1955; Church Advent, Cincinnati, Ohio, curate, 1955-58; University of Southern California, Los Angeles, chaplain, 1958-64; Washington Cathedral, Washington, D.C., canon, 1964—. Chairman, Washington Coalition for Clean Air, 1973-75. Consultant, National Institute of Health Volunteer Research Committee, 1974-76. *Military service:* British Army, Airborne, 1945-48; became lieutenant.

MEMBER: Council of Foreign Relations, Church Society for College Work.

WRITINGS:

(Editor) *The Vietnam War: Christian Perspectives,* Eerdmans, 1967.
(Editor) *This Little Planet,* introduction by Edmund Muskie, Scribner, 1970.
(Editor) *The New Genetics and the Future of Man,* Eerdmans, 1974.
(Editor) *The Charismatic Movement,* Eerdmans, 1974.
(Editor with Nancy S. Montgomery) *The Ordination of Women: Pro and Con,* Morehouse, 1975.
(Editor) *To Avoid Catastrophe: A Study in Future Nuclear Weapons Policy,* Eerdmans, 1977.
(Editor with Helen F. Reid) *A Hospice Handbook: A New Way to Care for the Dying,* Eerdmans, 1980.
(Editor) *American Character and Foreign Policy,* Eerdmans, 1986.

SIDELIGHTS: Michael Hamilton told *CA:* "I continue to be concerned with developing conferences and writing on the relation of the Judeo-Christian faith to whatever is new in the fields of politics, technology, medical ethics and social issues. Working for a just resolution of the Palestinian/Israeli conflict occupies a lot of my present energy and time."

AVOCATIONAL INTERESTS: Sailing, hiking.

*   *   *

HANSEN, Niles M(aurice) 1937-

PERSONAL: Born January 2, 1937, in Louisville, Ky.; son of Kristian and Alma (Jensen) Hansen; married Jo Drescher, August 22, 1959 (divorced, 1978), married Koren Sherrill, February 7, 1979; children: (first marriage) Karen, Eric, Laura; (second marriage) Stephen. *Education:* Centre College of Kentucky, B.A., 1958; Indiana University (now Indiana University at Bloomington), M.A., 1959, Ph.D., 1963.

ADDRESSES: Home—807 Rock Creek Dr., Austin, Tex. 78746. *Office*—Department of Economics, University of Texas at Austin, Austin, Tex. 78712.

CAREER: State University of Ghent, Ghent, Belgium, member of research staff in economics, 1961-62; University of Texas at Austin, assistant professor, 1963-66, associate professor of economics, 1966-67; University of Kentucky, Lexington, associate professor, 1967-68, professor of economics, 1968-69, associate director of Center for Developmental Change, 1967-69; University of Texas at Austin, professor of economics, 1969-75, Leroy G. Denman, Jr., Regents Professor in Economics, 1975—, director of Center for Economic Development, 1969-75. Member of committees, panels, research and study groups, and commissions, including United Nations Expert Group on Growth Center, 1969, and RAND Corp., 1974. Head of Urban and Regional Systems and area chairman for Human Settlements and Services, International Institute for Applied Systems Analysis, 1975-77. Visiting scholar of Centre d'Economie Regionale, Universite d'Aix-Marseille, 1988. Consultant to numerous institutions, government agencies, and professional organizations, including Commission on Population Growth and the American Future, 1971, National Area Development Institute, 1972, Agency for International Development, 1972, Office of Economic Opportunity, 1972, Brookings Institution, 1972, Agency for International Development, 1973, U.S. Department of Agriculture, 1979, and Radian Corp., 1979.

MEMBER: American Economic Association, Association for Comparative Economics, Association of Borderlands Scholars (member of council), Regional Science Association (president, Western chapter, 1981-82; vice-president), Southern Regional Science Association (president), Western Regional Science Association (president), Southern Economic Association.

AWARDS, HONORS: National Science Foundation fellow, 1965-66; Fulbright Fortieth Anniversary Distinguished Fellow in Turkey, 1987.

WRITINGS:

French Regional Planning, Indiana University Press, 1968.
France in the Modern World, Van Nostrand, 1969.
A Review of the Appalachian Regional Commission Program, Secretary of Commerce, 1969.
Rural Poverty and the Urban Crisis: A Strategy for Regional Development, Indiana University Press, 1970.
Financing Rural Development, National Area Development Institute, 1971.
(With N. David Huff, N. Dann Milne, Carol Pfrommer, and Richard YuKhin) *Economic Growth and Employment Opportunities for Disadvantaged Workers in the Tenco, Mississippi Area,* Southern Regional Council, 1971.
Intermediate-Size Cities as Growth Centers, Praeger, 1971.
(Editor and contributor) *Growth Centers and Regional Development,* Free Press, 1972.
(With Huff, Milne, Pfrommer, and YuKhin) *Planning for Growth and Development in Rural Areas in the Context of a National System of Regions,* Office of Economic Opportunity, 1972.
Location Preferences, Migration and Regional Growth, Praeger, 1973.

The Future of Nonmetropolitan America, Heath, 1973.

Evaluation of Studies Relevant to the Determination of Goals for Metropolitan Growth and Development, National Science Foundation, 1974.

(Editor and contributor) *Public Policy and Regional Economic Development; The Experience of Nine Western Countries,* Ballinger, 1974.

The Challenge of Urban Growth: The Basic Economics of City Size and Structure, Heath, 1975.

Cooperative Dispersed Urban Area Manpower Planning for Nonmetropolitan Populations, Manpower Administration, U.S. Department of Labor, 1975.

Improving Access to Economic Opportunity: Nonmetropolitan Labor Markets in an Urban Society, Ballinger, 1976.

(Editor) *Human Settlement Systems; International Perspectives on Structure, Change, and Public Policy,* Ballinger, 1977.

The Border Economy: Regional Development in the Southwest, University of Texas Press, 1981.

Contributor of articles and chapters to over thirty-five books, including J. Paelinck, editor, *Programming for Europe's Collective Needs,* North Holland Publishing, 1970, George L. Brinkman, editor, *The Development of Rural America,* University Press of Kansas, 1974, W. P. Avery, R. E. Lonsdale, and I. Volgyes, editors, *Rural Change and Public Policy: Eastern Europe, Latin America and Australia,* Pergamon, 1980, T. Kawashima and P. Korcelli, editors, *Human Settlement Systems: Spatial Patterns and Trends,* International Institute for Applied Systems Analysis (Austria), 1982.

Also author of papers and reports for national and local government agencies; also author of papers presented at more than twenty-five universities, institutes, and organizations. Contributor to *Britannica Book of the Year,* 1978, and to annals and proceedings; contributor of articles to such journals as *Land Economics, Journal of Human Resources, Social Research, Journal of Economic Issues,* and *Public Administration Review.* Advisory editor, *Social Science Quarterly;* member of editorial boards, *Growth and Change: A Journal of Regional Development, Review of Regional Studies, Journal of Borderlands Studies, Regional and Urban Economics,* and *International Regional Science Review.*

*   *   *

HANSEN, William F(reeman) 1941-

PERSONAL: Born June 22, 1941, in Fresno, Calif.; son of William Freeman and Helen (Jensen) Hansen; married Judith Friedman (divorced); married Marcia Jean Cebulska (a writer), August 14, 1972 (divorced); children: (second marriage) Inge Margrethe. *Education:* Attended Reed College, 1959-60, and Bakersfield College, 1960-61; University of California, Berkeley, A.B., 1965, Ph.D., 1970.

ADDRESSES: Home—317 South Rogers, Bloomington, Ind. 47403. *Office*—Department of Classical Studies, Indiana University, Bloomington, Ind. 47405.

CAREER: University of California, Berkeley, associate in classics, 1969-70; Indiana University at Bloomington, assistant professor, 1970-77, associate professor, 1977-85, professor of classical studies, 1985—, fellow of Folklore Institute, 1970—, associate dean of the faculties, 1986—.

MEMBER: International Society for Folk-Narrative Research, American Philological Association, American Folklore Society.

AWARDS, HONORS: Younger Humanist Fellow of National Endowment for the Humanities, 1972-73, for research in Copen-

hagen on the legend of Hamlet; American Council of Learned Societies fellowship, 1977-78, for research on Greek and Roman folktales.

WRITINGS:

The Conference Sequence: Patterned Narration Inconsistency in the Odyssey, University of California Classical Studies, 1972.

(Contributor) Linda Degh, Henry Glassie, and Felix Oinas, editors, *Folklore Today,* Research Center for Language and Semiotic Studies, Indiana University, 1976.

(Contributor) Oinas, editor, *The Heroic Epic and Saga,* Indiana University Press, 1978.

(Contributor) Burlakoff and Lindahl, editors, *Folklore on Two Continents,* Trickster Press, 1980.

(Contributor) Zygas and Vorrheis, editors, *Folklorica: Festschrift for Felix Oinas,* Indiana University, 1982.

Saxo Grammaticus and the Life of Hamlet, University of Nebraska Press, 1983.

(Contributor) Grant and Kitzinger, editors, *Civilization of the Ancient Mediterranean: Greece and Rome,* Scribner, 1988.

(Contributor) Edmunds, editor, *Approaches to Greek Myth,* Johns Hopkins University Press, 1989.

WORK IN PROGRESS: A Guide to International Folktales in Ancient Literature.

AVOCATIONAL INTERESTS: Herb gardening, pen and ink drawing.

*   *   *

HANSON, James Arthur 1940-

PERSONAL: Born August 29, 1940, in Bridgeport, Conn.; son of Arthur Christian (a gasoline station operator) and Alice Elizabeth (Rohrbach) Hanson; married Barbara Anne Kennedy (a high school teacher), 1965 (divorced, 1981); married Margaret Gall, 1981; children: (first marriage) Kristina Whitney; (second marriage) Matthew. *Education:* Yale University, B.A., 1961, M.A., 1963, Ph.D., 1967.

ADDRESSES: Office—World Bank, 700 19th St. N.W., Washington, D.C. 20431.

CAREER: Brown University, Providence, R.I., assistant professor, 1965-72, associate professor, 1972-79, professor of economics, 1980-81; World Bank, Washington, D.C., senior economist, 1981—. Consultant to Agency for International Development, Inter-American Development Bank, United National Economic Commission on Latin America, and Organization of American Societies.

MEMBER: American Economic Association, Econometric Society, Los Angeles Studies Association.

AWARDS, HONORS: Social Science Research Council fellowships, 1969, 1971-72; M.A., Brown University, 1973.

WRITINGS:

Growth in Open Economics, Springer-Verlag, 1971.

(Contributor) *Money and Politics in Latin America,* Los Angeles Center Publications, University of California, 1977.

(Editor with W. J. Behrman) *Short-Term Macroeconomic Policy in Latin America,* Ballinger, 1979.

Contractionary Devaluation, Substitution in Production and Consumption, and the Role of the Labor Market, World Bank, 1983.

Interest Rate Policies in Selected Developing Countries, 1970-1982, World Bank, 1985.

High Interest Rates, Spreads, and the Costs of Intermediation, World Bank, 1986.

WORK IN PROGRESS: Economic Development of Venezuela; Macro Policy Latin America Capital Markets and Development.

* * *

HARBAUGH, John W(arvelle) 1926-

PERSONAL: Born August 6, 1926, in Madison, Wis.; son of M. Dwight and Marjorie (Warvelle) Harbaugh; married Josephine Taylor, November 25, 1951 (died December 25, 1985); children: Robert, Dwight, Richard. *Education:* Attended Denison University, 1944-45; University of Kansas, B.S., 1948, M.S., 1950; University of Wisconsin, Ph.D., 1955. *Politics:* Republican.

ADDRESSES: Home—683 Salvatierra St., Stanford, Calif. 94305. *Office*—Department of Geology, Stanford University, Stanford, Calif. 94305.

CAREER: Stanford University, Stanford, Calif., assistant professor, 1955-61, associate professor, 1961-66, professor of geology, 1966—, chairman of department, 1969-72. Co-founder of Terrasciences, Inc., Lakewood, Colo.

MEMBER: Geological Society of America (fellow), American Association of Petroleum Geologists, Society of Economic Paleontologists and Mineralogists.

WRITINGS:

(With D. F. Merriam) *Computer Applications in Stratigraphic Analysis,* Wiley, 1968.
Stratigraphy and the Geologic Time Scale, W. C. Brown, 1968, 2nd edition, 1974.
(With Graeme Bonham-Carter) *Computer Simulation in Geology,* Wiley, 1970.
Guide to the Geology of Northern California, Kendall-Hunt, 1974.
(With J. H. Doveton and J. C. Davis) *Probability Methods in Oil Exploration,* Wiley-Interscience, 1977.
Historical Changes in Oil-Field Populations as a Method of Forecasting Field Sizes of Undiscovered Populations, Kansas Geological Survey, 1981.
(With Cushan Lin) *Graphic Display of Two- and Three-Dimensional Markov Computer Models in Geology,* Van Nostrand, 1984.
(With D. M. Tetzlaff) *Simulating Clastic Sedimentation,* Van Nostrand, 1989.

* * *

HARDIN, Charles M(eyer) 1908-

PERSONAL: Born August 29, 1908, in Lander, Wyo.; son of William E. (a lawyer) and Julia (Meyer) Hardin; married Sallie Gibson, December 1, 1933; children: Julia (Mrs. John Thomas Hansen). *Education:* University of Wyoming, A.B., 1930; University of Colorado, M.A., 1938; Harvard University, Ph.D., 1942.

ADDRESSES: Home—9919 Miller Dr., Davis, Calif. 95616. *Office*—Department of Political Science, University of California, Davis, Calif. 95616.

CAREER: High school teacher of English and French in Lander, Wyo., 1934-37; Harvard University, Cambridge, Mass., instructor in government, 1940-45; University of Chicago, Chicago, Ill., assistant professor, 1945-51, associate professor,

1952-57, professor of political science, 1958-60; Rockefeller Foundation, New York, N.Y., associate director of social sciences, 1961-64; University of California, Davis, professor of political science, 1964-76, director of International Agricultural Institute, 1965-70. Visiting fellow at Center for the Study of Democratic Institutions, summer, 1970. Member of President Lyndon B. Johnson's Task Force on Agriculture, 1964. Consultant to U.S. Department of Agriculture, 1945, 1949, Tennessee Valley Authority, 1948, International Bank for Reconstruction and Development, 1959, National Advisory Commission on Food and Fiber, 1966-67, and Ford Foundation, 1968.

AWARDS, HONORS: Best article award, *Journal of Farm Economics,* 1946, for "The Bureau of Agricultural Economics under Fire"; travel grant, Rockefeller Foundation, 1957; distinguished alumni award, University of Wyoming, 1977.

WRITINGS:

The Politics of Agriculture, Free Press, 1952.
Freedom in Agricultural Education, University of Chicago Press, 1955, reprinted, Arno, 1976.
Food and Fiber in American Politics, U.S. Government Printing Office, 1967.
(Contributor) Karl A. Fox and D. Gale Johnson, editors, *Readings in Agricultural Economics,* American Economic Association, 1969.
Presidential Power and Accountability: Toward a New Constitution, University of Chicago Press, 1974.
Constitutional Reform in America, Iowa State University Press, 1989.

SIDELIGHTS: Charles M. Hardin has been around the world twice and has worked in Pakistan and India. He has traveled through Latin America three times and has worked in Colombia, Chile, Peru, Mexico, and Brazil.

* * *

HAREVEN, Tamara K. 1937-

PERSONAL: Born May 10, 1937, in Cernauti, Rumania; daughter of Saul (a lawyer) and Mary (Hollinger) Kern. *Education:* Hebrew University of Jerusalem, B.A., 1960; University of Cincinnati, M.A., 1962; Ohio State University, Ph.D., 1965.

ADDRESSES: Office—Department of Individual and Family Studies, College of Human Resources, University of Delaware, Newark, Del. 19716; and Center for Population Studies, Harvard University, Cambridge, Mass. 02138.

CAREER: Dalhousie University, Halifax, Nova Scotia, assistant professor of history, 1965-67; Harvard University, Cambridge, Mass., fellow of Charles Warren Center for Studies in American History, 1967-69, associate professor, 1968-69; Clark University, Worcester, Mass., associate professor, 1969-76, professor of history, 1976-88, research associate, Center for Populations Studies, 1976—, director of family history project; University of Delaware, Newark, Unidel Professor of Family Studies and History, 1988—.

MEMBER: American Historical Association, Organization of American Historians, Phi Alpha Theta.

AWARDS, HONORS: Award from Yivo Institute for Jewish Research for best article of 1965, for "Un-American America and the *Jewish Daily Forward*"; New England Oral History Association award, 1978, for *Amoskeag: Life and Work in an American Factory-City,* and 1982, for *Family Time and Industrial Time;* Senior Fulbright fellow to India, 1978, and to Japan, 1987; Center for Advanced Study in the Behavior Sciences fellow, 1981-82; two-year research grant from National Institutes on Aging, 1987, for "Aging and Generational Relations: Cohort Change"; recipient of grants from the Rockefeller Foundation, Ford Foundation, and National Endowment for the Humanities.

WRITINGS:

Eleanor Roosevelt: An American Conscience, Quadrangle, 1968.
(Editor with Robert H. Bremner) *Children and Youth in America,* Harvard University Press, Volume I, 1970, Volume II, 1971, Volume III, 1974.
(Editor) *Anonymous Americans: Explorations in American Social History,* Prentice-Hall, 1971.
(Editor) *Family and Kin in American Urban Communities, 1780-1940,* F. Watts, 1977.
(Editor) *Transitions: The Family and the Life Course in Historical Perspective,* Academic Press, 1978.
(With Randolph Lagenbach) *Amoskeag: Life and Work in an American Factory-City,* Pantheon, 1978.
(Editor with Alice Rossi and Jerome Kagan) *The Family,* Norton, 1978.
(Editor with Maris Vinovskis) *Family and Population in Nineteenth-Century America,* Princeton University Press, 1978.
(Associate editor) *History of the Family and Kinship: A Select Bibliography,* Krauss Thompson, 1980.
Family Time and Industrial Time, Cambridge University Press, 1982.
(Editor with Kathleen J. Adams) *Aging and Life Course Transitions: An Interdisciplinary Perspective,* Guilford Press, 1982.
(Contributor) Marvin B. Sussman and Suzanne K. Steinmetz, editors, *Handbook of Marriage and the Family,* Plenum, 1987.
(Editor with Andrejs Plakans) *Family History at the Crossroads,* Princeton University Press, 1988.

Contributor of articles to *Journal of Social History, Journal of Marriage and the Family, Labor History, Journal of Interdisciplinary History,* and *Journal of Urban History.* Editor, *Journal of Family History,* 1975—.

WORK IN PROGRESS: A Social History of the American Family, for Dial; *The Silk Weavers of Kyoto.*

SIDELIGHTS: In a review of Tamara K. Hareven's book, *Amoskeag: Life and Work in an American Factory-City,* Milton Cantor writes in the *New Republic:* "Hareven, one of the most intelligent and prolific among contemporary historians of the family, has disclosed something of the life and work patterns of men and women in a great mill. In the course of it, she has also warned us about the insufficiency of simple formula, the complexity of men and societies, and we are in her debt for it." Benjamin DeMott, who declares the book to be a "no-frills history, solid and grainy," adds in the *Atlantic:* "Yet the lives here recorded really do breathe—attain, indeed, considerable cumulative impact before the end."

BIOGRAPHICAL/CRITICAL SOURCES:

PERIODICALS

Atlantic, January, 1979.
New Republic, December 23-30, 1978.

*   *   *

HARKAVY, Robert E(dward)   1936-

PERSONAL: Born November 19, 1936, in New York, N.Y.; son of Samuel S. (a chemical industry executive) and Helen R. (Riff) Harkavy; married Jane Frew, July 9, 1963; children: Michael. *Education:* Cornell University, B.A., 1958; attended University of Basel, 1959-60, and Harvard University, 1960-61; University of California, Berkeley, M.A., 1964; Yale University, Ph.D., 1973.

ADDRESSES: Home—P.O. Box 642, Lemont, Pa. 16851. *Office*—Department of Political Science, 107 Burrowes Building, Pennsylvania State University, University Park, Pa. 16802.

CAREER: Geigy Chemical Corp., Basel, Switzerland, laboratory technician, 1959; Chemical Fund, New York City, investment analyst, 1961; Crocker-Anglo Bank, San Francisco, Calif., investment analyst, 1961-62; U.S. Atomic Energy Commission, Washington, D.C., administrative assistant in Secretariat, 1966-68; Kalamazoo College, Kalamazoo, Mich., instructor, 1973-75; U.S. Arms Control and Disarmament Agency, Washington, D.C., foreign affairs officer for Non-Proliferation Bureau, 1975-76, and International Relations Bureaus, 1976-77; Cornell University, Ithaca, N.Y., senior research associate at Center for International Studies, 1977-78; Pennsylvania State University, University Park, associate professor, 1978-83, professor of political science, 1983—. U.S. International Communications Agency lecturer in Belgium, East and West Germany, and Yugoslavia, 1981, in Brazil and Mexico, 1982, and in Iceland, East and West Germany, Switzerland, Spain, Turkey, and Cyprus, 1988; visiting research professor at U.S. Army War College's Strategic Studies Institute, 1982-83; lecturer at colleges and universities, including Arizona State University, Lafayette College, U.S. Naval War College, Gettysburg College, U.S. Naval Postgraduate School, University of Pittsburgh, New School for Social Research, and University of Kiel; lecturer at Central Intelligence Agency; consultant to Stanford Research Institute, Hudson Institute, Congressional Research Service, and Office of the Secretary of Defense. *Military service:* U.S. Army, Artillery, 1958-59; became first lieutenant. U.S. Army Reserve, 1959-66.

MEMBER: International Institute for Strategic Studies, International Studies Association, American Political Science Association, Midwest Political Science Association, Inter-University Seminar on Armed Forces and Society, Phi Beta Kappa.

AWARDS, HONORS: Alexander von Humboldt fellow at University of Kiel, 1983-84; Fulbright research fellow, Sweden, 1985.

WRITINGS:

The Arms Trade and International Systems, Ballinger, 1975.
Spectre of a Middle Eastern Holocaust: The Strategic and Diplomatic Implications of the Israeli Nuclear Weapons Program (monograph), University of Denver, 1977.
Preemption and Two-Front Conventional Warfare: A Comparison of 1967 Israeli Strategy with the Pre-World War I German Schlieffen Plan (monograph), Leonard Davis Institute, Hebrew University of Jerusalem, 1978.
(Editor with Stephanie Neuman, and contributor) *Arms Transfers in the Modern World: Problems and Prospects,* Praeger, 1979.
(Editor with Edward A. Kolodziej, and contributor) *American Security Policy and Policy-Making: The Dilemmas of Using and Controlling Military Force,* Heath, 1980.
(Editor with Kolodziej, and contributor) *Security Policies of Developing States: Implications for Regional and Global Security,* Heath, 1981.
Great Power Competition for Overseas Bases: The Geopolitics of Access Diplomacy, Pergamon, 1982.

(Contributor) John J. Stremlau, editor, *The Foreign Policy Priorities of the Third World States,* Westview Press, 1982.

(Editor with Neuman) *The Lessons of Recent Wars in the Third World: Approaches and Case Studies,* Heath, 1985, Volume 2, . . . : *Comparative Dimensions,* 1987.

Bases Abroad, Oxford University Press, 1989.

Contributor to numerous books on American and foreign defense and security policies. Contributor of articles and reviews to political science journals, including *The Jerusalem Journal of International Relations, Third World Quarterly, International Organization,* and *Journal of International Affairs.*

WORK IN PROGRESS: A trade book on what can be learned from recent wars in the third world.

SIDELIGHTS: Robert E. Harkavy told *CA:* "If one were to look for an underlying driving force behind my scholarly interests (social scientists are no less prone than others to subjective forces), one would find a pervasive and consistent concern for the survival of Israel. Hence, I have written on arms transfers, nuclear proliferation, pariah states, the security policies of small countries, and the great powers' basing diplomacy. Each of these subjects, singly and in combination, are crucial to analyses of Israel's always-precarious defense policy. It is, of course, an interesting and open question as to whether such a compulsive concern produces analytic distortions, or, rather, is a necessary prerequisite to, or even the real wellspring of, understanding.

"I am presently involved in a large project, *The Lessons of Recent Wars in the Third World,* which has already spawned two volumes and a trade book in progress. There is, of course, the standard cliche about soldiers always fighting the 'last war,' which immediately conjurs the vivid image of the Maginot Line. But there is also the question of whether defense planning in one country attempts to divine lessons from wars in which they were not involved and then apply them to their own situations. Pakistan, in 1971, is claimed to have dreamed of pulling off a copy of Israel's 1967 blitzkrieg, in this case against India. Then too, there is the question of whether Soviet planners thought they could avoid a repeat of the U.S. Vietnam debacle in Afghanistan. Apparently, even with that 'lesson' in view, they have fallen into a similar trap.

"I have been asked a thousand times how I went from a chemistry major to a career as a political scientist, with an aborted M.B.A. in between. My father was a chemical engineer—I guess it took me until I was out of college to establish my own identity. But then, I went to college at a time when allegedly bright students were funneled into the 'hard' disciplines. I was not bad as a theoretical chemist, but was awful in the laboratory. Nobody who knows me now can imagine me a chemist. I often tell anxious Penn State undergraduates—so many caught up in the contemporary hypercareerism—that my story is not unusual, that many people hold jobs or pursue careers in their peak years which they could not have imagined when they graduated from college. But I sense that few of them are comforted in hearing that."

*   *   *

HARLAN, Glen
   See CEBULASH, Mel

HARRELL, Anne
   See NEGGERS, Carla A(malia)

*   *   *

HARRIS, Bill
   See HARRIS, William F., Jr.

*   *   *

HARRIS, H(arold) A(rthur)   1902-1974

PERSONAL: Born October 27, 1902, in Oxford, England; died August 29, 1974; son of George Washington (a college servant) and Myra (Taylor) Harris; married Dorothy Nita Rees, January 5, 1946. *Education:* Jesus College, Oxford, Diploma in Education (with distinction), 1926, M.A., 1932. *Religion:* Church of England.

ADDRESSES: Home—St. John's Home, St. Mary's Rd., Oxford OX4 1QE, England.

CAREER: St. David's University College, Lampeter, Wales, lecturer in English and classics, 1926-32, professor of classics, 1932-67. Visiting lecturer at University of Illinois, 1969, and University of Western Ontario, 1973. *Military service:* Home Guard, 1940-45; became second lieutenant.

MEMBER: International Council of Sport and Physical Education (corresponding member), Classical Association.

AWARDS, HONORS: Citation from American Academy of Physical Education, 1975, for "fascinating aspects of the ancient world researched and brought to life for present enjoyment."

WRITINGS:

Greek Athletes and Athletics, Hutchinson, 1964, Indiana University Press, 1966, reprinted, Greenwood Press, 1979.

Sport in Greece and Rome, Cornell University Press, 1972.

Hatletica Havonit Jehudim, Am Hassefer, 1972.

(Contributor) Horst Ueberhorst, editor, *Geschichte der Leibesuebungen* (title means "History of Sport"), Bartels & Wernitz, 1972.

Sport in Britain: Its Origins and Development, Stanley Paul, 1975.

Greek Athletics and the Jews, edited by Ian M. Barton and A. J. Brothers, University of Wales Press, 1976.

Contributor to *Journal of Hellenic Studies, Classical Review,* and *Greece and Rome.*

SIDELIGHTS: In a review of H. A. Harris's book *Greek Athletes and Athletics* Erich Segal writes in *Yale Review* that this book "is a useful and entertaining general introduction to sport of classical times. . . . [Harris] is especially good in his brief historical syntheses, which place the athletics he discusses in their proper context. His book is a judicious admixture of annals, analyses, and anecdotes, showing a thirst for accuracy and a zest for sport (he personally tested the relative merits of the ancient and modern javelins)."

BIOGRAPHICAL/CRITICAL SOURCES:

PERIODICALS

Yale Review, summer, 1967.*

HARRIS, Marion Rose (Young) 1925-
(Rose Young; pseudonym: Henry Charles)

PERSONAL: Born July 12, 1925, in Cardiff, South Wales; daughter of Robert Henry and Marion (Phillips) Young; married Kenneth Mackenzie Harris (the director of a furnishing company), August 18, 1943; children: Roger Mackenzie, Pamela Daphne, Keith Mackenzie. *Education:* Attended Gillingham School and Cardiff Technical College.

ADDRESSES: Home and office—Walpole Cottage, Long Dr., Burnham, Buckinghamshire SL1 8AJ, England.

CAREER: Writer. Private secretary to managing director of builder's merchant, 1942-46; free-lance journalist, 1946—; editor of Regional Feature Service, 1964-71; W. Foulsham & Co. Ltd., Slough, Buckinghamshire, England, editorial controller, 1974-83. Child care consultant for *Here's Health;* London correspondent for *Irish Leather and Footwear Journal* and *Futura* (fashion trade magazine). Furnishing consultant to builders, architects, and magazines, designing interiors for show houses at Ideal Homes Exhibition, Olympia, London, England, 1963-64, and for building estates in England.

MEMBER: Romantic Novelists Association, Society of Authors.

WRITINGS:

Fresh Fruit Dishes, Jenkins, 1963, reprinted, 1977.
Making a House a Home, Pan Books, 1963.
The Awful Slimmer's Book, Wolfe, 1967.
Teach Your Mum Flower Arranging, Wolfe, 1968.
(Contributor) *Dairy Book of Home Management,* Milk Marketing Board, 1969.
(Under pseudonym Henry Charles) *Twenty-Five Easy to Grow Vegetables: In Any Size Plot,* Foulsham, 1975.
(Under name Rose Young) *When the Clouds Clear,* International Publishing Co., 1975.
Captain of Her Heart, R. Hale, 1976.
(Under name Rose Young) *Love Can Conquer,* International Publishing Co., 1976.
(Under name Rose Young) *Secret of Abbey Place,* International Publishing Co., 1977.
Just a Handsome Stranger, Hamlyn, 1983.
The Queen's Windsor (nonfiction), Kensal Press, 1985.
Soldiers' Wives, Severn House Publishers, 1986.
Officers' Ladies, Severn House Publishers, 1987.
The Heart of the Dragon, Sphere Books, Book I: *Nesta,* 1988, Book II: *Amelda,* 1989, Book III: *Megan,* in press.

Also scriptwriter for British Broadcasting Corp. schools broadcast "Do Manners Matter," and for "Home This Afternoon" series. Contributor of short stories and articles to periodicals, including *Top Secretary, Homefinder, Cupid Chronicle, Home Overseas, Moneymaker,* and *Writer's Review.*

SIDELIGHTS: Marion Rose Harris told *CA:* "Fiction can be therapeutic. Transporting readers from their mundane daily round into a fantasy world can prove more beneficial than valium or any other sedative. Fiction often helps the reader to sort out problems or avoid some of life's pitfalls, so it could even be claimed that it has some educational value."

Harris adds that since 1986, she "has been publishing family sagas which have strong, factual backgrounds and are listed as 'general fiction.' "

HARRIS, Rosemary (Jeanne)

PERSONAL: Born in London, England; daughter of Arthur Travers (a marshal of the Royal Air Force) and Barbara D. K. (Money) Harris. *Education:* Attended Chelsea School of Art, London, and Courtauld Institute, London. *Politics:* Liberal. *Religion:* Christian.

ADDRESSES: Home—33 Cheyne Court, Flood St., London SW3 5TR, England. *Agent*—A. P. Watt & Son, 20 John St., London WC1N 2DR, England.

CAREER: Writer; picturer restorer; reader for Metro-Goldwyn-Mayer.

MEMBER: Society of Authors (deputy chairman, Children's Writers Group).

AWARDS, HONORS: Carnegie Medal for outstanding children's book, Library Association (England), 1968, for *The Moon in the Cloud;* Arts Council grant for research, 1971.

WRITINGS:

JUVENILES

The Moon in the Cloud (first book in trilogy), Faber, 1968, Macmillan (New York), 1970.
The Shadow on the Sun (second book in trilogy), Macmillan (New York), 1970.
The Seal-Singing, Macmillan (New York), 1971.
The Child in the Bamboo Grove, illustrations by Errol le Cain, Faber, 1971.
The Bright and Morning Star (third book in trilogy), Macmillan (New York), 1972.
The King's White Elephant, Faber, 1973.
The Flying Ship, Faber, 1975.
The Little Dog of Fo, Faber, 1976.
I Want to Be a Fish, Kestrel Books, 1977.
(Contributor) D. J. Denney, editor, *Young Winter's Tales #8,* Macmillan (London), 1978.
A Quest for Orion, Faber, 1978.
Beauty and the Beast, Faber, 1979.
Greenfinger House, Eel Pie, 1979.
Tower of the Stars, Faber, 1980.
The Enchanted Horse, Kestrel Books, 1981.
Janni's Stork, Blackie & Son, 1982.
Zed, Faber, 1982.
(Adaptor) *Heidi,* Benn, 1983.
Summers of the Wild Rose, Faber, 1987.
Colm of the Islands, Walker Books, 1989.

OTHER

The Summer House, Hamish Hamilton, 1956.
Voyage to Cythera, Bodley Head, 1958.
Venus with Sparrows, Faber, 1961.
All My Enemies, Faber, 1967, Simon & Schuster, 1972.
The Nice Girl's Story, Faber, 1968, published as *Nor Evil Dreams,* Simon & Schuster, 1973.
A Wicked Pack of Cards, Faber, 1969, Walker & Co., 1970.
Sea Magic and Other Stories of Enchantment, Macmillan (New York), 1974 (expanded version published in England as *The Lotus and the Grail: Legends from East and West,* Faber, 1974).
The Double Snare, Faber, 1974, Simon & Schuster, 1975.
Three Candles for the Dark, Faber, 1976.
(Editor) *Love and the Merry-go-round,* illustrations by Pauline Baynes, Hamish Hamilton, 1988.

Also author of television plays "Peronik," 1976, and "The Unknown Enchantment," 1981.

SIDELIGHTS: Rosemary Harris told *CA:* "There are many, many different things which turn someone into a writer by profession, rather than someone who writes a book or two on the side as a relief from other activities. I always wrote—but equally I always painted, and was drawn to music. Writing as a way of life is perhaps something that tends to happen, instead of being deliberately chosen—unless one starts off with serious intentions as a journalist, then gravitates to books.

"The turning point in my work was my first book for children, *The Moon in the Cloud,* which got the Carnegie Medal. It was a book that almost seemed to write itself, everything fell into place with such ease; but, looking back, I see that it owed a great deal to my years of training as a painter in Chelsea. It was certainly there that I got a lot of visual training which was a very strong element in that book. And it was in the sculpture class with F. E. McWilliam and Henry Moore that I learned to love the Egyptians—particularly the sculpture of the Old Kingdom. Curiously enough, several people have asked me if I was influenced by Thomas Mann's *Joseph and His Brethren,* and the answer is 'Yes, I was,' but only *after* I'd written *The Moon in the Cloud.* I didn't read Mann's great work until later on; then I think it was a strong influence on my writing two other books to complete the trilogy—*The Shadow on the Sun* and *The Bright and Morning Star.*"

AVOCATIONAL INTERESTS: Theater, music, photography.

BIOGRAPHICAL/CRITICAL SOURCES:

BOOKS

Something about the Author Autobiography Series, Volume 7, Gale, 1989.

PERIODICALS

New York Times Book Review, April 12, 1970.
Times Literary Supplement, July 20, 1970, March 27, 1981, November 26, 1982, March 29, 1987.

*   *   *

HARRIS, William F., Jr. 1933-
(Bill Harris)

PERSONAL: Born November 25, 1933, in Scranton, Pa.; son of William G. (a grocer) and Marjorie (Pierce) Harris; married second wife, Pamela Atkins, April, 1987; children: (first marriage) Michael, Ellen, Scott, Matthew. *Education:* Attended high school in North Bellmore, N.Y. *Politics:* Democrat. *Religion:* Episcopalian.

ADDRESSES: Home—322 East 18th St., New York, N.Y. 10003-2803.

CAREER: Crowell-Collier Publishing Co., New York City, in charge of sales promotion and public relations activities of magazines sold through schools, 1954-58; Dell Publishing Co., Inc., New York City, in charge of sales promotion and public relations for comic books, 1958-61; Western Publishing Co., Inc., New York City, editor of comic books, 1961-64; *New York Times,* New York City, editorial promotion copywriter, 1964-66; King Features Syndicate, New York City, creator and editor of Comic Book Division, 1966-69; *New York Times,* marketing services group manager and promotion copywriter, 1969-86. Licensed tour director in New York City, 1969—; director and

partner of tour agency ViewPoint International, 1981-1987. Involved in promotion of the Beatles film "Yellow Submarine."

WRITINGS:

New York, Mayflower, 1979.
United States of America, Mayflower, 1979.
Israel: The Promised Land, Mayflower, 1980.
Florida, Mayflower, 1980.
Hawaii, Mayflower, 1980.
Philadelphia, Mayflower, 1980.
Texas, Mayflower, 1981.
New England, Mayflower, 1981.
Boston, Mayflower, 1981.
Chicago, Mayflower, 1981.
Yellowstone and the Grand Tetons, Mayflower, 1981.
The Plaza Hotel, Poplar Books, 1982.
Washington, D.C., Abrams, 1982.
New York: City of Many Dreams, Crown, 1983.
New York at Night, Stewart, Tabori & Chang, 1983.
(Compiler with Mike Marqusee) *New York: An Anthology,* Little, Brown, 1985.
New York on the Water, World Yacht Enterprises, 1986.
History of the Presidents (from Johnson to Reagan), American Heritage Publishing, 1988.

PUBLISHED BY CRESCENT BOOKS

Colorado and the Rockies, 1983.
John F. Kennedy: A Tribute, 1983.
Canada, 1983.
The Landscapes of America, Volume 1, 1983, Volume 2, 1986.
The Lone Star State, 1984.
America: The Fifty States, 1984.
New York, 1984.
The American West, 1984.
Ghost Towns of the West, 1984.
Boston, 1984.
Philadelphia, 1984.
Chicago, 1984.
The Grand Canyon, 1985.
Virginia, 1985.
Pennsylvania, 1985.
The New England Coast, 1985.
Beautiful New England, 1985.
Williamsburg, 1985.
Iditarod: The Thousand Mile Marathon, 1985.
Wilderness of America, 1986.
Cowboys, 1986.
The Everglades, 1986.
New York from the Air, 1986.
Washington, D.C., 1986.
New England, 1986, 2nd edition, 1988.
Long Island, 1986.
Massachusetts, 1986.
Acadia National Park, 1986.
Homes of the Presidents, 1987.
Washington from the Air, 1987.
San Francisco from the Air, 1987.
Hawaii from the Air, 1987.
Grand Homes of the South, 1987.
Manhattan, 1987.
Maine, 1987.
New York State, 1987.
Texas, 1987.
Alaska, 1987.
Northern California, 1987.

The Balearic Islands, 1987.
Austria, 1987.
Canada's National Parks, 1987.
Rivers and Lakes of North America, 1987.
The Canary Islands, 1988.
California's National Parks, 1988.

Editor and writer of *Pan Am Welcome to New York,* a quarterly guide for international passengers arriving at Kennedy Airport. Writer for comic books, including *Phantom.* Contributor of articles to magazines, such as *New York Times, New York Alive, International Herald Tribune,* and *Eastern Review.*

WORK IN PROGRESS: NYC Access, guide to New York City for Simon & Schuster.

SIDELIGHTS: Bill Harris told *CA:* "Though I'm willing to admit there are other cities in the world, and even to write about them, I have to confess to a love affair with New York City that is almost unnatural. One of the most exciting days of my life was spent doing research for *New York at Night* when I watched a production at Radio City Music Hall from backstage and then spent the night aboard a tugboat in New York Harbor. I could live a happy life in Chicago, I think, and Venice is tempting. But there is only one New York, and it keeps getting better. The books I do are essentially picture books, the kind publishers call 'gift books' and their customers call 'coffee table books.' "

*   *   *

HARVEY, Nigel   1916-
(Hugh Willoughby)

PERSONAL: Born August 8, 1916, in Oxford, England; son of Godfrey Eric (a civil servant in India) and Stella Hope (Garratt) Harvey; married Barbara Anne Skemp; children: Charles Frazer, Geoffrey Rowland. *Education:* Exeter College, Oxford, M.A. (with honors), 1938; also attended Purdue University.

ADDRESSES: Home—41 Corringham Rd., Golders Green, London NW11, England.

CAREER: Ministry of Agriculture, Fisheries, and Food, London, England, member of staff, 1944-58; Agricultural Research Council, London, member of staff, 1958-76; full-time writer, 1976—. Agricultural history adviser to Old Fort William project in Ontario for National Heritage Ltd., 1974. Historic farm building adviser to Ministry of Agriculture, Fisheries, and Food, 1984. Chairman of Historic Farm, 1985.

MEMBER: Royal Institution of Chartered Surveyors (associate), Royal Agricultural Society of England (honorary member).

AWARDS, HONORS: Honorary librarian of Royal Agricultural Society of England, 1979.

WRITINGS:

The Story of Farm Buildings, National Federation of Young Farmers Clubs, 1953.
The Farming Kingdom, Turnstile, 1955.
Ditches, Dykes, and Deep Drainage, National Federation of Young Farmers Clubs, 1956.
(Under pseudonym Hugh Willoughby) *Amid the Alien Corn,* Bobbs-Merrill, 1958.
Farm Work Study, Farmer & Stockbreeder, 1958.
A History of Farm Buildings in England and Wales, David & Charles, 1970, 2nd edition, 1984.
Old Farm Buildings, Shire Publications, 1975, 3rd edition, 1987.

Fields, Hedges, and Ditches, Shire Publications, 1976, 2nd edition, 1987.
Farms and Farming, Shire Publications, 1976, 2nd edition, 1987.
Discovering Farm Livestock, Shire Publications, 1979.
(With Graham Cherry) *Effective Writing in Advisory Work,* Ministry of Agriculture, Fisheries, and Food, 1980.
The Industrial Archaeology of Farming in England and Wales, Batsford, 1980.
Trees, Woods, and Forests, Shire Publications, 1981.
(Editor) *Agricultural Research Centres: A World Directory of Organisations and Programmes,* Longmans, 1983.
Historic Farm Building Study: Sources of Information, Ministry of Agriculture, Fisheries, and Food, 1985.

Contributor to agriculture journals and to *New Statesman* and *Country Life.*

SIDELIGHTS: Nigel Harvey is a professional agriculturist writing on the history of his work. Some of his books are technical publications, but most are farming histories of interest to the general reader. *Amid the Alien Corn* is a collection of Harvey's letters from Purdue University to his family. He told *CA:* "My letters were never intended for publication, of course. When I got home, I had copies run-off, omitting personal matters, to give to friends and one of them took it to Bobbs-Merrill who offered to publish it." A reviewer for the *Christian Science Monitor* wrote, "Since he combines intellect with wit, his views make fast and easy reading, having for Americans all the fascination inherent in a chance to look over someone's shoulder and read private correspondence about ourselves."

According to Philip Riden writing in the *Times Literary Supplement,* Harvey's *Industrial Archaeology of Farming in England and Wales* describes "each stage in the farming process from 'The Winning of the Waste' through field, drainage, fertilizers, crops, stock, implements and machinery to the substantial section on farm buildings. . . . Harvey's style is plain and easy to follow; this is a book on technology which the non-technical can understand without difficulty."

BIOGRAPHICAL/CRITICAL SOURCES:

PERIODICALS

Christian Science Monitor, December 6, 1958.
Times Literary Supplement, November 21, 1980.

*   *   *

HASS, Robert   1941-

PERSONAL: Surname rhymes with "grass"; born March 1, 1941, in San Francisco, Calif.; son of Fred (in business) and Helen (Dahling) Hass; married Earline Leif (a psychotherapist), September 1, 1962; children: Leif, Kristin, Luke. *Education:* St. Mary's College of California, B.A., 1963; Stanford University, M.A., 1965, Ph.D., 1971.

ADDRESSES: Home—576 Santa Barbara Rd., Berkeley, Calif. 94707.

CAREER: State University of New York at Buffalo, assistant professor, 1967-71; St. Mary's College of California, Moraga, professor of English, 1971—. Visiting lecturer at University of Virginia, 1974, Goddard College, 1976, Columbia University, 1982, and University of California, Berkeley, 1983. Poet in residence, The Frost Place, Franconia, N.H., 1978.

AWARDS, HONORS: Woodrow Wilson fellow, 1963-64; Danforth fellow, 1963-67; Yale Series of Younger Poets Award from

Yale University Press, 1972, for *Field Guide;* U.S.-Great Britain Bicentennial Exchange Fellow in the Arts, 1976-77; William Carlos Williams Award, 1979, for *Praise;* Guggenheim Fellow, 1980; National Book Critics Circle Award in criticism, 1984, and Belles Lettres award, Bay Area Book Reviewers Association, 1986, for *Twentieth Century Pleasures: Prose on Poetry;* award of merit, American Academy of Arts and Letters, 1984; MacArthur Foundation grant, 1984.

WRITINGS:

POEMS

Field Guide, Yale University Press, 1973.
Winter Morning in Charlottesville, Sceptre Press, 1977.
Praise, Ecco Press, 1979.
(Contributor) *Five American Poets,* Carcanet New Press, 1979.
(Translator, with Robert Pinskey) Czeslaw Milosz, *The Separate Notebooks,* Ecco Press, 1983.
(Translator, with Czeslaw Milosz) Milosz, *Unattainable Earth,* Ecco Press, 1986.
(Translator with Louis Iribarne and Peter Scott) Milosz, *Collected Poems, 1931-1987,* Ecco Press, 1988.
The Apple Trees at Olema, Ecco Press, 1989.
Human Wishes, Ecco Press, 1989.

OTHER

Twentieth Century Pleasures: Prose on Poetry, Ecco Press, 1984.
(Editor) *Rock and Hawk: A Selection of Shorter Poems by Robinson Jeffers,* Random House, 1987.
(Co-editor with Bill Henderson and Jorie Graham) *The Pushcart Prize XII,* Pushcart Press, 1987.
(Editor with Charles Simic) Tomaz Salamun, *Selected Poems* (translations from the Slovene), Ecco Press, 1988.
(Editor) May Swenson and others, translators, *Selected Poems of Tomas Transtromer, 1954-1986,* Ecco Press, 1989.

Work represented in anthologies.

SIDELIGHTS: With his first collection of poems, *Field Guide,* Robert Hass won the 1973 Yale Series of Younger Poets Award and established himself, according to critics, as an important American poet. "He is a fine poet," Michael Waters relates in *Southwest Review,* "and his book is one of the very best to appear in a long time. . . . *Field Guide* is a means of naming things, of establishing an identity through one's surroundings, of translating the natural world into one's private history. This is a lot to accomplish, yet Robert Hass manages it with clarity and compassion." In the *Ontario Review* Linda W. Wagner agrees that "*Field Guide* is an impressive first collection. . . . Hass's view of knowledge is convincing. As we read the sonorous and generally regular poems, we are aware that the poet has achieved his apparent tranquility by living close to the edge. . . . One can be reminded only of the best of Hemingway."

Hass confirmed his ability with *Praise,* his second volume of poems. According to William Scammell in the *Times Literary Supplement,* these poems "unite freshness and wonder with a tough, inventive imagination." Writing in *Chicago Review* Ira Sadoff remarks that *Praise* "might even be the strongest collection of poems to come out in the late seventies." Sadoff notes that *Field Guide* "was intelligent and well-crafted; it tapped Hass's power of observation carefully and engagingly." Nevertheless the reviewer had "reservations" about *Field Guide* that "stemmed from some sense of chilliness that seemed to pervade a number of poems, as if the poems were wrought by an intellect distant from its subject matter." Sadoff continued: "I have no

such problems with *Praise.* . . . [It] marks Hass's arrival as an important, even pivotal, young poet."

Critic Robert Miklitsch, in his *Hollins Critic* review, expresses similar feelings about *Praise,* which he feels "marks the emergence of a major American poet. If his first book, *Field Guide,* . . . did not provoke such acclaim, the second book will." Still more applause comes from *Ontario Review* contributor Charles Molesworth, who writes that Hass is "slowly but convincingly becoming one of the best poets of his generation. . . . [*Praise*] is about language, its possibilities and its burdens, its rootedness in all we do and its flowering in all we hunger for and fear. . . . But the loving tentativeness, the need to see and to save, these are Hass's own gifts. He is that extremely rare person: a poet of fullness."

As Dick Davis notes in the *Times Literary Supplement,* Hass's "love for poetry, his intimate awareness of how it is made and the kinds of effects it is capable of, are obvious" in *Twentieth Century Pleasures: Prose on Poetry.* Other critics appreciate the book as well, honoring it with the National Book Critics Circle award, among others. Most readers commend Hass for the book's readability and inclusion of reflections taken from his personal life. "Mr. Hass's style balances conversational directness and eloquent complexity," notes *New York Times Book Review* contributor Anthony Libby. He concludes, "Mr. Hass believes that poetry is what defines the self, and it is his ability to describe that process that is the heart of this book's pleasure."

BIOGRAPHICAL/CRITICAL SOURCES:

BOOKS

Contemporary Literary Criticism, Volume 18, Gale, 1981.

PERIODICALS

Atlantic Monthly, June, 1979.
Chicago Review, winter, 1980.
Hollins Critic, February, 1980.
Los Angeles Times Book Review, November 18, 1984.
Nation, May 19, 1979.
New York Times Book Review, March 3, 1985.
Ontario Review, fall, 1974, fall-winter, 1979-80.
Southwest Review, June, 1975.
Times Literary Supplement, May 28, 1982, March 15, 1985.
Washington Post Book World, August 19, 1979.

*   *   *

HAUSER, Hillary 1944-

PERSONAL: Born September 4, 1944, in California; daughter of Carl Richard and Mabel (Hensel) Hauser. *Education:* University of Washington, Seattle, B.A., 1966.

ADDRESSES: Home—2421 Shelby St., P.O. Box 988, Summerland, Calif. 93067.

CAREER: TV Guide, Los Angeles, Calif., local editor, 1966-67, national programmer, 1967-68; *Skin Diver,* Los Angeles, assistant editor, 1968-71, special features editor, 1971—; *Ocean Science News,* Washington, D.C., West Coast editor, 1971-87; freelance writer, 1971—; *Santa Barbara News-Press,* Santa Barbara, Calif., reporter, 1981-87. U.S. correspondent, *Tauchen,* Republic of Germany, 1981—, and *New Zealand Dive,* 1983—. Member of Harbor Commission of Avalon, Catalina Island, 1971-72. Technical consultant for television films "Shark Kill" and "Trapped beneath the Sea."

MEMBER: Mensa.

AWARDS, HONORS: Winner of *Redbook* adventure writing contest, 1978; named Honorary Gold Master Instructor, Professional Association of Diving Instructors, 1978.

WRITINGS:

(Associate editor) *Ski World,* Petersen Publishing, 1973.
(Associate editor) Corky Fowler, *Skiing Techniques,* Petersen Publishing, 1973.
Women in Sports: Scuba Diving, Harvey House, 1976.
The Living World of the Reef, Walker & Co., 1978.
Book of Fishes, Photographic Book Co. (New York), 1984.
Diamonds (poems), Otto Press, 1984.
Call to Adventure, Bookmakers Guild, 1987.
Our Ocean World (juvenile), Bookmakers Guild, 1989.
(With mother, Mabel Hauser) *The Adventures of Antatole Ant,* Bookmakers Guild, 1989.

Author of monthly features, "Fish of the Month" and "News Briefs," in *Skin Diver,* 1968-76. Contributor to numerous periodicals, including *National Geographic, Reader's Digest, Esquire, Islands, Los Angeles Times Sunday Magazine,* and *Christian Science Sentinel.* Associate editor, *Ocean Realm,* 1988—; West coast editor, *Coastal Zone Management,* 1971-75.

WORK IN PROGRESS: Heart of a Sourdough, a tale of the Alaska gold rush of 1900.

SIDELIGHTS: Hillary Hauser told *CA:* "I think the main thing for aspiring writers to develop is a thick hide against rejections; if something doesn't sell the moment you send it out, keep it for a better day! My recently-published book, *Call to Adventure,* was rejected a number of times before I put it on the shelf sometime in 1981. I revived it in 1987, the year it was accepted and published, and we are going into a second printing of the book, about six months after the first edition came out! Even better than this story are the two books created by my mother in the late 1940s; over the years, they were tried on publishers, but never accepted. In 1989, these two books will be published—*The Adventures of Antatole Ant* and *The Truth about Santa Claus*—forty years after they were conceived (and twelve years after my mother, Mabel Hauser, passed over the Great Divide)! I think this proves that just because your ideas may be rejected at the outset doesn't mean they are not valid and valuable.

"With the recent flurry of book acceptances, I've embarked on a lecture career and very often find myself talking and listening to young people. Many of them want to know how and when I got started writing; I have had to confess to them that I was writing poems to sea lions and kelp when I was ten years old. I encourage these youthful listeners to listen to themselves, to follow their dreams, to take responsibility for what they want to do. Too often, these dreams are lost in the adult world of worry—about mortgages, insurance, and all the things everyone is 'supposed to do.' Even so-called 'juvenile delinquents' have a tremendous energy that can be channeled instead of battled. This philosophy is the reason I assembled *Call to Adventure;* in the book, supreme adventurers like Jacques Cousteau, Sir Edmund Hillary (first man up Mt. Everest), Robert Ballard (finder of the *Titanic*), and other exciting men and women tell of the obstacles they overcame in following their destinies. Writers must be willing to do the same."

HAYES, Joseph 1918-
(Joseph H. Arnold)

PERSONAL: Born August 2, 1918, in Indianapolis, Ind.; son of Harold Joseph and Pearl M. (Arnold) Hayes; married Marrijane Johnson (a free-lance writer); children: Gregory, Jason, Daniel. *Education:* Attended Indiana University, 1938-41.

ADDRESSES: Home—1168 Westway Dr., Sarasota, Fla. 33577.

CAREER: Playwright and novelist. Occasional producer of Broadway plays as partner in Erskine and Hayes productions.

MEMBER: Dramatists Guild, Authors League of America, Society of Stage Directors and Choreographers, Writers Guild of America (West), American Civil Liberties Union (chairman of Sarasota chapter).

AWARDS, HONORS: Charles H. Sergel Drama Prize, University of Chicago, 1948; Indiana Author's Day award in fiction, 1955, for *The Desperate Hours;* Antoinette Perry ("Tony") Award of American Theatre Wing, 1956, for play, "The Desperate Hours"; Edgar Allen Poe ("Edgar") Award of Mystery Writers of America, 1965, for best mystery screenplay, "The Desperate Hours"; D.H.L., Indiana University, 1971.

WRITINGS:

NOVELS

The Desperate Hours (Literary Guild selection; also see below), Random House, 1954, Carroll & Graf, 1985.
(With wife, Marrijane Hayes) *Bon Voyage,* Random House, 1957.
The Hours after Midnight, Random House, 1958.
Don't Go Away Mad, Random House, 1962.
The Third Day, McGraw, 1964.
The Deep End (also see below), Viking, 1967.
Like Any Other Fugitive, Dial, 1972.
The Long Dark Night, Putnam, 1974.
Missing and Presumed Dead, New American Library, 1976.
Island on Fire, Grosset, 1979.
Winner's Circle, Delacorte, 1980.
No Escape, Delacorte, 1982.
The Ways of Darkness, Morrow, 1986.

PLAYS

The Thompsons, Samuel French, 1944.
A Woman's Privilege, Samuel French, 1945.
The Bridegroom Waits, Samuel French, 1946.
Home for Christmas, Samuel French, 1946.
Too Young, Too Old, Baker Co., 1948.
"Leaf and Bough," produced on Broadway, 1949.
The Desperate Hours (based on his novel of the same title; produced on Broadway, 1955), Samuel French, 1956.
Calculated Risk (produced on Broadway, 1962), Samuel French, 1962.
"The Deep End" (based on his novel of the same title), produced on Broadway, 1969.
"Is Anyone Listening?," produced in Tallahassee, Fla., at Florida State University Theatre, February, 1971.
"Come into My Parlor," translation under the title "And Nothing but the Truth," first produced in West Berlin at the Renaissance Theatre, April 28, 1988.

Also author of screenplays, "The Young Doctors," 1962, "The Desperate Hours," and others.

PLAYS WITH WIFE, MARRIJANE HAYES, FOR AMATEUR PRODUCTION

And Came the Spring, Samuel French, 1944.
Too Many Dates, Samuel French, 1945.
Ask for Me Tomorrow, Samuel French, 1945.
Quiet Summer, Samuel French, 1945.
Come Rain, Come Shine, Samuel French, 1945.
Change of Heart, Samuel French, 1945.
Come Over to Our House, Samuel French, 1946.
Life of the Party, Samuel French, 1949.
June Wedding, Samuel French, 1949.
Curtain Going Up, Samuel French, 1950.
Once in Every Family, Samuel French, 1951.
Penny, Samuel French, 1951.
Mister Peepers, Samuel French, 1952.
Head in the Clouds, Samuel French, 1952.

UNDER PSEUDONYM JOSEPH H. ARNOLD

Sneak Date, Row, Peterson & Co., 1944.
Where's Laurie?, Row, Peterson & Co., 1946.

WORK IN PROGRESS: A novel dealing with the results, social and psychological, of a horrendous crime, not murder, untitled as yet.

SIDELIGHTS: Beginning with *The Desperate Hours,* the suspense story in which three fugitives take over a suburban household during their escape from an Indianapolis prison, playwright and novelist Joseph Hayes has written a dozen thrillers that have been adapted for stage and screen. Though his plots tend to be complicated, says Christopher Lehmann-Haupt of the *New York Times,* Hayes "is a master of economical storytelling, able to balance with the tip of his pen a dozen characters conniving at cross-purposes." Richard Sullivan of the *Chicago Sunday Tribune* called *The Desperate Hours* "A mighty well done piece of intense story telling" enhanced by extraordinary insight into his characters. Similarly impressed, John Raymond of the *New Statesman & Nation* found it an excellent first novel, "the most successful horror story that I have read for a long time." Of the author's twelfth novel, *The Ways of Darkness,* Lehmann-Haupt comments, "you have to be impressed at how long [Hayes] sustains such a high pitch of tension. . . . What's even more impressive is his ability to manipulate your concern. Whether he wants you counting the number of bullets left in the villain's pistol, or tracking the movements of the victim's drunken, homicidal father, Mr. Hayes has complete control."

Hayes believes that "those who claim only negative values in the world and then spend time and talent writing to convince that all is a void . . . deny their negative philosophy by the very creative act of writing." He adds: "The trend, in uncertain times, toward nihilism, in society and literature, seems destructive, the one feeding on the other. When have times ever been certain? How did all this whining start and where will it end? If one does not like the world as it is (and who could?), then his job is to change it—by criticism, protest, politics—and not to sit and wallow in his own sour juices."

MEDIA ADAPTATIONS: The film "Terror after Midnight" was based on Hayes's novel *The Hours after Midnight;* the novels *The Third Day* and *Bon Voyage* were made into films; "Come into My Parlor" is being made into a film produced by Raymond Girard and directed by the author.

BIOGRAPHICAL/CRITICAL SOURCES:

PERIODICALS

Best Sellers, November, 1985.
Chicago Sunday Tribune, February 28, 1954.
Chicago Tribune Book World, July 7, 1985.
New Statesman & Nation, October 2, 1954.
New Yorker, March 13, 1954.
New York Times, February 28, 1954, August 8, 1985, July 4, 1986.

*   *   *

HEALD, Tim(othy Villiers) 1944-
(David Lancaster)

PERSONAL: Born January 28, 1944, in Dorchester, Dorset, England; son of Villiers Archer John (a businessman) and Jean (Vaughan) Heald; married Alison Martina Leslie, March 30, 1968; children: Emma, Alexander, Lucy, Tristram. *Education:* Balliol College, Oxford, B.A. (with honors), 1965, M.A., 1984. *Politics:* Liberal.

ADDRESSES: *Home and office*—305 Sheen Rd., Richmond Surrey TW10 5AW, England. *Agent*—Richard Scott Simon, 43 Doughty St., London WC1N 2LF, England.

CAREER: *Sunday Times,* London, England, assistant diary columnist, 1965-67; *Town* magazine, London, features editor, 1967; *Daily Express,* London, feature writer, 1967-72; free-lance journalist and writer, 1972-77; *Weekend* magazine, Toronto, Ontario, associate editor, 1977-78; free-lance journalist and writer, 1978—.

MEMBER: PEN, Society of Authors (council of management, 1988—), Crime Writers Association (chairman, 1987-88), Annandale Society (former president), Marylbone Cricket Club, Royal Tennis Court.

WRITINGS:

MYSTERY NOVELS

Unbecoming Habits, Stein & Day, 1973.
Blue Blood Will Out, Stein & Day, 1974.
Deadline, Stein & Day, 1975.
Let Sleeping Dogs Die, Stein & Day, 1976.
Just Desserts, Scribner, 1979.
Murder at Moose Jaw, Doubleday, 1981.
A Small Masterpiece, Doubleday, 1982 (published in England as *Masterstroke,* Hutchinson, 1982).
Red Herrings, Doubleday, 1985.
Brought to Book, Doubleday, 1988.
Business Unusual, Macmillan (London), 1989.

OTHER

It's a Dog's Life, Elm Tree Books, 1971.
The Making of "Space 1999," Ballantine, 1976.
John Steed: An Authorized Biography, Weidenfeld & Nicolson, 1977.
(With Mayo Mohs) *H.R.H.: The Man Who Will Be King,* Arbor House, 1979, published with new prologue, Berkley Publishing, 1981.
Caroline R (novel), Arbor House, 1980 (published in England under pseudonym David Lancaster, Hutchinson, 1981).
Networks: Who We Know and How We Use Them, Hodder & Stoughton, 1983, published as *Old Boy Networks,* Ticknor & Fields, 1984.
Class Distinctions (novel), Hutchinson, 1984.

The Character of Cricket, Pavilion Books, 1986.
(Editor) *The Newest London Spy,* Muller, 1988.
(Editor) *The Rigby File,* Hodder & Stoughton, 1989.
150 Years of the Royal Warrant, Queen Anne Press, 1989.

Contributor of articles and reviews to numerous periodicals, including the *Daily Telegraph,* and to British Broadcasting Corp. Regular reviewer, London *Times,* 1973—; regular fiction reviewer, *Daily Telegraph,* 1974-77.

WORK IN PROGRESS: Novels; a nonfiction book.

SIDELIGHTS: Although Tim Heald has written several nonfiction works and mainstream novels and has had a notable career as a journalist, he is best known for his series of mystery novels featuring bumbling Board of Trade investigator Simon Bognor. As Carol Cleveland describes him in *Twentieth-Century Crime and Mystery Writers,* Heald's sleuth "is cousin to other fallible, physically unimpressive heroes of the 1970's. Bognor," she explains, " 'mindful as ever of the idiocy of his job,' is introduced unwillingly into various modern institutions chosen for their qualities of flamboyance, or anachronism, or both. He then passes through adventures that range from the pathetic to the ludicrous and back again." In the typical Bognor mystery, "Simon pokes around and stumbles on a solution, which, as his boss Parkinson would observe, is not too satisfactory but will have to do," *Washington Post Book World* reviewer Jean M. White notes. "But then you don't read Heald for deft solutions or action but for stylish wit and satire."

In addition, Heald has a flair for "creat[ing] vignettes that stick in the mind," as the *New York Times Book Review*'s Newgate Callendar comments, supplemented by what White calls "a delightful cast of characters." In the recent *Brought to Book,* for example, Bognor attends a publishing conference where a publisher/pornographer is found crushed to death by his own bookshelves. "In the world of opportunistic writers and megalomaniac takeovers it is only mildly surprising to find Russian submarines lurking [and] a psychopathic SAS poet" among other oddities, comments Harriet Waugh in the *Spectator.* In between these strange occurrences, Bognor "flits enthusiastically among more jokes, literary puns, *bon mots,* and jokes-within-jokes than" any of his literary predecessors, Marcel Berlins states in the London *Times.* The result, both critics agree, is "great fun."

Heald told *CA:* "I've always had a facility for words. I won essay prizes at school and started magazines and I've never considered anything else, except briefly, and absurdly, the British Foreign Office. The most important circumstance has always been luck—mostly good. I started at school, edited my first magazine at about age ten. I'd like to make a reasonable living out of writing and I'd like as many people as possible to read what I write and I'd like them to be entertained by it. I don't believe I have any amazingly important message to convey but at the same time I don't want my readers to treat my books as a sort of literary musack. I want them to be alert throughout!

"I'm influenced by everything I read but it would take a book to explain precisely how and why. I review thrillers for the London *Times* at the moment so my view of other writers is somewhat jaundiced (I am not able to be as selective as I would like). A very few impress me a lot, but much more strike me as being of marginal worth. There are almost certainly too many books being published but unfortunately if the total were to be cut back, the wrong books would suffer. I do think the majority of commercially successful books are appalling. . . . I'm afraid I have a low opinion of public taste (the mass market) and an even lower one of the literary sensibilities of the average publisher!"

MEDIA ADAPTATIONS: Some of Heald's mysteries have been adapted for television by Thames Television.

BIOGRAPHICAL/CRITICAL SOURCES:

BOOKS

Twentieth-Century Crime and Mystery Writers, St. James Press/St. Martin's, 1985.

PERIODICALS

New York Times Book Review, November 25, 1973, October 20, 1974.
Spectator, September 24, 1988.
Times (London), February 18, 1988.
Washington Post Book World, September 15, 1974.

* * *

HEATH, Catherine 1924-

PERSONAL: Born November 17, 1924, in London, England; daughter of Samuel Michael (an accountant) and Anna (de Boer) Hirsch; married Dennis Heath, July 19, 1949 (divorced, 1977); children: Anne Lindsay, Anthony David. *Education:* St. Hilda's College, Oxford, B.A. (with honors), 1946.

ADDRESSES: Home—17 Penarth Ct., Devonshire Ave., Sutton, Surrey, England. *Agent*—Curtis Brown Ltd., 162-168 Regent St., London W1, England.

CAREER: University of Wales, Cardiff, assistant lecturer in English literature, 1948-50; Carshalton College of Further Education, Carshalton, England, lecturer, 1964-70, senior lecturer in English, 1970-85. Member of social services committee, London Borough of Sutton, 1967-77.

MEMBER: International PEN, Amnesty International, Society of Authors.

WRITINGS:

Stone Walls (novel), J. Cape, 1973.
The Vulture (novel), J. Cape, 1974.
Joseph and the Goths (novel), J. Cape, 1975.
Lady on the Burning Deck (novel), J. Cape, 1978, Taplinger, 1979.
"Scorpio Male Seeks Libran Mate" (radio script), first produced by British Broadcasting Corp. (BBC-Radio), February 9, 1979.
Behaving Badly (novel; also see below), J. Cape, 1984, Taplinger, 1985.
"Behaving Badly" (four-part television screenplay adaptation of the novel), Humphrey Barclay Productions, 1989.

Contributor of drama criticism to *Plays International;* contributor to *New Poetry 3* and *Massachusetts Review.*

SIDELIGHTS: Catherine Heath "is consolidating a growing reputation as an important writer who is bringing her own distinctive gifts to the genre of English social comedy," declares Gerard Werson in the *Dictionary of Literary Biography.* Her style is characterized by its precision and her love of rules and order. As she once explained to *CA,* "I am a purist where language is concerned, believing that any artist must always love and have control of his medium." But Heath's tight control over her writing style is counterpointed by the content of her novels, which are concerned with the confusion of changing lifestyles and morality in today's society. Because of this subject, Heath's books often contain "a latent violence that is sometimes openly expressed by her characters in words and deeds," says Werson.

This deliberate contradiction between the content of her books and her choice of style results in what Werson considers to be a "considerable tragicomic force."

Having been compared by some critics to such authors as Barbara Pym and Molly Keene, Heath has been praised for her insight into human nature. "There's dark water under Catherine Heath's coruscating wit," remarks *Voice Literary Supplement* contributor Brett Harvey. "She understands sexual loneliness, jealousy, malice." Isabel Raphael similarly notes in her London *Times* review of *Behaving Badly* that "Catherine Heath understands the genuine affection behind family ties, as well as the ludicrously awful dilemmas of middle age, and looks on middle-age pretensions with a sharp and tolerant eye." Considering Heath's work to be on a par with the likes of Muriel Spark, Werson asserts that the author's "fiction is remarkable for its description of suffering, both real and imagined; for its apparently detached ironic statement of conflict, lack of fulfillment, and remorse; and for its comic perception of our struggle to survive."

MEDIA ADAPTATIONS: Radio adaptations have been produced by the British Broadcasting Corporation of *Joseph and the Goths,* 1977, *Lady on the Burning Deck,* 1979, and *Behaving Badly,* 1984.

BIOGRAPHICAL/CRITICAL SOURCES:

BOOKS

Dictionary of Literary Biography, Volume 14: *British Novelists since 1960,* Gale, 1983.

PERIODICALS

Los Angeles Times Book Review, April 21, 1985.
New York Times Book Review, April 28, 1985.
Spectator, September 23, 1978.
Times (London), April 5, 1984.
Times Literary Supplement, September 29, 1978, April 20, 1984.
Voice Literary Supplement, June, 1985.

*　　　*　　　*

HECKELMANN, Charles N(ewman) 1913-
(Charles Lawton)

PERSONAL: Born October 24, 1913; son of Edward (a metal lithographer) and Sophia (Hodum) Heckelmann; married Anne Auer, April 17, 1937; children: Lorraine (Mrs. Richard Kane), Thomas Edward. *Education:* University of Notre Dame, B.A. (maxima cum laude), 1934. *Religion:* Roman Catholic.

ADDRESSES: Home—10634 Green Trail Dr. S., Boynton Beach, Fla. 33436. *Agent*—Scott Meredith Literary Agency, Inc., 845 Third Ave., New York, N.Y. 10022.

CAREER: Brooklyn Daily Eagle, Brooklyn, N.Y., sports writer, 1934-37; Cupples & Leon Co., New York City, editor and production manager, 1937-41; Popular Library, Inc., New York City, editor-in-chief, 1941-58, vice-president, 1953-58; Monarch Books, Inc., New York City, president and editor-in-chief, 1958-65; David McKay Co., New York City, managing editor and director of subsidiary rights, 1968-71; Hawthorn Books, Inc., New York City, senior editor and rights director, 1971-72, editor-in-chief and vice-president, 1972-75; *National Enquirer,* Lantana, Fla., book editor, 1975-78.

MEMBER: Catholic Writers Guild of America (president, 1949-52), Western Writers of America (vice-president, 1955-57; president, 1964-65); National Cowboy Hall of Fame and Western Heritage Center.

WRITINGS:

Vengeance Trail, Arcadia House, 1944, reprinted, Popular Library, 1977.
Lawless Range, Arcadia House, 1945.
Six-Gun Outcast, Arcadia House, 1946.
Deputy Marshal, Arcadia House, 1947.
Guns of Arizona, Doubleday, 1949.
Outlaw Valley, Cupples & Leon, 1950.
Danger Rides the Range, Cupples & Leon, 1950.
Two-Bit Rancher, Doubleday, 1950.
Let the Guns Roar, Doubleday, 1950.
Fighting Ramrod, Doubleday, 1951.
Hell in His Holsters, Doubleday, 1952.
The Rawhider, Holt, 1952.
Hard Man with a Gun, Little, Brown, 1954.
Bullet Law, Little, Brown, 1955, reprinted, Popular Library, 1976.
Trumpets in the Dawn, Doubleday, 1958, reprinted, Popular Library, 1977.
The Big Valley, Whitman Publishing, 1966.
The Glory Riders, Avon, 1967.
Writing Fiction for Profit, Coward, 1968.
(Editor) *With Guidons Flying: Tales of the United States Calvary in the Old West by Members of the Western Writers of America,* Doubleday, 1970.
Stranger from Durango, Lancer Books, 1971.
Return of the Arapahoe, Popular Library, 1980.
Wagons to Wind River, Popular Library, 1982.

UNDER PSEUDONYM CHARLES LAWTON; YOUNG ADULTS

Clarkville's Battery, Cupples & Leon, 1937.
Ros. Hackney: Halfback, Cupples & Leon, 1937.
Jungle Menace: Starring Frank Buck, Cupples & Leon, 1937.
The Winning Forward Pass, Cupples & Leon, 1940.
Home Run Hennessey, Cupples & Leon, 1941.
Touchdown to Victory, Cupples & Leon, 1942.

OTHER

Contributor of short stories to magazines.

MEDIA ADAPTATIONS: The film productions of "Stranger from Santa Fe," 1947, "Frontier Feud," 1948, and "Deputy Marshal," 1949, are all based on Heckelmann's writings.

*　　　*　　　*

HELLMAN, Geoffrey T(heodore) 1907-1977

PERSONAL: Born February 13, 1907, in New York, N.Y.; died of cancer September 26, 1977, at his home in Manhattan; son of George S. and Hilda Emily (Josephthal) Hellman; married first wife, Daphne Bayne; married second wife, Katherine Henry, August 18, 1960 (died November 30, 1980); children: (first marriage) Daisy Paradis, (second marriage) Katherine Hellmann. *Education:* Yale University, A.B., 1928.

ADDRESSES: Home—New York, N.Y. *Office*—*New Yorker,* 25 West 43rd St., New York, N.Y. 10036.

CAREER: New Yorker, New York City, reporter and associate editor, 1929-31, staff writer, 1932-36, 1938-77; *Fortune,* New York City, associate editor, 1931-32; *Life,* New York City, associate editor, 1936-38. Columnist for *Yale Daily News,* 1927-28; staff writer for Office of the Coordinator of Inter-American Affairs, 1942-44. *Wartime service:* Consultant to U.S. Army Air Forces headquarters, 1944; member of history section of Office of Strategic Services, 1944-45.

MEMBER: Chi Delta Theta, Grolier Club (New York), Coffee House Club (New York), Century Club (New York), Dutch Treat Club (New York), Graduates Club (New Haven, Conn.), Elizabethan Club (New Haven; member of board of governors, 1926-27), Cosmos Club (Washington, D.C.).

WRITINGS:

Inquirendo Concerning a Peculiar Aberration or Detracking of the Collecting Impulse, Hawthorn House, 1933.
Motor-Car Touring Society of the City of New York, 1907-1919, privately printed, 1941.
AAK: A Profile (a profile of Alfred A. Knopf), privately printed, 1948, reprinted, 1986.
How to Disappear for an Hour, Dodd, 1947, illustrated by Steinberg, reprinted, Ayer Co., 1971.
Mrs. DePeyster's Parties and Other Lively Studies from the New Yorker, Macmillan, 1963.
Profile of a Museum, Art in America, 1965.
The Smithsonian: Octopus on the Mall, Lippincott, 1967, reprinted, Greenwood Press, 1977.
Bankers, Bones, and Beetles: The First Century of the American Museum of Natural History, Natural History Press, 1968.

Also author of *Onward and Upward with the Sciences: The Tail of Taxonomy,* 1964, and *Profile of a Museum,* 1965. Work represented in anthologies. Contributor of profiles and satire to popular magazines, including *New Yorker.*

SIDELIGHTS: For nearly half a century, Geoffrey T. Hellman wrote for the *New Yorker* magazine, leaving only twice to work briefly for *Fortune* and *Life.* Versatile and prolific, Hellman contributed acerbic pieces to "Talk of the Town," and was especially noted for his numerous, and humorous, profiles of personalities from Diego Rivera to Nelson Rockefeller. According to an obituary in *Time,* his depictions of the Smithsonian Institution and the American Museum of Natural History, *The Smithsonian: Octopus on the Mall* and *Bankers, Bones, and Beetles: The First Century of the American Museum of Natural History,* are "masterpieces of *New Yorker* prose." In an obituary written for the *New York Times,* Alden Whitman quoted Hellman's editor at the *New Yorker,* William Shawn: "Over a period of almost 50 years, Geoffrey Hellman wrote consistently blithe and funny factual pieces for the magazine—hundreds of them. In addition, he wrote scores of straight humor pieces. He was totally devoted to the idea of humor in factual writing, and never wrote a solemn or heavy piece. Erudite, imposing in appearance, aristocratic in manner, companionable, he became an institution at The New Yorker office. He was immensely informative on the prominent people and the aspects of natural history he chose to write about, but he always approached his information with high spirits and a sense of comedy. He was an enchanting stylist."

BIOGRAPHICAL/CRITICAL SOURCES:

PERIODICALS

Best Sellers, January 15, 1969.
National Review, December 31, 1968.
New York Times, February 4, 1969, September 28, 1977.
Time, October 10, 1977.

OBITUARIES:

PERIODICALS

AB Bookman's Weekly, January 30, 1978.
Newsweek, October 10, 1977.
New York Times, September 28, 1977.
Publishers Weekly, October 17, 1977.*

HERBERT, Don(ald Jeffrey) 1917-
(Mr. Wizard)

PERSONAL: Born July 10, 1917, in Waconia, Minn.; son of Herbert Geoffrey and Lydia (Peopple) Kemske; married Maraleita Dutton, October 12, 1939 (divorced, 1972); married Norma Nix Kasell, 1972; children: (first marriage) Jeffrey, Jay, Jill. *Education:* LaCross State Teachers College (now University of Wisconsin—LaCross), B.S., 1940.

ADDRESSES: Office—Prism Productions, Inc., P.O. Box 83, Canoga Park, Calif. 91305.

CAREER: Film and television producer-performer, writer. Actor and stage manager, Minnesota Stock Co., Minneapolis, 1940, New York City, 1941-42; radio actor on children's shows "Captain Midnight" and "Tom Mix," and writer, Chicago, Illinois, 1945-47; radio director for Community Fund, Chicago, 1948-49; co-producer and interviewer for radio program "It's Your Life," Congressional Industrial Health Association, 1949-50; originator and featured performer of television program "Watch Mr. Wizard," National Broadcasting Corp. (NBC), Chicago, 1951-52, New York City, 1952-65, 1971-72; announcer and television progress reporter for "General Electric Theatre," Columbia Broadcasting System (CBS), New York City, 1954-62; executive producer of series "Experiment: The Story of a Scientific Search," 1963-66, and educational film series "Science Close Up," 1964—; producer of video series for schools, "Assignment: Science"; producer and host of film "Nuclear Power Questions—and Answers," 1974; producer and star of "Mr. Wizard Close-Ups," (NBC), 1976; executive producer and on-camera reporter for syndicated science and engineering series, "How About," underwritten by National Science Foundation and General Motors Laboratories, 1979-86; creator and star of "Mr. Wizard's World," Nickelodeon Cable Network, 1983. Prism Productions, Inc., Canoga Park, Calif., television and film producer, 1951—. *Military service:* U.S. Air Force, became captain; awarded Distinguished Flying Cross, Air Medal with three oak leaf clusters.

MEMBER: National Academy of Television Arts and Sciences.

AWARDS, HONORS: Scholastic Broadcasting Award, 1951; New Jersey Science Teachers Award, 1951; Chicago Federated Advertising Club award, 1951; George Foster Peabody Award, 1953; awards from Institute for Education by Radio-TV, Ohio State University, 1953, 1954, 1955, 1957; Thomas Alva Edison Foundation National Mass Media Awards, 1955, 1963; special awards from Manufacturing Chemists Association, 1957, 1958; "Emmy" Award nominations for outstanding achievement in the field of children's programming, 1960, 1963.

WRITINGS:

(With Willie Watson and Betsy Taylor) *Mr. Wizard's Science Secrets,* illustrations by Robert A. Barker, Popular Mechanics Press, 1952, new and revised edition with revisions by Alexander Joseph, illustrations by Barker and Vivian Berger, Hawthorn Books, 1965.
Mr. Wizard's Experiments for Young Scientists, illustrations by Dan Noonon, Doubleday, 1959.
(With Hy Ruchlis) *Beginning Science with Mr. Wizard,* illustrations by Mel Hunter, Volume 1: *Water,* Volume 2: *Heat,* Volume 3: *Light,* Volume 4: *Flying,* Doubleday, 1960.
(With Fulvio Bardossi) *Kilauea: Case History of a Volcano,* illustrations by Joyce Ballantyne, Harper, 1968.
(With Ruchlis) *Mr. Wizard's 400 Experiments in Science,* Book-Lab (Brooklyn, N.Y.), 1968, revised edition, 1983.

(With Bardossi) *Secret in the White Cell: Case History of a Biological Search,* illustrations by Muriel Fabrizio, Ruth Mandelbaum, and Pauline Thomas, Harper, 1969.

Mr. Wizard's Supermarket Science, illustrations by Roy McKie, Random House, 1980.

Also author of *Mr. Wizard's Experiments in Chemistry,* 1970, *Crystal Growing,* and *Mr. Wizard's Mystery Garden.*

SIDELIGHTS: Don Herbert, described by C. K. Cole in a *Discover* profile as "the man who nursed the baby boom generation from meters and magnets to computers and chemistry," is familiar to millions of television viewers as Mr. Wizard. Originator and host of the award-winning children's television program "Watch Mr. Wizard," and creator of "How About," a series of eighty-second science news clips for adults, as well as "Experiment," a series of half-hour science specials, Herbert presents science to the general public in easily understood experiments generally disguised as fun. And according to Cole, no one is better at this than Herbert, "He stands alone."

Although Herbert was naturally suited to become Mr. Wizard, says Cole, he "did not set out to be the Pied Piper of science." Born and raised in a small Minnesota town, Herbert actually wanted to become a performer. By the time he entered high school, he was an accomplished magician, reports Cole; and after graduating from college with a double major in science and drama, he ventured to Broadway before returning to Wisconsin summer stock, where he played the romantic lead opposite "an ingenue named Nancy Davis—later Nancy Reagan." His theatrical career was interrupted, however, by World War II, in which Herbert piloted a B-24 bomber through more than fifty missions, earning an Air Medal and a Distinguished Flying Cross. With the war's end, Herbert settled in Chicago where he became a radio actor on such children's programs as "Captain Midnight," and an announcer on the "General Electric Theatre," hosted by Ronald Reagan.

However, Herbert's lifelong interest in what he calls "factual stuff—like science," recounts Cole, led him to present the idea for the program "Watch Mr. Wizard" to a Chicago television station. Suggesting that "the 'wizard' implied magic, but the 'Mr.' gave it respectability," Cole quotes Herbert as saying: "My idea of science turned everybody off, so we used magic tricks to get people interested. Then we did the science behind the magic." Using commonplace items to demonstrate the wonders of science has become Herbert's trademark, but it was originally necessitated by the show's low budget. In the estimation of Stuart Fischer in *Kids' TV: The First Twenty-five Years,* despite the its failure to attract "true commercial advertising support, this show proved to be one of television's most successful educational programs." During its long tenure at NBC, "Watch Mr. Wizard" earned numerous honors, including two "Emmy" Award nominations. In addition to spawning tens of thousands of fan clubs, the show provided the material for most of Herbert's books, which describe science experiments performable by young readers.

Engendering an interest in science in children who would later devote their college education to the field, "Watch Mr. Wizard" has also captivated adults, notes Cole, and has inspired the admiration of scientists as well. As an instance, Cole discusses one program of the "Experiment" series entitled "Secret of the White Cell," which explained the work of microbiologist James Hirsch: " 'Don is an absolute master of analogy,' Hirsch says. 'My work had to do with how white cells ingest bacteria from the environment, and it wasn't that easy to illustrate. But Don came up with a pie plate, a bolt and a puddle of mercury. You tipped the plate a little and that mercury seemed to gobble up that bolt. We showed it to 4th graders, and they understood it perfectly. Yet if you showed it to a group of scientists, they wouldn't be at all insulted.' " Herbert's experiments revolve around having fun, notes Cole. "People trust Don not to lead them into very deep water," states Herbert's associate Joe Walders to Cole. "And even when it is deep, they know they're not going to be there very long."

BIOGRAPHICAL/CRITICAL SOURCES:

BOOKS

Child Study Association of American, *The Children's Bookshelf,* Bantam, 1965.
Fischer, Stuart, *Kids' TV: The First Twenty-five Years,* Facts on File Publications, 1983.
Huck, Charlotte S., and D. A. Young, *Children's Literature in the Elementary School,* Holt, 1961.

PERIODICALS

Chicago Tribune, June 27, 1984.
Discover, March, 1984.*

* * *

HERZOG, Arthur (III) 1927-

PERSONAL: Born April 6, 1927, in New York, N.Y.; son of Arthur, Jr. and Elizabeth Lindsay (Dayton) Herzog; divorced; children: Matthew. *Education:* Attended University of Arizona, 1946; Stanford University, B.A., 1950; Columbia University, M.A., 1956. *Politics:* Democrat. *Religion:* None.

ADDRESSES: Home and office—P.O. Box 664, Times Square Station, New York, N.Y. 10036. *Agent*—Candida Donadio, 231 West 22nd St., New York, N.Y. 10011.

CAREER: Fawcett Publications, New York, N.Y., editor, 1954-57; full-time free-lance writer, 1957—. *Military service:* U.S. Navy, 1945-46.

MEMBER: Authors Guild, Authors League of America, PEN.

WRITINGS:

(Co-author) *Smoking and the Public Interest,* Consumers Union, 1963.
The War-Peace Establishment, Harper, 1965.
The Church Trap, Macmillan, 1968.
McCarthy for President, Viking, 1969.
The B.S. Factor, Simon & Schuster, 1973.
The Swarm, Simon & Schuster, 1974.
Earthsound, Simon & Schuster, 1975.
Orca, Simon & Schuster, 1976.
Heat, New American Library, 1976, revised edition, Tudor Books, 1989.
I.Q. 83, Berkley Publishing, 1977.
Make Us Happy, Crowell, 1978.
Glad to Be Here, Crowell, 1979.
Aries Rising, Richard Marek, 1980.
The Craving, Dell, 1982.
L.S.I.T.T., Arbor House, 1984, reprinted as *Takeover,* Berkley Publishing, 1987.
Vesco: From Wall Street to Castro's Cuba, the Rise, Fall and Exile of White Collar Crime, Doubleday, 1987.
How to Write Almost Everything Better, Carlton, 1987.
The Woodchipper Murder, Holt, 1989.

Contributor of articles to *Harper's, Esquire, New York Times,* and other publications.

WORK IN PROGRESS: A musical about a Manhattan developer intent on building the world's largest skyscraper.

SIDELIGHTS: "To connoisseurs of disaster, Arthur Herzog is a familiar name," notes *Washington Post* writer Joseph McLellan, referring to the author's numerous novels of calamity. *The Swarm,* one of his most popular books, follows a swarm of poisonous killer bees from South America to New York City. The novel, states McLellan, brings "a chilling sense of reality to a most unpromising subject." In *I.Q. 83,* Herzog presents a unique disaster in his story of a virus that drastically reduces the intelligence of its victims, leaving them virtually incapable of performing even ordinary tasks. "Once seeded in the imagination," comments Donald Goddard in the *New York Times Book Review,* "Arthur Herzog's vision of a world lapsing into imbecility roots itself at a deeper layer of unease than most armchair catastrophe-lovers are used to. Those frightened by the idea of killer sharks or fires in high buildings can still safely swim in backyard pools or live at peace in ranch-style homes," the critic explains. "But what precautions can they take against an invisible virus, spread like the common cold, that causes the mind to wrinkle up like a leaky balloon?" McLellan similarly concludes that "one can't help feeling that in this vision of catastrophe Arthur Herzog has produced a kind of terror impossible to attain with killer bees, sharks, earthquakes or towering infernos."

While readers may be most familiar with his novels, Herzog has also written several acclaimed nonfiction works. *Vesco: From Wall Street to Castro's Cuba, the Rise, Fall and Exile of the King of White Collar Crime,* for instance, traces the career of corporate raider Robert Vesco, whose illegal activities over ten years ago led to prosecution by the Securities and Exchange Commission and to perpetual exile in Latin America and the Caribbean. Reports about Vesco's past and present activities have varied greatly, leading to many myths and misconceptions; in his book, "Herzog has tracked [Vesco's associates] all down and made a herculean effort to separate fact from fiction, an effort complicated by the obvious relish with which Mr. Vesco multiplies fictions about himself," relates *New York Times Book Review* contributor Ron Rosenbaum. While his subject was elusive in granting an interview, the critic continues, Herzog's *Vesco* nevertheless "breaks new ground with its account of Mr. Vesco's exile years. It becomes a comic epic of nonstop scamming."

Robert Sherrill, however, finds Herzog's account of Vesco's business dealings disorienting, as he states in the *Washington Post:* "To me the corporate shenanigans are even more hopelessly confused than they were before. . . . A financial page junkie might get something out of [this] kind of reporting, but it leaves me gasping for air." But the critic admits that this confusion is due more to the author's subject matter than to his writing, explaining that "Herzog has done an awesome amount of research. And when he has a chance, he can come up with the kind of easy, flippant writing that those of us who grew up on Raymond Chandler enjoy a great deal. Herzog also has a fine talent for the compressed profile." "Herzog clarifies the financial complexities of Vesco's business deals as much as possible," asserts Charles Schlotter in the *West Coast Review of Books,* "and indicates when the truth is unknown, as it frequently is." The critic concludes that *Vesco* "is certainly the most complete and accurate account to date of [the businessman's] bewildering career."

MEDIA ADAPTATIONS: Orca was filmed by Paramount in 1977; *The Swarm,* directed by disaster king Irwin Allen, was produced by Warner Brothers in 1978.

BIOGRAPHICAL/CRITICAL SOURCES:

PERIODICALS

New York Times Book Review, July 2, 1978, October 25, 1987.
Wall Street Journal, December 10, 1987.
Washington Post, June 20, 1978, December 22, 1978, October 12, 1987.
West Coast Review of Books, Number 5, 1988.

*   *   *

HESS, Stephen 1933-

PERSONAL: Born April 20, 1933, in New York, N.Y.; son of Charles and Florence (Morse) Hess; married Elena Shayne, August 23, 1959 (divorced, 1979); children: Charles, James. *Education:* Attended University of Chicago, 1951-52; Johns Hopkins University, A.B., 1953, graduate study, 1953-55.

ADDRESSES: Home—3705 Porter St. N.W., Washington, D.C. 20016. *Office*—Brookings Institution, 1775 Massachusetts Ave. N.W., Washington, D.C. 20036. *Agent*—Elizabeth McKee, Harold Matson Co., Inc., 22 East 40th St., New York, N.Y. 10016.

CAREER: Mayor's Commission on Mass Transportation, Baltimore, Md., staff member, 1955-56; White House, Washington, D.C., staff assistant to the President, 1959-61; U.S. Senate, Washington, D.C., assistant to the minority whip, 1961; BIDCO (sale of factories in underdeveloped countries), Washington, D.C., secretary-treasurer, 1962-65; Institute for Policy Studies, Washington, D.C., associate fellow, 1965; Harvard University, Institute of Politics, John F. Kennedy School of Government, Cambridge, Mass., fellow, 1967-68; White House, Washington, D.C., deputy assistant to the President for urban affairs, 1969, national chairman of Conference on Children and Youth, 1969-71; Brookings Institution, Washington, D.C., senior fellow, 1972—. U.S. Representative to UNESCO General Conference in Paris, France, 1974, and to United Nations General Assembly, 1976; lecturer, Nigerian National Institute for Strategic and Policy Studies, 1979; faculty of government fellow, Harvard University, 1979-81.

Official participant in U.S. cultural missions to Japan, Hong Kong, Thailand, and Singapore in 1969, Venezuela in 1970, Rumania and Yugoslavia in 1971, India, Nepal, Turkey, and Iran in 1974, New Zealand, Australia, and Fiji in 1975, Greece, Italy, and Great Britain in 1976, Brazil in 1978, Argentina and Chile in 1980, and Federal Republic of Germany, Soviet Union and Spain in 1987. Member of National Academy of Public Administration; member of board of directors of International Writers Service, 1978—; member of visiting committee of Gerald R. Ford Institute of Public Service at Albion College, 1979—; member of numerous committees of other civic groups and institutions. Member of several committees and councils of the Republican Party. Consultant to foundations and agencies, including U.S. Information Agency, 1976, U.S. Office of Management and Budget, 1977, and the Russell Sage Foundation, 1980. Frequent commentator for British Broadcasting Corp., Canadian Broadcasting System, Public Broadcasting Service, and National Public Radio. *Military service:* U.S. Army, 1956-58.

MEMBER: Phi Beta Kappa, Johns Hopkins Club of Washington (vice-president, 1960-62).

AWARDS, HONORS: Named to *Time* magazine's list of 200 Young American Leaders, 1974; Lowell Mellett Award for Improving Journalism through Critical Evaluation, 1981, for *The Washington Reporters;* Outstanding Academic Book Award, American Library Association, 1986, for *The Ultimate Insiders.*

WRITINGS:

(With Malcolm Moos) *Hats in the Ring: The Making of Presidential Candidates,* Random House, 1960.
America's Political Dynasties: From Adams to Kennedy, Doubleday, 1966.
(With David S. Broder) *The Republican Establishment: The Present and Future of the G.O.P.,* Harper, 1967.
(With Milton Kaplan) *The Ungentlemanly Art: A History of American Political Cartoons,* Macmillan, 1968, revised edition, 1975.
(With Earl Mazo) *Nixon: A Political Portrait,* Harper, 1968, revised edition, 1969.
The Presidential Campaign: The Leadership Selection Process after Watergate, Brookings Institution, 1974, revised edition, 1978.
Organizing the Presidency (Fortune Book Club main selection and Book-of-the-Month Club alternate selection), Brookings Institution, 1976.
(Contributor) *The Presidency and the Congress,* University of Texas Press, 1979.
(Contributor) *Nominating a President: The Process and the Press,* Praeger, 1980.
The Washington Reporters, Brookings Institution, 1981.
The Government/Press Connection: Press Officers and Their Offices, Brookings Institution, 1984.
(Contributor) *The Impact of Mass Media,* Longman, 1985.
(Contributor) *Informing America: Who Is Responsible for What?,* Syracuse University Press, 1985.
(Contributor) *The Clash of Issues,* Prentice-Hall, 1986.
The Ultimate Insiders: U.S. Senators in the National Media, Brookings Institution, 1986.
(Contributor) *Mass Media,* Greenhaven, 1986.
(Contributor) *American Government,* Little, Brown, 1987.

Author of documentaries for educational television. Contributor to more than a dozen books on American government. Contributor to *Grolier's Encyclopedia Yearbook,* 1972; contributor of syndicated newspaper column to numerous periodicals, including *Boston Globe, Detroit News,* and *Philadelphia Inquirer;* contributor of articles to journals. Member of editorial board, *The Bureaucrat,* 1979-80, and *Presidential Studies Quarterly,* 1988—.

WORK IN PROGRESS: The Main Street Senate, on the interaction between senators and their local media; *Foreign Correspondents,* on foreign correspondents in the U.S. contrasted with U.S. coverage abroad; a revised edition of *Organizing the Presidency.*

SIDELIGHTS: In his book *The Washington Reporters,* political observer Stephen Hess explores the role Washington journalists play in the amount and depth of coverage that events in the capital receive in the national news media. According to Jonathan Friendly in a *New York Times* review, Hess "has assembled a statistical profile of the 1,250 newspaper, magazine, wire service, television and radio reporters and the way they work. It is not always a flattering picture, either of them or their editors." Although Hess often "buries us beneath a blizzard of statistics," says *Los Angeles Times* critic David Shaw, the book "has enough strengths to recommend it to anyone interested in the press."

BIOGRAPHICAL/CRITICAL SOURCES:

PERIODICALS

Christian Science Monitor, November 21, 1985.
Los Angeles Times, May 24, 1981.
Los Angeles Times Book Review, May 25, 1986.
New York Times, December 14, 1970, April 22, 1981.
New York Times Book Review, January 13, 1985.

Time, July 15, 1974.
Washington Post, April 12, 1981.
Washington Post Book World, October 7, 1984.
Washington Post/Potomac, August 23, 1970.

*   *   *

HEUER, Kenneth John 1927-

PERSONAL: Born January 30, 1927, in Yonkers, N.Y.; son of Lester Frederick and Ida Antoinette (Fechner) Heuer. *Education:* Attended Amherst College, 1945-48; New School for Social Research, B.A., 1961.

ADDRESSES: Home—1411 Petronia St., Key West, Fla. 33040.

CAREER: Head of science department at boys' preparatory school in New York City, 1948; American Museum, Hayden Planetarium, New York City, lecturer, 1948-53; Viking Press, Inc., New York City, science editor, 1953-60; Thomas Y. Crowell Co., New York City, science editor, 1960-61; Macmillan Publishing Co., Inc., New York City, editor in chief of trade science department, 1961-63; Charles Scribner's Sons, New York City, director of science book department, 1963-76, vice-president, 1974—. New York editor of Cornell University Press, 1980-82.

MEMBER: American Museum of Natural History (associate benefactor), Royal Astronomical Society (fellow).

AWARDS, HONORS: Science book award from National Science Teachers Association, 1978, for *Rainbows, Halos, and Other Wonders;* science book award from National Science Teachers Association and New York Academy of Sciences, 1981, for *Thunder, Singing Sands, and Other Wonders.*

WRITINGS:

Men of Other Planets, Pellegrini & Cudahy, 1951, revised edition, Collier Books, 1962.
The End of the World: Scientific Inquiry, Rinehart, 1953, revised edition published as *How the Earth Will Come to an End,* Collier Books, 1963.
Wonders of the Heavens, Dodd, 1954.
An Adventure in Astronomy, Viking, 1958.
City of the Stargazers, Scribner, 1972.
Rainbows, Halos, and Other Wonders: Light and Color in the Atmosphere, Dodd, 1978.
Thunder, Singing Sands, and Other Wonders: Sound in the Atmosphere, Dodd, 1981.
(Editor) *The Lost Notebooks of Loren Eiseley,* Little, Brown, 1987.

Contributor to magazines.

BIOGRAPHICAL/CRITICAL SOURCES:

PERIODICALS

English Journal, April, 1973, November, 1978.
Science Books and Films, May, 1973, May, 1979.
Scientific American, December, 1978.
Sky and Telescope, February, 1973, April, 1973, August, 1978.

*   *   *

HICKS, John V(ictor) 1907-

PERSONAL: Born February 24, 1907, in London, England; son of James and Harriett (Thomas) Hicks; married Marjorie Louise Kisbey (a musician and composer), December 22, 1936 (died

March 26, 1986). *Education:* Attended collegiate institute in Prince Albert, Saskatchewan, Canada.

ADDRESSES: Home—222 21st St. E., Prince Albert, Saskatchewan, Canada S6V 1M1.

CAREER: Worked as accountant in Saskatchewan Provincial Government; writer. Former organist at St. Alban's Cathedral, Prince Albert.

MEMBER: League of Canadian Poets, Saskatchewan Writers' Guild.

AWARDS, HONORS: Honorary fellow, University of Emmanuel College; D. Litt., University of Saskatchewan.

WRITINGS:

Now Is a Far Country (poems), Thistledown Press, 1978.
Winter Your Sleep (poems), Thistledown Press, 1980.
Silence like the Sun (poems), Thistledown Press, 1983.
Rootless Tree (poems), Thistledown Press, 1985.
Fives and Sixes (poems), Porcupine's Quill, 1986.
Side Glances: Notes on the Writer's Craft, Thistledown Press and Saskatchewan Writers' Guild, 1987.
Sticks and Strings: Poems New and Selected, Thistledown Press, 1988.

Work represented in anthologies, including *Anthology of Magazine Verse and Yearbook of American Poetry,* Monitor Book, 1980, 1981, 1986, and 1987. Contributor of poems to literature journals in the United States and Canada.

WORK IN PROGRESS: Rogueries and Recreations, poetry.

SIDELIGHTS: John V. Hicks told *CA:* "I am sure that becoming a poet is the natural result of a love of words and a wish to use them as others have used them. I am not aware that I ever consciously set out to 'write about' anything. Always the idea appears and explains itself. The more one trusts the subconscious the less one realizes what one is doing at the time. I write a certain amount of fiction too, and I find a story very often begins with a phrase or a whole sentence whispered in the mind's ear. I have always written at the typewriter, but a few years ago I found I could scribble on paper on a clipboard. This is certainly the handiest and most portable way of all. Either way works. I am one of those who wonder what on earth people who don't write or make music do."

BIOGRAPHICAL/CRITICAL SOURCES:

PERIODICALS

Globe & Mail, November 11, 1986.

*   *   *

HIGGINS, Colin   1941-1988

PERSONAL: Born July 28, 1941, in Noumea, New Caledonia; became a U.S. citizen; died August 5, 1988, from complications of AIDS; son of John Edward (a chief purser) and Joy (Kelly) Higgins. *Education:* Attended Sorbonne, University of Paris, 1965; Stanford University, B.A., 1967; University of California, Los Angeles, M.F.A., 1970.

ADDRESSES: Agent—Michael Ovitz, Creative Artists Agency, 1888 Century Park East, Los Angeles, Calif. 90067.

CAREER: Professional actor in California, 1960-70; screenwriter and director. *Military service:* U.S. Army, 1962-65.

AWARDS, HONORS: Writers Guild nomination for best comedy, 1976, for "Silver Streak," 1980, for "Nine to Five"; Edgar Award, Mystery Writers of America, 1978, for "Foul Play"; Hollywood Foreign Press nomination for best comedy/musical film, 1978, for "Foul Play," 1982, for "The Best Little Whorehouse in Texas."

WRITINGS:

"Harold and Maude" (screenplay), Paramount, 1971; play based upon screenplay produced on Broadway at Martin Beck Theatre, February, 1980 (novelization published as *Harold and Maude,* Lippincott, 1971).
."The Devil's Daughter" (television film), American Broadcasting Companies, Inc. (ABC-TV), January, 1973.
(With Dennis Cannon) "The Ik" (play; based on *The Mountain People* by Colin Turnbull), French translation by Jean-Claude Carrier first produced as "Les Iks" in Paris at Theatre des Bouffes du Nord, January, 1975; produced in English at Round House, London, January 15, 1976; produced in Washington, D.C., at George Washington University, October 20, 1976.
"Silver Streak" (screenplay), Twentieth Century-Fox, 1976.
"Foul Play" (screenplay), Paramount, 1978.
(With Patricia Resnik) "Nine to Five" (screenplay), Twentieth Century-Fox, 1980.
(With Larry L. King and Peter Masterson) "The Best Little Whorehouse in Texas" (screenplay based on the stage musical by King and Masterson), Universal, 1982.

Also contributor to anthologies.

SIDELIGHTS: Colin Higgins' untimely death brought an end to a long and successful career as a film writer and director. Though his later films have not been counted among modern-day masterworks—they have been criticized, in fact, for being formulaic—Higgins' debut movie, "Harold and Maude," is a genuine cult classic. Using the screenplay he wrote as a master's thesis, Higgins also directed this story of a bizarre love affair between the nineteen-year-old depressive Harold and the eighty-year-old eccentric Maude.

"Although it was not received well critically or at the box office," noted William Frankfather in a *Dictionary of Literary Biography* piece, the movie "did attract a strong following on college campuses. . . . Its appeal to students and young people seems to lie in its rejection of the establishment values represented by Harold's wealthy and domineering mother . . . and by the military, represented by Harold's uncle, a hawkish, one-armed general. Finding conventional values absurd, Harold repeatedly stages mock suicide attempts." As the story continues, Harold meets Maude, who is planning her actual suicide in time for her 80th birthday. A whirlwind affair ensues, with Maude showing Harold how much he has to live for. Then she ends her own life. "Though heartbroken by her suicide, [Harold] is converted to her love of life and learns to accept it—but on his own terms," as Frankfather said.

Higgins followed "Harold and Maude" with two action-adventure comedies, "Silver Streak" and "Foul Play," each of which owes a stylistic debt to Alfred Hitchcock. While they were both commercially successful, they did little to establish the director as an innovator. 1980 brought a feminist's revenge fantasy called "Nine to Five," wherein three mistreated secretaries seek revenge on their chauvinist boss. What begins as a series of lurid fantasies turns real as the secretaries kidnap their boss and hold him hostage. *Chicago Tribune* reviewer Gene Siskel praised the concept of the comedy, but complained that midway through the film the story takes a tiresomely slapstick twist. "The fantasies ran on too long and seemed like padding for a script that had nowhere to go," he remarked. "I guess what I wanted from 'Nine to Five' was a movie with zip, a slashing attack on the American corporate structure, where the still-favored position is the man on top." Still, "Nine to Five" was Higgins' biggest commercial success.

BIOGRAPHICAL/CRITICAL SOURCES:

BOOKS

Dictionary of Literary Biography, Gale, Volume 26: *American Screenwriters,* 1984.

PERIODICALS

Chicago Tribune, December 19, 1980, July 26, 1982.
Newsweek, December 13, 1976.
New York Times, July 19, 1978, February 8, 1980.
New York Times Book Review, September 26, 1971.
Time, December 13, 1976.

OBITUARIES:

PERIODICALS

Los Angeles Times, August 6, 1988.
New York Times, August 7, 1988.
Washington Post, August 7, 1988.*

*   *   *

HILTON, Suzanne 1922-

PERSONAL: Born September 3, 1922, in Pittsburgh, Pa.; daughter of Edwin P. (an insurance broker) and Helen (McFeely) McLean; married Warren Mitchell Hilton (an insurance engineer), June 15, 1946; children: Edwin Bruce, Diana Lester. *Education:* Attended Pennsylvania College for Women (now Chatham College), 1940-43; Beaver College, B.A., 1945. *Religion:* Methodist.

ADDRESSES: Home—301 Runnymede Ave., Jenkintown, Pa. 19046.

CAREER: Former researcher and copywriter for advertising department of Westminster Press, Philadelphia, Pa. Researcher and writer of local history.

MEMBER: Authors Guild, Philadelphia Children's Reading Round Table.

AWARDS, HONORS: How Do They Get Rid of It? and *How Do They Cope with It?* were selected books of the year by the Child Study Association; *The Way It Was—1876* was selected as one of the books of the year by *New York Times,* 1975; Legion of Honor, Chapel of Four Chaplains, 1978; award for nonfiction, Drexel University School of Library and Information Science, 1979; Golden Spur Award, Western Writers of America, 1981, for *Getting There: Frontier Travel without Power.*

WRITINGS:

YOUNG ADULT BOOKS

How Do They Get Rid of It? (Junior Literary Guild selection), Westminster, 1970.
How Do They Cope with It?, Westminster, 1970.
It's Smart to Use a Dummy (Junior Literary Guild selection), Westminster, 1971.
It's a Model World (Junior Literary Guild selection), Westminster, 1972.
Beat It, Burn It, and Drown It, Westminster, 1974.
The Way It Was—1876, Westminster, 1975.

Who Do You Think You Are?: Digging for Your Family Roots, Westminster, 1976.
Here Today and Gone Tomorrow (Junior Literary Guild selection), Westminster, 1978.
Getting There: Frontier Travel without Power (Junior Literary Guild selection), Westminster, 1980.
We, the People: The Way We Were, 1783-1793 (Junior Literary Guild selection), Westminster, 1981.
Faster than a Horse (Junior Literary Guild selection), Westminster, 1983.
The World of Young Tom Jefferson, Walker, 1986.
The World of Young George Washington, Walker, 1986.
The World of Young Herbert Hoover, Walker, 1987.
The World of Young Andrew Jackson, Walker, 1988.

OTHER

Also associate editor and contributor, *Montgomery County: The Second Hundred Years.* Contributor of short stories and articles to periodicals. Editor, Montgomery County (Pa.) Historical Society *Bulletin* and Old York Road Historical Society *Bulletin.*

WORK IN PROGRESS: Another book on history using resources from original manuscripts.

SIDELIGHTS: Suzanne Hilton told *CA:* "As a schoolchild, I never really liked history. Today I'm fascinated by it, trying to bring a new lively dimension to writing about the past. The people I write about really lived and still sound alive through their letters and diaries. I hope that my books can help spark young peoples' interest in what otherwise might be a dull task of memorizing dates. I have read several hundred diaries to pluck the most interesting tales written while the memory of an adventure was still ripe in the mind of the diary-writer.

"In just the same way, I find we can follow the young lives (just through teenage [years]) of our early presidents. History text books always skipped through those early years—as if they were totally unimportant. I have used genealogy, diaries, and eyewitness stories to learn more about the world that Jefferson, Washington, Hoover, and Andrew Jackson grew up in. What better way to prove 'the child is father to the man?' "

Hilton also mentions that she and her husband "often use a tired old VW camper to carry us from one interesting historical location to another for still more research and diary-snooping. We have been doing some genealogical research along the way as well."

AVOCATIONAL INTERESTS: Sailing and gunkholing up the little streams that run into Chesapeake Bay.

*   *   *

HINDE, Robert A(ubrey) 1923-

PERSONAL: Born October 26, 1923, in Norwich, England; son of Earnest Bertram (a physician) and Isabella (a nurse; maiden name, Taylor) Hinde; married Hester Coutts (divorced, 1971); married Joan Gladys Stevenson; children: two sons, four daughters. *Education:* University of London, B.Sc., 1948; St. John's College, Cambridge, B.A., 1948, M.A., 1950, Sc.D., 1958; Balliol College, Oxford, D.Phil., 1950.

ADDRESSES: Home—Park Lane, Madingley, Cambridgeshire, England.

CAREER: Cambridge University, Cambridge, England, curator at Ornithological Field Station, 1950-65, research fellow at St. John's College, 1951-54, steward, 1956-58, tutor, 1958-63, fellow, 1958—, Royal Society Research Professor, 1963—. Honorary director of Medical Research Council Unit on Development and Integration of Behaviour, 1970—. *Military service:* Royal Air Force, Coastal Command, 1941-45.

MEMBER: British Psychological Society (honorary fellow), Royal Society (fellow), American Academy of Arts and Sciences (honorary foreign member), American Ornithologists Union (honorary foreign member), National Academy of Sciences (honorary foreign associate member).

AWARDS, HONORS: Commander, Order of the British Empire, 1988.

WRITINGS:

Animal Behaviour: A Synthesis of Ethology and Comparative Psychology, McGraw, 1966, 2nd edition, 1970.
Social Behaviour and Its Development in Subhuman Primates, University of Oregon Press, 1972.
Biological Bases of Human Social Behaviour, McGraw, 1974.
Towards Understanding Relationships, Academic Press, 1979.
Ethology: Its Nature and Relations with Other Sciences, Oxford University Press, 1982.
Individuals, Relationships and Culture, Cambridge University Press, 1987.

EDITOR

Advances in the Study of Behaviour, Academic Press, Volume 1 (with D. S. Lehrman and E. Shaw), 1965, Volume 2 (with Lehrman and Shaw), 1969, Volume 3 (with Lehrman and Shaw), 1970, Volume 4 (with Lehrman and Shaw), 1974, Volume 5 (with Lehrman, Shaw, and J. S. Rosenblatt), 1974, Volume 6 (with Shaw, Rosenblatt, and C. Beer), 1976, Volume 7 (with Shaw, Rosenblatt, and Beer), 1976, Volume 8 (with Rosenblatt, Beer, and M. C. Busnel), 1978, Volume 9 (with Rosenblatt, Beer, and Busnel), 1979, Volume 10 (with Rosenblatt, Beer, and Busnel), 1979, Volume 11 (with Rosenblatt, Beer, and Busnel), 1980.
Bird Vocalizations, Cambridge University Press, 1969.
(With Gabriel Horn) *Short-Term Changes in Neural Activity and Behaviour,* Cambridge University Press, 1970.
Non-Verbal Communication, Cambridge University Press, 1972.
(With wife, Joan Stevenson Hinde) *Constraints on Learning,* Academic Press, 1973.
(With P. P. G. Bateson) *Growing Points in Ethology,* Cambridge University Press, 1976.
Primate Social Relationships, Blackwell Scientific Publications, 1983.
(With G. Prins and others) *Defended to Death,* Penguin, 1983.
(With A-N. Perret-Clermont and J. S. Hinde) *Social Relationships and Cognitive Development,* Clarendon Press, 1985.
(With J. S. Hinde) *Relationships with Families,* Clarendon Press, 1988.

OTHER

Contributor to scientific journals.

SIDELIGHTS: Robert A. Hinde told *CA:* "Having worked for some years on the effects of separation between mother and infant, using rhesus monkeys as experimental subjects, I have now focused on the nature of inter-individual relationships. My present research concerns the family and school relationships of preschool age children and their role in the development of personality."

BIOGRAPHICAL/CRITICAL SOURCES:

PERIODICALS

Times Literary Supplement, June 24, 1983, May 6, 1988.

*   *   *

HINKLE, Vernon 1935-
(H. V. Elkin)

PERSONAL: Born June 23, 1935, in Amsterdam, N.Y.; son of Vernon M. (a farmer) and Lovina (Lawrence) Hinkle; married Sally Applegate, June 3, 1956 (divorced, 1975); married Mary Sanders Shartle (a writer), September 8, 1978; children: Lawrence, Geneva. *Education:* Ithaca College, B.A., 1956; Yale University, M.F.A., 1961.

ADDRESSES: Home—470 West 24th St., New York, N.Y. 10011; and R.D. 1, Greenfield Center, N.Y. 12833.

CAREER: Polka Dot Playhouse, Bridgeport, Conn., director, 1958; Bradford College, Bradford, Mass., instructor, 1961-66, chairman of drama department, 1966-71; J. C. Penney Co., New York, N.Y., writer of internal communications, 1971-75, benefits communicator in personnel, 1975-77; free-lance writer, 1977—. Has given dramatic readings. Member of Theatre Artists Workshop of Westport (Conn.).

MEMBER: Dramatists Guild.

AWARDS, HONORS: Playwriting award, Ithaca College, 1953, for "Before Gabriel Blew"; faculty grant, Bradford College, 1966; named O'Neill Playwright, 1969.

WRITINGS:

NOVELS

(Under pseudonym H. V. Elkin) *Eagle Man,* Tower, 1978.
Music to Murder By, Tower, 1978.
(Under pseudonym H. V. Elkin) *Playground,* Tower, 1979.
(Under pseudonym H. V. Elkin) *Yellowstone,* Tower, 1980.
(Under pseudonym H. V. Elkin) *Mustang,* Tower, 1980.
(Under pseudonym H. V. Elkin) *Tiger's Chance,* Tower, 1980.
Murder after a Fashion, Leisure, 1986.

PLAYS

"Before Gabriel Blew" (one-act), first produced in Ithaca, N.Y., at Ithaca College, May 7, 1954.
"Musicians of Bremen" (one-act children's musical), with music by wife, Sally Applegate, first produced in Bradford, Mass., at Bradford College, December 11, 1963.
"Character in a Play" (one-act), first produced Off-Broadway at La Mama Experimental Theatre Club, August, 1965.
"The Concept" (two-act), first produced in Waterford, Conn., at O'Neill Theatre Center, July 9, 1969, rewritten as "Showcase," as yet unproduced.
"Edna" (one-act), first produced in Salina, Kan., at Kansas Wesleyan University, October 17, 1973.
"If I'm Dead, Start without Me" (two-act), first produced in Bridgeport, Conn., at Polka Dot Playhouse, September 10, 1982.

OTHER

Also author, under pseudonym H. V. Elkin, of a western series, four volumes, Tower, 1978-80; also author of plays for HB Studio, 1967 and 1970, American Renaissance Theatre, 1984-86, and Theatre Artists Workshop, 1986-88; also author of speeches, presentations, and industrial publications. Contributor to periodicals.

WORK IN PROGRESS: A novel, *Cloud Memory;* one-act plays, "Two Guys in the Woods," "Travel Play," "Close," and "King of the Laundry Room"; continuing playwriting for Theatre Artists Workshop.

SIDELIGHTS: Vernon Hinkle told *CA:* "Play became private fantasies on the farm where I was brought up, isolated from friends my own age. Sometimes, in later years, it became difficult to collaborate on a fantasy, as in theatre work. After some unhappy experiences trying, I started my first novel and enjoyed the privacy and control. Finally restless, I emerged from the novelist's cocoon with a new readiness to collaborate in theatre, even with some entrepreneuring spirit—a necessary quality for most playwrights who want to work in, not out of, the theatre.

"If my work is any one thing besides eclectic, it is mystery, in the sense that each piece (novel or play) is a puzzle or a quest for unknown answers. In this respect, I regard most fiction as mystery."

He adds: "I am motivated by 'organics' with all works in progress. The premise is that any creative unit has its own truth that resists superimposition of foreign elements. Solutions to all problems come from better familiarity with or insight into the work itself. Writer's block can be dissolved by continually re-reading what has already been written. Critiques are almost always helpful as clues to organic solutions, even though they may be, at face value, irrelevant."

*   *   *

HINTZ, (Loren) Martin 1945-

PERSONAL: Born June 1, 1945, in New Hampton, Iowa; son of Loren (a flier) and Gertrude (an office manager; maiden name, Russell) Hintz; married Sandra Lee Wright (a writer and literary agent), May 1, 1971; children: Daniel, Stephen, Kate. *Education:* College of St. Thomas, St. Paul, Minn., B.A., 1967; Northwestern University, M.A., 1968. *Politics:* Liberal. *Religion:* Roman Catholic.

ADDRESSES: Home and office—N55 W25837 Richmond Rd., Sussex, Wis. 53089.

CAREER: Case worker, American Red Cross, 1968-71; *Milwaukee Sentinel,* Milwaukee, Wis., reporter and editor, 1968-75; free-lance writer and photographer, 1975-88. Public relations director, William Eisner & Assoc. Instructor at University of Wisconsin—Milwaukee and Marquette University.

MEMBER: Society of American Travel Writers (vice chairman of central states chapter, 1978-79; chairman of central states chapter, 1979-83; member of national board, 1981-83; member of national membership committee, 1984-85), American Society of Journalists and Authors, Society of Children's Book Writers, Society of Professional Journalists (president, Milwaukee chapter, 1976), Circus Model Builders of America, Northwest Territorial Alliance (public relations officer), Midwest Travel Writers' Association, Clan Donald (Midwest district), Milwaukee Kickers (soccer club; member of board of directors, 1972-74), Milwaukee Press Club, Sigma Delta Chi (member of board of directors of Milwaukee chapter, 1972-74; president-elect, 1975-76; president, 1976).

AWARDS, HONORS: Kicker of the year award from Milwaukee Kickers, 1970; school bell award from Wisconsin Education Association, 1971, for educational news coverage; community service award from Inland Daily Press Association, 1974; has also received numerous photography, newspaper, and magazine writing awards from such groups as the central states chapter of Society of American Travel Writers, Midwest Travel Writers, and Council for Wisconsin Writers.

WRITINGS:

(With wife, Sandra Hintz) *We Can't Afford It,* Raintree, 1976.
The If I Can't Be Ordained, I'll Cook Book, Thomas More Press, 1978.
Computers in Our Society: Today and Tomorrow, F. Watts, 1983.
Cultural Geography: The Tropics, F. Watts, 1987.
History: Redevelopment Authority, City of Milwaukee, 1988.

CONTRIBUTOR

Four-Wheel Drive North American Trail Guide, Rand McNally, 1978.
Circus Workin's, Messner, 1980.
Tons of Fun, Messner, 1982.
The Universal Story, Universal Foods, 1982.

OTHER

Contributor to "Land of Enchantment" series, published by Childrens Press: *Land of Enchantment: Norway,* 1982; . . . *Finland,* 1983; . . . *West Germany,* 1983; . . . *Italy,* 1983; . . . *Chile,* 1984; . . . *Morocco,* 1984; . . . *Switzerland,* 1984; . . . *Argentina,* 1984; . . . *Sweden,* 1984, . . . *Ghana,* 1987; . . . *Hungary,* 1987. Contributor to various magazines and newspapers, including *Billboard, Amusement Business, Scouting, Midwest Living, Compass,* and *Wisconsin Trails.*

WORK IN PROGRESS: A collection of short stories; articles for periodicals.

SIDELIGHTS: Martin Hintz has played and coached soccer for the Milwaukee Kickers and has covered the World Cup Soccer Championships in Mexico and West Germany. He has written numerous articles as followups to his travels in Chile and Poland, as well as to other countries "in turmoil." During his college years, he worked for Royal American Shows, the largest carnival in the United States, and has used that experience as the basis for many short stories. Hintz has also been public relations director for the Milwaukee Irish Fest, the world's largest gaelic cultural celebration.

"All these experiences," Hintz told *CA,* "help keep the problems of society in perspective, as well as provide a basis for understanding our common humanity with all its joys and sorrows."

*   *   *

HODGES, Margaret Moore 1911-

PERSONAL: Born July 26, 1911, in Indianapolis, Ind.; daughter of Arthur Carlisle (a businessman) and Anna Marie (Mason) Moore; married Fletcher Hodges, Jr. (a museum curator), September 10, 1932; children: Fletcher III, Arthur Carlisle, John Andrews. *Education:* Vassar College, A.B. (with honors), 1932; Carnegie Institute of Technology (now Carnegie-Mellon University), M.L.S., 1958. *Religion:* Episcopalian.

ADDRESSES: Home—5812 Kentucky Ave., Pittsburgh, Pa. 15232. *Office*—Room 660, Library and Information Science Bldg., University of Pittsburgh, Pittsburgh, Pa. 15260.

CAREER: Carnegie Library of Pittsburgh, Pittsburgh, Pa., special assistant and children's librarian, 1953-64; Pittsburgh Public Schools, Pittsburgh, story specialist in compensatory education department, 1964-68; University of Pittsburgh, Graduate School of Library and Information Science, Pittsburgh, lecturer, 1964-68, assistant professor, 1968-72, associate professor, 1972-75, professor, 1975-77, professor emeritus, 1977—. Storyteller on program "Tell Me a Story," WQED-TV, 1965-76.

MEMBER: American Library Association, Pennsylvania Library Association, Distinguished Daughters of Pennsylvania (elected, 1970), Pittsburgh Bibliophiles, Pittsburgh Vassar Club.

AWARDS, HONORS: Carnegie Library staff scholarship, 1956-58; *The Wave* received Caldecott Award nomination, 1964, *New York Times* ten best picture books of the year award, 1964, and Silver Medal, Bienal (Brazil), 1965; *Lady Queen Anne: A Biography of Queen Anne of England* was selected as the best book for young adults by an Indiana author, 1970; *The Making of Joshua Cobb* was selected as a *New York Times* outstanding juvenile book, 1971; John G. Bowman Memorial grant, 1974; Distinguished Alumna, Carnegie Library School and Graduate School of Library and Information Science, 1976; Outstanding Pennsylvania Children's Author award, Pennsylvania School Librarians Association, 1977; *Saint George and the Dragon* received Caldecott Award, American Library Association, 1984, Carolyn W. Field Award for best children's book by a Pennsylvania author, 1984, *New York Times* Best Illustrated Children's Book Award, 1984, and *Horn Book* Honor Book award, 1985; "Margaret Hodges Day" citation from University of Pittsburgh School of Library and Information Science, 1985; Keystone State Reading Award, 1985; Margaret Hodges scholarship established, 1989.

WRITINGS:

(Editor) Kathleen Monypenny, *The Young Traveler in Australia,* Dutton, 1954.

(Editor) H. M. Harrop, *The Young Traveler in New Zealand,* Dutton, 1954.

(Editor) Lucile Iremonger, *The Young Traveler in the West Indies,* Dutton, 1955.

(Editor) Geoffrey Trease, *The Young Traveler in Greece,* Dutton, 1956.

One Little Drum, Follett, 1958.

(Editor with others) *Stories to Tell to Children,* Carnegie Library of Pittsburgh, 1960.

What's for Lunch, Charley?, Dial, 1961.

A Club against Keats, Dial, 1962.

The Secret in the Woods, Dial, 1963.

(Editor) *Tell It Again: Great Tales from around the World,* Dial, 1963.

The Wave, Houghton, 1964.

The Hatching of Joshua Cobb, Farrar, Straus, 1967.

Sing Out, Charley!, Farrar, Straus, 1968.

Lady Queen Anne: A Biography of Queen Anne of England, Farrar, Straus, 1968.

(Editor) *Constellation, a Shakespeare Anthology,* Farrar, Straus, 1968.

The Making of Joshua Cobb, Farrar, Straus, 1971.

The Gorgon's Head, Little, Brown, 1972.

Hopkins of the Mayflower: Portrait of a Dissenter, Farrar, Straus, 1972.

The Fire Bringer, Little, Brown, 1972.

Persephone and the Springtime, Little, Brown, 1973.

The Other World: Myths of the Celts, Farrar, Straus, 1973.

Baldur and the Mistletoe, Little, Brown, 1974.

The Freewheeling of Joshua Cobb, Farrar, Straus, 1974.

Knight Prisoner: The Tale of Sir Thomas Malory and His King Arthur, Farrar, Straus, 1976.

(Adaptor) *The Little Humpbacked Horse: A Russian Tale,* Farrar, Straus, 1980.

The High Riders, Scribner, 1980.

(Editor with Susan Steinfirst) Elva S. Smith, *The History of Children's Literature: A Syllabus with Selected Bibliographies,* 2nd edition, American Library Association, 1980.

The Avenger, Scribner, 1982.

(Adaptor) *St. George and the Dragon,* illustrations by Trina Schart Hyman, Little, Brown, 1984.

If You Had a Horse: Steeds of Myth and Legend, Scribner, 1984.

Making a Difference: The Story of an American Family, Scribner, 1989.

The Voice of the Great Bell, illustrations by Ed Young, Little, Brown, 1989.

The Arrow and the Lamp, the Story of Psyche, illustrations by Donna Diamond, Little, Brown, 1989.

Buried Moon, illustrations by Jamichael Henterly, Little, Brown, in press.

Contributor to journals.

SIDELIGHTS: Margaret Moore Hodges told *CA:* "My writing so far falls into three types: real life stories based on the adventures and misadventures of my three sons, the retelling of folk tales and myths in picture book format, and biography written to bring to life a few little-known or disregarded characters who have contributed in an important way to history. I have not been influenced by other writers, except that I read for pleasure the great writers of the past. I only wish their influence were apparent. Otherwise, I read what I need for background and research, but not much else. I suspect this is true of most writers."

AVOCATIONAL INTERESTS: Traveling, reading, gardening.

*   *   *

HOGE, Phyllis
      See THOMPSON, Phyllis Hoge

*   *   *

HORN, Pamela (Lucy Ray) 1936-

PERSONAL: Born May 2, 1936, in Derby, England; daughter of Gilbert Lawrence (a bank official) and Marjorie (Orton) Jones; married Clifford Alfred Horn (head of department of management and social studies at Oxford Polytechnic), March 30, 1963. *Education:* Attended Portsmouth Polytechnic, 1963-64; University of London, B.Sc., 1964; University of Leicester, Ph.D., 1968. *Religion:* Roman Catholic.

ADDRESSES: Home—Grey Roofs, 11 Harwell Rd., Sutton Courtenay, Abingdon, Oxford, England. *Office*—School of Education, Oxford Polytechnic, Headington, Oxford, England.

CAREER: Lecturer in shorthand and typewriting at Derby and District College of Technology, 1959-63; Oxford Polytechnic, Oxford, England, lecturer in economic and social history, 1967—.

MEMBER: Royal Society of Arts, Agricultural History Society, History of Education Society.

WRITINGS:

Joseph Arch: A Biography, Roundwood Press, 1971.

The Victorian Country Child, Roundwood Press, 1974.

(Editor) *Agricultural Trade Unionism in Oxfordshire, 1872-1881,* Oxfordshire Record Society, 1974.

The Rise and Fall of the Victorian Servant, St. Martin's, 1975.

Labouring Life in the Victorian Countryside, Hunter Press, 1976.

Education in Rural England, 1800-1914, St. Martin's, 1978.

Village Education in Nineteenth Century Oxfordshire: The Whitchurch School Logbook (1868-93) and Other Documents, Oxfordshire Record Society, 1979.

The Rural World, 1780-1850: Social Change in the English Countryside, St. Martin's, 1980.

A Georgian Parson and His Village: The Story of David Davies, 1742-1819, Beacon Publications, 1981.

William Marshall (1745-1818) and the Gregorian Countryside, Beacon Publications, 1982.

(Editor) George James Dew, *Oxfordshire Village Life: The Diaries of George James Dew (1846-1928), Relieving Officer,* Beacon Publications, 1983.

The Changing Countryside in Victorian and Edwardian England and Wales, Fairleigh Dickinson University Press, 1984.

(Editor) *Life in a Country Town: Reading and Mary Russell Mitford (1787-1855),* Beacon Publications, 1984.

Rural Life in England in the First World War, St. Martin's, 1984.

Life and Labour in Rural England, 1760-1850, Macmillan (Basingstoke, England), 1986.

(Editor) *Around Abingdon in Old Photographs,* Sutton Publishing, 1987.

(Contributor) James A. Mangan, editor, *Benefits Bestowed: Education and British Imperialism,* St. Martin's, 1988.

(Author of introduction) Samuel Adams and Sarah Adams, *The Complete Servant* (reprint of the 1825 edition), Southover Press, 1989.

The Victorian and Edwardian Schoolchild, Sutton Publishing, 1989.

Contributor to periodicals, including *Times Educational Supplement, Times Higher Educational Supplement, Times Literary Supplement, Historical Journal, History of Education Society Journal,* and *Countryman.*

SIDELIGHTS: Pamela Horn once told *CA:* "I am particularly concerned with nineteenth century rural life in Britain." She later added: "My interests have recently also been extended to cover elementary education and the role of women in the Victorian countryside."

AVOCATIONAL INTERESTS: Travel in Germany.

BIOGRAPHICAL/CRITICAL SOURCES:

PERIODICALS

Spectator, December 27, 1975, September 30, 1978.

Times Literary Supplement, September 3, 1971, February 14, 1975, November 28, 1975, February 18, 1977, January 25, 1985.

*   *   *

HUCK, Gabe (Donald Joseph) 1941-

PERSONAL: Born July 31, 1941, in Carroll, Iowa; son of Donald Joseph (a merchant) and Ruth Marie (a community worker; maiden name, Fachman) Huck; married Mary Jo Kircher (a potter), May 29, 1966; children: Jeremy, Sarah. *Education:* Immac-

ulate Conception Seminary (now Conception Seminary College), Conception, Mo., B.A., 1964; Catholic University of America, M.A., 1969. *Politics:* Democrat. *Religion:* Roman Catholic.

ADDRESSES: Home—542 Michigan, Apt. 3, Evanston, Ill. 60202. *Office*— Liturgy Training Publications, 1800 North Hermitage, Chicago, Ill. 60622.

CAREER: Liturgical Conference, Washington, S.C., editor, 1968-77; Liturgy Training Publications, Chicago, Ill., publisher and editor, 1977—.

MEMBER: Amnesty International, Bread for the World, Greenpeace, Liturgical Conference, Peace Museum.

WRITINGS:

Liturgy Needs Community, Paulist Press, 1972.

Liturgy with Style and Grace, Liturgy Training Publications, 1978.

A Book of Family Prayer, Seabury, 1978.

Teach Me to Pray, Sadlier, 1981.

The Three Days: Parish Liturgy in the Paschal Triduum, Liturgy Training Publications, 1981.

(Editor with Mary Ann Simcoe) *A Triduum Sourcebook,* Liturgy Training Publications, 1983.

How Can I Keep from Singing, Liturgy Training Publications, 1989.

The Communion Rite at Sunday Mass, Liturgy Training Publications, 1989.

Editor of *Liturgy,* 1968-75, *Major Feast and Seasons,* 1973-77, and *Liturgy 80,* 1977-89.

SIDELIGHTS: Gabe Huck told *CA:* "I work and write in the area of Christian (most often Roman Catholic) ritual and its practice, renewal, and place in the life of the individual and community. My position is in publishing, with some opportunity for writing and editing, as well as public speaking and occasional outside projects. Central to all of this is discovering how ritual expression in all its richness and variety can center the lives of our churches and households and strengthen us for the work of justice in our communities and our world.

"Rituals, like other basics of human society, can serve or enslave, can carry a people's meaning or grow hollow. Through the rituals of a people their 'way' is learned, not all at once but through the years of repetition. The problem today is that public ritual, as liturgy, is often seen as education, entertainment, or private devotion. Other rituals (daily prayer, fasting, seasonal observances) of households and individuals are crowded out by the needs and the pace created by contemporary society. Ritual provides a home, a place in which to create, from which to meet the world. It is not necessarily an agent of stability—at least not in the tradition of Jewish and Christian ritual. Ritual is far more likely to be an agent of justice and of change."

*   *   *

HUDSON, Meg
See KOEHLER, Margaret (Hudson)

J

JACOBS, Linda
See ALTMAN, Linda Jacobs

* * *

JACOBUS, Lee A. 1935-

PERSONAL: Born August 20, 1935, in Orange, N.J.; son of Ernest W. and Julia R. (Byrne) Jacobus; married Joanna J. Miller (a teacher of modern dance), April 5, 1958; children: Sharon Grania, James Diarmuid. *Education:* Brown University, A.B., 1957, A.M., 1959; Claremont University Center (now Claremont Graduate School), Ph.D., 1968.

ADDRESSES: Home—1 Meadow Wood Rd., Branford, Conn. 06405. *Office*—Department of English, University of Connecticut, U-25, Storrs, Conn. 06268.

CAREER: Mary C. Wheeler School, Providence, R.I., teacher of English, 1959-60; Western Connecticut State College, Danbury, instructor in English, 1960-66; University of Connecticut, Storrs, assistant professor, 1968-71, associate professor, 1971-77, professor of English, 1977—. Summer instructor at Phillips Exeter Academy, 1962, and Columbia University, 1967; visiting professor at Brown University, 1981.

MEMBER: Modern Language Association of America, American Committee for Irish Studies, Milton Society of America, James Joyce Society.

AWARDS, HONORS: Fellow of William Andrews Clark Memorial Library, University of California, Los Angeles, 1968; University of Connecticut Research Foundation grant, 1968, 1971, 1972; Connecticut Commission on the Arts grant, 1975-76; postdoctoral fellow, Yale University, 1982-83.

WRITINGS:

Improving College Reading, Harcourt, 1967, 5th edition, 1988.
(Editor) *Issues and Response,* Harcourt, 1968, revised edition, 1972.
(Editor) *Aesthetics and the Arts,* McGraw, 1968.
Developing College Reading, Harcourt, 1970, 3rd edition, 1984.
(Editor) *17 from Everywhere: Short Stories of the World,* Bantam, 1971.
(With F. David Martin) *Humanities through the Arts,* McGraw, 1975, 4th edition, 1990.
John Cleveland, Twayne, 1975.

(Contributor) Donald B. Gibson, editor, *Black American Poets,* Prentice-Hall, 1975.
Sudden Apprehension: Aspects of Knowledge in "Paradise Lost," Mouton, 1976.
The Sentence Book, Harcourt, 1977, 3rd edition, 1989.
(Editor) *The Longman Anthology of American Drama,* Longman, 1982.
(Editor) *A World of Ideas,* St. Martin's, 1983, 3rd edition, 1990.
Humanities: The Evolution of Values, McGraw, 1986.
The Bedford Introduction to Drama, St. Martin's, 1989.
Writing as Thinking, Macmillan, 1989.

Also author of plays. Contributor of articles to scholarly journals and of poems and short stories to literary magazines. Editor in chief, *LIT: Literature Interpretation Theory;* advisory editor, Longman, Inc., 1976—.

WORK IN PROGRESS: A play, *Long Division;* a book on Milton's use of Rhetoric and Logic.

SIDELIGHTS: Lee A. Jacobus told *CA:* "Lately, most of my writing has been in the field of college textbooks. The reason is that they grow naturally out of my teaching, which constantly presents me with opportunities for solving problems in ways that have not been tried before. I am committed to humanistic scholarship and values, and textbooks offer me a chance to touch many people at an age when they are likely to listen and learn. High quality texts are a kind of treasure, and I aim to add to that treasure as much as I can. Besides texts, I naturally write scholarship in the field of seventeenth-century English literature. In addition, I have been writing plays, two of which were performed in New York in an off-Broadway theater on 54th Street. I find playwriting to be the most natural form of writing I have ever done, and I am only sorry that it took me so long to try my hand at it. I have published poetry and fiction over the years, but it was not until I edited *The Longman Anthology of American Drama* that I became aware of the fact that I have some talent in that direction."

AVOCATIONAL INTERESTS: Music (a lifelong piano student), art, photography, "computer hacking."

* * *

JAFFE, Harold 1940-

PERSONAL: Born July 8, 1940, in New York, N.Y.; son of Lester and Blanche (Weber) Jaffe. *Education:* Grinnell College,

B.A., 1960; New York University, Ph.D. (with honors), 1967. *Politics:* "Progressive/Buddhist."

ADDRESSES: Home—3551 Granada Ave., San Diego, Calif. 92104. *Office*—Department of English, San Diego State University, San Diego, Calif. 92182.

CAREER: Long Island University, Brooklyn Center, Brooklyn, N.Y., assistant professor, 1965-71, associate professor of English, 1971-76; currently professor of creative writing and literature, San Diego State University, San Diego, Calif. Fulbright professor, University of Kerala, India, 1971-72; guest lecturer, New School for Social Research, 1972-73. *Military service:* U.S. Army Reserve, 1961-62.

MEMBER: Amnesty International, American Civil Liberties Union (ACLU), Greenpeace, Klan Watch, John Brown Anti-Klan Committee.

AWARDS, HONORS: Founder's Day Award, New York University, 1968; recipient of grants from National Endowment for the Arts, 1983 and 1988, and California Arts Council, 1989.

WRITINGS:

(Editor with John Tytell, and contributor) *The American Experience: A Radical Reader* (includes his one-act play, "Assassination"), Harper, 1970.
(Editor with Tytell) *Affinities: A Short Story Anthology,* Crowell, 1970.
(Editor) Richard Maurice Burke, *Walt Whitman,* Johnson Reprint, 1971.
Mole's Pity, Fiction Collective, 1979.
Mourning Crazy Horse: Stories, Fiction Collective, 1982.
Dos Indios (fiction), Thunder's Mouth, 1983.
(Editor with Lawrence McCaffery) *Writing and Politics,* San Diego State University, 1984.
Beasts: Fictions, Curbstone Press, 1985.
Madonna and Other Spectacles (fiction), PAJ Publications, 1988.
Eros in the Time of AIDS (fiction), City Lights, in press.

Also editor of *Central American Writing,* 1987. Contributor to literary journals, including *City Lights Review, Chicago Review, New Virginia Review, Mississippi Review,* and *New Directions in Prose Poetry.* Editor, *Fiction International,* 1983—.

WORK IN PROGRESS: Two novels, *Iago* and *Weird John Brown.*

SIDELIGHTS: In story collections such as *Beasts: Fictions,* Harold Jaffe presents "socio-political allegories of a relentlessly topical sort," comments James Kaufmann in the *Los Angeles Times Book Review.* "They drift sometimes into the fantastic, and they are stylistically prone to collage and other special effects." While this approach "too often [makes] strange or uneasy bedfellows," *New York Times Book Review* contributor Albert Mobilio believes that "political content and experimental technique mix powerfully" in Jaffe's work. Kaufmann, however, feels that "too many stories are top-heavy with message," which can weaken the author's prose. Nevertheless, as Mobilio concludes, "Jaffe is adventurous in taking on such large issues, and he succeeds because they are dramatized from a personal, often poetic perspective."

AVOCATIONAL INTERESTS: Skydiving, shark fishing, snorkeling, traveling to out-of-the-way places.

BIOGRAPHICAL/CRITICAL SOURCES:

PERIODICALS

Los Angeles Times Book Review, June 1, 1986.

New York Times Book Review, May 4, 1986, August 7, 1988.

*   *   *

JAFFEE, Mary L.
   See LINDSLEY, Mary F(rances)

*   *   *

JAMES, Amalia
   See NEGGERS, Carla A(malia)

*   *   *

JANKO, Richard 1955-

PERSONAL: Surname is pronounced Yanko; born May 30, 1955, in Weston Underwood, England; came to United States; son of Charles A. (an electrical engineer) and Helen (Murray) Janko; married Michele A. Hannoosh, 1984. *Education:* Trinity College, Cambridge, B.A., 1976, M.A., 1980, Ph.D., 1980.

ADDRESSES: Office—Department of Classics, University of California, Los Angeles, Calif. 90024.

CAREER: University of St. Andrews, St. Andrews, Scotland, lecturer in Greek, 1978-79; Cambridge University, Trinity College, Cambridge, England, research fellow in classics, 1979-82; Columbia University, New York, N.Y., 1982-87, began as assistant professor, became associate professor of classics; University of California, Los Angeles, professor of classics, 1987—. Assistant to archaeologists William Taylour, 1974-81, and Dimitrios U. Schilardi, 1982-84.

MEMBER: American Philological Association.

WRITINGS:

Homer, Hesiod, and the Hymns: Diachronic Development in Epic Diction, Cambridge University Press, 1982.
Aristotle on Comedy: Towards a Reconstruction of "Poetics II," Duckworth, 1984.
(Translator) Aristotle, *Poetics,* Hackett, 1987.
The Iliad: A Commentary, Volume 4: *Books 13-16,* Cambridge University Press, in press.

Contributor of numerous articles and reviews to scholarly publications, including *Glotta, Classical Quarterly, Hermes, Minos, Annual of the British School of Archaeology at Athens, Kadmos, Zeitschrift fuer Papyrologie und Epigraphik, Phoenix,* and *Mnemosyne.*

WORK IN PROGRESS: A book on Aristotle's theory of catharsis; additional commentary on Homer's *The Iliad.*

SIDELIGHTS: The focus of Richard Janko's *Homer, Hesiod, and the Hymns: Diachronic Development in Epic Diction* is the origin of the major Homeric hymns. The author establishes correlations between linguistic developments and relative dates of composition of the various works studied. According to a *Times Literary Supplement* review by Stephanie West, "no one seriously concerned with archaic Greek poetry can afford to ignore this book." West went on to say, "[Janko's] argumentation is always stimulating and ingenious, and the reader who has followed patiently through rugged tables of short dative-plurals and assorted genitives presently gains a vantage-point from which it even seems possible to discern some features of the prehistory of the epics."

Janko told *CA:* "I am fascinated by all periods of Greek life and culture, have traveled and done archaeological work in Greece, and am fluent in modern Greek. In *Aristotle on Comedy: Towards a Reconstruction of "Poetics II,"* I have identified a summary of the lost second book of Aristotle's *Poetics* (in a Tenth-Century Byzantine manuscript). This should prove of great interest to theorists of literature.

"I am now working on Aristotle's theory of catharsis, in the light of new papyrus fragments from Herculeneum; I was able to include a preliminary account of these in my annotated translation of Aristotle's *Poetics* and related texts, which is intended for students of philosophy, literature, and literary theory who know no Greek. My other current project is to contribute to the new Cambridge commentary on Homer's *Iliad.* There has been no full commentary on the *Iliad* since early this century, and we now know vastly more about Homeric poetry, with the decipherment of Mycenaean Greek, the progress of archaeology, and the study of oral-traditional epic poetry. My own volume will aim to do justice to all these exciting developments, but will place special emphasis on Homer's use of his sources, ancient scholarship on him and the state of the text."

BIOGRAPHICAL/CRITICAL SOURCES:

PERIODICALS

Times Literary Supplement, March 11, 1983.

*   *   *

JANSEN, Jared
  See CEBULASH, Mel

*   *   *

JENKINS, Roy (Harris)   1920-

PERSONAL: Born November 11, 1920, in Abersychan, Monmouthshire, Wales; son of Arthur (a member of Parliament) and Hattie (Harris) Jenkins; married Jennifer Morris (chairman of the National Trust), January 20, 1945; children: Charles, Cynthia, Edward. *Education:* Balliol College, Oxford, M.A. (with first class honors), 1941. *Politics:* Labour.

ADDRESSES: Home—2 Kensington Park Gardens, London W11, England; and St. Amand's House, East Hundred, Oxfordshire. *Office*—House of Lords, London SW1, England.

CAREER: Journalist and author; member of staff, Industrial and Commercial Finance Corp., Ltd., 1946-48; member of Parliament, London, England, 1948—; parliamentary private secretary to secretary of state for Commonwealth relations, 1949-50; Minister of Aviation, 1964-65; Home Secretary, 1965-67, 1974-76; Chancellor of the Exchequer, 1967-70; Deputy Leader of the Labour Party, 1970-72; president of the Commission of the European Communities, 1977-81; first leader of the Social Democratic Party, 1981-83; became Lord Jenkins of Hillhead, 1987; Chancellor, University of Oxford, 1987—. Governor, British Film Institute, 1955-58; director of financial operations, John Lewis Partnership, 1962-64; trustee, Pilgrim Trust, 1973—; director, Morgan Grenfell Holdings, Ltd., 1981-82. *Military service:* British Army, Royal artillery, 1944-46; became captain.

MEMBER: Royal Society of Literature (president, 1988—), Fabian Society (executive committee, 1949-61; chairman, 1957-58), Society of Authors (management committee, 1956-50), American Academy of Arts and Sciences.

AWARDS, HONORS: Charlemagne Prize, 1972; Robert Schuman Prize, 1972; Order of European Merit (Luxembourg), 1976;

Prix Bentinck, 1978; named Freeman, City of Brussels, 1980; Grand Cross, Order of Charles III (Spain), 1980. Recipient of twenty-three degrees, including L.L.D. from University of Leeds, 1971, Harvard University, 1972, University of Pennsylvania, 1973, University of Bath, 1978, University of Michigan, 1978, and University of Wales, 1979; D.Litt. from University of Glasgow, 1972, University of Warwick, 1978, and University of Reading, 1979; D.C.L., Oxford University, 1973; D.Sc., University of Aston in Birmingham, 1977; D.Univ. from University of Keele, 1977, and University of Essex, 1978.

WRITINGS:

(Editor) Clement Richard Attlee, *Purpose and Policy: Selected Speeches,* Hutchinson, 1947.
Mr. Attlee: An Interim Biography, Heinemann, 1948.
(With others) *Post-War Italy: A Report on Economic Conditions,* Fabian Books, 1950.
Fair Shares for the Rich, Tribune Publications, 1951.
(Contributor) *New Fabian Essays,* Fabian Books, 1952.
Pursuit of Progress: A Critical Analysis of the Achievement and Prospect of the Labour Party, Heinemann, 1953.
Mr. Balfour's Poodle: An Account of the Struggle between the House of Lords and the Government of Mr. Asquith, Heinemann, 1954, new edition published as *Mr. Balfour's Poodle: Peers Vs. People,* Chilmark, 1968.
Sir Charles Dilke: A Victorian Tragedy, Collins, 1958, revised edition published as *Victorian Scandal: A Biography of the Right Honourable Gentleman Sir Charles Dilke,* Chilmark, 1965.
The Labour Case, Penguin (Harmondsworth), 1959.
(With Douglas Jay) *The Common Market Debate,* Fabian International Bureau, 1962.
(Contributor) W. T. Rodgers, editor, *Hugh Gaitskell,* Thames & Hudson, 1964.
Asquith: Portrait of a Man and an Era, Chilmark, 1964 (published in England as *Asquith,* Collins, 1964).
Essays and Speeches, edited by Anthony Lester, Collins, 1967, Chilmark, 1968.
Afternoon on the Potomac: A British View of America's Changing Position in the World, Yale University Press, 1972.
British Foreign Policy since 1945, British Academy, 1972.
The Role of the European Community in World Affairs, Georgetown University School of Foreign Service, 1981.
(Editor) *Britain and the EEC,* Macmillan, 1983.
Truman, Harper, 1986.
Baldwin, Collins, 1987.
Gallery of Twentieth-Century Portraits, David & Charles, 1988.
European Diary, 1977-81, Collins, 1989.

SIDELIGHTS: British statesman Roy Jenkins has held a number of important positions in government. A member of Parliament since 1948, he has served as Minister of Aviation, Home Secretary, Deputy Leader of the Labour Party, and first Leader of the Social Democratic Party. In addition he has authored more than twenty books, including studies of British government and biographies of political figures. *Essays and Speeches,* say reviewers, shows the author's versatility and intelligence. Maurice Edelman writes in *Punch,* "Mr. Jenkins reveals himself as an urbane, sensible and civilized man, tolerant and liberal, who would have been much at home in an Age of Reason. There is nothing petty about this collection of occasional pieces and speeches which, apart from one or two historical essays, fall roughly into three headings—Great Men I've Known, Great Causes I've Espoused and Great Projects I've Handled."

Balancing his roles as statesman and author, Jenkins invests less of his time in research than other biographers, John Campbell notes in a London *Times* review, but this has not adversely affected the quality of the books. Of *Baldwin,* the biography of former prime minister Stanley Baldwin, Campbell observes, "because Mr Jenkins writes so well, even his reworking of familiar sources is immensely enjoyable to read; and because he is able to write out of his own experience of high office it is full of insights and judgments that are fresh, authoritative, and thoroughly his own." Personal experience also enhances *Gallery of Twentieth-Century Portraits.* Campbell suggests, "Perhaps in his exclusive concentration on biography—lovingly pinning his specimens with a finely-polished phrase and carefully ranking them in order of performance in their class—he is more like an entomologist than a historian, but it is a good dinner party game, and no one plays it better."

MEDIA ADAPTATIONS: Film rights to *Victorian Scandal: A Biography of the Right Honourable Gentleman Sir Charles Dilke* have been sold to Sam Spiegel, with John and Penelope Mortimer writing the screenplay.

BIOGRAPHICAL/CRITICAL SOURCES:

PERIODICALS

Chicago Tribune Book World, May 11, 1986.
Globe and Mail (Toronto), September 26, 1987.
Listener, November 23, 1967.
New Yorker, June 1, 1968.
New York Times Book Review, May 12, 1968, November 9, 1986.
Punch, January 10, 1968.
Times (London), March 5, 1987, December 17, 1988.
Times Literary Supplement, January 27, 1984, March 14, 1986, March 6, 1987, November 4, 1988, March 17, 1989.

*   *   *

JOHNS, Stephanie Bernardo   1947-
(Stephanie Bernardo)

PERSONAL: Born January 23, 1947, in Brooklyn, N.Y.; daughter of Stephen (a machinist) and Emily (a secretary; maiden name, Nader) Rizzo; married Anthony Bernardo, October 30, 1966 (divorced March 16, 1983); married G. Michael Johns, July 28, 1984; children: (first marriage) David; (second marriage) Christopher, Michael. *Education:* Attended John Carroll University, 1967-68; City College of the City University of New York, B.S., 1970, graduate study, 1970; graduate study at Montclair State College, 1973-76, and William Paterson College of New Jersey, 1976-77.

ADDRESSES: Home—32 Skyline Dr., Morristown, N.J. 07960.

CAREER: Columbia University, Lamont-Doherty Geological Observatory, Palisades, N.Y., research assistant in biological oceanography, 1970; *Encyclopedia Americana,* New York, N.Y., science research editor, 1970-72, free-lance science research editor, 1972-77; free-lance writer and researcher, 1977—. Free-lance researcher/writer for general books division of *Reader's Digest.*

WRITINGS:

(Under the name Stephanie Bernardo) *The Ethnic Almanac,* Doubleday, 1981.
(Under the name Stephanie Bernardo) *The Ultimate Checklist,* Doubleday, 1982.
The Allergy Guide to Brand Name Foods and Food Additives, New American Library, 1988.

Contributor to *What's What, Good Housekeeping Women's Almanac, The Book of Lists, The World Almanac Book of the Strange,* and *What's What of Sports.* Contributor to magazines and newspapers, including *Science Digest, Family Circle, New York, Signature, Next, Us, New York Post, Success, Diversion,* and *Town and Country.* Contributing editor of *Motor Boating and Sailing,* 1980—; research editor of *Technology,* 1982.

WORK IN PROGRESS: Collecting material for a book on fathers; guide to raising a brighter child.

SIDELIGHTS: Stephanie Bernardo Johns once told *CA:* "Growing up in an ethnic neighborhood—near Atlantic Avenue in Brooklyn Heights, an area that was primarily Arabic-speaking until twenty years ago—I was concerned about the heritage that was being lost. My mother Emily, who is of Lebanese descent, had married outside her ethnic group—something quite common in America. But I could see that I was losing something in terms of cultural preservation by being the product of an Italian-Lebanese household. What I had lost was the language of either set of grandparents. (Both my mother and father speak a second language; I speak only English.) I also noticed that my cousins on either side seemed much more involved in ethnic traditions—they belonged to ethnic churches such as Our Lady of Lebanon, and they practiced customs that were lost to my family. I wanted to preserve that cultural heritage in some small part, hence the germ of the idea for *The Ethnic Almanac.*

"I wanted people of every ethnic background and nationality to find some source of pride in my book. I examined almost every tradition, custom, hero, place name, holiday, etc., to learn the origin of what we identify as 'American.' I wanted to instill not only black pride, but Jewish pride, Lithuanian pride, Cuban pride, and more into the hearts of all Americans. Yet, the book is lighthearted and touched with humor. I think of it as a history book that is relevant to people's ethnic backgrounds. It is a storehouse of facts and interesting tidbits on bits of Americana that touch our lives every day. . . . It made me appreciate the hardships that my grandparents suffered, to come here as penniless immigrants embarking on a great adventure in a land they had only heard about.

"*The Ultimate Checklist* is a book of 'all the information you'll ever need to know.' From birth control to buying a layette, from cooking a chicken to planning a vacation. . . . There are practical lists as well: how to buy children's shoes; how to choose a divorce attorney; and what to expect at a house closing. *The Ultimate Checklist* was inspired by the numerous questions posed to the *Encyclopedia Americana,* where I worked as a researcher for several years. My job was to find any and all information that was *not* in the encyclopedia on the topics of health, medicine, agriculture, technology, and current events. It was the dream job of anyone who loves to read and loves libraries: Someone was paying me to read and research questions of topical interest. To my friends, I am the one they turn to for information on anything. My home is part research library. I enjoy the challenge of magazine writing and have been concentrating on science stories and nonfiction pieces for special interest magazines."

*   *   *

JOHNS, W(illiam) E(arle)   1893-1968
(William Earle, Jon Early)

PERSONAL: Born February 5, 1893, in Bengeo, Hertford, England; died June 21, 1968; son of William Richard Eastman

Johns; married Maude Hunt, 1914 (died, 1961); children: one son. *Education:* Educated at local grammar schools.

CAREER: Author, journalist, and columnist. Apprenticed to a Hertford surveyor, 1907-12; sanitary inspector, Swaffham, Norfolk, England, 1912-13; British Army, served in Norfolk Yeomanry, 1913-15, and in Machine Gun Corps in Egypt and Salonika, 1916-17; Royal Flying Corps, 1917-30, was shot down over France, September, 1918, and was a prisoner of war for the duration of World War I, Flying Officer, 1920-27, aviation illustrator, beginning 1927, retired as captain; lecturer, Air Defense Cadet Corps, 1939; Ministry of Information, London, England, writer, 1939-45. Air correspondent for several British and overseas newspapers and magazines.

WRITINGS:

(Editor) *Wings: A Book of Flying Adventures,* J. Hamilton, 1931.
(Editor) *The Modern Boy's Book of Aircraft,* Amalgamated Press, 1931.
(Under pseudonym William Earle) *Mossyface* (novel), Mellifont Press, 1932.
Fighting Planes and Aces (juvenile), J. Hamilton, 1932.
(With Harry M. Scholfield) *The Pictorial Flying Course,* J. Hamilton, 1932.
The Spy Flyers (novel), illustrated by Howard Leigh, J. Hamilton, 1933.
(Editor) *Thrilling Flights,* J. Hamilton, 1935.
The Raid (short stories), J. Hamilton, 1935.
Some Milestones in Aviation, J. Hamilton, 1935.
The Air V.C.'s, J. Hamilton, 1935.
Steeley Flies Again (novel), Newnes, 1936, revised edition, Latimer House, 1951.
Sky High (novel), Newnes, 1936, revised edition, Latimer House, 1951.
(Under pseudonym Jon Early) *Blue Blood Runs Thin* (novel), Newnes, 1936.
The Passing Show: A Garden Diary by an Amateur Gardener, My Garden, 1937.
Murder by Air (novel), Newnes, 1937, revised edition, Latimer House, 1951.
Desert Night (novel), J. Hamilton, 1938.
Champion of the Main (juvenile), illustrated by H. Gooderham, Oxford University Press, 1938.
The Murder at Castle Deeping (novel), J. Hamilton, 1938, revised edition, Latimer House, 1951.
Wings of Romance: A Steeley Adventure (novel), Newnes, 1939, revised edition, Latimer House, 1951.
Modern Boy's Book of Pirates (juvenile), Amalgamated Press, 1939.
The Unknown Quantity, J. Hamilton, 1940.
Sinister Service (juvenile), Oxford University Press, 1942.
King of the Commandos (juvenile), illustrated by Leslie Stead, University of London Press, 1943, reprinted, May Fair Books, 1963.
Comrades in Arms (juvenile), Hodder & Stoughton, 1947.
The Rustlers of Rattlesnake Valley (juvenile), Thomas Nelson, 1948.
Doctor Vane Answers the Call (short stories), Latimer House, 1950.
Short Stories, Latimer House, 1953.
Sky Fever, and Other Stories, Latimer House, 1953.
Adventure Bound (juvenile), illustrated by Douglas Relf, Thomas Nelson, 1955.
Adventure Unlimited (juvenile), illustrated by Relf, Thomas Nelson, 1957.
No Motive for Murder (novel), Hodder & Stoughton, 1958.

The Man Who Lost His Way (novel), Macdonald, 1959.
Adventures of the Junior Detection Club (juvenile), M. Parish, 1960.
Where the Golden Eagle Soars (juvenile), illustrated by Colin Gibson, Hodder & Stoughton, 1960.
Worlds of Wonder: More Adventures in Space (short stories), Hodder & Stoughton, 1962.
(With R. A. Kelley) *No Surrender,* Harrap, 1969.

"BIGGLES" SERIES; JUVENILE

The Camels Are Coming, J. Hamilton, 1932, published as *Biggles, Pioneer Air Fighter,* Armada, 1982.
The Cruise of the Condor: A Biggles Story, J. Hamilton, 1933, published as *Biggles in the Cruise of the Condor,* Thames, 1961.
. . . *of the Camel Squadron,* J. Hamilton, 1934, reprinted, Thames, 1961.
. . . *Flies Again,* J. Hamilton, 1934, reprinted, Thames, 1961.
. . . *Learns to Fly,* illustrated by Stead, Hodder & Stoughton, 1935, new edition, 1986.
. . . *Hits the Trail,* Oxford University Press, 1935.
. . . *in France,* Boys' Friend Library (London), 1935.
. . . *Flies East,* Hodder & Stoughton, 1935, reprinted, May Fair Books, 1963.
The Black Peril: A Biggles Story, J. Hamilton, 1935, published as *Biggles Flies East,* Boys' Friend Library, 1938, published as *Biggles and the Black Peril,* Thames, 1961.
. . . *in Africa* (also see below), Oxford University Press, 1936, reprinted, May Fair Books, 1965.
. . . *and Company,* Oxford University Press, 1936.
. . . *Flies West,* illustrated by Leigh and Alfred Sindall, Oxford University Press, 1937.
. . . *Air Commodore,* illustrated by Leigh and Sindall, Oxford University Press, 1937, reprinted, Collins, 1966.
. . . *Flies South,* Oxford University Press, 1938.
. . . *Goes to War* (also see below), Oxford University Press, 1938, reprinted, Severn House, 1980.
The Rescue Flight: A Biggles Story, Oxford University Press, 1938, published as . . . , *The Rescue Flight,* May Fair Books, 1965.
. . . *Flies North* (also see below), Oxford University Press, 1939.
. . . *in Spain* (also see below), Oxford University Press, 1939, reprinted, May Fair Books, 1963.
. . .—*Secret Agent,* Oxford University Press, 1940.
. . . *in the South Seas* (also see below), Oxford University Press, 1940.
. . . *in the Baltic* (also see below), Oxford University Press, 1940, reprinted, May Fair Books, 1963.
The Third Biggles Omnibus (contains *Biggles in Spain, Biggles Goes to War,* and *Biggles in the Baltic*), Oxford University Press, 1941.
. . . *Defies the Swastika,* Oxford University Press, 1941, reprinted, May Fair Books, 1965.
. . . *Sees it Through,* Oxford University Press, 1941.
Spitfire Parade: Stories of Biggles in War-Time, Oxford University Press, 1941.
. . . *Sweeps the Desert* (also see below), Hodder & Stoughton, 1942.
. . . *in the Jungle,* Oxford University Press, 1942.
. . . *"Fails to Return"* (also see below), illustrated by Stead, Hodder & Stoughton, 1943.
. . . , *Charter Pilot,* Oxford University Press, 1943, reprinted, May Fair Books, 1965.
. . . *in Borneo,* Oxford University Press, 1943.

. . . in the Orient (also see below), illustrated by Stead, Hodder & Stoughton, 1944, reprinted, May Fair Books, 1963.

Sergeant Bigglesworth, C.I.D. (also see below), illustrated by Stead, Hodder & Stoughton, 1946, reprinted, May Fair Books, 1963.

. . . Delivers the Goods (also see below), illustrated by Stead, Hodder & Stoughton, 1946.

Biggles' Second Case (also see below), illustrated by Stead, Hodder & Stoughton, 1948.

. . . Hunts Big Game, illustrated by Stead, Hodder & Stoughton, 1948, reprinted, Brockhampton Press, 1965.

. . . Breaks the Silence, illustrated by Stead, Hodder & Stoughton, 1949, new edition, 1983, published as *. . . in the Atlantic,* Armada, 1970.

. . . Takes a Holiday (also see below), illustrated by Stead, Hodder & Stoughton, 1949.

. . . Gets His Men (also see below), illustrated by Stead, Hodder & Stoughton, 1950, reprinted, May Fair Books, 1965.

. . . Goes to School, illustrated by Stead, Hodder & Stoughton, 1951.

Another Job for Biggles (also see below), illustrated by Stead, Hodder & Stoughton, 1951.

. . . Works It Out (also see below), illustrated by Stead, Hodder & Stoughton, 1951.

. . .—Air Detective, illustrated by Stead, Latimer House, 1952, reprinted, Dean & Son, 1967.

. . . Follows On, illustrated by Stead, Hodder & Stoughton, 1952.

. . . Takes the Case, illustrated by Stead, Hodder & Stoughton, 1952.

The First Biggles Omnibus (contains *Biggles Sweeps the Desert, Biggles in the Orient, Biggles Delivers the Goods,* and *Biggles "Fails to Return"*), Hodder & Stoughton, 1953.

. . . in the Blue, illustrated by Stead, Brockhampton Press, 1953.

. . . and the Black-Raider, illustrated by Stead, Hodder & Stoughton, 1953.

. . . in the Gobi, illustrated by Stead, Hodder & Stoughton, 1953.

. . . of the Special Air Police, illustrated by Stead, Thames, 1953.

. . . , Pioneer Air Fighter, illustrated by Stead, Thames, 1954, new edition, Armada, 1982.

. . . and the Pirate Treasure, and Other Biggles Adventures, illustrated by Stead, Brockhampton Press, 1954.

. . . Cuts It Fine, illustrated by Stead, Hodder & Stoughton, 1954.

. . . , Foreign Legionnaire, illustrated by Stead, Hodder & Stoughton, 1954.

Biggles' Chinese Puzzle, and Other Biggles Adventures, illustrated by Stead, Brockhampton Press, 1955.

. . . in Australia, illustrated by Stead, Hodder & Stoughton, 1955.

The Biggles Air Detective Omnibus (contains *Sergeant Bigglesworth, C.I.D., Biggles' Second Case, Another Job for Biggles,* and *Biggles Works It Out*), Hodder & Stoughton, 1956.

No Rest for Biggles (also see below), illustrated by Stead, Hodder & Stoughton, 1956.

. . . of 266, illustrated by Stead, Thames, 1956.

. . . Takes Charge, illustrated by Stead, Brockhampton Press, 1956.

. . . Makes Ends Meet, illustrated by Stead, Hodder & Stoughton, 1957.

. . . of the Interpol, illustrated by Stead, Brockhampton Press, 1957.

. . . on the Home Front, illustrated by Stead, Hodder & Stoughton, 1957.

. . . Presses On, illustrated by Stead, Brockhampton Press, 1958.

. . . Buries the Hatchet, illustrated by Stead, Brockhampton Press, 1958.

. . . on Mystery Island, illustrated by Stead, Hodder & Stoughton, 1958.

. . . in Mexico, illustrated by Stead, Brockhampton Press, 1959.

Biggles' Combined Operation, illustrated by Stead, Hodder & Stoughton, 1959.

. . . at World's End, illustrated by Stead, Brockhampton Press, 1959.

The Biggles Book of Heroes, M. Parish, 1959.

. . . and the Leopards of Zinn, illustrated by Stead, Brockhampton Press, 1960.

. . . Goes Home, illustrated by Stead, Brockhampton Press, 1960.

. . . and the Missing Millionaire, illustrated by Stead, Hodder & Stoughton, 1961.

. . . Forms a Syndicate, illustrated by Stead, Hodder & Stoughton, 1961, new edition, Chivers, 1986.

. . . and the Poor Rich Boy, illustrated by Stead, Brockhampton Press, 1961.

. . . Goes Alone, illustrated by Stead, Hodder & Stoughton, 1962.

Orchids for Biggles, illustrated by Stead, Brockhampton Press, 1962.

The Biggles Book of Treasure Hunting, illustrated by William Randall, M. Parish, 1962.

. . . Sets a Trap, illustrated by Stead, Hodder & Stoughton, 1962.

. . . and the Plane That Disappeared, illustrated by Stead, Hodder & Stoughton, 1963.

. . . Takes It Rough, illustrated by Stead, Brockhampton Press, 1963.

Biggles' Special Case, illustrated by Stead, Brockhampton Press, 1963.

. . . Flies to Work, illustrated by Stead, Hodder & Stoughton, 1963.

. . . Takes a Hand, illustrated by Stead, Hodder & Stoughton, 1963.

. . . and the Black Mask (also see below), illustrated by Stead, Hodder & Stoughton, 1964.

. . . Investigates, and Other Stories of the Air Police, illustrated by Stead, Brockhampton Press, 1964, new edition, Chivers, 1986.

. . . and the Lost Sovereigns, illustrated by Stead, Brockhampton Press, 1964, published as *. . . and the Last Treasure,* Hodder & Stoughton, 1978.

. . . and the Plot That Failed, illustrated by Stead, Brockhampton Press, 1965, new edition, Chivers, 1986.

. . . and the Blue Moon, illustrated by Stead, Brockhampton Press, 1965.

. . . Looks Back, illustrated by Stead, Hodder & Stoughton, 1965.

. . . Scores a Bull, illustrated by Stead, Hodder & Stoughton, 1965.

The Biggles Adventure Omnibus (contains *Biggles Gets His Men, No Rest for Biggles, Another Job for Biggles,* and *Biggles Takes a Holiday*), Hodder & Stoughton, 1965.

. . . and the Gun Runners, illustrated by Stead, Brockhampton Press, 1966.

. . . in the Terai, illustrated by Stead, Brockhampton Press, 1967.

. . . *and the Penitent Thief,* illustrated by Stead, Brockhampton Press, 1967.

. . . *Sorts It Out,* illustrated by Stead, Brockhampton Press, 1967.

. . . *and the Dark Intruder* (also see below), illustrated by Stead, Hodder & Stoughton, 1967.

. . . *in the Underworld,* illustrated by Stead, Brockhampton Press, 1968.

The Boy Biggles, illustrated by Stead, Dean & Sons, 1968.

. . . *and the Deep Blue Sea,* illustrated by Stead, Brockhampton Press, 1969.

. . . *and the Little Green God,* illustrated by Stead, Brockhampton Press, 1969.

. . . *and the Noble Lord,* illustrated by Stead, Brockhampton Press, 1969.

. . . *Sees Too Much,* illustrated by Stead, Brockhampton Press, 1970, new edition, Chivers, 1986.

. . . *of the Royal Flying Corps* (selection), edited by Piers Williams, Macdonald Purnell, 1978.

The Bumper Biggles Book, Chancellor Press, 1983.

The Best of Biggles: Five Thrilling Adventures (contains *Biggles in Africa, Biggles Flies North, Biggles in the South Seas, Biggles and the Black Mask,* and *Biggles and the Dark Intruder*), Chancellor Press, 1984.

"GIMLET" SERIES; ILLUSTRATED BY LESLIE STEAD

Gimlet Goes Again, University of London Press, 1944, reprinted, May Fair Books, 1963.

. . . *Comes Home,* University of London Press, 1946.

. . . *Mops Up,* Brockhampton Press, 1947, reprinted, May Fair Books, 1963.

Gimlet's Oriental Quest, Brockhampton Press, 1948, reprinted, May Fair Books, 1963.

. . . *Lends a Hand,* Brockhampton Press, 1949, reprinted, May Fair Books, 1964.

. . . *Bores In,* Brockhampton Press, 1950.

. . . *off the Map,* Brockhampton Press, 1951.

. . . *Gets the Answer,* Brockhampton Press, 1952.

. . . *Takes a Job,* Brockhampton Press, 1954.

"WORRALS" SERIES; ILLUSTRATED BY LESLIE STEAD

Worrals of the W.A.A.F., Lutterworth Press, 1941.

. . . *Flies Again,* Hodder & Stoughton, 1942.

. . . *Carries On,* Lutterworth Press, 1942.

. . . *on the War-Path,* Hodder & Stoughton, 1943.

. . . *Goes East,* Hodder & Stoughton, 1944.

. . . *of the Islands: A Story of the War in the Pacific,* Hodder & Stoughton, 1945.

. . . *in the Winds,* Hodder & Stoughton, 1947.

. . . *Down Under,* Lutterworth Press, 1948.

. . . *Goes Afoot,* Lutterworth Press, 1949.

. . . *in the Wastelands,* Lutterworth Press, 1949.

. . . *Investigates,* Lutterworth Press, 1950.

"REX CLINTON" SERIES; JUVENILE SCIENCE FICTION

Kings of Space: A Story of Interplanetary Exploration, illustrated by Stead, Hodder & Stoughton, 1954.

Return to Mars, illustrated by Stead, Hodder & Stoughton, 1955.

Now to the Stars, Hodder & Stoughton, 1956.

To Outer Space, illustrated by Stead, Hodder & Stoughton, 1957.

The Edge of Beyond, illustrated by Stead, Hodder & Stoughton, 1958.

The Death Rays of Ardilla, illustrated by Stead, Hodder & Stoughton, 1959.

To Worlds Unknown: A Story of Interplanetary Exploration, Hodder & Stoughton, 1960.

The Quest for the Perfect Planet, Hodder & Stoughton, 1961.

The Man Who Vanished into Space, Hodder & Stoughton, 1963.

OTHER

Also author of two plays, (with G. R. Ranier) "The Machine That Disappeared," 1942, and "The Charming Mrs. Nayther," 1942. Author of column "The Passing Show," for *My Garden* magazine, 1937-44; also columnist for *Modern Boy, Pearson's, Boys' Own Paper,* and *Girls' Own Paper.* Founder and editor, *Popular Flying,* 1932-39, and *Flying,* 1938-39.

MEDIA ADAPTATIONS: "Biggles—Adventures in Time," a 1988 film directed by John Hough, is based on W. E. Johns's books, featuring the character James Bigglesworth.

SIDELIGHTS: Drawing on his own experiences as a British pilot during World War I, W. E. Johns created his popular series character, flying ace James Bigglesworth, who appeared in approximately 100 "Biggles" books for children. An idealized champion of Britain and its values, Biggles led his friends Algy, Bertie, and Ginger on numerous adventures around the world as he fought international criminals for almost half a century. Using the same formula with which he had so much luck for Biggles, Johns also created three other series characters, Gimlet, Worrals, and Rex Clinton. Like the Biggles stories, the Gimlet books were a popular series about pilots, while Worrals of the Women's Auxiliary Air Force represented Johns's attempt to interest women readers in tales about airplanes.

The author's effort to enter the science fiction market was less successful, however, for he did not have the technical background which lent more realism to his series about airplane pilots. The result was that the Rex Clinton books contained numerous factual errors, such as a description of an Earth-sized planet becoming a nova. But despite such flaws in Johns's writing, his characters, especially Biggles, were well-loved by his readers. As Sheila Benson commented in a *Los Angeles Times* article, after his many adventures spanning several decades, Biggles has become "dear to the hearts of the British."

BIOGRAPHICAL/CRITICAL SOURCES:

BOOKS

Ellis, Peter Berresford, and Piers Williams, *Biggles: The Life of Captain W. E. Johns,* W. H. Allen, 1981.

Pearson, John, *Biggles: The Authorized Biography,* Sidgwick & Jackson, 1979.

PERIODICALS

Los Angeles Times, January 29, 1988.

OBITUARIES:

PERIODICALS

Time, June 28, 1968.*

*   *   *

JOHNSON, Natalie
  See ROBISON, Nancy L(ouise)

*   *   *

JONES, Eldred D(urosimi) 1925-

PERSONAL: Born January 6, 1925, in Freetown, Sierra Leone, West Africa; son of Eldred William and Ethline (Quinn) Jones;

married Marjorie Pratt, 1952; children: Esse-Mary, Iyamide. *Education:* Fourah Bay College, B.A., 1947; Corpus Christi College, Oxford, B.A., 1953; Oxford University, M.A., 1957; University of Durham, Ph.D., 1962. *Politics:* None. *Religion:* Christian.

ADDRESSES: Office—Department of English, Fourah Bay College, Private Moril Bay, Mount Aureol, Freetown, Sierra Leone, West Africa.

CAREER: Fourah Bay College, Freetown, Sierra Leone, lecturer, 1953-62, senior lecturer, 1962-64, professor of English and chairman of department, 1964-74, principal, 1974-85; University of Sierra Leone, Freetown, Sierra Leone, emeritus professor, 1986—. Chairman, Noma Award for publishing in Africa. Consultant, Association for the Study of Commonwealth Languages and Literatures.

MEMBER: International Shakespeare Association (member of executive committee), International Institute of Communication, Royal Society of Arts (fellow), National Theatre League (Sierra Leone; president, 1964), Globe Playhouse Trust (England; consulting member).

AWARDS, HONORS: First prize for best critical work, Festival of Negro Arts (Dakar, West Africa), 1966, for *Othello's Countrymen: The African in English Renaissance Drama;* member of the Order of the Republic of Sierra Leone, 1980; D.Litt., Williams College, 1985.

WRITINGS:

The Way to Write Successful Letters, Allen & Unwin, 1962.
Othello's Countrymen: The African in English Renaissance Drama, Oxford University Press, 1965.
(Compiler with Ronald Ridout) *Adjustments: An Anthology of African and Western Writing,* Edward Arnold, 1966.
(Editor with Christopher Fyfe) *Freetown: A Symposium,* Sierra Leone University Press, 1968.
The Elizabethan Image of Africa, University Press of Virginia, 1971.
(Editor) William Shakespeare, *Macbeth,* Macmillan, 1972.
Wole Soyinka, Twayne, 1973, 3rd edition, Heinemann Educational, 1988 (published in England as *The Writing of Wole Soyinka,* Heinemann, 1973).
(Compiler with Clifford N. Fyle) *A Krio-English Dictionary,* Oxford University Press, 1980.

Editor of annual, *African Literature Today,* Heinemann, 1966—, Africana Publishing, 1973—; general editor, "English for Schools and Colleges in West Africa" series, Macmillan, 1968-71; series editor, "New Perspectives on African Literature," Hans Zell Publishers, 1989—. African correspondent, *Shakespeare Quarterly,* 1967—.

WORK IN PROGRESS: Further research on African literature and Krio.

AVOCATIONAL INTERESTS: Acting and directing, cricket, tennis, music.

*   *   *

JORSTAD, Erling (Theodore) 1930-

PERSONAL: Born October 13, 1930, in Kenyon, Minn.; son of Oscar Edwin and Laura (Voxland) Jorstad; married Helen Haban (a college teacher), August 25, 1956 (divorced, 1979); married Ruth Arnold, 1987; children: (first marriage) Eric, Laura. *Education:* St. Olaf College, B.A., 1952; Harvard University, M.A., 1953; University of Wisconsin, Ph.D., 1957. *Religion:* Lutheran.

ADDRESSES: Home—1130 Highland Ave., Northfield, Minn. 55057. *Office*—Department of History, St. Olaf College, Northfield, Minn. 55057.

CAREER: St. Olaf College, Northfield, Minn., instructor, 1956-58, assistant professor, 1958-61, associate professor, 1961-69, professor of history, 1969—. Visiting professor of history at Chiang Mai University, Thailand, 1977. *Military service:* Minnesota National Guard, 1955-57; became second lieutenant.

MEMBER: American Historical Association, Organization of American Historians, American Association of University Professors, American Society of Church History, Society for Religion in Higher Education, Upper Midwest Historical Society (secretary, 1958-60), Phi Beta Kappa.

AWARDS, HONORS: Research fellowship, Minnesota Historical Society, 1959; grant-in-aid, American Association of State and Local History, 1960; research fellowship, Danforth Foundation, 1963-64; research grant, American Philosophical Society, 1970-71; recipient of several St. Olaf College faculty development grants.

WRITINGS:

The Politics of Doomsday: The Fundamentalists of the Far Right, Abingdon, 1970.
The Instant Giant: American Radicalism in the 1960s, College Notes, 1970.
Love It or Leave It?: A Dialog on Loyalty, Augsburg, 1972.
That New-Time Religion: The Jesus Revival in America, Augsburg, 1973.
The Holy Spirit in Today's Church, Abingdon, 1973.
Bold in the Spirit: Lutheran Charismatic Renewal in America, Augsburg, 1974.
The Politics of Moralism: The New Christian Right in America, Augsburg, 1981.
Evangelicals in the White House: The Cultural Maturation of Born Again Christianity, Edwin Mellen, 1981.
Being Religious in America: The Deepening Crisis over Public Faith, Augsburg, 1986.
The New Christian Right, 1981-1988, Edwin Mellen, 1987.
Holding Fast, Pressing On: Religion in the 80s, Greenwood Press, 1989.

Contributor to numerous periodicals, including *Christian Scholar, Ecumenist, Journal of American History, American Historical Review, Christianity Today, Fides et Historia,* and *Lutheran Quarterly.*

SIDELIGHTS: "My two major interests are religion and politics," Erling Jorstad told *CA.* "Since I am neither a politician nor a minister, I follow my interests by studying the relationship between these two fields. I write because I hope to reach a wide audience and because I find both my teaching and writing are enhanced by sustained scholarly research. Writing is a form of teaching; and in the classroom I have the opportunity to try out new ideas before starting the writing process on a new project. One major fringe benefit has been the large number of invitations to speak to various groups about my research. This is good not only for my ego and wallet, but it gives me the opportunity to realize that there really are people out there who have read my material. In turn, I learn from them what interests them, and often this helps shape the direction of my latest research project.

"My field of investigation is contemporary American religious life. This means I am writing instant history, something close to journalism. This creates some hazards, such as finding out someone else is bringing out a book before you are on the same subject. But it has rewards also, because it gives me a sense of engagement and participation in the current scene in America. I attempt to be as objective as possible and at the same time to put my scholarship to work for causes in which I believe."

AVOCATIONAL INTERESTS: Classical music, aquatic sports, bicycle touring.

JULIAN, Jane
   See WISEMAN, David

*   *   *

JUSTICIAR
   See POWELL-SMITH, Vincent (Walter Francis)

K

KALIA, Narendra Nath 1942-

PERSONAL: Born November 30, 1942, in Chintpurni, India; came to the United States in 1972; son of Pandit Ram Nath and Santosh (Kumari) Kalia. *Education:* University of Delhi, B.A. (with honors), 1963, M.A. (history), 1966; University of Waterloo, M.A. (political science), 1972; Syracuse University, Ph.D., 1978.

ADDRESSES: Home—333 Hoyt St., Buffalo, N.Y. 14213. *Office*—Department of Sociology, State University of New York College at Buffalo, 1300 Elmwood Ave., Buffalo, N.Y. 14222.

CAREER: University of Delhi, Delhi, India, lecturer in history, 1966-67; self-employed in business and sales in Toronto, Ontario, 1968-70; State University of New York College at Buffalo, professor of sociology, 1977—. Commentator on Voice of India radio program "Soch-Vichaar," broadcast in Toronto.

MEMBER: Canadian Association of South Asian Scholars, Society for the Scientific Study of Sex, Society for the Study of Social Problems, New York State Sociological Association, Western New York Professionals Working in Human Sexuality, Alpha Kappa Delta.

WRITINGS:

(Translator into Hindi) D. H. Lawrence, *Lady Chatterly's Lover,* Subodh Pocket Books (New Delhi), 1967.
(Translator into Hindi) Vladimir Nabokov, *A Kuprin's Yama: The Pit,* Subodh Pocket Books (New Delhi), 1967.
A Textbook of Indian History, Ranjit, 1968, 2nd edition, 1970.
Nau Baras (novel; title means "Nine Years"), Radha Krishna, 1975.
The Lies We Tell Our Children: Sexism in Indian Education, Vikas, 1979.
(Editor) *Pakistan Se Taza Ghazalen* (anthology of Pakistani Urdu poetry), Radha Krishna, 1980.
(Editor) *Pakistani Urdu Shayari,* Radhakrishna, Volume 1, 1984, Volume 2, 1985, Volume 3, 1986.
From Sexism to Equality: A Handbook in the Sociology of Education, New India Publications, 1986.

Contributor to Indian, American, and international periodicals. Member of advisory board of *Annual Editions.*

WORK IN PROGRESS: An article, "Symbols of Social Change: A Content-Analysis of Sociological Interrelations between Literature, Nation Building, Modernization, and Cultural Development."

SIDELIGHTS: Narendra Nath Kalia told *CA:* "Through a sociologist by profession, I study literature because literature makes humanness accessible in a way that typical social scientific data (survey, questionnaire, statistics) cannot.

"I received my initial graduate training in history, with an emphasis on cross-cultural perspectives. As a result, I find it difficult to discard Matthew Arnold's notion that in order to create the best culture (be it on the plains of Pakistan or in the classrooms in the U.S.) we must be in touch with the ethics of other cultures, and that only in literature do we find a record of the prescriptions and proscriptions—offered by the best and the brightest—on the human condition. A society's literature is also an implicit commentary on social life itself because poetry deals with concrete images and prose involves literary experiments reflecting the dilemmas and aspirations of an emerging middle class searching for an identity in the mass society.

"Just as the best works of literature are those that most accurately represent the society of which they are a product, the values of a genre are the microcosms of their civilization. Writers use the literary metaphor as it uses them. As readers, we express ourselves by identifying with the metaphors we cherish; as artists, we create metaphors to interpret out lives and longings. Metaphor is the radical mode for correlating our knowledge and experience through extended meanings in societal intercourse, and it also conveys the social truth incommunicable by other means. Aristotle had initiated the analysis of literature as the study of social communication by arguing that language functions in a dualism of literal and symbolic meanings. To qualitative sociologists, literature provides a necessary antidote to the scientific accounts of segmented human behavior and offers a fertile medium for mastering the group-individual duality in social behavior. Literature is the social scientist's willing ally: it conjugates with the scientific rigor to fructify the passionate wisdom of folk heritage."

*   *   *

KAMENETZ, Rodger 1950-

PERSONAL: Born January 20, 1950, in Baltimore, Md.; son of Irvin and Miriam Kamenetz; married Moira Crone (a fiction writer), October 15, 1979; children: Anya Miriam, Kezia Vida. *Education:* Yale University, B.A., 1970; Johns Hopkins University, M.A., 1972; Stanford University, M.A., 1975.

ADDRESSES: Home—3175 Hundred Oaks, Baton Rouge, La. 70808. *Office*—Department of English, Louisiana State University, Baton Rouge, La. 70803.

CAREER: Louisiana State University, Baton Rouge, director of creative writing program, 1983-86, associate professor of English, 1985—.

WRITINGS:

The Missing Jew (poems), Dryad, 1980.
Nympholepsy (poems), Dryad, 1984.
Terra Infirma, University of Arkansas Press, 1985.
Becoming a Father (essays), Poseidon Books, 1990.

Work represented in anthologies, including *Voices Within the Ark,* Avon, 1980. Contributor of poems to magazines, including *Antioch Review, Southern Review, Shenandoah, Grand Street, New Republic,* and *Mississippi Review.*

WORK IN PROGRESS: Morning, a collection of poems.

SIDELIGHTS: Writing in the *Sewanee Review,* Paul Ramsey praised Rodger Kamenetz's *The Missing Jew,* noting that the author "is a wonderfully pensive, able writer, sprucely rhythmical. The rhythms and Jewish speech-patterns remarkably blend. The patterns of development are many and satisfying: narrative, argument, thoughtful surprises, dialogue, questions and answers." And Andrei Codrescu commented in the *San Francisco Review of Books* that the "ear at work here is as good as W[illiam] C[arlos] Williams' in the early poems."

Kamenetz told *CA:* "*The Missing Jew* started as poems I wrote in the voice of my dead grandfather. I soon came to realize, by studying Jewish texts, particularly the Talmud, that I could hear echoes of his voice in those works, so I came to enlarge the scope of the book to include larger chunks of Jewish history and literature. I did not intend to be an exclusively ethnic writer. I think the specialization of Jewish literature in the West is absurd since so much of Western thought is Jewish thought. The title was partly inspired by a remark of a friend that the word 'Jew' was impossible to use in a poem, partly by the death of my grandfather, and partly by my own search for the Jew that was missing in me.

"*Nympholepsy* is about poetry and the erotic. I was trying to understand in this book why one writes poems at all—what is the compulsion, this nympholepsy, that seizes us with a desire for impossible things?

"In *Terra Infirma* I chose prose as a way of deepening my exploration of a difficult terrain: the death of my mother. I felt I wanted to lay bare everything in this book without the constriction of the formal considerations of poetry. I found, however, that prose offered formal challenges of its own so that I became equally fascinated with the process and the content. I call these writings essays, but in the radical sense." The book describes the author's ambiguous relationship with his mother, a strong-willed woman who loved her children possessively. *Newsweek* reviewer Gene Lyons commented that the combination "is an oddly haunting book—as impossible to summarize as it is to forget."

Kamenetz added, "In *Becoming a Father,* a series of linked essays, I ask the question, how did as unlikely a candidate as I become a father?

"I see my writing as in the figure of an ellipse. In geometry, an ellipse is a figure traced by keeping a set distance from two points, the foci. I find one focus in my experience and another focus in my reading. If I maintain the proper tension between the two, the pattern comes out nicely."

BIOGRAPHICAL/CRITICAL SOURCES:

PERIODICALS

Baltimore Jewish Times, February 16, 1979.
Newsweek, May 19, 1986.
Poetry Flash, April, 1981.
San Francisco Review of Books, December, 1980.
Sewanee Review, fall, 1980.
Southern Review, spring, 1986.

* * *

KARDISH, Laurence 1945-

PERSONAL: Born January 5, 1945, in Ottawa, Ontario, Canada; son of Samuel (a baker) and Tillie (Steinberg) Kardish; married Judith Leah Molot, August 10, 1967 (divorced); children: Naomi Frances. *Education:* Carleton University, B.A. (with honors), 1966; Columbia University, M.F.A., 1968.

ADDRESSES: Home—165 Christopher #5-Y, New York, N.Y. 10014. *Office*—Museum of Modern Art, 21 West 53rd St., New York, N.Y. 10019.

CAREER: Canadian Film Institute, Ottawa, Ontario, employed in Canadian film archives, National Film Theater, and Canadian Federation of Film Societies, 1965-66; Film-Makers Distribution Center, New York City, film distributor, 1967-68; Museum of Modern Art, New York City, assistant curator in film program, beginning 1968, currently associate curator for Department of Film Programming. Has toured Europe as part of a Museum of Modern Art program.

MEMBER: Canadian Film Institute, Playwrights Union of Canada, Film-Makers Co-Operative (New York City), Playwrights Co-Operative (Toronto).

AWARDS, HONORS: Canadian artists competition award for best narrative film, Art Gallery of Ontario, 1968, for "Slow Run."

WRITINGS:

Reel Plastic Magic: A Brief History of Filmmaking in America, Little, Brown, 1972.
Michael Balcon: The Pursuit of British Cinema, Museum of Modern Art, 1984.

PLAYS

"Goebbels Goebbeldygook," first performed in Ottawa, Ontario, at Carleton University, 1965.
Brussel Sprouts (first performed in Toronto at Factory Lab Theatre, February, 1972), Playwrights Co-Operative, 1969.
Little Steps to Heaven, Playwrights Co-Operative, 1973.

OTHER

Author of unpublished plays, including (with John Palmer) "Vesuvius Goes to Market," 1965, "Bronx Lullaby," 1969, and "Egg Cream," 1975; author, producer, and director of "Slow Run," an avant-garde screenplay, 1968; author of screenplay "Soft Passions," 1973. Contributor of articles to *New York Times* and *Film Comment.*

WORK IN PROGRESS: Various screenplays.*

KEENAN, Deborah (Anne) 1950-

PERSONAL: Born December 5, 1950, in Minneapolis, Minn.; daughter of Clifford A. (a chemical engineer) and Virginia (an English teacher; maiden name, Wells) Bowman; married second husband, Stephen M. Seidel, July 23, 1983; children: (first marriage) Brendan, Molly; (second marriage) Joseph. *Education:* Macalester College, B.A., 1973.

ADDRESSES: Home—1168 Laurel Ave., St. Paul, Minn. 55104.

CAREER: Poet in residence at a private school in St. Paul, Minn., beginning 1975; director of programming for COMPAS, a state arts organization, 1981-83; Milkweed Editions, Minneapolis, Minn., managing editor, 1985—.

WRITINGS:

On Stage: The Beatles, Creative Education Press, 1976.
On Stage: Barbra Streisand, Creative Education Press, 1976.
Household Wounds (poetry), New Rivers Press, 1981.
One Angel Then (poetry), Midnight Paper Sales Press, 1981.
(With Jim Moore) *How We Missed Belgium* (poetry), edited by Emilie Buchwald and R. W. Scholes, Milkweed Editions, 1984.
The Only Window That Counts (poetry), New Rivers Press, 1985.

Contributor of poems to literary magazines, including *Pequod* and *New England Review of Literature.*

WORK IN PROGRESS: A first novel; a fifth collection of poems.

SIDELIGHTS: Deborah Keenan told *CA* she writes "because it is difficult, necessary, and because the process keeps me sane."

AVOCATIONAL INTERESTS: Rock 'n' roll, gardening, the subject of grace.

*   *   *

KELLY, H(enry) A(nsgar) 1934-

PERSONAL: Born June 6, 1934, in Fort Dodge, Iowa; son of Harry Francis and Inez Ingeborg (Anderson) Kelly; married Marea Tancred, June 18, 1968; children: Sarah Marea, Dominic Tancred. *Education:* Attended Creighton University, 1952-53; St. Louis University, A.B., 1959, A.M. and Ph.L., 1961; Harvard University, Ph.D., 1965; postgraduate study at Boston College, 1964-66, and American Academy in Rome, 1966-67. *Politics:* "Independent, out of Democratic." *Religion:* Roman Catholic.

ADDRESSES: Home—1123 Kagawa St., Pacific Palisades, Calif. 90272. *Office*—University of California, Los Angeles, Department of English, 405 Hilgard St., Los Angeles, Calif. 90024.

CAREER: Society of Jesus (Jesuits), Wisconsin Province, scholastic seminarian, 1953-66; Harvard University, Society of Fellows, Cambridge, Mass., junior fellow, 1964-67; University of California, Los Angeles, assistant professor, 1967-69, associate professor, 1969-72, professor of English and medieval-renaissance studies, 1972—.

MEMBER: Medieval Academy of America (fellow), Medieval Association of the Pacific (president, 1988-90).

AWARDS, HONORS: Guggenheim fellow, 1971-72; National Endowment for the Humanities fellow, 1980-81.

WRITINGS:

The Devil, Demonology, and Witchcraft, Doubleday, 1968, revised edition, 1974 (published in England as *Towards the Death of Satan,* Geoffrey Chapman, 1968).
Divine Providence in the England of Shakespeare's Histories, Harvard University Press, 1970.
Love and Marriage in the Age of Chaucer, Cornell University Press, 1975.
The Matrimonial Trials of Henry VIII, Stanford University Press, 1976.
Canon Law and the Archpriest of Hita, Medieval and Renaissance Texts and Studies, 1984.
The Devil at Baptism: Ritual, Theology, and Drama, Cornell University Press, 1985.
Chaucer and the Cult of the Saint Valentine, E. J. Brill, 1986.
Tragedy and Comedy from Dante to Pseudo-Dante, University of California Press, 1989.

Contributor to professional journals, including *Church History, Journal of Religion, Modern Philology,* and *Ricardian.* Co-editor, *Viator: Medieval and Renaissance Studies* (annual of the Center for Medieval and Renaissance Studies, University of California, Los Angeles), 1970—.

WORK IN PROGRESS: Ideas of tragedy in the Middle Ages; a history of inquisitorial procedures.

*   *   *

KENNEDY, Joseph Charles 1929-
(X. J. Kennedy)

PERSONAL: Born August 21, 1929, in Dover, N.J.; son of Joseph Francis and Agnes (Rauter) Kennedy; married Dorothy Mintzlaff, January 31, 1962; children: Kathleen Anna, David Ian, Matthew Devin, Daniel Joseph, Joshua Quentin. *Education:* Seton Hall University, B.Sc., 1950; Columbia University, M.A., 1951; University of Paris, certificat, 1956; additional study at University of Michigan, 1956-62.

ADDRESSES: Home—4 Fern Way, Bedford, Mass. 01730. *Agent*—Curtis Brown, Ltd., 10 Astor Pl., New York, N.Y. 10003.

CAREER: University of Michigan, Ann Arbor, teaching fellow, 1956-60, instructor in English, 1960-62; Woman's College of University of North Carolina (now University of North Carolina at Greensboro), lecturer in English, 1962-63; Tufts University, Medford, Mass., assistant professor, 1963-67, associate professor, 1967-73, professor of English, 1973-79; free-lance writer, 1979—. Visiting lecturer, Wellesley College, 1964, and University of California, Irvine, 1966-67; Bruern fellow in American civilization, University of Leeds, 1974-75. *Military service:* U.S. Navy, 1951-55.

MEMBER: Modern Language Association, Children's Literature Association, National Council of Teachers of English, PEN, Authors Guild of America, John Barton Wolgamot Society, Phi Beta Kappa.

AWARDS, HONORS: Avery Hopwood Award, University of Michigan, 1959; Bread Loaf fellowship in poetry, 1960; Bess Hokin Prize, *Poetry* magazine, 1961; Lamont Award, Academy of American Poets, 1961, for *Nude Descending a Staircase: Poems, Song, a Ballad;* National Council on the Arts grant, 1967-68; Shelley Memorial Award, 1970; Guggenheim fellowship, 1973-74; Golden Rose Trophy, New England Poetry Club, 1974; *Knock at a Star: A Child's Introduction to Poetry* was a National Council of Teachers of English Teachers' Choice Book and a *School Library Journal* book of the year, both 1983; *Los Angeles Times* Book Award in poetry, 1985, for *Cross Ties: Selected Poems;* American Library Association Notable Book citation, 1986, for *The Forgetful Wishing Well: Poems for Young People;* L.H.D. from Lawrence University, 1988; Michael Braude Award for Light Verse, American Academy and Institute of Arts and Letters, 1989.

WRITINGS:

POETRY; UNDER PSEUDONYM X. J. KENNEDY

Nude Descending a Staircase: Poems, Song, a Ballad, Doubleday, 1961.

Growing into Love, Doubleday, 1969.

Bulsh, Burning Deck, 1970.

Breaking and Entering, Oxford University Press, 1971.

Emily Dickinson in Southern California, Godine, 1974.

Celebrations after the Death of John Brennan, Penmaen, 1974.

Hangover Mass, Bits Press, 1984.

Cross Ties: Selected Poems, University of Georgia Press, 1985.

OTHER; UNDER PSEUDONYM X. J. KENNEDY

(Editor with James E. Camp) *Mark Twain's Frontier* (textbook), Holt, 1963.

An Introduction to Poetry (textbook), Little, Brown, 1966, 7th edition, with instructor's manual written with wife, Dorothy M. Kennedy, Scott, Foresman, 1990.

(Editor with Camp and Keith Waldrop) *Pegasus Descending: A Book of the Best Bad Verse* (anthology), Macmillan, 1971.

(Editor) *Messages: A Thematic Anthology of Poetry,* Little, Brown, 1973.

(With Camp and Waldrop) *Three Tenors, One Vehicle* (song lyrics), Open Places, 1975.

One Winter Night in August and Other Nonsense Jingles (juvenile verse), Atheneum, 1975.

An Introduction to Fiction (textbook), with instructor's manual, Little, Brown, 1976, 4th edition, with instructor's manual with D. M. Kennedy, 1987.

Literature: An Introduction to Fiction, Poetry, and Drama (textbook), with instructor's manual, Little, Brown, 1976, 4th edition, with instructor's manual with D. M. Kennedy, 1987.

The Phantom Ice Cream Man: More Nonsense Jingles (juvenile verse), Atheneum, 1979.

(Editor) *Tygers of Wrath: Poems of Hate, Anger and Invective,* University of Georgia Press, 1981.

Did Adam Name the Vinegarroon? (juvenile verse), Godine, 1982.

(With D. M. Kennedy) *The Bedford Reader* (textbook), with instructor's manual, St. Martin's, 1982, 3rd edition, 1988.

(Compiler with D. M. Kennedy) *Knock at a Star: A Child's Introduction to Poetry,* Little, Brown, 1982.

(Translator from the French) *French Leave: Translations* (poetry), Robert L. Barth, 1983.

The Owlstone Crown (juvenile novel), Atheneum, 1983.

The Forgetful Wishing Well: Poems for Young People (juvenile verse), Atheneum, 1985.

Brats (juvenile verse), Atheneum, 1986.

Ghastlies, Gooks & Pincushions (juvenile verse), Macmillan, 1989.

(With D. M. Kennedy) *The Bedford Guide for College Writers,* with instructor's manual, St. Martin's, 1987, 2nd edition, 1990.

Poetry editor, *Paris Review,* 1961-64; co-editor, with D. M. Kennedy, *Counter/Measures,* 1971-74.

WORK IN PROGRESS: Poems; a comic novel; another novel for children; juvenile verse.

SIDELIGHTS: Although X. J. Kennedy has recently concentrated his literary efforts on writing college textbooks and children's verse, publication in 1961 of his first book of poetry, *Nude Descending a Staircase: Poems, Song, a Ballad,* established his reputation as a poet for adults. Poems from the collection had already won Kennedy the University of Michigan's Hopwood Award and *Poetry* magazine's Bess Hokin Prize, while the Academy of American Poets bestowed its Lamont Award on the volume itself. *Nude Descending a Staircase* reveals a poet who writes witty, satirical poems and—unlike the majority of his colleagues—uses traditional verse forms. This strict adherence to rhyme and measured rhythm has prevailed through all Kennedy's work, leading the poet, according to *National Review* contributor Loxley Nichols, to describe himself as "one of an endangered species."

Kennedy's thirty-year anthology of poetry, *Cross Ties: Selected Poems* (winner of the *Los Angeles Times* Book Award for poetry in 1985) is praised by critics for the two factors which attracted them to his first work: humor and dexterous use of poetic construction. In a *Christian Science Monitor* review of the volume, for example, Raymond Oliver calls Kennedy "the funniest poet alive" and claims "the secret of Kennedy's excellence is his mastery of traditional verse." *Poetry* contributor Roger Mitchell's critique of the book also highlights the same characteristics of Kennedy's work. "He is a satirist," Mitchell observes, "and few poets are funnier than he." And to those who might call Kennedy's poetry out-of-date or old-fashioned, Mitchell replies, "If [Kennedy] is driving a horse and buggy in the age of the automobile, it is an elegant, well-made buggy, and the animal is gorgeous and well-groomed." Nichols congratulates Kennedy for being different from the mass of poets: "His allegiance to traditional verse forms verifies that he is indeed a breed apart from many of his contemporaries. While not all are equally rewarding, the poems in *Cross Ties* are of a range and depth that demonstrate the viability and elasticity of a poetic voice that submits willingly to the stricture of meter and rhyme."

Commenting on his predilection for traditional poetic forms, Kennedy told *CA:* "As a poet, I have printed few lines that fail to rhyme and to scan metrically. Though I admire—envy!—poets who can dispense with such formalities, I find I need them. Many today dismiss the sonnet and other traditional forms as drab boxes for cramming with words. But to me the old forms are where the primitive and surprising action is. Writing in rhythm and rhyme, a poet is involved in a enormous, meaningful game, not under his ego's control. He is a mere mouse in the lion's den of the language—but with any luck, at times he can get the lion to come out."

BIOGRAPHICAL/CRITICAL SOURCES:

BOOKS

Contemporary Literary Criticism, Gale, Volume 8, 1978, Volume 42, 1987.

Dictionary of Literary Biography, Volume 5: *American Poets since World War II,* Gale, 1980.

PERIODICALS

Christian Science Monitor, August 7, 1985.

National Review, July 18, 1986.

Poetry, January, 1986.

KENNEDY, Paul (Michael) 1945-
(Paul M. Kennedy)

PERSONAL: Born June 17, 1945, in Wallsend, England; married; children: three sons. *Education:* University of Newcastle-upon-Tyne, M.A. (with first class honors), 1966; St. Antony's College, Oxford, D.Phil., 1970. *Politics:* "Wobbly." *Religion:* Roman Catholic.

ADDRESSES: Office—Department of History, Yale University, New Haven, Conn. 06520.

CAREER: University of East Anglia, Norwich, England, lecturer, 1970-75, reader, 1975-82, professor of history, 1982-83; Yale University, New Haven, Conn., J. Richardson Dilworth Professor of History, 1983—. Lecturer throughout the United States. Has made appearances on television shows, including the "Today Show" and "MacNeil-Lehrer Report."

MEMBER: Royal Historical Society (fellow), American Academy of Arts and Sciences (fellow).

AWARDS, HONORS: Fellow, Alexander von Humboldt Foundation, 1972; fellow, Institute for Advanced Study, Princeton University, 1978-79; honorary degrees from Yale University, Ohio University, and University of New Haven.

WRITINGS:

Pacific Onslaught, 7th December, 1941 to 7th February, 1943, Ballantine, 1972.
Pacific Victory, Ballantine, 1973.
(Under name Paul M. Kennedy) *The Samoan Tangle: A Study in Anglo-German-American Relations, 1878-1900,* Barnes & Noble, 1974.
(Under name Paul M. Kennedy) *The Rise and Fall of British Naval Mastery,* Scribner, 1976.
(Editor with J. A. Moses) *Germany in the Pacific and Far East, 1870-1914,* University of Queensland Press, 1977.
(Editor under name Paul M. Kennedy) *The War Plans of the Great Powers, 1880-1914,* Allen & Unwin, 1979.
(Under name Paul M. Kennedy) *The Rise of the Anglo-German Antagonism, 1860-1914,* Allen & Unwin, 1980.
The Realities behind Diplomacy: Background Influences on British External Policy, 1865-1980, Allen & Unwin, 1981.
(Editor with Anthony Nicholls) *Nationalist and Racialist Movements in Britain and Germany before 1914,* Macmillan, 1981.
Strategy and Diplomacy, 1870-1945: Eight Essays, Allen & Unwin, 1984.
The Rise and Fall of the Great Powers: Economic Change and Military Conflict from 1500 to 2000, Random House, 1988.

Contributor to history journals in England, Germany, Australia, Canada, and the United States.

SIDELIGHTS: The Rise and Fall of the Great Powers: Economic Change and Military Conflict from 1500 to 2000 is Paul Kennedy's lengthy, best-selling analysis of why countries gain and lose worldly power. According to *Los Angeles Times* critic Garry Abrams, "Kennedy's theory is that the rise and fall of most great countries and empires since 1500 share a pattern and that there is an inescapable linkage between wealth and military might. Major players on the world stage usually have begun the descent to lesser roles because they failed to prudently finance their military commitments and to match their military commitments to their capabilities."

The most talked-about section of the book, notes Abrams, is chapter eight, in which Kennedy suggests that the United

States's relative share of the world's wealth is declining when compared to its post-World War II stance. In Kennedy's opinion, both China and Japan are the countries to watch for in the years ahead. The author maintains, "If I'm going to preach about the lessons of history at all, it is that societies which did not invest in the future but invested too much either in defense or consumption were destined to be overtaken by those with a different set of priorities," quotes Abrams.

In his *Washington Post* review, Norman Podhoretz disagrees on several counts with the ideas represented in *The Rise and Fall of the Great Powers.* "Has [the United States's] decline really been caused by the economic factors that Kennedy and so many others keep harping on . . . ?" Podhoretz wonders. The reviewer also believes it is untrue "that a nation's power is necessarily a function of its economic and technological resources. As the case of Japan demonstrates, a nation can be economically strong and yet lack all other forms of power. As the case of the Soviet Union shows, a nation can be economically weak and yet command overwhelming military and political strength." Podhoretz maintains that Kennedy knows all of this but that as a liberal his ideas appeal to other liberals and Democrats: "For Democrats, the 'end of empire' idea has the benefit of redefining the issue of world power in economic terms, which conveniently moves the discussion away from military strength, an issue on which the Republicans have tended to have more credibility."

However, *New York Times* reviewer Christopher Lehmann-Haupt values Kennedy's book because the author "not only exploits his framework eloquently, he also makes use of it to dig deeper and explore the historical contexts in which some 'power centers' prospered—for instance, why in the 16th century the cluster of states in west-central Europe rose to economic and strategic pre-eminence while such imposing Oriental empires as Ming China or Tokugawa Japan did not." In his analysis, Kennedy surmises that the United States's *relative* erosion can be managed and need not be drastic. To this, Lehmann-Haupt responds that "some will call this conclusion defeatism and others will call it whispering happily in the dark. Whatever it may be, it demonstrates that while the body of this text may be for the occasional browser of good historical writing, its final section is for everyone concerned with the contemporary political scene."

BIOGRAPHICAL/CRITICAL SOURCES:

BOOKS

Bestsellers 89, Number 1, Gale, 1989.
Kennedy, Paul, *The Rise and Fall of the Great Powers: Economic Change and Military Conflict from 1500 to 2000,* Random House, 1988.

PERIODICALS

Economist, January 17, 1981.
Globe and Mail (Toronto), May 7, 1988.
Los Angeles Times, March 2, 1988, March 29, 1988.
New York Times, January 7, 1988, April 10, 1988, April 17, 1988.
New York Times Book Review, March 18, 1984.
Spectator, May 1, 1976, November 29, 1980.
Times Literary Supplement, February 7, 1975, January 30, 1981, May 22, 1981, March 16, 1984.
Tribune Books (Chicago), May 8, 1988.
Washington Post, February 25, 1988.

KENNEDY, Paul M.
See KENNEDY, Paul (Michael)

*   *   *

KENNEDY, X. J.
See KENNEDY, Joseph Charles

*   *   *

KETTLE, Peter
See GLOVER, Denis (James Matthews)

*   *   *

KEY, Jack D(ayton) 1934-

PERSONAL: Born February 24, 1934, in Enid, Okla.; son of Ernest Dayton and Janie (Haldeman) Key; married Virgie Ruth Richardson; children: Toni Ruth Janish, Scot Dayton, Todd Morgan. *Education:* Phillips University, B.A., 1958; University of New Mexico, M.A., 1960; University of Illinois—Urbana-Champaign, M.S., 1962.

ADDRESSES: Home—624 23rd St. N.E., Rochester, Minn. 55904. *Office*—Library, Mayo Clinic and Foundation, Rochester, Minn. 55905.

CAREER: Lovelace Foundation for Medical Education and Research, Albuquerque, N.M., assistant librarian, 1958-59, medical librarian, 1965-70; University of Illinois—Urbana-Champaign, staff supervisor at Graduate Library, 1960-62; University of Iowa, Iowa City, pharmacy librarian, 1962-64; Mayo Clinic and Foundation, Rochester, Minn., librarian, 1970—; Mayo Medical School, Rochester, instructor, 1973, assistant professor, 1973-81, associate professor of biomedical communications, 1981—. Alberta A. Brown Lecturer, Western Michigan University, 1979; participated in U.S. Navy Naval War College Conference, 1979; St. Ansgar Hospital Annual Memorial Lecturer, 1987. *Military service:* U.S. Navy, 1952-55.

MEMBER: Mystery Writers of America, Medical Library Association, American Institute of the History of Pharmacy, American Association of the History of Medicine, American Medical Writers Association, American Osler Society, Alcuin Society, Sigma Xi, Pi Sigma Alpha, Rotary International (historian, 1975-87; member of executive board, 1976-87; president and member of district advisory council, both 1979-80), Baker Street Irregulars (investiture, 1989), Ampersand Club, Norwegian Explorers.

AWARDS, HONORS: Marion Dorroh Memorial Scholar, New Mexico Library Association, 1960; Paul Harris Fellow, Rotary International, 1979; special author's award, *Minnesota Medicine,* 1980, for outstanding historical writing; first place award, *Mayflower Quarterly,* 1988, for historical article; Knight, Icelandic Order of the Falcon.

WRITINGS:

(Editor) *Library Automation: The Orient and South Pacific,* Association for Library Automation Research Communications Press, 1975.

(Editor) *Library Automation at the Mayo Clinic Library,* Association for Library Automation Research Communications Press, 1975.

(With C. G. Roland) *The Origin of the Vaccine Inoculation by Edward Jenner,* Majors, 1977.

William A. Hammond, M.D.: 1828-1900, John Davies, 1979.

(Editor with T. E. Keys) *Classics and Other Selected Readings in Medical Librarianship,* Robert E. Krieger, 1980.

(With Alvin E. Rodin) *Journal of a Quest for the Elusive Doctor Arthur Conan Doyle: May 12, 1982-June 18, 1982,* John Davies, 1982.

(With R. J. Mann) *Medical "Vanities,"* Majors, 1982.

(With B. E. Blustein) *William A. Hammond, M.D., 1828-1900: The Publications of an American Neurologist,* John Davies, 1983.

(With Keys and J. A. Callahan) *Classics of Cardiology,* Robert E. Krieger, Volume 3, 1983, Volume 4, parts 1 and 2 (with Callahan and D. C. McGoon), 1989.

(With Rodin) *Medical Casebook of Doctor Arthur Conan Doyle: From Practitioner to Sherlock Holmes and Beyond,* Robert E. Krieger, 1984.

(With Rodin) *Adventuring in England with Doctor Arthur Conan Doyle: Encounters with Sherlock Holmes, Disciples and Medicine,* KeyRod Literary Enterprises, 1986.

(Contributor with Callahan) *Cardiology: Fundamentals and Practice,* Yearbook Medical Publishers, 1987.

(With Rodin) *Aphorisms of Sherlock Holmes: Two Hundred Selections Collected from the Canonical Writings* (Centennial Commemorative Keepsake Edition), KeyRod Literary Enterprises, 1987.

(With Rodin) *Disguises in the Adventures of Sherlock Holmes: An Illustrated Analysis of Thirty Disguises from the Writings of Arthur Conan Doyle* (Centennial Commemorative Keepsake Edition), KeyRod Literary Enterprises, 1987.

(Contributor with Rodin) *The Baker Street Dozen,* Contemporary Books, 1987.

(With Rodin) *Lost Worlds in Time, Space and Medicine: The Science Fiction of Arthur Conan Doyle,* KeyRod Literary Enterprises, 1988.

(With Rodin) *Medicine, Literature and Eponyms: An Encyclopedia of Medical Eponyms Derived from Literary Characters,* Robert E. Krieger, 1989.

Also contributor to *Cultivating Sherlock Holmes,* Norwegian Explorers of Minnesota. Editor of monograph series "Automated Activities in Health Sciences Libraries," Association for Library Automation Research Communications Press, 1975-78. Author of columns, including "Key's Korner," *Moccasin Flower,* 1978—, and "Echoes from Our Past," *Minnesota Medicine,* 1982—. Contributor of more than 350 articles and reviews to history, library, and medical journals.

SIDELIGHTS: Jack D. Key and his co-author Alvin E. Rodin spent many years researching the life of Arthur Conan Doyle, the British physician who created the famous fictional detective Sherlock Holmes. The result of their study, *Medical Casebook of Doctor Arthur Conan Doyle: From Practitioner to Sherlock Holmes and Beyond,* explores the physician's career as an ophthalmologist. Key told a Rochester *Post-Bulletin* reporter that he and Rodin wanted to elevate Doyle from the position of an inadequate doctor who embraced writing as an alternative career, a view widely held. Instead the authors portray the physician as an important contributor to nineteenth-century medicine. For example, Key and Rodin claim in the book's introduction that Doyle's work in infectious diseases "reveals remarkable insight." *Medical Casebook of Doctor Arthur Conan Doyle* also investigates Doyle's use of disease in the Sherlock Holmes stories; the authors include an appendix of all the stories' characters and deaths.

BIOGRAPHICAL/CRITICAL SOURCES:

BOOKS

Key, Jack D. and Alvin E. Rodin, *Medical Casebook of Doctor Arthur Conan Doyle: From Practitioner to Sherlock Holmes and Beyond,* Robert E. Krieger, 1984.

PERIODICALS

Post-Bulletin (Rochester, Minn.), December 3, 1980, June 14, 1983.

*   *   *

KIMBRO, Harriet
See KOFALK, Harriet

*   *   *

KING, Stephen (Edwin) 1947-
(Steve King; pseudonyms: Richard Bachman, John Swithen)

PERSONAL: Born September 21, 1947, in Portland, Me.; son of Donald (a merchant sailor) and Nellie Ruth (Pillsbury) King; married Tabitha Jane Spruce (a novelist), January 2, 1971; children: Naomi Rachel, Joseph Hill, Owen Phillip. *Education:* University of Maine at Orono, B.Sc., 1970. *Politics:* Democrat.

ADDRESSES: Home—Bangor and Center Lovell, Me. *Office*—P.O. Box 1186, Bangor, Me. 04001. *Agent*—Arthur Greene, 101 Park Ave., New York, N.Y. 10178.

CAREER: Writer. Has worked as a janitor, a laborer in an industrial laundry, and in a knitting mill. Hampden Academy (high school), Hampden, Me., English teacher, 1971-73; University of Maine, Orono, writer in residence, 1978-79. Owner, Philtrum Press, a publishing house, and WZON-AM, a rock 'n' roll radio station, both in Bangor, Me. Has made cameo appearances in films "Knightriders," as Steven King, 1980, "Creepshow," 1982, "Maximum Overdrive," 1986, and "Pet Sematary," 1989; has also appeared in American Express credit card television commercial. Served as judge for 1977 World Fantasy Awards, 1978. Participated in radio honor panel with George A. Romero, Peter Straub, and Ira Levin, moderated by Dick Cavett on WNET in New York, October 30-31, 1980.

MEMBER: Authors Guild, Authors League of America.

AWARDS, HONORS: Carrie named to *School Library Journal's* Book List, 1975; World Fantasy Award nominations, 1976, for *'Salem's Lot,* 1979, for *The Stand* and *Night Shift,* 1980, for *The Dead Zone,* 1981, for "The Mist," and 1983, for "The Breathing Method: A Winter's Tale" in *Different Seasons;* Hugo Award nomination from World Science Fiction Society, and Nebula Award nomination from Science Fiction Writers of America, both 1978, both for *The Shining;* Balrog Awards, second place in best novel category for *The Stand,* and second place in best collection category for *Night Shift,* both 1979; *The Long Walk* was named to the American Library Association's list of best books for young adults, 1979; World Fantasy Award, 1980, for contributions to the field, and 1982, for story "Do the Dead Sing?"; Career Alumni Award, University of Maine at Orono, 1981; *Firestarter* was named to the American Library Association's list of best books for young adults, 1981; Nebula Award nomination, Science Fiction Writers of America, 1981, for story "The Way Station"; special British Fantasy Award for outstanding contribution to the genre, British Fantasy Society, 1982, for

Cujo; Hugo Award, World Science Fiction Convention, 1982, for *Stephen King's Danse Macabre;* named Best Fiction Writer of the Year, *Us* Magazine, 1982; Locus Award for best collection, Locus Publications, 1986, for *Stephen King's Skeleton Crew.*

WRITINGS:

NOVELS

Carrie: A Novel of a Girl with a Frightening Power (also see below), Doubleday, 1974, movie edition published as *Carrie,* New American Library/Times Mirror, 1975.

'Salem's Lot (Literary Guild alternate selection; also see below), Doubleday, 1975, television edition, New American Library, 1979.

The Shining (Literary Guild main selection; also see below), Doubleday, 1977, movie edition, New American Library, 1980.

The Stand, Doubleday, 1978, revised edition (includes cuts from King's original manuscript), illustrations by Berni Wrightson, 1990 (also published in a limited edition, Doubleday, 1990).

The Dead Zone (Literary Guild dual main selection), Viking, 1979, movie edition published as *The Dead Zone: Movie Tie-In,* New American Library, 1980.

Firestarter (Literary Guild main selection), Viking, 1980, reprinted with afterword by King, 1981 (also published in a limited, aluminum-coated, asbestos-cloth edition, Phantasia Press [Huntington Woods, Mich.], 1980).

Cujo, Viking, 1981 (also published in a limited edition, Mysterious Press, 1981).

Pet Sematary (Literary Guild dual main selection), Doubleday, 1983.

Christine (Literary Guild dual main selection), Viking, 1983 (also published with illustrations by Stephen Gervais in a limited edition, Donald M. Grant [West Kingston, R.I.], 1983).

(With Peter Straub) *The Talisman,* Viking Press/Putnam, 1984 (also published in a limited two-volume edition, Donald M. Grant, 1984).

The Eyes of the Dragon (young adult; Book-of-the-Month Club alternate selection), limited edition with illustrations by Kenneth R. Linkhauser, Philtrum Press, 1984, new edition with illustrations by David Palladini, Viking, 1987.

It (Book-of-the-Month Club main selection), Viking, 1986 (first published in limited German edition as *Es,* Heyne [Munich, West Germany], 1986).

Misery (Book-of-the-Month Club main selection), Viking, 1987.

The Tommyknockers (Book-of-the-Month Club main selection), Putnam, 1987.

The Dark Half (Book-of-the-Month Club main selection), Viking, 1989.

Also author of early unpublished novels: "Sword in the Darkness," also referred to as "Babylon Here"; "The Cannibals"; and "Blaze," a reworking of John Steinbeck's *Of Mice and Men.*

NOVELS UNDER PSEUDONYM RICHARD BACHMAN

Rage (also see below), New American Library/Signet, 1977.

The Long Walk (also see below), New American Library/Signet, 1979.

Roadwork: A Novel of the First Energy Crisis (also see below) New American Library/Signet, 1981.

The Running Man (also see below), New American Library/Signet, 1982.

Thinner, New American Library, 1984.

SHORT FICTION

Night Shift (story collection; also see below), introduction by John D. MacDonald, Doubleday, 1978, published as *Night Shift: Excursions into Horror,* New American Library/Signet, 1979.

Different Seasons (novellas; Book-of-the-Month Club main selection; contains: "Rita Hayworth and Shawshank Redemption: Hope Springs Eternal," published in a large-type edition as *Rita Hayworth and Shawshank Redemption: A Story from "Different Seasons,"* Thorndike Press, 1983; "Apt Pupil: Summer of Corruption"; "The Body: Fall from Innocence"; and "The Breathing Method: A Winter's Tale," published in a large-type edition as *The Breathing Method,* Chivers Press, 1984), Viking, 1982.

Cycle of the Werewolf (novella; also see below), illustrations by Berni Wrightson, limited portfolio edition published with "Berni Wrightson: An Appreciation," Land of Enchantment (Westland, Mich.), 1983, new edition, New American Library, 1985.

Stephen King's Skeleton Crew (story collection), illustrations by J. K. Potter, Viking, 1985 (also published in a limited edition, Scream Press, 1985).

My Pretty Pony, illustrations by Barbara Kruger, Knopf, 1989 (also published in a limited edition, Library Fellows of New York's Whitney Museum of American Art, 1989).

Also author of short story "Slade," a western, and, under pseudonym John Swithen, of short story "The Fifth Quarter."

"THE DARK TOWER" SERIES

The Dark Tower: The Gunslinger, illustrations by Michael Whelan, limited edition, Donald M. Grant, 1982, 2nd limited edition, 1984, published as *The Gunslinger,* New American Library, 1988.

The Drawing of Three, illustrations by Phil Hale, New American Library, 1989.

SCREENPLAYS

Stephen King's Creep Show: A George A. Romero Film (based upon King's stories: "Father's Day," "The Lonesome Death of Jordy Verrill," previously published as "Weeds," "The Crate," and "They're Creeping Up on You"; released by Warner Brothers as "Creepshow," 1982), illustrations by Berni Wrightson and Michele Wrightson, New American Library, 1982.

"Cat's Eye" (based upon King's stories: "Quitters, Inc.," "The Ledge," and "The General"), Metro Goldwyn Mayer/United Artists, 1984.

Silver Bullet (based upon King's novella *Cycle of the Werewolf,* also included; released by Paramount Pictures/Dino de Laurentiis's North Carolina Film Corp., 1985), illustrations by Berni Wrightson, New American Library/Signet, 1985.

(And director) *Maximum Overdrive* (based upon King's stories "The Mangler," "Trucks," and "The Lawnmower Man"; released by Dino de Laurentiis' North Carolina Film Corp., 1986), New American Library, 1986.

"Pet Sematary" (based upon King's novel of same title), Laurel Production, 1989.

Also author of teleplay "Sorry, Right Number" for "Tales from the Dark Side" series, and of screenplay "The Stand," based upon his novel of same title. Author of unproduced versions of screenplays, including "Children of the Corn," "Cujo," "The Dead Zone," "The Shotgunners," "The Shining," "Something Wicked This Way Comes," and "Daylight Dead," based upon

three stories from *Night Shift*—"Strawberry Spring," "I Know What You Need," and "Battleground."

OMNIBUS EDITIONS

Stephen King (contains *The Shining, 'Salem's Lot, Night Shift,* and *Carrie*), W. S. Heinemann/Octopus Books, 1981.

The Bachman Books: Four Early Novels (contains *Rage, The Long Walk, Roadwork,* and *The Running Man*), with introduction "Why I Was Richard Bachman," New American Library, 1985.

CONTRIBUTOR OF SHORT FICTION TO ANTHOLOGIES

Terry Carr, editor, *The Year's Finest Fantasy,* Putnam, 1978.

Charles L. Grant, editor, *Shadows,* Doubleday, Volume 1, 1978, Volume 4, 1981.

Grant, editor, *Nightmares,* Playboy, 1979.

Peter Haining, editor, *More Tales of Unknown Horror,* New English Library (London), 1979.

Ramsey Campbell, editor, *New Tales of the Cthulhu Mythos,* Arkham House 1980.

R. Chetwynd-Hayes, editor, *The 17th Fontana Book of Great Ghost Stories,* Fontana, 1981.

Jeff Frane and Jack Rems, editors, *A Fantasy Reader: The Seventh World Fantasy Convention Program Book,* Seventh World Fantasy Convention, 1981.

Campbell, editor, *New Terrors,* Pocket Books, 1982.

Grant, editor, *Terrors,* Playboy, 1982.

Stuart David Schiff, editor, *Death,* Playboy, 1982.

Tom Silberkleit and Jerry Biederman, editors, *The Do-It-Yourself Bestseller,* Doubleday, Dolphin, 1982.

Rusty Burke, editor, *Satyricon II Program Book,* Satyricon II/DeepSouthCon XXI, 1983.

Karl Edward Wagner, editor, *The Year's Best Horror Stories, Series XII,* DAW, 1984.

David G. Hartwell, editor, *The Dark Descent,* Doherty Associates, 1987.

J. N. Williamson, editor, *Masques II: All New Stories of Horror and the Supernatural,* Maclay & Associates, 1987.

Martin Harry Greenberg and Carol-Lynn Roessel Waugh, editors, *The New Adventures of Sherlock Holmes: Original Stories by Eminent Mystery Writers,* Carroll & Graf, 1987.

Douglas E. Winter, *Prime Evil: New Stories by the Masters of Modern Horror,* New American Library, 1988.

Dark Visions, Gollancz, 1989.

Also contributor of stories to numerous other anthologies, including "Squad D" to Harlan Ellison's forthcoming *The Last Dangerous Visions.*

CONTRIBUTOR

Dilys Winn, editor, *Murderess Ink: The Better Half of the Mystery,* Bell, 1979.

Kennedy Poyser, editor, *World Fantasy Convention '82,* Eighth World Fantasy Convention, 1982.

Tom Savini, *Grand Illusions,* Imagine, Inc., 1983, reprinted as *Bizarro,* Crown, 1983.

Robert Weinberg, editor, *World Fantasy Convention 1983,* Weird Tales Ltd., 1983.

Douglas E. Winter, editor, *Shadowings: The Reader's Guide to Horror Fiction, 1981-82,* Starmont House, 1983.

Sylvia K. Burack, editor, *The Writer's Handbook,* Writer, Inc., 1984.

Stephen King Goes to Hollywood, New American Library, 1987.

AUTHOR OF FOREWORD/INTRODUCTION

Mary Shelley, Bram Stoker, and Robert Louis Stevenson, *Frankenstein, Dracula, Dr. Jekyll and Mr. Hyde,* New American Library/Signet, 1978.

Joseph Payne Brennan, *The Shapes of Midnight,* Berkley, 1980.

John Farris, *When Michael Calls,* Pocket Books, 1981.

Charles L. Grant, *Tales from the Nightside,* Arkham House, 1981.

Bill Pronzini, Barry N. Malzberg, and Martin H. Greenberg, compilers, *The Arbor House Treasury of Horror and the Supernatural,* Arbor House, 1981.

Forrest J. Ackerman, *Mr. Monster's Movie Gold,* Donning (Virginia Beach/Norfolk, Va.), 1982.

Harlan Ellison, *Stalking the Nightmare,* limited edition, Phantasia Press, 1982, Berkley, 1984.

Tim Underwood and Chuck Miller, editors, *Fear Itself: The Horror Fiction of Stephen King,* Underwood-Miller, 1982.

Jessica Amanda Salmonson, editor, *Tales by Moonlight,* Robert L. Garcia (Chicago), 1983.

Mary Wollstonecraft Shelley, *Frankenstein, or The Modern Prometheus,* illustrations by Berni Wrightson, limited edition, Dodd, 1983.

Evan Hunter, *The Blackboard Jungle,* Arbor House, Library of Contemporary Americana, 1984.

Jim Thompson, *Now and On Earth,* limited edition, Dennis Macmillan (Belem, N.M.), 1986.

Underwood and Miller, editors, *Kingdom of Fear: The World of Stephen King,* Underwood-Miller, 1986.

Don Robertson, *Genuine Man,* Philtrum Press, 1988.

OTHER

(Under name Steve King) *The Star Invaders* (privately published stories), Triad, Inc., and Gaslight Books (Durham, Me.), 1964.

Another Quarter Mile: Poetry, Dorrance, 1979.

Stephen King's Danse Macabre (nonfiction), Everest House, 1981 (also published in limited edition).

The Plant (privately published episodes of a comic horror novel in progress), Philtrum Press (Bangor, Me.), Part I, 1982, Part II, 1983, Part III, 1985.

Black Magic and Music: A Novelist's Perspective on Bangor (pamphlet), Bangor Historical Society, 1983.

Stephen King's Year of Fear 1986 Calendar (color illustrations from novels and drawings from King's short stories published in horror magazines with accompanying text), New American Library, 1985.

Nightmares in the Sky: Gargoyles and Grotesques, photographs by f.Stop FitzGerald, Viking, 1988.

Also author of weekly column "King's Garbage Truck" for *Maine Campus,* February 20, 1969 through May 21, 1970, and of monthly book review column for *Adelina,* June through November, 1980. Contributor of short fiction and poetry to numerous magazines, including *Art, Castle Rock: The Stephen King Newsletter, Cavalier, Comics Review, Cosmopolitan, Ellery Queen's Mystery Magazine, Fantasy and Science Fiction, Gallery, Great Stories from Twilight Zone Magazine, Heavy Metal, Ladies' Home Journal, Magazine of Fantasy and Science Fiction, Maine, Maine Review, Marshroots, Marvel Comics, Moth, Omni, Onan, Playboy, Redbook, Reflections, Rolling Stone, Science Fiction Digest, Startling Mystery Stories, Terrors, Twilight Zone Magazine, Ubris, Whisper,* and *Yankee.*

WORK IN PROGRESS: A volume of four novellas entitled *Four after Midnight,* scheduled for publication in 1990; a horror novel entitled *Needful Things,* scheduled for publication in 1991; a psy-chological thriller entitled *Dolores Claiborne,* scheduled for publication in 1992; *The Cannibals: Livre Noir,* a detective story in French; a sequel to *'Salem's Lot;* original story for television to be broadcast in more than fourteen episodes.

SIDELIGHTS: "With Stephen King," muses Chelsea Quinn Yarbro in *Fear Itself: The Horror Fiction of Stephen King,* "you never have to ask 'Who's afraid of the big bad wolf?'—You are. And he knows it." Throughout a prolific array of novels, short stories, and screenwork in which elements of horror, fantasy, science fiction, and humor meld, King deftly arouses fear from dormancy. The breadth and durability of his popularity alone evince his mastery as a compelling storyteller. "Nothing is as unstoppable as one of King's furies, except perhaps King's word processor," remarks Gil Schwartz in *People* magazine, which selected King as one of twenty individuals who have defined the decade of the eighties. And although the critical reception of his work has not necessarily matched its sweeping success with readers, colleagues and several critics alike discern within it a substantial and enduring literary legitimacy. In *American Film,* for instance, Darrell Ewing and Dennis Meyers call him "the chronicler of contemporary America's dreams, desires, and fears." And fantasy writer Orson Scott Card, citing King's "brilliant" exploration of current American myths and legends, proclaims in a *Contemporary Authors* interview with Jean W. Ross: "If someone in the future wants to see what American life was like, what Americans cared about, what our stories were in the seventies and eighties, they'll read Stephen King." Moreover, says Card, in fifty years, King will be "regarded as the dominant literary figure of the time. A lot of us feel that way."

Credited with reviving the macabre in both fiction and film, "this maker of nightmares," says Andrew Klavan in the *Village Voice,* has finally become synonymous with the genre itself. A publishing marvel with nearly one hundred million copies of his work in print worldwide, not only is he the first writer to have had three, four, and finally five titles appear simultaneously on *New York Times'* bestseller lists, he remained on those lists continuously for more than a decade—frequently at the top for months at a stretch. Moreover, his recent *The Dark Half* commanded a record-shattering first printing for hardcover fiction of one and a half million copies. As David Streitfeld assesses it in the *Washington Post,* "King has passed beyond bestsellerdom into a special sort of nirvana reserved for him alone." Widely translated, King's work has also been regularly adapted for the screen and recorded on audio and video cassette, prompting Curt Suplee, in the *Washington Post Book World,* to call him "a one-man entertainment industry." While pointing out that King has not "single-handedly and overnight" transformed horror into the marketing sensation that it is, literary critic Leslie Fiedler concedes in *Kingdom of Fear: The World of Stephen King* that "no other writer in the genre [has] ever before produced so long a series of smash successes . . . so that he has indeed finally become—in his own words—a 'brand name.' " But as Paul Weingarten makes clear in the *Chicago Tribune Magazine,* "Stephen King, like any good brand name, delivers."

The genre of horror fiction, which boasts an avid and loyal readership, dates almost to the origins of the novel itself. Fiedler explains, for instance, that just as the portrayal of mundanity in Samuel Richardson's work represents a disavowal of the fantastic elements of Medieval and Renaissance Romance, "a kind of neo-fantastic fiction which abandoned the recognizable present in favor of an exotic past" emerged near the end of the eighteenth century as a partial reaction against the popular, sentimental, domestic novel. Consequently, in the aftermath of the French Revolution, continues Fiedler, "the fantastic was reborn in sinister form, as terrifying nightmare rather than idyllic dream," and was manifested in 1818 by the first and perhaps the best known of horror stories—Mary Wollstonecraft Shelley's *Frankenstein, Or the New Prometheus.* The novel was not critically well regarded during its time, though, and a similar reception awaited its progeny—Robert Louis Stevenson's *Dr. Jekyll and Mr. Hyde* and Bram Stoker's *Dracula.* Although the modern horror tale is founded in these three works, he notes in *Stephen King's Danse Macabre,* his study of the Gothic arts, especially literature, film, and television, "all three live a kind of half-life outside the bright circle of English literature's acknowledged classics."

While striking a deep and responsive chord within its readers, the genre of horror is frequently trivialized by critics who tend to regard it, when at all, less seriously than mainstream fiction. In an interview with Charles Platt in *Dream Makers: The Uncommon Men & Women Who Write Science Fiction,* King suspects that "most of the critics who review popular fiction have no understanding of it as a whole." Regarding the "propensity of a small but influential element of the literary establishment to ghettoize horror and fantasy and instantly relegate them beyond the pale of so-called serious literature," King tells Eric Norden in a *Playboy* interview, "I'm sure those critics' nineteenth-century precursors would have contemptuously dismissed [Edgar Allan] Poe as the great American hack." But as he contends in "The Horror Writer and the Ten Bears," his foreword to *Kingdom of Fear:* "Horror isn't a hack market now, and never was. The genre is one of the most delicate known to man, and it must be handled with great care and more than a little love." Furthermore, in a panel discussion at the 1984 World Fantasy Convention in Ottawa, reprinted in *Bare Bones: Conversations on Terror with Stephen King,* he predicts that horror writers "might actually have a serious place in American literature in a hundred years or so."

The genre survived on the fringe of respectability through movies and comic books, observes Fiedler, adding that during the repressive 1950s, "the far-from-innocent kids . . . fought back; surreptitiously indulging in the literature of horror, even as they listened to the rock music disapproved of by their fathers and mothers." Profoundly an offspring of the 1950s, King imparts the influence of its music and movies to the content and style of his fiction. In *Esquire,* Barney Cohen describes King's writing style as "American yahoo—big, brassy, and bodacious"; and according to Gary Williams Crawford in *Discovering Stephen King,* it derives not only from the American literary tradition of Realism, but the horror and science fiction film, and the horror comic book as well. King grew up with rock 'n' roll, played rhythm guitar in a rock band, and still enjoys playing—even though the family feline invariably leaves the room, he told the audience in a talk presented at a public library in Billerica, Massachusetts, reprinted in *Bare Bones.* As owner of a local rock radio station, he often works to the blare of its music, and laces much of his fiction with its lyrics. And as a lifelong fan of film, he conveys a cinematic immediacy to his books: "I see them almost as movies in my head," he explains to Michael Kilgore in a *Tampa Tribune* interview.

The first motion picture King remembers seeing is "The Creature from the Black Lagoon," but another film proved more portentous. He relates to Norden that he still has difficulty expressing how "terribly frightened and alone and depressed" he felt when, in 1957, a theatre manager interrupted "Earth vs. the Flying Saucers" to announce to the audience that the Soviet Union had launched the satellite "Sputnik": "At that moment, the fears of my fictional horror vividly intersected with the reality of potential nuclear holocaust; a transition from fantasy to a real

world suddenly became far more ominous and threatening." King believes that his entire generation is beset with terrifying itself because it is the first to mature under the threat of nuclear war; he adds in a *Penthouse* magazine interview with Bob Spitz that, consequently, it has been "forced to live almost entirely without romance and forced to find some kind of supernatural outlet for the romantic impulses that are in all of us." King suggests in *Danse Macabre* that "we make up horrors to help us cope with the real ones"; and, as he relates to Keith Bellows in a *Sourcebook* interview, "The more frightened people become about the real world, the easier they are to scare." Douglas E. Winter comments in the *Washington Post Book World* that "in a time of violence and confusion, it is little wonder then that so many readers have embraced the imaginative talents of Stephen King."

King's ability to comprehend "the attraction of fantastic horror to the denizen of the late 20th century" according to Deborah L. Notkin in *Fear Itself,* partially accounts for his unrivaled popularity in the genre. But what distinguishes him is the way in which he transforms the ordinary into the horrific. Pointing out in the *Atlantic* that horror frequently represents "the symbolic depiction of our common experience," Lloyd Rose observes that "King takes ordinary emotional situations—marital stress, infidelity, peer-group-acceptance worries—and translates them into violent tales of vampires and ghosts. He writes supernatural soap operas." But to Crawford, King is "a uniquely sensitive author" within the Gothic literary tradition, which he describes as "essentially a literature of nightmare, a conflict between waking life and the darkness within the human mind." Perpetuating the legacy of Edgar Allan Poe, Nathaniel Hawthorne, Herman Melville, Henry James, and H. P. Lovecraft, "King is heir to the American Gothic tradition in that he has placed his horrors in contemporary settings and has depicted the struggle of an American culture to face the horrors within it," explains Crawford, and because "he has shown the nightmare of our idealistic civilization."

Some critics, though, attribute King's extraordinary accomplishments simply to a deep and genuine enjoyment of, as well as respect for, the genre itself. According to Don Herron in *Discovering Stephen King,* for instance, "The fact that King *is* a horror fan is of more importance to his fiction than his past as a teacher, his aims as an artist, or even his ability as a craftsman." Herron suggests that although King's work may very well represent "a psychological mirror of our times," he doubts whether "the majority of fans or even his most intelligent critics read him for Deep Meaning." In Herron's estimation, most readers begin "a new Stephen King book with thrills of expectation, waiting for this guy who's *really* a horror *fan,* see, to jump out of the old closet and yell 'Boo!!!' "

"We value his unique ability to scare the living daylights out of us," says William F. Nolan in *Kingdom of Fear,* because "King, more than any other modern master of Dark Fantasy, knows how to activate our primal fears." Referring to himself as a "sort of Everyman" where fear is concerned, King admits to Kilgore that perhaps his books succeed because his own fears, some of which are the natural residue of childhood, are simply "very ordinary fears." Only through exercising his imagination, he adds, has he honed his "perceptions of them." Although he indicates to Norden that he never experienced anything paranormal as a child, he does recall being "terrified and fascinated by death—death in general and my own in particular—probably as a result of listening to all those radio shows as a kid and watching some pretty violent TV shows." Religion, too, provided its share of trepidations. "It scared me to death as a kid," he confesses to

Spitz. "I was raised Methodist, and I was scared that I was going to hell. The horror stories that I grew up on were biblical stories . . . the best horror stories ever written." As an adult, though, he shares a widespread anxiety over society's propensity toward self-destruction, frets about his family's security, is resolutely superstitious, and is prey to such pedestrian terrors as bugs, airplanes, and getting stuck in crowded elevators. He also retains a vigorous fear of the dark. "The dark is a big one," he admits in the talk presented at the Billerica library. "I don't like the dark." Or as he elaborates to Norden: "There's a lot of mystery in the world, a lot of dark, shadowy corners we haven't explored yet. We shouldn't be too smug about dismissing out of hand everything we can't understand. The dark can have *teeth,* man!"

"The desire to be scared is a childish impulse, belonging to innocence rather than to experience," writes Barbara Tritel in the *New York Times Book Review.* "Frightening escapist literature lets us escape not to a realm of existential terror . . . but to the realm of childhood, when, within some cozy setting, we were able to titillate ourselves with fear." And in Tritel's opinion, "King has understood and answered a profound and popular need." While most of his fiction is aimed at an adult audience, young people are especially drawn to it, and children are vital to it. Unlike his portrayals of women, which he acknowledges are at times weak, some of his strongest characters are children; and his realistic depictions of them have earned much critical praise. Lauding King's "energetic and febrile imagination," Richard R. Lingeman adds in the *New York Times* that he has "a radar fix on young people."

Observing that children suspend their disbelief easily, King argues in *Danse Macabre* that, ironically, they are actually "better able to deal with fantasy and terror *on its own terms* than their elders are." In an interview for *High Times,* for instance, he marvels at the resilience of a child's mind and the inexplicable, yet seemingly harmless, attraction of children to nightmare-inducing stories: "We start kids off on things like 'Hansel and Gretel,' which features child abandonment, kidnapping, attempted murder, forcible detention, cannibalism, and finally murder by cremation. And the kids love it." Adults are capable of distinguishing between fantasy and reality, but in the process of growing up, laments King in *Danse Macabre,* they develop "a good case of mental tunnel vision and a gradual ossification of the imaginative faculty"; thus, he perceives the task of the fantasy or horror writer as enabling one to become "for a little while, a child again." In *Time,* King discusses the prolonged obsession with childhood that his generation has had. "We went on playing for a long time, almost feverishly," he recalls. "I write for that buried child in us, but I'm writing for the grown-up too. I want grown-ups to look at the child long enough to be able to give him up."

Of his own childhood, King recounts to Norden that he was only two when his father (whose surname was originally Spansky, but was also known as Pollack before he legally changed his name to King) caroused his way out of the family one night, never to be heard from again. Several years thereafter, King discovered that his father had also had an affection for science fiction and horror stories, and had even submitted, albeit unsuccessfully, stories of his own to several men's magazines. With few resources after the departure of King's father, the family moved to the Midwest then back East to Connecticut before returning to Maine when King was about eleven to live with and help care for his ailing grandparents. Despite his mother's valiant efforts to provide for herself and two sons, King tells Norden that their's was a "pretty shirttail existence." Remembering being "prey to a lot of conflicting emotions as a child," King explains,

"I had friends and all that, but I often felt unhappy and different, estranged from other kids my age." Not surprisingly, throughout most of King's adolescence, the written word afforded a powerful diversion.

"Writing has always been it for me," King indicates in a panel discussion at the 1984 World Fantasy Convention in Ottawa, reprinted in *Bare Bones.* Science fiction and adventure stories comprised his first literary efforts. Having written his first story at the age of seven, King began submitting short fiction to magazines at twelve, and published his first story at eighteen. In high school, he authored a small, satiric newspaper entitled "The Village Vomit"; and in college, he penned a popular and eclectic series of columns called "King's Garbage Truck." He also started writing the novels he eventually published under the short-lived pseudonymous ruse of Richard Bachman—novels that focus more on elements of human alienation and brutality than supernatural horror. After graduation, King supplemented his teaching salary through various odd jobs, and by submitting stories to men's magazines. Searching for a form of his own, and responding to a friend's challenge to break out of the machismo mold of his short fiction, King wrote what he describes to Peck as "a parable of women's consciousness." Retrieving the discarded manuscript from the trash, though, King's wife Tabitha, a writer herself, suggested that he ought to expand it. And because King completed the first draft of *Carrie* at the time William Peter Blatty's *The Exorcist* and Thomas Tryon's *The Other* were being published, the novel was marketed as horror fiction, and the genre had found its juggernaut. Or, as Herron puts it in *Fear Itself,* "Like a mountain, King is there."

"Stephen King has made a dent in the national consciousness in a way no other horror writer has, at least during his own lifetime," states Alan Warren in *Discovering Stephen King.* "He is a genuine phenomenon." A newsletter—"Castle Rock"—has been published since 1985 to keep his ever-increasing number of fans well-informed; and Book-of-the-Month Club is reissuing all of his bestsellers as the Stephen King Library collection. In his preface to *Fear Itself,* "On Becoming a Brand Name," King describes the process as a fissional one in that a "writer produces a series of books which ricochet back and forth between hardcover and softcover at an ever increasing speed." Resorting to a pseudonym to get even more work into print accelerated the process for King; but according to Stephen P. Brown in *Kingdom of Fear,* although the ploy was not entirely "a vehicle for King to move his earliest work out of the trunk," it certainly triggered myriad speculations about, as well as hunts for, other possible pseudonyms he may also have used. In his essay "Why I Was Bachman" in *The Bachman Books: Four Early Novels by Stephen King,* King recalls that he simply considered it a good idea at the time, especially since he wanted to try to publish something without the attendant commotion that a Stephen King title would have unavoidably generated; also, his publisher believed that he had already saturated the market. King's prodigious literary output and multi-million-dollar contracts, though, have generated critical challenges to the inherent worth of his fiction; deducing that he has been somehow compromised by commercial success, some critics imply that he writes simply to fulfill contractual obligations. But as King tells Norden, "Money really has nothing to do with it one way or the other. I love writing the things I write, and I wouldn't and *couldn't* do anything else."

King writes daily, exempting only Christmas, the Fourth of July, and his birthday. He likes to work on two things simultaneously, beginning his day early with a two- or three-mile walk: "What I'm working on in the morning is what I'm *working* on," he says in a panel discussion at the 1980 World Fantasy Convention in Baltimore, reprinted in *Bare Bones*. He devotes his afternoon hours to rewriting. And according to his *Playboy* interview, while he is not particular about working conditions, he is about his output. Despite chronic headaches, occasional insomnia, and even a fear of writer's block, he produces six pages daily; "And that's like engraved in stone," he tells Moore.

Likening the physical act of writing to "autohypnosis, a series of mental passes you go through before you start," King explains to Peck that "if you've been doing it long enough, you immediately fall into a trance. I just write about what I feel I want to write about. I'm like a kid. . . . I like to make believe." King explains to Moore that although he begins with ideas and a sense of direction, he does not outline: "I'm never sure where the story's going or what's going to happen with it. It's a discovery." Neither does he prepare for his novels in any particularly conscious way: "Some of the books have germinated for a long time," he tells Christopher Evans in a *Minneapolis Star* interview. "That is to say, they are ideas that won't sink." Also, research follows the writing so as not to impede it: "Afterward," he comments to Moore, "I develop the soul of a true debater . . . and find out the things that support my side." Besieged by questions about where his ideas originate, King tells Norden, "Like most writers, I dredge my memory for material, but I'm seldom really explicitly autobiographical." And, while he indicates to Randi Henderson in a *Baltimore Sun* interview that his ideas often begin in a dreamlike fashion in which "disconnected elements . . . will kind of click together," he adds in his foreword to *Kingdom of Fear* that they can also come from his nightmares, "Not the nighttime variety, as a rule, but the ones that hide just beyond the doorway that separates the conscious from the unconscious."

King describes himself in *Waldenbooks Book Notes* as one of the eternal "Halloween people," replete with "vampire bat and a rattlesnake on my desk—both mercifully stuffed"; but a customary response when people first encounter him is that he does not seem weird enough. Noting that "they're usually disappointed," he tells Joyce Lynch Dewes Moore in *Mystery:* "They say, 'You're not a monster!' " And when he is asked, endlessly, "Why do you write that stuff?," he replies that aside from being "warped, of course," writing horror fiction serves as "a kind of psychological protection. It's like drawing a magic circle around myself and my family," he explains to the audience at the Billerica library. But King also approximates the role of horror writer to that of an "old Welsh sin eater" called upon to consume the sins of the dying so their souls might hurry unblemished into heaven; "I and my fellow horror writers are absorbing and defusing all your fears and anxieties and insecurities and taking them upon ourselves," King tells Norden. "We're sitting in the darkness beyond the flickering warmth of your fire, cackling into our caldrons and spinning out our spider webs of words, all the time sucking the sickness from your minds and spinning it out into the night."

Aware that "people want to be scared," as he relates to Abe Peck in a *Rolling Stone College Papers* interview, and truly delighted to be able to accommodate them, King rejects the criticism that he preys on the fears of others. As he explains to Jack Matthews in a *Detroit Free Press* interview, such people simply avoid his books just as those who are afraid of speed and heights, especially in tandem, shun roller coasters. And that, he declares to Paul Janeczko in *English Journal,* is precisely what he believes he owes his readers—"a good ride on the roller coaster." Regarding what he finds to be an essential reassurance that underlies and impels the genre itself, King remarks in *Danse Macabre*

that "beneath its fangs and fright wig," horror fiction is really quite conservative. The scare we experience from reading it is safe, he tells Henderson, because "there's a real element of, thank God it isn't me, in the situation." Comparing horror fiction with the morality plays of the late middle ages, for instance, he believes that its primary function is "to reaffirm the virtues of the norm by showing us what awful things happen to people who venture into taboo lands." Also, there is the solace in knowing that "when the lights go down in the theatre or when we open the book that the evildoers will almost certainly be punished, and measure will be returned for measure." But King admits to Norden that despite all the discussion by writers generally about "horror's providing a socially and psychologically useful catharsis for people's fears and aggressions, the brutal fact of the matter is that we're still in the business of public executions."

"Death is a significant element in nearly all horror fiction," writes Michael A. Morrison in *Fantasy Review*, "and it permeates King's novels and short stories." Noting in *Danse Macabre*, that a universal fear with which each of us must personally struggle is "the fear of dying," King explains to Spitz that "everybody goes out to horror movies, reads horror novels—and it's almost as though we're trying to preview the end." But he submits that "if the horror story is our rehearsal for death, then its strict moralities make it also a reaffirmation of life and good will and simple imagination—just one more pipeline to the infinite." While he believes that horror is "one of the ways we walk our imagination," as he tells Matthews, he does worry about the prospect of a mentally unstable reader patterning behavior after some fictional brutality. Remarking that "evil is basically stupid and unimaginative and doesn't need creative inspiration from me or anybody else," King tells Norden, for instance, that "despite knowing all that rationally, I have to admit that it is unsettling to feel that I could be linked in any way, however tenuous, to somebody else's murder."

King, who was absorbed as an adolescent by the capacity of evil to appear deceptively benign, separates the evil with which horror fiction is concerned into two types: that which resides within the human mind or heart and represents "an act of free and conscious will," and that which threatens from without and is "predestinate . . . like a stroke of lightning," he says in *Danse Macabre*. "He is obviously an intelligent, sensitive and voluptuously terrified man who writes horror stories as a way of worrying about life and death," observes Annie Gottlieb in the *New York Times Book Review*. "He knows that we have been set down in a frightening universe, full of real demons like death and disease, and perhaps the most frightening thing in it is the human mind." King recognizes, as he says in *Time,* that "there is a part of us that needs to vicariously exorcise the darker side of our feelings," and much of his fiction probes mental perturbation. Relating to Norden that one of his darkest childhood fears was of going suddenly and completely insane, King explains that writing is a way of exorcising his own nightmares and destructiveness: "Writing is necessary for my sanity. I can externalize my fears and insecurities and night terrors on paper, which is what people pay shrinks a small fortune to do." While the process is therapeutic for the writer, it seems to extend its benefits to the reader, as well. Summarizing what he finds as one of King's most important qualities as a writer, Clive Barker states in *Kingdom of Fear:* "He shows us . . . that on the journey which he has so eloquently charted, where no terror shows its face but on a street that we have ourselves trodden, it is not, finally, the stale formulae and the trite metaphysics we're taught from birth that will get us to the end of the ride alive; it is our intimacy with our dark and dreaming selves."

Although King has frequently referred to his own work as "the literary equivalent of a Big Mac and a large fries from McDonalds," Winter cites the general hallmarks of King's fiction as "effortless, colloquial prose and an unerring instinct for the visceral." Yet, because King likes to work within traditional themes, myths, and forms, however, some critics find his work derivative and contend that he ought to be concentrating his considerable creative energy and talent in areas traditionally deemed more literary or serious. King indicates to Norden that while he has never considered himself "a blazingly original writer in the sense of conceiving totally new and fresh plot ideas," what he tries to do is "to pour new wine from old bottles." Acknowledging that he has always viewed his own work as "more humdrum or more mundane than the sort of thing the really great writers do," King tells Moore that "you take what talent you have, and you just try to do what you can with it. That's all you can do."

Careful to keep his own fame in perspective, King tells Mel Allen in *Yankee* magazine, "I'm very leery of thinking that I'm somebody. Because nobody really is. Everybody is able to do something well, but in this country there's a premium put on stardom." Describing what he calls the "occupational hazard of the successful writer in America," King tells Kilgore that "once you begin to be successful, then you have to avoid being gobbled up. America has developed this sort of cannibalistic cult of celebrity, where first you set the guy up, and then you eat him." Pertaining to such disparaging critiques as a *Time* condemnation of him as a master of "postliterate prose," and an uncomplimentary *Village Voice* profile, King tells Norden: "People like me really do irritate people like them, you know. In effect, they're saying, 'What right do you have to entertain people. This is a serious world with a lot of serious problems. Let's sit around and pick scabs; *that's* art.'" But as Cohen points out, "People consume horror in order to be scared, not *arted*." King, however, suggests in *Danse Macabre* that horror actually "achieves the level of art simply because it is looking for something beyond art, something that predates art: it is looking for what I would call phobic pressure points. The good horror tale will dance its way to the center of your life and find the secret door to the room you believed no one but you knew of."

Although he does not necessarily feel that he has been treated unfairly by the critics, King expresses what it is like to witness the written word turned into filmed images that are less than generously received by critics. "Whenever I publish a book, I feel like a trapper caught by the Iroquois," he tells Peck. "They're all lined up with tomahawks, and the idea is to run through with your head down, and everybody gets to take a swing. . . . Finally, you get out the other side and you're bleeding and bruised, and *then* it gets turned into a movie, and you're there in front of the same line and everybody's got their tomahawks out again." Nevertheless, in his essay "Why I Was Bachman," he readily admits that he really has little to complain about: "I'm still married to the same woman, my kids are healthy and bright, and I'm being well paid for doing something I love." And despite the financial security and recognition, or perhaps because of its intrinsic responsibility, King strives to improve at his craft. "It's getting later and I want to get better, because you only get so many chances to do good work," he states in a panel discussion at the 1984 World Fantasy Convention in Ottawa. "There's no justification not to at least try to do good work when you make the money."

According to Warren in *Discovering Stephen King*, though, there is absolutely nothing to suggest that success has been detrimental to King; "As a novelist, King has been remarkably consistent." Noting, for instance, that "for generations it was given that brev-

ity was the soul of horror, that the ideal format for the tale of terror was the short story," Warren points out that "King was among the first to challenge that concept, writing not just successful novels of horror, but long novels." Moreover, says Warren, "his novels have gotten longer." King quips in the *Chicago Tribune Magazine* that his "philosophy has always been take a good thing and beat it 'til it don't move no more"; and although some critics fault him for overwriting, Warren suggests that "the sheer scope and ambitious nature of his storytelling demands a broad canvas." Referring to this as "the very pushiness of his technique," the *New York Times*' Christopher Lehmann-Haupt similarly contends that "the more he exasperates us by overpreparing, the more effectively his preparations eventually pay off."

"I just want to scare people," King remarks to Kilgore. "I'm very humble about that." And in Yarbro's estimation, "King knows how to evoke those special images that hook into all the archetypal forms of horror that we have thrived on since earliest youth." Recognized for the varied and vivid descriptions he consistently renders of the emotion he so skillfully summons, King claims no other technique for inducing fear than lulling a reader into complacency and then "turn[ing] the monsters loose," as he relates in a *Shayol* interview. To create a comfortably familiar world for the reader so that the horrors experienced within it will seem more real, he imbues his fiction with touchstones of reality—recognizable brand names, products, people, and events. King does, however, delineate a certain hierarchy of fear that he tries to attain, telling Norden: "There's terror on top, the finest emotion any writer can induce; then horror; and, on the very lowest level of all, the gag instinct of revulsion. Naturally, I'll try to terrify you first, and if that doesn't work, I'll try to horrify you, and if I can't make it there, I'll try to gross you out. I'm not proud. . . . So if somebody wakes up screaming because of what I wrote, I'm delighted. If he merely tosses his cookies, it's still a victory but on a lesser scale. I suppose the ultimate triumph would be to have somebody drop dead of a heart attack, literally scared to death. I'd say, 'Gee, that's a shame,' and I'd mean it, but part of me would be thinking, Jesus, that really *worked!*"

Influenced by the naturalistic novels of writers such as Theodore Dreiser and Frank Norris, King confesses to Janeczko that his personal outlook for the world's future is somewhat bleak; on the other hand, one of the things he finds most comforting in his own work is an element of optimism. "In almost all cases, I've begun with a premise that was really black," he says in a panel discussion at the 1980 World Fantasy Convention in Baltimore, reprinted in *Bare Bones*. "And a more pleasant resolution has forced itself upon that structure." But as Andrew M. Greeley maintains in *Kingdom of Fear*: "Unlike some other horror writers who lack his talents and sensitivity, Stephen King never ends his stories with any cheap or easy hope. People are badly hurt, they suffer and some of them die, but others survive the struggle and manage to grow. The powers of evil have not yet done them in." According to Notkin, though, the reassurance King brings to his own readers derives from a basic esteem for humanity itself, "For whether he is writing about vampires, about the death of 99 percent of the population, or about innocent little girls with the power to break the earth in half, King never stops emphasizing his essential liking for people."

"You have got to love the people in the story, because there is no horror without love and without feeling," King explains to Platt. "Horror is the contrasting emotion to our understanding of all the things that are good and normal." While stressing the importance of characterization, he regards the story itself as the most integral part of crafting fiction. "If you can tell a story, everything else becomes possible," he explains to Mat Schaffer in the *Boston Sunday Review,* reprinted in *Bare Bones.* "But without story, nothing is possible, because nobody wants to hear about your sensitive characters if there's nothing happening in your story. And the same is true with mood. Story is the only thing that's important." Harris speaks for several critics when he observes that King is at his best when he "is simply himself, and when he loses consciousness of himself as a writer—the way the old tale-teller around the campfire occasionally will—he can be outstanding." Praising King's "page-flipping narrative drive, yanking the reader along with eye-straining velocity," Brown describes his prose as "invisible," and points to those moments of pure transport in which "the reader is caught in the rush of events and forgets that words are being read. It is a quality as rare as it is critically underappreciated."

"There's unmistakable genius in Stephen King," begrudges Walter Kendrick in the *Village Voice,* adding that he writes "with such fierce conviction, such blind and brutal power, that no matter how hard you fight—and needless to say, I fought—he's irresistible." The less reserved critical affirmations of King's work extend from expressions of pragmatism to those of metaphor. Lehmann-Haupt, for example, a self-professed King addict, offers his evaluation of King's potential versus his accomplishments as a writer of horror fiction: "Once again, as I edged myself nervously toward the climax of one of his thrillers, I found myself considering what wonders Stephen King could accomplish if he would only put his storytelling talents to serious use. And then I had to ask myself: if Mr. King's aim in writing . . . was not entirely serious by some standard that I was vaguely invoking, then why, somebody please tell me, was I holding on to his book so hard that my knuckles had begun to turn white?" Winter assesses King's contribution to the genre in his study *Stephen King: The Art of Darkness* this way: "Death, destruction, and destiny await us all at the end of the journey—in life as in horror fiction. And the writer of horror stories serves as the boatman who ferries people across that Reach known as the River Styx—offering us a full dress rehearsal of death, while returning us momentarily to our youth. In the horror fiction of Stephen King, we can embark upon the night journey, make the descent down the dark hole, cross that narrowing Reach, and return again in safety to the surface—to the near shore of the river of death. For our boatman has a master's hand."

AVOCATIONAL INTERESTS: Reading (mostly fiction), jigsaw puzzles, playing the guitar ("I'm terrible and so try to bore no one but myself"), movies, bowling.

MEDIA ADAPTATIONS: Several of King's novels have been adapted for the screen or stage. *Carrie* was produced as a motion picture in 1976 by Paul Monash for United Artists with a screenplay by Lawrence D. Cohen, directed by Brian De Palma, featuring Sissy Spacek and Piper Laurie; it was released on video cassette by Columbia Broadcasting System/Fox Video the same year; it was also produced as a Broadway musical in 1988 by Cohen and Michael Gore, developed in England by the Royal Shakespeare Company, and featured Betty Buckley. *'Salem's Lot* was produced as a television miniseries in 1979 by Warner Brothers with a teleplay by Monash, featuring David Soul and James Mason. *The Shining* was filmed in 1980 by Warner Brothers/Hawks Films with a screenplay by director Stanley Kubrick and Diane Johnson, starring Jack Nicholson and Shelley Duvall. *Cujo* was filmed in 1983 by Warner Communications/Taft Entertainment with a screenplay by Don Carlos Dunaway and Lauren Currier, featuring Dee Wallace and Danny Pintauro. *The Dead Zone* was filmed in 1983 by Paramount Pictures with a screenplay by Jeffrey Boam, starring Christopher Walken.

Christine was filmed in 1983 by Columbia Pictures with a screenplay by Bill Phillips. *Firestarter* was produced in 1984 by Frank Capra, Jr., for Universal Pictures in association with Dino de Laurentiis with a screenplay by Stanley Mann, featuring David Keith and Drew Barrymore. "Stand by Me," based upon King's novella *The Body,* was filmed in 1986 by Columbia Pictures with screenplay by Raynold Gideon and Bruce A. Evans, and was directed by Rob Reiner. *The Running Man* was filmed in 1987 by Taft Entertainment/Barish Productions with a screenplay by Steven E. de Souza, starring Arnold Schwarzenegger. *Misery* is being produced as a film by director Reiner with a screenplay by William Goldman, scheduled for release in 1990. *It* is being produced as a six-hour miniseries scheduled for telecast by ABC-TV in 1990. *Apt Pupil: Summer of Corruption* is being developed for production by Richard Kobritz; and *The Talisman* has been optioned for a television miniseries.

Several of King's short stories have also been adapted for the screen. "The Woman in the Room" was filmed in 1983 by Darkwoods with a screenplay by director Frank Darabont, and was broadcast on public television in Los Angeles in 1985. "The Boogeyman" was filmed by Tantalus in 1982 and 1984 in association with the New York University School of Undergraduate Film with a screenplay by producer-director Jeffrey C. Schiro; it was released on video cassette with "The Woman in the Room" as "Two Mini-Features from Stephen King's Nightshift Collection" by Granite Entertainment Group in 1985. "Children of the Corn" was produced in 1984 by Donald P. Borchers and Terrence Kirby for New World Pictures with a screenplay by George Goldsmith. "The Word Processor of the Gods" was produced by George A. Romero and Richard Rubenstein for Laurel Productions in 1984 as "The Word Processor" with a teleplay by Michael Dowell and broadcast November 19, 1985 on "Tales from the Darkside" series and released on video cassette by Laurel Entertainment, Inc., 1985. "Gramma" was filmed on video cassette by CBS-TV in 1985 with a teleplay by Harlan Ellison and was broadcast on February 14, 1986 on "The Twilight Zone" series. "Creepshow 2," based upon "The Raft" and two unpublished stories by King ("Old Chief Woodn'head" and "The Hitchhiker"), was filmed in 1987 by New World Pictures with a screenplay by Romero. "Sorry, Right Number" has been adapted for the screen and broadcast on "Tales from the Darkside" series. "The Cat from Hell" is included in a four-segment anthology film entitled "Tales from the Darkside—The Movie," produced by Laurel Productions. "Graveyard Shift" has been optioned by George Demick.

King's screenplay "The Stand," based upon his novel of same title, has been optioned for a two-part film by Romero and Richard Rubenstein; his screenplay "Battleground" has been optioned by Martin Poll Productions for NBC-TV; "The Long Walk" has been optioned for a film production; a film based upon a treatment by King of "Training Exercise" is scheduled for production by Dino De Laurentiis's North Carolina Film Corporation; "Return to 'Salem's Lot" is an unproduced screenplay by Lawrence D. Cohen.

Unabridged readings of the novellas from *Different Seasons* ("Rita Hayworth and Shawshank Redemption: Different Seasons I," "The Body: Different Seasons II," "Apt Pupil: Different Seasons III," and "The Breathing Method: Different Season IV") were recorded on audio cassettes in 1984 by Recorded Books; readings by Frank Muller of stories from *Skeleton Crew* ("The Ballad of the Flexible Bullet," "Gramma," and "The Mist") were recorded for Recorded Books in 1985; and a set of six audio cassettes of *Night Shift,* read by Colin Fox, David Purdham, and Deidre Westervelt, has also been recorded. An abridged version by Sue Dawson of *Thinner* was recorded on two audio cassettes by Paul Sorvino for Listen for Pleasure in 1986. A dramatization of *The Mist* was performed on public radio in Boston, and a 90-minute adaptation written by Dennis Etchinson was recorded on audio cassette by Simon & Schuster Audioworks, 1986; it has also served as the basis of an "interactive fiction" software for a computer game of the same title, Mindscape, Inc. Audio cassettes of readings by David Purdham and Gale Garnett of "The Monkey," "Mrs. Todd's Shortcut," "The Reaper's Image," and "Gramma" were recorded by Warner Audio in 1986; and audio cassettes of readings of "Strawberry Spring," "The Boogeyman," "Graveyard Shift," "The Man Who Loved Flowers," "One for the Road," "The Last Rung on the Ladder," "I Know What You Need," "Jerusalem's Lot," and "I Am the Doorway" were recorded for Walden. Unabridged readings by King of *The Gunslinger* were recorded on four audio cassettes, and *The Drawing of Three* on eight audio cassettes for New American Library in 1988.

BIOGRAPHICAL/CRITICAL SOURCES:

BOOKS

Authors and Artists for Young Adults, Volume 1, Gale, 1989.

Beahm, George, editor, *The Stephen King Companion,* Andrews and McMeel, 1989.

Collings, Michael R., *Stephen King as Richard Bachman,* Starmont House, 1985.

Collings, *The Many Facets of Stephen King,* Starmont House, 1985.

Collings, and David Engebretson, *The Shorter Works of Stephen King,* Starmont House, 1985.

Collings, *The Annotated Guide to Stephen King: A Primary and Secondary Bibliography of the Works of America's Premier Horror Writer,* Starmont House, 1986.

Collings, *The Films of Stephen King,* Starmont House, 1986.

Collings, *The Stephen King Phenomenon,* Starmont House, 1987.

Contemporary Authors, New Revision Series, Gale, Volume 29, 1989.

Contemporary Literary Criticism, Gale, Volume 12, 1980, Volume 26, 1983, Volume 37, 1985.

Dictionary of Literary Biography Yearbook: 1980, Gale, 1981.

Horsting, Jessie, *Stephen King: At the Movies,* Signet/Starlog, 1986.

Kimberling, C. Ronald, *Kenneth Burke's Dramatism and Popular Arts,* Bowling Green State University Popular Press, 1982.

King, Stephen, *Stephen King's Danse Macabre,* Everest House, 1981.

Platt, Charles, *Dream Makers: The Uncommon Men & Women Who Write Science Fiction,* Berkley, 1983.

Schweitzer, Darrell, editor, *Discovering Stephen King,* Starmont House, 1985.

Underwood, Tim, and Chuck Miller, editors, *Fear Itself: The Horror Fiction of Stephen King,* Underwood-Miller, 1982.

Underwood and Miller, editors, *Kingdom of Fear: The World of Stephen King,* Underwood-Miller, 1986.

Underwood and Miller, editors, *Bare Bones: Conversations on Terror with Stephen King,* McGraw-Hill, 1988.

Winter, Douglas E., editor, *Shadowings: The Reader's Guide to Horror Fiction, 1981-1982,* Starmont House, 1983.

Winter, *Stephen King: The Art of Darkness,* New American Library, 1984.

PERIODICALS

American Film, June, 1986.

Atlantic, September, 1986.

Boston, October, 1980.

Boston Globe, October 10, 1980.

Boston Sunday Review, October 31, 1983.

Castle Rock: The Stephen King Newsletter, July, 1986.

Chernobog, Volume 18, 1980 (King issue).

Chicago Daily News, July 7, 1977.

Chicago Tribune, November 3, 1989.

Chicago Tribune Book World, June 8, 1980.

Chicago Tribune Magazine, October 27, 1985.

Cinefantastique, spring, 1981, Volume 12, numbers 2 and 3, 1982, Volume 15, number 2, 1985.

Detroit Free Press, November 12, 1982.

Detroit News, September 26, 1979.

English Journal, January, 1979, February, 1980, January, 1983, December, 1983, December, 1984.

Esquire, November, 1984.

Fangoria, December, 1979, June, 1980.

Fantasy Review, January, 1984.

Film Comment, May/June, 1981, May/June, 1986.

Film Journal, April 12, 1982.

Globe and Mail (Toronto), December 16, 1989.

High Times, January, 1981, June, 1981.

Horizon, February, 1978.

Los Angeles Times, April 23, 1978, December 10, 1978, August 26, 1979, September 28, 1980, May 10, 1981, September 6, 1981, May 8, 1983, November 20, 1983, November 18, 1984, August 25, 1985.

Los Angeles Times Book Review, August 29, 1982.

Macleans, August 11, 1986.

Miami Herald, March 24, 1984.

Minneapolis Star, September 8, 1979.

Mystery, March, 1981.

New Republic, February 21, 1981.

Newsweek, August 31, 1981, May 2, 1983.

New Yorker, January 15, 1979.

New York Times, March 1, 1977, August 14, 1981, August 11, 1982, April 12, 1983, October 21, 1983, November 8, 1984, June 11, 1985, April 4, 1987, January 25, 1988.

New York Times Book Review, May 26, 1974, October 24, 1976, February 20, 1977, March 26, 1978, February 4, 1979, September 23, 1979, May 11, 1980, May 10, 1981, September 27, 1981, August 29, 1982, April 3, 1983, November 6, 1983, November 4, 1984, June 9, 1985, February 22, 1987, December 6, 1987, October 29, 1989.

New York Times Magazine, May 11, 1980.

Parent's Magazine, January, 1982.

Penthouse, April, 1982.

People, March 7, 1977, December 29, 1980-January 5, 1981, May 18, 1981, January 28, 1985, fall, 1989.

Playboy, June, 1983.

Prevue, May, 1982.

Psychology Today, September, 1975.

Publisher's Weekly, January 17, 1977, May 11, 1984.

Rolling Stone, April, 1982.

Rolling Stone College Papers, winter, 1980, winter, 1983.

San Francisco Chronicle, August 15, 1982.

Saturday Review, September, 1981, November, 1984.

Self, September, 1981.

Shayol, summer, 1979, winter, 1982.

Sourcebook, 1982.

Tampa Tribune, August 31, 1980.

Time, August 30, 1982, July 1, 1985, October 6, 1986.

Tomb of Dracula, April, 1980, June, 1980.

TV Guide, June 13-19, 1981, December 5-11, 1981.

Twilight Zone Magazine, April, 1981, June, 1981, May, 1982.
USA Today, October 14, 1982, May 10, 1985.
Village Voice, April 29, 1981, October 23, 1984, March 3, 1987.
Voice Literary Supplement, September, 1982, November, 1985.
Waldenbooks Book Notes, August, 1983.
Washington Post, August 26, 1979, April 9, 1985, May 8, 1987.
Washington Post Book World, May 26, 1974, October 1, 1978, August 26, 1980, April 12, 1981, August 22, 1982, March 23, 1983, October 2, 1983, November 13, 1983, June 16, 1985.
Writer, July, 1986, July, 1988.
Writer's Digest, November, 1973, June, 1977, October, 1978.
Yankee, March, 1979.

—*Sketch by Sharon Malinowski*

* * *

KING, Steve
See KING, Stephen (Edwin)

* * *

KING, Tabitha (Jane) 1949-

PERSONAL: Born March 24, 1949, in Old Town, Me.; daughter of Raymond Geo (a social worker) and Sarah Jane (an administrative assistant; maiden name, White) Spruce; married Stephen E. King (a writer), January 2, 1971; children: Naomi Rachel, Joseph Hill, Owen Phillip. *Education:* University of Maine at Orono, B.A., 1971.

ADDRESSES: Home—Bangor and Center Lovell, Me. *Agent*—Richard Curtis, 164 East 64th St., New York, N.Y. 10021.

CAREER: Writer. Worked as waitress, 1972-73.

MEMBER: Writers Guild, PEN, Mystery Writers of America.

WRITINGS:

(Contributor) Dilys Winn, editor, *Murderess Ink: The Better Half of the Mystery,* Bell, 1979.
(Contributor) Charles L. Grant, editor, *Shadows,* Volume 4, Doubleday, 1981.
Small World (novel), Macmillan, 1981.
Caretakers (novel; Literary Guild alternate selection), Macmillan, 1983.
The Trap (novel; Doubleday Book Club selection; Literary Guild featured alternate selection), Macmillan, 1985.
Pearl (novel; Literary Guild alternate selection), New American Library, 1989.

SIDELIGHTS: Tabitha King, who has penned four very different novels primarily within the genre of suspense, discounts the notion that she vies for the readership of her husband, the enormously popular horror writer Stephen King; "He's like a river to my faucet," she tells *People*'s Mark Donovan. Referring to Stephen King's initial doubts about his wife's entrance into his literary domain, Donovan quotes King as saying, "Deep down I may have been a little jealous, with a small voice saying 'Hey, wait a minute. That's my toy.'" But although he "started reading *Small World* with trepidation, he finished it with pride," says Donovan: "'I knew she could write poetry,' marvels Stephen, 'but I never guessed she could write such a good novel right out of the box.'" Written over a period of several months on a pink electric typewriter presented to her as a thirtieth birthday present from her husband, *Small World* was written essentially for herself, Tabitha King explains in *Library Journal*. "But it pleases me no end that other people find it readable."

Small World concerns Dolly Douglas, middle-aged daughter of an American ex-president, and her fascination with miniatures. She teams up with Roger Tinker, a one-time researcher for the government and inventor of the minimizer, a device that shrinks all sorts of objects. Progressing from the miniaturization of valuable art objects, with which she furnishes the scale model of the White House presented to her while she lived there, to the shrinking of human beings as well, Dolly finally steals the device from Roger. "Perverse characters in odd situations make this an entertaining and quirky reading experience," writes a *Publishers Weekly* reviewer. Praising King's "exemplary" storytelling skills, Arlene Drack writes in *Best Sellers:* "She is witty, even picturesque in her language, with phrases and descriptions that literally made me laugh out loud." And although Tom Easton quibbles with its classification as a suspense novel, preferring science fiction instead, he remarks in an *Analog* review that it is "solid entertainment" and "a good story."

King's second novel, *Caretakers,* told in a series of flashbacks, brings together two aging acquaintances. Joe Nevers has lived his entire life in a small Maine village tending the homes of the summer people, including the upper-class Christopher family. When a blizzard prompts him to check on the last surviving member of this family, Torie Christopher, he finds her alone and terminally ill; out of their mutual unhappiness and need, they form a spiritual bond and end up caring for each other. Described by Barbara Parker in *Library Journal* as "a dark but moving tale, sensitively written, of one of the stranger ties that bind," the novel is about relationships, states Marcia A. Roman in *Best Sellers,* about how they "affect our lives," and also about how they "can shape our deaths and the meaning of those deaths." According to a *Harper's* reviewer, "King is at her best—and she is quite good—revealing the affection and devotion underneath the gruff banter of these two weatherbeaten friends who finally curl up to each other as death sets in." Susan Dooley comments in the *Washington Post Book World* that "King movingly portrays the pride and angry need they feel for each other." Some critics, however, find the flashback technique flawed; Dick Roraback in a *Los Angeles Times Book Review* piece, for example, regards the flashbacks as "splendid vignettes, some of them, teasing, goading, but ultimately distracting in their random order." However, as Judy Bass notes in the *New York Times Book Review,* "despite this, the novel works well because the author communicates the quiet nobility of Joe and Torie as they attempt to understand the past. Although overridingly tragic, 'Caretakers' yields glimpses of hope and courage." And according to a *West Coast Review of Books* contributor, "while not perfect, this careful study of a New England community proves [King] can keep up with the big folks."

In her third novel, *The Trap,* King turns to a tale of terror. It is a divided story about Liv Russell and her increasingly self-indulgent screenwriter husband Pat, who plans to move the family to California so that he can finish a violent film about Vietnam. When she retreats to the family's summer home in Maine to spend the winter sorting out the direction of her troubled marriage, she and her child are menaced by a gang of youths. Describing the novel as "a psychological study of a family in domestic crisis," as well as "a neat little thriller with violent overtones," a *Publishers Weekly* contributor praises the "engrossing" narrative and adds that "the suspense builds steadily." Although Chuck Moss, in a *Detroit News* review, finds that "marrying the trick-or-treat novel to feminist dogma has possibilities," he does not believe it is effective in *The Trap:* "The scariness isn't scary enough, the meaning isn't meaningful enough and if today's society is sick, well, what else is new?" However, according to a *West*

Coast Review of Books contributor, the novel "explores the theme of city versus country in a modern context." And in the opinion of a *Booklist* contributor, "Some finely drawn characterizations add depth to this overlong yet grimly involving novel."

Drawing upon Nathaniel Hawthorne's *The Scarlet Letter* and the daughter of Hester Prynne for inspiration, King's *Pearl* is about the daughter of an outcast. Born of her mother's affair with a black man, Pearl journeys to her mother's home in Maine where she claims her inheritance and establishes roots. A liberated woman, she successfully manages the town's diner and simultaneously maintains a relationship with two lovers. Although finding Pearl "an endearing character," Linda Simon suggests in the *Los Angeles Times Book Review* that "King has chosen to immerse her in romance rather than reality. When she is not sexually aroused, she is exhausted. . . . She is never called upon to make any difficult decisions or to encounter painful consequences." Ultimately, Simon concludes, the novel "is a predictable tale of a gutsy woman who finds the complications of her life wonderfully untangled, so that she can find love and live happily ever after." A *Publisher's Weekly* contributor observes, however, that although "Pearl's quiet wisdom and prodigious energy make her slightly more mythic than human . . . she remains an unforgettable character." And Simon speaks for several critics when she praises the "considerable affection" with which King creates the town residents. As Elizabeth Hand expresses it in the *Washington Post Book World:* "King paints a portrait of the Maine countryside so clearly that you can smell the rich thawing earth in its fields and graveyards."

Writing in the shadow of her husband's phenomenal success does not intimidate Tabitha King, nor does she worry about the criticism that she might be capitalizing on his substantial name. "When my husband and I first met," she indicates in *Library Journal,* "I was writing poetry and continued to do so for seven years after we married." Moreover, she remarks to Donovan, "I put 10 years into helping his career so if his name helps me with mine, I think it's legitimate." As Francis Koestler assesses it in the *Washington Post Book World,* though, Tabitha and Stephen King "have divided the world of literary goosebumps between them; his thrillers focus on the supernatural, hers on man's basest instincts. Both excel in their respective approaches."

BIOGRAPHICAL/CRITICAL SOURCES:

BOOKS

Winn, Dilys, editor, *Murderess Ink: The Better Half of the Mystery,* Bell, 1979.

PERIODICALS

Analog, November, 1982.
Best Sellers, September, 1981, November, 1983.
Booklist, May 1, 1981, April 1, 1985.
Detroit News, May 26, 1985.
Harper's, October, 1983.
Kirkus Reviews, February 1, 1985.
Library Journal, February 1, 1981, August, 1983.
Los Angeles Times Book Review, November 18, 1983, March 19, 1989.
New York Times Book Review, May 17, 1981, October 23, 1983.
People, May 18, 1981.
Publishers Weekly, February 6, 1981, July 29, 1983, February 15, 1985, September 9, 1988.
Washington Post Book World, October 2, 1983, May 5, 1985, December 11, 1988.

West Coast Review of Books, July/August, 1985.

—Sketch by Sharon Malinowski

*   *   *

KNAPP, Ronald Gary 1940-

PERSONAL: Born August 15, 1940, in Pittsburgh, Pa.; son of William H. and Thelma Ruth (Weber) Knapp; married May Tse (a librarian); children: Larissa, Jeffrey, Douglas. *Education:* Stetson University, B.A., 1962; University of Pittsburgh, Ph.S., 1968.

ADDRESSES: Home—5 Van Kleeck Ave., New Paltz, N.Y. 12561. *Office*—Department of Geography, State University of New York College at New Paltz, New Paltz, N.Y. 12561.

CAREER: State University of New York College at New Paltz, assistant professor, 1968-71, associate professor, 1971-78, professor of geography, 1978—, director of exchange program with Nanyang University, 1971-72, director of international education, 1982-83.

MEMBER: National Council for Geographic Education, Association for Asian Studies.

AWARDS, HONORS: Grant from American Philosophical Society, 1970; fellow of American Council of Learned Societies and Mellon Foundation, 1978; fellow of National Endowment for the Humanities, 1983-84; grant from the National Geographic Society Committee for Research and Exploration, 1987.

WRITINGS:

(Editor with B. Wallacker, A. Van Alstyne, and R. Smith; and contributor) *Chinese Walled Cities,* Chinese University of Hong Kong Press, 1979, University of Washington Press, 1980.
(Editor and contributor) *China's Island Frontier: Studies in the Historical Geography of Taiwan,* University Press of Hawaii, 1980.
(Contributor) Clifton W. Pannell, editor, *A Preface to East Asia: Geographical and Historical Approaches to Foreign Area Studies,* National Council for Geographic Education, 1981.
China's Traditional Rural Architecture: A Cultural Geography of the Common House, University of Hawaii Press, 1986.
China's Vernacular Architecture: House Form and Culture, University of Hawaii Press, 1989.
The Chinese House: Craft, Symbol, and the Folk Tradition, Oxford University Press, in press.

Contributor of articles and reviews to Asian studies and geography journals.

WORK IN PROGRESS: Research concerning village formation and transformation in rural China.

*   *   *

KNOX, James
See BRITTAIN, William (E.)

*   *   *

KOEHLER, Margaret (Hudson)
(Meg Hudson; pseudonyms: Maggi Charles, Russell Mead, Carole Standish)

PERSONAL: Born in New York, N.Y.; daughter of Erastus Mead (a physician) and Margaret (a nurse; maiden name, Giffen) Hudson; married Charles Russell Koehler (a journalist), May 24, 1947; children: Stephen Hudson, Richard Hudson. *Education:* Attended Syracuse University; studied languages, harp, and piano privately. *Religion:* Protestant.

ADDRESSES: Home—Orleans, Mass. *Agent*—Emilie Jacobson, Curtis Brown Ltd., Ten Astor Pl., New York, N.Y. 10003.

CAREER: Worked as a newspaper reporter in Georgia, New Jersey, New York, and Washington, D.C., and as a writer for a Washington, D.C., public relations firm; free-lance writer, 1960—.

MEMBER: American Society of Journalists and Authors, Authors Guild, Authors League of America, Mystery Writers of America, Romance Writers of America, National League of American Penwomen.

WRITINGS:

Visitors Guide to Cape Cod National Seashore, Chatham Press, 1973.
Recipes from the Portuguese of Provincetown, Chatham Press, 1973.
Recipes from the Russians of San Francisco, Chatham Press, 1974.
(Under name Meg Hudson) *The House on Kettle Hole Pond,* Bantam, 1979.
(Under pseudonym Carole Standish) *The Snow's Secret* (young adult novel), Scholastic, Inc., 1982.
(Under pseudonym Carole Standish) *Someone Is out There* (young adult novel), Scholastic, Inc., 1982.
(Under pseudonym Carole Standish) *The Mystery Cruise* (young adult novel), Scholastic, Inc., 1984.

ROMANCE NOVELS; UNDER NAME MEG HUDSON

Love's Sound in Silence, Harlequin, 1982.
Return to Rapture, Harlequin, 1983.
Though Hearts Resist, Harlequin, 1983.
To Love a Stranger, Harlequin, 1983.
Two Worlds, One Love, Harlequin, 1983.
A Charm for Adonis, Harlequin, 1983.
L'Espoir d'un Lendemain, Harlequin, 1983.
Beloved Stranger, Harlequin, 1984.
Chance Meeting, Harlequin, 1989.

OTHER

Also author of novels under pseudonym Maggi Charles; contributor of fact detective stories under pseudonym Russell Mead to *True Detective, Master Detective,* and *Official Detective;* contributor to more than thirty magazines.

WORK IN PROGRESS: The C Factor, a mainstream novel.

SIDELIGHTS: Margaret Koehler told *CA:* "I speak Spanish and French, and would like to speak twenty other languages as well; I feel that communication is probably the most vital thing in the world today, and in this respect professional writers must stand at and remain at the helm. Thus, travel is my favorite hobby, and is indulged in as much as is economically possible. Places visited are inevitably springboards for articles and books; fortunately this is an enthusiasm my husband shares."

* * *

KOFALK, Harriet 1937-
(Harriet Kimbro)

PERSONAL: Born October 12, 1937, in Paterson, N.J.; daughter of Harry R. F. (a decorator) and Ethelyn J. C. (a physician;

maiden name, Anderson) Kofalk; married Anthony S. Mixer, June 7, 1957 (divorced, 1965); married Robert R. Kimbro, August 7, 1967 (divorced, 1979); children: (first marriage) Randal Anthony, Jenene Margaret Kimbro Hunsaker. *Education:* University of New Mexico, B.A. (with honors), 1959.

ADDRESSES: Home—P.O. Box 2138, Santa Monica, Calif. 90406.

CAREER: Secretary in Denver, Colo., and Albuquerque, N.M., 1955-62; New Mexico Optometric Association, Albuquerque, executive secretary, 1962-65; American Optometric Association, St. Louis, Mo., administrative assistant, 1965-67; United Aircraft Corp., Redondo Beach, Calif., engineering assistant in systems analysis and evaluation, 1967-68; Kimbro Associates (association management business), Manhattan Beach, Calif., associate, 1970-72; Vogue Patterns, Elegance Division, Manhattan Beach, fashion staff director, 1972; Santa Fe Opera, Santa Fe, N.M., executive assistant, 1973-77; Eberline Instrument Co., Santa Fe, graphics manager, 1977-78; Lo-LoMai Springs Campground, Sedona, Ariz., staff member, 1978-79; RAND Corp., Santa Monica, Calif., department administrator of Publications, 1979-83, research administrator, 1985—; free-lance writer, 1983—.

MEMBER: American Association of University Women (branch first vice president, 1968-69), Haiku Society of America, National Audubon Society, Nature Conservancy, Sierra Club, Phi Kappa Phi, Phi Sigma Iota, Pi Lambda Theta.

AWARDS, HONORS: Honorable mention in Kansas Poetry Contest, 1981, for haiku; honorable mention from San Diego Historical Society Institute, 1984, for article "The Birds and Bees in Twin Oaks: Visit of a Naturalist in 1889," and 1986, for article "Bazaar del Mundo: Old Town's Cinderella or Her Pumpkin?"; second place from San Diego Historical Society Institute, 1988, for article "Woven Wind: The Silk Industry in San Diego County"; runner-up award in English haiku contest from Japan Air Lines, 1988; runner-up award in international haiku contest from Modern Haiku Association (Japan), 1988.

WRITINGS:

(Under name Harriet Kimbro) *Haiku,* privately printed, 1972.
(Under name Harriet Kimbro) *Good, You're in a Fowl Mood* (recipes), privately printed, 1973.
(Under name Harriet Kimbro) *Apple Encore* (folklore and recipes), Sunflower Press, 1977.
(Under name Harriet Kimbro) *Tamotzu in Haiku,* Sunstone Press, 1977.
Wisdom of the 80s, Friends of Wisdom, 1986.
Rainbows (haiku collection), Friends of Wisdom/Land of Enchantment Poetry Theater, 1987.
Working for Peace at RAND, RAND Corp., 1987.
Light (collection of poems), privately printed, 1988.
No Woman Tenderfoot: Florence Merriam Bailey, Pioneer Naturalist, Texas A&M University Press, 1989.
Home (collection of poems), privately printed, 1989.

Contributor of poems and articles to periodicals, including *Sunstone Review, Little Balkans Review, Harper's Weekly, New Mexico, New Mexico Architecture, Bird Watcher's Digest, Sew Business, Hai, Ko, Mainichi Daily News* (Tokyo), *Frogpond,* and *Christian Science Monitor.* Editor of newsletters of American Association of University Women, 1968, Southern California Society of Association Executives, 1970-72, and WING, 1983.

WORK IN PROGRESS: Shunpiking—choosing to travel the byways, a book of the inner and outer journey; *A Rainbow Is Really a Circle,* a book of nature poetry and photographs; continuing experiments with essays and poetry about our global home.

SIDELIGHTS: Harriet Kofalk told *CA:* "Writing has always been an important part of my life; I had twenty-five penpals while still in elementary school. The success of my free-lance efforts (poetry and magazine articles) led me away from the office-work world and toward concentrating on writing.

"Florence Merriam Bailey came into my life through a brief mention of her by conservationist Paul Brooks in a book review. Florence studied and wrote about live birds at the turn of this century, when it wasn't even considered proper for a lady to follow birds into the woods. As a fellow writer and birder, I wanted to know more about her. I found two of her books and learned that she had also written more than one hundred magazine articles on birds, and her biography began to take shape as my first book. Every serious writer needs a 'Florence,' an engrossing project that encourages you to write, opens new possibilities, and provides an enthusiasm that spurs writers on.

"Writing that book also helped me to find my own voice, and now my writing focuses on connecting my own inner experiences with the world of nature. Usually it evolves into poems, sometimes essays or children's stories. (Grandchildren are good audiences for whom to write.) I like to write both prose and poetry, and they mingle happily in writing about nature. Writing clarifies my own thinking about the natural world and I can then share something unique with others as well. The art of *reading* poetry is making a comeback. On a recent camping trip, the others in the group encouraged me to read all one evening, commenting that they rarely have opportunities to hear poetry. I also use reading as a writing technique, by reading material aloud to myself. If it reads well, it will be better to share with others—both on paper and orally.

"A friend recently called poetry 'the nectar of language,' the essence of life. Like the hummingbird, the American Indian symbol of joy, I draw nectar from all the flowers I can find, not only plants, but also people-flowers who each bloom in a unique form. This view of life creates the rainbow I cherish. We can each make out journey through life poetic, for poetry is all around us if we choose to see it. The publisher of *Tamotzu in Haiku* expressed my philosophy even before I had recognized it when he wrote in the cover note, 'Many of Harriet's friends feel that her life is poetry itself.'

"Writing provides its own motivation. The more I write, the more I want to write and the more I find to write about. Communicating ideas is the most important service we can render."

*   *   *

KOLON, Aleksandar 1947-

PERSONAL: Born June 3, 1947, in Zrenjanin, Yugoslavia; came to United States in 1975, naturalized in 1981; son of Danilo (a welder) and Andja (a seamstress; maiden name, Kerovic) Kolon; married Spomenka Krnjacic (a university professor), May 13, 1977 (divorced, 1978); married Una Vrbas (a librarian), November 8, 1980; children: (first marriage) Kirilo; (second marriage) Drina, Vardar. *Education:* Attended University of Belgrade; Wayne State University, B.A., 1980, M.A., 1984. *Politics:* Pragmatist. *Religion:* Gnostic.

ADDRESSES: Home—9568 Columbia, Redford, Mich. 48239.

CAREER: University of Belgrade, Belgrade, Yugoslavia, office assistant, 1967-68; Institute for Theoretical Literature, Belgrade,

intern, 1968-70, research assistant, 1970-73, deputy director, 1973-74; Bibliotheque Nikola Tesla, Paris, France, reference librarian, 1974-75; writer, 1975—.

MEMBER: Society of the Friends of Ancient and Historical Dubrovnik, Per Aspera Ad Acta, Society for Political Archaeology.

WRITINGS:

And Why with a Stone? (stories), Zoe Meiner Klein, 1976.
Liquid Poems, Micromegas, 1976.
In the World of Levers (poems), S. Slapschack Publishers, 1977.
Heaven's Doors (novel), Frontisterion, 1979.
In the Mines of King Tvrtko (novel), Boerjan, 1980.
Things That I Like (essays), Frontisterion, 1984.
In a Quandary (poems), S. Slapschack Publishers, 1985.
Things That I Used to Like (essays), Frontisterion, 1986.
Dancing in a Descending Elevator (poems), Grave Oeuvre, 1988.

WORK IN PROGRESS: Imaginary Authors, a bio-bibliographical guide to fictitious writers; a child's guide to Greek epic poetry.

SIDELIGHTS: Poet and essayist Aleksandar Kolon once told *CA:* "All fiction, as the admirable novelist Samson Ledic affirms, is meaningless. If this truth is obfuscated by such minor literary figures as [Jorge Luis] Borges and [Franz] Kafka, it finds its ultimate realization in the magisterial prose of M. Molybdenius, the author of *A Thanatological Theory of Meaning.*" Kolon more recently added that although he no longer writes fiction, he has not abandoned poetry, "Poetry distills what spirits cannot deaden."

AVOCATIONAL INTERESTS: "Greek philosophy before Thales, opera before Britten, origami, weightlifting."

*   *   *

KURTZMAN, Joel 1947-

PERSONAL: Born June 25, 1947, in Los Angeles, Calif.; son of Samuel (a dentist) and Roselle (a sculptor; maiden name, Rosencranz) Kurtzman; married Susan Gross (a literary agent), December 28, 1969. *Education:* University of California, Berkeley, A.B., 1971.

ADDRESSES: Office—*New York Times,* 229 West 43rd St., New York, N.Y. 10036. *Agent*—Felipa Brophy, Sterling Lord Agency, One Madison Ave., 22nd Floor, New York, N.Y. 10010.

CAREER: Writer; currently business and financial reporter, *New York Times,* New York, N.Y.

MEMBER: Authors Guild, Writers Guild West.

AWARDS, HONORS: Eisner Prize, Eisner Memorial Fund for creative achievement, for *Crown of Flowers.*

WRITINGS:

Crown of Flowers (novel), Dutton, 1970.
Sweet Bobby (novel), McGraw, 1974.
(With Phillip Gordon and J. P. Tarcher) *No More Dying: The Conquest of Aging and the Extension of Human Life,* ETC Publications, 1976.
(Editor with Ervin Laszlo) *The United States, Canada, and the New International Economic Order,* Pergamon, 1979.
(Editor with Laszlo) *Eastern Europe and the New International Economic Order: A Review of Four Representative Samples of Socialist Perspectives,* Pergamon, 1980.
(Editor with Laszlo) *Western Europe and the New International Economic Order,* Pergamon, 1980.

(Editor with Laszlo) *The Structure of the World Economy and Prospects for a New International Economic Order,* Pergamon, 1980.

(Editor with Laszlo and Toivo Miljan) *Food and Agriculture in Global Perspective: Discussion in the Committee of the Whole of the United Nations,* Pergamon, 1980.

(With Laszlo and A. K. Bhattacharya) *RCDC (Regional Cooperation among Developing Countries): The New Imperative of Development in the 1980s,* Pergamon, 1981.

(Editor with Laszlo) *Political and Institutional Issues of the New International Order,* Pergamon, 1981.

Futurecasting: Charting a Way to Your Future, ETC Publications, 1984.

The Decline and Crash of the American Economy, Norton, 1988.

Also author of screenplay, "Bobby's Axe."

SIDELIGHTS: Joel Kurtzman once told *CA:* "I want to be involved with my subject, I want to know how my characters breathe and move, what it looks like to see through their eyes. While researching and writing *Sweet Bobby,*" a novel about a young man severely traumatized by adolescence and war, "I worked in the violent wards of two mental hospitals. I needed to know my subjects firsthand." Kurtzman has more recently written nonfiction on scientific and economic subjects. He feels that "science is the true philosophy. The facts we know about the universe tell us both about where we live and about the human mind. Knowing about quarks and stars confirms Plato. The true dialectic is the equation between matter, energy, and mind. With nonfiction writing, I am interested in occupying the space between the actual and the possible. I want to observe things as they become. With fiction I want to straddle that point where the cosmos touches the heart."

BIOGRAPHICAL/CRITICAL SOURCES:

PERIODICALS

New York Times Book Review, February 24, 1974, July 24, 1988.

* * *

KUTTNER, Paul 1931-

PERSONAL: Born September 20, 1931, in Berlin, Germany; son of Paul (a physician) and Margarete (a piano teacher; maiden name, Fraenkel) Kuttner; married Myrtil Romegialli, September, 1956 (divorced, 1960); married Ursula Timmermann, 1963 (divorced, 1970); children: (second marriage) Stephen. *Education:* Attended schools in Berlin, Germany, and Bryanston School, Dorset, England. *Religion:* "Firm believer in the Divine Force that created Man, Nature, the Universe: a Life Force neither good nor evil and totally unrelated to all religious sects on earth."

ADDRESSES: Home—37-26 87th St., Jackson Heights, N.Y. 11372. *Office*—*Guinness Book of World Records,* 5th Floor, 387 Park Ave. S., New York, N.Y. 10016-8810.

CAREER: Der Weg (weekly newspaper), Bern, Switzerland, political, economic, and cultural reporter, and foreign correspondent in London, England, 1946-47; *News Chronicle,* London, U.S. correspondent, 1948; *What's On in London—The London Week,* London, columnist in Hollywood, Calif., 1948, and New York City, 1948-56; Bureau of Displaced Persons, Church World Service, New York City, social worker, 1948-53; Watson-Guptill Publications, Inc., New York City, salesperson, 1954-62;

Sterling Publishing Co., New York City, 1962-66, began as publicity director, became general manager; *Guinness Book of World Records,* New York City, publicity director, 1966—.

WRITINGS:

The Man Who Lost Everything (novel), Sterling, 1977.
Condemned (novel), Dawnwood Press, 1983.
Absolute Proof (novel), Dawnwood Press, 1984.
The Iron Virgin (novel), Dawnwood Press, 1986.
Headaches for History Buffs (nonfiction), Dawnwood Press, 1990.
Tough Questions . . . Amazing Answers!! (nonfiction), Dawnwood Press, in press.

TRANSLATOR FROM THE GERMAN; JUVENILES

Katharina Zechlin, *Creative Enamelling and Jewelry Making,* Sterling, 1965.
T. M. Schegger, *Make Your Own Mobiles,* Sterling, 1965.
A. Pfluger, *Karate: Basic Principles,* Sterling, 1967.
Susanne Strose, *Coloring Papers,* Sterling, 1968.
Strose, *Potato Printing,* Sterling, 1968.
Strose, *Candle Making,* Sterling, 1968.
Elmar Gruber, *Nail Sculpture,* Sterling, 1968.
Peter and Susanne Bauzen, *Flower Pressing,* Sterling, 1972.
Charles H. Paraquin, *Eye-Teasers: Optical Illusions and Puzzles,* Sterling, 1976.

SIDELIGHTS: Paul Kuttner once told *CA:* "Having been raised on the Spahn Ranch of *Mittel Europa* (Nazi Germany) in the 1930s, the melodrama and the tragedy of that era have left an indelible stamp on my mind, my writing, and the skepticism of my lifestyle. Melodrama: visiting my father at Berlin's Universum Film Aktiengesellschaft (UFA) movie studio where he was doctor-in-residence, watching Emil Jannings perform before the cameras, my filmed conversation with Hitler, and observing the political, racial, and cultural madness of the Nazi era in Berlin until 1939. Then the tragedy: my parents murdered in a concentration camp, my mother in the very last gassing operation in Auschwitz, according to the International Tracing Service; my sister, Annemarie, forced to live underground, and later dying of cancer; and I on my own at the age of eight, in England, where I spent my summer vacations with the chairman of Lloyd's of London and was wounded by a V-1 flying bomb in December, 1944. These early events influenced my life more than any single work or writer.

"In the end," Kuttner recalled, "it was literature—Shakespeare, Tolstoy, Shaw, Forster, Greene, Salinger, Hemingway, Wolfe, Goethe—which generously and mercifully opened my eyes to look at the world with a clearer vision. Literature let me see life from a less hunted and more tranquil, contemplative perspective. It, more than any person, became my balm—the motivating factor that finally triggered my determination to settle down after a restless life and two marriages and write, write, write." Kuttner more recently added: "If this proves a catharsis of sorts, a primary reason for my work is to let the reader vicariously feel the same emotions and see the same mind-pictures that stir my own fantasy and which move me so much that I must convey these light and deep thoughts, via the printed page, to friends and strangers alike in every corner of the globe."

The Man Who Lost Everything has been translated into Spanish.

AVOCATIONAL INTERESTS: Photography, amateur film directing, oil painting.

L

La FARGE, Oliver (Hazard Perry) 1901-1963

PERSONAL: Born December 19, 1901, in New York, N.Y.; son of Christopher Grant (an architect and lecturer) and Florence Bayard (a worker in nursing training schools; maiden name, Lockwood) La Farge; died August 2, 1963; married Wanden E. Mathews, September 28, 1929 (divorced, 1937); married Consuelo O. C. de Baca (a literary agent), October 14, 1939; children: (first marriage) Povy (daughter), Oliver Albee; (second marriage) John Pendaries. *Education:* Harvard University, B.A., 1924, M.A., 1929. *Religion:* Roman Catholic.

ADDRESSES: Home—Santa Fe, N.M.

CAREER: Tulane University, New Orleans, La., assistant professor of ethnology, 1926-28; Columbia University, New York, N.Y., research fellow in anthropology, 1931-33; teacher of writing technique, 1936-41. Director of Eastern Association in Indian Affairs, 1930-32, and of Intertribal Exhibition of Indian Arts, 1931; field representative for United States Indian Service, 1936; editorial advisor, Alliance Book Corp., 1940-41; appointed to ten-man advisory committee to the Government on Indian Affairs, 1949; member of U.S. Department of Interior's Committee on Indian Arts and Crafts; official advisor to the Hopi Indians. Trustee for W. E. B. DuBois Prize for Negro Literature, 1932-34; member of advisory board of the Laboratory of Anthropology, Santa Fe, N.M., 1935-41, 1946-63; member of awards committee of Opportunity Fellowships of John Hay Whitney Foundation. Participant in archaeology exhibitions to Arizona, Mexico, and Guatemala. *Military service:* U.S. Army Air Forces, 1942-45; became lieutenant colonel; received Legion of Merit award.

MEMBER: National Association on Indian Affairs (president, 1933-37), Association on American Indian Affairs (president, 1937-42, 1946-63), American Association for the Advancement of Science (fellow), American Anthropological Association, National Institute of Arts and Letters, PEN, Authors League of America (New York City), Century Club, Coffee House Club.

AWARDS, HONORS: Hemmenway fellow, 1924-26; Pulitzer Prize in fiction, 1929, for *Laughing Boy;* O. Henry Memorial Prize, 1931, for "Haunted Ground"; M.A., 1932, Brown University; Guggenheim fellowship for writing, 1941.

WRITINGS:

Laughing Boy (novel), Houghton, 1929, reprinted, Buccaneer Books, 1981.

(With Douglas Byers) *The Year Bearer's People,* Tulane University Press, 1931.

Sparks Fly Upward (novel), Houghton, 1931, reprinted, Popular Library, 1959.

Long Pennant (novel), Houghton, 1933.

All the Young Men (short stories; includes "Haunted Ground"), Houghton, 1935, reprinted, AMS Press, 1976.

The Enemy Gods (novel), Houghton, 1937, reprinted, University of New Mexico Press, 1975.

As Long as the Grass Shall Grow (nonfiction), Longmans, Green, 1940.

(Editor) *The Changing Indian,* University of Oklahoma Press, 1942.

The Copper Pot (novel), Houghton, 1942.

Raw Material (autobiography), Houghton, 1945.

Santa Eulalia: The Religion of a Cuchumatan Indian Town, University of Chicago Press, 1947.

The Eagle in the Egg, Houghton, 1949, reprinted, Arno, 1972.

Cochise of Arizona: The Pipe of Peace Is Broken (juvenile), illustrations by L. F. Bjorklund, Aladdin Books, 1953.

The Mother Ditch (juvenile), illustrations by Karl Larsson, Houghton, 1954.

Behind the Mountains, Houghton, 1956.

A Pictorial History of the American Indian, Crown, 1956, revised edition, 1974, special edition for young readers published as *The American Indian,* Golden Press, 1960.

A Pause in the Desert (short stories), Houghton, 1957.

(With Arthur N. Morgan) *Santa Fe: The Autobiography of a Southwestern Town,* University of Oklahoma Press, 1959.

The Door in the Wall (short stories), Houghton, 1965.

Winfield Townley Scott, editor, *The Man with the Calabash Pipe: Some Observations* (selections from the author's weekly newspaper column from 1950-63), Houghton, 1966.

(With others) *Introduction to American Indian Art,* two volumes, Rio Grande, 1985.

Author of a weekly newspaper column in *Santa Fe New Mexican,* 1950-63; contributor of articles and book reviews to many periodicals.

SIDELIGHTS: After winning a Pulitzer Prize in 1929 for his first novel, *Laughing Boy,* Oliver La Farge firmly established himself in American letters as an authority on American Indian culture. His background, ironically, did not point in that direction. Born of affluent parents in New York City, the young La Farge attended prestigious Groton School and, later, Harvard University, where he served on the editorial board of the *Harvard Advocate.* According to a *Dictionary of Literary Biography* piece by T. M. Pearce, it was during La Farge's university years that he visited Arizona on an archaeological field trip and used that setting for a short story about a "young Navajo who returns to his people after earning a college degree." Like that previous short story, the novel *Laughing Boy* concerns a young Navajo, the title character, a silversmith who "meets a young woman at a ritual dance," as Pearce described. "She tells him that she has lived in the American world as a servant to a missionary's wife, but he does not learn that she has also been intimate with a white rancher who lives near the Indian reservation. Her name is Slim Girl and her love for Laughing Boy helps her return to the Navajo world."

Following the success of *Laughing Boy,* La Farge continued his career as a writer, turning out several novels and nonfiction books covering Native American life. To Pearce, the author's fiction "[exhibited] his skill in devising plots and creating characters from a variety of backgrounds." In the opinion of *New York Times Book Review* critic Marshall Sprague, La Farge had produced "quiet, bittersweet tales written with fine economy of phrase and a kind of wistful delicacy."

BIOGRAPHICAL/CRITICAL SOURCES:

BOOKS

Dictionary of Literary Biography, Volume 9: *American Novelists, 1910-1945,* Gale, 1981.
Gillis, Everett A., *Oliver La Farge,* Steck-Vaughn, 1967.
La Farge, Oliver, *Raw Material,* Houghton, 1945.
McNickle, D'Arcy, *Indian Man: A Life of Oliver La Farge,* Indiana University Press, 1971.

PERIODICALS

New York Times Book Review, January 17, 1965.
Saturday Review, January 30, 1965.

OBITUARIES:

PERIODICALS

Newsweek, August 12, 1963.
New York Times, August 3, 1963.
Time, August 9, 1963.*

*   *   *

LANCASTER, David
    See HEALD, Tim(othy Villiers)

*   *   *

LANDON, Michael de L(aval)   1935-

PERSONAL: Born October 8, 1935, in Saint John, New Brunswick, Canada; son of Arthur Henry Whittington (a brigadier general in the Canadian Army) and Elizabeth Worthington (Fair) Landon; married Doris Lee Clay, December 31, 1959 (divorced, 1980); married Carole Marie Prather Casey (a businesswoman), February 28, 1981; children: (first marriage) Clay de Laval, Letitia Elizabeth. *Education:* Worcester College, Oxford, B.A. (with honors), 1958, M.A., 1961; University of Wiscon-

sin—Madison, M.A., 1962, Ph.D., 1966. *Politics:* Independent. *Religion:* Episcopalian.

ADDRESSES: Home—P.O. Box 172, University, Miss. 38677. *Office*—Department of History, University of Mississippi, University, Miss. 38677.

CAREER: Manor House School, Horsham, Sussex, England, history teacher, 1957; Dalhousie Preparatory School, Ladybank, Fife, Scotland, assistant master of history, 1957-58; Lakefield College School, Lakefield, Ontario, assistant master of French, 1958-60; University of Wisconsin—Madison, teaching assistant, 1961-63, project assistant, 1963-64; University of Mississippi, University, assistant professor, 1964-67, associate professor, 1967-72, professor of history, 1972—. Visiting associate professor, University of Wisconsin—Madison, 1971.

MEMBER: American Historical Association, American Society for Legal History (member of board of directors, 1982-84; secretary, 1988—), American Association of University Professors, Royal Historical Society (London; fellow), Conference on British Studies, Eta Sigma Phi, Phi Alpha Theta, Phi Kappa Phi, Oxford Society.

AWARDS, HONORS: American Philosophical Society research grant, 1966-67, 1973-74.

WRITINGS:

The Triumph of the Lawyers, University of Alabama Press, 1970.
The Honor and Dignity of the Profession: A History of the Mississippi State Bar, 1906-1976, University Press of Mississippi, 1979.
Erin and Britannia: The Historical Background to a Modern Tragedy, Nelson-Hall, 1981.

Contributor to *Per Se, Enlightenment Essays, Proceedings* of the American Philosophical Society, and other journals.

WORK IN PROGRESS: The Political Career of Sir John Maynard, Serjeant-at-Law, 1604-1690.

SIDELIGHTS: Michael de L. Landon wrote *CA:* "With my history of the Mississippi State Bar, published in 1979, I feel that I have achieved a mature writing style of my own with which I am reasonably content."

AVOCATIONAL INTERESTS: Gardening, cooking.

*   *   *

LANE, Jane
    See DAKERS, Elaine Kidner

*   *   *

LANG, Fritz   1890-1976

PERSONAL: Born December 5, 1890, in Vienna, Austria; died August 2, 1976, in Beverly Hills, Calif.; buried in Forest Lawn Cemetery, Hollywood Hills, Calif.; came to the United States, 1934; naturalized U.S. citizen, 1939; son of Anton (an architect) and Paula (Schlesinger) Lang; married Thea von Harbou (a novelist and screenwriter), 1920 (divorced, 1933). *Education:* Attended College of Technical Science in Vienna, 1908, and Academy of Graphic Arts in Munich, 1911; also studied painting in Paris, 1912-14.

CAREER: Screenwriter, director, and producer. Decla Bioscop Company (later merged with UFA), Berlin, Germany, 1918-34, began as story reader, became director; Metro-Goldwyn-Mayer,

Hollywood, Calif., director, 1934-37. Also founded several independent film companies. Director of films: "You Only Live Once," 1937; (and producer) "You and Me," 1938; "The Return of Frank James," 1940; "Western Union," 1941; "Man Hunt," 1941; (co-director) "Confirm or Deny," 1941; (co-director) "Moontide," 1942; "Ministry of Fear," 1944; "The Woman in the Window," 1944; (and producer) "Scarlet Street," 1945; "Cloak and Dagger," 1946; (and co-producer) "Secret beyond the Door," 1948; "House by the River," 1950; "An American Guerrilla in the Philippines," 1950; "Rancho Notorious," 1952; "Clash by Night," 1952; "The Blue Gardenia," 1953; "The Big Heat," 1953; "Human Desire," 1954; "Moonfleet," 1955; "While the City Sleeps," 1956; "Beyond a Reasonable Doubt," 1956. *Military service:* Served in Austrian Army during World War I; became lieutenant; wounded in action three times.

AWARDS, HONORS: Order of the Yugoslavian Flag with golden wreath, 1971; honorary professorship from University of Vienna, 1973; received award from Sorrento Film Festival, 1973, as "the best German film director"; received Commander's Cross Order of Merit and Golden Ribbon Motion Picture Art Award, both from Federal Republic of Germany; named officer of Order of Arts and Letters, government of France.

WRITINGS:

PUBLISHED SCREENPLAYS

(With wife, Thea von Harbou) *M* (also see below), Simon & Schuster, 1968.
(With von Harbou) *Metropolis* (also see below), Simon & Schuster, 1970.

SCREENPLAYS

"Die Hochzeit im Ekzentrikklub" (title means "Wedding in the Club of the Eccentrics"), Decla, 1917.
"Hilde Warren und der Tod" (title means "Hilde Warren and Death"), Decla, 1917.
"Joe Debbs," Decla, 1917.
"Die Rache ist mein" (title means "Revenge Is Mine"), Decla, 1918.
"Herren der Welt" (title means "Men of the World"), Decla, 1918.
"Bettler Gmb H," Decla, 1918.
(Co-author) "Wolkenbau und Flimmerstern" (title means "Castles in the Sky and Rhinestones"), Decla, 1919.
"Totentanz" (title means "Dance of Death"), Decla, 1919.
"Die Pest in Florenz" (title means "Plague in Florence"), Decla, 1919.
"Die Frau mit den Orchiden" (title means "The Woman with the Orchid"), Decla, 1919.
"Lilith und Ly," Decla, 1919.
(And director) "Halbblut," Decla, 1919, released in the United States as "The Weakling."
(And director) "Die Spinnen," Decla, Part 1: "Der Goldene See," 1919, Part 2: "Das Brillantenschiff," 1920, released in the United States as "The Spiders," 1978.
(And director) "Liliom," produced in France, 1934.
(With Bartlett Cormick, and director) "Fury," Metro-Goldwyn-Mayer, 1936.
(With Bertolt Brecht, and director and producer) "Hangmen Also Die!," United Artists, 1943.
(Co-author, director and producer) "Die Tausend Augen des Dr. Mabuse," Ajay Films, 1960, released in the United States as "The Thousand Eyes of Dr. Mabuse," also released as "Eye of Evil."

SCREENPLAYS; WITH WIFE, THEA VON HARBOU

(And director) "Das Wandernde Bild" (title means "The Wandering Image"), Decla, 1920.
(And director) "Kampfende Herzen," Decla, 1920.
(And director) "Der muede Tod: Ein Deutsches Volkslied in 6 Versen," Decla, 1921, released in the United States as "Between Two Worlds," 1923, released in England as "Destiny," also released as "The Three Lights."
"Das Indische Grabmal," Joe May Company/EFA, Part 1: "Die Sendung des Yoghi," 1921, Part 2: "Der Tiger von Eschnapur," 1921, remade by Lang as "Der Tiger von Eschnapur" and "Das Indische Grabmal," 1959, edited version released in the United States as "Journey to the Lost City," American-International, 1959, released in England as "Tiger of Bengal."
(And director) "Dr. Mabuse, der Spieler," Ullstein-UCO Films/UFA, Part 1: "Ein Bild der Zeit," 1921, Part 2: "Inferno-Menschen der Zeit," 1922, released in the United States as "Dr. Mabuse, the Gambler."
(And director) "Die Nibelungen," Part 1: "Siegfrieds Tod" (title means "Death of Siegfried"), 1924, Part 2: "Kriemhilds Rache" (title means "Kriemhild's Revenge"), UFA, 1924.
(And director) "Metropolis," UFA, 1927, released in the United States by Paramount, 1927.
(And director and producer) "Spione," Fritz Lang Film/UFA, 1928, released in the United States as "Spies," Metro-Goldwyn-Mayer, 1928, also released as "The Spy."
(And director and producer) "Die Frau im Mond," Fritz Lang Film/UFA, 1929, released in the United States as "Woman in the Moon," 1929, also released as "The Girl in the Moon" and "By Rocket to the Moon."
(And director) "M," Nero-Film, 1931, released in the United States by Paramount, 1933.
(And director) "Das Testament des Dr. Mabuse," Nero-Film, 1933, released in the United States as "The Last Will of Dr. Mabuse," 1935.

SIDELIGHTS: Considered to have been one of the cinema's finest directors, Fritz Lang specialized in films of suspense, conflict, and violence. His intense, no-frills narrative pace and striking visual sense were enormously influential in the adventure, science fiction, and thriller film genres. Among Lang's best known films were "Metropolis," a science fiction vision of a future dystopia, "M," a study of a child killer, and the Dr. Mabuse films, which feature the decadent mastermind of the criminal underworld. He also directed such popular suspense and crime movies as "Scarlet Street," "Fury," "The Big Heat," and "Ministry of Fear." Lang's own life, marked by war, political violence, and intrigue, was sometimes as dramatic as his cinematic work.

As a young man Lang attended art schools in Vienna and Munich, where he studied architecture. In 1910 he left his native Austria to travel around Europe, North Africa, and Asia, supporting himself by doing odd jobs and by selling his drawings to newspapers and magazines. Eventually he settled in Paris to study painting. During an exhibition of his paintings in Paris in 1914, Lang was informed that World War I had broken out. He was obliged to flee France, which was now at war with Austria, or face arrest as an alien. He escaped on the last train to Vienna, made his way back home, and joined the Austrian Army. Over the next two years he served at the front, and he was wounded in action three times.

While spending a year in a Viennese hospital recovering from a severe war injury, Lang began to write scripts, short stories, and ideas for films to pass the time. His work caught the attention of the director Joe May at the Decla Bioscop Company, a major German film studio. May bought and directed several of Lang's filmscripts. After recuperating from his injuries, Lang went to Berlin to work for Decla as a script reader, rising quickly to become a scenario writer. He also did some acting for the studio, including the role of Death in his own film "Hilde Warren und der Tod."

By 1919 Lang was directing films for Decla. His second directing effort, "Die Spinnen," later released in English as "The Spiders," was an adventure serial featuring a playboy detective who uncovers an international criminal conspiracy. The action takes place in the last remaining Incan temple in South America, in a secret cavern city hidden beneath San Francisco, and in a score of other exotic locales. Vincent Canby of the *New York Times* noted that the film had "dozens of pursuits and last-minute escapes" but was most interesting for its "matter-of-fact suggestion that paranoia is sanity." "Die Spinnen" proved to be hugely popular with German audiences.

In 1920 Lang married Thea von Harbou, a writer of thrillers and screenplays. (Some sources say that this was Lang's second marriage.) From then until their divorce in 1933 the couple wrote screenplays as a team, with Lang directing many of the scripts. His wife also wrote novelizations of some of their films. Their first successful collaboration was "Der Muede Tod: Ein Deutsches Volkslied in 6 Versen," released in the United States as "Between Two Worlds." Told in three episodes, the film presents variations on the same story of a young woman attempting to save her lover from death. Set in different historical periods, all three episodes lead "to the same conclusion: all the girl's efforts to save her lover lead him to his destruction," as Lotte H. Eisner wrote in *The Haunted Screen: Expressionism in the German Cinema and the Influence of Max Reinhardt.* Eisner was especially impressed with Lang's use of lighting to accentuate architectural details and his "intense feeling for the physical character of objects." In his review of the film for the *Spectator,* Bertram Higgins found it to be "one of the most original and impressive films that have ever been made."

With "Dr. Mabuse, der Spieler," released in English as "Dr. Mabuse, the Gambler," Lang turned to the crime genre for inspiration, recounting the evil machinations of a master criminal. Yet Dr. Mabuse is not alone in his criminality; the society of his time is also criminal. As Siegfried Kracauer commented in his *From Caligari to Hitler: A Psychological History of the German Film,* "the world [the film] pictures has fallen prey to lawlessness and depravity. A night-club dancer performs in a decor composed of outright sex symbols. Orgies are an institution, homosexuals and prostitute children are everyday characters. . . . Throughout the film Mabuse is stigmatized as a man of genius who has become Public Enemy No. 1. . . . [But when] Mabuse is wrecked . . . social depravity continues, and other Mabuses may follow."

The world of "Dr. Mabuse" was Lang's biting depiction of postwar German society, which was plagued by economic chaos, a loss of values, and political extremism. The first part of the two-part film was sub-titled "Image of Our Times," while the second part was sub-titled "Men of Our Times." German critics of the 1920s "recognized the unflattering but authentic reflection of their own day, of the inflation of the mad lost years when every vice and passion was rife," according to Eisner.

With "Die Nibelungen" Lang turned from contemporary society to the heroic past of German mythology. Like "Dr. Mabuse," however, "Die Nibelungen" is a two-part film; audiences were expected to view it on two consecutive evenings. And also like "Dr. Mabuse," it had a particular relevance for the German society of the post-war years. Talking to Gene D. Phillips of the *Village Voice* in the last interview he gave before his death in 1976, Lang explained his reasons for filming "Die Nibelungen." "By making the Siegfried legend into a film," he said, "I wanted to show that Germany was searching for an ideal in her past, even during the horrible time after the First World War in which the picture was made."

Based on a thirteenth-century German saga, "Die Nibelungen" recounted the adventures of such mythical characters as Siegfried, Brunhild, and Kriemhild. Knights, castles, sword fights, dragons, and beautiful maidens abound in the story. In creating certain scenes, Lang borrowed liberally from classic German paintings of these mythological tales, especially from the works of Arnold Boecklin. At times, the film seems to be a Boecklin painting come-to-life. Other scenes are designed so well by Lang, according to Eisner, that if stopped at the right moment they "might well be paintings in their own right."

Lang placed a heavy emphasis on creating a majestic mood in "Die Nibelungen." When filming scenes in castles or cathedrals, he grouped his actors in symmetrical patterns to create striking visual effects and an almost ceremonial atmosphere, and he subdued the dramatic element to accentuate the visual one. Speaking of the film in a review for the *Spectator,* Iris Barry noted that the film's actors behaved "with the passionlessness and dignity of actors in a pageant." Barry also reported that, for Lang, "the visual beauty of a film is just as important as its dramatic economy and effectiveness," and she found Lang's "use of tone, of sharp black and clear white and clean silver, . . . [to be] very accomplished and lovely." Writing in his book *The Film Till Now,* Paul Rotha ranked "Between Two Worlds" and "Die Nibelungen" as "supreme examples of the German art film."

After depicting the contemporary world in "Dr. Mabuse, the Gambler" and the world of the mythological past in "Die Nibelungen," Lang turned with "Metropolis" to the world of the next century. In this future world, men have built Metropolis, a glittering city reaching to the sky. But far below this city lies a subterranean factory town where dehumanized workers operate complex and dangerous machines. Those who work in the factory are not permitted to come to the surface, where the factory director and his family enjoy the sunshine, fresh air, and the beauty of vast pleasure gardens. When the girl Maria calls for justice and understanding for the workers, she gains the support of the factory director's son, who joins the rebellion. During the ensuing revolt, the workers wreck their machines and the factory director deliberately floods the cavern city.

"Metropolis" was probably the most detailed vision of the future that the silent films created. It was, according to Evelyn Gerstein in the *Nation,* "the first time the chill mechanized world of the future [had] been given reality." Lang's studio spent an unprecedented two million dollars on the film, building gigantic sets and hiring scores of extras. The scenes set in the underground factory, especially those in which workers move the hands of giant clock-like dials in a dark and foggy room, have been the inspiration for many later film sets. Shot in stark contrasts with lighting that lent a nightmarish quality to the film, "Metropolis" is recognized today as a milestone in the cinema.

Although "Metropolis" was a successful film, Lang was not happy with it. The conciliatory ending between the factory director and the rebellious workers was forced on him by his wife, who co-wrote the script, and by the studio. The work's later reputation as one of Adolf Hitler's favorite films further dampened Lang's enthusiasm for it. And he was bothered, too, that some of the dehumanizing factory conditions shown in the film later came true. Speaking to Peter Bogdanovich years later, Lang commented: "Should I say now that I like 'Metropolis' because something I have seen in my imagination comes true—when I detested it after it was finished?"

Lang's last German film was "M," the story of a psychopathic child killer who is eventually tracked down by both the police and the underworld. The story was inspired by the real-life child killer known as the Duesseldorf Monster, who had terrorized Germany in the 1920s. In Lang's treatment, the killer is portrayed as horrifying and pathetic by turns. As William Troy noted in the *Nation,* "No subject could be more inherently horrible, more dangerously open to a facile sensationalism of treatment. Yet such are the tact and the genius with which Fritz Lang has handled it that the result is something at once more significant than either the horror story, pure and simple . . ., or the so-called psychological 'document'. . . . The result is, in fact, a film which answers to most of the demands of classical tragedy."

Although a sound film, and the first sound film to be made in Germany, "M" used sound sparingly and with poignant effect. One such scene occurs when the killer's shadow drifts across the screen towards that of a little girl. The camera cuts to an empty dinner table and then back to the now-empty street where the killer and girl had been standing. All the while, the cries of the mother calling for her daughter are heard over the soundtrack. The cries become more urgent as the camera cuts rapidly between the two empty settings. Then, where the killer and girl had stood, Lang shows only a floating balloon, the device the murderer used to initially make the girl's acquaintance. The balloon drifts off aimlessly until it gets tangled in an overhead telegraph wire.

Played by actor Peter Lorre, who attained international recognition for his role, the murderer is "a somewhat infantile petty bourgeois who eats apples on the street and could not possibly be suspected of killing a fly," according to Kracauer. Lang reveals the killer's inner dementia through what Kracauer called "a brilliant pictorial device," that of surrounding him on several occasions with scores of inanimate objects which threaten to engulf him. These "mute objects" symbolize "the ascendancy of irrational powers," Kracauer explained, and define the murderer as "a prisoner of uncontrollable instincts."

Lang followed the murderer from his room, where he fights against but finally succumbs to his abhorrent desires, then out into the streets to stalk children, to being stalked in turn by both the police and the underworld. "M" builds to a tense sequence during which the killer is trapped in an empty office building at night, with search parties scouring the labyrinth of rooms for him. It has been called one of the most chilling climaxes in cinema history.

Gavin Lambert saw "M" as a culmination of Lang's early cinematic themes. Writing in *Sight and Sound,* Lambert found that "Dr. Mabuse," "The Spiders," and Lang's "The Spy" expressed the "idea of [a] demonic, almost abstract, power-organisation determined purposelessly to overthrow human society by acts of outrage and violence. . . . Finally, in *M,* the horrific life-and-death struggle is embodied in a single character, the child-murderer wretchedly trying to escape from his impulses and hallucinations. These films are not only Lang's most original and lasting achievements of his German period, but remain the most haunting melodramas of the cinema."

Soon after finishing "M," Lang was called to a meeting with Nazi propaganda minister Joseph Goebbels. Impressed with Lang's film work, and unaware of his political sympathies, Goebbels offered him the job of chief Nazi filmmaker. Lang agreed to think it over. Returning home, however, he immediately packed his bags and left for Paris. Lang was motivated to leave the country as much by his political beliefs as by his fear that the Nazis would discover his Jewish heritage. He left behind his wife, Thea von Harbou, who had recently joined the Nazi Party. As Andrew Sarris reported in the *Village Voice,* she "devoted herself thereafter to the Nazi cause." The couple divorced in 1933.

After a short time in France, Lang left for Hollywood to work with David O. Selznick of Metro-Goldwyn-Mayer. He was to direct only one film for MGM, the critically-acclaimed "Fury" in 1936, before leaving to free lance for a number of different studios. Lang also set up several film production companies of his own; his dislike for working by Hollywood rules often pushed him to finance his own work. Lang's insistence upon extensive preparation before the making of a film, a common practice among the early German filmmakers, ran counter to the more casual Hollywood ethos. Among film industry insiders Lang was known as a "difficult" director, a charge he contemptuously dismissed. In speaking with Mary Blume, who confronted him with the accusation, Lang said: "Difficult! Do you know what that means? It means you're a perfectionist. Hollywood hates perfectionists."

Over the next few decades Lang directed a number of successful Hollywood films which are still held in high esteem by critics today. These films include "Ministry of Fear," "The Woman in the Window," "Scarlet Street," "House by the River," "Rancho Notorious," "The Big Heat," and "Human Desire." His work ranged over the crime, western, and thriller genres. But some observers ranked his American films among Lang's lesser work, preferring the silent films he had made in Germany in the 1920s. These silent films, they argued, broke new ground and set standards that influenced scores of other filmmakers, while Lang's later efforts, although commendable, were necessarily more conventional. In Germany, too, Lang was able to direct his own scripts, while in America he was often obliged to direct the scripts of studio writers. In her study *Fritz Lang* Eisner claimed that "it is an academic question . . . whether Lang's German films or his American period are to be valued more highly. . . . There is, doubtless, a profound difference in perspective, but there is also a firm continuity of vision."

This cinematic vision is commented on by several critics who found a consistent outlook in all of Lang's films, whether made in Germany or America. "Lang's films," Eisner wrote in *Fritz Lang,* "like those of every great cinema creator, reveal a profound underlying unity. . . . [In Lang's films] character determines human fate: character is the demon of man. All Lang's American films will demonstrate this belief, with their recurrent questions: Where does guilt begin? What is innocence? What is good and what is evil?" Lambert claimed that "Fritz Lang's America is not essentially different from Fritz lang's Germany . . .; it is less openly macabre, its crime and terror exist on a comparatively realistic level, but both countries are really another country, a haunted place in which the same dramas constantly recur. . . . It is this persistent imaginative projection of an anxiety neurosis that gives Lang's films their unique power." Robert A. Armour saw a similar theme in Lang's films. He stated in his book *Fritz Lang:* "The dark struggles within and among his characters become statements of the dark side of our own personalities. . . . He understood how each of us is driven and confused by these conflicts. In the final analysis Fritz Lang was a first-rate entertainer who never allowed us to lose sight of his message. The dark struggle is a worthy theme, a theme that gives meaning to the visual images that dominate the films of Fritz Lang."

Francois Truffaut, writing in his *The Films in My Life*, attributed the dark vision of Lang's American films to the director's personal history. "Lang had to get out of Germany quickly in the face of Nazism," Truffaut wrote. "From then on, all of his work . . . will reflect this violent break." Many of Lang's Hollywood films are concerned with revenge, Truffaut pointed out, and tell stories of individuals who fight back after suffering a personal loss; this, Truffaut believed, was a reflection of Lang's own feelings after leaving Germany. By the 1950s Lang's films had become, according to Truffaut, "the bitterest in the history of film." Sarris explained that Lang was "never the sunny optimist . . . Lang prowled in the dark corners of the soul where destiny collided with depravity." The director openly acknowledged his obsession with the darker side of human nature. "I am profoundly fascinated by cruelty, fear, horror and death," he once said. "My films show my preoccupation with violence, the pathology of violence."

In the late 1950s Lang returned to Germany to make several films, including "Die Tausend Augen des Dr. Mabuse," released in the United States as "The Thousand Eyes of Dr. Mabuse." He also travelled to India to remake "Der Tiger von Eschnapur" and "Das Indische Grabmal," two films originally written with Thea von Harbou in the early 1920s. An English version of the film, drastically edited by the distributor, was released in the United States as "Journey to the Lost City." These last films were not critically appreciated. After appearing as himself in Jean Luc-Godard's "Contempt" in 1963, Lang retired from the film business to live quietly in Beverly Hills, California. From then until the time of his death in 1976, Lang's films were to undergo a revival among film aficionados. Many of his long unavailable silent films were finally released in the United States, while German filmmakers came to a new appreciation of his role in German cinematic history. In 1973 Lang was given a special award by the Sorrento Film Festival as "the best German film director."

John Russell Taylor of *Sight and Sound* quoted Lang as once saying, "I live through my eyes." Taylor went on to remark that "in the end it is [Lang's] power to embody his ideas visually which accounts for the lasting effect of his films." Upon Lang's death in 1976, *Newsweek* remembered him as a member of "the golden age of German expressionist films" who had "influenced hundreds of fellow directors." In an appreciation of Lang's career, Truffaut remarked that the director "was not only a genius, he was also the most isolated and the least understood of contemporary filmmakers."

Asked by Phillips which of his films he thought was best, Lang answered: "It is difficult for me to choose. . . . I like 'M,' my first sound picture, very much, and also 'Scarlet Street'. . ., but I cannot really say why. Somehow a certain film just seems to click, have all the right touches, and turn out the way I hoped that it would."

MEDIA ADAPTATIONS: "Metropolis" was adapted as a stage musical and produced in London in March, 1989.

BIOGRAPHICAL/CRITICAL SOURCES:

BOOKS

Armour, Robert A., *Fritz Lang*, Twayne, 1978.
Contemporary Literary Criticism, Volume 20, Gale, 1982.

Eisner, Lotte H., *The Haunted Screen: Expressionism in the German Cinema and the Influence of Max Reinhardt*, University of California Press, 1969.
Eisner, Lotte H., *Fritz Lang*, Oxford University Press, 1977.
Hunter, William, *Scrutiny of Cinema*, Wishart, 1932.
Jensen, Paul M., *The Cinema of Fritz Lang*, A. S. Barnes, 1968.
Kracauer, Siegfried, *From Caligari to Hitler: A Psychological History of the German Film*, Princeton University Press, 1947.
Rotha, Paul, *The Film Till Now*, J. Cape, 1930.
Truffaut, Francois, *The Films in My Life*, Simon & Schuster, 1978.

PERIODICALS

Film Comment, March-April, 1973, November-December, 1974.
Film Quarterly, winter, 1979-80.
Films and Filming, June, 1962.
Nation, March 23, 1927, April 19, 1933.
New York Times, November 8, 1979.
Sight and Sound, spring, 1950, summer, 1954, spring, 1955, summer, 1955, autumn, 1955, winter, 1961-62, summer, 1962, summer, 1967, autumn, 1975, spring, 1977, autumn, 1977.
Spectator, February 23, 1924, June 14, 1924, March 26, 1927.
Village Voice, August 16, 1976.

OBITUARIES:

PERIODICALS

Newsweek, August 16, 1976.
New York Times, August 3, 1976.
Time, August 16, 1976.
Washington Post, August 4, 1976.*

—*Sketch by Thomas Wiloch*

*   *   *

LANGER, Ellen J(ane) 1947-

PERSONAL: Born March 25, 1947, in New York, N.Y.; daughter of Norman J. (a pharmacist) and Sylvia (Tobias) Langer. *Education:* New York University, B.A., 1970; Yale University, Ph.D., 1974.

ADDRESSES: Home—Cambridge, Mass. *Office*—Department of Psychology, Harvard University, William James Hall 1340, Cambridge, Mass. 02138.

CAREER: New Century Publishing Co., New York City, freelance writer, 1969-70; Graduate School and University Center of the City University of New York, New York City, assistant professor of psychology, 1974-77; Harvard University, Cambridge, Mass., associate professor, 1977-81, professor of psychology, 1981—.

MEMBER: American Psychological Association, American Association for the Advancement of Science, Society of Experimental Social Psychologists, Phi Beta Kappa, Psi Chi, Sigma Xi.

AWARDS, HONORS: Award for distinguished contributions of psychology in the public interest, American Psychological Society, 1988.

WRITINGS:

(With Carol S. Dweck) *Personal Politics: The Psychology of Making It*, Prentice-Hall, 1973.
The Psychology of Control, Sage Publications, 1983.
Mindfulness, Addison-Wesley, 1989.

(Editor with Charles Alexander) *Higher Stages of Development,* Oxford University Press, 1989.

WORK IN PROGRESS: Research articles dealing with the elderly, deviance, health, and competence.

*   *   *

LANGGUTH, A(rthur) J(ohn) 1933-

PERSONAL: Born July 11, 1933, in Minneapolis, Minn.; son of Arthur J. and Doris (Turnquist) Langguth. *Education:* Harvard University, A.B., 1955.

ADDRESSES: Home—1922 Whitley Ave., Los Angeles, Calif. 90068. *Agent*—Lynn Nesbit, Janklow & Nesbit, 40 West 57th St., New York, N.Y. 10019.

CAREER: Cowles Publications, reporter in Washington, D.C., 1959; *Valley Times,* North Hollywood, Calif., reporter, 1960-63; *New York Times,* New York, N.Y., reporter, 1963-65; author. *Military service:* U.S. Army, 1956-58.

WRITINGS:

Jesus Christs (novel), Harper, 1968.
Wedlock (novel), Knopf, 1972.
Marksman (novel), Harper, 1974.
Macumba: White and Black Magic in Brazil, Harper, 1975.
Hidden Terrors: The Truth about U.S. Police Operations in Latin America, Pantheon, 1978.
Saki: A Life of Hector Hugh Munro, with Six Short Stories Never Before Collected, Simon & Schuster, 1981.
Patriots: The Men Who Started the American Revolution (Book-of-the-Month Club main selection), Simon & Schuster, 1988.

SIDELIGHTS: A. J. Langguth's *Patriots: The Men Who Started the American Revolution,* states Jody Powell in the *Los Angeles Times Book Review,* "is welcome even for those of us with an established addiction to history. It draws us back to the beginning of ours, an era that seldom receives the attention it deserves." Langguth, a former war reporter in Vietnam, wrote *Patriots* because he recognized a need for a popular history of the American Revolution. John A. Garraty portrays the book in the *New York Times Book Review* as telling "what happened, who did it, what effects followed, and why people today ought to know about these matters," while Powell declares that it "provided a spicy, toothsome respite" from dry historical writing.

Reviewers recognize that the book has some flaws; for instance, Powell notes that both George Rogers Clark's expedition against Fort Vincennes, in what is now Indiana, and the battles for the Carolinas during the late 1770s and early 1780s are ignored. They agree, however, that its strengths outweigh its weaknesses. Edwards Park writes in the *Washington Post Book World:* "I find *Patriots* a delight, and intend to use it the next time I get strung out on a Revolutionary War assignment." Harrison E. Salisbury comments in Chicago *Tribune Books* that Langguth's "narrative reads as though he was there at Valley Forge and Philadelphia. It couldn't have been done better if he had been."

BIOGRAPHICAL/CRITICAL SOURCES:

PERIODICALS

Los Angeles Times Book Review, March 13, 1988.
New York Times Book Review, April 24, 1988.
Tribune Books (Chicago), February 14, 1988.
Washington Post Book World, April 24, 1988.

LANGLEY, Noel 1911-1980

PERSONAL: Born December 25, 1911, in Durban, South Africa; became U.S. citizen, 1961; died November 4, 1980, in Desert Hot Springs, Calif.; son of Aubrey and Dora Langley; married Naomi Mary Legate, 1937 (divorced, 1954); married Pamela Deeming, 1959; children: (first marriage) three sons, two daughters. *Education:* University of Natal, B.A.

CAREER: Author, playwright, and writer-director of films produced in Britain and the United States. *Military service:* Canadian Navy, 1943-45; became lieutenant.

MEMBER: Writers Guild of America West.

AWARDS, HONORS: Donaldson Award (shared with Robert Morley), 1948, for "Edward, My Son."

WRITINGS:

Cage Me a Peacock (also see below), Barker, 1935, Morrow, 1937, reprinted, Penguin Books/Methuen, 1960.
There's a Porpoise behind Us, Barker, 1936, reprinted, Penguin, 1961, published as *So Unlike the English,* Morrow, 1937.
Tale of the Land of Green Ginger, Morrow, 1937, revised edition published as *The Land of Green Ginger,* illustrated by Edward Ardizzone, Penguin Books, 1966, reprinted, 1982.
Hocus Pocus, Methuen, 1941.
The Music of the Heart, Barker, 1946, reprinted, Mayflower, 1969.
The Cabbage Patch, Barker, 1947.
Nymph in Clover, Barker, 1948.
The True and Pathetic Story of Desbarollda the Waltzing Mouse, Drummond, 1948.
The Inconstant Moon, Barker, 1949.
(With Hazel Pynegar) *Somebody's Rocking My Dreamboat,* Barker, 1949.
Tales of Mystery and Revenge, Barker, 1950, reprinted, Mayflower, 1969.
(With Pynegar) *Cuckoo in the Dell,* Barker, 1951.
The Rift in the Lute, Barker, 1952.
Where Did Everybody Go?, Barker, 1960.
The Loner, Triton, 1967.
Edgar Cayce on Reincarnation, edited by Hugh Lynn Cayce, Hawthorn, 1968.
A Dream of Dragonflies, Macmillan, 1970.
(Editor) Jasper Swain, *On the Death of My Son,* Turnstone Books, 1974.

PLAYS

Farm of Three Echoes (first produced in London, 1935; produced in New York at Cort Theatre, November, 1939; also see below), Samuel French, 1940.
Three Plays: Farm of Three Echoes, For Ever, Friendly Relations (also see below), Miles, 1936.
Little Lambs Eat Ivy: A Light Comedy in Three Acts, (first produced, 1947; also produced as "The Walrus and the Carpenter"), Samuel French, 1950, reprinted, Mayflower, 1969.
(With Robert Morley) *Edward, My Son* (first produced in New York at Martin Beck Theatre, September, 1948; also see below), Samuel French, 1948.
"The Burning Bush" (adaptation), first produced in New York at Erwin Piscator Dramatic Workshop, December, 1949.
An Elegance of Rebels: A Play in Three Acts, Barker, 1960.

Also author of plays "Queer Cargo," 1934, "For Ever," 1934, "Friendly Relations," "No Regrets," 1937, "Cage Me a Peacock" (musical adaptation of his own book), 1948, "The Gentle Rain," and "Married Alive," 1952.

SCREENPLAYS

"Maytime," Metro-Goldwyn-Mayer (MGM), 1936.
"The Wizard of Oz," MGM, 1939.
"Florian," MGM, 1940.
"Unexpected Uncle," RKO, 1941.
"I Became a Criminal," Warner Brothers, 1947, originally titled "They Made Me a Fugitive," also titled "They Made Me a Criminal."
"Edward, My Son" (adapted from the play by the author and Morley), MGM, 1948.
"Adam and Evalyn," Universal, 1949, originally titled "Adam and Evelyne."
(With W. Somerset Maugham and R. C. Sherriff) "Trio," Paramount, 1950.
"Tom Brown's Schooldays," United Artists, 1951.
"A Christmas Carol," United Artists, 1951, originally titled "Scrooge."
"Ivanhoe," MGM, 1952.
"Pickwick Papers," Mayer-Kingsley, 1952.
"Knights of the Round Table," MGM, 1953.
"The Prisoner of Zenda," MGM, 1953.
"The Adventures of Sadie," Twentieth Century-Fox, 1954, originally titled "Our Girl Friday."
"Svengali," MGM, 1954.
"The Vagabond King," Paramount, 1956.
"The Search for Bridey Murphy," Paramount, 1956.
"The Circle," Kassler Films, 1957, originally titled "The Vicious Circle."

Also author of screenplays "Queer Cargo," "Shadows of Fire," "Father Knows Best," and "Snow White and the Three Stooges," for Twentieth Century-Fox, released in Britain as "Snow White and the Three Clowns."

SIDELIGHTS: Noel Langley was only twenty-six years old when producer Mervyn LeRoy asked him to write the film script for the MGM movie "The Wizard of Oz." Langley had already established himself as one of Hollywood's fastest scriptwriters—he produced a shooting script for the Nelson Eddy-Jeanette MacDonald hit picture "Maytime" in less than four days—and he produced a forty-three page adaptation of the novel by L. Frank Baum in only eleven days. Many of Langley's changes remain in the final version of the film; he introduced the Kansas farmhands who later appear in Oz as the Scarecrow and Tin Woodman, and Miss Gulch, the alter ego of the Wicked Witch of the West.

BIOGRAPHICAL/CRITICAL SOURCES:

BOOKS

Harmetz, Aljean, *The Making of "The Wizard of Oz,"* new edition, Delta, 1989.

PERIODICALS

New York Times, May 10, 1936, March 28, 1937, March 8, 1953.
Times Literary Supplement, December 14, 1935, December 18, 1937.

OBITUARIES:

PERIODICALS

Times (London), November 15, 1980.*

LANSDOWNE, J(ames) F(enwick)   1937-

PERSONAL: Born August 8, 1937, in Hong Kong; son of Ernest (an engineer) and Edith (Ford) Lansdowne; married Patricia Fraser McAfee, May 15, 1964 (divorced, 1973); married Helen Nicholson; children: (second marriage) Tristram, Emma. *Education:* Attended school in Canada.

ADDRESSES: Home—681 Transit Rd., Victoria, British Columbia, Canada. *Office*—941 Victoria Ave., Victoria, British Columbia, Canada V8S 4N6.

CAREER: Artist and writer. Art work has been exhibited at various galleries, including Smithsonian Institution, Washington, D.C., Audubon House, New York, N.Y., Oakland Museum, Oakland, Calif., Royal Ontario Museum, Toronto, Vancouver Art Gallery, Vancouver, British Columbia, and Tryon Galleries, London, England; work is also included in numerous permanent collections, including Montreal Museum of Fine Arts, Art Gallery Victoria, and Ulster Museum.

MEMBER: Federation of Canadian Artists, Royal Canadian Academy of Arts, Explorers Club (fellow), Canadian Nature Federation.

AWARDS, HONORS: Officer, Order of Canada.

WRITINGS:

(With John A. Livingston, and illustrator) *Birds of the Northern Forest,* McClelland & Stewart, 1966.
(With Livingston, and illustrator) *Birds of the Eastern Forest,* McClelland & Stewart, Part 1, 1968, Part 2, 1970.
(Self-illustrated) *Birds of the West Coast,* M. F. Feheley, Volume 1, 1976, Volume 2, 1980.
(Illustrator) S. Dillon Ripley, *Rails of the World,* David Godine, 1977.
(Illustrator) David Stokes, *A Guide to the Behavior of Common Birds,* Little, Brown, 1979.

SIDELIGHTS: J. F. Lansdowne is a well-known and respected artist specializing in capturing the beauty and gracefulness of birds in their natural environment. Several members of the British royal family, including Queen Elizabeth II, Prince Philip, and Prince Charles, have Lansdowne's art work in their collections. In a review of *Birds of the Northern Forest, Atlantic* critic Phoebe Adams writes that Lansdowne's work shows that he "has spent a great deal of time watching his subjects fly, perch, hop, scratch, and study inquisitive artists." Adams also remarks that in this book "the paintings record not only color but structure, volume, texture, characteristic, [and] motion."

BIOGRAPHICAL/CRITICAL SOURCES:

PERIODICALS

Atlantic, December, 1966.

*   *   *

LANT, Jeffrey Ladd   1947-

PERSONAL: Born February 16, 1947, in Maywood, Ill.; son of Donald Marshall (a credit manager) and Shirley Mae (Lauing) Lant. *Education:* Attended University of St. Andrew, 1967-68; University of California, Santa Barbara, B.A., 1969 (summa cum laude); Harvard University, M.A., 1970, Ph.D., 1975; Northeastern University, certificate, 1976.

ADDRESSES: Office—Jeffrey Lant Associates, Inc., 50 Follen St., Suite 507, Cambridge, Mass. 02138.

CAREER: Boston College, Chestnut Hill, Mass., coordinator of student services for evening college, 1976-78; Radcliffe College, Cambridge, Mass., assistant to president, 1978; Jeffrey Lant Associates, Inc. (consultants), Cambridge, founder and president, 1979—. Member of national advisory board, National Association of Independent Publishers.

AWARDS, HONORS: Official citations from Boston City Council, 1977, for work in adult continuing education, from Massachusetts House of Representatives, 1977, and from governor of Massachusetts, 1978, both for work with youth unemployment, from governor of Massachusetts, 1982, for services to business, from City of Cambridge, 1983, for service to nonprofit organizations, from City of Eureka, Calif., 1985, for services to small business, from City of Charleston, S.C., 1986, for services to nonprofit organizations, from City of Cape May, N.J., 1986, for services to small business, from State of Texas, 1988, for independent publishing services, and from City of Virginia Beach, Va., for services to adult education; Writer of the Year, Learning Resources Network, 1985.

WRITINGS:

Insubstantial Pageant: Ceremony and Confusion at Queen Victoria's Court, Taplinger, 1980.
Development Today: A Fund Raising Guide for Nonprofit Organizations, JLA Publications, 1980, 4th revised edition, 1990.
The Consultant's Kit: Establishing and Operating Your Successful Consulting Business, JLA Publications, 1982, 3rd edition, 1990.
(Editor) *Our Harvard: Reflections on College Life by Twenty-two Distinguished Graduates,* Taplinger, 1982.
The Unabashed Self-Promoter's Guide: What Every Man, Woman, Child, and Organization in America Needs to Know about Getting Ahead by Exploiting the Media, JLA Publications, 1983, 2nd revised edition, 1990.
Tricks of the Trade: The Complete Guide to Succeeding in the Advice Business, JLA Publications, 1986.
Money Making Marketing: Finding the People Who Need What You're Selling and Making Sure They Buy It, JLA Publications, 1987.
Money Talks: The Complete Guide to Creating a Profitable Workshop or Seminar in Any Field, JLA Publications, 1988, 2nd revised edition, 1989.
Cash Copy: How to Present Your Products and Services So Your Prospects Buy Them . . . Now!, JLA Publications, 1989.
How to Make a Whole Lot More Than $1,000,000 Writing, Commissioning, Publishing, and Selling "How-To" Information, JLA Publications, 1990.

Author of internationally-syndicated column "The Sure-Fire Business Success Column." Member of editorial board, *Limited Partnership Investment Review.*

SIDELIGHTS: Jeffrey Ladd Lant is known for his enterprise and initiative in creating his own consulting firm in 1979. Since then, his salary, according to the *Ann Arbor News,* "has multiplied . . . ten times over," and his business has expanded into the publishing world. Despite his phenomenal success, however, he advises others against simply abandoning their current positions to become consultants. "You'll never succeed as a consultant by just quitting your job," Lant tells the *Pittsburgh Business Times.* "Get so many clients first that you have to quit to handle them all."

Lant once told *CA:* "I'm interested in showing people, in detail, how America works and how to take advantage of circumstances. Each one of my books is an 'insider's' book—a look in-side an institution (like Harvard University or the Court of Queen Victoria, going back to my first book), or at a subject which is very much misunderstood: like setting up a consulting business or raising money for nonprofit organizations. *The Unabashed Self-Promoter's Guide* strips the media bare and will tell people and organizations how to exploit it for their own advantage. I've found that people have a hunger for this kind of information, and I shall continue to provide it."

Lant more recently wrote: "Over the past ten years I've written a book each year, each time devoting a good deal of attention to considering what my market really wants. Recently, I've been concentrating on providing marketing information, information that enables people to sell their products and services faster. With the entrepreneurial explosion of the last decade, hundreds of thousands of people have started businesses that they now must run profitably. I'm here to help them! That's what *Cash Copy: How to Offer Your Products and Services so Your Prospects Buy Them . . . Now!* and *Money Making Marketing* do. My latest book takes my research a step further. Now I provide information on just what it takes to create information products that my readers can use to profit from for years to come. In short, if I cannot yet provide a Fountain of Youth, at least I can tell them how to create a lifetime's Fountain of Income."

BIOGRAPHICAL/CRITICAL SOURCES:

BOOKS

Bailey, Geoffrey, *Maverick,* F. Watts, 1983.

PERIODICALS

Ann Arbor News, April 7, 1982.
Boston Globe, February 21, 1982, June 26, 1982.
Business Week, November 15, 1982.
Christian Science Monitor, December 22, 1980.
Pittsburgh Business Times, April 5, 1982.
Washington Post Book World, November 20, 1982.

*   *   *

LARSEN, Gaylord 1932-

PERSONAL: Born January 4, 1932, in Canova, S.D.; son of Victor D. (a school administrator) and Della R. (Nelson) Larsen; married K. Muriel Geiger, July 28, 1956; children: Gregory, Victor, Kathryn, Kenneth. *Education:* Sioux Falls College, B.A., 1953; University of California, Los Angeles, M.A., 1959. *Religion:* Protestant.

ADDRESSES: Home—1200 Seafarer St., Ventura, Calif. 93001. *Office*—Ventura College, 4667 Telegraph Rd., Ventura, Calif. 93003.

CAREER: American Broadcasting Companies, Inc. (ABC-TV), Los Angeles, Calif., film editor, 1960-61; Young & Rubicam Advertising, Los Angeles, network representative, 1961-68; Ventura College, Ventura, Calif., media specialist, 1971—. Producer of films, including "The Barrel," 1968, and "Agape," 1970, both for Gaylord Productions. *Military service:* U.S. Army, 1953-55.

MEMBER: Writers Guild of American West.

AWARDS, HONORS: Cornerstone Magazine award for best Christian fiction, 1983, for *Trouble Crossing the Pyrenees.*

WRITINGS:

The Kilbourne Connection (mystery), Bethany House, 1981.
Trouble Crossing the Pyrenees (mystery), Regal Books, 1983.
An Educated Death (novel), Ballantine/Epiphany, 1986.
The 180 Degree Murder (novel), Ballantine/Epiphany, 1987.

A Paramount Kill (novel), Dutton, 1988.
Atascadero Island (novel), Ballantine/Epiphany, 1989.
Dorothy and Agatha, Dutton, 1990.

Writer for television series "This Is the Life."

WORK IN PROGRESS: The Fourth Signature; The Girl in the Wall; "Pascal and I," a play.

SIDELIGHTS: Gaylord Larsen told *CA:* "I write from a Christian perspective, and I have an affinity for the mystery format. Working in such a genre I feel my first responsibility to the reader is to entertain. I try to construct an intriguing plot with interesting, if not always likable, characters and I plant enough questions along the way to keep the reader reading.

"Bringing off the mystery, of course, is the big trick. I try to give enough clues in the body of the story to give the reader a fighting chance to come up with the solution on his own. I write my stories backwards in the sense that I first determine the crime, who committed it, and why. Then I begin the story by following the detective or protagonist in a third person narrative, but keeping the vision quite limited to the protagonist's point of view. It is almost like writing two stories at once. We see on the written page what the protagonist knows, but between the lines and in the back of my head is the true story of what actually happened, which the guilty party is trying to keep hidden.

"A current trend in mystery writing is to make the storyline more like a standard novel, but bringing this off successfully is somewhat like walking a tightrope. A mystery requires a tight story line with frequent turns and developments while much of the standard novel is reflective and digressive. Not an easy pair to mix.

"My favorite authors of the genre are Raymond Chandler, Dorothy L. Sayers (quite a Christian writer in her own right), and Ross MacDonald. Chandler's essays on the mystery form are excellent and have helped my own development as a writer."

*   *   *

LARSON, Bruce 1925-

PERSONAL: Born in 1925, in Chicago, Ill.; married Hazel Fischer (an editor); children: Mark, Peter, Christine. *Education:* Lake Forest College, B.A. (with honors), 1949; Princeton Theological Seminary, B.D., 1952; Boston University, M.A., 1956; Eastern College, LL.D.; Seattle Pacific University, D.D.

ADDRESSES: Office—University Presbyterian Church, 4540 15th Ave. N.E., Seattle, Wash. 98105.

CAREER: Ordained Presbyterian minister in 1952; assistant minister of Presbyterian church in Binghampton, N.Y., 1952-55; minister of Presbyterian church in Pana, Ill., 1956-59; Faith at Work, Inc., Columbia, Md., field representative, 1959-62, executive director, 1962-68, president, 1968-73; founder and director of independent research project, Group Research and Individual Learning (GRAIL), 1973—; University Presbyterian Church, Seattle, Wash., senior pastor, 1980—. Visiting fellow, Princeton Theological Seminary, Princeton, N.J., 1975. Host of "Search," a national television series distributed by Communications Foundations, Inc., 1972—. Member of board of directors, Northwest Oncology Foundation; founding board member, Christian Conciliation Service of Puget Sound. Advisory board member, Habitat for Humanity.

AWARDS, HONORS: Lilly Endowment research grant, 1973-75.

WRITINGS:

Dare to Live Now!, Zondervan, 1965.
Setting Men Free, Zondervan, 1967.
Living on the Growing Edge, Zondervan, 1968.
(With Ralph Osborne) *The Emerging Church,* Word, Inc., 1970.
No Longer Strangers, Word, Inc., 1971, reprinted, 1985.
Ask Me to Dance, Word, Inc., 1972.
The One and Only You, Word, Inc., 1974.
(With Keith Miller) *The Edge of Adventure,* Word, Inc., 1974.
Thirty Days to a New You, Zondervan, 1974.
(With Miller) *Living the Adventure,* Word, Inc., 1975.
The Relational Revolution, Word, Inc., 1976.
The Meaning and Mystery of Being Human, Word, Inc., 1978.
(With Miller) *The Passionate People,* Word, Inc., 1979.
There's A Lot More to Health Than Not Being Sick, Word, Inc., 1981.
Believe and Belong, Word, Inc., 1981.
The Communicator's Commentary, Volume 3: *Luke,* edited by Lloyd Ogilvie, Word, Inc., 1984.
Wind and Fire, Word, Inc., 1984.
My Creator, My Friend, Word, Inc., 1986.
The Power to Make Things New: Messages by Bruce Larson, Lloyd John Ogilvie, Word, Inc., 1986.
Faith for the Journey, Revell, 1986.
A Call to Holy Living: Walking with God in Joy, Praise, and Gratitude, Augsburg, 1986.
The Presence: The God Who Delivers and Guides, Harper, 1988.
(With Sarah Henson) *Risk Management: Strategies for Managing Volunteer Programs,* MBA Publications, 1988.

SIDELIGHTS: Bruce Larson's books have been published in German, Chinese, Swedish, Afrikaans, Finnish, and Spanish.

*   *   *

LAWTON, Charles
See HECKELMANN, Charles N(ewman)

*   *   *

LEAS, Speed 1937-

PERSONAL: Born December 26, 1937, in Fresno, Calif.; son of Nathaniel (a contractor) and Ernestine (Burum) Leas; married Constance Stoppel; children: Jocelyn, Winston, Ellen, Nathaniel, Glenn. *Education:* University of California, Berkeley, B.A., 1960; Yale University, M.Div., 1963, M.S.T., 1964; University of California, Los Angeles, professional designation in training and development, 1973.

ADDRESSES: Office—Alban Institute, 17300 Bear Creek Rd., Boulder Creek, Calif. 95006.

CAREER: Ordained minister of United Church of Christ, 1964; University of California, Berkeley, campus minister at Plymouth House, 1959-60; minister of United Church of Christ in Los Angeles, Calif., 1964-67; Center of Metropolitan Mission In-Service Training, Los Angeles, director, 1967-73; Institute for Advanced Pastoral Studies, Bloomfield Hills, Mich., director of action research, 1973-77; Alban Institute, Boulder Creek, Calif., director of consultation, 1977—. Interim director, Joint Metropolitan Strategy and Action Coalition, 1969-70. Has lectured at School of Theology at Claremont, American Baptist Seminary of the West, and Fuller Theological Seminary. Has served on board of directors of Family Planning Centers of Los Angeles, Mafundi

Institute (culture and arts center), Los Angeles Council of Churches, and Learning-Earning Action Program.

MEMBER: Association for Creative Change (professional member), Society for Professionals in Dispute Resolution.

WRITINGS:

(Contributor) Malcolm Boyd, *The Underground Church,* Sheed, 1967.
(With Paul Kittlaus) *Church Fights: Managing Conflict in the Local Church,* Westminster, 1973.
Time Management: A Working Guide for Church Leaders, Abingdon, 1978.
(With Kittlaus) *The Pastoral Counselor in Social Action,* Fortress Press, 1981.
Leadership and Conflict, Abingdon, 1982.
Moving Your Church through Conflict, Alban Institute, 1987.

*   *   *

LEDERMANN, Walter 1911-

PERSONAL: Born March 18, 1911, in Berlin, Germany; son of William (a physician) and Charlotte (Apt) Ledermann; married Rushi Stadler (an analytical psychologist), March 15, 1946; children: Jonathan. *Education:* University of Berlin, state examination (mathematics and physics), 1933; University of St. Andrews, Ph.D., 1936; University of Edinburgh, D.Sc., 1940.

ADDRESSES: Home—10 Hove Park Rd., Hove, Sussex BN3 6LA, England. *Office*—Department of Mathematics, University of Sussex, Falmer, Brighton, England.

CAREER: St. Andrews University, St. Andrews, Scotland, lecturer in mathematics, 1938-46; University of Manchester, Manchester, England, lecturer, 1946-52, senior lecturer in mathematics, 1952-62; University of Sussex, Falmer, Brighton, England, reader, 1962-65, professor of mathematics, 1965-78, professor emeritus, 1978—. Visiting professor of mathematics at Notre Dame University, Ohio State University, Israel Institute of Technology (Haifa), National University of Mexico, and Aarhus (Denmark). Consultant to John Wiley & Sons (publishers).

MEMBER: Institute of Mathematics and Its Applications (member of council, 1973-75), Edinburgh Mathematical Society, Royal Society of Edinburgh, London Mathematical Society (member of council, 1967-78).

WRITINGS:

Introduction to the Theory of Finite Groups, Oliver & Boyd, 1949, 5th revised edition, 1964.
Complex Numbers, Routledge & Kegan Paul, 1958.
Integral Calculus, Routledge & Kegan Paul, 1964.
Multiple Integrals, Routledge & Kegan Paul, 1966.
Introduction to Group Theory, Longman, 1973, reprinted, 1989.
Introduction to Group Characters, Cambridge University Press, 1977, 2nd edition, 1987.

Editor, "Library of Mathematics," 25 volumes, Routledge & Kegan Paul, 1950—; chief editor, "Handbook of Applicable Mathematics," seven volumes with six guidebooks, Wiley, 1980—. Editor, *Journal of London Mathematical Society,* 1968-70, and *Bulletin of London Mathematical Society,* 1973-75. Some of Ledermann's works have been translated into Spanish, Italian, and German.

AVOCATIONAL INTERESTS: Amateur chamber music, foreign travel.

LEE, James Michael 1931-

PERSONAL: Born September 29, 1931, in New York, N.Y.; son of James (a certified public accountant) and Emma (Brenner) Lee; married Marlene Mayr, October 16, 1976; children: James Paul, Michael F. X., Patrick J. *Education:* St. John's University, A.M., 1956, Ed.D., 1958. *Politics:* Democrat. *Religion:* Roman Catholic.

ADDRESSES: Home—5316 Meadow Brook Rd., Birmingham, Ala. 35242. *Office*—School of Education, University of Alabama at Birmingham, University Station, Birmingham, Ala. 35294.

CAREER: Teacher in New York City secondary schools, 1955-59; lecturer at Seton Hall University, South Orange, N.J., and Hunter College (now of the City University of New York), New York City, 1959-60; St. Joseph College, West Hartford, Conn., assistant professor of education, 1959-62; University of Notre Dame, Notre Dame, Ind., assistant professor, 1962-65, associate professor, 1965-68, professor of education, 1968-77, chairman of department, 1966-71; University of Alabama at Birmingham, professor of education, 1977—, chairman of department of secondary education and educational foundations, 1977-79. Founder and publisher, Religious Education Press. Neighborhood Study Help Program, South Bend, Ind., vice president, and principal investigator of Office of Economic Opportunity study.

MEMBER: American Educational Research Association, Association of Professors and Researchers in Religious Education (member of executive committee, 1972-73, 1978), Religious Education Association (member of research committee, 1970—; member of board of directors, 1979—), Society for the Scientific Study of Religion, National Education Association, National Society for the Study of Education.

AWARDS, HONORS: Fulbright senior research scholar, University of Munich, 1974-75; Religious Education Association Lilly research teaching fellow, 1974-75.

WRITINGS:

Principles and Methods of Secondary Education, McGraw, 1963.
(Senior editor and contributor) *Seminary Education in a Time of Change,* Fides, 1965.
(With Nathaniel J. Pallone) *Guidance and Counseling in Schools: Foundations and Processes,* McGraw, 1966.
(Senior editor and contributor) *Readings in Guidance and Counseling,* Sheed, 1966.
(Editor and contributor) *Catholic Education in the Western World,* University of Notre Dame Press, 1967.
The Purpose of Catholic Schooling, National Education Association, 1968.
(Editor and contributor) *Toward a Future for Religious Education,* Pflaum, 1970.
The Shape of Religious Instruction: A Social-Science Approach, Religious Education Press, 1971.
The Flow of Religious Instruction: A Social-Science Approach, Religious Education Press, 1973.
Forward Together! A Training Program for Religious Educators, Thomas More Association, 1973.
(Editor) *The Religious Education We Need: Toward the Renewal of Christian Education,* Religious Education Press, 1977.
The Content of Religious Instruction, Religious Education Press, 1985.
(Editor and contributor) *The Spirituality of the Religious Educator,* Religious Education Press, 1985.

BIOGRAPHICAL/CRITICAL SOURCES:

PERIODICALS

Newsweek, May 3, 1965.

*   *   *

LEE, Warner
   See BATTIN, B(rinton) W(arner)

*   *   *

LEFKOWITZ, Bernard   1937-

PERSONAL: Born August 24, 1937, in New York, N.Y.; son of Edward and Ann (Fishbein) Lefkowitz; married Abigail Johnston (an illustrator), June 16, 1963. *Education:* City College (now of the City University of New York), B.A., 1959.

ADDRESSES: Home—New York, N.Y.

CAREER: New York Post, New York City, 1961-66, began as reporter, became assistant city editor; Peace Corps, Washington, D.C., evaluation officer with travel in Latin America, North Africa, the South Pacific, and Asia, 1968-69; free-lance writer in New York City, 1970—. Teacher at New School for Social Research, 1963-65, and City College of the City University of New York, 1970-71. Consultant to Ford Foundation, 1970-71.

AWARDS, HONORS: Silurian Society of New York Award, 1965, for best feature article; Edgar Allan Poe Award for best nonfiction, Mystery Writers of America, 1970, for *The Victims: The Wylie-Hoffert Murder Case and Its Strange Aftermath;* Ford Foundation grant.

WRITINGS:

(With Kenneth G. Gross) *The Victims: The Wylie-Hoffert Murder Case and Its Strange Aftermath,* Putnam, 1969 (published in England as *The Sting of Justice: The Wylie Hoffert Murder Case and Its Strange Aftermath,* W. H. Allen, 1971).
Breaktime: Living without Work in a Nine-to-Five World, Hawthorn, 1979.
Tough Change: Growing up on Your Own in America, Free Press, 1987.

Contributor of articles to *Look, Esquire, Nation, Village Voice,* and other publications.

BIOGRAPHICAL/CRITICAL SOURCES:

PERIODICALS

Chicago Tribune, August 30, 1979.
Los Angeles Times Book Review, July 29, 1979.
New York Times Book Review, August 5, 1979, June 5, 1988.
Saturday Review, June 28, 1969.
Washington Post, August 23, 1979.*

*   *   *

LEIGHTON, Frances Spatz

PERSONAL: Born in Geauga County, Ohio. *Education:* Attended Ohio State University.

ADDRESSES: Home—3636 16th St. N.W., Washington, D.C. 20010. *Office*—Metropolitan Sunday Newspapers, 1035 National Press Bldg., Washington, D.C. 20045. *Agent*—Oscar Collier, 875 Avenue of the Americas, New York, N.Y. 10001.

CAREER: Washington correspondent, *American Weekly,* 1950-63, *This Week* magazine, 1963-69, and Metropolitan Newspapers, Washington, D.C., 1965—. Worked as a writer for the International News Service.

MEMBER: National League of American Pen Women, National Press Club, American Newspaper Women's Club, National Women's Coalition, Washington Press Club, Writers League of Washington (president), White House Correspondent Association, Senate Periodical Correspondent Association, Art League.

AWARDS, HONORS: Edgar award, 1961.

WRITINGS:

AUTOBIOGRAPHIES

(With Francois Rysavy) *White House Chef: As Told to Frances Spatz Leighton,* Putnam, 1957.
(With Jane Rucker Barkley) *I Married the Veep,* Vanguard, 1958.
(With Louise Pfister) *I Married a Psychiatrist,* Citadel, 1961.
(With David Greer) *Bum Voyage,* Citadel, 1961.
(With Mini Rhea) *I Was Jacqueline Kennedy's Dressmaker,* Fleet Press, 1962.
(With Lillian Rogers Parks) *It Was Fun Working at the White House,* Fleet Press, 1969.
(With Mary Barelli Gallagher) *My Life with Jacqueline Kennedy,* McKay, 1969.
(With Traphes Bryant) *Dog Days at the White House: The Outrageous Memoirs of the Presidential Kennel Keeper,* Macmillan, 1975.
(With William Miller) *Fishbait: The Memoirs of the Congressional Doorkeeper,* Prentice-Hall, 1977.
(With Jerry Cammarata) *The Fun Book of Fatherhood; or, How the Animal Kingdom Is Helping to Raise the Wild Kids at Our House,* Corwin, 1978.
(With Hugh Alton Carter) *Cousin Beedie and Cousin Hot: My Life with the Carter Family of Plains, Georgia,* Prentice-Hall, 1978.
(With Parks) *My Thirty Years Backstairs at the White House,* Prentice-Hall, 1978.
(With June Allyson) *June Allyson,* Putnam, 1982.
(With Beverly Slater) *Stranger in My Bed,* Arbor House, 1984.

OTHER

(With Deborah Pierce) *I Prayed Myself Slim: The Prayer-Diet Book,* Citadel, 1960.
(With Rysavy) *White House Menus and Recipes* (cookbook), Avon, 1962.
(With Helen Baldwin) *They Call Her Lady Bird* (biography), Macfadden-Bartell, 1964.
(Editor) *The Johnson Wit,* Citadel, 1965.
The Memoirs of Senator Brown, a Capitol Cat, as Told to Frances Spatz Leighton (satire), Fleet Press, 1965.
(With Frank S. Caprio) *How to Avoid a Nervous Breakdown,* Meredith Press, 1969.
(With Rhea) *Sew Simply, Sew Right,* Fleet Press, 1969.
(With Rysavy) *A Treasury of White House Cooking,* Putnam, 1972.
(With John Cote Dahlinger) *The Secret Life of Henry Ford* (biography), Bobbs-Merrill, 1978.
(With Natalie Golos and Frances Golos Golbitz) *Coping with Your Allergies,* Simon & Schuster, 1979.
(With Ken Hoyt) *Drunk before Noon: The Behind the Scenes Story of the Washington Corps,* Prentice-Hall, 1979.
(With Louis Hurst) *The Sweetest Little Club in the World: The U.S. Senate,* Prentice-Hall, 1980.

(With John M. Szostak) *In the Footsteps of John Paul II: An Intimate Personal Portrait,* Prentice-Hall, 1980.

(With Parks) *The Roosevelts: A Family in Turmoil,* Prentice-Hall, 1981.

(With William S. Burroughs) *The Adding Machine: A Summation of Comments,* Seaver, 1984.

(With Oscar Collier) *How to Write and Sell Your First Novel,* Writers Digest, 1986.

The Search for the Real Nancy Reagan, Macmillan, 1987.

Contributor to journals, including *McCall's, Ladies' Home Journal,* and *Good Housekeeping.* Contributing editor to *Family Weekly.*

SIDELIGHTS: A long-time Washington correspondent for various magazines and newspapers, Frances Spatz Leighton has written and co-written about a dozen books concerning the White House and the people who have lived and worked there. Calling herself a "social historian" in a *Publishers Weekly* interview with Robert Dahlin, Leighton remarks that she has gotten much of her information from such unlikely people as the cooks and doormen who once worked at the White House. "Social historians are very happy to have these insights into public figures that no one else can give," she tells Dahlin. "What can a doorkeeper tell you?" she then added. "A lot."

Leighton's first book, *White House Chef: As Told to Frances Spatz Leighton,* was a collaborative effort with Francois Rysavy, who was in charge of the White House kitchen during the Eisenhower administration. "But the book contains not only menus," she relates to Dahlin. "It has anecdotes about the President's eating habits. It didn't quite make the best seller list and, oh, were the Eisenhowers furious at me. I revealed how incompatible they were and eating on little trays, watching TV. It was a unique book that kind of made me. Put me on the map." Since then, Leighton has published many similarly researched books, the most popular of which, *My Thirty Years Backstairs at the White House,* for which she enlisted the aid of one of the White House's domestic servants, made the best sellers list.

MEDIA ADAPTATIONS: My Thirty Years Backstairs at the White House was adapted as a television miniseries in 1979 entitled "Backstairs at the White House."

BIOGRAPHICAL/CRITICAL SOURCES:

PERIODICALS

Detroit News, November 16, 1979.
Los Angeles Times Book Review, June 14, 1987.
New York Times Book Review, July 12, 1987.
Publishers Weekly, October 1, 1979.
Washington Post Book World, July 14, 1981, August 12, 1984.*

*   *   *

LeMASTER, J(immie) R(ay) 1934-

PERSONAL: Born March 29, 1934, in Pike County, Ohio; son of Dennis (a truck driver) and Helen (Smith) LeMaster; married Donna Thompson, May 31, 1952; married second wife, Wanda May Ohnesorge, May 21, 1966; children: (first marriage) Lisa, Lynn, Lon. *Education:* Defiance College, B.S., 1959; Bowling Green State University, M.A., 1962, Ph.D., 1970. *Politics:* "Largely Republican." *Religion:* Presbyterian.

ADDRESSES: Home—201 Harrington Ave., Waco, Tex. 76706. *Office*—Department of English, Baylor University, Waco, Tex. 76789.

CAREER: High school English teacher in Stryker, Ohio, 1959-61, and Bryan, Ohio, 1961-62; Defiance College, Defiance, Ohio, instructor, 1962-65, assistant professor, 1965-69, associate professor, 1969-70, professor of English, 1970-77; Baylor University, Waco, Tex., professor of English and director of American studies, 1977—. Part-time instructor, Indiana University at Fort Wayne (now Indiana University/Purdue University at Fort Wayne), 1965-66. *Military service:* U.S. Navy, 1951-55.

AWARDS, HONORS: Litt.D., Defiance College, 1988.

MEMBER: American Studies Association, Modern Language Association of America, Conference of College Teachers of English, Mark Twain Circle of America, South Central Modern Language Association, American Studies Association of Texas, Texas Association of Creative Writing Teachers.

WRITINGS:

(Editor) *Poets of the Midwest,* Young Publications, 1966.
The Heart is a Gypsy (poems), South & West, 1967.
(Editor) *Morning in the Sun,* Defiance College Publications, 1968.
(Editor with Sanford Sternlicht) *Symposia Poets,* South & West, 1969.
Children of Adam (poems), South & West, 1971.
(Editor with William Chaney) *There Comes a Time,* Defiance College Publications, 1971.
Weeds and Wildflowers (poems), Defiance College Poetry Center, 1975.
(Editor) Jesse Stuart, *The World of Jesse Stuart: Selected Poems,* McGraw, 1975.
(Editor with Mary Washington Clarke) *Jesse Stuart: Essays on His Work,* University Press of Kentucky, 1977.
(Editor) *Jesse Stuart: Selected Criticism,* Valkyrie Press, 1978.
Jesse Stuart: A Reference Guide, G. K. Hall, 1979.
Jesse Stuart: Kentucky's Chronicler Poet, Memphis State University Press, 1980.
(Editor) John Clarke Jordan, *Making Sense of Grammar,* Columbia University Teachers College Press, 1980.
First Person, Second (poems), Tagore Institute of Creative Writing International, 1983.
(With E. Hudson Long) *The New Mark Twain Handbook,* Garland Publishing, 1985.
Purple Bamboo (poems), Tagore Institute of Creative Writing International, 1986.
(Editor with James D. Wilson) *The Mark Twain Encyclopedia,* Garland Publishing, 1991.

Also editor of *The Needle's Eye: Selections on Education from the Autobiographies of Jesse Stuart,* 1990. Contributor to literary journals.

SIDELIGHTS: J. R. LeMaster told *CA:* "My poems have always been a way of making sense of my life, a way of exploring and searching for a stay against chaos and confusion. For that reason my poems come out of crisis, although they come considerably after the crisis. More often than not the crisis is an imagined one, an emotional rather than an intellectual one, and the solution in the form of a poem is therefore an imagined solution. What is gained through writing poetry, I suspect, is imaginative control over the unknown."

*   *   *

LENT, John A(nthony) 1936-

PERSONAL: Born September 8, 1936, in East Millsboro, Pa.; son of John (a railroad worker) and Rose Marie (Marano) Lent;

married Martha Meadows, June 17, 1961 (divorced November 15, 1985); married Roseanne Kueny, July 9, 1988; children: (first marriage) Laura, Andrea, John Vincent, Lisa, Shahnon. *Education:* Ohio University, B.S.J. (with honors), 1958, M.S. (with highest honors), 1960; graduate study at University of Guadalajara, summer, 1961, and Syracuse University, 1962-64; University of Oslo, certificate, 1962; Sophia University, Tokyo, certificate, 1965; University of Iowa, Ph.D. (with highest honors), 1972.

ADDRESSES: Home—669 Ferne Blvd., Drexel Hill, Pa. 19026. *Office*—Department of Journalism, Temple University, Philadelphia, Pa. 19122.

CAREER: West Virginia Institute of Technology, Montgomery, instructor in English and journalism, and director of public relations, 1960-62, 1965-66; Wisconsin State University—Eau Claire (now University of Wisconsin—Eau Claire), assistant professor of journalism, 1966-67; Marshall University, Huntington, W. Va., assistant professor of journalism, 1967-69; Universiti Sains Malaysia, Penang, Malaysia, coordinator and lecturer in mass communications, 1972-74; Temple University, Philadelphia, Pa., associate professor, 1974-76, professor of communications, 1976—. Visiting lecturer, De La Salle College, Manila, Philippines, 1964-65; visiting associate professor, University of Wyoming, 1969-70. Participated in Indian Media Study Tour, New Delhi, summer, 1980. Has chaired and organized panels, lectured, presented papers, and spoken at national and international conferences and symposia in about 30 countries.

MEMBER: International Association for Mass Communication Research (chair of comic art and visual communications working groups), Association for Asian Studies, Asia Mass Communication Research and Information Centre, Latin American Studies Association, Caribbean Studies Association, Malaysia/Singapore/Brunei Studies Group (founding chairman), Philippine Study Group, Sigma Delta Chi, Sigma Tau Delta, Phi Alpha Theta, Kappa Tau Alpha.

AWARDS, HONORS: Fulbright scholar to Philippines, 1964-65; Bethany College (Bethany, W. Va.), Benedum Research Award, and Benedum Distinguished Professor Award, 1987; vice-chancellor research awards, Universiti Sains Malaysia; library collections at Ohio University and Alvina T. Burrows Institute named for Lent; two Broadcast Preceptor Awards, 1979; Outstanding Research Award, Temple University, 1988.

WRITINGS:

Journalism Study of New York Colleges and High Schools, Newhouse Communications Research Center, Syracuse University, 1963.
(Editor) *Readings on the Foreign Press,* West Virginia Institute of Technology, 1965.
Philippine Mass Communications Bibliography: First Cumulation of Sources on Areas of Advertising, Journalism, Newspaper, Magazine, Public Relations, Radio, Television, Movies, [Fort Worth], 1966.
Newhouse, Newspapers, Nuisances: Highlights in the Growth of a Communications Empire, Exposition Press, 1966.
Three Research Studies, West Virginia Institute of Technology, 1966.
Philippine Mass Communications: Before 1811, after 1966, Philippine Press, 1967.
(Editor) *The Asian Newspapers' Reluctant Revolution,* Iowa State University Press, 1971.

Asian Mass Communications: A Comprehensive Bibliography, School of Communications and Theater, Temple University, 1974.
(Contributor) Alan Wells, *Mass Communications: A World View,* National Press, 1974.
Commonwealth Caribbean Mass Communications, State University of New York Press, 1975.
Third World Mass Media and Their Search for Modernity: The Case of Commonwealth Caribbean, 1717-1976, Bucknell University Press, 1977.
(Editor) *Cultural Pluralism in Malaysia: Polity, Military, Mass Media, Education, Religion, and Social Class,* Center for Southeast Asian Studies, Northern Illinois University, 1977.
(Editor) *Broadcasting in Asia and the Pacific: A Continental Survey of Radio and Television,* Temple University Press, 1978.
(Editor) *Malaysian Studies: Present Knowledge and Research Trends,* Center for Southeast Asian Studies, Northern Illinois University, 1979.
Topics in Third World Mass Communications, Asian Research Service, 1979.
Development News, AMIC, 1979.
Caribbean Mass Communications: A Comprehensive Bibliography, African Studies Association, 1981.
(Editor) *Newspapers in Asia: Contemporary Trends and Problems,* Heinemann Educational, 1982.
New World and International Information Order: A Bibliography and Resource Guide, AMIC, 1982.
Women and Mass Media in Asia: An Annotated Bibliography, AMIC, 1985.
Malaysian Studies: Archaeology, Historiography, Geography and Bibliography, Northern Illinois University, 1985.
Comic Art: An International Bibliography, privately printed, 1986.
Global Guide to Mass Media, K.G. Saur, 1987.
Videocassette Recorders in the Third World, Longman, 1988.

Also contributor of chapters to numerous books; also co-author of filmstrip "Pied Type, a Load of Coal and the Laser"; also compiler of slide presentations on Asia and the Caribbean for Vis-Com, Inc., 1972, 1975. Book reviewer, *Choice.* Contributor of over 250 articles to more than one hundred periodicals, including *European Broadcast Review, Television Quarterly, Quill, Gazette* (Amsterdam), *Asian Studies, Silliman Journal* (Philippines), and *Estudios Orientales* (Mexico). Founding editor of *Berita: Newsletter of Malaysia/Singapore/Brunei Studies Group* and *Asian Studies at Temple Newsletter;* founding managing editor of *Witty World;* book review editor of *Asian Thought and Society* and *Studies in Latin American Popular Culture;* associate editor of *International Communications Bulletin,* 1970-72; assistant editor of *Media History Digest* and *Communication Booknotes;* bibliographer for *Journalism Quarterly,* 1969—; member of editorial board of periodicals, including *Crossroads, World Media Report, Philippine Research Bulletin, Human Rights Quarterly, Asian Profile, Indian Journal of Communication,* and *Journal of Pacific Rim Communication.*

WORK IN PROGRESS: Books on Asian films; research on transnationalizing telecommunications in Southeast Asia; Caribbean and Asian bibliographies on mass media; bibliography on women and mass media worldwide; Caribbean mass communications; popular culture in the Caribbean.

SIDELIGHTS: John A. Lent has traveled in Europe, Asia, Latin America, and the Caribbean. He developed and taught the first international communications courses at University of Wisconsin—Eau Claire, Marshall University, University of Wyoming, and Universiti Sains Malaysia. He has also supervised archaeological excavations in Canada, edited an underground newspaper, and helped organize FREE, a group for racial equality in West Virginia. Lent believes that writing comes from rigid discipline; he has now abandoned his earlier practice of writing all night in favor of a strict daytime schedule of 20-40 hours per week.

*   *   *

LESLIE, John Andrew 1940-

PERSONAL: Born August 2, 1940, in Calcutta, India; son of John Leslie (a solicitor, and wartime colonel and military judge) and Diana Elizabeth (Harris) Leslie; married Gillian Margaret Alliston (an economist and computer programmer), August 8, 1964; children: Thomas Kenneth, Katherine Susan. *Education:* Wadham College, Oxford, B.A., 1962, M.A., 1968, M.Litt., 1970.

ADDRESSES: Home—64 Forbes Ave., Guelph, Ontario, Canada N1G 1G4. *Office*—Department of Philosophy, University of Guelph, Guelph, Ontario, Canada N1G 2W1.

CAREER: University of Guelph, Guelph, Ontario, lecturer, 1968-70, assistant professor, 1970-76, associate professor, 1976-82, professor of philosophy, 1982—, chairman of University of Guelph/McMaster University joint doctoral program in philosophy, 1979-80. Professor at McMaster University, 1982—. Visiting fellow, research department of philosophy, Australian National University, 1987.

MEMBER: Canadian Philosophical Association, Canadian Society for the History and Philosophy of Science, American Philosophical Association, Philosophy of Science Association.

AWARDS, HONORS: Fellow of Social Science and Humanities Research Council of Canada, 1980-81.

WRITINGS:

(Contributor) John King-Farlow, editor, *The Challenge of Religion Today,* Neale Watson, 1976.
Value and Existence, Basil Blackwell, 1979.
(Contributor) Nicholas Rescher, editor, *Scientific Explanation and Understanding,* University Press of America, 1983.
(Contributor) Ernan McMullin, editor, *Evolution and Creation,* University of Notre Dame Press, 1984.
(Contributor) G. Coyne, editor, *Newton and the New Direction in Science,* Vatican Observatory, 1988.
(Contributor) R. Russell, editor, *Physics, Philosophy and Theology,* University of Notre Dame Press, 1988.
(Editor) *Physical Cosmology and Philosophy,* Macmillan, 1989.
Universes, Routledge & Kegan Paul, 1989.

Contributor to philosophy journals.

WORK IN PROGRESS: A book on risks to mankind's survival, *Risking the World's End.*

SIDELIGHTS: John Andrew Leslie told *CA:* "*Value and Existence* attempts to explain the universe not by reference to an Omnipotent Being existing outside the universe, but by reference to the universe's own ethical requiredness: the book argues that the ethical need for a good universe might itself be creatively powerful. In *Universes* I looked into the currently popular 'many worlds' cosmologies. This universe of ours seems extremely fine tuned to the production of intelligent life; very small changes in various physical and cosmological constants apparently would have made such life impossible. One possible explanation is that there are many worlds—sometimes called 'universes'—with conditions varying from world to world until sooner or later, somewhere or other, they favor the evolution of intelligent observers. An alternative explanation, one I considered in an article in the journal *Philosophy* some years ago, is that God created our universe with properties suited to intelligent life. But 'God' here may only be a name given to a creative ethical requirement."

BIOGRAPHICAL/CRITICAL SOURCES:

BOOKS

Mackie, J. L., *The Miracle of Theism,* Oxford University Press, 1982.

*   *   *

Le SUEUR, Meridel 1900-

PERSONAL: Born February 22, 1900, in Murray, Iowa; daughter of William Winston and Marion Lucy Wharton (mother later married to Alfred Le Sueur, who adopted the author); married Yasha Rabanoff, 1927 (deceased); children: Rachel Le Sueur, Deborah Le Sueur. *Education:* Attended high school in Fort Scott, Kan., and at American Academy of Dramatic Art. *Politics:* "My politics is that of life." *Religion:* "My religion, the world."

ADDRESSES: Home—1653 Victoria St., St. Paul, Minn. 55118.

CAREER: Writer; has been employed as a journalist and labor reporter. Actress during the 1920s, appeared in films "The Last of the Mohicans" and "The Perils of Pauline." Instructor in writing courses, University of Minnesota.

AWARDS, HONORS: Awarded second prize in Works Progress Administration (WPA) writing contest; recipient of *California Quarterly* annual award, a University of Minnesota grant, and a Bush Foundation grant.

WRITINGS:

Annunciation, Platen Press, 1935.
Salute to Spring and Other Stories, International Publishers, 1940, reprinted, 1983.
North Star Country, Duell, Sloan & Pearce, 1945, University of Nebraska Press, 1984.
Little Brother of the Wilderness: The Story of Johnny Appleseed, Knopf, 1947, Holy Cow, 1988.
Nancy Hanks of Wilderness Road: A Story of Abraham Lincoln's Mother, Knopf, 1949.
Sparrow Hawk (story of an Indian boy), Knopf, 1950, Holy Cow, 1987.
Chanticleer of Wilderness Road: A Story of Davy Crockett, Knopf, 1951, Holy Cow, 1989.
The River Road: A Story of Abraham Lincoln, Knopf, 1954.
Crusaders: The Radical Legacy of Marian and Arthur Le Sueur (biography of her parents), Blue Heron, 1955, reprinted, Minnesota Historical Society, 1984.
Corn Village: A Selection, Stanton & Lee, 1970.
Conquistadores, F. Watts, 1973.
The Mound Builders, F. Watts, 1974.
Rites of Ancient Ripening (poems), edited by Mary Ellen Shaw, Vanilla Press, 1975.
Harvest: Collected Stories (also see below), West End, 1977.
Song for My Time: Stories of the Period of Repression (also see below), West End, 1977.
Women on the Breadlines, West End, 1977.
The Girl (novel), West End, 1979, reprinted, 1985.
Harvest [and] *Song for My Time,* MEP Publications, 1982.

Ripening: Selected Work, 1927-1980, edited by Elaine Hedges, Feminist Press, 1982, 2nd edition, 1986.

(With John Crawford) *Worker Writers,* West End, 1982.

Word Is Movement: Journal Notes from Atlanta to Tulsa to Wounded Knee, Cardinal Press, 1984.

I Hear Men Talking and Other Stories, West End, 1984.

Also author of *We Sing Our Struggles: A Tribute to Us All,* edited by Mary McAnnally, Cardinal Press, and *America, Song We Sang Without Knowing: The Life and Ideas of Meridel Le Sueur,* Little Red Hen Press. Work represented in several anthologies, including *O. Henry Prize Short Stories,* 1946, and *O'Brien Best Stories.* Contributor of short stories and articles to magazines and newspapers. Editor, *Midwest,* 1935, and *People Together,* 1956.

WORK IN PROGRESS: The Dead Child, Memorial, and *The Green Corn Rebellion,* a prose symphony; *Corn: The Song of the Americas,* a narrative poem; "four short novels on Demeter and Persephone in the Midwest."

SIDELIGHTS: Meridel Le Sueur's long and controversial career as a writer began in the Midwest, a region that continues to influence her work. Although a highly regarded novelist and short story writer during the 1930s, Le Sueur's political views and activities were banned as "subversive" by Senator Joseph McCarthy in the early 1950s, resulting in over twenty years of literary obscurity. Since 1970, her books, frequently narrated from a woman's point of view, have found a new audience and popularity.

Le Sueur was born to Marion and William Wharton in Murray, Iowa, in 1900, and is the granddaughter of a Puritan temperance worker who had helped to open the state of Oklahoma. "In 1910, my mother had to kidnap us out of Texas to get away from our father," the author told *Publishers Weekly* interviewer John F. Baker. Like most women and children of that day, she explained, "We were property, [treated] worse than slaves." Le Sueur's mother later married Alfred Le Sueur, a lawyer who founded the Industrial Workers of the World. Writing in the *Nation,* Meredith Tax reports that the couple helped to bring Marxism to middle America by supporting the publication of socialist classics in the form of Haldeman-Julius Little Blue Books. "Ardent socialists, they saw 'a new world' opening before them in their Middle Western kitchen, where such eloquent radicals as Big Bill Haywood, Eugene Debs, Lincoln Steffens and Emma Goldman came and went," relates Blanche Gelfant in the *New York Times Book Review.* Labor union organizers who visited the Le Sueur home often and Indian women the young writer befriended as a girl helped her to develop the communal ideals expressed in her works.

Le Sueur's writings chiefly focus on the people, history, and traditions of her native Midwest. She wrote her first stories "as a little girl on a remaining patch of the American frontier," notes Patricia Hampl in *Ms.* magazine. "I first felt in my bones the immense contradictions of American Midwestern life," she told Hampl, "and also its hidden potential strength and beauty and, above all, the democratic traditions and history of the frontier" among the farmers and Indians of the area.

Le Sueur's works, especially those written during the 1930s, reflect these early concerns; they also exhibit a strong sense of social awareness and social protest. In 1928, after a brief career in Hollywood as an actress and stuntwoman, Le Sueur returned to the Midwest, a return which, Hampl points out, "coincided with the rebirth of activity among various populist and worker groups." Le Sueur became an active participant in this proletar-

ian movement. The commitment she made to writing during this time, as she recalls for Baker, was a commitment to exercise personal freedom and "to express the lives and thoughts of people who were unexpressed," she told Baker. She was one of the first women writers to break the code of silence about the hardships women faced on the American frontier: "My grandmother, who . . . never took a bath except in her shift, couldn't understand why I wanted to reveal what she had spent her life trying to conceal." According to a *Prairie Schooner* reviewer, Le Sueur's Midwestern depression-era stories cut through the "hypocrisy" of American culture and society. In a review of *Salute to Spring and Other Stories,* the reviewer writes, "American mythologies and truisms evaporate as she describes . . . an impoverished husband pressuring an unwilling wife to abort their child, an unemployed college honor student's death from starvation, striking factory workers gunned down by company men."

These initially well-received writings, as well as Le Sueur's association with the Communist party, later served to entangle her in what a critic for the *Worker Writer* calls the events of the "red scare." Hampl explains: "While she was writing the luminous short stories of lives lived in poverty and obscurity which gave her a national reputation, she was also reporting on the strikes, unemployment struggles, breadlines, and the plight of farmers in the Dakotas. . . . Hailed throughout the thirties as a major writer, she was blacklisted during the McCarthy years, because her identity as a radical . . . made her suspect."

As a result, for nearly thirty years Le Sueur found it difficult to publish her work. The *Worker Writer* reports: "Le Sueur gained only the attention of the bloodhounds sent out by the FBI, during the period of the 'Red scare' from 1946 to the mid-Fifties. She had to trade job for job . . . as the FBI visited and intimidated each new employer. Her writing was accepted only in the children's department of Alfred A. Knopf, under a nom de plume at *Seventeen* and *Mademoiselle,* and in the remaining publications of the Communist Party Press."

Since 1970, however, interest in Le Sueur's work has enjoyed a revival of sorts. She told *CA* that not only are her newer books being published, but her older ones have been "re-discovered" by a new generation of readers, particularly those involved with the "women's movement." Le Sueur considers "the young women now struggling to find their creative direction" to be "the people I was writing for [who finally] got born." She added: "I have written all my life of the struggles of the people of America, and the Midwest particularly. My two grandmothers and my mother were feminists and I have written of the life and struggles of women even before it was popular. I find the present the most exciting of my long career because of the visible field of expression in the Indian, Chicano, and women's movements. I am writing more and better, and have an audience—for the first time." More recently, she added, "At eighty five I have three books to finish before I leave this mortal coil. They are the culmination of my life's work and I have just received the Bush Foundation which grants me leisure and time to do this. I feel I am doing my best writing, the most living images and a real chorale of my whole life and my time. It will be like a symphony in three movements: *The Dead Child, Memorial,* and *The Green Corn Rebellion.* Maybe they should be printed together, as they all issue from the same root."

MEDIA ADAPTATIONS: "My People Are My Home," a film based on Le Sueur's work, was produced by the Women's Film Collective of Minnesota.

BIOGRAPHICAL/CRITICAL SOURCES:

BOOKS

Le Sueur, Meridel, *Crusaders: The Radical Legacy of Marian and Arthur Le Sueur,* Minnesota Historical Society, 1984.

PERIODICALS

Chicago Sunday Tribune, November 12, 1950.
Los Angeles Times Book Review, May 30, 1982.
Ms., August, 1975.
Nation, July 3, 1982.
New Republic, September 9, 1940.
New Yorker, June 1, 1940.
New York Herald Tribune Book Review, May 11, 1947, November 6, 1949, November 12, 1950, November 11, 1951, May 16, 1954.
New York Times, May 25, 1947, November 12, 1950, September 5, 1954.
New York Times Book Review, April 4, 1982.
Prairie Schooner, fall, 1977.
Publishers Weekly (interview), May 21, 1982.
San Francisco Chronicle, November 13, 1949.
Saturday Review of Literature, January 5, 1946, May 17, 1947.
Time, June 17, 1940.
Weekly Book Review, December 16, 1945.
Worker Writer, Volume 1, number 15, 1977.*

*   *   *

LIEBER, Robert J(ames) 1941-

PERSONAL: Born September 29, 1941, in Chicago, Ill.; married Nancy Lee Isaksen, June 20, 1964; children: Benjamin Yves, Keir Alexander. *Education:* University of Wisconsin, B.A. (with high honors), 1963; Harvard University, Ph.D., 1968.

ADDRESSES: Office—Department of Government, Georgetown University, Washington, D.C. 20057.

CAREER: University of California, Davis, assistant professor, 1968-72, associate professor, 1972-77, professor of political science, 1977-81, chairman of department, 1975-76 and 1977-80; Georgetown University, Washington, D.C., professor of government, 1982—. Visiting fellow, St. Antony's College, Oxford, 1969-70; fellow, Woodrow Wilson International Center for Scholars, 1980-81; guest scholar, Brookings Institution, 1980-81. Research associate, Harvard University Center for International Affairs, 1974-75, and Atlantic Institute, Paris, 1978-79. Coordinator of Middle East issues in Dukakis presidential campaign, 1987-88. Participant in Washington Institute's presidential study group on U.S. policy in the Middle East.

MEMBER: International Institute for Strategic Studies, American Political Science Association, Council on Foreign Relations. Phi Beta Kappa.

AWARDS, HONORS: NDEA Title IV fellowship in political science, University of Chicago, 1963-64; postdoctoral research training fellowship, Social Science Research Council, 1969-70; International Affairs fellowship, Council on Foreign Relations, 1972; Guggenheim fellowship, 1973; Rockefeller International Relations fellowship, 1978-79; Ford Foundation grant, 1981.

WRITINGS:

British Politics and European Unity: Parties, Elites, and Pressure Groups, University of California Press, 1970.
Theory and World Politics, Winthrop Publishers, 1972.
(Co-author) *Contemporary Politics: Europe,* Winthrop Publishers, 1976.

Oil and the Middle East War, Harvard University Center for International Affairs, 1976.
(Co-editor and contributor) *Eagle Entangled: U.S. Foreign Policy in a Complex World,* Longman, 1979.
(Editor and contributor) *Will Europe Fight for Oil?,* Praeger, 1983.
(Co-editor and contributor) *Eagle Defiant: U.S. Foreign Policy in the 1980s,* Little, Brown, 1983.
The Oil Decade: Conflict and Cooperation in the West, University Press of America, 1986.
(Co-editor and contributor) *Eagle Resurgent?: The Reagan Era in American Foreign Policy,* Little, Brown, 1987.
No Common Power: Understanding International Relations, Scott, Foresman/Little, Brown, 1988.

Contributor to periodicals, including *International Security, International Affairs* (London), *American Political Science Review, Politique Etrangere, Harpers, New York Times,* and *Washington Post.*

WORK IN PROGRESS: Writing on American foreign policy and U.S. relations with Western Europe and the Middle East.

SIDELIGHTS: Robert J. Lieber told *CA* that his "other credits include faculty and party politics, 'killer tennis,' and a walk-on part in the Alfred Hitchcock film classic 'North by Northwest.'"

*   *   *

LINDSLEY, Mary F(rances)
(Mary L. Jaffee)

PERSONAL: Born in New York, N.Y.; daughter of Guy Robert (an actor) and Florence (Everett) Lindsley; married Irving Lincoln Jaffee (a writer), January 26, 1963. *Education:* Hunter College (now Hunter College of the City University of New York), A.B., 1929; Columbia University, M.A., 1932. *Politics:* Independent. *Religion:* Roman Catholic.

ADDRESSES: Home—13361 El Dorado, Apt. 201H, Seal Beach, Calif. 90740.

CAREER: Hunter College (now Hunter College of the City University of New York), New York, N.Y., instructor, 1930-55, assistant professor, 1955-68, associate professor of English literature and creative writing, 1968-71; writer, 1971—. Conducted weekly radio talk show, "Prose and Poetry," California State University, Long Beach, 1978-80; participated in "Let's Rap," for KTTV-TV, 1982; has hour-long program reading her own poetry, public access television in Los Angeles and Long Beach areas, 1987—. Trustee and acting vice-president, World University, Tucson, Ariz., 1982—.

MEMBER: International Biographical Society (fellow), International Institute of Community Service (fellow), United Poets Laureate International, World Poetry Society, Poetry Society of America, Accademia Leonardo da Vinci (honorary representative; member of board of directors), Dickens Fellowship, New York Poetry Forum (California representative; life member), California Federation of Chaparral Poets (president of Orpheus chapter, 1974-76), Sherlock Holmes Society of Los Angeles.

AWARDS, HONORS: Accademia Leonardo da Vinci, bronze medal, 1965, silver medal, 1966; President Marcos Medal from the Philippines, 1968; United Poets Laureate International, golden laurel crown, 1968, 1969, 1973, and 1975, Laureate of Education, 1987; D.H.L. from Free University of Asia, 1969; trophy from California Olympiad of the Arts, 1972, 1976; medal from

Chinese Poetry Society, 1973; Order of Merit of Eight Chinese Virtues from World University, Hong Kong, 1973; D.L.A. from Great China Arts College of World University, 1973; Order of Merit of Six Chinese Arts, 1974; elected to Hall of Fame of Hunter College of the City University of New York, 1978; American Song Festival prize, 1981, for song lyrics; D.Litt. from World University, 1982; Dame of Merit, Sovereign Military Order of Saint John of Jerusalem, Knights of Malta, 1985; Einstein Academy, honorary Ph.D. and Einstein Medal for Continued Achievement, both 1986, and Marconi Medal for Continued Achievement, 1987; honorary Ph.D. from International Institute for Management (Taiwan), 1987; Medal of Honor from ABI (Raleigh, S.C.), 1987, for poetry; first, second, and third prizes in annual contest of California Federation of Chaparral Poets, 1988, for poetry.

WRITINGS:

POETRY

The Uncensored Letter and Other Poems, Island Press Cooperative, 1949.
Grand Tour and Other Poems, Philosophical Library, 1952.
Promenade, Accademia Leonardo da Vinci, 1965.
Pomp and Circumstance, Accademia Leonardo da Vinci, 1966.
Pax Romana, Accademia Leonardo da Vinci, 1967.
Selected Poems, Gaus, 1967.
Otma, Accademia Leonardo da Vinci, 1968.
Rosaria, Accademia Leonardo da Vinci, 1969.
Work Day of Pierre Toussaint, Accademia Leonardo da Vinci, 1970.
Circe and the Unicorn, Accademia Leonardo da Vinci, 1971.
The Masquers, Accademia Leonardo da Vinci, 1972.
One Life, Accademia Leonardo da Vinci, 1974.
Anarch's Hand, Accademia Leonardo da Vinci, 1974.
Night on the Saxon Shore, Accademia Leonardo da Vinci, 1975.
American Cavalcade, Dorrance, 1975.
Wasp in Amber, Accademia Leonardo da Vinci, 1976.
Marvelous Boy, Accademia Leonardo da Vinci, 1977.
Song of Mr. Cibber, Accademia Leonardo da Vinci, 1978.
Age of Reason, Triton Press, 1979.
A Narrow Mind, Accademia Leonardo da Vinci, 1980.
Dr. Burney's Daughter, Accademia Leonardo da Vinci, 1981.
Crisis in Counterpoint, Happy Publishers, 1982.
Georgina, Happy Publishers, 1982.
Bread, Water and Apples, Happy Publishers, 1983.
Shadows in the Tower, Happy Publishers, 1983.
Rubber Stamp, Happy Publishers, 1984.
Harvest Moon, Poets Press (India), 1985.
Simon's Boy, Tam's Books, 1986.
Devil in the Organ Loft, Tam's Books, 1986.
The Disappearing Man (Raoul Wallenberg), Tam's Books, 1987.
The Case for Arthur Nicholls, Tam's Books, 1987.
A House Not Built with Hands, Tam's Books, 1988.

SHORT STORIES

(Under name Mary L. Jaffee, with husband, Irving Lincoln Jaffee) *Beyond Baker Street,* Pontine, 1973.

PLAYS

(With Christine Solomon) "The Flim-flammers" (three-act), first produced in Seal Beach, Calif., 1974.

OTHER

Also author of *Centennial Child,* a five-volume novel about life on the stage in the late 1800s and early 1900s; also author, with Solomon, Laura Steele, and Ethol Pullen, of bicentennial program "California under Nine Flags," produced in Seal Beach, 1976. Author of weekly column "Magic Casements," in *Seal Beach Journal,* 1979-81; author of column in *Malibu Times,* 1985-88.

SIDELIGHTS: Mary F. Lindsley told *CA,* "I believe that an author has under all his humor the obligation to present the truth as he sees it; to ridicule and oppose what is evil, and to inspire his readers to ideals, constructive action, compassion, and, above all, hope."

AVOCATIONAL INTERESTS: Play production, photography, cartooning, travel (Europe and Asia).

* * *

LINDSTROM, Naomi (Eva) 1950-

PERSONAL: Born November 21, 1950, in Chicago, Ill.; daughter of Frederick B. (a sociology professor) and L. L. (a photographer) Lindstrom. *Education:* Attended Universidad Iberoamericana, 1970; University of Chicago, A.B., 1971; Arizona State University, M.A., 1972, Ph.D., 1974.

ADDRESSES: Home—Austin, Tex. *Office*—Department of Spanish and Portuguese, BAT110, University of Texas, Austin, Tex. 78712.

CAREER: Arizona State University, Tempe, instructor in Spanish, 1974-75; University of Texas at Austin, assistant professor, 1975-82, associate professor of Spanish and Portuguese, 1982—. Member of advisory board, Center for Mexican American Studies. Consultant, Fulbright Scholar Awards, Council on International Exchange of Scholars, and Women World Authors Project.

MEMBER: World Union of Jewish Studies, Instituto Internacional de Literatura Iberoamericana, International Pragmatics Association, Modern Language Association of America (chairperson of executive committee on twentieth-century Latin American literature), American Literary Translators Association, American Association of Teachers of Spanish and Portuguese, Latin American Studies Association, Latin American Jewish Studies Association, Southwest Council on Latin American Studies.

AWARDS, HONORS: Mellon Foundation fellowship, 1983-84; Dallas TACA Centennial fellowship, 1987-88.

WRITINGS:

Literary Expressionism in Argentina, Center for Latin American Studies, Arizona State University, 1977.
Macedonio Fernandez, Society for Spanish and Spanish American Studies, 1981.
(Contributor) Margaret Sayers Peden, editor, *The Latin American Short Story,* Twayne, 1983.
(Translator) Roberto Arlt, *The Seven Madmen,* David R. Godine, 1984.
(Translator) Lourdes Espinola, *Womanhood and Other Misfortunes,* Latitudes Press, 1985.
(Editor with Carmelo Virgillo) *Woman as Myth and Metaphor in Latin American Literature,* University of Missouri Press, 1985.
(Translator) Marjorie Agosin, *Women of Smoke,* Latin American Literary Review Press, 1988.
Women's Voice in Literature, Three Continents Press, 1989.
Jewish Issues in Argentine Literature: From Gerchunoff to Szichman, University of Missouri Press, 1989.
(Translator) Agosin, *Bonfires,* Bilingual Press, in press.

(Translator with Fred P. Ellison) Helena Parente Cunha, *Woman between Mirrors,* University of Texas Press, in press.

Contributor to literature and Latin American studies journals. Member of editorial board, University of Texas Press, *Studies in Latin American Popular Culture,* and *University of Texas Studies in Contemporary Spanish-American Fiction;* consultant, Longman Press. Contributing editor, *Chasqui.*

WORK IN PROGRESS: Studies on Argentine Literature, 1910-1950.

SIDELIGHTS: Naomi Lindstrom told *CA:* "My reason for turning to Latin American writing is that, in studying this literature, it is necessary to be aware of and deal with the question of relations between literature and society. I am drawn to this question because it is so difficult to handle in literary criticism. How is it possible to speak of literature's reflection of society without ignoring the characteristics that make it art?

"I began to study Latin American literature in the late 1960's. At that time, recent Latin American writing was greatly in vogue and departments could count on students signing up for certain courses just because of the glamorous aura surrounding such figures as Jorge Luis Borges and Gabriel Garcia Marquez. After this 'boom' of Latin American literature diminished, there were changes in the field. In research, critics were less bedazzled by the few superstars of 1960's writing and began to take more of a look at a greater variety of authors. There was also more of an effort to include neglected areas of writing, such as the work of women writers, writers who had not quite fit in with the main literary tendencies, and writers who had previously been considered not quite literary enough.

"My own critical work frequently is part of this effort to 'exhume' or 'rescue' the writers who have been bypassed in this way. I have a difficult time deciding how far I care to follow the movement to study marginal writers, though. Some of my colleagues would go so far as to include in their area of study illiterates who tape-recorded work and writers of dime novels, and I now view their work with some doubt and wonder.

"In looking for writers who have missed out on proper critical attention but are still within the category of literary workers, I have lately begun to look at the 'proletarian' wing of 1920's Argentine literature. My work so far has been chiefly on the proletarians' supposed rivals, the avant-garde writers of the same period. Certainly the 1920's avant-garde is full of enough radical literary rebels—following strange schemes for remaking literary expression—that one could spend an entire career studying them alone. But the more one looks at the proletarian works of the same years, the more it is evident that the less flashy and less manifesto-issuing proletarians were pursuing many of the same lines of experimentation as the avant-garde faction. Both groups, for instance, were concerned with retooling literary language in Spanish, which they found to be far too ornate, stuffy, and rhetorical. They were all interested in the possibilities of plain speaking, although the explanations they gave were usually unlike. The avant-garde tended to claim it wanted to look upon the beauty of a stark, derhetoricized language, while the proletarians claimed it was the duty of a socially conscious writer to write in a bare manner unlike the ornamentation of elite-class artists.

"I would like to examine texts produced by the proletarians to see the degree to which they utilized the same type of reform measures as the avant-garde. The problem involved would be to see how these writers really relied on art and its techniques to accomplish the innovations they sought, but at the same time not to lose from sight the fact that they were concerned with literature because of a belief it could help bring about changes in society. It is a classic research problem of how to juggle considerations of artistic style with those of literary writing as a social phenomenon."

*   *   *

LINENTHAL, Edward Tabor 1947-

PERSONAL: Born November 6, 1947, in Boston, Mass.; son of Arthur J. (a physician) and Eleanor (a political scientist; maiden name, Tabor) Linenthal; married Ulla Hannele Kuivanen (a microbiologist), 1974; children: Aaron Johannes, Jacob Arthur. *Education:* Western Michigan University, B.A., 1969; Pacific School of Religion, M.Div., 1973; University of California, Santa Barbara, Ph.D., 1979.

ADDRESSES: Home—937 Vine Ave., Oshkosh, Wis. 54901. *Office*—Department of Religion Studies, University of Wisconsin—Oshkosh, Oshkosh, Wis. 54901.

CAREER: University of California, Santa Barbara, lecturer in American religion, 1978-79; University of Wisconsin—Oshkosh, assistant professor, 1979-84, associate professor, 1984-89, professor of religious studies, 1989—, John McRosebush Professor, 1989-90. Post-doctoral fellow, Defense and Arms Control Studies Program, Massachusetts Institute of Technology, 1986-87. Executive director of Wisconsin Institute for the Study of War, Peace, and Global Cooperation, 1989—.

MEMBER: American Academy of Religion, American Society of Church History.

AWARDS, HONORS: Regents fellowship, University of California, Santa Barbara, 1978-79; distinguished teaching award, University of Wisconsin—Oshkosh, 1984-85.

WRITINGS:

Changing Images of the Warrior Hero in America: A History of Popular Symbolism, Edwin Mellen, 1983.
Symbolic Defense: The Cultural Significance of the Strategic Defense Initiative, University of Illinois Press, 1989.
(Editor and contributor with Ira Chernus) *A Shuddering Dawn: Religious Studies in the Nuclear Age,* State University of New York Press, 1989.

Contributor to *Religious Periodicals of the United States* and *Twentieth Century Shapers of American Popular Religion.* Also contributor to journals, including *Soundings, Journal of the American Academy of Religion, Bulletin of the Atomic Scientists, Southwestern Historical Quarterly, Fides et Historia, Christian Century,* and *Studies in Popular Culture.* Assistant editor of book review section of *Religious Studies Review,* 1981—.

WORK IN PROGRESS: Research on religions of the American presidents, martial space in America, and nuclear warfare and American culture.

SIDELIGHTS: Edward Tabor Linenthal told *CA:* "I have always been fascinated by the power of war in human experience, and much of my writing suggests ways we have symbolized war and warrior heroes. My book on American battlefields will examine a part of American patriotic religion that has been curiously neglected by students of American culture. These martial ceremonial centers are found throughout the nation and provide places for the celebration of patriotic orthodoxies as well as places where these orthodoxies are called into question. It is rich and exciting material to write about."

LISTON, Robert A. 1927-

PERSONAL: Born August 23, 1927, in Youngstown, Ohio; son of Benjamin Furman and Lola (Carder) Liston; married Jean Altman, September 8, 1950; children: Cynthia Kay, Stephen Ward, Felicia Kay. *Education:* Hiram College, A.B., 1949.

ADDRESSES: Home—423B East Sola St., Santa Barbara, Calif. 93101.

CAREER: Newspaperman in Marion, Ohio, 1954, and Mansfield, Ohio, 1954-56; *Baltimore News American,* Baltimore, Md., newspaperman, 1956-64; full-time free-lance writer. *Military service:* U.S. Army, Infantry, 1952-53; served in Korea.

AWARDS, HONORS: Christopher Book Award, 1974, for *The Right to Know: Censorship in America.*

WRITINGS:

Sargent Shriver: A Candid Portrait, Farrar, Straus, 1964.
Your Career in Law Enforcement, Messner, 1965, revised edition, 1973.
Your Career in Civil Service, Messner, 1966.
Your Career in Transportation, Messner, 1966.
Great Detectives, Platt and Munk, 1966.
Tides of Justice, Delacorte, 1966.
On-the-Job Training and Where to Get It, Messner, 1967, revised edition, 1973.
Your Career in Selling, Messner, 1967.
The Dangerous World of Spies and Spying, Platt and Munk, 1967.
(With Robert M. N. Crosby) *The Waysiders: Reading and the Dyslexic Child,* Delacorte, 1968 (published in England as *Reading and the Dyslexic Child,* Souvenir Press, 1969).
Downtown: Our Challenging Urban Problems, Delacorte, 1968.
Politics from Precinct to President, Delacorte, 1968.
What You Should Know about Pills, Pocket Books, 1968.
The Pros, Platt & Munk, 1968.
(With Surrey Marshe) *The Girl in the Centerfold,* Dell, 1969.
Slavery in America: The History of Slavery (Child Study Association book list), McGraw, 1970.
The American Poor (Child Study Association book list), Delacorte, 1970.
Greetings, You Are Hereby Ordered for Induction: The Story of the Draft, McGraw, 1970.
The Limits of Defiance: Strikes, Rights and Government, F. Watts, 1971.
Young Americans Abroad, Messner, 1971.
Dissent in America, McGraw, 1971.
Edge of Madness: Prisons and Prison Reform in America, F. Watts, 1972.
Slavery in America: The Heritage of Slavery, McGraw, 1972.
Who Shall Pay?: Taxes and Tax Reform in America, Messner, 1972, revised edition, 1976.
When Reason Fails: Psychotherapy in America, Macrae, 1972.
Presidential Power: How Much Is Too Much?, McGraw, 1972.
The American Political System, Parents Magazine Press, 1972.
The Right to Know: Censorship in America, F. Watts, 1973.
The United States and the Soviet Union: A Background Book on the Struggle for Power, Parents Magazine Press, 1973.
The Ugly Palaces: Housing in America, F. Watts, 1974.
Violence in America: A Search for Perspective, Messner, 1974.
Healing the Mind: Eight Views of Human Nature, Praeger, 1974.
Who Really Runs America?, Doubleday, 1974.
Who Stole the Sunset?: Dilemmas in Morality, Thomas Nelson, 1974.

Defense against Tyranny: A Balance of Power in Government, Messner, 1975.
We, the People?: Congressional Power, McGraw, 1975.
Getting in Touch with Your Government, Messner, 1975.
Promise or Peril?: The Role of Technology in Society, Thomas Nelson, 1976.
Patients or Prisoners?: The Mentally Ill in America, F. Watts, 1976.
By These Faiths: Religions for Today, Messner, 1977.
The Charity Racket, Thomas Nelson, 1977.
Why We Think as We Do, F. Watts, 1977.
Terrorism, Thomas Nelson, 1977.
Women Who Ruled: Cleopatra to Elizabeth II, Messner, 1978.
An Affair of State (novel), Pinnacle Books, 1978.
The Great Teams: Why They Win All the Time, Doubleday, 1979.
The Brandywine Exchange (novel), Tor Books, 1987.
The Seraphim Code (novel), Tor Books, 1988.
The Pueblo Surrender: A Covert Action by the National Security Agency, M. Evans, 1989.

Also author of more than twenty other novels under pseudonyms.

SIDELIGHTS: Robert A. Liston told *CA:* "I have had four distinct and overlapping literary careers: newspaperman, magazine journalist, nonfiction author, and novelist. In my twenties, when I began, my mentor, the late Sterling Noel, asked me why I wanted to write. 'To make some money,' I said. He replied, 'Kid, you'll make more money driving a bus.' Surely correct. In my forties I told someone I was motivated by glory. Surely a chimera. In my sixties I can now answer the question. Some writers speak of the search for completeness and of playing God in creating characters. I agree, but I would add: *for the love of it.* It is pure pleasure, the most fun thing I know to do. My son, a performer on the guitar, cannot imagine doing something where you receive no applause, no recognition. But then he is young."

Liston's books have been published in Britain and have been translated into Dutch, German, Swedish, Italian, and Japanese.

* * *

LONG, Robert 1954-

PERSONAL: Born October 15, 1954, in New York, N.Y.; son of Robert, Sr., and Mary (Gillick) Long. *Education:* Long Island University, B.A., 1977; Vermont College, M.F.A., 1984.

ADDRESSES: Home—25 Mudford Ave., Easthampton, N.Y. 11937. *Office*—Department of English, Southampton College, Southampton, N.Y. 11968. *Agent*—Ali Cole, 7 Sherrill Rd., Easthampton, N.Y. 11937.

CAREER: Southampton College, Southampton, N.Y., adjunct associate professor of English, 1979—.

WRITINGS:

Getting out of Town (poems), Street Press, 1978.
What It Is (poetry chapbook), Street Press, 1980.
(Editor) *Long Island Poets,* Permanent Press, 1986.
The Sonnets (poems), Illuminati, 1988.
What Happens (poems), Galileo Press, 1988.

Also contributor of poems to anthologies. Contributor to periodicals, including *New Yorker, Poetry, Partisan Review, Antioch Review,* and *American Scholar.*

WORK IN PROGRESS: Thirteen Stories; The Ruminations (poems).

LOOMES, Brian 1938-

PERSONAL: Born in 1938, in Leeds, England. *Education:* University of Leeds, B.A., 1962.

ADDRESSES: Home and office—Calf Haugh Farmhouse, Pateley Bridge, North Yorkshire, England.

CAREER: Antiques dealer, specializing in country clocks, 1966—.

MEMBER: Society of Genealogists (fellow).

WRITINGS:

Yorkshire Clockmakers, Dalesman Publishing, 1972, revised edition, George Kelsall, 1985.
The White Dial Clock, David & Charles, 1974.
Westmorland Clocks and Clockmakers, David & Charles, 1975.
Lancashire Clocks and Clockmakers, David & Charles, 1976.
Country Clocks and Their London Origins, David & Charles, 1976.
Watch and Clock Makers of the World, NAG Press, 1976, revised edition, 1989.
Complete British Clocks, David & Charles, 1978.
The Early Clockmakers of Great Britain, NAG Press, 1980.
Clocks: Guide to Dating and Valuation, Model & Allied Publications, 1980.
Grandfather Clocks and Their Cases, David & Charles, 1985.

Also author of television script "Sanctuary," 1980.

AVOCATIONAL INTERESTS: "Self-sufficiency, cultivation, gardening, and returning to the land."

*   *   *

LOPSHIRE, Robert M(artin) 1927-

PERSONAL: Born April 14, 1927, in Sarasota, Fla.; son of Conrad A. and Jessie (Martin) Davidson; adopted, 1931, by Roy Howard and Dorothy (DeLaGrange) Lopshire; married Jane Haller Ingalls, October 21, 1946 (divorced); married Selma Dorothy Stefel, February 21, 1974; children: Robert Martin, Jr., Howard Clyde, Terri Jane, Victoria Anne. *Education:* Attended Vesper George School of Art and School of Practical Art, both Boston, Mass., 1946-48.

ADDRESSES: Home—California.

CAREER: Free-lance artist and illustrator in Philadelphia, Pa., 1948-54, Boston, Mass., 1954-56, and New York City, 1956-59; Random House, New York City, creative art director, 1959-61; owner of advertising agency in Sergeantsville, N.J., 1961-64; writer. Consulting art director for companies in New York. *Military service:* U.S. Coast Guard, 1944-45, served in Pacific theatre; Air Sea Rescues, 1945-46, combat photographer; received invasion awards.

AWARDS, HONORS: I Want to Be Somebody New was chosen for the International Reading Association's Booklist of 1987.

WRITINGS:

Put Me in the Zoo, Random House, 1960.
How to Make Flibber, Etc., Random House, 1964, published as *The Beginner's Book of Things to Make: Fun Stuff You Can Make Yourself,* Beginner Books, 1977.
Beginner's Guide to Building and Flying Model Airplanes, Harper, 1967.
I Am Better Than You!, Harper, 1968.
It's Magic?, Macmillan, 1969.
Radio Control Miniature Aircraft, Macmillan, 1974.

How to Make Snop Snappers and Other Fine Things, Greenwillow, 1977.
The Biggest, Smallest, Fastest, Tallest Things You've Ever Heard Of, Crowell Junior Books, 1980.
ABC Games, Crowell Junior Books, 1986.
I Want to Be Somebody New, Beginner Books, 1986.
I Can Draw, Scholastic, Inc., 1988.

Illustrator of numerous children's books, including works by Kin Platt and Richard Margolis. Contributor to *World Book Encyclopedia;* contributor to magazines, including *Model Airplane News.*

WORK IN PROGRESS: Numerous children's book ideas.

SIDELIGHTS: Robert M. Lopshire told *CA:* "Two constant questions, when people find that I am a writer and artist, are: 'How did you get started?' and 'Where do you get your ideas?'

"There is no simple party-chatter answer to either question, as any writer or artist will be quick to admit. My feeling is that an artist or writer becomes so by a dedicated conviction that what boils within must be put down for others to see, study, and comment on. Many of us look forward to the acclaim—it bolsters our egos, or demolishes them so much that we try harder the next time if our work is snubbed.

"I would be dishonest if I said that I did not enjoy hearing that people like my work, but having chosen to write mainly for children, I have developed a bit different outlook. . . . I ignore the critics, be they kind or cutting. My audience is children—I write and draw for *them,* not the critics or any possible awards.

"I am personally offended by those writers I see pushing their books on television talk shows and the lecture circuits. (I turn down all such invitations.) A book, article, drawing, or painting should stand on its own for what it is . . . not as something sold by media or appearance hype. While I agree that the media should be used to inform of existing works, I find the public appearance of writers and artists promising more than they've done to be repugnant, just as I dislike the annual awards handed out to children's books that the children themselves never had a chance to vote for.

"Personally, the best award I've ever received was the news that one of my books was the most often stolen from a large metropolitan library system. I put a tremendous amount of effort into trying to give kids what *they* want . . . what better tribute could any writer ask for than a theft record? Of course, it would now seem only fitting that I do a book about why one should not go about stealing books from libraries!"

AVOCATIONAL INTERESTS: Model aircraft, painting, "stimulating young minds to think and go further than the immediate limits of their own small world."

*   *   *

LORD, Nancy
See TITUS, Eve

*   *   *

LOTTMAN, Eileen 1927-
(Harry Barney, Mike Cogan, Jessica Evans, Molly Flute, Samantha Mellors, Maud Willis)

PERSONAL: Born August 15, 1927, in Minneapolis, Minn.; daughter of Myer (a certified public accountant) and Goldye

(Cohn) Shubb; married Evan Lottman (a motion picture film editor), August 25, 1956; children: Jessica. *Education:* Attended University of Iowa, 1945-50.

ADDRESSES: Home—15 West 72nd St., New York, N.Y. 10023.

CAREER: Held numerous odd jobs, 1950-53; Arthur P. Jacobs Co., New York City, film press agent, 1953-64; G. P. Putnam's Sons, New York City, publicity director, 1964-68; Dell Publishing Co., New York City, publicity director, 1968-69; Bantam Books, New York City, editor, 1969-71; free-lance writer, 1971—. Instructor in screenwriting, Brooklyn College of the City University of New York, 1980-83. Member of executive board, Pen American Center.

WRITINGS:

NOVELS

The Hemlock Tree, Popular Library, 1975.
Summersea, Coward, 1975.
After the Wind, Dell, 1979.
(Under pseudonym Harry Barney) *The Package,* Dell, 1980.
The Brahmins, Delacorte, 1982.
(Co-translator from the French) Charlotte Wagner, *Sweet Cakes,* Pinnacle Books, 1983.

NOVELIZATIONS OF FILM AND TELEVISION SCRIPTS

(Under pseudonym Maud Willis) *The Devils' Rain,* Dell, 1975.
(Under pseudonym Maud Willis) *Doctors' Hospital,* Pocket Books, 1975.
The Bionic Woman: Welcome Home, Jaime, Berkeley Books, 1976.
The Bionic Woman: Extracurricular Activities, Berkeley Books, 1977.
(Under pseudonym Molly Flute) *Through the Looking Glass,* Dell, 1977.
The Greek Tycoon, Warner Books, 1978.
(Under pseudonym Jessica Evans) *Blind Sunday,* Scholastic Book Services, 1978.
(Under pseudonym Samantha Mellors) *The Orphan,* Jove, 1979.
All Night Long, Jove, 1980.
Rich and Famous, Bantam, 1981.
Dynasty, Bantam, 1983.
(Under pseudonym Mike Cogan) *Top Gun,* Pocket Books, 1987.
(Under pseudonym Mike Cogan) *The Presidio,* Pocket Books, 1988.

OTHER

Also author of four study guides on the making of films for Universal Pictures. Author of column "Under Covers," published in *Village Voice,* 1974-75, and of columns appearing in other periodicals, including *Publishers Weekly.* Contributor of numerous book reviews and articles to newspapers and magazines.

WORK IN PROGRESS: A screenplay; a novel.

*   *   *

LOVING, Jerome MacNeill 1941-

PERSONAL: Born December 25, 1941, in Philadelphia, Pa.; son of James Josephus and Nancy (MacNeill) Loving; married Cathleen Gervais Creighton (a teacher), July 3, 1965; children: David C., Alison Cameron. *Education:* Pennsylvania State University, B.A., 1964; Duquesne University, M.A., 1970; Duke University, Ph.D., 1973.

ADDRESSES: Office—Department of English, Texas A & M University, College Station, Tex. 77843.

CAREER: Texas A & M University, College Station, assistant professor, 1973-76, associate professor, 1976-81, professor of English, 1981—. Fulbright lecturer at Leningrad State University, 1978, and Sorbonne Nouvelle, University of Paris, 1989. Visiting professor at Sorbonne, University of Paris, 1984, and at University of Texas at Austin, 1986. *Military service:* U.S. Navy, 1964-67; served in Vietnam, 1966; became lieutenant junior grade.

MEMBER: International Association of University Professors of English, Modern Language Association of America (executive coordinator of American Literature Association, 1987—).

WRITINGS:

(Editor) *Civil War Letters of George Washington Whitman,* Duke University Press, 1975.
Walt Whitman's Champion: William Douglas O'Connor, Texas A & M University Press, 1978.
Emerson, Whitman, and the American Muse, University of North Carolina Press, 1982.
Emily Dickinson: The Poet on the Second Story, Cambridge University Press, 1986.
(Contributor) Emory Elliot, editor, *Columbia Literary History,* Columbia University Press, 1988.
(Editor) *Walt Whitman's Leaves of Grass,* Oxford University Press, 1990.

Contributor to history and literature journals.

WORK IN PROGRESS: Lost in the Customhouse: Authorship in the American Renaissance.

SIDELIGHTS: Jerome MacNeill wrote *CA:* "Criticism ought to focus more on the author's intellectual autonomy and less on the possibility that he or she is a cultural automaton."

*   *   *

LUCAS, George 1944-

PERSONAL: Born May 14, 1944, in Modesto, Calif.; son of George (a retail merchant) and Dorothy Lucas; *Education:* Modesto Junior College, A.A.; University of Southern California, B.F.A., 1966.

ADDRESSES: c/o Lucasfilm, Ltd., P.O. Box 2009, San Rafael, Calif. 94912.

CAREER: Director and writer of motion pictures, 1970—; executive producer of films, 1979—, including "The Empire Strikes Back," "Return of the Jedi," "Raiders of the Lost Ark," "Indiana Jones and the Temple of Doom," "Indiana Jones and the Last Crusade," "Willow," and "Tucker: The Man and His Dream." Assistant art editor and cameraman for director Francis Ford Coppola's "The Rain People," 1969; worked as a cameraman for director Saul Bass and as a film editor for the U.S. Information Agency; editor and cameraman for Coppola's "Finian's Rainbow." Founder, Lucasfilm, Ltd., San Rafael, Calif.

MEMBER: Writers Guild of America, Academy of Motion Picture Arts and Sciences, Screen Directors Guild.

AWARDS, HONORS: Third National Student Film Festival best film award, 1967-68, for "Electronic Labyrinth: THX 1138: 4EB"; best screenplay award from New York Film Critics and from National Society of Film Critics, Golden Globe award for best comedy, and nominations from Academy of Motion Picture Arts and Sciences for best screenplay, best director, and best film, all 1973, all for "American Graffiti"; best film award from Los Angeles Film Critics, nominations from Academy of Motion Picture Arts and Sciences for best director and best film, all 1977, and British Fantasy Award nomination, 1979, all for "Star Wars"; recipient of numerous other film awards.

WRITINGS:

American Graffiti (also see below), Grove, 1974.
Star Wars: From the Adventures of Luke Skywalker (also see below), Ballantine, 1976.

SCREENPLAYS

(With Walter Murch; and director) "THX-1138," Warner Brothers, 1970.
(With Gloria Katz and Willard Huyck; and director) "American Graffiti," Universal, 1973.
(And director) "Star Wars," Twentieth Century-Fox, 1977.
(With Lawrence Kasdan) "Return of the Jedi" (also see below), Lucasfilm, 1983.

OTHER

Author of original stories for films "More American Graffiti," 1979, "The Empire Strikes Back," 1980, (with Philip Kaufman) "Raiders of the Lost Ark," 1981, "Return of the Jedi," 1983, "Indiana Jones and the Temple of Doom," 1984, "Willow," 1988, and "Indiana Jones and the Last Crusade," 1989; author of original stories for television movies "The Ewok Adventure," 1985, and "Ewoks—The Battle for Endor," 1986.

SIDELIGHTS: "George Lucas has had a hand—as writer, producer, director, or all three—in five of the eight largest-grossing films of all time," according to *Los Angeles Times* contributor Charles Champlin. Lucas first achieved financial success with his movie "American Graffiti," which was released in 1973. The further success of the "Star Wars" trilogy ("Star Wars" alone has grossed over $400 million) and the Indiana Jones movies has allowed Lucas to establish his own film company, Lucasfilm, Ltd., a studio completely independent of Hollywood. "Ever since I was in film school, I've had this dream," he says in a biographical release from Lucasfilm. "It's the dream a lot of us from film school share, and the dream is to recreate the same kind of wonderful working environment we had in school together, a place where filmmakers and writers can gather and share ideas and study and help each other." The filmmaker adds: "I'm interested in making movies, not deals."

"As a teenager," the Lucasfilm biography relates, "Lucas's budding artistic ability manifested itself in the desire to become a photographer or artist, while his love of cars became a passion for auto racing. He pursued both interests simultaneously by taking art classes in school, and spending much of his free time rebuilding cars and working with pit crews at local races. But, neither dream was to be fulfilled in exactly the way he had hoped. His father was adamantly opposed to an art career, and his hopes of a racing career were dashed when the 18-year-old Lucas had a serious auto accident just before high school graduation.

"After a lengthy recovery period, Lucas entered Modesto Junior College where he majored in social sciences, with particular interest in anthropology, and sociology. He then attended USC Film School, graduating in 1966 with a B.F.A. degree. Close friendships developed with fellow students who are filmmakers today, including John Milius, Willard Huyck, Robert Dalva, Matthew Robbins, Hal Barwood, Walter Murch, Caleb Deschanel and Randal Kleiser. As a student, Lucas made eight short

films, including his most well known, entitled 'Electronic Labyrinth: THX 1138: 4EB.' This stark futuristic film follows every movement of a man on the run through the point of view of cameras and monitor screens placed along a blinding white corridor. It won the Best Film Award at the 3rd National Student Film Festival in 1967-68.

"In 1969," the biography continues, "Lucas moved to Mill Valley in Marin County, California. The move to the Bay Area was part of a dream he shared with Francis Coppola to establish an independent film production company. American Zoetrope was started with financing from Warner Bros., which then declined to finance the company's one project-in-development: 'Apocalypse Now,' written by John Milius, was to have been directed by George Lucas. In 1970, Zoetrope released its first film, 'THX 1138,' which was an expansion on the theme of [Lucas's] earlier student film. Directed by Lucas, 'THX' was shot in the Bay Area and edited at his Mill Valley home. The film was critically well-received, but was not a commercial success. Zoetrope's fortunes plummeted when Warner Bros. pulled the plug on the fledgling studio, leaving Coppola deeply in debt. The dream of having a self-supported center for Bay Area filmmakers seemed dead."

Lucas, nevertheless, went on to his next project. Departing from the science fiction genre, his second major film is a nostalgic look at teenage life in 1962, entitled "American Graffiti." Lucas directed the film with the help of friends Gary Kurtz and Coppola on a shoestring budget of $780,000. Universal executives disliked the loosely-plotted movie, but decided to release it in 1973. Two years later it had grossed $50 million and had won a Golden Globe award for best comedy, New York Film Critics and National Society of Film Critics awards for best screenplay, and five Oscar nominations.

The credibility which "American Graffiti" lent the director gave him the leverage to propose his idea for a science fiction movie called "Star Wars." After being refused by two studios, Lucas received $8.5 million in financial backing from 20th Century-Fox. His difficulty in getting a studio to support him was in part due to the original nature of the film about a civil war against an evil galactic empire. Explaining his motives for making "Star Wars" in the Lucasfilm biography, the producer comments: "I realized a whole generation was growing up without fairy tales. . . . I wanted to do a modern fairy tale, a myth. One of the criteria of the mythical fairy tale situation is an exotic faraway land, but we've lost all the fairy lands on this planet." He also remarks that "as a student of anthropology, I feel very strongly about the importance of mythology and fairy tales. Fairy tales deal with very basic ideals and morality. Folktales, religions and myths all were meant to teach man the right way to live. They are a psychological tool for teaching children."

Critics and audiences alike praised "Star Wars," which became the biggest box office success in movie history up to that time and won seven Oscars for art direction, sound, score, costume design, visual effects, editing, and sound effects editing. *New Yorker* reviewer Penelope Gilliatt calls the film "amazing" and "exuberantly entertaining," while a 1977 *Time* magazine article refers to it as "a grand and glorious film" that "is surely one of the swiftest two hours on celluloid." Lucas, though, is now less enthusiastic about "Star Wars." In a *Rolling Stone* interview, the director reveals, " 'Star Wars' is about twenty-five percent of what I wanted it to be."

Directing the production was also unsatisfying for Lucas. Shy and somewhat introverted, he "found the experience excruciatingly painful," he says in *Time*, ". . . and I've discovered what I knew all along: I am not a film director. I'm a film maker." He therefore switched to producing, letting others like Steven Spielberg and Irvin Kershner direct the movies he conceived. Two of the eight planned sequels to "Star Wars," "The Empire Strikes Back" and "Return of the Jedi," were well received in the theater, earning as much or more than "Star Wars." Some critics, however, believe these films are not equal to the original. London *Times* reviewer David Robinson, for example, fears that "special effects have more and more taken over from the human interest." But he also adds that " 'Return of the Jedi' remains a cunning and prodigal synthesis of every kind of popular myth."

The other popular films which Lucas has conceived and produced are the Indiana Jones movies "Raiders of the Lost Ark" and "Indiana Jones and the Temple of Doom"; another sequel, "Indiana Jones and the Last Crusade," was released in 1989. Like the "Star Wars" movies, Lucas hoped that these productions would help stimulate a renaissance of fantasy and adventure for modern film audiences. Sheila Benson writes in the *Los Angeles Times* how these movies recall "the combination of delight and shivery terror that Saturday-matinee movie serials produced." The films trace the exploits of archaeologist/adventurer Indiana Jones (played by Harrison Ford) through a series of cliff-hanging events, while he explores exotic lands during the 1930s.

After "Indiana Jones and the Temple of Doom," Lucas produced the unsuccessful movie "Howard the Duck," based on a comic book character, and the slightly more popular gothic fantasy "Labyrinth," before doing "Willow," another fantasy about the struggle between good and evil. Because fantasy stories have not sold well in theaters, critics have often speculated in their reviews of "Willow" whether distributor Metro-Goldwyn-Mayer/United Artists would suffer financially should the film fail. "Very little [has been] written about what the intention of the filmmaker was or whether it's art," Lucas complains in Kim Masters's *Chicago Tribune* article. "It's a genre that's never been a hit and it's about little people, which some people don't feel comfortable with," Lucas tells Masters. "I'm hoping this will sell because we've made an interesting movie," he concludes.

For the past few years, Lucas has concentrated on completing the building of Skywalker Ranch (his home near San Rafael, California) and further developing individual divisions within Lucasfilm, including animation, theater operations, post-production, retailing, and computer games. He has also been involved in making films with a more limited audience, including Akira Kurosawa's "Kagemusha" and the movie Lucas co-produced with Paul Schrader, "Mishima," "both of which won high critical praises," according to Champlin. Lucas has also ex-

ecutive-produced a 3-D musical short for Disney Studios, "Captain Eo," which stars Michael Jackson and is shown exclusively at Disney's amusement parks.

During his career, Lucas has become very involved in educational technology, toward which he applies the expertise of his companies. "Lucas' commitment to education has led the computer games division [of Lucasfilm] to explore the teaching potential of new technologies," reports the Lucasfilm biography. "The division is currently working with Apple Computer, the National Audubon Society, and the Smithsonian Institute on interactive projects for high school science instruction. The games division is also collaborating with the National Geographic Society to develop a multimedia historical geography curriculum for middle schools." Looking toward the future, the producer is presently working to expand the computer technology of Lucasfilm, Ltd. "We are nearing the 21st century yet filmmaking is still very crude," Lucas states. "Science is way beyond the film industry. Video and sound are presently more advanced. . . . The old film studios have never been interested in research and science . . . . I hope at [Lucasfilm] we can bring filmmaking into the 21st century."

AVOCATIONAL INTERESTS: Anthropology, sociology, social psychology, auto racing, comic and illustrator art, antique toys.

BIOGRAPHICAL/CRITICAL SOURCES:

BOOKS

Contemporary Literary Criticism, Volume 16, Gale, 1981.

PERIODICALS

Chicago Tribune, May 23, 1988.
Film Quarterly, spring, 1974.
Los Angeles Times, May 23, 1984, May 24, 1989.
Newsweek, May 31, 1971.
New Yorker, May 30, 1977.
New York Times, June 15, 1980, June 9, 1988.
Rolling Stone, August 25, 1977.
Time, May 30, 1977.
Times (London), June 3, 1983.
Washington Post, May 23, 1984, May 19, 1988.

—*Sketch by Kevin S. Hile*

*   *   *

LYNTON, Ann
    See RAYNER, Claire (Berenice)

M

MacALISTER, Ian
See ALBERT, Marvin H(ubert)

* * *

MacCRACKEN, Mary 1926-

PERSONAL: Born June 6, 1926, in Englewood, N.J.; daughter of Clifford Wilcox (an insurance broker) and Florence (Ferguson) Burnham; married Peter Thistle, 1945; married Calvin Dodd MacCracken (an inventor and engineer), June 25, 1969; children: (first marriage) Susan Lynn, Stephen Burnham, Nan Livingston. *Education:* Attended Wellesley College, 1943-45; Paterson State College, B.A., 1972, M.A., 1973. *Religion:* Presbyterian.

ADDRESSES: Home and office—325 Morrow Rd., Englewood, N.J. 07631.

CAREER: Teacher of emotionally disturbed children, 1965-70; supplemental teacher, 1970-73; private practice as learning disabilities specialist in Ridgewood, N.J., 1973-76; private practice as dyslexia specialist in Englewood, N.J., 1976—. Resource Room teacher, 1973-79.

MEMBER: Junior League, Englewood Field Club, Knickerbocker Country Club.

WRITINGS:

A Circle of Children, Lippincott, 1974.
Lovey, a Very Special Child, Lippincott, 1976 (published in England as *Lovey, a Child Reclaimed,* Deutsch, 1977).
City Kid, Little, Brown, 1981.
Turnabout Children: Overcoming Dyslexia and Other Learning Disabilities, Little, Brown, 1986.

SIDELIGHTS: In *Lovey: A Very Special Child,* Mary MacCracken "has written here a touching, moving true story about her class of four disturbed children," all of whom had been diagnosed as emotionally disturbed, Phillip Lopate describes in the *New York Times Book Review.* The focus is on Hannah, an eight-year-old labelled as severely psychotic and autistic, and MacCracken's efforts to reach the child. The result, as the critic notes, "is, in effect, a new version of the Miracle Worker taming the *wild child* and bringing her into civilized ways. However, Mrs. MacCracken locates the miracle in the children's efforts,

rather than her own," teaching her students self-worth and confidence. *Lovey* also contains the account of the author's own troubled past, an account which "deepen[s]" the book and "turns the story into a double journey," Lopate comments. While *Times Literary Supplement* contributor Sarah Curtis observes that "there is sentimentality in the way Mary MacCracken tells her story," she states that because of the teacher's methods in reaching her students, "it is appropriate that she evokes these [kinds of] feelings in her book." As Lopate concludes: "After all, one reads a book like this not for verbal felicities but for the wisdom and experience in it. When it comes to dealing with disturbed children, no one can match Mrs. MacCracken for her knowledge, compassion and delicate touch."

Lovey: A Very Special Child has been published in fourteen languages.

MEDIA ADAPTATIONS: Both *A Circle of Children* and *Lovey, a Very Special Child* were made into movies for broadcast on CBS-TV.

BIOGRAPHICAL/CRITICAL SOURCES:

PERIODICALS

Christian Science Monitor, April 13, 1981.
Los Angeles Times Book Review, July 5, 1987.
New York Times Book Review, October 17, 1976.
Times Literary Supplement, February 24, 1978.

* * *

MACKSEY, Kenneth J. 1923-
(Major K. J. Macksey)

PERSONAL: Born July 1, 1923, in Epsom, Surrey, England; son of Henry George and Alice (Nightingall) Macksey; married Joan Little, June 22, 1946; children: Susan, Andrew. *Education:* Received army schooling at Royal Military College, Sandhurst, 1943-44, and British Army Staff College, 1956. *Religion:* Church of England.

ADDRESSES: Home and office—Whatley Mill, Beaminster, Dorset, England. *Agent*—Watson Little Ltd., Suite 8, 26 Charing Cross Rd., London WC2H 0DG, England.

CAREER: Writer. British Army, Royal Tank Regiment, 1941-68, retired as major; Purnell's *History of the Second World*

War (weekly series) and *History of the First World War,* London, England, deputy editor, 1968-70. Consultant to the Canadian Army, 1980—.

MEMBER: Royal United Services Institute.

AWARDS, HONORS: Military: Military Cross. Literary: George Knight Clowes military essay prize, 1956, 1958.

WRITINGS:

To the Green Fields Beyond, Royal Tank Regiment, 1965.
The Shadow of Vimy Ridge, Kimber & Co., 1965.
Armoured Crusader: A Biography of Major-General Sir Percy Hobart, Hutchinson, 1967.
Afrika Korps, Ballantine, 1968.
(Under name Major K. J. Macksey) *Panzer Division: The Mailed Fist,* Ballantine, 1968.
The Crucible of Power: The Fight for Tunisia, Hutchinson, 1969.
Tank Force: Allied Armor in World War II, Ballantine, 1970.
Tank: A History of Armoured Fighting Vehicles, Macdonald, 1970.
Tank Warfare: A History of Tanks in Battle, Hart-Davis, 1971.
Beda Fomm, Ballantine, 1971.
Vimy Ridge, Ballantine, 1972.
The Guinness Guide to Tank Facts and Feats, Guinness Superlatives, 1972.
The Guinness History of Land Warfare, Guinness Superlatives, 1973.
Battle, Macdonald & Jane's, 1974.
The Partisans of Europe, Hart-Davis, 1975.
(Co-author) *The Guinness History of Sea Warfare,* Guinness Superlatives, 1975.
(Co-author) *The Guinness Guide to Feminine Achievements,* Guinness Superlatives, 1975.
Guderian: Panzer General, Macdonald & Jane's, 1975.
The Guinness History of Air Warfare, Guinness Superlatives, 1976.
The Guinness Book of 1952, Guinness Superlatives, 1976.
The Guinness Book of 1953, Guinness Superlatives, 1977.
The Guinness Book of 1954, Guinness Superlatives, 1978.
Kesselring: The Making of the Luftwaffe, Batsford, 1978.
Rommel: Campaigns and Battles, Arms & Armour Press, 1979.
The Tanks, 1945-1975, Arms & Armour Press, 1979.
Invasion, Arms & Armour Press, 1980.
The Tank Pioneers, Jane's Publishing, 1981.
History of the RAC, 1914-1975, Newtown Publications, 1983.
Commando Strike, Cooper, 1985.
First Clash, Arms & Armour Press, 1985.
Technology in War, Arms & Armour Press, 1986.
Godwin's Saga, Brassey's Defence Publishers, 1987.
Military Errors of World War II, Arms & Armour Press, 1987.
Tank versus Tank, Bantam, 1988.

Contributor to military journals.

WORK IN PROGRESS: Hitler: A Study in Command; Logistics.

SIDELIGHTS: About Kenneth Macksey's *First Clash,* John Melady of the Toronto *Globe & Mail* observes that this book, which deals with a hypothetical war in today's Europe, "has a ring of truth to it that is not always found in other 'what if' scenarios." Melady notes several problems and criticizes the book's presentation, cites examples of prose/dialogue weakness, and describes several inappropriate illustrations. He determines, however: "But notwithstanding all of the above problems, Macksey's book has its merits. . . . Read with care, it [*First Clash*] can finally capture the attention."

Macksey's *Military Errors of World War II* is a "fascinating examination of some of the most glaring major command errors made during the Second World War," according to Tony Foster in the Toronto *Globe & Mail.* Foster admires the "well written and concise text," commenting that Macksey's "pointed assessments are illuminating and at times amusing." The critic labels the maps and photographs "first class" and concludes that "Macksey has a firm grasp on his subjects and presents them with an unbiased and polished prose."

BIOGRAPHICAL/CRITICAL SOURCES:

PERIODICALS

Globe & Mail (Toronto), February 15, 1986, September 5, 1987.

*   *   *

MACKSEY, Major K. J.
See MACKSEY, Kenneth J.

*   *   *

MacLANE, Jack
See CRIDER, (Allen) Bill(y)

*   *   *

MacVICAR, Angus   1908-

PERSONAL: Born October 28, 1908, in Argyll, Scotland; son of Angus John (a minister) and Marsali (Mackenzie) MacVicar; married Jean Smith McKerral, June 24, 1936; children: Angus John. *Education:* University of Glasgow, M.A., 1930. *Religion:* Protestant.

ADDRESSES: Home—Achnamara, Southend, Campbeltown, Argyll, Scotland. *Agent*—A. M. Heath & Co. Ltd., 79 St. Martin's Ln., London, WC2N 4AA, England.

CAREER: Campbeltown Courier, Campbeltown, Argyll, Scotland, assistant editor, 1930-33; freelance writer, 1933—. *Military service:* British Army, 1939-45; became captain; mentioned in dispatches.

MEMBER: Society of Authors, Dunaverty Players Drama Club, Dunaverty Golf Club (Southend).

AWARDS, HONORS: Named honorary sheriff, Argyll County, 1967; honorary doctorate, Sterling University, 1985.

WRITINGS:

ADULT FICTION

The Purple Rock, Stanley Paul, 1933.
Death by the Mistletoe, Stanley Paul, 1934.
The Screaming Gull, Stanley Paul, 1935.
The Temple Falls, Stanley Paul, 1935.
Cavern, Stanley Paul, 1936.
The Crooked Finger, Stanley Paul, 1936.
The Ten Green Brothers, Stanley Paul, 1936.
Flowering Death, Stanley Paul, 1937.
Crime's Masquerader, Stanley Paul, 1939.
Eleven for Danger, Stanley Paul, 1939.
The Singing Spider, Stanley Paul, 1939.
Strangers from the Sea, Stanley Paul, 1939.
The Crouching Spy, Stanley Paul, 1941.
Death on the Machar, Stanley Paul, 1946.
The Other Man, Pemberton, 1947.
Greybreek, Stanley Paul, 1947.

Fugitives Road, Stanley Paul, 1949.
Escort to Adventure, Stanley Paul, 1952.
The Dancing Horse, John Long, 1961.
The Killings on Kersivay, John Long, 1962.
The Hammers of Fingal, John Long, 1963.
The Grey Shepherds, John Long, 1964.
Life-Boat—Green to White, Brockhampton Press, 1965.
Murder at the Open, John Long, 1965, Ian Henry, 1988.
The Canisbary Conspiracy, John Long, 1966.
Night on the Killer Reef, John Long, 1967.
Maniac, John Long, 1969.
Duel in the Glenfinnan, John Long, 1970.
The Golden Venus Affair, John Long, 1972.
The Painted Doll Affair, John Long, 1973.

ADULT NONFICTION

Rescue Call, Kaye & Ward, 1966.
Salt in My Porridge: Confessions of a Minister's Son, Jarrolds, 1971.
Heather in My Ears: More Confessions of a Minister's Son, Hutchinson, 1974.
Rocks in My Scotch: Still More Confessions of a Minister's Son, Hutchinson, 1977.
Silver in My Sporran: Confessions of a Writing Man, Hutchinson, 1979.
Bees in My Bonnet, Hutchinson, 1982.
Golf in My Galowses: Confessions of a Fairway Fanatic, Hutchinson, 1983.
Gremlins in My Garden: Confessions of a Harassed Horticulturist, Hutchinson, 1985.
Capers in My Kirk: Confessions of a Would-be Christian, Hutchinson, 1987.

CHILDREN'S FICTION

The Crocodile Men, Art & Educational, 1947.
The Black Wherry, Foley House Press, 1948.
Faraway Island, Foley House Press, 1949.
King Abbie's Adventure, Burke, 1950.
The Grey Pilot, Burke, 1951.
Stubby Sees It Through, Burke, 1951.
Tiger Mountain, Burke, 1952.
The Lost Planet (Children's Book Club selection), Burke, 1954.
Return to the Lost Planet, Burke, 1954.
Secret of the Lost Planet, Burke, 1955.
Dinny Smith Comes Home, Burke, 1955.
The Atom Chasers, Burke, 1956.
The Atom Chasers in Tibet, Burke, 1957.
Satellite 7, Burke, 1958.
Red Fire on the Lost Planet, Burke, 1959.
Peril on the Lost Planet, Burke, 1960.
Space Agent from the Lost Planet, Burke, 1961.
Space Agent and the Isles of Fire, Burke, 1962.
Kilpatrick—Special Reporter, Burke, 1963.
Space Agent and the Ancient Peril, Burke, 1964.
The High Cliffs of Kersivay, Harrap, 1964.
The Kersivay Kraken, Harrap, 1965.
The Cave of the Hammers, Kaye & Ward, 1966.
Super Nova and the Rogue Satellite, Brockhampton Press, 1969.
Super Nova and the Frozen Man, Brockhampton Press, 1970.

OTHER

Under Suspicion (one-act play), Brown, Son & Ferguson, c. 1962.
(With John C. Caldwell) *Let's Visit Scotland* (children's nonfiction), Burke, 1966, 4th revised edition, 1984.

Also author of plays "Minister's Monday," 1956, "Final Proof," 1957, "Mercy Flight," 1958, "Storm Tide," 1959, and "Stranger at Christmas," 1964. Author of features and documentaries for radio and television for adults and children; author of weekly radio comedy series, "The Glens of Glendale," 1954-59, and of television talk series, "Confessions of a Minister's Son," 1965-70. Adaptor of adult books, *The Singing Spider, Strangers from the Sea, The Canisbary Conspiracy,* and *Night on the Killer Reef,* and seventeen of his juvenile books for radio serials in Britain, many of which were broadcast in the United States, Germany, Malaya, and Scandinavia; adaptor of *The Lost Planet* and *Return to the Lost Planet* for television serials. Regular contributor of articles, short stories, and serials to British adult and juvenile magazines. MacVicar's books have been translated into many languages.

SIDELIGHTS: Angus MacVicar worked his way through college as a professional athlete. He still plays golf and "can score his age on his local course," he told *CA.*

* * *

MAHESHWARI, Shriram   1931-

PERSONAL: Born November 27, 1931, in India; son of Muniraj Maheshwari; married May 30, 1955, wife's name, Bimla; children: Manjula (daughter), Rajiv (son), Sanjiv (son), Anjula (daughter), Manish (son). *Education:* D.A.V. College, Kanpur, India, B.A., M.A. (economics), M.A. (political science); University of Delhi, Ph.D., 1965; University of Pennsylvania, M.G.A., 1964. *Religion:* Hinduism.

ADDRESSES: Office—Indian Institute of Public Administration, New Delhi, India.

CAREER: Agra University, Agra, India, lecturer, 1955-61; University of Delhi, Indian School of Public Administration, New Delhi, India, reader in public administration, 1965-73; Indian Institute of Public Administration, New Delhi, professor of political science and public administration, 1973—. Affiliated with Institute of Developing Economies, Tokyo. Visiting fellow, Maison des Sciences l'Hourire, Paris.

MEMBER: Indian Public Administration Association (past secretary-cum-treasurer; president).

WRITINGS:

(With A. Avasthi) *Public Administration,* Lakshmi Narain Agarwal, 1962, 7th edition, 1974.
The General Election in India, Chaitanya Publishing House, 1963.
Indian Administration, Orient Longman, 1968, 2nd edition, 1974.
The Evolution of Indian Administration, Lakshmi Narain Agarwal, 1970.
Local Government in India, Orient Longman, 1971.
Government through Consultation, Indian Institute of Public Administration, 1972.
The Administrative Reforms Commission, Lakshmi Narain Agarwal, 1972.
(Editor) *The Study of Public Administration,* Lakshmi Narain Agarwal, 1974.
Civil Service in Great Britain, Concept Publishing, 1976.
President's Rule in India, Macmillan (India), 1977.
Indian Parliamentary System, Lakshmi Narain Agarwal, 1981.
Electoral Politics in the National Metropolis, Ritu Publishers, 1982.
Administrative Reforms in India, Macmillan, 1982.
Open Government in India, Macmillan, 1983.
Rural Development in India, Sage Publications, 1986.

Higher Civil Service in Japan, Allied Publishers, 1987.

*   *   *

MAHY, Margaret 1936-

PERSONAL: Born March 21, 1936, in Whakatane, New Zealand; daughter of Francis George (a builder) and May (a teacher; maiden name, Penlington) Mahy; children: Penelope Helen, Bridget Frances. *Education:* University of New Zealand, B.A., 1958. *Politics:* "Anarchist." *Religion:* "Humanist."

ADDRESSES: Home—R.D. 1, Lyttelton, New Zealand. *Agent*—Alison Leach Agency, 10 Alma Sq., St. John's Wood, London NW8 9QD, England.

CAREER: Petone Public Library, Petone, New Zealand, assistant librarian, 1958-59; School Library Service, Christchurch, New Zealand, librarian in charge, 1967-76; Canterbury Public Library, Christchurch, children's librarian, 1976—; writer.

MEMBER: New Zealand Library Association.

AWARDS, HONORS: Esther Glenn Medal from New Zealand Library Association, 1969, for *A Lion in the Meadow,* 1973, for *The First Margaret Mahy Story Book,* and 1983, for *The Haunting;* Carnegie Medal, British Library Association, 1982, for *The Haunting,* and 1986, for *The Changeover: A Supernatural Romance;* Horn Book Honor List citation, *Horn Book,* 1985, for *The Changeover: A Supernatural Romance,* and 1987, for *The Catalogue of the Universe; 17 Kings and 42 Elephants* was named one of the year's ten best illustrated books in 1987 by the *New York Times Book Review.*

WRITINGS:

JUVENILES

A Lion in the Meadow, F. Watts, 1969.
A Dragon of an Ordinary Family, F. Watts, 1969.
Pillycock's Shop, F. Watts, 1969.
The Procession, F. Watts, 1969.
Mrs. Discombobulous, F. Watts, 1969.
The Princess and the Clown, F. Watts, 1971.
The Railway Engine and the Hairy Brigands, Dent, 1972.
The First Margaret Mahy Story Book, Dent, 1972.
The Boy with Two Shadows, F. Watts, 1972, Lippincott, 1989.
The Man Whose Mother Was a Pirate, Atheneum, 1972, Viking Kestrel, 1986.
The Second Margaret Mahy Story Book, Dent, 1973.
Clancy's Cabin, Dent, 1974.
The Bus under the Leaves, Dent, 1974.
Rooms to Let, F. Watts, 1974.
The Rare Spotted Birthday Party, F. Watts, 1974.
The Witch in the Cherry Tree, Parents' Magazine Press, 1974, Dent, 1984.
Stepmother, F. Watts, 1974.
The Third Margaret Mahy Story Book, Dent, 1975.
New Zealand: Yesterday and Today, F. Watts, 1975.
David's Witch Doctor, F. Watts, 1975.
Ultra-Violet Catastrophe, Parents' Magazine Press, 1975.
The Wind between the Stars, Dent, 1976.
The Boy Who Was Followed Home, F. Watts, 1976.
Leaf Magic (also see below), Parents' Magazine Press, 1976.
The Pirate Uncle, Dent, 1977.
The Nonstop Nonsense Book, Dent, 1977.
The Great Piratical Rambustification, Dent, 1978.
Raging Robots and Unruly Uncles, Dent, 1981.
The Haunting, Atheneum, 1982.
The Pirates' Mixed-Up Voyage, Dent, 1983.

Leaf Magic and Five Other Favourites, Dent, 1984.
The Chewing-Gum Rescue and Other Stories, Methuen, 1984.
The Changeover: A Supernatural Romance, Atheneum, 1984.
The Birthday Burglar [and] *A Very Wicked Headmistress,* Dent, 1984, illustrations by Margaret Chamberlain, Godine, 1988.
The Catalogue of the Universe, Atheneum, 1985.
Aliens in the Family, Scholastic, 1986.
17 Kings and 42 Elephants, illustrations by Patricia MacCarthy, Dial, 1987.
The Tricksters, Margaret K. McElderry Books, 1987.
Memory, Margaret K. McElderry Books, 1988.
The Door in the Air, Dent, 1988.
The Blood and Thunder Adventures on Hurricane Peak, Dent, 1989.

OTHER

Author of scripts "A Land Called Happy," "Woolly Valley," "Once upon a Story," and "The Margaret Mahy Story Book Theatre" for Television New Zealand, and the television series "Cuckooland" for the Gibson Group.

SIDELIGHTS: Children's author Margaret Mahy "has deserved her reputation as queen of the light fantastic with stories and picture-book texts which erupt with delightful visions," states *Times Literary Supplement* critic Sarah Hayes. And with *The Haunting,* a story of the ghostly possession of a young boy, Mahy "manages to combine a realistic approach to family life—in which how you feel about your parents and yourself is actually important—with a strong and terrifying line in fantasy," as Hayes notes. The critic concludes that in *The Haunting* "the strange pictures of the mind invade with terrible clarity the ordinary geography of daily life. And the warmth and closeness that underlie the vigorous family dialogues bear no trace of sentimentality: it is possible to believe, for once, that we are such stuff as dreams are made on."

The author of more than fifty books continues to elicit praise for her originality and use of vivid imagery. Of *The Tricksters,* Hayes remarks that Mahy "writes, as always, in a style which teeters on the brink of an abyss of her own invention," never far from whimsy in this story of tormented characters convened at a Florida beach house to celebrate Christmas. "The ability to combine a dazzling fantasy with painfully real emotions is a particular gift," says Hayes. Jan Dalley, writing in the *Times Literary Supplement,* points out that Mahy "continually pushes at the boundaries of [fairy-tale] conventions," and "roots out the sexism that used to be integral" to fiction for young readers.

BIOGRAPHICAL/CRITICAL SOURCES:

BOOKS

Children's Literature Review, Volume 7, Gale, 1984.

PERIODICALS

Los Angeles Times Book Review, May 31, 1987.
New York Times Book Review, July 13, 1986, May 17, 1987, November 8, 1987, January 22, 1989.
Times Literary Supplement, November 20, 1981, September 17, 1982, August 1, 1986, March 20, 1987, November 5, 1987, May 8, 1988, November 25, 1988.

*   *   *

MANHATTAN, Avro 1914-

PERSONAL: Born April 6, 1914, in Milan, Italy; son of Louis and Marie Antic (Roosevelt) Manhattan. *Education:* Studied for varying periods at the Sorbonne, University of Paris, at London School of Economics and Political Science, University of London, and at other universities. *Politics:* "Stubbornly independent." *Religion:* "Genuine believer in God, firm disbeliever in all established churches."

ADDRESSES: Home—24 Ansdell Ter., Kensington, London W.8, England.

CAREER: Former director of Radio Freedom, a station in England broadcasting to occupied Europe and partisans; worked for the political warfare department of the British Foreign Office, 1940-43; British Broadcasting Corp., London, England, writer of political commentaries, 1943-46; free-lance writer. Committee member, Federal Union, London; member of executive committee, Stopes Birth Control Clinic, London, 1954-59.

MEMBER: Royal Society of Literature, PEN, Society of Authors, Ethical Union, British Interplanetary Society (life member).

AWARDS, HONORS: Conferred title of baron by the King of Italy, 1953; created Knight Templar, Priory of England, 1974; Pioneer Award, American Atheists, 1976, for world-wide education in the matter of theo-politics; named Knight Commander of the Knights of Malta, 1981.

WRITINGS:

The Rumbling of the Apocalypse, Airoldi, 1934.
Towards the New Italy, preface by H. G. Wells, Lindsay Drummond, 1943.
Latin America and the Vatican, C. A. Watts, 1946.
The Vatican and the U.S.A., C. A. Watts, 1946.
Spain and the Vatican, C. A. Watts, 1946.
The Catholic Church against the Twentieth Century, C. A. Watts, 1947, 2nd edition, 1950.
The Vatican in Asia, C. A. Watts, 1948.
Religion in Russia, C. A. Watts, 1948.
The Vatican in World Politics, Gaer Associates, 1949.
Catholic Imperialism and World Freedom, C. A. Watts, 1952, reprinted, Ayer Co., 1972, 2nd edition, C. A. Watts, 1959.
Terror over Yugoslavia: The Threat to Europe, C. A. Watts, 1953.
The Dollar and the Vatican, Pioneer Press, 1956, 3rd edition, 1957.
Vatican Imperialism in the Twentieth Century, Zondervan, 1965.
Catholic Power Today, Lyle Stuart, 1967.
Catholic Terror in Ireland, Paravision Publications, 1971, 4th edition, Attic Press, 1972.
The Vatican Billions: Two Thousand Years of Wealth Accumulation, Attic Press, 1972.
The Vatican-Moscow Alliance: A Dangerous New Partnership, Ralston-Pilot, 1977.
The Dream Universe: Time, Dreams, and the New Cosmology, Ralston-Pilot, 1981.
The Vatican-Moscow-Washington Alliance: Startling Revelations of Dangerous New Partnerships, Chick, 1982, 5th edition, 1986.
The Vatican Billions: From Caesar to the Space Age, Chick, 1983.
Vietnam—Why Did We Go?: The Shocking Story of the Catholic Church's Role in Starting the Vietnam War, Chick, 1984, 4th edition, 1986.
Poems from Manhattan: A Book of Poetry, Paravision Books, 1984, 2nd edition, 1985.
Murder in the Vatican, Ozark Mountain Publications, 1985, 2nd edition, 1986.

The Vatican Holocaust: The Sensational Account of the Most Horrifying Massacre of the Twentieth Century, Ozark Mountain Publications, 1986.
(And illustrator) *The Dawn of Man: An Epic of Our Ancestors before Man's Discovery of Fire,* Paravision Books, 1986.

WORK IN PROGRESS: 2000 Years of World History: The Popes, a panoramic view of major world events in the West, Asia, and the Americas, with specific references to the religious motivations of major world religions; *The Secret Life of a Sex Revolutionary,* the life and work of Dr. Marie Stopes, the pioneer of birth control; *The Presidential Web,* a satirical epic about the contemporary American presidency.

SIDELIGHTS: Avro Manhattan was a friend of George Bernard Shaw, actress Lillah MacCarthy, and H. G. Wells. He cooperated with Wells in drafting and distributing a Bill of Human Rights, intended as a basis for a new world community after World War II. Manhattan once told *CA:* "What made me write political books? A verbal challenge with H. G. Wells after the latter wrote a book called *Crux Ansata,* which I thought very inadequate. My motivation for writing is idealism, creativity, poetry, and the urge to polemics. How do I view contemporary writers and their works? Never read any. In my opinion, the contemporary scene is creative decadence with legions of literary lemmings yearning for the void. My advice to aspiring writers is to maintain vision, idealism, hard work and determination."

One of Manhattan's more recent works is a book which took him 40 years to complete: *The Dawn of Man: An Epic of Our Ancestors before Man's Discovery of Fire.* The author describes this major effort as "written mostly in poetical prose—now and then interspersed with poetry." Another book, *The Presidential Web,* took him 20 years to complete and satirizes politics in the United States, the Soviet Union, and the world.

AVOCATIONAL INTERESTS: Astronomy, ants and termites, painting, sculpture, writing poetry.

* * *

MANNING, Harvey (Hawthorne) 1925-

PERSONAL: Born July 16, 1925, in Seattle, Wash.; son of Harvey Simpson (a logger) and Katherine (a farmer; maiden name, Hawthorne) Manning; married Betty Lorraine Williams (a librarian), May 20, 1947; children: Penelope, Rebecca, Claudia, Harvey. *Education:* University of Washington, B.A., 1946. *Politics:* "Radical-conservative anarchist." *Religion:* "Animist-pantheist."

ADDRESSES: Home and office—15819 Southeast 44th St., Bellevue, Wash. 98006.

CAREER: Worked in warehouse in Seattle, Wash., 1947; University of Washington, Seattle, chemistry stockroom clerk, 1947-50; Black & Decker, Seattle, electric tools repairman, 1951; *Post-Intelligencer,* Seattle, in sales control, 1952-54; KISW-FM, Seattle, manager, 1954-56; KXA-Radio, Seattle, time salesman, 1956-57; Macmillan Co., New York City, traveler, 1957; Paper Editions, Inc., San Francisco, traveler, 1958; Rinehart Co., New York City, college traveler, 1958-61; Holt, Rinehart & Winston, Inc., New York City, college traveler, 1960-61; Military Manuals, Renton, Wash., Atlas F editor, 1961; Martin-Marietta, Moses Lake, Wash., Titan I writer, 1961; University of Washington, Seattle, writer and editor, 1967-71; writer. Chief editor of Mountaineers Books, 1955-71.

MEMBER: Audubon Society, Sierra Club, National Parks Association, Wilderness Society, Boy Scouts of America, Olympic

Park Associates, Friends of Columbia Gorge, Friends of the Earth, Friends of Nisqually Delta, Federation of Western Outdoor Clubs, Mount St. Helen's Protective Society, Washington Environmental Council, Washington Native Plants Society, Washington Wilderness Alliance, Mountaineers of Seattle (chairman of climbing committee, 1951; chairman of safety committee, 1954; chairman of literary fund committee; trustee, 1960-70), Newcastle Historical Society, Issaquah Alps Trails Club (founding president, 1979-89).

AWARDS, HONORS: Became Eagle Scout in Boy Scouts of America, 1940; service award from Mountaineers of Seattle, 1963; Outstanding Environmentalist Award from Governor of Washington, 1983; numerous "Writer's Day" awards from State of Washington.

WRITINGS:

High Worlds of the Mountainclimber, with photographs by Bob Spring and Ira Spring, Superior, 1959.

(Co-editor) *Mountaineering: The Freedom of the Hills,* Mountaineers, 1960, revised edition, 1967.

The North Cascades, with photographs by Tom Miller, Mountaineers, 1964.

The Wild Cascades: Forgotten Parkland, with photographs by Ansel Adams and others, Sierra Books, 1965.

The North Cascades National Park, with photographs by B. Spring and I. Spring, Superior, 1969.

(With I. Spring) *Fifty Hikes in Mount Rainier National Park,* with photographs by B. Spring and I. Spring, Mount Rainier National History Association, 1969.

(With B. Spring and I. Spring) *The Key to Our Environment: Cool, Clear Water,* Superior, 1970.

(With I. Spring) *One Hundred Two Hikes in the Alpine Lakes, South Cascades, and Olympics,* with photographs by B. Spring and I. Spring, Mountaineers, 1971.

Backpacking: One Step at a Time, with cartoons by Bob Cram and photographs by Keith Gunnar, REI Press, 1971, revised edition, Vintage Books, 1986.

(Contributor) *Wilderness U.S.A.,* National Geographic Society, 1973.

(With I. Spring) *Wilderness Trails Northwest: A Hiker's and Climber's Overview-Guide to National Parks and Wilderness Areas in Wyoming, Montana, Idaho, Northern California, Oregon, Washington, British Columbia, and Canadian Rockies,* Touchstone, 1974, revised edition, Mountaineers, 1981.

(With Kenneth Brower) *Cry Crisis: A Rehearsal in Alaska,* edited by Hugh Nash, Friends of the Earth, 1974.

(With B. Spring and I. Spring) *National Parks of the Northwest,* Superior, 1975.

Footloose: Walks and Hikes around Puget Sound, Mountaineers, Volume 1, 1977, Volume 2, 1978, Volume 3, 1978, Volume 4, 1979, new edition, 1987-89.

Oregon Wildlife Areas, with photographs by B. Spring and I. Spring, Superior, c. 1978.

Mountain Flowers, with photographs by B. Spring and I. Spring, Mountaineers, c. 1979.

Northwest Outdoor Vacations, photographs by I. Spring, Writing Works, 1982.

Washington Wilderness: The Unfinished Work, photographs by Pat O'Hara, Mountaineers, 1984.

(With I. Spring) *One Hundred Hikes in the South Cascades and Olympics,* Mountaineers, 1987.

Walking the Beach to Bellingham, Madrona, 1987.

Fifty Years of Climbing Together, Recreational Equipment, Inc., 1988.

(With I. Spring) *One Hundred Hikes in Alpine Lakes,* Mountaineers, 1988.

(With I. Spring) *One Hundred Hikes in Glacier Peak Area,* Mountaineers, 1989.

(With I. Spring) *One Hundred Hikes in the North Cascades,* Mountaineers, 1989.

(With I. Spring) *Walks in the Sun and Flowers of Washington's Steppe,* Mountaineers, 1990.

Contributor to periodicals, including *Backpacking Magazine, Issaquah Alpiner, Mountain Gazette, Summit, Ascent, Mountaineer,* and *Interim.* Editor of *Wild Cascades,* North Cascades Conservation Council, 1961-71, and *University of Washington Magazine,* 1961-71; Northwest editor of *Not Man Apart,* 1971-75.

WORK IN PROGRESS: "Books, pamphlets, broadsides."

SIDELIGHTS: Harvey Manning has written numerous books on nature. His *Backpacking: One Step at a Time* is a funny yet sensible guide to backpacking, with tips on walking and enjoying nature. A reviewer in the *New York Times Book Review* described *Backpacking* as a "hearty, opinionated book."

Manning told *CA:* "If a person decides quite early in life to try to be a writer, it is helpful to spend a little time in 'creative writing' courses, preferably in high school only. One does better to take Latin, or grammar, or copy-editing if a course can be found (most writers cannot rigidly enforce a style guide—and neither can very many professional editors).

"A hopeful writer should avoid any gainful employment that demands use of the brain; better to sell one's body, doing manual labor, than one's mind. However, the hoper should not suppose that the world will recognize it owes him a living.

"What defeats most hopeful writers is a lack of patience. They tend to be very lazy people and easily distracted, forever looking for a wealthy patron who will keep them in ease while they expand their souls. Except for the rare writer with genius and discipline (and enough energy or outside help to keep body and soul together while learning the craft), the hoper does best spending a lot of years mainly living—and learning something to write about.

"My writing career, such as it has been, developed from fortuitous circumstances. I was a fairly literate climber at a time when a textbook on climbing was needed. The book became a classic and gave me credentials to be a wilderness writer, which led to a publisher's offer to write a text on backpacking when it was entering the fad stage. Oddly enough, the climbing book also got me a job as a university writer-editor.

"As a youth I was impelled toward writing by exhibitionism. Now, in age, when I really don't give a damn what anybody thinks of me and mainly would like to be let alone to go walking in the woods, I write for the same reason that others throughout the world throw homemade grenades into police headquarters. There are just one hell of a lot of bastards who need to be blown up. Disliking bad noises, I use the typewriter."

BIOGRAPHICAL/CRITICAL SOURCES:

PERIODICALS

New York Times Book Review, July 14, 1974.

*   *   *

MARA, Jeanette
See CEBULASH, Mel

MARRIN, Albert 1936-

PERSONAL: Born July 24, 1936, in New York, N.Y.; son of Louis and Frieda (Funt) Marrin; married Yvette Rappaport (a teacher), November 22, 1959. *Education:* City College (now City College of the City University of New York), B.A., 1958; Yeshiva University, M.S.Ed., 1959; Columbia University, M.A., 1961, Ph.D., 1968.

ADDRESSES: Home—750 Kappock St., Bronx, N.Y. 10463. *Office*—Department of History, Yeshiva University, 500 West 185th St., New York, N.Y. 10033. *Agent*—Toni Mendez, Inc., 141 East 56th St., New York, N.Y. 10022.

CAREER: William Howard Taft High School, New York City, social studies teacher, 1959-68; Yeshiva University, New York City, assistant professor of history, 1968-78, professor and chairman of history department, 1978—; writer, 1968—. Visiting professor, Yeshiva University, 1967-68, and Touro College, 1972—.

MEMBER: American Historical Association, Phi Alpha Theta (president of Alpha Mu chapter, 1957-58).

AWARDS, HONORS: Notable Children's Trade Book selection, National Council for Social Studies and Children's Book Council, 1985, and *Boston Globe/Horn Book* Honor Book for nonfiction, all for *1812: The War Nobody Won.*

WRITINGS:

War and the Christian Conscience: Augustine to Martin Luther King, Jr., Regnery, 1971.
The Last Crusade: The Church of England in the First World War, Duke University Press, 1973.
Nicholas Murray Butler, Twayne, 1976.
Sir Norman Angell, Twayne, 1979.

JUVENILE HISTORY

The Airman's War: World War II in the Sky, Atheneum, 1982.
Overlord: D-Day and the Invasion of Europe, Atheneum, 1982.
Victory in the Pacific, Macmillan, 1983.
War Clouds in the West: Indians and Cavalrymen, 1860-1890, Atheneum, 1984.
The Sea Rovers: Pirates, Privateers, and Buccaneers, Atheneum, 1984.
The Secret Armies: Spies, Counterspies, Saboteurs in World War II, Macmillan, 1985.
1812: The War Nobody Won, Atheneum, 1985.
The Yanks Are Coming: The United States in the First World War, Atheneum, 1986.
Aztecs and Spaniards: Cortes and the Conquest of Mexico, illustrated by Richard Rosenblum, Atheneum, 1986.
Hitler: A Portrait of a Tyrant, Viking, 1987.
Struggle for a Continent: The French and Indian Wars, Macmillan, 1987.
The War for Independence: The Story of the American Revolution, Macmillan, 1988.

WORK IN PROGRESS: A book about Mao Tse-tung.

AVOCATIONAL INTERESTS: Travel (Europe).*

*   *   *

MARTIN, F(rancis) X(avier) 1922-

PERSONAL: Born October 2, 1922, in County Kerry, Ireland; son of Conor John (a physician) and Catherine (Fitzmaurice) Martin. *Education:* Augustinian College, Dublin, Ireland, L.Ph., 1944; University College, Dublin, National University of Ireland, B.A., 1949, M.A., 1952; Pontifical Gregorian University, Rome, Italy, B.D., 1951; Peterhouse, Cambridge, Ph.D., 1959.

ADDRESSES: Home—Augustinian House of Studies, Dublin 16, Ireland. *Office*—Department of Medieval History, University College, National University of Ireland, Dublin 4, Ireland.

CAREER: Entered Augustinian Order, 1941, ordained Roman Catholic priest, 1952; National University of Ireland, University College, Dublin, assistant lecturer in history, 1959-62, professor of medieval history, 1962—. Visiting professor, La Trobe University, Melbourne, Australia, 1972; visiting fellow, Australian National University, 1983. Definitor, Anglo-Irish Augustinian Province. Member of Irish Manuscripts Commission, 1963—. National Library of Ireland, trustee, 1971—, chairman of council of trustees, 1977-82.

MEMBER: Royal Irish Academy, Kildare Street/University Club (Dublin).

AWARDS, HONORS: Dublin Millennium Medal, 1987.

WRITINGS:

The Irish Augustinians in Rome, edited by J. F. Madden, [Rome], 1956.
The Problem of Giles of Viterbo, 1469-1532, Augustinian Historical Institute (Louvain), 1960.
Friar Nugent: A Study of Francis Lavalin Nugent, 1569-1635, Agent of the Counter-Reformation, Methuen, 1962.
1916: Myth, Fact, and Mystery, Studia Hibernica, 1968.
No Hero in the House: Diarmait MacMurchada and the Coming of the Normans to Ireland, 1169, National University of Ireland, 1977.

EDITOR

(With J. A. Watt and J. B. Morrall, and contributor) *Medieval Studies; Presented to Aubrey Gwynn, S.J.,* Three Candles, 1961.
The Irish Volunteers, 1913-1915: Recollections and Documents, Duffy, 1963.
The Howth Gun-Running, 1914: Recollections and Documents, Browne & Nolan, 1964.
(And contributor) *1916 and University College, Dublin,* Brown & Nolan, 1966.
(With T. W. Moody, and contributor) *The Course of Irish History,* Mercier Press, 1967, new enlarged edition, 1984.
(And contributor) *Leaders and Men of the Easter Rising: Dublin 1916,* Cornell University Press, 1967.
(With F. J. Byrne, and contributor) *The Scholar Revolutionary: Eoin MacNeill, 1867-1945, and the Making of the New Ireland,* Irish University Press, 1973.
M. J. Morrin, *John Waldeby, c.1315-c.1372: Augustinian Preacher and Writer,* Augustinian Historical Institute (Rome), 1975.
(With Moody and Byrne) *A New History of Ireland,* Oxford University Press, Volume III, 1976, Volume VIII, 1983, Volume IX, 1984, Volume IV, 1986, Volume II, 1987, Volume V, 1989.
Michael Tierney, *Eoin MacNeill: Scholar and Man of Action, 1867-1945,* Oxford University Press, 1980.
Lambert Simnel: Crowning of a King, Christ Church Cathedral, Dublin, 1989.

OTHER

(Contributor) Isidorus a Villapadierna, editor, *Miscellanea Melchor de Pobladura,* [Rome], 1964.

(Contributor) Desmond Williams, editor, *The Irish Struggle, 1916-1926,* Routledge & Kegan Paul, 1966.

(Contributor) *Miscellanea Historiae Ecclesiasticae,* Volume II, [Louvain], 1967.

(Contributor) E. Kamenka, editor, *Nationalism: The Nature and Evolution of an Idea,* Australian National University Press, 1973, 2nd edition, Edward Arnold (London), 1976.

(Contributor) B. O'Farrell, editor, *The Irish Parliamentary Tradition,* Gill & Macmillan, 1973.

(Contributor) C. Mayer and W. Eckermann, editors, *Scientifica Augustiniana,* Augustinus Verlag, 1975.

(Translator from the Latin, and author of historical notes with A. B. Scott) Giraldus Cambrensis, *Expugnatio Hibernica: The Conquest of Ireland,* Royal Irish Academy, 1978.

General editor of "Medieval" series (booklets), Dublin Historical Association. Co-editor of "Course of Irish History" programs, Radio Telefis Eireann (RTE), 1966, and consulting editor and contributor to series of sixteen talks on the Anglo-Norman "invasion" of Ireland, RTE, 1969. Contributor to *International Bibliography of Historical Sciences, New Catholic Encyclopedia,* and *Dictionnaire de Spiritualite.* Contributor of articles on medieval, Renaissance, Counter-Reformation, and modern Irish history to a variety of periodicals.

WORK IN PROGRESS: A biography of the life and time of Giles of Viterbo, 1469-1532.

BIOGRAPHICAL/CRITICAL SOURCES:

PERIODICALS

Books Ireland, December, 1984.
Irish Independent, June 8, 1984.
Irish Press, June 8, 1984.
Irish Times, June 8, 1984, June 12, 1984, November 8, 1984.*

*   *   *

MARTIN, Ruth
    See RAYNER, Claire (Berenice)

*   *   *

MARTIN, Steve   1945-

PERSONAL: Born August, 1945, in Waco, Tex.; son of Glenn (a realtor) and Mary (Lee) Martin; married Victoria Tennant (an actress), 1986. *Education:* Attended Long Beach State College and University of California at Los Angeles.

ADDRESSES: Home—Beverly Hills, Calif. *Office*—P. O. Box 929, Beverly Hills, Calif. 90213. *Agent*—Marty Klein, Agency for the Performing Arts, 9000 Sunset Blvd., Suite 1200, Los Angeles, Calif. 90069; (public relations) Paul Bloch, Rogers & Cowan, 10000 Santa Monica Blvd., Los Angeles, Calif. 90067.

CAREER: Comedian, actor, and writer. Partner in the Aspen Film Society and 40 Share Productions. Worked at Disneyland and Knott's Berry Farm in the early 1960s; performer in coffeehouses, c. 1963; comedy writer for television programs, including "The Smothers Brothers Comedy Hour," 1968, "The John Denver Rocky Mountain Christmas Show," 1975, and "Van Dyke and Company," 1975, and for performers, including Glen Campbell, Ray Stevens, Pat Paulsen, John Denver, and Sonny and Cher; has made numerous guest appearances on television programs, including "The Tonight Show Starring Johnny Carson," "Dinah!," "The Merv Griffin Show," "The Dick Cavett Show," and "Saturday Night Live"; executive producer, "Do-

mestic Life" (television series), Columbia Broadcasting System (CBS), 1984; actor in motion pictures, including "The Absent Minded Waiter," 1977, "The Jerk," 1979, "Pennies from Heaven," 1981, "Dead Men Don't Wear Plaid," 1982, "The Man with Two Brains," 1983, "The Lonely Guy," 1984, "All of Me," 1984, "Little Shop of Horrors," 1986, "Three Amigos!," 1986, "Roxanne," 1987, "Planes, Trains, and Automobiles," 1987, "Dirty Rotten Scoundrels," 1988, and "Parenthood," 1989.

MEMBER: Screen Actors Guild, American Guild of Variety Artists, American Federation of Television and Radio Artists.

AWARDS, HONORS: Emmy Award, National Academy of Television Arts and Sciences, 1969, for best achievement in comedy, variety, or music for "The Smothers Brothers Comedy Hour"; Emmy Award nomination, 1975, for best writing in a comedy, variety, or music special for "Van Dyke and Company"; Georgie Award, American Guild of Variety Artists, 1977; Academy Award nomination, Academy of Motion Picture Arts and Sciences, 1977, for "The Absent-Minded Waiter"; Jack Benny Award, University of California at Los Angeles, 1978, for entertainment excellence; Grammy Award, National Academy of Recording Arts and Sciences, 1978, for "Let's Get Small," and 1979, for "A Wild and Crazy Guy"; National Society of Film Critics Award and New York Film Critics Circle Award, both 1984, both for role in "All of Me."

WRITINGS:

Cruel Shoes (humorous sketches; Literary Guild alternate selection; Playboy Book Club featured alternate), Press of the Pegacycle Lady, 1977, revised and enlarged edition, Putnam, 1979.

"The Absent-Minded Waiter" (screenplay), Paramount, 1977.

"Let's Get Small" (recording), Warner Bros., 1977.

"Steve Martin: A Wild and Crazy Guy" (television special), National Broadcasting Corp. (NBC), 1978.

"A Wild and Crazy Guy" (recording), Warner Bros., 1978.

"King Tut" (recording), Warner Bros., 1978.

"Comedy Is Not Pretty" (recording; also see below), Warner Bros., 1979.

(With Carl Reiner) "The Jerk" (screenplay), Universal, 1979.

"Comedy Is Not Pretty" (television special), NBC, 1980.

"Steve Martin's Best Show Ever" (television special), NBC, 1981.

"The Steve Martin Brothers" (recording), Warner Bros., 1982.

(With Reiner and George Gipe) "Dead Men Don't Wear Plaid" (screenplay), Universal, 1982.

(Co-writer) "The Man with Two Brains" (screenplay), Warner Bros., 1983.

(With Lorne Michaels and Randy Newman; and executive producer) "Three Amigos!" (screenplay), Orion, 1986.

(And executive producer) "Roxanne" (screenplay; based on "Cyrano de Bergerac" by Edmond Rostand), Columbia, 1987.

SIDELIGHTS: "Well, EXCUUUSE MEEEE!!!" Steve Martin would roar during his stand-up comedy routine, his entire body shaking with indignation, and the audience, many sporting giant bunny ears or a fake arrow through the head, would erupt with howls, cheers, and an ovation comparable to those heard at rock concerts. The bizarre incongruity of a junior-executive type wearing balloons on his head, latex nose and glasses, and a white, custom-tailored, three-piece suit struck the perfect chord with American audiences in the 1970s. Martin's sudden attacks of "happy feet" took him lurching across the stage; he twisted balloons into absurd shapes, then named them "Puppy dog! Venereal disease! The Sistine Chapel!"; he performed magic tricks that didn't quite work. But most of all, Martin parodied the whole idea of a comedian standing on stage telling jokes. Playing the part of a "wild and crazy guy," Martin became one of the hottest stand-up comics of the decade. His first two comedy albums won Grammy Awards and sold millions of copies; he scored a hit single with the absurd song "King Tut"; and the book *Cruel Shoes,* his collection of humorous sketches, was a national bestseller. By 1979 Martin had graduated to films, making the box office smash "The Jerk" and following with a string of other films throughout the 1980s. His performance in 1984's "All of Me" earned popular acclaim as well as awards from the National Society of Film Critics and the New York Film Critics Circle. "Roxanne" showed him capable of touching character portrayals, while "Planes, Trains and Automobiles" gave Martin the chance to play the straight man. Over the course of two decades, Martin has "evolved from a cooly absurdist stand-up comic to a fully formed, amazingly nimble comic actor," notes Janet Maslin in the *New York Times.*

Martin's fascination with the entertainment world stems back to his childhood. He was stagestruck at the age of three and grew up idolizing such comedians as Laurel and Hardy, Jerry Lewis, and Red Skelton. "The first day I saw a movie," he told *Newsweek*'s Tony Schwartz, "I knew that's what I wanted to do." By the age of five, he was memorizing Red Skelton's television skits and performing them at school show-and-tells. When his family moved to California, he hiked over to the new Disneyland amusement park and got a part-time job selling guidebooks, magic tricks, and Frontierland rodeo ropes. "I had mystical summer nights there," he recalls. "Fireworks, lights in the trees, a dance band playing music from the '40s."

During working hours he would sneak away to watch an old vaudevillian comic, Wally Boag, at Disneyland's Golden Horseshoe Revue. The comedian performed a routine of songs, jokes, and balloon tricks that Martin committed to memory. Soon he was performing the tricks he sold, twirling a lasso, playing the banjo, and appearing in a Boag production called "It's Vaudeville Again." After eight years at the Magic Kingdom, Martin left for nearby Knott's Berry Farm to act in melodrama at the Birdcage Theatre and perform his own fifteen-minute routines of comedy, magic, and banjo music.

Martin's budding career was cut short by his discovery of education. He fell in love with Stormy, an actress in the Birdcage company, who persuaded him to read Somerset Maugham's *The Razor's Edge.* "It was all about a person who questions life," Martin told Schwartz. "I read it and I can remember afterward sitting in a park and Stormy saying, 'Knowledge is the most important thing there is.'" Convinced, Martin enrolled at Long Beach State College where he studied philosophy for the next three years. But when he came across the arguments of Ludwig Wittgenstein concerning semantics, and the philosopher's contention that nothing is absolutely true, his interest in philosophy waned. Martin concluded that "the only logical thing was comedy because you don't have to explain it or justify it." He transferred to the University of California and changed his major to theatre.

Martin's first big break in show business came when he submitted some of his written material to Mason Williams, the head writer for CBS-TV's "The Smothers Brothers Comedy Hour." At the time, Martin was broke, living in a maid's quarters in Bel Air, struggling as a performer at small clubs and coffeehouses, and studying television writing at UCLA. Williams invited him to join the writing staff of the show, one of the highest-rated shows on television at the time. "I didn't have any *idea* what I was doing there," he admitted. "So young and inexperienced in such a big-league job. But I was too busy repressing it all to deal with it." CBS cancelled the show in 1968, but Martin and the show's other ten writers won an Emmy for their work. The award tripled Martin's value as a writer, and he was soon making $1,500 a week writing for entertainers like Glen Campbell, Ray Stevens, Pat Paulsen, John Denver, and Sonny and Cher. Still, his ambition was to work onstage: "I decided to stop writing for other people and perform full-time again," he told Kathy Lowry of *New Times.* "I was bored with writing all that formula stuff. I wanted to deal directly with the audience."

The early 1970s was a dismal period in Martin's career. He took his stand-up act on the road, playing every small club he could find and opening for rock groups whose drugged, impatient audiences shouted him off the stage. "Back then they didn't know what a comedian was," Martin told Janet Coleman in *New York.* He later satirized the period in one of his routines: a marijuana-smoking hippie is watching Martin perform, nods slowly, then drawls, "These guys are *good.*" Coleman recounts that Martin is "still annoyed by the ritual sloppiness and inattention of the 'love generation' audience."

Success as a stand-up comedian came when Martin developed a distinctive stage persona. When doing his act, Martin became a parody of a comedian, a satire on the idea of a professional comic. His character was shallow and slick, desperate for acceptance, full of insincere show-business asides to the audience, and unaware of his own stupidity. Balloon gags, juggling, banjo playing, and rabbit ears were all used in a purposely hokey attempt to get laughs. Pauline Kael describes Martin's stand-up act in the *New Yorker:* "Onstage, he puts across the idea that he's going to do some cornball routine, and then when he does it it has quotation marks around it, and that's what makes it hilarious. He does the routine straight, yet he's totally facetious."

His usual performance began with Martin walking out in his six-hundred-dollar white suit, an expensive banjo slung over his shoulder, and announced: "Hi, I'm Steve Martin, and I'll be out in *just* a minute!" For a few moments, he goofed in the spotlight, hummed to himself, looked around aimlessly. He was "waiting for the drugs to take effect," he explained. Then, "Okay, you paid the money, you're expecting to see a professional show, so let's not waste any more time, here we go with Professional Show Business, let's go, hey!" He steps back, starts tuning the banjo, plucking one string then another, turning a peg or two, then moves up and smashes his nose into the microphone. "Okay, we're moving now, eh folks? Yes, these are the good times and we're having them, ah ha ha ha."

"I mean," David Felton wonders in *Rolling Stone,* "what *is* this shit? Here's one of the hottest comedians in the business . . . and he's standing up there like a *jerk,* an *idiot,* a f——ing *asshole!* And that's the whole point." Lowry explains: "Steve Martin just wants to get a laugh; he doesn't much care about being profound or pricking society's conscience." Schwartz claims that "Martin's style is a pie in the faces of Lenny Bruce, Dick Gregory, Mort Sahl and all the iconoclastic comics who dominated the stand-up scene in the '60s." Martin agrees. Speaking to *U.S. News & World Report,* he revealed: "The '60s was a time of humorlessness in America. Everybody was so dead earnest. . . . During this time, the cheapest way to get a laugh was to make a political joke. . . . When I made my breakthrough in comedy in the early 1970s, politics was very much on everybody's mind. I saw it as my job to take it off their minds and so left politics out of my comedy. I think that was a big part of my success.

There was no moralizing, no left, no right; it was just about a human being."

Martin transferred his stage persona to the screen in 1979's "The Jerk," a film that grossed over seventy million dollars at the box office. Playing the white son in a poor black family (obviously an adopted son, but Martin doesn't realize it), he goes on to win and lose a fortune with a crazy invention. Audiences loved the movie, but critics found it wanting, expecting it to be somehow more "relevant" or provocative. Martin's next few efforts were also met with critical coolness. Audience appeal was also limited. "Pennies from Heaven," a lush musical set in the Thirties, lost money; "Dead Men Don't Wear Plaid," a spoof of the hard-boiled detective genre which incorporated scenes from vintage movies, was a box office disappointment. As Martin said of this period to Kenneth Turan in *Rolling Stone,* "It was like a dog scratching around to find a place to sit, getting up and down, walking around five or six times, before finally settling somewhere. That's the way I kept walking, trying to find the right screen persona to sit in. Something I like playing. Something I can do again."

It was only with "All of Me," in which Martin co-starred with Lily Tomlin, that he discovered a comfortable screen character. Ironically for the comic who had made his reputation as a "wild man," Martin's new character was a normal fellow who is beset with unusual problems. In the film, Martin plays a lawyer who becomes possessed by the spirit of a dead woman. One side of his body is controlled by the woman, the other side by him. Martin's amazing ability to portray this absurd physical condition—half male and half female—drew widespread critical praise and won him two major film awards as well. "To see his physical contortions in *All of Me,*" writes Turan, "to watch him trying to play both sexes simultaneously . . . is so boggling that audiences are often far too flabbergasted to laugh at all. Had he been born in another century, Martin might have been burned at the stake for witchcraft or demonic possession." In addition to the film's physical humor, Jack Barth writes in *Film Comment,* "*All of Me* is Martin's first comedy to subjugate gags to story and characterization. . . . [It] is also the first Martin film to deliver a satisfying ending." The result pleased the filmgoing public as well as the critics. "All of Me," notes Turan, was "the Number One film in America, with reviews to match."

Martin further developed his new screen character in subsequent films, particularly in "Roxanne," a gentle, updated version of the classic "Cyrano de Bergerac." Martin plays a small town fireman with an absurdly long nose. Called upon to assist a friend in wooing the new woman in town, Martin falls in love with her himself. Writing in the *Chicago Tribune,* Dave Kehr calls the film "a romantic comedy of grace, buoyancy and surprising emotional depth, filled with civilized pleasures." Tom Shales in the *Washington Post* reports that "critics have adored the writing, but have also likened Martin's comedic agility onscreen to Charlie Chaplin's. There have been references to things like 'comic genius' bursting forth." In her review for the *Los Angeles Times,* Sheila Benson notes: "I can't think of a current movie in which every element is in such balance: Martin seems unfettered, expansive, utterly at ease, capable of any physical feat. . . . There's a tenderness to him that's magnetic." David Ansen in *Newsweek* concludes: " 'Roxanne' is a charmer. Sweet-spirited, relaxed, it's a sun-dappled romantic comedy. . . . This is the culmination of a long quest to exorcise [Martin's] stage persona as a wild and crazy guy."

By the late 1980s Martin had left his stand-up "wild and crazy" image behind him. He had become, in the words of Richard Cor-

liss of *Time,* "this decade's most charming and resourceful comic actor." A wide variety of film comedy roles were suddenly available to him. In "Planes, Trains and Automobiles" Martin played the straight man to John Candy, in "Dirty Rotten Scoundrels" he played a conman with Michael Caine, and in "Parenthood" he was a middle-class father. And all three films, in pleasant contrast to several earlier Martin efforts, were solid box office hits.

Although he is now one of comedy's most successful stars, Martin lives quietly in Beverly Hills. He avoids the film industry's nightlife, and he is known as an art collector, a vegetarian, and a man who cherishes his privacy. Speaking to *U.S. News & World Report,* Martin muses on the entertainment industry: "One thing about show business is that you only get what you earn. If Prince sells out a concert, it's not as though the money is coming from the government. He says, 'I'm going to charge $15 . . . to get in, and you don't have to come if you don't want to.' It's very capitalistic, democratic and fair."

AVOCATIONAL INTERESTS: Reading old magic books, art books, museum catalogs, and the *New Yorker* magazine; playing horseshoes; skiing.

BIOGRAPHICAL/CRITICAL SOURCES:

BOOKS

Contemporary Literary Criticism, Volume 30, Gale, 1984.
Lenburg, Greg, Randy Skretvedt and Jeff Lenburg, *Steve Martin: The Unauthorized Biography,* St. Martin's, 1980.

PERIODICALS

American Film, June, 1982, November, 1988, August, 1989.
Chicago Tribune, June 19, 1987, July 13, 1987.
Esquire, March 27, 1979.
Film Comment, January, 1979.
Films in Review, February, 1988.
Los Angeles Times, December 27, 1984, June 19, 1987, June 28, 1987, June 30, 1987.
Newsweek, January 31, 1977, April 3, 1978, June 22, 1987.
New Times, September 2, 1977.
New York, August 22, 1977.
New Yorker, June 27, 1983.
New York Times, January 14, 1980, May 21, 1982, June 19, 1987, July 12, 1987.
People, May 1, 1978, July 6, 1987.
Rolling Stone, December 1, 1977, July 27, 1978, November 30, 1978, April 5, 1979, November 8, 1984.
Time, October 31, 1977, June 15, 1987, August 24, 1987.
U.S. News & World Report, June 17, 1985.
Washington Post, September 15, 1977, June 3, 1979, June 23, 1979, June 19, 1987.

—*Sketch by Thomas Wiloch*

*   *   *

MARWICK, Arthur 1936-

PERSONAL: Born February 29, 1936, in Edinburgh, Scotland; son of William Hutton (a lecturer) and Maeve (Brereton) Marwick. *Education:* University of Edinburgh, M.A. (first class honours), 1957; Balliol College, Oxford, B.Litt., 1960.

ADDRESSES: Home—67 Fitzjohn's Ave., London NW 3, England. *Office*—Department of History, Open University, Bletchley, Buckinghamshire, England.

CAREER: University of Aberdeen, Aberdeen, Scotland, assistant lecturer in history, 1959-60; University of Edinburgh, Edinburgh, Scotland, lecturer in history, 1960-69, director of studies, 1964-69; Open University, Bletchley, England, professor of history, 1969—, dean of arts, 1978-84. Visiting professor, State University of New York at Buffalo, 1966-67, Stanford University, 1984-85; visiting scholar, Hoover Institution, 1984-85; directeur d'etudes invite, L'Ecole des hautes etudes en sciences sociales, Paris, 1985.

MEMBER: Royal Historical Society (fellow).

AWARDS, HONORS: D.Litt., Edinburgh University, 1981.

WRITINGS:

The Explosion of British Society, 1914-1962, Pan Books, 1963.
Clifford Allen: The Open Conspirator, Oliver & Boyd, 1964.
The Deluge: British Society and the First World War, Bodley Head, 1965, Little, Brown, 1966.
Britain in the Century of Total War: War, Peace, and Social Change, 1900-1967, Little, Brown, 1968.
The Nature of History, Macmillan, 1970, Knopf, 1971, new revised edition, Macmillan, 1989.
(Contributor) Karl Miller, editor, *Memoirs of a Modern Scotland,* Faber, 1970.
War and Social Change in the Twentieth Century, Macmillan, 1976.
The Home Front: The British and the Second World War, Thames & Hudson, 1976.
Women at War, 1914-1918, Fontana, 1977.
Class: Image and Reality in Britain, France, and the USA since 1930, Oxford University Press, 1980.
(Editor) *Illustrated Dictionary of British History,* Thames & Hudson, 1980.
British Society since 1945, Penguin, 1982, revised edition, 1989.
Britain in Our Century: Images and Controversies, Thames & Hudson, 1984.
(Editor) *Class in the Twentieth Century,* St. Martin's, 1986.
Beauty in History: Society, Politics, and Personal Appearance, c. 1500 to the Present, Thames & Hudson, 1988.

Contributor of articles and reviews to learned and popular journals.

WORK IN PROGRESS: Editing and contributing to *Literature and Society: Some Major Issues; British Culture since 1965; The International Cultural Revolution of the 1960s.*

SIDELIGHTS: Class and society in the twentieth century is the subject of much of Arthur Marwick's research, culminating in such titles as *Class: Image and Reality in Britain, France and the USA since 1930* and *British Society since 1945.* The author often uses quotes from members of various social stations to illustrate his theses; in Shirley Robin Letwin's *Spectator* review of *Class,* the critic notes some examples: "A nightwatchman, whose wife was described as a prostitute, looks down on the owner of his lodging house as 'working-class.' But a [driver] regards the owner of [a liquor shop], who takes lodgers, as a privileged 'boss.' A stable boy, in awe of his 'boss,' the greatest man in town, nevertheless invites him home to dinner, only to discover that [the boss] uses the word 'yis,' which establishes that he is really 'working-class.' A housepainter describes himself as 'working-class,' but an engineer's turner, on the other hand, insists that he is an 'artisan.'"

In *British Society since 1945* Marwick contends that "from the point of view of the vast majority of the British people, as little interested as ever in major national concerns, the most significant changes in values were probably those related to sexual mores and social relationships." The author "does not ignore

structural questions, like the rediscovery of poverty and the new dimensions of social inequality, but nor does he dwell on them," according to *Times Literary Supplement* critic Peter Clark. "[Marwick] prefers to illuminate his themes obliquely with the anecdotal insight and the telling quotation. He has achieved his aim in breaking new ground and now that he has done so it will be easier for others to follow."

Marwick told *CA* that a more recent book, *Beauty in History: Society, Politics, and Personal Appearance, c. 1500 to the Present,* "against the vociferous opposition of cultural theorists and some feminists, opens up a new area of historical research, the social and political implications of personal appearance, male and female." He added: "In evaluating beauty we should not, as all previous writers have done, look simply at what painters *painted,* as fashion writers *decreed,* nor even at one or two individual beauties and what was *said* about them; we must look at what people actually *did.*"

BIOGRAPHICAL/CRITICAL SOURCES:

BOOKS

Marwick, Arthur, *Class: Image and Reality in Britain, France, and the USA since 1930,* Oxford University Press, 1980.
Marwick, Arthur, *British Society since 1945,* Penguin, 1982, revised edition, 1989.

PERIODICALS

Listener, July 31, 1980.
New York Review of Books, December 16, 1969.
New York Times, December 27, 1965.
Spectator, June 14, 1980.
Times (London), June 19, 1980.
Times Literary Supplement, July 23, 1982, January 11, 1985.

*   *   *

MARX, Anne

PERSONAL: Born in Bleicherode, Germany; came to the United States in 1936, naturalized in 1938; daughter of Jakob (a physician) and Susanne (Weinberg) Loewenstein; married Frederick E. Marx (a real estate consultant), February 12, 1937; children: Thomas J., Stephen L. *Education:* Graduated from University of Heidelberg Medical School; University of Berlin Medical School, M.S., 1933; attended Orthopedic Clinic of University of Frankfurt am Main, 1934-35.

ADDRESSES: Home—315 The Colony, Tallwood Lane, Hartsdale, N.Y. 10530.

CAREER: Fairleigh Dickinson University, Madison, N.J., staff member of poetry workshop, 1962-64; Iona College, Writers' Conference, New Rochelle, N.Y., director of poetry workshop, 1964-70; Wagner College, New York City Writers' Conference, fellow, 1965; principal speaker, Arkansas Writers' Conference and South & West Conventions, 1966-71; Poetry Society of America Poetry Workshop, New York City, guest critic, 1970-71; Council for the Arts in Westchester, Inc., Westchester, N.Y., chairman of poetry division, 1970; New York Public Library, Donnell Library Center, New York City, director of poetry reading series, 1970-74. Workshop leader or speaker at National League of American Pen Women conventions, 1974-87, and National Federation of State Poetry Societies conventions, 1976, 1981, and 1982. Workshop leader and/or reader at poetry festivals in Louisiana, New York, and Indonesia. Chairman, Biennial Poetry Festival, Lincoln Center, New York City; organizer of poetry readings celebrating the Biennial Birthday of the

Statue of Liberty, remembering the Holocaust, and representing The Arts in Judaism.

MEMBER: Poetry Society of America (fellow, 1964; member of executive board, 1965-70; vice-president, 1970-72), Poetry Society of Great Britain, National League of American Pen Women (president of Westchester County branch, 1962-64; North Atlantic regional chairman, 1964-66; national poetry editor, 1974-78; New York State letters chairman, 1978-80; New York State President, 1982-84; national 2nd vice-president, 1984-86), Academy of American Poets, National Federation of State Poetry Societies, Composers, Artists and Authors of America, Inc. (poetry editor, 1974-78), Poetry Society of Pennsylvania, New York Poetry Forum.

AWARDS, HONORS: Poetry awards from National Federation of Women's Clubs, 1957, 1958, 1959, and National Federation of State Poetry Societies, 1962, 1965, 1966; National Sonnet prizes, 1959, 1968; American Weave Chapbook Award, 1960, for *Into the Wind of Waking;* annual Braithwaite Contest, 1960; Countess d'Esternaux gold medal, 1965; Greenwood Prize (Great Britain), 1966; South & West Publications award, 1966, for *By Grace of Pain;* award, Ivan Franko Memorial Competition, 1966; *Atlantic* Award, 1967; Mason Sonnet Prizes, World Order of Narrative Poets, 1970, 1971, 1972, 1974, 1975, 1980; Cecil Hemley Memorial Prize, Poetry Society of America, 1974; named Poet of the Year, New York Poetry Forum, 1981; World Order of Narrative Poets prizes, 1981-86; Della Miller Memorial Prize, 1982; Song Lyric Award from composer De Lisa, 1983; biennial and annual poetry prizes in National League of American Pen Women competitions, 1985-88; biennial award for Excellence in Service, 1986, and Distinguished Service Award, 1988, both from National League of American Pen Women.

WRITINGS:

POETRY

Ein Buechlein: German Lyrics, Kaufman Verlag, 1935.
Into the Wind of Waking, foreword by John Holmes, American Weave Press, 1960.
The Second Voice, Fine Editions Press, 1963.
By Grace of Pain, South & West Publications, 1966.
By Way of People, Golden Quill Press, 1970.
A Time to Mend: Selected Poems, 1960-1970, Living Poets Library, 1973.
Hear of Israel and Other Poems, Golden Quill Press, 1975.
40 Love Poems for 40 Years, Highmarks House, 1977.
Face Lifts for All Seasons: New Poems, Golden Quill Press, 1980.
45 Love Poems for 45 Years, Highmarks House, 1982.
A Further Semester: New Poems, William Bauhan, 1985.

OTHER

Holocaust: Hurts to Healings, Crossroads Agency (Texas), 1984, bilingual edition published as *Wunden und Narben / Hurts to Healings,* The World of Books, Ltd., 1986.

Also co-editor of *Pegasus in the Seventies* (anthology), 1975. Contributor to more than twenty anthologies, including *American Women Poets,* Olivant Press, *The Study and Writing of Poetry: American Women Poets Study Their Craft,* Whitston Publishing, 1982, *Great Poems,* Collins & World, 1983, and *The Courage to Grow Old,* Ballantine, 1989. Contributor to *Ukranian Review, Christian Science Monitor, Croton Review, New York Times, Negative Capability,* and other periodicals. Contributing editor, *Pen Woman,* 1986-88.

WORK IN PROGRESS: Revising a collection of articles on poetry; a book of new poems on illness and recovery.

SIDELIGHTS: Anne Marx once told *CA:* "As a bilingual poet, I am especially intrigued with the mystery of language communicating in the unique way we call poetry. Born and educated in Germany, I always knew poetry to be a spontaneous activity for me. Being expelled from my homeland meant giving up not only a beloved language but also the writing of poetry, my most meaningful means of communication. It took twenty years until English became my most natural voice, the preferred tool for writing. The differences in my two languages, as well as in my two backgrounds, intrigue me now. Aided by a thorough early foundation in Latin, a fair command of French, and by my present extensive annual travel abroad, I am searching for new ways to overcome language barriers, especially in poetry. Translations are never enough."

More recently, she wrote, "Now, a number of years later, I realize that translations—done knowledgeably and lovingly—can indeed become a bridge. A German professor did a superb job of translating my Holocaust poems and circulating them in my hometown and in other parts of Germany. The surprising and moving reaction of young people identifying with me at this time, when my recollections were presented to them in their mother language, became a revelation of the power of the word, the right word at the right time. For me, this cycle beginning with my first small collection of German lyrics is completed with the publication of this bilingual volume [*Wunden und Narben / Hurts to Healings*]."

BIOGRAPHICAL/CRITICAL SOURCES:

PERIODICALS

Beaux Arts, spring, 1957.
Book Exchange (London), November, 1970.
Encore, November, 1975, January, 1976.
Essence, winter, 1967-68.
Il Giornale Dei Poetei, April, 1976.
New York Times, March 1, 1981.
Pen Woman, May, 1969, June, 1983, November, 1988.
Poet Lore, spring, 1968, winter, 1971, summer, 1974.
Poetry Society Bulletin, October, 1959, October, 1963, November, 1964, November, 1966, November, 1968, November, 1970.
Villager, October, 1960, February, 1971.
Wormser Zeitung (Germany), March, 1983, November, 1986.

*   *   *

MASON, George E(van) 1932-

PERSONAL: Born March 9, 1932, in Cortland, N.Y.; son of Evan E. and Norma (Barnes) Mason; married Gloria M. Gulino, July 3, 1953; children: Victoria, Joseph, Elizabeth, William, Christopher. *Education:* Cortland State Teachers College (now State University of New York College at Cortland), B.S., 1953; Syracuse University, M.S., 1958, Ph.D., 1963. *Politics:* Democrat.

ADDRESSES: Home—405 Riverhill, Athens, Ga. 30606. *Office*—College of Education, University of Georgia, Athens, Ga. 30602.

CAREER: Elementary teacher in North Syracuse, N.Y., 1955-57; Board of Cooperative Educational Services, Theresa, N.Y., reading specialist, 1957-60; Florida State University, Tallahassee, associate professor and head of department of elementary education, 1963-66; University of Georgia, Athens, associate professor, 1966-71, professor of reading, 1971—, head of department, 1973-78. *Military service:* U.S. Army, 1953-55.

MEMBER: International Reading Association, National Reading Conference, College Reading Association (president, 1984-85), Organization of Teacher Educators in Reading.

WRITINGS:

(With Edwin H. Smith) *Teaching Reading in Adult Basic Education,* Florida State Department of Education, 1965.

(With William D. Sheldon) *Winner's Circle,* Allyn & Bacon, 1970.

On the Level, Allyn & Bacon, 1975.

Full Count, Allyn & Bacon, 1975.

A Primer on Teaching Reading, F. E. Peacock, 1981.

(With Jay S. Blanchard and Danny B. Daniel) *Computer Applications in Reading,* International Reading Association, 1979, revised edition, 1983.

Scoring Higher on Tests (set of hectograph masters), J. Weston Walch, 1983.

(Editor with Blanchard) *The Computer in Reading and Language Arts,* Haworth Press, 1987.

The Language Experience Recorder, Plus (computer program), Teacher Support Software, 1987.

Sentence Starters (computer program), Teacher Support Software, 1987.

Stories from Planet Z (computer program), Teacher Support Software, 1987.

(With Shelley Wepner) *Reading Realities* (computer program), Teacher Support Software, 1988.

Author of column "The Printout" in *Reading Teacher,* 1983-86.

WORK IN PROGRESS: Development of a descriptor list for a computer database of reading/language arts lessons for Educational Products Information Exchange.

SIDELIGHTS: George E. Mason told *CA,* "I'm an active barbershopper (member of SPEBSQSA) and sing regularly with a registered quartet, 'The Seldom-Asked Four.' "

*　　*　　*

MATEJIC, Mateja 1924-

PERSONAL: Born February 19, 1924, in Smederevo, Yugoslavia; came to the United States in 1956, naturalized citizen, 1961; son of Dragoljub and Milica (Jelenkovic) Matejic; married Ljubica Nebrigic, June 13, 1949; children: Predrag, Milica, Vida, Nenad, Dragana. *Education:* Theological Seminary, Eboli, Italy, Diploma, 1946; Wayne State University, B.A., 1963; University of Michigan, Ph.D., 1967.

ADDRESSES: Home—1404 Norma Rd., Columbus, Ohio 43229. *Office*—Ohio State University, 1841 Millikin Rd., Columbus, Ohio 43210.

CAREER: Ordained Eastern Orthodox priest, 1951; priest at Orthodox churches in displaced persons camps, West Germany, 1951-56; parish priest in Monroe, Mich., 1956-57; parish priest at St. Steven of Dechani Serbian Orthodox Church, 1967—; Case Western Reserve University, Cleveland, Ohio, assistant professor of Slavic languages and literature, 1967-68; Ohio State University, Columbus, assistant professor, 1968-71, associate professor, 1971-74, professor of Slavic languages and literature, 1974-89, professor emeritus, 1989—, director of Hilandar Research Project, 1969-89, senior research associate of project, 1989—. Director of Kosovo Publishing Co., 1976—.

MEMBER: American Serbian Academic Society, American Association for the Advancement of Slavic Studies, American Association of Teachers of Slavic and East European Languages, Association of Writers in Bulgaria, Association of Writers in Serbia (honorary member).

AWARDS, HONORS: Woodrow Wilson fellowship, 1963; received second degree St. Klimet of Ochrida Medal from Patriarch of Bulgaria, 1978; 1300 Years of Bulgarian State Medal, 1985; Medal of Merit from University of Sofia, 1988.

WRITINGS:

Phrase Book: Serbian-English, Young Men's Christian Association (Hamburg, West Germany), 1950.

Biography of Saint Sava, Kosovo Publishing, 1976.

Hilandar Slavic Codices, Ohio State University Press, 1976.

Glorifying Saint Sava, Kosovo Publishing, 1977.

(Editor with Dragan Milivojevic) *An Anthology of Medieval Serbian Literature in English,* Slavica, 1980.

The Holy Mount and Hilandar Monastery, Hilandar Research Project, 1983.

Slavic Manuscripts from the Fekula Collection: A Description, Kosovo Publishing, 1983.

(With Vasa Mihailovich) *A Comprehensive Bibliography of Yugoslav Literature in English Translation: 1594-1980,* Slavic, 1984.

(Translator) Hrizostrom of Hilandar, *Officer for Saint Sava the Third,* Hilandar Research Project, 1986.

(With Dimitrije Bogdanovic) *Slavic Codices of the Great Lavra Monastery: A Description,* Centre International d'Information sur les Sources de l'Histoire Balkanique et Mediterraneene, 1988.

Relationships between the Russian and the Serbian Churches through the Centuries, Resource Center for Medieval Slavic Studies, Ohio State University, 1988.

Prayerbook for Orthodox Christians, Diocese of Sumadija, 1988.

IN SERBO-CROATIAN

Pesme (title means "Poems"), Iskra, 1964.

Ljermontovljev Demon i Njegoseva Luca Mikrokozma (title means "Lermontov's 'Demon' and Njegos's 'Rays of Microcosm' "), Avala, 1964.

(With Borivoje Karapandzich) *Na stazama izbeglickim: Srpsko pesnistvo u izbeglistvu, 1945-1968* (title means "On the Path of Exiles: Serbian Poetry in Exile, 1945-1968"), Srpska misao, 1969.

Hilandarski rukopis (title means "Hilandar Manuscript"), Kosovo Publishing, 1982.

OTHER

Contributor of more than two hundred articles, poems, and reviews to journals. Editor of *Path of Orthodoxy,* 1968—.

SIDELIGHTS: A Serbian Orthodox priest, Mateja Matejic became director of the Hilandar Research Project at Ohio State University in 1969. Located on Mt. Athos in Greece, Hilandar Monastery has housed Serbian monks and scholars since its founding in 1198. It also possesses a wealth of art and historic documents, including rare manuscripts that date back to the eleventh century. The manuscripts, which consist largely of imperial edicts and ecclesiastical codices, contain much folklore and secular literature as well. Concerned with the loss to Serbian culture that would result if these irreplaceable materials were ever destroyed, Matejic made arrangements to microfilm the contents of Hilandar Monastery's library for Ohio State University. The microfilm collection comprises approximately five hundred thousand pages of manuscript, most of which is written in one of the Slavic languages. Matejic's *Hilandar Slavic Codices* is a checklist of the Hilandar Slavic Manuscripts and provides a title, date, language, genre, and description for each of the documents.

* * *

MATILAL, Bimal Krishna 1935-

PERSONAL: Born June 1, 1935, in Calcutta, India; son of Hare Krishna and Parimal (Chakravorty) Matilal; married Karabi Chatterjee, May 8, 1958; children: Tamal, Anvita. *Education:* University of Calcutta, B.A. (with honors), 1954, M.A., 1956; Harvard University, A.M., 1963, Ph.D., 1965. *Religion:* Hinduism.

ADDRESSES: Office—Oriental Institute, Oxford University, Oxford OX1 2JD, England.

CAREER: Government Sanskrit College, Calcutta, India, lecturer in Sanskrit literature, 1957-62; University of Toronto, Toronto, Ontario, assistant professor, 1965-67, associate professor, 1967-71, professor of Indian philosophy, 1971-77; Oxford University, Oxford, England, Spalding Professor of Eastern Religions and Ethics, 1977—. Visiting associate professor, University of Pennsylvania, 1969-70; visiting professor, University of California, 1979, Victoria University of Wellington, New Zealand, and University of Chicago, 1983. S. N. Das Gupta Memorial Lecturer, Cambridge University, 1978; Stephanos Ghosh Lecturer, Calcutta University, 1980; S. G. Deuskan Lecturer, Calcutta, 1986. Visiting senior fellow, University of London, 1971-72; Shastri senior fellow, Shastri Indo-Canadian Institute, 1973; fellow, All Souls College, Oxford, 1976-81; visiting fellow, Harvard University, 1982 and 1988. Delegate, Third International Congress for Logic, Methodology and Philosophy of Science, Amsterdam, 1967.

MEMBER: International Congress of Orientalists, American Oriental Society, Society for Asian and Comparative Philosophy (vice-president, 1973—), Asiatic Society (Calcutta).

AWARDS, HONORS: University of Toronto overseas research fellowship.

WRITINGS:

The Navya-Nyaya Doctrine of Negation, Harvard University Press, 1968.
Epistemology, Logic and Grammar in Indian Philosophical Analysis, Mouton, 1971.
Sasadhara's Nyaya-Siddhanta-Dipa, L.D. Institute of Indology (Ahmedabad, India), 1976.
Jan Gonda, editor, *Nyaya-Vaisesika,* Volume 6: *A History of Indian Literature,* Harrassowitz, 1977.
The Central Philosophy of Jainism, L.D. Institute of Indology, 1981.
Logical and Ethical Issues in Religious Beliefs, Calcutta University Press, 1982.
Logic of Language and Reality: Introduction to Classical Indian Philosophy, Motilal Banarsidass, 1985.
(Editor) *Analytical Philosophy in Comparative Perception,* D. Reidel, 1985.
Perception: An Essay on Classical Indian Theory of Knowledge, Oxford University Press, 1986.
(Editor) *Buddhist Logic and Epistemology,* D. Reidel, 1986.
Niti, Yukti O Dharma (title means "Reason, Morality, and Religion"), Ananda (Calcutta), 1987.
Confrontation of Cultures, C.S.S.S. Calcutta, 1988.
Philosophy of Language in India, Oxford University Press (Delhi), in press.

Also author of radio play for All India Radio, 1961; editor, "Studies of Classical India" series, D. Reidel, 1978—. Contributor to journals in Europe, the United States, and India. Founder-editor, *Journal of Indian Philosophy,* twelve volumes, D. Reidel, 1970—.

WORK IN PROGRESS: The Indian Ethos: Epics and Ethics, a large monograph for Oxford University Press.

BIOGRAPHICAL/CRITICAL SOURCES:

BOOKS

The Contribution of Canadian Universities to an Understanding of Asia and Africa: A Bibliographical Directory of Scholars, 2nd edition, Canadian National Commission for UNESCO, 1967.

PERIODICALS

Times Literary Supplement, October 10, 1986.

* * *

MAY, Elaine Tyler 1947-

PERSONAL: Born September 17, 1947, in Los Angeles, Calif.; daughter of Edward T. (a physician) and Lillian (an art historian and family-planning educator; maiden name, Bass) Tyler; married Larry L. May (a historian and author), March 7, 1970; children: Michael Edward, Daniel David, Sarah Lillian. *Education:* University of California, Los Angeles, A.B. (cum laude), 1969, M.A., 1970, Ph.D., 1975.

ADDRESSES: Home—88 Arthur Ave. S.E., Minneapolis, Minn. 55414. *Office*—American Studies Program, 104 Scott Hall, University of Minnesota, Minneapolis, Minn. 55455.

CAREER: U.S. Senate, Washington, D.C., research intern with Committee on Intergovernmental Relations, 1969; California State University, Fullerton, instructor in history, 1971-72; California State University, Los Angeles, instructor in history, 1972-73; Princeton University, Princeton, N.J., instructor, 1974-76, assistant professor of history, 1976-78; University of Minnesota, Minneapolis, assistant professor, 1978-81, associate professor of American studies, 1981-89, professor of American studies and history, 1989—, associate dean, College of Liberal Arts, 1987—, member of women's studies governing council. Public speaker; humanities commentator for Minnesota Public Radio, 1981; project director, organizer, and moderator.

MEMBER: American Historical Association, Organization of American Historians, American Studies Association, American Association for the Advancement of the Humanities, National Organization for Women, Social Science History Association, Women Historians of the Midwest.

AWARDS, HONORS: Research fellow at Princeton University, 1975-77, Princeton Inn fellow, 1976; Mellon fellow at Harvard University, 1981-82; research scholar at Radcliffe College, 1982; fellow of American Council of Learned Societies, 1983-84; grant from National Endowment for the Humanities, 1983.

WRITINGS:

Great Expectations: Marriage and Divorce in Post-Victorian America, University of Chicago Press, 1980.
(Contributor) Michael Gordon, editor, *The American Family in Social-Historical Perspective,* 3rd edition, St. Martin's, 1983.
(Contributor) Stanley I. Kutler and Stanley N. Katz, editors, *The Promise of American History: Progress and Prospects,* Johns Hopkins University Press, 1983.

Homeward Bound: American Families in the Cold War Era, Basic Books, 1988.

(Contributor) Larry May, editor, *Recasting America: Culture and Politics in the Age of Cold War,* University of Chicago Press, 1989.

(Contributor) Steven Fraser and Gary Gerstle, editors, *The Rise and Fall of New Deal Liberalism,* Princeton University Press, 1989.

Contributor of more than a dozen articles and reviews to history and women's studies journals and newspapers.

SIDELIGHTS: Elaine Tyler May once told *CA:* "Everywhere we turn we find people bemoaning, or celebrating, the imminent collapse of the American family. And yet, the cry has been heard before. In the midst of every era that has undergone tremendous social change, the family has appeared threatened. The family continues to survive, although it is continually transformed, through each major historical upheaval. My work is prompted in part by an effort to understand these changes and the massive popular concern over the fate of the family.

"As a historian, I find it fascinating to see the same concerns emerge in different historical contexts. Why is the 'emancipation of women,' for example, continually blamed for the erosion of the family? As a feminist as well as a spouse and a mother, I find it imperative that the emancipation of women not be on a collision course with the survival of the family. In my own research and writing, I have found that the problems of family life are more the result of the failure of feminist goals than they are a result of their success. Although historians are not in the business of making predictions, it is my own feeling that once feminist goals are achieved in the public as well as in the private institutions of American life, we will find true mutuality and equality in the home. On that day in the hopefully near future, perhaps we will stop worrying about the collapse of American families. Families at that point will be intact because they will express the desires of the individuals within them—whether those families are united by marriage, blood, or friendship. We will then find a new meaning of 'family life' altogether."

*   *   *

MAY, Robert Stephen 1929-
(Robin May)

PERSONAL: Born December 26, 1929, in Deal, Kent, England; son of Robert Cyril (a naval surgeon) and Mary (Robertson) May; married Dorothy Joan Clarke, June 7, 1958 (died August 8, 1975); married Maureen Frances Fillipkiewicz, December 4, 1976; children: Michael Robert, Elizabeth Magda, David Peter. *Education:* Attended Central School of Speech and Drama, 1950-53. *Religion:* Church of England.

ADDRESSES: Home—23 Malcolm Rd., Wimbledon, London S.W. 19, England. *Agent*—Rupert Crew Ltd., Kings Mews, London WC1N 2JA, England.

CAREER: Actor, under name Robin May, in British Isles, 1953-63; commercial artists' agent in London, England, 1963-66; free-lance writer and journalist in London, 1966—; I.P.C. Magazines Ltd., London, feature writer and sub-editor of *Look and Learn,* beginning 1970. *Military service:* Royal Artillery, 1948-50; became second lieutenant.

MEMBER: National Union of Journalists, Society of Authors, Western Writers of America, English Westerners, Kansas Historical Society, Montana Historical Society, New York State Historical Association, South Dakota Historical Society, Wyoming Historical Society, Ontario Historical Society.

WRITINGS:

UNDER NAME ROBIN MAY

Operamania, Vernon & Yates, 1966.
Theatremania, Vernon & Yates, 1967.
(Compiler) *The Wit of the Theatre,* Frewin, 1969.
Who's Who in Shakespeare, Elm Tree, 1972.
Companion to the Theatre, Lutterworth, 1973.
Who Was Shakespeare?, David & Charles, 1974.
Wolfe's Army, Osprey, 1974.
The British Army in the American Revolution, Osprey, 1974.
The Wild West, Look-In, 1975.
The Gold Rushes, Luscombe, 1977, Hippocrene, 1978.
(With Joseph G. Rosa) *Gunlaw,* Contemporary Books, 1977 (published in England as *Gunsmoke,* New English Library, 1977).
The Story of the Wild West, Hamlyn, 1979.
(With Rosa) *Cowboy,* New English Library, 1980.
Behind the Baton, Muller, 1981.
Indians, Bison Books, 1982.
Gunfighters, Bison Books, 1983.
William the Conqueror and the Normans, Wayland, 1984.
Canute and the Vikings, Wayland, 1984.
Plains Indians of North America, Wayland, 1984.
History of the American West, Hamlyn, 1984.
Hallowe'en, Wayland, 1984.
Alfred the Great and the Saxons, Wayland, 1984.
Julius Caesar and the Romans, Wayland, 1984
Daniel Boone and the American West, Wayland, 1985.
A Plains Indian Warrior, Wayland, 1986.
A Colonial American Merchant, Wayland, 1986.
A Plantation Slave, Wayland, 1986.
History of the Theatre, Hamlyn, 1986.
A Guide to the Opera, Hamlyn, 1987.
(With Rosa) *Buffalo Bill and His Wild West: A Pictorial Biography,* University Press of Kansas, 1989.

SIDELIGHTS: Robert Stephen May told *CA:* "I am very lucky. I earn most of my living writing about my two favorite subjects, the American West and the performing arts. I write for young people as well as adults—an excellent way to achieve clarity and conciseness."

*   *   *

MAY, Robin
See MAY, Robert Stephen

*   *   *

MAYNES, E(dwin) Scott 1922-

PERSONAL: Born October 6, 1922, in Meriden, Conn.; son of Edwin (a cost estimator) and E. Janet (Scott) Maynes; married Blanche Rivero, November 11, 1953; children: Lisa, Philip, Christina. *Education:* Springfield College, B.S., 1947; Wesleyan University, M.A., 1949; University of Michigan, Ph.D., 1956. *Politics:* Democrat. *Religion:* Unitarian.

ADDRESSES: Home—112 North Sunset Dr., Ithaca, N.Y. 14850. *Office*—Department of Consumer Economics and Housing, Cornell University, Ithaca, N.Y. 14853.

CAREER: University of Michigan, Survey Research Center, Ann Arbor, assistant study director, 1949-53, study director,

1953-56; University of Minnesota, Minneapolis, assistant professor, 1956-60, associate professor, 1960-68, professor of economics, 1968-74, director of research, 1972-74; Cornell University, Ithaca, N.Y., professor of consumer economics and housing, 1974—, chairman of department, 1976-81. Visiting professor, University of California, San Diego, 1971-73. Member of board of directors of various financial institutions and consumer organizations. Consultant to various international institutes and councils. *Military service:* U.S. Army Air Forces, 1943-45; became sergeant.

MEMBER: American Economic Association, American Council on Consumer Interests (board member, 1980-82), Consumers Union of the United States (board member, 1968-77; treasurer, 1972-75), Ithaca Memorial Society (president, 1986-88).

WRITINGS:

(Editor with C. Arthur Williams) *Fault or No-Fault,* University of Minnesota Press, 1971.
Decision-Making for Consumers, Macmillan, 1976.
(Editor with ACCI Research Committee) *The Frontier of Research in the Consumer Interest,* American Council on Consumer Interests, 1988.

Contributor to professional journals. Member of editorial board, *Journal of Consumer Affairs,* 1974—, *Journal of Consumer Research,* 1977-83, and *Journal of Consumer Policy,* 1977—.

WORK IN PROGRESS: Consumer Product and Testing Organizations, an International Comparison, a monograph to be completed in 1991.

*   *   *

MAYS, Buddy (Gene) 1943-

PERSONAL: Born September 11, 1943, in Albuquerque, N.M.; son of Carl (an electrician) and Ethel (Boggus) Mays; married Mary Helen Now, October 20, 1973 (divorced June 1, 1977). *Education:* Attended New Mexico State University, 1967-70. *Politics:* None.

ADDRESSES: Home and office—P.O. Box 44, Truth or Consequences, N.M. 87901.

CAREER: Free-lance writer and photographer. *Albuquerque Tribune,* Albuquerque, N.M., photographer, 1970-72; Philmont Scout Ranch, Cimarron, N.M., instructor in mountaineering, 1972; KOAT-TV, Santa Fe, N.M., reporter, 1974-75. *Military service:* U.S. Coast Guard, 1961-65; received Gold Lifesaving Medal and expert rifleman medal.

MEMBER: Society of American Travel Writers.

AWARDS, HONORS: Pulitzer Prize nomination, 1977, for feature photography on the American cowboy in the Southwest; best black and white portfolio, Society of American Travel Writers International Photo Competition, 1985; runner-up for best color photo, Lowell Thomas Travel Journalism Awards, 1985.

WRITINGS:

Wildwaters, Chronicle Books, 1977.
A Pilgrim's Notebook Guide to Western Wildlife, Chronicle Books, 1977.
People of the Sun, University of New Mexico Press, 1979.
Ancient Cities of the Southwest, Chronicle Books, 1982.
Children of the Ancients, Chronicle Books, 1984.
Bed and Breakfast, Colorado, Chronicle Books, 1985.
RVing America's Backroads: Texas, Trailer Life Books, 1989.

RVing America's Backroads: New York, Trailer Life Books, 1989.

Also contributor to books. Contributor of articles and photographs to numerous periodicals, including *Time, Forbes, Travel-Holiday, Outdoor Life, Sports Afield, San Francisco Examiner,* and *New York Daily News.*

SIDELIGHTS: Buddy Mays told *CA:* "My present journalistic world revolves around travel, and most of my books, articles, and photographs deal with this subject. During the past five years, I've visited, photographed, and written about more than 40 countries and the wonders therein, and I'm still surprised and astonished by what I see and record. The world is a wondrous and wonderful place; if I can communicate to others less fortunate than myself (from a traveler's point of view) some of my own enthusiasm and experience about faraway places, than I have succeeded as a travel journalist."

*   *   *

McCLAIN, John O. 1942-

PERSONAL: Born January 30, 1942, in Spokane, Wash.; married Donna I. Dempster, 1980. *Education:* Washington State University, B.S., 1964; Yale University, M.S., 1965, Ph.D., 1970.

ADDRESSES: Office—S. C. Johnson Graduate School of Management, Malott Hall, Cornell University, Ithaca, N.Y. 14853.

CAREER: Sikorsky Helicopter, Stratford, Conn., research engineer, 1965-67; Cornell University, Ithaca, N.Y., assistant professor, 1970-75, associate professor, 1976-81, professor of production and quantitative methods, 1982—, coordinator of Sloan Program in Hospital and Health Services Administration, 1980-82. Consultant in production and inventory control and health services management. *Military service:* U.S. Army, 1960. U.S. Army Reserve, 1960-68; became sergeant.

MEMBER: Operations Research Society of America, Institute of Management Science, American Production and Inventory Control Society.

WRITINGS:

(With Joseph L. Thomas) *Operations Management: Production of Goods and Services,* Prentice-Hall, 1980, 2nd edition, 1985.
(With R. Conway, W. Maxwell, and S. Worona) *A User's Guide to XCELL,* Scientific Press, 1987.
(With L. J. Thomas and D. Edwards) *Cases in Operations Management: Using the XCELL Factory Modeling System,* Scientific Press, 1987.

Also author, with Thomas, of *Instructor's Guide to Cases in Operations Management,* 1987. Contributor to business, management, and health care journals.

WORK IN PROGRESS: Research on multi-item, multi-stage production in capacity bottleneck facilities; research on the costs and benefits of work-in-process inventory; research on different quality control methods in manufacturing.

*   *   *

McFEE, Michael 1954-

PERSONAL: Born June 4, 1954, in Asheville, N.C.; son of William Howard (a postal clerk) and Lucy (Farmer) McFee; married Belinda Anne Pickett (a clerk), June 16, 1978; children:

Philip Pickett. *Education:* University of North Carolina, B.A. (summa cum laude), 1976, M.A., 1978.

ADDRESSES: Home—2514 Pickett Rd., Durham, N.C. 27705.

CAREER: Duke University, Durham, N.C., instructor in continuing education, 1982-83; North Carolina State University at Raleigh, lecturer in English, fall, 1983; University of North Carolina, Chapel Hill, visiting lecturer in poetry, spring, 1984; University of North Carolina, Greensboro, visiting instructor, fall, 1985; visiting assistant professor at Cornell University, summer session, 1986-88; visiting poet, Lawrence University, winter, 1988. Judge of Academy of American Poets annual prize, 1978, 1981; writer in residence, Weymouth Cultural Center, 1983; poet in residence, Mary Arden Festival, Wake Forest University, 1983; afternoon poet, Duke University Writers' Conference, summers, 1986-88. Gives poetry readings.

MEMBER: National Book Critics Circle, Phi Beta Kappa.

AWARDS, HONORS: Discovery/*Nation* Award from *Nation* and the Poetry Center of the 92nd Street YMCA, 1980, for a manuscript of ten poems; scholar at Bread Loaf Writers' Conference and Reynolds Homestead Writers' Conference, both 1980; first prize from *Crucible,* 1980, for long poem "Roll for the Rump of the Year"; Pushcart Prize from Pushcart Press editors, 1981-82, for "Silo Letter in the Dead of a Warm Winter"; North Carolina Arts Council fellowship in poetry, 1985-86; Ingram Merrill Foundation fellowship in poetry and fiction, 1986; National Endowment for the Arts fellowship in poetry, 1987-88.

WRITINGS:

(Contributor) Jeffrey Richards, editor, *An Introduction to Film Criticism,* 3rd edition, Department of English, University of North Carolina, 1977.
(Contributor) *Pushcart Prize VI: Best of the Small Presses,* Pushcart, 1981.
Plain Air (poems), University Presses of Florida, 1983.
(Editor) *The Spectator Reader,* Spectator Publications, 1985.
Vanishing Acts (poems), Gnomon Press, 1989.

Work represented in anthologies, including *No Business Poems,* 1981; *New North Carolina Poetry: The Eighties,* edited by Stephen E. Smith, Green River, 1982; *Anthology of Magazine Verse and Yearbook of American Poetry; Lightyear,* 1984-89; *The Bedford Introduction to Literature,* 1987. Contributor of several hundred poems, articles, and reviews to magazines, including the *New Yorker, Poetry, Hudson Review, Nation, Georgia Review, Parnassus, Ploughshares,* and *Southern Poetry Review.* Poetry editor of *Carolina Quarterly,* 1977-79; book editor of *Spectator,* 1980—; book critic for National Public Radio, WUNC-FM, Chapel Hill, N.C., 1982—.

WORK IN PROGRESS: A third collection of poems, as yet untitled; *Pisgah,* a novel.

SIDELIGHTS: "I'm from the North Carolina mountains," Michael McFee once told *CA:* "The geography of the mountains, and, increasingly, their people, figure prominently in my writings. In ridge and relative I admire a clarity and yet convolution of line, a crabbed spaciousness—their 'plain air.' I was lucky to be influenced by several excellent expatriate Carolina writers: Robert Morgan, whose dense mountain baroque style taught me to load every rift with more ore, and A. R. Ammons. From discovering his books on a half-price table in Chapel Hill, to imitating them in my undergraduate honors manuscript, to writing a master's thesis on his long poems, Ammons has been a constant presence, his work a model of the balance possible between mind and world.

"My jobs have included housepainter, yard man, muffler plant worker, architectural draftsman, librarian, research aide, editor, journalist, critic, teacher, and poet. I stubbornly resisted an M.F.A. in creative writing because of the political gamesmanship and still view the academy with very mixed feelings—hence, the hodgepodge of odd jobs. I dislike pretentiousness, whether in professors, poets, or postmen. One of my poems ends: 'The elemental rule of life and art / Is simple as this: *Question airs.*' My motto is adopted from Melville: 'O Time, Strength, Cash, and Patience!'

"I suppose my poetry could be described as local and loyal, literal, and often playful. The imagists were right: concentration is of the essence in poetry (and in life as well). Shelley called poetry 'a means of redeeming from decay the visitations of the divinity in man,' which is true enough. But it is also—and increasingly—a means of redeeming us from the mundane decay of each day. Poetry is one way to halt, for a moment, that dissipation, that erosion of concentration that characterizes our lives. About the fiction in progress there is little to say so far, except that it seems a new approach (through character, scene, and story) to a familiar subject—the changing and yet enduring nature of the mountains, epitomized in Pisgah."

BIOGRAPHICAL/CRITICAL SOURCES:

PERIODICALS

Durham Morning Herald, February 5, 1984.

*   *   *

McMASTER, Beth 1935-

PERSONAL: Born April 15, 1935, in Peterborough, Ontario, Canada; daughter of John (a manufacturer and financier) and Stella (a secretary; maiden name, Shearer) Brown; married Stuart McMaster (a teacher), August 24, 1956; children: Kim, Brent, Rick. *Education:* Attended Teachers College (Peterborough), 1954; Trent University, B.A., 1983.

ADDRESSES: Home—R.R. 2, Peterborough, Ontario, Canada K9J 6X3. *Agent*—c/o Simon & Pierre Publishing, P.O. Box 280, Adelaide St., Toronto, Ontario, Canada M5C 2J4.

CAREER: Worked as elementary school teacher in Rockcliffe Airport, Ottawa, Ontario, 1954-57; *Peterborough Examiner,* Peterborough, Ontario, writer and reporter, 1963-68; Haliburton School of Fine Arts, Haliburton, Ontario, teacher of creative writing, 1972-73; Sir Standford Fleming College, Peterborough, teacher of creative writing, 1973-74; playwright. Member of Peterborough District United Way Board, 1978-82.

MEMBER: Canadian Child and Youth Drama Association, Playwrights Canada, Eastern Ontario Drama League (chairman, 1977-78), Peterborough Theatre Guild (president, 1975-76; honorary life member).

AWARDS, HONORS: Award from Nova Scotia Drama League, 1972, for "Stick with Molasses"; award from Touring Players Foundation, 1973, for "Which Witch Is Which?"; award from Ontario Multicultural Theatre Association, 1976, for "When Everybody Cares"; Peterborough Cultural Achievement Award, 1981.

WRITINGS:

When Everybody Cares (one-act play; first produced by SHARE Touring Co., in July, 1977), Simon & Pierre, 1976.
Beyond Escape (two-act play; first produced in Lindsay, Ontario, at Kawartha Summer Theatre, July, 1987), Playwright's Union of Canada, 1987.

ONE-ACT PLAYS FOR CHILDREN

The Magic Ring (first produced in Peterborough, Ontario, at Peterborough Theatre Guild, May, 1969), Simon & Pierre, 1974.

The Haunted Castle (first produced at Peterborough Theatre Guild, May, 1970), Simon & Pierre, 1974.

Stick with Molasses (first produced at Peterborough Theatre Guild, May, 1971), Playwright's Canada, 1973.

Which Witch Is Which? (first produced at Peterborough Theatre Guild, May, 1972), Simon & Pierre, 1973.

The Doll Said "Ouch" (first produced at Peterborough Theatre Guild, December, 1973), Simon & Pierre, 1977.

A Flumpet, a Trumpet (first produced at Peterborough Theatre Guild, June, 1974), Simon & Pierre, 1975.

Stripes for Christmas (first produced at Peterborough Theatre Guild, December, 1974), Simon & Pierre, 1977.

Happy Christmas (first produced at Peterborough Theatre Guild, December, 1975), Simon & Pierre, 1977.

Put on the Spot (first produced at Peterborough Theatre Guild, June, 1976), Simon & Pierre, 1976.

Happy Holly (first produced at Peterborough Theatre Guild, December, 1976; broadcast by CHEX-TV, December, 1976), Simon & Pierre, 1981.

Christmas Cards (first produced at Peterborough Theatre Guild, December, 1977; broadcast by CFTO-TV and CHEX-TV, December, 1977), Simon & Pierre, 1981.

Robena's Rose Coloured Glasses (first produced at Peterborough Theatre Guild, May, 1978), Simon & Pierre, 1986.

Magic Icicles (first produced at Peterborough Theatre Guild, December, 1978; broadcast by CHEX-TV, December, 1978), Simon & Pierre, 1982.

Super Santa Clone (first produced at Peterborough Theatre Guild, December, 1979; broadcast by CHEX-TV, December, 1979), Simon & Pierre, 1983.

"Polly Meets Pestford Plaque," first produced in Peterborough at County Dental Services, May, 1980.

"All Aboard for Happy Smiles," first produced in Cobourg, Ontario, at Cobourg Dental Services, May, 1981.

The Naciwonki Cap (first produced at Peterborough Theatre Guild, December, 1981; broadcast by CHEX-TV, December, 1981), Simon & Pierre, 1982.

"Mighty Murphy Saves the Day," first produced in Peterborough at County Dental Services, May, 1982.

Let's Hear It for Christmas! (first produced at Peterborough Theatre Guild, December, 1983), Simon & Pierre, 1986.

"Cat's Cradle," first produced in Peterborough at Adam Scott Collegiate Institute, March, 1984.

Twice Six Plus One (first produced in Lindsay at Kawartha Summer Theatre, 1985), Playwright's Union of Canada, 1989.

ONE-ACT PUPPET PLAYS FOR CHILDREN

"Whose Hat's That?," first produced in Peterborough at Lansdowne Place, November, 1982.

"Sing a Song for Christmas," first produced at Lansdowne Place, November, 1983.

"Reindeer Number Nine," first produced at Lansdowne Place, November, 1983.

"I Want to Be a Dinosaur," first produced in Kingston, Ontario, at Cataraqui Town Center, November, 1988.

OTHER

Work represented in anthologies, including *A Collection of Canadian Plays,* Volume 4, Simon & Pierre, 1973, and *Popular Performance Plays of Canada,* Volumes 1 and 2, Simon & Pierre, 1981.

WORK IN PROGRESS: A second adult two-act thriller, "Colour Me Dead," about a cyanide murder; a children's play, "Bradley Bradley and the Octopus," to be produced by the Peterborough Theatre Guild, December, 1989.

SIDELIGHTS: Beth McMaster once told *CA:* "When I began to write for children there was very little that was good for them to see in live performance. My own children saw some very bad theatre. Today the situation is much improved. But because of the great influence of television on children, the need for entertainment that involves input from them is an even more important reason for writing audience participation plays. And in spite of the advocates of subtlety and absurdity, I believe there is still a place in theatre (both adult's and children's) for good entertainment that has a clear, identifiable theme and story line. Most of my plays have a character-building message ('The Naciwonki Cap' exemplifies the power of positive thinking. ['Naciwonki' is 'I know I can' spelled backwards]; 'Which Witch Is Which?' says everyone makes mistakes, don't be afraid to admit you have). Children need reassurance that their feelings and fears are normal and acceptable.

"It's important to me that my plays don't 'talk down' to children. I try, without being didactic, to give them something positive to take home. I keep their interest with lots of action and by involving them in resolving the play's problem. Over the years, I've sorted out what kids like—they like a chase (as in 'Which Witch Is Which?'); they like to see the villain ridiculed rather than destroyed (as in 'The Haunted Castle'); they love to see children put something over on adults (as in 'Stripes for Christmas'); they love 'super' figures (as in 'Super Santa Clone'); they have little interest in romance (I found that out during the production of 'The Magic Ring'); they love music (it's in all my plays, written by Dick Beck, Monica Palmer, or Clifford Maynes).

"It has been said that because the female characters in many of my plays are very strong, they promote women's liberation. That pleases me for I have never seen women as anything but male contemporaries. But a more practical reason for the female leads is the fact that in amateur theatre the chances of casting a strong female are much better. Children shower attention on the villain in my plays. I think they all see a bit of themselves in him, and the fact that his evil ways lead to his downfall reinforces what they have been told by their parents, teachers, and most immediately by the 'guide figure' in the play. They have the reassurance that the universe is unfolding as it should. More and more my plays tend to zero in on relationships—relationships with ourselves and with others. In 'Whose Hat's That?' a boy learns to accept his own name; 'Reindeer Number Nine' finds out that there is a place in life for a follower.

"But for me the most important contribution my playwriting can make is to spark in children an interest in theatre—to light up their imaginations so that when they are the taxpayers and the business people and the politicians, they will say with conviction, 'Yes, live theatre is worthwhile. Let's support it.'" McMaster more recently added that "authors have to be aware of the financial struggle that theatres everywhere experience. My work is aimed at summer theatre audiences. The plays are gripping, fast-moving thrillers with a minimal cast (four to six) and one set. They are challenging to write but they are being produced and enjoyed—and that's the real test."

MEAD, Russell
See KOEHLER, Margaret (Hudson)

*   *   *

MEBANE, Mary E(lizabeth) 1933-

PERSONAL: Born June 26, 1933, in Durham County, N.C.; daughter of Samuel Nathaniel (a farmer) and Carrie (a factory worker; maiden name, Brandon) Mebane. *Education:* North Carolina College at Durham (now North Carolina Central University), B.A. (summa cum laude), 1955; University of North Carolina, M.A., 1961, Ph.D., 1973.

CAREER: Martin County (N.C.) public schools, English and music teacher, 1955-56; Pinehurst (N.C.) public schools, English, music, and library teacher, 1957; Durham City (N.C.) public schools, English and social studies teacher, 1957-60; North Carolina College at Durham (now North Carolina Central University), 1960-65, began as instructor, became assistant professor of English; South Carolina State College, Orangeburg, associate professor of English, 1967-74; University of South Carolina, Columbia, associate professor of English, 1974-77; University of Wisconsin—Madison, lecturer in composition, 1980-83.

MEMBER: International PEN, International Platform Association, Authors Guild, Authors League of America, Modern Language Association of America, National Council of Teachers of English, College Language Association, South Atlantic Modern Language Association.

AWARDS, HONORS: Southern Fellowships Fund fellowships, 1965, 1966; Woodrow Wilson Career Teaching fellowship, 1968; Southern Fellowship Fund dissertation year grant, 1971; Distinguished Alumnus Award in Literature, University of North Carolina at Chapel Hill, 1982; Milwaukee Artists Foundation grant, 1983; creative writing fellowship grant, National Endowment for the Arts, 1983.

WRITINGS:

(Contributor) R. Baird Shuman, editor, *A Galaxy of Black Writing,* Moore Publishing, 1970.
(Contributor) Harrison E. Salisbury, editor, *The Eloquence of Protest: Voices of the Seventies,* Houghton, 1972.
"Take a Sad Song" (two-act play), first produced in Columbia, S.C., at Playwrights' Corner, February, 1975.
(Contributor) Louis D. Rubin, Jr., editor, *Southern Panorama,* Louisiana State University Press, 1979.
Mary: An Autobiography, Viking, 1981.
Mary, Wayfarer (autobiography), Viking, 1983.

Contributor to *New York Times.*

SIDELIGHTS: In a *Los Angeles Times* review of Mary E. Mebane's *Mary: An Autobiography,* Carolyn See observes that "this is not primarily a black story, but another telling of the Ugly Duckling fable." Mebane grew up on an impoverished farm in North Carolina in the 1930s and 40s, when racial prejudice there was still at a peak. "Historically, my lifetime is important," Mebane writes in her second autobiography, *Mary, Wayfarer,* "because I was part of the last generation born into a world of total legal segregation in the Southern United States." *Mary* and *Mary, Wayfarer* chronicle her struggle to escape the trap of poverty and prejudice. However, her ambition to do so, as she relates, was far from an easy task, since Mebane not only had to contend with racial prejudice, but also had to overcome a family environment in which she was shown no affection or support from either her parents or her siblings.

In her autobiographies, Mebane releases her frustration against those who always opposed her efforts to make something of herself. Reviewing *Mary,* See remarks that this work is, therefore, "in many ways a grudge book" against her family, whites, and even other blacks. *Mary* is not a militant book that portrays the world as white against black, nor is it, as See phrases it, "a Booker T. Washington 'credit to her race' chronology." Instead, Mebane sees racial prejudice as a problem that both whites and blacks help to promote. "Where 'Mary' departs from the ordinary black chronicle," observes See, "is that it portrays the blacks—98% of them—. . . as even worse [than whites]. Everyone, *everyone,* in the society not only accepts his awful lot, his ignorance, his oppression, but clings to it, tenaciously." Some critics, like *Voice Literary Supplement*'s Margo Jefferson, object to the author's point of view. "She often writes," complains Jefferson, "as though no one but Mary Mebane emerged from such a background so unappreciated, with such gifts. And while this may be an emotional truth, it is not a factual one." Jonathan Yardley, however, praises *Mary, Wayfarer* in a *Washington Post* review as "a persistently stimulating, surprising book. It is also, as was 'Mary' before it, absorbing and moving."

Mebane managed to escape her allotted place in life through education—specifically, by earning a Ph.D. at the University of North Carolina at Chapel Hill, where she first experienced an integrated setting. "For the first time in my life my work was recognized" at the university, she reflects in *Mary, Wayfarer,* "and I was given some support—this in an environment that I had been taught to suspect as totally and unrelentingly hostile and threatening." With her degrees from North Carolina College and the University of North Carolina, she was able to become a successful teacher and lecturer in public schools and universities. Mebane's life, Yardley therefore concludes, is a "tribute, above all else, to her courage and her unshakable belief in the power of education to redeem, liberate and exalt."

Mebane once told *CA:* "It is my belief that the black folk are the most creative, viable people that America can produce. They just don't know it."

AVOCATIONAL INTERESTS: Reading.

BIOGRAPHICAL/CRITICAL SOURCES:

BOOKS

Mebane, Mary E., *Mary: An Autobiography,* Viking, 1981.
Mebane, Mary E., *Mary, Wayfarer,* Viking, 1983.
Rush, T. G., and Carol F. Myers, editors, *Black American Writers Past and Present: A Biographical and Bibliographical Dictionary,* Scarecrow, 1975.

PERIODICALS

Chicago Tribune Book World, May 10, 1981.
Esquire, February, 1976.
Los Angeles Times, March 16, 1981.
New York Times Book Review, March 29, 1981.
Voice Literary Supplement, June, 1983.
Washington Post, June 8, 1983.*

*   *   *

MEIER, Gerald M(arvin) 1923-

PERSONAL: Born February 9, 1923, in Tacoma, Wash.; son of Max and Bessie (Nagle) Meier; married Gilda Slot, October 23, 1954; children: David, Daniel, Jeremy, Andrew. *Education:* Reed College, B.A., 1947; Oxford University, B.Litt., 1952; Harvard University, Ph.D., 1953.

ADDRESSES: Home—774 Santa Ynez, Stanford, Calif. 94305. *Office*—Graduate School of Business, Stanford University, Stanford, Calif. 94305.

CAREER: Williams College, Williamstown, Mass., instructor in economics, 1952-54; Wesleyan University, Middletown, Conn., assistant professor, 1954-58, professor of economics, 1958-63, Chester D. Hubbard Professor of Economics and Social Sciences, 1959-63; Stanford University, Stanford, Calif., professor of international economics, 1963—. Yale University, visiting professor, 1959-61, Russell Sage Foundation resident, 1976-77; Stanford University, Brookings National Research Professor, 1961-62, visiting professor, 1962.

MEMBER: American Economic Association, American Association of Rhodes Scholars, Royal Economic Society, Phi Beta Kappa.

AWARDS, HONORS: Rhodes Scholar, Oxford University, 1952; Guggenheim fellowship, 1957-58.

WRITINGS:

(With Robert E. Baldwin) *Economic Development: Theory, History, Policy,* Wiley, 1957.

International Trade and Development, Harper, 1963, revised edition published as *The International Economics of Development: Theory and Policy,* Harper, 1968.

Leading Issues in Development Economics: Selected Materials and Commentary, Oxford University Press, 1964, 2nd edition published as *Leading Issues in Development Economics: Studies in International Poverty,* 1970, 3rd edition published as *Leading Issues in Economic Development,* 1976, 5th edition, 1989.

Problems of Trade Policy, Oxford University Press, 1973.

(Editor) *International Economic Reform: Collected Papers of Emile Despres,* Oxford University Press, 1973.

Problems of Cooperation for Development, Oxford University Press, 1974.

Problems of a World Monetary Order, Oxford University Press, 1974, 2nd edition, 1982.

Employment, Trade, and Development: A Problem in International Development, Sijthoff, 1977.

International Economics: The Theory of Policy, Oxford University Press, 1980.

(Editor) *Pricing Policy for Development Management,* Johns Hopkins University Press, 1982.

Emerging from Poverty, Oxford University Press, 1984.

(Editor) *Pioneers in Development,* Oxford University Press, 1984.

(Editor) *Pioneers in Development, Second Series,* Oxford University Press, 1987.

New Political Economy and Development Policymaking, Institute of Contemporary Studies, 1990.

WORK IN PROGRESS: The Concept of "Fairness" in Trade Policy.

SIDELIGHTS: Gerald M. Meier told *CA:* "[I am] now interested in how economists, political scientists, and policymakers are undertaking a critical reassessment of the development record. What has gone right? What has gone wrong? and what are the appropriate policies needed to allow other countries to emerge from poverty? I am especially concerned with trade policy, foreign investment, and external debt."

MELLORS, Samantha
See LOTTMAN, Eileen

*   *   *

MERCER, James L(ee) 1936-

PERSONAL: Born November 7, 1936, in Sayre, Okla.; son of Fred Elm (an oilfield worker) and Ora Lee (Davidson) Mercer; married Karolyn Lois Prince (an attorney), November 16, 1962; children: Tara Lee Mercer Wales, James Lee Mercer, Jr. *Education:* Attended Sayre Junior College, 1959-60; University of Nevada, B.S., 1964, M.B.A., 1966; University of North Carolina, Certificate in Municipal Administration, 1971; attended Cornell University, 1979.

ADDRESSES: Home—1119 Aurora Ct., Dunwoody, Ga. 30338. *Office*—Mercer, Slavin and Nevins, Inc., 3374 Hardee Ave., Atlanta, Ga. 30341.

CAREER: Pacific Telephone Co., Sacramento, Calif., management trainee, 1965-66; General Dynamics Corp., Pomona, Calif., production control supervisor, 1966-67; Litton Systems, Inc., Ingalls Shipbuilding Division, Pascagoula, Miss., assistant to vice president, general manager, and nuclear submarine project manager, 1967-70; assistant city manager of the city of Raleigh, N.C., 1970-73; Public Technology, Inc., Washington, D.C., national program director, 1973-76; Battelle Memorial Institute, Atlanta, Ga., general manager of southern operations, 1976-79; Korn/Ferry International (executive research firm), Atlanta, vice president and partner, 1979-81; James Mercer & Associates, Inc. (management consultants), Atlanta, president, 1981-86; Georgia Institute of Technology, Atlanta, senior research associate and director of Industrial Extension Division, 1981-83; Coopers & Lybrand (certified public accountants), Atlanta, director of governmental consulting, 1983-84; Wolfe & Associates (management consultants), Atlanta, regional vice president, 1984-86; Mercer, Slavin & Nevins, Inc. (management consultants), Atlanta, president, 1986—.

Ad-hoc instructor in management, economics, and business communications at Mississippi Gulf Coast Junior College, Gautier, 1967-70; ad-hoc instructor of graduate seminar in management systems at North Carolina State University, Raleigh, 1972-73. Founding member of board of directors of University of Nevada Foundation, Reno, of advisory council of School of Business, California Polytechnic State University, San Luis Obispo, 1980—, and of advisory board and master of public administration program at University of South Carolina and College of Charleston, 1987—. Seven-term member of Atlanta Chamber of Commerce loaned executive steering committee. Nine-term member of University of Nevada Alumni Association's executive committee. Chairman of Raleigh Civic Center Study Commission; consultant to National Science Foundation; industry expert advisor to I.B.M., Southern Bell, and WANG Laboratories. Lecturer and seminar leader on subjects related to management and public adminstration. *Military service:* U.S. Navy, 1955-59.

MEMBER: International City Management Association, American Institute of Industrial Engineers (past chapter president), American Society for Public Administration, Technology Transfer Society (member of board of directors and secretary/treasurer), Beta Gamma Sigma.

AWARDS, HONORS: George C. Franklin Memorial Award from North Carolina League of Municipalities, 1971, for contributions in public administration; two service awards and key to city of Raleigh, N.C., 1973.

WRITINGS:

(Contributor) Donald E. Cunningham, John R. Craig, and Theodore W. Schlie, editors, *Technological Innovation: The Experimental R & D Incentives Program,* Westview, 1977.

(With Edwin H. Koester) *Public Management Systems,* American Management Association, 1978.

(Contributor) Peter Szanton, editor, *Not Well Advised,* Russell Sage Foundation, 1981.

(Editor with Ronald J. Philips) *Public Technology: Key to Improved Government Productivity,* American Management Association, 1981.

(Editor with Jules J. Duga) *Technology and Productivity in Urban Government: The 1980's,* Battelle Press, 1981.

(With Susan W. Woolston and William V. Donaldson) *Managing Urban Government Services: Strategies, Tools, and Techniques for the Eighties,* American Management Association, 1981.

(Contributor) Milton Leontiades, editor, *Management Policy: Readings and Cases,* Random House, 1983.

Strategic Planning for Public Managers, Quorum Books, 1990.

Public Employee Involvement Processes, Quorum Books, 1990.

Contributor of nearly two hundred articles and reviews to business and management journals, including *Harvard Business Review.*

SIDELIGHTS: James L. Mercer told *CA:* "Private businesses, states, and local governments across America are caught in a squeeze between high costs and stable or declining sales or revenues. I have devoted my career and my writings to bringing the practical benefits of science, technology, and business systems to bear on the high-priority needs of business, industry, state, and local governments. My future writings will continue to reflect this theme in an attempt to assist businesses and governments to become more self-sufficient and their programs more cost-effective in the 1990's and beyond."

*   *   *

MERRITT, E. B.
  See WADDINGTON, Miriam

*   *   *

MILLER, Arthur   1915-

PERSONAL: Born October 17, 1915, in New York, N.Y.; son of Isidore (a manufacturer) and Augusta (Barnett) Miller; married Mary Grace Slattery, 1940 (divorced, 1956); married Marilyn Monroe (an actress), June, 1956 (divorced, 1961); married Ingeborg Morath (a photojournalist), 1962; children: (first marriage) Jane Ellen, Robert Arthur; (third marriage) Rebecca Augusta, Daniel. *Education:* University of Michigan, A.B., 1938.

ADDRESSES: Agent—International Creative Management, 40 West 57th St., New York, N.Y. 10019.

CAREER: Writer, 1938—. Associate of Federal Theater Project, 1938; author of radio plays, 1939-44; dramatist and essayist, 1944—. Also worked in an automobile parts warehouse, the Brooklyn Navy Yard, and a box factory. Resident lecturer, University of Michigan, 1973-74.

MEMBER: Dramatists Guild, Authors League of America, National Institute of Arts and Letters, PEN (international president, 1965-69).

AWARDS, HONORS: Avery Hopwood Awards from the University of Michigan, 1936, for "Honors at Dawn," and 1937, for "No Villain: They Too Arise"; Bureau of New Plays Prize from Theatre Guild of New York, 1938; Theatre Guild National Prize, 1944, for *The Man Who Had All the Luck;* Drama Critics Circle Awards, 1947, for *All My Sons,* and 1949, for *Death of a Salesman;* Antoinette Perry Awards, 1947, for *All My Sons,* 1949, for *Death of a Salesman,* and 1953, for *The Crucible;* Donaldson Awards, 1947, for *All My Sons,* 1949, for *Death of a Salesman,* and 1953, for *The Crucible;* Pulitzer Prize for drama, 1949, for *Death of a Salesman;* National Association of Independent Schools award, 1954; L.H.D. from University of Michigan, 1956, and Carnegie-Mellon University, 1970; Obie Award from *Village Voice,* 1958, for *The Crucible;* American Academy of Arts and Letters gold medal, 1959; Anglo-American Award, 1966; Emmy Award, National Academy of Television Arts and Sciences, 1967, for *Death of a Salesman;* Brandeis University creative arts award, 1969; George Foster Peabody Award, 1981, for *Playing for Time;* John F. Kennedy Award for Lifetime Achievement, 1984.

WRITINGS:

PLAYS

"Honors at Dawn," produced in Ann Arbor, Mich., 1936.

"No Villain: They Too Arise," produced in Ann Arbor, Mich., 1937.

"The Man Who Had All the Luck," produced on Broadway at Forest Theatre, November 23, 1944.

All My Sons (three-act; produced on Broadway at Coronet Theatre, January 29, 1947; also see below), Reynal, 1947, reprinted, Chelsea House, 1987.

Death of a Salesman (two-act; produced on Broadway at Morosco Theatre, February 10, 1949; also see below), Viking, 1949, reprinted, Chelsea House, 1987, published as *Death of a Salesman: Text and Criticism,* edited by Gerald Weales, Penguin, 1977.

(Adaptor) Henrik Ibsen, *An Enemy of the People* (produced on Broadway at Broadhurst Theatre, December 28, 1950), Viking, 1951.

The Crucible (four-act; produced on Broadway at Martin Beck Theatre, January 22, 1953), Viking, 1953, published as *The Crucible: Text and Criticism,* edited by Weales, Viking, 1977.

A View from the Bridge, [and] *A Memory of Two Mondays* (produced together on Broadway at Coronet Theatre, September 29, 1955; also see below), Viking 1955, published separately, Dramatists Play Service, 1956, revised version of *A View from the Bridge* (produced Off-Broadway at Sheridan Square Playhouse, January 28, 1965; also see below), Cresset, 1956, reprinted, Penguin, 1977.

After the Fall (produced on Broadway at American National Theatre and Academy, January 23, 1964), Viking, 1964, reprinted, Penguin, 1980.

Incident at Vichy (produced on Broadway at American National Theatre and Academy, December 3, 1964), Viking, 1965.

The Price (produced on Broadway at Morosco Theatre, February 7, 1968; also see below), Viking, 1968, reprinted, Penguin, 1985.

The Creation of the World and Other Business (produced on Broadway at Shubert Theatre, November 30, 1972), Viking, 1972.

Up from Paradise, with music by Stanley Silverman (musical version of *The Creation of the World and Other Business;* first produced in Ann Arbor, Mich. at Trueblood Theatre, directed and narrated by Miller, April, 1974; produced Off-Broadway at Jewish Repertory Theater, October 25, 1983), Viking, 1978.

The Archbishop's Ceiling (produced in Washington, D.C., at Eisenhower Theatre, Kennedy Center for the Performing Arts, April 30, 1977), Dramatists Play Service, 1976.

The American Clock (first produced in Charleston, S.C., at Dock Street Theatre, 1980; produced on Broadway at Harold Clurman Theatre, 1980), Viking, 1980.

Elegy for a Lady [and] *Some Kind of Love Story* (one-acts; produced together under title "Two-Way Mirror" in New Haven, Conn., at Long Wharf Theatre, 1983), published separately by Dramatists Play Service, 1984.

Playing for Time (stage adaptation of screenplay; produced in England at Netherbow Art Centre, August, 1986; also see below), Dramatic Publishing, 1985.

Danger: Memory! Two Plays: "I Can't Remember Anything" and "Clara" (one-acts; produced on Broadway at Mitzi E. Newhouse Theatre, Lincoln Center for the Performing Arts, February 8, 1987), Grove, 1987.

SCREENPLAYS

(With others) "The Story of G.I. Joe," produced by United Artists, 1945.

"The Witches of Salem," produced by Kingsley-International, 1958.

The Misfits (produced by United Artists, 1961; also see below), published as *The Misfits: An Original Screenplay Directed by John Huston,* edited by George P. Garrett, Irvington, 1982.

"The Price" (based on play of same title), produced by United Artists, 1969.

"The Hook," produced by MCA, 1975.

Fame (also see below), produced by National Broadcasting Company (NBC-TV), 1978.

"Playing for Time," produced by Columbia Broadcasting System (CBS-TV), 1980.

FICTION

Focus (novel), Reynal, 1945, reprinted with introduction by the author, Arbor House, 1984.

The Misfits (novella; also see below), Viking, 1961.

Jane's Blanket (juvenile), Collier, 1963.

I Don't Need You Anymore (stories), Viking, 1967.

"The Misfits" and Other Stories, Scribner, 1987.

NONFICTION

Situation Normal (reportage on the army), Reynal, 1944.

In Russia, with photographs by wife, Inge Morath, Viking, 1969.

In the Country, with photographs by Morath, Viking, 1977.

Robert A. Martin, editor, *The Theatre Essays of Arthur Miller,* Viking, 1978.

Chinese Encounters, with photographs by Morath, Farrar, Straus, 1979.

Salesman in Beijing, with photographs by Morath, Viking, 1984.

Timebends: A Life (autobiography), Grove, 1987.

OMNIBUS VOLUMES

(Also author of introduction) *Arthur Miller's Collected Plays* (contains "All My Sons," "Death of a Salesman," "The Crucible," "A Memory of Two Mondays," and "A View from the Bridge"), Viking, 1957.

Harold Clurman, editor, *The Portable Arthur Miller* (includes "Death of a Salesman," "The Crucible," "Incident at Vichy," "The Price," "The Misfits," "Fame," and "In Russia"), Viking, 1971.

(Also author of introduction) *Collected Plays, Volume II,* Viking, 1980.

CONTRIBUTOR

William Kozlendko, compiler, *One-hundred Non-Royalty Radio Plays,* Greenberg, 1941.

Edwin Seaver, editor, *Cross-Section 1944,* Fischer, 1944.

Erik Barnous, editor, *Radio Drama in Action,* Farrar & Rinehart, 1945.

Margaret Mayorga, editor, *The Best One-Act Plays of 1944,* Dodd, 1945.

Joseph Liss, editor, *Radio's Best Plays,* Greenberg, 1947.

H. William Fitelson, editor, *Theatre Guild on the Air,* Rinehart, 1947.

One-Act: Eleven Short Plays of the Modern Theatre, Grove, 1961.

Six Great Modern Plays, Dell, 1964.

Poetry and Film: Two Symposiums, Gotham, 1973.

OTHER

Contributor of essays, commentary, and short stories to periodicals, including *Collier's, New York Times, Theatre Arts, Holiday, Nation, Esquire,* and *Atlantic.* The University of Michigan at Ann Arbor, the University of Texas at Austin, and the New York Public Library have collections of Miller's papers.

SIDELIGHTS: Arthur Miller is widely recognized as a preeminent playwright of the modern American theatre. Miller's realistic dramas explore the complex psychological and social issues that plague humankind in the wake of the Second World War: the dangers of rampant materialism, the struggle for dignity in a dehumanizing world, the erosion of the family structure, and the perils besetting human rights. Several of Miller's best-known plays—*All My Sons, Death of a Salesman,* and *The Crucible*—have been performed for well over forty years, and according to Benjamin Nelson in *Arthur Miller: Portrait of a Playwright,* they "continue to endure, . . . in fact gaining in strength and impact." Nelson sees the many plays in the Miller canon as "stunning dramatic achievements." Viewers, he notes, "are jolted by the immediate emotional impact of something real, something vibrantly alive exploding at them with a burst of meaning and a ring of truth. The impact is hardly accidental. Miller's plays are products of a meticulous craftsman with an unerring sense of the theater and the ability to create meaningful people in striking situations." In an era marked by theatrical experimentation, much of it at the expense of theme and message, Miller has concentrated on portraying life as it is lived and on proving, in his own words, that "we are made and yet are more than what made us." Walter Kerr observes in *Twentieth Century Interpretations of "The Crucible"* that Miller has "not only the professional crusader's zeal for humanity, but the imaginative writer's feel for it—how it really behaves, how it moves about a room, how it looks in its foolish as well as its noble attitudes."

An earnest sense of social responsibility is one earmark of an Arthur Miller play. For the playwright, writes Neil Carson in *Arthur Miller,* "man is inescapably social, . . . and it is impossible to understand an individual without understanding his society. . . . Miller focuses on the point of intersection between the inner and outer worlds." Whether Miller's plays are set in America or abroad, he reveals characters who are the products of their environments, as well as societies that may support individuals or imprison them, or both. Conflicts arise sometimes from a character's assault on the prevailing order and sometimes from his too willing acceptance of shallow values. *New York Times* contributor Mel Gussow contends that in play after play, Miller "holds man responsible for his—and for his neighbor's—actions. Each work is a drama of accountability." This is not to suggest that Miller serves as a political reformer who seeks to overthrow established mores; rather, he explores the inescapable bonds between human beings and the terrible tolls exacted when people deny those bonds. Nelson feels that this "intense desire of one man to carry on a continuing and meaningful dialogue with other men" establishes Miller "not as a writer ahead of his time or above his time, but profoundly of his time." In *Arthur Miller: A Collection of Critical Essays,* Tom F. Driver writes: "The foremost asset Arthur Miller possesses as a playwright is his knowledge that the theatre must dedicate itself to public matters. He has an acute sense of his audience as persons to be addressed, never merely spectators to be tolerated."

If the plays begin at the point where a character's personal, social, and economic selves meet, they ultimately explore the character's dawning recognition of his moral imperatives. *Los Angeles Times* correspondent Judith Szarka claims that the author's most famous works confront issues raised "when a character is forced to consider the morality of his actions or the validity of his motivating ideals. Whether the protagonist accepts guilt or denies it, transcends the dissolution of cherished ideals or is destroyed along with them, reveals that person's priorities and instincts." Carson observes that Miller "seems almost medieval in his concern with such topics as conscience, presumption, despair and faith. Miller is quintessentially an explorer of the shadowy region between pride and guilt. His characters are a peculiar combination of insight and blindness, doubt and assertiveness, which makes them alternately confront and avoid their innermost selves." Some Miller characters are victorious in their struggles for selfhood; others cannot make the leap of recognition and are consigned to despair. The playwright champions those who achieve essential dignity through an awareness of the dignity of others. Nelson suggests that in most Miller dramas "the possibility of responsibility and action is restored. . . . And because this possibility permeates his work, Arthur Miller is one of the most rebellious writers in modern drama. His continuing exploration of the ramifications of determinism and free will, guilt and responsibility, drift and action, represents his revolt against a theater singing dirges of woe."

The nuclear family offers a favorite context for Miller's dramas. According to Allan Lewis in *American Plays and Playwrights of the Contemporary Theater,* much of Miller's work consists of family plays "in which the social issue is revealed through the personal dilemma. The family is a microcosm of a world beyond, and the behavior of an individual in love, sex, or parental relations is evidence of the choices imposed by social necessity." Carson also declares that one of Miller's strengths "is his penetrating insight into familial relationships." Many of Miller's fictitious families revolve around a dominant though not necessarily admirable father, a devoted but beleaguered mother, and two sons who quietly compete for parental approval. In *Arthur Miller: A Collection of Critical Essays,* Harold Clurman writes: "The shock which shatters Miller's dramatic cosmos always begins with the father's inability to enact the role of moral authority the son assigns to him and which the father willy-nilly assumes. The son never altogether absolves the father for his defection nor is the father ever able to forgive himself for it. Each bears a heavy burden of responsibility to the other." Nelson likewise sees Miller's plays as "personal courts of inquiry in which victimized sons eventually become the unwilling prosecutors of their fathers. The climactic moment in each drama involves a son's agonized and essentially futile attempt to make his father face truth. . . . In each situation, the father's degradation serves as the ironic but crucial prerequisite for his son's possible salvation." The parents need not even be alive and active in the drama to exert an influence, because Miller's characters are deeply rooted in the past. *Encounter* essayist Ronald Hayman notes that the plays "cannot move forwards without moving backwards" to crucial prior moments that are then "made to exist as if they have been preserved in amber."

Although none of Miller's theatre work is specifically autobiographical, it has been strongly influenced by his particular life experiences. An early influential event was the Great Depression of the 1930s. Miller was born in New York City in 1915, and until 1929 he lived the comfortable life of an upper middle class businessman's son. Then the stock market collapsed, and his father, a coat manufacturer, was forced out of work. First his parents sold their luxury items, one by one, to pay the bills. Later the family had to move from the spacious Harlem apartment of Miller's youth to a tiny house in Brooklyn. Miller told the *New York Times* that the Depression "occurred during a particularly sensitive moment" for him. "I was turning 14 or 15 and I was without leaders," he said. "This was symptomatic not just of me but of that whole generation. It made you want to search for ultimate values, for things that would not fall apart under pressure." Like many others at the time, Miller was attracted to the tenets of socialism; Clurman suggests that the young man realized "it was not financial stress alone that shook the foundations of American life at that time but a false ideal which the preceding era, the Twenties, had raised to the level of a religious creed: the ideal of Success." Miller saw how his father's fate was shared on every side by those who had had blind faith in the so-called American Dream, and as a thoughtful man he sought an alternative vision of an ideal society.

Lacking funds for college tuition, and not having earned the grades to merit a scholarship, Miller determined to work until he could afford to enter a university. His job at a Manhattan auto parts warehouse exposed him to yet another troubling social conundrum: anti-Semitism. Being Jewish, he was hired only reluctantly, and occasional comments by his fellow employees let him know that his faith was held against him. Eventually he overcame the prejudice and made friends at the warehouse, but the experience enhanced his desire to change some of society's damaging attitudes. While he was saving portions of his salary for college, Miller read voraciously on his own and spent the routine hours at his job thinking about what he had read. Nelson contends that Miller's reading before college brought him "the first sense that writing could be a way of communicating, of defining experience, shaping chaos, making some kind of sense out of apparent senselessness."

In the midst of the Depression Miller entered the University of Michigan where, to quote Nelson, "the atmosphere was one of challenge rather than despairing finality." An undistinguished high school student, Miller had to prove himself capable of college work in his first year. That accomplished, he matured into a good scholar who spent his spare hours writing for the college newspaper and working as a custodian in a research laboratory that housed several hundred mice. During a mid-semester break in his sophomore year, he turned his hand to playwrighting in hopes of winning a prestigious (and lucrative) Avery Hopwood Award from the university. His first play, "Honors at Dawn," won the award in 1936. The next year he won again with "No Villain: They Too Arise." Both dramas tackled themes that would later fuel his major works: the sins committed in the name of "free enterprise," sibling rivalry, and moral responsibility to family and community. *Modern American Playwrights* author Jean Gould writes: "In his plays Arthur Miller was to question and to sit in judgment against the false values of the past and present, as yet a distant outcome of his college years, but already clearly outlined in his early manuscript plays."

The Hopwood Awards and a Bureau of New Plays Prize from the Theatre Guild of New York enabled Miller to find writing jobs right out of college. In 1938 he worked briefly for the Federal Theater Project, then he began to turn out radio dramas. Although radio work paid well, Miller yearned to do plays for the stage. He got his chance in 1944, when his work "The Man Who Had All the Luck" had its Broadway premier. An investigation of man's ability to determine his own fate, the play serves as "a kind of simple alphabet of ideas that will be developed later," according to Sheila Huftel in *Arthur Miller: The Burning Glass*. "The Man Who Had All the Luck" folded shortly after its opening, and Miller went on to other non-theatrical projects. One of these, a nonfiction book entitled *Situation Normal,* examined the lives and attitudes of ordinary soldiers going to battle in World War II. The other, a novel called *Focus,* explored the irrationality of anti-Semitism. *Focus* was a modest success on the book market; Huftel observes that the work "is a dramatist's novel: tense in construction and dynamic in climax. The reader is driven by it as tragedy commands an audience, partly by technique but mainly by intensity." Despite the lackluster showing of his first Broadway play and the success of his novel, Miller felt drawn back to the theatre. By 1947 he had crafted a major play from the bare bones of a true wartime incident.

All My Sons is Miller's first successful "drama of accountability." In the play, an aging businessman comes to the anguished recognition that his responsibility extends beyond his immediate family to the wider world of humankind. Having sold defective merchandise to the army, and having lied to protect his business when the merchandise caused war planes to crash in battle, the businessman learns that he has in fact caused the death of one of his own sons. His other son, also a war veteran, savagely rebukes him for his warped sense of morality. In *Arthur Miller: A Collection of Critical Essays,* Gerald Weales notes that the businessman, Joe Keller, is "an image of American success, who is destroyed when he is forced to see that image in another context—through the eyes of his idealist son." The son, Chris, has learned from his war experiences that relatedness is not particular but universal; he is shocked by his father's unscrupulous renunciation of that knowledge. Huftel writes that in *All My Sons,* "Miller is concerned with consciousness, not crime, and with bringing a man face to face with the consequences he has caused, forcing him to share in the results of his creation." In his introduction to *Arthur Miller's Collected Plays,* the author himself suggests that the play lays siege to "the fortress of unrelatedness. It is an assertion not so much of a morality in terms of right and wrong, but of a moral world's being such because men cannot walk away from certain of their deeds."

Some critics have faulted *All My Sons* for its heavy-handed message. In *Arthur Miller: A Collection of Critical Essays,* for instance, M. W. Steinberg comments that the characters "exist mainly to illustrate the unhappy consequences of a disaster generated by a selfish, materialistic society which respects economic success as it flaunts underlying moral law." Other reviewers have praised the manner in which Miller presents his story, however. Nelson writes: "More than any of Miller's subsequent plays, *All My Sons* is a drama in the service of a message. Fortunately the message is dramatic and substantial, and the play is rooted in enough human conflict and complexity so that it never deteriorates into an illustrated editorial." Gould likewise styles the work "a sincere, moving, at times gripping drama of ideas." *All My Sons* won numerous awards and established Miller as a young playwright of promise. The drama has been revived many times and has been filmed as a movie and as a teleplay. Directing his remarks to the continuing pertinence of the story, *Washing-*

ton Post contributor Joseph McLellan concludes that *All My Sons* is "rather a period piece" now, but even so, "the passions with which it deals—family loyalty, greed, self-deception, cowardice and remorse—are timeless, and it builds them into a structure like that of a classic tragedy."

With the box office proceeds from *All My Sons* Miller bought a farm in rural Connecticut. There he built himself a studio and began to work on another drama. It was produced in 1949 under the title *Death of a Salesman,* and it received overwhelming critical and public acclaim. The play centers on the emotional deterioration of Willy Loman, an aging and not too successful salesman who can hardly distinguish between his memories of a brighter past and his setbacks in the dismal present. In the course of the play Willy grapples with the loss of his job and the failure of his two grown sons to achieve wealth, and with it, presumably, happiness. Nelson writes of Willy: "Shot through with weaknesses and faults, he is almost a personification of self-delusion and waste, the apotheosis of the modern man in an age too vast, demanding and complex for him. . . . He personifies the human being's desire, for all his flaws, to force apart the steel pincers of necessity and partake of magnificence." Willy does aspire to greatness for himself and his sons, but he champions a success ethic that is both shallow and contradictory—the cult of popularity, good looks, and a winning personality. "From the conflicting success images that wander through his troubled brain comes Willy's double ambition—to be rich and to be loved," notes Weales. Facing ruin, Willy still cannot relinquish his skewed values, and he becomes a martyr to them. His sons must come to terms with their father's splintered legacy and determine the essence of his ultimate worth. *New York Times* contributor Frank Rich observes that *Death of a Salesman* "is most of all about fathers and sons . . . . The drama's tidal pull comes from the sons' tortured attempts to reconcile themselves to their father's dreams."

Because Willy struggles valiantly for money and recognition, and then fails on both accounts, some critics see *Death of a Salesman* as an indictment of the American system. In *Newsweek,* Jack Kroll suggests that the drama is "a great public ritualizing of some of our deepest and deadliest contradictions. It is a play about the misplaced energy of the basic human material in American society." The message Miller sends in the work is not so simple, however. Nelson writes: "One of the strengths of *Death of a Salesman* is its refusal to pin blame exclusively on a person, an institution, or even on an entire society. Although Willy Loman's destruction is partly the fault of his family and the failure of certain values propounded by society, it is no less his own doing." Indeed, while Willy adheres to an adolescent code of values, his son Biff and his neighbor Charley represent alternative reactions to family and society. According to R. H. Gardner in *The Splintered Stage: The Decline of the American Theater,* the play is "an affirmation of the proposition that persistent application of one's talents, small though they may be, pays off. And this, after all, is the substance of the American dream." Willy's tragic decline is given added poignancy by the suggestion that he might have become an expert carpenter had he not pursued the chimeras of wealth and popularity.

From its debut performance onwards, *Death of a Salesman* has drawn tears from its audiences. Critical debate rages, however, over Willy Loman's stature as a tragic hero. In the classic definition of tragedy, the hero is a person of high stature brought low by the recognition of an insurmountable character flaw. Some scholars feel that Willy does not fit that mold—that he is pitiable but not tragic. For instance, Eric Mottram contends in *Arthur Miller: A Collection of Critical Essays* that Willy represents "what happens to an ordinarily uneducated man in an unjust competitive society in which men are victimized by false gods. His fate is not tragic. There is nothing of the superhuman or providential or destined in this play. Everyone fails in a waste of misplaced energy." Others have suggested that Willy cannot be considered a tragic hero because he never confronts his faulty values. Nelson writes: "Although the play's power lies in its stunning ability to elicit . . . sympathy, the intensely idiosyncratic portrait of Willy Loman is a constant reminder that the meaning of his drama depends upon our clear awareness of the limitations of Willy's life and vision." Conversely, *Dictionary of Literary Biography* essayist Jeffrey Helterman finds Willy well in the tradition of William Shakespeare's and Henrik Ibsen's tragic creations. "Acting destructively because of misconceived ideals is the stuff of tragedy," Helterman declares. In his introduction to *Arthur Miller's Collected Plays,* Miller comments on his character's inherent tragedy: "Willy Loman has broken a law without whose protection life is insupportable if not incomprehensible to him and to many others; it is the law which says that a failure in society and in business has no right to live. . . . The law of success is not administered by statute or church, but it is very nearly as powerful in its grip upon men."

On one point most critics agree: *Death of a Salesman* is one of the significant accomplishments of modern American letters. In *The Forties: Fiction, Poetry, Drama,* Lois Gordon calls it "the major American drama of the 1940s" and adds that it "remains unequalled in its brilliant and original fusion of realistic and poetic techniques, its richness of visual and verbal texture, and its wide range of emotional impact." *New York Times* columnist Frank Rich concludes that *Death of a Salesman* "is one of a handful of American plays that appear destined to outlast the 20th century. In Willy Loman, that insignificant salesman who has lost the magic touch along with the shine on his shoes after a lifetime on the road, Miller created an enduring image of our unslaked thirst for popularity and success." According to John Gassner in the *Quarterly Journal of Speech,* Miller "has accomplished the feat of writing a drama critical of wrong values that virtually every member of our middle-class can accept as valid. It stabs itself into a playgoer's consciousness to a degree that may well lead him to review his own life and the lives of those who are closest to him. The conviction of the writing is, besides, strengthened by a quality of compassion rarely experienced in our theatre."

Miller rose to prominence during a particularly tense time in American politics. In the early 1950s many national leaders perceived a threat of communist domination even within the borders of the United States, and public figures from all walks of life fell under suspicion of conspiring to overthrow the government. Miller and several of his theatre associates became targets for persecution, and in that climate the playwright conceived *The Crucible.* First produced in 1953, *The Crucible* chronicles the hysterical witch-hunt in seventeenth-century Salem, Massachusetts, through the deeds of one courageous dissenter, John Proctor. As John Gassner notes in *Twentieth Century Interpretations of "The Crucible,"* Miller's motivation "plainly included taking a public stand against authoritarian inquisitions and mass hysteria. . . . It is one of Miller's distinctions that he was one of the very few writers of the period to speak out unequivocally for reason and justice." If Miller began his researches into the Salem witch trials with the communist-hunting trials in mind, he soon uncovered a deeper level for his prospective drama. In his autobiography, *Timebends: A Life,* Miller writes: "The political question . . . of whether witches and Communists could be equated was no longer to the point. What was manifestly parallel was the guilt, two centuries apart, of holding illicit, suppressed feelings of alienation and hostility toward standard, daylight society as defined by its most orthodox proponents." What Miller reveals in *The Crucible,* to quote *University College Quarterly* essayist John H. Ferres, is the tenet that "life is not worth living when lies must be told to one's self and one's friends to preserve it."

Early reviewers of *The Crucible* saw the play—and often denounced it—as an allegory for the McCarthy hearings on communism. That view has been revised significantly in the wake of the work's continuing popularity. "For a play that was often dismissed as a political tract for the times, *The Crucible* has survived uncommonly well," states Ferres. Robert A. Martin offers a similar opinion in *Modern Drama.* The play, writes Martin, "has endured beyond the immediate events of its own time. . . . As one of the most frequently produced plays in the American theater, *The Crucible* has attained a life of its own; one that both interprets and defines the cultural and historical background of American society. Given the general lack of plays in the American theater that have seriously undertaken to explore the meaning and significance of the American past in relation to the present, *The Crucible* stands virtually alone as a dramatically coherent rendition of one of the most terrifying chapters in American history." In *Twentieth Century Interpretations of "The Crucible,"* Phillip G. Hill speaks to the play's pertinence. To quote Hill, the work remains "a powerful indictment of bigotry, narrow-mindedness, hypocrisy, and violation of due process of law, from whatever source these evils spring." Edward Murray concludes in *Arthur Miller, Dramatist* that *The Crucible* "remains one of Miller's best plays and one of the most impressive achievements of the American theater."

The eight-year period following the first production of *The Crucible* was extremely hectic and ultimately dispiriting for Miller. In 1955 he divorced his first wife, and the following year he married actress Marilyn Monroe. At the same time, his supposed communist sympathies caused his expulsion from a scriptwriting project based on New York City's Youth Board, and he was denied a passport renewal by the State Department. Shortly after his celebrated second marriage, Miller was subpoenaed to appear before the House Un-American Activities Committee, where he was queried about his political beliefs. Miller admitted to the Committee that he had attended a few informal Communist Party meetings many years earlier, but he refused to name others who had attended the meetings even when the Committee insisted he do so. Helterman writes: "In a classic case of life imitating art, Miller took the precise position Proctor took before his Puritan judges. Just as Proctor is willing to implicate himself but refuses to name other dabblers with witchcraft, so Miller named himself, but refused to identify any others involved in communist-front activities." Miller was charged with contempt of Congress and was tried and convicted in 1957. His conviction was overturned on appeal the next year. Nelson concludes: "In a time when men and women were being enticed and coerced into giving up their cores and identities, the author of *The Crucible* remained himself. It was a knowledge and a victory that reached far beyond any court decision."

Just before Miller's political problems began in earnest, he brought another production to Broadway. It consisted of two one-act plays, *A Memory of Two Mondays* and *A View from the Bridge.* Both are set in working-class Manhattan; *A Memory of Two Mondays* dramatizes a young man's escape from the crushing boredom of work in a warehouse, and *A View from the Bridge* chronicles the death of a misguided Italian longshoreman. Of the two, *A View from the Bridge* has had a longer and more varied theatrical life. After critics found the one-act version lacking in motive and detail, Miller expanded the work to two acts. The longer production had a successful run in London and has been revived several times in New York. In *A View from the Bridge,* writes Helterman, Miller "creates his contemporary classical tragedy." Eddie Carbone, the hero, accepts two illegal immigrants into the home he shares with his wife and his young niece. When one of the immigrants falls in love with the niece, Eddie reacts with irrational anger. Only he cannot see that his protectiveness towards the girl is a form of jealousy born of his own submerged sexual feelings for her. Eventually Eddie breaks the most important unwritten law of his ethnic community—he turns the immigrants over to the authorities for deportation. The decision marks Eddie for inglorious death, a high price for lack of self-knowledge. *Washington Post* contributor David Richard concludes that the expanded version of *A View from the Bridge* "gives the chase to some elemental emotions and it is willing to tell a raw, compelling story about human beings in deep conflict. That willingness makes all the difference. There's matter here for actors to sink their teeth into; reason for them to square off, eyes blazing, on the sidewalk."

Marriage to one of Hollywood's biggest stars brought Miller numerous unforeseen problems. The couple found themselves hounded by reporters at every turn, and Monroe relied on Miller to help her make business and artistic decisions. Helterman observes: "Despite her deference to his work habits, Miller soon fell into Monroe's orbit rather than vice versa." This difficulty was compounded by Monroe's deep-seated emotional problems and her barbiturate dependency, both of which predated her marriage to Miller. Still Miller found many admirable and poignant qualities in his famous wife, and he wrote a movie script, *The Misfits,* that reflected some of those qualities. Filmed in 1961, *The Misfits* gave Monroe a chance to perform a role with depth. Although the movie was not a box-office success, it has been praised in retrospect for its script and for John Huston's directing. Mottram suggests that the screenplay "is Miller's most detailed and ambitious work, and if the film was not a masterpiece, at least Huston and the actors never betrayed the seriousness of the writer's demands." *The Misfits* explores the last breaths of the wild West cowboy myth through three luckless drifters and an anguished divorcee who search for permanence in a world of purposeless flux. "Threatened with isolation, personal and social, these people and this way to life define instability," notes Sheila Huftel. "This film script is like a city built on shifting sand; through it a search is going on for something stable in the face of change, for a way to live, and for a way out of chaos." Shortly after *The Misfits* finished shooting, Monroe filed for divorce, and Miller was plunged back into the relative obscurity he needed in order to write plays.

The Misfits and subsequent works such as *After the Fall* and *Incident at Vichy* introduced a new theme in Miller's work—man's hopeless alienation from himself and others. *Critical Quarterly* contributor Kerry McSweeney maintains that the horrors of World War II as well as his more personal problems caused Miller to reject his vision of possible social harmony among humankind. "His characters now grope alone for values to sustain their dissipating lives and each value, once discovered, slips again into ambiguity," writes McSweeney. "Most frightening of all is the realization that human corruption, once attributed to conscious deviation from recognizable moral norms, is now seen as an irresistible impulse in the heart of man. The theme of universal guilt becomes increasingly and despairingly affirmed." Also affirmed, however, is the possibility of redemption through an understanding of self and an abrogation of destructive impulses—a realization achieved with great difficulty. According to Clurman, the

proposition that people can still relate one to another "takes on a new meaning; a new light is shed on the injunction of human responsibility. Each of us is separate and in our separateness we must assume responsibility even in full awareness of that separateness." Quentin, the protagonist of *After the Fall,* is the first Miller character to tackle these issues.

"*After the Fall* is the testimony of a life—a mind made visual," observes Huftel. The drama consists of a series of recollections from the mind of Quentin, an attorney facing the consequences of his actions for the first time. To quote Helterman, the play's action "is expressionistic throughout, using an open space in which various people and events come and go, always confronting Quentin's judging mind. In this episodic structure the recurrent matter to be resolved is the nature of guilt, the limits of personal responsibility for the lives of others, and the means of expiation for crimes real or imagined. Three crises in Quentin's life are vividly presented: Nazi death camps, the suicide of Quentin's beautiful but neurotic wife, Maggie, and Quentin's confrontation with the anti-Communist House Committee on Un-American Activities." Confessional in nature, *After the Fall* "resolved many of the problems which had vexed Miller throughout his writing career," according to C. W. E. Bigsby in *Twentieth Century Literature.* "It served to exorcise his personal sense of guilt but, more significantly, provided evidence that he had finally evolved a consistent concept of the relation between human freedom and human limitations."

When *After the Fall* was first produced in 1964, it met with round condemnation from the critics. Many of them felt that the play unfairly exploited Miller's relationship with Marilyn Monroe, and her subsequent suicide, for the purpose of high drama. Nelson calls the attacks on the play "blatantly unfair" and adds that by concentrating on the work's parallels to Miller's actual life "many critics and viewers wholly missed the genuine stature of the finest play Miller had written since *The Crucible.*" Robert Hogan likewise contends in *Arthur Miller* that *After the Fall* "was so obviously based on Miller's life that its true merits were at first difficult to see. . . . At any rate, *After the Fall* is Miller's most intellectually probing play." Huftel's description of the work sums up its impact. "It is as if someone took his life and tore it up in front of you, the while explaining why he was doing it. It seems incredible that any hope at all can be pulled out of such darkness. For this reason, people may see the pain, but not the point—see that every hope is blasted with insight, and yet that insight is all that will save you." Clurman, among other retrospective viewers, concludes that this work from the author's recollected past is "a signal step in the evolution of Arthur Miller as man and artist."

Nazi atrocities continued to dominate Miller's thematics in his next play, *Incident at Vichy.* Returning to stark realism, the work explores human reactions to irrational and unavoidable sadism. Nelson suggests that the drama exposes "not the villainy of the Nazis—which is scarcely worth reiterating—but the involvement of human beings with justice and injustice, self-preservation and commitment to others, which make for some of the conditions responsible for Nazism's growth and, by strong implication, for its possible resurrection." *Incident at Vichy* highlights one man's sacrificial gesture to save the life of a Jewish doctor otherwise destined for the extermination camps. In Nelson's words, one movement of the play "is toward despair, toward the loss of hopes, illusions, and rationalizations, toward the inadequacy of reason and logic as well as faith, toward the erosion of any value that might possibly endow the word humanity with some positive meaning." In the core of the work, Nelson continues, Miller "is grappling with *complicity,* not *equality,* in evil. . . . He is not claiming that we are all equally guilty of injustice in the world, but rather that very few of us, for all our avowed decency, are wholly innocent." *Incident at Vichy* is another of Miller's plays that has been revived and restaged many times in New York and elsewhere. In a *New York Times* review, Richard F. Shepard concludes: "This is Arthur Miller at his most searching and provocative, peeling the leaves of motivation as though they were coming off of an artichoke, always more remaining to shroud the core. It is a play that makes you think."

In 1969 Miller wrote *The Price,* one of his most successful Broadway plays. The work reprises his family dramas, this time with two middle-aged brothers who meet in an attic to dispose of their deceased parents' furniture. Old jealousies and self-righteous alibis flare as the brothers compare lives and bemoan lost opportunities. Helterman finds *The Price* "a most traditional piece of theater, harking back to *All My Sons,* not only in its theme of defining the price one pays for the choices in life, but also in its technique of the characters uncovering the past by retelling events to reveal one incompletely understood motive after another in their present lives." Nelson elaborates: "Illusions and rationalizations are punctured by the verbal rapiers the two men wield against each other until at the end of the duel each has been laid bare to the bone of reality and forced to see some of the truths he has attempted to conceal. And each then departs, having gained some new awareness but still essentially powerless to alter the role he has played for more than half his life." Speaking to the play's power to move viewers, *Modern Drama* correspondent Orm Oeverland writes: "Two hours in an attic with old furniture and four people—and the experience in the theater is of something organic, something that comes alive and evolves before us on the stage." Nelson likewise calls *The Price* a "powerful and provocative" work and concludes that it is "a play of the heart and for the heart, and although it advocates very few truths, it unmistakably and hauntingly has caught many."

Miller's more recent stage works have enjoyed longer runs in England than in the United States. This is due in great part to the costs of mounting a Broadway production; plays must be fantastic successes immediately or they are forced to fold. In his autobiography Miller addresses this difficulty: "The problem is not that the American theatre has no place for great plays but rather that it doesn't support good ones, the ground from which the extraordinary spring." *The American Clock,* Miller's 1980 portrait of the Great Depression, is one production that fared better in London than it did in New York. During the show's pre-Broadway run Miller tinkered with it endlessly, endeavoring to satisfy the demands of directors and producers. Still the show failed. The London production returned faithfully to Miller's original concept, and the play was a hit. Watching it in London, Miller writes in *Timebends,* he "felt the happy sadness of knowing that my original impulse had been correct in this work; but as had happened more than once before, in the American production I had not had the luck to fall in with people sufficiently at ease with psychopolitical themes. . . . I had hopelessly given way and reshaped a play for what I had come to think of as the Frightened Theatre." Several other Miller plays, including *Danger, Memory!* and *The Archbishop's Ceiling* have met with similar fates.

Miller has done relatively little work for movies or television, principally because he likes to maintain artistic control over his scripts. When he does write for the mass media, such as in his teleplay "Playing for Time," he invests the production with the same seriousness to be found in his stage dramas. "Playing for Time," first aired in 1980, tells the true story of Fania Fenelon, an inmate of Auschwitz whose position in the camp orchestra saves her from death. According to Helterman, the "portrayal of individual courage in the face of brutal dehumanization is even more searing than in *Incident at Vichy.* . . . That his heroine is able to unify multiple attitudes and that she has in fact survived to tell her story marks a decidedly positive conclusion to this most harrowing of scripts." *New York Times* reviewer John J. O'Connor writes: " 'Playing for Time' is totally uncompromising in its depictions of hope and despair, of generosity and viciousness, of death and survival in the bizarre, nightmare world of a concentration camp. . . . This is a powerful production featuring the best script Mr. Miller has written in years. . . . Perhaps the program itself can be watched for a glimmering of the truth, a truth that may be denied to those of us who did not directly experience the monumental inhumanity of an aspiring 'master race.' "

Ever active and energetic, Miller has become an international traveller and spokesman for human rights and artistic freedom. As the first international president of PEN he opened the Soviet Bloc nations to that organization and offered its support to imprisoned and persecuted writers. *New York Times Book Review* contributor Roger Shattuck observes that Miller "was the only American famous enough and courageous enough in 1966 to inject new vitality into PEN International." Indeed, Miller resuscitated the dwindling organization and has seen it grow in prominence and power. He has also seen his best-known plays produced in such unlikely locales as Moscow and Beijing, where *Death of a Salesman* was one of the first American dramas to be performed. Miller directed the Beijing production of *Salesman* himself, with the help of translators. In *The New Consciousness, 1941-1968,* Helterman writes: "That [Miller] was able to motivate [Chinese] actors who had survived the cultural revolution and that a play so embedded in American capitalism was able to reach the audience in the capital of communism is testimony that the play's true message is more personal and human than sociological." Miller claims in *Timebends* that the Chinese reaction to *Death of a Salesman* confirmed "what had become more and more obvious over the decades in the play's hundreds of productions throughout the world: Willy was representative everywhere, in every kind of system, of ourselves in this time . . . not simply as a type but because of what he wanted. Which was to excel, to win out over anonymity and meaninglessness, to love and be loved, and above all, perhaps, to *count.* "

Willy Loman may not have won out over anonymity, but his creator certainly has. Respect for Miller's artistic accomplishment has come from all quarters and is renewed each time a Miller work is revived. Tom F. Driver lists the playwright's special strengths: an "acute awareness of the 'public' nature of theatre, the desire to see and report life realistically, an unwillingness to settle for a merely positivist version of reality, and a desire to see a theatre of 'heightened consciousness.' " Driver adds: "By putting these concerns before the public, Arthur Miller has shown that his sights are higher than those of any of his competitors at the Broadway box office. The fact that such concerns exist in a playwright of his prominence is proof that our theatre is still alive." Robert W. Corrigan addresses the same idea in his contribution to *Arthur Miller: A Collection of Critical Essays.* As Corrigan sees it, Miller's "passionate concern that attention be paid to the aspirations, worries, and failures of all men—and, more especially, of the little man who is representative of the best and worst of an industrialized democratic society—has resulted in plays of great range and emotional impact. . . . Miller's own sense of involvement with modern man's struggle to be himself is revealed in his own growth as an artist and has made him one of the modern theatre's most compelling and important spokesmen." *American Drama and Theater in the 20th Century* essayist William Heyen concludes that Miller's characters "will be asking us for a long time how we must live in the world. Their presence, their humanity as they strain to realize themselves, is staggering."

Arthur Miller "lives the life of a country squire on 400 acres of Connecticut countryside, where he gardens, mows, plants evergreens, works as a carpenter, and writes four to six hours every morning," according to Helterman in the *Dictionary of Literary Biography*. Miller is married to photojournalist Ingeborg Morath; together they have produced several nonfiction books about their worldwide travels. Miller has had much to say about the art of playwrighting over the years, both from a personal and a judgmental standpoint. Reflecting on his own career, he told the *New York Times*: "There's an intensification of feeling when you create a play that doesn't exist anywhere else. It's a way of spiritually living. There's a pleasure there that doesn't exist in real life. You get swept up in a free emotional life—and you can be all those other people. . . . That's when you're most alive."

MEDIA ADAPTATIONS: All My Sons was filmed as a movie by Universal in 1948 and as a television special by the Corporation for Public Broadcasting in 1987; *Death of a Salesman* was filmed as a movie by Columbia in 1951 and as a television special by CBS-TV in 1985; *The Crucible* was filmed in France by Kingsley-International in 1958; *A View from the Bridge* was filmed by Continental in 1962; *After the Fall* was filmed as a television special by NBC-TV in 1969.

AVOCATIONAL INTERESTS: Carpentry, farming.

BIOGRAPHICAL/CRITICAL SOURCES:

BOOKS

Authors in the News, Volume 1, Gale, 1976.

Bhatia, S. K., *Arthur Miller,* Heinemann, 1985.

Bigsby, C. W. E., *Confrontation and Commitment: A Study of Contemporary American Drama, 1959-66,* University of Missouri Press, 1968.

Bigsby, C. W. E., *A Critical Introduction to Twentieth-Century American Drama,* Cambridge University Press, 1984.

Bogard, Travis, and William I. Oliver, editors, *Modern Drama,* Oxford University Press, 1965.

Brown, John Russell and Bernard Harris, editors, *American Theatre,* Edward Arnold, 1967.

Brustein, Robert, *The Third Theatre,* Knopf, 1969.

Carson, Neil, *Arthur Miller,* Grove, 1982.

Cohn, Ruby, *Dialogue in American Drama,* Indiana University Press, 1971.

Cole, Toby, editor, *Playwrights on Playwrighting,* Hill & Wang, 1961.

Contemporary Literary Criticism, Gale, Volume 1, 1973, Volume 2, 1974, Volume 6, 1976, Volume 10, 1979, Volume 15, 1980, Volume 26, 1983.

Corrigan, Robert W., editor, *Arthur Miller: A Collection of Critical Essays,* Prentice-Hall, 1969.

Dekle, Bernard, *Profiles of Modern American Authors,* Charles E. Tuttle, 1969.

Dictionary of Literary Biography, Volume 7: *Twentieth-Century American Dramatists,* Gale, 1981.

Downer, Alan S., editor, *The American Theatre Today,* Basic Books, 1967.

Duprey, Richard A., *Just off the Aisle: The Ramblings of a Catholic Critic,* Newman Press, 1962.

Evans, Richard, *Psychology and Arthur Miller,* Dutton, 1969.

Ferres, John H., editor, *Twentieth Century Interpretations of "The Crucible,"* Prentice-Hall, 1972.

French, Warren, editor, *The Forties: Fiction, Poetry, Drama,* Everett/Edwards, 1969.

Gardner, R. H., *The Splintered Stage: The Decline of the American Theater,* Macmillan, 1965.

Gassner, John, *Dramatic Soundings: Evaluations and Retractions Culled from 30 Years of Dramatic Criticism,* Crown, 1968.

Gilman, Richard, *Common and Uncommon Masks: Writings on Theatre 1961-1970,* Random House, 1971.

Gould, Jean, *Modern American Playwrights,* Dodd, 1966.

Hayashi, T., *Arthur Miller and Tennessee Williams,* McFarland, 1983.

Hogan, Robert, *Arthur Miller,* University of Minnesota Press, 1964.

Huftel, Sheila, *Arthur Miller: The Burning Glass,* Citadel, 1965.

Hurrell, John D., editor, *Two Modern American Tragedies: Reviews and Criticism of "Death of a Salesman" and "A Streetcar Named Desire,"* Scribner, 1961.

Lewis, Allan, *American Plays and Playwrights of the Contemporary Theatre,* Crown Publishers, 1970.

Madden, David, editor, *American Dreams, American Nightmares,* Southern Illinois University Press, 1970.

Martin, Robert, editor, *Arthur Miller: New Perspectives,* Prentice-Hall, 1982.

Martine, James J., editor, *Critical Essays on Arthur Miller,* G. K. Hall, 1979.

Miller, Arthur, *Arthur Miller's Collected Plays,* Viking, 1957.

Miller, Arthur, *Collected Plays, Volume II,* Viking, 1980.

Miller, Arthur, *Timebends: A Life,* Grove, 1987.

Moss, Leonard, *Arthur Miller,* Twayne, 1967.

Murray, Edward, *Arthur Miller, Dramatist,* Ungar, 1967.

Murray, Edward, *The Cinematic Imagination: Writers and the Motion Pictures,* Ungar, 1972.

Nelson, Benjamin, *Arthur Miller: Portrait of a Playwright,* McKay, 1970.

The New Consciousness, 1941-1968, Gale, 1987.

Porter, Thomas, *Myth and Modern American Drama,* Wayne State University Press, 1969.

Rahv, Philip, *The Myth and the Powerhouse,* Farrar, Straus, 1965.

Sheed, Wilfrid, *The Morning After,* Farrar, Straus, 1971.

Twentieth Century Interpretations of "Death of a Salesman," Prentice-Hall, 1983.

Tynan, Kenneth, *Curtains,* Atheneum, 1961.

Vogel, Dan, *The Three Masks of American Tragedy,* Louisiana State University Press, 1974.

Wager, Walter, editor, *The Playwrights Speak,* Delacorte, 1967.

Warshow, Robert, *The Immediate Experience: Movies, Comics, Theatre and Other Aspects of Popular Culture,* Doubleday, 1962.

Weales, Gerald, *American Drama since World War II,* Harcourt, 1962.

Weber, Alfred and Siegfried Neuweiler, editors, *Amerikanisches Drama und Theater im 20. Jahrhundert: American Drama and Theater in the 20th Century,* Vandenhoeck & Ruprecht, 1975.

Welland, Dennis, *Arthur Miller,* Grove, 1961, revised edition published as *Miller: The Playwright,* Methuen, 1979, reprinted, 1983.

White, Sidney, *Guide to Arthur Miller,* Merrill, 1970.

PERIODICALS

American Theatre, May, 1986.

Atlantic, April, 1956.

Book Week, March 8, 1964.

Catholic World, May, 1950.

Chicago Tribune, September 30, 1980, April 20, 1983, February 17, 1984, April 30, 1985, November 27, 1987.

Chicago Tribune Books, November 15, 1987.

College English, November, 1964.

Commentary, February, 1973.

Commonweal, February 19, 1965.

Critical Quarterly, summer, 1959.

Criticism, fall, 1967.

Dalhousie Review, Volume XL, 1960.

Detroit Free Press, March 5, 1967.

Detroit News, November 25, 1973.

Educational Theatre Journal, October, 1958, October, 1969.

Emory University Quarterly, Volume XVI, 1960.

Encounter, May, 1957, July, 1959, November, 1971.

Esquire, October, 1959, March, 1961.

Globe & Mail (Toronto), May 19, 1984.

Harper's, November, 1960.

Horizon, December, 1984.

Hudson Review, September, 1965, summer, 1968.

Life, December 22, 1958.

Listener, September 27, 1979.

Literary Criterion, summer, 1974.

Los Angeles Times, April 10, 1981, November 27, 1982, March 26, 1983, June 10, 1984, June 15, 1984, May 26, 1986, February 14, 1987, November 15, 1987.

Los Angeles Times Book Review, November 8, 1987.

Maclean's, September 16, 1985.

Michigan Quarterly Review, summer, 1967, fall, 1974, spring, 1977, summer, 1985.

Modern Drama, March, 1975, December, 1976, September, 1977, September, 1984.

Nation, July 19, 1975.

New Leader, November 3, 1980.

New Republic, May 27, 1972, July 19, 1975, May 6, 1978.

New Statesman, February 4, 1966.

Newsweek, February 3, 1964, December 11, 1972, July 7, 1975, November 16, 1987.

New York, May 15, 1972, July 7, 1975.

New Yorker, July 7, 1975.

New York Herald Tribune, September 27, 1965.

New York Review of Books, March 5, 1964, January 14, 1965.

New York Times, February 27, 1949, October 9, 1955, July 6, 1965, June 17, 1979, May 27, 1980, September 30, 1980, November 16, 1980, June 12, 1981, January 30, 1983, February 4, 1983, February 10, 1983, February 13, 1983, October 23, 1983, October 26, 1983, March 30, 1984, May 9, 1984, October 5, 1984, September 15, 1985, February 9, 1986, February 16, 1986, February 1, 1987, February 9, 1987, November 2, 1987.

New York Times Book Review, October 14, 1979, June 24, 1984, November 8, 1987.

New York Times Magazine, February 13, 1972.

Observer, March 2, 1969.

Paris Review, summer, 1966, summer, 1968.

Plays and Players, July, 1986.

Publishers Weekly, November 6, 1987.

Quarterly Journal of Speech, October, 1949.

Renascence, fall, 1978.

Saturday Review, January 31, 1953, June 4, 1966, July 25, 1970.

Sewanee Review, winter, 1960.

Studies in Short Fiction, fall, 1976.

Theatre Arts, June, 1947, April, 1953, October, 1953.

Theatre Journal, May, 1980.

Time, December 6, 1976, October 15, 1984, August 18, 1986, May 4, 1987, November 23, 1987.

Times (London), April 21, 1983, April 3, 1984, July 4, 1984, July 5, 1984, September 5, 1984, April 19, 1985, August 8, 1986, August 28, 1986, October 31, 1986, December 20, 1986, February 14, 1987, February 19, 1987, March 5, 1987.

Times Literary Supplement, December 25-31, 1987.

Tulane Drama Review, May, 1958, Volume IV, number 4, 1960.

Twentieth Century Literature, January, 1970.

University College Quarterly, May, 1972.

Virginia Quarterly Review, summer, 1964.

Washington Post, October 26, 1969, October 1, 1979, October 16, 1980, October 26, 1980, December 15, 1980, February 13, 1983, February 19, 1984, February 27, 1984, March 2, 1984, February 22, 1987, November 23, 1987.

Wilson Library Bulletin, May, 1965.

—*Sketch by Anne Janette Johnson*

*   *   *

MILLER, Linda Lael   1949-

PERSONAL: Maiden name rhymes with "sale"; born June 10, 1949, in Spokane, Wash.; daughter of Grady Eugene (a U.S. Park Service foreman) and Hazel (Bleecker) Lael; married Rick M. Miller (a shipyard painter), October 12, 1968 (divorced July, 1987); children: Wendy Diane. *Education:* Attended high school in Northport, Wash. *Politics:* Independent. *Religion:* Methodist.

ADDRESSES: Home and office—2295 Woods Rd. S.E., Port Orchard, Wash. 98366. *Agent*—Irene Goodman, Irene Goodman Literary Agency, 521 Fifth Ave., 17th Floor, New York, N.Y. 10017.

CAREER: Rockwood Clinic, Spokane, Wash., clerk, 1968-71; Aetna Insurance Co., Spokane, clerk, 1978-79; Pan American World Airways, Bangor, Wash., clerk, 1980-81; writer.

AWARDS, HONORS: Most Sensual Historical Romance Award, *Romantic Times* Reviewer's Choice, 1987, for *Wanton Angel.*

WRITINGS:

Fletcher's Woman, Pocket Books, 1983.

Desire and Destiny, Pocket Books, 1983.

Snowflakes on the Sea, Silhouette, 1984.

Banner O'Brien, Tapestry, 1984.

Willow, Tapestry, 1984.

Part of the Bargain, Silhouette, 1985.

Corbin's Fancy, Tapestry, 1985.

State Secrets, Silhouette, 1985.

Memory's Embrace, Tapestry, 1986.

Ragged Rainbows, Silhouette, 1986.

Lauralee, Pocket Books, 1986.

Wanton Angel, Pocket Books, 1987.

Moonfire, Pocket Books, 1988.

Angelfire, Pocket Books, in press.

The Used-to-Be Lovers, Silhouette, in press.

Contributor of about thirty stories to confession magazines and *Woman's World.*

SIDELIGHTS: Linda Lael Miller told *CA:* "I consider Norman Vincent Peale's books invaluable to anyone, writer or non-writer. I've read them all. I read a lot of history, of course, and books on the writing craft. I would love to travel and intend to."

MILLER, Rex 1929-

PERSONAL: Born May 18, 1929, in Jacksonville, Ala.; son of James Otho (a textile worker) and Leila Beatrice (Thompson) Miller; married Patricia Ann Navara (a teacher), August 22, 1953; children: Martin Rex, Matthew Ronald, Mark Richard. *Education:* Iowa State Teachers College (now University of Northern Iowa), B.A., 1953; Colorado State College of Education (now University of Northern Colorado), M.A., 1956; University of Buffalo (now State University of New York College at Buffalo), Ed.D., 1961.

ADDRESSES: Home—110 White Cedar Dr., East Amherst, N.Y. 14051. *Office*—Department of Industrial Arts Education, State University of New York College at Buffalo, 507 Upton Hall, Buffalo, N.Y. 14222.

CAREER: KWWL-Radio, Waterloo, Iowa, engineer and announcer, 1951-53; teacher of history and industrial arts at public schools in Allison, Iowa, 1953-54; teacher of industrial arts and safety at public schools in Ankeny, Iowa, 1954-57; State University of New York College at Buffalo, assistant professor, 1957-60, associate professor, 1960-65, professor of industrial arts education, 1965—. Member of adult education faculty at Seneca Vocational School, 1958-60, and at public schools in West Seneca, N.Y., 1960-61. Visiting professor at Old Dominion University, summer, 1965, Washington State University, summer, 1967, and Bemidji State College, summer, 1974; adjunct professor at State University of New York at Buffalo, 1976-80. Director of teacher workshops in the United States, West Germany, England, Spain, Belgium, Turkey, and Canada; director of National Defense Education Act Institute for Electronics for Junior High School Teachers, 1967. Public speaker. Announcer and engineer for KCBC-Radio, 1954, and KFKA-Radio, 1956; engineering technical writer for Tri-Graphics, Inc., 1962; editor at McKnight Publishing Co., 1963, and at Radatron Corp., 1973. Judge at Monroe County Industrial Arts Fair, 1973. Inventions and patents include 3-E Experimenter, J-E Experimenter, and C-22 Communicator, all for McKnight Publishing, and Project R Kits, for Radatron Corp. Consultant to Sylvania Education Corp., Eothen Films Ltd., and Theodore Audel. *Military service:* U.S. Air Force, radio mechanic and instructor, 1947-51; became staff sergeant.

MEMBER: International Technology Education Association (life member; chairman of Industrial Arts Clubs committee, 1959-60, 1963-69), American Council on Technology Teacher Education (life member), National Education Association, New York State Technology Education Association (life member), Western New York Technology Education Association, Epsilon Pi Tau.

AWARDS, HONORS: Laureate citation, Epsilon Pi Tau, 1969; certificate of appreciation, American Industrial Arts Student Association, 1976; alumni achievement award, University of Northern Iowa, 1977; distinguished service award and award of distinction, American Industrial Arts Association, both 1979.

WRITINGS:

Energy, Electricity, and Electronics: Applied Activities, McKnight, 1963, textbook, laboratory manual, and professional edition, 1964.
Selected Readings for Industrial Arts, McKnight, 1963.
Experiences with Electrons, with laboratory manual and teacher's manual, McKnight, 1966.
Let's Communicate, Tarot Publishing, 1971.
Communications, Electricity, and Electronics, McKnight, 1971.

Metal Technology, with laboratory manual and instructor's guide, Sams, 1975.
Communications: Industry and Careers, Prentice-Hall, 1976.
Communications: Electricity and Electronics, Prentice-Hall, 1976.
Outboard Motors and Boating, Audel, 1977.
Electric Motors, Audel, 1977, revised edition, 1983.
Industrial Electricity, with student workbook and teacher's answer key, Charles A. Bennett, 1978, 2nd edition, 1982, teacher's guide, 1980.
Basic Electricity, Charles A. Bennett, 1978.
Machinist's Library: Machine Shop, Audel, 3rd edition, 1978, 4th edition, 1983.
Machinist's Library: Toolmaker's Handy Book, Audel, 3rd edition, 1978, 4th edition, 1983.
Machinist's Library: Basic Machine Shop, Audel, 3rd edition, 1978, 4th edition, 1983.
Experiments for Electricity and Electronics, with teacher's manual, 2nd edition, Bobbs-Merrill, 1979.
Croxton's Raid (history), Old Army Press, 1979.
Mathematics for Electricity and Electronics, with answer key, Glencoe, 1980.
Residential Electrical Wiring, with student guide and teacher's manual, Charles A. Bennett, 1981.
Carpentry Fundamentals, with workbook and teacher's manual, McGraw, 1981.
Energy, Electricity, and Electronics, with laboratory manual, South-Western, 1982, teacher's manual, 1983.
Refrigeration and Air Conditioning, with student's guide and teacher's guide, Charles A. Bennett, 1983.
Home Appliance Servicing, Bobbs-Merrill, 1983.
Small Gasoline Engines, Audel, 1984.
Fractional Horsepower Electric Motors, Bobbs-Merrill, 1984.
Painting and Decorating, Bobbs-Merrill, 1984.
Mechanists' Library, Bobbs-Merrill, 4th edition, 1984.
Air Conditioning: Home and Commercial, Bobbs-Merrill, 1984.
Refrigeration: Home and Commercial, Bobbs-Merrill, 1984.
Electronics the Easy Way, Barron's, 1984, new edition, 1988.
Mathematics for Electricians and Electronic Technicians, G. K. Hall, 1985.
The Forgotten Regiment (a Civil War history of the 55th Alabama Infantry Regiment), Patrex Press, 1987.
Fundamentals of Industrial Robots and Robotics, PWS Kent, 1988.
Electricity for Heating, Air Conditioning and Refrigeration, Harcourt, 1988.
Industrial and Residential Electricity, Glencoe, 1988.

Author of film series "From Atoms to Transistors," released by Encyclopaedia Britannica Educational Corp. in 1970. Contributor of more than one hundred articles to education and industrial arts journals and newspapers.

SIDELIGHTS: Rex Miller told *CA:* "I write because I like to write. I like to put technical things together for the benefit of others. My writing is mostly technical in nature—however, I do enjoy the research and writing of Civil War history books.

"Industrial arts offers an opportunity for a person to become skilled in a number of technical areas. Teaching industrial arts students at the college level provides stimulation and demands keeping up to date on the latest technical developments.

"High school teachers of technology education are turned out at our college well-versed in woodworking, metalworking, ceramics, plastics, drafting, electronics, graphic arts, and power mechanics. They offer the high school student an opportunity to keep in tune with the developing technological world. The future will demand more technically-oriented people, and technology education teachers will have to provide the training and education needed to aid in advancing the nation toward technical literacy.

"My textbooks and technical trade books are but one way of making sure that teachers and learners have the materials needed to understand the society in which they are living and reaping the benefits thereof. Being able to extend to others the benefits of technical competence is reward enough for me. The financial rewards aren't exactly meager and are also a source of motivation."

*　*　*

MILLER, Wilma H(ildruth) 1936-

PERSONAL: Born March 8, 1936, in Dixon, Ill.; daughter of William A. (an electrician) and Ruth (Hanson) Miller. *Education:* Northern Illinois University, B.S., 1958, M.S., 1961; University of Arizona, Ed.D., 1967. *Religion:* Protestant.

ADDRESSES: Home—302 North Coolidge, Normal, Ill. 61761. *Office*—Specialized Educational Development, Illinois State University, Normal, Ill. 61761.

CAREER: Elementary school teacher in Dixon, Ill., 1958-63, and Tucson, Ariz., 1963-64; Wisconsin State University (now University of Wisconsin—Whitewater), Whitewater, assistant professor of reading, 1965-68; Illinois State University, Normal, associate professor, 1968-72, professor of education, 1972—. Visiting professor at Western Washington State College (now Western Washington University), 1970.

MEMBER: International Reading Association, American Educational Research Association, Illinois Association for Higher Education, Kappa Delta Pi, Pi Lambda Theta.

AWARDS, HONORS: Citation of merit, International Reading Association, 1968, for doctoral dissertation; summer fellowship, Illinois State University, 1970.

WRITINGS:

Identifying and Correcting Reading Difficulties in Children, Center for Applied Research in Education, 1971.
(Editor) *Elementary Reading Today: Selected Articles,* Holt, 1972.
The First R: Elementary Reading Today, Holt, 1972, 2nd edition, 1977.
Diagnosis and Correction of Reading Difficulties in Secondary School Students, Center for Applied Research in Education, 1973.
Reading Diagnosis Kit, Center for Applied Research in Education, 1974, 3rd edition, 1985.
Reading Correction Kit, Center for Applied Research in Education, 1975, 2nd edition, 1982.
Corrective Reading Skills Activity File, Center for Applied Research in Education, 1977.
Reading Activities Handbook, Holt, 1980.
Teaching Elementary Reading Today, Holt, 1983.
Reading Teacher's Complete Diagnosis and Correction Manual, Center for Applied Research in Education, 1988.
Reading Comprehension Activities Kit, Center for Applied Research in Education, in press.

Contributor to periodicals, including *Reading Teacher, Elementary English, Elementary School Journal, Clearinghouse,* and *Illinois School Research.* Editor, *Reading Clinic,* 1975-77.

MILLS, Daniel Quinn 1941-

PERSONAL: Born November 24, 1941, in Houston, Tex.; son of Daniel Monroe (an engineer) and Louise (Quinn) Mills; married Joyce Smith, 1971; children: Lisa Ann, Shirley Elizabeth. *Education:* Ohio Wesleyan University, B.A., 1963; Harvard University, Ph.D., 1968.

ADDRESSES: Office—Harvard School of Business Administration, Harvard University, Boston, Mass. 02163.

CAREER: Massachusetts Institute of Technology, Cambridge, assistant professor, 1968-71, associate professor, 1971-74, professor of management, 1974-76; Harvard University, Harvard School of Business Administration, Cambridge, professor of business administration, 1976—. Chairman of construction industry stabilization committee, U.S. Department of Labor, 1973-74; member, National Commission of Employment Policy.

MEMBER: American Economic Association, Industrial Relations Research Association.

WRITINGS:

Industrial Relations and Manpower in Construction, MIT Press, 1972.
Government, Labor, and Inflation: Wage Stabilization in the United States, University of Chicago Press, 1976.
Labor-Management Relations (includes instructor's manual), McGraw, 1978, 4th edition, 1988.
Employment and Unemployment Statistics in Collective Bargaining, National Commission on Employment and Unemployment Statistics, 1978.
(Editor with Julian E. Lange) *The Construction Industry: Balance-Wheel of the Economy,* Lexington Books, 1979.
Industrial Relations in Transition, Wiley, 1984.
(With Malcolm Lovell, George Lodge, and Bruce Scott) *Competitiveness and the U.S. Economy,* Howard University Press, 1984.
The New Competitors: A Report on American Managers from the Harvard Business School, Wiley, 1985.
Not Like Our Parents: How the Baby Boom Is Changing, Morrow, 1987.
The IBM Lesson: The Profitable Art of Full Employment, Times Books, 1988.
The Radical Executive, Wiley, 1990.

Contributor to business and management journals.

SIDELIGHTS: Daniel Quinn Mills once told *CA:* "I have always been interested in the way individuals in our society relate to large organizations and in how organizations deal with other organizations. My work began with government activities, then focused on unions. Now it is centered on management. Writing is both a way to communicate ideas and to receive feedback.

"There has been major change in the relationship of individuals and organizations in the past twenty years. Legislation has conveyed greater protections and rights on the individual vis-a-vis the large organizations with which he or she is associated. And individuals have become more independent of organizations in their thinking. Even where people belong to voluntary associations such as trade associations, other business groups, unions, or religious bodies, they are now less dependent on the organization for information, attitudes, and guidance. Instead, individuals rely on the mass media, particularly television, for what they seem to consider less-biased news. As a result, nongovernmental organizations are less able to commit themselves and their members to positions on important issues. To some authors this appears to create a greater decentralization of power in America.

But what results is instead a vacuum in which very small and un-representative groups may be able to acquire substantial political and economic power. It is a far more fluid political and social environment, one with both strengths and dangers."

BIOGRAPHICAL/CRITICAL SOURCES:

PERIODICALS

Los Angeles Times Book Review, February 7, 1988.

* * *

MISHAN, E(zra) J(oshua) 1917-

PERSONAL: Born November 15, 1917, in Manchester, England; son of David (a businessman) and Freda (Choueke) Mishan; married Ray Blesofsky, October, 1951; children: David, Freda, Joseph, Rachel. *Education:* University of London, M.Sc., 1949; University of Chicago, Ph.D., 1951.

ADDRESSES: Home—22 Gainsborough Gardens, London NW 11, England.

CAREER: University of London, London School of Economics and Political Science, London, England, professor of economics, 1956-77; writer, 1975—. Visiting professor at American University, 1970-72, and University of Maryland, 1974-75; lecturer at Johns Hopkins University, 1971.

WRITINGS:

The Costs of Economic Growth, Praeger, 1967, revised edition published as *Technology and Growth: The Price We Pay,* 1970.
Welfare Economics: An Assessment, North Holland, 1969.
Twenty-One Popular Economic Fallacies, Penguin, 1969.
Cost-Benefit Analysis, Praeger, 1971, 3rd edition, Allen & Unwin, 1982.
Making the World Safe for Pornography, Alcove Press, 1973.
The Economic Growth Debate, Allen & Unwin, 1977.
Pornography, Psychedelics, and Technology, Allen & Unwin, 1981.
Economic Efficiency and Social Welfare, Allen & Unwin, 1981.
Introduction to Normative Economics, Oxford University Press, 1982.
What Political Economy Is All About, Cambridge University Press, 1983.
Economic Myths and the Mythology of Economics, Wheatsheaf, 1986.

Contributor of more than one hundred articles to professional economic journals; also contributor of popular articles to bank reviews, newspapers, and to magazines, including *Encounter, Salisbury Review,* and *Political Quarterly.*

WORK IN PROGRESS: Narcot Drugs: The Problem and the Solution; Why Personal Freedom in the West Must Decline; Spaceship Earth: A Planet Out of Control.

SIDELIGHTS: E. J. Mishan's book, *The Costs of Economic Growth,* "was one of the first to alert the public and the economics profession," writes Leonard Silk in the *New York Times Book Review,* "to the perils of continuous economic and technological advance." In subsequent books Mishan continues to examine the consequences of economic growth, drawing attention to its ill effects on society. But Mishan told *CA:* "Since retirement I spend much more time figure sculpting. Economics remains a hobby, though a fascinating one. In the last few years I find solace in writing on highly contentious topics, such as race in Britain, capital punishment, women's so-called liberation, and in ways that

run counter to the 'Established Enlightenment.' At the same time I strive to keep abreast of local and global doom-confirming developments, both ecological and social. The question I return to every so often is that of the primal or root causes both of the decay of Western civilization and of the impending destruction of the planet itself. Just when the modern world entered the orbit of self-destruction, and just why it cannot move away from that path, are surely absorbing questions."

BIOGRAPHICAL/CRITICAL SOURCES:

PERIODICALS

New Statesman, July 7, 1967.
New York Times, November 21, 1971.
New York Times Book Review, February 5, 1978, December 7, 1980.
Spectator, June 28, 1969, September 20, 1969.

* * *

MIZRUCHI, Mark S(heldon) 1953-

PERSONAL: Born December 10, 1953, in New Haven, Conn.; son of Ephraim Harold (a sociologist) and Ruth (Tractenberg) Mizruchi; married Katherine Ann Teves (a concert pianist), June 17, 1981; children: Joshua Aaron. *Education:* Washington University, St. Louis, Mo., A.B., 1975; State University of New York at Stony Brook, M.A., 1977, Ph.D., 1980.

ADDRESSES: Home—403 West 115th St., Apt. 41, New York, N.Y. 10025. *Office*—Department of Sociology, Columbia University, New York, N.Y. 10027.

CAREER: State University of New York at Stony Brook, lecturer in sociology, 1978-80; Yeshiva University, Albert Einstein College of Medicine, Bronx, N.Y., biostatistician at Scientific Computing Center, 1980-87, assistant professor of psychiatry and biostatistics, 1981-87; Columbia University, New York, N.Y., assistant professor of sociology, 1987—.

MEMBER: International Network for Social Network Analysis, American Sociological Association, Academy of Management, Eastern Sociological Society.

AWARDS, HONORS: Presidential Young Investigator Award, National Science Foundation, 1988.

WRITINGS:

The American Corporate Network, 1904-1974, Sage Publications, 1982.
(Editor with Michael Schwartz) *Intercorporate Relations: The Structural Analysis of Business,* Cambridge University Press, 1987.

Contributor of articles and reviews to periodicals, including *Administrative Science Quarterly, American Sociological Review, American Journal of Sociology, Sociological Methodology, Academy of Management Review, Social Networks,* and *American Journal of Psychiatry.*

WORK IN PROGRESS: A structural analysis of political behavior among large American corporations; a longitudinal study of organizational responses to capital dependence; models of centrality and power in social networks; an examination of organizational structure and performance; the impact of housing costs on local economies.

MOHL, Raymond A(llen) 1939-

PERSONAL: Born October 8, 1939, in Tarrytown, N.Y.; son of Raymond and Eileen (Mcfadden) Mohl; married Nancy Engle (a teacher), December 24, 1960 (divorced April, 1980); married Sandra M. Knott (a librarian), July, 1980; children: (first marriage) Raymond J., Nancy A. *Education:* Hamilton College, B.A., 1961; Yale University, M.A.T., 1962; New York University, M.A., 1965, Ph.D., 1967.

ADDRESSES: Home—3939 Fifth Ave. N.E., Apt. B-203, Boca Raton, Fla. 33431. *Office*—History Department, Florida Atlantic University, Boca Raton, Fla. 33431.

CAREER: Valhalla High School, Valhalla, N.Y., social studies teacher, 1962-64; New York University, New York, N.Y., instructor in history, 1966; Indiana University Northwest, Gary, assistant professor, 1967-70, associate professor of history, 1970; Florida Atlantic University, Boca Raton, assistant professor, 1970-71, associate professor, 1970-74, professor of history, 1974—. Lecturer in American urban history at Public Service Institute, Chicago, 1967, and at N.D.E.A. Institute for Advanced Study in History, Indiana University, Indianapolis (now Indiana University-Purdue University at Indianapolis), 1968; Fulbright lecturer, Tel Aviv University, 1978-79, University of Western Australia, 1983, and University of Goettingen, 1987. Visiting professor, Florida State University and London Study Centre, 1982. Has presented papers at meetings of professional organizations.

MEMBER: American Historical Association, Organization of American Historians, American Urban History Association, Immigration History Society, Social Welfare History Group, Southern Historical Association, Florida Historical Society, Phi Kappa Phi, Phi Alpha Theta.

AWARDS, HONORS: Council on Research in Economic History research grant, 1968; American Philosophical Society research grant, 1969; Danforth associate award, 1970; research fellowship, American Council of Learned Societies, 1970-80; National Endowment for the Humanities fellowship, 1972-73, 1984-85; grant in aid, Immigration Research Center, University of Minnesota, 1975; grant in aid, American Association for State and Local History, 1984-85; Webb-Smith essay prize, University of Texas at Arlington, 1988. Numerous research grants and fellowships from Indiana University, 1968, 1969, 1970, and Florida Atlantic University, 1971, 1973, 1975, 1976-77, 1980.

WRITINGS:

(Editor with Neil Betten) *Urban America in Historical Perspective,* Weybright, 1970.
Poverty in New York, 1783-1825, Oxford University Press, 1971.
(Editor with James F. Richardson, and contributor) *The Urban Experience,* Wadsworth, 1972.
(With Ronald D. Cohen) *The Paradox of Progressive Education,* Kennikat, 1979.
The New City: Urban America in the Industrial Age, 1860-1920, Harlan Davidson, 1985.
Steel City: Urban and Ethnic Patterns in Gary, Indiana, 1906-1950, Holmes & Meier, 1986.
The Making of Urban America, Scholarly Resources, 1988.
Searching for the Sunbelt, University of Tennessee Press, 1989.

CONTRIBUTOR

Richard L. Watson, Jr., and William H. Cartwright, editors, *American History and Culture,* National Council for the Social Studies, 1972.

James B. Lane and David Goldfield, editors, *The Enduring Ghetto,* Lippincott, 1973.
Norris Hundley, Jr., editor, *The Chicano,* American Bibliographic Center-Clio Press, 1975.
Barbara Sicherman and Carol Hurd Green, editors, *Notable American Women: The Modern Period,* Harvard University Press, 1980.
Bernard J. Weiss, editor, *American Education and the European Immigrant,* University of Illinois Press, 1982.
Walter Trattner, editor, *Social Welfare or Social Control?,* University of Tennessee Press, 1983.
Richard M. Bernard and Bradley R. Rice, editors, *Sunbelt Cities,* University of Texas Press, 1983.
Randall M. Miller and George E. Rozzelta, editors, *Shades of the Sunbelt: Essays on Ethnicity, Race, and the Urban South,* Greenwood Press, 1988.
M. Mark Stolarik, editor, *Forgotten Doors: The Other Ports of Entry to the United States,* Balch Institute Press, 1988.
John D. Buenker, editor, *The Historical Dictionary of the Progressive Era,* Greenwood Press, 1989.
Paul S. George, editor, *A Guide to the History of Florida,* Greenwood Press, 1989.
Francesco Cordasco, editor, *Dictionary of American Immigration History,* Garland Publishing, 1989.
Robert B. Fairbanks and Kathleen Underwood, editors, *Essays on Sunbelt Cities and Recent Urban America,* Texas A & M University Press, 1989.
Betten and Michael Austin, editors, *The Roots of Community Organizing,* Temple University Press, 1990.

OTHER

General editor of "American Urban Studies" series, Kennikat, 1972-83. Abstractor for *Historical Abstracts* and *America: History and Life.* Contributor to numerous professional journals, including *History Today, Journal of American History, Journal of American Ethnic History, Ethnicity, Educational Forum, Migration World, Urban Geography, Journal of Ethnic Studies, Amerikastudien,* and *Current History;* also contributor of reviews to numerous periodicals. *Journal of Urban History,* editor, 1973-77, associate editor, 1977—.

WORK IN PROGRESS: A History of Race and Ethnicity in Miami; British Urban Planning in Palestine, 1918-1948; Urbanization in Australia.

*   *   *

MONTALE, Eugenio 1896-1981

PERSONAL: Born October 12, 1896, in Genoa, Italy; died September 12, 1981, of heart failure in Milan, Italy; son of Domenico (a manufacturer of marine products) and Giuseppina (Ricci) Montale; married Drusilla "la Mosca" Tanzi, 1958 (died, 1963). *Education:* Attended schools in Genoa, Italy.

ADDRESSES: Home—Via Bigli, 15, Milan, Italy (winters); Forte dei Marmi, Italy (summers).

CAREER: Free-lance poet and critic in Genoa, Italy, 1922-26; Bemporad (publishing house), member of editorial staff, Florence, Italy, 1927-28; Gabinetto Vieusseux Library, Florence, curator, 1928-38; free-lance writer in Milan, Italy, 1938-48; *Corriere della Sera,* Milan, literary editor, 1948-73, and music critic, 1955-81. *Military service:* Italian Army, 1915-18, became lieutenant.

AWARDS, HONORS: Premio dell'Antico Fattore, 1932, for *La casa dei doganieri e altri versi;* Premio Manzotto, 1956, for *La bufera e altro;* Dante Medal (Italy), 1959; Feltrinelli prize of the Accademia dei Lincei, 1963, 1964; named Senator of the Republic, 1967; Calouite Bulbenkian Prize (Paris), 1971; Nobel Prize in Literature, 1975; honorary degrees from University of Milan, University of Rome, Cambridge University, Basel University, and Nice University.

WRITINGS:

POETRY

Ossi di seppia (also see below), Gobetti (Turin), 1925, reprinted, Mondadori, 1983, translation by Antonio Mazza published as *The Bones of Cuttlefish,* Mosaic Press, 1983.

La casa dei doganieri e altri versi (title means "The Customs House and Other Poems"; also see below), Antico Fattore (Florence), 1932.

Le occasioni (includes poems originally published in *La casa dei doganieri e altri versi;* also see below), Einaudi (Turin), 1939, reprinted, Mondadori, 1970, translation by William Arrowsmith published as *The Occasions,* Norton, 1987.

Finisterre (also see below), Collana di Lugano (Lugano), 1943.

Poesie, Mondadori, Volume I: *Ossi di seppia,* 1948, reprinted, 1968, Volume II: *Le occasioni,* 1949, Volume III: *La bufera e altro* (also see below), 1957.

La bufera e altro (includes poems published in *Finisterre*), Neri Pozza (Venice), 1956, translation by Charles Wright published as *The Storm and Other Poems,* Oberlin College, 1978, translation by Arrowsmith published as *The Storm and Other Things,* Norton, 1986.

Poems, translation by Edwin Morgan, School of Art, University of Reading (England), 1959.

Poesie di Montale (bilingual edition), with English adaptations of Montale's poems by Robert Lowell, Lanterna (Bologna), 1960.

Accordi e pastelli, Strenna per gli Amici, 1962.

Satura (collection of five poems), [Verona], 1963, translation by Donald Sheehan and David Keller published as *Satura: Five Poems,* Francesco, 1969, revised Italian edition published with "Xenia"(sequence of poems; also see below) as *Satura: 1962-1970* (also see below), Mondadori, 1971.

Poesie: Poems (bilingual edition), translation and introduction by George Kay, Edinburgh University Press, 1964, published as *Selected Poems of Eugenio Montale,* Penguin, 1969.

Selected Poems (bilingual edition), intoduction by Glauco Cambon, New Directions, 1965.

Il colpevole, V. Scheiwiller (Milan), 1966.

Provisional Conclusions: A Selection of the Poetry of Eugenio Montale, 1920-1970 (bilingual edition), translation by Edith Farnsworth, Regenery, 1970.

Xenia, translation by Ghan Singh, Black Sparrow Press, 1970.

Trentadue variazioni, G. Lucini, 1973.

Diario del '71 e del '72 (also see below), Mondadori, 1973.

Motetti: The Motets of Eugenio Montale (bilingual edition; poems originally included in *Le occasioni*), translation by Lawrence Kart, Grabhorn Hoyem Press, 1973.

Selected Poems (Italian text), edited with English introduction, notes, and vocabulary by Singh, with a preface by the author, Manchester University Press, 1975.

New Poems (selections from *Satura: 1962-1970* and *Diario del '71 e del '72*), translation and introduction by Singh, with an essay by F. R. Leavis, New Directions, 1976.

Xenia and Motets (bilingual edition), translation by Kate Hughes, Agenda Editions, 1977.

Tutte le poesie (title means "All the Poems"), Mondadori, 1977, revised edition, 1984.

L'opera in versi (title means "Poetical Works"; two volumes), edited by Rosanna Bettarini and Gianfranco Contini, Einaudi, 1980.

It Depends: A Poet's Notebook (bilingual edition), translation of *Quaderno di quattro anni* (also see below) and introduction by Singh, New Directions, 1980.

Altre versi e poesie disperse (anthology), Mondadori, 1981, translation by Jonathan Galassi published as *Otherwise: Last and First Poems of Eugenio Montale* (bilingual edition), Random House, 1984.

Also author of *Quaderno di quattro anni* (title means "Notebook of Four Years"), 1977.

PROSE

La solitudine dell'artista, Associazione Italiana per la Liberta della Cultura (Rome), 1952.

La farfalla di Dinard (short articles, prose poems, and memoirs), Neri Pozza, 1956, expanded edition, Mondadori, 1960, translation by Singh published as *The Butterfly of Dinard,* London Magazine Editions, 1970, University Press of Kentucky, 1971.

Eugenio Montale/Italo Svevo: Lettere, con gli scritti de Montale su Svevo (title means "Eugenio Montale/Italo Svevo: Letters, with Montale's Writings on Svevo"), De Donato, 1966, published as *Italo Svevo-Eugenio Montale: Carteggio* (title means "Italo Svevo-Eugenio Montale: Correspondence"), Mondadori, 1976.

Auto da fe: Cronache in due tempi (title means "Act of Faith: Chronicles from Two Periods"), Il Saggiatore (Milan), 1966.

Fuori di case (title means "Away from Home"; travel pieces), R. Riccardi (Milan), 1969.

La poesia non esiste (title means "Poetry Does not Exist"), All'insegna del Pesce d'Oro (Milan), 1971.

Nel nostro tempo, Rizzoli (Milan), 1972, translation by Alastair Hamilton published as *Poet in Our Time,* Urizen Books, 1976.

Sulla poesia (title means "On Poetry"), edited by Giorgio Zampa, Mondadori, 1976.

Selected Essays, translation and introduction by Singh, with foreword by the author, Carcanet New Press, 1978.

Montale comenta Montale (title means "Montale Speaks on Montale"), edited by Lorenzo Greco, Pratiche (Parma), 1980.

Prime alla Scala (title means "Openings at the Scala"; collected writings on music), Mondadori, 1981.

Lettere a Salvatore Quasimodo (correspondence), Bompiani, 1981.

I miei scritti sul 'Mondo': Da Bonsanti a Pannunzio, edited by Giovanni Spadolini, Le Monnier (Florence), 1981.

The Second Life of Art: Selected Essays of Eugenio Montale, translation, introduction, and notes by Galassi, Ecco Press, 1982.

Quaderno genovese (title means "Genoan Diary"; memoirs), Mondadori, 1983.

TRANSLATOR INTO ITALIAN

Herman Meville, *La storia di Billy Budd,* [Milan], 1942.

Eugene O'Neill, *Strano interludio,* Edizione Teatro dell'Universita (Rome), 1943.

Quaderno di traduzioni (translations of Shakespeare, T. S. Eliot, Gerard Manley Hopkins, and others), Edizioni della Meridiana, 1948.

Shakespeare, *Amleto, principe di Danimarca,* Cederna (Milan), 1949.

John Steinbeck, *Al dio sconosciuto,* [Milan], 1954.

Troilo e Cressida: Opera in tre atti (translation of Christopher Hassall's libretto), Carisch (Milan), 1956.

Angus Wilson, *La cicuta e dopo,* [Milan], 1956.

Jorge Guillen, *Jorge Guillen: Tradotto da Eugenio Montale,* All'insegna del Pesce d'Oro, 1958.

Also translator of *La battaglia,* by Steinbeck, 1940, *Il mio mundo e qui,* by Dorothy Parker, 1943, Shakespeare's *La commedia degli errori, Racconto d'inverno,* and *Timone d'Atene,* three volumes, 1947, *La tragica storia del dottor Faust,* by Christopher Marlowe, 1951, and *Proserpina e lo straniero,* by Omar Del Carlo, 1952.

CONTRIBUTOR

Mario Praz, editor, *Teatro,* [Milan], 1942.

A. Obertello, editor, *Teatro elizabettiano,* [Milan], 1951.

E. F. Accorocca, editor, *Ritratti su misura,* Socalizio del libro (Venice), 1960.

G. Macchia, editor, *Teatro francese del grande secolo,* [Turin], 1960.

Gianandrea Gavazzeni, editor, *I nemici della musica,* All'insegna del Pesce d'Oro, 1965.

OTHER

(Author of preface) Camillo Sbarbaro, *Poesia e prosa,* Mondadori, 1979.

Contributor to numerous anthologies. Also contributor of essays, critical pieces, and other articles and reviews to many literary journals, magazines, and newspapers, such as *Solaria* (Florence), *Botteghe Oscure* (Rome), *Gazetta del Popolo* (Turin), and to several foreign publications. Co-founder and literary critic for *Primo Tempo* (literary magazine; Turin), beginning 1921.

SIDELIGHTS: Despite the fact that Eugenio Montale produced only five volumes of poetry in his first fifty years as a writer, when the Swedish Academy awarded the Italian poet and critic the 1975 Nobel Prize for Literature they called him "one of the most important poets of the contemporary West," according to a *Publishers Weekly* report. One of Montale's translators, Jonathan Galassi, echoed the enthusiastic terms of the Academy in his introduction to *The Second Life of Art: Selected Essays of Eugenio Montale* in which he referred to Montale as "one of the great artistic sensibilities of our time." In a short summary of critical opinion on Montale's work, Galassi continued: "Eugenio Montale has been widely acknowledged as the greatest Italian poet since [Giacomo] Leopardi and his work has won an admiring readership throughout the world. His . . . books of poems have, for thousands of readers, expressed something essential about our age."

Montale began writing poetry while a teenager, at the beginning of what was to be an upheaval in Italian lyric tradition. Describing the artistic milieu in which Montale began his life's work, D. S. Carne-Ross noted in the *New York Review of Books:* "The Italian who set out to write poetry in the second decade of the century had perhaps no harder task than his colleagues in France or America, but it was a different task. The problem was how to lower one's voice without being trivial or shapeless, how to raise it without repeating the gestures of an incommodious rhetoric. Italian was an intractable medium. Inveterately mandarin, weighed down by the almost Chinese burden of a six-hundred-year-old literary tradition, it was not a modern language." Not only did Italian writers of the period have to contend with the legacy of their rich cultural heritage, but they also had to deal with a more recent phenomenon in their literature: the influence of the prolific Italian poet, novelist, and dramatist, Gabriele D'Annunzio, whose highly embellished style seemed to have become the only legitimate mode of writing available to them. "Montale's radical renovation of Italian poetry," according to Galassi, "was motivated by a desire to 'come closer' to his own experience than the prevailing poetic language allowed him."

Montale explained his effort to cope with the poetic language of the day and the final outcome of this struggle in his widely-quoted essay, "Intentions (Imaginary Interview)," included in *The Second Life of Art.* "I wanted my words to come closer than those of the other poets I'd read," Montale noted. "Closer to what? I seemed to be living under a bell jar, and yet I felt I was close to something essential. A subtle veil, a thread, barely separated me from the definitive *quid.* Absolute expression would have meant breaking that veil, that thread: an explosion, the end of the illusion of the world as representation. But this remained an unreachable goal. And my wish to come close remained musical, instinctive, unprogrammatic. I wanted to wring the neck of the eloquence of our old aulic language, even at the risk of a counter-eloquence."

For Montale coming close meant a private focus in his poetry that caused many critics to label his work as obscure or hermetic. He is often named along with Giuseppe Ungaretti and Salvatore Quasimodo as one of the founders of the poetic school known as hermeticism, an Italian variant of the French symbolist movement. Montale himself denied any membership in such a group, and observed in his essay "Let's Talk about Hermeticism" (also included in Galassi's anthology): "I have never purposely tried to be obscure and therefore do not feel very well qualified to talk about a supposed Italian hermeticism, assuming (as I very much doubt) that there is a group of writers in Italy who have a systematic non-communication as their objective."

Whether hermetic or not, Montale's poetry is difficult. Noting the demanding quality of Montale's work, Soviet poet and critic Joseph Brodsky stated in a *New York Review of Books* essay that the "voice of a man speaking—often muttering—to himself is generally the most conspicuous characteristic of Montale's poetry." Many of Montale's poems are undiscernible to most casual readers, just as the meaning of the words of a man talking to himself is difficult for another to grasp. Problems in comprehension arise because Montale, in an effort to eliminate in his verse what *Parnassus: Poetry in Review* contributor Alfred Corn called "the merely expository element in poetry," sought not to talk about an occurrence in his poems but to simply express the feelings associated with the event. According to Corn, "this approach to poetic form allows for great condensation and therefore great power; but the poems are undeniably difficult." Montale's chief interpreter in recent years, Ghan Singh, examined Montale's poetic complexities in *Eugenio Montale: A Critical Study of His Poetry, Prose, and Criticism,* remarking: "Of all the important twentieth-century Italian poets Montale is the one in whose case it is most difficult to proceed by explicating, through definite formulations and statements, what a particular poem is about. In other words, what comes out through the reading of the poem and what was in the poet's mind when he wrote it, seldom lend themselves to a condensed summary."

In *Three Modern Poets: Saba, Ungaretti, Montale,* Joseph Cary echoed the thoughts of other critics on Montale's verse in general while pointing in particular to the obscurity of Montale's *The Occasions.* "As Montale himself has written," Cary observed, "it is a short step from the intense poem to the obscure one. We are not talking of any grammatical-syntactical ellipsis here but of the nature of the poet's dramatic methods, his procedural assumptions. To be plunged, with minimal or no preparation, *in medias res,* which is to say, into the midst of an occasion dense with its own particular history, cross-currents, associations and emotional resonances, seems to me to be a fair description of the difficulties typically encountered in certain of the *Occasioni* poems."

Corn and Carne-Ross regard Montale's group of twenty brief poems, "Motets" (originally included in the collection, *The Occasions*), as a leading example of Montale's condensed form of poetry. "Even a hasty reading," wrote Carne-Ross, "reveals their singular formal mastery (they have been compared to Mallarme's octosyllabic sonnets); even a prolonged reading is often baffled by these impenetrable little poems. The images are always sensuously lucid . . . , but they often point back to some 'occasion' which it is impossible to reconstruct, and as a result we do not know how to relate the images to each other or to the poem as a whole." Montale's technique in "Motets" is comparable to that used in the poetic sequence "Xenia" (included in the English translation of *Satura: 1962-1970*), written after the death of the poet's wife in 1963. Brodsky contended that in these later poems "the personal note is enforced by the fact that the poet's persona is talking about things only he and [his wife] had knowledge of—shoehorns, suitcases, the names of hotels where they used to stay, mutual acquaintances, books they had both read. Out of this sort of *realia,* and out of the inertia of intimate speech, emerges a private mythology which gradually acquires all the traits appropriate to any mythology, including surrealistic visions, metamorphoses, and the like."

The image of a man talking to himself can be used not only to allude to the opaque quality of Montale's verse but also to refer to what, according to critics, is a dominant characteristic of his poetry, that of the poet talking to an absent other. So frequently did Montale address his poems to a female—named or unnamed—that John Ahern observed in the *New York Times Book Review* that the reader could "surmise that for Montale life, like art, was quintessentially speech to a woman." "Motets" and "Xenia," for example, are addressed to absent lovers; the first to Clizia, the second to his dead wife, known as "la Mosca." Glauco Cambon studied the similarities and differences between the two sequences of poems in his *Books Abroad* essay on Montale in which Cambon referred to "one central feature of Montale's style, the use of a sometimes unspecifiable Thou to elicit self-revelation on the part of the lyrical persona." Elsewhere in the same piece Cambon commented: "Obviously la Mosca fulfills in *Xenia* a function analogous to that of Clizia in 'Motets' and in various other poems from *Le Occasioni* and *La Bufera:* to provide a focal Thou that draws the persona out, to conquer his reticence about what really matters, to embody the unseizable reality of what is personal. Distance, absence, memory are a prerequisite of such polar tension, as they were for Dante and Petrarch. In Clizia's case distance is geographic, while in la Mosca's case it is metaphysical, being provided by death."

Cambon is only one of many critics who made a comparison between Montale and the great early fourteenth-century Italian poet, Dante. Singh, for example, observed "Montale's use of Dante's vocabulary, style, and imagery," but also noted that "if while deliberately using a distinctly Dantesque word or phrase, Montale succeeds in making it do something quite different, it is because his thought and sensibility, his mode of analyzing and assessing his own experience, and the nature of his explorations into reality are as profoundly different from Dante's as they are characteristically modern." Both Arshi Pipa, who wrote a book-length study of Montale's resemblance to Dante entitled *Montale and Dante,* and Galassi concluded that one of the ways Montale was able to break with tradition and renovate Italian literature

was by actually paying homage to that same tradition. "Montale's solution to the problem of tradition, certainly one of the most successful solutions achieved by a poet in our century," Galassi explained, "involved an innovative appropriation of the Italian literary past to serve his own very personal contemporary purposes. To Pipa, who sees Montale's relationship to Dante as the central issue in understanding this aspect of Montale's achievement in renewing Italian literature, 'he has continued tradition in poetry by recreating it, and this he has done by going back to its origin, where he has established contact with one who may well be called the father of the nation.' "

When parallels are drawn between Montale and writers outside the Italian tradition, they are most often between Montale and T. S. Eliot. "Comparison between the two poets is inevitable," according to Galassi, "for both turn to a re-evaluation of tradition in their search for an authentic means of giving voice to the existential anxiousness of twentieth-century man." A London *Times* writer observed that both poets possessed similar styles and "a common predilection for dry, desolate, cruel landscapes." This tendency is evident in the poem, "Arsenio" from *The Bones of Cuttlefish,* for example, which Carne-Ross called "in a real sense Montale's *Waste Land*," referring to one of Eliot's best-known poems. "Arsenio," like much of Montale's early work, depicts the rugged, tormented Ligurian coastline of Cinque Terre, the part of the Italian Riviera where Montale was born and to which he returned every summer of his youth. The starkness of the area can be seen in Mario Praz's translation of the first lines of "Arsenio," which appears in *The Poem Itself:* "The whirlwinds lift the dust/ over the roofs, in eddies, and over the open spaces/ deserted, where the hooded horses/ sniff the ground, motionless in front/ of the glistening windows of the hotel." Praz maintained that the book's suggested "the dry, desolate purity of [Montale's] early inspiration: white cuttlefish bones stranded on the margin of the beach, where the sea casts up all its drift and wreckage. The white cuttlefish bones lie helpless among the sand and weeds; a wave every now and then disturbs and displaces them, giving them a semblance of motion and life." In this description of perceived motion or life amidst symbols of death critics find another relationship between "Arsenio" and "The Waste Land." While both poems are filled with desolate description, they both also embrace a desire for redemption or rebirth.

Other critics, such as Singh and Wallace Craft, see more differences between the two poets than similarities. In a *Books Abroad* essay on Montale published shortly after the poet won the Nobel Prize, Craft recognized that with similar intent Montale and Eliot both described nature as a series of fragmented images. The critic then went on to examine the dissimilarities between the two writers. "Both Eliot and Montale explored this fragmented world," observed Craft, "in order to fathom the mystery of human life. It must be pointed out, however, that Eliot emerges from his existential wilderness or wasteland to find resolution in the framework of Christianity. Montale's quest, on the other hand, never leads to final answers. The fundamental questions regarding life, death and human fate posed in the early poetry are deepened, repeated but not resolved in later verse."

Although his poetry was largely responsible for Montale's worldwide fame, he received considerable critical attention in the United States with the posthumous publication of Galassi's translation of a compilation of his essays, *The Second Life of Art: Selected Essays of Eugenio Montale.* Even though in the last three decades of his life Montale came to be regarded—mainly due to his position as literary editor for Milan's *Corriere della Sera*—"as the Grand Old Man of Italian criticism," according to a London *Times* writer, this book of essays was one of the first collections of the Italian's critical prose to appear in English. Galassi saw these essays as both "selections from an unwritten intellectual autobiography" of Montale and "the rudiments of a context in which to view Montale's greatest work, his poetry."

BIOGRAPHICAL/CRITICAL SOURCES:

BOOKS

Almansi, Guido and Bruce Merry, *Eugenio Montale,* Edinburgh University Press, 1978.
Burnshaw, Stanley, editor, *The Poem Itself,* Horizen Press, 1981.
Cambon, Glauco, *Eugenio Montale,* Columbia University Press, 1972.
Cary, Joseph, *Three Modern Poets: Saba, Ungaretti, Montale,* New York University Press, 1969.
Contemporary Literary Criticism, Gale, Volume 7, 1977, Volume 9, 1978, Volume 18, 1981.
Montale, Eugenio, *The Second Life of Art: Selected Essays of Eugenio Montale,* edited and with an introduction by Jonathan Galassi, Ecco Press, 1982.
Pipa, Arshi, *Montale and Dante,* University of Minnesota Press, 1968.
Singh, Ghan, *Eugenio Montale: A Critical Study of His Poetry, Prose, and Criticism,* Yale University Press, 1973.
West, Rebecca J., *Eugenio Montale: Poet on the Edge,* Harvard University Press, 1981.

PERIODICALS

Books Abroad, winter, 1947, summer, 1957, winter, 1967, autumn, 1971, winter, 1976.
Los Angeles Times Book Review, February 24, 1985.
Nation, October 9, 1976.
New Republic, July 17, 1976, February 25, 1985.
New York Review of Books, October 20, 1966, June 1, 1972, June 9, 1977, February 17, 1983.
New York Times Book Review, May 30, 1976, November 14, 1982, November 18, 1984, February 23, 1986.
Parnassus: Poetry in Review, spring-summer, 1977.
Saturday Review of Literature, July 18, 1936.
Times Literary Supplement, January 27, 1978, September 4, 1981, October 16, 1981, January 8, 1982, November 8, 1982, August 5, 1983.
Village Voice, November 10, 1975.
Washington Post Book World, January 2, 1983.
World Literature Today, autumn, 1981, spring, 1984.

OBITUARIES:

PERIODICALS

AB Bookman's Weekly, October 19, 1981.
Newsweek, September 28, 1981.
New York Times, September 14, 1981.
Publishers Weekly, September 25, 1981.
Time, September 28, 1981.
Times (London), September 14, 1981.
Washington Post, September 14, 1981.*

—*Sketch by Marian Gonsior*

*   *   *

MORGAN, Bill   1949-

PERSONAL: Born April 28, 1949, in Beaver, Pa.; married Judy A. Matz. *Education:* University of Pittsburgh, B.A., 1972, M.L.S., 1973.

ADDRESSES: Home—1202 Lexington Ave., Apt. 100, New York, N.Y. 10028.

CAREER: Artist, 1973—.

MEMBER: Bibliographic Society of America.

WRITINGS:

Lawrence Ferlinghetti: A Comprehensive Bibliography, Garland Publishing, 1982.
(Editor) *Kanreki,* Lospecchio Press, 1986.
(Editor with Bob Rosenthal) *Best Minds: A Tribute to Allen Ginsberg,* Lospecchio Press, 1986.

Also designer of edition of Allen Ginsberg's *Old Love Story,* for Lospecchio Press.

WORK IN PROGRESS: A bibliography of Allen Ginsberg, completion expected in 1991; a bibliography of Peter Orlovsky, completion expected in 1991.

*   *   *

MORRISON, David (Douglas)   1940-

PERSONAL: Born June 26, 1940, in Danville, Ill. *Education:* University of Illinois, B.A., 1962; Harvard University, M.A., 1964, Ph.D., 1969.

ADDRESSES: Home—Box 446, Cupertino, Calif. 95015. *Office*—Space Science Division, NASA Ames N245-1, Moffett, Calif. 94035.

CAREER: University of Hawaii at Manoa, Honolulu, assistant astronomer at Institute for Astronomy, 1969-73, associate astronomer, 1973-79, professor of astronomy, 1979-88, chairman of graduate program in astronomy, 1979-80, vice-chancellor for research and graduate education, 1983-85, director of NASA Infrared Telescope Facility, 1986-88; National Aeronautics and Space Administration (NASA), assistant deputy director and staff scientist at Planetary Division, Office of Space Science, 1976-78, program scientist and vice-chairman of project science group for Galileo Mission, 1977-78, acting deputy associate administrator for space science, 1981, member of Project Voyager Imaging Science Team, 1978-89, interdisciplinary scientist for Project Galileo, 1979—, chairman of Solar System Exploration Committee, 1983-85, interdisciplinary scientist for comet rendezvous mission, 1986—, chief of Space Science Division, NASA Ames Research Center, 1988—.

MEMBER: International Astronomical Union, American Association for the Advancement of Science (fellow; chairman of Astronomy Division, 1984-85), American Astronomical Society (member of council, 1983-85; chairman of Planetary Division, 1980-81), American Geophysical Union, Meteoritical Society, Committee on Space Research, Astronomical Society of the Pacific (member of board of directors, 1977-83; president, 1982-84), Cosmos Club.

AWARDS, HONORS: Awards from National Aeronautics and Space Administration include Sustained Superior Performance Award, 1978, Group Achievement Award, 1981, and Superior Achievement Award, 1981; Asteroid 2410 Morrison was named in Morrison's honor, 1981.

WRITINGS:

(Editor with D. M. Hunten) *The Saturn System,* National Aeronautics and Space Administration, 1978.
(Editor with W. C. Wells) *Asteroids: An Exploration Assessment,* National Aeronautics and Space Administration, 1978.

(With Jane Samz) *Voyage to Jupiter,* National Aeronautics and Space Administration, 1980.
Voyages to Saturn, National Aeronautics and Space Administration, 1982.
(Editor and contributor) *Satellites of Jupiter,* University of Arizona Press, 1982.
(With G. Abell and S. C. Wolff) *Exploration of the Universe,* Saunders, 1987.
(With T. C. Owen) *The Planetary System,* Addison-Wesley, 1988.
(With Abell and Wolff) *Realm of the Universe,* Saunders, 1988.
(With C. R. Chapman) *Cosmic Catastrophes,* Plenum, 1989.
(With Wolff) *Frontiers of Astronomy,* Saunders, 1990.
Voyage to Uranus, National Aeronautics and Space Administration, 1990.

CONTRIBUTOR

T. Gehrels, editor, *Jupiter,* University of Arizona Press, 1976.
J. A. Burns, editor, *Planetary Satellites,* University of Arizona Press, 1977.
Gehrels, editor, *Asteroids,* University of Arizona Press, 1979.
C. G. Wynn-Williams and D. P. Cruikshank, editors, *Infrared Astronomy,* D. Reidel, 1981.
Gehrels and M. S. Matthews, editors, *Saturn,* University of Arizona Press, 1983.

OTHER

Contributor of about one hundred articles to scientific journals, including *Nature, Science,* and *Sky and Telescope.* Member of editorial board of *Icarus,* 1975-77, associate editor, 1977—; associate editor of *Journal of Geophysical Research,* 1978-80; editor of *Satellites of Jupiter,* 1979-82; member of editorial board of *Reviews of Geophysics and Space Physics,* 1981-83.

*   *   *

MOURSUND, David G. 1936-

PERSONAL: Surname is pronounced *More*-sun; born November 3, 1936, in Eugene, Ore.; son of Andrew F. (a professor) and Lulu (Vorleck) Moursund; married Janet Peck (a professor), August 12, 1961; children: Elizabeth Ann, David Andrew, Russell Alan, Jennifer Lee. *Education:* University of Oregon, B.A., 1958; University of Wisconsin—Madison, M.A., 1960, Ph.D., 1963.

ADDRESSES: Home—532 East 39th Pl., Eugene, Ore. 97405. *Office*—Department of Computer and Information Science, University of Oregon, Eugene, Ore. 97403.

CAREER: Michigan State University, East Lansing, assistant professor, 1963-66, associate professor of mathematics, 1966-67; University of Oregon, Eugene, associate professor, 1967-76, professor of computer science, 1976—, research associate, Computer Center, 1967-70, head of department of computer science, 1969-75. Founder and president, International Council for Computers in Education, Inc., 1979—. Member of advisory board, Apple Education Foundation; consultant. *Military service:* U.S. Army, 1958-59; became second lieutenant.

MEMBER: Association for Computing Machinery, American Mathematical Association, Phi Beta Kappa.

WRITINGS:

(With Charles Duris) *Elementary Theory and Application of Numerical Analysis,* McGraw, 1967, reprinted, Dover, 1988.
How Computers Do It, Wadsworth, 1969.

Problem Analysis and Solution Using FORTRAN IV, Wadsworth, 1970.
(Editor with Dunlap) *Computers in Education Resource Handbook,* University of Oregon Press, 1973, 5th revised edition, 1977.
BASIC Programming for Computer Literacy, McGraw, 1978.
(With Karen Billings) *Are You Computer Literate?,* Dilithium, 1979.
(With Billings) *Problem Solving with Calculators,* Dilithium, 1979.
School Administrator's Introduction to Instructional Use of Computers, International Council for Computers in Education, 1980, 3rd revised edition, 1983.
Calculators in the Classroom: With Applications for Elementary and Middle School Teachers, Wiley, 1981.
An Introduction to Computers in Education for Elementary and Middle School Teachers, International Council for Computers in Education, 1981.
The Parent's Guide to Computers in Education, International Council for Computers in Education, 1983.
The Computer Coordinator, International Council for Computers in Education, 1985.
High Tech-High Touch: A Computer Education Leadership Development Workshop, International Council for Computers in Education, 1985.
Computers and Problem Solving: A Workshop for Educators, International Council for Computers in Education, 1986.
Collected Editorials, International Council for Computers in Education, in press.

Also author of booklets on education computing for International Council for Computers in Education. Editor in chief, *Computing Teacher,* 1979—.*

*   *   *

MOURSUND, Janet (Peck) 1936-

PERSONAL: Surname is pronounced *More*-sun; born May 14, 1936, in Berwyn, Ill.; daughter of Russell (a rural mail carrier) and Hazel (Roder) Peck; married David Moursund (a professor of computer science), August 12, 1961; children: Elizabeth Ann, David Andrew, Russell Alan, Jennifer Lee. *Education:* Knox College, B.A., 1958; University of Wisconsin—Madison, M.S., 1961, Ph.D., 1963. *Politics:* Independent. *Religion:* Lutheran.

ADDRESSES: Home—532 East 30th Pl., Eugene, Ore. 97405. *Office*—Division of Counseling and Educational Psychology, University of Oregon, Eugene, Ore. 97403.

CAREER: Michigan State University, East Lansing, assistant professor of psychology, 1963-67; University of Oregon, Eugene, assistant professor, 1967-70, associate professor of educational psychology, 1970—.

MEMBER: American Psychological Association.

WRITINGS:

Us People, Brooks-Cole, 1972.
Evaluation: An Introduction to Research Design, Brooks-Cole, 1973.
Learning and the Learner, Brooks-Cole, 1976.
(With James Geiwitz) *Approaches to Personality: An Introduction to People,* Brooks-Cole, 1978.
The Process of Counseling and Therapy, Prentice-Hall, 1985.
(With Richard Erskine) *Integrative Psychotherapy in Action,* Sage Publications, 1988.

AVOCATIONAL INTERESTS: Conservation, population control, ecology.

*　　*　　*

Mr. Wizard
See HERBERT, Don(ald Jeffrey)

*　　*　　*

MUDE, O.
See GOREY, Edward (St. John)

*　　*　　*

MUNNELL, Alicia H(aydock) 1942-

PERSONAL: Born December 6, 1942, in New York, N.Y.; daughter of Walter Howe and Alicia (Wildman) Haydock; married Henry Scanlon Healy (a lawyer), February 2, 1980; children: (previous marriage) Thomas Clark, Jr., Hamilton Haydock. *Education:* Wellesley College, B.A., 1964; Boston University, M.A., 1966; Harvard University, Ph.D., 1973.

ADDRESSES: Home—6 West Cedar Street, Boston, Mass. 02108. *Office*—Federal Reserve Bank of Boston, 600 Atlantic Ave., Boston, Mass. 02106.

CAREER: New England Telephone Co., Boston, Mass., staff assistant in Business Research Division, 1964-65; Brookings Institution, Washington, D.C., research assistant in economic studies program, 1966-68; Federal Reserve Bank of Boston, Boston, fiscal economist, 1973—, assistant vice-president, 1976-78, vice-president, 1979-84, senior vice-president and director of research, 1984—. Assistant professor of economics, Wellesley College, 1974; member of associated staff, Brookings Institution, 1975—.

Member of Massachusetts governor's task force on unemployment compensation, 1975, and of advisory group to National Commission for Employment Policy, 1980-82. Member, Massachusetts Retirement Law Commission, 1976-82, and Commission to Review Massachusetts Anti-Takeover Laws, 1988—. Member of advisory committee for Massachusetts pension funding, 1976, and Urban Institute HUD Grant on State-Local Pensions, 1978-81; staff director of National Planning Association joint committee on public pensions, 1978; member of advisory board for National Aging Policy Center on Income Maintenance, Brandeis University, 1980-84; member of technical advisory board of joint study committee on public pension fund investment, California state legislature, 1982; member of Carnegie Commission on College Retirement, 1984-86; member of board of directors of Pension Rights Center, 1984—. Member of National Academy of Sciences Institute of Medicine committee to plan a major study of national long-term care policies, 1984-87, of research advisory committee for Ford Foundation project on social welfare policy and the American future, 1985-88, and of advisory committee for Harvard University consortium on long-term care, 1986-87. Member, International Institute of Public Finance, 1986—; co-founder and president of National Academy of Social Insurance, 1986—; member of research advisory board, Economic Policy Institute, 1988—; member of program review committee, Brigham and Women's Hospital, 1988—. Has presented testimony before several congressional subcommittees on social security, 1984, 1985, 1988.

MEMBER: National Academy of Sciences Institute of Medicine, American Economic Association, American Association of Retired Persons, Boston Economic Club (secretary-treasurer, 1986-87; vice president, 1987-88; president, 1988-89), Phi Beta Kappa.

AWARDS, HONORS: The Future of Social Security was named an outstanding business book of the year by *Library Journal*, 1977, and an outstanding book in industrial relations and labor economics by the industrial relations section at Princeton University, 1977, and received an honorable mention in the Wright-Kulp Book Awards, University of Texas, 1979; *The Economics of Private Pensions* was named an outstanding book in industrial relations and labor economics by the industrial relations section at Princeton University, 1983; named to Academy of Distinguished Alumni, Boston University, 1985; Alumnae Achievement Award, Wellesley College, 1989.

WRITINGS:

The Impact of Social Security on Personal Savings, Ballinger, 1974.
(With Robert W. Eisenmenger, Joan T. Poskanzer, Richard F. Syron, and Steven J. Weiss) *Options for Fiscal Reform in Massachusetts,* Federal Reserve Bank of Boston, 1975.
The Future of Social Security, Brookings Institution, 1977.
Pensions for Public Employees, National Planning Association, 1979.
The Economics of Private Pensions, Brookings Institution, 1982.
(Editor) *Lessons from the Income Maintenance Experiments,* Federal Reserve Bank of Boston, 1987.

CONTRIBUTOR

Joseph A. Pechman, Henry J. Aaron, and Michael K. Taussig, editors, *Social Security: Perspectives for Reform,* Brookings Institution, 1968.
Pechman, editor, *Setting National Priorities: The 1978 Budget,* Brookings Institution, 1977.
Ann M. Connolly, editor, *Funding Pensions: Issues and Implications for Financial Markets,* Federal Reserve Bank of Boston, 1977.
Barbara Risman Herzog, editor, *Aging and Income,* Human Sciences Press, 1978.
Financing Social Security, American Enterprise Institute for Public Policy Research, 1979.
The Economics of Taxation, Brookings Institution, 1980.
Capital Formation in the United States, Federal Reserve Board, 1980.
Retirement Policy in an Aging Society, Duke University Press, 1980.
(With Laura E. Stiglin) *A Challenge to Social Security: The Changing Roles of Women and Men in American Society,* Academic Press, 1981.
Saving for Retirement, American Council of Life Insurance, 1981.
(With Stiglin) *Readings in Labor Economics and Labor Relations,* 3rd edition, Academic Press, 1982.
Setting National Priorities: The 1984 Budget, Brookings Institution, 1983.
Myron H. Ross, editor, *The Economics of Aging,* W. E. Upjohn Institute for Employment Research, 1985.
Yung-Ping Chen and George F. Rohrlich, editors, *Checks and Balances in Social Security,* University Press of America, 1986.
(With Nancy Altman and James Verdier) *Renewing the Promise: Medicare and Its Reform,* Oxford University Press, 1988.
Social Security and Economic Well-Being across Generations, American Association of Retired Persons, 1988.

Social Security's Looming Surpluses: Prospects and Policy Implications, American Enterprise Institute, 1989.

OTHER

Contributor to proceedings, and to *World Book Encyclopedia* and *Academic American Encyclopedia.* Also contributor of articles and book reviews to numerous magazines, newspapers, and professional journals.

*   *   *

MURPHY, John W(illiam) 1948-

PERSONAL: Born November 3, 1948, in Youngstown, Ohio; son of William H. and Margurite V. (Locke) Murphy; married Karen Callaghan, November 10, 1980; children: Sarah Beth. *Education:* Kent State University, B.A., 1972; Ohio University, M.A., 1974; attended Fordham University, 1975-76; Ohio State University, Ph.D., 1981.

ADDRESSES: Home—8034 Camino Ct., Miami, Fla. 33143. *Office*—Department of Sociology, University of Miami, Coral Gables, Fla. 33124.

CAREER: Community Action Against Addiction, Cleveland, Ohio, director of research program and evaluation, 1976-79; Muskingum College, New Concord, Ohio, assistant professor of sociology, 1979-81; Arkansas State University, State University, assistant professor of sociology, 1982—. Instructor at Cuyahoga Community College, 1977-79; research assistant at Academy for Contemporary Problems, 1979-80; assistant professor at Capital University, Columbus, Ohio, 1982; director of program evaluation for Ohio State University's health careers opportunity program, 1982; fellow at Red Feather Institute, Livermore, Colo., summer, 1982. Public speaker, conference organizer.

MEMBER: North American Society for Social Philosophy (member of board of directors), American Sociological Society, National Humanistic Sociology Council (Midwestern representative, 1981-82), Viktor Frankl Society, Jean Gebser Circle, Humanistic Sociological Society, North Central Sociological Association (chairman of committee on applied sociology, 1978-80).

WRITINGS:

(Contributor) Stephen Skousgaard, editor, *Phenomenology and the Understanding of Human Destiny,* University Press of America, 1981.
The Social Philosophy of Martin Buber, University Press of America, 1982.
(Contributor) Scott T. McNall, editor, *Current Perspectives in Social Theory,* JAI Press, 1982.
(With Joseph J. Pilotta) *Qualitative Methodology: Theory and Application; A Guide for the Social Practitioner,* Kendall/Hunt, 1983.
(With Pilotta, Tricia Jones, and Elizabeth Wilson) *Responsible Organizations: Control without Coercion,* Ablex, 1984.
(Editor with Pilotta and Algis Mickunas) *The Underside of High-Tech: Technology and the Deformation of Human Sensibilities,* Greenwood Press, 1986.
(Editor with John T. Pardeck) *Technology and Human Productivity,* Greenwood Press, 1986.
(Contributor) *Festschrift fuer Chaim Perelman,* D. Reidel, 1987.
(Editor with Pardeck) *Technology and Human Services Delivery,* Haworth, 1988.
Postmodern Social Analysis and Criticism, Greenwood Press, 1989.

Contributor of more than eighty articles and reviews to sociology journals, including *New Orleans Review* and *Human Studies.* Co-editor of *Applied Sociologist,* 1979-81.

SIDELIGHTS: John W. Murphy told *CA:* "I wrote a book on Martin Buber primarily because I have had a long-time interest in his work. Additionally, he is a humanist, and I also ascribe to the tenets of humanism. My views parallel his to the extent that we offer a similar view of social philosophy, particularly when addressing the issue of social order. Our image of social life can be characterized as 'responsible order' simply because it is based on human action and not abstract theoretical principles. I am presently attempting to apply this rendition of social order to areas such as the legal system, the workplace, and politics. Currently this theoretical viewpoint is referred to as the democratization of social life."

*   *   *

MYERS, J(ohn) William 1919-

PERSONAL: Born December 1, 1919, in Huntington, W.Va.; son of Condon William (an engraver) and Mary Olive (Fox) Myers; married Nancy Hortense Paxton, July 6, 1942 (died, 1954); married Helen File Fleming, November 28, 1981; children: Martha Ann (Mrs. Philip L. Parks), Lenora Ellen (Mrs. James Johns), Nancy Louise (Mrs. Gerald D. Smith), John Charles. *Education:* Ohio Wesleyan University, B.A., 1951; Bowling Green State University, M.A., 1952. *Politics:* Liberal Democrat.

ADDRESSES: Home—105 Fulton St., Lyons, Ohio 43533.

CAREER: Ordained a minister in Methodist Church, 1948; minister, Ohio Annual Conference of the Methodist Church, 1944-54; transferred to the Unitarian Church, 1956; minister, Horton Unitarian Universalist Church, Horton, Mich.; minister, Jersey Universalist Church, 1974-78; Lyons Unitarian Universality Church, Lyons, Ohio, minister, 1978-81. Journeyman letterpress and lithographic printer, editor, publisher, book designer, and free-lance writer, 1954—. Lecturer on poetry and religion.

MEMBER: American Academy of Poets, Poetry Society of America, Catholic Poetry Society of America, American Translators Association, Ohio Poetry Society, Poetry Society of Virginia.

AWARDS, HONORS: Nomination for Pulitzer Prize in Poetry, 1964, for *Green Are My Words;* London Literary Circle award, 1967, for poem "Prayer for a House I Never Had."

WRITINGS:

POETRY

Evening Exercises, Humanist Education Press, 1956.
These Mown Dandelions, Ohio Poetry Review Press, 1959.
My Mind's Poor Birds, Elgeuera Press, 1963.
Alley to an Island, New Merrymount Press, 1963.
Green Are My Words, New Merrymount Press, 1964.
Sun Bands and Other Poems, Georgetown Press, 1964.
Anatomy of a Feeling, New Merrymount Press, 1966.
Variations on a Nightingale, New Merrymount Press, 1968.
A Greene County Ballad, New Merrymount Press, 1972.
The Sky Is Forever, New Merrymount Press, 1974.
Something Will Be Mine, New Merrymount Press, 1976.
Annotations 1951, New Merrymount Press, 1977.
Stones of Promise, New Merrymount Press, 1977.
(Translator of Freidrich Nietzsche's text to the Frederick Delius choral work) *A Mass of Life,* New Merrymount Press, 1980.

Homage to Dionysius: Selected Poems of Friedrich W. Nietzsche in Translation, New Merrymount Press, 1982.

Juliet and God (poetic play), New Merrymount Press, 1983.

Apprentice to the Muse: First Poems, New Merrymount Press, 1986.

Painful Knowledge: Homage to Schopenhaur, Poems after the Aphorisms, New Merrymount Press, 1987.

Amphion in Appalachia, New Merrymount Press, 1987.

Rediscovered Country, New Merrymount Press, 1988.

OTHER

Also translator from the German of poetry of Johann W. Von Goethe, Friedrich Hoelderlin, Joseph von Eichendorff, Friedrich Rueckert, Edward Moerike, Reiner Kunze, Gottfried Keller, Richard Dehmel, Stefan Anton George, Hermann Hesse, Franz Werfel, and Karl Krolow. Reviewer for *Chicago Sun-Times.* Contributor of poems and bibliographies to over sixty periodicals, including *Bitterroot, Twentieth-Century Literature, Descant, New York Herald Tribune, Cardinal Poetry Quarterly, South and West,* and *Laurel Review.* Editor, *Mid-Lakes Humanist* (American Humanist Association publication), 1956-59, *Ohio Poetry Review,* 1957-59, *Anthropos, the Quarterly of Humanist Poetry,* 1958-59, Ohio Poetry Society *Bulletin,* 1958-59, and *Poetry Dial,* 1959-61; poetry editor, *Humanist,* 1961-62; advisory and contributing editor, *Dasein: The Quarterly Review,* 1962—.

WORK IN PROGRESS: Opus Guyandotte, a collection of poems; *A Long Time Learning,* an autobiography; *White Rocks: A Poetic Legend.*

SIDELIGHTS: J. William Myers told *CA:* "As I approach what are doubtless the last decades of my life there is a perspective—to chase a metaphor is the enduring thing. So I desire, down deep, to fly above this time of cheap ethics, unbelievable illiteracy and a fear of man's demise, to live in the hope something of mine will sing beyond the ruin. This means I have purposed to make use of the symbol knowing it to be a symbol and never to be mistaken for reality."

AVOCATIONAL INTERESTS: Cooking, baking, making wines.

BIOGRAPHICAL/CRITICAL SOURCES:

PERIODICALS

Adrian Telegram, February 9, 1980.
Columbus Dispatch, May 22, 1969.
Newark Advocate, May 1, 1978.
Observer-Reporter (Washington, Pa.), June 23, 1969.
Record-Outlook (McDonald, Pa.), November 18, 1971.

N

NEGGERS, Carla A(malia) 1955-
(Anne Harrell, Amalia James)

PERSONAL: Born August 9, 1955, in Belchertown, Mass.; daughter of Leonardus C. (a machinist) and Florine (a teacher; maiden name, Harrell) Neggers; married Joe B. Jewell (a United Methodist minister), July 23, 1977; children: Katherine Rye, Zachary Wynne. *Education:* Boston University, B.S. (magna cum laude), 1977.

ADDRESSES: Home—990 Hoosick Rd., Troy, N.Y. 12180. *Office*—Denise Marcil Literary Agency, Inc. 685 West End Ave., New York, N.Y. 10025.

CAREER: American Heart Association, Boston, Mass., public relations associate, 1975-77; staff writer, L. W. Robbins Associates, 1977; free-lance writer, 1978—. Presents writers' workshops; guest on television and radio programs.

MEMBER: International Women's Writing Guild, Romance Writers of America, Authors Guild, Authors League of America.

AWARDS, HONORS: Reviewer's Choice Award, *Romantic Times,* 1985, for *The Uneven Score,* 1988, for *All in a Name;* Reviewer's Choice Award nominations, *Romantic Times,* 1983, for best Bantam Loveswept, 1986 and 1987, both for best Harlequin Temptation, 1988, for best romance series writer.

WRITINGS:

(Under pseudonym Amalia James) *Midsummer Dreams* (romance novel), Bantam, 1982.
(Under pseudonym Amalia James) *Tangled Promises* (romance novel), Bantam, 1982.
(Under pseudonym Amalia James) *Dream Images* (romance novel), Bantam, 1983.
Dancing Season (romance novel), Avon, 1983.
Matching Wits (romance novel), Bantam, 1983.
Outrageous Desire (romance novel), Dell, 1983.
Heart on a String (romance novel), Bantam, 1983.
A Touch of Magic (romance novel), Bantam, 1984.
Delinquent Desire (romance novel), New American Library, 1984.
The Venus Shoe (romantic suspense), Avon, 1984.
The Knotted Skein (romantic suspense), Avon, 1984.
Southern Comfort (romance novel), Dell, 1984.

The Uneven Score (romantic suspense), Avon, 1985.
Apple of My Eye (romance novel), Dell, 1985.
Interior Designs (romance novel), Dell, 1985.
Captivated (romance novel), Harlequin, 1986.
Trade Secrets (romance novel), Harlequin, 1987.
Claim the Crown, Harlequin, 1987.
Family Matters (romance novel), Harlequin, 1988.
All in a Name (romance novel), Harlequin, 1988.
A Winning Battle (romance novel), Harlequin, 1989.
Finders Keepers (romance novel), Harlequin, 1989.
(Under pseudonym Anne Harrell) *Minstrel's Fire,* Berkley Publishing, 1989.
(Under pseudonym Anne Harrell) *Betrayals,* Berkley Publishing, 1990.

SIDELIGHTS: Carla A. Neggers once told *CA:* "I began writing romances in 1981 after my first novel, a romantic suspense, had been rejected sixteen times. Romantic suspense, it seemed, was out. So over a spicy lunch in Manhattan my agent suggested I try writing a book without a corpse in it. This hadn't really occurred to me. 'Try a straight romance,' she said. To which I said, 'You mean a formulaic story about a pretty, virginal, innocent twenty-year-old who's swept off her feet by a tall, dark, macho, handsome and worldly forty-year-old man? *Yuck!*' She asked me if I'd ever read a series romance. I admitted I hadn't. So she, being a patient woman, loaded me up with books and told me to call her.

"I read the books and realized the market was much more open to new ideas and new twists than I'd ever imagined. The heroines weren't all virgins! They were *over twenty-five!* They had *careers!* The heroes weren't all brooding violent types! Sure, there were books that I despised, but weren't there mysteries I despised? Why should I have to like every romance? So I said to myself: 'if I can write a romance with characters I like and situations I find amusing, I'll do it.' So I wrote, I sold, and I've been having lots of fun being a 'romance writer.'

"Meanwhile, of course, I'm still partial to my corpses, and when publishers started thinking about bringing back romantic suspense, there I was with my much-rejected novel. I revised it and sold it to Avon, who had rejected it way back when. So I always tell new writers to *persevere.*

"I write because I like to create characters and tell stories. Not all my stories are light-hearted romances or mysteries. Some will sell, some won't. But I know I have to stretch myself and take risks . . . as a writer and as a person."

AVOCATIONAL INTERESTS: Reading, counted cross-stitch embroidery, exercise, cooking, gardening.

BIOGRAPHICAL/CRITICAL SOURCES:

PERIODICALS

Boston Herald, January 23, 1983.
Boy Meets Girl, January 28, 1983.
Los Angeles Times Book Review, October 14, 1984, January 6, 1985.

*   *   *

NEIPRIS, Janet
   See WILLE, Janet Neipris

*   *   *

NELSON, Richard K(ing) 1941-

PERSONAL: Born December 1, 1941, in Madison, Wis.; son of Robert King (a state employee) and Florence (Olson) Nelson. *Education:* University of Wisconsin, B.S., 1964, M.S., 1968; University of California, Santa Barbara, Ph.D., 1971.

CAREER: University of California, Santa Barbara, research fellow in anthropology, 1968-71; University of Hawaii, Honolulu, assistant professor of anthropology, 1971-72; Memorial University of Newfoundland, St. Johns, assistant professor of anthropology, 1972-73; University of Alaska, Fairbanks, research associate, 1973-77; University of California, Santa Barbara, visiting lecturer, 1978; University of California, Santa Cruz, visiting lecturer, 1979; University of Alaska, visiting professor, 1980, affiliate associate professor, 1982—; self-employed writer/researcher, 1982—. Member of field expeditions to Kodiak Island, Alaska, 1961, Anangula Island in the Aleutians, 1963, and four extended ethnographic field studies among Alaskan Eskimos and Athabaskan Indians.

WRITINGS:

Alaskan Eskimo Exploitation of the Sea Ice Environment, Arctic Aeromedical Laboratory, U.S. Air Force, 1966.
Hunters of the Northern Ice, University of Chicago Press, 1969.
Hunters of the Northern Forest, University of Chicago Press, 1973.
(Co-author) *Kuuvangmiit: Contemporary Subsistence Living in the Latter Twentieth Century,* National Park Service, 1977.
(Co-author) *Tracks in the Wildland: A Portrayal of Koyukon and Nunamiut Subsistence,* National Park Service, 1978.
Shadow of the Hunter: Stories of Eskimo Life, University of Chicago Press, 1980.
Harvest of the Sea: Coastal Subsistence in Modern Wainwright, North Slope Borough (Barrow, Alaska), 1982.
Make Prayers to the Raven: A Koyukon View of the Northern Forest, University of Chicago Press, 1983.
The Athapaskans: People of the Boreal Forest, University of Alaska Museum (Fairbanks), 1983.
(Co-author) *Interior Alaska: A Journey through Time,* Alaska Northwest Publishing, 1986.
The Island Within, North Point Press, 1989.

SIDELIGHTS: Richard K. Nelson told *CA:* "I never really chose to be a writer. It evolved as an outgrowth of my professional work in anthropology and my experiences among Alaskan Eskimos and Athabaskan Indians.

"As an undergraduate college student, I joined two summer research projects in Alaska. In 1964-65, I spent a year with Eskimo people in the North Slope village of Wainwright, studying their methods of hunting and travel on the sea ice, recording their knowledge of the animals and the surrounding environment. This experience made a different person of me and shaped the entire course of my life. After returning home, I sequestered myself in a basement office at the University of Wisconsin and wrote two voluminous ethnographic reports. I never considered that they might become a book, until I had a completely unexpected meeting with an editor from the University of Chicago Press. I never formally submitted a manuscript (because my major professor asked the editor to look at it), and I knew nothing of how publishers review submissions, so I felt no stress or anxiety as the process took place. Then came an offer to publish my consolidated reports as a book, eventually titled *Hunters of the Northern Ice.* The book was later accepted in lieu of a masters thesis.

"My second book, *Hunters of the Northern Forest,* describes the subsistence life and environmental knowledge of Kutchin Athabaskan Indians, who live near the Arctic Circle in Alaska's forested interior. I spent a year living with Kutchin people, then returned home and wrote the manuscript in about six months, working seven days a week, twelve hours a day. Although it was submitted for my doctoral thesis at the University of California, my goal from the outset was to publish the material as a book. And this time, I suffered through months of anxiety and self-doubt as I awaited the publisher's decision.

"I wrote my next book—*Shadow of the Hunter*—over a period of five or six years, working whenever I could find a bit of spare time. This project grew from a desire to change my approach as a writing anthropologist: to give a more sensory account of Eskimo people and their arctic environment, to present accurate information in a readable style, and to allow myself a chance for creative expression. After finishing the manuscript, it took years before I had enough courage to show it to a publisher. What has gratified me most about this book are the favorable comments it has received from Eskimo people and the place it has found in some Alaskan schools where Eskimo children are taught about their own traditions. This book has also been translated into Japanese.

"*Make Prayers to the Raven* is based on a years' work with the Koyukon Athabaskan Indians, recording their traditional knowledge of the Alaskan forest and their beliefs about proper behavior toward nature. I thoroughly enjoyed living with the Koyukon people, and their teachings on living respectfully in the natural world profoundly have influenced the way I've conducted my own life. In this book, I tried to express my own feelings about Koyukon people and their traditions, while also staying within the bounds of scientific description. I believe the traditions recorded in *Make Prayers to the Raven* should not only be read as ethnography but as universally important perspectives on living in right relationship with our environment. Because of this, I feel it is the most significant work I've done. A documentary television series based on the book, titled 'Make Prayers to the Raven,' was recently produced for the Public Broadcasting System and will be shown worldwide by the B.B.C.

"My latest book, called *The Island Within,* is an exploration of my own relationship to the natural community of an island near my home, drawing perspectives from Koyukon teachings and from western ecological science. It's by far the most personal and challenging work I've ever done, and therefore the most enjoyable. As with everything I've written, my first goal in this book is to explore the ways of living in close and harmonious relationship to nature, and to pass along the wisdom inherent in traditional cultures such as [those of] the Alaskan Eskimos and Indians.

"Although I never thought of being an author until I was an adult, I've come to love writing and now center my life around it. Writing is the most solitary work imaginable, and spending long days alone is sometimes extremely difficult. But as I move toward more creative writing, I find the enjoyment considerably outweighs the hardship. The greatest rewards for me are in the daily work of writing, the fulfillment of dealing with words and expressing my feelings about the world outside myself, and the sense of doing something to educate others about the places where I've lived and the people who have taught me. This means much more than holding a book in my hands and thinking, 'I wrote this.'

"I have gone from a person who never intended to write to one who never intends to stop writing. I've found the most important things about writing are: to believe that I can do it, to accept huge sacrifices and little pay, to spend some time writing every day, to write about what means the most to me and what I know best, and to remember that I am writing to serve my subject rather than to serve myself."

MEDIA ADAPTATIONS: Make Prayers to the Raven was adapted as a television documentary series of the same name by P.B.S. and will be distributed by the B.B.C.

*   *   *

NEUBERGER, Egon 1925-

PERSONAL: Born February 27, 1925, in Zagreb, Yugoslavia; naturalized U.S. citizen; son of Paul (a lawyer) and Ann (Freund) Neuberger; married Florence Perlmutter (a computer specialist), December 22, 1949; children: Leah Ruth, Marc Joseph. *Education:* Cornell University, B.A., 1947; Harvard University, M.A., 1949, Ph.D., 1958.

ADDRESSES: Home—Five Somerset Ct., East Setauket, N.Y. 11733. *Office*—Department of Economics, State University of New York, Stony Brook, N.Y. 11794.

CAREER: U.S. Department of State, Washington, D.C., economic analyst, 1949-54, economic officer at U.S. Embassy in Moscow, 1952-53; National Bureau of Economic Research, Washington, D.C., economist, 1954; Massachusetts Institute of Technology, Cambridge, visiting fellow at Center for International Studies, 1956-57; Amherst College, Amherst, Mass., assistant professor of economics, 1957-60; RAND Corp., Santa Monica, Calif., economist, 1961-67; University of California, Los Angeles, adjunct associate professor of economics, 1963-65; State University of New York at Stony Brook, professor of economics, 1967—, dean of social and behavioral sciences, 1982-88. Visiting professor, University of Michigan, 1965-66; Columbia University, visiting professor, 1967-68, and senior fellow at Russian Institute and Research Institute on International Change, 1975-76; research scholar, Indiana University, 1969-75; visiting scholar, Wiener Institut fuer Internationale Wirtschaftsvergleiche; academic visitor, London School of Economics and Political Science, 1982; visiting senior scholar, Birckbeck College, University of London, 1982; visiting research professor, Ecole des Hautes Etudes en Sciences Sociales, 1982; visiting professor, University of Paris, 1990. Research consultant, Yale University, Institution for Social and Policy Studies, 1980. Has lectured at numerous universities, including Oxford University, Harvard University, Yale University, Cornell University, Columbia University, and

London School of Economics. Member of U.S. delegation of trade experts to the U.S.S.R., 1963. Member of selection committee for the Frank E. Seidman Distinguished Award, 1981-82. *Military service:* U.S. Army, 1943-46; served in Europe.

MEMBER: American Economic Association, American Association for the Advancement of Slavic Studies, Association for Comparative Economic Studies (member of executive committee, 1974-76; vice president, 1989; president, 1990), Association for the Study of the Grants Economy (member of advisory board, 1972—), Omicron Delta Epsilon (member of executive board, 1969—; trustee, 1970-73; president, 1980-81).

AWARDS, HONORS: Awarded fellowships from Ford Foundation, 1954-57, Social Science Research Council, 1959, American Philosophical Association, 1959, International Research and Exchanges Board, 1971, 1974-75, American Academy of Science, 1972, American Council of Learned Societies, 1974-75, and others; winner of International Competition on Research on Soviet Union and Eastern Europe, Ford Foundation, 1975; awarded grants from Social Science Research Council, 1982, National Endowment for the Humanities, 1982-84, Exxon Education Foundation, 1982-85, and others.

WRITINGS:

The USSR and the West as Market for Primary Products: Stability, Growth, and Size, RAND Corp., 1963.
(Editor with Alan A. Brown, and contributor) *International Trade and Central Planning: An Analysis of Economic Interactions,* University of California Press, 1968.
(Editor with Brown and M. Palmatier, and contributor) *Perspectives in Economics: Economists Look at Their Fields of Study,* McGraw, 1971.
(Editor with Brown and J. A. Licari, and contributor) *Urban and Social Economics in Market and Planned Economies,* Volume 1: *Policy, Planning, and Development,* Volume 2: *Housing, Income and Environment,* Praeger, 1974.
(With W. J. Duffy) *Comparative Economic Systems: A Decision-Making Approach,* Allyn & Bacon, 1976.
(Editor with Brown, and contributor) *Internal Migration: A Comparative Perspective,* Academic Press, 1977.
(With Juan Lara) *The Foreign Trade Practices of Centrally Planned Economies and Their Impact on U.S. International Competitiveness,* National Planning Association, 1977.
(Editor with Laura D. Tyson, and contributor) *The Impact of International Economic Disturbances on the Soviet Union and Eastern Europe: Transmission and Response,* Pergamon, 1980.

CONTRIBUTOR

Morris Bornstein, editor, *Plan and Market: Reform in Eastern Europe,* Yale University Press, 1973.
John P. Hardt, editor, *Reorientation and Commercial Relations of the Economies of Eastern Europe,* Joint Economic Committee, United States Congress, 1974.
Klaus-Detlev Grothuser, editor, *Sudosteuropa Handbuch,* Volume 1: *Jugoslawien,* Vandenhoeck & Ruprecht, 1975.
Judith L. Thornton, editor, *Economic Analysis of Soviet-Type Systems,* Cambridge University Press, 1976.
F. L. Altmann, O. Kyn, and H.-J. Wagener, editors, *On the Measurement of Factor Productivities: Theoretical Problems and Empirical Results,* Vandenhoeck & Ruprecht, 1976.
Hardt, editor, *East European Economies Post-Helsinki,* Joint Economic Committee, United States Congress, 1977.
Steven Rosefielde, editor, *World Communism at the Crossroads,* Martinus Nijhoff (The Hague), 1980.

Hardt, editor, *East European Economic Assessment,* Part 2: *Regional Assessment,* Joint Economic Committee, United States Congress, 1981.

Mary Jean Bowman, editor, *Collective Choice in Education,* Kluwer Nijhoff, 1981.

Frank H. Stephen, editor, *The Performance of Labour-managed Firms,* Macmillan, 1982.

Bornstein, editor, *Comparative Economic Systems: Models and Cases,* Irwin, 6th edition, 1989.

Fundamentals of Pure and Applied Economics, Harwood Academic Press, in press.

J. Dutta and Z. Zhongli, editors, *China's Economic Revolution,* JAI Press, in press.

OTHER

Author of other RAND publications on Soviet economics and foreign aid. Contributor to *Encyclopedia of Economics,* McGraw, 1982. Contributor to economic journals, including *American Economic Review, Quarterly Journal of Economics, Review of Economics and Statistics, Journal of Comparative Economics, Southern Economic Journal, Public Choice,* and *Economia Internazionale.* Founding editor, "Irving Fisher Award Monograph" series and "Frank W. Taussig Award Article" series, Omicron Delta Epsilon, 1969-83. Board of Editors, *Journal of Comparative Economics,* 1985-88.

*   *   *

NEUMEYER, Peter F(lorian) 1929-

PERSONAL: Born August 4, 1929, in Munich, Germany (now West Germany); son of Alfred and Eva Maria (Kirchheim) Neumeyer; married Helen Snell (an editor and music professor), December 27, 1952; children: Zachary Thomas, Christopher Muir, Daniel Patrick. *Education:* University of California, Berkeley, B.A., 1951, M.A., 1955, Ph.D., 1963.

ADDRESSES: Home—7968 Windsor Dr., La Mesa, Calif. 92041. *Office*—Department of English, San Diego State University, San Diego, Calif. 92182.

CAREER: Worked while attending school as dishwasher, lifeguard, swimming teacher, camp counselor, and truck driver; teacher in Santa Rosa, Calif., and Orinda, Calif., public schools, 1957-61; University of California, Berkeley, instructor in English, 1962-63; Harvard University, Cambridge, Mass., assistant professor of education, 1963-69; State University of New York at Stony Brook, associate professor of English, 1969-75; West Virginia University, Morgantown, professor of English and chairman of department, 1975-78; San Diego State University, San Diego, Calif., professor of English, 1978—. Former president, Medford (Mass.) Educational Council; representative for Project Plan, Three Village Schools, Setauket, N.Y.

MEMBER: Modern Language Association of America, Philological Association of the Pacific Coast.

AWARDS, HONORS: First prize for poem "Gulls," *Rebel* magazine, 1964; Scholarship Award, Children's Literature Association, 1983; National Endowment for the Humanities travel awards and summer fellowship; also recipient of several regional poetry awards.

WRITINGS:

JUVENILES

(With Edward Gorey) *Donald and the . . .,* Addison-Wesley, 1969.

(With Gorey) *Donald Has a Difficulty,* Fantod Press, 1970.

(With Gorey) *Why We Have Day and Night,* Young Scott Books, 1970, reprinted, Borgo, 1989.

The Faithful Fish, Young Scott Books, 1971.

Dream Cat, Green Tiger, 1982.

(Translator) Hans Baumann, *Mischa and His Brothers,* Green Tiger, 1985.

(Adaptor) *The Phantom of the Opera,* Gibbs, 1988.

OTHER

(Editor) *Twentieth Century Interpretations of "The Castle,"* Prentice-Hall, 1969.

(Contributor) Ralph Smith, editor, *Aesthetic Concepts and Education,* University of Illinois Press, 1970.

(Editor with William C. Carpenter) *Elements of Fiction: An Introduction to the Short Story,* W. C. Brown, 1974.

Homage to John Clare: A Poetical and Critical Correspondence, Peregrine Smith, 1980.

(Editor with Harold Darling) *Image and Maker: An Annual Dedicated to the Consideration of Book Illustration,* Green Tiger, 1984.

Contributor of more than sixty articles to professional journals; contributor of poems, essays, and regular book reviews to magazines and journals.

WORK IN PROGRESS: Research on children and literature, on the work of Franz Kafka, and on contemporary poetry.

SIDELIGHTS: "*Tristram Shandy* is the book that first suggested to me the possibilities in literature," Peter Neumeyer told *CA.* "I read the book in an otherwise dull sophomore survey course in English literature. I several times veered to other majors . . . tried anthropology and Law School. I was mighty happy to return to Chaucer, and to people who wanted to talk about books. Probably a long history of back ailments, laying me up for great stretches of time, forced me to write—for had I never been flat on my back, I would have spent absolutely all my time doing what I love still above all other things: hiking, fishing, swimming, and best of all, riding great ocean rollers in to shore. What is important? Probably to listen. Listen. Observe. That way you come close to understanding, perhaps loving. . . ."

Neumeyer added that his books "were written really because they had to get out of me—so, written for me—and people who have as peculiar a sense of humor or as quirky a sense of what is important as I do, may find them entertaining. They certainly weren't written specifically with children in mind. In fact, I personally don't think *Donald and the . . .* or *Donald Has a Difficulty* or *Why We Have Day and Night* are children's books at all. They're books without too many words, beautifully illustrated by Edward Gorey. Somebody other than the author decided to give them card catalogue numbers that classified them as children's books. *Why We Have Night and Day* is much influenced by the writing of Franz Kafka, on whom I do research. The last page of that book is very important, and is misprinted. It is all white. It was intended to be all black. That was pretty much the point of the book. Librarians who get it should write on the last page of the book, 'Color me black,' and let some child do it."

BIOGRAPHICAL/CRITICAL SOURCES:

PERIODICALS

New York Review of Books, April 10, 1969.
Saturday Review, April 17, 1971.

NEVINS, (Joseph) Allan 1890-1971

PERSONAL: Born May 20, 1890, in Camp Point, Ill.; died of cerebral vascular arterial sclerosis, March 5, 1971, in Menlo Park, Calif.; son of Joseph Allan and Emma (Stahl) Nevins; married Mary Fleming Richardson, December 30, 1916; children: Anne Elizabeth (Mrs. John Loftis), Meredith (Mrs. William Mayer). *Education:* University of Illinois, A.B., 1912, M.A. 1913.

ADDRESSES: Home—Killingworth, Conn.; and 445 Prospect Square, Pasadena, Calif. *Office*—Henry E. Huntington Library, San Marino, Calif.; and *American Heritage,* 551 Fifth Ave., New York, N.Y.

CAREER: University of Illinois, Urbana, instructor in English, 1912-13; *New York Evening Post,* New York City, editorial writer, 1913-23; *The Nation,* New York City, editorial writer, 1913-18; *New York Sun,* New York City, literary editor, 1924-25; *New York World,* New York City, editorial staff, 1925-31; Cornell University, Ithaca, N.Y., professor of history, 1927-28; Columbia University, New York City, associate professor, 1928-31, DeWitt Clinton Professor of History, 1931-58, founder and director of Oral History Project, 1948, professor emeritus, 1958-71; Huntington Library, San Marino, Calif., senior research associate, 1958-71. Special representative, Office of War Information in Australia and New Zealand, 1943-44; chief public affairs officer, American Embassy, London, England, 1945-46; special representative, United States Information Services, India and Japan, 1965. Harmsworth Professor, Oxford University, 1940-41, 1964-65. Visiting professor, California Institute of Technology, 1937-38, and Hebrew University of Jerusalem, 1952. Chairman, Civil War Centennial Commission, 1961-66. Trustee, Woodrow Wilson International Center for Scholars, Smithsonian Institution, 1969-71.

MEMBER: American Historical Association (president, 1960), Society of American Historians (president, 1950-61), American Academy of Arts and Letters (president, 1966-68), Council on Foreign Relations, New York State Historical Society (corresponding member), Athenaeum Club (London), Century Club and Lotus Club (both New York), National Press Club (Washington, D.C.).

AWARDS, HONORS: Pulitzer Prizes for biography, 1932, for *Grover Cleveland: A Study in Courage,* and 1937, for *Hamilton Fish: The Inner History of the Grant Administration;* Scribner Centenary Prize and Bancroft Prize, both 1947, both for *The Ordeal of the Union;* gold medal for history and biography from National Institute of Arts and Letters, 1957; gold medals from New York Historical Society, 1958, Commonwealth Club of California, 1960, and Rice University, 1962; Fletcher Pratt Award from Civil War Round Table of New York, 1960, for *The War for the Union: War Becomes Revolution, 1862-1863;* California Literature Medal, 1961, for *The War for the Union,* Volume 1: *The Improvised War, 1861-1862,* and Volume 2: *War becomes Revolution, 1862-1863;* honored by the creation of the Allan Nevins Chair of Economic History at Columbia University, 1965; Golden Plate Award from American Academy of Achievement, 1966; Alexander Hamilton Award from Columbia University, 1968; National Book Award, 1972, for *The War for the Union,* Volume 3: *The Organized War, 1863-1864* and Volume 4: *The Organized War to Victory, 1864-1865.* Honorary degrees from 28 colleges and universities, including Litt.D., Union College, 1935, Dartmouth College, 1936, Trinity College, 1948, University of Illinois, 1953, University of Southern California, Oxford University, and Birmingham University, 1965; LL.D., Washington and Lee University, 1935, Miami University, 1937, Dartmouth College, 1958, Columbia University, 1960, University of California, 1962, Occidental College, 1967, and Long Island University, 1968; L.H.D., Illinois College, 1953.

WRITINGS:

Illinois, Oxford University Press, 1917.

The Evening Post: A Century of Journalism, Boni & Liveright, 1922, reprinted, Russell & Russell, 1968.

The American States during and after the Revolution, 1775-1789, Macmillan, 1924, reprinted, Quadrangle, 1971.

The Emergence of Modern America, 1865-1878, Macmillan, 1927, reprinted, Scholarly Press, 1972.

Fremont, the West's Greatest Adventurer, Harper & Brothers, 1928.

Henry White: Thirty Years of American Diplomacy, Harper & Brothers, 1930.

Master's Essays in History: A Manual of Instructions and Suggestions, Columbia University Press, 1930.

Grover Cleveland: A Study in Courage, Dodd, 1932, reprinted, 1964.

History of the Bank of New York and Trust Company, 1784-1934, privately printed, 1934, reprinted, Arno, 1976.

The Tempo of Political Change (pamphlet), Roswell Park Committee on Publications, University of Buffalo, 1934.

Abram S. Hewitt, with Some Account of Peter Cooper, Harper & Brothers, 1935, reprinted, Octagon, 1967.

Hamilton Fish: The Inner History of the Grant Administration, Dodd, 1936, revised edition, Ungar, 1957.

The Gateway to History, Heath, 1938, 3rd edition, Quadrangle Books, 1963.

Fremont, Pathmaker of the West, Appleton, 1939, 4th edition, Ungar, 1962.

John D. Rockefeller: The Heroic Age of American Enterprise, Scribner, 1940, reprinted, Kraus, 1969.

America in World Affairs, Oxford University Press, 1941.

This Is England Today, Scribner, 1941.

(With Henry Steele Commager) *America: The Story of a Free People,* Little, 1942, published as *The Pocket History of the United States,* Pocket Books, 1943, 8th revised edition, 1987.

A Brief History of the United States, Clarendon Press, 1942.

A Select Bibliography of the History of the United States, Wyman, 1942.

(With J. B. Brebner) *The Making of Modern Britain: A Short History,* Norton, 1943.

(With Frank Weitenkampf) *A Century of Political Cartoons: Caricature in the United States from 1800-1900,* Scribner, 1944, reprinted, Octagon, 1975.

(With Commager) *A Short History of the United States,* Modern Library, 1945, 6th edition, Knopf, 1976.

Old America in a Young World, Newcomen Society, 1945.

Sail On: The Story of the American Merchant Marine, United States Lines, 1946.

The Ordeal of the Union (also see below), Scribner, Volume 1: *Fruits of Manifest Destiny, 1847-1852,* 1947, Volume 2: *A House Dividing, 1852-1857,* 1947.

10 Million Readers, 23 Million Books (pamphlet), U.S. Government Printing Office, 1948.

The Emergence of Lincoln, Scribner, Volume 1: *Douglas, Buchanan, and Party Chaos, 1857-1859,* 1950, Volume 2: *Prologue to Civil War, 1859-1861,* 1950.

The United States in a Chaotic World: A Chronicle of World Affairs, 1918-1933, Yale University Press, 1950.

The New Deal and World Affairs: A Chronicle of World Affairs, 1933-1945, Yale University Press, 1950.

(With Jeannette Mirsky) *The World of Eli Whitney,* Macmillan, 1952.

Study in Power: John D. Rockefeller, Industrialist and Philanthropist, Scribner, 1953, abridged edition by William Greenleaf, 1959.

The Statesmanship of the Civil War, Macmillan, 1953, revised edition, Collier, 1962.

Kansas and the Stream of American Destiny (pamphlet), University of Kansas Press, 1954.

(With Frank Ernest Hill) *Ford,* Scribner, Volume 1: *The Times, the Man, the Company,* 1954, Volume 2: *Expansion and Challenge, 1915-1933,* 1957, Volume 3: *Decline and Rebirth,* 1959, all reprinted, Arno, 1976.

The American Arts and American Freedom, University of Illinois, 1958.

The War for the Union, Scribner, Volume 1: *The Improvised War, 1861-1862,* 1959, Volume 2: *War Becomes Revolution, 1862-1863,* 1960, Volume 3: *The Organized War, 1863-1864,* 1971, Volume 4: *The Organized War to Victory, 1864-1865,* 1971.

The Nomination of Abraham Lincoln: New Forces and New Men, Chicago Historical Society, 1960.

(With others) *Energy and Man: A Symposium,* Appleton, 1960.

The State Universities and Democracy, University of Illinois Press, 1962, reprinted, Greenwood Press, 1977.

Herbert H. Lehman and His Era, Scribner, 1963.

A History of the American People from 1492, Oxford University Press, 1965, 2nd edition, 1970.

James Truslow Adams: Historian of the American Dream, University of Illinois Press, 1968.

The Ordeal of the Union: Selected Chapters Compiled and Introduced by E. B. Long, Scribner, 1973.

Ray Allen Billington, editor, *Allan Nevins on History,* Scribner, 1975.

EDITOR

Ponteach; or, The Savages of America; a Tragedy by Robert Rogers; with an Introduction and a Biography of the Author by Allan Nevins, Caxton Club [Chicago], 1914, reprinted, B. Franklin, 1971.

American Social History as Recorded by British Travellers, Holt, 1923, revised edition published as *America through British Eyes,* Oxford University Press, 1948, revised and enlarged edition, P. Smith, 1968.

Philip Hone, *Diary, 1828-1851,* two volumes, Dodd, 1927, reprinted in one volume as *The Diary of Philip Hone,* Arno, 1970.

American Press Opinion, Washington to Coolidge: A Documentary Record of Editorial Leadership and Criticism, 1785-1927, Heath, 1928, reprinted, Kennikat, 1969.

Charles Dickens, *David Copperfield,* two volumes, Macmillan, 1928.

John Quincy Adams, *Diary, 1794-1845,* Longmans, Green, 1928, reprinted as *The Diary of John Quincy Adams,* Ungar, 1969.

Polk: The Diary of a President, 1845-1849, Longmans, Green, 1929.

Walter Lippmann, *Interpretations, 1931-1932,* Macmillan, 1932.

Grover Cleveland, *Letters, 1850-1908,* Houghton, 1933, reprinted as *The Letters of Grover Cleveland,* Da Capo, 1970.

(With Lippmann) *A Modern Reader: Essays on Present-Day Life and Culture,* Heath, 1936.

Brand Whitlock, *Little Lion, Mieke,* Appleton, 1937.

Abram Stevens Hewitt, *Selected Writings,* Columbia University Press, 1937, reprinted, Kennikat, 1965.

(With Commager) *The Heritage of America,* Little, 1939, revised edition, 1949.

(With Claude Mitchell Simpson, Jr.) *American Reader,* Heath, 1941.

(With Louis M. Hacker) *The United States and Its Place in World Affairs, 1918-1943,* Heath, 1943.

(With John A. Krout) *The Greater City: New York, 1898-1948,* Columbia University Press, 1948, reprinted, Greenwood Press, 1981.

(With Milton Halsey Thomas) George Templeton Strong, *Diary,* four volumes (also see below), Macmillan, 1952, reprinted as *The Diary of George Templeton Strong,* Octagon, 1974.

Frederic R. Coudert, *Half Century of International Problems: A Lawyer's Views,* Columbia University Press, 1954.

James Fenimore Cooper, *The Leatherstocking Saga,* Pantheon, 1954.

John Charles Fremont, *Narratives of Exploration and Adventure,* Longmans, Green, 1956.

Times of Trial, Knopf, 1958.

John F. Kennedy, *Strategy of Peace,* Harper, 1960.

Auguste Laugel, *The United States during the Civil War,* Indiana University Press, 1961.

Strong, *Diary of the Civil War, 1860-1865 (originally appeared as Volume 3 of his Diary),* Macmillan, 1962.

Charles Shiels Wainwright, *A Diary of Battle, 1861-1865,* Harcourt, 1962.

(With Irving Stone) *Lincoln: A Contemporary Portrait,* Doubleday, 1962.

John Dos Passos and others, *Lincoln and the Gettysburg Address,* University of Illinois Press, 1964.

John Wallace, *Carpet Bag Rule in Florida,* University of Florida Press, 1964.

Kennedy, *The Burden and the Glory* (compiled from notes from his public statements and addresses; foreword by Lyndon B. Johnson), Harper, 1964.

History of the United States from the Compromise of 1850, abridged edition, University of Chicago Press, 1966.

(Author of foreword) Nicholas Roosevelt, *Theodore Roosevelt: The Man as I Knew Him,* Dodd, 1967.

(With others) *Civil War Books,* Louisiana State University Press, Volume 1, 1967, Volume 2, 1969.

(With Harold Hyman) *Heard 'round the World,* Knopf, 1969.

OTHER

(Contributor) *A Sense of History: The Best Writing from the Pages of American Heritage,* American Heritage/ Houghton, 1985.

Also author of *Life of Robert Rogers,* 1914, and *American Foreign Policy in the Light of Its Recent History,* 1941. General editor of "American Political Leaders" series, "Chronicles of America" series, Heath's "College and University History" series, and University of Michigan's "History of the Modern World" series. Consultant on numerous other books. Contributor to professional journals and popular periodicals, including *Nation* and *Saturday Review.* Founder, editor, and member of board of directors of *American Heritage* magazine. Nevins's papers are collected at the Butler Library, Columbia University, and the Huntington Library, San Marino, California.

SIDELIGHTS: Historian Allan Nevins was one of modern America's most prolific and impassioned academicians. Prior to his illness and death in 1971, he authored more than fifty full-length books and edited more than one hundred others, most while he taught full-time as DeWitt Clinton Professor of History at Columbia University. *Dictionary of Literary Biography* contributor Richard M. McMurry called Nevins "one of the most versatile, probably the greatest, and certainly the most prolific of twentieth-century American historians," a scholar who "maintained a healthy lifelong interest and involvement in the world beyond the university, especially in literature and politics." Nevins believed that a knowledge of history should be a major part of every citizen's life and that history books and biographies should be written with the aim of educating the widest possible audience. He brought a background in journalism to bear upon his historical works, and he was awarded numerous prestigious prizes, including two Pulitzers, in recognition of the accessibility of his writings. In a *New York Times Book Review* retrospective, C. Vann Woodward noted that Nevins's books, "far from amateurish, were scholarly and exhaustive in research. . . . But the heroic subject, full of color, drama and emotion, lent itself to the narrative tradition he admired and cultivated, and he was at his best with it. Here was history as 'heritage,' hallowed with nostalgia, sustaining national pride, healing rather than divisive. It was also history as romantic entertainment in the grand manner." *New York Herald Tribune Book Review* correspondent John Kenneth Galbraith similarly observed that Nevins allowed "color and drama to derive from his materials." In fact, Galbraith concluded, "it is hard to see how history could be better written."

Nevins was born and raised on a 220-acre farm near Camp Point, Illinois. His parents were no-nonsense farm folk who expected their children to help with the chores and to read serious literature. From an early age Nevins immersed himself in the works he found in his parents' library; later he sold apples and rabbits in order to buy books. When he finished high school in 1908 he decided to pursue a career in journalism. He won a complete scholarship to the University of Illinois, majored in English, and helped to write and edit the school newspaper, the *Illini.* He earned a Bachelor's degree in 1912 and remained at Illinois another year, teaching English and working for his Master's degree. Armed with his academic credentials, he travelled to New York City in 1913 and landed a staff position writing editorials and literary articles for the *Nation* and its sister publication, the *Evening Post.* Nevins had never found history a compelling subject while in college, but once he moved to New York—and settled near Columbia University—he began to spend his spare time in libraries, doing research on American history. "Whatever the reason for his interest in history," McMurry wrote, "Nevins devoted more and more time to it. When his day's work at the paper was finished, Nevins . . . dashed from the office to the New York Public Library. There he labored until closing time when he emerged with an armload of books to carry home and work with late into the night."

Journalism began to lose its appeal for Nevins as history and research consumed him. In 1927 he took his first teaching job, at Cornell University. The next year he was hired as an associate professor at Columbia, a position he held concurrently with a post at the *New York World* until 1931. Finally he quit journalism altogether in 1931 and became a professional academic historian. By that time he had already published several well-received works, including *The Evening Post: A Century of Journalism, The American States during and after the Revolution, 1775-1789,* and *The Emergence of Modern America, 1865-1878.* Nevins may have retired from active journalism, but he never eschewed the journalistic style of prose writing and reporting for a heavier, more pedantic tone. His personal goal was to be a thorough scholar who also wrote well; to be accurate yet imaginative. "Vitality and breadth the best university men do not need to learn," Nevins claimed in the *Saturday Review.* "But as the

world of journalism would gladly take gifts of expertness and exactness from academic sources, so the universities can learn something from the journalistic tradition. One lesson it might well learn is the importance of presenting facts and ideas in attractive garb. . . . Too often the academic tribe simply does not take the trouble to make its work decently alluring."

Not all scholars appreciated Nevins's approach, or, for that matter, his scorn of "ivory tower" methodology. *New Republic* contributor Peter Gay contended that Nevins "enjoyed a supreme self-confidence that permitted him to treat ambiguous issues as clearcut, unresolved issues as settled. It was this self-assurance in face of an uncertain past that enabled Nevins to publish so much. . . . Doubt, or facing problems through, would have spoiled and tarnished his shiny tale of alluring adventure and romance." Conversely, McMurry commended Nevins's balanced view of history and attributed his vast amount of publications to physical stamina, iron discipline, and singlemindedness. "Nevins sought by thorough research to develop in detail the personalities and characters of his subjects, to evaluate them fairly against the broad background of their times, and to combine scholarship, interpretation, and good literary style," McMurry wrote. Nevins "was not blind to the shortcomings of those whose lives he studied, and his books were reasonably balanced accounts. The praise and awards that the books received attested to Nevins's success."

In 1932 Nevins won a Pulitzer Prize for his biography *Grover Cleveland: A Study in Courage.* Reviewers found much to praise in the 832-page work. In the *Saturday Review,* W. A. White called the book "a scholar's work and yet there is no lack of swift movement, no sense of erudition for its own sake, no failure to dramatize an event sharply, when the event requires dramatization." The critic added: "But above all, this is not one of those 'smarty' books written by men who study their subjects diligently in order to strafe them intelligently. . . . The story of [Cleveland] has grown out of the material under the author's hands; which is an ideal way to make a biography; and the tale that is told here, if it is finally a hero tale and it is—is well told, convincingly and with charm, intelligently, and never shrinking from unpleasant truth." *New Republic* correspondent William MacDonald noted: "Mr. Nevins' book is a distinguished piece of political biography, exhaustive, apparently in its research, scholarly and skillful in its management of a great wealth and variety of material, and frank as well as judicious in awarding honors and demerits." "Now and then an historical or biographical work appears which merits the term definitive; Allan Nevins's life of Grover Cleveland belongs in that category," maintained E. F. Brown in *Current History.* "This biography carries greater authority than any previous account of Grover Cleveland. It is hard to believe that another study of his career will be needed."

Nevins won his second Pulitzer Prize in 1937, for *Hamilton Fish: The Inner History of the Grant Administration.* In his review of the work for *Books* magazine, MacDonald wrote that Fish's obscurity "has now been dispelled by an illuminating and impressive biography which meets with distinction every test of thoroughness, understanding and candor that criticism can apply." The book had a greater function for Nevins, however. It helped to heighten his interest in the era of the American Civil War, an interest that would lead him to write eight lengthy volumes on the events before and during the great nineteenth century conflict. Nevins was disturbed by the preponderance of military histories of the Civil War. He wanted to redress the imbalance by considering the political, social, administrative, cultural, and economic elements of American life during the period. McMurry claimed that the historian "was especially interested in describing how the changes wrought by the conflict acted as a catalyst to prepare the nation for its industrial future."

The eight books, published under series titles *The Ordeal of the Union, The Emergence of Lincoln,* and *The War for the Union,* were among Nevins's most notable—and controversial—publications. McMurry expressed the opinion that reviews of the series reflected the critics' own regional biases, not Nevins's, and added that many reviewers "praised the thoroughness of his research, the breadth of his coverage, and his literary grace and pointed out that in almost every chapter he had been able to increase historians' knowledge of the period." Perhaps by virtue of this work on the Civil War—the last two volumes of which were published posthumously in 1971—Nevins was made chairman of the Civil War Centennial Commission in 1961. Under Nevins's leadership, according to McMurry, the commission "sponsored a fitting commemoration" with the accent on education rather than on tawdry exploitation of the violent battles.

Nevins's other abiding interest was the history of the industrial development of the United States. He disputed the negative attitude of some academic historians toward such industrialists as John D. Rockefeller and Henry Ford; indeed, he saw America's industrial development as a positive and timely occurrence. To quote McMurry, Nevins argued that industrialization "had raised the American standard of living and lowered the cost of manufactured goods. The conduct of big businesses had often been more ethical and less dishonest than that of their smaller competitors who had been so beloved by earlier historians. Most important, Nevins maintained, the businessmen had forged a great industrial power from an agricultural republic just in time to insure victory over Germany in World War I and World War II." *New York Times* contributor Albin Krebs contended that this Nevins thesis "was calmly accepted, except by some of the younger, muckraking historians of the period." It was equally acceptable to corporations and the families of industrial magnates, who gave Nevins unprecedented access to private papers. Nevins's two best-known works in this vein were *John D. Rockefeller: The Heroic Age of American Enterprise,* published in 1940, and the three-volume biography *Ford: The Times, the Man, the Company, Expansion and Challenge, 1915-1933,* and *Decline and Rebirth.*

By many accounts, including McMurry's, Nevins was an indefatigable worker who juggled a full load of teaching and graduate student sponsorship, several simultaneous book projects, and civilian service to the American government. He also was instrumental in launching and running two pioneering enterprises—*American Heritage* magazine, the first history periodical for general readers, and Columbia's Oral History Project, a program that tape-recorded interviews with prominent Americans. When he reached mandatory retirement age at Columbia in 1958 he became a senior research associate at the Huntington Library, where, according to McMurry, he "ran up the stairs . . . because the elevator was so slow that it wasted valuable time that could be devoted to writing." While at the Huntington, Nevins completed the last three volumes of his Civil War series, with the help of some assistants, as well as five other full-length books. In 1965 Columbia created the Allan Nevins Chair of Economic History in his honor, using a half million dollar endowment Nevins himself donated to the school, saved over the years from book royalties. Nevins died of a year-long illness in 1971, ending what Woodward called a "remarkable career." Woodward also wrote: "Allan Nevins was a one-man history-book industry, a phenomenon of American productivity without parallel in the field." According to R. B. Harwell in the *Chicago Sunday Tribune,* Nevins

outshone "any rival historian in the breadth of his familiarity with the materials of history. . . . His judgements on men and events [were] clear, concise, and authoritative." McMurry concluded: "American letters in general and American history in particular, . . . will always be fuller, richer, and better because of Allan Nevins and the 'history of interest and importance' that he discovered and about which he wrote so much and so well."

AVOCATIONAL INTERESTS: Golf and fishing.

BIOGRAPHICAL/CRITICAL SOURCES:

BOOKS

The American Historian: A Social-Intellectual History of the Writing of the American Past, Oxford University Press, 1960.
Billington, Ray Allen, editor, *Allan Nevins on History,* Scribner, 1975.
Davis, Elizabeth Logan, *Fathers of America,* Revell, 1958.
Dictionary of Literary Biography, Volume 17: *Twentieth-Century American Historians,* Gale, 1983.
Wish, Harvey, editor, *American Historians,* Oxford University Press, 1962.

PERIODICALS

American Historical Review, October, 1953, July, 1954, April, 1959.
Best Sellers, November 1, 1968, August 15, 1971.
Books, October 23, 1932, October 25, 1936, October 20, 1940.
Boston Transcript, January 4, 1933, November 21, 1936, October 15, 1940.
Chicago Sunday Tribune, October 15, 1950, September 15, 1957, August 30, 1959, November 20, 1960.
Christian Science Monitor, January 4, 1941, October 14, 1950, May 21, 1953, March 4, 1954, September 19, 1957, September 3, 1959, December 8, 1960, October 20, 1962.
Commonweal, September 29, 1950.
Current History, January, 1933.
Nation, September 24, 1938, November 9, 1940, December 2, 1950, May 30, 1953.
New Republic, November 16, 1932, January 20, 1937, October 12, 1938, December 9, 1940, October 11, 1975.
New Statesman, August 22, 1953, June 2, 1967.
New Yorker, March 27, 1954.
New York Herald Tribune Book Review, October 15, 1950, May 24, 1953, February 28, 1954, September 15, 1957, September 13, 1959.
New York Times, October 16, 1932, November 29, 1936, August 28, 1938, November 17, 1940, October 15, 1950, June 28, 1953, September 27, 1953, February 28, 1954, September 15, 1957.
New York Times Book Review, August 30, 1959, December 26, 1971.
San Francisco Chronicle, November 5, 1950, April 11, 1954, November 24, 1957.
Saturday Review, October 22, 1932, October 31, 1936, September 10, 1938, October 26, 1940, December 27, 1941, October 14, 1950, May 23, 1953, February 27, 1954, September 14, 1957, June 21, 1958, August 29, 1959, November 20, 1971.
Spectator, August 20, 1954, May 2, 1958.
Time, October 26, 1936, October 28, 1940, July 21, 1958.
Times Literary Supplement, September 25, 1953, November 26, 1954, May 9, 1958, March 11, 1960, April 24, 1969.
Yale Review, winter, 1941, December, 1957.

OBITUARIES:

PERIODICALS

Newsday, March 6, 1971.
New York Times, March 6, 1971.
Publishers Weekly, March 22, 1971.
Time, March 15, 1971.
Washington Post, March 6, 1971.

—Sketch by Anne Janette Johnson

*   *   *

NIEMEYER, Gerhart 1907-

PERSONAL: Born February 15, 1907, in Essen, Germany (now West Germany); came to the United States, 1937; naturalized U.S. citizen, 1943; son of Victor and Kaethe (Ley) Niemeyer; married Lucie Lenzner, September 18, 1931; children: A. Hermann, Lucian L., Paul V., Lisa M., Christian B. *Education:* Attended Cambridge University, 1925-26, and Munich University, 1926-27; Kiel University, LL.B., 1930, J.U.D., 1932.

ADDRESSES: Home—806 East Angela Blvd., South Bend, Ind. 46617.

CAREER: Madrid University, Madrid, Spain, lecturer in law, 1933-34, head of classes for Federation of Spanish Associations for International Studies and member of research faculty of Institute of Studies in International Economics, 1934-36; Princeton University, Princeton, N.J., lecturer, 1937-39, assistant professor of politics, 1940-44; Oglethorpe University, Atlanta, Ga., professor of political science and head of division, 1944-50; foreign affairs officer, U.S. Department of State, 1950-53; research analyst, Council on Foreign Relations, 1953-55; University of Notre Dame, Notre Dame, Ind., professor of political science, 1955-76, emeritus professor of government, 1976—. Visiting professor or faculty member at numerous colleges and universities, including Yale University, 1942, 1946, 1954-55, University of Munich, 1962-63, and Hillsdale College, 1976-82. Member of task force on foreign policy, Republican National Committee, 1965-68. Ordained in Episcopal Church as deacon, 1973, priest, 1980, and canon, 1987.

MEMBER: American Political Science Association, American Society of Political and Legal Philosophy.

WRITINGS:

Law without Force, Princeton University Press, 1941.
An Inquiry into Soviet Mentality, Praeger, 1956.
Facts on Communism, Volume 1: *The Communist Ideology,* U.S. Government Printing Office, 1959.
Handbook on Communism, Praeger, 1962.
Communists in Coalition Governments, American Enterprise Institute for Public Policy Research, 1963.
Deceitful Peace, Arlington House, 1971.
Between Nothingness and Paradise, Louisiana State University Press, 1971.
(Translator) Eric Voegelin, *Anamnesis,* University of Notre Dame Press, 1978.
Aftersight and Foresight: Selected Essays, foreword by William F. Buckley, Jr., University Press of America, 1988.

Associate editor, *Modern Age,* 1965—.

AVOCATIONAL INTERESTS: Chamber music.*

NOAH, Harold J(ulius) 1925-

PERSONAL: Born January 21, 1925, in London, England; son of Abraham and Sophia (Cohen) Noah; married Norma Mestel, October 20, 1945; married second wife, Helen Claire Chisnell, October 14, 1966; children: Deborah Ann Susan, Carolyn Anne Elizabeth, Adam Pierre Michael, David Harold Michael. *Education:* London School of Economics and Political Science, B.Sc., 1946, graduate study, 1959-60; King's College, London, Teacher's Diploma, 1949, Academic Diploma, 1954; Columbia University, Ph.D., 1964.

ADDRESSES: Home—560 Riverside Dr., New York, N.Y. 10027. *Office*—468 Bardy Hall, State University of New York at Buffalo, Buffalo, N.Y. 14260.

CAREER: Labour Party, London, England, research assistant, 1946-48; Southwest London College of Commerce, London, instructor in economics, 1948-49; Henry Thornton School, London, 1949-60, began as assistant master, became head of economics department; Fairleigh Dickinson University, Madison, N.J., assistant professor of economics, 1960-61; Columbia University, New York, N.Y., instructor, 1962-64, assistant professor, 1964-66, associate professor of comparative education, 1966-69, professor of economics and education, 1969—, Arthur I. Gates Professor of Economics and Education, 1981-83, Gardner Cowles Chair of Education, 1983-87, director of Institute of Philosophy and Politics of Education, Teachers College, 1974—, dean of Teachers College, 1976-81; State University of New York at Buffalo, Buffalo, professor of education, 1987—. Member of several committees; visiting fellow of Institut fuer Bildungsforschung in der Max-Planck-Gesellschaff, 1964-65; consultant, New Jersey Commission of Education, 1969-71, and Organization for Economic Cooperation and Development, Paris, France, 1971-82.

MEMBER: Royal Economic Society, American Economic Association, American Association for the Advancement of Slavic Studies, Comparative and International Education Society (president, 1973-74), Comparative Education Society in Europe, Association for Comparative Economics, National Academy of Education, American Educational Research Association.

AWARDS, HONORS: Fulbright grant, 1958-59; Ford Foundation grant, 1969-72.

WRITINGS:

Financing Soviet Schools, Teachers College Press, 1967.
(Translator and editor) *The Economics of Education in the U.S.S.R.,* Praeger, 1969.
(With Max A. Eckstein) *Toward a Science of Comparative Education,* Macmillan, 1969.
(With Eckstein) *Scientific Investigations in Comparative Education,* Macmillan, 1969.
Germany: Review of National Policies, Organization for Economic Cooperation and Development, 1972.
(With Eckstein) *Metropolitanism and Education: A Comparative Study* (monograph), Institute of Philosophy and Politics of Education, Teachers College, Columbia University, 1973.
Canada: Review of National Politics, Organization for Economic Cooperation and Development, 1976.
(With A. H. Passow and others) *The National Case Study: An Empirical Comparative Study of Twenty-One Educational Systems,* Almqvist & Wiksell, 1976.
(With Joel Sherman) *Education Financing and Policy Goals for Primary Schools: General Report,* Organization for Economic Cooperation and Development, 1979.

(With Eckstein) *International Study of Business/Industry Involvement in Education,* Institute of Philosophy and Politics of Education, Teachers College, Columbia University, 1987.

CONTRIBUTOR

Lesley L. Browder, editor, *Emerging Patterns of Administrative Accountability,* McCutcheon, 1971.

Marxism, Communism, and Western Society: A Comparative Encyclopedia, Verlag Herder, 1971.

Elliot W. Eisner and Elizabeth Vallance, editors, *Conflicting Concepts of Curriculum,* McCutcheon, 1973.

Reginald Edwards and others, editors, *Relevant Methods in Comparative Education,* UNESCO Institute of Education, 1973.

Richard W. Lindholm, editor, *Property Taxation and the Finance of Education,* [Wisconsin], 1973.

Walter Ackerman and others, editors, *Erziehung in Israel,* Volume II, Klett-Cotta, 1982.

E. B. Gumbert, editor, *Patriarchy, Party, Population, and Pedagogy,* Georgia State University, 1986.

Hermann Roehrs, editor, *Tradition and Reform of the University in International Perspective,* Peter Lang Verlag, 1987.

OTHER

Also contributor and sections editor of *International Encyclopedia of Education,* Pergamon. Contributor to periodicals. *Comparative Education Review,* associate editor, 1964-66, editor, 1966-71, member of editorial board, 1973-79; member of editorial advisory board, *Slavic Review,* 1967-69; *Soviet Education,* editor, 1970-78, chairman of editorial advisory board, 1979—. Guest editor, *Some Aspects of Comparative Education: A Festschrift in Honour of Edmund King* and *Compare* (periodical), 1981.

SIDELIGHTS: Toward a Science of Comparative Education has been published in a Spanish edition. Harold J. Noah speaks French, German, and Russian.

*   *   *

NOFZIGER, Margaret 1946-

PERSONAL: Born May 9, 1946, in San Francisco, Calif.; daughter of James C. Nofziger and Marjorie (Goodwin) Shore; married Thomas P. Dotzler (an historic preservation artisan); children: Asa, Lubitza. *Education:* Attended San Francisco State College (now University), 1964-67.

ADDRESSES: Office—MND Publishing, Inc., P.O. Box 210813, Nashville, Tenn. 37221.

CAREER: Book Publishing Co., Summertown, Tenn., general manager, editor, and staff writer, 1971-84, president, 1984-85; MND Publishing, Inc., Nashville, Tenn., president, 1986—.

MEMBER: National Family Planning and Reproductive Health Association.

WRITINGS:

A Co-operative Method of Natural Birth Control, Book Publishing, 1976.

The Fertility Question, Book Publishing, 1982.

Signs of Fertility: The Personal Science of Natural Birth Control, MND Publishing, 1988.

NOLAN, Chuck
See EDSON, J(ohn) T(homas)

*   *   *

NORTH, Robert
See WITHERS, Carl A.

*   *   *

NOVAK, Michael 1933-

PERSONAL: Born September 9, 1933, in Johnstown, Pa.; son of Michael John and Irene Louise (Sakmar) Novak; married Karen Laub (a painter and printmaker), June 29, 1963; children: Richard, Tanya, Jana. *Education:* Stonehill College, A.B. (summa cum laude), 1956; Gregorian University (Rome, Italy), B.T. (cum laude), 1958; attended Catholic University, 1958-60; Harvard University, M.A., 1965.

ADDRESSES: Office—American Enterprise Institute for Public Policy Research, 1150 17th Street, N.W., Washington, D.C. 20036. *Agent*—Donald Cutler, Sterling Lord Agency, Inc., 660 Madison Ave., New York, N.Y. 10021.

CAREER: Stanford University, Palo Alto, Calif., assistant professor of humanities, 1965-68; State University of New York, Old Westbury, associate professor of philosophy and religious studies, 1968-73, provost, Disciplines College, 1969-71; Rockefeller Foundation, New York, N.Y., associate director of humanities, 1973-74; Syracuse University, Syracuse, N.Y., Ledden-Watson Distinguished Professor of Religious Studies, 1977-79; American Enterprise Institute for Public Policy Research, Washington, D.C., George Frederick Jewett Scholar in Religion and Public Policy, 1978—. Visiting professor at Union Theological Seminary, 1966, Carleton College, 1970, Immaculate Heart College, Hollywood, Calif., 1971, and University of California, Santa Barbara, 1972; visiting W. Harold and Martha Welch Professor of American Studies at the University of Notre Dame, 1987-88. Senior policy advisor to R. Sargent Shriver, 1970; speechwriter for R. Sargent Shriver, 1970, 1972, and for Edmund Muskie, 1971; member of staff, George McGovern's presidential campaign, 1972. Fellow of Institute for Society, Ethics and the Life Sciences, 1969—. Advisor on programs in medicine and ethics, Joseph P. Kennedy, Jr., Foundation, 1971. Judge for National Book Awards, 1971, and DuPont Broadcast Journalism Award, 1971-80. Founder and member of board of directors, Ethnic Millions Political Action Committee, 1974; chief of United States delegation to the United Nations Human Rights Commission, Geneva, Switzerland, 1981 and 1982; member of Presidential Commission on Cultural Diversity, 1978-84, Board for International Broadcasting, 1984—, and Presidential Commission on Ethnic Justice, 1985-87.

MEMBER: Society for Values in Higher Education (member of central committee, 1969-72), American Academy of Religion (program director, 1968-72), Council on Foreign Relations, Council on Religion and International Affairs.

AWARDS, HONORS: Kent fellow, 1961—; named "most influential professor" by the senior classes at Stanford University, 1967 and 1968; Hastings Institute fellow, 1970-76; "man of the year" citation from the city of Johnstown, Pa., and Faith and Freedom Award from Religious Heritage Association, both 1978; Medal of Freedom and Friend of Freedom commendation, both 1981; theology award from Catholic Press Association, 1987, for *Will It Liberate?: Questions about Liberation Theology.*

Honorary degrees include LL.D., Keuka College, 1970, Le-Moyne College, 1976; L.H.D., Davis and Elkins College, 1971, Stonehill College, 1977; Litt.D., Sacred Heart College, 1977, Muhlenberg College, 1979, D'Youville College, 1981, and Boston University, 1981.

WRITINGS:

The Tiber Was Silver (novel), Doubleday, 1961.

A New Generation: American and Catholic, Herder & Herder, 1964.

The Open Church: Vatican II: Act II, Macmillan, 1964.

(Editor) *The Experience of Marriage,* Macmillan, 1964.

Belief and Unbelief, Macmillan, 1965.

A Time To Build, Macmillan, 1967.

(Editor) *American Philosophy and the Future,* Scribner, 1968.

A Theology for Radical Politics, Herder & Herder, 1969.

Naked I Leave (novel), Macmillan, 1970.

The Experience of Nothingness, Harper, 1970.

Ascent of the Mountain, Flight of the Dove: An Invitation to Religious Studies, Harper, 1971, revised edition, 1978.

Politics: Realism and Imagination, Herder & Herder, 1971.

The Rise of the Unmeltable Ethnics: Politics and Culture in the Seventies, Macmillan, 1972.

(With wife, Karen Laub-Novak) *A Book of Elements,* Herder & Herder, 1972.

Choosing Our King: Powerful Symbols in Presidential Politics, Macmillan, 1974.

The Joy of Sports: End Zones, Bases, Baskets, Balls, and the Consecration of the American Spirit, Basic Books, 1976.

The Guns of Lattimer, Basic Books, 1978.

(Editor) *Capitalism and Socialism: A Theological Inquiry,* American Enterprise Institute for Public Policy Research, 1979.

The Spirit of Democratic Capitalism, Simon & Schuster, 1982.

Moral Clarity in the Nuclear Age, T. Nelson, 1983.

Confession of a Catholic, Harper, 1983.

Freedom with Justice: Catholic Social Thought and Liberal Institutions, Harper, 1984.

Will It Liberate?: Questions about Liberation Theology, Paulist Press, 1987.

CONTRIBUTOR

Leonard Liek and David Hawke, editors, *American Colloquy,* Bobbs-Merrill, 1963.

Edward Schilleback, editor, *Concilium Dogma,* Volume I: *The Church and Mankind,* Paulist Press, 1964.

William Birmingham, editor, *What Catholics Think about Birth Control,* Sheed & Ward, 1965.

Daniel Callahan, editor, *Generation of the Third Eye,* Sheed & Ward, 1965.

Voluntary Associations: A Study of Groups in Free Societies, John Knox Press, 1966.

Mitchell Cohen and Dennis Hale, editors, *The New Student Left: An Anthology,* Beacon Press, 1966.

Elwyn A. Smith, editor, *Church-State Relations in Ecumenical Perspective,* Duquesne University Press, 1966.

Sister M. Charles Borromeo, editor, *The New Nuns,* New American Library, 1967.

Bernard Murchland, editor, *The Meaning of the Death of God,* Random House, 1967.

Conspiracy, Harper, 1973.

H. Wheeler, editor, *Beyond the Punitive Society,* W. H. Freeman, 1973.

Television as a Social Force, Praeger, 1975.

Marvin Barrett, editor, *The Fifth Alfred I. DuPont-Columbia University Survey of Broadcast Journalism,* Crowell, 1975.

OTHER

Contributor to scholarly and general publications, including *Commentary, Harper's, New Republic,* and *Commonweal.* Contributor to the *Washington Star,* 1976; syndicated newspaper columnist, 1976-80, 1984—. Associate editor, *Commonweal,* 1966-69; contributing editor, *Christian Century,* 1967-80, *Christianity and Crisis,* 1968-74; member of editorial board, *Motive,* 1966-68, *Journal of Ecumenical Studies,* 1967—, *Worldview,* 1971, and *National Review.* Member of board of advisors, *American Report,* 1970. Founder and member of editorial board, *The World,* 1982—; co-founder of *Crisis* magazine, 1982; publisher, 1987—.

SIDELIGHTS: Social philosopher Michael Novak told the *New York Times* that he tries "to interpret the American experience in theological terms" in order to produce "a philosophy-theology of the American way of life." Novak, who is a resident scholar at the American Enterprise Institute in Washington, D.C., writes books, articles, and newspaper columns that examine the relationship between the principles of democratic capitalism and Judeo-Christian teachings. He is one of a very few Catholic scholars who defends capitalism on theological and moral grounds and who finds capitalistic societies most conducive to human spiritual growth. *Washington Post Book World* contributor Harvey Cox feels that Novak "has demonstrated his capacity for astute theological analysis" through more than twenty books dealing with such diverse subjects as ethnic identity, sports, nuclear arms, economics, and liberation theology. As William McGurn notes in the *Wall Street Journal,* Novak enters a "heated debate" as ". . . a bridge between two groups who often do not realize how mutually dependent they are. He is at once a theologian who appreciates how wealth is generated and sustained, and an economist who understands the moral virtues that make this possible."

Michael Novak was born and raised in Johnstown, Pennsylvania, the grandson of Slovak immigrants. He was devoutly religious from an early age, and at fourteen he became a junior seminarian in the Congregation of Holy Cross. Planning to enter the priesthood, he attended Stonehill College in Massachusetts and then the Gregorian University in Rome, earning Bachelor's degrees in philosophy and theology. Shortly before his ordination in 1960 he obtained a dispensation from his religious vows in order to continue his studies in the secular community. Novak told the *New York Times* that he left priesthood training because he wanted to be a writer and "didn't see how I could do the independent thinking and travelling I wanted to do, and do it in community and under obedience." Still, the Catholic church remained his major early focus; his first novel, *The Tiber Was Silver,* takes place in Rome, and his journalism of the period concerns American Catholics' opinions and the church reforms set in motion by Vatican Council II. While working on his Master's degree at Harvard, Novak wrote several books, including the essay collection *A New Generation: American and Catholic,* and a firsthand account of Vatican II, *The Open Church.* In 1965 he went to Stanford University as an assistant professor of humanities.

At Stanford, where he was a very popular teacher, Novak became involved with protests against the Vietnam War and other radical platforms. His writings from 1965 through 1970 analyze the mood of alienation and disorientation prevalent in that era and propose "a new inwardness of human experience and a new belief in man which despite all setbacks makes us struggle to change community," to quote *Christian Century* reviewer Charles C. West. Having undergone personal crises of faith himself, his books offer a case for Christian theism as one avenue to self-knowledge. Works such as *A Theology for Radical Politics, The Experience of Nothingness, Belief and Unbelief,* and *Ascent of the Mountain, Flight of the Dove: An Invitation to Religious Studies* are, according to Sidney Hook in *Commentary,* honest attempts "to meet the challenge of naturalism without sacrificing or diluting . . . faith." *New York Times Book Review* correspondent J. M. Cameron finds *Belief and Unbelief* "a moving and perceptive account of the difficulties of a Christian in the present climate of opinion. . . . It expresses, without mitigating, the perplexities of those Christians—roughly, the 'progressives' in any Christian establishment—who are faintly astonished to find themselves closer to unbelievers than to their believing fellows on a variety of crucial moral issues, typically today those concerned with civil rights and warfare." In a *Chicago Tribune Book World* piece on *The Experience of Nothingness,* Charles Frankel calls Novak "a philosopher of the rising generation [who] makes the effort to explore the current mood . . ., to speak for that mood, and to go beyond it to the expression of an ideal which might turn this mood from a purely negative one into an affirmative program."

From 1968 to 1973 Novak worked as an associate professor of philosophy and religious studies at the State University of New York, Old Westbury campus. During those years his focus was broadening to include social, political, and cultural questions. He served as an advisor and speechwriter for several Democratic politicians, including R. Sargent Shriver, Edmund Muskie, and George McGovern. Concurrently he published a controversial book, *The Rise of the Unmeltable Ethnics,* in which he praised ethnic diversity and called for a "new cultural pluralism" to challenge the established "elite Protestant politics." *Chronicle Review* contributor Richard W. Fox finds the work "an impassioned plea for a new liberalism based on a recognition of cultural diversity in white America. . . . It remains the most illuminating introduction to the personal, communal, and political meanings of 'the new ethnicity.' " Some reviewers have reacted adversely to the level of passion Novak employs in *The Rise of the Unmeltable Ethnics.* In the *New York Times Book Review,* Garry Wills writes: "There is something dismaying about an immoral book written by a very moral man. . . . Nothing is quite so strange as a naturally pleasant person who feels it is his duty to be unpleasant, to call civility an Anglo-Saxon deceit." Wills concludes that the book serves as a contribution to the "rapidly growing literature on the social uses of hatred." *American Political Science Review* essayist Lawrence H. Fuchs also suggests that in *The Rise of the Unmeltable Ethnics* "the passion gets out of hand occasionally," but adds that few students of the ethnicity of American politics "would quarrel with many of Novak's major assertions: political unity depends in part upon cultural pluralism."

Choosing Our King, published in 1972, and *The Joy of Sports: End Zones, Bases, Baskets, Balls, and the Consecration of the American Spirit,* published in 1976, both offer analyses of the religious and psychological symbolism behind secular American institutions. *Choosing Our King* "refers to the President as king, high priest, and prophet," according to George E. Reedy in the *National Review,* with special emphasis on the failed 1972 campaign of George McGovern. In *The Joy of Sports,* to quote *New Leader* reviewer Ben Yagoda, Novak reveals "that the limits and disciplines of sports, like the formal rituals of religion, can momentarily free us from the irredeemable impurities of earthly life." Fox feels that these two works, along with *The Rise of the Unmeltable Ethnics,* have marked "the emergence of a thinker who [is] reflecting deeply upon the American experience and

searching for a voice and style with which to speak not only to the 'educated,' but also to ordinary Americans like the members of Eastern European ethnic groups, from whose world he came." Reedy likewise concludes that Novak's work "serves the highest purpose of writing—to make people think."

Novak was doing some intense thinking himself in the mid to late 1970s. In fact, he underwent a fundamental ideological metamorphosis from a supporter of socialist ideals to a defender of democratic capitalism. "I used to think socialism was a good idea, but nobody has made it work yet," Novak told *Time* magazine. "I moved to the realization that the idea itself is wrong." Novak faced economic reality, he said in the *Rocky Mountain News,* and then had to admit that socialism "doesn't work very well. In politics, it produces tyranny; in economics, it produces poverty." Anne Husted Burleigh notes in *Modern Age* that Novak's change of ideology has altered his theology as well. "Novak's movement from left to right across the theological spectrum, documented in a superb and sober . . . book, *Confession of a Catholic,* corresponds to the change of heart he has undergone in politics and economics," Burleigh writes. "One supposes that, as he grew in his understanding of how a limited government-free market political economy works and how it can protect moral-cultural values, he became increasingly disenchanted with the pronounced gnostic and Marxist tone assumed in the last twenty years by a substantial wing of the church." This theme is elucidated in Novak's more recent books, including *The Spirit of Democratic Capitalism, Moral Clarity in the Nuclear Age,* and *Freedom with Justice: Catholic Social Thought and Liberal Institutions.*

Published in 1982, and translated into more than a half-dozen foreign languages, *The Spirit of Democratic Capitalism* remains one of Novak's best-known books. The work "pronounces democratic capitalism the best of all political-economic systems, in ideal as well as in results," according to a *New York Times* reviewer. Furthermore, argues the author, despised though it is, capitalism offers the best actual hope for alleviating poverty and suppressing tyranny—it allows even the humblest citizen to improve his or her station in society. "Novak argues that democracy and a free economy are the natural embodiment of the ideals of liberty and individual worth that are the foundation of the Judeo-Christian tradition," Walter Isaacson writes in *Time.* Isaacson concludes: "The marriage of pluralism and productivity best realizes the Christian ideal of *caritas,* or the compassionate love of fellow human beings." Novak's thesis takes into account the inherent dangers of democratic capitalism—materialism and greed—but concludes that the system is the only one that "renders sinful tendencies as productive of good as possible." *New Republic* essayist Charles Krauthammer calls *The Spirit of Democratic Capitalism* "a sophisticated and often original defense of Western democratic capitalism, and a hymn to its spirit of freedom and pluralism. Novak's book is certain at least to inspire those now just beginning to lay siege to the heretofore sacrosanct citadel of liberation theology and its claim that 'Christianity is the religion of which socialism is the practice.' " Isaacson similarly concludes that Novak's "carefully woven theological and political argument succeeds in its overall mission: to remind readers that democratic capitalism is not only a system that truly works but at its best is a living embodiment of its own ideals."

Moral Clarity in the Nuclear Age, Freedom with Justice, and *Will It Liberate?: Questions about Liberation Theology* are all meant to influence international Catholic thought on such issues as socialism, national defense, and human rights. According to Walter Goodman in the *New York Times,* Novak's "plain objective is to provide ammunition to those within his church's hierarchy who oppose Marxist-tinged doctrines, exemplified by the liberation theology movement that is enjoying considerable influence in Latin America." *New York Times Book Review* contributor Aaron Wildavsky likewise observes that Novak "aims to describe Catholic social thought in modern times, to make manifest the contributions as well as errors of popes and theologians, revealing their ready acceptance of political rights and their halting appreciation of economic productivity, to critique 'liberation theology' and to begin the task of devising a Catholic economic theology." Most critics agree that Novak's arguments in support of democracy, capitalism, nuclear arms as deterrents to war, and limited central government have influenced the tenor of several controversial pastoral letters from Catholic bishops in recent years. To quote *Commonweal* essayist R. A. Schroth, Novak's assertions on public policy and theology have "helped transform the church."

In addition to his full-length works, Novak writes a syndicated newspaper column, a regular column for the *National Review,* and numerous articles for periodicals. He is a founding director of the Ethnic Millions Political Action Committee, and he has entered public service as chief delegate to the 1981 and 1982 sessions of the United Nations Human Rights Commission in Geneva, Switzerland. Novak, who sees himself primarily as a teacher who can excite learned debate, lives in Washington, D.C., with his wife and three children. Although his work has sometimes been criticized for its opinionated tone, most observers concede that Novak's influence as a political/theological philosopher has been considerable. Fox concludes: "Michael Novak is a writer of rare versatility and power. . . . His work is rivalled by few contemporary authors—not just in sheer volume, but in range, in diversity of form, and in depth of insight."

BIOGRAPHICAL/CRITICAL SOURCES:

BOOKS

Bunzel, John H., editor, *Political Passages: Journeys of Change through Two Decades, 1968-1988,* Free Press, 1988.
Contemporary Issues Criticism, Volume 1, Gale, 1982.
Novak, Michael, *Confessions of a Catholic,* Harper, 1983.

PERIODICALS

America, March 14, 1964, November 6, 1965, May 3, 1969, September 12, 1970.
American Political Science Review, June, 1974.
American Scholar, winter, 1972-73.
Best Sellers, July 1, 1971.
Book Week, June 28, 1964.
Book World, May 31, 1970.
Chicago Tribune Book World, May 31, 1970.
Christian Century, January 12, 1966, March 12, 1969, July 30, 1969, April 11, 1973.
Christianity Today, July 10, 1987.
Chronicle Review, February 5, 1979.
Commentary, April, 1966, June, 1972, July, 1974, July, 1982.
Commonweal, March 20, 1964, August 21, 1964, September 6, 1968, June 13, 1969, February 18, 1972.
Critic, October, 1964.
Fortune, May 17, 1982.
Library Journal, June 1, 1964.
Los Angeles Times, October 1, 1982.
Los Angeles Times Book Review, December 30, 1984.
Modern Age, spring/summer, 1984.
Nation, November 9, 1970, April 24, 1982, May 18, 1985.
National Review, May 24, 1974, August 6, 1976, December 31, 1985.
New Leader, July 19, 1976.
New Republic, November 25, 1972, May 30, 1974, January 6, 1979, June 16, 1982, May 4, 1987.
Newsweek, April 24, 1972.
New York Review of Books, December 20, 1983.
New York Times, April 29, 1972, May 9, 1982, December 5, 1984.
New York Times Book Review, May 26, 1966, April 23, 1972, April 7, 1974, June 13, 1976, January 28, 1979, July 17, 1983, December 9, 1984.
Rocky Mountain News, June 24, 1984.
Saturday Review, January 6, 1968, March 23, 1974, June 26, 1976.
Time, May 8, 1972, June 28, 1976, May 10, 1982.
Times Literary Supplement, December 2, 1983.
U.S. News and World Report, November 26, 1984.
Village Voice, September 6, 1976.
Wall Street Journal, February 20, 1985.
Washington Post, May 11, 1983.
Washington Post Book World, June 6, 1976, May 9, 1982, February 24, 1985, April 5, 1987.

—*Sketch by Anne Janette Johnson*

O

O'CONNOR, Elizabeth (Anita) 1921-

PERSONAL: Born April 11, 1921, in Spring Lake, N.J.; daughter of William J. (a plumbing and heating contractor) and C. Marie O'Connor. *Education:* Attended Riverdale Country School for Girls. *Politics:* Independent. *Religion:* Protestant.

ADDRESSES: Office—Church of the Saviour, 2025 Massachusetts Ave. N.W., Washington, D.C. 20036.

CAREER: Worked in public relations prior to 1953; Church of the Saviour, Washington, D.C., writer and counsellor, 1953—. Consultant and workshop leader to the seven Church of the Saviour Faith Communities. Founder and president of Sarah's Circle, a housing program for the elderly.

WRITINGS:

Call to Commitment: The Story of the Church of the Saviour, Harper, 1963.
Journey Inward, Journey Outward, Harper, 1968.
Our Many Selves, Harper, 1971.
Eighth Day of Creation: Gift and Creativity, Word Publishing, 1971.
Search for Silence, Word Publishing, 1972, revised edition with foreword by N. Gordon Cosby, LuraMedia, 1986.
The New Community, Harper, 1976.
Letters to Scattered Pilgrims, Harper, 1979.
Cry Pain, Cry Hope: Thresholds to Purpose, Word Publishing, 1987.

SIDELIGHTS: In many of her writings, Elizabeth O'Connor draws from her experiences as a worker for Washington D.C.'s Church of the Saviour, an inner-city congregation focused on community needs. Among the projects conducted by Church of the Savior are Jubilee Housing (involved in slum renovation), School of Christian Living, World Peacemakers, For Love of Children (FLOC), The Potter's House (a coffee house), and The Servant Leadership School.

BIOGRAPHICAL/CRITICAL SOURCES:

PERIODICALS

America, February 19, 1977.
Christian Century, March 12, 1980.

O'DELL, Scott 1898-1989

PERSONAL: Born May 23, 1898, in Los Angeles, Calif.; died October 15, 1989, in Mount Kisco, N.Y., of prostate cancer; son of Bennett Mason and May Elizabeth (Gabriel) O'Dell; married first wife, Jane Rattenbury; married second wife, Elizabeth Hall; children: Susan Anderson, David Mason. *Education:* Attended Occidental College, 1919, University of Wisconsin, 1920, Stanford University, 1920-21, and University of Rome, 1925.

ADDRESSES: Agent—McIntosh & Otis, Inc., 310 Madison Ave., New York, N.Y. 10017.

CAREER: Former cameraman and technical director for Paramount Studios. Had once worked as a farmer. Full-time writer, 1934-89. *Military service:* U.S. Air Force and U.S. Army.

AWARDS, HONORS: Rupert Hughes Award, 1960, John Newbery Medal, 1961, Southern California Council on Literature for Children and Young People notable book award, 1961, Hans Christian Andersen award of merit, 1962, William Allen White Award, 1963, German Juvenile International Award, 1963, and Nene Award, 1964, all for *Island of the Blue Dolphins;* Newbery honor award, 1967, and German Juvenile International Award, 1968, both for *The King's Fifth;* Newbery honor awards, 1968, for *The Black Pearl,* and 1971, for *Sing Down the Moon;* Hans Christian Andersen Medal for lifetime achievement, 1972; University of Southern Mississippi medallion, 1976; Regina Medal, 1978; *Focal* Award, Los Angeles Public Library, 1981; Florida State Historical Association award, 1985, for *Alexandra;* Scott O'Dell Award for Historical Fiction, 1987, for *Streams to the River, River to the Sea: A Novel of Sacagawea;* School Library Media Specialist of Southeastern New York award for contribution to children's literature, 1989; Northern Westchester Center for the Arts award, 1989.

WRITINGS:

Representative Photoplays Analyzed: Modern Authorship, Palmer Institute of Authorship, 1924.
Woman of Spain: A Story of Old California (novel), Houghton, 1934.
Hill of the Hawk (novel), Bobbs-Merrill, 1947.
(With William Doyle) *Man Alone,* Bobbs-Merrill, 1953.
Country of the Sun: Southern California, an Informal History and Guide, Crowell, 1957.
The Sea is Red: A Novel, Holt, 1958.

(With Rhoda Kellogg) *The Psychology of Children's Art,* Communications Research Machines, 1967.

FOR CHILDREN

Island of the Blue Dolphins, Houghton, 1960, reprinted, Dell, 1987.
The King's Fifth, Houghton, 1966.
The Black Pearl, Houghton, 1967.
The Dark Canoe, Houghton, 1968.
Journey to Jericho, Houghton, 1969.
Sing Down the Moon, Houghton, 1970.
The Treasure of Topo-el-Bampo, Houghton, 1972.
The Cruise of the Arctic Star, Houghton, 1973.
Child of Fire, Houghton, 1974.
The Hawk That Dare Not Hunt by Day, Houghton, 1975.
Zia, Houghton, 1976.
The 290, Houghton, 1976.
Carlota, Houghton, 1977.
Kathleen, Please Come Home, Houghton, 1978.
The Captive, Houghton, 1979.
Sarah Bishop, Houghton, 1980.
The Feathered Serpent, Houghton, 1981.
The Spanish Smile, Houghton, 1982.
The Amethyst Ring, Houghton, 1983.
The Castle in the Sea, Houghton, 1983.
Alexandra, Houghton, 1984.
The Road to Damietta, Houghton, 1985.
Streams to the River, River to the Sea: A Novel of Sacagawea, Houghton, 1986.
The Serpent Never Sleeps: A Novel of Jamestown and Pocahontas, Houghton, 1987.
Black Star, Bright Dawn, Houghton, 1988.
My Name is Not Angelica, Houghton, 1989.

OTHER

Former book columnist for the *Los Angeles Times.* Former book editor for the *Los Angeles Daily News.*

WORK IN PROGRESS: Thunder Rolling in the Mountains.

SIDELIGHTS: An author of over two dozen children's books, which often deal with historical subjects from his native Southern California, Scott O'Dell was best known for his first juvenile novel, *Island of the Blue Dolphins.* Discussing the theme of this book, O'Dell told *CA* that it develops the idea of "Albert Schweitzer's reverence for all life. And the belief that we must learn to forgive our enemies, that the hopes of civilization itself, obscure as they are, cannot be realized without this act of identification. In my twenty-five other books for the young the same theme appears." These works deal with such themes as racial conflict, greed, and coming to terms with one's enemies, using a style that is characterized by simple, laconic sentences. The quality of O'Dell's work is substantiated by the numerous awards he earned, including the Newbery Medal, Hans Christian Anderson award of merit, and five other awards for *Island of the Blue Dolphins,* and a Newbery honor award and German Juvenile International Award for his second most acclaimed book, *The King's Fifth.*

Island of the Blue Dolphins is a fictionalized account of the true story of an Indian girl who was stranded on an island off the California coast in the mid-nineteenth century. O'Dell's reverence-for-life theme is illustrated by how the girl Karana manages to develop a friendship with Rontu, the leader of a pack of wild dogs who killed her younger brother, and with Tutok, a girl of the enemy Aleut tribe. Karana's ability to set aside her hatred and fear for the Aleuts, Rontu, and the other creatures of the is-

land allows her to survive the dangers and solitude of her secluded home. "It is Karana's loneliness and isolation," explains Malcolm Usrey in his *Dictionary of Literary Biography* entry about the author, "that give the book one of its most powerful and universal themes, that all people need to be with others, to love and be loved. As O'Dell himself said in his Newbery Award acceptance speech, 'The human heart, lonely and in need of love, is a vessel which needs replenishing.' " The universality of these themes lends *Island of the Blue Dolphins* "the timeless, enduring quality of a classic," remarks a *Chicago Tribune* reviewer. "Reading it should be a deeply moving experience for anyone over 10."

The 1976 sequel to *Island of the Blue Dolphins, Zia,* contrasts its predecessor by dealing with the theme of racial prejudice and its destructive capabilities. The story relates how Karana's niece, Zia Sandoval, and her brother Mando leave Santa Barbara Mission in search of their aunt. Their efforts are thwarted, however, when they are captured by whalers for whom they are forced to work. They eventually escape only to be captured and imprisoned by the Spanish for not helping to find other Indians, who have also left the mission. Karana is eventually found, but she, too, is mistreated by the Spanish. Running away and hiding in a cave, she later dies from an unexplained illness.

Although Ethel L. Heins feels that *Zia* is not as powerful a book as *Island of the Blue Dolphins,* she notes in *Horn Book* that it is not fair to compare the two, since they were not written for the same purpose. *Zia* "is told with simplicity and occasional flashes of humor and has its own individuality," Heins affirms. *New York Times Book Review* contributor Barbara Wersba similarly believes that " 'Zia' is a completely fresh creation, rich in character and action." "What draws one into this book, and probably accounts for the popularity of *Island of the Blue Dolphins,* as well," says Joyce Milton in a *Washington Post Book World* article, "is O'Dell's short, loaded sentences which force the reader to participate." Comparing the two novels, Milton holds that "the two books seem to prove that truth is not only stranger but, well, truer."

Another O'Dell novel about racial conflict, *Sing Down the Moon,* won the author a Newbery honor award in 1971. In these pages, O'Dell tells the tragic story of the Long Walk, the 10,000 mile trek which American soldiers forced the Navajos to march in 1864. "As in his other novels dealing with the relationship of Indians and Americans," explains Usrey, "O'Dell has created a powerful and moving story, made poignant by his restraint and simplicity, reflecting the stoic, proud, and quiet or passive strength of Bright Morning," the protagonist. In comparison to *Island of the Blue Dolphins,* however, author John Rowe Townsend notes in his book *A Sense of Story: Essays on Contemporary Writers for Children,* "a style which was admirably suited to the lonely setting of a Pacific Island is less appropiate for a story that is full of people and harsh, clashing action." Zena Sutherland expresses the opposite opinion about O'Dell's style in *Sing Down the Moon.* In the *Bulletin of the Center for Children's Books* she writes that the novelist's simple style makes the tragedy of the Navajo's plight all the more "vivid."

The kind of exploitation against American Indians shown in *Sing Down the Moon* arises again as a theme in O'Dell's trilogy about the Spanish conquistadors. The books, *The Captive, The Feathered Serpent,* and *The Amethyst Ring,* center around sixteen-year-old seminarian Julian Escobar, a fictional character in a tale filled with historically accurate facts about Spain's bloody victories over the Aztecs, Incas, and Mayas. Escobar is marooned in Mexico, where he finds the Mayan civilization in a state of decline. He assumes the role of the Mayan god Kukulcan and attempts to restore the civilization's former grandeur, while also dreaming of glory and wealth for himself. The conquistadors, however, defeat the Mayas, as well as the Incas and Aztecs, and Escobar returns to Spain to join the religious order of the Brothers of the Poor.

The spiritual evolution that Escobar undergoes as a result of his experience is a central theme of the trilogy. After his ideals about the use of power and his visions of glory are lost with the fall of the City of the Seven Serpents to Cortes, his growing sympathy for the Indians becomes complete. He even falls in love with an Incan princess. By the end of *The Amethyst Ring* Escobar has given up his desire to be a priest, as well as his dreams of wealth. It is this development in Escobar's character, according to a *Kirkus Reviews* article, which is "the compelling focus of a trilogy crackling with intrigue, historical spectacle, and the conflict of cultures that confounds [Escobar's] loyalties."

The thoroughly-researched historical background of O'Dell's trilogy is what impresses some critics more than Escobar's character. *Washington Post Book World* reviewer Leon Garfield, for instance, feels that *The Captive* is "well constructed, well researched, contains many interesting items of unfamiliar knowledge, and displays unimpeachable moral worth," but he adds that "it is not very readable." Usrey similarly comments that the trilogy is not successful because "O'Dell fails to make his historical epic real and alive for readers." Jack Forman's *New York Times Book Review* article also points out some problems with plot devices, such as how Escobar learns to communicate with the Mayas so quickly. But overall he asserts that "there's no better introduction to the rich and remote Mayan culture than through such a well-told tale" as this.

O'Dell's *The Black Pearl*, which won him another Newbery honor award in 1968, deals again with the subjects of greed and religion. The author weaves a tale of superstition versus reality in "one of the most exciting and suspenseful of all O'Dell's novels," as Usrey assesses it. Although not as "moving" as *Island of the Blue Dolphins*, *Washington Post Book World* contributor Polly Goodwin considers *The Black Pearl* to be a "curiously compelling story." The novel is set in the seaside town of La Paz in Baja California, where a boy named Ramon Salazar finds a precious black pearl in a lagoon that is the home of the legendary sea creature, Manta Diablo. Ramon's father mistakenly believes that he can buy God's protection for his fleet of ships by giving the pearl to the town priest. When the ships and his father are lost in a storm anyway, Ramon decides to throw it back into the lagoon. Gaspar Ruiz, the last survivor of the lost fleet, convinces Ramon to try and sell the pearl, only to be killed for his efforts by Manta Diablo. In the end, Ramon gives the pearl to the Madonna as an offering of his love. "The most important theme of [*The Black Pearl*]," Usrey says, "is that a gift of great price must be made out of love, not out of selfishness."

Selfishness in the form of avarice reappears as a theme in *The King's Fifth*, which tells how a young mapmaker named Esteban de Sandoval is convinced by the greedy Captain Mendoza to help him find Indian gold. Interested at first only in his career as a mapmaker, Esteban eventually becomes so corrupted that he helps Mendoza flood an entire Indian city in order to get the promised treasure. They obtain a fortune in the process, but their efforts come to nothing in the end. Mendoza is killed by his own dog, the expedition's soldiers die or abandon them, and their Indian guide and interpreter deserts them as well. When Esteban's last companion, Father Francisco, dies in the desert, he is finally convinced of the gold's evil and abandons it. As a result, however, he is imprisoned for not giving the King his legal share of the money.

Winner of O'Dell's first Newbery honor award and the German Juvenile International Award, *The King's Fifth* is a "colorful and dramatic tale of the Conquistadors," according to Walter Havighurst's review in *World Journal Tribune Book Week*. "Though they go in the name of Christianity and to convert the Indians, [the Spaniards'] motives are made clear," says Usrey. He continues, "O'Dell reflects a fairly recent trend in fiction for children; that is not to slight or bend the truth in favor of the European conquerors." But even though the author emphasizes the cruel treatment of the Indians by their conquerors in this book, the story "is not simplified into a contest of the good against the bad," maintains Havighurst. Even the novel's worst characters have some good qualities, while the good characters suffer from certain limitations. Overall, Viguers echoes the view of other critics when she writes that "the writing [in *The King's Fifth*] is subtly beautiful, often moving, and says more than may be caught in one reading." Among the books that O'Dell had written by the early 1970s, Townsend avers that "*The King's Fifth*—a sombre, almost stately novel—is best of all."

Despite the many books set in historical southwestern America that O'Dell wrote, to say that his works are limited to this area would be misleading. In addition to his books for adults, the author penned several children's novels set in modern times, such as *Child of Fire* and *Kathleen, Please Come Home*. The former deals in large part with the conflict between two gang members in Del Mar, California, and the latter is concerned with a young girl's drug addiction. O'Dell also wrote historical novels about, among other things, St. Francis of Assisi (*The Road to Damietta*), a real-life character living during the American Revolution (*Sarah Bishop*), and the smuggling of William Tyndale's translation of the New Testament into England (*The Hawk That Dare Not Hunt by Day*).

In 1985, O'Dell won the Florida State Historical Association award for *Alexandra*, another novel set in modern times, but in this case the action occurs in a Greek community in the Florida Keys. The book deals with contemporary issues such as feminism and the smuggling of cocaine into the United States. *Washington Post Book World* critic Deborah Churchman calls *Alexandra* "a tightly written book on deep subjects from an author who's demonstrated in most of his 18 other novels . . . that he knows how to handle the depths." Some of the author's novels, too, are not concerned so much with expressing a theme or studying an issue as they are with relating a tale of pure adventure. In 1988, for example, O'Dell published *Black Star, Bright Dawn*, a story about the Iditarod dogsled race between Anchorage and Nome, Alaska. A *Publishers Weekly* reviewer claims that this book is "exciting to read and infused with dignity." Another novel of adventure by the author, *Streams to the River, River to the Sea: A Novel of Sacagawea*, concerns the famous Lewis and Clark expedition through the Louisiana Territory. For this book O'Dell won the Scott O'Dell Award for Historical Fiction in 1987. This award, the author told *CA*, was established by himself in 1981 to be given to books which "acquaint young readers with their past and then persuades them that history, especially their own, has relevance to the lives they will lead and the choices they will be forced to make."

In addition to making children aware of their past, the author wrote "to make them aware of man's inhumanity but also of the possibilities for endurance, resourcefulness, and moral courage," says Usrey. *Island of the Blue Dolphins* and *The King's Fifth* are examples of this goal O'Dell had for his books. Since their publication critics have often weighed his later books against these first two. Townsend considers these early books to be the author's best, saying in 1971 that "subsequent O'Dell books . . . have been slighter." Since that time, however, the author's continual accumulation of awards until his death in 1989 attests to his unwaning skills as a writer of children's books. But even if this were not the case, affirms Usrey, O'Dell's "contributions to literature for children would be significant if he had written no other books besides *Island of the Blue Dolphins . . .* and *The King's Fifth.*"

MEDIA ADAPTATIONS: Island of the Blue Dolphins was filmed by Universal in 1964; *The Black Pearl* was filmed in 1976; *The King's Fifth* was animated for television in 1982 under the title "Mysterious Cities of Gold."

BIOGRAPHICAL/CRITICAL SOURCES:

BOOKS

Children's Literature Review, Gale, Volume 1, 1976, Volume 16, 1989.
Contemporary Literary Criticism, Volume 30, Gale, 1984.
Dictionary of Literary Biography, Volume 52: *American Writers for Children since 1960: Fiction,* Gale, 1986.
Georgiou, Constantine, *Children and Their Literature,* Prentice-Hall, 1969.
Kingston, Carolyn T., *The Tragic Mode in Children's Literature,* Columbia University Teachers College Press, 1974.
Meigs, Cornelia, editor, *A Critical History of Children's Literature,* Macmillan, 1969.
Townsend, John Rowe, *Written for Children: An Outline of English Language Children's Literature,* Lippincott, 1965.
Townsend, John Rowe, *A Sense of Story: Essays on Contemporary Writing for Children,* Lippincott, 1971.

PERIODICALS

Bulletin for the Center for Children's Books, January, 1971.
Chicago Tribune, May 8, 1960.
Elementary English, April, 1975.
Horn Book, April, 1960, December, 1966, October, 1967, December, 1968, June, 1976, December, 1977, April, 1982.
Kirkus Reviews, March 15, 1978, January 15, 1980, April 15, 1983.
Los Angeles Times Book Review, July 20, 1986.
New York Herald Tribune Book Review, May 8, 1960.
New York Times Book Review, March 27, 1960, November 5, 1967, October 18, 1970, November 3, 1974, February 22, 1976, May 2, 1976, April 30, 1978, February 24, 1980, May 4, 1980, January 10, 1982.
Publishers Weekly, March 11, 1988.
San Francisco Chronicle, May 8, 1960.
Times Literary Supplement, July 15, 1977.
Washington Post Book World, November 5, 1967, May 2, 1976, March 9, 1980, January 9, 1983, January 13, 1985.
World Journal Tribune Book Week, December 18, 1966.

OBITUARIES:

PERIODICALS

New York Times, October 17, 1989.
Washington Post, October 18, 1989.

—*Sketch by Kevin S. Hile*

OLEYAR, Rita Balkey
    See BALKEY, Rita

*   *   *

ORBIS, Victor
    See POWELL-SMITH, Vincent (Walter Francis)

*   *   *

ORENSTEIN, Frank (Everett)   1919-

PERSONAL: Born June 22, 1919, in New York, N.Y.; son of Charles and Cecile (Kobliner) Orenstein. *Education:* Dartmouth College, B.A., 1940; University of Chicago, M.A., 1942.

ADDRESSES: Home—P.O. Box 244, Gardiner, N.Y. 12525.

CAREER: U.S. Department of State, Washington, D.C., senior project director for Voice of America evaluation staff, 1950-52, chief of evaluation staff for International Educational Exchange program, 1952-56; McCann Erickson, New York City, manager of television and print research and project director of market and motivation research, 1956-60; Newspaper Advertising Bureau, New York City, vice president and director of research, 1960-77; writer, 1977—. *Military service:* U.S. Army, 1942-46.

MEMBER: Mystery Writers of America, American Association for Public Opinion Research, American Sociological Association, Market Research Council, Newspaper Research Council.

AWARDS, HONORS: Sidney Goldish Award, International Newspaper Promotion Association, 1975, for "a significant, continuing contribution to newspaper research."

WRITINGS:

Murder on Madison Avenue, St. Martin's, 1983.
One Man in the Gray Flannel Shroud, St. Martin's, 1984.
A Candidate for Murder, St. Martin's, 1987.
Paradise of Death, St. Martin's, 1988.
A Killing in Real Estate, St. Martin's, 1989.

WORK IN PROGRESS: Off with the Old.

*   *   *

ORESICK, Peter (Michael)   1955-

PERSONAL: Surname is pronounced O-*res*-sick; born September 8, 1955, in Ford City, Pa.; son of Peter (a glassworker) and Mary (a glassworker; maiden name, Gernat) Oresick; married Stephanie Lane Flom (a park naturalist), November 26, 1977; children: William, Jacob. *Education:* University of Pittsburgh, B.A., 1977, M.F.A., 1981. *Religion:* Catholic.

ADDRESSES: Home—6342 Jackson St., Pittsburgh, Pa. 15206.

CAREER: Poet. Keystone Oaks School District, Pittsburgh, Pa., teacher of English, 1977-78; Pennsylvania Council on the Arts, Artists in Schools and Communities Program, Harrisburg, Pa., poet, 1977-84; Pittsburgh Public Schools, Pittsburgh, teacher of English, 1978-81; University of Pittsburgh Press, Pittsburgh, promotion and marketing manager, 1985—. Part-time instructor in writing, University of Pittsburgh, 1982-83.

AWARDS, HONORS: Academy of American Poets Prize, University of Pittsburgh, 1980; fellowship in writing, Pennsylvania Council on the Arts, 1984.

WRITINGS:

The Story of Glass (poetry), West End Press, 1977.

(Contributor) Roger Gaess, editor, *Leaving the Bough: 50 American Poets of the 80s,* International Publishers, 1982.
Other Lives (poetry), Adastra Press, 1985.
An American Peace (poetry), Shadow Press U.S.A., 1985.

Contributor to magazines, including *Poetry East, Michigan Quarterly Review, Minnesota Review,* and *Poetry Northwest.*

WORK IN PROGRESS: Two books, *Working Classics: Poems on Industrial Life* and *American Poetry Now: A Field Guide.*

SIDELIGHTS: Peter Oresick grew up in Ford City, Pennsylvania, a mill town that borders on the Allegheny River north of Pittsburgh. His grandparents were Ukrainian-Ruthenian immigrants who had settled there as glassworkers around the turn of the century. Oresick's first work, *The Story of Glass,* is described by *Pitt News* reviewer Martha H. Garvey as "often a verbal photo album" of members of his family, the plant they worked in for three generations (Pittsburgh Plate Glass), and Ford City, a town that, according to Garvey, "sleeps, eats, and breathes glass." Oresick once told *CA* that "after the publication of *The Story of Glass,* I felt my writing was locked in the treadmill of my personal history. I began doing translations as a way out, and I wrote poems about characters who interested me. The result is *Other Lives.* This obsession with character led me to an interest in plot, and now narrative poetry."

BIOGRAPHICAL/CRITICAL SOURCES:

PERIODICALS

Daily World, May 13, 1977.
Pitt News, March 18, 1977.

*   *   *

ORIANS, Gordon H(owell) 1932-

PERSONAL: Born July 10, 1932, in Eau Claire, Wis.; son of Howard Lester (a clergyman) and Marion (Senty) Orians; married Elizabeth Newton, June 25, 1955; children: Carlyn Elizabeth, Kristin Jean, Colin Mark. *Education:* University of Wisconsin, B.S., 1954; graduate study at Oxford University, 1954-55; University of California, Berkeley, Ph.D., 1960.

ADDRESSES: Office—Department of Zoology and Institute for Environmental Studies, University of Washington, Seattle, Wash. 98195.

CAREER: University of Washington, Seattle, assistant professor, 1960-64, associate professor, 1964-68, professor of zoology, 1968—, director of Institute of Environmental Studies, 1976-86. *Military service:* U.S. Army, 1967; became second lieutenant.

MEMBER: American Association for the Advancement of Science, Organization for Tropical Studies (president, 1988—), National Academy of Sciences (elected, 1989), American Ornithologists Union (fellow), American Society of Naturalists (vice-president, 1987-88), Ecological Society of America, Society for the Study of Evolution, Animal Behavior Society, Association for Tropical Biology, Cooper Ornithological Society, Royal Dutch Academy of Sciences (fellow).

AWARDS, HONORS: Fulbright fellowship, 1954-55; Guggenheim fellowship, 1973-74; Brewster Medal, American Ornithologists Union.

WRITINGS:

The Study of Life (textbook), Allyn & Bacon, 1969, 2nd edition, 1973.
(Contributor) D. S. Farner and J. R. King, editors, *Avian Biology,* Volume 1, Academic Press, 1971.

(With E. W. Pfeiffer, J. B. Neilands, Alje Vennema, and A. H. Westing) *Harvest of Death: Chemical Warfare in Vietnam and Cambodia,* Free Press, 1972.
(Editor with Otto T. Solbrig) *Convergent Evolution in Warm Deserts: An Examination of Strategies and Patterns in Deserts of Argentina and the United States,* Academic Press, 1977.
Some Adaptations of Marsh-Nesting Blackbirds, Princeton University Press, 1980.
(With William K. Purves) *Life: The Science of Biology,* Sinauer, 1983, 2nd edition, 1987.
Blackbirds of the Americas, University of Washington Press, 1985.

Also author, with Eric L. Charnov, of *Optimal Foraging: Some Theoretical Explanations,* 1973. Contributor to proceedings and to professional journals, including *Science, Ecology, American Naturalist, Auk, Condor, Evolution, Systematic Zoology,* and *Journal of Animal Ecology.*

*   *   *

OSTRIKER, Alicia (Suskin) 1937-

PERSONAL: Born November 11, 1937, in New York, N.Y.; daughter of David (a civil service employee) and Beatrice (Linnick) Suskin; married Jeremiah P. Ostriker (a professor of astrophysics), December, 1958; children: Rebecca, Eve, Gabriel. *Education:* Brandeis University, B.A., 1959; University of Wisconsin, M.A., 1961, Ph.D., 1964. *Religion:* Jewish.

ADDRESSES: Home—33 Philip Dr., Princeton, N.J. 08540. *Office*—Department of English, Rutgers University, New Brunswick, N.J. 08903.

CAREER: Rutgers University, New Brunswick, N.J., assistant professor, 1965-68, associate professor, 1968-72, professor of English, 1972—.

AWARDS, HONORS: National Council on the Humanities summer grant, 1968; National Endowment for the Arts fellowship, 1976-77; New Jersey Arts Council fellowship, 1980-81; Rockefeller Foundation fellowship, 1982; Guggenheim Foundation fellowship, 1984-85; William Carlos Williams prize, Poetry Society of America, 1986, for *The Imaginary Lover;* Strousse Poetry prize, *Prairie Schooner,* 1986.

WRITINGS:

Vision and Verse in William Blake, University of Wisconsin Press, 1965.
Songs (poetry), Holt, 1969.
Once More Out of Darkness, and Other Poems (chapbook), Berkeley Poets Workshop and Press, 1974.
(Editor) *William Blake: Complete Poems,* Penguin, 1977.
A Dream of Springtime (poems), Smith/Horizon Press, 1979.
(Contributor) *Shakespeare's Sisters,* Indiana University Press, 1979.
The Mother/Child Papers (poems), Momentum, 1980, reprinted, Beacon Press, 1986.
(Contributor) *The State of the Language,* University of California Press, 1980.
A Woman under the Surface: Poems and Prose Poems, Princeton University Press, 1982.
Writing Like a Woman (essays), University of Michigan Press, 1983.
(Contributor) *Claims for Poetry,* University of Michigan Press, 1983.
The Imaginary Lover (poems), Pittsburgh University Press, 1986.

Stealing the Language: The Emergence of Women's Poetry in America, Beacon Press, 1986.

Contributor of poems and essays to literary reviews and magazines, including *New Yorker.*

SIDELIGHTS: Feminist critic Alicia Ostriker has published six books of poetry and several books on the relationship between gender and literature. In 1986, the Poetry Society of America gave this recipient of numerous fellowships and grants the Williams Carlos Williams prize for *The Imaginary Lover.* Ostriker "is at her best when most urbane and ironic" in these poems that look back at marriage from the perspective of mid-life, says *Times Literary Supplement* contributor Clair Wills. "The actions are melodramatic, but the recording consciousness is steady," Patricia Hampl relates in the *New York Times Book Review.* Since the poems often reflect on disappointment or loss, they have an elegiac tone. More noticeable, however, "is Mrs. Ostriker's tendency to locate a sustaining force for the rest of life—a force that is both passionate and honorable," Hampl observes. This is evident in lines from "Everywoman Her Own Theology," in which Ostriker declares: "Ethically, I am looking for / An absolute endorsement of loving-kindness." At times, says Hampl, the poems lack music, but charm the reader with their "candor and thoughtfulness."

In *Stealing the Language: The Emergence of Women's Poetry in America,* Ostriker asserts that women writers have produced poetry that is "explicitly female in the sense that the writers have chosen to explore experiences central to their sex." Furthermore, in their search to find an aesthetic that accommodates this expression, Ostriker claims that women poets are "challenging and transforming the history of poetry. They constitute a literary movement comparable to romanticism or modernism in our literary past."

These claims have evoked a wide range of response from reviewers. Frieda Gardner, writing in the *Women's Review of Books,* agrees that women have brought new subject matter to American poetry; the "thematic landscape" of literature now includes poems on "women's quests for self-definition, on the uses and treachery of anger, . . . female eroticism and, most impressively, on women poets' sweeping revision of Western mythology," Gardner relates. However, "lots of male poets grew fat on the 'butter and sugar' Ostriker calls peculiarly feminine," Mary Karr points out in a *Poetry* review. Daisy Aldan, writing in *World Literature Today,* concurs, taking exception to Ostriker's assumptions that women's poetry is naturally more visceral and necessarily less sophisticated in form and thought than that of men. Reviewers also question if poetry by women is unified by the concentrated "drive for power" that Ostriker sees in it. Nonetheless, states Karr, "those predisposed to feminist criticism will eagerly take up these pages. At the other extreme, certain critics and philosophers will shudder at the very thought of women generating language, a practice they interpret as exclusively masculine."

BIOGRAPHICAL/CRITICAL SOURCES:

BOOKS

Ostriker, Alicia, *The Imaginary Lover,* University of Pittsburgh Press, 1986.
Ostriker, Alicia, *Stealing the Language: The Emergence of Women's Poetry in America,* Beacon Press, 1986.

PERIODICALS

Georgia Review, fall, 1987.
National Forum, summer, 1987.

New York Times Book Review, July 20, 1986, June 7, 1987.
Poetry, February, 1987.
Times Literary Supplement, July 10, 1987.
Women's Review of Books, April, 1987.
World Literature Today, spring, 1987.

* * *

OZER, Mark N(orman) 1932-

PERSONAL: Born January 17, 1932, in Cambridge, Mass.; son of Samuel Louis and Naomi (Smith) Ozer; married Ann E. Teitler, September 29, 1957 (divorced, 1978); married Martha Louise Ross (a project director), August 12, 1979; children: Katherine A., Elizabeth M., Mark P., Emily J., Nicole A. *Education:* Harvard University, B.A., 1953; Boston University, M.D., 1957.

ADDRESSES: Home—1919 Stuart Ave., Richmond, Va. 23220. *Office*—McGuire Veterans Administration Medical Center, Richmond, Va. 23249.

CAREER: Stanford University Hospital, San Francisco, Calif., medical intern, 1957-58; Stanford University Hospital and San Francisco General Hospital, San Francisco, medical resident, 1958-59; Mt. Sinai Hospital, New York, N.Y., neurology resident, 1959-60 and 1962-64; fellow at Washington School of Psychiatry, 1964-65; Children's Hospital of the National Medical Center, Washington, D.C., associate neurologist and director of learning studies program, 1965-74; clinical practice of neurology, 1975-83; McGuire Veterans Administration Medical Center, Richmond, Va., assistant chief, SCI Service, 1983—. Howard University, Washington, D.C., instructor in neurology, 1964-65; George Washington School of Medicine, Washington, D.C., instructor, 1965-68, assistant professor of neurology, 1968-72, associate professor of child health and development, 1972-83. Assistant clinical professor of psychiatry and pediatrics at University of Maryland School of Medicine, 1967-74; lecturer in maternal and child health at University of Michigan School of Public Health, 1968-70. Consulting neurologist at numerous institutions, including National Children's Center, Washington, D.C., 1965-72; conducts workshops. *Military service:* U.S. Air Force, 1960-62; neurologist at U.S.A.F. Hospital, London, England.

MEMBER: International Medical Society, International Neuropsychological Society, Congress of Rehabilitation Medicine, American Academy of Neurology, American Society of Cybernetics (president, 1976-77), American Academy of Aphasia, Society of Neuroscience, American Association of the History of Medicine, Gerontological Society of America, Society for Health and Human Values, Society for Behavioral Medicine.

AWARDS, HONORS: Fellowship from National Institute of Mental Health, 1964-65.

WRITINGS:

(Editor and contributor) *A Cybernetic Approach to the Assessment of Children,* Westview, 1979.
Solving Learning and Behavior Problems of Children, Jossey-Bass, 1980.
The Ozer Method: A Breakthrough Problem-Solving Technique for Parents and Children, Morrow, 1982.
The Dialogue of Education: Problem Solving in Today's Schools, Special Child Publications, 1984.
Spinal Cord Injury: A Guide for Patient and Family, Raven Press, 1987.
The Management of Persons with Spinal Cord Injury, Demos Publications, 1988.

Patient Participation in Program Planning, F. A. Davis, 1989.

CONTRIBUTOR

M. B. Bender, editor, *The Approach to Diagnosis in Modern Neurology,* Grune, 1967.

Jerome Hellmuth, editor, *Disadvantaged Child,* Volume 2: *Head Start and Early Intervention,* Special Child Publication, 1968.

(With E. A. Weinstein and others) M. T. Sarno, editor, *Aphasia: Selected Readings,* Appleton-Century-Crofts, 1972.

Cybernetic Technique in Brain Research and the Educational Process, American Society for Cybernetics, 1973.

S. A. Kirk and J. M. McCarthy, editors, *Learning Disabilities,* Houghton, 1975.

Ronald W. Mandersheid and Frances E. Mandersheid, editors, *Systems Science and the Future of Health,* Groome Center (Washington, D.C.), 1976.

Charles Peters and Nathaniel Peters, editors, *Reading Problems in Perspective,* Addison-Wesley, 1977.

Peter Mittler, editor, *Research to Practice in Mental Retardation,* Volume 2: *Education and Training,* University Park Press, 1977.

C. Dechert, editor, *Sistema paradigmi societa* (title means "The Systems Paradigm"), Franco Angeli Editore, 1978.

R. Piazza and I. Newman, editors, *Readings in Individualized Educational Programs,* Special Learning Corp. (Guilford, Conn.), 1979.

R. Ochroch, editor, *The Diagnosis and Treatment of Minimal Brain Dysfunction in Children: A Clinical Approach,* Human Sciences, 1981.

Manual for Allied Health Professionals for Work with Handicapped Children, American Society of Allied Health Professionals (Washington, D.C.), 1981.

G. E. Lasker, editor, *Applied Systems and Cybernetics,* Volume 4: *Systems Research in Health Care,* Pergamon, 1981.

OTHER

Contributor of more that sixty articles to psychology and medical journals, including *Cortex, Psychological Bulletin, Journal of Learning Disabilities,* and *Journal of Childhood Education International.* Member of board of editors for *Journal of Learning Disabilities* and *Behavioral and Brain Sciences.*

WORK IN PROGRESS: Management of Persons with Chronic Neurological Disabilities; Managing Your Own Health.

SIDELIGHTS: Mark N. Ozer told *CA:* "I have been interested throughout my career in the interaction of brain and behavior and the means by which physicians can help patients to learn about themselves—their own ways of thinking (as in education) and the ways by which their own bodies function (as in health). I have had a commitment to doing this in the aggregate, as well as for individual patients. That is the reason for my books and other writing for professionals and the public at large."

P

PADGETT, Ron 1942-
(Harlan Dangerfield)

PERSONAL: Born June 17, 1942, in Tulsa, Okla.; married; children: one son. *Education:* Columbia University, A.B., 1964.

ADDRESSES: Home—342 East 13th St., New York, N.Y. 10003.

CAREER: Worked as an auto mechanic and drove transcontinental cargo transport before 1962; St. Mark's-in-the-Bowery, New York City, poetry workshop instructor, 1968-69; poet in various New York City Poets in the Schools programs, 1969-76; writer in the community, South Carolina Arts Commission, 1976-78; St. Mark's Poetry Project, New York City, director, 1978-81; Teachers and Writers Collaborative, New York City, director of publications, 1982—. Co-founder, Full Court Press (publishers), New York City, 1973.

AWARDS, HONORS: Boar's Head Poetry Prize and George E. Woodberry Award, Columbia University, both 1964; Gotham Book Mart Avant-Garde Poetry Prize, 1964; recipient of numerous fellowships and grants, including Fulbright fellowship, 1965-66, and Guggenheim fellowship, 1986.

WRITINGS:

POETRY COLLECTIONS

In Advance of the Broken Arm, "C" Press, 1964.
(With Ted Berrigan and Joe Brainard) *Some Things,* "C" Press, 1964.
2/2 Stories for Andy Warhol, "C" Press, 1965.
Sky, Goliard Press, 1966.
(With Berrigan) *Bean Spasms,* Kulcher Press, 1967.
Tone Arm, Once Press, 1967.
(With Brainard) *100,000 Fleeing Hilda,* Boke, 1967.
(With Tom Clark) *Bun,* Angel Hair Books, 1968.
Great Balls of Fire, Holt, 1969.
(With Jim Dine) *The Adventures of Mr. and Mrs. Jim and Ron,* Cape Gouliard Press, 1970.
Sweet Pea, Aloes, 1971.
Poetry Collection, Strange Faeces Press, 1971.
(With Brainard) *Sufferin' Succotash* [bound with *Kiss My Ass* by Michael Brownstein], Adventures in Poetry, 1971.
(With Berrigan and Clark) *Back in Boston Again,* Telegraph, 1972.

(With Dine) *Oo La La,* Petersburg Press, 1973.
Crazy Compositions, Big Sky, 1974.
(With others) *The World of Leon,* Big Sky, 1974.
Toujours l'amour, SUN, 1976.
Arrive by Pullman, Generations (Paris), 1978.
Tulsa Kid, Z Press, 1979.
Triangles in the Afternoon, SUN, 1980.
How to Be a Woodpecker, Toothpaste Press, 1983.

EDITOR

(With Berrigan) Tom Veitch, *Literary Days,* "C" Press, 1964.
(With David Shapiro) *An Anthology of New York Poets,* Random House, 1970.
(With Bill Zavatsky) *The Whole Word Catalogue 2,* Teachers and Writers Collaborative/McGraw, 1976.
(With Nancy Larson Shapiro) *The Point: Where Teaching and Writing Intersect,* Teachers and Writers Collaborative, 1983.
The Complete Poems of Edwin Denby, Random House, 1986.
The Teachers and Writers Handbook of Poetic Forms, Teachers and Writers Collaborative, 1987.

OTHER

(With Berrigan) *Seventeen: Collected Plays,* "C" Press, 1965.
(Translator) Guillaume Apollinaire, *The Poet Assassinated,* Holt, 1968.
(Translator) Pierre Cabanne, *Dialogues with Marcel Duchamp,* Viking, 1970.
(Adaptor with Johnny Stanton) Henry Caray, *Chrononhotonothologos,* Boke, 1971.
Antlers in the Treetops (novel), Coach House Press, 1973.
(Translator with Zavatsky) Valery Larbaud, *The Poems of A. O. Barnabooth,* Mushinsha (Tokyo), 1974.
(Translator) Blaise Cendrars, *Kodak,* Adventures in Poetry, 1976.
(Translator) Appollinaire, *The Poet Assassinated and Other Stories,* North Point Press, 1984.
(With Raymond Roussel) *Among the Blacks* (memoir), Avenue B, 1988.

Contributor, sometimes under pseudonym Harlan Dangerfield, to magazines and journals.

SIDELIGHTS: "Ron Padgett is the grand old *young* man of the New York School of poets," asserts *Village Voice* contributor

Aram Saroyan, a school which, as Gilbert Sorrentino describes it in the *New York Times Book Review,* "relies on highly sophisticated, urban statement, seemingly artless when it is most artificial, and ingenuous when it is most shrewd." The critic explains: "The poems defy criticism by proffering the reader a brilliantly polished but false naivete. This is consciously done." Padgett's poems in particular "defy explanation and specification, appearing incoherent on the surface," Caroline G. Bokinsky notes in a *Dictionary of Literary Biography* essay, "but once the surface is penetrated, the private world of the poet emerges. Ron Padgett brilliantly transforms mundane experience into the subject of the poetry," Bokinsky continues, "through subtle humor, wordplay, and a childlike fascination with the world."

In *Triangles in the Afternoon* and *Tulsa Kid,* for example, Padgett's poems deal with such commonplace things as Cheez-Its, chocolate milk, and kitchen matches, as *New York Times Book Review* contributor Donna Brook observes. The critic believes that "for both what he discusses and how he goes about discussing it . . ., Ron Padgett can be called a champion of American language and experience." "Padgett has an ability to play games with his free-flowing imagination," claims Bokinsky, "allowing him to grab an image and take off with it. . . . Padgett seeks in the mundane something that will excite the imagination: banal, trite, everyday words and phrases of language can be exciting," the critic adds. "I feel good about Padgett's work," Brook states, "the way it wakes, shakes, and charms, and I carry it around even when I don't coherently defend it to myself." As Bokinsky summarizes, the poet "never ceases from exploring the mystery of the commonplace while giving pleasure as he illuminates the trivial."

BIOGRAPHICAL/CRITICAL SOURCES:

BOOKS

Dictionary of Literary Biography, Volume 5: *American Poets since World War II,* Gale, 1980.
Kostelanetz, Richard, editor, *The New American Arts,* Horizon, 1966.

PERIODICALS

American Book Review, March/April, 1981.
New York Times Book Review, March 31, 1968, September 19, 1976.
Village Voice, December 7, 1967, January 24, 1977.

*   *   *

PALEY, Vivian Gussin 1929-

PERSONAL: Born January 25, 1929, in Chicago, Ill.; daughter of Harry A. (a physician) and Yetta (Meisel) Gussin; married Irving Paley (in public relations), June 20, 1947; children: David Robert. *Education:* University of Chicago, B.A., 1947; Tulane University, B.A., 1950; Hofstra University, M.A., 1962. *Religion:* Jewish.

ADDRESSES: Home—5422 South Blackstone, Chicago, Ill. 60615. *Office*—Laboratory School, University of Chicago, 1362 East 59th St., Chicago, Ill. 60637.

CAREER: Teacher in New Orleans, La., 1952-56, and Great Neck, N.Y., 1963-70; University of Chicago, Chicago, Ill., teacher at Laboratory School, 1971—.

AWARDS, HONORS: Erikson Institute Award for service to children, 1987; MacArthur Foundation fellowship, 1989.

WRITINGS:

White Teacher, Harvard University Press, 1979.
Wally's Stories: Conversations in the Kindergarten, Harvard University Press, 1981.
Boys and Girls: Superheroes in the Doll Corner, University of Chicago Press, 1984.
Mollie Is Three: Growing Up in School, University of Chicago Press, 1986.
Bad Guys Don't Have Birthdays: Fantasy Play at Four, University of Chicago Press, 1988.
Teaching Young Children, Harvard University Press, 1990.

SIDELIGHTS: In her books about the behavior and thought of preschoolers, "which should be required reading wherever children are growing," Vivian Gussin Paley "does not presume to *understand* pre-school children, or to theorize," observes Penelope Leach in the *New York Times Book Review.* "Her strength lies equally in knowing that she does not know and in trying to learn," explains the critic, adding that in *Mollie Is Three: Growing Up in School,* Paley "avoids the arrogance of adult to small child; of teacher to student; of writer to reader." By relating anecdotes from her kindergarten classroom at the University of Chicago's Laboratory School, Paley's "revealing, often humorous" works say "less about teaching than . . . about the emergence of creativity, sex roles and self-confidence," comments *Los Angeles Times Book Review* writer Alex Raksin. *Wally's Stories: Conversations in the Kindergarten,* for example, is "a book exceptionally modest in manner and unusually substantial in matter," states D. J. Enright in the *Times Literary Supplement;* in her detailing of the stories children invent, "Paley has given a vivid and credible picture of how five-year-olds think. An entertaining picture, too," Enright concludes, "and a strangely inspiriting one."

Paley told *CA:* "My point of view is that of the classroom teacher, not often heard because few classroom teachers write books or articles. It is subjective and personal. The teacher observes the child in ways that are quite different from the psychologist and academic researcher, who watch and measure human behavior in the classroom. The teacher watches, becomes involved in, and practices human behavior in the classroom.

"As a writer I am primarily interested in the attitudes and beliefs of teacher and child. This hidden current influences and often supersedes the formal curriculum but is seldom examined or discussed openly.

"When I began writing *White Teacher,* I thought I knew certain children best because our backgrounds were similar. I have since discovered that all the children have more in common with one another than any one of them has with me. The major source of incongruity is between their thinking and mine."

BIOGRAPHICAL/CRITICAL SOURCES:

PERIODICALS

Los Angeles Times Book Review, August 17, 1986, May 1, 1988.
New Republic, May 26, 1979.
New York Times Book Review, July 6, 1986, April 3, 1988.
Times Literary Supplement, July 10, 1981.

*   *   *

PARKER, Hershel 1935-
(Samuel Willis)

PERSONAL: Born November 26, 1935, in Comanche, Okla.; son of Lloyd (a botanist) and Martha (Costner) Parker; married

Joanne Johnson (an English professor), June 29, 1963 (divorced, 1979); married Heddy Richter (a librarian), 1981; children: (first marriage) Alison, Sabrina. *Education:* Lamar State College (now Lamar University), B.A., 1959; Northwestern University, M.A., 1960, Ph.D., 1963.

ADDRESSES: Office—Department of English, University of Delaware, Newark, Del. 19716.

CAREER: Telegraph operator for Kansas City Southern Railway, 1952-59; University of Illinois at Urbana-Champaign, assistant professor, 1963-65; Northwestern University, Evanston, Ill., assistant professor, 1965-68; University of Southern California, Los Angeles, associate professor, 1968-70, professor of English, 1970-70; University of Delaware, Newark, H. Fletcher Brown Professor, 1979—.

MEMBER: Modern Language Association of America (member of Hubbell Award committee), Melville Society, Center for Editions of American Authors (member of executive committee, 1971-74).

AWARDS, HONORS: Woodrow Wilson fellowship, 1959-60; Guggenheim fellowship, 1974-75; University of Southern California Creative Scholarship and Research Award, 1977; fellowship from Center for Advanced Study, University of Delaware, 1981-82.

WRITINGS:

EDITOR

Gansevoort Melville's 1846 London Journal and Letters from England, 1845, New York Public Library, 1966.
The Recognition of Herman Melville: Selected Criticism since 1846, University of Michigan Press, 1967.
(With Harrison Hayford) Herman Melville, *Moby-Dick: An Authoritative Text* (includes reviews and letters by Melville, analogues and sources, and criticism), Norton, 1967.
(And contributor with Hayford and G. Thomas Tanselle) *The Writings of Herman Melville,* Northwestern University Press and Newberry Library, Volume 1: *Typee: A Peep at Polynesian Life,* 1968, Volume 2: *Omoo: A Narrative of Adventures in the South Seas,* 1968, Volume 3: *Redburn: His First Voyage; Being the Sailor-Boy Confessions and Reminiscences of the Son-of-a-Gentleman, in the Merchant Service,* 1969, Volume 4: *Mardi and a Voyage Thither,* 1970, Volume 5: *White-Jacket; or, The World in a Man-of-War,* 1970, Volume 6: *Pierre,* 1971, Volume 6: *Moby-Dick,* 1988.
(With Hayford) *Moby-Dick as Doubloon: Essays and Extracts, 1851-1970,* Norton, 1970.
Melville, *The Confidence-Man: His Masquerade; An Authoritative Text* (includes backgrounds and sources, reviews, criticism, and annotated bibliography), Norton, 1971.
Shorter Works of Hawthorne and Melville, C. E. Merrill, 1972.
(With Steven Mailloux) *Checklist of Melville Reviews,* Melville Society, 1975.
Norton Anthology of American Literature, Volume 1, Norton, 1979, 3rd edition, 1989.
(With Brian Higgins) *Critical Essays on Herman Melville's "Pierre; or, The Ambiguities,"* G. K. Hall, 1983.
Flawed Texts and Verbal Icons: Literary Authority in American Fiction, Northwestern University Press, 1984.
(With Jay Leyda) *The New Melville Log,* three volumes, Gordion Press, forthcoming.

OTHER

(Compiler with Tyrus Hillway) *Directory of Melville Dissertations,* Melville Society, 1962.

Contributor of articles to *American Literature, Studies in Short Fiction, New York Historical Society Quarterly, Modern Language Quarterly, Nineteenth-Century Fiction, Papers of the Bibliographical Society of America, Mississippi Quarterly, Studies in the Novel,* and other literary journals; formerly contributed articles under the pseudonym Samuel Willis to periodicals. Contributor of the Melville chapter to the annual volume of *American Literary Scholarship,* 1972-80. Guest editor of *Studies in the Novel,* spring, 1978.

WORK IN PROGRESS: Continuing work on *The Writings of Herman Melville* for Northwestern University Press and Newberry Library; *Clarel;* a biography of Herman Melville for Norton.

SIDELIGHTS: Hershel Parker told *CA:* "What I have been doing for the past ten years or so is defining a biographical-bibliographical-textual-aesthetic approach to literature, moving from the textual evidence amassed in the 1960s to its aesthetic implications—implications which have gone largely unnoticed because of the pervasive dominance of the New Critical distrust of biographical evidence, a distrust that has survived to prejudice even deconstructionist theorists (such as Jonathan Culler) and feminist theorists (such as Annette Kolodny) against the possibility of discovering authorial intention. I have been working to bring textual scholarship, criticism, and theory into relationship with the work being done by cognitive psychologists at Cornell, such as James J. Gibson, and the work being done on the creative process, especially that by Dr. Albert Rothenberg, the Yale clinical psychiatrist.

"I am particularly interested in demonstrating how so much criticism and theory has gone to waste because it does not take account of textual evidence and does not take account of the way the human mind is designed to make sense even of texts which literally are nonsensical, or which contain only skewed authorial meaning, or which contain meanings which are adventitious, never intended by the author or anyone else. I have been arguing for this new literary approach in many articles and finally in . . . *Flawed Texts and Verbal Icons: Literary Authority in American Fiction.* The title [of the book was] tentative . . . [for some time] because of the difficulty of getting in both the fact that many standard texts are drastically flawed, flawed even to the point of being in places unintelligible, and also the fact that the direction of the creative process is always toward the sort of formal unity which would delight a New Critic; because of the difficulty of getting in the fact of the authority of the author and the fact that authority is frequently lost, in part; and finally because much of the book is devoted to examining the efforts of readers to make sense of what does not make sense."

More recently, Parker added: "I'm glad I did the work which led to *Flawed Texts and Verbal Icons,* but that phase is done, and since 1987 I have been working again full-time on Melville's life. In reaction to the joint triumph of critical theory (which ignores research) and the New Historicism (which vaunts itself on zestful narrative rather than truth-telling), I have happily returned to archival research in the great Melville collections (and many other collections). There is nothing in the world I would rather be doing than completing *The New Melville Log* and writing *The Life of Herman Melville.*"

BIOGRAPHICAL/CRITICAL SOURCES:

PERIODICALS

Times Literary Supplement, February 15, 1985.

PARKIN, David 1940-

PERSONAL: Born November 5, 1940, in Watford, Hertford-shire, England; son of Cecil Joseph (a clerk) and Rose (Johnson) Parkin; married Monica Lacey; children: Nathan Charo, Sasha Louise, Andrew Jesse. *Education:* School of Oriental and African Studies, B.A. (with first class honors), 1962, Ph.D., 1965.

ADDRESSES: Home—55 Southover, Lewes, Sussex, England. *Office*—School of Oriental and African Studies, University of London, London W.C.1, England.

CAREER: University of London, School of Oriental and African Studies, London, England, lecturer, 1964-76, reader, 1976-81, professor of African anthropology, 1981—. Senior research fellow, University College, Nairobi, Kenya, 1968-69; lecturer in social anthropology, Sussex University, 1971-72; visiting professor, University of California, Berkeley, spring, 1980.

MEMBER: International African Institute, Royal Anthropological Institute, Association of Social Anthropologists (chairman).

AWARDS, HONORS: Rivers Medal, Royal Anthropological Institute, 1985.

WRITINGS:

Neighbours and Nationals in an African City Ward, University of California Press, 1969.
Palms, Wine and Witnesses, Chandler, 1972.
(Contributor) W. H. Whiteley, editor, *Language in Kenya,* Oxford University Press, 1974.
(Editor) *Town and Country in Central and Eastern Africa,* Oxford University Press, 1975.
The Cultural Definition of Political Response: Lineal Destiny along the Luo, Academic Press, 1978.
(Editor) *Semantic Anthropology,* Academic Press, 1982.
Speaking of Arts: A Giriama Impression, Indiana Africa, 1982.
(Editor) *The Anthropology of Evil,* Basil Blackwell, 1985.
(Co-editor with David Nayamwaya) *Transformations of African Marriage,* Manchester University Press, 1987.

Also co-editor of *Swahili Language and Society,* 1985. Contributor to *Africa, Man,* and other journals. Co-editor, *Africa,* 1976-80.

WORK IN PROGRESS: Writing on the economic and ritual life of the Giriama of Kenya; research on socio-linguistics in Nairobi, and on Islam in East Africa.

SIDELIGHTS: David Parkin, who is competent in French, German, Swahili, Luo, and Giriama, told *CA:* "I believe that anthropology truly does, as is often claimed, tell us about ourselves through our understanding of other cultures, and that is why I am committed to the subject. Certainly, anthropology is a better way of reaching out to the 'other' than nuclear missiles. No politician would ever accept these as alternatives, and it is unlikely that humanistic anthropological writings have significant impact at all. They certainly don't sell. But we persevere, nevertheless, and will continue to do so."

BIOGRAPHICAL/CRITICAL SOURCES:

PERIODICALS

New York Times Book Review, October 6, 1985.
Times Literary Supplement, July 8, 1983, July 19, 1985.

PARTRIDGE, Frances (Catherine) 1900-

PERSONAL: Born March 15, 1900, in London, England; daughter of William Cecil (an architect) and Margaret (Lloyd) Marshall; married Ralph Partridge, March 2, 1933 (died, 1960); children: Lytton Burgo (deceased). *Education:* Newnham College, Cambridge, graduated with honors, 1921. *Politics:* "Liberal and pacifist." *Religion:* None.

ADDRESSES: Home—16 West Halkin St., London SW1X 8JL, England. *Agent*—Gill Coleridge, Rogers, Coleridge & White, 20 Powis Mews, London W.11, England.

CAREER: Translator and author. Worked at a bookstore, 1921-28.

MEMBER: International PEN, Royal Literary Society (fellow), London Library, London Medical Orchestra.

WRITINGS:

(Editor with husband, Ralph Partridge) *The Greville Memoirs, 1814-1860,* eight volumes, Macmillan, 1938.
A Pacifist's War, Hogarth Press, 1978.
Love in Bloomsbury: Memories, Little, Brown, 1981 (published in England as *Memories,* Gollancz, 1983).
(With Julia Strachey) *Julia: A Portrait of Julia Strachey by Julia Strachey and Frances Partridge,* Little, Brown, 1983.
Everything to Lose: Diaries, 1945-1960, Little, Brown, 1985.
Friends in Focus: A Life in Photographs, Chatto & Windus, 1987.
A Bloomsbury Album, Little, Brown, 1987.

TRANSLATOR FROM THE SPANISH

Mercedes Ballesteros de Gailbrois, *Nothing Is Impossible,* Harvill, 1956.
Vincent Blasco-Ibanez, *Blood and Sand,* Elek, 1958.
Blasco-Ibanez, *The Naked Lady,* Elek, 1959.
Miguel A. Asturias, *The President,* Atheneum, 1963.
Jose L. Aranguren, *Human Communication,* McGraw, 1967.
Pedro L. Entralgo, *Doctor and Patient,* McGraw, 1969.
Alejo Carpentier, *War of Time,* Knopf, 1970.
Rita Guibert, *Seven Voices,* Knopf, 1973.
Carpentier, *Reasons of State,* Knopf, 1976.

TRANSLATOR FROM THE FRENCH

Iovleff Bornet, *Something to Declare,* Harvill, 1957.
Joseph Dessel, *The Enemy in the Mouth,* Hart-Davis, 1961.
Gabriel Estivals, *A Gap in the Wall,* Collins, 1963.
Raymond Cogniat, *Seventeenth-Century Painting,* Viking, 1964.
Vassily Photiades, *Eighteenth-Century Painting,* Viking, 1964.
Olivier Beigbeider, *Ivory,* Putnam, 1965.
Pierre Nordon, *Conan Doyle: A Biography,* J. Murray, 1966, Holt, 1967.
Jacques Bonssard, *The Civilization of Charlemagne,* McGraw, 1967.
Gilbert Martineau, *Napoleon's St. Helena,* J. Murray, 1968, Rand McNally, 1969.
Martineau, *Napoleon Surrenders,* J. Murray, 1974.
Martineau, *Napoleon's Last Journey,* J. Murray, 1976.
Martineau, *Madame Mere,* J. Murray, 1978.

OTHER

Translator of magazine articles from French and Spanish. Contributor to *New Statesman, Spectator,* and *Times Literary Supplement.*

SIDELIGHTS: A translator of books in Spanish and French for many years, Frances Partridge gave up this work at the age of 70 to write original works based on the diaries she kept while living in the company of members of the famous Bloomsbury group. Members of this group of British intellectuals included Virginia Woolf and her husband, Leonard, Lytton Strachey, E. M. Forster, John Meynard Keynes, Vanessa and Clive Bell, Duncan Grant, and others who followed an idealistic philosophy influenced by G. E. Moore's *Principia Ethica.* Partridge (then Frances Marshall) became involved with the Bloomsburyites when she fell in love with Ralph Partridge, who was married to Dora Carrington. Dora and Ralph Partridge lived, in turn, with Lytton Strachey, in a well-known *menage a trois* at Ham Spray in Hampshire. This arrangement ended when Strachey died of cancer and Dora subsequently committed suicide. Soon afterwards, Ralph Partridge married Frances and the two lived happily until his death in 1960.

The story behind this and other affairs among the Bloomsburyites has since become the subject of many, often gossipy, books. But critics note that Frances Partridge has provided a new perspective to the lives of these people in her personal accounts. Caroline Moorehead, for example, describes *Love in Bloomsbury* in the London *Times* as "a book about friendship, among people who really cared about friends, about its rules and limits and the determining power of its influence." *New York Times* critic Anatole Broyard adds that Partridge "is natural, unassuming and observing, neither a spy, a gossip nor one of the charmed circle herself, but someone who was always there and deeply interested in the others."

Each of Partridge's books about the Bloomsbury group covers a different period and subject of its history. *A Pacifist's War* covers the years during World War II, *Love in Bloomsbury: Memories* involves the times between world wars, and *Julia: A Portrait of Julia Strachey by Julia Strachey and Frances Partridge,* focuses on one of the group's most enigmatic, personally troubled members, who was a long-time friend of Partridge. *Everything to Lose: Diaries, 1945-1960* is somewhat less concerned with Bloomsbury, centering on the life the author enjoyed with her husband after World War II. In a *Spectator* article concerning all these books, Moorehead feels that "if John Updike is the poet of unhappy marriage, Frances Partridge is that of friendship, an attachment whose rules and demands she understands and conveys extraordinarily well. Furthermore, she lacks the malice of some of the Bloomsbury writers; she can be mocking and exigent but she is not merciless. It is her own particular and very agreeable voice that leaves its mark on every page."

However, because the author often goes into such great detail about the daily lives of the Bloomsbury group, some reviewers have found parts of Partridge's books to be slow reading. *Times Literary Supplement* contributor Margaret Forster remarks that the descriptions of Robert Kee's love affairs are uninteresting to read, "as are the commonplace comings and goings of most of [Partridge's] friends." But, Forster adds, "there is also . . . the inspiring theme of Partridge's love for her husband." Other critics, such as *Washington Post Book World* reviewer Stanley Weintraub, praise the author for the writing skills she demonstrates in her diaries. "Nothing of Frances Partridge's other writing evidences the verve for vivid description of her diaries," says Weintraub. "From the opening pages her knack for capsulizing sensory impressions is remarkable," the reviewer concludes.

Partridge's books about Bloomsbury are significant, according to *New York Times Book Review* critic Samuel Hynes in his review of *Love in Bloomsbury,* in that the author has written more than an account of life among British intellectuals in the early twentieth century, "she has [also] written a social history of what happened to young persons of her sex and class in England in

a time of great social change." Partridge's portrayal of these people succeeds, opines Jean Strouse in *Newsweek,* because "there is no reverential talk of genius, no poppycock about intellect's finest hour. Instead, she draws deft sketches from her personal impressions of the 'Bloomsburies.' " "Frances Partridge," concludes *New York Times Book Review* contributor Caryn James, "has outlived the ghostly presences of Bloomsbury and refused to become a living relic of her era. Still assessing, still irreverent, she is Bloomsbury's living legacy."

AVOCATIONAL INTERESTS: Music (plays violin in an amateur orchestra and attends operas and concerts), collecting and identifying wild flowers, reading (particularly history, memoirs, philosophy, and biographies).

BIOGRAPHICAL/CRITICAL SOURCES:

PERIODICALS

Los Angeles Times Book Review, September 13, 1981, September 4, 1983.
Newsweek, October 5, 1981.
New York Times, September 30, 1981, August 26, 1983.
New York Times Book Review, September 27, 1981, October 16, 1983, May 4, 1986.
Spectator, February 21, 1981, December 7, 1985.
Times (London), January 29, 1981.
Times Literary Supplement, August 4, 1978, February 13, 1981, May 13, 1983, October 25, 1985.
Washington Post Book World, April 13, 1986.

*   *   *

PATRICK, Robert   1937-

PERSONAL: Born September 27, 1937, in Kilgore, Tex. *Education:* Attended Eastern New Mexico University, three years.

ADDRESSES: Home—c/o La Mama, 74A East Fourth St., New York, N.Y. 10003.

CAREER: Playwright, actor, director, and songwriter. Worked as dishwasher, autopsy typist, accounts receivable correspondent, astrologer, and reporter. Caffe Cino, New York City, waiter, doorman, and stage manager, 1961-63; Old Reliable Theatre Tavern, New York City, playwright-in-residence, 1967-71.

MEMBER: New York Theatre Strategy, Playwrights Cooperative, Actors Studio.

AWARDS, HONORS: Show Business best Off-Off Broadway playwright award, 1968-69, for "Joyce Dynel," "Fog," and "Salvation Army"; nominated for *Village Voice* "Obie" award, 1973; Glasgow Citizens' Theatre International play contest, first prize, 1973, for "Kennedy's Children"; Rockefeller Foundation playwright-in-residence grant, 1973; Creative Artists Public Service grant, 1976; International Thespian Society Founders Award, 1979.

WRITINGS:

Untold Decades: Seven Comedies of Gay Romance, St. Martin's, 1988.

PLAYS

"The Haunted Host" (also see below), first produced Off-Off-Broadway at Caffe Cino, November 29, 1964.
"Mirage" (also see below), first produced Off-Broadway at La Mama, July 8, 1965.
"The Sleeping Bag," first produced at Playwrights' Workshop, June, 1966.

"Indecent Exposure," first produced Off-Off-Broadway at Caffe Cino, September 27, 1966.

"Halloween Hermit," first produced Off-Off-Broadway at Caffe Cino, October 31, 1966.

"Cheesecake" (also see below), first produced Off-Off-Broadway at Caffe Cino, 1966.

"Lights, Camera, Action" (also see below), first produced Off-Off-Broadway at Caffe Cino, June 8, 1967.

"The Warhol Machine," first produced Off-Off-Broadway at Playbox Studio, July 18, 1967.

"Still-Love" (also see below), first produced Off-Off-Broadway at Playbox Studio, July 18, 1967.

"Cornered" (also see below), first produced at Theatre Gallery, January 26, 1968.

"Un Bel Di," first produced at Theatre Gallery, January 26, 1968.

"Help, I Am" (also see below), first produced at Theatre Gallery, January 26, 1968.

"Camera Obscura," first produced Off-Off-Broadway at Caffe Cino; produced Off-Broadway at Cafe au Go Go, May 8, 1968.

"The Arnold Bliss Show" (also see below), first produced Off-Off-Broadway by New York Theatre Ensemble, April 1, 1969.

"A Bad Place to Get Your Head," first produced at St. Peters Church, July 14, 1970.

"Bread-Tangle," first produced at St. Peters Church, July 14, 1970.

"Picture Wire," first produced at St. Peters Church, August 13, 1970.

"I Am Trying to Tell You Something," first produced at The Open Space, August, 1970.

"Shelter," first produced Off-Off-Broadway at Playbox Studio, November, 1970.

"The Richest Girl in the World Finds Happiness" (also see below), first produced Off-Broadway at La Mama, December 24, 1970.

"Hymen and Carbuncle" (also see below), produced Off-Off-Broadway by the Dove Company, 1970.

"A Christmas Carol," first produced Off-Broadway at La Mama, December 22, 1971.

"Youth Rebellion," first produced at Sammy's Bowery Follies, February, 1972.

Play by Play (first produced Off-Broadway at La Mama, December 20, 1972), Samuel French, 1975.

"Something Else" (also see below), first produced Off-Off-Broadway by New York Theatre Ensemble, January, 1973.

"Ludwig and Wagner" (also see below), first produced Off-Broadway at La Mama, February, 1973.

"Mercy Drop" (also see below), first produced at W.P.A. Theatre, March, 1973.

"Simultaneous Transmissions," first produced at Kranny's Nook, March 1, 1973.

"The Track of the Narwhal," first produced in Boston, Mass. at Boston Conservatory, April 28, 1973.

Kennedy's Children (first produced at Clark Center, May 30, 1973; produced on the West End at Arts Theatre Club, May, 1975; produced on Broadway at Golden Theatre, November 3, 1975), Samuel French (London) 1975, Random House, 1976.

"Cleaning House" (also see below), first produced at W.P.A. Theatre, June 27, 1973.

"Hippy as a Lark," first produced at Stagelights II, June, 1973.

"Blue Is for Boys," produced in Hollywood, Calif., at Deja Vu, September, 1973, produced Off-Broadway at Corner Loft Studio, January, 1987.

"The Golden Circle," first produced by Spring Street Company, September 26, 1973.

"Love Lace" (also see below), first produced at Pico Playhouse, 1974.

"How I Came to Be Here Tonight," first produced Off-Broadway at La Mama Hollywood, March 21, 1974.

"Orpheus and Amerika," first produced in Los Angeles, Calif. at Odyssey Theatre, April, 1974.

"Fred and Harold, and One Person," first produced in London, England, 1976.

"My Dear, It Doesn't Mean a Thing," first produced in London, 1976.

My Cup Runneth Over (first produced in Brooklyn, N.Y., at Everyman Theatre, November 3, 1977), Dramatists Play Service, 1979.

"Judas," first produced in Santa Monica, Calif., April, 1978.

"T-Shirts," first produced in Minneapolis, Minn., at Out-and-About Theatre, October 19, 1978.

Mutual Benefit Life (first produced by Production Company, October, 1978), Dramatists Play Service, 1979.

"Bank Street Breakfast" (also see below), first produced by the Fourth E, February, 1979.

"Communication Gap," first produced in Greensboro, N.C., 1979.

"The Family Bar" (also see below), first produced in Hollywood at Deja Vu, 1979.

"Big Sweet," first produced in Richmond, Va., January, 1984.

"No Trojan Women," produced in Wallingford, Conn., July, 1985.

"Explanation of a Xmas Wedding," produced at Theatre for the New City, December 29, 1987.

Also author of "Diaghilev and Nijinsky" (also see below).

PLAYS; ALL FIRST PRODUCED OFF-OFF BROADWAY AT OLD RELIABLE THEATRE TAVERN

"See Other Side," April 1, 1968.

"Absolute Power over Movie Stars," May 13, 1968.

"Preggin and Liss" (also see below), June 17, 1968.

"The Overseers," July 1, 1968.

"Angels in Agony," July 1, 1968.

"Salvation Army," September 23, 1968.

"Dynel," December 16, 1968.

"Fog," January 20, 1969.

"I Came to New York to Write" (also see below), March 24, 1969.

"Joyce Dynel" (also see below), April 7, 1969.

"The Young Aquarius," April 28, 1969.

"Oooooooops!," May 12, 1969.

"Lily of the Valley of the Dolls," June 30, 1969.

"One Person" (also see below), August 29, 1969.

"Angel, Honey, Baby, Darling, Dear," July 20, 1970.

"The Golden Animal," July 20, 1970.

COLLECTIONS

Robert Patrick's Cheep Theatricks! (contains "I Came to New York to Write," "The Haunted Host," "Joyce Dynel," "Cornered," "Still-Love," "Lights, Camera, Action," "Help, I Am," "The Arnold Bliss Show," "One Person," "Preggin and Liss," and "The Richest Girl in the World Finds Happiness"), edited by Michael Feingold, Winter House, 1972.

One Man, One Woman (contains "Mirage," "Cleaning House," "Cheesecake," "Something Else," "Love Lace," and "Bank Street Breakfast") Samuel French, 1975.
Mercy Drop and Other Plays (contains "Mercy Drop," "Ludwig and Wagner," "Diaghilev and Nijinsky," "Hymen and Carbuncle," and "The Family Bar"), Calamus Books, 1980.

OTHER

Also author of "Sketches," first produced in 1966, "Silver Skies," "Tarquin Truthbeauty," and "The Actor and the Invader," all produced in 1969, "La Repetition" and "Sketches and Songs," both produced in 1970, "Songs," produced in 1972, "Imp-Prisonment" and "The Twisted Root," both produced in 1973, and several other plays variously produced 1979-85, including "All in the Mind," "The Sane Scientist," "Twenty-four Inches," "The Spinning Tree," "Report to the Mayor," and "Bread Alone." Contributor to anthologies, including *Collision Course, New American Plays 3, The Off-Off Broadway Book,* and *West Coast Plays 5.* Contributor to periodicals, including *Saturday Review, Astrology Today, Playbill, Gaysweek,* and *New York.*

WORK IN PROGRESS: Temple Slave, a novel.

SIDELIGHTS: Robert Patrick is one of the theatre's most prolific playwrights. With some seventy Off-Broadway one-act and full-length works to his credit, Patrick is still best known primarily for one work—"Kennedy's Children"—that made it to Broadway. "Patrick is something of a maverick, an urchin in a middle-aged body, a Texas drifter with an obsession for story telling," according to Maggie Hawthorn in a *Seattle Post-Intelligencer* article. "[He] is, by his own admission, voluble. He loves to talk about the theater, about people, about himself, about America." He is also one of the early proponents of gay drama—"many gay theatres in America and abroad have opened with [my] work," as the author tells *CA.*

"Kennedy's Children" depicts the barroom confessions of five representatives of the sixties, yet, according to Patrick, the play is not primarily concerned with the era. As Patrick notes to Robert Berkvist of the *New York Times,* the play's theme "is the loss of heroes. And it's not about the sixties, it's about now, about why we have become what we are." As Patrick was completing the work, he goes on to say, he found that the characters "were each a different aspect of the lost-hero theme: one had killed his hero, another had seen his hero betrayed, another had tried to be a hero."

"A play is primarily a shared experience which exists only in performance," Patrick once told *CA.* "Its immediacy is its special quality. Unlike films and literature, which record experiences that once happened, a play presents an event. Its *reality* makes it a powerful moral and psychological tool. Theatrical artists who do not communicate consciously, communicate helplessly and unconsciously."

MEDIA ADAPTATIONS: "My Cup Runneth Over" was produced for public television. "Kennedy's Children," which has been translated into some forty languages, has been produced on television in several countries.

BIOGRAPHICAL/CRITICAL SOURCES:

BOOKS

Authors in the News, Volume 2, Gale, 1976.
Feingold, Michael, editor, *Robert Patrick's Cheep Theatricks!,* Winter House, 1972.
Poland, Albert, and Bruce Mailman, editors, *The Off-Off Broadway Book,* Bobbs-Merrill, 1972.

PERIODICALS

Newsweek, November 17, 1975.
New York Times, May 4, 1975, September 3, 1975, November 9, 1975, June 23, 1978, January 29, 1987, December 29, 1987.
Seattle Post-Intelligencer, April 18, 1976.
Time, November 17, 1975.

*   *   *

PAUL, Sheri
See RESNICK, Sylvia (Safran)

*   *   *

PAULSEN, Gary 1939-

PERSONAL: Born May 17, 1939, in Minneapolis, Minn.; son of Oscar and Eunice Paulsen; married third wife, Ruth Ellen Wright (an artist), May 5, 1971; children: James Wright. *Education:* Attended Bemidji College, 1957-58; and University of Colorado, 1976. *Politics:* "As Solzhenitsyn has said, 'If we limit ourselves to political structures we are not artists.' " *Religion:* "I believe in spiritual progress."

ADDRESSES: Home—Leonard, Mich. *Agent*—Jonathan Lazear, 430 First Ave. N., Milwaukee, Wis. 55401.

CAREER: Has worked variously as a teacher, electronics field engineer, soldier, actor, director, farmer, rancher, truck driver, trapper, professional archer, migrant farm worker, singer, and sailor; currently a full-time writer. *Military service:* U.S. Army, 1959-62; became sergeant.

AWARDS, HONORS: Central Missouri Award for Children's Literature, 1976; *The Green Recruit* was chosen one of New York Public Library's Books for the Teen Age, 1980, 1981 and 1982, and *Sailing: From Jibs to Jibing* was chosen in 1982; *Dancing Carl* was selected one of American Library Association's Best Young Adult Books, 1983, and *Tracker* was selected in 1984; *Dogsong* was chosen one of Child Study Association of America's Children's Books of the Year, and was a Newbery Honor Book, 1986; Society of Midland Author Award, 1985, for *Tracker; Hatchet* was named a Newbery Honor Book, 1987.

WRITINGS:

NONFICTION

The Special War, Sirkay, 1966.
Some Birds Don't Fly, Rand McNally, 1969.
The Building a New, Buying an Old, Remodeling a Used Comprehensive Home and Shelter Book, Prentice-Hall, 1976.
Farm: A History and Celebration of the American Farmer, Prentice-Hall, 1977.
Hiking and Backpacking, Simon & Schuster, 1978.
Successful Home Repair: When Not to Call the Contractor, Structures, 1978.
Canoeing, Kayaking and Rafting, Simon & Schuster, 1979.
Money Saving Home Repair Guide, Ideals, 1981.
Beat the System: A Survival Guide, Pinnacle Books, 1983.

CHILDREN'S BOOKS

Mr. Tucker, Funk & Wagnall, 1968.
(With Dan Theis) *The Man Who Climbed the Mountain,* Raintree, 1976.
The Small Ones, Raintree, 1976.
The Grass Eaters, Raintree, 1976.
Dribbling, Shooting, and Scoring Sometimes, Raintree, 1976.

Hitting, Pitching, and Running Maybe, Raintree, 1976.
Tackling, Running, and Kicking—Now and Again, Raintree, 1977.
Riding, Roping, and Bulldogging—Almost, Raintree, 1977.
The Golden Stick, Raintree, 1977.
Careers in an Airport, Raintree, 1977.
The CB Radio Caper, Raintree, 1977.
The Curse of the Cobra, Raintree, 1977.
Running, Jumping and Throwing—If You Can, Raintree, 1978.
Forehanding and Backhanding—If You're Lucky, Raintree, 1978.
Downhill, Hotdogging and Cross-Country—If the Snow Isn't Sticky, Raintree, 1979.
Facing Off, Checking and Goaltending—Perhaps, Raintree, 1979.
Going Very Fast in a Circle—If You Don't Run out of Gas, Raintree, 1979.
Launching, Floating High and Landing—If Your Pilot Light Doesn't Go Out, Raintree, 1979.
Pummeling, Falling and Getting Up—Sometimes, Raintree, 1979.
Track, Enduro and Motocross—Unless You Fall Over, Raintree, 1979.
TV and Movie Animals, Messner, 1980.
Sailing: From Jibs to Jibing, Messner, 1981.
The Crossing, PLB, 1987.
Hatchet, Orchard Books, 1987.
The Island, Orchard Books, 1988.
Voyage of the Frog, Orchard Books, 1989.

NOVELS

The Implosion Effect, Major Books, 1976.
The Death Specialists, Major Books, 1976.
The Foxman, Thomas Nelson, 1977.
Winterkill, Thomas Nelson, 1977.
Tiltawhirl John, Thomas Nelson, 1977.
C. B. Jockey, Major Books, 1977.
The Day the White Deer Died, Thomas Nelson, 1978.
Hope and a Hatchet, Thomas Nelson, 1978.
The Green Recruit, Independence Press, 1978.
The Spitball Gang, Elsevier/Nelson, 1980.
The Sweeper, Harlequin, 1981.
Clutterkill, Harlequin, 1982.
Popcorn Days and Buttermilk Nights, Lodestar Books, 1983.
Dancing Carl, Bradbury, 1983.
Tracker, Bradbury, 1984.
Dogsong, Bradbury, 1985.
Sentries, Bradbury, 1986.
Murphy (western), Walker & Co., 1987.
Murphy's Gold (western), Walker & Co., 1988.
Murphy's Herd (western), Walker & Co., 1989.
Night Rituals, Donald I. Fine, Inc., 1989.

OTHER

"Communications" (one-act play), first produced in New Mexico by a local theatre group, 1974.
"Together-Apart" (one-act play), first produced in Denver, Colo., at Changing Scene Theatre, 1976.
The Madonna Stories (short stories), Van Vliet & Co., 1989.

Also author of more than two hundred short stories and articles.

SIDELIGHTS: Most of Gary Paulsen's novels and how-to books are aimed at a younger audience, and many of the works feature an outdoors theme, one familiar to the author. He has, for instance, worked as a field engineer, a trapper, and a rancher. At one point, Paulsen ran the grueling Iditarod dogsled race in Alaska, and used the experience to write *Dogsong,* a story of a boy's coming of age on the northern tundra. "We can feel the cold snow and ice upon his body," says *Best Sellers* critic Eugene J. Linehan. "He discards use of snowmobiles or modern guns. It is a return to tribal lore which teaches [the boy] how to find food; even to reverence the dead animal which provides such. And mixed into the action is a dream which also teaches him to interpret life. There is poetic majesty in the descriptions without a touch of condescension to the young."

Noting that coming-of-age adventures seem to be the author's forte (in such other novels as *Hatchet* and *The Crossing*), *New York Times Book Review* writer Edwin J. Kenney, Jr., finds that another Paulsen novel, *The Island,* "is significantly different from these earlier books because it is essentially a meditative novel that subordinates, indeed practically stops, external action to concentrate on the reflections of a 14-year-old boy about the world around him and his relation to it." The central figure in *The Island,* the young Wil Neuton, moves with his parents to an isolated house in Wisconsin's north woods, where Wil discovers a small island drifting in a lake. The land "becomes his secret, his home, his center, from which he begins truly to see, to know and to be," as Kenney describes. In the critic's view, "it may well be that for young readers action is more powerful than symbol, the epic world more revelatory than the lyric. Nevertheless, [Paulsen] has evocatively presented the mysteriousness of the spiritual quest through the unconscious for wholeness and authenticity."

BIOGRAPHICAL/CRITICAL SOURCES:

PERIODICALS

Best Sellers, July, 1985.
Los Angeles Times, December 12, 1987.
New York Times Book Review, May 22, 1988.
Writer's Digest, January, 1980.

*   *   *

PAUL VI, Pope   1897-1978

PERSONAL: Full name, Giovanni Battista Enrico Antonio Maria Montini; born September 26, 1897, in Concesio, Italy; died August 6, 1978, in Castel Gandolfo, Italy; son of Giorgio (an attorney and newspaper editor) and Giudetta (Alghisi) Montini. *Education:* Attended Lombard Seminary, University of Rome, Pontifical Gregorian University, and Pontifical Ecclesiastical Academy.

ADDRESSES: Home and office—Palazzo Apostolico Vaticano, Vatican City, Italy.

CAREER: Ordained Roman Catholic priest, 1920; secretary to apostolic nunciature, Warsaw, Poland, 1923; document writer, Secretariat of State, Vatican, 1924; national spiritual adviser, Italian Federation of Catholic University Students, 1925-35; professor of history and pontifical diplomacy, 1931-37; adviser to Pope Pius XII, 1944-52; appointed substitute secretary of state for ordinary (internal) affairs, 1952; consecrated archbishop of Milan, 1954; created cardinal, 1958; elected pope, June 21, 1963, papal reign, 1963-78.

WRITINGS:

Ecclesiam Suam (encyclical letter; title means "The Paths of the Church"), America Press, 1964.
Su la Madonna e su i santi (1955-1962), Arcivescovado di Milano, 1965.

Dialogues: Reflections on God and Man, Simon & Schuster, 1965.
On the Development of Peoples (encyclical letter; translated from the original Latin text, *Populorum Progressio*), Paulist/Newman, 1967.
Humanae Vitae (encyclical letter; title means "On Human Life"), Paulist/Newman, 1968.
What Must God Be Like?, Dimension Books, 1975.
Mary, God's Mother and Ours, St. Paul Editions (Boston), 1979.

Also author of several other encyclical letters, including "Mysterium Fidei" (title means "The Mystery of Faith") and "Sacerdotalis Caelibatus" (title means "On Priestly Celibacy"); also author of reports and proceedings of the Second Vatican Council.

SIDELIGHTS: Pope Paul VI was the 262nd successor to the seat of St. Peter in Rome. A priest with minimal experience as a pastor, Paul became the supreme pastor to the world's Roman Catholics in 1963 during a period of great change and controversy brought about by the reforms of the Second Vatican Council. He came to the papacy with a reputation of being a liberal and yet will be remembered as a conservative who, in matters of priestly celibacy and birth control, followed strict Catholic traditions.

Perhaps Paul's most important contribution to his church came in the area of ecumenism. During his fifteen-year papacy, Paul opened communication channels with non-Christian peoples and with other Christian denominations. During his 1964 trip to the Holy Land, Paul met with the spiritual leader of Eastern Orthodoxy, Patriarch Athenagoras I. Their meeting began a series of exchanges between the two religious leaders that resulted in the annulment of excommunications passed by both churches in 1054. Many sources refer to this incident as the high point of Paul's reign as pope. He subsequently met with the archbishop of Canterbury in 1966. This event was the first meeting between the two leaders of these Christian churches since King Henry VIII's break with Rome during the sixteenth century.

In order to carry out these diplomatic missions, Paul embarked on a series of lengthy trips the like of which had never before been undertaken by a pope in Catholic history. He traveled to sixteen countries on six continents, becoming the first reigning pope to visit the United States. The message that Paul took to these countries was one of world peace and an end to the sufferings of the poor in Third World nations. In 1967, he issued the encyclical *Populorum Progressio* ("On the Development of Peoples"), in which he called for an end to the "dehumanizing value system that allowed rich countries to exploit poor countries."

As progressive as he was in these matters, Paul was just as conservative in other areas. Advised by some bishops to take a strong stand against artificial methods of birth control, Paul issued the controversial encyclical *Humanae Vitae* ("On Human Life"). While many Catholics expected their pope to take a liberal stance on the issue of birth control because of his awareness of the problems of overpopulation in the world's poorer countries, Paul stated in the encyclical that church approval of artificial means of birth control would open "a wide and easy road toward conjugal infidelity and the general lowering of morality." The pope's words caused a split within the church. Many priests openly denounced the document and several Western bishops expressed their disappointment in the pope's decision. Although he always considered dissent healthy, Paul suffered personal anguish at the criticism of this encyclical. For many, this is the major issue that will forever be linked with Paul's papacy.

Personally, Paul was a man who enjoyed classical music in his apartments at the Vatican. He was fluent in French and Italian, and knew Portuguese, Spanish, German, and English, in addition to Latin and other classical languages. He considered himself a disciple of the French Thomistic philosopher Jacques Maritain. Paul also enjoyed modern art and redecorated the papal residence employing modern pieces. He established a collection of modern art in the Vatican Museum.

BIOGRAPHICAL/CRITICAL SOURCES:

BOOKS

Barrett, William E., *Shepherd of Mankind,* Doubleday, 1964.
Clancy, John G., *Apostle for Our Time: Pope Paul VI,* Kenedy, 1963.
Four Popes: Keepers of the Faith since 1958, Ideal Publishing Corp., 1978.
Pope Paul VI and the Holy Land, translation by Aileen O'Brien, Herder & Herder, 1964.

PERIODICALS

Christianity Today, August 22, 1969.
New Statesman, November 22, 1968.
Newsweek, August 7, 1967, September 2, 1968, August 21, 1978.
McCall's, February, 1974.
Time, August 30, 1968, November 22, 1968, August 21, 1978.

OBITUARIES:

PERIODICALS

New York Times, August 7, 1978.
Washington Post, August 7, 1978.*

*   *   *

PEISSEL, Michel (Francois)   1937-

PERSONAL: Surname is pronounced Pay-sell; born February 11, 1937, in Paris, France; son of Georges (a diplomat) and Simone (Ladeuille) Peissel; married Marie Claire deMontaignac, June, 1963; married Mildred (Missy) Lynard Allen, 1981; children: (first marriage) Oliver, Jocelyn; (second marriage) Octavia, Morgan. *Education:* Attended University of Ottowa and Harvard Business School, 1958-59; Sorbonne, University of Paris, Ph.D., 1969.

ADDRESSES: Home—Calle del Puig, Cadaques 17488, Gerona, Spain.

CAREER: Explorer and writer. Participated in an expedition down the Quintana-Roo coast of the Yucatan Peninsula, Mexico, 1958, led an anthropological expedition to the Mount Everest area of the Himalayas, 1959, and a second Quintana-Roo expedition, 1961; one of the few westerners to enter Mustang, a feudal kingdom between Tibet and Nepal, where he spent the spring of 1964; made an expedition across Bhutan (another Himalayan country), 1968; led an expedition through Nepal by hovercraft, 1972; participated in an expedition in quest of Mayan waterways, 1975; did field work in Ladakh and Zanskar regions in the Himalayas, 1975-78; participated in filming expedition to Zanskar to make four-part British Broadcasting Corporation documentary "The Last Place on Earth," 1978; led International Ganges Hovercraft Expedition, 1980; explored southeastern Tibet, 1986; reconstituted a Mayan nautical journey down the Yucatan coast, 1988.

WRITINGS:

The Lost World of Quintana-Roo, Dutton, 1963.
Tiger for Breakfast, Dutton, 1966.

Mustang: The Forbidden Kingdom, Dutton, 1967 (published in England as *Mustang: A Lost Tibetan Kingdom,* Collins, 1968).

Lords and Lamas: A Solitary Expedition across the Secret Himalayan Kingdom of Bhutan, Heinemann, 1970.

Bhoutan: Royaume d'Asie inconnu, Editions B. Ai. l Sarl, 1971.

Cavaliers of Kham: The Secret War in Tibet, Heinemann, 1972, published as *The Secret War in Tibet,* Little, Brown, 1973.

The Great Himalayan Passage: Across the Himalayas by Hovercraft, Collins, 1974, published as *The Great Himalayan Passage: The Story of an Extraordinary Adventure on the Roof of the World,* Little, Brown, 1975.

Himalaya Continent Secret, Flammarion, 1977.

The Mayan Gates of Gold, Laffont, 1978.

Zanskar: The Hidden Kingdom, Dutton, 1979.

The Ants Gold, Collins, 1984.

The Himalayan World and Its Culture (illustrated), Perlinger, 1985.

La Tibetaine, Laffont, 1988.

(With wife, Missy Allen) *Dictionary of Dangers,* Thorson's, 1989.

The Journey of the Itza, Laffont, 1990.

Contributor of about 150 feature stories to periodicals, including *Geo, L'Express, National Geographic, McCalls, Europa, Time,* and *Gazetta Illustrada.*

SIDELIGHTS: Michel Peissel's *Zanskar: The Hidden Kingdom* concerns a medieval Buddhist community of 12,000 that still thrives in a valley in the western Himalayas. According to Jan Morris in *Spectator,* part of the region's history includes "a prophecy that Zanskar would one day be a meeting place for fairies. If M. Peissel were not an explorer of high reputation, one might be tempted to suppose that he had made the whole place up." Peissel's work on his explorations in the Yucatan Peninsula, *The Lost World of Quintana-Roo,* has been published in France, Sweden, Spain, Czechoslovakia, U.S.S.R., and England. *Mustang: The Forbidden Kingdom* has been translated into French, German, Russian, and Spanish for a total of eighty-one editions in fifteen countries.

BIOGRAPHICAL/CRITICAL SOURCES:

PERIODICALS

Books and Bookmen, April, 1968.
L'Express, November 20, 1972.
Listener, December 26, 1968.
New Statesman, September 15, 1967.
New Yorker, August 5, 1967.
New York Times Book Review, June 25, 1967.
Observer Review, August 11, 1968.
Paris Match, July, 1988.
Spectator, February 16, 1980.
Time, March 5, 1984.
Times (London), February 9, 1972, June 7, 1972, December 14, 1972.
Wall Street Journal, January 2, 1980.

*　　*　　*

PEMPEL, T. J. 1942-

PERSONAL: Born December 15, 1942, in Valley Stream, N.Y.; son of Thomas D. and Agnes (Haran) Pempel; separated; children: Aaron Kennedy, Sean McDowell. *Education:* Columbia University, B.A. (cum laude), 1966, M.A., 1969, Certificate in East Asian Studies, 1969, Ph.D., 1972; attended University of Michigan, 1968.

ADDRESSES: Home—150 Turkey Hill Rd., Ithaca, N.Y. 14850. *Office*—Department of Government, B-47 McGraw Hall, Cornell University, Ithaca, N.Y. 14853.

CAREER: New York City Urban Corps, New York, N.Y., field director, 1966; member of political research staff of Howard J. Samuel's New York gubernatorial campaign, 1969-70; Cornell University, Ithaca, N.Y., assistant professor, 1972-77, associate professor, 1977-81, professor of government, 1981—, director of China-Japan program, 1980-85. Member of Tokyo's Center for Japanese Social and Political Ideas, 1971—; member of Upstate New York Japan Seminar, 1972—; member of Social Science Research Council Joint Committee for Japanese Studies, 1978-83; consultant to U.S. Department of State. *Military service:* U.S. Marine Corps, 1960-64.

MEMBER: American Political Science Association, Association for Asian Studies, Phi Beta Kappa.

AWARDS, HONORS: Fulbright fellow in Japan, 1970-71, 1975-76; Cornell University grants for China and Japan, 1972, 1973, 1975, 1976; National Science Foundation grant, 1974-77; grants from U.S. Office of Education, 1975-77, National Endowment for the Humanities, 1975-78, Social Science Research Council, 1977-78, 1984-85, Ford Foundation, 1979-81, Henry Luce Foundation, 1979-81, National Resource Center, 1981-83, Japan Foundation, 1985-86.

WRITINGS:

(Editor of English translation) *Bibliography on Higher Education and the Student Problem in Japan,* Kokusai Bunka Shinkokai, 1972.

(Editor of English translation) *Educational Standards in Japan,* Ministry of Finance Press (Tokyo, Japan), 1973.

(Editor of English translation) *Research Documents on Comparative Higher Education,* Hiroshima University, 1976.

(With Douglas Ashford and Peter J. Katzenstein) *Bibliography of Comparative Public Policy in Britain, West Germany, and France,* American Society for Public Administration, 1976.

(Editor and contributor) *Policymaking in Contemporary Japan,* Cornell University Press, 1977.

(With Ashford and Katzenstein) *Comparative Public Policy: A Cross National Bibliography,* Sage Publications, 1978.

Patterns of Japanese Policymaking, Westview, 1978.

Policy and Politics in Japan: Creative Conservation, Temple University Press, 1981.

(With Thomas Ilgen) *Trading Technology: Europe and Japan in the Middle East,* Praeger, 1986.

Japan: Dilemmas of Success, Foreign Policy Association, 1986.

(Editor and contributor) *Uncommon Democracies: The One-Party Dominant Regimes,* Cornell University Press, 1989.

CONTRIBUTOR

Andrew Cordier, editor, *Columbia University Essays in International Affairs,* Volume 3, Columbia University Press, 1968.

Nagai Michio, editor, *Nan no tame no kyoiku ka?* (title means "Education for What?"), Toyo Keizai Shimposha, 1971.

Raymond Bowers and others, editors, *Communications for a Mobile Society,* Sage Publications, 1978.

Katzenstein, editor, *Between Power and Plenty,* University of Wisconsin Press, 1978.

Louis Maisel and Joseph Cooper, editors, *Patterns of Evolution and Decay,* Sage Publications, 1978.

Philippe Schmitter and Gerhard Lehmbruch, editors, *Trends toward Corporatist Intermediation,* Sage Publications, 1979.

Robert Ward and Sakamoto Yoshikazu, editors, *Policy and Planning during the Allied Occupation of Japan,* Princeton University Press, 1982.

Yasonori Sone and Tadao Tomita, editors, *Sekai seiji no naka no Nihon seiji* (title means "Japanese Politics in the Context of World Politics"), Yuhikaku, 1983.

Ezra Suleiman and Carlos Alba, editors, *The Role of Higher Civil Servants in Politics,* Holmes & Meier, 1984.

Takeshi Ishida and Ellis Krauss, editors, *Democracy in Japan,* University of Pittsburgh Press, 1989.

Francis Castles, editor, *Comparative History of Public Policy,* Oxford University Press, 1989.

Also contributor to *Encyclopedia of Japan.*

OTHER

Co-editor of series "Policy and Politics in Industrial States," Temple University Press. Contributor of about twenty articles and reviews to political science and Asian studies journals. Contributing editor of *Japan Interpreter,* 1975—; member of editorial board of *China-Japan Research Papers,* 1973—.

WORK IN PROGRESS: Research on party-bureaucratic relations in one-party dominant democracies; research on comparative public policy, the role of higher civil servants in central government, and political management of economic change in postwar Japan.

* * *

PERRY, Barbara Fisher
See FISHER, Barbara

* * *

PETERFREUND, Stuart (Samuel) 1945-

PERSONAL: Born June 30, 1945, in Brooklyn, N.Y.; son of Harold (an automobile dealer) and Gloria (Doller) Peterfreund. *Education:* Cornell University, B.A., 1966; University of California, M.F.A., 1968; University of Washington, Seattle, Ph.D., 1974.

ADDRESSES: Home—P.O. Box 1H63, Stunley, Mass. 01464. *Office*—Department of English, Northeastern University, Boston, Mass. 02115.

CAREER: Wiltwyck School for Boys, Inc., Yorktown, N.Y., group care worker and psychological researcher, 1970-71 (period included civilian public service as conscientious objector to military duty, 1969-71); University of Arkansas at Little Rock, assistant professor of English, 1975-78; Northeastern University, Boston, Mass., assistant professor, 1978-82, associate professor of English, 1982—; poet. Poet in residence, Southern Literary Festival, 1977.

MEMBER: Modern Language Association of America, Society for Literature and Science, Wordsworth-Coleridge Association, Byron Society, Keats-Shelley Society, Pi Delta Epsilon.

AWARDS, HONORS: First prize in *Writer's Digest* Poetry Contest, 1970, for "Rainstorm in the Country"; Southern Federation of State Arts Agencies fellow, 1977; National Endowment for the Humanities fellow in residence, 1979, 1983, 1988; first prize in Worcester County Poetry Association Contest, 1989.

WRITINGS:

The Hanged Knife (poems), Ithaca House, 1970.

Harder Than Rain (poems), Ithaca House, 1977.
Interstatements (poems), Curbstone, 1986.

Contributor to anthologies, including *Quickly Aging Here: Some Poets of the 1970s,* edited by Geof Hewitt, Doubleday-Anchor, 1969, *A Government Job at Last: An Anthology of Work Poems, Mostly Canadian,* edited by Tom Wayman, McLeod, 1976, *X-1: An Anthology of Experimental Fiction,* edited by Harry Smith, 1976, *Storie di ordinaria poesia,* edited by Riccardo Duranti, Savelli, 1982, and *New England Poetry: A Sampler,* edited by Paul Ruffin, 1988. Contributor of more than one hundred poems to literary magazines, including *Beloit Poetry Journal* and *Shenandoah.* Assistant editor, *Epoch,* 1964-66, 1969; editor, *Worcester Review,* 1988—.

WORK IN PROGRESS: Another collection of poems; research on eighteenth- and early nineteenth-century British literature, literature and science, and critical theory.

SIDELIGHTS: Stuart Peterfreund once told *CA:* "It seems to me that the best poets of the younger American school (40 and over, recent corpses allowed) such as Berryman, Logan, Merwin, Justice, Simpson, and Roethke, are men who have acknowledged the raw deal they got by being born (something Lowell has never gotten over), have made of the world a positive, though not necessarily optimistic vision, which they have justified by somehow withdrawing from the darkness and allowing themselves to be re-born into their own, visionary worlds. And when I speak of visionary I don't mean mystical, I mean metaphorical. And it is easier to live in the metaphor than in the darkness, as well as being far more productive. The projectivists, the New York poets, the *kayak* surrealists all fail for me because they never make the value judgement necessary in the creation of the metaphor for darkness. They show instead, how science can kill poetry: by recording process without questioning the 'why.'

"At any rate, in my own writing, I find it necessary to control reality. And the only reality I can control is the one I make for *me.* It's not the most exciting of all worlds. It's memories of my mother and grandfathers, the few girls I have loved, good friends I get drunk and riot with every time I see them, the several times we ruled the world. It's sitting and drinking wine, listening to classical music on the radio very late at night in New York, knowing that I'm alive. It's stumbling through the dark and loving it for a minute, the way you love a city you've visited because you know your way around. And in the dark, if you can find your way, you're doing all right. There are many ways to do it, the best of them being to sing.

"I am committed to the position that language has no absolute authority, but that language is the only authority there is. The position stresses the responsibility I take upon myself to read and write in as moral way as possible. The position also stresses my commitment to a career based both in criticism and creative activity. I make no fundamental distinction between the need to read well and the need to write powerfully, nor do I make any fundamental distinction between the creative reading that leads to the literary text and the creative writing reading that leads to the critical text."

Peterfreund recently added: "I don't retreat any or all of the foregoing, but as a middle-aged, monogamous homeowner, father of a young child, and so on, I may have outlived it."

* * *

PETERSEN, P(eter) J(ames) 1941-

PERSONAL: Born October 23, 1941, in Santa Rosa, Calif.; son of Carl Eric (a farmer) and Alice (a farmer; maiden name, Winters) Petersen; married Marian Braun (a nurse), July 6, 1963; children: Karen, Carla. *Education:* Stanford University, A.B., 1962; San Francisco State College (now University), M.A., 1964; University of New Mexico, Ph.D., 1972.

ADDRESSES: Home—1243 Pueblo Court, Redding, Calif. 96001. *Office*—Department of English, Shasta College, Box 6006, Redding, Calif. 96099. *Agent*—Ellen Levine Literary Agency, Inc., 432 Park Ave. S., Suite 1205, New York, N.Y. 10016.

CAREER: Shasta College, Redding, Calif., instructor in English, 1964—.

MEMBER: Society of Children's Book Writers.

AWARDS, HONORS: National Endowment for the Humanities fellowship, 1976-77; American Library Association's list of best books for young adults included, in 1982, *Would You Settle for Improbable?,* and in 1983, *Nobody Else Can Walk It for You.*

WRITINGS:

JUVENILES

Would You Settle for Improbable?, Delacorte, 1981.
Nobody Else Can Walk It for You, Delacorte, 1982.
The Boll Weevil Express, Delacorte, 1983.
Here's to the Sophomores, Delacorte, 1984.
Corky and the Brothers Cool, Delacorte, 1985.
Going for the Big One, Delacorte, 1986.
Good-bye to Good Ol' Charlie, Delacorte, 1987.
The Freshman Detective Blues, Delacorte, 1987.
How Can You Hijack a Cave?, Delacorte, 1988.
The Fireplug Is First Base, Dutton, 1990.

SIDELIGHTS: P. J. Petersen once told *CA:* "I had been writing for more than twenty years when I sold my first novel. Prior to that, I had sold nothing—not even a greeting card verse. Having had no commercial success, I wrote the novel for my daughter Karen. If I hadn't been able to sell it, I intended to give her the manuscript as a present from a loving father. I think it was my commitment to her that made the book a success.

"My novels deal with the difficult ethical problems that young people face. *Would You Settle for Improbable?* involves the difficulty of changing destructive behavior patterns. *Nobody Else Can Walk It for You* concerns responses to violence. In *The Boll Weevil Express,* a runaway has to decide between two unsatisfactory ways to live. Although I try to avoid preaching, my own preferences can be seen in the approach to life taken by my central characters—the ones who keep trusting and hoping and caring, even though they're often hurt and disappointed.

"As a child I loved listening to the dramatic programs on the radio: 'The Whistler,' 'Suspense,' 'The Fat Man.' Naturally, much of my elementary school writing was in the form of radio plays. As I look over my novels, I can see the influence of this background. My books are primarily told through dialogue, with very little description or analysis."

*   *   *

PETRAKIS, Harry Mark 1923-

PERSONAL: Born June 5, 1923, in St. Louis, Mo.; son of Mark E. (an Eastern Orthodox priest) and Stella (Christoulakis) Petrakis; married Diane Perparos, September 30, 1945; children: Mark, John, Dean. *Education:* Attended University of Illinois, 1940-41. *Politics:* "Uneasy Democrat."

ADDRESSES: Home and office—80 East Rd., Dune Acres, Chesterton, Ind. 46304.

CAREER: Has worked as laborer, steelworker, real estate salesman, speech writer, and sales correspondent; free-lance writer and lecturer, 1960—. Teacher at writing workshops, including Indiana University Writer's Conference, 1964-65, 1970, 1974, Illinois Wesleyan University, 1978-79, Ball State University, 1978, 1980, University of Wisconsin—Rhinelander, 1978-80, and University of Rochester, 1979-80; teacher of workshop classes in the novel and short story in Winnetka and Highland Park, Ill. McGuffey Visiting Lecturer, Ohio University, winter, 1971; writer in residence, Chicago Public Library, 1976-77, and Chicago Board of Education, 1978-79. Judge, Nelson Algren short story contest, 1987.

MEMBER: Authors Guild, Authors League of America, PEN, Writers Guild of America—West.

AWARDS, HONORS: Atlantic "Firsts" Award, and Benjamin Franklin citation, both 1957, both for short stories; awards from Friends of American Writers, Society of Midland Authors, and Friends of Literature, all 1964, all for *The Odyssey of Kostas Volakis;* National Book Award nominations for fiction, 1965, for *Pericles on 31st Street,* and 1966, for *A Dream of Kings;* L.H.D., University of Illinois, 1971, Governor's State University, 1979, Hellenic College, 1984, and Roosevelt University, 1987; Carl Sandburg Award, Friends of the Chicago Public Library, 1983, for *Days of Vengeance.*

WRITINGS:

FICTION

Lion at My Heart, Atlantic-Little, Brown, 1959.
The Odyssey of Kostas Volakis, McKay, 1963.
Pericles on 31st Street (short stories), Quadrangle, 1965.
A Dream of Kings, McKay, 1966.
The Waves of Night and Other Stories, McKay, 1969.
In the Land of Morning, McKay, 1973.
The Hour of the Bell, Doubleday, 1976.
A Petrakis Reader (short stories), Doubleday, 1978.
Nick the Greek, Doubleday, 1979.
Days of Vengeance, Doubleday, 1983.
Collected Stories, Lake View Press, 1986.

OTHER

The Founder's Touch: The Life of Paul Galvin of Motorola, McGraw, 1965.
(Contributor) Elizabeth Janeway, editor, *The Writer's World,* McGraw, 1969.
Stelmark: A Family Recollection (autobiography), McKay, 1970.
Reflections: A Writer's Life, a Writer's Work, Lake View Press, 1984.

Also author of television and film adaptations of his short stories, including "Pericles on 31st Street," and "The Judge," 1961-62; author of scripts for film adaptations of *A Dream of Kings,* 1969, and *In the Land of Morning,* 1974; adaptor of teleplay for "The Blue Hotel," 1978. Contributor of short stories to *Atlantic, Harper's Bazaar, Saturday Evening Post,* and other publications. Contributor of articles and reviews to *New York Times, Chicago Tribune, Saturday Review,* and *Life.*

WORK IN PROGRESS: "A novel sequel to *A Dream of Kings* bringing the protagonist, Leonidas Matsoukas, back to America after five years in a Greek Junta prison," titled *Ghost of the Sun.*

SIDELIGHTS: Author of seven novels, several short story collections, and memoirs, Harry Mark Petrakis specializes in interpreting the immigrant experience in America. Basing his stories on recollections of people and events in Chicago's Greek community, Petrakis combines a classically tragic outlook on life with an unquenchable enthusiasm for what few pleasures the gods offer man in exchange for all his pain and suffering. While Petrakis is frequently classified as an "ethnic" or "provincial" writer and compared to *Zorba the Greek* author Nikos Kazantzakis, *West Coast Review of Books* writer Ira Festel asserts that "Petrakis' real subjects are the eternal problems with which the human race has been wrestling since antiquity: the inevitable process of aging, and the approaching confrontation with death; the universal need to love and to be loved . . . ; and above all, the need to make accommodation with an often meaningless life." Other reviewers, however, feel that Petrakis's writing is characterized by his ability to use local settings and characters to produce a larger meaning; "Like it or not," notes Robert Gish in Chicago *Tribune Books,* "Petrakis succeeds precisely because he is an ethnic and a regional writer who, like other masters of the tale, takes a culture, an ethnic heritage, a local setting and an ambiance, and projects them into the realm of the universal." The critic adds that "for Petrakis, a job, a courtship, a marriage, a family are simple but momentous things; just as making love, growing old, and dying demand the wiles, the courage, and the dauntless spirit of Odysseus."

Petrakis creates this type of modern Hellenic hero in *A Dream of Kings* through the character of Leonidas Matsoukas, a Greek-American immigrant intent on returning to his native land, where the healing sun may cure his dying son. By reading the novel and "meeting Matsoukas and sharing his experiences," Daniel Stern notes in the *Saturday Review,* one is reminded "that passion is not dead, humor is not dead, devotion is not dead. (Speaking, pardonably, for the moment as a novelist, it also demonstrates that the novel is not dead.)" Calling Matsoukas "a Homeric hero behind on his rent in a Chicago slum," *New York Times Book Review* contributor John Wakeman similarly observes a mythical aspect in *A Dream of Kings:* "Not for the first time, [Petrakis] asks us to believe that a man can be godlike, then reminds us that the most godlike man is only human. And he invites us to join him in celebrating this inextinguishable humanity." While the critic faults Petrakis for a "clumsy and overheated" style, he nevertheless suggests that the novel is "Mr. Petrakis' most ambitious affirmation of the humanistic credo he shares with his acknowledged master, the Cretan novelist Nikos Kazantzakis." Stern also observes that Matsoukas is "a sort of Zorba the Greek-American," adding that "here perhaps, is the only flaw. There is a touch of familiarity in it all. Petrakis has not chosen to travel a new path." Despite this, the critic concludes that Petrakis "proves that when you travel in your own style you can make the journey your own. *A Dream of Kings* is essentially a small book. But it is also in many ways a small wonder. Steeped in Hellenisms, full of the richness of a deeply experienced Greco-American life, it is a beautiful tale."

"The quality Petrakis has that makes him different from most other American novelists is his ability to give his stories an epic, mythic atmosphere, apparently without even trying, when he is writing about ordinary people in everyday situations," comments the *Washington Post*'s Joseph McLellan. "That quality distinguished 'A Dream of Kings,' which is probably his best-known work, and it can be felt also in 'Days of Vengeance.' " Set in the early nineteenth century, *Days of Vengeance* follows the quest of a young Cretan shepherd, Manolis, as he travels to America seeking to avenge the murder of his older brother; ranging from the immigrant neighborhoods of Chicago to railroad camps in the Far West, the novel is told through the voices of

the murderer and a priest, as well as Manolis's own. "In Mr. Petrakis's practiced hands, the troublesome technique of shifting viewpoints serves both to advance the novel's narrative and to enhance its suspense," remarks Johanna Kaplan in the *New York Times Book Review.* "But his vision of human nature is not an enlarging one, nor does it entertain complexity. Too often this constricting view of life results in a sameness of tone, so that the characters are not made distinctive but become mere agents of plot." *Los Angeles Times* book editor Art Seidenbaum similarly states that *Days of Vengeance* "is what we used to call 'slick fiction' because the narrative is smooth and individuals stay at the surface even if they work in mines."

McLellan, however, while conceding some faults, maintains that *Days of Vengeance* is superior to the average quest story: "This is not exactly one of the classics of our time, but it is a well-crafted novel that keeps the reader going eagerly from one page to the next and also conveys the sense that human life has important, unseen dimensions." And in a *Chicago Tribune Book World* review, Elie Wiesel echoes previous assessments of Petrakis's work, noting that *Days of Vengeance* "recalls the work of the distinguished Greek writer Nikos Kazantzakis. Crete and its impassioned beings. Thirst for freedom, the power of desire. The implacable law of certain family traditions, the inexorable advance and fulfillment of avenging fate. All these themes can be found in Petrakis' disturbing story, which is told with the talent we have come to expect of him." The critic concludes that "this magnificent novel," even though it is compared to the work of Kazantzakis, instead "reminds me of Petrakis, who is true to himself."

In addition to his short fiction and novels, Petrakis has published his memoirs of growing up in Chicago in *Stelmark: A Family Recollection. New York Times* reviewer Thomas Lask sees a similarity between this memoir and the author's other work: " 'Stelmark' is only a series of chapters out of the life of the author, but they are done with such discernment and convey so successfully the substance and meaning of each incident that these random jottings are transformed into a pungent and heartwarming autobiography. As in his novels and short stories, Petrakis combines down-to-earth, concrete particulars with the spiritual and emotional values they embody." While Peter Sourian criticizes Petrakis for simplifying his own emotions and reactions to his recollections, the critic notes in the *New York Times Book Review* that "each tale makes a relatively simple but nonetheless important moral point drawn from concrete experience and with an earnest emotional involvement which is sometimes a little humorless but most often really attractive." The critic adds that each of the episodes of *Stelmark* contains "a good deal of unobtrusively sophisticated craftsmanship." And *Saturday Review* contributor Naid Sofian concludes that Petrakis's memoir "is a wise and human book and superior to most others in its genre."

"A reader can always look forward with confidence to certain qualities in the work of Harry Mark Petrakis," asserts Lask in a review of *In the Land of Morning.* "The structure will be firm, the writing concrete, the details tangible, the approach to existence earthy, sensuous and ultimately tragic. His prose is fluent and supple, splendidly adapted to the needs of his fiction. And he is so sparing of his means that his books in retrospect appear to be longer and larger than they are." Part of Petrakis's success, suggests L. J. Davis in the *Washington Post Book World,* is that he tells his "old, old story . . . as though it has never been told before, as though he just this minute thought it up. He sometimes treats the English language this way, but no matter," continues the critic, remarking that "in everything Petrakis writes, there is freshness and charm, but there is something that has all but vanished in these surly times. It is the sheer delight he takes in his craft, the pleasure of the storytelling itself." "If one wishes to write, that is an individual journey with different discoveries for each person," Petrakis told Eugene Kennedy in a *Chicago Tribune Book World* interview. "If from these discoveries one can evoke revelations—little, not overwhelming—these are moments of prophecy. A reader will say, yes, this is a part of life, these people are real. If it makes them reflect on their life, then that is the work of the writer," the author added. "One must become aware of these essential . . . [elements] of life. So we can wish for others [and for ourselves] what Homer wished for his friends, the banquet, the song, and the harp, friendship, warm baths, sleep and love."

BIOGRAPHICAL/CRITICAL SOURCES:

BOOKS

Contemporary Literary Criticism, Volume 3, Gale, 1975.
Petrakis, Harry Mark, *Stelmark: A Family Recollection,* McKay, 1970.
Petrakis, Harry Mark, *Reflections: A Writer's Life, a Writer's Work,* Lake View Press, 1984.

PERIODICALS

Atlantic, August, 1959, December, 1966.
Chicago Tribune, February 8, 1987.
Chicago Tribune Book World, November 4, 1979, August 7, 1983, November 27, 1983.
Los Angeles Times, September 7, 1983.
New York Times, October 22, 1966, October 24, 1970, March 10, 1973, December 10, 1976.
New York Times Book Review, June 28, 1959, October 2, 1966, June 29, 1969, September 13, 1970, March 11, 1973, August 28, 1983.
Saturday Review, August 8, 1959, October 1, 1966, June 28, 1969, October 3, 1970.
Tribune Books (Chicago), January 4, 1987.
Washington Post, September 9, 1983.
Washington Post Book World, January 6, 1980.
West Coast Review of Books, May, 1978.

—*Sketch by Diane Telgen*

*   *   *

PETTIGREW, Thomas Fraser 1931-

PERSONAL: Born March 14, 1931, in Richmond, Va.; son of Joseph Crane (a mechanical engineer) and Janet (Gibb) Pettigrew; married Ann Hallman (a physician and public health specialist), February 25, 1956; children: Mark Fraser. *Education:* University of Virginia, A.B., 1952; Harvard University, M.A., 1955, Ph.D., 1956. *Politics:* "Ardent Democrat." *Religion:* Episcopalian.

ADDRESSES: Home—524 Van Ness Ave., Santa Cruz, Calif. 95060; and (April through August) Spinozastraat 21 II, 1018 HE Amsterdam, Netherlands. *Office*—Stevenson College, University of California, Santa Cruz, Calif. 95064; and (April through August) Psychologie Fakulteit, Universiteit van Amsterdam, Weesperplein 8, 1018 XA Amsterdam, Netherlands.

CAREER: University of North Carolina at Chapel Hill, assistant professor of psychology, 1956-57; Harvard University, Cambridge, Mass., assistant professor, 1957-62, lecturer, 1962-64, associate professor, 1964-68, professor of social psychology, 1968-80, professor of sociology, 1974-80; University of California, Santa Cruz, professor of social psychology, 1980—; University of Amsterdam, Netherlands, professor of social psychology, 1986—. Member, White House Task Force on Education, 1967; member of board, Race Relations Information Center, 1969-72. Chairman, Episcopal Presiding Bishop's Advisory Committee on Race Relations, 1961-63; member, Massachusetts Governor's Advisory Committee on Civil Rights, 1962-64; consultant to U.S. Office of Education, 1965-68, and U.S. Commission on Civil Rights, 1966-71; member of research advisory committee, Children's Television Workshop, 1970-74; consultant to Systems Development Corp., Educational Testing Service, and numerous public school systems.

MEMBER: European Association of Social Psychology, Society for the Psychological Study of Social Issues (president, 1967-68), American Psychological Association (fellow), American Sociological Association (council member, 1979-82), Society for the Study of Social Problems, Western Psychological Association, Pacific Sociological Association, Phi Beta Kappa.

AWARDS, HONORS: Guggenheim fellowship, 1967-68; National Science Foundation senior scientist fellowship, 1974; Center for Advanced Study in the Behavioral Sciences fellowship, 1975-76; Sydney Spivak Award for race relations research, American Sociological Association, 1978; Netherlands Institute for Advanced Study fellowship, 1984-85; Kurt Lewin Award in Social Psychology, Society for the Psychological Study of Social Issues, 1987; co-recipient of Gordon Allport Intergroup Research Award, Society for the Psychological Study of Social Issues, 1988; faculty research award, University of California, Santa Cruz, 1989.

WRITINGS:

(With E. Q. Campbell) *Christians in Racial Crisis: A Study of the Little Rock Ministry,* Public Affairs Press, 1959.
Negro American Intelligence, Anti-Defamation League of B'nai B'rith, c. 1964.
(Editor with Daniel C. Thompson) *Negro American Personality,* Society for the Psychological Study of Social Issues, 1964.
A Profile of the Negro American, Van Nostrand, 1964.
Epitaph for Jim Crow, Anti-Defamation League of B'nai B'rith, 1964.
(With H. E. Freeman, H. M. Hughes, R. Morris, and L. G. Watts) *The Middle-Income Negro Family Faces Urban Renewal,* Brandeis University, 1964.
Racially Separate or Together?, McGraw, 1971.
(Editor) *Racial Discrimination in the United States,* Harper, 1975.
(Editor) *Sociology of Race Relations: Reflections and Reform,* Free Press, 1980.
(With G. Fredrickson, D. Knobel, N. Glazer, and R. Veda) *Prejudice,* Harvard University Press, 1982.
(With D. Alston) *Tom Bradley's Campaigns for Governor,* Joint Center for Political Studies, 1988.

Contributor to periodicals. Member of editorial boards, *Journal of Social Issues,* 1959-64, *Integrated Education,* 1963-84, *Phylon,* 1965—, *Education and Urban Society,* 1968—, *Social Psychology Quarterly,* 1977-80, *Political Behavior,* 1978—, *Ethnic and Racial Studies,* 1978—, *Review of Personality and Social Psychology,* 1980-85, and *Social Behaviour,* 1989—.

WORK IN PROGRESS: New Patterns of Racism: Black-White Relations since the 1960s; a new edition of G. W. Allport's *The Nature of Prejudice.*

SIDELIGHTS: Thomas Fraser Pettigrew told *CA:* "I continue to study and write about race relations, because it remains one of our nation's most serious domestic problems, but now that I live half of each year in Europe, my analyses are becoming more comparative: What is unique to black-white problems in the U.S.? And what do they share with other intergroup problems in the world?"

*   *   *

PHIPPS, William E(ugene) 1930-

PERSONAL: Born January 28, 1930, in Waynesboro, Va.; son of Charles Henry (a clergyman) and Ruth (Patterson) Phipps; married Martha Ann Swezey, December 21, 1954; children: Charles, Anna, Ruth. *Education:* Davidson College, B.S., 1949; Union Theological Seminary, B.D., 1952; University of St. Andrews, Ph.D., 1954; University of Hawaii, M.A., 1963.

ADDRESSES: Home—Lincoln Ave., Elkins, W.Va. 26241. *Office*—Davis and Elkins College, Elkins, W.Va. 26241.

CAREER: Presbyterian clergyman. Peace College, Raleigh, N.C., professor of Bible, 1954-56; Davis and Elkins College, Elkins, W.Va., professor of religion and philosophy and chairman of department, 1956—. *Military service:* U.S. Army Reserve, 1955-63; became first lieutenant.

MEMBER: American Academy of Religion, American Association of University Professors, West Virginia Philosophical Society (president, 1968-69), Phi Alpha Theta, Rotary.

WRITINGS:

Was Jesus Married?: The Distortion of Sexuality in the Christian Tradition, Harper, 1970.
The Sexuality of Jesus: Theological and Literary Perspectives, Harper, 1973.
Recovering Biblical Sensuousness, Westminster, 1975.
Paul against Supernaturalism, Philosophical Library, 1987.
Death: Confronting the Reality, John Knox, 1987.
Cremation Concerns, C. C Thomas, 1989.
Genesis and Gender, Praeger, 1989.

Contributor to religion journals and to the *New York Times.*

WORK IN PROGRESS: A publication "that focuses on the humanity of Jesus."

SIDELIGHTS: William E. Phipps told *CA:* "I think that significant personal qualities are best revealed when someone expresses opinions about the opposite sex. Thus, I have used this index of character in searching scriptures and theological writings. In theory, most religious figures hold that inequity is iniquity, but few are fully conscious of the gender injustices that are embedded in the cultural patterns that they accept."

BIOGRAPHICAL/CRITICAL SOURCES:

PERIODICALS

Christian Century, November 25, 1970, March 3, 1971, April 28, 1971.

*   *   *

PIG, Edward
See GOREY, Edward (St. John)

*   *   *

POLKING, Kirk 1925-

PERSONAL: Born December 21, 1925, in Covington, Ky.; daughter of Henry (a salesman) and Mary (Hull) Polking. *Edu-*

cation: Studied in evening courses at American University, 1944, and periodically at University of Cincinnati and Xavier University, 1944—. *Politics:* Independent. *Religion:* Roman Catholic.

ADDRESSES: Home—529 Constitution Sq., Cincinnati, Ohio 45255. *Office*—F & W Publishing Co., 1507 Dava Ave., Cincinnati, Ohio 45207.

CAREER: U. S. War Department, Washington, D.C., administrative assistant, 1943-45; F & W Publishing Co., Cincinnati, Ohio, editorial assistant on *Modern Photography* and *Writer's Digest,* 1948-52, circulation manager of *Farm Quarterly,* 1952-57; free-lance writer, 1957-63; F & W Publishing Co., editor of *Writer's Digest,* 1963-73, editor of *Artist's Market,* 1973-75, director of Writer's Digest School, 1976—.

MEMBER: Author's Guild, National Federation of Press Women, National League of American Pen Women, Women in Communications.

AWARDS, HONORS: Headliner Award, Women in Communications, 1970.

WRITINGS:

Let's Go with Lewis and Clark, Putnam, 1963.
Let's Go with Henry Hudson, Putnam, 1964.
Let's Go See Congress at Work, Putnam, 1966.
Let's Go to an Atomic Energy Town, Putnam, 1968.
(Editor with others) *The Beginning Writer's Handbook,* Writer's Digest, 1968, revised edition published as *The Beginning Writer's Answer Book,* 4th revised edition, 1987.
(Editor) *How to Make Money in Your Spare Time by Writing,* Cornerstone Library, 1971.
The Private Pilot's Dictionary and Handbook, Arco, 1974, 2nd edition, 1986.
(Editor with Leonard Mergnus) *Law and the Writer,* Writer's Digest, 1978.
(Editor) *Freelance Jobs for Writers,* Writer's Digest, 1980.
Oceans of the World: Our Essential Resource, Putnam, 1983.
(Editor) *Beginner's Guide to Getting Published,* Writer's Digest, 1987.
(Editor) *The Writer's Friendly Legal Guide,* Writer's Digest, 1989.

Editor or co-editor, *The Writer's Market,* 1964-71.

WORK IN PROGRESS: New home study courses in writing; juvenile books.

AVOCATIONAL INTERESTS: Flying (obtained private pilot's license in 1968).

*   *   *

POLLARD, Jack 1926-

PERSONAL: Born July 31, 1926, in Sydney, New South Wales, Australia; son of John Hume (a tailor) and Grace (Griffiths) Pollard; married Barbara Anne Broadbent (a journalist), March 29, 1958; children: James, John, Katharine, Louise. *Education:* Attended school in Sydney, Australia. *Politics:* Liberal. *Religion:* Church of England.

ADDRESSES: Home and office—7 Selwyn St., Wollstonecraft, Sydney, New South Wales, Australia. *Agent*—Paul R. Reynolds, Inc., 12 East 41st St., New York, N.Y. 10017.

CAREER: Writer and editor of sports books, 1965—. *Sydney Daily Telegraph,* Sydney, Australia, member of staff, 1940-43; foreign correspondent for Australian newspapers, 1947-56; K.

G. Murray Ltd. (magazine chain), Sydney, executive editor, 1959-65; Pollard Publishing Co., Sydney, owner, 1969—. Adviser on outdoor and sporting books to several Australian publishers. *Military service:* Australian Army, 1943-46, mainly assigned to army newspapers; became sergeant.

MEMBER: Australian Jockey Club, New South Wales Cricketers' Club, Rugby Club (New South Wales).

AWARDS, HONORS: Bi-Centenary Award for best cricket book, English Cricket Society, 1983, for *Australian Cricket: The Game and the Players;* has earned several Australian Book Week commendations.

WRITINGS:

Meet the Kangaroos: Introducing the 1948/49 Australian Rugby Team, Hotspur Publishing, 1949.

Penny Arcade (novel), Muller, 1956.

(With Lew Hoad) *The Lew Hoad Story,* Prentice-Hall, 1958 (published in England as *My Game,* Hodder & Stoughton, 1958).

Advantage Receiver, Muller, 1960.

The Roughrider: The Story of Lance Skuthorpe, Lansdowne Press, 1962, published as *The Horse Tamer,* Pollard Publishing, 1970.

(With Rodney George Laver) *How to Play Winning Tennis,* Pelham Books, 1964, published as *How to Play Championship Tennis,* Macmillan, 1965.

(With John Williams Raper) *The Johnny Raper Rugby League Book,* K. G. Murray, 1965.

Keith Miller on Cricket (as told to Pollard), Pelham Books, 1965.

(With Bruce Devlin) *Play Like the Devil,* Angus & Robertson, 1967.

(With Don Talbot) *Swimming to Win,* Pelham, 1967, Hawthorne, 1969.

The Ampol Book of Sporting Records, Pollard Publishing, 1968, 2nd edition published as *Ampol's Australian Sporting Records,* 1969, 3rd edition published as *Ampol's Sporting Records,* 1971, 6th edition, 1981.

Jack Pollard's Australian Fishing, Angus & Robertson, 1969, revised edition, 1989.

Pictorial History of Australian Horse Racing, Paul Hamlyn, 1971.

Havesome Book of Nutty Records, Pollard Publishing, 1978.

Australian Cricket: The Game and the Players, edited by Ian Moir, Hodder & Stoughton (Sydney), 1982, revised and enlarged edition, 1989.

Pictorial History of Australian Cricket, Dent, 1983, 2nd revised and enlarged edition, 1989.

Australian Rugby Union: The Game and the Players, Angus & Robertson (Sydney), 1984.

The Formative Years of Australian Cricket, 1803-1893 (sports history; first volume in a series), Angus & Robertson, 1987.

The Turbulent Years of Australian Cricket, 1893-1917 (sports history; second volume in a series), Angus & Robertson, 1987.

Australian Horse Racing, Angus & Robertson, 1988.

The Bradman Years of Australian Cricket, 1918-1948 (sports history; third volume in a series), Angus & Robertson, 1988.

The Bradman to Packer Years, 1948-1988 (sports history; fourth volume in a series), Angus & Robertson, 1989.

The Highest, Most and Best of Australian Cricket, 1850-1989 (sports history; fifth volume in a series), Angus & Robertson, 1989.

EDITOR

Cricket—the Australian Way, N. Kaye, 1961, 10th edition, 1980.

Lawn Bowls—the Australian Way, Lansdowne Press, 1962.

Swimming—Australian Style, Lansdowne Press, 1963.

Lawn Tennis—the Australian Way, Lansdowne Press, 1963, 2nd edition, 1971.

The Australian Surfrider, K. G. Murray, 1963, revised edition published as *The Surfrider,* K. G. Murray, 1965, Taplinger, 1968.

High Mark: The Complete Book on Australian Football, K. G. Murray, 1964, 2nd edition, 1967.

Six and Out: The Legend of Australian Cricket, Lansdowne Press, 1964.

Birds of Paradox: Birdlife in Australia and New Zealand, Lansdowne Press, 1967.

How to Ride a Surfboard, Pollard Publishing, 1972.

After Stumps Were Drawn, Collins, 1985.

COMPILER

This is Rugby League, Lansdowne Press, 1962, 2nd edition published as *Rugby League—the Australian Way,* 1970.

Gregory's Australian Guide to Bowls, 2nd edition, Gregory Publishing (Sydney), 1963.

Gregory's Australian Fishing Guide, Gregory Publishing, 2nd edition, 1963, 4th edition, 1965.

Gregory's Australian Guide to Hunting and Shooting, Gregory Publishing, 1963.

Straight Shooting, K. G. Murray, 1963, 2nd revised edition, 1967.

Gregory's Australian Guide to Golf, 2nd edition, Gregory Publishing, 1964.

Gregory's Australian Guide to Camping and Caravans, Gregory Publishing, 1964.

Gregory's Guide to Rugby League, Gregory Publishing, 1965.

Horses and Horsemen: Wild Bush Horses, Thoroughbreds and the Men Who Rode Them, Lansdowne Press, 1966.

One for the Road: Stories of Racetrack, Trials, Pioneer, Veteran, Vintage and Outback Motoring in Australia and New Zealand, Angus & Robertson, 1966, Tri-Ocean, 1967.

The Scream of the Reel, Lansdowne Press, 1966.

Wild Dogs, Working Dogs, Pedigrees and Pets, Lansdowne Press, 1968.

OTHER

Contributor and editorial adviser to Australian editions of *World Book Encyclopedia.* Contributor to Australian magazines, including *Bulletin* and *Australian Cricketer;* contributor to various Australian city newspapers.

WORK IN PROGRESS: A golf pictorial book for Hodder & Stoughton.

SIDELIGHTS: Cricket is Jack Pollard's perennial love, although he is regarded as a world authority on lawn tennis, the origins of Australia's three football codes, soccer, Rugby, and Australian Rules; he has covered nine Wimbledons, five British Open gold championships, and numerous international rugby matches. His books have been published in England and New Zealand, as well as in Australia, and many are available in the United States through Sportshelf & Soccer Associates. Some of his books have been translated into Japanese, German, Dutch, and Italian.

BIOGRAPHICAL/CRITICAL SOURCES:

PERIODICALS

Times Literary Supplement, August 12, 1965, January 13, 1984, November 16, 1984.

*   *   *

POLOMA, Margaret Mary 1943-

PERSONAL: Born August 27, 1943, in Los Angeles, Calif.; daughter of Steven (a machinist) and Helen (Matyas) Poloma. *Education:* Notre Dame College of Ohio, B.A., 1965; Case Western Reserve University, M.A., 1966, Ph.D., 1970. *Religion:* Roman Catholic.

ADDRESSES: Home—2872 Silver Lake Blvd., Silver Lake, Ohio 44224. *Office*—Department of Sociology, University of Akron, Akron, Ohio 44325-1905.

CAREER: Cleveland State University, Cleveland, Ohio, instructor in sociology, 1969-70; University of Akron, Akron, Ohio, assistant professor, 1970-77, associate professor, 1977-81, professor of sociology, 1981—.

MEMBER: American Sociological Association, Society for the Scientific Study of Religion (secretary, 1986-89), Association for Sociology of Religion (member of executive committee, 1980-83), Religious Research Association (director at large, 1986-88).

WRITINGS:

Contemporary Sociological Theory, Macmillan, 1979.
The Charismatic Movement: Is There a New Pentecost?, Twayne, 1982.
(With Charles De Santo) *Social Problems: Christian Perspective,* Hunter Textbooks, 1985.
The Assemblies of God at the Crossroads: Charisma and Institutional Dilemmas, University of Tennessee Press, 1989.

Co-editor of *Sociological Focus,* 1975-80; editor of *Christian Sociologists Newsletter,* 1977-86.

WORK IN PROGRESS: With Brian F. Pendleton, *Religiosity and Well-Being: Exploring Neglected Dimensions of Quality of Life Research;* research on divine healing as an alternative to traditional medical practices.

SIDELIGHTS: Margaret Mary Poloma informed *CA:* "Undoubtedly the experience that has most colored my recent professional involvements and writings is my 1975 conversion, during which I accepted Jesus Christ as my Savior and Lord. Not unlike the scientists of seventeenth-century England, whose writings were analyzed by sociologist Robert Merton, I desire that my career as a social scientist primarily gives glory to God. It is through prayer that I seek to determine the research and writing path of God's design and prayer that strengthens me to carry out my work.

"My own religious experiences have led me to work with other sociologists who are seeking to develop a Christian perspective in sociology. Much like the humanist, feminist, or black perspectives that are already part of the sociological enterprise, the Christian perspective attempts to alert the discipline to biases in it. Sociology's atheistic roots, although often blanketed with 'value-free' assertions, have prevented it from understanding certain aspects of human behavior that have failed to align with its values."

PORTER, Darwin (Fred) 1937-

PERSONAL: Born September 13, 1937, in Greensboro, N.C.; son of Numie Rowan (a builder) and Hazel Lee (an artist; maiden name, Phillips) Porter. *Education:* University of Miami, Coral Gables, Fla., B.A., 1959. *Politics:* Independent.

ADDRESSES: Home—75 St. Marks Pl., Staten Island, N.Y. 10301. *Office*—Prentice Hall Press, One Gulf & Western Plaza, New York, N.Y. 10023.

CAREER: Miami Herald, Miami, Fla., bureau chief, 1959-60; Haggart Associates, New York City, vice president, 1961-64; Arthur Frommer, Inc. (publishers), New York City, editor, 1964-67; Frommer-Pasmantier Publishing Corp., New York City, editor, 1967-80; Prentice-Hall Press, New York City, editor, 1980—.

MEMBER: Society of American Travel Writers, Smithsonian Association, Sigma Delta Chi.

AWARDS, HONORS: International Film and Television Festival of New York Silver Award, 1977, for "Chemical Transfer."

WRITINGS:

Butterflies in Heat (novel; also see below), Manor, 1976.
Marika, Arbor House, 1977.
"Chemical Transfer" (industrial film screenplay), Tim David Marketing Services, Inc., 1977.
"Butterflies in Heat" (screenplay; based on his novel), Jerry B. Wheeler Productions, 1979.
Venus: A Novel Suggested by the Life of Anais Nin, Arbor House, 1982.
Sister Rose (novel), Antelope, 1983.

EDITOR OF TRAVEL GUIDES

(With Stanley Mills Haggart) *England on $5 a Day,* A. Frommer, 1964, revised editions published as *England on $5 and $10 a Day,* 1966, *England on $10 a Day,* 1973, *England on $10 and $15 a Day,* 1975, *England on $15 a Day,* 1977, *England and Scotland on $20 a Day,* Frommer-Pasmantier, 1980, (as sole editor) *England and Scotland on $25 a Day,* 1982, *England on $35 a Day,* 1986, *England on $40 a Day,* Prentice-Hall, 1988, and *England on $50 a Day,* 1990.
(With Haggart) *Spain on $5 a Day,* A. Frommer, 1966, revised editions published as *Spain on $5 and $10 a Day,* 1971, *Spain and Morocco on $5 and $10 a Day,* 1973, *Spain and Morocco on $10 a Day,* 1975, *Spain and Morocco on $10 and $15 a Day,* 1977, Frommer-Pasmantier, 1979, *Spain and Morocco Plus the Canary Islands on $20 a Day,* 1981, (as sole editor) *Spain and Morocco Plus the Canary Islands on $25 a Day,* 1983, *Spain and Morocco Plus the Canary Islands on $35 a Day,* 1985, *Spain and Morocco on $40 a Day,* Prentice-Hall, 1987, new edition, 1989.
(With Haggart) *Scandinavia on $5 and $10 a Day,* A. Frommer, 1967, revised editions published as *Scandinavia on $10 a Day,* 1971, *Scandinavia on $15 a Day,* 1975, *Scandinavia on $15 and $20 a Day,* 1977, *Scandinavia on $20 a Day,* 1979, *Scandinavia on $25 a Day,* Frommer-Pasmantier, 1981, (as sole editor) *Scandinavia on $35 a Day,* 1985, *Frommer's Scandinavia on $50 a Day,* Prentice-Hall, 1987, and *Frommer's Scandinavia on $60 a Day,* 1989.
(With Haggart) *Arthur Frommer's Dollarwise Guide to Italy,* Frommer-Pasmantier, 1969, revised editions published as *Frommer's Dollarwise Guide to Italy,* 1981, and (as sole editor) *Frommer's Dollarwise Italy,* Prentice-Hall, 1989, new edition, 1990.

TWA's Budget Guide to Los Angeles, Trans World Airlines, 1969, revised editions published as *Getaway Guide to Los Angeles,* Frommer-Pasmantier, 1971, and (with Haggart and Rena Bulkin) *Arthur Frommer's Guide to Los Angeles,* 1977, new edition, 1979.

(With Haggart) *Arthur Frommer's Dollarwise Guide to England,* Frommer-Pasmantier, 1969, revised editions published as *Arthur Frommer's Dollarwise Guide to England and Scotland,* 1979, (as sole editor) *Frommer's Dollarwise Guide to England and Scotland,* Prentice-Hall, 1987, and *Frommer's Dollarwise England and Scotland,* 1989, new edition, 1990.

(With Haggart) *Arthur Frommer's Dollarwise Guide to Portugal,* Frommer-Pasmantier, 1970, revised editions published as *Arthur Frommer's Dollarwise Guide to Portugal, Madeira, and the Azores,* 1980, (as sole editor) Frommer's Dollarwise Portugal, Madeira, and the Azores, Prentice-Hall, 1990.

Getaway Guide to London, Frommer-Pasmantier, 1970.

(With Haggart) *TWA's Budget Guide to Madrid* (also see below), Frommer-Pasmantier, 1970.

(With Haggart) *TWA's Budget Guide to Lisbon* (also see below), Frommer-Pasmantier, 1970.

(With Haggart) *Arthur Frommer's Dollarwise Guide to France,* Frommer-Pasmantier, 1971, revised editions (as sole editor) published as *Frommer's Dollarwise Guide to France,* 1983, and *Frommer's Dollarwise France,* Prentice-Hall, 1989.

(With Haggart) *Getaway Guide to Lisbon/Madrid* (includes revised editions of *TWA's Budget Guide to Lisbon* and *TWA's Budget Guide to Madrid*), Frommer-Pasmantier, 1971, revised editions published as *Getaway Guide to Lisbon-Madrid-Malaga,* 1974, *Trans World Getaway Guide to Lisbon/Madrid/Costa del Sol,* 1975, *Arthur Frommer's Guide to Lisbon/Madrid/Costa del Sol,* 1977, and *Frommer's Guide to Lisbon, Madrid, and the Costa del Sol,* 1981, new edition, (as sole editor) Prentice-Hall, 1989.

(With John Godwin) *Getaway Guide to Paris,* Frommer-Pasmantier, 1971, revised editions (with Haggart) published as *Arthur Frommer's Guide to Paris,* 1977, and *Frommer's Guide to Paris,* 1981, new edition (as sole editor), Prentice-Hall, 1989.

(With Haggart) *Arthur Frommer's Dollarwise Guide to Germany,* Frommer-Pasmantier, 1972, revised editions (as sole editor) published as *Frommer's Dollarwise Guide to Germany,* 1982, and *Frommer's Dollarwise Germany,* Prentice-Hall, 1990.

(With Haggart) *Transworld Getaway Guide to Rome,* Frommer-Pasmantier, 1975, revised editions published as *Arthur Frommer's Guide to Rome,* 1977, and *Frommer's Guide to Rome,* 1981, new edition (as sole editor), Prentice-Hall, 1989.

(With Haggart and Godwin) *Arthur Frommer's Guide to London,* Frommer-Pasmantier, 1977, revised edition (with Haggart) published as *Frommer's Guide to London,* 1981, new edition (as sole editor), Prentice-Hall, 1989.

(With Haggart) *Arthur Frommer's Dollarwise Guide to the Caribbean, Including Bermuda and The Bahamas,* Frommer-Pasmantier, 1980, revised editions (as sole editor) published as *Frommer's Dollarwise Guide to the Caribbean,* 1986, and *Frommer's Dollarwise Caribbean,* Prentice-Hall, 1990.

(With Haggart) *The Caribbean Bargain Book,* Frommer-Pasmantier, 1980.

Frommer's Dollarwise Guide to Switzerland and Liechtenstein, Frommer-Pasmantier, 1984, revised edition published as *Frommer's Dollarwise Switzerland and Liechtenstein,* Prentice-Hall, 1990.

Frommer's Dollarwise Guide to Austria and Hungary, Frommer-Pasmantier, 1985, revised edition published as *Frommer's Dollarwise Austria and Hungary,* Prentice-Hall, 1989.

Frommer's Dollarwise Guide to Bermuda and The Bahamas, Frommer-Pasmantier, 1986, revised edition published as *Frommer's Dollarwise Bermuda and The Bahamas,* Prentice-Hall, 1990.

Frommer's Scotland and Wales on $35 a Day, Frommer-Pasmantier, 1986, revised editions published as *Frommer's Scotland and Wales on $40 a Day,* Prentice-Hall, 1988, and *Frommer's Scotland and Wales on $50 a Day,* 1990.

OTHER

Also author of screenplay, "The Last Resort." Editor, *Travel Bulletin,* 1983-85.

SIDELIGHTS: Darwin Porter told *CA* that he lives in a "historic, twenty-room and seven-gabled house with verandas" on a street where Theodore Dreiser once lived and Henry James used to vacation. He writes that his "globetrotting goal is to set a world record: to write about 311 island groups or countries, from the North Pole to Ogasawara-gunto in the Bonin Islands off Japan." Several of Porter's travel guides have been translated into French, Italian, and Spanish.

As a journalist, Porter's notable assignments have included coverage of Cuban guerilla training camps in 1960 and interviews with such subjects as Eleanor Roosevelt, Robert Frost, Tennessee Williams, Harry S. Truman, Richard Nixon, Sophie Tucker, Adlai Stevenson, and Lucille Ball.

*   *   *

POSEY, Carl A(lfred, Jr.) 1933-

PERSONAL: Born September 13, 1933, in Ancon, Canal Zone, Panama; American citizen born abroad; came to U.S. annually before 1951; son of Carl A. Posey (a civil engineer) and Margaret Elizabeth Posey Dalton (a statistician; maiden name, Stapleton); married Catherine Elizabeth Ann Wadia; children: Megan, Robin, Carl A. III, Honor. *Education:* Texas A & M University, A.B., 1962. *Religion:* None.

ADDRESSES: Home and office—P.O. Box 19894, Alexandria, Va. 22320. *Agent*—Jack Stewart, 133 West 17th St., New York, N.Y. 10011.

CAREER: Houston Chronicle, Houston, Texas, artist and copywriter, 1955-56; Douglas Aircraft Co., Long Beach, Calif., technical writer, 1956-58; John I. Thompson Co., Washington, D.C., technical writer, 1958-60; General Dynamics/Astronautics, San Diego, Calif., engineering writer, 1962-63, publications editor, 1963; U.S. Coast and Geodetic Survey, Washington, D.C., writer and editor, 1963-66; National Oceanic and Atmospheric Administration, Washington, D.C., public affairs officer in Washington, 1966-71, and in Boulder, Colo., 1971-81; International Institute for Applied Systems Analysis, Laxenburg, Austria, head of communications, 1981-82; free-lance writer, 1983; National Optical Astronomy Observatories, Tuscon, Ariz., director of public information, 1984-87; Time-Life Books, Alexandria, Va., text editor, 1988—. *Military service:* U.S. Army, 1952-54.

MEMBER: Authors Guild, Authors League of America.

AWARDS, HONORS: Silver medal from U.S. Department of Commerce, 1976; National Magazine Award, 1986, for "The Inspectors," published in *Science 85.*

WRITINGS:

Kiev Footprint (suspense novel), Dodd, Hale, 1983.

Prospero Drill (suspense novel), Hale, 1984, St. Martin's, 1986.
Dead Issue (suspense novel), Hale, 1985, published as *Red Danube*, St. Martin's, 1986.
Benchley's Chip (suspense novel), Hale, 1989.

WORK IN PROGRESS: The Senator's Will, a suspense novel; various articles and short stories.

SIDELIGHTS: Carl A. Posey commented: "After a long career illuminating science and technology for the interested general public, I find myself writing fiction in which science plays an important role—not science fiction, but fiction with a large helping of science in it. And, as a private pilot, I add a lot of aviation to these tales.

"For example, *Kiev Footprint* is in many respects a standard chase novel, but one in which science plays a major part. The conspiracies in the novel involve clandestine uses of the space shuttle, space weaponry of the type proposed in President Reagan's 'star wars' speech, and such timely events as cosmonauts with docking and reentry problems. *Prospero Drill* is about a hurricane-modification experiment gone sour, in which a scientist, obsessed with carrying out the seeding experiment he has worked for so long to develop, goes against his agency and his government to do it—all the while being manipulated by larger powers who understand and use his obsession.

"*Dead Issue* (*Red Danube* in the U.S.), set in Vienna and other European places, looks at the kind of science one finds in international think tanks where East and West mingle and cooperate in an odd mix of deep seriousness and frivolity. The novel explores the dark side of such institutions, in which computers probe computers, information is passed eastward, and no one is quite what he seems. It also examines the relationship of superpowers, of 'the incurably violent with the incurably paranoid,' as one character puts it.

"*Benchley's Chip,* as the title implies, touches on microchip technology, which provides the motive for a violent story involving children and tough men and women on both sides. It is set mostly in Bulgaria and Vienna and in one of its subplots, extends the action of *Dead Issue. The Senator's Will* is about grand families, powerful men, astronomy, copper, drugs, and ideologies, and set in the American southeast and Chile."

AVOCATIONAL INTERESTS: Flying (has private pilot's license).

*   *   *

POTTER, Faith
See TOPEROFF, Sam

*   *   *

POTTER, (Ronald) Jeremy 1922-

PERSONAL: Born April 25, 1922, in London, England; son of Alistair Richardson and Mairi Chalmers (Dick) Potter; married Margaret Newman (a novelist, under name Margaret Potter and pseudonyms Anne Betteridge and Anne Melville), 1950; children: Jocelyn, Jonathan. *Education:* Queen's College, Oxford University, M.A., 1953.

ADDRESSES: Home—The Old Pottery, Larkins Lane, Headington, Oxford OX3 9DW, England.

CAREER: New Statesman, 1951-69, began as manager, became deputy chairman; Independent Television Publications Ltd.,

managing director, 1970-79, chairman, Independent Television Books, 1971-79; Hutchinson Ltd., director, 1978-84, deputy chairman, 1981-82, chairman, 1982-84; writer and publisher. Director, London Weekend Television Ltd., 1979—, Page & Moy PLC, 1979-89, and Constable & Co., 1980—. Appeals chairman, Newsvendors' Benevolent Institution, 1979. Captain, Hampstead Hockey Club, 1954-57; World Amateur over 60s Champion, Real tennis, 1986-88. *Military service:* Indian Army, intelligence officer.

MEMBER: Royal Society of Authors (fellow), Richard III Society (chairman, 1971—), Periodical Publishers Association (president, 1978-79), Twickenham Arts Council (chairman, 1967-68); Garrick Club, MCC Club, Puritans Hockey Club.

WRITINGS:

(Translator with Kennedy McWhirter) Hans Becker (a pseudonym), *Devil on My Shoulder,* Jarrods, 1955.
Hazard Chase (novel), Constable, 1964, reprinted, 1989.
Death in the Office (novel), Constable, 1965.
Foul Play (novel), Constable, 1967.
The Dance of Death (novel), Constable, 1968, Walker & Co., 1969.
A Trail of Blood (novel), Constable, 1970, McCall Publishing, 1971.
Going West (novel), Constable, 1972.
Disgrace and Favour: A Novel of Tudor and Stuart Times, Constable, 1975.
Death in the Forest (novel), Constable, 1977.
Good King Richard? An Account of Richard III and His Reputation, 1483-1983, Constable, 1983.
Pretenders, Constable, 1986, published as *Pretenders to the English Throne,* Barnes & Noble, 1987.
Independent Television in Britain, Volume 3: *Politics and Control, 1968-80,* Macmillan, 1989.

AVOCATIONAL INTERESTS: Reading, writing, Real tennis.

*   *   *

POURNELLE, Jerry (Eugene) 1933-
(Wade Curtis)

PERSONAL: Born August 7, 1933, in Shreveport, La.; son of P. Eugene (a radio station owner) and R. Ruth (Lewis) Pournelle; married Roberta Jane Isdell (a reading specialist), July 18, 1959; children: Alexander, Francis Russell, Phillip, Richard Stefan. *Education:* Attended University of Iowa, 1953-54; University of Washington, B.S., 1955, M.S., 1957, Ph.D. (psychology), 1960, Ph.D. (political science), 1964. *Politics:* Republican. *Religion:* "Anglo-Catholic."

ADDRESSES: Home—3960 Laurel Canyon Blvd., Suite 372, Studio City, Calif. 91604. *Agent*—Eleanor Wood, Spectrum Agency, 432 Park Ave. S., Suite 1205, New York, N.Y. 10016.

CAREER: University of Washington Medical School, Seattle, research assistant, 1954-57; Boeing Corp., Seattle, aviation psychologist and systems engineer, 1957-64; Aerospace Corp., San Bernadino, Calif., manager of special studies, 1964-65; systems scientist, North American Aviation, 1964-65; research specialist and proposal manager, American Rockwell Corp., 1965-66; Pepperdine University, Los Angeles, Calif., professor of history and political science, 1966-69; executive assistant to mayor of Los Angeles and director of research, Los Angeles, 1969-70; freelance writer, lecturer, and consultant, 1969—. Member of Republican Board of Governors, San Bernardino Co., 1960-64;

chairman of board, Seattle Civic Playhouse, 1962-63; member of board of directors, Ocean Living Institute. Adviser to numerous futurist and space-oriented organizations. *Military service:* U.S. Army, 1950-52.

MEMBER: Science Fiction Writers of America (president, 1973-74), Mystery Writers of America, American Institute of Aeronautics and Astronautics, Operations Research Society of America (fellow), American Association for the Advancement of Science (fellow), American Academy of Arts and Sciences (fellow), American Rocket Society, Institute for Strategic Studies, American Security Council, University Professors for Academic Order (director, 1971), Society for Creative Anachronism, Military and Hospitaler Order of St. Lazarus of Jerusalem (officer).

AWARDS, HONORS: Bronze Medal from American Security Council, 1967; Republic of Estonia Award of Honor, 1968; John W. Campbell Award for Best New Writer of 1972, World Science Fiction Convention, 1973; Evans-Freehafer Award, 1977; Nebula Award nomination (with Larry Niven), Science Fiction Writers of America, 1977, for *Inferno;* Hugo nomination (with Niven), World Science Fiction Convention, 1978, for *Lucifer's Hammer;* American Book Award nomination, science fiction hardcover, 1980, for *Janissaries.*

WRITINGS:

SCIENCE FICTION

A Spaceship for the King, DAW, 1972, revised and expanded version published as *King David's Spaceship,* Pocket Books, 1980.
Escape from the Planet of the Apes (novelization of screenplay), Award, 1974.
(With Larry Niven) *The Mote in God's Eye,* Simon & Schuster, 1974.
Birth of Fire, Laser (Toronto), 1976, Pocket Books, 1978.
(With Niven) *Inferno,* Pocket Books, 1976.
West of Honor, Laser, 1976, Pocket Books, 1978.
The Mercenary, Pocket Books, 1977.
(With Niven) *Lucifer's Hammer,* Playboy Press, 1977.
High Justice (short stories), Pocket Books, 1977.
Exiles to Glory, Ace Books, 1978.
Janissaries, Ace Books, 1979.
(With Niven) *Oath of Fealty,* Phantasia Press, 1981.
(With Roland Green) *Janissaries: Clan and Crown,* Ace Books, 1982.
(With Niven) *Footfall,* Ballantine, 1985.
(With Green) *Janissaries III: Storms of Victory,* Ace Books, 1987.
(With Niven and Steven Barnes) *The Legacy of Heorot,* Simon & Schuster, 1987.
Mercenary Prince, Baen, 1989.

EDITOR

20/20 Vision, Avon, 1974.
(And contributor) *Black Holes,* Fawcett, 1979.
(With John F. Carr, and contributor) *The Endless Frontier,* Ace Books, 1979.
(With Carr) *The Survival of Freedom,* Fawcett, 1981.
(With Carr) *The Endless Frontier 2,* Ace Books, 1981.
(With Carr) *Nebula Award Stories 16,* Holt, 1982.
(With Carr, and contributor) *There Will Be War,* Tor Books, 1983.
(With Carr, and contributor) *There Will Be War: Men of War, Volume II,* Tor Books, 1984.

(With Carr) *There Will Be War: Blood and Iron, Volume III,* Tor Books, 1985.
(With Carr) *Imperial Stars: Stars at War,* Baen, 1985.
(With Carr) *Silicon Brains,* Ballantine, 1985.
(With Carr) *Science Fiction Yearbook 1984,* Baen, 1985.
(With Carr) *There Will Be War: Day of the Tyrant, Volume IV,* Tor Books, 1985.
(With Jim Baen and Carr) *Far Frontiers 1-7,* Baen, 7 volumes, 1985-86.
(With Carr) *There Will Be War: Warrior!, Volume V,* Tor Books, 1986.
(With Carr) *Republic and Empire: Imperial Stars, Volume II,* Baen, 1987.
(With Carr) *There Will Be War: Guns of Darkness, Volume VI,* Tor Books, 1987.
(With Carr) *Warworld, Volume I: The Burning Eye,* Baen, 1988.
(With Carr) *There Will Be War: Call to Battle, Volume VII,* Tor Books, 1988.
(With Carr) *There Will Be War: Armageddon, Volume VIII,* Tor Books, 1989.

NONFICTION

(With Stefan T. Possony) *The Strategy of Technology: Winning the Decisive War,* Dunellen, 1970.
(Contributor) Reginald Bretnor, editor, *The Craft of Science Fiction,* Harper, 1976.
That Buck Rogers Stuff, edited by Gavin Claypool, Extequer, 1977.
(With R. Gagliardi) *The Mathematics of the Energy Crisis,* Intergalactic Publishing, 1978.
A Step farther Out (essays), W. H. Allen, 1980, Ace Books, 1983.
(With Dean Ing) *Mutual Assured Survival: A Space-Age Solution to Nuclear Annihilation,* Baen, 1984.
The User's Guide to Small Computers, Baen, 1985.
Adventures in Microland, Baen, 1985.

OTHER

(Under pseudonym Wade Curtis) *Red Heroin* (novel), Berkley Publishing, 1969, reprinted under name Jerry Pournelle, Ace Books, 1985.
(Under pseudonym Wade Curtis) *Red Dragon* (novel), Berkley Publishing, 1971, reprinted under name Jerry Pournelle, Ace Books, 1985.

Also author of *Human Temperature Tolerance in Astronautic Environments,* 1959, *Stability and National Security,* 1968, *Congress Debates Viet Nam,* 1971, and *The Right to Read,* 1971. Contributor of non-fiction articles to *Analog, Galaxy, Info World,* and *American Legion.* Author of column "Notes from Chaos Manor," *Byte;* science columnist, *Galaxy Science Fiction Magazine;* computer columnist, *Popular Computing.*

SIDELIGHTS: "Of all the SF writers running around loose, Jerry Pournelle may just be the best qualified, on paper, to deal with all the intellectual demands that science fiction can make on a writer," asserts Bud Foote in the *Detroit News.* The critic elaborates: "[Pournelle] holds undergraduate degrees in history and engineering, doctorates in psychology and political science. And in spite of all that education, he can write." In addition, Pournelle worked in the space industry during its heyday in the early 1960s, spending two years as chief of the Experimental Stress Program of Boeing's Human Factor Laboratories. Consequently, when the market for space research dropped in the late 1960s, "it was a natural move to make" to become a science fiction writer, as the author told Jeffrey M. Elliot in *Science Fiction Voices Number Three: Interviews with Science Fiction Writers.*

Pournelle added that "in fact, I used to tell Robert Heinlein and Poul Anderson, both of whom I've known for over twenty years, that I did the same work they did, except I didn't have to create characters to go with it. It wasn't really a big jump from that to writing science fiction, especially since I had done considerable research on alternative futures and technologies."

Charles Platt believes that Pournelle's work reflects his diverse background; in *Dream Makers Volume II: The Uncommon Men and Women Who Write Science Fiction,* Platt characterizes Pournelle's fiction as demonstrating "beyond debate the benefits that technology can bring. He argues from a broader historical perspective than most of us maintain. And he is, in the end, an idealist," continues the critic. "He seems to feel no equivocation; there is right, and there is wrong, and you defend your principles with all the physical and mental resources that you possess." One work which exemplifies his emphasis on the advantages of science is *King David's Spaceship,* which follows the attempts of a planet to regain technological proficiency and thus qualify to join a rejuvenated galactic empire. Situated in Pournelle's "future history," an elaborate framework of events covering over one thousand years, *King David's Spaceship* also presents the problems facing the Imperial Navy, which is unsure how to manage the situation. Calling the work similar to "the old-fashioned science fiction of 30 years ago," *Washington Post Book World* contributors Alexei and Cory Panshin believe that "this novel is a romp, a technological fairy tale, but it can't be taken seriously for a moment. Even to partake of its exuberance, you must close your eyes, promise not to think, and turn the clock back." While Foote also compares the novel to the conventional science fiction of years past, he believes that Pournelle improves on the genre: "Like all of Pournelle's soldier books, [*King David's Spaceship*] is the polished-up, historically-savvy, intellectually reputable great-grandson of space opera, and it has a lot of the charm of space opera without the lousy writing, bogus history, and knee-jerk anthropocentrism of the bad-old good-old days."

Although he has enjoyed success writing solo, it is Pournelle's collaborations with Larry Niven which have brought him the most recognition; as Niven remarked to Platt, "I would say that we're the most successful collaboration in science-fiction history." The team began with *The Mote in God's Eye,* a novel situated in Pournelle's future history, and later novels established the duo as a crossover phenomenon on the bestseller charts; *Lucifer's Hammer,* for example, has over three million copies in print. Relating the aftermath of a comet striking the earth, *Lucifer's Hammer* "is one of the most ambitious disaster novels to date," writes Richard Freeman in the *New York Times Book Review.* "For all its portentous length, the narrative pace seldom flags, and the stick-figure characters are sufficiently animated." Another collaboration, *Oath of Fealty,* presents a similarly epic tale, relating the efforts of Todos Santos, a completely self-contained and self-sustaining city, to beat back the attempts of terrorists and jealous outsiders to destroy it. "To keep the pages turning, [the] cardboard characters are involved in a pitched battle with environmentalists, a jailbreak, a kidnaping, confrontations with petty crooks and Los Angeles politicians, and sexual encounters," describes David N. Samuelson in the *Los Angeles Times,* adding that "this melodrama punctuates the conflict between old and new life styles." While he also faults *Oath of Fealty* for being somewhat one-dimensional, *Science Fiction and Fantasy Book Review* contributor Lawrence I. Charters believes that the novel differs from most escapist science fiction: "Readers interested in nice, safe non-controversial escapism may be troubled by *Oath of Fealty.* Most SF dealing with explosive political or social issues is placed in the far future." Charters explains that

"*Oath* does not provide this soothing distance; try as you might, the world about you and the world you are reading about seem uncomfortably close." The critic concludes that "*Oath of Fealty* is, without question, a book worth reading, and arguing about."

Typical of Pournelle and Niven's other collaborations, *Footfall* "is a structural hybrid that shouldn't work but does," observes Gerald Jonas of the *New York Times Book Review.* "On the one hand, it is a big, fat 'crossover' novel clearly aimed at an audience more familiar with the formulas of mass-market fiction. . . . On the other hand, its science fiction elements are handled with a skill found only in the best of the genre." The account of an alien invasion of earth by elephant-like "Snouts," *Footfall* presents a detailed and complex view of an alien race and their society. Noting that the authors "are the cutting edge in a revival of the exuberant space-opera adventure," *Chicago Tribune Book World* contributors James Park Sloan and Eugene Sloan observe that Pournelle "is the master of plot and adventure, while Niven . . . provides the leavening of hard science. 'Footfall' holds the two in delicate balance." In detailing the structure of the alien "herd," the novel "also sees humankind afresh through the lens of alien eyes," note the critics; because "many scenes are laid within the alien viewpoint," *Magazine of Fantasy and Science Fiction* critic Algis Budrys similarly finds *Footfall* "fascinating because we see many ramifications of the basic proposition." Tim Sullivan, however, echoes criticisms of other Pournelle-Niven epics, commenting in the *Washington Post Book World* that the novel "is at least twice as long as it ought to be, and it is extremely heavy-handed." But *Science Fiction Review*'s Richard E. Geis, calling the work "extraordinarily powerful" and "gut tensing, emotional bedrock stuff" asserts that *Footfall* is "impossible to put down." The critic adds that the book "*is* probably the finest novel of alien invasion ever written." " 'Footfall' is a whopper of escapist adventure," conclude the Sloans. "[It is] a story that will delight both Trufans and members of the Mundane herd who don't normally read science fiction."

Pournelle and Niven join with another science fiction writer, Steven Barnes, for *The Legacy of Heorot,* an intricate reworking of the Beowulf legend. Although *Los Angeles Times Book Review* contributor Mary Dryden believes that "the idea of reworking the Beowulf legend on a science fiction theme appears specious, if not ludicrous," she asserts that *The Legacy of Heorot* "undertakes that presumptuous exercise not only without disappointment but with substantial success." Set on Tau Ceti Four, a colony planet of seemingly simple ecology and few dangers, the novel follows the attempts of the settlers to deal with the sudden appearance of a dangerous and lethal predator, which they call a "Grendel." "Typically, science fiction monsters are crudely imagined, about on the level of King Kong or Godzilla," states Phyllis Magida in the Chicago *Tribune Books.* In contrast, notes the critic, *The Legacy of Heorot*'s "Grendels are far more sophisticated," with complex body mechanisms that allow for rapid attack and escape. The novel is more than a story of resisting invasion, however; after the settlers seem to have beaten back these monsters, their problems are complicated by the discovery that the destruction of the Grendels is disturbing the planet's ecology and further endangering the settlement's status.

Despite this complex setting and situation, notes Magida, "the action develops in one smooth, fast line and culminates in a long, relentless battle—violent, but so well imagined that it comes alive in the mind's eye." And Dryden praises the authors for the intricacy and success of their literary parallel: " 'The Legacy of Heorot' is riddled with science fiction jargon, yet opens each chapter with quotations from classical literature and philosophy. . . . At every turn of the plot, there are point and counterpoint. The authors have taken great pains to produce a convincing story analogous to the legend of Beowulf in its symbolic representation of good and evil, the familiar and the unknown." In addition, the struggle of *Heorot*'s colonists to overcome the dangers of their planet while preserving its ecology mirrors the themes that Pournelle presents throughout his work. As the author told Elliot, "My work reflects my own view of the world, particularly my view of science and technology. As I see it, not all technology is good, but it's certainly not all bad. It affords you a host of choices." Pournelle further characterized this theme: " 'While science gives you choices, those choices represent both good and bad.' In many of my stories, though, the wrong choice is made, which is the way things work in real life."

When asked why his collaboration with Niven has been so successful, Pournelle told Elliot, "It's simple: we cover each other's spots. As I mentioned earlier, Larry has an overly fertile imagination. He comes up with some great ideas, but he's not always capable of executing them in the context of a realistic story. . . . On the other hand, I'm not as good at coming up with these fantastic attention-getters. Larry's much better at that than I am. I tend to do the nuts-and-bolts work, making sure that all the loose ends are well thought out. The end result," concluded Pournelle, "is that we usually come up with a product that neither of us could have created separately." Whether writing in tandem with Niven or alone, however, Pournelle feels that his work is designed to entertain his readers. "I see myself as the modern-day counterpart of the chap in the Bronze Age who used to wander around from camp fire to camp fire with a lyre in his hand," the author told Elliot. "He would see this group of guys sitting around a camp fire, and he'd say, 'Boys, if you'll fill up my cup with some of that wine, and cut me off a chunk of that roast boar, I'll tell you a story about a virgin and a bull that you just won't believe.' Well, that's what I do for a living. I sing songs for my supper and, fortunately, I get a pretty good supper out of it. Hopefully, they're pretty good songs, too."

AVOCATIONAL INTERESTS: Sailing, backpacking, computers, war gaming.

BIOGRAPHICAL/CRITICAL SOURCES:

BOOKS

Elliot, Jeffrey M., *Science Fiction Voices Number Three: Interviews with Science Fiction Writers,* Borgo Press, 1980.
Platt, Charles, *Dream Makers Volume II: The Uncommon Men and Women Who Write Science Fiction,* Berkley Publishing, 1983.

PERIODICALS

Analog, December, 1979.
Chicago Tribune Book World, March 22, 1981, October 13, 1985.
Detroit News, April 19, 1981.
Los Angeles Times Book Review, November 8, 1981, February 24, 1985, August 2, 1987.
Magazine of Fantasy and Science Fiction, August, 1985.
New York Times, February 26, 1985.
New York Times Book Review, January 12, 1975, November 13, 1977, September 8, 1985.
Publishers Weekly, March 8, 1985.
Science Fiction and Fantasy Book Review, April, 1982.
Science Fiction Review, February, 1976, May, 1985.
Tribune Books (Chicago), July 12, 1987.

Washington Post Book World, April 26, 1981, December 27, 1981, July 28, 1985.

—*Sketch by Diane Telgen*

* * *

POWELL-SMITH, Vincent (Walter Francis) 1939- (Francis Elphinstone, Justiciar, Victor Orbis, Santa Maria)

PERSONAL: Surname is pronounced Pole-Smith; born April 28, 1939, in Westerham, Kent, England; son of Alfred Vincent (a businessman) and Catherine May (Berry) Powell-Smith; married Gabrielle Anne Marson, January 1, 1966 (divorced, 1973); married Margaret Gillian Plenderleith, December 15, 1973; children: (first marriage) Amanda Jane, Helena Alexia. *Education:* Attended International Faculty of Comparative Law, Luxembourg, 1960; University of Birmingham, LL.B. (honors), 1962; Gray's Inn, London, Dip.Com., 1963, LL.M., 1968, D.Litt., 1971, M.Sc., 1976.

ADDRESSES: Home—Old Post House, Theddingworth, Leicestershire LE17 6QP, England. *Office*—21 De Montfort St., Leicestershire LE1 7FZ, England; and 21 Montague St., Portman Square, London W1, England.

CAREER: Hammersmith College of Art and Building, London, England, assistant lecturer, 1963-64; John Hilton Bureau of the News of the World Ltd., Cambridge, England, legal adviser, 1964-65, consultant legal adviser, 1965-75; Leicester Polytechnic, Leicester, England, lecturer in law, 1966-68; University of Aston, Birmingham, England, lecturer in law, 1968—, director of studies, School of Business Administration, 1975—. Visiting lecturer, University of Bradford, 1970—. Vice-chancellor and former registrar, Order of the Crown of Stuart; registrar, Memorial of Merit of King Charles the Martyr. Member, Minister's Joint Advisory Committee on Safety and Health in the Construction Industries. Consultant, Professional, Business and Industrial Management Studies and Productivity Services (International) Ltd., 1975—; legal adviser and consultant to various companies; former special lecturer and adviser to Construction Industry Training Board.

MEMBER: Royal Society of Arts (fellow), Philosophical Society of England (fellow), Society of Public Teachers of Law, Royal Commonwealth Society, Faculty of Building (fellow; member of council), National Federation of Master Steeplejacks and Lightning Conductor Engineers (secretary, 1970—), National Federation of Demolition Contractors (secretary, 1971—), Demolition Industry Conciliation Board (joint secretary, 1971—), Demolition and Dismantling Industry Register (joint registrar, 1974—), Institute of Explosive Engineers (secretary, 1974—), Society of Antiquaries of Scotland (fellow), Heraldry Society, Stair Society; honorary member of several literary and foreign societies.

AWARDS, HONORS: Recipient of numerous foreign decorations, including Bronze Medal of Merite Civique, Silver Medal of Renaissance Francaise, Knight's Cross of Merite National Francais, and Medaille d'Argent, Arts-Sciences-Lettres, Commandeur de l'Education Sociale, from France; Grand Collar of Order of St. Agatha of Paterno, from Marshal; Lateran Cross, first class, from the Vatican; Officer of the Order of Lippe.

WRITINGS:

The Law of Boundaries and Fences, Butterworth & Co., 1967, 2nd edition, 1975.
A Modern View of the Law for Builders and Surveyors, Pergamon, 1967.

(With W. S. Whyte) *The Building Regulations Explained and Illustrated for Residential Buildings,* Crosby Lockwood Staples, 1967, 7th edition (with M. J. Billington) published as *Whyte and Powell-Smith's The Building Regulations Explained and Illustrated,* Collins, 1986.

(Editor) Blackwell, *The Law of Meetings,* Butterworth & Co., 9th edition, 1967.

Questions and Answers on "A" Level Law, Butterworth & Co., 1967, 2nd edition, 1971.

Know Your Contract Cases, Butterworth & Co., 1968.

(With R. S. Sim) *Casebook on Contract,* Butterworth & Co., 1968, 2nd edition, 1972.

(With R. S. Sim) *Land Law Casebook,* Butterworth & Co., 1968.

(With Paul Barber) *British Constitution Notebook,* Butterworth & Co., 1968.

(With R. S. Sim) *Casebook on Industrial Law,* Butterworth & Co., 1969.

(With Barber) *Tort Notebook,* Butterworth & Co., 1969.

(Editor) Alfred Frank Topham, *Topham's Real Property: An Introductory Explanation of the Law Relating to Land,* Butterworth & Co., 11th edition, 1969.

(With Barber) *Contract Notebook,* Butterworth & Co., 1969.

The Transport Act 1968, Butterworth & Co., 1969.

The Law and Practice Relating to Company Directors, Butterworth & Co., 1969.

Questions and Answers on General Principles of English Law, Butterworth & Co., 1969.

(With R. S. Sim) *Questions and Answers on Company Law,* Butterworth & Co., 1969.

(Editor) *The Law Students' Annual,* Butterworth & Co., 1969-72.

(Author of supplement) Alfred E. Emden, *Emden and Gill's Building Contracts and Practice,* Butterworth & Co., 7th edition, 1972.

Contract, Butterworth & Co., 4th edition, 1973, 6th edition, 1982.

(With G. Biggs) *Episcopal Heraldry in England and Wales,* Skilton, 1975.

A Protection Handbook: Questions and Answers on the Employment Protection Act 1975, Alan Osborne Ltd., 1976.

Contractors' Guide to the Joint Contracts Tribunal's Standard Forms of Building Contract, IPC Building and Contract Journals, 5th edition, 1978, 6th edition, 1983.

(With John Sims) *Building Contract Claims,* Granada, 1983, 2nd edition, BSP Professional, 1989.

(With Michael Furmston) *A Building Contract Casebook,* Granada, 1984, revised edition, BSP Professional, 1989.

(With Jeremy Brown Houghton) *Horse and Stable Management,* Granada, 1984, Chapters 1-9 reprinted as *The Systems of the Horse,* Howell Book, 1987.

(With David Chappell) *Building Contract Dictionary,* Architectural Press, 1985.

(With Chappell) *Building Contracts Tabulated and Compared,* Architectural Press, 1985.

(With J. Sims) *Determination and Suspension of Construction Contracts,* Collins, 1985.

(With J. Sims) *Contract Documentation for Contractors,* Collins, 1985.

(With Chappell) *JCT Intermediate Form of Contract,* Architectural Press, 1985.

(With Chappell) *JCT Minor Works Form of Contract: An Architect's Guide to the Agreement for Minor Building Works,* Architectural Press, 1986.

(Editor with Furmston) *You and the Law,* Hamlyn, 1988.

(With Douglas Stephenson) *Civil Engineering Claims,* BSP Professional, 1989.

Also author of *C. L. Berry: The Young Pretender's Mistress,* 1974, *The Demolition Contracting Industry,* 1974, and (with Chappell) *Building Contracts Compared and Tabulated,* 1987; editor of *Summer's Treatise on Ghosts,* 1975. Regular contributor to *New Law Journal, Contract Journal,* and *Protection;* occasional contributor, sometimes under pseudonyms Francis Elphinstone, Victor Orbis, Santa Maria, and Justiciar, to other legal and literary journals, including *Daily Telegraph* and *Financial Times.* Legal correspondent, *Contract Journal,* 1974—; editorial adviser, Butterworth & Co.

WORK IN PROGRESS: Modern Construction Law, for Crosby Lockwood Staples; *The British Demolition Industry; Kings across the Water,* for Skilton.

AVOCATIONAL INTERESTS: "Heraldry and genealogy, mediaevalism, traditionalist studies. Interested also in wine and food, foreign travel, notably in Europe. I am an armchair gardener and a would-be golfer."*

*   *   *

POYER, David 1949-
(David Andreissen)

PERSONAL: Born November 26, 1949, in DuBois, Pa.; son of Charles and Margaret Poyer; divorced. *Education:* U.S. Naval Academy, B.S. (with merit), 1971.

ADDRESSES: Home—Washington, D.C.

CAREER: U.S. Navy, surface line officer on frigates and amphibious ships, 1971-77; transferred to U.S. Naval Reserve, 1977; present rank, commander; free-lance writer, 1977—. Founding member of Tidewater Writers Workshop.

MEMBER: Authors Guild, Authors League of America, U.S. Naval Institute, American Society of Naval Engineers, U.S. Naval Academy Alumni Association, SERVAS.

WRITINGS:

White Continent (adventure novel), Jove, 1980.
The Shiloh Project (adventure novel), Avon, 1981.
(Under pseudonym David Andreissen) *Star Seed* (science fiction novel), Donning, 1982.
The Return of Philo T. McGiffin (comic novel), St. Martin's, 1983.
(Editor) *Command at Sea,* 4th edition, U.S. Naval Institute Press, 1983.
Stepfather Bank (science fiction novel), St. Martin's, 1987.
The Dead of Winter (novel), Tor Books, 1988.
The Med (sea novel), St. Martin's, 1988.
Hatteras Blue (sea novel), St. Martin's, 1989.

Contributor of stories to magazines, including *Analog, Galileo, Isaac Asimov's Science Fiction Magazine, Mike Shayne's Mystery Magazine,* and *Unearth.*

WORK IN PROGRESS: The Gulf, a long novel about the U.S. Navy in the Persian Gulf, the second volume of a series.

SIDELIGHTS: David Poyer once told *CA:* "I was born in a small town in northwestern Pennsylvania, in the hills, and named after David Copperfield. My sister, my brother, and I grew up in vicious poverty but always with books around, thanks to our mother. I knew I would write someday, but I needed to see something of the world first. With this in mind, I applied to the Naval Academy—a free education and certainly an opportunity to travel. Much to my surprise, I was accepted. I sweated my way through and graduated in 1971. I spent the next six years at sea, married, divorced, and finally asked for transfer to the Reserves. It was time to try for the dream.

"For five years after that, I did the garret-and-starvation routine in Norfolk, Virginia, trying to write novels. Times were rough at first, since my novels returned to my mailbox as surely and as rapidly as homing pigeons. I like to tell the story about raiding demolished buildings for the Civil Defense rations in the basements. A little moldy, but nutritious. . . . Eventually I found a steady market in regional magazines and made several sales to the mystery and science fiction nations. I became a partner in a small guidebook publishing company. At that point, I began writing novels again. The seasoning helped, and *White Continent* and *Shiloh Project* sold.

"It is hard to see one's work from the outside; nevertheless I'll try. I admire strong stories with characters who must decide between good and evil—and situations where the choice is not as easy as it may sound. I don't like fantasy, and my work leans toward realism. I value accurate backgrounds, believable characters, and realistic dialogue and dislike wordiness, schlock, and digression. My goal is very simple—to write a novel, someday, that will satisfy me."

Poyer recently added: "Since then, aside from brief periods as an engineer or consultant, I've worked as a novelist. Gradually success has come, in terms of sales and recognition. But even more heartening is the feeling that I'm still improving, still learning the craft (but with a long way to go yet). I love the profession of fiction. There's no other way I'd rather spend my life—relieved at intervals, of course, with some sailing."

*   *   *

PRESTON, Ivy (Alice) Kinross 1914-

PERSONAL: Born November 11, 1914, in Timaru, Canterbury, New Zealand; daughter of Andrew (a farmer) and Lily (Ward) Kinross; married Percival Edward James Preston (a farmer), October 14, 1937 (died, 1956); children: David Robin, Peter Ronald, Diane Jeane, Lynnette Ruth. *Education:* Attended schools in Canterbury, New Zealand. *Politics:* Labour. *Religion:* Presbyterian.

ADDRESSES: Home—95 Church St., Timaru, New Zealand.

CAREER: Novelist.

MEMBER: P.E.N., New Zealand Women Writers Society, Romantic Novelists' Association (London), Romance Writers of America, South Island Writers Association, Timaru Writers Guild.

WRITINGS:

The Silver Stream (autobiography), Pegasus Press, 1959.
Where Ratas Twine, Wright & Brown, 1960.
None So Blind, Wright & Brown, 1961.
Magic in Maoriland, Wright & Brown, 1962.
Rosemary for Remembrance, R. Hale, 1962.
Island of Enchantment, R. Hale, 1963.
Tamarisk in Bloom, R. Hale, 1963.
Hearts Do Not Break, R. Hale, 1964.
The Blue Remembered Hills, R. Hale, 1965.
The Secret Love of Nurse Wilson, R. Hale, 1966.
Enchanted Evening, R. Hale, 1966.
Hospital on the Hill, R. Hale, 1967.
Nicolette, R. Hale, 1967.

Red Roses for a Nurse, R. Hale, 1968.
Ticket of Destiny, R. Hale, 1969.
April in Westland, R. Hale, 1969.
A Fleeting Breath, R. Hale, 1970, Beagle Books, 1971.
Interrupted Journey, R. Hale, 1970, Beagle Books, 1971.
Portrait of Pierre, R. Hale, 1970, Beagle Books, 1971.
Petals in the Wind, R. Hale, 1971.
Release the Past, R. Hale, 1972.
Romance in Glenmore Street, R. Hale, 1973, Ace Books, 1978.
Voyage of Destiny, R. Hale, 1973.
Moonlight on the Lake, R. Hale, 1974.
The House above the Bay, R. Hale, 1975.
Sunlit Seas, R. Hale, 1975.
Where Starts May Lead, R. Hale, 1976.
One Broken Dream, R. Hale, 1977.
Mountain Magic, R. Hale, 1978.
Summer at Willowbank, R. Hale, 1979.
Interlude in Greece, R. Hale, 1980.
Nurse in Confusion, R. Hale, 1981.
Enchantment at Hillcrest, R. Hale, 1982.
Fair Accuser, R. Hale, 1985.
To Dream Again, R. Hale, 1985.
Flight from Heartbreak, R. Hale, 1986.
Stranger from the Sea, R. Hale, 1986.
Threads of Destiny, R. Hale, 1987.
Tumult of the Heart, R. Hale, 1988.

Also author of *Elizabeth Ward, Pioneer* (biography) and *Landscapes of the Past* (autobiography), both privately printed.

WORK IN PROGRESS: Spring at Granite Peaks, a novel for R. Hale.

SIDELIGHTS: Ivy Kinross Preston told *CA:* "Although I have always loved to write I began writing books seriously when I was left a widow with four children to bring up and educate. Having begun my career the wrong way round with an autobiography, now at nearly the end of my life, I have written another autobiography updating the first and including family history for the use of my descendants, including six grandchildren.

"With my family self-supporting I can now indulge my love of travel, and I have visited all the countries I only dreamed of as a struggling writer.

"Writing is my pleasure and my torment, my delight and my despair. I think I agree with the Yorkshire writer John Wainwright who, when asked what he would like to be if he wasn't a writer, replied, 'Dead.' That's dedication. I have a motto above my desk that says: 'Writing is easy; all you do is sit and stare at a blank sheet of paper while drops of blood form on your forehead.' Sometimes that almost seems true, but I wouldn't want any other career."

Preston's books have been translated into French, Italian, Dutch, Norwegian, Greek, Danish, and German; some of her novels have also appeared in Nigerian editions.

BIOGRAPHICAL/CRITICAL SOURCES:

BOOKS

Preston, Ivy Kinross, *The Silver Stream* (autobiography), Pegasus Press, 1959.

PERIODICALS

Christchurch Star, December 1, 1960.
New Zealand Weekly News, July 15, 1959.
New Zealand Women's Weekly, January 23, 1963.
Timaru Herald, July 7, 1963, December 12, 1963.

PRUDE, Agnes George de Mille 1905-
(Agnes de Mille)

PERSONAL: Born 1905, in New York, N.Y.; daughter of William C. (a film producer and playwright) and Anna (George) de Mille; married Walter Foy Prude, June 14, 1943; children: Jonathan. *Education:* University of California, Los Angeles, A.B. (cum laude); studied dancing under Koslov, Marie Rambert, Antony Tudor, and Tamara Karsavina in London, 1922-38.

ADDRESSES: Home—25 East Ninth St., New York, N.Y. 10009. *Agent*—Harold Ober Associates, Inc., 40 East 49th St., New York, N.Y. 10017.

CAREER: Choreographer, director, dancer, author. First appeared as a dancer in MacKlin Marrow's production of Mozart's "La Finta Giardiniera," New York City, 1927; made her concert debut at the Republic Theatre, New York City, 1928; toured the United States, England, France, and Denmark as a dance recitalist and choreographer, 1928-42; joined the Ballet Theatre as choreographer, New York City, 1939, dancing in and directing her own compositions; headed the Agnes de Mille Dance Theatre, 1953-54, touring 126 cities; toured with American Ballet Theater at Royal Opera House, Covent Garden, London, 1956, dancing in her own compositions "Three Virgins and the Devil" and "Rodeo"; appeared on "Omnibus" television shows as lecturer and dancer, 1956-57; headed Agnes de Mille Heritage Dance Theatre, 1973-75. Choreographed the films, "Romeo and Juliet," 1936, "Oklahoma!," 1955; choreographed over 14 musicals, including "Oklahoma!," 1943, "One Touch of Venus," 1943, "Bloomer Girl," 1944, "Carousel," 1945, "Brigadoon," 1947, and "Paint Your Wagon," 1951; directed and choreographed "Allegro," 1947; directed "Rape of Lucretia," 1949, and "Out of This World," 1950; choreographed numerous ballets for companies, including Ballet Russe de Monte Carlo, 1942, the Royal Winnipeg Ballet, 1972, and the American Ballet Theatre; danced with the Royal Winnipeg Ballet in "The Rehearsal," her own composition. Member, National Advisory Council of the Performing Arts, 1965-66.

MEMBER: Society for Stage Directors and Choreographers (vice president, 1965-66; president, 1965-67), Merriewold Country Club (New York).

AWARDS, HONORS: Donaldson awards, 1943, 1945, and 1947; New York Critics awards, 1943, 1944, 1945; Mademoiselle merit award, 1944; Woman of the Year, American Newspaper Woman's Guild, 1946; Antoinette Perry award (Tony) for best choreographer, 1947 and 1962; Lord and Taylor award, 1947; Dancing Masters award of merit, 1950; *Dance* magazine award, 1957; Woman of the Year, American National Theatre and Academy, 1962; Capezio award, 1966; Handel Medallion, 1976; Kennedy Award, 1981; National Medal of Arts, 1986. Litt.D. from Mills College, 1952, Russell Sage College, 1953, Clark University, 1962, Franklin and Marshall College, 1965, Western Michigan University, 1967, and Nasson College, 1970; D.H.L. from Smith College, 1954, Western College, 1955, Hood College, 1957, and Goucher College, 1961; D.F.A. from Northwestern University, 1960, and University of California, Los Angeles, 1964; other honorary doctorates from Dartmouth College, 1974, Duke University, 1975, University of North Carolina, 1980, New York University, 1981, and The Julliard School, 1989.

WRITINGS:

UNDER NAME AGNES DE MILLE

Dance to the Piper: Memoirs of the Ballet (autobiography; also see below), Hamish Hamilton, 1951, published as *Dance to the Piper,* Little, Brown, 1952, reprinted, State Mutual Book, 1987.

And Promenade Home (autobiography; also see below), Little, Brown, 1958, reprinted, Da Capo, 1980.

(Contributor) Jack D. Summerfield and Lorlyn Thatcher, editors, *The Creative Mind and Method: Exploring the Nature of Creativeness in American Arts, Sciences, and Professions,* University of Texas Press, 1960.

To a Young Dancer: A Handbook, Little, Brown, 1962 (published in England as *To a Young Dancer: A Handbook for Dance Students, Parents, and Teachers,* Putnam, 1963).

The Book of the Dance, Golden Press, 1963.

Lizzie Borden: A Dance of Death, Little, Brown, 1968.

Russian Journals, Dance Perspectives Foundation, 1970.

(Contributor) Walter Terry, *The Dance in America,* revised edition, Harper, 1971.

Speak to Me, Dance with Me, Little, Brown, 1973.

Where the Wings Grow: A Memoir of Childhood, Doubleday, 1978.

Dance to the Piper and Promenade Home: A Two-Part Autobiography, Da Capo, 1979.

America Dances, Macmillan, 1980.

Reprieve: A Memoir, foreword and notes by Fred Plum, Doubleday, 1981.

Contributor to periodicals, including *Atlantic Monthly, Theatre Arts, Good Housekeeping, Esquire, Vogue, Horizon,* and *McCall's;* contributor to the *New York Times.*

WORK IN PROGRESS: Two memoirs.

SIDELIGHTS: Best known by her maiden name, Agnes de Mille, Agnes George de Mille Prude is the niece of the well-known producer Cecil B. de Mille, the daughter of writer/director William C. de Mille, and the granddaughter of political economist Henry George. De Mille has made a name for herself in her own right, however, as the famous choreographer of such musicals as "Carousel," "Brigadoon," and "Oklahoma!," and of ballets like "Three Virgins and a Devil," "Rodeo," and "Fall River Legend." Her work in these productions presents a unique blend of classical technique with the more modern rhythms of American dance, drawing as well from the innovative choreography styles developed by Martha Graham. Sometimes called "America's first lady of dance," according to Eileen Simpson's *New York Times Book Review* article, President Ronald Reagan awarded de Mille the National Medal of Arts in 1986 for her lifetime achievements in the theater.

From the beginning, de Mille's sole aspiration in life was to be a dancer. After graduating from the University of California, Los Angeles, she studied in New York City and, more thoroughly, in London under the tutelage of Marie Rambert and others. She had some success in touring with companies in America and Europe, but it was not until she choreographed "Three Virgins and a Devil" in 1941, and, most notably, "Rodeo," in 1942, that she received her greatest recognition. This early part of her career as a dancer is partly described in de Mille's autobiography, *Speak to Me, Dance with Me.*

Although many of the choreographer's books deal either with dancing, as in *The Book of Dance* and *America Dances,* or with her work as a dancer, as in *Dance to the Piper: Memoirs of the Ballet* and *And Promenade Home,* some of de Mille's writings focus more on her personal life. *New York Times* contributor Anna Kesselgoff calls one of these works, *Where the Wings Grow: A Memoir of Childhood,* "Agnes de Mille's finest book." This autobiography recalls the author's childhood summers, which were spent at her parents' New York estate. Several critics have noted de Mille's talent for portraying "the passionate quality of memory itself" in this account of the past, as Deborah Jowitt notes in the *New York Times Book Review*. And *Newsweek* reviewer Margo Jefferson goes so far as to say that *Where the Wings Grow* "is nearly as valuable a piece of Americana as [de Mille's] landmark choreography of 'Rodeo' and the dances for 'Oklahoma!' "

In 1975, shortly before a performance by her dance company in New York, de Mille suffered a massive stroke. While in the hospital, she endured several smaller strokes and a heart attack, and her friends and family feared she would never recover. But with the help of her husband, she rediscovered her ambition to continue her work and overcame many of her physical limitations. This period of despair and triumph in her life is recorded in her 1981 autobiography, *Reprieve: A Memoir*. Balanced with objective comments by Dr. Fred Plum, her neurologist, de Mille's book is "a touchingly candid account of the psychic crisis that was brought on by the seemingly interminable period of physical helplessness," says Simpson. Richard F. Shepard adds in his *New York Times* article that "Miss de Mille is an honest writer, and she does not write in self-pity. She well describes the despair of a person along in years who dreads the loss of her career."

Still paralyzed on her right side and forced to use a wheelchair, de Mille returned to the stage in 1977 and has managed to conduct performances regularly since then. She has done four more ballets, including her production of "The Informer" in 1988 with the American Ballet Theatre, the company with which she began a long association in the 1940s. The current artistic director of the American Ballet Theatre, Mikhail Baryshnikov, describes de Mille to Walter Price in a *Los Angeles Times* article as "a trip and a challenge. She has an incredible mind. She knows her sub-

jects 200 percent. . . . She accomplishes more from that wheelchair than most other choreographers do running around all over the stage." "I know it's a cliche," Baryshnikov also tells Price, "but it's a true one that Agnes de Mille is the most American of all choreographers."

AVOCATIONAL INTERESTS: Tennis, gardening.

BIOGRAPHICAL/CRITICAL SOURCES:

BOOKS

Cole, Edwin, editor, *Dance Memoranda,* Duell, 1947.
de Mille, Agnes, *Speak to Me, Dance with Me,* Little, Brown, 1973.
de Mille, Agnes, *Where the Wings Grow: A Memoir of Childhood,* Doubleday, 1978.
de Mille, Agnes, *And Promenade Home,* Da Capo, 1980.
de Mille, Agnes, *Reprieve: A Memoir,* Doubleday, 1981.
de Mille, Agnes, *Dance to the Piper,* State Mutual Book, 1987.
Hazeltine, Alice Isabel, compiler, *We Grew Up in America,* Abingdon, 1954.
McConnell, *Famous Ballet Dancers,* Crowell, 1955.
Stoddard, *Famous American Women,* Crowell, 1970.

PERIODICALS

Dance, October, 1971.
Los Angeles Times, February 28, 1988, May 12, 1988.
Newsweek, January 30, 1978.
New York Times, February 8, 1978, October 23, 1981, May 8, 1988, May 12, 1988.
New York Times Book Review, May 6, 1973, February 5, 1978, February 1, 1981, February 27, 1981.
Time, February 25, 1974.

Q

QUARRY, Nick
See ALBERT, Marvin H(ubert)

*　　*　　*

QUEBEDEAUX, Richard (Anthony) 1944-

PERSONAL: Born October 16, 1944, in Los Angeles, Calif.; son of Thomas Crawford (an electrical engineer) and Annette (Scheyer) Quebedeaux. *Education:* University of California, Los Angeles, B.A. (with honors), 1966, M.A., 1970; Harvard University, S.T.B. (cum laude), 1968; Oxford University, D. Phil., 1975. *Politics:* Democrat. *Religion:* United Church of Christ.

ADDRESSES: Home—2236 Channing Way, Berkeley, Calif. 94704-2164.

CAREER: Free-lance writer, 1971—. United Campus Ministry to the University of California at Santa Barbara, Isla Vista, Calif., interim program coordinator, 1974; Southern California Conference of the United Church of Christ, Pasadena, Calif., staff intern, 1974-75; United Church Board for Homeland Ministries, New York, N.Y., consultant on church renewal, 1975-77; Unification Theological Seminary, Barrytown, N.Y., consulting coordinator of ecumenical conferences, 1978-82, lecturer on religion and society, 1980—. Member of Southern California Commission of United Ministries in Higher Education, 1974-75. Senior consultant, International Religious Foundation, 1982—.

MEMBER: American Society of Authors and Journalists, Harvard Club (New York).

AWARDS, HONORS: Ecumenical scholarship, World Council of Churches, 1969-70, for Mansfield College, Oxford.

WRITINGS:

The Young Evangelicals, Harper, 1974.
The New Charismatics: The Origins, Development, and Significance of Neo-Pentecostalism, Doubleday, 1976.
The Worldly Evangelicals, Harper, 1978.
I Found It!: The Story of Bill Bright and Campus Crusade for Christ, Harper, 1979.

(Author of introduction) Arthur C. Piepkorn, *Profiles in Belief, Volume IV: Evangelical, Fundamentalist, and Other Christian Bodies,* Harper, 1979.
(Editor with Rodney Sawatsky) *Evangelical-Unification Dialogue,* Rose of Sharon Press, 1979.
By What Authority: The Rise of Personality Cults in American Christianity, Harper, 1982.
(Editor) *Lifestyle: Conversations with Members of the Unification Church,* Rose of Sharon Press, 1982.
The New Charismatics II, Harper, 1983.
(Contributor) Glen Evans, editor, *The Complete Guide to Writing Nonfiction,* Writer's Digest Books, 1983.
(Contributor) Ursula King, editor, *Women in the World's Religions: Past and Present,* Paragon House, 1987.
(Contributor) Charles H. Lippy and Peter W. Williams, editors, *Encyclopedia of the American Religious Experience,* Scribner, 1988.
(Contributor) William R. Garrett, editor, *The Social Consequences of Religious Faith,* Paragon House, 1989.
Prime Sources of California and Nevada Local History: 160 Rare and Important City, County and State Directories, 1850-1906, Arthur H. Clark, in press.

Contributor of articles and reviews to periodicals, including *Christianity and Crisis, Journal of Current Social Issues, Christian Science Monitor, The World and I, Christian Century, American Journal of Sociology,* and *New Conversations.*

SIDELIGHTS: New York Times reviewer Kenneth A. Briggs describes Richard Quebedeaux's *The Worldly Evangelicals* as "the best analysis of a huge segment of America's religious life that has come along since the revivalistic boom began a few years ago. Besides providing insightful and useful information, it is written with flair and coy humor."

BIOGRAPHICAL/CRITICAL SOURCES:

PERIODICALS

New York Times, November 17, 1978.
Wittenburg Door, June-July, 1978, February-March, 1981.

R

RADLAUER, Edward 1921-

PERSONAL: Born March 3, 1921, in Kentucky; son of Kurt and Hulda Radlauer; married Ruth Shaw (a writer and editor), June 28, 1947; children: David, Robin, Daniel. *Education:* University of California, Los Angeles, B.A., 1947, graduate study, 1949-50; Whittier College, M.A., 1956.

ADDRESSES: Office—Radlauer Productions, Inc., P.O. Box 1637, Whittier, Calif. 90609; and P.O. Box 1237, Idyllwild, Calif. 92349.

CAREER: Employed by California Department of Employment, 1948-49; teacher, reading specialist, and principal, 1950-68; writer, 1968—.

AWARDS, HONORS: With Ruth Shaw Radlauer, shared Dorothy Mackenzie Award for Service to Children and Reading, Southern California Council on Literature for Children and Young People, 1983.

WRITINGS:

JUVENILES

(With wife, Ruth Shaw Radlauer) *About Missiles and Men,* Melmont, 1959.
(With R. S. Radlauer) *About Atomic Power for People,* Melmont, 1960.
(With R. S. Radlauer) *Atoms Afloat: The Nuclear Ship Savannah,* Abelard, 1963.
Drag Racing: Quarter Mile Thunder, Abelard, 1966.
(With R. S. Radlauer) *Father Is Big,* Bowmar, 1967.
(With R. S. Radlauer) *What Is a Community?,* Children's Press, 1967.
Slot Car Racing, Bowmar, 1967.
(With R. S. Radlauer) *Get Ready for School,* Children's Press, 1967.
(With R. S. Radlauer) *Water for Your Community,* Children's Press, 1968.
(With R. S. Radlauer) *Evening,* Bowmar, 1968.
(With R. S. Radlauer) *Colors,* Bowmar, 1968.
(With R. S. Radlauer) *Whose Tools Are These?,* Children's Press, 1968.
Motorcycles: Whirling Wire Wheels, Abelard, 1969, revised edition, Bowmar, 1975.
(With R. S. Radlauer) *Quarter Midget Challenge* (fiction), Children's Press, 1969.

Minibike Challenge (fiction), Children's Press, 1970.
Snowmobiles, Bowmar, 1970.
Motorcycle Challenge (fiction), Children's Press, 1972.
Dragstrip Challenge, Children's Press, 1972.
Cats!, Bowmar, 1976.
Wheels!, Bowmar, 1976.
Racing!, Bowmar, 1976.
Kickoff!, Bowmar, 1976.
Drag Racing Then and Now, Children's Press, 1983.
Dirt Riders, Children's Press, 1983.
Motorcycles Then and Now, Children's Press, 1985.
(With wife, R. S. Radlauer) *Earthquakes,* Children's Press, 1987.

ILLUSTRATED WITH OWN PHOTOGRAPHS

Drag Racing, Bowmar, 1967, revised edition, 1975.
Karting: Fun on Four Wheels, Bowmar, 1967, revised edition, 1975.
The Mighty Midgets, Bowmar, 1967, revised edition, 1975.
Teen Fair, Bowmar, 1967, revised edition published as *Teen Fair Car Show,* 1975,
(With R. S. Radlauer) *Horses,* Bowmar, 1968, revised edition, 1975.
Surfing, Bowmar, 1968, revised edition, 1975.
Custom Cars, Bowmar, 1968, revised edition, 1974.
Drag Racing Funny Cars, Bowmar, 1968, revised edition, 1975.
Dune Buggy Racing, Bowmar, 1968.
Dune Buggies, Bowmar, 1968, revised edition, 1975.
Drag Strip Challenge (fiction), Children's Press, 1969.
Karting Challenge (fiction), Children's Press, 1969.
(With R. S. Radlauer) *We Go on Wheels,* Children's Press, 1970.
(With R. S. Radlauer) *Horses Pix Dix: A Picture Dictionary,* Bowmar, 1970.
VW Bugs, Bowmar, 1970, revised edition, 1974.
Drag Racing Pix Dix: A Picture Dictionary, Bowmar, 1970.
Minibikes, Bowmar, 1970, revised edition, 1975.
Motorcycle Racing, Bowmar, 1970, revised edition, 1975.
(With R. S. Radlauer) *Buggy-Go-Round,* F. Watts, 1971.
(With R. S. Radlauer) *On the Drag Strip,* F. Watts, 1971.
(With R. S. Radlauer) *Scramble Cycle,* F. Watts, 1971.
(With R. S. Radlauer) *On the Sand,* F. Watts, 1972.
(With R. S. Radlauer) *Horsing Around,* F. Watts, 1972.
(With R. S. Radlauer) *Chopper Cycle* (fiction), F. Watts, 1972.
(With R. S. Radlauer) *Bonneville Cars,* F. Watts, 1973.

(With R. S. Radlauer) *Horse Show Challenge* (fiction), Children's Press, 1973.

(With R. S. Radlauer) *Motorcycle Mutt,* F. Watts, 1973.

(With R. S. Radlauer) *On the Water,* F. Watts, 1973.

(With R. S. Radlauer) *Salt Cycle,* F. Watts, 1973.

Motorcyclopedia, Bowmar, 1973.

(With R. S. Radlauer) *Foolish Filly,* F. Watts, 1974.

(With R. S. Radlauer) *Racing on the Wind,* F. Watts, 1974.

Bicycles, Bowmar, 1974, revised edition, 1975.

(With son, Daniel Radlauer) *Race Car Drivers School,* F. Watts, 1975.

(With Daniel Radlauer) *Pursuit School,* F. Watts, 1975.

(With Daniel Radlauer) *Motorcycle Moto Cross School,* F. Watts, 1975.

Rodeo School, F. Watts, 1976.

(With R. S. Radlauer) *Gymnastics School,* F. Watts, 1976.

"READY, GET SET, GO" SERIES

Fast, Faster, Fastest, Children's Press, 1973.

Motorcycle Mania, Children's Press, 1973.

Soap Box Racing, Children's Press, 1973.

(With other Radlauers) *Ready, Get Set, Whoa!,* Children's Press, 1974.

Wild Wheels, Children's Press, 1974.

Flying Mania, Children's Press, 1974.

(With son, David Radlauer) *Model Airplanes,* Children's Press, 1976.

Racing Numbers, Children's Press, 1976.

Shark Mania, Children's Press, 1976.

(With David Radlauer) *Skateboard Mania,* Children's Press, 1976.

Boats, Children's Press, 1977.

Model Cars, Children's Press, 1977.

Monkey Mania, Children's Press, 1977.

(And photographer with daughter, Robin Radlauer) *Soccer,* Children's Press, 1978.

CB Radio, Children's Press, 1978.

(With David Radlauer) *Model Trains,* Children's Press, 1979.

(With Robin Radlauer) *Bicycle Motorcross,* Children's Press, 1979.

Dinosaur Mania, Children's Press, 1979.

(With R. S. Radlauer) *Hot Rod Mania,* Children's Press, 1980.

Monster Mania, Children's Press, 1980.

Roller Skate Mania, Children's Press, 1980.

Trucks, Children's Press, 1980.

Minibike Racing, Children's Press, 1980.

(With R. S. Radlauer) *Miniatures,* Children's Press, 1980.

(With R. S. Radlauer) *Dolls,* Children's Press, 1980.

"MANIA" SERIES

(With R. S. Radlauer) *Baseball Mania,* Children's Press, 1980.

(With R. S. Radlauer) *Chopper Cycle Mania,* Children's Press, 1980.

(With R. S. Radlauer) *Pet Mania,* Children's Press, 1980.

(With R. S. Radlauer) *Bird Mania,* Children's Press, 1981.

(With R. S. Radlauer) *Clown Mania,* Children's Press, 1981.

(With R. S. Radlauer) *Reptile Mania,* Children's Press, 1981.

(With R. S. Radlauer) *Contest Mania,* Children's Press, 1981.

(With R. S. Radlauer) *Cowboy Mania,* Children's Press, 1981.

(With R. S. Radlauer) *Horse Mania,* Children's Press, 1981.

Volcano Mania, Children's Press, 1981.

Truck Mania, Children's Press, 1982.

(With R. S. Radlauer) *Dog Mania,* Children's Press, 1982.

(With R. S. Radlauer) *Low Rider Mania,* Children's Press, 1982.

Minibike Mania, Children's Press, 1982.

Parade Mania, Children's Press, 1982.

"GEMINI" SERIES

Some Basics about Bicycles, Children's Press, 1978.

Some Basics about Motorcycles, Children's Press, 1978.

Some Basics about Skateboards, illustrations by Robin Radlauer, Children's Press, 1978.

Some Basics about Vans, with own photographs, Children's Press, 1978.

Some Basics about Hang Gliding, Children's Press, 1979.

Some Basics about Running, Children's Press, 1979.

Some Basics about Classic Cars, Children's Press, 1980.

Some Basics about Water Skiing, Children's Press, 1980.

Some Basics about Wind Surfing, Children's Press, 1980.

(With R. S. Radlauer) *Some Basics about Women's Gymnastics,* Children's Press, 1980.

Some Basics about Radio Control Cars, Children's Press, 1981.

Some Basics about Rock Climbing, Children's Press, 1981.

Some Basics about Corvettes, Children's Press, 1981.

Some Basics about Karate, Children's Press, 1981.

Some Basics about Minitrucks, Children's Press, 1982.

(With R. S. Radlauer) *Some Basics about Women's Basketball,* Children's Press, 1982.

"WINNER" SERIES

(With R. S. Radlauer) *Minibike Winners,* Children's Press, 1982.

(With R. S. Radlauer) *Motorcycle Winners,* Children's Press, 1982.

(With R. S. Radlauer) *Karting Winners,* Children's Press, 1982.

Soap Box Winners, Children's Press, 1983.

(With R. S. Radlauer) *Guide Dog Winners,* Children's Press, 1983.

(With R. S. Radlauer) *BMX Winners,* Children's Press, 1984.

"RADLAUER MODEL" SERIES

Model Trucks, Children's Press, 1983.

Model Fighter Planes, Children's Press, 1983.

Model Rockets, Children's Press, 1984.

Model Warships, Children's Press, 1984.

"TECH TALK" SERIES; WITH R. S. RADLAUER

Radio Tech Talk, Children's Press, 1984.

(And with B. Mather and J. Mather) *Computer Tech Talk,* Children's Press, 1984.

(And with B. Mather and J. Mather) *Satellite Tech Talk,* Children's Press, 1984.

(And with B. Mather and J. Mather) *Robot Tech Talk,* Children's Press, 1984.

Nuclear Tech Talk, Children's Press, 1985.

Truck Tech Talk, Children's Press, 1986.

Auto Tech Talk, Children's Press, 1987.

OTHER

Also author of six reading board games for Bowmar. Also photographer of *Mammoth Cave National Park,* written by R. S. Radlauer for Children's Press; photographic contributor to several other books written by R. S. Radlauer for Children's Press, including *Acadia National Park* and *Zion National Park,* both 1978, *Haleakala National Park* and *Hawaii Volcanoes National Park,* both 1979, *Grand Teton National Park* and *Bryce Canyon National Park,* both 1980, *Virgin Islands National Park, Carlsbad Caverns National Park,* and *Denali National Park and Preserve,* all 1981, and *Shenandoah National Park,* 1982.

SIDELIGHTS: Edward Radlauer told *CA:* "For many years we met the needs of the less able student, the poor and slow reader who was left out of the college-oriented curriculum. Now that people involved with United States science and industry agree that our schools need to emphasize education in the scientific and technological areas, our recent books put emphasis on these areas of the school curriculum."

*　　*　　*

RADLAUER, Ruth Shaw 1926-

PERSONAL: Born August 18, 1926, in Midwest, Wyo.; daughter of Tracy Nichols (an industrial relations employee) and Ruth (a real estate agent; maiden name, Preston); married Edward Radlauer (a writer), June 28, 1947; children: David, Robin, Daniel. *Education:* University of California, Los Angeles, B.A.

ADDRESSES: Home—La Habra, Calif. *Office*—Radlauer Productions, Inc., P.O. Box 1637, Whittier, Calif. 90609.

CAREER: Elementary teacher in Norwalk, Calif., 1950-51; substitute teacher in elementary schools in Norwalk, La Habra, and East Whittier, Calif., 1953-69; special education teacher in La Puente, Calif., 1966-67; Whittier Union High School District, Whittier, Calif., adult education teacher of parent education and creative writing, 1968-71; Elk Grove Books (a division of Children's Press), Whittier, editor, 1971—.

MEMBER: Authors Guild, Authors League of America, Writers' Club of Whittier.

AWARDS, HONORS: With Edward Radlauer, shared Dorothy Mackenzie Award for Service to Children and Reading, Southern California Council on Literature for Children and Young People, 1983.

WRITINGS:

Fathers at Work, Melmont, 1958, published as *About Men at Work,* 1967.
Women at Work, Melmont, 1959.
Of Course, You're a Horse, Abelard, 1959.
Mothers Are That Way, Abelard, 1960.
About Four Seasons and Five Senses, Melmont, 1960.
(Self-illustrated) *Good Times Drawing Lines,* Melmont, 1961.
Good Times with Words, Melmont, 1963.
Stein, the Great Retriever, Bobbs-Merrill, 1964.
(With Marjorie Pursel) *Where in the World Do You Live?,* Franklin Publishing, 1965.
From Place to Place, Franklin Publishing, 1965.
Food from Farm to Family, Franklin Publishing, 1965.
Clothes from Head to Toe, Franklin Publishing, 1965.
What Can You Do with a Box?, Children's Press, 1967.
Yellowstone National Park, Children's Press, 1975.
Yosemite National Park, Children's Press, 1975.
Everglades National Park, Children's Press, 1975.
Great Smoky Mountains National Park, Children's Press, 1976, updated edition, 1985.
Mesa Verde National Park, Children's Press, 1976, updated edition, 1984.
Grand Canyon National Park, Children's Press, 1976.
Rocky Mountain National Park, Children's Press, 1977.
Glacier National Park, Children's Press, 1977.
Olympic National Park, Children's Press, 1978.
(And photographer with husband, Edward Radlauer) *Acadia National Park,* Children's Press, 1978.
Mammoth Cave National Park, with photographs by E. Radlauer, Children's Press, 1978.
(And photographer with E. Radlauer) *Zion National Park,* Children's Press, 1978.

(And photographer with E. Radlauer) *Haleakala National Park,* Children's Press, 1979.
(And photographer with E. Radlauer) *Hawaii Volcanoes National Park,* Children's Press, 1979.
(And photographer with E. Radlauer) *Bryce Canyon National Park,* Children's Press, 1980.
(And photographer with E. Radlauer) *Grand Teton National Park,* Children's Press, 1980.
(And photographer with E. Radlauer and Henry M. Anderson) *Virgin Islands National Park,* Children's Press, 1981.
(And photographer with E. Radlauer and Rick McIntyre) *Denali National Park and Preserve,* Children's Press, 1981.
(And photographer with E. Radlauer) *Carlsbad Caverns National Park,* Children's Press, 1981.
Volcanoes, Children's Press, 1981.
(And photographer with E. Radlauer) *Shenandoah National Park,* Children's Press, 1982.
(With Anderson) *Reefs,* Children's Press, 1983.
(With Charles H. Steinbridge) *Planets,* Children's Press, 1984.
(With Steinbridge) *Comets,* Children's Press, 1984.
(With Lisa Sue Gitkin) *The Power of Ice,* Children's Press, 1985.
(With Carolynn Young) *Voyagers One and Two: Robots in Space,* Children's Press, 1987.
Molly, Prentice-Hall, 1987.
Breakfast by Molly, Simon & Schuster, 1988.
Molly at the Library, Simon & Schuster, 1988.

WITH HUSBAND, EDWARD RADLAUER

About Missiles and Men, Melmont, 1959.
About Atomic Power for People, Melmont, 1960.
Atoms Afloat: The Nuclear Ship Savannah, Abelard, 1963.
What Is a Community?, Children's Press, 1967.
Get Ready for School, Children's Press, 1967.
Father is Big, Bowmar, 1967.
Whose Tools Are These?, Children's Press, 1968.
Water for Your Community, Children's Press, 1968.
Colors, Bowmar, 1968.
Evening, Bowmar, 1968.
Horses, Bowmar, 1968, revised edition, 1975.
Quarter Midget Challenge, Children's Press, 1969.
Horses Pix Dix: A Picture Dictionary, Bowmar, 1970.
We Go On Wheels, Children's Press, 1970.
Buggy-Go-Round, F. Watts, 1971.
On the Drag Strip, F. Watts, 1971.
Scramble Cycle, F. Watts, 1971.
Chopper Cycle, F. Watts, 1972.
Horsing Around, F. Watts, 1972.
On the Sand, F. Watts, 1972.
Bonneville Cars, F. Watts, 1973.
Motorcycle Mutt, F. Watts, 1973.
On the Water, F. Watts, 1973.
Salt Cycle, F. Watts, 1973.
Horse Show Challenge (fiction), Children's Press, 1973.
Foolish Filly, F. Watts, 1974.
Racing on the Wind, F. Watts, 1974.
Gymnastics School, F. Watts, 1976.
Some Basics about Women's Gymnastics, Children's Press, 1980.
Hot Rod Mania, Children's Press, 1980.
Miniatures, Children's Press, 1980.
Dolls, Children's Press, 1980.
Baseball Mania, Children's Press, 1980.
Chopper Cycle Mania, Children's Press, 1980.
Pet Mania, Children's Press, 1980.
Bird Mania, Children's Press, 1981.
Clown Mania, Children's Press, 1981.

Reptile Mania, Children's Press, 1981.
Contest Mania, Children's Press, 1981.
Cowboy Mania, Children's Press, 1981.
Horse Mania, Children's Press, 1981.
Dog Mania, Children's Press, 1982.
Low Rider Mania, Children's Press, 1982.
Some Basics about Women's Basketball, Children's Press, 1982.
Karting Winners, Children's Press, 1982.
Minibike Winners, Children's Press, 1982.
Motorcycle Winners, Children's Press, 1982.
Guide Dog Winners, Children's Press, 1983.
BMX Winners, Children's Press, 1984.
Radio Tech Talk, Children's Press, 1984.
(And with B. Mather and J. Mather) *Computer Tech Talk,* Children's Press, 1984.
(And with B. Mather and J. Mather) *Satellite Tech Talk,* Children's Press, 1984.
(And with B. Mather and J. Mather) *Robot Tech Talk,* Children's Press, 1984.
Nuclear Tech Talk, Children's Press, 1985.
Truck Tech Talk, Children's Press, 1986.
Auto Tech Talk, Children's Press, 1987.
Earthquakes, Children's Press, 1987.

WORK IN PROGRESS: Revisions of all national park books.

SIDELIGHTS: Ruth Shaw Radlauer told *CA:* "I had access to a typewriter when I was seven years old, so I started writing plays which were adaptations of *Cinderella* and the like. I did not set out to be a writer until after I'd taught first grade. I couldn't find the books I wanted for my class, especially in the field of social studies. While I preferred to write fantasy or humor in verse, I got my start in social studies books for primary grades.

"When the State of California adopted a series of my books, my sometime collaborator, Ed Radlauer, began to look upon our writing more seriously. As a school administrator, Ed saw a great need, and we set out to supply it: reading material with a high impact of colorful reality and interest, written with a reluctant or non-bookish reader in mind. This led to our 'Reading Incentives Series' and other similar books on subjects like motorcycles, horses, drag racing, and minibikes."

AVOCATIONAL INTERESTS: Horses, music, hiking, sewing, bread-baking, basket-making.

*   *   *

RAFFEL, Burton 1928-

PERSONAL: Surname is pronounced Raf-*fel;* born April 27, 1928, in New York, N.Y.; son of Harry L. (a lawyer) and Rose (Karr) Raffel; married; wife's name, Elizabeth; children: Brian, Blake (deceased), Stefan, Kezia, Shifra, Wendy. *Education:* Brooklyn College (now Brooklyn College of the City University of New York), B.A., 1948; Ohio State University, M.A., 1949; Yale University, J.D., 1958.

ADDRESSES: Home—765 Harrison St., Denver, Colo. 80206. *Office*—Department of English, University of Denver, Denver, Colo. 80208. *Agent*—Peter Livingston, 143 Collier St., Toronto, Ontario M4W 1M2, Canada.

CAREER: Admitted to the Bar of the State of New York. Brooklyn College (now Brooklyn College of the City University of New York), Brooklyn, N.Y., fellow and lecturer in English, 1950-51; Ford Foundation English Language Teacher Training Program, Makassar, Indonesia, instructor, 1953-55; Milbank,

Tweed, Hadley & McCloy (attorneys), New York City, attorney, 1958-60; Foundation Library Center, New York City, editor of *Foundation News,* 1960-63; State University of New York at Stony Brook, instructor, 1964-65, assistant professor of English, 1965-66; State University of New York at Buffalo, associate professor of English, 1966-68; University of Texas at Austin, visiting professor, 1969-70, professor of English and classics and chairman of graduate program in comparative literature, 1970-71; Ontario College of Art, Toronto, Ontario, senior tutor (dean), 1971-72; York University, Toronto, visiting professor of humanities, 1972-75; University of Denver, Denver, Colo., professor of English, 1975—. Visiting professor of English, Haifa University, Israel, 1968-69, and Emory University, spring, 1974; Vanier Lecturer, University of Ottawa, 1978. Free-lance writer and editor; radio and television broadcaster. Founding trustee, Theatre in the Street.

MEMBER: National Humanities Faculty.

AWARDS, HONORS: Two American Philosophical Society grants for a study of modern Indonesian poetry, 1964; two Research Foundation of the State of New York grants for a study of the translation process; Frances Steloff Prize, 1978, for story in *Panache;* nominated for Citizens Chair, University of Hawaii, 1978-79.

WRITINGS:

TRANSLATOR

(And author of introduction) *Poems from the Old English,* University of Nebraska Press, 1960, 2nd edition, 1964.
(And author of introduction) *Beowulf,* New American Library, 1963, published with an afterword by Raffel, University of Massachusetts Press, 1971.
(With Nurdin Salam) *Chairil Anwar: Selected Poems,* New Directions, 1963.
(And editor) *An Anthology of Modern Indonesian Poetry,* University of California Press, 1964, revised edition, State University of New York Press, 1968.
(And editor and author of introduction) *From the Vietnamese: Ten Centuries of Poetry,* October House, 1968.
(And editor and author of introduction) *The Complete Poetry and Prose of Chairil Anwar,* State University of New York Press, 1970.
(And author of introduction) *Sir Gawain and the Green Knight,* New American Library, 1970.
(And compiler and author of introduction and notes) *Russian Poetry under the Tsars: An Anthology,* State University of New York Press, 1971.
(And editor) *Poems: An Anthology,* New American Library, 1971.
(With Alla Burago) *Selected Works of Nikolai S. Gumilev,* State University of New York Press, 1972.
(With Burago) *Complete Poetry of Osip Emilievitch Mandelstam,* State University of New York Press, 1973.
Selected Odes, Epodes, Satires, and Epistles of Horace, New American Library, 1973.
(And author of introduction) *Horace: Ars Poetica,* State University of New York Press, 1974.
(With Harry Aveling, and author of introduction) *Ballads and Blues: Selected Poetry of W. S. Rendra,* Oxford University Press (Kuala Lumpur), 1974.
(With N. N. Bich and W. S. Merwin) *A Thousand Years of Vietnamese Poetry,* Knopf, 1975.
(And author of introduction) *Lyrics from the Greek,* Writers Workshop, 1978.

Salvador Espriu, *The Bull Hide/La pell de brau,* Writers Workshop, 1978, 2nd edition, Marlboro Press, 1987.

(With Burago) *Selected Poems of Alexander Pushkin,* Writers Workshop, 1979.

The Essential Horace, North Point Press, 1983.

(With Zuxin Ding) *Gems of Chinese Poetry,* Liaoning University Press, 1986.

Chretian de Troyes, *Yuain,* Yale University Press, 1987.

OTHER

(With Robert Creeley, Joseph Slotkin, and Matthew Carney) *Short Story 3,* Scribner, 1960.

The Development of Modern Indonesian Poetry, State University of New York Press, 1967.

Mia Poems, October House, 1968.

The Forked Tongue: A Study of the Translation Process, Mouton, 1971.

Introduction to Poetry, New American Library, 1971.

Why Re-Create?, National Humanities Faculty (Concord, Mass.), 1973.

Guide to Paperback Translation in the Humanities, National Humanities Faculty, 1976.

Four Humours (poems), Writers Workshop, 1979.

Robert Lowell, Ungar, 1981.

T. S. Eliot, Ungar, 1982.

How to Read a Poem, Meridian, 1984.

Changing the Angle of the Sun-Dial (poems), Northwoods, 1984.

(Editor) *Forty-One Stories of O. Henry,* Signet, 1984.

American Victorians: Explorations in Emotional History, Archon Books, 1984.

(Editor) *Signet Classic Book of American Stories,* Signet, 1985.

Ezra Pound: Prime Minister of Poetry, Archon Books, 1985.

Possum and Ole Ez in the Public Eye: Contemporaries and Peers on T. S. Eliot and Ezra Pound, 1892-1972, Archon Books, 1985.

Grice (poems), Trilobite Press, 1985.

Evenly Distributed Rubble (poems), Moonsquilt Press, 1985.

After Such Ignorance (novel), Writers Workshop, 1986.

Man as A Social Animal (poems), Writers Workshop, 1986.

(Editor) *Signet Classic Book of Contemporary Stories,* Signet, 1986.

Politicians, Poets, and Con Men: Emotional History in Late Victorian America, Shoe String, 1986.

(With wife, Elizabeth Raffel) *Founder's Fury* (novel), Pocket Books, 1987.

Co-author of screenplay, "The Legend of Alfred Packer," 1979. Contributor of articles, short stories, poetry, and criticism to periodicals, including *Panache, Hudson Review, Virginia Quarterly Review, London Magazine,* and *Prairie Schooner;* also contributor to legal journals. Member of editorial board, *Literature East and West,* 1967-70; editor, *Denver Quarterly,* 1976-77.

WORK IN PROGRESS: An introductory college literature text; a study of poetic translation; more novels, plays, and poems.

SIDELIGHTS: Burton Raffel once told *CA:* "Writing fiction has become an increasingly chancy business in the past decade or so. Writing and publishing poetry is a good deal less chancy, perhaps because there are so many lively small presses and because, in any case, there are no financial rewards involved (or expected). I have published a total of five stories in small magazines in the past few years, and one long novel, written in collaboration with my wife, with a major New York publisher, one short novel with a small press; more 'commercial' magazines, and more commercial book publishers, are at the moment not keen on literary writers in general and this writer in particular. (I have no

less than eight novels, of varying lengths, complete and sitting in my files; I have three completed volumes of poetry in those same files.)

"Although my work has attracted some critical attention, it has gotten virtually no attention from publishers. I have, I think, a reasonably good overall perspective on the situation of the writer in America in the 1980s—and I do not like what I see. I find myself more and more discouraged, both as to my own prospects and the prospects of serious writers in general. The quality of judgment exhibited by commercial publishers (and the quality of the editors making those judgments) seems to me sharply in the decline. I hope there will be at least some improvement in this coming decade, but I have no very great belief that my prayers will be answered. Like most serious writers, I go on writing because I have no choice, not because either the rewards or the satisfactions are large. [To put it] bluntly, they are not at all large, and most often they are non-existent."*

*   *   *

RAJNEESH, Acharya   1931-1990
(Bhagwan Shree Rajneesh)

PERSONAL: Born December 11, 1931, in Kutchwara, India; died January 19, 1990, in Poona, India; son of Swami Dev Teertha (a businessman) and Saraswati (Devi) Bharati. *Education:* Jabalpur University, B.A., 1955; University of Saugar, M.A., 1957.

CAREER: Former professor of philosophy; Zen, Taoist, and Tantric master.

WRITINGS:

The Mysteries of Life and Death, translated from the Hindi by Malini Bisen, Motilal Banarsidass (India), 1978.

UNDER NAME BHAGWAN SHREE RAJNEESH

Towards the Unknown, Jeevan Jagruti Kendra, 1969.

The Gateless Gate, Jeevan Jagruti Kendra, 1971.

Seeds of Revolution, Jeevan Jagruti Kendra, 1972.

Lead Kindly Light, Jeevan Jagruti Kendra, 1972.

I Am the Gate, Jeevan Jagruti Kendra, 1972, 2nd edition, 1976.

The Eternal Message, Jeevan Jagruti Kendra, 1973.

The Book of Secrets: Vigyana Bhairava Tantra, Volume 1, Rajneesh Foundation, 1974, 2nd edition, 1975, Harper, 1976, Volume 2, Rajneesh Foundation, 1975, Harper, 1979, Volumes 3-5, Rajneesh Foundation, 1976.

The Way of the White Clouds, Rajneesh Foundation, 1975, revised edition published as *My Way: The Way of the White Clouds,* Rajneesh Foundation, 1978.

No Water, No Moon, Rajneesh Foundation, 1975, 2nd edition, 1978.

The Mustard Seed: The Gospel according to Thomas, Rajneesh Foundation, 1975, 2nd edition, 1978, Harper, 1978.

Roots and Wings, Rajneesh Foundation, 1975.

. . . And the Flowers Showered, Rajneesh Foundation, 1975, De Vorss, 1978.

Tantra, the Supreme Understanding: Tilop's "Song of Mahamudra," Rajneesh Foundation, 1975, published in the United States as *Only One Sky,* Dutton, 1976.

Tantra: The Complete Understanding, Rajneesh Foundation, 1975.

Neither This nor That: Sosan, Rajneesh Foundation, 1975.

Yoga, the Alpha and Omega: Patanjali, Rajneesh Foundation, Volumes 1-3, 5, 1976, Volumes 4, 6-8, 1977, Volumes 9-10, 1978.

Just like That, Rajneesh Foundation, 1976.

Hammer on the Rock, Rajneesh Foundation, 1976, Grove, 1979.

The Hidden Harmony: The Fragments of Heraclitus, Rajneesh Foundation, 1976.

When the Shoe Fits: The Sayings of Chuang Tzu, Rajneesh Foundation, 1976, De Vorss, 1978.

Returning to the Source, Rajneesh Foundation, 1976.

Tao, the Three Treasures: The Tao Te Ching of Lao Tzu, Rajneesh Foundation, Volumes 1-3, 1976, Volume 4, 1977.

The Ultimate Alchemy: Atma Pooja Upanishad, Rajneesh Foundation, Volume 2, 1976, Volume 1, 1977.

Until You Die, Rajneesh Foundation, 1976.

The Grass Grows by Itself, Rajneesh Foundation, 1976, De Vorss, 1978.

Come Follow Me: The Four Gospels, Rajneesh Foundation, Volume 1, 1976, Volumes 2-4, 1977.

Vedanta, Seven Steps to Samadhi: Akshya Upanishad, Rajneesh Foundation, 1976.

The True Sage, Rajneesh Foundation, 1976.

Nirvana: The Last Nightmare, Rajneesh Foundation, 1976.

The Empty Boat: The Stories of Chuang Tzu, 1976.

Meditation: The Art of Exstasy, Harper, 1976 (published in India as *Meditation: The Art of Inner Ecstasy,* Rajneesh Foundation, 1977).

Above All, Don't Wobble, Rajneesh Foundation, 1977.

The Supreme Doctrine: Kenopanishad, Rajneesh Foundation, 1977.

Nothing to Lose but Your Head, Rajneesh Foundation, 1977.

The Search: The Ten Zen Bulls, Rajneesh Foundation, 1977.

Dang Dang Doko Dang, Rajneesh Foundation, 1977.

Ancient Music in the Pines, Rajneesh Foundation, 1977.

The Beloved: The Baul Mystics, Rajneesh Foundation, Volume 1, 1977, Volume 2, 1978.

Be Realistic: Plan for a Miracle, Rajneesh Foundation, 1977.

A Sudden Clash of Thunder, Rajneesh Foundation, 1977.

The Psychology of the Esoteric, Harper, 1977.

The Cypress in the Courtyard, Rajneesh Foundation, 1978.

Get Out of Your Own Way, Rajneesh Foundation, 1978.

The New Alchemy: To Turn You On—Mabel Collins' "Light on the Path," Rajneesh Foundation, 1978.

The Discipline of Transcendence: The Sutra of Forty-two Chapters, four volumes, Rajneesh Foundation, 1978.

Ecstasy, the Forgotten Language: Kabir, Rajneesh Foundation, 1978.

The Art of Dying, Rajneesh Foundation, 1978.

Beloved of My Heart, Rajneesh Foundation, 1978.

A Rose Is a Rose Is a Rose, Rajneesh Foundation, 1978.

Dance Your Way to God, Rajneesh Foundation, 1978.

The Great Nothing, Rajneesh Foundation, 1978.

God Is Not for Sale, Rajneesh Foundation, 1978.

The Divine Melody: Kabir, Rajneesh Foundation, 1978.

The Path of Love: Kabir, Rajneesh Foundation, 1978.

The Heart Sutra: The Prajnaparamita Hridayam Sutra, Rajneesh Foundation, 1978.

The Passion for the Impossible, Rajneesh Foundation, 1978.

Tao, the Pathless Path: The Sayings of Lieh Tzu, Rajneesh Foundation, Volume 2, 1978, Volume 1, 1979.

Zen: The Path of Paradox, Rajneesh Foundation, Volume 1, 1978, Volumes 2-3, 1979.

The Shadow of the Whip, Rajneesh Foundation, 1978.

This Very Body the Buddha: Hakuin's "Song of the Meditation," Rajneesh Foundation, 1978.

The Supreme Understanding, Sheldon Press, 1978.

Dimensions beyond the Known, Sheldon Press, 1978.

The Tantra Vision: The Royal Song of Saraha, Volumes 1-2, Rajneesh Foundation, 1979.

The Diamond Sutra: The Vajrachchedika Prajnaparamita Sutra, Rajneesh Foundation, 1979.

The Rajneesh Nothing Book (blank pages), Rajneesh Foundation, 1979.

Blessed Are the Ignorant, Rajneesh Foundation, 1979.

Walk without Feet, Fly without Wings, and Think without Mind, Rajneesh Foundation, 1979.

The Buddha Disease, Rajneesh Foundation, 1979.

This Is It, Rajneesh Foundation, 1979.

The Revolution: Kabir, Rajneesh Foundation, 1979.

Take It Easy: Ikkyu, Rajneesh Foundation, Volume 1, 1979, Volume 2, 1980.

From Sex to Superconsciousness, Rajneesh Foundation, 1979.

Sufis: The People of the Path, Rajneesh Foundation, Volume 1, 1979, Volume 2, 1980.

The Zero Experience, Rajneesh Foundation, 1979.

For Madmen Only—Price of Admission: Your Mind, Rajneesh Foundation, 1979.

A Cup of Tea: Letters, Rajneesh Foundation, 1980.

The Secret, Rajneesh Foundation, 1980.

The Sun Rises in the Evening, Rajneesh Foundation, 1980.

The Perfect Master, Rajneesh Foundation, Volume 1, 1980, Volume 2, 1981.

What Is, Is, What Ain't, Ain't, Rajneesh Foundation, 1980.

The Open Secret, Rajneesh Foundation, 1980.

The Sun behind the Sun behind the Sun, Rajneesh Foundation, 1980.

Turn On, Tune In, and Drop the Lot, Rajneesh Foundation, 1980.

Zorba the Buddha, Rajneesh Foundation, 1980.

The Ninety-nine Names of Nothingness, Rajneesh Foundation, 1980.

Don't Just Do Something, Sit There, Rajneesh Foundation, 1980.

Far beyond the Stars, Rajneesh Foundation, 1980.

The Fish in the Sea Is Not Thirsty, Rajneesh Foundation, 1980.

The Further Shore, Rajneesh Foundation, 1980.

I Say unto You: The Four Gospels, Rajneesh Foundation, Volume 1, 1980, Volume 2, 1983.

Let Go!, Rajneesh Foundation, 1980.

The Madman's Guide to Enlightenment, Rajneesh Foundation, 1980.

The Open Door, Rajneesh Foundation, 1980.

The Sound of Running Water, Rajneesh Foundation, 1980.

Hallelujah!, Rajneesh Foundation, 1981.

Only Losers Can Win in This Game, Rajneesh Foundation, 1981.

Believing the Impossible before Breakfast, Rajneesh Foundation, 1981.

Be Still and Know, Rajneesh Foundation, 1981.

The Guest, Rajneesh Foundation, 1981.

The NO Book (No Buddha, No Teaching, No Discipline), Rajneesh Foundation, 1981.

Philosophia Perennis, two volumes, Rajneesh Foundation, 1981.

When the Shoe Fits, Rajneesh Foundation, 1981.

Zen: Zest, Zip, Zap and Zing, Rajneesh Foundation, 1981.

The White Lotus, Rajneesh Foundation, 1981.

The Sound of One Hand Clapping, Rajneesh Foundation, 1981.

Walking in Zen, Sitting in Zen, Rajneesh Foundation, 1982.

The Secret of the Secrets, Rajneesh Foundation, Volume 1, 1982, Volume 2, 1983.

The Book of the Books, Rajneesh Foundation, Volume 1, 1982, Volume 2, 1983, Volume 3, 1984.

Don't Bite My Finger, Look Where I'm Pointing, Rajneesh Foundation, 1982.

The Goose Is Out, Rajneesh Foundation, 1982.

The Book of Wisdom, Rajneesh Foundation, Volume 1, 1983, Volume 2, 1984.

The Tongue-Tip Taste of Tao, Rajneesh Foundation, 1983.

The Sacred Yes, Rajneesh Foundation, 1983.

Won't You Join the Dance?, Rajneesh Foundation, 1983.

Don't Look before You Leap, Rajneesh Foundation, 1983.

God's Got a Thing about You, Rajneesh Foundation, 1983.

Guida Spirituale, Rajneesh Foundation, 1983.

Theologia Mystica, Rajneesh Foundation, 1983.

Hsin Hsin Ming: The Book of Nothing, Rajneesh Foundation, 1983.

The Orange Book, Rajneesh Foundation, 1983.

Philosophia Ultima, Rajneesh Foundation, 1983.

Rajneeshism: An Introduction to Bhagwan Shree Rajneesh and His Religion, Rajneesh Foundation, 2nd edition, 1983.

Tantra, Spirituality and Sex, Rajneesh Foundation, 1983.

Tao: The Three Treasures, Rajneesh Foundation, 1983.

You Ain't Seen Nothing Yet, Rajneesh Foundation, 1984.

Yoga: The Science of the Soul, three volumes, 1984.

Zen: The Special Transmission, Rajneesh Foundation, 1984.

Snap Your Fingers, Slap Your Face, and Wake Up!, Rajneesh Foundation, 1984.

And Now, and Here, Rajneesh Foundation, Volume 1, 1984, Volume 2, 1985.

Beware of Socialism, Rajneesh Foundation, 1984.

The Book: An Introduction to the Teachings of Bhagwan Shree Rajneesh, three volumes, Rajneesh Foundation, 1984.

I Am That, Rajneesh Foundation, 1984.

In Search of the Miraculous, Volume 1, Rajneesh Foundation, 1984.

The Long and the Short of the All, Rajneesh Foundation, 1984.

The Perfect Way, Rajneesh Foundation, 1984.

The Shadow of the Bamboo, Rajneesh Foundation, 1984.

Tao: The Golden Gate, Rajneesh Foundation, Volume 1, 1984, Volume 2, 1985.

The Rainbow Bridge, Rajneesh Foundation, 1985.

This Very Place the Lotus Palace, Rajneesh Foundation, 1985.

The Rajneesh Bible, Volume 1, Rajneesh Foundation, 1985.

Beyond Enlightenment, Rajneesh Foundation, 1986.

The Last Testament, Rajneesh Foundation, 1986.

The Rajneesh Upanishad, Rajneesh Foundation, 1986.

The Messiah: Commentaries by Bhagwan Shree Rajneesh on Kahlil Gibran's "The Prophet," Rebel Publishing House (Cologne), 1987.

Author of more than a hundred books in Hindi, all published by Rajneesh Foundation, beginning 1975. Author of *Sannyas* and *Rajneesh Newsletter.*

WORK IN PROGRESS: The First Principle; The Wisdom of the Sands; Unio Mystica; The Book of the Books, Volume 4; *Don't Let Yourself Be Upset by the Sutra, Rather Upset the Sutra Yourself; The Rajneesh Bible,* Volumes 2-3; *Rajneesh Neo-I Ching; The Wild Geese and the Water.*

SIDELIGHTS: Bhagwan Shree Rajneesh, whose hundreds of books have been translated into Japanese, Dutch, Italian, French, German, Spanish, and Portuguese, first came to the United States in 1981. Establishing a large commune in Oregon, the mystic from India set out to teach people Rajneeshism, an "eclectic blend of Eastern mysticism and Western philosophy and psychology," according to a *Chicago Tribune* article by Rogers Worthington. The community, dubbed Rajneeshpuram, soon grew into a 2,000 acre city with a population of over 6,000. Local Oregonians, however, were upset by the religious practices of Rajneeshpuram's inhabitants, who were encouraged to practice free sex in order to promote emotional health.

Despite the local distaste for the religious sect's sexual practices, Worthington reports that "a 1983 survey done by a team from the University of Oregon [demonstrated that] Rajneeshees scored much higher in satisfaction and self-esteem, and lower in stress and blood pressure than a comparable group of adults in Portland." Nevertheless, Rajneesh's activities were brought to the attention of the federal government. The religious leader was soon charged with 35 counts of deliberate violations against immigration laws. On a plea bargain, he admitted his guilt in two of the charges and was deported back to his native India in 1985.

About his many books, Rajneesh's associate, Ma Yoga Asha, told *CA* in 1982: "The books . . . published by Rajneesh Foundation International provide a unique record of Bhagwan's attempt, during those seven years of discourses [before he came to the United States], to explore all the avenues of verbal communication; to say all that can possible be said by way of guidance to the spiritual seeker. These books include not only his discourses, but also a series of intimate dialogues between the Master and individual disciples, that used to take place at the ashram every evening."

In a 1985 letter to *CA,* Rajneesh's publisher, Swami Anand Rama, quoted the religious leader as saying: "My effort is not just to help individuals—obviously that's what I am doing—but deep down it is an effort to create the situation, the background, the essential context in which a new man can arise with love in the heart, with light in the soul, with intelligence, with awareness, and can transform the whole earth into a paradise. That miracle is possible."

BIOGRAPHICAL/CRITICAL SOURCES:

BOOKS

Bharti, Ma Satya, *The Ultimate Risk,* Wildwood House, 1979.

Divya, Ma Prem, *Lord of the Full Moon: Life with Bhagwan Shree Rajneesh,* Rajneesh Foundation, 1979.

Gunther, Bernard, *Dying for Enlightenment,* Harper, 1979.

Prasad, R. C., *The Mystic of Feeling,* Motilal Banarsidass, 1970, 2nd edition, 1978.

PERIODICALS

Chicago Tribune, October 19, 1984.*

*   *   *

RAJNEESH, Bhagwan Shree
See RAJNEESH, Acharya

*   *   *

RANDALL, Bob 1937-

PERSONAL: Birth-given name, Stanley B. Goldstein; born August 20, 1937, in New York, N.Y.; son of Jerome (in sales) and Bessie (Chiz) Goldstein; married Ruth Gordon, March 11, 1962; children: one daughter, one son. *Education:* New York University, A.B., 1958.

ADDRESSES: Office—Bob Randall Productions, Box 2483, New Preston, Conn. 06777.

CAREER: Marschalk Advertising Agency, New York City, copywriter, 1963-73; actor, 1959-62; playwright, television writer, and novelist, 1972—. Producer and headwriter for series

"Kate and Allie," Columbia Broadcasting System (CBS), 1984-88; affiliated with Bob Randall Productions, 1988—.

MEMBER: Writers Guild of America, Dramatists Guild.

AWARDS, HONORS: Drama Desk most promising playwright award, 1972, for *6 Rms Riv Vu;* Edgar Allan Poe Award, 1977, for *The Fan;* winner of numerous awards for television series "Kate and Allie," including Writers Guild of America award and Humanities Award, both 1987.

WRITINGS:

"Brief Sublet" (two-act play), 1970, revised as *6 Rms Riv Vu* (first produced in New York City at the Helen Hayes Theatre, October 17, 1972), Doubleday, 1973.
"The Magic Show" (musical), first produced in New York City at Cort Theatre, May 28, 1974.
The Fan (novel; Literary Guild selection), Random House, 1977.
The Next (novel), Warner Books, 1981.
The Calling (novel), Simon & Schuster, 1981.

Author of "Annie and the Seven Hoods," a comedy revue. Also author of teleplays, including "Mo and Joe," and creator of series "On Our Own," both for CBS.

WORK IN PROGRESS: "Last Man on the List," a screenplay; "Elliot's Mother," a play; "People Don't Do Things Like That," a comedy-thriller.

SIDELIGHTS: In his first novel, *The Fan,* Bob Randall unfolds his plot through a series of letters written by Sally Ross, an actress; Jake, her ex-husband; Douglas Breen, a demented fan of Miss Ross's; and investigators of Breen's bizarre letters. As the story progresses, the correspondence between Sally and Jake becomes more loving and intense, while the fan letters from Breen to Sally become increasingly personal and threatening. A bestseller, *The Fan* was critically acclaimed by such reviewers as David Brudnoy, who wrote in *National Review:* "The book is a quick read; an intelligent treatment of an unusual subject; an alarming story; and, as everybody's grandmother used to say, it's a caution." Nora Johnson of the *New York Times Book Review* described *The Fan* as "a riveting tale of love, fear and urban woe." Randall's subsequent novels *The Next* and *The Calling* are also tales of suspense. However, the writer is perhaps best known for a work not often associated with his name: the television series "Kate and Allie." The story of two divorced New York women banding together to rear their children, the comedy has enjoyed a long run on CBS and garnered several awards for Randall.

MEDIA ADAPTATIONS: The Fan was adapted as a motion picture, starring Lauren Bacall, James Garner, and Maureen Stapleton, by Paramount in 1981. *6 Rms Riv Vu* was made into a television production.

BIOGRAPHICAL/CRITICAL SOURCES:

PERIODICALS

National Review, July 22, 1977.
New York Times Book Review, May 8, 1977.
Times Literary Supplement, September 2, 1977.
Village Voice, May 9, 1977.

*   *   *

RANSOME, Arthur (Michell) 1884-1967

PERSONAL: Born January 18, 1884, in Leeds, Yorkshire, England; died June 3, 1967, in Manchester, England; son of Cyril Ransome (a college history professor); married Ivy Constance Walker, 1909 (marriage dissolved); married Eugenia Shelepin, 1924; children: (first marriage) Tabitha. *Education:* Educated at Rugby School.

ADDRESSES: Home—Suffolk, England.

CAREER: Writer, critic, and journalist. Worked as a war correspondent in Russia for *Daily News* and *Manchester Guardian* during World War I and the Russian Revolution.

AWARDS, HONORS: Carnegie Medal, 1936, for *Pigeon Post;* Litt.D., University of Leeds, 1952; Commander, Order of the British Empire, 1953; *The Fool of the World and the Flying Ship* was named an American Library Association Notable Book and appeared on the *Horn Book* Honor List, both 1968; honorary M.A., University of Durham.

WRITINGS:

NONFICTION

Bohemia in London, Dodd, 1907, 2nd edition, Stephen Swift, 1912, reprinted, Oxford University Press, 1984.
A History of Story-Telling: Studies in the Development of Narrative, T.C. & E.C. Jack, 1909, reprinted, Norwood, 1977.
Edgar Allan Poe: A Critical Study, M. Secker, 1910, reprinted, P. West, 1977.
Oscar Wilde: A Critical Study, M. Secker, 1912, reprinted, Folcroft, 1972.
Portraits and Speculations, Macmillan, 1913, reprinted, Folcroft, 1972.
Russia in 1919, B.W. Huebsch, 1919 (published in England as *Six Weeks in Russia in 1919,* Allen & Unwin, 1919).
The Crisis in Russia, B.W. Huebsch, 1921.
"Racundra's" First Cruise (Sailing on the Eastern Baltic), B.W. Huebsch, 1923, reprinted, David & Charles, 1988.
The Chinese Puzzle, Allen & Unwin, 1927.
Rod and Line: Essays together with Aksakov on Fishing (includes extracts from the works of S. T. Aksakov), J. Cape, 1929, reprinted, Sphere Books, 1967.
Mainly about Fishing, Black, 1959.
The Autobiography of Arthur Ransome, edited by Rupert Hart-Davis, J. Cape, 1976.

JUVENILES

Nature Books for Children, Anthony Treherne, 1906.
(Reteller) *Old Peter's Russian Tales* (also see below), F.A. Stokes, 1917, new edition, Puffin, 1974.
(Reteller) *Aladdin and His Wonderful Lamp in Rhyme,* Nisbet, 1920.
(Reteller) *The Soldier and Death : A Russian Folk Tale Retold by Arthur Ransome,* B.W. Huebsch, 1922, reprinted, Edmund Ward, 1962.
(Reteller) *The Fool of the World and the Flying Ship* (excerpt from *Old Peter's Russian Tales*), Farrar, Straus, 1968.
The War of the Birds and the Beasts and Other Russian Tales, J. Cape, 1984.

"SWALLOWS AND AMAZONS" SERIES; JUVENILES

Swallows and Amazons, J. Cape, 1930, 2nd edition with new illustrations, 1931, U.S. edition with new illustrations, Lippincott, 1931, new edition with illustrations by the author, Penguin, 1968.
Swallowdale, J. Cape, 1931, U.S. edition with new illustrations, Lippincott, 1932, new edition, Penguin, 1968.

Peter Duck, self-illustrated, J. Cape, 1932, revised edition with additional illustrations by Helene Carter, Lippincott, 1933, reprinted, Penguin, 1968.

Winter Holiday, J. Cape, 1933, Lippincott, 1934, reprinted, Penguin, 1968.

Coot Club (also see below), J. Cape, 1934, Lippincott, 1935, reprinted, Salem House, 1980.

Pigeon Post, J. Cape, 1936, Lippincott, 1937, reprinted, Salem House, 1980.

We Didn't Mean to Go to Sea, self-illustrated, J. Cape, 1937, Macmillan, 1938, reprinted with a new introduction by Beryl B. Beatley, Gregg, 1981.

Secret Water, self-illustrated, J. Cape, 1939, Macmillan, 1940, reprinted, Salem House, 1980.

The Big Six (also see below), self-illustrated, J. Cape, 1940, Macmillan, 1941, reprinted, Salem House, 1980.

Missee Lee, self-illustrated, J. Cape, 1941, Macmillan, 1942, reprinted, Salem House, 1980.

The Picts and the Martyrs; or, Not Welcome at All, self-illustrated, Macmillan, 1943, reprinted, Salem House, 1980.

Great Northern?, J. Cape, 1947, Macmillan, 1948, reprinted, J. Cape, 1982.

Swallows and Amazons For Ever (abridged edition of *Coot Club* and *Big Six*), Puffin, 1983.

Coots in the North & Other Stories, introduced and edited by Hugh Brogan, Cape, 1988.

EDITOR

The World's Story Tellers, T.C. & E.C. Jack, 1908.

The Book of Friendship: Essays, Poems, Maxims, & Prose Passages, T.C. & E.C. Jack, 1909.

The Book of Love: Essays, Poems, Maxims, & Prose Passages, T.C. & E.C. Jack, 1910.

John MacGregor, *The Voyage Alone in the Yawl Rob Roy,* Hart-Davis, 1954.

OTHER

The Souls of the Streets, and Other Little Papers, Brown, Langham, 1904.

The Stone Lady: Ten Little Papers and Two Mad Stories, Brown, Langham, 1905.

The Imp and the Elf and the Ogre, Nisbet, 1910.

The Hoofmarks of the Faun, Martin Secker, 1911.

(Author of preface and appendix) Remy de Gourmont, *A Night in the Luxembourg,* Stephen Swift, 1912.

The Elixir of Life, Methuen, 1915.

The Soldier and Death, B.W. Huebsch, 1922.

(Translator) Yuri N. Libedinsky, *A Week,* Allen & Unwin, 1923.

(Author of foreword) Richard T. MacMullen, *Down Channel,* Allen & Unwin, 1931.

(Author of introduction) Joshua Slocum, *Sailing Alone Around the World and Voyage of the Liberdade,* Hart-Davis, 1948.

SIDELIGHTS: *Swallows and Amazons,* the first volume of Arthur Ransome's "Swallows and Amazons" series, was his greatest success as a writer. He completed work on the volume at age forty-five, after recovering from an illness which ended his work as a foreign correspondent. Based in part on Ransome's childhood memories of holidays spent at Lake Windermere in northwest England, the story concerns true-to-life children, who are likeable and understandable, and who do things every child likes to do. According to a *New Statesman* reviewer, the work appealed to both adults and children. "The outward aspect of the book will please the grown-up eye," the critic noted, "and may raise an expectation that the children in it are psychologically studied for adult reading. But the child-reader will be delighted to find nothing so uninteresting to him as child-psychology, and the things that do interest him treated on a real and serious plane. The ideal reader should certainly be not too old for make-believe about a miniature desert-island."

Swallowdale, the second volume in the same series, was also praised for its appeal to all age groups. Anne T. Eaton, a *New York Times* contributor, wrote: "Like its predecessor, *Swallows and Amazons,* [it] meets the test of a good book for children, for it can be read with pleasure by adults as well as boys and girls. The book is full of adventure, not artificial excitement, but the kind that a child who has not been too much interfered with will find for himself anywhere, though, in this instance, an island for camping, a sail boat, and a sympathetic and sensible mother furnish an ideal starting point for imaginative play."

In statements published in Ransome's 1976 autobiography and elsewhere, it was obvious that Ransome thoroughly enjoyed his profession. For instance, in Hugh Shelley's sketch of the author published in *Three Bodley Head Monographs,* Shelley quoted Ransome as saying: "You write not *for* children but for yourself, and if, by good fortune, children enjoy what you enjoy, why then you are a writer of children's books. . . . No special credit to you, but simply thumping good luck." Ransome's British readers have responded to his work with similar enthusiasm: *Swallows and Amazons* has sold over 300,000 copies in hardback in the nearly sixty years since it was originally published, while the entire series has sold over 2.5 million copies in hardback and as many in paperback. In the same period of time, no Ransome novel has ever been allowed to go out of print. Forty years after the last of the original twelve volumes of the series was published, a posthumous thirteenth volume based on an uncompleted manuscript appeared. This late addition to the Ransome canon, entitled *Coots in the North & Other Stories,* prompted London *Times* contributor J. P. Crowther to remark: "Ransome's success and the staying power of his literature has elevated him to a point attained by so few writers, where even his waste basket is rifled for the gems it may contain. It might be unfair to the writer, but it is still the sincerest form of flattery."

A collection of Ransome's papers are housed in the Ransome Room at Abbot Hall in Kendal, England.

MEDIA ADAPTATIONS: Swallows and Amazons was made into a film by Richard Pilbrow in 1974; there have been two British television series based on Ransome's work.

AVOCATIONAL INTERESTS: Fishing, sailing, fairy tales.

BIOGRAPHICAL/CRITICAL SOURCES:

BOOKS

Children's Literature Review, Volume 8, Gale, 1985.

Hardyment, Christina, *Arthur Ransome and Captain Flint's Trunk,* J. Cape, 1984.

Lewis, Kathleen, editor, *Three Bodley Head Monographs,* Bodley Head, 1960.

Ransome, Arthur, *The Autobiography of Arthur Ransome,* edited by Rupert Hart-Davis, J. Cape, 1976.

PERIODICALS

New Statesman, August 2, 1930.

New York Times, February 14, 1932, May 14, 1933.

Times (London), October 29, 1988.

Times Literary Supplement, January 6-12, 1989.

OBITUARIES:

PERIODICALS

New York Times, June 6, 1967.
Publishers Weekly, June 26, 1967.*

*   *   *

RAWLS, James J(abus) 1945-

PERSONAL: Born November 10, 1945, in Washington, D.C.; son of Jabus W. (an engineer) and Jane Kathleen (Brumfield) Rawls; married Linda Joyce Higdon, December 29, 1967; children: Benjamin Jabus, Elizabeth Jane Kathleen. *Education:* Stanford University, B.A. (with distinction), 1967; University of California, Berkeley, M.A., 1969, Ph.D., 1975. *Politics:* Democrat. *Religion:* Episcopalian.

ADDRESSES: Home—166 France St., Sonoma, Calif. 95476. *Office*— Department of History, Diablo Valley College, Pleasant Hill, Calif. 94523.

CAREER: San Francisco State University, San Francisco, Calif., instructor in history, 1971-75; Diablo Valley College, Pleasant Hill, Calif., instructor in history, 1975. Visiting professor at University of California, Berkeley, 1989; consultant to Oakland Museum, KQED-TV, and National Endowment for the Humanities.

MEMBER: American Historical Association, California Historical Society, Friends of Bancroft Library.

AWARDS, HONORS: Fellow Award, California Historical Society, 1988; National Teaching Excellence Award, University of Texas, 1989.

WRITINGS:

(Editor and author of introduction) *Dan DeQuille of the Big Bonanza,* Book Club of California, 1980.
(With Walton Bean) *California: An Interpretive History,* McGraw, 1983, new edition, 1988.
Indians of California: The Changing Image, University of Oklahoma Press, 1984.
(With Philip Weeks) *Land of Liberty: A United States History,* Holt, 1985.
(Editor and author of introduction) *California: A Place, a People, a Dream,* Chronicle Books, 1986.
(Editor and author of introduction) *New Directions in California History,* McGraw, 1988.
(Author of foreword) *California Architecture: Historic American Buildings Survey,* Chronicle Books, 1988.
(Contributor) *A Guide to the History of California,* Greenwood Press, 1989.

Contributor to *Worldmark Encyclopedia of the States.* Contributor of articles and reviews to history journals and regional magazines, including *American West.* Review editor of *California History.*

WORK IN PROGRESS: Research for an article on Indian-Chinese relations during the Gold Rush; the changing images of the old Spanish missions of California; writing for young people on history and social studies.

SIDELIGHTS: James J. Rawls told CA: "My interest in the history of the West and of California probably stems as much from my residency here as anything else. I see about me in California the culmination of the nation's westering. The expectations, hopes, dreams, and ambitions of many Americans have been fulfilled or challenged here at the continent's edge. I am frequently struck by the tension within California between dream and reality, expectation and result.

"My largest research project thus far has been for *Indians of California: The Changing Image.* I was fascinated by the shifting images of the Indians—created by white observers—over the decades of contact. The evolution of imagery was fueled by the changing needs of the white population. Needing to discredit early Hispanic claims to the land, American observers saw the Indians as victims of Hispanic mistreatment; needing a cheap labor force themselves, they viewed the Indians as a useful class of laborers; needing unimpeded access to the resources of the Golden State during the gold rush, they treated the Indians simply as obstacles to be eliminated. I believe that no other writer has traced this peculiar evolution of images."

BIOGRAPHICAL/CRITICAL SOURCES:

PERIODICALS

Los Angeles Times Book Review, June 24, 1984.

*   *   *

RAYNER, Claire (Berenice) 1931-
(Sheila Brandon, Berry Chetwynd, Ann Lynton, Ruth Martin, Isobel Saxe)

PERSONAL: Born January 22, 1931, in London, England; married Desmond Rayner (a literary agent, manager, and painter), June 23, 1957; children: Amanda, Adam, Jay. *Education:* Studied nursing at Royal Northern Hospital, London; studied midwifery at Guy's Hospital.

ADDRESSES: Home—Holly Wood House, Roxborough Ave., Harrow-on-the-Hill, Middlesex HA1 3BU, England. *Agent*—Desmond Rayner, Holly Wood House, Roxborough Ave., Harrow-on-the-Hill, Middlesex HA1 3BU, England; and Aaron M. Priest, Aaron M. Priest Literary Agency, 565 Fifth Ave., New York, N.Y. 10017.

CAREER: Writer and broadcaster. Nurse and midwife at hospitals in London, England, including Royal Free Hospital and Whittington Hospital, 1954-60. Presenter of BBC-1 television series, "Claire Rayner's Casebook," 1980-84; co-presenter of Thames Television program, "Kitchen Garden"; presenter of BBC-Wales radio program, "Contact"; creator of six videotapes, "In Company with Claire Rayner." Has appeared frequently on British radio and television programs; makes weekly appearances on TV-AM program "Good Morning Britain." Lecturer throughout the United Kingdom.

MEMBER: Freedom of the City of London.

AWARDS, HONORS: Named one of the women "most British women would regard as a role model" in a national survey, 1988; honorary fellowship, Polytechnic of North London; Best Specialist Columnist of the Year award, *Publisher.*

WRITINGS:

NONFICTION

Mothers and Midwives, Allen & Unwin, 1962.
What Happens in the Hospital, Hart-Davis, 1963.
The Calendar of Childhood: A Guide for All Mothers, Ebury Press, 1964.
Your Baby, Hamlyn, 1965.
Careers with Children, R. Hale, 1966.
Housework the Easy Way, Transworld, 1967.
Shall I Be a Nurse?, Wheaton, 1967.

Home Nursing and Family Health, Transworld, 1967.
101 Facts an Expectant Mother Should Know, Dickens Press, 1967.
Essentials of Outpatient Nursing, Arlington Books, 1967.
For Children: Equipping a Home for a Growing Family, Macdonald for Council of Industrial Design, 1967.
101 Key Facts of Practical Baby Care, Dickens Press, 1967.
(Under pseudonym Ann Lynton) *Mothercraft,* Corgi, 1967.
A Parent's Guide to Sex Education, Corgi, 1968, Dolphin Books, 1969.
People in Love: A Modern Guide to Sex in Marriage, Hamlyn, 1968, revised edition published as *About Sex,* Fontana Books, 1972.
Protecting Your Baby, Richardson Merrell, 1971.
Woman's Medical Dictionary, Corgi, 1971.
When to Call the Doctor—What to Do Whilst Waiting, Corgi, 1972.
The Shy Person's Book, Wolfe, 1973, McKay, 1974.
Childcare Made Simple, W. H. Allen, 1973, 2nd edition, Heinemann, 1983.
Where Do I Come From?: Answers to a Child's Questions about Sex, Arlington Books, 1974.
(Contributing editor) *The Rand McNally Atlas of the Body and Mind,* Rand McNally, 1976 (published in England as *The Mitchell Beazley Atlas of the Body and Mind,* Mitchell Beazley, 1976).
(With Keith Fordyce) *Kitchen Garden,* ITP Ltd., 1976.
(With Fordyce) *More Kitchen Garden,* ITP Ltd., 1977.
Family Feelings: Understanding Your Child from Zero to Five, Arrow, 1977.
Claire Rayner Answers Your 100 Questions on Pregnancy, BBC Publications, 1977.
(With Fordyce) *Claire and Keith's Kitchen Garden,* Arrow, 1978.
The Body Book, Barron, 1978.
Related to Sex, Paddington Press, 1979.
(With Fordyce) *Greenhouse Gardening,* Hamlyn, 1979.
Everything Your Doctor Would Tell You If He Had the Time, Putnam, 1980.
Claire Rayner's Lifeguide: A Commonsense Approach to Modern Living, New English Library, 1980.
Baby and Young Child Care: A Practical Guide for Parents of Children Aged Zero-Five Years, Purnell, 1981, published as *Child Care from Birth to Age Five,* H. P. Books, 1983.
Growing Pains and How to Avoid Them, Heinemann, 1984.
Claire Rayner's Marriage Guide: How to Make Yours Work, Macmillan, 1984.
The Getting Better Books, Deutsch, 1985.
Woman, Hamlyn, 1986.
When I Grow Up, Virgin Books, 1986.
Safe Sex, Sphere Books, 1987.
Claire Rayner Talking, Southdown Press (Australia), 1988.
The Don't Spoil Your Body Book, Bodley Head, 1989.

NOVELS

Shilling a Pound Pears, Hart-Davis, 1964.
The House on the Fen, Transworld, 1967, reprinted, Linford Mystery, 1989.
Starch of Aprons, R. Hale, 1967, published as *The Hive,* Corgi, 1968, reprinted, Piatkus Books, 1983.
Lady Mislaid, Corgi, 1968.
Death on the Table, Corgi, 1969.
The Meddlers, Simon & Schuster, 1970.
A Time to Heal, Simon & Schuster, 1972.
The Burning Summer, Allison & Busby, 1972.

Sisters, Hutchinson, 1978.
Reprise, Hutchinson, 1980.
The Running Years, Delacorte, 1981.
Family Chorus, Hutchinson, 1984.
The Virus Man, Hutchinson, 1985.
Lunching at Laura's, Arrow, 1986.
Jubilee (Book One of "The Poppy Chronicle"), Weidenfeld & Nicolson, 1987.
Flanders (Book Two of "The Poppy Chronicle"), Weidenfeld & Nicolson, 1988.
Maddie, M. Joseph, 1988.
Clinical Judgements, M. Joseph, 1989.

"THE PERFORMERS" SERIES

Gower Street, Simon & Schuster, 1973.
The Haymarket, Simon & Schuster, 1974.
Paddington Green, Cassell, 1975.
Soho Square, Cassell, 1976.
Bedford Row, Putnam, 1977.
Long Acre, Putnam, 1978.
Charing Cross, Putnam, 1979.
The Strand, Putnam, 1980.
Chelsea Reach, Weidenfeld & Nicolson, 1982.
Shaftesbury Avenue, Weidenfeld & Nicolson, 1983.
Piccadilly, Weidenfeld & Nicolson, 1985.
Seven Dials, Weidenfeld & Nicolson, 1986.

NOVELS UNDER PSEUDONYM SHEILA BRANDON

The Final Year, Corgi, 1962, reprinted, Ulverscroft, 1983.
Cottage Hospital, Corgi, 1963, reprinted, Linford Romance, 1986.
Children's Ward, Corgi, 1964, reprinted, Linford Romance, 1986.
The Lonely One, Corgi, 1965, reprinted, Linford Romance, 1986.
The Doctors of Downlands, Corgi, 1968, reprinted, Linford Romance, 1987.
The Private Wing, Corgi, 1971.
Nurse in the Sun, Corgi, 1972.

OTHER

(Under pseudonym Isobel Saxe) *Desperate Remedies,* Corgi, 1968.

Woman's Own, regular columnist under house pseudonym Ruth Martin, nine years, under name Claire Rayner, 1975-88; regular columnist, *Woman,* 1988—; author of regular column, "Problem Page," for *Petticoat, Sun, Sunday Mirror,* and *Today.* Contributor to magazines and newspapers, including *Lancet, Medical World, Nursing Times, Nursing Mirror,* and *Design.* Many of Rayner's books have been translated.

WORK IN PROGRESS: Further volumes of "The Poppy Chronicles."

*   *   *

REES, Dilwyn
See DANIEL, Glyn (Edmund)

*   *   *

REESE, Carolyn Johnson 1938-
(Lyn Reese)

PERSONAL: Born January 10, 1938, in South Orange, N.J.; daughter of Wharton Vail (engineer) and Caroline (a teacher;

maiden name, Stafford) Johnson; married Charles H. Reese (a systems engineer), September 23, 1961; children: Vail Charles, Nicholas Stafford. *Education:* Mount Holyoke College, B.A., 1960; Stanford University, M.A., 1961; graduate study at University of California, Berkeley, 1962-63.

ADDRESSES: Home—1030 Spruce St., Berkeley, Calif. 94707.

CAREER: Crestmont School, Richmond, Calif., co-founder, 1969-72; curriculum developer and resource teacher for women's studies program for public schools of Berkeley, Calif., 1972-78; director of mathematics and science sex desegregation project for public schools of Novato, Calif., 1980-81. Curriculum specialist for Far West Laboratory for Educational Research, 1976-77; consultant to Berkeley High School department of history, 1983; director of education program for California Historical Society, 1986-88; co-director of New Directions Curriculum Developers, 1988-89.

MEMBER: Najda: Women Concerned about the Middle East, Math-Science Network for Women, Western Women Historians Association, California Council for Social Studies, Institute for History Study.

AWARDS, HONORS: Women Educators Curriculum Award, American Educational Research Association, 1982, for *In Search of Our Past; I'm On My Way Running: Women Speak on Coming of Age* was named one of 1983's best books for young adults by the American Library Association.

WRITINGS:

UNDER NAME LYN REESE

Sources of Strength: Women and Culture; A Teacher's Guide, U.S. Department of Health, Education, and Welfare, 1979.

In Search of Our Past: Six Units in Women's History, U.S. Department of Health, Education, and Welfare, 1979.

(Editor with Jean Wilkinson and Phyllis Koppelman) *I'm on My Way Running: Women Speak on Coming of Age,* Avon, 1983.

Two Voices from Nigeria: Through the Literature of Chinua Achebe and Buchi Emecheta, Stanford University Press, 1985.

Women in the World: Student Resources, Scarecrow Press, 1987.

(Author of teacher's guide) *On Location: Travels to California's Past* (video series), California Historical Society, 1988.

(Author of teacher's guide) *Hearts and Hands: Women's Quilts in American History* (video), Ferrero Films, 1989.

(Author of teacher's guide) *Visions toward Tomorrow: A History of the East Bay Afro-American Community* (video), Northern California Afro-American Center, 1989.

Contributor to *California Historical Quarterly.*

WORK IN PROGRESS: Creating a series of young adult short stories about women in diverse periods of world history.

SIDELIGHTS: Lyn Reese told *CA:* "Since the early 1970s, I have been developing educational materials which highlight the important role of women in history. As much as possible I try to present history by using short stories or first person accounts. In this way, I let women speak for themselves. I've found that students relate well to the voices of real people, and that it helps young women sharpen their perceptions of themselves as women and begin to see the universality of the female experience. The intent of our cross-cultural anthology on female coming-of-age [*I'm on My Way Running: Women Speak on Coming of Age*], for example, [is to use] many first person narratives to discuss themes that link the concerns of young women everywhere. It

begins with selections about first menstruation, the clearest sign of a girl's entry into womanhood, and then looks at the impact of sexuality, the increased concern with appearance, and the intensification of the mother-daughter relationship. The last chapter demonstrates girls' desires for adventure and includes the stories of some who have broken with tradition.

"Most of my writing is done in collaboration with others. The collective process can be laborious and lengthy, yet I feel that group input enhances the final product and mutual support lightens the day. Currently, I am responding to the increased interest in using literature to teach historical topics and contemporary issues. In California, sixth and seventh grade teachers are now expected to incorporate literature into classes which cover world history topics to the Middle Ages. There is, however, a dearth of age-appropriate materials and I am trying to bridge the gap with a series of short stories about women from these early periods. Each of my stories includes a brief teacher background essay and follow-up questions and activities. Since I have desktop publishing equipment, I layout my own work and look for a publisher to provide the printing and distribution. I am close, however, to attempting to market my material myself!"

*   *   *

REESE, Lyn
  See REESE, Carolyn Johnson

*   *   *

REESE, (John) Terence   1913-

PERSONAL: Born August 28, 1913, in Epsom, England; son of John (a confectioner and hotelier) and Anne (a hotelier; maiden name, Hutchings) Reese; married Alwyn Sherrington (in business), 1970. *Education:* Attended Bradfield College and New College, Oxford.

ADDRESSES: Home—18a Woods Mews, Park Ln., London W.1, England.

CAREER: Writer and bridge expert. Bridge correspondent for *Evening News,* London, England, 1948-80, *Observer,* London, 1950—, *Lady,* 1954—, and *Standard,* 1980—.

AWARDS, HONORS: Winner of numerous British, European, and world bridge championships.

WRITINGS:

(With Hubert Phillips) *The Elements of Contract,* British Bridge World, 1937, 2nd edition, revised, Eyre & Spottiswoode, 1948.

Reese on Play: An Introduction to Good Bridge, Edward Arnold, 1947, 2nd edition, R. Hale, 1975.

(With Phillips) *How to Play Bridge,* Penguin Books, 1945, revised edition, Parrish, 1958.

(With Phillips) *Bridge with Mr. Playbetter,* Batchworth Press, 1952.

The Expert Game, Edward Arnold, 1958, new edition, R. Hale, 1973.

Master Play, the Expert Game: Contract Bridge, Coffin, 1960, published as *Master Play in Contract Bridge,* Dover, 1974.

Play Bridge with Reese, Sterling, 1960.

Modern Bidding and the Acol System, Nicholson & Watson, 1960.

Bridge, Penguin Books, 1961, new edition, Hodder & Stoughton, 1980.

Develop Your Bidding Judgment, Sterling, 1962, published as *Bidding a Bridge Hand,* Dover, 1972.

The Game of Bridge, Constable, 1962.

(With Anthony Watkins) *Poker, Game of Skill,* Faber, 1962, Merrimack Book Service, 1964.

Learn Bridge with Reese, Faber, 1962, revised edition, Hamlyn/American, 1978.

(With Watkins) *Secrets of Modern Poker,* Sterling, 1964.

Bridge for Bright Beginners, Sterling, 1964.

Your Book of Contract Bridge, Faber, 1965, Transatlantic, 1971.

(Editor) Ely Culbertson, *Contract Bridge Self-Teacher,* revised edition, Faber, 1965.

(Editor) Culbertson, *Contract Bridge Complete,* 7th edition, revised, Faber, 1965.

(Editor) Alfred Sheinwold, *Improve Your Bridge,* Jenkins, 1965.

(Editor) Josephine Murphy Culbertson, *Contract Bridge Made Easy the New Point Count Way,* Faber, 1966.

Story of an Accusation, Heinemann, 1966, Simon & Schuster, 1967.

(With Boris Schapiro) *Bridge Card by Card,* Hamlyn/American, 1969.

(Adapter from the French) Benito Garozzo and Leon Yallouze, *The Blue Club* (with foreword by Omar Sharif), Faber, 1969.

Precision Bidding and Precision Play, W. H. Allen, 1972, Sterling, 1973, 2nd edition, R. Hale, 1980.

Advanced Bridge (adapted from *Play Bridge with Reese* and *Develop Your Bidding Judgment),* Sterling, 1973.

(With Robert Brinig) *Backgammon: The Modern Game,* W. H. Allen, 1975, Sterling, 1976.

Play These Hands with Me, W. H. Allen, 1976.

Bridge by Question and Answer, Arthur Barker, 1976.

Bridge at the Top (autobiography), Merrimack Book Service, 1977.

Begin Bridge with Reese, Sterling, 1977.

Winning at Casino Gambling: An International Guide, Sterling, 1978.

The Most Puzzling Situations in Bridge Play, Sterling, 1978.

(With Jeremy Flint) *Trick Thirteen* (novel), Weidenfeld & Nicolson, 1979.

(With Patrick Jourdain) *Squeeze Play Made Easy: Techniques for Advanced Bridge Players,* Sterling, 1980 (published in England as *Squeeze Play Is Easy,* Allen & Unwin, 1980).

Bridge Tips by World Masters, R. Hale, 1980, Crown, 1981.

(With Eddie Kantar) *Defend with Your Life,* Merrimack Book Service, 1981.

(Adapter from the French) *Omar Sharif's Life in Bridge,* Faber, 1982.

Teach Yourself Bridge, Hodder & Stoughton, 1982.

(With David Bird) *Miracles of Card Play,* Gollancz, 1982.

(With Bird) *How the Experts Do It,* Faber, 1982.

(With Bird) *The Modern Game,* Faber, 1983.

(With Bird) *Unholy Tricks,* Gollancz, 1984.

(With Julian Pottage) *Positive Defence,* Gollancz, 1985.

What Would You Bid?, Faber, 1986.

(With Martin Hoffman) *Play It Again, Sam,* Devyn Press, 1986.

(With Pottage) *Positive Declarer's Play,* Gollancz, 1986.

Master Plays in a Single Suit, Gollancz, 1987.

(With Bird) *Doubled and Venerable,* Gollancz, 1987.

Bridge for Ambitious Players, Gollancz, 1988.

Master Deceptive Plays, Gollancz, 1988.

(With Bird) *The Hidden Side of Bridge,* Gollancz, 1988.

WITH ALBERT DORMER

Bridge Player's Dictionary, Sterling, 1959, revised and enlarged edition, 1963, adaptation published as *Bridge Conventions, Finesses and Coups,* Sterling, 1965.

Blueprint for Bidding: The Acol System Applied to American Bridge, Sterling, 1961.

The Acol System Today, Edward Arnold, 1961, revised edition published as *Bridge, the Acol System of Bidding: A Modern Version of the Acol System Today,* Pan Books, 1978.

The Play of the Cards, Penguin Books, 1967, new edition, R. Hale, 1977.

Bridge for Tournament Players, R. Hale, 1968.

How to Play a Good Game of Bridge, Heinemann, 1969.

How to Play a Better Game of Bridge, Stein & Day, 1969.

Practical Bidding and Practical Play, Sterling, 1973.

The Complete Book of Bridge, Faber, 1973, Saturday Review Press, 1974.

The Bridge Player's Alphabetical Handbook, Merrimack Book Service, 1981.

WITH ROGER TREZEL

Safety Plays in Bridge, Fell, 1976.

Elimination Play in Bridge, Fell, 1976.

Blocking and Unblocking Plays in Bridge, Fell, 1976.

Snares and Swindles in Bridge, Fell, 1976.

When to Duck, When to Win in Bridge, Fell, 1978.

Those Extra Chances in Bridge, Fell, 1978.

The Art of Defence in Bridge, Gollancz, 1979.

Master the Odds in Bridge, Gollancz, 1979.

The Mistakes You Make at Bridge, Gollancz, 1984.

OTHER

Former editor of *British Bridge World* magazine.

WORK IN PROGRESS: Editions of his work to be published in French, German, Italian, Danish, Swedish, Portuguese, Japanese, Dutch, and Hebrew.

SIDELIGHTS: Terence Reese told *CA:* "Since 1976 I have played very little bridge and prefer to lose my money at backgammon. Tournament bridge is being ruined by the World Bridge Federation with its ghastly regulations, screens, and so forth." He added in 1988, "It *has* been ruined, since players nowadays are permitted to use whatever artificial methods they please."

BIOGRAPHICAL/CRITICAL SOURCES:

BOOKS

Reese, Terence, *Bridge at the Top* (autobiography), Merrimack Book Service, 1977.

PERIODICALS

Life, June 4, 1965.

McCall's, September, 1965.

Nation, September 18, 1967.

New Statesman, December 30, 1966.

Time, June 4, 1965.

Times Literary Supplement, April 13, 1967.

*   *   *

REICH, Sheldon 1931-

PERSONAL: Born September 5, 1931, in Brooklyn, N.Y.; son of Hyman David and Molly (Gubman) Reich; married Dorothy Kashdan, June, 1951 (divorced, 1979); married Shirley Gish (a writer), November 2, 1980 (divorced, 1985); children: Robin Reich Bowen, Jonathan, Adam. *Education:* University of Miami, Coral Gables, Fla., A.B., 1954; New York University, M.A., 1957; University of Iowa, Ph.D., 1966.

ADDRESSES: Home—710 North Alamo Ave., Tucson, Ariz. 85711. *Office*—Department of Art History, University of Arizona, Tucson, Ariz. 85721.

CAREER: Oklahoma State University, Stillwater, assistant professor of art history, 1957-60; University of Arizona, Tucson, assistant professor, 1960-65, associate professor, 1966-67, professor of art history, 1967-68; University of Cincinnati, Cincinnati, Ohio, professor of art history and head of department, 1968-72; University of Arizona, professor of art history, 1972—. Research fellow at National Museum of American Art, 1971-72. *Military service:* U.S. Air Force, 1950-51; became airman first class.

MEMBER: College Art Association of America, American Association of University Professors, Mid-American College of Art Association.

AWARDS, HONORS: Helen Wurlitzer Foundation of New Mexico grant, 1983.

WRITINGS:

John Marin Drawings, 1886-1951, University of Utah Press, 1969.
John Marin: A Stylistic Analysis and a Catalogue Raisonne, two volumes, University of Arizona Press, 1970, revised edition published as *John Marin: A Catalogue Raisonne,* University of Missouri Press, 1990.
A. H. Maurer, Smithsonian Institution Press, 1973.
Francisco Zuniga, Sculptor: Conversations and Interpretations, University of Arizona Press, 1980.
Keith Crown Watercolors, University of Missouri Press, 1986.
James G. Davis, Tucson Museum of Art, 1988.
Andrew Dasburg: His Life and Art, Bucknell University Press/Associated University Presses, 1989.

Author of exhibition catalogs. Contributor of articles and reviews to art journals.

SIDELIGHTS: Sheldon Reich once told *CA:* "I don't consider myself an author in the creative meaning of the word. Writing is simply the medium through which I convey what I have learned about the art of others. I'm best known as an expert on early twentieth-century American art, but in many ways I receive more pleasure from the work I do that relates to living artists. Coming in direct contact with artists like Francisco Zuniga, Isabel Bishop, and others not yet quite as well known, is stimulating. When occasionally I brood about art being a peripheral concern in the modern world—a sense communicated in part by the emphasis on science in the academic environment in which I have spent my entire adult life—it helps enormously to meet these powerful, dedicated painters and sculptors who have few, if any, such doubts about the contribution they are making to the quality of modern life."

*   *   *

RESNICK, Sylvia (Safran) 1927-
(Sheri Paul)

PERSONAL: Born February 22, 1927, in Chicago, Ill.; daughter of Abe (a tailor) and Sarah (an actress; maiden name, Green) Safran; married Max Resnick (an aeronautical designer), July 9, 1948; children: Barry Paul. *Education:* Attended Wright Junior College, 1945, and Los Angeles Junior College, 1946. *Religion:* Jewish.

ADDRESSES: Home—22732 Kittridge St., West Hills, Calif. 91307. *Agent*—Helen McGrath, 1406 Idaho Ct., Concord, Calif. 94521.

CAREER: Free-lance writer, 1964-67; *Movie Life,* New York, N.Y., Hollywood editor, 1967-69; *Rona Barrett's Hollywood,* Hollywood, Calif., associate editor, 1970-72; *Bestways,* La Canada, Calif., feature writer and beauty editor, 1973-77; free-lance writer, 1977—.

MEMBER: California Writer's Club, Independent Writers of Southern California.

WRITINGS:

FOR YOUNG ADULTS

Debbie Preston, Teenage Reporter: The Case of the Gypsy's Warning (novel), New American Library, 1972.
Debbie Preston and the Hollywood Mystery (novel), New American Library, 1972.
Debbie Preston and the Donny Osmond Mystery (novel), New American Library, 1973.
The Partridge Family Cookbook, Curtis Books, 1973.
The Walton Family Cookbook, Bantam, 1976.
Kristy McNichol (biography), Xerox Education Publications, 1979.

OTHER

Heat Wave (novel), Chariot Publishing, 1961.
Willing Flesh (novel), Chariot Publishing, 1962.
Burt Reynolds: An Unauthorized Biography, St. Martin's, 1983.

Author of columns "Las Vegas Go-Round," *TV Star Parade,* 1967-70, "Daytime Television News" and "Film Reviews," *Rona Barrett's Hollywood,* 1970-72, "Film Reviews," *Hollywood Now,* 1972, "Your Beauty," *Bestways,* 1973-77, and "The Selective Traveller," *Maine Sunday Telegram,* 1982-86; also author of column "A Word to the Wives," 1958-59, and a semi-monthly beauty column for *Hair* magazine. Contributor, sometimes under pseudonym Sheri Paul, to magazines and newspapers, including *Photoplay, Chicago Tribune, Los Angeles Herald Examiner, San Francisco Herald Examiner, Milwaukee Sentinel,* and *Ft. Lauderdale Sun-Sentinel.*

WORK IN PROGRESS: Longings, a novel; *A Matter of the Heart,* for Harlequin American Romance.

SIDELIGHTS: Sylvia Resnick told *CA:* "I feel that writers have an obligation to reflect an aura of hope, especially in the climate of uncertainty and noncommitment in which we presently live. Although I write about the everyday lives of my characters, often presenting them with real and tragic problems, in the end I must always leave them and my readers with *hope.* I think that there is too much of the negative being published: dwelling on and elaborating on sensational crimes in the name of literature. Readers should be involved with the characters in a book, but in a way that is enriching rather than merely titillating or shocking.

"When I was a child, the books of Pearl Buck and Louisa May Alcott were my mainstay. They were not works of pure sweetness and light, but they were uplifting and inspiring in their positive influence, in which the family was of uppermost importance even in the midst of strife and war or the sorrows of sickness and death. I am no Pollyanna, but I do feel I have a responsibility to use whatever talents I have to do whatever little or (hopefully) much I can to uplift while entertaining with words.

"Travel is my second love, and whenever there is enough time and money I am off on a trip. Although I have a passion for antiquity, it is primarily centered on the people of the past, rather than the things. The remnants of other times in the form of furniture, art, and especially old houses set up a chain reaction that eventually spins a story about the people to whom those objects belonged. And whenever I travel I manage to get to know as much as I can about one or more of the natives. I love people, and am excited by meeting with them and with the past that has shaped all of us.

"Another of my activities is the study of metaphysics and its entire scope of the mental and spiritual. I have taken classes in learning how to expand my psychic awareness, which I found fascinating. I believe very deeply in the need of all of us to return to the basics of caring for one another, and perhaps this can be made possible through an expansion of spiritual consciousness, tuning in to one another in a positive way."

AVOCATIONAL INTERESTS: Cooking, reading, dancing, watching old movies.

*   *   *

RICHARDS, Jeffrey (Michael) 1945-

PERSONAL: Born November 5, 1945, in Birmingham, England; son of Joseph Leslie (a works manager) and Peggy (North) Richards. *Education:* Jesus College, Cambridge, B.A., 1967, M.A., 1972.

ADDRESSES: Office—Department of History, University of Lancaster, Bailrigg, Lancashire LA1 4YG, England.

CAREER: University of Lancaster, Lancaster, England, lecturer in Byzantine history, 1969-81, senior lecturer in history, 1981—, reader in history, 1987—. Lecturer at York University, Edinburgh University, Imperial War Museum, and other universities and organizations.

MEMBER: British Film Institute, British Society of Sports History, Association of University Teachers, Ecclesiastical History Society, Sherlock Holmes Society, Cambridge Union Society, John Buchan Society, Henty Society.

AWARDS, HONORS: Grants from Wolfson Foundation and British Academy.

WRITINGS:

Visions of Yesterday, Routledge & Kegan Paul, 1973.
Swordsmen of the Screen, Routledge & Kegan Paul, 1977.
The Popes and the Papacy in the Early Middle Ages, 476-752, Routledge & Kegan Paul, 1979.
Consul of God: The Life and Times of Pope Gregory the Great, Routledge & Kegan Paul, 1980.
A Social History of Britain in Postcards, 1870-1920, Longman, 1980.
(Editor and author of introduction) James Greenwood, *The Seven Curses of London,* Blackwell, 1981.
(With Anthony Aldgate) *British Cinema and Society, 1930-1970,* Barnes & Noble, 1983 (published in England as *Best of British: Cinema and Society, 1930-1970,* Blackwell, 1983).
Age of the Dream Palace: Cinema and Society in Britain, 1930-1939, Routledge & Kegan Paul, 1984.
(With John M. MacKenzie) *The Railway Station: A Social History,* Oxford University Press, 1986.
(With Aldgate) *Britain Can Take It: British Films and the Second World War,* Blackwell, 1986.
Thorold Dickinson: The Man and His Films, Croom Helm, 1986.
(Editor with Dorothy Sheridan) *Mass Observation at the Movies,* Routledge & Kegan Paul, 1987.
Happiest Days: The Public Schools in English Fiction, Manchester University Press, 1988.
(Editor) *Imperialism and Juvenile Literature,* Manchester University Press, 1989.

CONTRIBUTOR

Bill Nichols, editor, *Movies and Methods,* California University Press, 1977.
John Tulloch, editor, *Conflict and Control in the Cinema,* Macmillan, 1978.
James Curran and Vincent Porter, editors, *British Cinema History,* Weidenfeld & Nicolson, 1983.
John K. Walton and James Walvin, editors, *Leisure in Britain, 1780-1939,* Manchester University Press, 1983.
MacKenzie, editor, *Imperialism and Popular Culture,* Manchester University Press, 1986.
Charles Barr, editor, *All Our Yesterdays,* British Film Institute, 1986.
J. A. Mangan and Walvin, editors, *Manliness and Morality,* Manchester University Press, 1987.
P. Taylor, editor, *Britain and the Cinema and the Second World War,* Macmillan, 1988.

OTHER

Editor of "Cinema and Society" series, for Routledge & Kegan Paul. Arts columnist, *Daily Telegraph,* 1987—. Contributor of articles and reviews to magazines, including *Focus on Film, Silent Picture, Cultures, Economist,* and *Encounter.* Member of editorial board, *Historical Journal of Film, Radio, and Television.*

WORK IN PROGRESS: History of medieval minority groups; study of the life and work of British actor Sir Henry Irving.

SIDELIGHTS: Jeffrey Richards told *CA:* "I have two main research interests: the relationship between Papacy and Empire in the early Byzantine period, and the relationship between cinema and society in Britain and America. My basic view on the first is that, contrary to the widely held view that mutual hostility existed between Papacy and Empire, Papal Rome was a loyal subject to the Eastern Emperor in Constantinople until the fall of Ravenna to the Lombards. This view underlies both *The Popes and the Papacy in the Early Middle Ages, 476-752* and the biography of Pope Gregory I, *Consul of God: The Life and Times of Pope Gregory the Great.*

"I am concerned in the area of cinema to explore the nature of film as artifact rather than as art, a product of its environment, a reflection and influence on that environment. This idea has underlain my film books and is the underlying theme of a series of books I am editing for Routledge & Kegan Paul under the general heading 'Cinema and Society.' "

AVOCATIONAL INTERESTS: Railway station architecture, "supporting my local football team, Aston Villa."

BIOGRAPHICAL/CRITICAL SOURCES:

PERIODICALS

New York Times Book Review, November 9, 1986.
Times Literary Supplement, December 14, 1973, November 11, 1977, December 21, 1979, August 15, 1980, November 18, 1983, August 17, 1984, June 27, 1986, August 12-18, 1988.

*   *   *

RICHSTATTER, Thomas 1939-

PERSONAL: Born October 14, 1939, in Topeka, Kan.; son of Otto Joseph (a linoleum mechanic) and Rose Mary (Sack) Richstatter. *Education:* Duns Scotus College, B.A., 1962; attended St. Leonard College, 1962-66; University of Notre Dame, M.A., 1971; Institut Superieur de Liturgie de Paris, M.S.L., 1976; Institut Catholique de Paris, S.T.D., 1976.

ADDRESSES: Office—St. Meinrad School of Theology, St. Meinrad, Ind. 47577.

CAREER: Entered Order of Friars Minor (Franciscans), 1958, ordained Roman Catholic priest, 1966; St. Francis Seminary, Cincinnati, Ohio, instructor in religion, 1966-71; pastor of Roman Catholic community in Paris, France, 1973-76; St. Leonard College, Centerville, Ohio, instructor in sacramental theology, 1976-81; Washington Theological Union, Washington, D.C., instructor in sacramental theology, 1981-83; St. Meinrad School of Theology, St. Meinrad, Ind., associate professor of sacramental-liturgical theology, 1984—. Instructor at Catholic University of America, 1981-83; adjunct professor at St. Vincent Regional Seminary, 1984. Member of Franciscan Committee for Liturgical Research, 1978—; executive secretary of Federation of Diocesan Liturgical Commissions, 1981-83; adviser to Bishops' Committee on the Liturgy, 1981-83. Member of board of trustees of National Shrine of the Immaculate Conception, 1981-83.

MEMBER: Societas Liturgica, North American Academy of Liturgy, Canon Law Society of America.

WRITINGS:

Liturgical Law Today: New Style, New Spirit, Franciscan Herald, 1977.
(Contributor) *Pastoral Care of the Sick: Rites of Anointing and Viaticum,* Publications Office, United States Catholic Conference, 1984.
(Contributor) *The Code of Canon Law: A Text and Commentary,* Paulist Press, 1985.
(Contributor) Bernard J. Lee, editor, *Alternative Futures for Worship,* Volume 3: *Eucharist,* Liturgical Press, 1987.
Would You Like to Be Anointed?, St. Anthony Messenger Press, 1987.
The Reconciliation of Penitents: A Study of the Structural Elements of the Communal Rite of Penance, Federation of Diocesan Liturgical Commissions, 1987.
Before You Say "I Do": Four Things to Remember When Planning Your Wedding Liturgy, St. Anthony Messenger Press, 1989.
(Contributor) *Catholic Update,* St. Anthony Messenger Press, 1990.
Scriptural Meditations for Ministers of Communion, Pastoral Press, 1990.
What's Happened to Catholic Devotions?, St. Anthony Messenger Press, 1991.

OTHER

Author of a television series "The Sacraments: The Church at Prayer," Cable TV Communications Office, Roman Catholic Diocese of Cincinnati, 1981, and of tape cassette series, "Today's Liturgy: New Style, New Spirit," 1978, "The Sacraments: The Church at Prayer," 1981, and "Praying Your Way through Lent," 1986, all published by St. Anthony Messenger Press. Consultant on film, "The Challenge of Change: The Visual Dimension of Worship," Pretty Pictures, 1983. Contributor to *New Catholic Encyclopedia.* Contributor to religious magazines. Editor of *Federation of Diocesan Liturgical Commissions Newsletter,* 1981-83.

SIDELIGHTS: Thomas Richstatter wrote *CA:* "It's easy to write for colleagues and professionals—the challenge today is to make the very best scholarship and historical research available to the ordinary people in the pew and to allow the results of scholarship to be applied in the parishes and tested by the masses. Popularization is more than 'making it simple,' it is an art."

*   *   *

RICHTER, Hans   1888-1976

PERSONAL: Born 1888, in Berlin, Germany; died February 1, 1976, in Locarno, Switzerland; came to the United States, 1941; became U.S. citizen; married. *Education:* Attended Berlin Academy of Fine Arts, 1908; Weimer Academy of Art, master's degree, 1909.

CAREER: Painter, filmmaker, actor, and writer. Collaborator on *Die Aktion* (journal), 1914; member of Dada group in Zurich, Switzerland, 1916-18; publisher and editor of *G* (art magazine), 1923-26; *Textil-Zeitung,* Berlin, Germany, chief designer, 1925; Lichtbildbuhne, Berlin, artistic advisor, 1926-27; *Taegliche Rundschau,* Berlin, film and music critic, 1927-28; Central-Film, Zurich, chief producer, 1937-38; Frobenius-Film, Basel, Switzerland, chief producer, 1939; City College (now City College of the City University of New York), New York, N.Y., director of Institute of Film Techniques, 1942-56. One-man art exhibitions in Munich, Zurich, New York, San Francisco, Chicago, Berlin, Washington, D.C., Milan, Amsterdam, Paris, Geneva, and other cities. *Military service:* German Army, 1914-16; wounded in action.

AWARDS, HONORS: International Prize for Film, Venice Film Festival, 1947, for "Dreams That Money Can Buy"; R. J. Flaherty Award, 1956 and 1966; Cross of Merit, German Government, 1964 and 1973; Art Prize of the City of Berlin, 1967; Berlin International Film Festival Award, 1971.

WRITINGS:

Film-Gegner von heute, Film-Freunde von morgen, Verlag H. Reckendorf (Berlin), 1929.
Film gesteren, heden, morgen, [Amsterdam], 1935.
The Political Film, [New York], 1941.
(Contributor) Frank Stauffacher, editor, *Art in Cinema,* San Francisco Museum of Art, 1947.
(Contributor) Roger Maurell, editor, *Experiment in the Film,* Grey Walls Press, 1949.
Dada Profile, Verlag Die Arche (Zurich), 1961.
Dada, Kunst und Antikunst (memoir), M. DuMont Schauberg, 1964, translation by David Britt published as *Dada: Art and Anti-Art,* McGraw, 1965.
Plastic Arts of the Twentieth Century, edited by Marcel Joray, Editions du Griffon, 1965.
Hans Richter (autobiographical), Editions du Griffin, 1965.
Cinquante ans de dadaisme, 1916-1966, Goethe Institut, 1970.
Hans Richter by Hans Richter, edited by Cleve Gray, Holt, 1971.
(Illustrator) *Peinture et cinema,* Goethe Institut, 1971.
The World between the Ox and the Swine: Dada Drawings by Hans Richter, Museum of Art, Rhode Island School of Design, 1971.
Begegnungen von Dada bis heute: Briefe, Dokumente, M. DuMont Schauberg, 1973.
Der Kampf um den Film, [Munich], 1976, translation by Ben Brewster published as *The Struggle for the Film: Towards a Socially Responsible Cinema,* edited by Jurgen Romhild, St. Martin's, 1986.
Opera Grafica dal 1902 al 1969, La nuova Foglio (Pollenza, Italy), 1976.
Hans Richter, 1888-1976: dessins et portraits dada, Le Musee (Les Sables-d'Olonne), 1978.

SCREENPLAYS

"Rhythm 21," 1921; "Rhythm 23," 1923; "Rhythm 25," 1925; "Filmstudie," 1926; "Inflation," 1927; "Vormittagsspuk" (title means "Ghosts before Breakfast"), 1927; "Rennsymphonie" (title means "Race Symphony"), 1928; "Zweigroschenzauber" (title means "Two-Penny Magic"), 1929; "Alles dreht sich, alles bewegt sich" (title means "Everything Turns, Everything Revolves"), 1929; "Nachmittag zu den Wettrennen," 1929; "Sturm uber la Sarraz," 1929; "Everyday," 1930; "Neues Leben," 1930; "Europa Radio," 1931; "Hallo Everybody," 1933; "Vom Blitz zum Fernsehbild," 1936; "Eine kleine Welt im dunkelem," 1938; "Die Enstehung der Farbe," 1938; "Die Eroberung des Himmels," 1938; "Hans im Glueck," 1938; "Die Boerse," 1939; "The Movies Take a Holiday," 1944; "Dreams That Money Can Buy," 1947; "Minotaur," 1954; "8 x 8: A Chess Sonata," 1957; "Dadascope," 1957; "Passionate Pastime," 1957; "From Dada to Surrealism," 1961; "Alexander Calder: From the Circus to the Moon," 1963; "Dadascope: Part II," 1967. The documentary "Forty Years of Experiment, Part 1," 1961, is composed of films and film fragments by Richter from the 1920s.

OTHER

Also author of several exhibition catalogues. Contributor to *College Art Journal, Hollywood Quarterly, Saturday Review, Die Form, De Stijl, Film-Kurier, Cercle et Carre, Film Culture,* and *Filmmakers Newsletter.*

SIDELIGHTS: Best known for his experimental films "Dreams That Money Can Buy," "Rhythm 21," and "Ghosts before Breakfast" (originally "Vormmittagspuk"), Hans Richter was a pioneer in abstract film and animation. He was also a world-renowned painter and a major participant in the anarchistic art movement known as Dada. His memoir *Dada: Art and Anti-Art* gives a detailed history of the people and ideas behind the controversial group.

Richter first became interested in modern art while still in school, where he studied painting and carpentry; at that time carpentry was thought to be a necessary prelude to a career as an architect. In 1912 he discovered the German magazine *Der Sturm,* the country's leading Expressionist journal, an event he later marked as a turning point in his development. In 1914 he became involved with *Die Aktion* magazine and with the circle of avant-garde artists associated with the Cafe des Westens in Berlin. *Die Aktion* dedicated an entire issue to Richter's work that same year.

After an 18-month stint in the German Army during the First World War, which ended when he was wounded in action, Richter and his new wife (a nurse he met while recovering in the hospital) went to Zurich to meet two of Richter's friends from the army. (The three young men had vowed that, if they survived the war, they would meet in Zurich in 1916. All of them did survive.) During the visit, Richter was introduced to Tristan Tzara, Francis Picabia, Hugo Ball, and other artists who were working together in a Zurich cafe under the group name Cabaret Voltaire. Under this name the group presented a variety of experimental artistic works. Within days, Richter had joined them.

The Cabaret Voltaire was composed of artists from all over Europe who had settled in Switzerland to avoid the raging war. Their anger and frustration over what they saw as a senseless slaughter led them to an artistic revolt against the causes of the war. These "causes," they believed, included such things as rational thinking, religion, nationalism, and urban civilization. As Richter explained it in an article for *Saturday Review,* "The whole dead-earnest Reality—the war, the generals, the govern-

ments, the schools, the arts, all that they had experienced in their young lives, everything that was called Sense—looked like a dying Non-Sense. And, comparatively, the so-called Non-Sense became a form of living, of living protest, a protesting Sense."

As their artistic rebellion grew, the Cabaret Voltaire performers labeled themselves followers of "Dada," a word that has been given several meanings and origins by members of the group. Hans Arp credited Tzara with having fabricated the word; Richard Huelsenbeck claimed that it was a French word for hobbyhorse; and Hugo Ball explained that "Dada is foolery, foolery extracted from the emptiness in which all the higher problems are wrapped, a gladiator's gesture, a game played with the shabby remnants . . . a public execution of false morality."

Whatever the word's origin, Dada came to represent a kind of artistic anti-art which overturned the assumptions of most recognized artistic standards. Dadaists, as the Cabaret Voltaire artists soon called themselves, experimented with simultaneously-read works, with poems created by chance occurrence, with collage and cut-up techniques, and with the random, the primitive, and the deliberately unartistic. Chance played a major role in their creations, as did the use of unconventional materials and found objects. Poetry readings were punctuated by screams and shouts, grating sound effects, and obscenities directed at the audience. Music was created on a variety of objects; lectures resembled nothing more than shouted arguments; plays were staged with actors wearing costumes of cardboard tubing and chanting phonetic poems in voices like a priest conducting high mass. The Dadaists also published magazines, booklets of poems and drawings, and manifestoes. Many Dada events, because of their openly offensive, satiric, and aggressive nature, ended in nasty brawls with hostile members of the public. As what George Heard Hamilton of *Saturday Review* called "a charter member" of Dada, Richter participated in the most important events in the group's short-lived history. His artwork and manifestoes appeared in the Dada publications and exhibitions, and he delivered lectures, painted scenery and backdrops, and performed in the many events.

Though Dada in Zurich was a brief phenomenon, lasting only until the end of the First World War, it had several postwar offshoots in other European cities. More importantly, Dada has also had a seminal influence on the artistic thought of this century and inspired a score of other art movements. Because of the Dadaists' willingness to throw out all previously-held beliefs, they were able to see the artistic process in a way that no other art movement had. Richter explained in his *Dada: Art and Anti-Art* that "the freedom not to care a damn about anything . . . brought us all the more closer to the source of all art, the voice within ourselves." In his *Saturday Review* article, Richter described Dada as the "creative impulse and source of many valid expressions of twentieth-century spirit and art."

With the end of the war, Richter returned to Germany and began to work on some of the ideas he had developed during his involvement with Dada. The role of chance had particularly caught his attention, and Richter sought to find a way to harness chance for artistic purposes. He collaborated with Viking Eggeling, a Swedish artist he had met in Zurich. As Richter explained in an article for the *Saturday Review,* "Eggeling and I searched into what we called later 'a universal language of form.' If there was a 'Law of Chance,' then there should be, by the same logic, a 'Law of Rule'—to make the 'Law of Chance' meaningful: abstract art free *and* disciplined."

Richter saw music as a possible model for a disciplined use of chance. He and Eggeling began to work on a new sort of painting which fused the rhythmic nature of music with the artist's spontaneity. Drawing sequences of abstract designs on long sheets of paper, the two men created a kind of scroll painting which revealed itself in a moving, rhythmical manner as the paper was unrolled. The fluctuating variations of the designs on the unrolling scrolls, and the way they forced the eye to move, were of special interest to the two artists.

These scroll paintings soon gave way to experiments with animated films in which abstract figures moved and danced. "Rhythm 21" was the first of Richter's films and one of his most important. Based on one of the scroll paintings completed in 1923, the film consists of moving squares expanding and contracting so that a rhythmic pulse of form is created. The square of the screen itself becomes a part of the developing design. "Rhythm 21" is described by Inez Hedges in *Languages of Revolt: Dada and Surrealist Literature and Film* as a film in which the audience is made to "question the illusion of foreground and background in film, since the relationships between the shapes are continually changing. The film breaks the frame of visual illusion by undercutting the viewer's traditional orientation toward the screen image, usually stabilized by the presentation of visual information from a coherent perspective." Writing in *Films in Review*, Herman G. Weinberg gave a historical perspective on the film work of Richter and Eggeling. According to Weinberg, "the first purely abstract films were Hans Richter's *Rhythm 21* and Viking Eggeling's *Diagonal Symphony*, both produced in 1921 in Berlin. . . . All who now work in the experimental film field are in direct line of descent from those Richter and Eggeling experiments."

In 1927 Richter turned from experiments with abstract film to more surreal film work. The first of these, "Ghosts before Breakfast," is a whimsical film in which everyday objects revolt against their owners. Hats fly in formation through the air; neckties refuse to be tied; necklaces wriggle like snakes; men's beards appear and disappear as they please. As Hedges remarked, the film "overturns received notions of causality." Werner Haftmann, in his postscript to *Dada: Art and Anti-Art,* called "Ghosts before Breakfast" "one of the first Surrealist films. The 'characters' are everyday objects incited to incongruous juxtapositions and demented sequences of actions by a 'revolt against routine.' " With the success of the film, Richter gave up painting for many years to devote his time to filmmaking.

During the 1930s Richter made short subjects, documentaries, industrial films, and even commercials. In England, he worked with Sergei Eisenstein on "Everyday"; he spent several months filming "Metall" in Germany and the Soviet Union (it was never completed); and, after leaving Germany with the rise of Hitler, he wandered throughout Europe for a time before spending several years producing films for two Swiss companies. Richter also acted in a dozen films shot in Germany and Switzerland and wrote books of film theory.

In 1941 Richter came to the United States and became director of the Institute of Film Techniques at City College in New York City, a position he was to hold for thirteen years. During World War II, many of Richter's European friends came to America. Such artists as Max Ernst, Man Ray, and Marcel Duchamp, fleeing from Nazi-occupied Europe, found themselves in New York at this time. Richter gathered together many of these artists to make the film "Dreams That Money Can Buy," a full-length work filmed between 1944 and 1947. Richter served as producer of the complete film, while the individual dream sequences were directed by his friends.

"Dreams That Money Can Buy" tells the story of Joe, the Dream Detective, who sells dreams to amnesiacs, a business that eventually overwhelms him. Produced on a budget of $25,000 furnished by Peggy Guggenheim, the film was shot in a Manhattan loft. Since many of Richter's film collaborators were surrealists, the film has an incongruous, otherworldly quality. Most of the individual dreams are based on paintings done by the artists. Marcel Duchamp's sequence is a cinematic version of his famous "Nude Descending a Staircase," for example, while Max Ernst recreated a flooded bedroom scene from his collage novel *Une Semaine de Bonte.* Although many critics of the time were less than enthusiastic about "Dreams That Money Can Buy," it has gained a reputation as one of the better experimental films of the 1940s. Weinberg called it "a kind of summation, an apotheosis of a tradition, [and] a confirmation of [Richter's film] theories."

Interest in the Dada art movement was renewed in the 1960s with the advent of Pop Art, Op Art, and Happenings, all of which reflected Dada's spirit of irreverence, satire, and spontaneity. Since little of value had been written about the movement's ideas and participants, Richter decided to produce a historical record of Dada's goals and achievements. His book *Dada: Art and Anti-Art* is a chronicle not only of his own experience with Dada in Zurich, but of later manifestations of the movement in Berlin, Paris, and elsewhere. He also traced Dada's continuing influence on other art movements since the First World War. According to Hamilton, Richter's account was written "with the authority of one who was there but also with tolerance, sympathy, and humor. . . . He is also a scrupulous historian." Hilton Kramer of the *New York Times Book Review* described the book as a "delightfully written, well-illustrated account."

In the 1960s Richter returned to his scroll paintings of the 1920s, creating several works that unrolled horizontally or vertically, and which emphasized the flowing motion of colors. Throughout the 1960s and early 1970s these works were exhibited in one-man shows at American and European galleries; *Newsweek* reported that Richter's paintings had "commanded new appreciation" in his later years. His works are found in the Museum of Modern Art in New York, the National Galerie in Berlin, the Musee d'Art Moderne in Paris, the Galleria Nazionale d'Arte Moderna in Rome, and in other museums throughout the world.

BIOGRAPHICAL/CRITICAL SOURCES:

BOOKS

Hedges, Inez, *Languages of Revolt: Dada and Surrealist Literature and Film,* Duke University Press, 1983.
Lippard, Lucy R., editor, *Dadas on Art,* Prentice, 1971.
Richter, Hans, *Dada: Art and Anti-Art,* McGraw, 1965.
Richter, Hans, *Hans Richter,* Editions du Griffin, 1965.
Richter, Hans, *Hans Richter by Hans Richter,* edited by Cleve Gray, Holt, 1971.
Sanesi, Roberto, *The Pictorial Language of Hans Richter,* [Milan], 1975.

PERIODICALS

Art in America, January, 1968, July, 1969.
Arts Magazine, September, 1959.
Christian Science Monitor, June 2, 1966.
Dance, February, 1947.
Film Culture, winter, 1963-64, summer, 1966.
Films in Review, December, 1951.
Hollywood Quarterly, fall, 1949.
Library Journal, May 1, 1966.
New York Times Book Review, December 4, 1966.
Saturday Review, February 1, 1958, April 2, 1966.

Theatre Arts, February, 1948.
Time, February 16, 1968.

OBITUARIES:

PERIODICALS

Newsweek, February 16, 1976.
New York Times, February 3, 1976.
Time, February 16, 1976.*

—Sketch by Thomas Wiloch

* * *

RISSMAN, Art
    See SUSSMAN, Susan

* * *

RISSMAN, Susan
    See SUSSMAN, Susan

* * *

ROBERTS, Brian   1930-

PERSONAL: Born March 19, 1930, in London, England; son of Henry Albert (an engineer) and Edith (Watts) Roberts. *Education:* St. Mary's College, Twickenham, England, Teacher's Certificate, 1955; University of London, Diploma in Sociology, 1958. *Religion:* Roman Catholic.

ADDRESSES: Home—North Knoll Cottage, 15 Bridge Street, Frome, Somerset BA11 1BB, England. *Agent*—John Farquharson, Ltd., Suite 1914, 250 West 57th St., New York, N.Y., 10107.

CAREER: Free-lance writer. Teacher in England and South Africa, 1958-67. *Military service:* Royal Navy, 1949-53.

WRITINGS:

Ladies in the Veld, J. Murray, 1965.
Cecil Rhodes and the Princess, Lippincott, 1969.
Churchills in Africa, Taplinger, 1971.
The Diamond Magnates, Scribner, 1972.
The Zulu Kings, Scribner, 1974.
Kimberley: Turbulent City, David Philip (Capetown), 1976.
The Mad Bad Line: The Family of Lord Alfred Douglas, Hamish Hamilton, 1981.
Randolph: A Study of Churchill's Son, Hamish Hamilton, 1984.
Cecil Rhodes: Flawed Colossus, Norton, 1988.

Contributor to newspapers and magazines in England and South America.

WORK IN PROGRESS: A book concerning the adventures of women during the Anglo-Boer War.

SIDELIGHTS: Brian Roberts has written several books on South African history and the people involved in making that history. *Cecil Rhodes and the Princess,* his 1969 book, is a dual biography of Cecil Rhodes, a British colonial administrator who made a fortune in African diamonds, and Catherine Radziwill. Radziwill was a Polish-born princess whose unsuccessful attempts to win Rhodes's affection resulted in political and social scandal. A *Times Literary Supplement* reviewer comments that "this is the first detailed study of Princess Radziwill to have been written, and the record of her early political and journalistic intrigues provides an illuminating background to her later activities in South Africa. For this, and for his exploration behind the public image of Rhodes to discover the person of flesh, blood and even emotion, Mr. Roberts has delved deeply. The result is an absorbing, controversial dual biography."

"After writing in diverting style on Cecil Rhodes and Princess Radziwill," says another *Times Literary Supplement* critic, Roberts "has chosen a more . . . important South African theme" for his next book, *Churchills in Africa.* As history of the period of the 1890s and the early 1900s, "when South Africa cast its strongest spell, . . . it makes a good story, and Mr. Roberts has told it well, in a fluent style and with an impartiality that is rare," the reviewer comments.

In his next volume on South African history, *The Diamond Magnates,* Roberts writes about the four fortune hunters of the 1870s who ultimately founded the world's largest diamond mining company, DeBeer's of South Africa. Roberts "has produced a most readable and well-researched study of what were indeed the Klondyke days," says a *Times Literary Supplement* reviewer. The reviewer adds that Roberts presents "an entertaining and well-documented account of this group of men as they fought each other for supremacy."

In his 1974 book, Roberts writes a history of the Zulu nation in southeast Africa during the nineteenth century. *The Zulu Kings,* says Alden Whitman in a *New York Times Book Review* article, "is the first tempered account we have . . . of the rise of the Zulu nation. It is an impressive feat, not only for its scholarship and its attention to oral tradition, but also for its grasp of the Zulu experience and its evocation of the Zulu ethos."

Brian Roberts commented, "I think that biography, or books dealing with historical events, can be every bit as entertaining as a novel. There is no need to distort or take liberties with facts to make a nonfiction book readable. Indeed a true story is often as colourful as anything a novelist can create and well-researched, real-life characters can be depicted in depth without any imaginative touches. This is what I try to do."

BIOGRAPHICAL/CRITICAL SOURCES:

PERIODICALS

Chicago Tribune, June 20, 1988.
New York Times, August 5, 1969.
New York Times Book Review, July 20, 1975.
Observer Review, July 6, 1969, November 20, 1970.
Times (London), April 19, 1984.
Times Literary Supplement, July 31, 1969, August 1, 1971, October 6, 1972, April 13, 1984.
Washington Post Book World, July 22, 1973.

* * *

ROBINSON, Barbara Webb   1927-

PERSONAL: Born October 24, 1927, in Portsmouth, Ohio; daughter of Theodore L. and Grace (Mooney) Webb; married John F. Robinson, 1949; children: Carolyn, Marjorie. *Education:* Allegheny College, B.A., 1948.

ADDRESSES: Home—2063 Fox Creek Rd., Berwyn, Pa. 19132.

CAREER: Free-lance writer.

AWARDS, HONORS: Breadloaf fellow, 1962; Georgia Children's Book Award, 1976, and Young Hoosier Book Award, 1978, both for *The Best Christmas Pageant Ever.*

WRITINGS:

JUVENILE

Across from Indian Shore, Lothrop, 1962.
Trace through the Forest, Lothrop, 1965.
The Fattest Bear in the First Grade, Random House, 1969.

The Best Christmas Pageant Ever (also see below), illustrated by Judith Gwyn Brown, Harper, 1972, reprinted, 1988.

Temporary Time, Temporary Places, Harper, 1982.

The Best Christmas Pageant Ever (play adaptation of book of the same title; first produced in Seattle, Wash., at the Children's Theater), Samuel French, 1982.

"The Best Christmas Pageant Ever" (television screenplay adaptation of book of the same title), Schaefer-Karpf, 1983.

My Brother Louis Measures Worms, and Other Louis Stories, Harper, 1988.

OTHER

Contributor of short stories to *McCall's, Good Housekeeping, Redbook, Ladies' Home Journal,* and *Toronto Star Weekly.*

* * *

ROBISON, Nancy L(ouise) 1934-
(Natalie Johnson)

PERSONAL: Born January 20, 1934, in Compton, Calif.; daughter of Iver and May (Ingersoll) Johnson; married Robert B. Robison (a fire department administrator), August 14, 1954; children: Jeff, Todd, Eric, Glenn. *Education:* Attended University of California, Los Angeles, and Pasadena City College, 1951, 1972-75.

ADDRESSES: Home—Calif.

CAREER: Film and television actress and model in Los Angeles, Calif., 1950-74; full-time writer, 1974—; writer, producer, and hostess of cable television show "Author to Author," 1983-85.

MEMBER: Society of Children's Book Writers, California Writers Club, Southern California Council on Writing for Children and Young People.

AWARDS, HONORS: UFO Kidnap! was selected as a Children's Choice book by the Children's Book Council of New York in 1979.

WRITINGS:

JUVENILE

Where is Zip?, Ginn, 1974.

Hang Glider Mystery, Lantern Press, 1976.

Department Store Model Mystery, Scholastic Book Services, 1977.

Where Did My Little Fox Go?, Garrard, 1977.

The Missing Ball of String, Garrard, 1977.

Hang Gliding (nonfiction), Harvey House, 1978.

Tracy Austin: Teen Tennis Champ (nonfiction), Harvey House, 1978.

UFO Kidnap!, illustrated by Edward Frascino, Lothrop, 1978.

The Other Place (science fiction), illustrated by Jean Drescher, Walker & Co., 1978.

On the Balance Beam (nonfiction), edited by Kathy Pacini, illustrated by Rondi Anderson, Albert Whitman, 1978.

Space Hijack! (science fiction), illustrated by Frascino, Lothrop, 1979.

The Lizard Hunt, illustrated by Lynn Munsinger, Lothrop, 1979.

Baton Twirling (nonfiction), Harvey House, 1979.

Nancy Lopez: Wonder Woman of Golf (nonfiction), Childrens Press, 1979.

Janet Guthrie: Race Car Driver (nonfiction), Childrens Press, 1979.

Mystery at Hilltop Camp, Garrard, 1979.

Games to Play in the Pool, Lothrop, 1980.

Izoo, illustrated by Frascino, Lothrop, 1980.

Kurt Thomas: International Winner (nonfiction), Childrens Press, 1980.

Ballet Magic, Albert Whitman, 1981.

Cheerleading, Harvey House, 1981.

(Under pseudonym Natalie Johnson) *Jenny,* Tempo Books, 1981.

Plumber's Line, Scholastic Book Services, 1981.

U. and M.E., edited by Howard Schroeder, illustrated by Paul Furan, Crestwood House, 1981.

Ponies, edited by Schroeder, Crestwood House, 1983.

Hunters and Jumpers, edited by Schroeder, Crestwood House, 1983.

Janet Jackson: In Control (nonfiction), Dillon, 1987.

YOUNG ADULT

Love, Lost and Found, Dutton, 1983.

Laughter in the Rain, Dutton, 1984.

One Kiss, Dutton, 1984.

Run for Love, Dutton, 1984.

Julie and the Jogger, Dutton, 1984.

More than Just Friends, Dutton, 1984.

OTHER

Dear Son, about Your Wedding: A Guide for the Groom-to-Be, Simon & Schuster, 1989.

Author of privately-printed cookbook, *Cookie Smorgasbord.* Contributor of over 100 stories and articles to magazines, including *Jack and Jill, Christian Science Monitor, Young World,* and *Boston Research;* contributor to *Pennywhistle Press* and other newspapers.

WORK IN PROGRESS: Ten Tall Soldiers, a picture book for Henry Holt; *Buffalo Bill, a Man of the West,* for F. Watts; *A Tale of Two Tails,* a picture book; *A Man with Sixteen Watches,* a book about hiking in the Alps; *The Great Piginelli,* a juvenile book about "a pig who believes he's an opera star, when he's really a supernumerary."

SIDELIGHTS: Nancy L. Robison once told *CA:* "I come from a Scandinavian background. My grandmother on my mother's side was a vaudeville actress and later a motion picture and television actress. She also wrote plays, so I came by my acting and writing careers naturally. When I was three years old I was adopted from the family into another one.

"My first article was published when I was fifteen, and it had to do with my experiences as a television actress. At this time I couldn't choose between careers. I loved to act and I loved to write, but writing meant I had to sit still and I wasn't ready to do that. I pursued a career in the theatre. It wasn't until 1974 that I got serious about writing children's books, and now I enjoy it so much I write every day.

"At this time I still haven't written the book I want to write or feel I am capable of writing. I suppose when I do write it my career will be over, so I'll just keep putting it off until I'm ready to retire.

"I enjoy travel and have been to Mexico, England, Scotland, and Wales, Norway, Sweden, Denmark, France, Belgium, and Germany. I find travel educational and plan to do more."

AVOCATIONAL INTERESTS: Tennis, skiing, hiking, sailing, ice skating, tap dancing, swimming, knitting, baking breads and pastries.

RODRIGUEZ O(RDONEZ), Jaime E(dmundo) 1940-

PERSONAL: Born April 12, 1940, in Guayaquil, Ecuador; came to the United States in 1948; naturalized citizen, 1973; son of Luis A. (an Ecuadorean army officer and military writer) and Beatriz (Ordonez) Rodriguez; married Linda G. Alexander (an historian), November 24, 1965. *Education:* University of Houston, B.A., 1965, M.A., 1966; University of Texas, Ph.D., 1970. *Politics:* Democrat.

ADDRESSES: Office—Department of History, University of California, Irvine, Calif. 92717.

CAREER: California State University, Long Beach, assistant professor of history, 1963-73; University of California, Irvine, assistant professor, 1973-75, associate professor, 1975-81, professor of history, 1981—, distinguished faculty lecturer, 1979-80, dean of graduate studies and research, 1980-86. Honorary fellow at National University of Mexico's Institute for Historical Research, 1979—. Member of Conference on Latin American History (chairman of Andean studies committee, 1976; chairman of Mexican studies committee, 1979-80); member of council of Smithsonian Institution, 1988. *Military service:* U.S. Army, Medical Corps, 1959-62.

MEMBER: Congress of Mexican and United States Historians (member of U.S. organizing committee, 1981-91), American Historical Association, Latin American Studies Association, National Chicano Council on Higher Education, American Academy of Franciscan History (associate member), Council of Graduate Schools of the United States, National Association of State Universities and Land-Grant Colleges, National Council of University Research Administrators, National Academy of History of Ecuador (corresponding member), Centro de Estudios Historicos del Guayas (corresponding member), Pacific Coast Council on Latin American Studies (vice-president, 1979; president, 1980).

AWARDS, HONORS: Organization of American States fellowship for Mexico, summer, 1968; Social Science Research Council fellowship for Ecuador, 1971-72; University of California faculty fellowships for Ecuador, summers, 1975 and 1978, fellowships for Mexico, summers, 1976, 1977, 1979, 1986, 1987, and 1988; Mellon Foundation fellowship, 1980-81; Hubert Herring Memorial Award from Pacific Coast Council on Latin American Studies, 1980, for *The Forging of the Cosmic Race;* Fulbright grant for Mexico, 1982.

WRITINGS:

(Contributor) Richard Greenleaf and Michael Meyer, editors, *Research in Mexican History,* University of Nebraska Press, 1973.

(Translator) Romeo Flores Caballero, *Counterrevolution,* University of Nebraska Press, 1974.

The Emergence of Spanish America: Vicente Rocafuerte and Spanish Americanism, 1808-1832, University of California Press, 1975.

Estudios sobre Vicente Rocafuerte (title means "Studies about Vicente Rocafuerte"), Archivo Historico del Guayas, 1975.

(Editor) *Andean Field Research Guide,* Duke University Press, 1977.

El nacimiento de Hispanoamerica (title means "The Birth of Spanish America"), Fondo de Cultura Economica, 1980.

(With Colin M. MacLachlan) *The Forging of the Cosmic Race: A Reinterpretation of Colonial Mexico,* University of California Press, 1980.

(Editor with John Te Paske, William Sater, and Leon Campbell) *Research Guide to Andean History,* Duke University Press, 1981.

Down from Colonialism: Mexico's Nineteenth-Century Crisis, Chicano Studies Research Center, University of California, Los Angeles, 1983.

(Editor and contributor) *The Mexican and the Mexican Experience in the Nineteenth Century,* Bilingual Press, 1988.

(Editor) *La formacion de un Republicano* (title means "The Making of a Republican"), Volume IV: *Obras completas de Servando Teresa de Mier* (title means "The Complete Works of Servando Teresa de Mier"), Universidad Nacional Autonoma de Mexico, 1988.

(Editor and contributor) *The Independence of Mexico and the Creation of the New Nation,* Latin American Center, University of California, Los Angeles, 1989.

Contributor to Latin American studies journals. Editor of *Mexican Studies/Estudios Mexicanos;* Mexico-area editor for *Americas,* 1978-86; member of editorial board of *New Scholar,* 1978-86, and *Journal of Interamerican Studies and World Affairs,* 1982-88.

WORK IN PROGRESS: A Socioeconomic History of the First Federal Republic of Mexico, 1824-1834; A Study of the Ideological Process of Mexican Independence; A Socioeconomic History of Quito, Ecuador, 1750-1850.

SIDELIGHTS: Jaime E. Rodriguez O. told *CA:* "My work seeks to explain Spanish America's failure to modernize in the early nineteenth century. At the time Western Europe and the United States were being transformed into modern industrial societies, the newly-independent nations of Spanish American were crippled by economic depression and extreme political instability. Scholars have generally argued that this failure to modernize stemmed from the feudal Spanish colonial structure which did not prepare Spanish Americans for self-government. According to this view, after independence Spanish American leaders rejected colonial traditions and adopted foreign systems of government unsuited to their nations' needs, causing Spanish America's nineteenth-century crisis.

"I examined some of the problems of nation-building in Spanish America in a series of studies and concluded that independence was not a sharp break with the past and that Spanish American leaders had not blindly accepted alien forms of government. Instead, I demonstrated the continuity of the Spanish and Spanish American reform tradition and its influence upon the leaders of the new countries. With Professor Colin M. MacLachlan of Tulane University, I examined Mexico's colonial epoch to test the validity of the neo-feudal thesis. We concluded that colonial Mexico had not been a feudal but a capitalist society; that the region developed a complex, balanced, and integrated economy which transformed the area into the most dynamic part of the Spanish empire; and that it was one of the few regions in the world where racial and cultural intermingling created a new society.

"I am presently engaged in two studies to explain the post-independence period: an analysis of Mexico's early nineteenth-century economy to explain why one of the Western Hemisphere's most prosperous areas plunged into a prolonged economic depression in the first half of the nineteenth century; and a second work, a study of Quito, Ecuador, during the years 1750-1850, to examine the way in which a peripheral area of Spanish America made the transition from colony to independent nation."

ROME, Anthony
 See ALBERT, Marvin H(ubert)

* * *

ROSE, Phyllis
 See THOMPSON, Phyllis Hoge

* * *

ROSEN, Gerald 1938-

PERSONAL: Born December 24, 1938, in New York, N.Y.; son of Sol (a retail liquor dealer) and Eve (Berger) Rosen; married Charlotte Mayer (a typesetter), March 27, 1962 (divorced, 1976); married Marijke Wittkampf, 1981. *Education:* Rensselaer Polytechnic Institute, B.E.E., 1960; Wharton School, M.B.A., 1962; University of Pennsylvania, A.M., 1966, Ph.D., 1969. *Politics:* "Left individualist." *Religion:* "American Buddhist."

ADDRESSES: Home—489 Utah St., San Francisco, Calif. 94110. *Office*—Department of English, California State College, Sonoma, Rohnert Park, Calif. 94928.

CAREER: Magid Liquor Store, New York, N.Y., manager, 1967-71; California State College, Sonoma, Rohnert Park, instructor in writing and literature, 1971-80, university writer in residence, 1980—. *Military service:* U.S. Army, 1962-65; became first lieutenant.

MEMBER: Beta Gamma Sigma.

WRITINGS:

Blues for a Dying Nation (novel), Dial, 1972.
The Carmen Miranda Memorial Flagpole (novel), Presidio Press, 1977.
Zen in the Art of J. D. Salinger (nonfiction), Creative Arts Books, 1977.
Dr. Ebenezer's Book and Liquor Store (novel), St. Martin's, 1980.
Growing up Bronx (novel), North Atlantic Books, 1984.

Contributor to *Partisan Review, American Quarterly, San Francisco Review of Books, Carte Segrete, Paragone,* and other journals.

WORK IN PROGRESS: A novel, *The Rebirth of an American Wife.*

SIDELIGHTS: In works such as *Blues for a Dying Nation* and *The Carmen Miranda Memorial Flagpole,* Gerald Rosen uses humor to examine contemporary culture's fascination with violence and war. *Blues for a Dying Nation,* for instance, follows a young accountant who enlists in the Army and eventually joins a motley group of revolutionaries; the result, as William Crawford Woods describes it in the *New York Times Book Review,* is a kind of " 'Catch-22' with all the stops pulled out—and much of the substance as well." Nevertheless, the critic remarks that "this magical mystery tour of a first novel is a fairy tale of revolution no less vital for being so fashionable in its concerns." Less ambitious than its predecessor, *The Carmen Miranda Memorial Flagpole* covers similar ground in relating the exploits of two brothers, both Vietnam veterans, one of whom is slowly losing his mind. "The novel is a relentless, continual, unending torrent of wisecracks and one-line jokes," notes *New York Times Book Review* contributor Sheldon Frank; calling it "a book that is both hilarious and devastating," the critic concludes that *The Carmen Miranda Memorial Flagpole* "is an exceptional novel." And while *Growing up Bronx* does not deal directly with a specific

military incident or group, it also presents "scenes of violence, the novel's funniest, [which] raise some serious questions about the relation between domestic abuse, violence on the streets and in the schools, and the 'official venom' of a war," Martha B. Tack observes in the *New York Times Book Review.* While his novel "doesn't offer any sure-fire answers," the critic states that Rosen "has written a humorous, touching novel about Jewish boyhood in urban America during the nuclear age."

Rosen told *CA* that he is interested in "Zen, humor, sports, jazz, rock and classical music, and meditation. My writing has been influenced by artists like Jean Luc Godard, Janis Joplin, Jimi Hendrix, Charlie Parker, J. S. Bach, Sakyamuni, and Jan Vermeer, besides other writers. The purpose of my writing is to lead the reader to question the way he has been taught to see the world. My jokes are armed and should be considered dangerous."

BIOGRAPHICAL/CRITICAL SOURCES:

BOOKS

Klinkowitz, Jerome, *The Practice of Fiction in America,* Iowa State University Press, 1980.

PERIODICALS

Chicago Tribune Book World, August 10, 1980.
New York Times Book Review, May 21, 1972, September 18, 1977, January 13, 1985.
Publishers Weekly, September 7, 1984.

* * *

ROSEN, R. D.
 See ROSEN, Richard (Dean)

* * *

ROSEN, Richard (Dean) 1949-
 ## (R. D. Rosen)

PERSONAL: Born February 18, 1949, in Chicago, Ill.; son of Sol A. and Carolyn (Baskin) Rosen; married Diane McWhorter (a journalist); children: Lucy. *Education:* Attended Brown University, 1967-68; Harvard University, B.A., 1972. *Religion:* Jewish.

ADDRESSES: Home—166 E. 96th St., Apt. 10-B, New York, N.Y. 10128. *Agent*—(literary) Robert Lescher, 155 E. 71st St., New York, N.Y. 10021; (television) Arthur Kaminsky, Athletes & Artists, 421 Seventh Ave., New York, N.Y. 10001.

CAREER: Writer. *Boston Phoenix,* Boston, Mass., staff writer and arts editor, 1972-76; *Boston Magazine,* Boston, staff writer and columnist, 1977-78; WGBH-TV, Boston, television news reporter and columnist, 1978-79; *The Real Paper,* Boston, editor-in-chief, 1979-80; WGBH-TV, Boston, television reporter, writer, actor-producer of national humor special, "The Generic News," and director-producer of "Enterprise" documentary, 1982-84; National Broadcasting Company (NBC-TV), New York, N.Y., staff writer for "Saturday Night Live" comedy series, 1985; Home Box Office (HBO), Los Angeles, Calif., cast member and writer for "Not Necessarily the News," 1989-90. Associate, "I Have a Dream" Project, East Harlem, N.Y., 1986-87.

MEMBER: Writers Guild of America, Mystery Writers of America.

AWARDS, HONORS: Academy of American Poets prize, 1970; three Emmy Awards (New England region), 1984; Edgar Allan

Poe Award for best first mystery novel, from Mystery Writers of America, 1985, for *Strike Three, You're Dead.*

WRITINGS:

(Under name R. D. Rosen) *Me and My Friends, We No Longer Profess Any Graces: A Premature Memoir,* Macmillan, 1971.
(Under name R. D. Rosen) *Psychobabble: Fast Talk and Quick Cure in the Era of Feeling,* Atheneum, 1977.

MYSTERIES

(Under name R. D. Rosen) *Strike Three, You're Dead,* Walker, 1984.
Fadeaway, Harper, 1986.
Saturday Night Dead, Viking, 1988.

SCRIPTS

(Under name R. D. Rosen) "The Generic News," Public Broadcasting System (PBS), 1983.
(Under name R. D. Rosen) "Workout," Public Broadcasting System (PBS), 1984.

OTHER

Contributor to numerous periodicals, including *New York Times, New York, Sports Illustrated, New Republic, New Times,* and *Psychology Today.*

SIDELIGHTS: R. D. Rosen, whose first novel *Strike Three, You're Dead* won the prestigious Edgar Allan Poe award, is a veteran journalist, television writer, producer, and performer. Rosen's career has included stints with WGBH-TV, Boston's public broadcasting station, and the popular "Saturday Night Live" comedy series on NBC. He has also authored two books of nonfiction (in one of which he coined a new term, "psychobabble"), and even penned some poetry. Since 1984, he has become known for his mystery novels, all featuring a ballplayer-turned-detective named Harvey Blissberg.

Strike Three, You're Dead introduces Blissberg, an aging center fielder for the fictitious Providence Jewels. When his roommate is found murdered, Blissberg undertakes his own investigation, during which he himself becomes a target for murder. Rosen drew upon his extensive knowledge of major league baseball—and his own experiences as a player—in order to add realism to the novel. To quote Bob Wiemer in *Newsday,* the resulting work is "the literary equivalent of an in-the-park home run." *New York Times* columnist Newgate Callendar calls *Strike Three, You're Dead* "an entertaining and well-written book," adding: "Mr. Rosen can write. His dialogue is smart and sophisticated and his characters altogether three-dimensional. Clearly the author loves baseball, but he does not get sentimental about it. His approach is entirely professional." The Mystery Writers of America found *Strike Three, You're Dead* the best first mystery novel of the year in 1985.

In subsequent books, Blissberg has retired from baseball and is a full-time gumshoe. *Fadeaway* concerns the violent deaths of two professional basketball players, both found in Boston's Logan Airport. Called in to track the murderer, Blissberg uncovers a sordid trail of drug abuse and recruiting violations. *Washington Post Book World* contributor Jean M. White notes that in *Fadeaway* Rosen "writes with a light, sure touch. He has done his homework on the drug problem and recruiting pressures in basketball. . . . The ending is a corker." *Saturday Night Dead* follows Blissberg onto the set of a late-night comedy show where the reigning executive is suddenly killed. A *Publisher's Weekly* reviewer writes of the work: "The story's skillful contrasts of

edged satire and pathos make it irresistible, the third triumph for Blissberg and his creator."

CA INTERVIEW

CA interviewed R. D. Rosen by telephone on February 10, 1989, at his home in New York, New York.

CA: Your career covers an interesting range of activities: writing poetry, book reviews, restaurant criticism, television pieces, social criticism, mysteries; written and broadcast journalism; television acting, directing, and production. Did you start out with such a scope of ambitions?

ROSEN: When I was a teenager trying to fall asleep at night, contemplating what I was going to do when I grew up, the only ambition I remember articulating to myself was that I would like to do a different thing every day of the week. Back then it was, I would like to be a doctor on Monday, a baseball player on Tuesday—that sort of thing. I realize, looking back, that I've come relatively close to fulfilling that fantasy. I don't do a different thing every day of the week, but I've managed to dart around, to write in a number of forms. I've got a restless little brain.

CA: In an article for Change, *Stu Cohen quoted you on the influence of your friend James Atlas, to whom (along with your family) you dedicated your first book,* Me and My Friends, We No Longer Profess Any Graces. *Would you comment on his inspiration to you, past and present, in your writing?*

ROSEN: Only to say that we are very good friends, have been since our mothers pushed our strollers together in the playground. When we were adolescents, he began writing poetry and, I think in the competitive spirit of our relationship, I started to write poetry. Of course it wouldn't have worked if I hadn't already been inclined to write or had some ability in that area. As teenagers we used to give each other poems to critique. I clearly remember calling him when we were high school sophomores; I had written a poem in the style of Dickinson, which I read him along with an actual Dickinson poem, and insisted he guess which was which. Once we even wrote a sonnet together on a train, alternating lines. His influence was partly that he made it seem all right to want to be a writer. In those years I was spending most of my time playing sports and painting. So he was a good model. He took literature much more seriously than I did. Jim was the sort of sixteen-year-old who knew that the aging W. H. Auden was reading at a nearby college. On the other hand, I was the sort of sixteen-year-old who knew the names of the promising rookies in the Chicago White Sox spring training camp.

CA: Until you started writing the mysteries—the first of which, Strike Three, You're Dead, *won you a 1985 Edgar Award—your best known work may have been the word psychobabble. You lamented in a piece in the* New Republic *that the 1977 book of the same name wasn't greatly noticed and you rarely got credit for fathering the word.*

ROSEN: Yes. I'd be a wealthy man if I were able to copyright a word and exact a small payment from everyone who uttered it. I have now invented another word. I don't want to predict how popular this one is going to be, but I just published an article in *New York Magazine* called "Bullcrit," which is a term that applies to a phenomenon that's particularly prevalent in New

York, in which people talk about books as if they've read them. They haven't. Generally they've read the reviews or maybe heard about the reviews, or they know somebody who knows somebody who's read the reviews.

CA: They would never dream of saying, "I haven't read the book."

ROSEN: No, of course not. In a culturally competitive community like New York, you would never do that. But the irony is that if there's no intellectual or social advantage to having read a book, as long as it's widely accepted that you can talk about it even if you know nothing about it, why make the investment of reading a book? Also, socially, if you've read the book and you've made that kind of commitment, there's a tendency to feel that you have to defend the book; it's a way of defending your investment. But if you haven't read the book, you can say anything you want about it, true or false. It gives you greater latitude socially. It's a way of being a literary critic without incurring the inconvenience of reading book-length material. I call it the "Sacredness of the Secondhand." But you were asking me about psychobabble.

CA: I was interested partly in the fact that your first two books were written during a time of great social ferment, and many people who were your age during those years were too caught up in it to see it objectively. How did you come by the detachment to do it so well?

ROSEN: Literary detachment may to some extent be genetic, but certainly a lot of it comes from having at a young age an ability—sometimes a crippling ability—to see the world through language and to love books and love reading and to have your playfulness often take the form of toying with language. The circumstances of childhood may suppress or exaggerate that ability. It's a mixed blessing. You can develop some real skills as a writer and thinker. On the other hand, it separates you from direct action. I think many writers face this struggle especially as they grow older; they have to balance their purpose as a writer and a thinker with the moral and existential requirements of being a human being moving through time and space, acting on the world and being acted on. Writing can too easily become a refuge. In most writers, I suspect, there's a deeply rooted and nurtured dissatisfaction with the world, and a wish to improve on it, organize it imaginatively, rearrange it passionately. This is not something you learn; it's something you are from a young age, and the best strategy is to make your peace with this nature, prize it, and carry it beyond its sometimes narcissistic frame into the wider world.

CA: How much psychobabbling would you say is going on now compared to the sixties and seventies, the period you were writing about in the book?

ROSEN: Writing the book answered a personal need to understand what was going on and to understand certain things about myself and the relationship between language and self-knowledge. I was a psychobabbler, too, in my own way. After I wrote it, I began slowly to separate myself from the whole issue. I spent as little time as possible around graduates of Est! I'm sure psychobabble flourishes in some circles, but I would say there's less of it now. It's been replaced by other kinds of babble, including *acquisibabble*. There seems to be more talk about what one does and what one has these days. A line I hear a lot in New York is "You know, I'm very good at what I do." I want to turn and respond, "Who asked you?" In certain circles there's a real pressure always to assert your competence, your successfulness, your income.

Ten years ago, people in my generation—I'm almost forty now—were still heavily under the influence of the values of the sixties. And as I get older, it seems to me that the mini-generation that I'm part of, that section of the baby boom that went to college in the late sixties and early sixties, was very special in that we were much less materialistic at that stage than many previous generations and almost every subsequent generation. There were good expressions of our nonmaterialism, but psychobabble was one of the unfortunate by-products, one of the sloppier examples of our self-infatuation. Everything then was so different from how twenty-five and thirty-year-olds see it now. The self-infatuation that kids seems to have today is really all about acquisitiveness and status. I had a conversation recently with Sid Blumenthal, a good friend who's a political writer my age; we came of age as writers in Boston. And he said he'd begun to feel really naive, because he takes offense at some of the excesses of the decade. I sometimes feel that way, too.

CA: Through the 1970s and well into the eighties you were not only writing books, but also doing that multitude of other things I mentioned at the beginning. Your work in journalism includes stints at the Boston Phoenix, Boston Magazine, *and the* Real Paper. *How did you go, first, from poetry to journalism, and then into television?*

ROSEN: I stopped writing poetry when I was in college, probably because I didn't think I had the ability to be a great poet. I no longer thought in stanzas. I discovered prose while I was still in college. That not only seemed more interesting to me and suited my temperament better, but it was lucrative. I wrote my first book when I was twenty-one. I liked the idea of poetry in prose. I went into journalism because, although I don't have the proverbial printer's ink in my veins, writing journalism—particularly at that time in the early seventies in Boston, where you had two very vibrant alternative weeklies—was a terrific compromise between being an academic and being a newspaper reporter. It enabled you to bring to the writing of journalism a lot of the post-graduate obsessions and intellectualism and poetry that you can't get into a daily newspaper. I've often thought that I was really fortunate to be able to latch onto the world of alternative journalism, because it gave me an opportunity to learn about the world, to learn a trade, and to publish without having to give up all those little sensibilities that newspaper and magazine journalism tends to sand off.

When I went into television in my late twenties, that was partly because my temperament is sort of split. I don't like to spend all of my time writing. There's part of me that's something of a businessman and likes to collaborate with other people, and those are aspects of my character that writing doesn't address. Writing is not a business in the true sense of the word. You produce a manuscript, you produce a book, and then if you're lucky you sell it to a publisher but you cease to have anything to do with it: you have no control over the manufacturing of it, the marketing of it. That can be a little frustrating and infantilizing. You're very dependent. You go from a world of almost narcissistic purity in which you control your book to a situation where you've given it up for adoption, for money, to people that you don't know. Going into TV was a way to express that other side of my character, to work on shorter-term, collaborative projects. In the case of television journalism, I not only wrote the material and performed it, but I was in the editing room when it was edited and I wrote the leads that the anchorman read when he presented it. In some ways, it can be a much more vertically integrated process.

CA: You must always be doing several things at a time.

ROSEN: I stagger them. When I'm working on a book, that's basically all I want to do. Writing a novel can be very captivating and very time-consuming. But then I go through periods when I'm not writing a novel and I'm working on video-related projects or trying to develop other ideas or working on shorter humor pieces. I just try to keep things hopping.

CA: You've written humor for television's "Saturday Night Live" and you wrote, directed, and acted in the PBS humor special "The Generic News." Any thoughts about what makes humor work on television, what special qualities are required?

ROSEN: Sometimes I think the best humor is just social criticism with a punchline. Humor is so idiosyncratic. It's a wonderful mystery in a way, though it can be reduced to certain mechanistic laws, and some humor is more mechanistic than others. Sometimes the most wonderful humor is kind of opaque; it has a certain genius to it, like S. J. Perelman's writing or the best of the "Saturday Night Live" sketches over the years.

CA: Did you lose any "Saturday Night Live" friends when your third mystery, Saturday Night Dead, *was published?*

ROSEN: I was only there for a couple of months, because it just wasn't my cup of tea. So I didn't really make that many friends to lose.

CA: Your mysteries are a treat indeed. How did you come up with your unusual detective, Harvey Blissberg?

ROSEN: I just observed the old rule that you should write about what you know. When I sat down to plan my first mystery, I thought about what I knew, and I know a lot about baseball. In fact, when I think about the things I've written over the years, I realize that baseball has found its way into almost every form. I've written journalism and poetry about baseball. I've written pieces that were odes to Fenway Park. I've drawn baseball parks. Baseball was sewn into my character at an early age, so I wasn't surprised when baseball popped into my head as the setting for my first novel. I played enough baseball to know what it was like from the inside; I knew how baseball players talk; I understood the rules of the game. I understood the poetry of the game. Harvey Blissberg evolved out of that.

CA: Harvey's brother Norm is a great character. He exemplifies something you said in "The Story of Baseball" in Me and My Friends, We No Longer Profess Any Graces: *"Baseball gives the spectator what is so dearly lacking in his life—a sense of being the manipulator, the employer."*

ROSEN: Its advantage for the spectator is that the action is so observable; all the moments are widely spaced, so you can always tell or have explained to you what's happening on the field, sometimes before it happens. Try doing that at a football or basketball or hockey game! Baseball is a more ruminative, more democratic game for spectators. However, I'm no longer the fan I used to be.

CA: I have the feeling that you find the mysteries almost as much fun to write as readers do to read, and yet it's obvious that a lot of hard, careful work goes into them. How much of a story do you know when you start out?

ROSEN: If you get on a train in New York to go to Boston, you know you'll end up in Boston, and you know that you'll go through New Haven and New London and Providence. But you don't know or you can't remember what some of the little towns in between look like, and you can't predict whether you'll actually stay on the train straight through: you might get off in New London on the spur of the moment, rent a car, take a little side trip into Connecticut. That's sort of how it is when I write a book. Judging from what other writers have told me about what they do, I think I'm a little more compulsive about outlining books than most people. I don't do it in great detail, but I want to know where I'm heading, and I want to know where the major stops are along the way. But inevitably what happens is that I get to Providence and I look out the window and see some fantastic something and I decide to get off the train. I'll meet somebody and somebody will tell me a story. I'll spend some time in Rhode Island before I get back on the train. I almost always end up in Boston, but there are a lot of surprises and happy accidents along the way. It's also true in my case that toward the end of the first draft one of the characters suddenly tells me something I should have known all along.

CA: One of your particular strengths as a writer is dialogue, both the snappy line and authentic-sounding ethnic speech patterns. Do you listen a lot to people and make notes of things that might be useful in your fiction?

ROSEN: More and more I'm aware of listening carefully and taking notes. But I've always been fascinated by speech; I'm truly fascinated by what people say. Just the other day I was meeting with some people I'm doing a project with, and one of them used a colloquial expression I'd never heard before. I whipped out a little leather-bound pad of paper I keep in my pocket at all times and I wrote it down. He said, "What are you doing?" and I said, "I just thought that was great. I've got to write it down." It sounds banal, but there's a terrific amount of natural poetry to the way people speak when they're not thinking about what they say. I don't think I wrote a lot of that down when I was younger, but now I'm much more aware of trying to capture these things before I forget them, because I think they're pretty precious. I'm not sure where my sensitivity to the way people speak and express themselves comes from originally, but it was certainly that sensitivity at work when I wrote *Psychobabble*, because that's really about distortions in speech and thinking, about language as disguise. It shows a lot in the humor I do, the satire where I ape advertising or news diction. That comes to mind because I'm working on a humor book that is kind of an advertising parody, a sort of existential catalogue. Some people are fascinated by rocks. I'm fascinated by what comes out of people's mouths, and why.

CA: How much has the journalism and television experience helped you in writing the fiction?

ROSEN: Immensely. Having experience in other professions is very valuable for a writer. You always want to be writing about something. You don't want to be writing about different versions of yourself or different versions of what the inside of your brain looks like. The things I find most fascinating about novels sometimes are what they have to say about what other people do for a living. I would rather read about an RC Cola salesman, to cite a novel I read recently, than read about another divorce in the making. I think what people do is very interesting, so my experience in journalism, although it's clearly related to being a writer, gave me a larger frame of reference. I'm afflicted, and blessed, by curiosity about what people *do*.

BIOGRAPHICAL/CRITICAL SOURCES:

BOOKS

Contemporary Literary Criticism, Volume 39, Gale, 1987.

PERIODICALS

Change, April, 1978.
Chicago Tribune Books, July 3, 1988.
Eagle [Providence], October 21, 1984.
New Republic, August 22, 1981, August 29, 1981.
Newsday, August 19, 1984.
New Yorker, November 24, 1986.
New York Times, October 28, 1984.
Publishers Weekly, May 11, 1984, April 22, 1988.
Sports Illustrated, April 18, 1985.
Washington Post Book World, January 20, 1985, November 16, 1986.
Wilson Library Bulletin, November, 1984.

—*Interview by Jean W. Ross*

* * *

ROSENBERG, Stephen N(icholas) 1941-

PERSONAL: Born February 27, 1941, in New York, N.Y.; son of Edward P. (a businessman) and Ruth (an attorney; maiden name, Jochnowitz) Rosenberg; married Barbara Horowitz (a fund raiser), January 30, 1966; children: Jordana, Amanda. *Education:* Cornell University, B.A., 1963; Yeshiva University, M.D., 1967; Harvard University, M.P.H., 1969. *Religion:* Jewish.

ADDRESSES: Home—233 East 69th St., New York, N.Y. 10021. *Office*—Division of Health, Policy, and Management, Columbia University, 600 West 168th St., New York, N.Y. 10032.

CAREER: Highland General Hospital, Oakland, Calif., intern, 1968; New York City Department of Health, New York City, deputy director of Medicaid program, 1970-73; senior public health physician, 1975—; San Bernardino County Public Health Department, San Bernardino, Calif., director, 1973-74; Columbia University, New York City, assistant professor, 1974-82, associate professor of public health, 1982—; New York City Employee Benefits Program, medical director, 1983—. Attending physician at Presbyterian Hospital, 1977—. Clinical instructor at Albert Einstein College of Medicine, 1969-73; visiting associate professor at Hunter College Institute of Health Sciences, 1972-73; lecturer at California State College, San Bernardino, 1973-74; adjunct associate professor in biomedical program at City College of the City University of New York, 1978-81.

MEMBER: American Public Health Association, American College of Preventive Medicine (fellow), Scientists' Institute for Public Information (fellow).

WRITINGS:

The Brenda Maneuver (novel), New Market Press, 1982.
The Johnson & Johnson First Aid Book, Warner Books, 1985.

WORK IN PROGRESS: A second medical mystery—"less comical but scary as hell"; an exploration of the collapse of the American health care system in the 1980s.

SIDELIGHTS: Stephen N. Rosenberg drew heavily upon his own experiences as a public health professional in a major city health department to write the comic mystery novel *The Brenda Maneuver.* The story centers on Dr. Nicholas Kaminsky, an offi-

cial with a penchant for comedy whose job is to assure the quality of all health care services provided in New York City that are paid for in total or in part with city or federal funds. In the course of his usually mundane duties, Kaminsky uncovers one of the largest health care frauds in the history of the city and then, with the help of a deputy district attorney and a policewoman, turns amateur detective in an attempt to unmask the perpetrators. While critic Alan Cheuse finds fault with Rosenberg's use of humor, he commends other aspects of the author's first novel, writing in the *New York Times Book Review* that the work "offers a great deal of entertaining health care lore," and adding that its readers will be "treated to a vigorous rendering of fresh new mystery material."

The Johnson & Johnson First Aid Book has been published in French, Italian, Greek, Hebrew, and Afrikaans editions. "The last of these, with illustrations unchanged from the original edition, may be the only book in Afrikaans that shows whites and blacks rescuing each other from fire, drowning, etc.," as Rosenberg recently told *CA.* He also adds that "the first aid book—much more than the novel—shows the influence of Dickens, Jerome Weidman, and the stuff you read on the back of cereal boxes."

BIOGRAPHICAL/CRITICAL SOURCES:

PERIODICALS

Los Angeles Times Book Review, December 19, 1982.
New York Times Book Review, January 16, 1983.

* * *

ROSENBLUM, Mort 1943-

PERSONAL: Born June 12, 1943, in Milwaukee, Wis.; son of Martin and Mary (Rakita) Rosenblum; married Randi Slaughter (a writer), October 16, 1971 (divorced). *Education:* University of Arizona, B.A., 1965; graduate study at Columbia University, 1976-77. *Religion:* Jewish.

ADDRESSES: Office—Associated Press, 162 rue du Faubourg St. Honore, 75008 Paris, France. *Agent*—Carol Mann Literary Agency, 55 Fifth Ave, New York, N.Y. 10003.

CAREER: Associated Press, New York City, correspondent in Kinshasa, Zaire, 1967-68, and Lagos, Nigeria, 1968-70, bureau chief in Singapore, 1970-73, Buenos Aires, Argentina, 1973-76, and Paris, France, 1977-79; *International Herald Tribune,* Paris, editor-in-chief, 1979-81; Associated Press, New York City, special correspondent in Paris, 1981—. Member of Council on Foreign Relations.

MEMBER: Overseas Press Club, Anglo-American Press Club.

AWARDS, HONORS: Edward R. Murrow fellow, 1976-77; University of Arizona Centennial Medal; has received five Pulitzer Prize nominations.

WRITINGS:

Coups and Earthquakes: Reporting the World for America, Harper, 1978.
Mission to Civilize: The French Way, Harcourt, 1986.
(With Doug Williamson) *Squandering Eden: Africa at the Edge,* Harcourt, 1987.
Back Home: A Foreign Correspondent Rediscovers America, Morrow, 1989.

Contributor to *Foreign Affairs, New York Review of Books,* and *Nouvelles Litteraires.*

WORK IN PROGRESS: A novel.

SIDELIGHTS: As a foreign correspondent and former bureau chief in Paris for the Associated Press, Mort Rosenblum has traveled extensively throughout Africa, Asia, and South America. He uses these experiences in his books to discuss his profession and the countries he has visited during his career. In his first book, *Coups and Earthquakes: Reporting the World for America,* Rosenblum warns against the philosophy held by many American newspaper editors that the only foreign events which concern Americans are natural disasters and military coups. Instead, the author believes that the American people desire detailed foreign news coverage and that, as Caroline Seebohm says in the *New York Times Book Review,* "failing to present the people with efficient first-hand reporting from abroad is both irresponsible and undemocratic."

Rosenblum attempts to follow his own advice by providing accurate reporting in his next two books, *Mission to Civilize: The French Way* and *Squandering Eden: Africa at the Edge,* the latter of which he co-wrote with Doug Williamson. These publications consider Africa and other Third World countries and how their people and environments have been affected by government. In *Mission to Civilize,* the author discusses the effects of French colonialization around the world, focusing on France's diplomatic relations with its former colonies. Commenting on this work, *New York Times Books Review* contributor William R. Carlson writes that Rosenblum "deftly weaves an impressive array of facts and observations, drawn from his many years as a journalist, around the idea that France, unlike the other great colonial powers, has managed to remain a global power, thanks to its own projection of itself as a civilizing force." The countries in Africa are focused upon in *Squandering Eden: Africa at the Edge.* In this book, Rosenblum's knowledge of politics is combined with Williamson's concern for the environment to produce what Michael Parks calls in the *Los Angeles Times Book Review,* "a profoundly disturbing book" about the plight of Africa's people and wildlife.

Although some reviewers, such as *Businees Week* correspondent John Rossant, accuse Rosenblum of sometimes being "a little too glib, as in his thumbnail romp through French history" in *Mission to Civilize,* his skill as a reporter has often been noted. James Brooke, for example, comments in the *New York Times Book Review* that "unburdened with sentimentality, 'Squandering Eden' puts in sharp focus the grim outlook for Africa"; and *New York Times* contributor John Gross asserts that the author is "exceptionally fair-minded" in *Mission to Civilize.* Rosenblum, concludes Rossant, "has a keen reporter's eye and a humorous, sometimes devilish pen."

More recently, the author has taken advantage of his experience as a world traveler, who has been outside the United States for some 20 years, to offer a new perspective of his native country. *Back Home: A Foreign Correspondent Rediscovers America,* compares Rosenblum's memories of America with what he actually finds upon his return. Looking at his country as if it were another foreign land about which he is reporting, the author experiences a combination of affection and disappointed surprise, especially when it comes to the racism which still remains despite years of social change. The result of this revelation, as one *Publishers Weekly* contributor observes, is that "the underlying dark note in Rosenblum's narrative is prominent albeit illuminating."

BIOGRAPHICAL/CRITICAL SOURCES:

PERIODICALS

Business Week, December 22, 1986.
Los Angeles Times Book Review, July 5, 1987, November 1, 1987.

New York Times, December 19, 1986.
New York Times Book Review, October 21, 1979, June 21, 1981, December 21, 1986, November 29, 1987, February 7, 1988.
Publishers Weekly, June 9, 1989.
Times Literary Supplement, November 18, 1988.
Washington Post Book World, August 26, 1979, January 4, 1987.

*   *   *

ROSENSTIEL, Leonie 1947-

PERSONAL: Born December 28, 1947, in New York, N.Y.; daughter of Raymond (an investor) and Annette (an anthropologist; maiden name, Bitterman) Rosenstiel. *Education:* Julliard School of Music, certificate, 1964; Barnard College, B.A., 1968; Columbia University, M.A., 1970, M.Phil., 1974; Mexican National Institute of Fine Arts, diploma, 1975.

ADDRESSES: Office—Research Associates International, 340 East 52nd St., New York, N.Y. 10022.

CAREER: Barnard-Columbia Chamber Music Society, New York City, founder and director, 1965-67; *Current Musicology,* New York City, associate editor, 1969-71, special projects editor, 1971-73; instructor in music at adult school in Manhasset, N.Y., 1974-76; Caribbean Network System, New York City, associate producer, 1977; Research Associates International, New York City, president, 1980—; Authors Aid Associates, New York City, vice-president, 1980—. Founder, director, Manhasset Chamber Ensemble, 1974-76. Alumni trustee, Professional Children's School, 1972-74. Consulting editor, DaCapo Press, 1976; writer of record liner notes for Gemini Hall and Spectrum records, 1976—; free-lance editorial consultant to publishers, 1977—.

MEMBER: International Musicological Society, Authors Guild, Authors League of America, American Musicological Society, Music Library Association, Sonneck Society, Columbia University Graduate Faculty Alumni Association.

AWARDS, HONORS: New York State Regents scholar and fellow, 1964-69; honorable mention, Mesa de Trabajo de los Medios Masivos de Communicacion, 1975, for article "Music and Communication in Colombia, 1800-1936"; American Council of Learned Societies grant, 1978; Rockefeller Foundation grant, 1978-79; American Philosophical Society grant; honorable mention, Instituto de Bellas Artes, Mexico.

WRITINGS:

(Translator) *Music Handbook,* Colorado College Music Press, 1976.
The Life and Works of Lili Boulanger, Fairleigh Dickinson University Press, 1978.
(Contributor) *Twentieth-Century Music,* J. Calder, 1979.
(Contributor) *The First International Conference on Music and Communication,* UNESCO, 1979.
(General editor and contributor) *The Schirmer History of Music,* Schirmer Books, 1982.
Nadia Boulanger: A Life in Music, Norton, 1982.
(Editor with Arthur Orrmont) *Literary Agents of North America,* Author Aid, 1983—.
(Editor with Orrmont) *Freelancers of North America,* Author Aid, 1984—.

SIDELIGHTS: Leonie Rosenstiel once told *CA:* "I have traveled widely throughout the United States, Canada, Latin America, and Europe, observing people and customs rather than simply seeing places."

AVOCATIONAL INTERESTS: Reading, yoga, listening to people, writing letters, good conversation.

BIOGRAPHICAL/CRITICAL SOURCES:

PERIODICALS

Los Angeles Times Book Review, October 17, 1982.
New York Times, June 18, 1982.
New York Times Book Review, May 23, 1982.
Times Literary Supplement, July 1, 1983.
Washington Post Book World, July 3, 1982.*

*　　　*　　　*

ROTH, Charles E(dmund)　1934-

PERSONAL: Born January 14, 1934, in Danbury, Conn.; son of Charles Henry (in business) and Emma (in business; maiden name, Beers) Roth; married Betty Jane King (a teacher), December 22, 1956 (died August 1, 1988); children: C. Douglas (died June 1, 1987), Richard A., Barbara Ellen, Amy Jane. *Education:* Attended Wesleyan University, 1951-53; University of Connecticut, A.B., 1956; Cornell University, M.S., 1961.

ADDRESSES: Office—Massachusetts Audubon Society, South Great Rd., Lincoln, Mass. 01773.

CAREER: Ardsley Public Schools, Ardsley, N.Y., science teacher, 1956-59; Rye Nature Center, Rye, N.Y., director, 1961-62; Massachusetts Audubon Society, Lincoln, Mass., director of education, chief of interpretive services and director of educational services, 1962—. Consultant to U.S. Office of Education and Office of Environmental Education, 1972-77; instructor in philosophy of environmental education at Antioch College, 1978-82; adjunct professor of environmental science, University of Massachusetts, 1975-85.

MEMBER: Alliance of Environmental Education (founding member, member of executive committee, 1974—; president, 1976-77 and 1981-82), Littleton Conservation Commission (chair, 1973-74).

AWARDS, HONORS: Conservation education award from Massachusetts Wildlife Federation, 1966; New England Environmental Education Alliance award, 1980, for outstanding service to environmental education; Project WILD Director's award, 1987; Distinguished Service Award to an individual, North American Association for Environmental Education, 1987.

WRITINGS:

(Author of foreword) Thornton Burgess, *Mother West Wind's Neighbors,* Grosset, 1968.
(Illustrator) Allen R. Keith, *The Mammals of Martha's Vineyard,* Dukes County Historical Society, 1969.
The Most Dangerous Animal in the World (juvenile), Addison-Wesley, 1971.
(Contributor) Mrs. James Oliver and others, editors, *Museums and the Environment: A Handbook for Education,* American Association of Museums, 1971.
(With Miriam Dickey) *Who's Who in Urban America,* Massachusetts Audubon Society, 1972.
(With Dickey) *Beyond the Classroom,* Massachusetts Audubon Society, 1972.
(Editor with Warren Little) *Environmental Education in Massachusetts,* Massachusetts Audubon Society/Fund for Preservation of Natural Areas, 1972.
(Contributor) Robert H. McCabe, editor, *Man and Environment,* Prentice-Hall, Volume 1, 1972, Volume 2, 1974.

Walking Catfish and Other Aliens (juvenile), Addison-Wesley, 1973.
(Contributor) Don Albrecht and Noel McInnes, editors, *What Makes Education Environmental?,* Data/Courier/Environmental Educators, 1974.
(Contributor) John H. Noyes and Donald R. Progulske, editors, *Wildlife in an Urbanizing Environment,* University of Massachusetts Co-op Extension, 1974.
(With R. Joseph Froelich) *The Farm Book* (juvenile), Addison-Wesley, 1977.
Then There Were None, Addison-Wesley, 1977.
(And illustrator)*An Introduction to the Mammals of Massachusetts,* Massachusetts Audubon Society, 1978.
(With Linda Lockwood) *Strategies and Activities for Using Communities as Environmental Education Sites,* ERIC/Science, Mathematics, and Environmental Clearinghouse, 1979.
(And illustrator)*The Wildlife Observer's Guidebook,* Prentice-Hall, 1982.
The Plant Observer's Guidebook, Prentice-Hall, 1984.
The Sky Observer's Guidebook, Prentice-Hall, 1986.
(And illustrator)*Wildlife in Massachusetts* (text and coloring book), Project WILD (Massachusetts), 1988.
(With C. Cervoni, T. Wellnitz, and E. Arms) *Schoolground Science Activities,* Massachusetts Audubon Society, 1989.

Contributor of more than one hundred entries to *Encyclopedia Britannica Junior;* contributor of numerous articles to magazines, including *Massachusetts Wildlife, Massachusetts Audubon* (now *Sanctuary*), *Audubon, The Environmentalist, Ranger Rick, Nature Study,* and *World Wildlife.*

SIDELIGHTS: Charles E. Roth's writings reflect his primary interests in animal behavior, environmental education, and natural history. His 1982 book, *The Wildlife Observer's Guidebook,* instructs nature enthusiasts in note-taking and in capturing and marking animals, and explains "how to turn a backyard or beach or woodlot into an inexhaustible mine of satisfying experience," notes David Graber of the *Los Angeles Times Book Review.* Roth's books for young readers focus on environmental issues, ecology, and the relationship between human beings and their environment. In *The Most Dangerous Animal in the World,* humans play the title role as Roth explores the dangers in human beings' abilities to change and alter their surroundings. Ecological balance is the topic of *Walking Catfish and Other Aliens,* in which the author examines various creatures not native to North America who now thrive on the continent and affect, for better or worse, the balance of nature. *The Farm Book* is an educational guide to a New England farm throughout which, according to Jane Resh Thomas of the *New York Times Book Review,* "children will not only find lessons . . . but imaginative pleasures of their own."

Roth told *CA:* "I like to share knowledge with others but more importantly I like to empower people by helping them learn how to find out about this fascinating planet on their own. These are my primary motivations behind the hard work of writing a book. A secondary motivation is that writing for others helps me to learn. I have a love affair with nature and it occupies much of my thought—both pleasurable and disturbing (as I see us continually destroy it and thus ourselves). I am equally concerned with humankind's changing role in natural ecosystems and what that tells us about being human."

AVOCATIONAL INTERESTS: Wildlife painting and carving, nature photography.

BIOGRAPHICAL/CRITICAL SOURCES:

PERIODICALS

Los Angeles Times Book Review, August 22, 1982.
New York Times Book Review, February 26, 1978.

*   *   *

RUCKMAN, Ivy 1931-

PERSONAL: Born May 25, 1931, in Hastings, Neb.; daughter of Joy Uberto (a teacher and tree surgeon) and Lena Chloe (Osgood) Myers; married Edgar Baldwin Heylmun, December 17, 1955 (divorced, 1963); married Stuart Allan Ruckman (a dentist), June 6, 1965 (died, 1983); children: Kimberly Sue, William Bret, Stuart Andrew. *Education:* Hastings College, B.A., 1953; graduate study at University of Utah, 1963.

ADDRESSES: Home—3698 Golden Hills Ave., Salt Lake City, Utah 84121.

CAREER: High school English teacher in Casper, Wyo., 1953-57; Skyline High School, Salt Lake City, Utah, English teacher, 1962-65, creative writing instructor, 1970-72.

MEMBER: Society of Children's Book Writers, Southeastern Advocates of Literature for Young People, Utah Children's Literature Association, Friends of the Salt Lake County Library System, Manuscripters.

AWARDS, HONORS: First place in Utah Fine Arts Contest, 1982, for *What's an Average Kid Like Me Doing Way Up Here?;* Utah Children's Book Award nomination, 1982, for *Melba the Brain;* Mountain Plains Library Association Literary Contribution Award, 1985, for body of work; Utah Children's Book Award nomination, 1988, for *This Is Your Captain Speaking;* Maud Hart Lovelace Book Award, 1988, for *Night of the Twisters.*

WRITINGS:

FOR YOUNG PEOPLE

Who Needs Rainbows?, Messner, 1969.
Encounter, Doubleday, 1978.
Melba the Brain, Westminster, 1979.
What's an Average Kid Like Me Doing Way Up Here?, Delacorte, 1983, revised edition, Dell, 1988.
In a Class By Herself, Harcourt, 1983.
The Hunger Scream, Walker, 1983.
Night of the Twisters, Harper, 1984.
This Is Your Captain Speaking, Walker & Co., 1987.
No Way Out, Harper, 1988.
Who Invited the Undertaker?, Harper, 1989.

OTHER

Editor of class-written television play for ABC-TV series "Room 222." Contributor of short stories to periodicals *Jack and Jill, Cricket,* and *Ranger Rick.*

WORK IN PROGRESS: A sequel to *Melba the Brain.*

SIDELIGHTS: Ivy Ruckman told *CA:* "As often happens in a family, two children may develop such an affinity they seem to think interchangeably. This was true for my brother William and me. We were children during the depression years, a fortunate time for us: make-believe was all the pleasure we could afford. We were poor in material things, but we didn't know or care. We had each other and considered ourselves the best company. While our parents and the five older children dealt with dust storms, drought, and anxiety, our whole existence was play. Left to our own devices, unhampered by balls or trikes, we entered imaginary worlds yet to be invaded by TV or comic books.

"On a typical afternoon an upended stool became a ship's parapet, a rag mop displayed the colors. The longest stirring spoon in the kitchen stood by for an oar. The Captain and his First Mate, thus grandly appointed, rolled out to sea with solemn purpose—the capture of pirates. Together William and I built igloos in the Arctic tundra, stalked big game in steaming jungles while black panthers stalked us; we performed daring feats on a slender bar and did acrobatics on the broad-backed workhorses who always looked astonished to find themselves the dappled darlings of the circus ring. Christmas opulence, our contemporaries will remember, consisted of one or two gifts and a sack of nuts and candy from church. One year the two of us exchanged Woolworth 'diamond' rings, then spent the entire holidays slinking about the house as jewel thieves.

"If our shoes didn't always fit during those magic years, we nonetheless had books. Our mother read *Robinson Crusoe* to us before I was old enough to understand it. Our real bonanza, however, was to be found in the trash that our father hauled from people in town who owned and discarded books. A broad sampling came our way—everything from an ancient copy of Washington Irving to a volume called *White Slavery in America.* We also salvaged bookkeeping ledgers from the trash pile if they contained empty pages for drawing or writing, and once, heavy medical tomes from a doctor's effects, accompanied by a human foot preserved in a specimen jar, which Daddy locked in the shed. This treasure was ultimately viewed by every skeptical kid in the neighborhood and, as I remember, became something of a status symbol for my brother and me.

"When three older brothers joined the Navy and World War II became a reality to our family, William and I took matters into our own hands. We rolled out a huge map on the cellar floor and located Germany. (Later we repeated the process with Japan.) 'They won't win,' William assured me. 'See? They're smaller than we are.' I believed him, the way I always did. As far as I was concerned, the war was as good as won.

"Later, during our teens, we took a serious turn, devoting our energies to saving the drunken and downtrodden. We joined the Salvation Army. We played in the band and testified on the street corner. I learned the beat of the gospel tunes and solicited souls through the piano and the street organ. We gave our lives to God. It was William, I recall, who paid for my first black Salvation Army bonnet so that I could look as holy as I felt. I couldn't say, now, which of us outshone the other in piety. Though we continued to share interests in biology and Shakespeare, by the time we received degrees from Hastings College we had different goals. For the first time, we went separate ways. William became a cardiovascular surgeon; I became a high school English teacher. However, nothing has contributed so much to my 'writer's reservoir' as those early years spent skipping along after my creative and capricious brother.

"Now I have my own family: Kim, an English teacher; Bret, who attends the University of Colorado; and Stuart, who is my toughest critic. Their interests and enthusiasms naturally contribute to my work. The characters in my books take on many of their mannerisms, much of their speech, and even end up usurping their activities. Today I am lecturing and writing full-time, specializing in middle-grade and young adult novels. By habit I have become a peripatetic, which means I never stay put, I have a desk and a home office, but I end up writing everywhere—in the car, at auto repair shops, cross-legged on the porch swing, while lunching out. I do my best thinking and planning in the bathtub or the swimming pool. My husband, Allan, built a platform for me alongside our stream because I enjoy writing outdoors so much and because the properties of water seem to free my mind for creative thinking.

"For me, the writing itself is very difficult. If I can produce two to four pages of prose in a day, I feel I've done well (at top speed one day I wrote thirteen pages of a novel; another time, creeping like a snail, I produced one paragraph). Because the *sound* of one's writing is so important, I rely heavily on my 'ear' for realistic dialogue, for the flow of my prose, for the sentence balance I want to achieve. The hardest part of writing, as I see it, is getting a story to work in the first place; the revising, or 'fine tuning,' is the most enjoyable. First and foremost, however, I want my characters to live and I want the reader to care about what happens to them. I become very much involved in the lives of my fictional 'children.' I succeed as a writer, I feel, only to the extent readers share my involvement.

"Though my travels have taken me as far as Europe, the Orient, the British Isles, and Mexico, now when I pack I'm more often flying somewhere to speak to readers in the schools or to meet with librarians or writers' groups. Although I'd really rather write than talk about writing, I suspect I have the best of both worlds most of the time."

* * *

RUE, Leslie W(aits) 1944-

PERSONAL: Born December 28, 1944, in Bryn Mawr, Pa.; son of William H. and Harriett (Waits) Rue; married Passie McCarty, April 20, 1968; children: two daughters, one son. *Education:* Georgia Institute of Technology, B.I.E. (with honors), 1967, M.S.I.E., 1969; Georgia State University, Ph.D., 1973.

ADDRESSES: Home—2829 Arden Rd. N.W., Atlanta, Ga. 30327. *Office*—Department of Management, Georgia State University, Atlanta, Ga. 30303.

CAREER: Delta Airlines, Atlanta, Ga., methods analyst, 1967; Georgia State University, Atlanta, instructor in quantitative methods, 1972-73; Indiana University, Bloomington, assistant professor of administrative and behavioral studies, 1973-74; Georgia State University, professor of management, 1974—. *Military service:* U.S. Army, operations research project leader, analyst, and programmer for Management Systems Support Agency at the Pentagon, 1969-70, and data processing officer at headquarters in Seoul, Korea, 1970.

MEMBER: Academy of Management, Southern Management Association, Alpha Pi Mu, Phi Eta Sigma, Phi Kappa Phi, Sigma Iota Epsilon.

WRITINGS:

(With Robert M. Fulmer) *The Practice and Profitability of Long-Range Planning* (monograph), Planning Executives Institute, 1973.

(With William Lindsay) *Environmental Complexity on Long-Range Planning* (monograph), Planning Executives Institute, 1976.

(With Lloyd L. Byars) *Management: Theory and Application,* Irwin, 1977, 5th edition, 1989.

(With Byars) *Personnel Management: Concepts and Application,* Saunders, 1979.

(With Byars and Norman R. Harbaugh) *Readings and Cases in Personnel Management,* Saunders, 1979.

(With Byars) *Supervision: Key Link to Productivity,* Irwin, 1982, 2nd edition, 1986.

(With George R. Terry) *Self Review in Supervision,* Learning Systems Co., 1982.

(With Terry) *Self Review in Management,* Learning Systems Co., 1982.

(With Byars) *Human Resource and Personnel Management,* Irwin, 1984, 2nd edition, 1987.

(With Phyllis G. Holland) *Strategic Management and Business Policy,* McGraw, 1986, 2nd edition, 1989.

Contributor of more than thirty articles to business and management journals. Member of editorial advisory council, *Business,* 1978-80; member of editorial review board, *Journal of Management.*

* * *

RUIZ, Ramon Eduardo 1921-

PERSONAL: Born September 9, 1921, in Pacific Beach, Calif.; son of Ramon and Dolores (Urueta) Ruiz; married Natalia Marrujo (a teacher), October 14, 1944; children: Olivia Teresa, Maura Natalia. *Education:* San Diego State College (now University), B.A., 1947; Claremont Graduate School, M.A., 1948; University of California, Berkeley, Ph.D., 1954. *Politics:* Independent.

ADDRESSES: Home—P.O. Box 1775, Rancho Santa Fe, Calif. 92067. *Office*—Department of History, University of California, San Diego, Calif.

CAREER: University of Oregon, Eugene, instructor, 1955-56, assistant professor of history, 1956-57; Southern Methodist University, Dallas, Tex., assistant professor of Spanish, 1957-58; Smith College, Northampton, Mass., assistant professor, 1958-60, associate professor, 1960-63, professor of history, 1963-69; University of California, San Diego, professor of history, 1970—. *Military service:* U.S. Army Air Forces, 1943-46; served in Pacific theater; became second lieutenant.

MEMBER: American Historical Association, Conference on Latin American History, Phi Beta Kappa.

AWARDS, HONORS: Huntington Library fellow, 1958; American Philosophical Society fellow, 1959; Fulbright scholar in Mexico, 1965-66; *Cuba: The Making of a Revolution* was named one of the twenty-one best history books of 1968 by *Washington Post Book World* and *Chicago Tribune;* Hubert C. Herring Best Book prize, Pacific Coast Council on Latin American Studies, 1981, for *The Great Rebellion: Mexico, 1905-1924;* fellow, Center for Advanced Study in the Behavioral Sciences, Stanford, Calif., 1984-85.

WRITINGS:

(Editor) *An American in Maximilian's Mexico,* Huntington Library, 1959.

Mexico, the Challenge of Poverty and Illiteracy, Huntington Library, 1963.

(Editor) *The Mexican War—Was it Manifest Destiny?,* Holt, 1963.

Cuba: The Making of a Revolution, University of Massachusetts Press, 1968.

(With John William Tebbel) *South by Southwest: The Mexican-American and His Heritage,* Doubleday, 1969.

(With James David Atwater) *Out from Under: Benito Juarez and the Struggle for Mexican Independence,* Doubleday, 1969.

(Editor) *Interpreting Latin American History,* Holt, 1970.

Labor and the Ambivalent Revolutionaries: Mexico, 1911-1923, Johns Hopkins Press, 1976.

(Editor, with Robert Detweiler) *Liberation in the Americas,* Campile Press, 1978.

The Great Rebellion: Mexico, 1905-1924, Norton, 1980.

The People of Sonora and Yankee Capitalists, University of Arizona Press, 1988.

A History of the Mexican People, Norton, 1990.

SIDELIGHTS: "The prevailing American view of the Mexican Revolution is of an oppressed people rising up against foreign bosses, military dictatorship, and feudalism, recovering national pride, establishing popular rule, . . . and providing justice for the worker; in short, 'the first of the 20th-century social revolutions,' " writes John Womack, Jr., in his *New Republic* review of Ramon Eduardo Ruiz's *The Great Rebellion: Mexico, 1905-1924.* The "chief merit [of the book]," Womack says, "is its central thesis, that far from a 'radical change' of Mexican society the revolution was 'essentially a face-lifting of Mexican capitalism, . . . one of the last bourgeois protests of the 19th century, and not . . . the precursor of the socialist explosions of the 20th century.' "

While the critic finds that Ruiz's "thesis is not original," he states that *The Great Rebellion* "is the first major statement by an eminent American historian of Mexico that the real revolution was not a triumph of 'the people' at large, but a long, violent, specifically bourgeois reform, which crushed other popular uprisings for the sake of better business." And although Womack cites "several faults" in the book, including the author's discussion of the difference between "a rebellion" and a "revolution" and his omission of Mexico's financial history during the conflict, the reviewer immediately concludes that the work "deserves wide circulation. More than a reinterpretation of the Mexican Revolution, Ruiz implicitly offers important wisdom on contemporary Mexico."

BIOGRAPHICAL/CRITICAL SOURCES:

BOOKS

Ruiz, Ramon Eduardo, *The Great Rebellion: Mexico, 1905-1924,* Norton, 1980.

PERIODICALS

Nation, July 22, 1968.
New Republic, July 20, 1968, February 14, 1981.
New York Times Book Review, November 16, 1980.
Washington Post Book World, August 18, 1968.

*   *   *

RULE, Jane (Vance) 1931-

PERSONAL: Born March 28, 1931, in Plainfield, N.J.; daughter of Arthur Richards (a businessman) and Jane (Packer) Rule. *Education:* Mills College, B.A., 1952.

ADDRESSES: *Home*—The Fork, R.R. 1, Galiano, British Columbia, Canada V0N 1P0. *Agent*—Georges Borchardt, Inc., 136 East 57th St., New York, N.Y. 10022.

CAREER: Writer. Concord Academy, Concord, Mass., teacher of English, 1954-56; University of British Columbia, Vancouver, assistant director of International House, 1958-59, lecturer in English, 1959-70, visiting lecturer in creative writing, 1973-74. Has worked variously as a typist, teacher of handicapped children, change girl in a gambling house, and store clerk, mostly for background material.

MEMBER: Phi Beta Kappa.

AWARDS, HONORS: Canadian Authors' Association, best novel of 1978 award, for *The Young in One Another's Arms,* and best short story of 1978 award, for "Joy"; Literature Award, Gay Academic Union, 1978; award of merit, Fund for Human Dignity, 1983.

WRITINGS:

The Desert of the Heart (novel), Macmillan Co. of Canada, 1964, World Publishing, 1965, reprinted, Naiad Press, 1983.
This Is Not for You (novel), McCall Publishing Co., 1970.
Against the Season (novel), McCall Publishing Co., 1971, Naiad Press, 1984.
(Contributor) *Best Short Stories of 1972,* Oberon, 1972.
(Contributor) *Contemporary Voices,* Prentice-Hall, 1972.
(Contributor) *New Canadian Short Stories,* Oberon, 1975.
(Contributor) *Stories from Pacific and Arctic Canada,* Macmillan, 1975.
(Contributor) *After You're Out,* Links Books, 1975.
Theme for Diverse Instruments (short stories), Talonbooks, 1975.
Lesbian Images (criticism), Doubleday, 1975.
The Young in One Another's Arms (novel), Doubleday, 1977.
Contract with the World (novel), Harcourt, 1980.
Outlander (short stories and essays), Naiad Press, 1981.
(Contributor) Bob Weaver, editor, *Small Wonders,* CBC, 1982.
(Contributor) Ed Jackson and Stan Persky, editors, *Flaunting It,* Pink Triangle Press, 1982.
Inland Passage and Other Stories, Naiad Press, 1985.
A Hot-Eyed Moderate (essays), Naiad Press, 1985.
Memory Board (novel), Macmillan, 1987.
After the Fire (novel), Macmillan, 1989.

Author of column "So's Your Grandmother," in *Body Politic.* Contributor of reviews and articles to literature journals and other periodicals, including *Redbook, Chatelaine, San Francisco Review, Housewife, Canadian Literature, Queen's Quarterly,* and *Globe and Mail.*

SIDELIGHTS: Jane Rule is a lesbian novelist who was born in New Jersey, lived in England at one period, and currently lives in Canada. Since the age of fifteen, by which time she had already grown to the height of six feet, she has found women more attractive than men. Her novels and stories make lesbian characters interesting against the backdrop of ordinary middle-class life. "The voice that speaks in Rule's work is characterized, above all, by honesty and tolerance," writes Constance Rook in the *Dictionary of Literary Biography,* "and the attractiveness of her work is very much a function of that voice."

"Jane Rule is a sensitive, lyrical novelist with an almost painterly mastery of the intricacies of human relationships," comments Nancy Wigston in Toronto's *Globe and Mail.* Of *Memory Board,* for example, a novel in which a set of opposite-sex twins try to untangle their various sexual relationships from the perspective of old age, also explores "those perennially confused issues of parent-child relationships, of personal and social guilts, of family responsibilities and resentments, of the uneasy hold that the dead may still exert on the living," notes *Globe and Mail* contributor Janette Turner Hospital. Hospital says Rule "explores these many knots with wit, a probing intelligence and a bracing and unsentimental style."

Rule's gifted storytelling carries the reader along through her "low-key" fictions, say critics such as Linda Cahill. She suggests in *Globe and Mail* that by avoiding loud apologetics and melodrama, Rule means to say that homosexuality is "no more or less than one of the ways human beings express their love." Consequently, there is "something soothing, even comforting in Jane Rule's best work," Cahill concludes.

MEDIA ADAPTATIONS: The Desert of the Heart was made into a feature film entitled "Desert Hearts" by Desert Heart Productions, 1984.

AVOCATIONAL INTERESTS: Civil liberties and international aid programs, gardening, collecting paintings.

BIOGRAPHICAL/CRITICAL SOURCES:

BOOKS

Contemporary Literary Criticism, Volume 27, Gale, 1984.
Dictionary of Literary Biography, Volume 60: *Canadian Writers since 1960, Second Series,* Gale, 1987.
Rule, Jane, *Lesbian Images* (autobiographical essays), Doubleday, 1975.
Rule, Jane, *A Hot-Eyed Moderate* (autobiographical essays), Naiad Press, 1985.

PERIODICALS

Canadian Fiction Magazine, autumn, 1976 (interview).
Chicago Tribune, June 6, 1986.
Globe and Mail, August 18, 1984, October 5, 1985, May 3, 1986, October 17, 1987.
Los Angeles Times Book Review, October 5, 1980.
New York Times, April 4, 1986.

*   *   *

RUSSELL, Colin Archibald 1928-

PERSONAL: Born July 9, 1928, in London, England; son of Archibald Lennard (an insurance manager) and J. Winifred (Price) Russell; married Shirley P. Sinclair, September 3, 1954; children: Caroline S., Jeremy C., Catherine J., Helena K. *Education:* University College, Hull, B.Sc., 1949; University of London, M.Sc., 1958, Ph.D., 1962, D.Sc., 1978. *Religion:* Protestant.

ADDRESSES: Home—64 Putnoe Lane, Bedford MK41 9AF, England. *Office*—Open University, Milton Keynes MK7 6AA, England.

CAREER: Kingston Technical College, Surrey, England, assistant lecturer in chemistry, 1950-59; Harris College, Preston, Lancashire, England, lecturer, 1959-61, senior lecturer, 1961-68, principal lecturer in organic chemistry, 1968-70; Open University, Milton Keynes, England, senior lecturer, 1970-72, reader, 1972-81, professor of history of science and technology, 1981—.

MEMBER: Royal Society of Chemistry (fellow; past chairman of historical group), British Society for History of Science (president, 1986-88), Society for the History of Alchemy and Early Chemistry, Royal Institution of Great Britain.

WRITINGS:

(With N. E. Edwards and K. J. Dean) *The Physics and Chemistry of Baking,* Maclaren, 1963, 3rd edition, Applied Science Publishers, 1979.
(Contributor) D. S. L. Cardwell, editor, *John Dalton and the Progress of Science,* Manchester University Press, 1968.
(Contributor) T. I. Williams, editor, *A Biographical Dictionary of Scientists,* Black, 1969, 2nd edition, 1973.
(Revisor) F. W. Gibbs, *Organic Chemistry Today,* Pelican, 1970.
The History of Valency, Leicester University Press, 1971.
(Author of introduction, commentary, and notes) J. J. Berzelius, *Essai sur la theorie des proportions chimiques,* Johnson Reprint, 1972.

(With D. C. Goodman) *Science and the Rise of Technology since 1800,* John Wright, 1972.
(Editor) *Science and Religious Belief: A Selection of Recent Historical Studies Readings,* University of London Press, 1973.
(Contributor) O. B. Ramsay, editor, *Van't Hoff—Le bel centennial,* American Chemical Society, 1975.
(With N. C. Coley and G. K. Roberts) *Chemists by Profession: The Origins and Rise of the Royal Institute of Chemistry,* Royal Institute of Chemistry, 1977.
(Contributor) W. F. Bynum, E. J. Browne, and R. Pater, editors, *The Dictionary of the History of Science,* Macmillan, 1981.
Science and Social Change in Britain and Europe, 1700-1900, Macmillan, 1983.
(Editor) *Recent Developments in the History of Chemistry,* Royal Society of Chemistry, 1985.
Cross-Currents: Interactions between Science and Faith, Eerdmans, 1985.
Lancastrian Chemist: The Early Years of Sir Edward Frankland, Open University Press, 1986.
(Contributor) D. J. Jeremy, editor, *Dictionary of Brinners Biography,* Butterworth, 1986.
(Contributor) S. B. Ferguson and D. F. Wright, editors, *New Dictionary of Theology,* IVP, 1988.
(With P. J. Morris) *Archives of the British Chemical Industry,* British Society for History of Science, 1989.

Also author of about twenty-five correspondence texts for Open University. Has written television and radio programs produced for Open University, ITV, and the BBC. Contributor to professional journals, including *Annals of Science, Journal of the Chemical Society, British Journal for the History of Science, Science and Christian Belief, Chemistry in Britain, Ambix,* and *Nature.*

WORK IN PROGRESS: Research on the history of nineteenth-century chemistry, especially organic chemistry and on interactions between science and religion; biographical studies of Victorian chemists, especially Sir E. Frankland.

*   *   *

RUTMAN, Leo 1935-

PERSONAL: Born September 23, 1935, in New York, N.Y.; son of Lucien (a singer) and Paula (Gesunterman) Rutman; married Bette Levine, August 11, 1988; children: (previous marriage) Kristofer. *Education:* Hofstra University, B.A., 1959; additional study in drama at Columbia University, Brandeis University, and Yale University. *Religion:* Jewish.

ADDRESSES: Home—41 Whittington Rd., White Plains, N.Y. 10607. *Agent*—Bob Talian, International Creative Management, 40 West 57th St., New York, N.Y. 10019.

CAREER: Novelist and playwright. Lecturer in English at Hunter College of the City University of New York and Fordham University; lecturer in theatre department at Lehman College of the City University of New York. Affiliated with New School for Social Research. *Military service:* U.S. Army, 1954-56.

AWARDS, HONORS: Sam S. Shubert Award from Columbia University, 1966-67, for playwriting; Playwright-in-Residence Award from Brandeis University, 1967-68; Joseph S. Levine Film Fellowship from Yale University, 1968-69.

WRITINGS:

PLAYS

They Got Jack (two-act; first produced Off-Broadway at New Theatre, 1966), Yale University Press, 1969.

"Interlude at a Shoe Shine Stand" (one-act), first produced Off-Off Broadway at 13th Street Theatre, 1967.

"Where Is Che Guevara?" (two-act), first produced Off-Broadway at Actors Studio, 1970.

Gott ist Tot! Killed Along with James Bond in a Four Car Collision on the Los Angeles Freeway (three-act), L'Action Theatrale, 1972.

"Twenty Years after the Man in the Iron Mask," first produced Off-Off Broadway at the Theatre for the New City, 1977.

Also author of "Jesus Is a Junkie," produced Off-Off Broadway at Theatre for the New City, "A Night Wind" (an autobiographical play), "The Life and Death of Rogue Robbie Kilkenny" (a play about Robert Kennedy), "America in Heat," "Night Whispers," and "Leon Trotsky."

OTHER

5 Good Boys (novel), Viking, 1982.
Spear of Destiny, D. I. Fine, 1988.
American Reich, Ballantine, 1990.

Also author of "The World Is Mine at Six O'Clock Tonight" (a rock musical), "South" (filmscript), and *Good Men Die in the Sunlight* (novel).

WORK IN PROGRESS: Eddie Purple and *The Second Coming of the Last Judgment,* both for Ballantine.

S

SABAR, Yona 1939-

PERSONAL: Born February 25, 1939, in Zakho, Iraq; emigrated to Israel, 1951; came to the United States in 1965, naturalized U.S. citizen, 1976; son of Rahamim and Miriam (Hamu) Sabar; married Stephanie Kruger; children: Ariel, Ilan. *Education:* Hebrew University of Jerusalem, B.A., 1963; Yale University, Ph.D., 1970. *Religion:* Jewish.

ADDRESSES: Office—Department of Near Eastern Languages and Cultures, University of California, Los Angeles, Calif. 90024.

CAREER: University of California, Los Angeles, assistant professor, 1972-76, associate professor, 1976-82, professor of Hebrew, 1982—.

WRITINGS:

A Neo-Aramaic Midrash on Beshallah (Exodus), Otto Harrassowitz Press, 1976.
(Editor and translator) *The Folk Literature of the Kurdistani Jews: An Anthology,* Yale University Press, 1982.
The Book of Genesis in Neo-Aramaic, Hebrew University Press, 1983.
Homilies (Midrashim) in the Neo-Aramaic of the Kurdistani Jews, Israel Academy of Sciences and Humanities, 1984.
The Book of Exodus in Neo-Aramaic, Hebrew University Press, 1988.

WORK IN PROGRESS: Study on dialects and literature of Kurdistani Jews.

SIDELIGHTS: Yona Sabar told *CA:* "The community of Kurdistani Jews, like many other small ethnic groups in the world, are losing their unique identity, their Aramaic language (spoken for over three thousand years), and their heritage. Therefore, as a native of this community, I made it my mission to preserve as much as possible of their linguistic, spiritual, and literary traditions and folklore for the community of interested scholars and other educated people."

*   *   *

SACKLER, Howard (Oliver) 1929-1982

PERSONAL: Born December 19, 1929, in New York, N.Y.; died of pulmonary thrombosis October 14 (some sources say October 13), 1982, in Ibiza, Spain; son of Martin and Ida Sackler; married Greta Lynn Lungren, December 1, 1963; children: Molly, Daniel. *Education:* Brooklyn College (now Brooklyn College of the City University of New York), B.A., 1950.

ADDRESSES: Home—Sta. Eulalia del Rio, Ibiza, Spain. *Agent*—Jay Harris, 555 Fifth Ave., New York, N.Y. 10017.

CAREER: Playwright and screenwriter, 1950-82. Director of Caedmon Records, New York, N.Y., and London, England, 1953-68. Theatre director in New York, London, Dublin, and Los Angeles of plays, including "The Family Reunion," 1954, "Women of Trachis," 1954, "Purgatory" and "The Words upon the Windowpane," 1955, "Hamlet," 1957, "Krapp's Last Tape" and "Chin, Chin," 1960, "Suzanna Andler," 1973, and "Duchess of Malfi," 1976. Director of film, "A Midsummer Night's Dream," 1961, and of television program, "Shakespeare: Soul of an Age," first broadcast by the National Broadcasting Company (NBC), 1964.

AWARDS, HONORS: Rockefeller Foundation grant, 1953; Littauer Foundation grant, 1954; Maxwell Anderson Award, 1954; Sergel Award, 1959; Pulitzer Prize for drama, New York Drama Critics Circle Award, and Antoinette Perry Award (Tony), all 1969, all for *The Great White Hope.*

WRITINGS:

Want My Shepherd: Poems, Caedmon, 1954.
"Uriel Acosta," first produced in Berkeley, Calif., 1954.
"Mr. Welk and Jersey Jim" (also see below), first produced in New York at Actors Studio Theatre, 1960.
"The Yellow Loves," first produced in Chicago, 1960.
A Few Enquiries (four one-acts: *Sarah, The Nine O'Clock Mail, Mr. Welk and Jersey Jim,* and *Skippy;* first produced together in Boston by Theatre Company, 1965), Dial, 1970.
"The Pastime of Monsieur Robert," first produced in London at Hampsted Theatre, 1966.
The Great White Hope (first produced in Washington, D.C. at Arena Stage, 1967, produced in New York at Alvin Theatre, 1968), Dial, 1968.
(Contributor) Edward Parone, editor, *New Theatre in America,* Dell, 1974.
"Semmelweiss," first produced in Buffalo, N.Y. at Studio Arena Theatre, November 4, 1977.
"Goodbye Fidel," first produced in New York at Ambassador Theatre, 1980.

SCREENPLAYS

"Desert Padre," RKO, 1950.
"Fear and Desire," Stanley Kubrick Productions, 1953.
"Killer's Kiss," United Artists, 1955.
"A Midsummer Night's Dream" (adapted from the Czechoslovakian film version), Showcorporation, 1961.
"The Great White Hope," Twentieth Century Fox, 1970.
"Bugsy," United Artists, 1973.
"Jaws II," Universal, 1976.
(With Paul Theroux and Peter Bogdanovich) "Saint Jack," New World Productions, 1979.

OTHER

Also author of "Medea" and "Klondike," plays. Contributor of poetry to *Hudson Review, Poetry, Commentary,* and *New Directions.* Sackler's papers are at the Humanities Research Center, University of Texas, Austin.

WORK IN PROGRESS: "Bert & Eddie," a play.

SIDELIGHTS: The late Howard Sackler was an award-winning playwright whose works combined historical incident, free verse, and intense character study. The author is best remembered for his drama *The Great White Hope,* a sweeping chronicle of a black boxer that in 1969 earned the prestigious "triple crown" of theatrical citations—the Pulitzer Prize, the New York Drama Critics Circle Award, and the Antoinette Perry Award. Sackler, who considered himself a poet as well as a dramatist, was also a noted director and producer who engineered numerous recordings of classical plays. His sudden death in 1982 marked the end of a thirty-two year period of involvement with stage and screen.

Sackler started writing for the theatre in his mid-twenties. Before that he composed poetry under the tutelage of W. H. Auden and provided screenplays for budding director Stanley Kubrick. Sackler was particularly drawn to T. S. Eliot's verse drama, so his first play, "Uriel Acosta," was written in verse. A one-act based on the life of an Inquisition-era Portuguese Jew, "Uriel Acosta" won the 1954 Maxwell Anderson Award from the University of California at Berkeley. *Dictionary of Literary Biography* contributor Robert W. Hungerford wrote: "By the time his first play was produced in 1954, and with the publication of a book of his poetry *[Want My Shepherd],* and the production of three of his screenplays, Sackler's writing career was off to a commendable beginning for a man who was barely twenty-five."

In 1953 Sackler became founding director of Caedmon Records. Working primarily from London, he engineered more than two hundred recordings of well-known plays, often employing England's most respected actors and actresses for the readings. A sample of Caedmon's output includes "Hamlet," featuring Paul Scofield, "Romeo and Juliet," featuring Albert Finney and Claire Bloom, and "Cyrano de Bergerac," featuring Sir Ralph Richardson. Hungerford has suggested that Sackler's association with Caedmon "marks a contribution of considerable significance to twentieth-century drama."

The Caedmon project occupied Sackler throughout much of the late 1950s, but in the 1960s he returned to playwrighting. His first major work, *A Few Enquiries,* was produced in 1965. A series of four one-acts, *A Few Enquiries* offers quirky pieces on accidental death, submerged guilt, neurosis, and fantasy. "What makes these plays—and Sackler—so unusual is that they are classical and poetic while being modern in their treatment of reality and their sense of the stage," Martin Gottfried noted in his introduction to the published plays. "They are literary, yet production-oriented. In short, Sackler is an artist, speaking in a unique voice without trying to fit into one school of playwrighting or another. His plays aren't naturalistic, but neither are they abstract. They work in the spaces of surrealism, where reality can be heightened or lowered, and so they must be read that way."

For many years Sackler had been fascinated by the career of Jack Johnson, a turn-of-the-century boxer who became the first black heavyweight champion. Sackler decided to use Johnson's troubled life as the basis for a play, and in 1967 he completed *The Great White Hope.* The title refers to the hopes white fans pin on the black champion's opponents—a black titleholder is an affront to white supremacy. Johnson, renamed "Jackson" in the play, must confront not only his foes in the ring but the hostilities of American society at large. In a review in *The Nation,* Julius Novick observed that Sackler "has gotten hold of a vitally significant piece of history, has realized just why it is significant, and has put that significance, in vivid human terms, on the stage. . . . The play demands of us, in urgently dramatic terms, that we examine the whole [racial] question and our stake in it."

The Great White Hope swept the major theatrical awards in 1969 and made stars of its author and its lead actor, James Earl Jones. *Hudson Review* contributor John Simon contended that the staged work "generates considerable excitement. . . . The play has energy and variety. It knows when to hurtle and when to sashay forward, there is humor in it, and it does generate a growing sense of entrapment and doom." During a 1989 revival of the drama, *Chicago Tribune* critic Richard Christiansen stated: "The real triumph of the play comes not so much in its bigness as in its brilliant, single-minded use of [Johnson's] story to show the brutal, deadly effects of racial hatred. . . . The production moves swiftly and seamlessly, and the high-energy performances, although sometimes difficult to hear in the heat of the hubub, are handled with accurate detail and understanding, right down to every small but crucial role."

Subsequent Sackler plays continued to draw upon historical incident for theme and setting. "Semmelweiss," first produced in 1977, concerns the gradual nervous collapse of a nineteenth-century physician, a true-life pioneer of sterilization techniques. "Goodbye Fidel," produced in 1980, chronicles the rise of Fidel Castro in Cuba through citizens affected by his policies. Neither of these two plays enjoyed commercial success, but critics expressed admiration for "Semmelweiss," in particular. *New York Times* contributor Mel Gussow, for instance, praised the moments in the work "that are so graphic that they are almost unbearable to watch." Gussow added: "this is a play that incites an audience to feelings beyond compassion; we want to demand action."

Sackler died of pulmonary thrombosis at his home in Ibiza, Spain late in 1982. He was at work on several plays at the time, including "Klondike," based on the Alaskan gold rush. None of his unfinished plays have been produced, but his finished works, especially *The Great White Hope* and "Semmelweiss," continue to grace the stage in America and England. Gottfried concluded that for the theatre—his favorite medium—Sackler "[used] language with care, the structures with confidence, at a time when both language and structure [were] both suspect and rare. He [was] disciplined in a period of anarchy, [wrote] for actors in a period of performers. He [was] his own man, as any artist must be."

BIOGRAPHICAL/CRITICAL SOURCES:

BOOKS

Contemporary Literary Criticism, Volume 14, 1980.

Dictionary of Literary Biography, Volume 7: *Twentieth-Century American Dramatists,* Gale, 1981.

Funke, Lewis, *Playwrights Talk about Writing: 12 Interviews with Lewis Funke,* Dramatic Publishing, 1975.

Sackler, Howard, *A Few Enquiries,* Dial, 1970.

PERIODICALS

Chicago Tribune, January 13, 1989.

Harper's, January, 1969.

Hudson Review, winter, 1968-69.

Nation, January 15, 1968.

National Review, December 17, 1968.

New Republic, October 26, 1968.

New York Review of Books, February 1, 1968.

New York Times, October 13, 1968, November 24, 1977, April 29, 1979, April 24, 1980, May 22, 1981.

Time, June 1, 1981.

Times (London), November 6, 1985.

Village Voice, October 10, 1968.

Washington Post, October 11, 1978, October 22, 1978.

Western Humanities Review, autumn, 1969.

OBITUARIES:

PERIODICALS

New York Times, October 15, 1982.

Times (London), October 18, 1982.

Washington Post, October 16, 1982.*

—*Sketch by Anne Janette Johnson*

*   *   *

SAFA, Helen M. Icken   1930-

PERSONAL: Surname is accented on second syllable; born December 4, 1930, in Brooklyn, N.Y.; daughter of Gustav F. (self-employed) and Erna (Keune) Icken; married Manouchehr Safa-Isfahani (with United Nations), December 23, 1962; children: Mitra; stepchildren: Kaveh, Arya. *Education:* Cornell University, B.A., 1952; Columbia University, M.A., 1958, Ph.D., 1962. *Politics:* Democrat. *Religion:* Protestant.

ADDRESSES: Home—2021 Northwest 15th Ave., Gainesville, Fla. 32605. *Office*—Center for Latin American Studies, University of Florida, Gainesville, Fla. 32611.

CAREER: New York City Board of Education, New York, N.Y., research assistant, 1954; training and evaluation officer, Puerto Rican Department of State, Technical Cooperation Administration, 1954-55; information analyst, Commonwealth of Puerto Rico, Social Programs Administration, 1955-56; consultant in Research Office, New York State Division of Housing, 1956-57; consultant in Research Office, Commonwealth of Puerto Rico, Urban Renewal and Housing Administration, 1959-60; Inter-American Housing and Planning Center, Pan American Union, Bogata, Colombia, temporary consultant, 1961; Syracuse University, Syracuse, N.Y., assistant professor of anthropology and senior research associate of Youth Development Center, 1962-67; Rutgers University, New Brunswick, N.J., associate professor, 1967-72, professor of anthropology and urban planning, 1972-74, associate director, then director of Latin American Institute, 1970-74, New Brunswick Chairperson of Anthropology, 1974-80, graduate director, 1974-76; University of Florida, Gainesville, director of Center for Latin American Studies and professor of anthropology, 1980-85, professor of anthropology and Latin American studies, 1985—. Has coordinated and participated in numerous conferences throughout the

world, 1973—; member of review boards, panels, and delegations, 1974—. Fulbright program, member of advisory screening committee, 1974-77, chairperson, 1983-86; member of Inter-American Foundation doctoral fellowship committee, 1987-90.

MEMBER: International Congress of Americanists, American Anthropological Association (fellow), Society for Applied Anthropology (fellow), Latin American Studies Association (member of executive committee, 1974-77; president, 1983-84), American Ethnological Society, National Organization for Women, Phi Beta Kappa.

AWARDS, HONORS: Grant from National Institute of Mental Health, 1963, 1969-70, 1980-83; grant from U.S. Office of Education, 1966-67; collaborative research grant from Social Science Research Council, 1976-77; grant from Smithsonian Foreign Currency Program, 1978-79; grant from Wenner-Gren Foundation for Anthropological Research conference grant, 1980 and 1985; collaborative grant from National Science Foundation; named distinguished professor, University of Utrecht, Netherlands, 1987, and Northwestern University, 1990; fellow, Kellogg Institute for International Studies, University of Notre Dame, 1989.

WRITINGS:

The Urban Poor of Puerto Rico: A Study in Development and Inequality, Holt, 1974.

(Editor with Brian DuToit) *Migration and Development,* Mouton, 1975.

(Editor with DuToit) *Migration and Ethnicity,* Mouton, 1975.

(Editor with Gloria Levitas) *Social Problems in Corporate America,* Harper, 1975.

(Editor with June Nash) *Sex and Class in Latin America,* Praeger, 1976.

(Editor) *Toward a Political Economy of Urbanization in Third World Countries,* Oxford University Press (New Delhi), 1982.

(Editor with Nash) *Women and Change in Latin America: New Directions in the Study of Sex and Class in Latin America,* J.F. Bergin, 1985.

(Editor with Eleanor Leacock) *Women's Work: Development and the Division of Labor by Gender,* Bergin & Garvey, 1986.

CONTRIBUTOR

Irwin Deutscher and E. Thompson, editors, *Among the People: Encounters with the Urban Poor,* Basic Books, 1968.

Anuario Indigenista, Volume XXXIX, Inter-American Indian Institute, 1969.

Murray Wax, editor, *Anthropological Perspectives on Education,* Basic Books, 1971.

Peter Orleans and Russell Ellis, editors, *Urban Affairs Annual Review,* Volume V, Sage Publications, 1971.

Charles O. Crawford, editor, *The Family: Structure and Function in Health Crises,* Macmillan, 1971.

Family and Social Change in the Caribbean, Institute of Caribbean Studies, University of Puerto Rico, 1973.

S. L. Bailey and R. T. Hyman, editors, *Perspectives on Latin America,* Bobbs-Merrill, 1974.

Boxandall, Gordon, and Reverby, editors, *America's Working Women,* Vintage Book, 1977.

D. Shimkin and others, editors, *Anthropology for the Future,* University of Illinois, 1978.

Women and National Development, University of Chicago Press, 1978.

I. Horowitz, J. Leggett, and M. Oppenheimer, editors, *The American Working Class: Perspectives for the 1980s,* Dutton, 1979.

D. Mortimer and R. S. Bruce-Laporte, editors, *Female Immigrants to the United States: Caribbean, Latin American, and African Experiences,* Smithsonian Institution, 1981.

J. Nash and M. P. Fernandez Kelly, editors, *Women and the International Division of Labor,* State University of New York Press, 1983.

N. El-Sanabary, editor, *Women and Work in the Third World,* Center for the Study, Education, and Advancement of Women, University of California, Berkeley, 1983.

Jack Hopkins, editor, *Latin America: Perspectives of a Region,* Holmes & Meier, 1985.

Steve Sanderson, editor, *The Americas in the International Division of Labor,* Holmes & Meier, in press.

H. P. Smith and J. Feagin, editors, *The Capitalist City: Global Restructuring and Communist Affairs,* Basil Blackwell, 1987.

Leith Mullings, editor, *Cities in the United States,* Columbia University Press, 1987.

E. Acosto-Belen and B. Sjostrom, editors, *The Hispanic Experience in the United States,* Praeger, 1988.

OTHER

Also contributor, June Nash and Juan Corradi, editors, *Ideology and Social Change in Latin America,* 1975. Contributor to numerous periodicals, including *American Anthropologist, Contemporary Sociology, Cultural Survival, Caribbean Studies, Human Organization,* and *Latin American Perspectives.* Guest editor, *American Behavioral Scientist,* March-April, 1972.

*   *   *

St. JOHN THOMAS, David
See THOMAS, David St. John

*   *   *

SALISBURY, Harrison E(vans) 1908-

PERSONAL: Born November 14, 1908, in Minneapolis, Minn.; son of Percy Pritchard and Georgianna (Evans) Salisbury; married Mary Hollis, April 1, 1933 (divorced); married Charlotte Young Rand, 1964; children: (first marriage) Michael, Stephan. *Education:* University of Minnesota, A.B., 1930.

ADDRESSES: Home—Box 70, Taconic, Conn. 06079. *Agent*—Curtis Brown, 10 Astor Place, New York, N.Y. 10003.

CAREER: Minneapolis Journal, Minneapolis, Minn., reporter, 1928; United Press, reporter, London manager, Moscow manager, and foreign editor, 1930-48; *New York Times,* correspondent in Moscow, 1949-54, reporter in New York City, 1955-61, national editor, 1962-64, assistant managing editor, 1964-70, associate editor and editor of opinion-editorial page, 1971-75.

MEMBER: American Academy and Institute of Arts and Letters (president, 1975-77), Authors League of America (president, 1980-85), National Press Club (Washington, D.C.), Century Association (New York).

AWARDS, HONORS: Pulitzer Prize in international reporting, 1955, for articles on the Soviet Union.

WRITINGS:

Russia on the Way, Macmillan, 1946.
American in Russia, Harper, 1955 (published in England as *Stalin's Russia and After,* Macmillan [London], 1955).

The Shook-up Generation, Harper, 1958.
To Moscow—and Beyond: A Reporter's Narrative, Harper, 1960.
Moscow Journal: The End of Stalin, University of Chicago Press, 1961.
The Northern Palmyra Affair, Harper, 1962.
A New Russia?, Harper, 1962.
The Key to Moscow, Lippincott, 1963.
Russia, Atheneum, 1965 (published in England as *The Soviet Union,* Encyclopaedia Britannica Educational Corp., 1967).
Orbit of China, Harper, 1967.
(Editor and contributor) *The Soviet Union: The First Fifty Years,* Harcourt, 1967 (published in England as *Anatomy of the Soviet Union,* Thomas Nelson, 1967).
Behind the Lines—Hanoi, December 23, 1966-January 7, 1967, Harper, 1967.
(Editor) Andrei Sakharov, *Progress, Coexistence, and Intellectual Freedom,* Norton, 1968.
War between Russia and China, Norton, 1969 (published in England as *The Coming War between Russia and China,* Secker & Warburg, 1969).
The 900 Days: The Siege of Leningrad, Harper, 1969, reprinted with a new introduction, Da Capo Press, 1985 (published in England as *The Siege of Leningrad,* Secker & Warburg, 1969).
(Editor) Georgi K. Zhukov, *Marshal Zhukov's Greatest Battles,* Harper, 1969.
The Many Americas Shall Be One, Norton, 1971.
(Author of commentary) Emil Schulthess, *Soviet Union,* Harper, 1971.
(Editor) *The Eloquence of Protest: Voices of the 70's,* Houghton, 1972.
(Editor and contributor, with James A. Keith and Ida Prince Nelson) *Project WERC Resource Book,* Teacher Assist Center, 1972.
(Editor with David Schneiderman) *The Indignant Years: Art and Articles from the Op-Ed Page of the New York Times,* Crown/Arno Press, 1973.
To Peking—and Beyond: A Report on the New Asia, Quadrangle, 1973.
(Editor and author of foreword) Sakharov, *Sakharov Speaks,* Knopf, 1974.
The Gates of Hell, Random House, 1975.
Travels around America, Walker, 1976.
Black Night, White Snow: Russia's Revolutions, 1905-1917, Doubleday, 1978.
Russia in Revolution, Holt, 1979.
(Editor) *Russian Society since the Revolution,* Ayer Co., 1979.
Without Fear or Favor: The New York Times and Its Times, New York Times, 1980, published as *Without Fear or Favor: An Uncompromising Look at the New York Times,* Ballantine, 1981.
China: 100 Years of Revolution, Holt, 1983.
A Journey for Our Times: A Memoir, Harper, 1983.
(Editor and author of introduction) *Vietnam Reconsidered: Lessons from a War,* Harper, 1984.
The Long March: The Untold Story, Harper, 1985.
A Time of Change: A Reporter's Tale of Our Time, Harper, 1988.
The Great Black Dragon Fire: The Chinese Inferno, Little, Brown, 1989.
Tiananmen Diary: Thirteen Days in June, Little, Brown, 1989.

SIDELIGHTS: During his long career, Pulitzer Prize-winning journalist Harrison E. Salisbury has specialized in covering the Soviet Union and China. He has served as the Moscow manager for United Press and as Moscow correspondent for the *New York Times,* and he has written a number of books on recent Soviet and Chinese history. In the course of his work he has traveled to Siberia, Central Asia, Outer Mongolia, Tibet, North Vietnam and North Korea. He was the first western reporter allowed to visit Hanoi during the Vietnam War. For his book *The Long March: The Untold Story,* Salisbury retraced the arduous seven thousand mile march of the Red Chinese Army, a march that cost some eighty thousand lives. Called a "battle-scarred old reporter" by James Yuenger in *Tribune Books,* Salisbury explains in an article for *Modern Maturity:* "I am a writer. I like to write and report and have since I was in college. There is nothing I would rather do."

After leaving college in 1930, Salisbury worked for the United Press in Chicago, covering the trial of gangster Al Capone. He was soon transferred overseas to handle first the London and then the Moscow office. During the Second World War he covered the Eastern Front for United Press, reporting on the fighting between Soviet and Nazi troops. Following the war Salisbury became the Moscow correspondent for the *New York Times,* a position he held until 1954. It was during this time that Salisbury's name became "synonymous with the Soviet Union, whose politics, totalitarian leadership, and, above all, its people, preoccupied him for some 40 years," according to Robert Manning in the *New York Times.* Upon returning home in 1954 following Soviet dictator Joseph Stalin's death, Salisbury wrote a series of articles about Kremlin politics and Stalin's crimes; these articles won him the Pulitzer Prize in 1955.

Because of the extensive censorship practiced in the Soviet Union in the 1940s and 1950s, Salisbury's stories while he was a reporter there were often cut before they were allowed to be sent out of the country. It was not until he returned to the United States that he was able to speak openly about many aspects of Soviet life. His experiences in the Soviet Union were recounted in a string of books during the 1950s and 1960s, including such titles as *Stalin's Russia and After, To Moscow—and Beyond: A Reporter's Narrative,* and *Moscow Journal: The End of Stalin.*

In *A Journey for Our Times: A Memoir,* Salisbury writes about his years in the Soviet Union, a country that, Robert MacNeil notes in the *New York Times,* "has dominated much of his adult life." Salisbury explains in the book: "I've been interested in Russia as a whole, the Russianness of Russia rather than the Soviet phase, which seems to me to be an aberration and not as interesting as the culture and tradition and the marvelous Russian literature and the nature of the people and the country." *A Journey for Our Times* covers the problems Salisbury experienced both with the Soviet censors and with his editors back home. The Soviets withheld information from him; the editors sometimes revised his stories. Salisbury also recounts his fear in 1950 that the KGB was trying to kill him with a paralyzing drug, and the possibility in 1953, just before Stalin's death, that he would be put on trial. "When [Salisbury] warms up, when he writes about what moves him," MacNeil says in his review of the book, " 'A Journey for Our Times' is superb."

Salisbury's career after his return to the United States is recounted in *A Time of Change: A Reporter's Tale of Our Time,* his second volume of memoirs. In this book he tells of covering the civil rights era and the Vietnam War, among other major stories of the 1960s. His stories about Birmingham, Alabama, during the height of civil rights turbulence, in which he warned that the city was about to explode in violence, earned him 42 charges of criminal libel and a $10 million suit against him and the *New York Times.* Salisbury and the *Times* won dismissal of the cases. During the Vietnam War, he was the first American reporter allowed to visit North Vietnam, where his stories of American

bombing raids over Hanoi drew criticism from hardliners back home. He was also the first reporter allowed into Communist Albania, North Korea, and Mongolia. Aside from his travels abroad, Salisbury recounts the office politics at the *New York Times* during the 1960s and 1970s, providing what Yuenger calls "gossip of an intriguing order."

To Arnold R. Isaacs of the *Washington Post Book World, A Time of Change* is "zesty, fast-paced, a tumbling, kaleidoscopic succession of places and events and personalities and details set down vividly but not always thoughtfully or originally. . . . Most readers . . . will come away from this book with a new respect for the craft of those, like Salisbury, who undertake to observe and explain complicated, turbulent events not from a safe distance or after they have passed, but from close up and as they occur." Yuenger concludes that *A Time of Change,* along with the first volume of Salisbury's memoirs, "should be required reading for every young reporter who wants to know how it's done."

At the age of 75, Salisbury received permission to retrace the historic Long March of the Red Chinese Army, a journey of some 7,400 miles across some of the most rugged terrain in China. The Long March began in 1934 when the Red Army, chased by the much larger armies of Nationalist leader Chaing Kai-Shek, sought to escape being wiped out. When they finally reached the western Chinese province of Shaanxi after a grueling, year-long journey, only 4,000 survivors remained of the original 86,000 soldiers. The Long March has assumed legendary stature in modern Chinese history because of the important role played by Mao Zedong, later to become leader of Red China, and other prominent Chinese communists.

In *The Long March: The Untold Story,* Salisbury tells of the hardships and misery of the Long March, comparing the historic trek to his own journey over the same terrain fifty years later. Accompanied by his wife, Charlotte, and his close friend John S. Service, Salisbury followed the route of the Long March by jeep, mule, and even on foot. He also interviewed many of the original Long March participants to obtain their insights into the event, and he spoke to local historians and government officials. "Only, I felt, by traveling those 7,400 miles could I write an accurate account of the Long March," Salisbury explains in *Modern Maturity.* "Only so could I convey some small sense of the ordeal of the men and women who made the march." Salisbury's book, Judith Shapiro writes in the *New Republic,* "provides a fascinating glimpse into Maoist China's myth of its origins." Michel Oksenberg, writing in the *New York Times Book Review,* calls *The Long March* "an engrossing and revealing account . . . the best to date."

Called by Connie Lauerman in the *Chicago Tribune* "a reporter's reporter, at once tough and compassionate, worldly and naive," Salisbury is often ranked among the best known and most respected of American journalists. Peter S. Prescott in *Newsweek* describes him as "the most distinguished of postwar foreign correspondents." Yuenger finds Salisbury to be "an extraordinary piece of work—passionately romantic and coldly cynical, quick to take offense or dispense praise, relentlessly catty . . ., yet wisely tolerant of man's foibles. He wears his heart on his typewriter. And he has proven, time and time again, that he is one hell of a journalist."

CA INTERVIEW

CA interviewed Harrison E. Salisbury by telephone on August 1, 1988, at his home in Taconic, Connecticut.

CA: You've just gotten back from a trip to China, a country you've written about recently in your second memoir, A Time of Change, *and* The Long March. *Was the trip related to your work?*

SALISBURY: Yes. I'm doing another book on China. This one deals with the Deng Xiaoping period. It's set against the background of the terrible chaos in which China found itself at the time Mao died as the result of the insanity of many of his later policies. I've spent six of the last ten months in China working on the book, including interviews with a great many of the top Chinese who were involved in the events both before and after Mao's death and have been involved in the new politics which have brought about so many changes in China.

I have also traveled extensively there in order to see the changes at the grass roots, to inspect the large industrial establishments since they've gone on virtually a profit-making basis and to look at some of the small new factories and enterprises started by individuals under the program of encouraging private enterprise. I've seen every possible aspect of Chinese life. For *The Long March,* Mrs. Salisbury and I spent four months in China in 1984, during which we were traveling through back country. While we were gathering information on the Long March, which occurred fifty years ago, I was also getting a great deal of contemporary information, because that's where I first realized the profound effects of the new policies in agriculture, where the peasants have been turned loose to make money and are doing it with great vigor and pleasure. I've covered in these two long stays about two-thirds of all the provinces of China.

This mountain of material I now have in hand will be going into the new book; I'm just sitting down to sort it out and catalogue it so I can write with facility.

CA: As you said in A Time of Change, *"the US-USSR-China triangle" weighs very heavily on the world's future. From your recent observations, what do you feel the U.S. should be doing—or doing better—to promote a good working relationship among the three countries?*

SALISBURY: So far as China is concerned, we have an excellent relationship. It was founded very firmly by Mr. Nixon and the late Premier Zhou and Mao Zedong, and it has developed quite soundly. I think at this point we should make an effort to assess a little bit more accurately what we can do to assist in deepening our relationship over the long term. This means basically measures which will intensify our industrial and economic interchange with China. We already have gotten up to being the number two trading partner of China, which is a very important position to be in. And since China is going to be vastly expanding her economy over the next twenty years, there are a good many things we can do and are in fact beginning to do to widen that trade. The Chinese have to be able to export to this country in order to buy here, and there are certain areas in which we could make that easier for them. I think that's the most important thing to do, and maybe the second most important thing would be enhancing our contribution to China's education. They're desperately in need of more trained people in the sciences and various other areas for high-tech. But the basic lines of our policy vis-a-vis China are quite well set.

So far as the Soviet Union is concerned, we are on a very good course there with the various initiatives Mr. Reagan has made, with the cooperation of Mr. Gorbachev and indeed sometimes started by him, in methods of reducing the arms race and bringing nuclear weaponry under control. That great field has really been opened up; they've made enormous progress and its effects have flowed back very powerfully into the relationship between the two countries.

I think probably the most important thing we can do now is to begin to deepen our understanding of what's been happening in the Soviet Union, the extent to which they have abandoned a great deal of the old excess and worn-out baggage of Marxism, and appreciate more fully the extent to which they are moving on, not in capitalist terms, but toward creating what would be a kind of mixed economy such as we haven't seen in the world, a mixture of some of their socialist ideas and a lot of our private-enterprise ideas. That certainly is a very favorable circumstance for us, and I don't believe there's a deep understanding of that in the U.S. as a whole. I think many people here have very strong prejudices against the Soviet Union that come out of years of antagonism and were intensified in the early years of the Reagan administration, in which he was conducting such strong propaganda against the "Evil Empire," which he has now embraced. We have some homework to do there. And then—this is for the next administration—there'll have to be some serious thought given to the course of our long-term relationship with the Soviets, particularly in continuing the momentum that has been set up in negotiations on these life-or-death problems of nuclear weapons and things of that kind.

CA: How much of a chance do you feel Gorbachev's reforms have of lasting?

SALISBURY: This is still a gamble, because he has very powerful opposition at home, as I think everybody is well aware now. There's a very strong conservative or reactionary group in the Soviet Union which is not at all pleased with his opening things up and his new aspect both at home and abroad, but most particularly at home, because that's where these things are concentrated. I believe that the party conference he had in June, with its remarkable publicity and openness, the spectacle of the leaders arguing amongst themselves carried on nationwide television; the very great lengths he's gone to in sweeping away the worst aspects that remained of the Stalin regime; rehabilitation of all of the people who for sixty years were considered to be traitors and criminals—all this has given him a support within the country in general which he did not have before.

Whether that is going to be powerful enough to enable him to go ahead with this dreadfully difficult task of dismantling the bureaucracy, with bringing light into all the dark corners of the country, all these things that he thinks (and I think quite rightly) are necessary if Russia is really to join the modern technological world and not be left way behind, I don't yet know. I cannot help but realize that the entrenched forces of reaction in the Soviet Union are very powerful. There's nothing so powerful as a bureaucracy which has been in existence and strengthened constantly over a period of fifty or sixty years. That's what he's up against, and he has not until now had what I would call a strong popular mandate. I think he's getting on; I think the party congress went further than anything before to give him popular support. But he's got to keep going, and you can see that he understands this and realizes it very well by the statements in which he's constantly saying, We have to keep up the momentum, we've got to put these various measures into law, we have to start carrying them out. I would say that it's still a gamble on whether he can put it across, but that the odds are slowly, slowly moving in his favor. I'm more optimistic this year than I was last year, and last year I was a little more optimistic than I was the year before.

CA: Censorship of the outgoing news was a great problem for you during your 1949-1954 stay in Russia, as you detailed in your first memoir, A Journey for Our Times. *How much censorship takes place now in Russia and China?*

SALISBURY: So far as actual outgoing censorship is concerned, the Chinese have never had any. The Russians abolished their censorship in 1958, so it hasn't been operative there either for a long time. I emphasize outgoing censorship because there are two kinds. If you have internal censorship, which both countries have had to an extraordinary extent, the facts about what's happening in the country are not known, either to the people in the country or to the outside world, because you can't get at them. In the case of the Soviet Union, when they abolished outgoing censorship, they did not abolish any of the internal controls on news. In the Khrushchev period there was a substantial amount of openness, because it served Khrushchev's policies, and he himself talked volubly about everything known to man. You could write a great deal when you traveled around, and a certain number of people would talk to you; but internal censorship was still there, so it was extremely difficult. Many things happened in that period that we just didn't know about. When Brezhnev came in, things went back several degrees. Again, no external censorship, but still great control on news inside the country.

What's happening now under what Mr. Gorbachev calls *glasnost* is a spirited effort to stimulate the press and radio and television inside the Soviet Union to report practically everything that's going on in the country. They are certainly not up to the standard of press and media reporting that we have in this country, but as compared with anything that's ever been seen before in Russia and the Soviet Union, it's a field day. It may well be that there's enough momentum so that it will continue in that direction, although I still have to have my fingers crossed as to how far any press can go which is essentially owned and controlled by the government. But this particular government wants very much to use the press to open things up. This is seen as being positive as far as Gorbachev's program is concerned. They encourage it; they stimulate it; and we benefit from it because there's practically nothing we can't find out now in the Soviet Union and very little that they don't report themselves. That's like night and day as far as my experience has been concerned.

On the Chinese side, it's somewhat different. Although they've never had external censorship, they are masters at keeping what's going on to themselves. If information is not fed into some chain of individuals or institutions where foreigners have a chance at getting it, they're not going to know about it. Even if you travel around the country—and there's no one, I think I can say with due modesty, who has traveled in China as much as I have in recent years—you may not find out about things. Although I have found that, if you get out there, you do find out a hell of a lot that's been going on which is not known in Beijing, certainly not in the foreign colony and probably not to the government itself, because China is a very compartmented country.

But there are lots of restrictions on travel. I've been very, very fortunate in being able to gain support from people at the top, which has enabled me to travel in a way that no one else has. As a result of that, I could probably sit down now and tell Deng Xiaoping about conditions in the country that he doesn't know anything about. But that kind of situation doesn't really mean that the country has opened up—either to itself, which is the number one requisite, or to the outside. The press corps in Beijing is constantly bumping up against rigidity—they can't go here, they can't go there, people won't talk to them, all that kind of thing. That's where bureaucratic practices that are not formal-

ized in any code, not written down as any kind of law, are in many cases far more forbidding than formal rules of censorship.

CA: The 900 Days: The Siege of Leningrad, *which was both a critical and a popular success, surely involved mountains of research in getting the material and painstaking work in shaping it as you did. What were the biggest hurdles in writing that book?*

SALISBURY: I first saw Leningrad four or five days after the siege was lifted. I spent about ten days there, became acquainted with the people, talked to many of them. I got the story in crude outline, as much as one could at that time, and reported what I could report. In wartime, with the allied nature of our relationship with Russia, it was possible to do lots of things that it was impossible to do later. (Even so, there was very strict censorship then, and the censors removed from my reports for the United Press many things which I later was able to put into the book.)

But after the war, and when I went back in 1949 for the *New York Times,* I found that the situation was entirely different. It was almost impossible to get information of any kind, particularly about things that were not regarded positively by Stalin—and Leningrad was not, because it was a dark crime on his record. When I came back to the United States in 1954, after Stalin's death, I began to try to collect materials and write *The 900 Days.* But I encountered so many difficulties—not only lack of cooperation, but a hostile attitude on the part of the Soviet authorities—that after around 1959 I had just about given up. I had concluded that I would never be able to get enough material to write the kind of book I wanted to write.

At that point I shifted and wrote a novel called *The Northern Palmyra Affair,* which deals with Leningrad. I thought this was probably as close as I would be able to get to telling the Leningrad story. But almost immediately thereafter, I had a very lucky break—or maybe it was the changing times. Back in the Soviet Union, I went to Leningrad and got the Union of Soviet Writers to assemble for me a group of writers and poets who had lived through the siege or had been in Leningrad either before or after it. We spent a day together, in which they told me about their personal experiences and referred me to books they or others had written, the kind of materials that I needed for my book. That was of extraordinary assistance to me, and out of that grew several other things; for example, I was able to establish contact with two or three historians, including a man named Pavlov, who was the general in charge of rationing and supplies in Leningrad and who was marvelously helpful to me. All of a sudden things opened up.

Another great assistance was that, as a result of Khrushchev's policy of trying to get a more realistic account of the war (and actually to blacken Stalin's reputation), he encouraged the military commanders to write their memoirs. These memoirs, particularly in the very first years in which they were being written, were very revealing. Like military men everywhere, these all had stories to tell: stories of fights they'd had with other commanders, rows they'd had with Stalin, the obstacles that had been placed in their paths—and of course they were always right and the other guy was wrong. But if you put them all together, they made a mosaic that told a great deal about what happened up in Leningrad. With the aid of these things and the further guidance and help of several Leningrad historians, I was, to my utter joy, able to put *The 900 Days* together and write a fairly comprehensive and realistic book about this extraordinary feat of heroism and the tragedies that the city underwent. I brought that out in 1969, which was the twenty-fifth anniversary of the lifting of the siege.

CA: Were Russian readers able to get the book?

SALISBURY: It was, as you said, a critical success and a very popular book in this country, and it should have been an equal critical and popular success in the Soviet Union under any normal conditions. But conditions were not normal. The Soviet authorities responded to the book with vitriolic attacks, and even went so far as to publish a full-page article in *Pravda,* their leading newspaper, which was signed by Marshall Georgi Zhukov, though I'm sure he didn't write it. It was an attack on me as perpetrating pro-Nazi propaganda, depriving the Russians of their just laurels for their great victory and denigrating the Communist party.

The principal reason for this was that I had exposed in the book the terrible intrigues that went on and the errors that were made inside the party, particularly by Stalin and the top leadership. I had not given great credit to the party; I had given credit to the people, which was where it belonged. They couldn't stand that, so they denounced me, and the book was banned in Russia and never published there. Harper and Row, at my suggestion, did bring out a small paperback edition translated into very poor Russian, which was basically for Russians to buy when they were in this country and take back to the Soviet Union with them. Many people did do that.

I'm happy to say that several Soviet writers have told me in the last few months that, under the present conditions of *glasnost,* one of the major magazines is going to publish excerpts from it, and maybe they'll even think of publishing the book. I think it's possible as things stand now that they might do it. It would be a pleasure to see the book published there. And it would be good for the people of Leningrad, because, to this day, no book of this kind has been written on the subject by a Soviet author. There have been several vivid and wonderful things written such as personal experiences, and two writers whom I know went around and collected interviews with a number of survivors and published a volume of these interviews. I might say they had a two- or three-year fight with the censorship board before they could get that published, and that was only eight or nine years ago; so you can see how the pall of censorship still hangs over Leningrad. But maybe in the next year or so *The 900 Days* will appear in Russia, and that would be a marvelous event.

CA: In your two memoirs, you quote from journals you kept along the way. How much were you able to draw from them in reconstructing your life in such detail, and how big a part did memory play?

SALISBURY: I did and do keep journals. They are not in the form of neat volumes, one a year, or anything of that kind; they're much more apt to be very careful note-keeping and impressions which I jot down, usually, when I'm abroad working on some story. When I don't do that, I write very detailed letters about anything I haven't written in stories, and I have been fortunate enough to keep all of my notebooks and copies of my stories since before the time of World War II. So I have a vast store of material that I can use to flesh out my recollections. My memory of many events is very clear and vivid, but we all suffer from lapses. I think the most frequent failing of memory is a tendency to superimpose two similar events, and I judge this not only by my own, but by having interviewed lots of people for historical works. I found it to be true when I was interviewing editors and reporters for the book I did about the *New York Times, Without Fear or Favor.* All of them are trained observers, and yet I found that there was a tendency in many of them, on a topic like the publishing of the Pentagon Papers, when there were all kinds of

dramatic events falling one on top of the other, to consolidate two episodes into one. I know that I have that problem as well, but I have enough material to sort out the facts in almost every instance, and certainly in every instance of any consequence.

I had one great disappointment as far as writing the memoirs was concerned. From the start of my newspaper career, when I left Minneapolis and went to Chicago and then all the way onward, I had made a habit of writing home at least once a week about what I was doing and my impressions and things of that kind. My mother had very carefully preserved all of this correspondence. When I sat down to write my first volume of memoirs, I believed it was all out in Minneapolis with my sister, who still lived in the old family house. To my horror, I discovered that she didn't have it, and there was no record of what had happened to it. Fortunately, I found a few odd letters here and there which I was able to use quite well in fleshing out certain reminiscences. But the great bulk of them dealing with my newspaper career in Chicago and in Washington during the New Deal were gone, destroyed or lost—I just don't know what happened to them. That was a blow, because there was lots of good naive material in them that I would have liked to rely on.

In all of my memoir writing I have acted as a newspaper reporter reporting on myself. I haven't depended on my recollections; I've written or talked to anyone I could think of who was in on various events that I was in on and gotten their impressions. Fortunately, I have been quite lucky in that I have always been a rather prolific letter-writer, and several of my old friends turned up stocks of letters which were helpful. The fine-grained detail in the memoirs is due to that technique, I think. I don't know whether people writing their memoirs always do that or whether they just sit down and write what they remember. But, being a reporter, I felt that I should find out from other observers what I was doing.

CA: In Without Fear or Favor *you detailed the* New York Times*'s difficult decision to publish the Pentagon Papers and commented that that event symbolized "the metamorphosis of the* Times *from a newspaper that recorded the action to one that has become, like it or not, a very considerable part of the action." Would you comment on the question of how far papers should go to be a part of the action?*

SALISBURY: If a paper is going to get involved in a major piece of investigative reporting, I think the most important thing is for it to be aware that its involvement does, in some measure, transform the event itself. Newspapers have, generally speaking, been oblivious to the fact that the very presence of the paper or its publication of material may change the course of particular events. This is especially true since events like the Pentagon Papers, Watergate, and, to a lesser extent, the Iran-contra affair. The newspapers have a tendency to put something in the paper and walk away from it. The consequences may linger; they may have a lot of effect on events, and it's important for the papers to understand that.

This was certainly true in two great stories in which the *New York Times* was involved. One was the civil rights struggle in the South, and the other was Vietnam. The *Times* was involved in the civil rights struggle almost more than it realized, simply by having reporters in places where events were going on—and sometimes the event didn't happen *because* the *Times* reporter was there. There was almost a formula in the days when Claude Sitton was covering the South that if the civil rights activists got into terrible trouble in some remote area and looked as though they might be mobbed by deputy sheriffs, they would try to put in a telephone call to Claude and tell him what was happening, and he'd say, "I'll be right there." Then the word would go out to the deputies that the *Times* was coming, and it was sort of like calling out the cavalry. This modified the atmosphere in many ways.

Unfortunately, Turner Catledge, who was the managing editor at that time and deeply interested in this story, had the view that reporters did not belong in it. He felt they were invisible witnesses, and what happened to them and their response and all the rest of it was not to be published in the *Times*. I think Turner was wrong. I don't think reporters should aggrandize themselves, but if Sitton arrived at 2 a.m. at some little place in Mississippi where a siege of a motel housing civil rights activists was under way, and the shooting stopped when he got there, I think that should be reported. But that never happened.

CA: In your very personal 1976 book Travels around America, *you compared our past with our present and concluded, despite serious problems, on a note of optimism. What are your greatest concerns for the country as we approach the twenty-first century?*

SALISBURY: If I had to narrow it down to one concern, it would be education. I happen to believe that education is the key to everything, and our educational system certainly has gone backward in the popular area. I'm not just talking about the core cities and the deterioration of urban education, which almost entirely can be traced to race problems. I'm talking about education across the board and the dedication of people to good education.

Before we had a public-school system, we had a tradition in this country that education was brought in with the people who came over. I don't think there was anyone in the first hundred or two hundred years of immigration who didn't put education first. I grew up in an immigrant area where education was regarded as the golden ladder; it was the way you made your way in the world. I still believe it is the golden ladder for everyone, and I see on every side chintziness about appropriations, teachers who are just time-servers, pupils who are there because they're compelled to be there, families who have no concern or feeling of responsibility toward the next generation—or their own, for that matter. And this is all accompanied by enormous expenditures on junk. We're the world's greatest consumers of junk, beginning with food and running through everything in our society, but we worry about ten cents for education. Unless we get off that stance, we're going to be moving down the ladder instead of up. We still put the money in at the top; our high-tech education and high-tech research are really the best in the world. We have a better education than the Japanese, with whom we're often compared; they feed off of our educational and scientific achievements. But how long that's going to endure, I just don't know. I worry about it every single day.

I give a smaller version of this lecture to the Chinese: I say that, whatever they do, they should put more money into education. If they want to get up and going in the world, education is the way to do it. And it's cheap. It doesn't cost anything compared with this crazy armament expenditure, the lousy, graft-ridden stuff they pour the money out for in Washington. For one-tenth of the military budget we could get a thousand times the bang, if we put it in education.

BIOGRAPHICAL/CRITICAL SOURCES:

BOOKS

Salisbury, Harrison E., *A Journey for Our Times: A Memoir,* Harper, 1983.

Salisbury, Harrison E., *A Time of Change: A Reporter's Tale of Our Time,* Harper, 1988.

PERIODICALS

Chicago Tribune, August 3, 1983.
Los Angeles Times Book Review, April 3, 1988.
Modern Maturity, October-November, 1986.
Nation, May 24, 1980.
National Review, March 6, 1981.
New Republic, June 28, 1980, December 16, 1985.
Newsweek, June 6, 1983, October 14, 1985.
New York Times, June 8, 1983.
New York Times Book Review, May 18, 1980, May 15, 1983, September 29, 1985, March 20, 1988.
Publishers Weekly, October 19, 1984.
Tribune Books (Chicago), February 21, 1988.
Washington Post, June 11, 1980.
Washington Post Book World, March 6, 1988.

—*Sketch by Thomas Wiloch*

—*Interview by Jean W. Ross*

*   *   *

SANTA MARIA
  See POWELL-SMITH, Vincent (Walter Francis)

*   *   *

SAROYAN, Aram   1943-

PERSONAL: Born September 25, 1943; son of William (a writer) and Carol (Marcus) Saroyan (now Matthau); married Gailyn McClanahan, October 9, 1968; children: Strawberry, Cream, Armenak. *Education:* Attended the University of Chicago, New York University, and Columbia University.

ADDRESSES: Home—Thousand Oaks, Calif. *Agent*—c/o Wendy Weil, Wendy Weil Agency, 747 Third Ave., New York, N.Y. 10017.

CAREER: Writer. Publisher and editor of *Lines* (magazine), 1964-65.

AWARDS, HONORS: Poetry Award, National Endowment for the Arts, for the poem "lighght."

WRITINGS:

(With Jenni Caldwell and Richard Kolmar) *Poems* (also see below), Acadia, 1963.
In (poetry), Bear Press (LaGrande, Ore.), 1965.
Works (poetry), Lines (New York), 1966.
Aram Saroyan, Lines (Cambridge, Mass.), 1967, Random House, 1968.
Pages, Random House, 1969.
Words and Photographs, Big Table Publishing, 1970.
Cloth: An Electric Novel, Big Table Publishing, 1971.
The Rest: Poetry, Telegraph Books, 1971, Blackberry Books, 1986.
Poems (includes the work in *Poems,* Acadia, 1963), Telegraph Books, 1972, Blackberry Books, 1986.
The Street: An Autobiographical Novel, Bookstore Press, 1974.
O My Generation and Other Poems, Blackberry Books, 1976.
Genesis Angels: The Saga of Lew Welch and the Beat Generation, Morrow, 1979.
Last Rites: The Death of William Saroyan, Morrow, 1982.
William Saroyan (an illustrated biography), Harcourt, 1983.

Trio: Oona Chaplin, Carol Matthau, Gloria Vanderbilt; Portrait of an Intimate Friendship, Linden Press/Simon & Schuster, 1985.
The Romantic (novel), McGraw, 1988.

Contributor of poetry and prose to *New York Times Sunday Magazine, New York Times Book Review, Village Voice, Nation, Rolling Stone, Paris Review,* and *Poetry.*

SIDELIGHTS: The son of Armenian-American playwright William Saroyan, Aram Saroyan has received both critical acclaim and censure for his minimalist poetry and his nonfiction about his famous parents. Like the poems of Robert Creeley, Saroyan's first poems, published by *Poetry* magazine and small presses, are lean, direct statement poems aimed at containing the most meaning in the fewest words. Later poems using the visual effects of letters on the page (concrete poetry) extend Creeley's aesthetic, in which the form of a poem self-consciously reflects its content. Saroyan's emphasis on the visual aspect of written language also shows the influence of the young Saroyan's work in photography as the student of well-known photographers Richard Avedon and Hiro. Ted Berrigan was the poet who encouraged Saroyan to be more experimental with language for the sake of learning during the 1960s, and smoking marijuana became a part of Saroyan's writing process for a short time. Conflict with his father over this controversial practice was one of many fights that brought attention to the young poet. For example, twenty years of argument that extended from the literary community to the White House followed after Robert Duncan chose Saroyan's one-word poem "lighght" for a National Endowment for the Arts Poetry Award.

Saroyan studied the works of Lew Welch, another important contributor to his development as a writer, when working on *Genesis Angels: The Saga of Lew Welch and the Beat Generation.* In his essay in *Contemporary Authors Autobiography Series,* Saroyan calls Welch a steadying influence whose ideas helped him to develop the ability to compose longer works. A writer must have a disciplined side to balance the wild, creative side; writing *Genesis Angels* challenged him to achieve that kind of balance, he explains. The book's purpose was to celebrate the experiences of the Beat generation; yet, because it chronicles the suicides of several artists in the movement—including Welch's disappearance into the desert with a gun—Saroyan struggled through three revisions of the ending in order "to give the proper weight to this dark side of the story."

The most pervasive influence in Saroyan's work came from his father in the form of emotional imperatives to build a stable marriage and family life, which eluded the elder Saroyan. Having stopped writing poetry in order to devote his time to his family, the younger Saroyan eventually turned to writing prose about the importance of family relationships. The biographies of his parents, like his father's works, are survival oriented and therapeutic; in all his books, Saroyan moves toward a better understanding of himself and others. While William exorcised sufferings related to his Armenian heritage, Aram confronts the anguish related to his parents' early divorce and separation from his father.

Last Rites: The Death of William Saroyan and *William Saroyan* express this darker side of the author's personal past. Critics call both books "diatribes" for exposing the elder Saroyan's least admirable traits; regarding *Last Rites,* Anatole Broyard of the *New York Times* points out, "We have only the son's word for this version, and before I was very deep in the book I began to wish I could hear the father's side, too." On the other hand, *Los Angeles Times* contributor Carolyn See finds *William Saroyan* "at once so marvelously fascinating you can't put it down, and so unbearably painful you can't hold it in your hands." What it reveals about both authors, she says, "ends up shedding light on others as well."

If the portraits in the Saroyan biographies is sometimes harsh, the author offers this softer commentary in his *Contemporary Authors Autobiographical Series* essay: "In my books about my father, I grappled with a figure whose public and private sides reflected a profound ambivalence. Here was a man whose deepest wound—his father's death and his own subsequent confinement in an orphanage from the age of three to the age of eight—had somehow alchemized in him an amazing strength of character. In the thirties, in the midst of the Great Depression, the young man who had been an orphan wrote stories of such sweetness and high spirits that they helped to keep hope alive in an ailing nation, and catapulted the writer to the literary equivalent of a movie star." The playwright's decision to survive his personal pain was perhaps more important to him than the price it extracted from family members, Saroyan speculates: "The paradox of my father's life was that in denying his own pain, he seemed helpless not to perpetuate it in others' lives." This is a characteristically American problem, he asserts. Saroyan's study of his father's life led him to realize "that there was no easy moral judgment to be extracted: that he did what he had to do, some of it wonderful, some of it sad and painful indeed. . . . It was useful and perhaps even healing to study and think about his life, to reflect on it; that while his own life may have made it impossible for he himself to do this, a part of his legacy to me was a life far less painful than his own: one from which I could turn around and try to take some measure of our history as a family."

Before leaving family history as a subject for nonfiction, Saroyan wrote *Trio: Oona Chaplin, Carol Matthau, Gloria Vanderbilt; Portrait of an Intimate Friendship.* His account of his mother Carol's experiences with Gloria Vanderbilt and the wife of Charlie Chaplin is most interesting, according to reviewers, when it includes figures such as Truman Capote or Oona's husband, who returned from exile in 1972 to receive a special academy award. Saroyan explains the absence of sensational detail in his autobiographical essay: "The important thing was to try to render these women as I had actually known them and also as I might imaginatively expand that knowing."

Continuing concern with family values figures in Saroyan's first novel, *The Romantic,* "a brief, elegant study in self-reflection" that, at times, "resembles a minimalist, hip Harlequin novel for men," notes Stuart Schoffman in the *Los Angeles Times Book Review.* The main character James, a family man and screenwriter, indulges in adultery, which he "experiences in a state of permanent apology," as Schoffman puts it. Fulfilling the intent stated in the title, the narrator of *The Romantic* confesses and is forgiven by his wife. He embraces the routines of family life, if for no other reason than his knowledge that children are the world's future. He realizes, too, says Schoffman, "that his solutions, however sublime, are only the next round of romantic panacea, just as trite and transitory as the celebrities and brand names with which this book of modern problems is peppered. But the answers will do for now, maybe for always."

BIOGRAPHICAL/CRITICAL SOURCES:

BOOKS

Contemporary Authors Autobiography Series, Volume 5, Gale, 1988.

PERIODICALS

Chicago Tribune, September 1, 1985.
Chicago Tribune Book World, September 5, 1982, July 31, 1983.
Detroit News, August 11, 1985.
Globe and Mail (Toronto), August 17, 1985.
Los Angeles Times, August 22, 1983, December 18, 1988.
Los Angeles Times Book Review, July 1, 1979, August 15, 1982,
     August 4, 1985, December 18, 1988.
Newsweek, April 22, 1968.
New York Times, August 14, 1982.
New York Times Book Review, April 29, 1979, August 1, 1982,
     December 18, 1988.
Poetry, June, 1967.
Time, September 16, 1985.
Washington Post, August 7, 1985.
Washington Post Book World, August 15, 1982.

—Sketch by Marilyn K. Basel

*   *   *

SAROYAN, William 1908-1981
(Sirak Goryan)

PERSONAL: Born August 31, 1908, in Fresno, Calif.; died May 18, 1981, of cancer and cremated in Fresno; half of his ashes interred in Fresno, the remaining half interred near Yerevan, Armenia, U.S.S.R., May 29, 1981; son of Armenak (a Presbyterian preacher and writer) and Takoohi (Saroyan) Saroyan; married Carol Marcus, February, 1943 (divorced, November, 1949); remarried Carol Marcus, 1951 (divorced, 1952); children: Aram, Lucy. *Education:* Left high school at age fifteen.

CAREER: Short story writer, playwright, novelist. Began selling newspapers at the age of eight for the *Fresno Evening Herald;* while still in school he worked at various jobs, including that of telegraph messenger boy; after leaving school he worked in his uncle's law office, then held numerous odd jobs, including that of grocery clerk, vineyard worker, postal employee, and office manager of San Francisco Postal Telegraph Co. Co-founder of Conference Press, 1936. Organized and directed The Saroyan Theatre, August, 1942 (closed after one week). Writer in residence, Purdue University, 1961. *Military service:* U.S. Army, 1942-45.

AWARDS, HONORS: O. Henry Award, 1934, for "The Daring Young Man on the Flying Trapeze"; Drama Critics Circle Award, 1940, for "The Time of Your Life"; Pulitzer Prize, 1940, for "The Time of Your Life"—declined by the author on the principle that business should not judge the arts; Academy Award, 1943, for the screenplay "The Human Comedy"; California Literature Gold Medal, 1952, for *Tracy's Tiger;* American Book Award nomination, 1980, for *Obituaries.*

WRITINGS:

The Daring Young Man on the Flying Trapeze, and Other Stories (also see below), Random House, 1934, reprinted, Yolla Bolly, 1984.
A Christmas Psalm, Gelber, Lilienthal, 1935.
Inhale and Exhale (stories; also see below), Random House, 1936, reprinted, Books for Libraries Press, 1972.
Those Who Write Them and Those Who Collect Them, Black Archer Press, 1936.
Three Times Three (stories; also see below), Conference Press, 1936.
Little Children (stories), Harcourt, 1937.
A Gay and Melancholy Flux (compiled from *Inhale and Exhale* and *Three Times Three*), Faber, 1937.

Love, Here Is My Hat, and Other Short Romances, Modern Age Books, 1938.
The Trouble with Tigers (stories), Harcourt, 1938.
A Native American, George Fields, 1938.
Peace, It's Wonderful (stories), Modern Age Books, 1939.
3 Fragments and a Story, Little Man, 1939.
The Hungerers: A Short Play, S. French, 1939.
My Heart's in the Highlands (play; produced on Broadway at Guild Theatre, April 13, 1939; first published in *One-Act Play Magazine,* December, 1937; also see below), Harcourt, 1939.
The Time of Your Life (play; produced on Broadway at Booth Theatre, October 25, 1939; produced in London, England, by Royal Shakespeare Company, 1982; also see below; also includes essays), Harcourt, 1939, acting edition, S. French, 1941, R.S.C. acting edition, Methuen, 1983.
Christmas, 1939, Quercus Press, 1939.
"A Theme in the Life of the Great American Goof" (ballet-play; also see below), produced in New York City at Center Theatre, January, 1940.
Subway Circus (play), S. French, 1940.
The Ping-Pong Game (play; produced in New York, 1945), S. French, 1940.
A Special Announcement, House of Books, 1940.
My Name Is Aram (stories; Book-of-the-Month Club selection), Harcourt, 1940, revised edition, 1966.
The Beautiful People (play; produced under the author's direction on Broadway at Lyceum Theatre, April 21, 1940), Harcourt, 1941.
Love's Old Sweet Song (play; first produced on Broadway at Plymouth Theatre, May 2, 1940; also see below), S. French, 1941.
Three Plays: My Heart's in the Highlands, The Time of Your Life, Love's Old Sweet Song, Harcourt, 1940.
Saroyan's Fables, Harcourt, 1941.
The Insurance Salesman and Other Stories, Faber (London), 1941.
Harlem as Seen by Hirschfield, Hyperion Press, 1941.
Hilltop Russians in San Francisco, James Ladd Delkin, 1941.
The People with Light Coming Out of Them (radio play; first broadcast, 1941), The Free Company (New York City), 1941.
Jim Dandy, A Play, Little Man Press (Cincinnati), 1941, reprinted as *Jim Dandy: Fat Man in a Famine,* Harcourt, 1947.
"Across the Board on Tomorrow Morning," first produced in Pasadena, Calif., at Pasadena Playhouse, February, 1941; produced in New York at Theatre Showcase, March, 1942; produced under the author's direction on Broadway at Belasco Theatre, on the same bill with "Talking to You," August, 1942.
Hello Out There (play; first produced in Santa Barbara, Calif., at Lobeto Theatre, September, 1941; produced on Broadway at Belasco Theatre, September, 1942), S. French, 1949.
Razzle-Dazzle (short plays; includes "A Theme in the Life of the Great American Goof"), Harcourt, 1942.
"Talking to You" (play), produced on Broadway at Belasco Theatre, August, 1942.
"The Good Job" (screenplay based on his story "A Number of the Poor"), Loew's, Inc., 1942.
48 Saroyan Stories, Avon, 1942.
The Human Comedy (novel; also see below), Harcourt, 1943, revised edition, 1966.
"The Human Comedy," (scenario based on *The Human Comedy*), Metro-Goldwyn-Mayer, 1943.

Thirty-One Selected Stories, Avon, 1943.

Fragment, Albert M. Bender, 1943.

Get Away Old Man (play; produced on Broadway at Cort Theatre, November, 1943), Harcourt, 1944.

Someday I'll Be A Millionaire Myself, Avon, 1944.

Dear Baby (stories), Harcourt, 1944.

(With Henry Miller and Hilaire Hiler) *Why Abstract?,* New Directions, 1945, reprinted, Haskell House, 1974.

The Adventures of Wesley Jackson (novel; also see below), Harcourt, 1946.

The Saroyan Special: Selected Short Stories, Harcourt, 1948, Books for Libraries Press, 1970.

The Fiscal Hoboes, Press of Valenti Angelo, 1949.

Sam Ego's House (play; also see below), S. French, 1949.

A Decent Birth, a Happy Funeral (play; also see below) S. French, 1949.

Don't Go Away Mad, and Two Other Plays: Sam Ego's House [and] *A Decent Birth, a Happy Funeral,* Harcourt, 1949.

The Assyrian, And Other Stories, Harcourt, 1950.

The Twin Adventures: The Adventures of William Saroyan, A Diary; The Adventures of Wesley Jackson, A Novel, Harcourt, 1950.

"The Son" (play), produced in Los Angeles, Calif., 1950.

(Author of introduction) Khatchik Minasian, *The Simple Songs of Khatchik Minasian,* Colt Press, 1950.

Rock Wagram (novel), Doubleday, 1951.

Tracy's Tiger (fantasy), Doubleday, 1951, revised edition, Ballantine, 1967.

The Bicycle Rider in Beverly Hills (autobiography), Scribner, 1952, Ballantine, 1971.

The Laughing Matter (novel), Doubleday, 1953.

"Opera, Opera" (play), produced in New York at Amato Theatre, December, 1955.

Mama I Love You (novel; listed in some sources under the working title "The Bouncing Ball"), Atlantic-Little, Brown, 1956, reprinted, Dell, 1986.

The Whole Voyald and Other Stories, Atlantic-Little, Brown, 1956.

Papa You're Crazy (novel), Atlantic-Little, Brown, 1957.

"Ever Been in Love with a Midget?" (play), produced in Berlin, 1957.

The Cave Dwellers (play; produced on Broadway at Bijou Theatre, October 19, 1957), Putnam, 1958.

The Slaughter of the Innocents (play; produced in The Hague, Netherlands, 1957), S. French, 1958.

The William Saroyan Reader, Braziller, 1958.

Once Around the Block (play), S. French, 1959.

"The Paris Comedy; or, The Secret of Lily" (play; produced in Vienna, Austria, 1960), published as *The Dogs, or The Paris Comedy, and Two Other Plays: Chris Sick, or Happy New Year Anyway, Making Money,* and *Nineteen Other Very Short Plays,* Phaedra, 1969.

Sam, the Highest Jumper of Them All, or The London Comedy (play; produced in London under the author's direction, 1960), Faber, 1961.

(With Henry Cecil) "Settled Out of Court" (play), produced in London, 1960.

"High Time along the Wabash" (play), produced in West Lafayette, Ind., at Purdue University, 1961.

"Ah, Man" (play), music by Peter Fricker, produced in Adelburgh, Suffolk, England, 1962.

Here Comes, There Goes, You Know Who (autobiography), Simon & Schuster, 1962.

My Lousy Adventures with Money, New Strand (London), 1962.

Boys and Girls Together (novel), Harcourt, 1963.

Me (juvenile), Crowell-Collier, 1963.

Not Dying (autobiography), Harcourt, 1963.

One Day in the Afternoon of the World (novel), Harcourt, 1964.

After Thirty Years: The Daring Young Man on the Flying Trapeze (includes essays), Harcourt, 1964.

Best Stories of William Saroyan, Faber, 1964.

Deleted Beginning and End of a Short Story, Lowell-Adams House Printers (Cambridge, Mass.), 1965.

Short Drive, Sweet Chariot (reminiscences), Phaedra, 1966.

My Kind of Crazy and Wonderful People, Harcourt, 1966.

(Author of introduction) *The Arabian Nights,* Platt & Munk, 1966.

Look at Us; Let's See; Here We Are; Look Hard, Speak Soft; I See, You See, We All See; Stop, Look, Listen; Beholder's Eye; Don't Look Now but Isn't That You? (Us? U.S.?), Cowles, 1967.

I Used to Believe I Had Forever, Now I'm Not So Sure, Cowles, 1968.

(Author of foreword) Barbara Holden and Mary Jane Woebcke, *A Child's Guide to San Francisco,* Diablo Press, 1968.

Horsey Gorsey and the Frog (juvenile), illustrated by Grace Davidian, R. Hale, 1968.

Letters from 74 rue Taitbout, or Don't Go, but If You Must, Say Hello to Everybody, World, 1968, published as *Don't Go, but If You Must, Say Hello to Everybody,* Cassell, 1970.

Man with the Heart in the Highlands, and Other Stories, Dell, 1968.

Days of Life and Death and Escape to the Moon, Dial, 1970.

(Editor and author of introduction) *Hairenik, 1934-1939: An Anthology of Short Stories and Poems* (collection of Armenian-American literature), Books for Libraries Press, 1971.

Places Where I've Done Time, Praeger, 1972.

The Tooth and My Father, Doubleday, 1974.

"The Rebirth Celebration of the Human Race at Artie Zabala's Off-Broadway Theater" (play), first produced in New York City, July 10, 1975.

An Act or Two of Foolish Kindness, Penmaen Press & Design, 1976.

Sons Come and Go, Mothers Hang In Forever, Franklin Library, 1976.

Morris Hirschfield, Rizzoli International, 1976.

Chance Meetings, Norton, 1978.

(Compiler) *Patmuatsk'ner / Uiliem Saroyean; Hayats'uts' Hovhannes Sheohmelean* (selected Armenian stories), Sewan, 1978.

Two Short Paris Summertime Plays of 1974: Assassinations and Jim, Sam and Anna, Santa Susana Press, 1979.

Obituaries, Creative Arts, 1979.

Births, introduction by David Kherdian, Creative Arts, 1981.

My Name Is Saroyan (short stories; autobiographical), edited by James H. Tashjian, Coward-McCann, 1983.

The New Saroyan Reader: A Connoisseur's Anthology of the Writings of William Saroyan, edited by Brian Derwent, Creative Arts, 1984.

The Circus (juvenile), Creative Education, 1986.

The Armenian Trilogy, California State University Press, 1986.

The Pheasant Hunter: About Fathers and Sons, Redpath Press, 1986.

Madness in the Family, edited by Leo Hamalian, New Directions, 1988.

Also author of the plays "Something about a Soldier," "Hero of the World," and "Sweeney in the Trees," all produced in stock, 1940. Plays represented in anthologies, including *Famous American Plays of the 1930s,* edited by Harold Clurman, and *One Act: Eleven Short Plays of the Modern Theatre,* edited by Samuel

Moon. Writer of song lyrics, including "Come On-a My House" with Ross Bagdasarian, in 1951. Contributor to *Overland Monthly, Hairenik* (Armenian-American magazine), *Story, Saturday Evening Post, Atlantic, Look, McCall's,* and other periodicals. *The Human Comedy* and *The Adventures of Wesley Jackson* have been translated into Russian.

SIDELIGHTS: William Saroyan's career began in 1934 with the publication of *The Daring Young Man on the Flying Trapeze, and Other Stories.* From that time on, he wrote prolifically, producing a steady stream of short stories, plays, novels, memoirs, and essays. His career can be divided into five phases. From 1934 to 1939 he wrote short stories; from 1939 to 1943 his energies were directed toward playwriting; the years 1943-1951 saw the appearance of his first two novels (*The Human Comedy* and *The Adventures of Wesley Jackson*), as well as plays and short fiction; between 1951 and 1964 Saroyan published a series of novels dealing with marriage and the family; and finally, from 1964 until his death in 1981, Saroyan devoted himself primarily to the exploration of his past through autobiographical writings.

It is through the short story genre that Saroyan made his initial impact as a writer. During this first creative period, Saroyan published eight volumes; in the preface to *The Assyrian, and Other Stories,* he estimated that during these years he wrote "five hundred short stories, or a mean average of one hundred per annum." These early collections project a wide variety of thematic concerns, yet they are united in their portrayal of America between the two world wars. Saroyan's first books reflect the painful realities of the Depression of the 1930s. The young writer without a job in his first famous story "The Daring Young Man on the Flying Trapeze" goes to be interviewed for a position and finds that "already there were two dozen young men in the place." The story "International Harvester" from the 1936 collection *Inhale and Exhale* also gives a bleak vision of complete economic collapse: "Shamefully to the depths fallen: America. In Wall Street they talk as if the end of this country is within sight."

Readers clearly saw their troubled lives vividly portrayed in Saroyan's stories; though they depicted the agony of the times, the stories also conveyed great hope and vigorously defiant good spirits. However, as Maxwell Geismar remarked in *Writers in Crisis: The American Novel, 1925-1940,* "the depression of the 1930s, apparently so destructive and so despairing," was actually a time of "regeneration" for the major writers of the period. Furthermore, "the American writer had gained moral stature, a sense of his own cultural connection, a series of new meanings and new values for his work." The crisis these writers were experiencing was, of course, more than merely economic. A deep cultural schism had rocked Europe since Friedrich Nietzsche's nineteenth-century apocalyptic prophecies and affected such American writers as Henry Miller, whose *Tropic of Cancer* appeared in the same year as Saroyan's first collection of short fiction.

Between 1939 and 1943, Saroyan published and produced his most famous plays. Works such as *My Heart's in the Highlands, The Beautiful People,* and "Across the Board on Tomorrow Morning" were well received by some critics and audiences; *The Time of Your Life* won the Pulitzer Prize as the best play of the 1939-1940 season, but Saroyan refused the award on the grounds that businessmen should not judge art. Although championed by critics like George Jean Nathan, Saroyan had a strained relationship with the theatrical world. From the time his first play appeared on Broadway, critics called his work surrealistic, sentimental, or difficult to understand. His creation of a fragile, fluid,

dramatic universe full of strange, lonely, confused, and gentle people startled theatergoers accustomed to conventional plots and characterization. His instinctive and highly innovative sense of dramatic form was lost on many audiences. These plays were a wonderful amalgam of vaudeville, absurdism, sentiment, spontaneity, reverie, humor, despair, philosophical speculation, and whimsy. His plays introduced a kind of rambunctious energy into staid American drama. His "absurdity" bore a direct relationship to his sorrow at observing the waste of the true, vital impulses of life in the contemporary world. His artist figures—Joe, Jonah Webster, Ben Alexander—all feel within themselves the dying of the old order and the painful struggle to give birth to a new consciousness.

In 1941, after two active years on Broadway, Saroyan traveled to Hollywood to work on the film version of *The Human Comedy* for Metro-Goldwyn-Mayer. When the scenario was completed, it was made into a successful motion picture. From the beginning of his career, Saroyan had committed himself to celebrating the brotherhood of man, and in *The Human Comedy* he preached a familiar sermon: love one another, or you shall perish. This portrayal of love's power in small-town America offered consolation to millions ravaged by the suffering and death brought on by World War II.

Saroyan went on to publish four novels between 1951 and 1964: *Rock Wagram, The Laughing Matter, Boys and Girls Together,* and *One Day in the Afternoon of the World.* Each novel explores in fictional form the troubled years of Saroyan's own marriage to Carol Marcus and that marriage's aftermath. These thinly disguised transcriptions of Saroyan's own life might be termed the "fatherhood novels," for they are linked thematically through the author's concern with founding a family. Each Armenian-American protagonist in these novels is searching for (or has already found) a wife and children, his emblems of human community. Edward Krickel, in a 1970 *Georgia Review* article, correctly points out that sex and love in Saroyan's novels are not ends in themselves, but rather "lead to family and the honorable roles of parent and grandparent, in short the traditional view. Children are the glory of the relationship." In the novels, as in the plays and short stories, the family symbolizes the family of humanity in microcosm and localizes the desire for universal brotherhood that had always marked Saroyan's vision. The Webster family in *The Beautiful People,* the Macauleys in *The Human Comedy,* the Alexanders in *My Heart's in the Highlands,* and the Garoghlanians in *My Name Is Aram* all were his imaginary families before he sought to become a father himself and realize his dreams.

During the 1930s and 1940s, Saroyan reached the peak of his fame; by the mid-1950s his reputation had declined substantially. Many critics have dismissed Saroyan for not being what they wanted him to be, rather than considering the writer's virtues and faults on his own terms. Saroyan was aware early in his career that he was being neglected, as is apparent from his reaction in *Razzle-Dazzle* to the critical reception of the plays: "As it happened first with my short stories, my plays appeared so suddenly and continued to come so swiftly that no one was quite prepared to fully meet and appreciate them, so that so far neither the short stories nor the plays have found critical understanding worthy of them. If the critics have failed, I have not. I have both written and criticized my plays, and so far the importance I have given them, as they have appeared, has been supported by theatrical history. If the critics have not yet agreed with me on the value of my work, it is still to be proved that I am not the writer I say I am. I shall some day startle those who now regard me as nothing more than a show-off, but I shall not startle myself." What he said of his short stories and plays proved to be true of the novels and autobiographical writings as well.

Peter Collier, in a *New York Times Book Review* essay, attributed the critical devaluation to the fact that "the generation of academic critics had now come to power who were overseeing the development of the kind of dense, cerebral literature which justified their profession." Saroyan's often flippant and antiacademic tone was not calculated to endear him to the professors. Another complaint commonly voiced by critics was Saroyan's tendency toward "escapism." Philip Rahv found Saroyan's role as lover of mankind irritating; in the *American Mercury* Rahv wrote that in *The Human Comedy* Saroyan insisted "evil is unreal," although the world was obviously mired in pain and tragedy. Linked to this charge of escapism was Saroyan's nonpolitical stance; he supported no 'ism' and was therefore accused of lacking a social conscience. This attitude put him out of favor with the proletarian writers of the 1930s who were eager to enlist him in their cause. Although Saroyan always affirmed the brotherhood of man, he recognized no authorities, no leaders, no programs to save the world.

Among the negative comments about Saroyan's works is the charge that he was a simple-minded, sentimental romantic whose naive optimism did not reflect the terrible realities of the age. However, the angst of the twentieth century pervades his work; his brooding depression appears not only in the later books but also in an early play, *The Time of Your Life*. Saroyan's lonely and and pathetic characters sense the oncoming fury of World War II, and the knowledge that life is poised at the rim of disaster haunts their dialogue. Commentators have almost completely ignored this darker, despairing existential side of Saroyan's work.

Though the alienation and melancholy that characterize much of Saroyan's work are typical of twentieth-century literature, the feeling of rootlessness that pervades his imagination finds an important source in his Armenian heritage. In 1896, twelve years before Saroyan's birth, 200,000 Armenians were massacred by the Turks. In 1915, the Turks deported the Armenian population of 2,500,000 to Syria and Mesopotamia; more than a million and a half Armenians were killed during this process. The Armenian migration began in earnest; of those who escaped deportation, many fled to Russia and the United States. Armenak and Takoohi Saroyan were among the thousands who came to America during the first wave of the massacres. William, the only one of their four children to be born in America, was born in Fresno, California.

In California's San Joaquin Valley, Saroyan's parents found a region similar to their native land. Although Armenians would establish communities in other parts of America, California attracted the greatest number because it was the ideal region for a predominantly agricultural people. Although California seemed idyllic, the racial conflicts that had driven the Armenians to their newfound land continued. In the autobiographical *Here Comes, There Goes, You Know Who*, Saroyan remarked: "The Armenians were considered inferior, they were pushed around, they were hated, and I was an Armenian. I refused to forget it then, and I refuse to forget it now, but not because being an Armenian had, or has, any particular significance." Because the Armenians were not really absorbed into American life, isolated within their own communities, it is no accident that Saroyan's work conveys a powerful sense of not being at home in the world.

If the Armenian people were symbolically homeless in their American exile, Saroyan himself, after the age of three, was literally homeless. The death of his father in 1911 surely contributed to his lifelong obsession with death and estrangement. Saroyan's mother was forced to place him in an orphanage, and it is evident from his autobiographical writings that his childhood was often profoundly unhappy. Midway through his career, Saroyan wondered, as he says in *Here Comes, There Goes, You Know Who:* "Well, first of all, just where was my home? Was it in Fresno, where I was born? Was it in San Jose, where my father died? Was it in Oakland, where I spent four very important years? . . . Home was in myself, and I wasn't there, that's all . . . I was far from home." The poverty of his early life drove him to literature, and to the quest for meaning: "I took to writing at an early age to escape from meaninglessness, uselessness, unimportance, insignificance, poverty, enslavement, ill health, despair, madness, and all manner of other unattractive, natural, and inevitable things. I have managed to conceal my madness fairly effectively," he wrote in *Here Comes, There Goes, You Know Who*.

Saroyan returned obsessively throughout his career to the theme of "madness," to a consideration of the possible reasons for his sorrow and psychic dislocation. He revealed a kind of "race-melancholy" underlying the Armenian temperament. In the late story "The Assyrian," he explored the dark side of his sensibility under the guise of an Assyrian hero, Paul Scott: "The longer he'd lived, the more he'd become acquainted with the Assyrian side, the old side, the tired side, the impatient and wise side, the side he had never suspected existed in himself until he was thirteen and had begun to be a man." Another foreign alter ego, the Arab in *The Time of Your Life*, repeats to himself: "No foundation. All the way down the line"—at once expressing the pain of the exile and Saroyan's own sense of disorder and spiritual emptiness.

Saroyan also identified this madness with illness, which was, he declared in *The Bicycle Rider in Beverly Hills*, "an event of the soul more than of the body." He asserted in the same volume, "I have been more or less ill all my life," a statement remarkable for both its extremism and its honesty. In *Days of Life and Death and Escape to the Moon*, a late memoir, he drew together various aspects of his own self-analysis in reexamining the past: "Most of the time illnesses of one sort or another came to me regularly, all the year round. I can't believe it is all from the sorrow in my nature, in my family, in my race, but I know some of it is." Saroyan was thus aware that his psychology derived from his Armenian heritage, the effects of his family life, and some quality inherent in his own personality.

If Saroyan was not at home in the world as it was, he was very much at home in his own imaginative recreation of it in his work. There may not be "real" homes and families like the one depicted in Saroyan's play *The Beautiful People*, but that is beside the point. As Wallace Stevens pointed out, the artist must *create* nobility, must press back against the world's chaos to create a livable sphere of existence. For Saroyan, art was a way toward health, toward reconciliation, toward psychic regeneration. He observed in the preface to *Don't Go Away Mad, and Two Other Plays* that he needed to write "because I hate to believe I'm sick or half-dead; because I want to get better; because writing is my therapy."

Deeply aware of the fragmentation and spiritual anarchy of life in the modern world, Saroyan exhibited a driving impulse toward joy, self-realization, and psychic integration. In the introduction to *Three Plays* he remarked that "the imperative requirement of our time is to restore faith to the mass and integrity to the individual. The integration of man is still far from realized. In a single age this integration can be immeasurably improved, but it is impossible and useless to seek to imagine its full achievement. Integration will begin to occur when the individual is uninhibited, impersonal, simultaneously natural and cultured, without hate, without fear, and rich in spiritual grace." Saroyan's work, then, records the attempt to integrate the divided self.

Following the final dissolution of his marriage in 1952 Saroyan turned increasingly to the exploration of his past through a series of autobiographies, memoirs, and journals. Although he continued to publish plays and fiction, autobiography became his main form of self-expression. This impulse reflected a shift in emphasis from art to life, from "doing" to "being," from the creation of works to the creation of self. Saroyan sought in memory a key to his identity, a meaningful pattern underlying the chaos of experience. In *The Bicycle Rider in Beverly Hills,* he wrote: "I want to think about the things I may have forgotten. I want to have a go at them because I have an idea they will help make known how I became who I am." Like Whitman, Thomas Wolfe, and Henry Miller, Saroyan obsessively focused on his own responses, emotions, and experiences in search of the psychological matrices of his behavior and personality. The writings of his final phase, however, are not only an important source of biographical insights—they also represent some of his best prose.

There is in these last writings a vibrant joy, a deep pleasure taken in small details of daily living. Saroyan buys cheap second-hand books in a Paris shop, brings home basil plants to his apartment, delights in solitude and reading. He writes of casual long walks, visits to libraries, meetings with dear friends. Musing over the strange disjunctions of a long life, he remembers many people: family, writers, former teachers, childhood comrades.

Saroyan's search in these last years was the search of his youth. His continuing antipathy toward authority, repression, and the fettering of the human spirit made him an influence on writers of the Beat Generation, who responded to his innovative, hip, casual, jazzy voice. Beginning his career in San Francisco, meeting ground of the spiritual East and expansive West, Saroyan wrote of beautiful people and preached love not war; he had been a flower-child of the 1930s. It is thus no accident that he was a literary godfather to such writers as Jack Kerouac and J. D. Salinger.

In his last work published during his lifetime, *Obituaries,* he wrote: "My work is writing, but my real work is being." He was, in Rahv's conception, a literary "redskin." As Stephen Axelrod explains in *Robert Lowell: Life and Art,* Rahv believed that "American literature composes itself into a debate between 'palefaces' and 'redskins.' The 'palefaces' (Henry James, T. S. Eliot, and Allen Tate would belong to this part) produce a patrician art which is intellectual, symbolic, cosmopolitan, disciplined, cultured. The 'redskins' (Walt Whitman and William Carlos Williams would tend to belong here) produce a plebian art which is emotional, naturalistic, nativist, energetic, in some sense *un*cultured. . . . All such formulations attest to a basic bifurcation [or, rift] in American literature between writers who experience primarily with the head and those who experience primarily with the blood." Saroyan wanted to feel the world directly, intuitively—like D. H. Lawrence, "with the blood." Saroyan's work is thus a great deal more complex than many commentators have acknowledged. His writing is a blend of the affirmative, mystical, and rambunctious qualities of the American romantic sensibility and of the profound sadness that finds its source in the tragic history of the Armenian people. On the one hand, Saroyan was thoroughly American in his persistent expansiveness, verve and spontaneity. Yet he was also the Armenian grieving for his lost homeland, speaking for those lost in an alien culture.

Precisely this sense of man's essential aloneness links Saroyan's work directly to the main currents of modern philosophical thought and to the major modernist writers; he has acknowledged his deep love for the work of both Samuel Beckett and Eugene Ionesco. One of the few observers to have discerned this important aspect of Saroyan's work was Edward Hoagland, who, in a 1970 *Chicago Tribune Book World* essay, called Saroyan "brother at once to Thomas Mann and to [Beckett,] the author of *Krapp's Last Tape.*" The existential strain was noted by Thelma Shinn, who remarked in *Modern Drama* that his work may be seen as the record of the search for meaning within the self. The difficulty of this quest for true meaning was also emphasized by William Fisher, who argued in his *College English* essay that in mid-career Saroyan's "novels and plays became strange battlegrounds where belief struggled with skepticism." These articles are among the few devoted to a serious consideration of Saroyan's place in modern literature.

MEDIA ADAPTATIONS: A film version of *The Human Comedy* starring Mickey Rooney was released in 1943; United Artists made a film based on *The Time of Your Life* starring Jimmy Cagney in 1948; an opera version of *Hello Out There* prepared by composer Jack Beeson was widely performed in 1953; a television adaptation of *The Time of Your Life* was produced on "Playhouse 90," October, 1958; "Ah, Sweet Mystery of Mrs. Murphy" was produced by NBC-TV, 1959; "The Unstoppable Gray Fox" was produced by CBS-TV, 1962; *My Heart's in the Highlands* was adapted for opera by Beeson and broadcast on television March 18, 1970; selections from *The Dogs, or The Paris Comedy, and Two Other Plays: Chris Sick, or Happy New Year Anyway, Making Money, and Nineteen Other Very Short Plays* were presented on television by NET Playhouse on December 8, 1970; a musical version of *The Human Comedy* was produced on Broadway by Joseph Papp in 1986.

BIOGRAPHICAL/CRITICAL SOURCES:

BOOKS

Aaron, Daniel, *Writers on the Left,* Oxford University Press, 1977.

Agee, James, *Agee on Film,* McDowell, Obolensky, 1958.

Axelrod, Stephen Gould, *Robert Lowell: Life and Art,* Princeton University Press, 1978.

Balakian, Nona, *The Armenian-American Writer,* AGBU, 1958.

Balakian, Nona, *Critical Encounters,* Bobbs-Merrill, 1978.

Calonne, David Stephen, *William Saroyan: My Real Work Is Being,* University of North Carolina Press, 1983.

Contemporary Literary Criticism, Gale, Volume 1, 1973, Volume 8, 1978, Volume 10, 1979, Volume 29, 1984, Volume 34, 1985.

Dictionary of Literary Biography, Gale, Volume 7: *Twentieth-Century American Dramatists,* 1981, Volume 9: *American Novelists, 1910-1945,* 1981.

Dictionary of Literary Biography Yearbook: 1981, Gale, 1982.

Esslin, Martin, *The Theatre of the Absurd,* Doubleday, 1961.

Floan, Howard, *William Saroyan,* Twayne, 1966.

Geismar, Maxwell, *Writers in Crisis: The American Novel, 1925-1940,* Hill and Wang, 1966.

Gifford, Barry, and Lawrence Lee, *Saroyan: A Biography,* Harper, 1984.

Gold, Herbert, *A Walk on the West Side: California on the Brink,* Arbor House, 1981.

Kazin, Alfred, *Starting Out in the Thirties,* Vintage, 1980.

Kherdian, David, *A Bibliography of William Saroyan: 1934-1964,* Howell, 1965.

Krutch, Joseph Wood, *The American Drama since 1918*, Braziller, 1957.

Lipton, Lawrence, *The Holy Barbarians*, Messner, 1959.

Martin, Jay, *Always Merry and Bright: The Life of Henry Miller*, Penguin, 1980.

McCarthy, Mary, *Sights and Spectacles*, Farrar, 1956.

Saroyan, Aram, *William Saroyan*, Harcourt, 1983.

Saroyan, Aram, *Last Rites: The Death of William Saroyan*, Harcourt, 1983.

Saroyan, William, *The Daring Young Man on the Flying Trapeze, and Other Stories*, Random House, 1934, reprinted, Yolla Bolly, 1984.

Saroyan, William, *Inhale and Exhale*, Random House, 1936, reprinted, Books for Libraries Press, 1972.

Saroyan, William, *The Time of Your Life*, Harcourt, 1939.

Saroyan, William, *Three Plays*, Harcourt, 1940.

Saroyan, William, *Razzle-Dazzle*, Harcourt, 1942.

Saroyan, William, *Don't Go Away Mad, and Two Other Plays*, Harcourt, 1949.

Saroyan, William, *The Assyrian, and Other Stories*, Harcourt, 1950.

Saroyan, William, *The Bicycle Rider in Beverly Hills* (autobiography), Scribner, 1952, Ballantine, 1971.

Saroyan, William, *Here Comes, There Goes, You Know Who* (autobiography), Simon & Schuster, 1962.

Saroyan, William, *Not Dying* (autobiography), Harcourt, 1963.

Saroyan, William, *Days of Life and Death and Escape to the Moon* (memoir), Dial, 1970.

Saroyan, William, *Obituaries*, Creative Arts, 1979.

Stevens, Wallace, *The Necessary Angel: Essays on Reality and the Imagination*, Knopf, 1951.

Straumann, Heinrich, *American Literature in the Twentieth Century*, Harper, 1965.

Trilling, Diana, *Reviewing the Forties*, Harcourt, 1978.

Weales, Gerald C., *American Drama since World War II*, Harcourt, 1962.

Wilson, Edmund, *The Boys in the Back Room: Notes on California Novelists*, Colt Press, 1941.

PERIODICALS

American Mercury, September, 1943.

Chicago Tribune Book World, July 5, 1970.

College English, March, 1955.

Commonweal, November 4, 1942.

Detroit Free Press, May 22, 1981.

Georgia Review, fall, 1970.

Los Angeles Times, May 19, 1981, June 7, 1981.

Modern Drama, September, 1972.

New Republic, March 1, 1943, March 9, 1953.

New York Times Book Review, April 2, 1972, August 15, 1976, May 20, 1979, August 21, 1983.

Pacific Spectator, winter, 1947.

Punch, January 31, 1973.

Quarterly Journal of Speech, February, 1944.

Saturday Review of Literature, December 28, 1940.

Theatre Arts, December, 1958.

Times Literary Supplement, June 22, 1973.

Virginia Quarterly Review, summer, 1944.

OBITUARIES:

PERIODICALS

Detroit News, May 24, 1981.

Newsweek, June 1, 1981.

New York Times, May 19, 1981.

Publishers Weekly, June 5, 1981.

Time, June 1, 1981.

Washington Post, May 19, 1981.*

—Sidelights by David Stephen Calonne

* * *

SAXE, Isobel
See RAYNER, Claire (Berenice)

* * *

SAY, Allen 1937-

PERSONAL: Born August 28, 1937; son of Masako Moriwaki; married Deirdre Myles, April 18, 1974; children: Yuriko (daughter). *Education:* Studied at Aoyama Gakuin, Tokyo, Japan, three years, Chouinard Art Institute, one year, Los Angeles Art Center School, one year, University of California, Berkeley, two years, and San Francisco Art Institute, one year.

ADDRESSES: Home—San Francisco, Calif.

CAREER: EIZO Press, Berkeley, Calif., publisher, 1968; commercial photographer and illustrator, 1969—; writer.

AWARDS, HONORS: Named to the *Horn Book* honor list, 1984, and Christopher Award, 1985, both for *How My Parents Learned to Eat*; Boston Globe/Horn Book Award, 1988, and Caldecott Honor Book, 1989, both for *The Boy of the Three Year Nap*.

WRITINGS:

(And illustrator) *Dr. Smith's Safari*, Harper, 1972.

(And illustrator) *Once under the Cherry Blossom Tree: An Old Japanese Tale*, Harper, 1974.

(And illustrator) *The Feast of Lanterns*, Harper, 1976.

The Innkeeper's Apprentice (young adult), Harper, 1979.

(And illustrator) *The Bicycle Man*, Houghton, 1982.

(And illustrator) *A River Dream*, Houghton, 1988.

(And illustrator) *The Lost Lake*, Houghton, 1989.

El Chino, Houghton, 1990.

ILLUSTRATOR

Brother Antoninus, *A Canticle to the Waterbirds*, EIZO Press, 1968.

Wilson Pinney, editor, *Two Ways of Seeing*, Little, Brown, 1971.

Eve Bunting, *Magic and Night River*, Harper, 1978.

Annetta Lawson, *The Lucky Yak*, Parnassus Press, 1980.

Thea Brow, *The Secret Cross of Lorraine*, Houghton, 1981.

Ina R. Friedman, *How My Parents Learned to Eat*, Houghton, 1984.

Dianne Snyder, *The Boy of the Three Year Nap*, Houghton, 1988.

AVOCATIONAL INTERESTS: Fly Fishing.

BIOGRAPHICAL/CRITICAL SOURCES:

PERIODICALS

New York Times Book Review, May 5, 1974, October 24, 1982.

Washington Post Book World, May 19, 1974, May 4, 1975.

* * *

SCHROEDER, Oliver Charles, Jr. 1916-

PERSONAL: Born April 19, 1916, in Cleveland, Ohio; son of Oliver Charles and Mabel Isa (Wheaton) Schroeder; married Gladys Marie Schuneman, July 17, 1942; children: James Oliver,

Jill Marie. *Education:* Western Reserve University (now Case Western Reserve University), A.B., 1938; Harvard University, J.D., 1941. *Religion:* Christian.

ADDRESSES: Home—3375 Seaton Rd., Cleveland Heights, Ohio 44118. *Office*—Law-Medicine Center, Case Western Reserve University, 134 Gund Hall, Cleveland, Ohio 44106.

CAREER: Admitted to the Ohio Bar, 1941; private practice of law in Cleveland, Ohio, 1941-43; Cleveland Transit Service, Cleveland, attorney, 1946-48; Case Western Reserve University, Cleveland, member of faculty of law, 1948-86, director of Law-Medicine Center, 1953-86, became Albert J. Weatherhead III and Richard W. Weatherhead Professor of Law and Criminal Justice. Presented "The Law and Medicine," a weekly program for Physicians Radio Network. Director of Christian Board of Publications, 1967-86; member of board of directors of Inarco Corp., 1971-79; member of board of trustees of National Benevolent Association, 1980-84; chairman of board of trustees of Forensic Sciences Foundation, 1976-85. Cleveland Heights City Council, member, 1965-77, mayor, 1972-74. *Military service:* U.S. Navy, 1943-67; became captain.

MEMBER: American Bar Association, American Academy of Forensic Sciences (president, 1963-64), Ohio State Bar Association, Bar Association of Greater Cleveland.

AWARDS, HONORS: Award for outstanding research and service in law and government, Ohio State Bar Foundation, 1981; Gradwohl Medal, American Academy of Forensic Sciences, 1987.

WRITINGS:

International Crime and the U.S. Constitution, Western Reserve Press, 1950.
Homicide in an Urban Community, C. C Thomas, 1960.
Lawyer Discipline: The Ohio Story, Ohio State Bar Foundation, 1967.
The Dynamics of Technology, Press of Case Western Reserve University, 1972.
Dental Jurisprudence, P.S.G. Publishing, 1980.
Ohio Criminal Law, two volumes, Banks-Baldwin, 1981.
Manual for Death Investigation, Forensic Sciences Foundation, 1985.
Utilization of Forensic Sciences by Police Organizations, Forensic Sciences Foundation, 1985.
The State of the Art in Forensic Sciences, Forensic Sciences Foundation, 1986.

*   *   *

SCHUH, G(eorge) Edward   1930-

PERSONAL: Born September 13, 1930, in Indianapolis, Ind.; son of George Oscar Edward (a farmer) and Viola May (Lentz) Schuh; married Maria Ignez Angeli, May 23, 1965; children: Audrey Marie, Susan Marie, Tanya Marie. *Education:* Purdue University, B.S., 1952; Michigan State University, M.S., 1954; University of Chicago, M.A., 1958, Ph.D., 1961. *Politics:* Independent. *Religion:* United Church of Christ.

ADDRESSES: Home—8400 Demontreville Tr. N., Lake Elmo, Minn. 55042. *Office*—Humphrey Center, 301 19th Ave. S., Minneapolis, Minn. 55455.

CAREER: Purdue University, Lafayette, Ind., instructor, 1959-61, assistant professor, 1961-62, associate professor, 1962-65, professor of agricultural economics, 1965-79, director of Center for Public Policy and Public Administration, 1977-78;

Department of Agriculture, Washington, D.C., deputy undersecretary for international affairs and commodity programs, 1978-79; University of Minnesota, St. Paul, professor of agricultural and applied economics and head of department, 1979-84; World Bank, Washington, D.C., director of agricultural and rural development, 1984-87; University of Minnesota, dean of Hubert H. Humphrey Institute for Public Affairs, 1987—. Honorary professor, University of Vicosa, Brazil, 1965. Director, National Bureau of Economic Research, 1977-84; member of board of directors, Economics Institute, 1979-84, and Minneapolis Grain Exchange, 1980-83. Agriculture program advisor, Ford Foundation, Rio de Janeiro, Brazil, 1966-72; senior staff economist, President's Council of Economic Advisers, 1974-75; deputy under secretary for international affairs and commodity programs, U.S. Department of Agriculture, 1978-79. *Military service:* U.S. Army, 1954-56; became sergeant.

MEMBER: International Association of Agricultural Economists, American Agricultural Economics Association (fellow; director, 1977-80; president-elect, 1980-81; president, 1981-82), American Association for the Advancement of Science (fellow), American Academy of Arts and Sciences (fellow), Econometric Society, American Economics Association, Brazilian Society of Agricultural Economists, Sigma Xi, Gamma Sigma Delta, Phi Tau Sigma.

AWARDS, HONORS: Awards from American Agricultural Economics Association, 1961, for best Ph.D. thesis, 1971, for best published research, 1974, for best journal article, 1979, for contributions to policy analysis, and 1988, for publication of enduring value.

WRITINGS:

(With Eliseu R. Alves) *The Agricultural Development of Brazil,* Praeger, 1970.
Research on Agricultural Development in Brazil, Agricultural Development Council, 1970.
(With Rubens Araujo Dias, Constantino Fraga, and Phil Warnken) *The Development of Paulista Agriculture,* Secretariat of Agriculture (Sao Paulo, Brazil), 1972.
(Editor with Paulo Cidade Araujo) *Readings in Agricultural Development,* University of Sao Paulo, 1974.
(Contributor) Claudio Roberto Contador, editor, *Tecnologia e desenvolvimento agricola,* IREA/INPES (Rio de Janeiro, Brazil), 1975.
The Modernization of Brazilian Agriculture: An Interpretation, Ohio State University, 1975.
(With Helio Tollini) *Costs and Benefits of Agricultural Research: The State of the Arts,* World Bank, 1979.
(With Ignez Guatimosim Vidigal Lopes) *Alocacao do tempo de familia ruais des baixa renda no Brasil: Um modelo de engajamento em empregos multiplos* (title means "Time Allocation of Low Income Rural Brazilian Households"), Ministerio da Agricultura, Comissao de Financiamento da Producao (Brasilia, Brazil), 1979.
(Editor with D. Gale Johnson) *The Role of Markets in the World Food Economy,* Westview, 1983.
(With Cidade Araujo) *Desenvolvimento da agricultura, estudios de casos,* Livraria Pioneira (Sao Paulo), 1983.
The United States and the Developing Countries: An Economic Perspective, National Planning Association, Committee on Changing International Realities, 1986.
(Editor with Jennifer L. McCoy) *Food, Agriculture, and Development in the Pacific Basin: Prospects for International Collaboration in a Dynamic Economy,* Westview, 1986.

Contributor to agricultural economics journals.

WORK IN PROGRESS: Theory of Agricultural Development in Latin America; Labor Absorption in Brazil.

*   *   *

SCHULLERY, Paul (David) 1948-

PERSONAL: Surname is pronounced Shul-air-ee; born July 4, 1948, in Middletown, Pa; son of Stephen Emil (a Lutheran minister) and Judith Catherine (a teacher; maiden name, Murphy) Schullery; married Dianne Patricia Russell (an editor), June 11, 1983 (divorced December, 1988). *Education:* Wittenberg University, B.A., 1970; Ohio University, M.A., 1977. *Religion:* Lutheran.

ADDRESSES: Home—P.O. Box 665, Yellowstone National Park, Wyo. 82190.

CAREER: National Park Service, Yellowstone National Park, Wyo., ranger-naturalist, summers, 1972-77, historian-archivist, winters, 1974-77; Museum of American Fly Fishing, Manchester, Vt., executive director, 1977-82; freelance writer and research consultant, Livingston, Mont., 1982-86; Yellowstone National Park, National Park Service Research Division, technical writer, 1988—. Member of board of trustees, Museum of American Fly Fishing, 1982—. Consulting researcher, Mount Rainier National Park, 1983.

MEMBER: American Association for the Advancement of Science, National Parks and Conservation Association (member of council of advisers, 1987—), Greater Yellowstone Coalition, Theodore Roosevelt Association, Trout Unlimited, Federation of Fly Fishers (senior adviser, 1980—; senior vice-president, 1982-83).

AWARDS, HONORS: Special Achievement Award for supervisory work from National Park Service, Yellowstone National Park, 1977; award for graphic arts excellence from Printing Industries of America, 1980 and 1981, and from Consolidated Papers, Inc., 1981, all for journal *American Fly Fisher;* overall National Park Service award for excellence in interpretive publications and first place award in Competition of the Conference of National Park Cooperating Associations, both 1984, both for *Freshwater Wilderness: Yellowstone Fishes and Their World; The Bears of Yellowstone* was named one of the outstanding books of 1986 by *Montana* magazine.

WRITINGS:

(Editor) *Old Yellowstone Days,* Colorado Associated University Press, 1979.
The Bears of Yellowstone, Yellowstone Library and Museum Association, 1980, new edition, Roberts Rinehart, 1986.
(Editor) *The Grand Canyon: Early Impressions,* Colorado Associated University Press, 1981.
(Editor) *American Bears: Selections from the Writings of Theodore Roosevelt,* Colorado Associated University Press, 1983.
(With John D. Varley) *Freshwater Wilderness: Yellowstone Fishes and Their World,* Yellowstone Library and Museum Association, 1983.
Mountain Time (memoir), Schocken, 1984.
(With C. Beasley, C. W. Buchholtz, and S. Trimble) *The Sierra Club Guides to the National Parks: The Rocky Mountains and the Great Plains,* Stewart, Tabori & Chang, 1984.
(Editor) *Theodore Roosevelt: Wilderness Writings,* Peregrine Smith, 1986.
(Editor and author of new material) Freeman Tildon, *The National Parks,* foreword by William Penn Mott, revised edition, Knopf, 1986.

(Editor) *Island in the Sky: Pioneering Accounts of Mount Rainier,* Mountaineers-Books, 1987.
(With D. Despain, D. Houston, and M. Meagher) *Wildlife in Transition: Man and Nature on Yellowstone's Northern Range,* Roberts Rinehart, 1987.
American Fly Fishing: A History, Nick Lyons, 1987.
(With Bud Lilly) *Bud Lilly's Guide to Western Fly Fishing,* Nick Lyons, 1987.
(With Lilly) *A Trout's Best Friend,* Pruett, 1987.
The Bear Hunter's Century, Dodd, 1988, reprinted, Stackpole, 1989.

Nature columnist and associate editor, *Country Journal,* 1986-88. Contributor to magazines, including *Country Journal, American West, Field and Stream, National Parks, Outdoor Life, Gray's Sporting Journal,* and *New York Times Book Review.* Editor, *American Fly Fisher,* 1978-83.

WORK IN PROGRESS: A collection of fishing essays and stories for book publication; collection of natural history essays; articles and reports on natural resource-related issues in Yellowstone National Park, particularly the 1988 fires and their political and ecological meanings.

SIDELIGHTS: Paul Schullery wrote to *CA:* "My work has been in several related areas—conservation history, modern conservation, natural history, sporting history, and modern outdoor sports. Fishing and hunting in North America have not been subjected to one percent of the scholarly scrutiny that has been given to organized games, partly because games, such as football and baseball, are more completely recorded both as far as statistics of the games themselves and as far as the numbers of spectators involved. Field sports, or blood sports, have been passed by in modern scholarship, resulting in a lack of public and scholarly understanding of their place in American culture. Drawn to these activities by my own recreational interests as well as by my related enthusiasms for nature and conservation, I have attempted to encourage the study of field sports by scholars, and have located several fellow enthusiasts with whom I share this project. My essay 'Hope for the Hook and Bullet Press' in the *New York Times Book Review* in 1985 was an attempt to bring the field of 'outdoor writing' to the attention of more people as a legitimate type of writing with a long and fascinating history. It was also an attempt to cast a sympathetic yet critical eye on that field, and thus was a source of some controversy among outdoor writers.

"I have also enjoyed writing about my own outdoor activities; my book *Mountain Time* is a memoir of my years as a Yellowstone Park ranger, and mixes personal anecdote with examination of the place of wilderness recreation in American life and history."

AVOCATIONAL INTERESTS: Hiking, nature photography, guitar playing.

*   *   *

SCHULZ, David A. 1933-

PERSONAL: Born April 17, 1933, in St. Louis, Mo.; son of Jonathan H. (in real estate) and Bertha Stella (Renick) Schulz; married Helene Alice Robertson, August 31, 1957; children: Lisa Mariah, Allison Lee. *Education:* Princeton University, A.B., 1954; Protestant Episcopal Theological Seminary in Virginia, B.D., 1960; Washington University, St. Louis, Mo., M.A., 1965, Ph.D., 1968. *Politics:* Independent.

ADDRESSES: Office—Department of Sociology, University of Delaware, Newark, Del. 19716.

CAREER: Field geologist, American Zinc Co., 1956-57; ordained Episcopal priest, 1961; Grace Episcopal Church, Kirkwood, Mo., curate, 1961-62; Washington University, St. Louis, Mo., lecturer, 1964-67; Pennsylvania State University, University Park, assistant professor of sociology, 1967-70; University of Delaware, Newark, associate professor of sociology and urban affairs, 1970—. *Military service:* U.S. Army, 1954-56.

MEMBER: American Sociological Association, Society for the Study of Social Problems, American Association for the Advancement of Science, National Council on Family Relations, Sex Information and Education Council, Groves Conference, Eastern Sociological Society.

AWARDS, HONORS: Bobbs-Merrill Award, 1965; National Science Foundation institutional grant, 1968.

WRITINGS:

Coming up Black: Patterns of Ghetto Socialization, Prentice-Hall, 1968.
The Changing Family: Its Function and Future, Prentice-Hall, 1972, 3rd edition, 1982.
(With Stanley F. Rodgers) *Marriage, the Family, and Personal Fulfillment,* Prentice-Hall, 1975, 3rd edition, 1985.
(With Robert A. Wilson) *Urban Sociology,* Prentice-Hall, 1978.
Human Sexuality, Prentice-Hall, 1979, 3rd edition, 1988.
(Editor with John M. Byrne and Marvin B. Sussman) *Families and the Energy Transition,* Haworth Press, 1985.

Contributor to sociology journals. Book review editor, *Journal of Marriage and the Family,* 1968-74.*

*   *   *

SCHWARTZ, Sheila (Ruth) 1929-

PERSONAL: Born March 15, 1929, in New York, N.Y.; daughter of Mark (a lawyer) and Sylvia (Schwartz) Frackman; divorced; children: Nancy Lynn (deceased), Jonathan, Elizabeth. *Education:* Adelphi University, B.A., 1946; Columbia University, M.A., 1948; New York University, Ed.D., 1964.

ADDRESSES: Home—5 Spies Rd., New Paltz, N.Y. 12561. *Office*—Department of Education, State University of New York, New Paltz, N.Y. 12561.

CAREER: Hofstra University, Hempstead, N.Y., instructor, 1958-60; City College of the City University of New York, New York. N.Y., instructor, 1962-63; State University of New York College at New Paltz, professor of English education, 1963—. Part-time professor of English in Associate in Arts Program, New York University, 1963—. Member of faculty, Hawaii Project English, 1972. Director of Hi/Lo Review and of Children's Book Reviews Service. President, New York State Conference on English Education.

MEMBER: PEN, Authors League of America, National Council of Teachers of English, National Association for Humanities Education (former president, Northeast branch), Adolescent Literature Association (president and founding member), New York State English Council (fellow; past president).

AWARDS, HONORS: Fulbright fellow at University College, Cork, Ireland, 1977; awards from New York State English Council, 1979, for excellence in teaching and excellence in letters; award from Adolescent Literature Association, 1980, for contributions to adolescent literature.

WRITINGS:

(With Gabriel Reuben) *How People Lived in Ancient Greece and Rome,* Benefic, 1967.
(With daughter, Nancy Lynn Schwartz) *How People Live in Mexico,* Benefic, 1969.
Teaching the Humanities: Selected Readings, Macmillan, 1970.
Earth in Transit, Dell, 1976.
Teaching Reading through Adolescent Literature (videotape series), Prentice-Hall, 1978.
Growing up Guilty (young adult novel), Pantheon, 1978.
Like Mother, Like Me, Pantheon, 1978.
Teaching Adolescent Literature, Hayden, 1979.
The Solid Gold Circle (novel), Crown, 1981.
One Day You'll Go, Scholastic Book Services, 1982.
Best Intentions, Crown, 1982.
(With N. L. Schwartz) *The Hollywood Writers' Wars,* Knopf, 1982.
Jealousy, Scholastic Book Services, 1983.
Sorority, Warner Books, 1987.
Bigger Is Better, Crosswinds, 1987.
The Most Popular Girl, Crosswinds, 1988.

OTHER

Contributor of more than one hundred twenty-five articles and reviews to periodicals, including *New York Times Book Review* and *Psychology Today.*

WORK IN PROGRESS: In Brotherly Love, a novel.

SIDELIGHTS: Sheila Schwartz told *CA:* "The world of books has always been my favorite, reading and writing my favorite activities. I can still remember being praised in elementary school for my writing and trudging from room to room to read my work, at my teacher's behest, to other classes. I do not ever remember playing with dolls. Whenever I was asked what I wanted for birthdays, it was always books, books, and more books. I used to spend much of my free time in our small local library, and the first part-time job I got was working there. I was fired soon after, though, for getting lost in the stacks. I could not resist picking up a book that excited my imagination and beginning to read it right there on the spot.

"But life came between me and my writing. I got married, had three children, taught school, and began to work on my doctorate. I wrote articles, did book reviews, and began to publish small nonfiction books as the children got older. One of my proudest literary achievements at that time was the fact that my daughter Nancy wrote *How People Live in Mexico* with me when she was only seventeen.

"The years passed. I obtained my doctorate, became a college teacher, and still I was not writing fiction. Nancy went out to Hollywood to work as a screenwriter, the other two children went to college, my marriage broke up, and in 1976, I had a big empty house and a big empty heart. Finally there was room for fiction. My first young adult novel was *Growing up Guilty,* about a fat, homely girl in Brooklyn at the onset of World War II. Was the girl me? Emotionally yes, but in actuality no.

"My next novel was *Like Mother, Like Me,* which dealt with the relationship between a teenage girl and her recently separated mother. Nancy liked this book so much that she wrote the screenplay for it, and it was presented on CBS and starred Kristy McNichol and Linda Lavin. But Nancy did not live to see it on television. Suddenly, out of nowhere, this beautiful, brilliant girl complained of headaches. The CAT scan revealed a brain tumor, and she died two weeks later in 1978. . . . I not only lost my beloved daughter, I lost my dearest friend, my literary collaborator.

"At the time of her death, Nancy had been working on *The Hollywood Writers' Wars,* a history of the blacklist in Hollywood. The day after her death I was at work to complete the book, so there would be one book in libraries with her name on it. I have two other children, and it is their love plus my writing work that have enabled me to survive. I work every day, . . . and feel fortunate that life has given me work and love."

MEDIA ADAPTATIONS: Like Mother, Like Me was adapted for CBS-TV by Sheila Schwartz's daughter, Nancy.

*   *   *

SEGY, Ladislas 1904-

PERSONAL: Born February 10, 1904, in Budapest, Hungary; immigrated to the United States, 1936; naturalized U.S. citizen, 1941; married.

ADDRESSES: Home—35 West 90th St., New York, N.Y. 10024. *Office*—Segy Gallery, 50 West 57th St., New York, N.Y. 10019.

CAREER: Began collecting African and modern French art in Paris in the 1920s, later exhibiting African sculpture in Paris and Berlin; continued collecting after arrival in United States in 1936; Segy Gallery, New York, N.Y., owner and director, 1950—. Has exhibited African art in nearly 400 museums and universities in the United States and Canada. Lecturer at numerous museums and universities, including Columbia University, New York University, Parsons School of Design, University of Michigan, Brandeis University, and Yale University; has also lectured in South America, 1956, in conjunction with a U.S. Department of State program.

AWARDS, HONORS: Litt.D., Central State College (now University; Wilberforce, Ohio), 1953.

WRITINGS:

African Sculpture Speaks, Wyn, 1952, 4th revised edition, Da Capo Press, 1975.
African Sculpture, Dover, 1958, reprinted, 1975.
African Art Studies, Volume 1, Wittenborn, 1960.
The Yorubi Ibeji Statue, Verlag fuer Recht und Gesellschaft (Basel, Switzerland), 1970.
The Mossi Doll: An Archetypal Fertility Figure, Tribus (Stuttgart, West Germany), 1972.
Masks of Black Africa, Dover, 1975.

Contributor of research and story structure for "Buma: African Sculpture Speaks," Encyclopedia Britannica Films, 1951. Contributor to professional journals and museum bulletins in Europe and the United States, including *Phylon, Journal of Negro History, Etc.: A Review of General Semantics, Midwest Journal, Acta Tropica* (Basel), and *Anthropos* (West Germany).

WORK IN PROGRESS: Four books: *Being and Meaning: Creativity and the Mystical Participation, The Identity of the Self, The Meaning of Jacques Lipschitz's Sculpture,* and *African Fertility Cults: Phallic, Snake and Storm;* journal articles.

BIOGRAPHICAL/CRITICAL SOURCES:

PERIODICALS

Saturday Review, December 6, 1969.
Washington Post Book World, May 2, 1976.*

SEMONCHE, John E(rwin) 1933-

PERSONAL: Surname is pronounced Sem-*on*-chee; born February 9, 1933, in Alpha, N.J.; son of John (a machinist) and Anna (Luchachek) Semonche; married Barbara Potts (a newspaper librarian), June 16, 1962; children: Laura Vera-Anne. *Education:* Brown University, A.B., 1954; Northwestern University, M.A., 1955, Ph.D., 1962; Duke University, L.L.B., 1967.

ADDRESSES: Home—2650 University Dr., Durham, N.C. 27707. *Office*—Department of History, School of Law, University of North Carolina, Chapel Hill, N.C. 27514.

CAREER: Admitted to Bar of State of North Carolina, 1967; University of North Carolina, Chapel Hill, instructor, 1960-63, assistant professor, 1963-68, associate professor, 1968-72, professor of history, 1973—, lecturer in law, 1967—. *Military service:* U.S. Navy, 1955-58; became lieutenant, j.g.

MEMBER: American Historical Association, Organization of American Historians, North Carolina Bar Association.

WRITINGS:

Ray Stannard Baker: A Quest for Democracy in Modern America, 1870-1918, University of North Carolina Press, 1969.
Charting the Future: The Supreme Court Responds to a Changing Society, 1890-1920, Greenwood, 1978.
Religion and Constitutional Government in the United States: A Historical Overview with Sources, Signal Books, 1985.

Contributor to journals, including *American Journal of Legal History, Los Angeles Law Review,* and *North Carolina Law Review.*

WORK IN PROGRESS: A study of how and why the U.S. Supreme Court is able to make policies within the confines of a democratic society; a historical play set in the 1890s; research on constitutional and legal history.

SIDELIGHTS: John E. Semonche told *CA:* "Scholars who research the historical past too often limit their potential readership by obscuring the human drama behind a less than lively prose style and a tendency to overconceptualize their subject. Narratives can be analytical and still capture the drama that makes history a subject of popular interest. For instance, since so much of the writing on the Supreme Court is institutionally oriented, I sought in my recent work to humanize the subject and view the Court within the complex society it served. The result should be a more readable and accessible book. For any writer the task should be the same—attempting to widen the arena of his/her communication."*

*   *   *

SEVELA, Efraim 1928-

PERSONAL: First name spelled Ephraim in some sources; born March 8, 1928, in Bobruisk, U.S.S.R.; son of Joel E. (a sportsman) and Rachel (Gelfand) Sevela; married Julia Gendelstein (an actress), September 19, 1958; children: Maria, Danial. *Education:* Attended University of Minsk, 1945-48.

ADDRESSES: Home—West Germany.

CAREER: Writer. Worked as a journalist in Vilna, U.S.S.R., and as a script writer and film director in Moscow, U.S.S.R.

MEMBER: Union of Soviet Filmmakers.

WRITINGS:

WORKS IN ENGLISH

Legends from Invalid Street (stories), translation by Anthony Kahn, Doubleday, 1974.

Truth Is for Strangers: A Novel about a Soviet Poet, translation by Antonina W. Bouis, Doubleday, 1976, published in the original Russian as *Viking,* Black Sea Book Store, 1981.

Farewell, Israel! (nonfiction), translation by Edmond Browne, Gateway Editions, 1977.

Pochemu net raia na zemie (novel), Stav (Jerusalem), 1982, translation by Richard Lourie published as *Why There Is No Heaven on Earth,* Harper, 1982.

The Standard Bearer, translation by Donald Arthur, Benjamin Barrett, and Lourie, Icarus, 1983.

OTHER

Ostanovite samolet—ia slezu!, (title means "Stop the Plane—I'll Get Off!"), Stav, 1977.

Muzhkoi razgovor v russkoi bane (stories), Grand (Tel Aviv), 1980.

Prodai tvoyu mat, Stav, 1981.

Zub mudrosti (fiction), Stav, 1981.

Popugai govoryashchii na idish (stories) Stav, 1982.

Mama: Kinopovest (fiction), Stav, 1982.

Toiota Korolla, privately published, 1984.

Vse ne kak u lyudei, privately published, 1984.

Also author of plays and eight feature filmscripts in Russian.

WORK IN PROGRESS: Last Convulsions; a children's book for Harper.

SIDELIGHTS: In 1971, Efraim Sevela and twenty-three other Soviet Jews staged a sit-in to protest the country's restrictive emigration policies. Much to the demonstrators' surprise, the government did not punish them but instead allowed them and many other Jews to emigrate to Israel. For Sevela and his fellows, however, the joy of victory soon turned to disillusionment when they found that life in Israel failed to meet their expectations. "This collective despair fuels Sevela's polemic [*Farewell, Israel!*], which asserts that . . . Israel is a land of indolent wastefulness, discrimination, and insufferable arrogance," describes Alan L. Miller in *National Review.* While a *Booklist* reviewer observes that some of Sevela's accusations "result simply from his false hopes and shattered dreams," he admits that "many of the criticisms leveled at Israel appear just." Sevela has met with a better response for his fiction, which frequently deals with Jewish life in pre-World War II Russia. About *Why There Is No Heaven on Earth,* for example, *New York Times Book Review* contributor Wallace Markfield states that Sevela's work "is one of the most beautifully written and deeply felt novels that I have encountered about the half-chivalric, half-criminal universe that young boys inhabit." The critic concludes that the novel "is done so quietly and simply, so effectively, that one forgets the art."

BIOGRAPHICAL/CRITICAL SOURCES:

BOOKS

Sevela, Efraim, *Farewell, Israel!,* translation by Edmond Browne, Gateway Editions, 1977.

PERIODICALS

Booklist, December 1, 1977.
Commentary, February, 1978.
National Review, March 31, 1978.
New York Times Book Review, April 25, 1982.*

SHANOR, Donald Read 1927-

PERSONAL: Born July 11, 1927, in Ann Arbor, Mich.; son of William Wilson (an engineer) and Katherine (an English teacher; maiden name, Read) Shanor; married Constance Collier (a science editor), November 24, 1951; children: Rebecca Read, Elizabeth Lynne. *Education:* Northwestern University, B.S., 1951; Columbia University, M.A., 1964. *Politics:* Liberal Democrat.

ADDRESSES: Home—285 Riverside Dr., New York, N.Y. 10025. *Office*—Graduate School of Journalism, Columbia University, New York, N.Y. 10027. *Agent*—A. L. Hart, Fox-Chase Agency, Public Ledger Bldg., Independence Sq., Philadelphia, Pa. 19106.

CAREER: During his early career was factory and railroad worker; American Forces Network, Frankfurt, Germany, editor/reporter, 1952-54; United Press International, editor/reporter in Frankfurt, Germany, London, England, New York City, and at the United Nations, 1954-65; Columbia University, New York City, lecturer in journalism, 1965-67; *Chicago Daily News,* Chicago, Ill., correspondent in Eastern and Western Europe and the Mideast, 1967-71; Columbia University, 1971—, began as associate professor, became Godfrey Lowell Cabot Professor of Journalism and International Affairs. *Military service:* U.S. Navy, 1945-46.

MEMBER: Society of Professional Journalists, American Council on Germany.

AWARDS, HONORS: Finalist for H. L. Mencken Award, for *Behind the Lines: The Private War against Soviet Censorship;* grant, U.S. Institute of Peace, 1988-89.

WRITINGS:

The New Voice of Radio Free Europe (monograph), Columbia University Press, 1967.

Soviet Europe, Harper, 1975.

The Soviet Triangle: Russia's Relations with China and the West in the Eighties, St. Martin's, 1980.

(Co-author) *News from Abroad and the Foreign Policy Public,* Foreign Policy Association, 1980.

Behind the Lines: The Private War against Soviet Censorship, St. Martin's, 1985.

(With wife, Constance C. Shanor) *The Chinese Century,* St. Martin's, 1989.

Contributor to periodicals, including *Atlantic Monthly, New Leader, New York Times,* and *Baltimore Sun.* Contributing editor, *World Press Review,* 1973—; advisory editor, *Columbia Journalism Review,* 1971—.

WORK IN PROGRESS: The Independent Peace Movement in the German Democratic Republic.

SIDELIGHTS: Donald Read Shanor told *CA* that the kind of writing he is currently doing doesn't differ greatly from what he was producing as a daily journalist, except in one all-important aspect: now he can measure his time devoted to research and reporting in months and even years instead of hours or days. "Where the daily journalist may have at best a five-minute scan of the clips or their electronic equivalent for background, [I] can take the time to do a complete 'ghost draft' of [my] chapters, writing a draft of the book on the basis of the information already available. The next step, however, is crucial: going out and doing the reporting and further original research, using the ghost draft only as a way of beginning to learn the subject, as a key to knowing what questions to ask. In the final version, almost all of the ghost draft disappears (hence its name), since it is superseded by better, newer, more focused information and writing."

AVOCATIONAL INTERESTS: Carpentry, hiking.

*   *   *

SHAW, Timothy Milton 1945-

PERSONAL: Born January 27, 1945, in Frimley, England; son of Arnold J. (a civil servant) and Margaret E. (a teacher) Shaw; married Susan M. Sturt, July 8, 1967 (divorced, 1981); married B. Jane L. Parpart (a professor), September 2, 1983; children: Benjamin, Amanda; (stepchildren) Laura Parpart, Lee Parpart. *Education:* University of Sussex, B.A., 1967; University of East Africa, M.A., 1969; Princeton University, M.A., 1971, Ph.D., 1975.

ADDRESSES: Home—6138 Linden St., Nova Scotia, Canada B3H 2K8. *Office*—Centre for Foreign Policy Studies, Dalhousie University, Halifax, Nova Scotia, Canada B3H 4H6.

CAREER: Dalhousie University, Halifax, Nova Scotia, assistant professor of political science, 1972-73; University of Zambia, Lusaka, lecturer in international politics, 1973-74; Dalhousie University, assistant professor, 1974-77, associate professor of political science, 1977-78, associate of Centre for Foreign Policy Studies, 1972—, director of Centre for African Studies, 1977-78; Carleton University, Ottawa, Ontario, visiting associate professor of political science, 1978-79; University of Ife, Ile-Ife, Nigeria, visiting senior lecturer in international relations, 1979-80; Dalhousie University, associate professor, 1980-82, professor of political science, 1982—, director of Centre for African Studies, 1983-89; visiting professor in African political economy, University of Zimbabwe, 1989. Director of International Development Studies, 1985—. Consultant to United Nations Economic Commission for Africa, UNICEF, International Development Research Centre, North-South Institute, and Ward University Service of Canada.

MEMBER: International Studies Association, Canadian Association for African Studies, Canadian Political Science Association, African Association of Political Scientists, African Studies Association, African Association of Political Science.

WRITINGS:

Dependence and Underdevelopment: The Development and Foreign Policies of Zambia, Ohio University Papers in International Studies, 1976.
(With Douglas G. Anglin) *Zambia's Foreign Policy: Studies in Diplomacy and Dependence,* Westview, 1979.
Towards an International Political Economy for the 1980s: From Dependence to (Inter)dependence, Centre for Foreign Policy Studies, Dalhousie University, 1980.
(With Anglin) *Alternative Sources of Event Data on Zambian Foreign Policy,* Maxwell School of Citizenship and Public Affairs, Syracuse University, 1981.
The Political Economy of Zambia and the Future of Southern Africa, Nigerian Institute of International Affairs, 1981.
Africa's International Affairs: An Analysis and Bibliography, Centre for Foreign Policy Studies, Dalhousie University, 1983.
Towards a Political Economy for Africa: The Dialectics of Dependence, Macmillan, 1985.
Southern Africa in Crisis, Centre for Foreign Policy Studies, 1986.

Also author of, with Julius O. Ihonvbere and E. John Inegbedion, *Nigeria: Africa's Major Power,* Westview; and, with Ihonvbere, *Towards a Political Economy of Nigeria.*

EDITOR AND CONTRIBUTOR

(With Kenneth A. Heard) *Cooperation and Conflict in Southern Africa: Papers on a Regional Subsystem,* University Press of America, 1976.
(With Anglin and Carl G. Widstrand) *Conflict and Change in Southern Africa: Papers from a Scandinavian-Canadian Conference,* University Press of America, 1978.
(With Anglin and Widstrand) *Canada, Scandinavia, and Southern Africa,* Africana, 1978.
(With Heard) *The Politics of Africa: Dependence and Development,* Africana, 1979.
Alternative Futures for Africa, Westview, 1982.
(With Sola Ojo) *Africa and the International Political System,* University Press of America, 1982.
(With Olajide Aluko) *Nigerian Foreign Policy: Alternative Perceptions and Projections,* St. Martin's, 1983.
(With Aluko) *The Political Economy of African Foreign Policy: Comparative Analysis,* St. Martin's, 1984.
(With Aluko) *Southern Africa in the 1980s,* Allen & Unwin, 1985.
(With Aluko) *Africa Projected: From Recession to Renaissance by the Year 2000?,* Macmillan, 1985.
(With Adebayo Adedeji) *Economic Crisis in Africa,* Lynne Riemer, 1985.
(With Ibrahim Msabaha) *Confrontation and Liberation in Southern Africa,* Westview, 1987.
(With Naomi Chasan) *Coping with Africa's Food Crisis,* Lynne Riemer, 1988.
(With J. Carisson) *NICS and the Political Economy of South: South Relations,* Macmillan, 1988.
(With Julius Nyangoro) *Corporations in Africa,* Westview, 1989.
(With others) *Economic History of Southern Africa* (two volumes), Frank Cass, 1990.
(With Ralph I. Onwuka) *Africa and World Politics into the 1990s.* Macmillan, 1989.

OTHER

Contributor to African studies, development studies, and political science journals.

WORK IN PROGRESS: Research on the political economy of Nigeria, on change—conflicted and cooperative—in Southern Africa, and on alternative development strategies and scenarios for Africa.

SIDELIGHTS: Timothy Milton Shaw told *CA:* "Despite Naipaul's dismissive assertion that 'Africa has no future,' this Third World continent remains both perplexing and promising. It challenges many assumptions and is still an untapped cornucopia. I fell in love with the misleadingly named 'dark continent' in the late 1960s and have since returned at least once every year. Africa offers a rich diversity of experiences—a spectrum of political economies and ideologies—which can best be approached and understood through a 'radical' perspective. My current research and writing focuses on contradictions within this continent, with their implications for foreign policies and future projections. There are increasingly antagonistic tensions between classes, countries, and genders that affect prospects for production and accumulation: will the remaining ten years of this century be characterized by expansion or regression? Will Africa's immense human and natural resources be mobilized for its development or others? Can the continent turn around its decline and become more self-reliant and self-maintaining? As Pliny remarked in the first century A.D., '*Ex Africa semper aliquid novi,*' something new is always coming out of Africa."

BIOGRAPHICAL/CRITICAL SOURCES:

PERIODICALS

New Statesman, January 25, 1980.

* * *

SHEED, Wilfrid (John Joseph) 1930-

PERSONAL: Born December 27, 1930, in London, England; came to the United States in 1940; son of Francis Joseph (an author and publisher) and Maisie (an author and publisher; maiden name Ward) Sheed; married Miriam Ungerer; children: Elizabeth Carol, Francis, Marion. *Education:* Lincoln College, Oxford, B.A. 1954, M.A., 1957. *Religion:* Roman Catholic.

ADDRESSES: Home—Sag Harbor, N.Y. 11963. *Agent*—Lantz-Donadio, 111 West 57th St., New York, N.Y. 10019.

CAREER: Jubilee, New York, N.Y., movie reviewer, 1959-61, associate editor, 1959-66; *Commonweal,* New York City, drama critic and book editor, 1964-71; *Esquire,* New York City, movie critic, 1967-69; *New York Times,* New York City, columnist, 1971—. Visiting lecturer in creative arts, Princeton University, 1970-71; Book of the Month Club judge, 1972—; reviewer for numerous publications.

MEMBER: PEN.

AWARDS, HONORS: National Book Award nomination, 1966, for *Office Politics,* and 1971, for *Max Jamison;* "best fiction book of 1970" citation from *Time* magazine, 1971, for *Max Jamison;* Guggenheim fellowship and National Institute and American Academy award in literature, both 1971.

WRITINGS:

FICTION

Joseph (juvenile), Sheed, 1958.
A Middle Class Education: A Novel, Houghton, 1960.
The Hack (novel), Macmillan, 1963, reprinted, Vintage Books, 1980.
Square's Progress: A Novel, Farrar, Straus, 1965.
Office Politics: A Novel, Farrar, Straus, 1966.
The Blacking Factory & Pennsylvania Gothic: A Short Novel and a Long Story, Farrar, Straus, 1968.
Max Jamison: A Novel, Farrar, Straus, 1970 (published in England as *The Critic: A Novel,* Weidenfeld & Nicolson, 1970).
People Will Always Be Kind (novel), Farrar, Straus, 1973.
Transatlantic Blues (novel), Dutton, 1978.
The Boys of Winter (novel), Knopf, 1987.

NONFICTION

(Editor) G. K. Chesterton, *Essays and Poems,* Penguin, 1958.
The Morning After: Selected Essays and Reviews, Farrar, Straus, 1971.
Three Mobs: Labor, Church, and Mafia, Sheed, 1974.
Muhammad Ali: A Portrait in Words and Photographs, New American Library, 1975.
(Author of introduction) James Thurber, *Men, Women and Dogs,* Dodd, 1975.
The Good Word & Other Words, Dutton, 1978.
Clare Boothe Luce, Thorndike Press, 1982.
Frank & Maisie: A Memoir with Parents, Simon & Schuster, 1985.
(Editor) *Sixteen Short Novels,* Dutton, 1986.

(Author of text) *The Kennedy Legacy: A Generation Later,* Viking, 1988.

OTHER

Also author of *Vanishing Species of America,* 1974. Contributor to numerous periodicals, including *New York Times Book Review, Esquire, Sports Illustrated,* and *Commonweal.*

SIDELIGHTS: Novelist and critic Wilfrid Sheed has been a prominent man of letters in America for nearly thirty years. *Time* correspondent John Skow calls Sheed "almost certainly the best American reviewer of books," an elegant writer who is also "a novelist of wit and intelligence." Sheed, who was raised both in England and the United States, is often cited as an essayist who is penetrating but not pompous—"an acute and twinkling observer, adept at both irony and slapstick farce, compassionate to a fault and a most clever and accomplished stylist," to quote Eliot Fremont-Smith in the *New York Times.* The author may be slightly better known for his reviews, but he has also penned almost a dozen works of fiction, many of which draw upon his personal experiences from childhood to maturity. *Washington Post Book World* columnist Jonathan Yardley finds Sheed "a novelist of depth, complexity and compassion. . . . Sheed gets better with each new novel, and there are few writers of whom that can be said." All of Sheed's works share two essential components, according to his critics: they display finely-wrought prose and subtle, ironic humor. In *Newsweek,* Peter S. Prescott contends that Sheed "is a very funny man, but (especially in recent years) his wit has been used in the service of humaneness, a kind of domestic service to the family of man."

Sheed may have seemed destined for a literary life from his birth. Four years before he was born his parents, Frank Sheed and Maisie Ward Sheed, established the prestigious publishing firm of Sheed & Ward, "one of the most respected religious publishers in the world," according to Walter W. Ross III in the *Dictionary of Literary Biography.* Thus Sheed and his sister grew up surrounded by the important Catholic writers and thinkers of their day; both children were encouraged to excel in their studies and to enjoy vigorous exercise. When Sheed was nine the Second World War erupted, and the family moved to America, settling in Torresdale, Pennsylvania. Sheed spent his early teen years there, fascinated by American sports, especially baseball. His own budding athletic talent was squelched abruptly at fourteen when he contracted the dreaded polio, an event that shadowed the rest of his youth. Having recovered after a long convalescence, Sheed returned to England to attend preparatory school and Oxford University. Where he had been considered British in Pennsylvania, he was now looked on as an American in his native land. This too contributed to his conception of himself, both in his actions and in his philosophy.

Sheed told the *New York Times Book Review* that he "picked up . . . writing on the very day" his father died, as a meager consolation for the loss. Soon he was supporting himself by doing book and movie reviews for magazines and writing fiction in his spare time. "I guess I just sort of backed into writing," he told *Publishers Weekly.* "Probably I do not understand the craft at all, and how difficult it is. Theoretically, I may not even approve of the kind of writing I do and such a markedly personal style, but I didn't seem to have a heck of a lot of choice in the matter. I have taken off from family experiences sometimes as if they were daydreams." Indeed, much of Sheed's fiction contains autobiographical elements, although the author admits that he alters incidents immensely. "I use settings I know," he said. "I wait until things have distilled, fomented. The boyhood episodes in my novels are less and less based on anything that really happened."

Still, many of Sheed's early novels deal with themes that mirror his youth. *A Middle Class Education,* his first novel, is a satire on school life in England and America. *The Blacking Factory* and *Pennsylvania Gothic* explore childhood isolation in rural Pennsylvania, and *People Will Always Be Kind* concerns a teenager stricken with polio. One theme remains more or less constant throughout all of Sheed's fiction: his protagonists, regardless of age, are prone to self-analysis of the most intense sort. As *New York Times* contributor Christopher Lehmann-Haupt puts it, Sheed's works are studies "in agonized self-consciousness."

Several of Sheed's best known novels, including *Office Politics, The Hack, Max Jamison,* and *The Boys of Winter,* deal with the wry and sometimes sordid worlds of journalism and publishing. According to John Blades in a Chicago *Tribune Books* review, Sheed "comes from a publishing family, and few writers cover the territory so confidently, or write about it with so much vim and vitriol, such malicious afore- and afterthought." For instance, *Office Politics,* which was nominated for the National Book Award in 1966, analyzes a vicious power struggle that ensues among members of a magazine staff after the editor-in-chief becomes ill. In an essay for *Wisconsin Studies in Contemporary Literature,* Richard Lehan writes that *Office Politics* "uses the drab world of New York City to intensify the drab, sordid, meaningless routine that turns young men into cynics and romantic expectation into despair." *New York Times* commentator Charles Poore suggests that Sheed "has a splendid gift for dramatizing the search-and-destroy diabolism of outrageous fortune. His characters are multidimensional without hazing off into the pretentiously symbolic."

Not every reviewer finds Sheed's characters so multidimensional. In a *New York Review of Books* essay, Robert Towers contends that Sheed's novels "read more like demonstrations than imaginative works of fiction. . . . His novels seem stronger in documentation than in invention and regularly give the *appearance* of autobiography only slightly transmuted—even when the characters and their circumstances are obviously 'made up.' They have trouble progressing beyond their initial premise or situation into a freely moving story, with the result that their denouements are often unconvincing . . . or melodramatic." *Village Voice* contributor James Wolcott likewise sees Sheed's fiction as working in a "self-created void: the characters are store-window mannequins, the scenery consists of painted back-drops. Nothing is at stake, no giddy risks are taken, so the jokes become only curlicues in his elegant doodling." Other critics have responded warmly to Sheed's work. A *Time* reviewer writes: "Sheed constructs a bright, cutting prose from the dross of everyday slang. He wields that prose with a subtle ear for speech rhythms and a sardonic eye for the tell-tale gesture. . . . His protagonists are ordinary guys desperately trying to fend off the world's idiocies and evils long enough to define themselves and do the decent thing. They rarely succeed completely." In the *New Republic,* Yardley maintains that Sheed has moved "toward a fiction which, while the dazzle remains, has gained measurably in depth and subtlety. . . . Even at his darkest, he is a joy to read. His wit and perceptiveness are marvelous. . . . It is a measure of his achievement that we only rarely feel that the glitter is for its own sake."

Max Jamison, published in 1970, is one of Sheed's most successful novels. In another case of thinly-veiled autobiography, the book spotlights a Broadway theatre critic whose life is consumed by his work. *Saturday Review* correspondent Robert Cromie calls it "a darkly engaging book, which may be read purely as entertainment, or, as I am sure Sheed intended it should, as a sympathetic, occasionally ribald, always engrossing portrait of

a tragi-comic man, mired in a profession he no longer respects or truly enjoys, a man doomed to boredom and despair, with only an occasional slight flash of pleasure in prospect to keep him alive until the fall of the final curtain." *Max Jamison* also received a nomination for the National Book Award and has been generally well-received by critics. *Commonweal* essayist David Lodge finds in the work "impressive evidence of the mature poise and skill Wilfrid Sheed has achieved as a novelist," and a *National Observer* contributor calls the book "one of the most unhappily accurate accounts of a critic's day-to-day life ever committed to paper." In a *New Republic* review, Yardley finds the unhappy Max "nonetheless a curiously admirable character for whom, in the end, one grieves. His pomposity is maddening, but in his insistence upon 'standards' there is an old-fashioned deference to tradition which one must honor; he is a man of genuine if dubiously exercised integrity. For all his stiffness, his infuriating withdrawal from the turmoil and pain of life, he inspires sadness and sympathy."

Transatlantic Blues, Sheed's 1978 novel, concerns the travails of a continent-hopping television personality with roots in England and America. *New York Times Book Review* correspondent Julian Moynahan finds the work "fictional autobiography structured as a general confession in the old Catholic sense of the term. . . . It turns out to be a tale of growing up between two countries and is one we have been waiting for from Wilfrid Sheed. . . . That isn't, of course, to pretend that the book is Sheed's own confession." According to Walter Clemons in *Newsweek, Transatlantic Blues* "is a rich mess of a novel, the funniest and freest Sheed has written. The miserable [protagonist] Chatworth is endowed with a ripped-open version of a transatlantic style Sheed has made his own, in which Oxonian clarity joins with American lowdown colloquial. . . . Chatworth's confessional prose is rawer and speedier, edgier and more combative than anything we have heard from Sheed before. At full throttle it is exciting and explosively funny." Many observers have found Sheed's use of first person narration in the book more conducive to his humor and prose style. *Critic* essayist Laurence P. Smith calls the book "clearly Sheed's finest novel to date. . . . His voice seems less coldly detached, revealing an emotional concern for his characters that his sardonic, cutting style has often obscured. *Transatlantic Blues* is a novel filled with so much humor that the temptation is to speak of nothing else. It is rich in the irony, parody, satire and witty verbal gymnastics that have earned Sheed his reputation as a leading novelist of manners. Yet his vision is the entire sad human predicament. . . . It is humor with a serious purpose." Smith elaborates: "Between the laughs are the leads, the themes and insights which help to explain the chaos within every man. Tear-washed eyes, from laughter or grief, may offer the clearest view of the truth, or at least of one's own soul."

Nine years separate the publication dates of *Transatlantic Blues* and *The Boys of Winter,* a tragi-comic novel about struggling authors and their editors set in the rural reaches of Long Island. As Herbert Gold notes in the *New York Times Book Review,* the subject of the tale "is not so much the life of literature as careerism—also sex and softball—in an exurban Long Island colony." Sheed makes forays into the jealousies between competing fiction writers, the vagaries of the book business, and the macho antics of grown men let loose on a softball diamond. Gold writes that *The Boys of Winter* "brings Grub Street to contemporary times and the exurbs—and it's funny. Finally it does the satirist's good work of demolition, but it also, alas, tells much of the truth about literary politicking. . . . The gloomy conditions of publishing are not rubbed in our faces, and the implications are among the subtexts adroitly not emphasized. There is a nostalgia for times when the Word really did seem haunted and holy." *Los Angeles Times Book Review* contributor Art Seidenbaum concludes: "Anyone unfortunate enough to earn or learn a living in the book business will relish the back-biting behind the back-slapping in this artful novel about the wiles of writers, editors, publishers and hangers-on. Every character, as a matter of fiction, is a hanger-on here, trying to survive over somebody else's live body."

Sheed began his career as a critic writing reviews for popular periodicals, and even now he prefers a more colloquial and less academic style for his criticism—and a popular rather than academic forum. "The ideal critic, after all, is not an Aristotle or Solon or Lionel Trilling, stuffing laws down the artists' and readers' throats," writes Mitchell S. Ross in the *Chicago Tribune Book World,* "he is a stimulator, even an agitator, whose first responsibility is to rouse his readers and irritate the cogitative cells, a task at which Sheed succeeds brilliantly. . . . His is the sort of critic who makes the ordinary labels of reviewers seem trivial—which is to say, the only kind of critic who really counts. . . . If this is not criticism, then nothing being written today is worthy of that great classification." Sheed's essays and reviews have appeared in such disparate places as *Sports Illustrated, Life, Esquire,* and the *New York Times Book Review.* The best of them are collected in two works, *The Morning After: Selected Essays and Reviews* and *The Good Word and Other Words.* Morris Freedman describes Sheed's criticism in the *New Republic:* "Mr. Sheed writes to order, mostly pithy essays on movies, plays or books, in the pages of [magazines]. The formal demands of this occasional writing, like those of the heroic couplet itself, force a concentration on the epigram, the compact summation, the striking generalization. . . . To this highly professional skill Sheed fortunately brings the restraint of common sense, balance and, most importantly, a sense of responsibility." George Stade puts it another way in the *New York Times Book Review.* "The bright, quick sentences flash through the reader's head, depositing pictures and patterns that only fade behind the rush of new ones, the sequence and sum by no means altogether without subtlety," Stade comments. ". . .Sheed is not the kind of bullying guide who in a fit of naive vanity wants to put the skeptical tourist in his place. There are no significant pauses before dark solemnities or pointed gestures toward an ineffable murk."

Sheed's fiction is widely respected, but his criticism has made his national name. According to Thomas Edwards in the *New York Times Book Review,* Sheed's work "is much in demand at the quality and slick publications alike, and one sees how his shameless lack of sham would tickle the 'inside' world of writers, editors, publishers and professional reviewers, where the pretense that the game of literature is deadly serious, somehow less political, commercial and self-advancing than the other games in town, must get positively suffocating." *Time* commentator John Skow claims that Sheed is not a critic but a reviewer, "and in his weight class, one of the best in America. He has the good taste to know that glibness is slightly shabby. . . . Sheed's opinions seem right most of the time, but not so invariably right as to be insufferable. Too much rightness shuts off debate and stifles the thought process. Sheed provides a good mixture of wisdom and nonsense." In a *New Republic* assessment, Ross concludes that Sheed's works of criticism "stand beside the works of the academics like . . . fresh and crusty loaves beside stacks of Wonder Bread."

In recent years Sheed has added full-length biographies to his list of publications. Both *Clare Boothe Luce* and *Frank and Maisie: A Memoir with Parents* are intimate accounts of their subjects, less scholarly than personal. In a *Chicago Tribune Book World* review of *Clare Boothe Luce,* Ronald Steel finds the work "a brilliantly written pastiche," adding: "Sheed is a masterly prose stylist, as addictive as chocolates, and as biting at one-liners as the lady herself. . . . Although he doesn't unveil what makes Clare tick, he does make her human. And in doing so he shows one way that an intelligent and ambitious woman made it in America in the days before affirmative action." Likewise, *New York Times* contributor John Gross notes that in *Frank and Maisie* Sheed "has not attempted to provide a full-scale portrait of his parents. Instead, he has written an account of what it was like to grow up as one of their two children. . . . But the book is Frank and Maisie's, beyond a doubt, and a very eloquent memorial to them it is—both entertaining and deeply felt, full of wry insights into the contradictions of human nature, a demonstration (if one is needed) that love and what in the end can only be called filial piety are no barrier to the incisiveness that readers of Mr. Sheed's novels and journalism have come to expect of him."

Transatlantic novelist, respected critic, and gentle biographer, Sheed has enjoyed a lengthy stay in the literary sphere. *Nation* essayist Vivian Mercier contends that Sheed has "made it," not with a bestseller, "but as a critic and novelist and something more than either—a man of letters." In his *Chicago Tribune Book World* piece, Ross writes: "The man is a natural critic who happens to write novels. A natural critic? Yes, and much more; indeed, a naturalness beautifully embellished. This is a critic with a thousand phrases on his sleeve, a playful adventurer among books. This is a man who does not need the framework of a story in order to impose his imagination upon us; Sheed is the rare critic who can stamp his personality on every page he writes. Why does the man bother with novel-writing when his talent for criticism is so great? . . . He can do the job with some skill . . . and so he continues doing it." Stade comments that in Sheed's various works, "the prose, the pace, the humor are pleasures neither old-fashioned nor new-fangled, but simply unique. . . . So is a certain quality of moral intelligence, one graced by an unflappable and chastened sanity, a charity precise and unsentimental." In the *Washington Post Book World,* Webster Schott concludes of Sheed: "He is one of our brightest reflectors. Let's urge him on in our mutual education."

Sheed is quoted on his occupation in the *Dictionary of Literary Biography.* "Circumstances have obliged me to do a good deal of reviewing (the last refuge of the light essayist): books, plays, etc.," he said. "I find this work painful, but it serves a couple of selfish purposes. It enables me to work out various aesthetic ideas, while unloading my little burden of didacticism in a safe place; and it gives me a certain thin-lipped benignity towards my own critics, when they turn the cannon round and aim it in my direction." Sheed told the *New York Times Book Review* that, as an experience, "fiction is more rewarding, even if it dumps you out of a flying door into a mudbath. But, whatever the word on that, one's nonfiction gains tremendously from having known the pressure, just as a political commentator would gain from running for office. Whatever you can still do when you can't be fastidious is your essence."

AVOCATIONAL INTERESTS: Baseball, softball, boxing.

BIOGRAPHICAL/CRITICAL SOURCES:

BOOKS

Contemporary Literary Criticism, Gale, Volume 2, 1973, Volume 4, 1975, Volume 10, 1979.
Dictionary of Literary Biography, Volume 6: *American Novelists since World War II, Second Series,* Gale, 1980.

Sheed, Wilfrid, *Frank and Maisie: A Memoir with Parents,* Simon & Schuster, 1985.

PERIODICALS

America, November 9, 1963.
Atlantic, May, 1973, March, 1978.
Chicago Tribune Book World, December 17, 1978, February 7, 1982.
Commonweal, January 24, 1969, May 8, 1970, June 24, 1977, April 14, 1978.
Critic, summer, 1978, December, 1978.
Horizon, Autumn, 1971.
International Fiction Review, January, 1974.
Kenyon Review, Volume 31, number 2, 1969.
Life, April 18, 1969.
Los Angeles Times, October 30, 1985.
Los Angeles Times Book Review, July 19, 1987, August 28, 1988.
Nation, December 20, 1971, February 20, 1982.
National Observer, October 28, 1968, May 11, 1970.
National Review, February 9, 1971.
New Leader, November 4, 1968.
New Republic, May 23, 1970, October 2, 1971, May 5, 1973, January 21, 1978.
New Statesman, January 18, 1974.
Newsweek, October 4, 1971, January 16, 1978, February 22, 1982, August 24, 1987.
New Yorker, November 30, 1968, March 13, 1978, December 9, 1985.
New York Review of Books, May 17, 1973, October 30, 1975, January 26, 1978, November 8, 1979, April 1, 1982, May 8, 1986.
New York Times, August 23, 1965, September 19, 1968, May 7, 1970, April 11, 1973, September 15, 1975, January 13, 1978, December 21, 1978, February 10, 1982, October 15, 1985, July 30, 1987.
New York Times Book Review, August 22, 1965, September 8, 1968, May 3, 1970, October 10, 1971, April 8, 1973, September 21, 1975, January 15, 1978, January 21, 1979, February 21, 1982, November 10, 1985, August 2, 1987.
People, August 31, 1987.
Publishers Weekly, February 6, 1978.
Saturday Review, September 4, 1965, September 14, 1968, June 6, 1970, January 20, 1979, July, 1982.
Spectator, January 26, 1974.
Sports Illustrated, November 11, 1968.
Time, September 20, 1968, January 6, 1975, September 8, 1975, January 27, 1978, December 25, 1978, February 22, 1982, November 18, 1985, August 3, 1987.
Times (London), August 5, 1982.
Times Literary Supplement, November 4, 1965, February 9, 1967, August 14, 1969, July 31, 1970, January 18, 1974, November 23, 1979, October 1, 1982, May 30, 1986.
Tribune Books (Chicago), July 19, 1987.
Village Voice, August 26, 1971, January 23, 1978.
Washington Post Book World, January 7, 1968, September 22, 1968, April 29, 1973, February 5, 1978, December 24, 1978, February 14, 1982, January 5, 1986, August 19, 1987, October 16, 1988.
Wisconsin Studies in Contemporary Literature, summer, 1967.*

—*Sketch by Anne Janette Johnson*

SHIPMAN, David 1932-

PERSONAL: Born November 4, 1932, in Norwich, England; son of Alfred Herbert and Edith (Deeks) Shipman. *Education:* Attended Merton College, Oxford, 1954-55.

ADDRESSES: Agent—Frances Kelly Agency, 111 Clifton Rd., Kingston-upon-Thames, Surrey KT2 6PL, England.

CAREER: Victor Gollancz Ltd., and Methuen & Co Ltd., London, England, assistant sales manager, 1955-61; representative in Europe for U.S. publisher, Curtis Circulation, 1961-63; freelance European representative for several British publishers, 1964-66; writer and film historian, 1968—. Guest lecturer on cinema, University of East Anglia, 1972.

WRITINGS:

The Great Movie Stars: The Golden Years, Crown, 1970, revised edition, Hill & Wang, 1981.
The Great Movie Stars: The International Years, Angus & Robertson, 1972, St. Martin's, 1973, revised edition, Hill & Wang, 1981.
Brando, Doubleday, 1974, revised and enlarged edition published as *Marlon Brando,* Sphere Books, 1989.
The Story of Cinema, Volume I: *From the Beginnings to "Gone with the Wind,"* Hodder & Stoughton, 1982, St. Martin's, 1984, Volume II: *From "Citizen Kane" to the Present Day,* St. Martin's, 1984.
The Good Film and Video Guide, Hodder & Stoughton/ Consumers' Association, 1984, revised edition, 1986.
A Pictorial History of Science Fiction Films, Hamlyn, 1985.
Caught in the Act: Sex and Eroticism in the Movies, Elm Tree Books, 1985.
Movietalk: Who Said What about Whom in the Movies, Bloomsbury, 1988.

Associate editor, *Films and Filming,* 1983.

WORK IN PROGRESS: Revisions of *The Great Movie Stars* and *The Story of Cinema.*

* * *

SHULMAN, Frank Joseph 1943-

PERSONAL: Born September 20, 1943, in Boston, Mass.; son of Murray (a civil engineer) and Edna (Altman) Shulman; married Anna See-Ping Leon, 1985. *Education:* Harvard University, A.B. (magna cum laude), 1964; additional study at Hebrew University of Jerusalem, 1964-65, and Inter-University Center for Japanese Language Studies, 1967-68; University of Michigan, M.A. (East Asian studies), 1968, M.A. (library science), 1969, doctoral candidate, 1974—.

ADDRESSES: Home—9225 Limestone Place, College Park, Md. 20740-3943. *Office*—c/o East Asia Collection, McKeldin Library, University of Maryland, College Park, Md. 20742-7011.

CAREER: University of Michigan, Center for Japanese Studies, Ann Arbor, bibliographer and librarian, 1970-75; University of Maryland, McKeldin Library, College Park, curator of East Asia Collection and Gordon W. Prange Collection, 1976—. Library consultant to the Groupe d'Etudes et de Documentation sur le Japon Contemporain, Ecole Pratique des Hautes Etudes, 1974; consultant to Woodrow Wilson International Center for Scholars at the Smithsonian Institution.

MEMBER: International Association of Orientalist Librarians, Association for Asian Studies (member of executive group of committee on East Asian libraries, 1982-83; member of board of directors, 1983-86; member of executive committee, 1985-86; chairman of council of conferences, 1985-86), Independent Scholars of Asia, European Association for Japanese Studies, Association for the Bibliography of History, Middle East Librarians' Association, Mid-Atlantic Region/Association for Asian Studies (vice-president, 1980-81), Asiatic Society of Japan, Japan-American Society of Washington, D.C., Phi Kappa Phi, Beta Phi Mu.

AWARDS, HONORS: Awarded grants for bibliographical work by Memorial Foundation for Jewish Culture, 1973 and 1984, Committee on Research Materials on Southeast Asia of the Association for Asian Studies, 1974, Japan-United States Friendship Commission, 1978, Henry Luce Foundation, 1980 and 1983, Japan Foundation, 1982, and Joseph Meyerhoff Fund, Inc., 1983.

WRITINGS:

EDITOR AND COMPILER

Japan and Korea: An Annotated Bibliography of Doctoral Dissertations in Western Languages, 1877-1969, American Library Association, 1970.

Doctoral Dissertations on South Asia, 1966-1970: An Annotated Bibliography Covering North America, Europe and Australia, Center for South and Southeast Asian Studies, University of Michigan, 1971.

(With Leonard H. D. Gordon) *Doctoral Dissertations on China: A Bibliography of Studies in Western Languages, 1945-1970,* University of Washington Press, 1972.

American and British Doctoral Dissertations on Israel and Palestine in Modern Times, Xerox University Microfilms, 1973.

(With Robert Ward) *Allied Occupation of Japan, 1945-1970: An Annotated Bibliography of Western-Language Materials,* American Library Association, 1974.

(With Teresa S. Yang and Thomas C. Kuo) *East Asian Resources in American Libraries,* Paragon, 1977.

Doctoral Dissertations on China, 1971-1975: A Bibliography of Studies in Western Languages, University of Washington Press, 1978.

(With Archie R. Crouch) *Mid-Atlantic Directory to Resources for Asian Studies,* Mid-Atlantic Region, Association for Asian Studies, 1980.

Doctoral Dissertations on Japan and on Korea, 1969-1979: An Annotated Bibliography of Studies in Western Languages, University of Washington Press, 1982.

Burma: An Annotated Bibliographical Guide to International Doctoral Dissertation Research, 1898-1985, University Press of America, 1986.

Japan (World Bibliographical Series, Volume 103), Clio Press, 1990.

CONTRIBUTOR

Lawrence H. Redford, editor, *Occupation of Japan: Impact of Legal Reform,* MacArthur Memorial, 1978.

John A. Lent, editor, *Malaysian Studies: Present Knowledge and Research Trends,* Center for Southeast Asian Studies, Northern Illinois University Press, 1979.

Redford, editor, *Occupation of Japan: Economic Policy and Reform,* MacArthur Memorial, 1980.

(With Hong-nack Kim) *Papers of the First International Conference on Korean Studies, 1979,* Academy of Korean Studies, 1980.

Ronald A. Morse, editor, *Korean Studies in America: Options for the Future,* University Press of America, 1983.

Morse, editor, *Southeast Asian Studies: Options for the Future,* University Press of America, 1984.

Morse, editor, *Japan and the Middle East in Alliance Politics,* University Press of America, 1986.

Kenneth W. Berger, editor, *Asian Studies in the Southeast: A Twenty-five Year Retrospect,* Southeast Conference, Association for Asian Studies, 1987.

OTHER

Advisory editor for reference book series on Asian studies for G. K. Hall & Co., 1977-83. Contributor of numerous articles and book reviews to professional journals, including *Journal of Asian Studies, Library Quarterly, Journal of Korean Affairs, Journal of the Association of Teachers of Japanese,* and many others. Editor for doctoral dissertations, *Newsletter of the Association for Asian Studies,* 1969-71, and *Asian Studies Professional Review,* 1971-74; assistant editor, *Bibliography of Asian Studies* of the Association for Asian Studies, 1970-71; editor, *Doctoral Dissertations on Asia: An Annotated Bibliographical Journal of Current International Research,* 1975—.

WORK IN PROGRESS: Doctoral Dissertations on China and on Inner Asia, 1976-1985; Doctoral Dissertations in Jewish Studies and Related Subjects, 1945-1990: A Bibliography on Jewish History and Civilization, the Old Testament, the Ancient Near East, the State of Israel, and Contemporary Jewish Affairs, for Greenwood Press; Doctoral Dissertations on Southeast Asia, 1968-1990: An Annotated Bibliography of International Research, for University of Michigan; The Allied Occupation of Japan: A Bibliography of Western-Language Publications from the Years 1970-1990, for Center for Japanese Studies, University of Michigan; An Annotated Guide to Academic Newsletters, Association Bulletins, and Outreach News-Notes on Asia.

SIDELIGHTS: Frank Joseph Shulman has long been interested in the subject of Japan's postwar economic and political relations with the Middle East and in the history of the Jews and Jewish communities in East, Southeast, and South Asia. He has a very extensive personal library collection on Asia, and is the founder and curator of the Asian Studies Newsletter Archives, a public service-oriented but privately maintained archival collection of over one thousand academic and cultural newsletters and association bulletins dealing with Asian affairs and Asian studies.

*   *   *

SILVER, Gerald A(lbert) 1932-

PERSONAL: Born June 5, 1932, in Omaha, Neb.; son of Harry and Rose (Albert) Silver; children: Steven, Barbara, Richard, Larry. *Education:* Los Angeles City College, A.A., 1953; Los Angeles State College of Applied Arts and Sciences (now California State University, Los Angeles), B.A., 1955; California State College at Los Angeles (now California State University at Los Angeles), M.A., 1965; University of California, Los Angeles, Ed.D., 1969.

ADDRESSES: Home—4944 Gaviota Ave., Encino, Calif. *Office*—Editorial Enterprises, 4944 Gaviota Ave., Encino, Calif. 91436.

CAREER: Silver Star Printing Co., Los Angeles, Calif., owner, 1950-61; Los Angeles City College, Los Angeles, 1961—, began as assistant professor, currently professor of business adminstration; writer and photographer, 1962—. Instructor of technical writing seminars in Los Angeles. Has appeared on television and has had speaking engagements at professional meetings and at various educational institutions.

WRITINGS:

Printing Estimating, American Technical Society, 1970.

Modern Graphic Arts Paste-up, American Technical Society, 1973, 2nd edition, Van Nostrand 1983.

Simplified BASIC Programming, McGraw, 1974, 3rd edition, 1988.

Computer Algorithms and Flowcharting, McGraw, 1975.

Professional Printing Estimating, North American Publishing, 1975, 2nd edition, 1984.

Simplified ANSI Fortran IV Programming, Harcourt, 1976.

Introduction to Systems Analysis, Prentice-Hall, 1976.

Data Processing for Business, Harcourt, 1977, 3rd edition, 1981.

Small Computers Systems for Business, McGraw, 1978.

Introduction to Modern Business, McGraw, 1978.

Social Impact of Computers, Harcourt, 1979.

A Moneymaking Guide to Printing Estimating, Printing Industries Association, 1979.

Graphic Layout and Design, Van Nostrand, 1981.

Introduction to Management, West Publishing, 1981.

(With Myrna Silver) *Weekend Fathers,* Stratford Press, 1981.

Introduction to Printing Estimating, Kendall/Hunt, 1982.

A Moneymaking Guide to Printing Estimating, Printing Industries Association, 1984.

Second Loves, Praeger, 1985.

Learning Computer Programming, Boyd & Fraser, 1986.

Computer-Aided Estimating, Graphic Arts Technical Foundation, 1986.

Computers and Information Processing, Harper, 1986.

Data Communications for Business, Boyd & Fraser, 1987.

Systems Analysis and Design, Addison Wesley, 1989.

Introduction to Desktop Publishing, W. C. Brown, 1989.

Contributor of section on computers to *Compton's Encyclopedia,* 1983. Contributor to professional journals.

AVOCATIONAL INTERESTS: Electronics, cinematography, foreign travel.

*   *   *

SIMPSON, Alan 1912-

PERSONAL: Born July 23, 1912, in Gateshead, Durham, England; became U.S. citizen, 1954; son of George Hardwick and Isabella (Graham) Simpson; married Mary McQueen McEldowney, 1938; children: Barbara Simpson Flynn Waller, Carol Simpson Stern, Rupert. *Education:* Worcester College, Oxford, B.A. (first class honors), 1933; Merton College, Oxford, M.A., 1935, D.Phil., 1940.

ADDRESSES: Home—Yellow Gate Farm, Little Compton, R.I. 02837-0908.

CAREER: University of St. Andrews, Fife, Scotland, senior lecturer in modern British history and American history, 1938-46; University College Law School, Dundee, Scotland, lecturer in constitutional law, 1938-46; University of Chicago, Chicago, Ill., assistant professor, 1946-54, associate professor of history, 1954-59, Thomas E. Donnelley Professor of History and dean of the College, 1959-64; Vassar College, Poughkeepsie, N.Y., president and professor of history, 1964-77. Member of board of trustees, Colonial Williamsburg, 1968-82. *Military service:* British Army, Royal Artillery, 1939-45; became major.

MEMBER: American Historical Association, American Antiquarian Society, Century Club (New York).

AWARDS, HONORS: University of Chicago Quantrell Award for excellence in teaching; Book Prize, Institute of Early American History and Culture; LL.D., Colgate University and Knox College; Litt.D., National College of Education, Rhode Island College, and University of Rochester.

WRITINGS:

(Co-editor and author of introduction) *The People Shall Judge: Readings in the Formation of American Policy,* two volumes, University of Chicago Press, 1949.

Puritanism in Old and New England, University of Chicago Press, 1955.

The Wealth of the Gentry, 1540-1600: East Anglian Studies, University of Chicago Press, 1961, reprinted, 1976.

(Editor with wife, Mary Simpson) Benjamin Church, *Diary of King Philip's War,* Pequot Press, 1975.

Helen Lockwood's College Years, 1908-1912, Vassar College, 1977.

(Editor and author of introduction with M. Simpson) *I Too Am Here: Letters of Jane Welsh Carlyle,* Cambridge University Press, 1977.

The Mysteries of the "Frenchman's Map" of Williamsburg, Virginia, Colonial Williamsburg, 1984.

(With M. Simpson and Ralph Connor) *Jean Webster, Storyteller,* Tymor Associates, 1984.

Also author of monographs. Contributor of articles on colonial history to *Colonial Williamsburg Journal.*

WORK IN PROGRESS: Studies in the rise of the Carter and Burwell families of Virginia.

*   *   *

SIMPSON, Dick 1940-

PERSONAL: Born November 8, 1940, in Houston, Tex.; son of Warren Weldon and Ola Ela (Felts) Simpson; married second wife, Sarajane Avidon, March 23, 1987. *Education:* Attended Agricultural and Mechanical College of Texas (now Texas A&M University), 1959-60; University of Texas, B.A., 1963; Indiana University, M.A., 1964, Ph.D., 1968; McCormick Theological Seminary, M.Div., 1984. *Politics:* Independent.

ADDRESSES: Home—2501 West Lunt, Chicago, Ill. 60645. *Office*—Department of Political Science, University of Illinois at Chicago Circle, Box 4348, Chicago, Ill. 60680.

CAREER: University of Illinois at Chicago Circle, assistant professor, 1967-72, associate professor of political science, 1972—. Ordained minister of United Church of Christ, 1984. Illinois state campaign manager for Eugene McCarthy, 1968; alderman of the 44th Ward, City of Chicago, 1971-79; transition team co-chair for Mayor Harold Washington, 1983. Founder and executive director, Independent Precinct Organization; executive director, Clergy and Laity Concerned, 1987-89. Humanities Institute fellow, University of Illinois, 1985-86. Producer of films, "By the People," 1970, and "Give Us This Day," 1972.

MEMBER: American Political Science Association, National Association of Neighborhoods (member of national board), Lakeview Citizens Council, Campaign Against Pollution (member of steering committee).

AWARDS, HONORS: Foreign Area fellowship for research in Africa, 1966-67; Silver Circle Award for excellence in teaching, University of Illinois, 1971.

WRITINGS:

Who Rules?: An Introduction to the Study of Politics, Swallow Press, 1970.

(Contributor) Victor Olorunsola, editor, *The Politics of Cultural Sub-Nationalism in Africa,* Doubleday, 1972.

Winning Elections: A Handbook in Participatory Politics, Swallow Press, 1972, revised edition, 1982.

Chicago's Future in a Time of Change, Stipes, 1976, revised edition, 1988.

(With George Beam) *Strategies for Change: How to Make the American Political Dream Work,* Swallow Press, 1976.

(With Beam) *Political Action: The Key to Understanding Politics,* Swallow Press, 1984.

Chicago City Council Reform, City Club of Chicago, 1989.

The Politics of Compassion and Transformation, Swallow Press, 1989.

SIDELIGHTS: Dick Simpson told *CA:* "I believe that study, teaching, and political action should inform each other, that reflection should govern both the practice of politics and the study of politics. After the fashion of Plato's philosopher-kings, I have thought that knowledge and ruling are best developed together. Thus, I merge three full-time jobs into a single career—I am a full-time student of politics, a full-time professor, and a full-time politician. Each experience adds depth and substance to the other. My writing is focused on the real world of politics but as seen in the perspective of political theory. In recent years I have gone further to attempt to combine the study of politics and religion. This is reflected in my latest book, *The Politics of Compassion and Transformation.*"

*　　*　　*

SIMPSON, Dorothy 1933-

PERSONAL: Born June 20, 1933, in Blaenavon, Monmouthshire, Wales; daughter of Robert Wilfrid (a civil servant) and Gladys (a teacher of elocution; maiden name, Jones) Preece; married Keith Taylor Simpson (a barrister), July 22, 1961; children: Mark Taylor, Ian Robert, Emma Morag. *Education:* University of Bristol, B.A. (with honors), 1954, teaching diploma, 1955. *Religion:* Christian.

ADDRESSES: Home—Leeds, England. *Agent*— Anne McDermid, Curtis Brown Ltd., 162-168 Regent St., London W1R 5TA, England.

CAREER: Teacher of English and French at Dartford Grammar School for Girls, Dartford, England, 1955-59, and Erith Grammar School, Erith, England, 1959-61; Senacre School, Maidstone, Kent, England teacher of English, 1961-62; marriage guidance counsellor, 1969-82; writer, 1975—.

MEMBER: Crime Writers Association, Society of Authors, Mystery Writers of America.

AWARDS, HONORS: Silver Dagger Award from Crime Writers Association of Great Britain, 1985, for *Last Seen Alive.*

WRITINGS:

MYSTERY NOVELS

Harbingers of Fear (suspense novel), Macdonald & Janes, 1977.

"INSPECTOR THANET" SERIES; PUBLISHED BY SCRIBNER

The Night She Died, 1981.
Six Feet Under, 1982.
Puppet for a Corpse, 1983.
Close Her Eyes, 1984.
Last Seen Alive, 1985.
Dead on Arrival, 1986.
Element of Doubt, 1987.
Suspicious Death, 1988.

Dead by Morning, 1989.

OTHER

Contributor to *Ellery Queen's Mystery Magazine* and *Alfred Hitchcock's Mystery Magazine.*

WORK IN PROGRESS: More books in the "Inspector Thanet" series; additional crime stories.

SIDELIGHTS: It was mid-life for Dorothy Simpson before she wrote her first book, *Harbingers of Fear.* Accepted by the first publisher it was submitted to, this suspense novel was generally well-received by British readers. Although her husband sensed her literary ability and for years urged her to try her hand at writing, Simpson felt uninspired to toil away on a book. However, as she explained to *CA:* "I began to write after a long illness in 1975, which gave me plenty of time for reflection and reassessment. I was fortunate in that my first book found an agent immediately, and a publisher and serialization in a major women's magazine."

Following this initial success, Simpson wrote three books that were all rejected by various publishers. As a result, Simpson took a serious look at her talents, assessed her strengths, and decided to devote her next efforts to creating an intriguing murder mystery staged around an engaging sleuth. After months of molding and planning, Inspector Luke Thanet and his loyal assistant, Sergeant Lineham were created to solve the murder in *The Night She Died.*

Described as "an absolutely first rate mystery" by *Publishers Weekly, The Night She Died* was greeted enthusiastically by reviewers and readers not only in Simpson's homeland of England but in the United States as well. In a *Washington Post Book World* review of *The Night She Died* Jean M. White states that "Simpson neatly interweaves past and present with deft double-plotting. Her characters take on real-life dimension, notably Inspector Thanet, a policeman with a bad back, an interesting wife, and a compassionate curiosity about human beings. This is a first-rate job from a writer with subtlety and an unobtrusive literate style." Since *The Night She Died,* Simpson has added eight more books to her "Inspector Thanet" series and has built a following of loyal readers who eagerly await each new book.

Much of the reason for her success can be attributed to the popularity of Inspector Thanet himself. Simpson portrays Thanet as an average British policeman. Although he seems blessed with great detective skills, he still is very human—besieged with the problems of everyday life, such as experiencing and coping with a chronic bad back, the joys and tribulations of fatherhood, and the efforts needed to maintain a good marriage.

"Detective Inspector Luke Thanet [is] a man of gentle mien, he is inclined to use psychology and tact, rather than showboat heroics, when pursuing his murder inquiries," comments a critic for the *New York Times Book Review.* And Douglas Hill remarks in Toronto's *Globe and Mail:* "Thanet comes across as gentle, human, civilized; his approach to [a] particular crime [and] specific people, leads to a rewarding psychological synthesis. Just don't read Simpson after a dose of the neo-Hammett, shoot-'em-up, down-and-dirty school of detective writing. Then you may be disappointed with Luke Thanet and his quiet ways. That would be a pity."

Reviewers have frequently compared Simpson's mystery novels with those of fellow countrywomen Agatha Christie and Margery Allingham. Like these two detective novelists, Simpson presents a meticulously designed mystery with a cast of characters and vividly detailed local settings as developed and integral as her plot. Charles Champlin writes in the *Los Angeles Times Book Review:* "The country village murder cases as Christie and Allingham used to write them, complete with manor house, eccentric vicar and a map for a frontispiece, are an endangered species. But Dorothy Simpson writes them fondly and well."

CA INTERVIEW

CA interviewed Dorothy Simpson by telephone on November 30, 1988, at her home near Maidstone, in Kent, England.

CA: You began to write after an illness in 1975, you've told Contemporary Authors *earlier. Was writing something you'd thought for a long time of trying?*

SIMPSON: No, it wasn't. My husband had been trying to persuade me to write for a very long time. He's a barrister, and he says he thinks I'd make the worst witness in the world because I can never answer a question with a straight "yes" or "no"; I always have to give the background. I have to tell a story. So he'd been trying for years to get me to write. Eventually, after this long period of enforced rest, I decided I ought to try it.

CA: And how did you settle on the mystery genre?

SIMPSON: I'd always been very interested in mysteries, I'd always enjoyed reading them, and that was why I decided to try it.

CA: Your first book, unlike the ones that followed, was not a Luke Thanet story. How did you decide after the first book that you'd like to have a series hero?

SIMPSON: I wrote the first book, a suspense novel called *Harbingers of Fear,* which immediately found a publisher and was serialized in one of the major magazines over here. This was my first attempt and I thought, Fine, wonderful; there's nothing to this writing business. I'm all set for a long and happy career! I then wrote three suspense novels which were not published—as soon as I had finished one, I would start the next. But when I got to the fourth one after *Harbingers of Fear,* I'd almost got to the end, but I wasn't very happy with it, and I thought I really should reassess what I was doing and see if perhaps I should try a new direction. It was at that moment that I saw how this particular book I was working on at the time could be turned into a detective novel. In fact, this book became *The Night She Died,* my first detective novel. And in it, the woman who had been the heroine of this suspense novel I'd been trying to write was actually dead at the beginning—she became the victim. Knowing that, people who have read *The Night She Died* can see why there's almost a book within a book: you take a leap backwards in time. In a way, I was using that suspense novel as a rich source of background material for the detective novel.

But it was interesting in that, because the victim was so important in that story and in fact almost became alive through the interviews that Thanet did with all the people he met and talked to, I set the pattern for my following books, in which the victim really does become the central character of the story even though he or she is dead. People have said that this is something I do. Someone said that Thanet solves the crime by recreating the emotional past of the victim. I think this is true to quite a high degree. In fact, the victims in my books very often are people who have suffered some kind of trauma in childhood and have become damaged personalities through this. It damages their relationships right through their lives, and then at a certain point

the violence rebounds upon them: because of what's happened to them in the past, they themselves meet a violent end. I think I did this purely by chance initially, but it is something I have continued to do since. And it is something that I believe—that trauma in childhood can have a very severe, profound, and long-lasting effect. I suppose this is the way it comes through my work.

CA: One of the nice things about Thanet is that he's part of a family instead of a loner. How did Luke Thanet and his wife and children develop in your mind before you began writing about them?

SIMPSON: When I thought how to turn that particular suspense novel into a detective novel, I said to myself, In case this detective novel is taken and becomes successful, I will deliberately lay the foundations for a series. I really thought quite a lot about this in terms of the background to use, the characters, and so on. And one of the things I obviously had to think about to quite a high degree was the character of my detective, which is extremely important. I wanted him to be somebody I liked and wouldn't get tired of. I didn't want to be like Agatha Christie, who wanted to kill Hercule Poirot off, and like Arthur Conan Doyle, who did indeed kill off Sherlock Holmes at one point and then had to resuscitate him.

I also very deliberately set out to write about a good marriage but with the sort of problems that normal people experience. I knew that I was taking a risk in this because it's so much easier to write arrestingly about bad things, wicked things, evil things—there's so much more drama in them. But I felt that these positive things, good relationships in particular, were extremely important to me, and that if I couldn't write about the things I believed in, I didn't want to write at all. So I decided to give Luke Thanet a good marriage but with the sort of problems that readers of the books would be able to identify with, and this would apply to the children as well. I did work as a marriage guidance counselor for about thirteen years, and I felt that through the training and the study and the actual work itself, I had learnt a lot about marriage and about the relationships between people and their motivations. These were all things I very much wanted to bring in. I particularly wanted to show Thanet and his wife working through these problems that afflict everybody. Also, in the Thanets' marriage, I hoped to deal with something which I think is one of the big changes in marriage in this century, the fact that so many more women work and how this affects their relationships with their husbands. This is very much an ongoing thing, and I don't think anybody has found a solution to it even yet. Fashions come and fashions go, but this was something I tried to deal with in the books, coming to a crisis in *Element of Doubt.*

CA: Yes, when Joan Thanet, in her capacity as a probation officer, finds that one of her young clients is a suspect in a murder case her husband is investigating.

SIMPSON: Yes. I felt I had to bring this particular problem to a resolution in that book. I'd been building up to it for a number of books. But even so, as everybody knows, the problems that afflict ordinary people continue to come and continue to change, and I feel there should still be plenty of material left for future books!

CA: Does your husband ever help with such details as police procedure, or maybe serve as a first reader for the books?

SIMPSON: No, he doesn't. I have taken advice on the police procedure from people in the police. There is a superintendent in the

Kent police who has always helped me with my queries. My husband, of course, will answer any queries I make of him, but his work is rather more technical court work, and I don't get into that in the books. Usually I go to whichever expert I think is necessary at the time. If I need an expert on fire control, for example, as I did at the end of *Close Her Eyes,* then I'll go to the fire department. And I've always found that people are very helpful. I think everybody is pleased to share their expertise with somebody who genuinely wants to talk about it.

CA: All of your characters, not only the Thanets and your central figures, are quite interesting in their own right, and you have a way of capturing them in just a few sentences. Are you by chance a life-long people watcher?

SIMPSON: Never consciously. I know there are writers who say they go out in the streets and study people. I don't consciously observe, but I think I must absorb a lot without even realizing it. The people in my books are not actually based on anybody; they are just vividly imagined, I think. And I think it's extremely important in a detective novel that minor characters should not be just vehicles for the conveyance of information, which is really what they are. When Thanet goes to see somebody, he goes because I want the reader to learn something from that particular witness. It's very easy to let minor characters just be stereotypes. On the wall of my study I used to have a little notice saying, "Remember: every minor character must be interesting." I haven't got it any longer, because I have dinned it into myself so hard. I do try, even with the people that Thanet just meets quite casually, to make them come alive or be idiosyncratic in some way so that they are more real to the reader. I think you've got to believe in these people yourself; you must create a credible world. This is where a book will succeed or fail. If you don't believe in it, I don't think readers will believe in it either.

CA: There's a very fine sense of place in the books. Are your fictional settings usually drawn from actual ones? Do you sketch them out, or anything of that sort?

SIMPSON: I have a very keen visual sense. I'm very fond of landscape, of architecture. The county in which I live, Kent, is the setting for my books. The town of Sturrenden is entirely imaginary. But, because the architecture and the way I write about it is based on Kentish towns and Kentish buildings and Kentish building materials and so on, people in Kent have various ideas of where it is. Some say it's Sevenoaks, some say it's Cranbrook, and one critic of my last book said that Sturrenden was obviously a very thinly disguised Sandwich. Now, I have never been to Sandwich. But this reader recognized in Sturrenden these absolutely archetypal Kentish things. And everybody does this; they all have a different theory.

It's the same with the villages. In *Six Feet Under* I think people in my own village were convinced that it was their village. But, in fact, all my settings are imaginary, except that I do name real places. I occasionally use a real place. For example, the medical center in *Puppet for a Corpse* actually exists. And it really was the first in Kent and it did come into being because of the dedication of this old doctor who, when he died, left the land for it to be built on. I didn't know when I wrote it, but his now elderly widow is still alive, and she was absolutely thrilled that the medical center was immortalized in this book. Generally speaking, though, the whole thing is imagined. The landscape is Kentish, but it is not usually a specific place.

CA: When you begin a book, how much do you know? Do you know the whole plot, essentially?

SIMPSON: It depends what you mean by "begin." If you mean begin writing, yes, absolutely. If you mean when I begin work on a book, at that point all I have is an idea why the murder happened and who committed it. Once I have that germ of an idea, I spend two or three months working on the plot. By now I have worked out a routine for preparing a book. I know that there are approximately twenty decisions that I have to make. I will go through them and work on each of them steadily. One of the most important things I do—the most important thing, really—is build up the victim's circle of relationships. Obviously one has to have a number of suspects, and I have to find credible motives why these various people might want to get rid of the victim. That is very, very important.

Then there are all sorts of other things. For example, I have to decide on the development of the Thanets' life in a particular book, and in Lineham's life as Thanet's sergeant. After I've been working steadily for two or three months through the great list of decisions I have to make, I have amassed an enormous amount of information. It is from that information that I begin working out my first synopsis, and then my second, and then my third. When I get to my final synopsis, I've probably got about ten pages, say half a page per chapter, with a very detailed account of exactly what will happen during the book.

But that doesn't mean to say that I have thought about where it will happen or how it will happen or anything else that will actually flesh the story out. Some people say that if you have it all worked out in advance, it must be terribly boring to write. But it's not, for two reasons. One is that a good detective novel is extremely complex, and if I were trying to work it out as I went along, I would be very worried indeed in case the thing went wrong or things didn't fit. I think it's extremely important to get the right sequence of events. The other thing is that when I've got the final synopsis and I actually sit down to write chapter one, that is the point at which my imagination really comes into play, and where I will start to work very hard using whatever writing skill I possess to make the thing come alive. When I give talks I often say to people, "At this point I could hand out the synopsis for any of my books to twenty people in the audience and say, 'Go away and write a book,' and you'd all come back with a completely different book." So, although I do put an enormous amount of work into preparation, it is in the actual writing of that first draft that I make it individually mine.

CA: So there are sometimes surprises for you too?

SIMPSON: Yes. I usually leave the last seven, eight, or nine chapters flexible, so there will be space for any interesting developments, or perhaps a character will become more developed. When I get to a particular point, I will work those chapters out.

CA: Crime writers, like almost all novelists, are very much publicized and popularized in this country. Is it the same there?

SIMPSON: No, it's not. Take Ruth Rendell, for instance. Since some of her books have been on television, she has become more widely known. But even she, who is an excellent writer, hasn't until relatively recently become what you might almost call a household name. No, over here crime writers are not universally known, and certainly they don't receive anything like the kind of publicity that I understand they do in the United States.

CA: The mystery or crime novel seems to be especially loved here now, and there are obviously good crime writers in both our countries. Do you have any thoughts about why the genre is so popular?

SIMPSON: I think it always has been popular, but I think I was very lucky in that I started writing my detective novels at a time when two things happened. One, there was the emergence of a group of really excellent new crime writers over here, and I think their very quality increased the popularity of the genre. I was lucky in that I was carried along on the same wave. Another thing which I think served to increase the popularity over here was the introduction of Public Lending Right. When the first Public Lending Right sums were paid out, there was great shock in the publishing world when they realized just how popular the crime writers were in the libraries. I think it was this realization that has resulted in more crime writers being published in paperback over here. But I believe it's a genre that will continue to be popular—it's very difficult to say how popular, of course—because a lot of people do find detective novels very satisfying. They present a very firm scale of values with which people feel comfortable; they always have a resolution, which people like; they do present a certain challenge, which, again, people enjoy. From the point of view of the detective story writer, you can't lose. If you manage to outwit the reader, he's always pleasantly surprised and says, "Oh, what a good book! I never would have guessed." And if you don't outwit him, he's very pleased with himself for having beaten you at your own game.

CA: And, as other people have said, the form doesn't limit the writer in subject matter or setting. You can go in any direction with it.

SIMPSON: This is what I realized when I was thinking about the suspense novel that I wasn't satisfied with. I suddenly saw at that point that it is possible within the crime novel to say or do whatever you want. You can find your own individual way, use your own individual voice, and be yourself as a writer in the mystery.

CA: Are there other kinds of writing you'd like to try your hand at?

SIMPSON: I've written some short stories, all of which came out in the United States. Until recently there's been a practically nonexistent market over here, so they always go to *Ellery Queen's Mystery Magazine* or *Alfred Hitchcock's Mystery Magazine.* But even those I don't seem to have had time to do lately; I seem to have been extremely busy with writing Thanet books. I haven't seriously contemplated any other writing because it does seem to take all my available time to write these novels. I certainly could never write a novel about a psychopath, because I wouldn't want to waste my time living with a psychopath inside my head, so to speak, for a year, which is roughly the length of time it takes me to write a book. So we'll just have to see.

CA: So far as you know now, will the Thanets go on indefinitely?

SIMPSON: I hope so. I don't tend to look beyond the book on which I'm working; if I'm working on a Thanet book, then the Thanet series is going on. I think it is pointless really to look ahead. Up until now I've always found that I've finished one and had a break and then I've had an idea for the next one.

BIOGRAPHICAL/CRITICAL SOURCES:

PERIODICALS

Booklist, December 1, 1986.
Globe and Mail (Toronto), March 25, 1989.
Listener, July 2, 1987.
Library Journal, January, 1987.
Los Angeles Times Book Review, January 1, 1989.
New York Times Book Review, January 1, 1989.
Publishers Weekly, May 1, 1981, August 2, 1985, January 29, 1988.

Times, April 25, 1986.
Times Literary Supplement, May 28, 1982, April 5, 1985.
Washington Post Book World, June 21, 1981, November 17, 1985.

—*Interview by Jean W. Ross*

*   *   *

SKINNER, Ainslie
  See GOSLING, Paula

*   *   *

SKLAREW, Myra 1934-

PERSONAL: Born December 18, 1934, in Baltimore, Md.; daughter of Samuel (a biochemist) and Anne (a librarian; maiden name, Wolpe) Weisberg; married Bruce Sklarew (a psychoanalyst), 1955 (divorced, 1976); children: Deborah, Eric. *Education:* Tufts University, B.S., 1956; Johns Hopkins University, M.A., 1970.

ADDRESSES: Office—Corporation of Yaddo, Box 395, Saratoga Springs, New York 12866.

CAREER: Pianist with dance band in Long Island, N.Y., 1949; typist in female admissions of Central Islip State Hospital, lab technician working in chemical assays and cholesterol studies at National Dairy Research Laboratory, bookkeeper for a beer company, all 1952-54; Yale University School of Medicine, New Haven, Conn., research assistant in Department of Neurophysiology, 1955-57; Outdoor Nursery School, Maryland, assistant teacher, 1961-62; president, 1964-65, and adviser to board, 1965-66, of Montgomery County Council of Cooperative Nursery Schools; National Institute of Mental Health and Home Study, Inc., Maryland, tutor with Infant Education Project, 1966-67; American University, Washington, D.C., instructor, 1970-73, professorial lecturer, 1973-76, member of administrative staff, 1976, assistant professor, 1977-81, associate professor of literature, 1981-87, director of master of fine arts degree program in creative writing, 1980-87; Corporation of Yaddo, Saratoga Springs, New York, president, 1987—.

Instructor at College of General Studies of George Washington University, 1970-71. Member of poetry advisory committee of Folger Library; member of literature panel of District of Columbia Commission for the Arts and Humanities. Lecturer or panel member for American Film Institute, Library of Congress, Symposium on Science and Literature, and Folger Seminar. Has given over one hundred poetry readings at colleges, schools, and organizations throughout the United States and in Israel, including Library of Congress, Folger Shakespeare Library, Smithsonian Institution, and Tennessee Poetry Circuit.

MEMBER: Poetry Society of America, Academy of American Poets, Poets and Writers.

AWARDS, HONORS: Di Castagnola Award from Poetry Society of America, 1972, and poetry award from National Jewish Book Council, 1977, both for *From the Backyard of the Diaspora;* Gordon Barber Award, 1980, for poem "Somnambulist"; National Endowment for the Arts fellowship, 1981; four-time winner of PEN Syndicated Fiction Award.

WRITINGS:

POETRY

In the Basket of the Blind, Cherry Valley, 1975.
From the Backyard of the Diaspora, Dryad, 1976, new edition, 1981.

The Science of Goodbyes, University of Georgia Press, 1982.
Blessed Art Thou, No-One, Chowder Chapbooks, 1982.
Travels of the Itinerant Freda Aharon, Water Mark, 1985.
Altamira, Washington Writers, 1987.

OTHER

Like a Field Riddled by Ants (stories), Lost Roads, 1987.

Poetry recorded for "Contemporary Poet's" series of the Library of Congress. Contributor of more than three hundred poems, articles, and reviews to magazines and newspapers, including *Quest, New Republic, Moment, New York Times,* and *Carolina Quarterly.* Founder and member of editorial board, *DELOS,* a translation magazine.

WORK IN PROGRESS: The Refusal, a novel; a book of children's stories; a collection of poems for Jewish holy days.

SIDELIGHTS: Myra Sklarew's *The Science of Goodbyes,* her first major work since the mid-seventies, has met with critical acceptance. Inge Judd commented in the *Library Journal* that the work is "one of the most appealing, strikingly intelligent books" that she had read in a while. Gardner McFall for the *Washington Review* additionally remarked that "though one is first struck by the content of this book and the intellect shaping it, it is important to mention that the poet's clarity and simplicity of style hauntingly support and do justice to her ideas."

Sklarew wrote to *CA* that "we live in a time when the imagination is swamped by the real events of our world. Nietzsche said that we have art so we shall not die of reality. For those of us who live in countries which are oppressed or which are undergoing radical change, the life of the mind is barely given a chance. Yet we do see significant works coming out of South Africa, out of Central Europe, Central America, the Middle East. If one could encompass the current world through one's art . . . what a great work or series of works could be done. One has only to look at the nineteenth century to study the great resistance to change before Darwin and a dozen others brought us into a new realm. While we read of barbarism or witness it, we also read and learn of the remarkable work being done in basic scientific research. More has been discovered in the last fifty or sixty years in science than in the whole history of science. This miracle is happening right under our noses but mostly we are too overwhelmed by political events to pay attention. Again, as artists, the opportunity to explore the world of science is just beginning. In America, such diversity exists among the practitioners of art, that few giants have emerged. Some decry this democratization of the arts; I applaud it. Imagine a whole society tempered and governed by literature, music, paintings and sculpture, by the vision and world view of artists. Imagine America with a paint brush in its hand instead of a gun. I'll live there."

BIOGRAPHICAL/CRITICAL SOURCES:

PERIODICALS

Jerusalem Post, August 21, 1970.
Library Journal, January, 1976, August, 1976, May 1, 1982.
Sewanee Review, summer, 1977.
Small Press Review, May, 1976.
Washington Post Magazine, December 5, 1982.
Washington Review, October-November, 1982.

* * *

SKURZYNSKI, Gloria (Joan) 1930-

PERSONAL: Born July 6, 1930, in Duquesne, Pa.; daughter of Aylmer Kearney and Serena (Decker) Flister; married Edward Joseph Skurzynski (an aerospace engineer), December 1, 1951; children: Serena, Janine, Joan, Alane, Lauren. *Education:* Attended Mt. Mercy College, Pittsburgh, Pa., 1948-50. *Religion:* Roman Catholic.

ADDRESSES: Home—2559 Spring Haven Dr., Salt Lake City, Utah 84109.

CAREER: Author of books for young people. Statistical clerk for U.S. Steel Corp., Pittsburgh, Pa., 1950-52.

AWARDS, HONORS: Golden Kite Award, Society of Children's Book Writers, 1979, for *Bionic Parts for People;* Christopher Award, Horn Book Honor Book, and American Library Association (ALA) Booklist Reviewer's Choice Award, all 1979, for *What Happened in Hamelin;* ALA Booklist Reviewer's Choice Award and ALA Best Books for Young Adults Award, both 1982, both for *Manwolf;* School Library Journal Best Books of 1983 Award, ALA Best Books for Young Adults Award, and Golden Kite Award, all 1983, all for *The Tempering;* Golden Spur Award, Western Writers of America, 1984, for *Trapped in the Slickrock Canyon.*

WRITINGS:

FOR YOUNG PEOPLE

The Magic Pumpkin, Four Winds, 1971.
The Remarkable Journey of Gustavus Bell, Abingdon, 1973.
The Poltergeist of Jason Morey, Dodd, 1975.
In a Bottle with a Cork on Top, Dodd, 1976.
Two Fools and a Faker, Lothrop, 1977.
Bionic Parts for People (Junior Literary Guild selection), Four Winds, 1978.
Martin by Himself, Houghton, 1979.
What Happened in Hamelin, Four Winds, 1979.
Honest Andrew, Harcourt, 1980.
Safeguarding the Land, Harcourt, 1981.
(Contributor) *Three Folktales,* Houghton, 1981.
Manwolf, Clarion Books, 1981.
The Tempering, Clarion Books, 1983.
The Minstrel in the Tower, Random House, 1988.
Dangerous Ground, Bradbury, 1989.
Class Act, Fawcett, 1990.

"THE MOUNTAIN WEST ADVENTURE" SERIES; FOR YOUNG PEOPLE

Lost in the Devil's Desert, Lothrop, 1982.
Trapped in the Slickrock Canyon, Lothrop, 1984.
Caught in the Moving Mountains, Lothrop, 1984.
Swept in the Wave of Terror, Lothrop, 1985.

MEDIA ADAPTATIONS: A film adaptation of *What Happened in Hamelin* was telecast by CBS-TV on "Storybreak" in 1987.

* * *

SMALL, Melvin 1939-

PERSONAL: Born March 14, 1939, in New York. N.Y.; son of Herman Z. and Ann (Ashkenazy) Small; married Sarajane Miller, October 23, 1958; children: Michael, Mark. *Education:* Dartmouth College, B.A., 1960; University of Michigan, M.A., 1961, Ph.D., 1965.

ADDRESSES: Home—1815 Northwood, Royal Oak, Mich. 48073. *Office*—History Department, Wayne State University, Detroit, Mich. 48202.

CAREER: Wayne State University, Detroit, Mich., assistant professor, 1965-70, associate professor, 1970-75, professor of history, 1976—, chairman of department, 1979-86. Visiting assistant professor, University of Michigan, summer, 1968; visiting professor, Aarhus University, Aarhus, Denmark, 1972-74, 1983.

MEMBER: American Historical Association, Organization of American Historians, Society for Historians of American Foreign Relations, Peace Science Society (member of executive council, 1976-79), Council of Peace Research in History (member of council, 1987—).

AWARDS, HONORS: Fellow, Center for Advanced Study in the Behavioral Sciences, 1969-70; American Council of Learned Societies, study fellow, 1969-70, grant, 1983; grant, Lyndon B. Johnson Library, 1982, 1988; grant, Canadian government, 1987.

WRITINGS:

(Editor) *Public Opinion and Historians,* Wayne State University Press, 1970.
(With J. David Singer) *The Wages of War,* Wiley, 1972.
Was War Necessary?, Sage Books, 1980.
(With Singer) *Resort to Arms,* Sage Books, 1982.
(Editor with Singer) *International War,* Dorsey, 1985, revised edition, 1989.
Johnson, Nixon, and the Doves, Rutgers University Press, 1988.

CONTRIBUTOR

James N. Rosenau, editor, *International Politics and Foreign Policy,* Free Press, 1969.
Francis A. Beer, editor, *Alliances,* Holt, 1970.
Julian R. Friedman and others, editors, *Alliances in International Politics,* Allyn & Bacon, 1970.
James Short and Marvin Wolfgang, editors, *Collective Violence,* Aldine, 1972.
William Coplin and Charles Kegley, editors, *Analyzing International Relations,* Praeger, 1975.
Alexander De Conde, editor, *Dictionary of the History of American Foreign Policy,* Scribner, 1978.
Paul Loren, editor, *Diplomacy: New Approaches in History, Theory, and Policy,* Free Press, 1979.
Kegley and Pat McGowan, editors, *Challenges to America,* Sage Books, 1979.
John M. Carroll and George C. Herring, editors, *Modern American Diplomacy,* Scholarly Resources, 1986.
Alan Sabrosky and Charles Gochman, editors, *Prisoners of War,* Heath, 1989.

OTHER

Contributor to journals in his field.

WORK IN PROGRESS: The Media and the Anti-Vietnam War Movement.

*   *   *

SMART, (Roderick) Ninian 1927-

PERSONAL: Born May 6, 1927, in Cambridge, England; son of William Marshall (a professor) and Isabel (Carswell) Smart; married Libushka Clementina Baruffaldi, July 17, 1954; children: Roderick, Luisabel, Caroline, Peregrine. *Education:* Oxford University, B.A., 1951, B. Phil. and M.A., both 1954. *Politics:* Social Democrat. *Religion:* Church of England.

ADDRESSES: Office—Department of Religious Studies, University of California, Santa Barbara, Calif. 93106.

CAREER: University College of Wales, Aberystwyth, assistant lecturer, 1952-55; University of London, King's College, Lon-

don, England, lecturer in the history and philosophy of religion, 1956-61; University of Birmingham, Birmingham, England, H. G. Wood Professor of Theology, 1961-67; University of Lancaster, Lancaster, England, professor of religious studies, 1967-82; University of California, Santa Barbara, professor of religious studies, 1976—, elected J. F. Rowny Professor of Comparative Religions, 1988. Visiting professor at University of Wisconsin, 1965, Princeton University, 1972, Otago University, 1972, University of Queensland, 1980, University of Cape Town, 1982, and Harvard University, 1983. Visiting lecturer in philosophy, Yale University, 1955-56; visiting lecturer, Banaras Hindu University, summer, 1960; Teape Lecturer, University of Delhi, 1964; Gifford Lecturer, University of Edinburgh, 1979-80. Editorial consultant, "The Long Search" series, BBC-TV. *Military service:* British Army, Intelligence Corps, 1945-48; served overseas in Ceylon (now Sri Lanka); became captain.

MEMBER: Aristotelian Society, Athenaeum Club (London).

WRITINGS:

Reasons and Faiths, Routledge & Kegan Paul, 1958.
A Dialogue of Religions, S.C.M. Press, 1960.
(Editor) *Historical Selections in the Philosophy of Religion,* Harper, 1962.
Philosophers and Religious Truth, S.C.M. Press, 1964, 2nd edition, 1969.
Doctrine and Argument in Indian Philosophy, Allen & Unwin, 1964.
The Teacher and Christian Belief, James Clarke, 1966.
Secular Education and the Logic of Religion, Faber, 1968.
The Yogi and the Devotee, Allen & Unwin, 1968.
The Religious Experience of Mankind, Scribner, 1969.
Buddhism and the Death of God, University of Southampton, 1970.
The Philosophy of Religion, Random House, 1970, 2nd revised edition, 1976.
The Concept of Worship, Macmillan, 1972.
The Phenomenon of Religion, Macmillan, 1973.
The Science of Religion and the Sociology of Knowledge: Some Methodological Questions, Princeton University Press, 1974.
Mao, Collins, 1974.
The Long Search, BBC Publications, 1977.
(With Donald Harder) *New Movements in the Study and Teaching of Religious Education,* M. Temple Smith, 1978.
In Search of Christianity, Harper, 1979.
Beyond Ideology: Religion and the Future of Western Civilization, Harper, 1981.
(Editor with Richard Hecht) *Sacred Texts of the World: A Universal Anthology,* Crossroad (New York), 1982.
Worldviews: Crosscultural Explorations in Human Beliefs, Scribner, 1983.
Concept and Empathy, New York University Press, 1986.
Religion and the Western Mind, State University of New York Press, 1986.
The World's Religions, Prentice-Hall, 1989.

Also author of *The Phenomenon of Christianity,* 1979. Contributor to philosophy and theology journals.

WORK IN PROGRESS: A book on religions and ideologies.

SIDELIGHTS: In his book *In Search of Christianity,* Ninian Smart "is intrigued by his quarry's quick-change artistry as found around the world," notes Huston Horn in the *Los Angeles Times Book Review.* "[Smart] observes the heterogeneous array of Christian dogmas and customs and certitudes and hunches with the affectionate and wondering trust one feels at Pasadena's New Year's Rose Parade: Like high priests, the white-suited tournament officials insist there really is a conceptual theme beneath all the floral trappings; it's up to the beholder to believe. . . . Smart says: 'It is not possible to define an essence of Christianity, beyond saying that the faith relates to Christ.' But . . . the face of Christ . . . has seldom for long retained shape and focus. Thus, Smart suspects, it is possible finally to speak only of Christianities, and only of sociologies of the various Christianities. . . . 'The beginning of understanding it,' he concludes, 'is noticing its strangeness.' "

Smart told *CA:* "I have tried in my writings to illuminate problems of philosophy and the history and nature of religion and religions. When I have the ideas I usually write fast. *The Concept of Worship* was written in eight days in Princeton in 1971. But sometimes I do a lot of revision. Though some of the stuff is technical I believe in clarity. I write best in my wife's home in North Italy; the sun seems to warm the brain."

AVOCATIONAL INTERESTS: Cricket, painting.

BIOGRAPHICAL/CRITICAL SOURCES:

PERIODICALS

Christian Century, May 7, 1969.
Commonweal, April 4, 1969.
Los Angeles Times, February 3, 1983.
Los Angeles Times Book Review, September 16, 1979.
New York Times Book Review, February 9, 1969, July 16, 1969.

*   *   *

SMIL, Vaclav 1943-

PERSONAL: Born December 9, 1943, in Plzen, Czechoslovakia; son of Vaclav (a policeman) and Marie (Kaspar) Smil; married Eva Fidler (a physician), December 14, 1967; children: David. *Education:* Carolinum University, R.N.Dr., 1965; Pennsylvania State University, Ph.D., 1972.

ADDRESSES: Office—Department of Geography, University of Manitoba, Winnipeg, Manitoba, Canada R3T 2N2.

CAREER: Environmental affairs and energy consultant, 1966-69; University of Manitoba, Winnipeg, Manitoba, assistant professor, 1972-76, associate professor, 1976-80, professor of geography, 1980—. Consultant to World Bank, Rockefeller Foundation, U.S. Congress, U.S. Agency for International Development, and International Development Research Center. *Military service:* Czechoslovak Army, Military Geographic Institute, 1966-67.

WRITINGS:

Energy and the Environment, University of Manitoba, 1974.
China's Energy, Praeger, 1976.
(Editor with W. E. Knowland) *Energy in the Developing World: The Real Energy Crisis,* Oxford University Press, 1980.
(With Paul Nachman and T. V. Long II) *Energy Analysis in Agriculture,* Westview, 1983.
Biomass Energies: Resources, Links, Constraints, Plenum, 1983.
The Bad Earth Environmental Degradation in China, M. E. Sharpe, 1983.
Carbon-Nitrogen-Sulfur: Human Interference in Grand Biospheric Cycles, Plenum, 1985.
Energy, Food, Environment: Realities, Myths, Options, Oxford University Press, 1987.
Energy in China's Modernization: Advances and Limitations, M. E. Sharpe, 1988.

General Energetics, Wiley, 1990.

Contributor of more than 130 articles to scientific and business journals. Contributing editor of *Current History.*

WORK IN PROGRESS: China's Environment; The Third Planet: An Inquiry into the Earth's Prospects.

SIDELIGHTS: Vaclav Smil told *CA:* "I cannot imagine that I could be pursuing a traditional scientific career devoted to a well-defined, circumscribed topic to be visited in ever-increasing depths for several decades spanning the completion of Ph.D. and retirement as professor emeritus. I am too fascinated by countless links among unruly, complex, fuzzy and changing realities to try to be *the* expert responsible for a particular pigeonhole. My books and papers reflect this deep personal bias: I have written on topics ranging from the greenhouse effect, grand biospheric cycles, and acid rain to the Oriental perception of beauty and Japanese economic efficiency, from Iowa corn farming and the OPEC oil maneuvering to coronary heart disease, Western mortality, and the Chinese food. And yet these disparate items are all linked by my interest in the behavior of complex systems, in following, unravelling and exposing the connectedness of environment and human actions. And most of the time these writings carry the common denominator of energy, whose conversion is the existential foundation of every happening in the universe. So far, *Energy Food Environment* has been the best embodiment of this roaming search.

"But this holistic approach, although it has been making some inroads in the contemporary scientific writings, is running against the strengthening trend of narrow specialization: checking the increasingly impenetrable titles of papers appearing even in general science journals is the easiest way to confirm this perhaps inevitable but certainly unfortunate shift. I intend to continue writing against this current: it is often difficult (as the book publishers ask: 'And what is precisely the intended market?'— and do not like to hear any well-educated person who wants to ponder some complex wholes) but always interesting. My goal will remain to explore the complexities of fundamental civilizational relationships involving energy, food, environment, economy, culture, and public policy—and to offer some commonsensical suggestions about the ways to proceed. I hope that during the next decade I will do as well as in the 1980s."

*   *   *

SMILEY, Jane (Graves) 1949-

PERSONAL: Born September 26, 1949, in Los Angeles, Calif.; daughter of James Laverne (in U.S. Army) and Frances Nuelle (a writer; maiden name, Graves) Smiley; married John Whiston, September 4, 1970 (divorced, November, 1975); married William Silag (an editor), May 1, 1978 (divorced, February, 1986); married Stephen Mortensen (a screenwriter), July 25, 1987; children: (second marriage) Phoebe Graves Silag, Lucy Gallagher Silag. *Education:* Vassar College, B.A., 1971; University of Iowa, M.A., 1975, M.F.A., 1976, Ph.D., 1978. *Politics:* "Skeptical." *Religion:* "Vehement agnostic."

ADDRESSES: Agent—Molly Friedrich, Aaron Priest Agency, 122 East 42nd St., New York, N.Y. 10168. *Office*—Department of English, Iowa State University, Ames, Iowa 50011.

CAREER: Iowa State University, Ames, professor of English, 1981—. Visiting assistant professor at University of Iowa, spring, 1981.

MEMBER: Authors Guild, Authors League of America.

AWARDS, HONORS: Fulbright fellowship, 1976-77; grant from National Endowment for the Arts, 1978, and 1987; Friends of American Writers Prize, 1981, for *At Paradise Gate;* O. Henry Award, 1982, 1985, and 1988; *The Age of Grief* was nominated for the National Book Critics Circle Award, 1987.

WRITINGS:

Barn Blind (novel), Harper, 1980.
At Paradise Gate (novel), Simon & Schuster, 1981.
Duplicate Keys (mystery novel), Knopf, 1984.
The Age of Grief (story collection), Knopf, 1987.
Catskill Crafts: Artisans of the Catskill Mountains (nonfiction), Crown, 1987.
The Greenlanders (novel), Knopf, 1988.
Ordinary Love and Good Will (novellas), Knopf, 1989.

Work represented in anthologies, including *The Pushcart Anthology, Best American Short Stories, 1985,* and *Best of the Eighties.* Contributor of stories to *Redbook, Atlantic, Mademoiselle, Fiction, TriQuarterly,* and *Playgirl.*

SIDELIGHTS: Before publishing *The Greenlanders,* a massive saga of Scandinavian life in the 14th century, Jane Smiley had written three novels and a story collection set in the contemporary world. Whatever the setting, all of her books share a concern for families and their troubles. As Joanne Kaufman remarks in *People,* Smiley "has an unerring, unsettling ability to capture the rhythms of family life gone askew." Smiley also possesses what Jane Yolen in the *Washington Post* calls a "spare, yet lyric" prose. In addition, Yolen finds Smiley to be "a true story-teller."

The theme of family life was present in Smiley's first book, *Barn Blind,* a "pastoral novel of smooth texture and—like the Middle Western summer in which it is set—rich, drowsy pace," as Michael Malone describes it in the *New York Times Book Review.* The story revolves around Kate Karlson, a rancher's wife, and her strained relationships with her four teenaged children. "Smiley handles with skill and understanding the mercurial molasses of adolescence, and the inchoate, cumbersome love that family members feel for one another," according to Malone.

In her next book, *At Paradise Gate,* Smiley looked again at conflict between family members. In this story, elderly Anna Robinson faces the imminent death of her husband, Ike. The couple have had a rough marriage; Ike is an emotionally cold and violent person. When Anna's three daughters arrive to visit their dying father, old sibling rivalries are unearthed, tensions between the parents are renewed, and Anna must confront the failures and triumphs of her life. The story, explains Valerie Miner in the *New York Times Book Review,* "is not so much about Ike's death as about Anna's life—a retrospective on her difficult past and a resolution of her remaining years." *At Paradise Gate,* Susan Wood maintains in the *Washington Post,* "is a sensitive study of what it means to grow old and face death, and of the courage to see clearly what one's life has meant."

Smiley took a different tack with *Duplicate Keys,* a mystery novel set in Manhattan; and yet even in this book her concern for family relations holds firm. Laura Marcus of the *Times Literary Supplement* calls *Duplicate Keys* a story about "marriages, affairs, friendships, growing up and growing older. . . . Smiley demonstrates a considerable sensitivity in the treatment of love and friendship." Lois Gould in the *New York Times Book Review* calls the book only incidently a mystery. "More important and far more compelling," Gould notes, "is the anatomy of friendship, betrayal, the color of dusk on the Upper West Side, the aroma of lilacs in Brooklyn's Botanic Garden, of chocolate tortes

at Zabar's, and the bittersweet smell of near success that is perhaps the most pungent odor in town." Alice Cromie in the *Chicago Tribune Book World* concludes that *Duplicate Keys* is "a sophisticated story of friendships, loves, jealousies, drugs, celebrities and life in the fastest lane in Manhattan."

In 1987 Smiley published *The Age of Grief,* a collection of five stories and a novella, focusing on the joys and sorrows of married life. The title novella, according to Kaufman, "is a haunting view of a marriage from the inside, a tale told by a betrayed husband full of humor and sadness and sound and quiet fury." Michiko Kakutani, writing in the *New York Times,* finds that the novella "opens out, organically, from a comic portrait . . . into a lovely and very sad meditation on the evanescence and durability of love." Speaking of the book as a whole, Roz Kaveney writes in the *Times Literary Supplement* that "one of the major strengths of this quiet and unflashy collection . . . is that in [Smiley's] stories things actually do happen. These events are entirely in keeping with her strong vein of social realism, but they have too a quality of the unpredictable, a quality which gives an uninsistent but pervasive sense of the pain and surprise which lie beneath even the most conventional of lives." Anne Bernays, in her review for the *New York Times Book Review,* concludes: "The stories are fine; the novella is splendid." John Blades in the *Chicago Tribune* finds that Smiley "speaks most confidently and affectingly [about] the delicate mechanics of marriage and family life, the intricate mysteries of love."

In 1988 Smiley published *The Greenlanders,* a "prodigiously detailed, haunting novel," as Howard Norman describes it in the *New York Times Book Review.* A 500-page historical novel set in 14th century Greenland, the novel took Smiley five years to research and write. *The Greenlanders* is "a sprawling, multi-generational, heroic Norse narrative," according to Richard Panek in *Tribune Books.* Based on old Viking sagas and, in particular, on surviving accounts of the colonies the Vikings established in Greenland, the story blends fact and fiction to create a modern novel with a traditional flavor. As Norman explains, the book "employs a 'folkloristic' mode—with its stories overlapping other stories, folded into yet others." The technique, Yolen finds, presents "more than an individual's story. It is the community's story, the land's." By telling the community's story, Smiley contrasts the tragic failure of the Greenland colonies to survive with our contemporary society and its problems. "The result," Panek writes, "is a novel that places contemporary conflicts into the context of the ages."

As in her other novels, Smiley also focuses on family relations in *The Greenlanders,* tracing the effects of a curse on several generations of the Gunnarsson family, well-to-do farmers in Greenland. "Family matters . . .," Yolen states, "become both the focus and the subtext of the novel: the feuds, the curses, the marriages, the passions and the brutal deaths." Norman notes the complexity of the novel, citing the "hundreds of episodes and tributary episodes: the seasonal seal hunts and rituals, the travels over hazardous yet awe-inspiring terrain, the births and deaths. . . . Given the vast template of History, it is impressive how Ms. Smiley is able to telescope certain incidents, unravel personalities in a few paragraphs, [and] delve into a kind of folkloric metaphysics." Norman concludes that Smiley "is a diverse and masterly writer."

CA INTERVIEW

CA interviewed Jane Smiley by telephone on January 20, 1989, at her home in Ames, Iowa.

CA: The Greenlanders, published in 1988, is your fifth book of fiction and quite different from the earlier ones, but the one you've said you knew first you were going to write. How did The Greenlanders *begin in your mind and lead you through all the other writing?*

SMILEY: I knew that I wanted to write that before I wrote the other books because I was in Iceland in 1976 and I thought that would be quite an interesting story to tell. But I also knew already that I was going to be a writer; I had been in the Iowa Writers' Workshop and I had written a number of stories. Also, when I was in Iceland that year, maybe because I was so alone, I came up with other ideas. One was for *Barn Blind* and one was for *At Paradise Gate.* I knew that, of the three ideas, *The Greenlanders* was a much more complicated and demanding one. So I kept it in my mind. I was aware that there was a remote possibility someone else would glom onto it before I wrote my book, but I decided it would be better to start with something I was more familiar with. And so I started with *Barn Blind* and then went on to *At Paradise Gate.* In the summer of eighty I came up with the idea for *Duplicate Keys.* I recognized that I didn't have a whole lot of experience in plotting something and in getting the action going, so I decided to use *Duplicate Keys,* which is a murder mystery with a fairly tightly wrapped plot, to learn how to plot and to have more action.

CA: I wondered if you had taken on Duplicate Keys *as a deliberate challenge in handling the mystery form.*

SMILEY: I was always a lover of mysteries and I always wanted to write one. I knew I would write a mystery, but I didn't think I would be a mystery writer per se. And of all the more tightly plotted genres, mysteries were the one that I was most familiar with. So when I thought about what I would need to do in order to write something with a plot, it seemed natural to write a mystery rather than a romance or something else.

CA: Because all the pieces really have to fit.

SMILEY: That's right. And that was the hard part and the learning part, plugging all the holes in the plot. I really learned a lot from that book, although as I was writing it and after I wrote it I felt a little defensive about it, as if I had compromised my gift.

CA: The Norse sagas were part of your inspiration for The Greenlanders, *you told* Publishers Weekly.

SMILEY: Yes. When I first started doing graduate work in Old Norse, I had already taken Old English and Middle English and I liked medieval literature a lot. But when I started reading Old Norse I felt a real affinity for the literature and the world view that it described, which contains at the same time a kind of bleakness and a comic quality. The classic Viking death scene involves a horrible injury combined with very intense fatalism combined with a kind of dismissal of the injury. In the sagas, they're always holding their guts in with their hands. There's an absurdity to that that's simultaneously entrancing and ridiculous. But if you're in the mood—and the sagas do put you in the mood—it's more entrancing to think that people could be as stoic as that. I'm not at all that way, but I felt an affinity for that worldview. Also, the Norse people were really the only people we know of who imagined the end of the world in a tragic way rather than a comic way. They never imagined salvation; in their mythology they imagined the world being destroyed by the forces of evil. I think that's a worldview that people in our era

must feel an affinity with because it coincides so closely with what we imagine our world could end like, with the destruction of everything and the triumph of the forces of evil. Plus these sagas were prose rather than poetry, so they spoke to me over a long distance and a long period of time. I felt a great affinity with them. I first wanted to write a dissertation on them, but, since I am not basically an academic sort of person, I couldn't bring myself to do that. I guess the sincerest form of love is the kind of reproduction that I finally did.

CA: There's a wealth of everyday detail in The Greenlanders *that makes the stories come alive—bits about food and clothing, and such interesting things as the fact that people usually carried their own spoons with them when they went traveling or visiting. Were such details hard to come by?*

SMILEY: Surprisingly, no, because of my time in Iceland. I know exactly where I got that detail about the spoons. A friend of mine took me out into the countryside in Iceland, and we went down to the south coast where there was a little folk museum. The Icelanders are extremely careful in some ways of their heritage; they all are literate and they read the sagas, and they are careful of preserving old things from the saga times and since. One of the displays was a group of spoon cases, and I remember reading that spoons were very valuable—they were usually carved out of horn and were the only eating utensil that a person would have apart from a knife—and people would carry them with them. My favorite moment with the spoons in *The Greenlanders* was when the prophet's wife reports that Christ had his spoon too when he came to visit them.

CA: The Greenlanders is not only a good book but a very handsome one—the print, jacket, endpapers, and design are especially well done, I think.

SMILEY: Yes, they did quite a good job, I thought.

CA: Your first novel, Barn Blind, *would seem to indicate that you have a great knowledge of horses and riding, and a closeness to the land. Are these things part of your background?*

SMILEY: I was obsessed with horses my whole childhood, and I spent a lot of time riding and I owned a couple of horses. I would say that was my first and maybe ultimately my strongest obsession in some ways. I don't feel it anymore, but I felt it very strongly then. I had pretty much gotten over it by the time I wrote *Barn Blind,* but there was plenty of stuff to draw on.

CA: One of the things you do extremely well in your fiction is depict the dynamics of family life, particularly its tensions. Barn Blind *is a good example, as are your second novel,* At Paradise Gate, *and the title story of* The Age of Grief. *Both the novels also portray marriages in which one spouse seems to love far more than the other. Would you talk about your concern with these themes?*

SMILEY: I guess when I was writing those things, I wasn't so aware of the dynamics. I think most writers put down on paper what they think to be the natural pattern of life, especially earlier in their careers, and then they're sort of surprised to discover how unusual or weird or even unpleasant other people think these patterns are. I feel the tensions of family life are the interesting things to talk about since I accept the closeness of family life as a given. So I talk about the tensions, assuming in my mind that there's this underlying intimacy or commitment to one another. I'm always surprised to discover that people think the characters are cold or somehow abnormal in their affections.

"The Age of Grief" is about a particular time in a particular marriage when the husband suspects that something is going on with the wife, that she's being unfaithful or that she's somehow showing less commitment to the marriage. And yet I think if I had chosen to write about another time in that same marriage, the dynamics might have been different. I don't think that marriage is necessarily a marriage in which the husband loves the wife more than the wife loves the husband. A lot of elderly women loved *At Paradise Gate*. I got an award for it called the Friends of American Writers Prize, and when I went to Chicago to accept the award, most of the people greeting me were elderly women. They adored that book, and my grandmother liked it too. I think there was a kind of realism in the way that marriage was depicted and the way that these people's commitment over the years had survived ups and downs in their feelings that these older women recognized to be valid, and which I assume everybody sees as a facet of marriage—that people's feelings modulate and change and go through different phases, and that gives the relationship and the commitment a lot more complexity as it changes and grows over the years. So I didn't feel that the older couple in *At Paradise Gate* had had an unusually bad marriage or that they should have separated or anything like that. I just felt that the woman in whose consciousness the story is going is an exceptionally realistic and honest person who can recognize both that things weren't perfect and that she also loved her husband very much and that she's going to miss him a great deal when he's gone.

CA: It was interesting how, even while she knew she was going to miss him terribly, she was at the same time planning things she would do alone and enjoy—how she would become her own person in a way she hadn't been before.

SMILEY: Yes. I felt Anna Robinson was enough of a realist that there would be these simultaneous feelings of forward and backward looking. Her husband had been sick a long time, so she knew that this was only the final moment in a long play. She expected his illness to result in death, so it wasn't as if she was unprepared for that.

CA: I thought you did an admirable job with her, and also with Kate Karlson in Barn Blind, *who was not to me a likable character at all but was quite believable.*

SMILEY: Kate Karlson wasn't very likable to me either, but one of the things I wanted to do was portray a character whose likability had nothing to do with whether she was right or wrong, with the truth of her perceptions. I think there is a kind of coldness in her, but one of the things that fascinates me in some of my characters is the question: if a person has real talent or real genius or a real obsession with something and is very good at it, then how does that affect their personality and the people around them, and what are the claims that they can make in the name of their talent against the other people around them, who are maybe more ordinary and don't have any particular talent? What's the moral weight of genius? I think that's an interesting question, and I explore it from time to time.

CA: Reviewing The Age of Grief *in the* Chicago Tribune, *John Blades said that "Smiley . . . often seems to struggle for meanings, for shadings, and it is this uncertainty that gives her work its subtle strength." Does a story sometimes begin for you as a kind of exploration of feelings?*

SMILEY: Yes, that's true. Everything I write, I write in a sort of investigative mode, and to me an interesting character is a per-

son who is trying to figure out what's right and trying to reconcile everything that they are told with what their feelings are. I think my characters are usually trying to come up with some right way to act, or even to think or be, in the face of a lot of confusing input.

CA: You've done fiction of just about every conventional length now. Is there a single form you're more comfortable with, or do you enjoy them all just about equally?

SMILEY: I enjoy them all. Every time I'm writing a particular form, I think, Gosh, this is really nice; I like this form. At the moment I'm writing a short story, which I haven't done in about a year and a half, and I was thinking this morning of how pleasing it was to have it suddenly develop and blossom and be finished. There's a kind of freedom in using that form. But my recent work, and a book that's going to be published in September, is a book of two novellas. And when I'm writing novellas, I think, This form offers you a lot of freedom, and isn't it nice to be able to be a little meditative or to develop one character fully or to have a little space but not so much. I like all the forms, and I like being able to shift back and forth among them.

CA: From your point of view as a former student of a writing workshop and as a teacher, what's your feeling about workshop study for beginning writers?

SMILEY: I have a commitment to the workshop way of teaching, and that's how I teach. I think it's good for students because it does a lot of things for their psyches, for their work, and for their careers. For their psyches, it gives them a sense that they aren't isolated and that there's always somebody they can show their work to; they have an audience and the audience has a face. In some ways writing for a workshop is kind of like writing for publication when you're first starting out. It helps them deliver the work and make it less a part of themselves; they don't have to feel so profoundly umbilically attached to it. I think it's good for their work in that, for most students, it provides a structured way to keep producing and practicing that isn't involved so much in constantly having to drum up the initiative to do it. And I think it's good for their careers in that it's easy to make contacts with somebody. It's a network that is now attached—democratically attached—to an institution that everybody has access to, the institution of higher learning. A person can go into any junior college or any state university and find a way onto the ladder. I like that. I think that's very good. It's no longer *them* in New York and us in Rochester, Minnesota, and they are so far away from us that we can never make contact with them, or we have to go to them.

I think, though, that the individual student's workshop experience can be not so good because it so much depends on the teacher and the type of class that the teacher runs and what the teacher thinks about it. There are many writers who feel that teaching workshops is a distraction and a burden that prevents them from doing their own work, and that they might as well be working in a factory. I think the students of those writers are getting a raw deal. I don't feel that way myself. I find that my teaching has enabled me to abstract ideas and theories and methods from my writing that otherwise wouldn't have become conscious; they would have stayed semiconscious and I would have been just sort of sliding along on them all these years. There are a fair number of times when I come home and I'm looking at a piece of work that I'm having trouble with, and some principle that I've annunciated a thousand times in the classroom comes back to me. Then I realize that I have not followed my own principle and that if I analyze my own story in the way that I analyze my students' stories, or that I ask them to analyze their stories, I can actually use it to make the story better. So, for me, the combination of teaching and writing has involved a melding of theory and practice. For me it's been quite good. And I think that my students have benefited from the fact that I am ready to analyze and contemplate the act of writing and then talk about that to them. There are a lot of writers who are more unconscious than that and more instinctive, and for them it's harder to bring things to the students that the students might be able to use.

I think the institution of the workshop around the country has its good and bad aspects, but I think its major good aspect is helping beginning writers not feel so isolated and giving them some structure, and also in enabling anybody who can get into the classroom to get on the ladder somehow. That's a much more democratic and widespread political effect that I think eventually will rebound to the benefit of American literature.

CA: Some good writers have already come out of writers' workshops.

SMILEY: I think that's true. Mostly when New York editors are clamoring against the workshops and saying that they aren't any good, what they are saying is that they haven't created greatness. But I don't think you can know. I'm on the upper side of the generation of workshop writers, and I don't know that people achieve greatness in their work until they're older than I am. So I don't know that the workshop experiment has had its full run yet. But we'll see.

CA: You're married to a screenwriter, Stephen Mortensen. Is there any chance of a joint effort that would turn some of your books into movies?

SMILEY: There's always a chance, but I don't know. He works on his own ideas, and I don't really feel that my ideas are that adaptable to the screen. I don't feel that they have enough action, and they often rely on peculiarly narrative effects to work. I wouldn't mind writing a screenplay, but whenever I sit down to try and do something in that form, my instincts are so different that it always comes out bad. What you discover is that you're not a good *writer.* You're a good novelist or a good prose writer, but somehow this idea of being a good writer, which you always thought you were since high school, turns out not to be true.

CA: Can you talk about what your readers are likely to get from you after the novellas?

SMILEY: I'm about to start another big novel, another one about life in the country—this one is about a farm in Iowa. I think it'll be another big, bleak, apocalyptic tome, not quite as long as *The Greenlanders* and in a very different form, but as weighty.

CA: Any thoughts about your writing that you'd like to add?

SMILEY: I always feel that my novels have an underlying political purpose. For *The Greenlanders,* I wanted to raise people's consciousnesses about the effect of conflict in a society that is different from ours but actually like ours. But this underlying political idea never comes across. The aesthetic ideas and the interactions of the characters and the movement of the language always overwhelm whatever I originally thought my message was. I guess that's my secret and I'm telling the world now.

CA: The writing turns into such good fiction that it hides your message!

SMILEY: Well, at least such complicated fiction. And maybe that should be my goal. We want fiction to mimic the complexity of life, and I suppose I should be glad when it does. But then I'm sort of appalled when I read that certain writers or publications whose politics I disagree with adore my work; I never know quite what to think about that. But that's OK.

BIOGRAPHICAL/CRITICAL SOURCES:

PERIODICALS

Chicago Tribune, November 6, 1987.
Chicago Tribune Book World, July 8, 1984.
Los Angeles Times Book Review, March 18, 1984, October 18, 1987.
New York Times, August 26, 1987.
New York Times Book Review, August 17, 1980, November 22, 1981, April 29, 1984, September 6, 1987, May 15, 1988.
People, January 18, 1988.
Publishers Weekly, April 1, 1988.
Times (London), February 4, 1988.
Times Literary Supplement, August 24, 1984, March 18, 1988.
Tribune Books (Chicago), April 3, 1988.
Washington Post, October 27, 1981, May 13, 1988.

—*Sketch by Thomas Wiloch*

—*Interview by Jean W. Ross*

*   *   *

SMITH, Brian C(live) 1938-

PERSONAL: Born January 23, 1938, in London, England; son of Cyril (a sales representative) and Hilda (a secretary; maiden name, Padengtion) Smith; married Jean Baselow (a teacher), August, 1960; children: Rebecca, David. *Education:* University of Exeter, B.A., 1959, Ph.D., 1970; McMaster University, M.A., 1963.

ADDRESSES: Home—67 Warminster Rd., Bath BA2 6RU, England. *Office*—School of Humanities and Social Sciences, University of Bath, Claverton Down, Bath BA2 7AY, England.

CAREER: University of Exeter, Exeter, England, assistant lecturer in politics, 1963-65; Ahmadu Bello University, Zaria, Nigeria, lecturer in public administration, 1965-66; University of Exeter, lecturer in politics, 1966-70; Civil Service College, London, England, lecturer in public administration, 1970-72; University of Bath, Bath, England, senior lecturer, 1972-80, reader in public administration, 1980—. Chairman of public administration committee of Joint University Council for Social and Public Administration, 1980-83.

MEMBER: Political Studies Association, Royal Institute of Public Administration.

WRITINGS:

Regionalism in England, Acton Society Trust, 1965.
Field Administration, Routledge & Kegan Paul, 1967.
Advising Ministers, Routledge & Kegan Paul, 1969.
(With Jeffrey Stanyer) *Administering Britain,* Martin Robertson, 1976.
Policy Making in British Government, Martin Robertson, 1976.
(With D. C. Pitt) *Government Departments: An Organisational Perspective,* Routledge & Kegan Paul, 1981.
(Editor with Pitt) *The Computer Revolution in Public Administration,* Harvester Press, 1984.
Decentralisation, Allen & Unwin, 1985.
Bureaucracy and Political Power, Harvester Press, 1987.

Editor, *Public Administration Bulletin,* 1970-76, and *Public Administration and Development,* 1984—.

WORK IN PROGRESS: Research on inter-governmental relations, administrative theory, and development administration.

SIDELIGHTS: Brian Smith told *CA:* "Tutors and colleagues have been more important to my career than individual writers. To my tutor at Exeter, Derek Crabtree, I owe a debt of gratitude not only for introducing me to the history of political ideas but also for his example of tolerant and rational thought. My head of department at Exeter from 1963 to 1970, H. Victor Wiseman, gave a degree of professional encouragement and personal friendship unusual for someone in such a position. I learn more about the subject that interests me most, the territorial dimension of politics, from my good friend Jeffrey Stanyer than from anyone else. At the University of Bath my colleague Geof Wood has taught me that it is not too late to develop an intellectual foundation to a radical position in political analysis. I have been particularly fortunate in my colleagues throughout my career, and if I have achieved anything, I owe it to them."

*   *   *

SMITH, Herbert F(rancis) 1922-

PERSONAL: Born December 31, 1922, in Buffalo, N.Y.; son of John Francis (a mechanic) and Clara (Otto) Smith. *Education:* Attended Canisius College, 1949, St. Philip Neri School for Delayed Vocations, Boston, 1950, and Loyola Seminary, Shrub Oak, N.Y.; Fordham University, M.A., 1961; Woodstock College, Woodstock, Md., S.T.B., 1963. *Politics:* Democrat.

ADDRESSES: Home and office—Jesuit Community, St. Joseph's University, 5600 City Ave., Philadelphia, Pa. 19131.

CAREER: American Radio Institute, Buffalo, N.Y., instructor in radio-television, 1948-50; entered Society of Jesus (Jesuits), 1951, ordained Roman Catholic priest, 1962; teacher of math, English, and religion at Roman Catholic high school in Baltimore, Md., 1958-59; director of spiritual programs and retreats, 1965-75; producer-director and writer for "Who Will Believe Our Report?" broadcast on WIBF-FM Radio, 1976-88. Regular speaker for "International Sacred Heart" radio program, 1973-85. Regional secretary and Philadelphia Archdiocesan director of the Apostleship of Prayer, 1988—.

MEMBER: Fellowship of Catholic Scholars.

WRITINGS:

Living for Resurrection, Joseph F. Wagner, 1970.
The Lord Experience, Liturgical Press, 1973.
God Day by Day, Our Sunday Visitor, 1973.
The Pilgrim Contemplative: Early Years, Liturgical Press, 1977.
The Pilgrim Contemplative: Mature Years, Liturgical Press, 1977.
(With Joseph A. DiIenno) *Sexual Inversion: The Question, with Catholic Answers,* Daughters of St. Paul, 1979, revised edition published as *Homosexuality,* 1989.
Hidden Victory: A Novel of Jesus, St. Joseph's University Press, 1984.
Natural Family Planning: Why It Succeeds, Daughters of St. Paul, 1987.
Prayer and Personality Development, Dimension, 1989.
Sunday Homilies, Alba House, 1989.

Author of column, "The Sunday Mass in Focus," in *Catholic Standard and Times* and *Magnificat,* 1967-69. Contributor to *Catholic Encyclopedia for School and Home.* Contributor to religious publications and newspapers.

WORK IN PROGRESS: Research in family life; more homilies for a second edition of *Sunday Homilies.*

SIDELIGHTS: Herbert F. Smith told *CA:* "I'm of the breed of wayfarers and explorers of the Absolute. My journey is interior, in the uncharted realms of the spirit. My bodily passages across America are external expressions of the inner travels—mere epiphenomena. My struggles are with more than human powers. I have gone from knowing Christ to knowing that Christ is Mystery and life is a mysterious evolution that carries us into His depths. I have captured what I could of this mystery in *The Pilgrim Contemplative.*

"My journey to Israel in late 1977, and eight months there beginning *Hidden Victory: A Novel of Jesus,* was another profound journey, experiencing another culture, a modern one, yet rooted and intermingled with storied soil where every stone has memories. 'And now my feet are standing within your walls, O Jerusalem!' To walk through Bethlehem and old Nazareth, float high in the Dead Sea, and splash in the gentle waves of the Sea of Galilee-all not so different from two millenia ago—was the dream of an author fulfilled. It was the experience behind *Hidden Victory* that led a reader to tell me yesterday, 'It's like being there.' I hope it is, and it should be, because I have been there researching with head and feet, as I had been there for a lifetime before, and 2,000 years ago—in mind and heart and mystery. There with the Master."

*   *   *

SMITH, John David 1949-

PERSONAL: Born October 14, 1949, in Brooklyn, N.Y.; son of Leonard Calgut (a businessman) and Doris (Woronock) Smith. *Education:* Baldwin-Wallace College, A.B. (cum laude), 1971; University of Kentucky, A.M., 1973, Ph.D., 1977.

ADDRESSES: Office—Department of History, Box 8108, North Carolina State University, Raleigh, N.C. 27695-8108.

CAREER: Louis A. Warren Lincoln Library and Museum, Fort Wayne, Ind., curator, 1977-79; Historic Columbia Foundation, Columbia, S.C., director, 1979-80; Southeast Missouri State University, Cape Girardeau, instructor, 1980-81, assistant professor of history, 1981-82; North Carolina State University, Raleigh, assistant professor, 1982-87, associate professor of history, 1987—. Member of associate faculty, Indiana University-Purdue University, Fort Wayne, 1978-79; lecturer, University of South Carolina, 1979-80; visiting assistant professor, University of Kentucky, summer, 1981; visiting associate professor, School of Library and Information Science, University of North Carolina at Chapel Hill, 1986—. Member of board of directors, Friends of the North Carolina State Archives, 1983—; member of International Council on Archives Committee on Professional Training and Education, 1986—.

MEMBER: American Historical Association, Organization of American Historians, Society of American Archivists, Southern Historical Association.

AWARDS, HONORS: American Council of Learned Societies fellowship, 1981-82; James Still fellowship, Andrew W. Mellon Foundation, 1982; Albert J. Beveridge Travel Grant, American Historical Association, 1983, 1987; Outstanding Academic Book award, American Library Association, 1983, for *Black Slavery in the Americas: An Interdisciplinary Bibliography, 1865-1980;* National Endowment for the Humanities grant, 1986.

WRITINGS:

(Editor with William Cooper, Jr.) *Window on the War: Frances Dallam Peter's Lexington Civil War Diary,* Fayette County Historic Commission, 1976.

(Contributor) *A Man for the Ages,* Louis A. Warren Lincoln Library and Museum, 1978.

(Compiler) *Black Slavery in the Americas: An Interdisciplinary Bibliography, 1865-1980,* two volumes, Greenwood Press, 1982.

An Old Creed for the New South: Proslavery Ideology and Historiography, 1865-1918, Greenwood Press, 1985.

(Editor with Randall M. Miller) *The Dictionary of Afro-American Slavery,* Greenwood Press, 1988.

William Hannibal Thomas and "The American Negro," University of Georgia Press, 1990.

(Editor with John C. Inscoe) *The Labor and Legacy of Ulrich Bonnell Phillips: An Anthology of Historical Criticism,* Greenwood Press, in press.

Author of pamphlets on historical subjects; contributor of articles and reviews to history journals and newspapers.

* * *

SMITH, Peter C(harles Horstead) 1940-

PERSONAL: Born October 15, 1940, in North Elmham, Norfolk, England; son of Ernest Gordon and Eileen (Horstead) Smith; married Patricia Ireson, July 27, 1963; children: Paul David, Dawn Tracey.

ADDRESSES: Home—"Foxden," 12 Brooklands Rd., Riseley, Bedford MK44 1EE, England.

CAREER: Novelist and author of books on military and naval history. General Post Office, London, England, overseas telegraph officer, 1965-70; W. & J. MacKay Ltd., London, manager of printing sales office, 1970-72; Photo Precision Ltd., St. Ives, Cambridge, England, editor, 1972-74; *Cape Sun,* London, editor and journalist, 1974-75; tutor and instructor in communication skills, British Telecomms, 1976—.

MEMBER: Society of Authors, Royal Marines Historical Society, American Aviation Historical Society.

WRITINGS:

Destroyer Leader, William Kimber, 1968.
Task Force 57, William Kimber, 1969.
Pedestal, William Kimber, 1970.
Hard Lying, William Kimber, 1971, Naval Institute Press, 1972.
Stuka at War, Ian Allan, 1971, Arco, 1972.
British Battle Cruisers, Almark, 1971.
(With Edwin Walker) *War in the Aegean,* William Kimber, 1972.
Heritage of the Sea, Balfour, 1972.
Royal Navy Ships' Badges, Balfour, 1973.
Royal Air Force Squadron Badges, Balfour, 1973.
(Editor) *Destroyer Action* (anthology), William Kimber, 1974.
Per Mare per Terram, Balfour, 1974.
(With Walker) *Battles of the Malta Striking Forces,* Ian Allan, 1974.
(Editor) *The Haunted Sea* (anthology), William Kimber, 1975.
The Story of the Torpedo Bomber, Almark, 1975.
Arctic Victory, William Kimber, 1975.
Midway, New English Library, 1976.
Fighting Flotilla, William Kimber, 1976.
(Editor) *Undesirable Properties,* William Kimber, 1977.
The Great Ships Pass, Naval Institute Press, 1977.

(Editor) *The Phantom Coach,* William Kimber, 1979.
Hit First, Hit Hard, William Kimber, 1979.
(Editor) *Haunted Shores,* William Kimber, 1980.
Action Imminent, William Kimber, 1980.
Impact!, William Kimber, 1981.
(With John R. Dominy) *Cruisers in Action,* William Kimber, 1981.
Dive Bomber!: An Illustrated History, Naval Institute Press, 1982.
Rendezvous Skerki Bank (novel), New English Library, 1982.
Hold the Narrow Sea: Naval Warfare in the English Channel, 1939-45, Naval Institute Press, 1984.
(Editor) *Uninvited Guests: Thirteen Unwelcome Visitors,* William Kimber, 1984.
H.M.S. Wild Swan, William Kimber, 1985.
Into the Assault: Famous Dive-Bomber Aces of the Second World War, University of Washington Press, 1985.
Vengeance!: Vultee Vengeance Dive Bomber, Airlife, 1986, Smithsonian Institution Press, 1988.
Jungle Dive: Bombers at War, J. Murray, 1987.
Victoria's Victories: Seven Classic Battles of the British Army, Spellmount, 1987, Hippocrene, 1988.
Pedestal: Malta Convoy of August 1942, William Kimber, 1987.
Massacre at Tobruk: The Story of Operation Agreement, William Kimber, 1987.
(With Derek Oakley) *The Royal Marines,* Spellmount, 1988.
Dive Bombers in Action, Sterling Pub., 1988.
Battleship Royal Sovereign, William Kimber, 1988.

Also author of *Strike from the Sky* and *Eagle's War;* ghostwriter of numerous books on historic places. Contributor to military history magazines, including *Warship International, Navy International, Army Quarterly, Military History,* and *World War II.*

WORK IN PROGRESS: A book of short stories, *Behind the Black Curtain;* two novels, *Death Wing Staffeln* and *Slug!;* factual histories, *Stuka Squadron, T-G: A Celebration, Sailors in Dock,* and *Into the Minefields.*

AVOCATIONAL INTERESTS: Military and naval history, London, science fiction, original rock 'n' roll recordings.

* * *

SMITH, Richard P(aul) 1949-

PERSONAL: Born March 9, 1949, in Bremerton, Wash.; son of James G. and Betty V. (a cashier; maiden name, Yelle) Smith; married Lucy J. LaFaive (an administrative assistant), May 15, 1976. *Education:* Northern Michigan University, B.S., 1971.

ADDRESSES: Home and office—814 Clark St., Marquette, Mich. 49855.

CAREER: Free-lance writer and photographer, 1973—.

MEMBER: Outdoor Writers Association of America, Michigan Outdoor Writers Association.

AWARDS, HONORS: Named communicator of the year by Michigan United Conservation Clubs and received writer of the year award from Upper Peninsula Michigan Writers, both 1978, both for weekly column in the *Marquette Mining Journal;* award from Bass'n Gal Writing Competition, 1982, for an article about a woman trapper; Eagle Rare Journalism Award from Eagle Rare Bourbon and Outdoor Writers Association of America, 1983, for an article about the wolves of Michigan's Isle Royale.

WRITINGS:

ILLUSTRATED WITH OWN PHOTOGRAPHS

Deer Hunting, Stackpole, 1978, 2nd edition, 1980.
Animal Tracks and Signs of North America, Stackpole, 1982.
The Book of the Black Bear, Winchester Press, 1985.
Hunting Rabbits and Hares, Stackpole, 1986.
Michigan Big Game Records, privately printed, 1986.
Tracking Wounded Deer, Stackpole, 1988.

OTHER

Author of weekly column in *The Delta Reporter* and of a monthly column in *Michigan Out-of-Doors.* Contributor to magazines, including *Outdoor Life, Field and Stream, Sports Afield, American Hunter, Bowhunter,* and *Petersen's Hunting.* Field editor of *Deer and Deer Hunting;* editor of *Buck Fox.*

SIDELIGHTS: Richard P. Smith wrote *CA:* "I am an outdoor person, and I write about many of my experiences with wildlife. I thought I could write articles on outdoor subjects as good as any being published. My life revolves around the outdoors and wildlife. There are few days that go by when I'm not photographing wildlife or some other aspect of the outdoors—hunting, fishing, or camping. Or I'm writing or sorting through photos in my office. I have always been actively involved in the outdoors, which led to my becoming an outdoor writer and photographer. Many of my personal experiences find their way into my books and magazine articles.

"As a hunter, I am part of the life-and-death struggle that goes on in the outdoors daily, and not just an observer. I'm a predator just as the wolf, mountain lion, and coyote are, and am just as important in the scheme of things. Hunters are true conservationists, making use of renewable natural resources and at the same time insuring a future supply of those resources.

"Sport hunting is often misunderstood and probably misnamed. Hunters hunt for recreation and, in most cases, meat. It is possible to enjoy a day of hunting (recreation) without seeing game that is sought. It is not necessary to kill anything to have hunted. The kill, when it does occur, accounts for a small fraction of the time spent hunting. Few people, if any, hunt for sport, and they certainly don't kill for sport."

* * *

SNYDER, Gary (Sherman) 1930-

PERSONAL: Born May 8, 1930, in San Francisco, Calif.; son of Harold Alton and Lois (Wilkie) Snyder; married Alison Gass, 1950 (divorced, 1951); married Joanne Kyger (a poet), 1960 (divorced, 1964); married Masa Uehara, August 6, 1967; children: (third marriage) Kai, Gen. *Education:* Reed College, B.A. (in anthropology and literature), 1951; attended Indiana University, 1951; University of California, Berkeley, graduate study in Oriental languages, 1953-56. *Politics:* Radical. *Religion:* Buddhist of the Mahayana-Vajrayana line.

CAREER: Poet and translator, 1959—. Worked as seaman, logger, trail crew member, and forest lookout, 1948-56; lecturer at University of California, Berkeley, 1964-65. Visiting lecturer at numerous universities and writing workshops. Member of United Nations Conference on the Human Environment, 1972; former chairman of California Arts Council.

MEMBER: American Academy and Institute of Arts and Letters.

AWARDS, HONORS: Scholarship from First Zen Institute of America, 1956, for study in Japan; National Institute and American Academy poetry award, 1966; Bollingen Foundation grant, 1966-67; Frank O'Hara Prize, 1967; Levinson Prize from *Poetry* magazine, 1968; Guggenheim fellowship, 1968-69; Pulitzer Prize in poetry, 1975, for *Turtle Island.*

WRITINGS:

POETRY

Riprap (also see below), Origin Press, 1959.
Myths & Texts, Totem Press, 1960, reprinted, New Directions, 1978.
Riprap & Cold Mountain Poems (the *Cold Mountain* poems are Snyder's translations of poems by Han-Shan), Four Seasons Foundation, 1965, reprinted, 1977.
Six Sections from Mountains and Rivers without End, Four Seasons Foundation, 1965, revised edition published as *Six Sections from Mountains and Rivers without End, Plus One,* 1970.
A Range of Poems (includes translations of the modern Japanese poet, Miyazawa Kenji), Fulcrum (London), 1966.
Three Worlds, Three Realms, Six Roads, Griffin Press, 1966.
The Back Country, New Directions, 1968.
The Blue Sky, Phoenix Book Shop, 1969.
Regarding Wave, New Directions, 1970.
Manzanita, Kent State University Libraries, 1971.
Plute Creek, State University College at Brockport, 1972.
The Fudo Trilogy: Spel against Demons, Smokey the Bear Sutra, The California Water Plan (also see below), illustrated by Michael Corr, Shaman Drum, 1973.
Turtle Island, New Directions, 1974.
All in the Family, University of California Library, c. 1975.
Smokey the Bear Sutra (chapbook), 1976.
Songs for Gaia, illustrated by Corr, Copper Canyon, 1979.
Axe Handles, North Point Press, 1983.
Left Out in the Rain: New Poems 1947-1986, North Point Press, 1986.

PROSE

Earth House Hold: Technical Notes and Queries to Fellow Dharma Revolutionaries (essays), New Directions, 1969.
(Contributor) *Ecology: Me,* Moving On, 1970.
The Old Ways: Six Essays, City Lights, 1977.
On Bread & Poetry: A Panel Discussion between Gary Snyder, Lew Welch and Philip Whalen, edited by Donald M. Allen, Grey Fox, 1977.
He Who Hunted Birds in His Father's Village: The Dimensions of a Haida Myth (undergraduate thesis), preface by Nathaniel Tarn, Grey Fox, 1979.
The Real Work: Interviews & Talks, 1964-1979, edited with introduction by Scott McLean, New Directions, 1980.
Passage through India (autobiography), Grey Fox, 1983.

CONTRIBUTOR TO ANTHOLOGIES

Donald Hall, editor, *Contemporary American Poetry,* Penguin Books, 1962.
Walter Lowenfels, editor, *A New American Anthology,* International Publications, 1964.
Fernando Pivano, editor, *Poesia degli Ultima Americani,* Feltrinelli Editore (Milan), 1964.
Allen, editor, *12 Poets & 1 Painter,* Four Seasons Foundation, 1964.
Paris Leary and Robert Kelly, editors, *A Controversy of Poets,* Doubleday, 1965.
(Contributor of translations of Han-Shan) A. C. Graham, editor, *Poems of the Late T'ang,* Penguin Books, 1966.

Howard McCord, editor, *The Only Journal of the Tibetan Kite Society,* Tribal Press, 1970.

OTHER

The New Religion (sound recording), Big Sur Recordings, 1967.

Contributor to numerous periodicals, including *Janus, Evergreen Review, Black Mountain Review, Yugen, Chicago Review, Jabberwock, San Francisco Review, Big Table, Origin, Kulchur, Journal for the Protection of All Beings, Nation, City Lights Journal, Yale Literary Magazine, Beloit Poetry Journal,* and *Poetry.* The University of California, Davis, holds a collection of Snyder's manuscripts.

WORK IN PROGRESS: A long poem, *Mountains and Rivers without End,* begun in 1956, dramatically structured after a *No* play and titled after a Chinese sideways scroll painting.

SIDELIGHTS: Gary Snyder is one of the rare modern poets who has bridged the gap between popular appeal and serious academic criticism. Snyder began his career in the 1950s as a noted member of the "Beat Generation," and since then he has explored a wide range of social and spiritual matters in both poetry and prose. Snyder's work blends physical reality—precise observations of nature—with inner insight received primarily through the practice of Zen Buddhism. *Southwest Review* essayist Abraham Rothberg notes that the poet "celebrates nature, the simple, the animal, the sexual, the tribal, the self. . . . He sees man as an indissoluble part of the natural environment, flourishing when he accepts and adapts to that natural heritage, creating a hell on earth and within himself when he is separated from it by his intellect and its technological and societal creations." While Snyder has gained the attention of readers as a spokesman for the preservation of the natural world and its earth-conscious cultures, he is not simply a "back-to-nature" poet with a facile message. In *American Poetry in the Twentieth Century,* Kenneth Rexroth observes that although Snyder proposes "a new ethic, a new esthetic, [and] a new life style," he is also "an accomplished technician who has learned from the poetry of several languages and who has developed a sure and flexible style capable of handling any material he wishes." According to Charles Altieri in *Enlarging the Temple: New Directions in American Poetry during the 1960s,* Snyder's achievement "is a considerable one. Judged simply in aesthetic terms, according to norms of precision, intelligence, imaginative play, and moments of deep resonance, he easily ranks among the best poets of his generation. Moreover, he manages to provide a fresh perspective on metaphysical themes, which he makes relevant and compelling."

Snyder's emphasis on metaphysics and his celebration of the natural order remove his work from the general tenor of Beat writing. *Dictionary of Literary Biography* contributor Dan McLeod explains that while authors such as Allen Ginsberg and Neal Cassady "represented in their different ways rather destructive responses to the alienation inherent in modern American technocracy, the example of Snyder's life and values offered a constructive, albeit underground, alternative to mainstream American culture." No less searing in his indictments of Western values than the other Beat writers, Snyder has proposed "a morality that is unharmful, that tends toward wholeness. An ethics not of the trigger or fist, but of the heart," to quote *New Republic* reviewer Timothy Baland. Snyder has looked to the Orient and to the beliefs of American Indians for positive responses to the world, and he has tempered his studies with stints of hard physical labor as a logger and trail builder. In the *Southwest Review,* Roger Jones calls Snyder "one of the century's *healthiest* writers," a poet who "perceives man as completely situated within the schemes of natural order, and sees as a necessity man's awareness that he is as real and as whole as the world—a perception muddled by the metaphysical notion of the world as a mere stage for the enactment of our eternal destinies." Charles Molesworth elaborates on this premise in his work *Gary Snyder's Vision: Poetry and the Real Work.* Molesworth sees Snyder as "a moral visionary who is neither a scourge nor a satirist; . . . he has spoken as a prophet whose 'tribe' is without definite national or cultural boundaries."

Altieri believes that Snyder's "articulation of a possible religious faith" independent of Western culture has greatly enhanced his popularity, especially among younger readers. If that is so, Snyder's themes have also been served by an accessible style, drawn from the examples of Japanese haiku and Chinese verse. In a book entitled *Gary Snyder,* Bob Steuding remarks that Snyder "has created a new kind of poetry that is direct, concrete, non-Romantic, and ecological. . . . Snyder's work will be remembered in its own right as the example of a new direction taken in American literature." *Nation* contributor Richard Tillinghast writes: "In Snyder the stuff of the world—'content'—has always shone with a wonderful sense of earthiness and health. He has always had things to tell us, experiences to relate, a set of values to expound. . . . He has influenced a generation." McLeod finds Snyder's "poetic fusion of Buddhist and tribal world views with ecological science" a "remarkable cross-cultural achievement—an utterly appropriate postmodernist expression of a post-industrial sensibility." Robert Mezey puts it more simply in the *Western Humanities Review* when he concludes: "This missionary is really a joyful poet, and the gratitude and celebration at the heart of his view of life often overwhelm the necessity to teach and explain. So the teaching is done silently, which is the best way to do it."

Born and raised in the American West, Snyder lived close to nature from earliest childhood. Even at a very young age he was distressed by the wanton destruction of the Pacific Northwestern forests, and he began to study and respect the Indian cultures that "seemed to have some sense of how a life harmonious with nature might be lived," according to Rothberg. Snyder went to public schools in Seattle and Portland, and he augmented his education by reading about Indian lore and pioneer adventures. Wild regions continued to fascinate him as he matured; he became an expert mountain climber and learned back-country survival techniques. A visit to the Seattle Art Museum introduced him to Chinese landscape painting, and he developed an interest in the Orient as an example of a high civilization that had maintained its bonds to nature. After high school Snyder divided his time between studies at the prestigious Reed College—and later Indiana University and the University of California, Berkeley—and work as a lumberjack, trail maker, and firewatcher in the deep woods. The balance between physical labor and intellectual pursuits informs his earliest writing; McLeod feels that the unlikely juxtaposition makes Snyder either "the last of an old breed or the beginning of a new breed of backwoodsmen figures in American literature." In *Alone with America: Essays on the Art of Poetry in the United States since 1950,* Richard Howard describes Snyder's youth as "the rapturous life of a cosmic bum."

In the autumn of 1952 Snyder moved to the San Francisco Bay area in order to study Oriental languages at Berkeley. He was already immersed in Zen Buddhism and had begun to write poetry about his work in the wilderness. McLeod contends that the four years Snyder spent in San Francisco "were of enormous importance to his . . . growth as a poet." He became part of a community of writers, including Philip Whalen, Allen Ginsberg, and Jack Kerouac, who would come to be known as the Beat Generation and who would be heralded as the forerunners of a counter-culture revolution in literature. If Snyder was influenced by his antisocial contemporaries, he also exerted an influence on them. Kerouac modeled his character Japhy Ryder in *The Dharma Bums* on Snyder, and the poet encouraged his friends to take an interest in Eastern philosophy as an antidote to the ills of the West. McLeod notes, however, that although "he is clearly one of its major figures, Snyder was out of town when the Beat movement was most alive on the American scene." Having been awarded a scholarship by the First Zen Institute of America, Snyder moved to Japan in 1956 and stayed abroad almost continuously for the next twelve years. Part of that time he lived in an ashram and devoted himself to strenuous Zen study and meditation. He also travelled extensively, visiting India and Indonesia, and even venturing as far as Istanbul on an oil tanker, the *Sappa Creek*. His first two poetry collections, *Riprap* and *Myths & Texts*, were published in 1959 and 1960.

Snyder's early poems represent a vigorous attempt to achieve freedom from the "establishment" mores of urban America. *Sagetrieb* contributor Thomas Parkinson describes the works as moments in which "action and contemplation become identical states of being, and both states of secular grace. From this fusion wisdom emerges, and it is not useless but timed to the event. The result is a terrible sanity, a literal clairvoyance, an innate decorum." The poems in *Riprap* and *Myths & Texts* are miniature narratives captured from the active working life of the author; Rothberg contends that in them Snyder wants "to be considered a poet of ordinary men, writing in a language shaped in their idiom." Audiences responded to Snyder's portrayals of the vigorous backwoods visionary whose joy flows from physical pursuits and contemplation of the wild world. In the *Los Angeles Times Book Review*, Schuyler Ingle writes: "I could sense [Snyder] in his lines, all long-haired and denim-clad, laced-up high-top logger boots. He was an educated, curious man comfortable with his own sexuality." Rothberg too detects the education underlying the hardier roles. According to the critic, Snyder "cannot quite conceal the intellect or learning in his work, which everywhere reveals his considerable knowledge of anthropology, linguistics, Zen Buddhism, history, and other arcane lore."

Unquestionably, Snyder's involvement with Buddhism has been important to his poetry from the outset. As Julian Gitzen notes in *Critical Quarterly*, Snyder "was attracted to Buddhism because its teachings conformed to and re-enforced his native personality, interests and beliefs." Much of the poet's work "manifests a . . . movement out to an awareness of self in cosmos complemented by the perception of cosmos contained within the self," to quote Altieri. In *American Poetry since 1960: Some Critical Perspectives*, Alan Williamson also states that Snyder's canon "suggests a process of meditation or spiritual exercise, clearing the path from temporal life to the moment of Enlightenment—the sudden dropping-away of the phenomenal world in the contemplation of the infinite and eternal, All and Nothingness." The aim, according to Parkinson, is "not to achieve harmony with nature but to create an inner harmony that equals to the natural external harmony." *Criticism* essayist Robert Kern declares that the resulting poems "are almost celebrations of those moments when the mind's resistances have been overcome and the difficult transition has been made from ordinary consciousness to a state in which the mind has dropped its symbolic burden of words, books, abstractions, even personal history and identity—whatever might stand in the way of a direct, unhampered perception of things."

The structure of Snyder's poetry is influenced by the intellectual dilemma of using language—the medium of rational dis-course—to disclose deeper, extra-rational states of being. *Dictionary of Literary Biography* essayist Alex Batman observes that Snyder realizes mere words may be inadequate for the articulation of his discoveries. The poet overcomes this problem by producing verse "based on the Oriental haiku—sharp, uncomplicated images that, like many Oriental paintings, form sketches that the reader's imagination must fill in." Gitzen writes: "Snyder's poems in general possess [an] air of spontaneity, almost as though they were hastily written notes for poems, rather than finished constructions. Such unpolished form harmonizes with the Zen aesthetic." The critic adds, however, that spontaneous and simple though the works may seem, they are in fact "the result of conscious and painstaking effort." Batman likewise finds Snyder's pieces "deceptively simple rather than superficially simplistic." Altieri comments that for the skeptic or half-believer, "the real miracle is the skill with which Snyder uses the aesthetic devices of lyrical poetry to sustain his religious claims. His basic achievement is his power to make his readers reflect on the ontological core of the lyrical vision by calling attention to the way it can be things or processes themselves, and not merely the elements of a poem, which mutually create one another's significance and suggest a unifying power producing, sustaining, and giving meaning to these relationships." Steuding concludes that the "Buddhist perception of oneness . . . creates a poetry of immediacy and startling originality."

Buddhism is by no means the sole departure point for Snyder's work, however. Well-versed in anthropology and the lore of so-called "primitive" cultures, the author reveres myth and ritual as essential demonstrations of man-in-nature and nature-in-man. In *The American West*, Thomas W. Pew, Jr., writes: "Snyder, like a handful of other writers since Carl Jung, has discovered the similarities of myth, religion, and his own personal dream content as well as the product of his meditations and has fashioned that collective material into words that set off little explosions in our thought process and our own deeper memory." Harking back to the Stone Age, Snyder sees the poet as a shaman who acts as a medium for songs and chants springing from the earth. McLeod explains: "The poet-shaman draws his songs from the [Earth] Mother Goddess and through the magic power of image, metaphor, music, and myth creates the artistic patterns that express the most deeply held knowledge and values of the community. Embodied in literary form, this knowledge and these values may survive and evolve, sustaining the group generation after generation." McLeod states further that myth and ritual are for Snyder "far more than reflections of experience. . . . They are also a means whereby we can shape and control experience through the sympathetic magic inherent in the metaphysical connections that link myth and ritual to the quotidian world."

It is not surprising, therefore, that Snyder draws on the traditions of oral literature—chants, incantations, and songs—to communicate his experiences. *Denver Quarterly* contributor Kevin Oderman observes that the poet "writes out of a tradition of self-effacement, and his yearnings are for a communal poetry rooted in place." Scott McLean also addresses this idea in his introduction to Snyder's *The Real Work: Interviews & Talks, 1964-1979*. "All of Gary Snyder's study and work has been directed toward a poetry that would approach phenomena with a disciplined clarity that would then use the 'archaic' and the 'primitive' as models to once again see this poetry as woven through all the parts of our lives," McLean writes. "Thus it draws its substance and forms from the broadest range of a people's day-to-day lives, enmeshed in the facts of work, the real trembling in joy and grief, thankfulness for good crops, the health of a child, the warmth of the lover's touch. Further, Snyder seeks to recover a poetry that could sing and thus relate us to: magpie, beaver, a mountain range, binding us to all these other lives, seeing our spiritual lives as bound up in the rounds of nature." McLean concludes that in terms of the human race's future, "Snyder's look toward the primitive may vouchsafe one of the only real alternative directions available." Addressing himself more specifically to the poetry, Jones admits in *Southwest Review* that Snyder's shamanistic role is an important one for modern letters "as poetry seems to base itself less in sound than in the medium of print."

Many of Snyder's poems aim specifically at instilling an ecological consciousness in his audience. Jones observes that the poet advocates "peaceful stewardship, economy, responsibility with the world's resources, and, most importantly, sanity—all still within the capabilities of modern societies, and bound up in the perception of the world and its life-sources as a glorious whole." This theme pervades Snyder's 1974 Pulitzer Prize-winning volume, *Turtle Island,* a work in which the poet manages "to locate the self ecologically in its actions and interactions with its environment, to keep it anchored to its minute-by-minute manifestations in (and as a part of) the physical world," to quote Robert Kern in *Contemporary Literature.* According to Gitzen, Snyder assumes that "while man neither individually nor as a species is essential to nature . . . nature is essential to the existence of all men. Consideration for our own welfare demands that we abandon efforts to dominate nature and assume instead an awareness of our subjection to natural law. . . . Snyder repeatedly seeks to impress upon his readers the awesome immensity of space, time, energy, and matter working together to generate a destiny beyond the reach of human will." Some critics, such as *Partisan Review* contributor Robert Boyers, find Snyder's commitment "programmistic and facile," a simplistic evocation of the "noble savage" as hero. Others, including *New York Times Book Review* correspondent Herbert Leibowitz, applaud the poet's world view. "Snyder's sane housekeeping principles desperately need to become Government and corporate policy," Leibowitz writes. "He is on the side of the gods."

"The curve of Snyder's career has been from the factlike density of perceptual intensity to the harmonious patternmaking of the immanently mythic imagination," Molesworth states. "Such a course of development has taken Snyder deeper and deeper into the workings of the political imagination as well." Snyder's more recent works reflect a growing concern for the environment and the plight of the American Indian as well as the new insights engendered by his domestic responsibilities. McLeod notes that a "shift from the examination of the self to the exercise of social responsibility is clearly reflected in the development of Snyder's writing which has moved from the still, almost purely meditative lyrics in *Riprap,* to the celebration of the human family as a vital part of a broad network of relationships linking all forms of life in *Regarding Wave,* to the eco-political poems and essays in *Turtle Island.*" *Axe Handles,* Snyder's 1983 collection, returns to the domestic environment—especially the relationship between father and sons—as a central motif. *Poetry* magazine reviewer Bruce Bawer contends that the work "conveys a luminous, poignant vision of a life afforded joy and strength by a recognition of the essential things which give it meaning. It is, to my tastes, Snyder's finest book." One ongoing project spans the poet's entire career—a long poem, *Mountains and Rivers without End,* titled after a Chinese sideways scroll painting. Finished portions of the piece have been published, and in them, Steuding claims, "one finds directness and simplicity of statement, clarity and brilliance of mind, and profundity and depth of emotional range.

In these instances, Snyder's is a poetry of incredible power and beauty."

In addition to his many volumes of verse, Snyder has published books of prose essays and interviews that can be read "not only as partial explanation of the poetry but as the record of an evolving mind with extreme good sense in treating the problems of the world," according to Parkinson. Snyder's prose expands his sense of social purpose and reveals the series of interests and concerns that have sparked his creative writing. Parkinson suggests that Snyder is distinguished "not only as a poet but as a prose expositor—he has a gift for quiet, untroubled, accurate observation with occasional leaps to genuine eloquence. He has taken to himself a subject matter, complex, vast, and permanently interesting, a subject so compelling that it is not unreasonable to assert that he has become a center for a new set of cultural possibilities."

Critics and general readers alike have responded to Snyder's "new set of cultural possibilities." Steuding proposes that the writer's work "truly influences one who reads him thoroughly to 'see' in a startling new way. Presenting the vision of an integrated and unified world, this heroic poetic effort cannot but help to create a much needed change of consciousness." Robert Mezey notes that Snyder "has a compelling vision of our relationship with this living nature, which is our nature, what it is and what it must be if we/nature survive on this planet, and his art serves that vision unwaveringly." According to Halvard Johnson in the *Minnesota Review,* the "unique power and value of Snyder's poetry lies not simply in clearly articulated images or in complex patterns of sound and rhythm, but rather in the freedom, the openness of spirit that permits the poems simply to be what they are, what they can be. . . . They respond to the rhythms of the world." Molesworth offers perhaps the most succinct appraisal of Gary Snyder's poetic vision. "Snyder has built a place for the mind to stay and to imagine more far-reaching harmonies while preserving all the wealth of the past," Molesworth concludes. "This, of course, is the world of his books where he is willing and even eager to give us another world both more ideal and more real than our own. The rest of the work is ours."

In an essay published in *A Controversy of Poets,* Snyder offers his own assessment of his art. "As a poet," he writes, "I hold the most archaic values on earth. They go back to the late Paleolithic: the fertility of the soil, the magic of animals, the power-vision in solitude, the terrifying initiation and rebirth; the love and ecstasy of the dance, the common work of the tribe. I try to hold both history and wilderness in mind, that my poems may approach the true measure of things and stand against the unbalance and ignorance of our times."

BIOGRAPHICAL/CRITICAL SOURCES:

BOOKS

Allen, Donald M., editor, *The New American Poetry,* Grove, 1960.

Almon, Bert, *Gary Snyder,* Boise State University Press, 1979.

Altieri, Charles, *Enlarging the Temple: New Directions in American Poetry during the 1960s,* Bucknell University Press, 1979.

Charters, Samuel, *Some Poems/Poets: Studies in American Underground Poetry since 1945,* Oyez, 1971.

Contemporary Literary Criticism, Gale, Volume 1, 1973, Volume 2, 1974, Volume 5, 1976, Volume 9, 1978, Volume 32, 1985.

Cook, Bruce, *The Beat Generation,* Scribner, 1971.

Dictionary of Literary Biography, Gale, Volume 5: *American Poets since World War II,* 1980, Volume 16: *The Beats: Literary Bohemians in Postwar America,* 1983.

Faas, Ekbert, editor, *Towards a New American Poetics: Essays & Interviews,* Black Sparrow Press, 1978.

Howard, Richard, *Alone with America: Essays on the Art of Poetry in the United States since 1950,* Atheneum, 1969.

Kherdian, David, *A Biographical Sketch and Descriptive Checklist of Gary Snyder,* Oyez, 1965.

Leary, Paris and Robert Kelly, editors, *A Controversy of Poets,* Doubleday, 1965.

McCord, Howard, *Some Notes to Gary Snyder's "Myths & Texts,"* Sand Dollar, 1971.

McNeill, Katherine, *Gary Snyder,* Phoenix, 1980.

Molesworth, Charles, *Gary Snyder's Vision: Poetry and the Real Work,* University of Missouri Press, 1983.

Rexroth, Kenneth, *Assays,* New Directions, 1961.

Rexroth, Kenneth, *American Poetry in the Twentieth Century,* Herder & Herder, 1971.

Shaw, Robert B., editor, *American Poetry since 1960: Some Critical Perspectives,* Dufour, 1974.

Sherman, Paul, *Repossessing and Renewing,* Louisiana State University Press, 1976.

Synder, Gary, *The Real Work: Interviews & Talks, 1964-1979,* edited with introduction by Scott McLean, New Directions, 1980.

Steuding, Bob, *Gary Snyder,* Twayne, 1976.

PERIODICALS

Alcheringa, autumn, 1972.
American Poetry Review, November, 1983.
American West, January-February, 1981.
Beloit Poetry Journal, fall-winter, 1971-72.
Boundary II, Volume 4, 1976.
Colorado Quarterly, summer, 1968.
Contemporary Literature, spring, 1977.
Critical Quarterly, winter, 1973.
Criticism, spring, 1977.
Denver Quarterly, fall, 1980.
Epoch: A Magazine of Contemporary Literature, fall, 1965.
Far Point, Volume 4, 1970.
Holiday, March, 1966.
Iowa Review, summer, 1970.
Journal of Modern Literature, Volume 2, 1971-72.
Kansas Quarterly, spring, 1970.
Los Angeles Times, November 28, 1986.
Los Angeles Times Book Review, July 1, 1979, November 23, 1980, November 13, 1983, December 28, 1986.
Minnesota Review, fall, 1971.
Nation, September 1, 1969, November 19, 1983.
New Republic, April 4, 1970.
New Statesman, November 4, 1966.
New York Review of Books, January 22, 1976.
New York Times Book Review, May 11, 1969, June 8, 1969, March 23, 1975.
Partisan Review, summer, 1969, winter, 1971-72.
Poetry, June, 1971, June, 1972, September, 1984.
Prairie Schooner, winter, 1960-61.
Sagetrieb, spring, 1984.
Saturday Review, October 11, 1969, April 3, 1971.
Sixties, spring, 1962, spring, 1972.
Southern Review, summer, 1968.
Southwest Review, spring, 1971, winter, 1976, spring, 1982.
Spectator, December 25, 1971.
Sulfur 10, Volume 4, number 1, 1984.

Tamkang Review, spring, 1980.
Times Literary Supplement, December 24, 1971, May 30, 1980.
Village Voice, November 17, 1966, May 1, 1984.
Washington Post Book World, December 25, 1983.
Western American Literature, fall, 1968, spring, 1980, fall, 1980, spring, 1981.
Western Humanities Review, spring, 1975.
World Literature Today, summer, 1984.

—*Sketch by Anne Janette Johnson*

*   *   *

SODERSTROM, Edward Jonathan 1954-

PERSONAL: Born November 17, 1954, in Grand Rapids, Mich.; son of Edward Carl and Anne (Spangenburg) Soderstrom; married Gail Louise DeWitt (an educational programs director), June 25, 1977; children: Rachelle Louise, Kari Anne, Luke Edward. *Education:* Hope College, B.A. (magna cum laude), 1976; Northwestern University, Ph.D., 1980.

ADDRESSES: Home—100 Holbrook Lane, Oak Ridge, Tenn. 37830. *Office*—Martin Marietta Energy Systems, P.O. Box 2008, Oak Ridge, Tenn. 37831-6259.

CAREER: Oak Ridge National Laboratory, Oak Ridge, Tenn., research associate in social impact analysis group of Energy Division, 1975, 1980-84, technology transfer research group leader, 1984-85; Martin Marietta Energy Systems, Oak Ridge, Tenn., director of technology applications, 1984—. Consultant to Practical Concepts, Inc., Environmental Protection Agency, and National Science Foundation.

MEMBER: American Psychological Association, Evaluation Research Society, Licensing Executive Society, Phi Beta Kappa, Psi Chi.

AWARDS, HONORS: Presidential scholar, 1972, research award from Sigma Chi fraternity, 1976; post-doctoral fellow of National Science Foundation, 1980.

WRITINGS:

Social Impact Assessment: Experimental Methods and Approaches, Praeger, 1981.

(Contributor) R. G. Post, editor, *Waste Isolation in the U.S. and Elsewhere: Technical Programs and Public Communications,* Volume 2: *Low Level Waste,* University of Arizona Press, 1982.

(Contributor) P. L. Hofman, editor, *Advances in the Science and Technology of the Management of High-Level Nuclear Waste,* Office of Nuclear Waste Isolation, 1982.

(Contributor) A. Eskesen, editor, *The Restructuring Economy,* Bentley College, 1982.

(Contributor) G. R. Gilbert, editor, *Making and Managing Policy: Formulation, Analysis, and Evaluation,* Dekker, 1984.

(With others) *Impacts of Hazardous Technology: Restarting Three Mile Island Unit One,* State University of New York Press, 1986.

(Contributor) R. W. Lake, editor, *Resolving Locational Conflict,* Center for Urban Political Research, 1987.

(Contributor) A. Furino, editor, *Cooperation and Competition in the Global Economy: Issues and Strategies,* Ballinger, 1988.

Contributor to technical journals.

SIDELIGHTS: Edward Jonathan Soderstrom told *CA:* "At the same time the United States is enjoying a period of relative economic stability, our nation faces a serious challenge to its future competitiveness. Our competitive preeminence in world commerce has eroded over the past decade. We are being challenged in the trading arena by our European trading partners and emerging nations of industrial significance in Asia and Latin America. Sustaining our competitiveness over the long term is all-important in maintaining our standard of living, advancing our foreign policy aims, and our national security.

"The primary reason that past efforts at technology transfer had only limited success is lack of recognition that such transfers are not unidirectional, but rather an exchange between two parties. Consequently, for any transfer to be successful, consonant with the principles of a capitalistic economy such as the United States', both parties to the exchange must, in some way, benefit or 'profit.' This 'profit' must take the form of a tangible return on the investments of both parties to the transfer. One way to achieve this goal is to create a framework of incentives for private sector firms to invest in the commercial development of federally-developed technologies, and to make government-developed technologies readily available to the commercial sector under licensing terms that are attractive to them. Over the past five years, I have been working to move Oak Ridge National Laboratory in this direction by increasing our emphasis on technology transfer through such mechanisms as granting commercially attractive licenses. Energy Systems pursued an aggressive licensing program in accordance with accepted commercial practices.

"The results of these initiatives are worth noting. More than $600,000 in license fees and royalties have been received, and nearly $20 million of commercial product sales have resulted from Energy Systems' technology licensing efforts of the past two years. This encouraging start indicates good prospects for future increases in U.S.-based commercial production from federally funded technologies developed at Oak Ridge."

*   *   *

SOUCY, Robert J(oseph) 1933-

PERSONAL: Born June 25, 1933, in Topeka, Kan.; son of William Joseph (a fruit peddler) and Bernice Winifred (Riley) Soucy; married Barbara Jeanne Stone (a teacher), May 30, 1958; married Sharon Fairchild (a teacher), 1986; children: (first marriage) Anne Marie, Alissa Bernice. *Education:* Washburn University, A.B., 1955; University of Kansas, M.A., 1958; University of Wisconsin, Ph.D., 1963.

ADDRESSES: Home—258 East College, Oberlin, Ohio 44074. *Office*—Department of History, Oberlin College, Oberlin, Ohio 44074.

CAREER: Harvard University, Cambridge, Mass., instructor in history, 1963-64; Kent State University, Kent, Ohio, assistant professor of history, 1964-66; Oberlin College, Oberlin, Ohio, assistant professor, 1966-70, associate professor, 1970-77, professor of history, 1977—. *Military service:* U.S. Air Force, 1958-60; became lieutenant.

MEMBER: International Psychohistorical Association, American Historical Association, French Historical Studies Society.

AWARDS, HONORS: Grants from American Council of Learned Societies, National Endowment for the Humanities, and American Philosophical Society, 1969-70, 1988-89.

WRITINGS:

Fascism in France: The Case of Maurice Barres, University of California Press, 1972.

(Contributor) Stephen Ward, editor, *The War Generation,* Kennikat, 1974.
Fascist Intellectual: Drieu La Rochelle, University of California Press, 1979.
French Fascism: The First Wave, 1924-1933, Yale University Press, 1986.

Contributor to history journals.

WORK IN PROGRESS: French Fascism: The Second Wave, 1933-39.

BIOGRAPHICAL/CRITICAL SOURCES:

PERIODICALS

New York Times Book Review, April 20, 1986.
Times Literary Supplement, June 6, 1980.

*   *   *

SOUZA, Raymond D(ale) 1936-

PERSONAL: Born March 11, 1936, in Attleboro, Mass.; son of Joseph B. (a worker in a jewel factory) and Linda (Pimental) Souza; married Martha Heckmaster (a teacher of Spanish), December 23, 1966; children: Richard, Robert. *Education:* Attended University of Massachusetts, 1954-56; Drury College, B.A. (magna cum laude), 1958; University of Missouri, M.A., 1960, Ph.D., 1964.

ADDRESSES: Home—1732 West 21st St. Ter., Lawrence, Kan. 66044. *Office*—Department of Spanish and Portuguese, University of Kansas, Lawrence, Kan. 66046.

CAREER: High School teacher of Spanish in Salem, Mo., 1958-59; Kent State University, Kent, Ohio, instructor in Spanish, 1961-62; University of Kansas, Lawrence, assistant professor, 1963-68, associate professor, 1968-73, professor of Spanish, 1973—, chairman of department, 1968-71, chairman of summer school in Guadalajara, Mexico, Exxon Intra-University Visiting Professor of Linguistics and Philosophy, 1981-82.

MEMBER: Instituto Internacional de Literatura Iberoamericana, Association of North American Columbanists (president, 1987-89), Modern Language Association of America, American Association of Teachers of Spanish and Portuguese, American Numismatic Association, Kansas Foreign Language Association.

AWARDS, HONORS: Ford Foundation research grants, 1966 and 1968; American Philosophical Society grant, 1968; Tinker Foundation research grant, summer, 1982.

WRITINGS:

Major Cuban Novelists: Innovation and Tradition, University of Missouri Press, 1976.
(Contributor) Juan Valencia and Edward Coughlin, editors, *Homanje a Octavio Paz,* Editorial Universitaria Potosina, 1976.
(Contributor) Raymond L. Williams, editor, *Aproximaciones a Gustavo Alvarez Gardeazabal,* Plaza y Janes (Bogota), 1977.
(Contributor) Gaston F. Fernandez, editor, *La narrativa de Carlos Alberto Montaner,* Planeta/Universidad (Madrid), 1978.
(Contributor) Justo C. Ulloa, editor, *Jose Lezama Lima: Textos Criticos,* Universal (Miami), 1979.
(Contributor) Mechtild Strausfeld, editor, *Aspekte von Jose Lezama Limas "Paradiso,"* Suhrkamp Verlag, 1979.
Lino Novas Calvo, Twayne, 1981.
The Poetic Fiction of Jose Lezama Lima, University of Missouri Press, 1983.

(Contributor) Williams, editor, *Ensayos de literatura columbiana,* Plaza y Janes, 1985.

(Contributor) Daniel Maratos and Marnesba D. Hill, editors, *Escritores de la diaspora cubana/Cuban Exile Writers: A Bibliographical Handbook,* Scarecrow, 1986.

La historia en la novela hispanoamerican moderna, Tercer Mundo Editores (Bogota), 1988.

Contributor of about forty articles and twenty reviews to language and Spanish studies journals.

WORK IN PROGRESS: A book on Guillermo Cabrera Infante.

SIDELIGHTS: Raymond D. Souza told *CA:* "My research and publications deal with Spanish-American literature, and I am particularly interested in prose fiction and poetry as well as literary theory. I became involved in writing about Spanish-American literature because the subject interests me and I enjoy communicating my findings to others. I have never been able to separate teaching from research because I find that a dynamic relationship exists between these two activities. Discoveries and knowledge gained in research inevitably find expression in class, and new ideas uncovered while teaching have resulted in exciting research."

Souza's *Major Cuban Novelists: Innovation and Tradition* "is indeed a highly useful introduction and important contribution to the study of the Cuban novel," according to Jorge A. Marban in the *International Fiction Review.* Marban notes that in this survey of the Cuban novel from the mid-1800s to 1969, the author "strives at clarity, conciseness, and meaningful simplicity when discussing complex and difficult matters." Critics also value Souza's studies of Lino Novas Calvo and Jose Lezama Lima. "There are few critics who know Novas Calvo the man and Novas Calvo the writer as well as Professor Souza; the fruit of that intimate knowledge is this highly recommended Twayne book [*Lino Novas Calvo*]," writes Myron I. Lichtblau in *Hispania.*

Of *The Poetic Fiction of Jose Lezama Lima, International Fiction Review* contributor David William Foster comments, "[it] is an excellent example of a critical approach to a complex work of fiction that falls into neither the sort of reductionist interpretation—plot summaries and thematic paraphrasings—that are often the lot of contemporary narratives nor into the deconstructionist 'paratextualizing' that are often intriguing intellectual constructs but leave one with a (sinful) nostalgia for the text under scrutiny. As a consequence, Souza has made a valuable contribution to the criticism on *Paradiso* that will satisfy the demands of both major critics of Lezama Lima's work and the nonspecialist reader." Furthermore, notes Ramon Magrans in the *Kentucky Romance Quarterly,* Souza "has proven the author's conviction that order and unity do exist in this world although they are not always apparent in our time-bound universe." Magrans calls this reading of Lezama Lima's works "a major accomplishment."

AVOCATIONAL INTERESTS: Numismatics, sailing.

BIOGRAPHICAL/CRITICAL SOURCES:

PERIODICALS

Hispania, December, 1982.
International Fiction Review, Number 4, 1977, Volume 12, number 2, 1985.
Kentucky Romance Quarterly, Volume 32, number 4, 1985.
World Literature Today, summer, 1977.

SPACHE, Evelyn B(ispham) 1929-

PERSONAL: Born August 15, 1929, in Sarasota, Fla.; married Charles Schoonover, 1951; married second husband, George D. Spache, October 29, 1967; children: (first marriage) Raymond, Margo. *Education:* Florida Southern College, B.S., 1951; University of Florida, M.A., 1959. *Religion:* Presbyterian.

ADDRESSES: Home—4042 Wilshire Circle E., Sarasota, Fla. 34238. *Office*—Spache Educational Consultants, Inc., 4042 Wilshire Circle E., Sarasota, Fla. 34238.

CAREER: Elementary teacher in Sarasota, Fla., public schools, 1951-53, 1956-63; teacher in Gainesville, Fla., public schools, 1953-54; Wee Wisdom Nursery School, Gainesville, director, 1954-56; Florida Southern College, Lakeland, assistant professor of education, 1963-65; Jacksonville University, Jacksonville, Fla., assistant professor of education, 1965-70; University of South Florida, Tampa, professor of reading, beginning 1972—. Secretary and treasurer, Spache Educational Consultants, Inc., 1973—; president, E. Spache Investments, Inc., 1981—. Instructor at Provincial Summer School, Halifax, Nova Scotia, 1969. Consultant to School of Education, Johannesburg, South Africa, 1966.

MEMBER: International Reading Association, Association for Childhood Education International, American Association of University Women, American Reading Forum, National Reading Conference, Florida Reading Council, Delta Kappa Gamma.

WRITINGS:

(With husband, George D. Spache) *Reading in the Elementary School,* 2nd edition (Evelyn Spache was not associated with first edition), Allyn & Bacon, 1969, 5th edition, 1986.
Reading Activities for Child Involvement, Allyn & Bacon, 1972, 3rd edition, 1982.
Concepts and Inquiry: Vocabulary Building Exercises, Allyn & Bacon, 1975.
Puzzlers to Teach Phonics, Instructor Publications, 1976.
Puzzlers to Teach Vocabulary Books, Instructor Publications, 1976.
Reproducible Skills and Concept Ideas: Reading Activities for Child Involvement, Allyn & Bacon, 1978.
(With G. D. Spache and others) *Project Achievement: Reading,* Books A-G, Scholastic, Inc., 1982-86.
(With Alice White) *Computerized Placement Appraisal,* Instructional Communications Technology, 1989.

Also author, with Robert Ruddell, of "Pathfinder" series, Allyn & Bacon, 1977.*

*   *   *

SPAULDING, Douglas
See BRADBURY, Ray (Douglas)

*   *   *

SPAULDING, Leonard
See BRADBURY, Ray (Douglas)

*   *   *

SPICKER, Stuart Francis 1937-

PERSONAL: Born May 14, 1937, in New York, N.Y.; son of Mark and Ella (Goldfaden) Spicker; married Lorraine Langlois, October 26, 1984; children: Edana Lynn, Aaron Jon, Glenn

David. *Education:* Queens College (now Queens College of the City University of New York), B.A., 1959; New School for Social Research, M.A., 1962; University of Colorado, Ph.D., 1968.

ADDRESSES: Home—1 Harte Ct., Farmington, Conn. 06117. *Office*—Department of Community Medicine and Health Care, Health Center, School of Medicine, University of Connecticut, Farmington, Conn. 06032.

CAREER: University of Alabama, University, part-time instructor in philosophy, 1963-64; U.S. Air Force Academy, Colorado Springs, Colo., instructor in behavioral sciences, 1964-65, instructor in philosophy, 1965-66, assistant professor of philosophy, 1967; University of Wyoming, Laramie, assistant professor of philosophy, 1967-69; Lea College, Albert Lea, Minn., associate professor of philosophy and behavioral sciences, 1970-71; Coe College, Cedar Rapids, Iowa, associate professor of philosophy and chairman of department, 1971-73; University of Connecticut, Health Center, Farmington, associate professor, 1973-78, professor of community medicine and philosophy, 1978—. Part-time instructor at University of Colorado, 1965-66, and Southern Colorado State College, 1966-67; visiting associate professor at University of Texas, Medical Branch, autumn, 1974. Program associate, National Science Foundation Technical Assessment and Risk Analysis Division, 1982-83. Consultant to Israel Ministry of Defense on Joint Clinical Research Project on Brain Injured Veterans. *Military service:* U.S. Air Force, 1962-67; became captain.

MEMBER: American Philosophical Association (Eastern Division), American Association of University Professors, Aristotelian Society, Institute of Society, Ethics, and the Life Sciences, Metaphysical Society of America, Society for Health and Human Values, Society for Phenomenology and Existential Philosophy, British Society for Phenomenology, Royal Institute of Philosophy, Southern Society for Philosophy and Psychology, Sigma Xi.

AWARDS, HONORS: Fellowship from National Endowment for the Humanities to Cambridge, England, 1969-70; awards from Council for Philosophical Studies, 1968, 1974; fellowship from Institute on Human Values in Medicine to University of Vermont, summer, 1973; grant from National Endowment for the Humanities, 1974-75; grants from Connecticut Humanities Council, 1974-75, 1975-76, 1976-77; grant from F.I.P.S.E., U.S. Department of Education, 1987-89.

WRITINGS:

(Editor and author of introduction) *The Philosophy of the Body: Rejections of Cartesian Dualism,* Quadrangle, 1970.
Temporality: Husserl and Merleau-Ponty, Man & World, 1974.
(Editor with H. T. Engelhardt, and contributor) *Evaluation and Explanation in the Biomedical Sciences,* D. Reidel, 1975.
(Contributor) I. R. Lawson and S. R. Ingman, editors, *The Language of Geriatric Care: Implications for Professional Review,* State of Connecticut, 1975.
(Editor with Engelhardt, and author of introduction) *Philosophical Dimensions of the Neuro-Medical Sciences,* D. Reidel, 1976.
(Editor with Engelhardt, and contributor) *Philosophical Medical Ethics: Its Nature and Significance,* D. Reidel, 1977.
(Editor with Engelhardt, and author of introduction) *Mental Health: Philosophical Perspectives,* D. Reidel, 1977.
(Editor and author of introduction) *Organism, Medicine, and Man: Natura Naturata—Essays in Honor of Hans Jonas on His Seventy-fifth Birthday,* D. Reidel, 1978.

(Editor with Kathleen M. Woodward and David D. Van Tassel) *Aging and the Elderly: Humanistic Perspectives in Gerontology,* Humanities, 1978.
(Editor) *Organism, Medicine, and Metaphysics,* Junk Publishers (Netherlands), 1978.
(Editor with Sally Gadow) *Nursing, Images and Ideals: Opening Dialogue with the Humanities,* Springer Publishing, 1980.
(With Ingman) *Vitalizing Long-Term Care: The Teaching Nursing Home and Other Perspectives,* Springer Publishing, 1984.

Also editor with Engelhardt, and author of introduction, of *Philosophical Foundations of Clinical Judgment,* D. Reidel. Co-editor of "Philosophy and Medicine" series, Kluwer, 35 volumes, 1973—. Editor, with others, of *Proceedings* of Trans-Disciplinary Symposium on Philosophy and Medicine, 1975-79, 1981; co-editor and author of introduction of *Proceedings of the New England Conference on Humanities in Clinical Medicine.* Contributor to *Encyclopedia of Bioethics.* Contributor of articles and reviews to scholarly journals, including *Journal of the British Society of Phenomenology.* Associate editor, *Journal of Medicine and Philosophy,* 1985—; consulting editor of *Connecticut Medicine,* 1976—; editor, *Hospital Ethics Committee Forum,* 1989.

WORK IN PROGRESS: The Bounds of the Body: An Examination of the Metaphysical Foundations of Medicine.

* * *

SPIEGEL, Richard Alan 1947-

PERSONAL: Born January 24, 1947, in New York, N.Y.; son of Morris (a real estate broker) and Sylvia (in newspaper advertising; maiden name, Iskowitz) Spiegel; married Barbara Fisher, June 21, 1983; stepchildren: Athelantis. *Education:* Syracuse University, B.A., 1967; New York University, M.A., 1981.

ADDRESSES: Home—393 St. Pauls Ave., Staten Island, N.Y. 10304. *Office*—250 West 18th St., New York, N.Y. 10011.

CAREER: Teacher at community center in New York City, 1967-68; U.S. Peace Corps, Washington, D.C., teacher in Liberia, 1968-69; teacher at international school in Vilstern, Netherlands, 1970-71; teacher at public schools in Charlotte Amalie, Virgin Islands, 1971-72; Scribblers, New York City, director and editor of *Scribblers Sheet,* 1972-75; Bard Press, New York City, publisher and editor, 1974-80; Waterways Project, New York City, co-director, 1979—. Producer of poetry and folk music programs on cable television, 1972-75; play reader for playwright development program of Public Theater, 1975-76; director of New York Poetry Festival, 1976-78; member of New York City Board of Education Alternative High School and Program Sites.

AWARDS, HONORS: National Endowment for the Arts fellow, 1978.

WRITINGS:

POEMS

Icarus, Bard Press, 1975.
Lust's Last, Bard Press, 1976.
Harbor, Bard Press, 1979.
Syg's Saga, Bard, 1981.

EDITOR; JUVENILE; WITH WIFE, BARBARA FISHER

Poetry Hunter, No. 1, Ten Penny Players, 1981.
More Poetry Hunter, Ten Penny Players, 1981.
Still More Poetry Hunter, Ten Penny Players, 1981.
Subway Slams, Ten Penny Players, 1981.

In Search of a Song, Ten Penny Players, Volume 1: *PS-114,* Volume 2: *PS-276,* 1981, Volume 3: *Jefferson Market Library,* 1982, Volume 4, by Adrienne Day, 1983, Volume 5, by New York Book Fair, 1983, Volume 6, by Roxanne Mennella, 1984, Volume 7, by Sarah Wilkins, 1984, Volume 8: *Inner Clockwork,* 1985.

Greenwich Village Lore and Chinatown Tales, Ten Penny Players, 1983.

Menella and Wilkins, *Dolls,* Ten Penny Players, 1984.

Yearning to Breathe Free, Ten Penny Players, 1984.

Fairies, Elves, and Gnomes, Ten Penny Players, 1985.

Streams I, New York City Board of Education, 1987.

Streams II, New York City Board of Education, 1988.

Streams III, New York City Board of Education, 1989.

Streams IV, New York City Board of Education, 1990.

OTHER

Contributor to anthologies, including *From Hudson to the World,* Hudson River Sloop Clearwater, 1978; and *More than a Gathering of Dreamers,* Coordinating Council of Literary Magazines, 1980. Contributor of poems to periodicals, including *Jewish Currents, Dodeka, Home Planet News, AIM, Public Press,* and *Poet.* Member of editorial board, *American Review,* 1974-77; co-editor with Fisher of *Waterways: Poetry in the Mainstream,* 1979-89, *Forward Face,* Cranio-Facial Unit of New York University Hospital, and *Newsletter* of the Active New York City Committee on the Handicapped Parent.

WORK IN PROGRESS: Poor John, a long poem.

SIDELIGHTS: The Waterways Project is a series of small press book fairs, poetry readings, and workshops. It also operates a literary arts program within the New York City Board of Education, serving students in drug rehabilitation centers, prisons, shelters for the homeless, and alternative high schools.

Richard Alan Spiegel told *CA:* "In order to create audiences for literature it is necessary to involve people in the processes of literature, processes that include authoring and publishing."

*   *   *

SPINELLI, Jerry 1941-

PERSONAL: Born February 1, 1941, in Norristown, Pa.; son of Louis A. (a printer) and Lorna Mae (Bigler) Spinelli; married Eileen Mesi (a writer), May 21, 1977; children: Kevin, Barbara, Lana, Jeffrey, Molly, Sean, Ben. *Education:* Gettysburg College, A.B., 1963; Johns Hopkins University, M.A., 1964; attended Temple University, 1964.

ADDRESSES: Home—331 Melvin Rd., Phoenixville, Pa. 19460. *Agent*—Mrs. Ray Lincoln, Ray Lincoln Literary Agency, Four Surrey Rd., Melrose Park, Pa. 19126.

CAREER: Chilton Co. (magazine publisher), Radnor, Pa., editor, 1966-89. *Military service:* U.S. Naval Air Reserve, 1966-72.

WRITINGS:

JUVENILES

Space Station Seventh Grade, Little, Brown, 1982.
Who Put That Hair in My Toothbrush?, Little, Brown, 1984.
Night of the Whale, Little Brown, 1985.
Jason and Marceline, Little, Brown, 1986.
Dump Days, Little, Brown, 1988.
Maniac Magee, Little, Brown, 1990.

OTHER

(Contributor) Lee Gutkind, editor, *Our Roots Grow Deeper Than We Know: Pennsylvania Writers—Pennsylvania Life,* University of Pittsburgh Press, 1985.

(Contributor) Virginia A. Arnold and Carl B. Smith, editors, *Noble Pursuits,* Macmillan, 1988.

Work represented in anthologies, including *Best Sports Stories of 1982,* Dutton.

SIDELIGHTS: Jerry Spinelli told *CA:* "For most of my kid years, we lived in a brick row house in the West End. I did the usual kid stuff: rode my bike, played chew-the-peg, flipped baseball cards, skimmed flat stones across Stony Creek, cracked twin popsickles, caught poison ivy, wondered about girls, thought stuff that I would never say out loud.

"When I was sixteen, my high school football team won a big game. That night I wrote a poem about it. The poem was published in the local newspaper, and right about then I stopped wanting to become a Major League shortstop and started wanting to become a writer. But first I became a grownup. And I thought, as most grownups do: Okay, now on to the important stuff. So I tried writing grownup novels about important stuff. Nobody wanted them.

"In my thirties I married another writer, Eileen Spinelli. Not only did she bring a wagonload of published poems and stories to the marriage, she brought half-a-dozen kids. Instant fatherhood. One night one of our angels snuck into the refrigerator and swiped the fried chicken that I was saving for lunch the next day. When I discovered the chicken was gone, I did what I had done after the big football victory: I wrote about it.

"I didn't know it at the time, but I had begun to write my first published novel, *Space Station Seventh Grade.* By the time it was finished, hardly anything in it had to do with my grownup, 'important' years. It was all from the West End days. And I had begun to see that in my own memories and in the kids around me, I had all the material I needed for a schoolbagful of books. I saw that each kid is a population unto him- or herself, and that a child's bedroom is as much a window to the universe as an orbiting telescope or a philosopher's study.

"And I saw that each of us, in our kidhoods, was a Huckleberry Finn, drifting on a current that seemed tortuously slow at times, poling for the shore to check out every slightest glimmer in the trees. . . . And the current flows faster and faster, adulthood's delta looms, and one day we look to get our bearings and find that we are out to sea. And now we know what we did not know then: what an adventure it was!"

BIOGRAPHICAL/CRITICAL SOURCES:

PERIODICALS

Los Angeles Times, May 9, 1987.
Washington Post Book World, January 13, 1985.

*   *   *

SPITZER, Robert J(ames) 1953-

PERSONAL: Born September 12, 1953, in Utica, N.Y.; son of William H. (a New York State lottery director) and Virginia (a political consultant; maiden name, Moak) Spitzer. *Education:* State University of New York College at Fredonia, B.A. (summa cum laude), 1975; Cornell University, M.A., 1978, Ph.D., 1980.

ADDRESSES: Home—29 Clinton St., Homer, N.Y. 13077. *Office*—Department of Political Science, State University of New York College at Cortland, P.O. Box 2000, Cortland, N.Y. 13045.

CAREER: Eisenhower College, Seneca Falls, N.Y. (now Rochester Institute of Technology), instructor in political science, 1978-79; Cornell University, Ithaca, N.Y., instructor in political science, 1979; State University of New York College at Cortland, assistant professor, 1979-84, associate professor, 1984-89, professor of political science, 1989—, chairman of department, 1983-89. Visiting professor at Cornell University, 1980, 1988, 1989 and State University College of Technology, Utica-Rome, 1985, 1986, 1988. Adjunct professor at Tompkins-Cortland Community College, 1982-83. Member of New York State Commission on the Bicentennial of the U.S. Constitution, 1986-1989 and New York State Ratification Celebration Committee for U.S. Constitution Bicentennial, 1987-88.

MEMBER: American Political Science Association, Policy Studies Organization, Center for the Study of the Presidency, Presidency Research Group, New York Political Science Association, Phi Sigma Alpha, Phi Beta Kappa, Phi Alpha Theta.

AWARDS, HONORS: National Endowment for the Humanities research grant, 1986.

WRITINGS:

The Presidency and Public Policy: The Four Arenas of Presidential Power, University of Alabama Press, 1983.

(Contributor) Peter W. Colby, editor, *New York State Today,* State University of New York Press, 1984, revised edition, 1989.

(Contributor) Susan Bursell, editor, *Criminal Justice,* Greenhaven Press, 1986.

The Right to Life Movement and Third Party Politics, Greenwood Press, 1987.

(Contributor) Raymond Tatalovich and Byron Daynes, editors, *Social Regulatory Policy: Recent Moral Controversies in American Politics,* Westview Press, 1988.

The Presidential Veto: Touchstone of the American Presidency, State University of New York Press, 1988.

(Contributor) Thomas Cronin, editor, *Inventing the American Presidency: Early Decisions and Critical Precedents,* University Press of Kansas, 1989.

(Contributor) Michael Nelson, editor, *The Congressional Quarterly Guide to the Presidency,* Congressional Quarterly, 1989.

President and Congress, McGraw, 1990.

Also contributor of articles and reviews to political science journals and newspapers, including *American Political Science Review, American Journal of Political Science, Policy Studies Journal, Journal of Politics, American Politics Quarterly, Congress and the Presidency, Rochester Times Union, Syracuse Post Standard,* and *Des Moines Register.* Copy editor of *Administrative Science Quarterly,* 1982-83.

SIDELIGHTS: Robert J. Spitzer told *CA:* "My concern in the study of the presidency centers on the lack of agreement over how the institution does and should work. Most argue that the 'success' or 'failure' of a presidency (however one might define these terms) is determined mostly by the president's personal skill, initiative, political experience, and the like. These factors are important, but I argue that there are a whole set of factors that shape what the president does and how well he does it that are external to his personal skills. My study is an attempt to identify these factors, to show how presidential actions and outcomes are shaped by factors common to all presidents, whether liberal or conservative, Republican or Democrat.

"Let me add a word about writing. Most of the people I know find the writing process difficult-to-agonizing. I must confess, if sheepishly, that I enjoy writing. Even in my field of political science, I find the writing a creative and stimulating process. Teaching and administrative duties limit the time I can devote to writing, but it is always psychically rewarding."

*   *   *

SPROUL, R(obert) C(harles)   1939-

PERSONAL: Born February 13, 1939, in Pittsburgh, Pa.; son of Robert C. (a certified public accountant) and Mayre (Yardis) Sproul; married Vesta Ann Voorhis, June 11, 1960; children: Sherrie Sproul Dick, Robert Craig. *Education:* Westminster College, New Wilmington, Pa., B.A., 1961; Pittsburgh Theological Seminary, B.D., 1964; Free University of Amsterdam, Drs., 1969.

ADDRESSES: Home—Orlando, Fla. *Office*—Department of Theology/Apologetics, Reformed Theological Seminary, 5422 Clinton Blvd., Jackson, Miss. 39209.

CAREER: Ordained United Presbyterian minister, 1965; ordained minister of Presbyterian Church of America, 1976; Westminster College, New Wilmington, Pa., instructor in philosophy and theology, 1965-66; Gordon College, Wenham, Mass., assistant professor of theological studies, 1966-68; Conwell School of Theology (now Conwell Theological Seminary), South Hamilton, Mass., assistant professor of philosophical theology, 1968-69, visiting professor of apologetics, 1971-81; College Hill United Presbyterian Church, Cincinnati, Ohio, minister of theology, 1969-71; Ligonier Valley Study Center (now Ligonier Ministries), Stahlstown, Pa., president, 1971—; Reformed Theological Seminary, Jackson, Miss., professor of systematic theology and apologetics, 1980—, John Dyer Trimble, Sr. chair, 1987—. Director of Coalition for Christian Outreach, Inc., 1971-76, Prison Fellowship, Inc., 1978-84, Evangelism Explosion III International, 1980-81, and Serve International, Inc., 1982—; member of executive committee of International Council on Biblical Inerrancy, 1977-83.

MEMBER: Philosophical Theological Society.

AWARDS, HONORS: Litt.D. from Geneva College, 1976; Angel Award, 1984, for *Johnny Come Home.*

WRITINGS:

The Symbol, Presbyterian & Reformed Publishing, 1973, reprinted as *Basic Training: Plain Talk on the Key Truths of the Faith,* Zondervan, 1982.

The Psychology of Atheism, Bethany Fellowship, 1974, reprinted as *If There Is a God, Why Are There Atheists?,* Bethany House, 1978.

God's Inerrant Word, Bethany House, 1975.

Discovering the Intimate Marriage, Bethany House, 1975.

Objections Answered, Regal Books, 1978, reprinted as *Reason to Believe,* Zondervan, 1982.

Knowing Scripture, Inter-Varsity Press, 1978.

Stronger than Steel, Harper, 1980.

In Search of Dignity, Regal Books, 1983.

Who Is Jesus?, Tyndale, 1983.

Ethics and the Christian, Tyndale, 1983.

Johnny Come Home, Regal Books, 1984, reprinted as *Thy Brother's Keeper,* Wolgemuth & Hyatt, 1988.

Classical Apologetics, Zondervan, 1984.

Effective Prayer, Tyndale, 1984.
God's Will and the Christian, Tyndale, 1984.
The Holiness of God, Tyndale, 1985.
The Intimate Marriage, Tyndale, 1986.
Lifeviews, Fleming Revell, 1986.
Chosen by God, Tyndale, 1986.
One Holy Passion, T. Nelson, 1987.
Pleasing God, Tyndale, 1988.
Surprised by Suffering, Tyndale, 1989.

SIDELIGHTS: R. C. Sproul told *CA:* "Of all the avenues of communication which I use—teaching, lecturing, preaching, radio, videotape, television—I like writing the best. It is the first priority, the passion of my life. I have said on occasion, 'Lock me in my study and throw away the key and I will be happy.' But a strong sense of duty will not allow me this luxury. Writing has such a 'finished' character to it. It is the best means I have of expressing the good, the true, and the beautiful which is what my writing is all about. I am convinced that these things can only be defined and understood from a comprehensive understanding of the Christian faith, so that provides both my motivation and my working framework. And published works have the possibility of enduring through time, of speaking not only to this generation but to the next.

"Authors who have captured my mind by the sheer scope and integrity of their thought include Martin Luther, John Calvin, and Jonathan Edwards. In terms of style I am awed by William Manchester."

*   *   *

STALEY, Thomas F(abian) 1935-

PERSONAL: Born August 13, 1935, in Pittsburgh, Pa.; son of Fabian Richard and Mary (McNulty) Staley; married Carolyn O'Brien, September 3, 1960; children: Thomas Fabian, Caroline Ann, Mary Elizabeth, Timothy X. *Education:* Regis College, A.B. and B.S., both 1957; University of Tulsa, M.A., 1958; University of Pittsburgh, Ph.D., 1962.

ADDRESSES: Home—2528 Tanglewood Trail, Austin, Tex. 78703. *Office*—Harry Random Humanities Research Center, P.O. Drawer 7219, University of Texas, Austin, Tex. 78713.

CAREER: Rollins College, Winter Park, Fla., assistant professor of English, 1961-62; University of Tulsa, Tulsa, Okla., assistant professor, 1962-67, associate professor, 1967-69, professor of English, 1969-88, Trustees' Professor of Modern Literature, 1977-88, dean of graduate school, 1969-77, acting vice president for academic affairs, 1977, provost, 1983-88; University of Texas at Austin, director of Harry Ransom Humanities Research Center and professor of English, 1988—. Fulbright professor in Italy, 1966-67, spring, 1971; visiting professor at University of Pittsburgh, 1967, 1970, and State University of New York at Buffalo, summer, 1974. Chair/co-chair of International James Joyce Symposium, 1967, 1969, 1971, 1973, and 1977; president of James Joyce Foundation, 1969-73 (member of board of directors, 1967—). Chairman of board of directors of Undercroft Montessori School, 1969-70, and Marquette School, 1969-70; director of Graduate Institute of Modern Letters, 1970-77; member of board of directors of Cascia Hall Preparatory School. Member of advisory board of Tulsa Arts and Humanities Council, 1970-79; member of Tulsa City-County Library Commission, 1974; member of Institute for the Humanities at Salado.

MEMBER: American Association of University Professors, Modern Language Association of America, Anglo-Irish Studies Association, American Committee for Irish Studies, James Joyce Society, South Central Modern Language Association (section chairman, 1965-66, 1968-69, 1970-71, 1975-76), Midwest Association of Graduate Schools, Friends of the Tulsa County Library (member of board of directors, 1971-83), Tulsa Tennis Club.

AWARDS, HONORS: Danforth associate, 1962-66, senior associate, 1967—; American Council of Learned Societies grant, 1969.

WRITINGS:

(Editor) *James Joyce Today: Essays on the Major Works,* Indiana University Press, 1966.
(Contributor) Lester Zimmerman, editor, *Jonathan Swift: Tercentenary Essays* (monograph), University of Tulsa, 1967.
(Editor with H. J. Mooney, Jr., and contributor) *The Shapeless God: Essays on the Modern Novel,* University of Pittsburgh Press, 1968.
James Joyce's Portrait of the Artist, Littlefield, 1968.
(Editor with Zimmerman) *Literature and Theology* (monograph), University of Tulsa, 1969.
(Editor with James R. Baker) *Dubliners: A Critical Handbook,* Wadsworth, 1969.
(Editor) *Italo Svevo: Essays on His Work* (monograph), University of Tulsa, 1969.
(Contributor) W. T. Zyla, editor, *James Joyce: His Place in World Literature,* Texas Tech Press, 1969.
(Editor with Bernard Benstock, and contributor) *Approaches to Ulysses: Ten Essays,* University of Pittsburgh Press, 1970.
(Editor) *Ulysses: Fifty Years,* University of Indiana Press, 1974.
(Contributor) Richard Finneran, editor, *Anglo-Irish Literature: A Review of the Research,* Modern Language Association of America, 1976.
Dorothy Richardson, Twayne, 1976.
(With Benstock) *Approaches to Joyce's Portrait: Ten Essays,* University of Pittsburgh Press, 1976.
Jean Rhys: A Critical Study, Macmillan, 1979.
Twentieth-Century Women Novelists, Macmillan, 1982.
(Editor) *Dictionary of Literary Biography,* Gale, Volume 34: *British Novelists, 1890-1929: Traditionalists,* 1985, Volume 36: *British Novelists, 1890-1929: Modernists,* 1985.
An Annotated Critical Bibliography of James Joyce, St. Martin's, 1989.

WORK IN PROGRESS: "Religious Elements and Thomistic Encounters: Noon on Joyce and Aquinas," in collection of essays on Joyce for University of Illinois Press; *A Joyce Companion,* for Macmillan.

*   *   *

STANDISH, Carole
See KOEHLER, Margaret (Hudson)

*   *   *

STAUFFER, Helen Winter 1922-

PERSONAL: Born January 4, 1922, in Mitchell, S.D.; daughter of Fred Bernhard and Lila (Erie) Winter; married Mitchell H. Stauffer, March 30, 1944; children: Susan, Sally, Robin, Melody. *Education:* Kearney State College, B.A. (magna cum laude), 1964, M.S., 1968; University of Nebraska, Ph.D., 1974.

ADDRESSES: Office—Department of English, Kearney State College, 905 West 25th St., Kearney, Neb. 68847.

CAREER: High school English teacher in Grand Island, Neb., 1964-67; Kearney State College, Kearney, Neb., instructor, 1968-72, assistant professor, 1972-74, associate professor, 1974-76, professor of English, 1976—. *Military service:* U.S. Navy, Women Accepted for Volunteer Emergency Service (WAVES), 1942-44.

MEMBER: Modern Language Association of America, National Education Association, Western Literature Association (president, 1980), Nebraska Council of Teachers of English, Phi Theta Kappa, Pi Delta Phi, Sigma Tau Delta, Delta Tau Kappa, Alpha Delta Kappa, Kappa Delta Pi.

AWARDS, HONORS: Grants from Nebraska State College Research Council, 1972, 1973, 1975-76, 1982, 1987, and 1988; grant from National Endowment for the Humanities, 1976; Mary Major Crawford Award from Kearney State College.

WRITINGS:

(Contributor) Merrill Lewis and L. L. Lee, editors, *Women, Women Writers, and the West,* Whitston Publishing, 1980.
(Contributor) Fred Erisman and Richard W. Etulain, editors, *Fifty Western Writers,* Greenwood Press, 1982.
Mari Sandoz: Story Catcher of the Plains, University of Nebraska Press, 1982.
(Editor with Susan J. Rosowski) *Women and Western American Literature,* Whitston Press, 1982.
(Editor and author of introduction) *Welded Women: Poems of Nancy Westerfield,* Kearney State College Press, 1983.
(Contributor) Vine DeLoria, Jr., editor, *Sender of Words: Essays in Memory of John G. Neihardt,* Howe Brothers, 1984.
(Contributor) Susan Pierce, editor, *Perspectives: Women in Nebraska History,* Nebraska Department of Education and Nebraska State Council for Social Studies, 1984.
(Contributor) Everett Albert, editor, *Great Plains Chautauqua Tabloid,* Kansas, Nebraska, South Dakota, and North Dakota Committees for the Humanities, 1985, new edition, 1986.
(Contributor) J. Golden Taylor and others, editors, *Literary History of the American West,* Western Literature Association and Texas Christian University Press, 1987.

Contributor to periodicals, including *Great Plains Quarterly, Prairie Schooner, Kansas Heritage, Western American Literature, Platte Valley Review, Georgia Historical Quarterly,* and *New Mexico Historical Review.*

WORK IN PROGRESS: Editing the letters of Mari Sandoz for a book tentatively entitled *The Western Writer and the Eastern Establishment: Selected Letters of Mari Sandoz, 1924-1966.*

SIDELIGHTS: Helen Winter Stauffer told *CA:* "My study of Sandoz began with admiration for *Crazy Horse,* her biography of the Oglala Sioux war chief who fought generals Crook and Custer in the Indian wars on the Plains in the 1870s. Her ability to recreate the man and his time was impressive; her understanding of her protagonist and his milieu suggests extensive knowledge of and sympathy for another culture than her own. As I made inquiries into Sandoz's use of sources I discovered that she had access to special information most other researchers overlooked or did not know about. In the process of locating that information and examining Sandoz's use of it, I myself became enthusiastic about Plains history, geography, and sociology. Although I appreciated Sandoz's first book, *Old Jules,* the biography of her father who was important in the settlement of the northwestern Nebraska frontier, it was not until I began the study of *Crazy Horse* and began to read Sandoz's voluminous correspondence that I appreciated the fact that Mari Sandoz had

herself led an interesting life: a childhood on a violent frontier, years of frustration and near-starvation in Lincoln, Nebraska, before she published, [then] later years of success, living in New York City, but longing always for the West.

"Although the role of women in the West was not a major issue for Sandoz (with the exception of Gulla Slogum and Miss Morissa, Sandoz's protagonists are usually male), my study of her work led me to an interest in other western women writers and, further, to other experiences of women who helped to develop the country. All too much western literature uses the old mythic plots that tend to treat the female as an adjunct to the male hero. The women's journals and diaries now being published make it clear that female heroes did and do exist, and their stories often refute the idea that there can be little interesting in a female, whether she lives only in fiction or in real life."

Stauffer adds, "As an offshoot of my interest in Sandoz and other western women writers, I portrayed Mari Sandoz for eight weeks in the summer of 1985 for the Great Plains Chautauqua, and played the role of Libbie Custer in 1986 and 1987."

*   *   *

STEBBINS, Robert A(lan)   1938-

PERSONAL: Born June 22, 1938, in Rhinelander, Wis.; son of William N. (a business executive) and Dorothy (Guy) Stebbins; married Karin Y. Olson, January 11, 1964; children: Paul, Lisa, Christi. *Education:* Macalester College, B.A., 1961; University of Minnesota, M.A., 1962, Ph.D., 1964. *Politics:* None. *Religion:* None.

ADDRESSES: Home—144 Edgemont Estates Dr., N.W., Calgary, Alberta, Canada T3A 2M3. *Office*—Department of Sociology, University of Calgary, Calgary, Alberta, Canada T2N 1N4.

CAREER: Presbyterian College, Clinton, S.C., associate professor of sociology, 1964-65; Memorial University of Newfoundland, St. John's, assistant professor, 1965-68, associate professor of sociology and chairman of department of sociology and anthropology, 1968-73; University of Texas at Arlington, professor of sociology, 1973-76; University of Calgary, Calgary, Alberta, professor of sociology and chairman of department, 1976—. President, St. John's Symphony Orchestra, 1968-69. *Military service:* Minnesota National Guard, 1956-64; became staff sergeant.

MEMBER: International Sociological Association, Canadian Sociology and Anthropology Association (president, 1987-88), American Sociological Association, Society for the Study of Symbolic Interaction, Society for the Study of Social Problems (member of publications committee, 1976-79), Pacific Sociological Association, International Society of Bassists.

AWARDS, HONORS: Canada Council leave fellowship, 1971-72; National Endowment for the Humanities summer stipend, 1976; Calgary Institute for the Humanities fellow, 1987-88.

WRITINGS:

Commitment to Deviance: The Nonprofessional Criminal in the Community, Greenwood Press, 1971.
The Disorderly Classroom: Its Physical and Temporal Conditions, Memorial University of Newfoundland, 1974.
Teachers and Meaning, E. J. Brill, 1975.
Amateurs: On the Margin between Work and Leisure, Sage Publications, 1979.

(Editor with William B. Shaffir and Allan Turowetz) *Fieldwork Experience: Qualitative Approaches to Social Research,* St. Martin's, 1980.

(Editor with Turowetz and Michael Rosenberg) *The Sociology of Deviance,* St. Martin's, 1982.

The Magician: Career, Culture, and Social Psychology in a Variety Art, Irwin, 1984.

Sociology: The Study of Society, Harper, 1987.

Canadian Football: The View from the Helmet, University of Western Ontario, 1987.

Deviance: Tolerable Differences, McGraw-Hill/Ryerson Press, 1988.

Contributor of articles to journals in the United States, Canada, and Europe. Member of editorial board, *Canadian Review of Sociology and Anthropology,* 1970-73; associate editor, *Journal of Jazz Studies,* 1973-82.

WORK IN PROGRESS: The Laugh Makers: Stand-Up Comedy as Art, Business, and Life-Style.

SIDELIGHTS: Robert A. Stebbins told *CA:* "With the completion of the study of Canadian stand-up comics, I am now in a position to start on the synthesis of eight field studies undertaken since 1974 of amateurs and professionals in art, science, sport, and entertainment. That synthesis will examine, at a somewhat more abstract level, the interplay between those two categories of work and leisure and the lifestyles of those who pursue careers as pastimes or occupations in the four areas. My interest in the synthesis will include the ways in which the central activity intersects with family roles and leisure or occupational roles and the thrills and disappointments and costs and rewards connected with these activities."

*   *   *

STEGLICH, W(infred) G(eorge) 1921-

PERSONAL: Born September 21, 1921, in Giddings, Tex.; son of Gustav E. (a custodian) and Meta (Behnken) Steglich; married Ruth Edwards, May 30, 1948; children: Carolyn Sue, Catherine Ann, James Edwards. *Education:* Concordia College, Oakland, Calif., A.A., 1940; Concordia Seminary, St. Louis, Mo., B.A., 1942, diploma in theology, 1946; attended Washington University, St. Louis, 1942-43; University of Texas, M.A., 1945, Ph.D., 1951; attended Florida State University, 1955-56. *Politics:* Independent. *Religion:* Lutheran.

ADDRESSES: Home—3926 Briarcrest Dr., Norman, Okla. 73072. *Office*—Department of Sociology, University of Oklahoma, Norman, Okla. 73069.

CAREER: University of Texas at Austin, instructor in sociology, 1946-48; University of New Mexico, Albuquerque, instructor in sociology, 1948-49; Colorado State University, Fort Collins, assistant professor, 1949-52, associate professor of sociology, 1952-57, chairman of sociology section, 1954-57; Texas Technological College (now Texas Tech University), Lubbock, associate professor, 1957-59, professor of sociology, 1959-68, head of department of sociology and anthropology, 1960-68; University of Texas at El Paso, professor of sociology and head of department, 1968-76; University of Oklahoma, Norman, professor of sociology and chairperson of department, 1976—. Visiting professor, University of Texas at Austin, summer, 1961, and California State University, Hayward, summer, 1973. Member of advisory committees of various educational research groups.

MEMBER: American Sociological Association (fellow), Population Association of America, American Association for the Advancement of Science, Southwestern Sociological Association (president, 1962-63), Southwestern Social Science Association (president, 1975-76), Southern Sociological Association, Oklahoma Sociological Association, Alpha Kappa Delta, Pi Gamma Mu.

AWARDS, HONORS: Research grant, Hogg Foundation for Mental Health, 1959-62; visiting fellow, Episcopal Theological Seminary of the Southwest, 1964.

WRITINGS:

(Contributor) Reuben Hahn, editor, *Present-Day Issues in the Light of Faith,* Missouri Synod, Lutheran Church, 1959.

(Author of teacher's manual) Francis Merrill, *Society and Culture: An Introduction to Sociology,* Prentice-Hall, 1961, 4th edition, 1969.

(Contributor) Lawrence L. Graves, editor, *The History of Lubbock,* West Texas Museum Association, 1962.

(Contributor) Mhyra S. Minnis and Walter J. Cartwright, editors, *Sociological Perspectives: Readings in Deviant Behavior and Social Problems,* W. C. Brown, 1968.

Student Guide to Sociology, Prentice-Hall, 1969.

(Contributor) C. L. Ainsworth, editor, *Teachers and Counselors for Mexican American Children,* Southwest Education Development Corp., 1969.

(With Margaret Snooks) *American Social Problems: An Institutional View,* Goodyear Publishing Co., 1980.

Contributor to proceedings; contributor of articles and reviews on sociology to various journals.

WORK IN PROGRESS: Common Concepts in General Sociology; research on mortality and infant mortality in the Spanish surname population; research on the demography of the U.S.-Mexican border.*

*   *   *

STEIN, Herman D(avid) 1917-

PERSONAL: Born August 13, 1917, in New York, N.Y.; son of Charles and Emma (Rosenblum) Stein; married Charmion Kerr (a social worker), September 15, 1946; children: Karen Lou Gelender, Shoshi Stein Bennett, Naomi Elizabeth. *Education:* College of the City of New York (now City College of the City University of New York), B.S.S., 1939; Columbia University, M.S., 1941, D.S.W., 1958.

ADDRESSES: Home—3211 Van Aken Blvd., Shaker Heights, Ohio 44120. *Office*—Case Western Reserve University, 436 Pardee, 2040 Adelbert Rd., Cleveland, Ohio 44106.

CAREER: Jewish Family Service, New York City, caseworker and director of public relations, 1941-45; Columbia University School of Social Work, New York City, instructor, 1945-47; American Joint Distribution Committee, Paris, France, deputy director of budget and research and director of welfare department, 1947-50; Columbia University School of Social Work, instructor to associate professor, 1950-64, professor, 1958-64, director of research center, 1959-62; Case Western Reserve University, Cleveland, Ohio, dean and professor, School of Applied Social Sciences, 1964-68, provost of social and behavioral sciences, 1967-71, university provost and vice president, 1968-72 and 1986-88, university professor, 1972—. Faculty member, Smith College, summers, 1951-62; visiting professor, University of Hawaii, 1971-72; lecturer, Harvard University School of Public Health, 1971-83. Founder and director, Global Currents Lectures, Case Western Reserve University, 1983-87. Consultant to business firms, international governmental organizations, social service organizations, and state and local governments, 1952—; member of advisory committees, National Institute of Mental Health, 1959-71; member of board, Mobilization for Youth, 1961-64; chairman, Mayor's Commission on the Crisis in Welfare in Cleveland, 1967-68; senior advisor to executive director, UNICEF, 1976-82.

MEMBER: International Conference on Social Welfare, International Association of Schools of Social Work, Council on Social Work Education, National Association of Social Workers, American Sociological Society, Society for Applied Anthropology, Society for the Study of Social Problems, Society for Psychological Study of Social Issues, Council on International Programs, Club of Rome (associate member).

AWARDS, HONORS: L.H.D., Hebrew Union College-Jewish Institute of Religion, 1969; distinguished service award, Council on Social Work Education, 1970; Rene Sand Award, International Council on Social Welfare, 1984.

WRITINGS:

Careers for Men in Family Social Work, Family Welfare Association of America, 1946.
The Story of the Jewish Board of Guardians, Jewish Board of Guardians, 1947.
Measuring Your Public Relations, National Publicity Council, 1952.
(With Richard A. Cloward) *Social Perspectives on Behavior,* Free Press of Glencoe, 1958.
(Contributor) Marshall Sklare, editor, *The Jews,* Free Press of Glencoe, 1958.
The Curriculum Study of Columbia University School of Social Work, School of Social Work, Columbia University, 1961.
(With John M. Martin and Alex Rosen) *The Swastika Daubings and Related Incidents of Winter 1960,* School of Social Work, Columbia University, 1961.
(With Joseph L. Blau, Nathan Glazer, Oscar Handlin, and Mary F. Handlin) *The Characteristics of American Jews,* Jewish Education Committee Press, 1965.
(Editor) *Planning for the Needs of Children in Developing Countries,* United Nations Childrens Fund, 1965.
(Editor) *Social Theory and Social Invention,* Case Western Reserve University Press, 1968.
(Editor) *The Crisis in Welfare in Cleveland: Report of the Mayor's Commission,* Case Western Reserve University Press, 1969.
(With Irwin T. Sanders) *Social Work Education, Family Planning, and Population Dynamics: Summary and Critique of an International Conference,* Council on Social Work Education, 1971.
(With Avis L. Kristenson) *The Professional School and the University: The Case of Social Work,* Council on Social Work Education, 1971.
(Editor) *Organization and the Human Services: Cross-Disciplinary Reflections,* Temple University Press, 1981.

Contributor to books and encyclopedias. Contributor of more than one hundred articles and monographs to professional and scientific journals; contributor of reviews to various journals.

WORK IN PROGRESS: Studies of African social development.

SIDELIGHTS: Herman D. Stein has lived in or travelled on missions to all the countries of western Europe, to northern and eastern Africa, including Egypt, to western Africa, including the Ivory Coast, Togo, Burkina Faso, and Nigeria, to Israel and Bra-

zil, in addition to India, Thailand, the Phillipines, Indonesia, and other Asian countries. He is fluent in French and Hebrew.

*   *   *

STEINER, Barbara A(nnette)   1934-
(Alix Ainsley, Anne Daniel; Kate D'Andrea, Annette Cole, joint pseudonyms)

PERSONAL: Born November 3, 1934, in Dardanelle, Ark.; daughter of Hershel Thomas (a collector and dealer of Indian relics) and Rachel Julia (an antiques dealer; maiden name, Stilley) Daniel; married Kenneth E. Steiner (an electrical engineer), August 4, 1957 (divorced January, 1980); children: Rachel Anne, Rebecca Sue. *Education:* Henderson State Teachers College (now Henderson State College), Arkadelphia, Ark., B.S.E., 1955; University of Kansas, M.S.E., 1959; attended University of Colorado, 1973 and 1975. *Religion:* Protestant.

ADDRESSES: Home—Boulder, Colo.

CAREER: Writer. Elementary school teacher in the public schools of Independence, Mo., 1955-57, Lawrence, Kan., 1957-58, Wichita, Kan., 1958-59, and Nederland, Colo., 1966-68; local church librarian, 1969-74. Actor in local religious drama productions, 1971-75; member of task force for Boulder Council of Churches, 1971-75; youth group director, 1972-74.

MEMBER: Society of Children's Book Writers (vice-president of Rocky Mountain Chapter, 1976-77, president, 1977-78, regional advisor, 1980-85; member of national board, 1984-88, 1989-92), Audubon Society, National Wildlife Association, Colorado Authors League, Evergreen Art Association (president, 1962-63), Evergreen Home Demonstration Club (president, 1961-62), Boulder Tennis Association (secretary, 1970, vice-president, 1977).

AWARDS, HONORS: Top Hand award, 1972, and best juvenile article award, 1973, both from Colorado Authors league; best juvenile nonfiction book citation, Colorado Authors League, outstanding science book for children citation, National Science Teachers Association and Children's Book Council, both 1973, both for *Biography of a Polar Bear;* Top Hand award, 1977, for *Biography of a Kangaroo Rat,* 1981, for juvenile poetry, 1984, for *Hat Full of Love,* 1986, for *Oliver Dibbs to the Rescue,* 1986, for *Is There a Cure for Sophomore Year?,* and *Creative Writing: A Guide for Teaching Young People,* 1987, for *Oliver Dibbs and the Dinosaur Cause;* Children's Book Award citation, 1982, for *But Not Stanleigh,* 1984, for *Stanleigh's Wrong-Side-Out Day,* and 1988, for *Oliver Dibbs to the Rescue;* Dorothy Canfield Fisher award nomination, 1989, for *Tessa.*

WRITINGS:

Biography of a Polar Bear, Putnam, 1972.
Biography of a Wolf, Putnam, 1973.
Your Hobby: Stamp Collecting, Schmitt, Hall & McCreary, 1973.
Biography of a Desert Bighorn, Putnam, 1975.
Biography of a Kangaroo Rat, Putnam, 1977.
Biography of a Killer Whale, Putnam, 1978.
Biography of a Bengal Tiger, Putnam, 1979.
But Not Stanleigh, Childrens Press, 1980.
Stanleigh's Wrong-Side-Out Day, Childrens Press, 1982.
Secret Love (young adult), Scholastic Book Services, 1982.
Searching Heart (young adult), Scholastic Book Services, 1982.
Hat Full of Love (young adult), Tempo Books, 1983.
See You in July (young adult), Silhouette Press, 1984.
Tia and Keith (young adult), Warner Books, 1984.

The Secret of the Dark (young adult), Scholastic Book Services, 1984.
(With Kathleen Phillips) *Creative Writing: A Handbook for Teaching Young People,* Libraries Unlimited, 1985.
(Under pseudonym Alix Ainsley) *House of the Whispering Aspens,* Zebra, 1985.
Oliver Dibbs to the Rescue ("Oliver Dibbs" series) Macmillan, 1986.
Is There a Cure for Sophomore Year?, Signet, 1986.
Life of the Party, Dell, 1986.
The Night Before, Fawcett, 1986.
Sweet Revenge, Fawcett, 1986.
If You Love Me, Bantam, 1986.
Oliver Dibbs and the Dinosaur Cause ("Oliver Dibbs" series), Macmillan, 1986.
(Under pseudonym Alix Ainsley) *Echoes of Landre House,* Zebra, 1987.
Sunny Side Up, Field Publications, 1987.
Everybody Loves a Clown, Field Publications, 1987.
Sneaking Around, Field Publications, 1987.
Kristin's Song, Field Publications, 1988.
(With Kathleen Phillips) *Catching Ideas: Creative Writing Activity Book,* Libraries Unlimited, 1988.
Love Match, Willowisp, 1988.
Puppy Love, Willowisp, 1988.
Tessa (young adult), Morrow Junior Books, 1988.
The Photographer, Avon Books, 1989.
Whale Brother, Walker & Co., 1989.
Dolby and the Woof-Off ("Oliver Dibbs" series), Morrow Junior Books, 1990.
Ghost Cave, Harcourt, 1990.
Desert Trip, Sierra Club Books, 1990.

Also author of "Hardy Boys Casefiles" number 20, *Witness to Murder,* Archway, 1988, and of "Cassandra Best, Teen Detective," number 4, *Treasure Beach,* Grosset & Dunlap, 1989. Contributor, sometimes under pseudonyms, of over sixty articles, stories, plays, and poems to children's and teen magazines and religious publications, including *Humpty Dumpty, Ranger Rick, Woman's Day, Childlife,* and *Starwind.*

WORK IN PROGRESS: If You Were an Aborigine Child, a picture book; "Foghorn Jones" series of junior adventure novels; a fourth Oliver Dibbs book; *Journal Keeping for Children,* with Kathleen Phillips.

SIDELIGHTS: "While I still write for teens," Barbara A. Steiner told *CA,* "I am writing more and more for younger children now. I have discovered that I can write humor, and am having a good time writing the Oliver Dibbs series. Oliver is very interested in animals and animal causes as am I. In the *Dinosaur Cause,* Oliver even fought for extinct animal causes, getting Stegosaurus elected Colorado state fossil.

"I am very pleased to announce the publication of *Tessa* from Morrow Junior Books. The book took five years to write, because I was writing from some of the truths in my life, my childhood, and often it is difficult to go back in time. However, I have always wished I could have dug Indian relics with my father in the river bottoms of Arkansas. Tessa does this in the novel. Sometimes when you write a book about your own life, you can go back and live parts of it over again, doing some of the things you wished you had done. This book deals again with one of my favorite themes, teen rights, the right to choose, make one's own mistakes, decisions. Tessa's decision held no easy answers."

AVOCATIONAL INTERESTS: Tennis, backpacking, photography, birding, travelling, needlework (especially quilting), stamp collecting, American Indian masks and Navajo rugs, scout badge teaching (especially creative writing and drama), speaking to school children about being an author.

*   *   *

STEWART, Desmond (Stirling)   1924-1981

PERSONAL: Born April 20, 1924, in Leavesden, England; died June 12, 1981, in London, England; son of Roy Mackenzie (a physician) and Agnes Maud (Stirling) Stewart. *Education:* Trinity College, Oxford, M.A. (with honors), 1946, B.Litt., 1948. *Religion:* Church of England.

ADDRESSES: Agent—Anthony Sheil Associates Ltd., 2/3 Morwell St., London WC1B 3AR, England.

CAREER: University of Baghdad, Baghdad, Iraq, assistant professor of English, 1948-56; inspector of English in Islamic schools in Beirut, Lebanon, 1956-58; writer, 1958-81. Former Middle East correspondent for *Spectator,* London, England.

MEMBER: Royal Society of Literature (fellow).

WRITINGS:

FICTION

Leopard in the Grass, Euphorion Books, 1951, Farrar, Straus, 1952.
The Memoirs of Alcibiades, Euphorion Books, 1952.
The Unsuitable Englishman, Farrar, Straus, 1954.
A Woman Besieged, Heinemann, 1959.
The Men of Friday, Heinemann, 1961.
The Sequence of Roles (trilogy), Chapman & Hall, Book 1: *The Round Mosaic,* 1965, Book 2: *The Pyramid Inch,* 1966, Book 3: *The Mamelukes,* 1968.
The Vampire of Mons, Harper, 1976.

NONFICTION

(With John Haylock) *New Babylon: A Portrait of Iraq,* Collins, 1956.
(With Gerald Hamilton) *Emma in Blue: A Romance of Friendship,* Wingate, 1957, Roy, 1958.
Young Egypt, Wingate, 1958.
Turmoil in Beirut: A Personal Account, Wingate, 1958.
(With the editors of *Life* magazine) *The Arab World* (juvenile), Time-Life, 1962, revised edition, 1968.
(With the editors of *Life* magazine) *Turkey* (juvenile), Time-Life, 1965, revised edition, 1969.
Cairo, Phoenix House, 1965, A. S. Barnes, 1966, published as *Cairo: 5500 Years,* Crowell, 1968, published as *Great Cairo: Mother of the World,* Hart-Davis, 1969, reprinted, Columbia University Press, 1985.
(With the editors of Time-Life Books) *Early Islam,* Time-Life, 1967.
Orphan with a Hoop: The Life of Emile Bustani, Chapman & Hall, 1967.
(With the editors of Newsweek Book Division) *The Pyramids and Sphinx,* Newsweek, 1971.
The Middle East: Temple of Janus, Doubleday, 1971.
Theodore Herzl: Artist and Politician, Doubleday, 1974.
(With the editors of Newsweek Book Division) *The Alhambra,* Newsweek, 1974.
T. E. Lawrence, Harper, 1977.
Mecca, photographs by Mohamed Amin, Newsweek, 1980.
The Foreigner: A Search for the First Century Jesus, Hamish Hamilton, 1981.
The Palestinians: Victims of Expediency, Quartet Books, 1982.

TRANSLATOR

Plato, *Socrates and the Soul of Man,* Beacon Press, 1951.
A. R. Sharkawi, *Egyptian Earth,* Heinemann, 1962.
Fathi Ghanem, *The Man Who Lost His Shadow,* Houghton, 1966, reprinted, Three Continents, 1981.

Also translator of many Arabic poems into English.

OTHER

The Besieged City (poems), Fortune Press, 1945.

Contributor to *Nation, Spectator, Holiday, Poetry, Encounter, New Statesman,* and other Arab and English publications.

SIDELIGHTS: A novelist and nonfiction writer, Desmond Stewart was "an expert on the secular history of the Middle East," according to *Times Literary Supplement* reviewer Humphrey Carpenter. In an obituary in the London *Times,* Francis King similarly remarks that Stewart was "an accomplished Arabist, equally effective as an interpreter of the Arabs to the British and of the British to the Arabs." Many of the author's novels were set in the Middle East, but his most ambitious work, *The Sequence of Roles,* takes place in Great Britain, and parallels the decline of a Scottish-Irish family with that of the British Empire.

Stewart was fluent in Arabic, could read German, Spanish, and Turkish, and had a working knowledge of Greek, Latin, Italian, and French.

BIOGRAPHICAL/CRITICAL SOURCES:

PERIODICALS

Los Angeles Times Book Review, November 30, 1980.
Nation, August 16, 1971.
New York Review of Books, September 29, 1977.
New York Times Book Review, December 3, 1967, May 30, 1976, November 6, 1977.
Observer Review, June 25, 1967.
Spectator, September 3, 1965, June 9, 1967, February 28, 1976, July 9, 1977, December 19, 1981.
Times Literary Supplement, July 1, 1965, July 15, 1965, June 15, 1967, December 1, 1972, February 27, 1976, January 13, 1978, April 9, 1982.
Washington Post Book World, May 9, 1976.

OBITUARIES:

PERIODICALS

Times (London), June 22, 1981.

[Sketch reviewed by brother, M. E. Lenfestey]

*　　*　　*

STINE, G(eorge) Harry 1928-
(Lee Correy)

PERSONAL: Born March 26, 1928, in Philadelphia, Pa.; son of George Haeberle (an eye surgeon) and Rhea Matilda (O'Neil) Stine; married Barbara A. Knauth, June 10, 1952; children: Constance Rhea, Eleanor Ann, George Willard. *Education:* Attended University of Colorado, 1946-50; Colorado College, B.A., 1952.

ADDRESSES: Home—616 West Frier Dr., Phoenix, Ariz. 85021. *Agent*—Scott Meredith Literary Agency, Inc., 845 Third Ave., New York, N.Y. 10022.

CAREER: White Sands Proving Ground, White Sands, N.M., chief of controls and instruments section in propulsion branch, 1952-55, chief of Range Operations Division and Navy flight safety engineer, 1955-57; Martin Co., Denver, Colo., design specialist, 1957; Model Missiles, Inc., Denver, president and chief engineer, 1957-59; Stanley Aviation Corp., Denver, design engineer, 1959-60; Huyck Corp., Stamford, Conn., assistant director of research, 1960-65; consulting engineer and science writer in New Canaan, Conn., 1965-73; Flow Technology, Inc., Phoenix, Ariz., marketing manager, 1973-76; science writer and consultant, 1976—.

MEMBER: American Institute of Aeronautics and Astronautics (associate fellow), Instrument Society of America, Academy of Model Aeronautics, National Aeronautic Association, National Association of Rocketry (founder; president, 1957-67; honorary trustee), American Society of Aerospace Education, Science Fiction Writers of America, L-S Society, National Fire Protection Association, British Interplanetary Society (fellow), New York Academy of Sciences, Theta Xi, Explorers Club (New York City; fellow).

AWARDS, HONORS: Special award, American Rocket Society, 1957, for founding and editing *Missile Away!;* Bendix Trophy, National Association of Rocketry, 1964, 1965, 1967, and 1968; Silver Medal, American Space Pioneer, U.S. Army Association, 1965; Silver Medal, payload category, First International Model Rocket Competition, Dubnica, Czechoslovakia, 1966; special award, National Association of Rocketry, 1967; first recipient of annual award in Model Rocketry Division, Hobby Industry Association of America, 1969.

WRITINGS:

Rocket Power and Space Flight, Holt, 1957.
Earth Satellites and the Race for Space Superiority, Ace Books, 1957.
Man and the Space Frontier, Knopf, 1962.
(Contributor) Frederick Pohl, editor, *The Expert Dreamers,* Doubleday, 1962.
The Handbook of Model Rocketry, Follett, 1965, 5th edition, Arco, 1983.
(Contributor) George W. Early, editor, *Encounters with Aliens,* Sherbourne, 1969.
The Model Rocket Manual, Sentinel, 1969.
Model Rocket Safety, Model Products Corp., 1970.
(Contributor) Ben Bova, editor, *The Analog Science Fact Reader,* Sherbourne, 1974.
The Third Industrial Revolution, Putnam, 1975.
(Contributor) Bova, editor, *A New View of the Solar System,* St. Martin's, 1976.
The New Model Rocketry Manual, Arco, 1977.
Shuttle into Space, Follett, 1978.
The Space Enterprise, Ace Books, 1980.
Space Power, Ace Books, 1981.
Confrontation in Space, Prentice-Hall, 1981.
The Hopeful Future, Macmillan, 1983.
The Silicon Gods, Dell, 1984.
Bits, Bytes, Bauds, and Brains, Arbor House, 1984.
Handbook for Space Colonists, Holt, 1985.
On the Frontiers of Science: Strange Machines You Can Build, Atheneum, 1985.
The Corporate Survivors, Amacom, 1986.
The Business Guide to Space, Holt, in press.
ICBM, Crown, in press.
Zahedan! (fiction), Zebra Books, in press.
Operation Steel Band (fiction), Zebra Books, in press.
The Bastaard Rebellion (fiction), Zebra Books, in press.

UNDER PSEUDONYM LEE CORREY

Starship through Space, Holt, 1954.
Contraband Rocket, Ace Books, 1955.
Rocket Man, Holt, 1956.
Star Driver, Ballantine, 1980.
Shuttle Down, Ballantine, 1981.
Space Doctor, Ballantine, 1981.
The Abode of Life, Pocket Books, 1982.
Manna, DAW Books, 1983.
A Matter of Metalaw, DAW Books, 1986.

OTHER

Also author of six technical papers, five filmscripts, and four television scripts. Science fiction short stories are represented in anthologies, including *Science Fiction, '58: The Year's Greatest Science Fiction and Fantasy,* edited by Judith Merrill, Gnome, 1958, *The Sixth Annual of the Year's Best Science Fiction,* edited by Merrill, Simon & Schuster, 1961, and *Analog Six,* edited by John W. Campbell, Doubleday, 1968. Contributor to *Collier's Encyclopedia.* Author of columns "Conquest of Space," in *Mechanix Illustrated,* 1956-57, and "The Alternate View," in *Analog,* 1980—. Contributor of over 200 science fiction stories, non-fiction articles on science, and articles on model rocketry to periodicals, including *Omni, Science Digest, Saturday Evening Post, Astounding,* and *Magazine of Fantasy and Science Fiction.* Editor and founder, *Missile Away!,* 1953-57, *Model Rocketeer,* 1958-64, and *Flow Factor,* 1973-76; senior editor, *Aviation/Space,* 1982—.

WORK IN PROGRESS: "Too many authors talk about the stories they are going to do tomorrow. I prefer to discuss only what I have done."

SIDELIGHTS: "I had the good fortune to grow up in Colorado Springs, Colorado, on one of the last physical frontiers on the North American continent, the American West," G. Harry Stine told *CA.* "I also had the good fortune to choose a father who was an eye surgeon, who was an amateur scientist, and who surrounded me with books from as early as I can remember. In concert with my father, a number of men instilled in me a consuming curiosity about the universe around me. Once I asked one of them what I could ever do to repay him. I have been repaying him ever since because he said, 'There is no way that you can repay me directly and personally. The only thing that you can do to repay me is to do the same thing for the next generation. The obligation is always toward the future.'

"I write the sort of thing that I would like to read. I write it the way I would like to read it. I write entertainment. I am competing for the reader's time and money; if he doesn't like what I write, he will not spend his time and plunk down his hard-earned money a second time."

Stine is optimistic about the future; he believes that "the human race is going to survive. We will use the accumulated knowledge of centuries plus our rational minds to solve the problems that seem to beset us at the moment. . . . They are really no worse than the problems that faced other generations in the past. The current problems seem worse because they are current and because we have not yet solved them. What is difficult to us was impossible to our parents and will be commonplace to our children. We will indeed slay the dragons of war, intolerance, and pollution. We will marry the princess of outer space. And we will live happily ever after among the stars. We now have or will soon have the capability to do anything we want to do; we must only be willing to pay for it and to live with all the consequences.

"Like it or not, we live in a technological reality. One can escape it only be regressing through centuries of human history. I have attempted to master or at least understand as much about technology as possible. I have operated or am at least aware of how to operate every possible human transportation machine; for example, I have operated railroad trains, horses, automobiles, boats, and airplanes. I am a licensed pilot, own an airplane, and fly regularly. I hope someday to fly in a rocket-powered space vehicle . . . or in any sort of space vehicle. I greatly admire the fictitious man who, when asked if he could fly a helicopter, replied, 'I don't know; I've never tried.'

"The human race has a long way yet to go, and there are a lot of things left to do. According to a recent U.N. survey, nearly half the people in the world cannot read or write their native language; in the 'literate' United States of America, there are 21,000,000 people who are illiterate. Over 100,000,000 Americans have never been up in an airplane. Ninety per cent of the people on Earth have never been more than 25 miles from their birthplace, nor do they expect to travel beyond their village during their lifetimes."

*   *   *

STONE, Clarence N.   1935-

PERSONAL: Born March 9, 1935, in Chester, S.C. *Education:* University of South Carolina, A.B. (magna cum laude), 1957; Duke University, M.A., 1960, Ph.D., 1963.

ADDRESSES: Home—10610 Glenwild Rd., Silver Spring, Md. *Office*—Department of Government and Politics, 2149 Lefrak Hall, University of Maryland, College Park, Md. 20742.

CAREER: University of Nevada, Las Vegas, instuctor in political science, 1960-62; Westminster College, New Wilmington, Pa., instuctor in political science, 1962-63; Emory University, Atlanta, Ga., assistant professor of political science, 1963-68; University of Maryland, College Park, 1968—, began as associate professor, became professor of government, politics, and urban studies.

MEMBER: American Political Science Association, Urban Affairs Association, Southern Political Science Association (president, 1980-81), Phi Beta Kappa, Pi Sigma Alpha.

AWARDS, HONORS: Fellow of American Political Science Association, 1966-67; Chastain Award from Southern Political Science Association, 1977, for *Economic Growth and Neighborhood Discontent;* grant from National Endowment for the Humanities, 1980.

WRITINGS:

Economic Growth and Neighborhood Discontent: System Bias in the Urban Renewal Program of Atlanta, University of North Carolina Press, 1977.
(With Robert K. Whelan and William J. Murin) *Urban Policy and Politics in a Bureaucratic Age,* Prentice-Hall, 1979, 2nd edition, 1986.
(With Heywood T. Sanders) *The Politics of Urban Development,* University Press of Kansas, 1987.
Regime Politics: Governing Atlanta, 1946-1988, University Press of Kansas, 1989.

CONTRIBUTOR

Carl Beck, editor, *Law and Justice,* Duke University Press, 1970.
Ernest A. Chaples, Jr., editor, *Resolving Political Conflict in America,* McCutchan, 1971.

Stephen J. Wayne, editor, *Investigating the American Political System,* Schenkman, 1974.
Charles T. Goodsell, editor, *The Public Encounter: Where State and Citizen Meet,* Indiana University Press, 1981.
Janet K. Boles, editor, *The Egalitarian City,* Praeger, 1986.
Robert Waste, editor, *Community Power,* Praeger, 1987.
G. William Domhoff and Thomas R. Dye, editors, *Power Elites and Organizations,* Sage, 1987.

OTHER

Contributor to scholarly journals.

*　　*　　*

STRYJKOWSKI, Julian 1905-

PERSONAL: Born April 27, 1905, in Stryj, Poland (now in U.S.S.R.). *Education:* University of Lwow, D.Ph., 1932.

ADDRESSES: Home—Wyzwolenia 2/47, Warsaw, Poland.

CAREER: Writer.

AWARDS, HONORS: Award from Alfred Jurzykowski Foundation (New York), 1980.

WRITINGS:

Bieg do Fragala (short stories; title means "Course to Fragala"), Czytelnik, 1951.
Pozegnanie z Italia (title means "Farewell to Italy"), Czytelnik, 1954.
Glosy w ciemnosci (first novel in "Galician Trilogy"; title means "Voices in the Dark"), Czytelnik, 1956.
Imie wlasne: Opowiadania (short stories), Czytelnik, 1961.
Czarna roza (short stories; title means "The Black Rose"), Czytelnik, 1962.
Austeria (second novel in "Galician Trilogy"), Czytelnik, 1966, translation by Celina Wieniewska published as *The Inn,* Harcourt, 1971.
Na Wierzbach nasze skrzypce (short stories; title means "On Willows Our Fiddles"), Czytelnik, 1974.
Sen Azrila (third novel in "Galician Trilogy"; title means "Azril's Dream"), Czytelnik, 1975.
Przybysz z Narbony (novel; title means "The Visitor from Narbona"), Czytelnik, 1977.
Wielki strach (novel; title means "Great Fear"), Czytelnik, 1980.
Tommaso del cavaliere, Czytelnik, 1982.
Odpowiedz (first book in biblical triptych; title means "Answer"), Czytelnik, 1982.
Krol Dawid zyje (second book in biblical triptych; title means "King David Is Alive"), Czytelnik, 1984.
Juda Makabi (third book in biblical triptych; title means "Judas Maccabaeus"), Czytelnik, 1986.

Also author of plays "Dziedzictwo" (title means "Heir"), first produced in 1955, and "Sodoma" (title means "Sodom"), first produced in 1963. Editor, *Tworczsc* (literary monthly), Warsaw, 1954. Stryjkowski's books have been translated into fourteen languages.

SIDELIGHTS: Polish-born Jewish author Julian Stryjkowski, who for years felt he had "nothing to write about," commented to *CA:* "In 1943 I was in Russia and it was in Russia where I heard the news of the dramatic fate of the insurrection in the Warsaw Ghetto. The Jewish people did not exist any more. . . . I told myself . . . *now* I must write. Not about the Warsaw Ghetto, since I wasn't there. What I must do is to try, within my modest means, to write an epitaph, lay a tombstone, erect a mon-ument to the Jewish insurgents, and the whole Jewish nation. I must save from oblivion as much as I can. And with a tremendous effort of memory—I began to bring back to life what seemed the irretrievably lost Atlantis of my childhood, with all the details, scenery and men and women now dead that I could evoke. The Jewish people and its past became the main theme of my writing."

BIOGRAPHICAL/CRITICAL SOURCES:

PERIODICALS

New York Times Book Review, April 2, 1972.
Times Literary Supplement, March 10, 1972.
World Literature Today, winter, 1982.

*　　*　　*

STUART, Ian 1927-
(Malcolm Gray)

PERSONAL: Born May 6, 1927, in Royston, England; son of Leslie Charles (a schoolmaster) and Olive Margaret (Wilson) Stuart; married Audrey Joyce Allen, March 7, 1953; children: Bruce Graham, Neil Charles. *Education:* Educated in England. *Religion:* Church of England.

ADDRESSES: Home—218 Watford Rd., St. Albans, Hertfordshire AL2 3EA, England.

CAREER: Formerly a bank manager; full-time writer, beginning 1984.

MEMBER: International Association of Crime Writers, Crime Writers Association, Society of Authors, Mystery Writers of America, PEN.

WRITINGS:

The Snow on the Ben, Ward, Lock, 1961.
Golf in Hertfordshire, William Carling, 1972.
Death from Disclosure, R. Hale, 1976.
Flood Tide, R. Hale, 1977.
Sand Trap, R. Hale, 1977.
Fatal Switch, R. Hale, 1978.
A Weekend to Kill, R. Hale, 1978.
Pictures in the Dark, R. Hale, 1979.
The Renshaw Strike, R. Hale, 1980.
End on the Rocks, R. Hale, 1981.
The Garb of Truth, R. Hale, 1982, Doubleday, 1984.
Thrilling-Sweet and Rotten, R. Hale, 1983, Doubleday, 1985.
A Growing Concern, Doubleday, 1987.
Sandscreen, Doubleday, 1987.
The Margin, Doubleday, 1988.

UNDER PSEUDONYM MALCOLM GRAY

Look Back on Murder, Ross Anderson, 1985, Doubleday, 1986.
Stab in the Back, Doubleday, 1986.
A Matter of Record, Doubleday, 1987.
An Unwelcome Presence, Doubleday, 1989.

OTHER

Contributor to *Mystery Guild Anthology,* 1980, *John Creasey Crime Collection,* 1981 and 1986, and *Ellery Queen's Prime Comics,* numbers 4 and 5. Also contributor of short stories, serials, and articles to periodicals.

SIDELIGHTS: Ian Stuart explained to *CA* that the books written under his own name are "crime novels with topical plots." His *Sandscreen,* for instance, which a *New York Times Book Re-*

view contributor admires for its "powerful buildup to a smash ending," concerns "a plot by Arab terrorists to assassinate the U.S. president in London," says Stuart, "and *The Margin* [concerns] a conspiracy to illegally cream off the profits of an illicit arms sale to South Africa." He describes the books written under the pseudonym of Malcolm Gray as "fairly 'cosy' detective stories." Several of Stuart's books have been translated for publication in Scandinavia, Germany, and South America.

BIOGRAPHICAL/CRITICAL SOURCES:

PERIODICALS

New York Times Book Review, March 8, 1987.

*   *   *

SUID, Murray 1942-

PERSONAL: Surname rhymes with "fluid"; born May 16, 1942, in Cleveland, Ohio; son of Ben (a shop owner) and Jean (a shop owner; maiden name, Reiter) Suid; married Roberta Koch (an editor), April 1, 1967; children: Anna Lisa. *Education:* Brandeis University, B.A., 1964; Harvard University, M.Ed., 1967.

ADDRESSES: Home and office—1111 Greenwood Ave., Palo Alto, Calif. 94301. *Agent*—Curtis Brown Ltd., Ten Astor Pl., New York, N.Y. 10003.

CAREER: High school teacher of English and mathematics in Lenox, Mass., 1965-66; Philadelphia Public Schools, Philadelphia, Pa., junior high school English teacher 1967-68, curriculum writer, 1968-72; Education Today, Inc., *Learning* magazine, Palo Alto, Calif., staff writer, 1972-76; free-lance writer, 1976—. Workshop leader, Learning Institute, 1978—; lecturer, San Jose State University Department of Journalism.

AWARDS, HONORS: Special jury prize, Marburg Film Festival, and Eagle Award, Council on International Nontheatrical Events, both 1972, both for short film, "The J-Walker."

WRITINGS:

Painting with the Sun: A First Book of Photography, Dynamic Learning Corp., 1970.
(With Marcus Foster and wife, Roberta Suid) *Making Schools Work,* Westminster, 1971.
(With Jim Morrow) *Moviemaking Illustrated,* Hayden, 1973.
(With R. Suid) *Happy Birthday to U.S.: A Bicentennial Activity Book,* Addison-Wesley, 1975.
"How to Make Movies Your Friends Will Want to See Twice" (film), Benchmark Films, 1975.
(With Morrow) *Media and Kids: A Handbook for Teachers,* Hayden, 1976.
(With R. Suid, Buff Bradley, and Jean Eastman) *Married, Etc.: A Sourcebook for Couples,* Addison-Wesley, 1976.
(With R. Suid, Bradley, and Jan Berman) *Single: Living Your Own Way,* Addison-Wesley, 1977.
(With Ron Harris) *Made in America,* Addison-Wesley, 1978.
The Thinking Person's Self Help Guide to Reasonable Rules for Writing, Think Ink, 1980.
Demonic Mnemonics, Fearon Teacher Aids, 1981.
The Creativity Catalog, Fearon Teacher Aids, 1982.
For the Love of Words, Monday Morning Books, 1983.
(With others) *For the Love of Editing,* Monday Morning Books, 1983.
(With Wanda Lincoln) *For the Love of Letter Writing,* Monday Morning Books, 1983.
For the Love of Speaking and Listening, Monday Morning Books, 1983.

The Teacher-Friendly Computer Book, Monday Morning Books, 1984.
(With daughter, Anna Suid) *Holiday Crafts,* Monday Morning Books, 1985.
(Editor with Lincoln) *Teacher Quotation Book,* Dale Seymour, 1986.
For the Love of Research, Monday Morning Books, 1986.
For the Love of Sentences, Monday Morning Books, 1986.
For the Love of Stories, Monday Morning Books, 1986.
Book Factory, Monday Morning Books, 1988.
Greeting Cards, Monday Morning Books, 1988.
Recipes for Writing, Addison-Wesley, 1989.
Your Smart House, Parasol Press, 1990.

Also author of film "The J-Walker," 1972; author of multimedia series "Interaction," Houghton, 1974. Co-author of column "Ask about Learning," *Philadelphia Inquirer,* 1971-72. Editor, *K-Eight,* 1971-72.

WORK IN PROGRESS: Great Flying Saucer Hoax and *Moving to Mars,* two novels.

SIDELIGHTS: Murray Suid told *CA* that his current interests include "creating books for children and adults, developing educational products—kindergarten through college—especially in the areas of language arts and social studies, developing educational products for the home, and writing and producing films."

He added that "my greatest interest is in taking readers 'behind the scenes'—showing how inventors work, how marriages work (or don't work), how TV shows are made, etc. Much of my writing is based on interviews. I also am interested in showing readers how to do things."

The author later stated: "I hope my books encourage competence, especially in young readers. I want to help demystify contemporary phenomena and institutions—everything from television to marriage."

*   *   *

SUSSMAN, Susan 1942-
(Susan Rissman; Art Rissman, pseudonym)

PERSONAL: Born April 22, 1942, in Chicago, Ill.; daughter of Emmanuel A. (a judge) and Edie (Leavitt) Rissman; married Barry Sussman (president of a fabric company), September 21, 1963; children: Sy, Aaron, Rachel. *Education:* University of Illinois, B.A., 1963. *Religion:* Jewish.

ADDRESSES: Home—Evanston, Ill. *Office*—Noyes Cultural Center, 927 Noyes St., Evanston, Ill. 60201. *Agent*—Jane Jordan Browne Multimedia Product Development, Inc., 410 South Michigan Ave., Room 724, Chicago, Ill. 60605.

CAREER: Free-lance journalist, 1963-82; associated with Noyes Cultural Center, Evanston, Ill.

MEMBER: Children's Reading Round Table, Midwest Authors Guild, Off Campus Writers Workshop, Society of Midland Authors (program chair), Society of Children's Book Writers.

WRITINGS:

(Contributor) Margaret Branson and Evarts Erickson, editors, *Urban America,* Scott, Foresman, 1970.
Hippo Thunder (juvenile), Albert Whitman, 1982.
There's No Such Thing as a Chanukah Bush, Sandy Goldstein (juvenile), Albert Whitman, 1983.
Don't Say Goodbye (young adult), Dell, 1985.
Casey the Nomad (juvenile), Albert Whitman, 1985.

Sweet Talk (young adult), Dell, 1986.
Night after Night (young adult), Dell, 1986.
Just Friends (young adult), Fawcett/Ballantine), 1986.
Lies (People Believe) about Animals, Albert Whitman, 1987.
Big Friends, Little Friends (juvenile), Houghton, 1989.
The Dieter, Pocket Books, 1989.
Hanukkah: Eight Lights around the World (juvenile), Albert Whitman, 1989.

Author of "Notes from the Locker Room," a column in *Racquetball.* Contributor of articles and stories to newspapers and magazines, including *Ellery Queen Mystery Magazine.* Has also written under name Susan Rissman and pseudonym Art Rissman.

WORK IN PROGRESS: Susan Sussman once told *CA:* "I received my first rejection slip from the *Saturday Evening Post* when I was eleven years old. I had been writing long before that, but didn't think to publish until then. I was finally published six long years later. I have written for everyone from preschool-age children to adults, and find myself comfortable in both fiction and nonfiction. I love writing for children and believe it is an important area for a writer. Sometimes, however, something else floats up from the murky depths, as 'The Breaking," in *Ellery Queen Mystery Magazine,* and it must be written down."

*   *   *

SWAINSON, Donald 1938-

PERSONAL: Born November 23, 1938, in Baldur, Manitoba, Canada; son of Ingolfur and Liney (Oleson) Swainson; married Eleanor Garson (a credit counselor), 1963; children: Eirik, Andrew. *Education:* University of Manitoba, B.A., 1960; University of Toronto, M.A., 1961, Ph.D., 1969. *Religion:* Anglican.

ADDRESSES: Office—Department of History, Queen's University, Kingston, Ontario, Canada K7L 3N6.

CAREER: Queen's University, Kingston, Ontario, lecturer, 1963-65, assistant professor, 1965-70, associate professor, 1970-79, professor of history, 1979—. Senior officer of Planning and Priorities Committee of cabinet for government of Manitoba, 1972-73.

MEMBER: Canadian Historical Association, Manitoba Historical Society, Ontario Historical Society.

WRITINGS:

Ontario and Conderation, Centennial Commission of Canada, 1967.
(With Christopher Ondaatje) *The Prime Ministers of Canada, 1867-1968,* Pagurian, 1968, 2nd edition, 1975.
(Editor) *Historical Essays on the Prairie Provinces,* McClelland & Stewart, 1970.
J. C. Dent: The Last Forty Years, McClelland & Stewart, 1971.
John A. Mcdonald: The Man and the Politician, Oxford University Press, 1971, 2nd edition, Quarry Press, 1989.
(Editor) *Oliver Mowat's Ontario,* Macmillan, 1972.
Macdonald of Kingston, Thomas Nelson, 1979.
(With wife, Eleanor Swainson) *The Buffalo Hunt,* Peter Martin Associates, 1980.
Garden Island: A Shipping Empire, Marine Museum of the Great Lakes at Kingston, 1984.
(With Brian Osborne) *The Sault Sainte Marie Canal,* Parks Canada, 1986.
(With Osborne) *History of Kingston,* Butternut Press, 1989.

Contributor to history journals. Member of editorial board of *Whig-Standard.*

WORK IN PROGRESS: The Conservative Tradition in Canada.

SIDELIGHTS: Donald Swainson told *CA:* "My focus is on national politics and the regional societies and political cultures that have evolved in Ontario and the prairie region. *The Conservative Tradition in Canada* is a project that will, I hope, help to explain crucial elements in the political evolution of Canada's national party system."

*   *   *

SWITHEN, John
See KING, Stephen (Edwin)

T

TARN, Nathaniel 1928-

PERSONAL: Born June 30, 1928, in Paris, France; son of Marcel and Yvonne (Suchar) Tarn; married Janet Rodney, 1981; children: (first marriage) Andrea, Marc. *Education:* Cambridge University, B.A. (with honors), 1948, M.A., 1952; graduate study at Sorbonne, University of Paris, 1949-51; University of Chicago, M.A., 1952, Ph.D., 1957; additional graduate study at London School of Economics and Political Science.

ADDRESSES: Home—P. O. Box 566, Tesuque, New Mexico 87574.

CAREER: Writer. Anthropologist in Guatemala, Burma, and other countries, 1952-79; Jonathan Cape Ltd. (publishers), London, England, founder and director of Cape Goliard Press and Editor of Cape Editions. 1967-69; Rutgers University, Rutgers College, New Brunswick, N.J., professor of comparative literature, 1970-84, professor emeritus, 1984—. Lecturer at colleges and universities, including University of Chicago and University of London, 1952-67; visiting professor at State University of New York at Buffalo and Princeton University, 1969-70.

AWARDS, HONORS: Guiness Prize for poetry, 1963; Wenner Gren Foundation fellowship in anthropology and literature, 1979-81; Commonwealth of Pennsylvania fellowship in poetry, 1983; Rockefeller Foundation fellowship, Bellagio, Italy, 1988.

WRITINGS:

Old Savage/Young City (poems), J. Cape, 1964, Random House, 1965.
(With Richard Murphy and Jon Silkin) *Penguin Modern Poets No. Seven: Richard Murphy, Jon Silkin, Nathaniel Tarn,* Penguin, 1965.
(Translator) Pablo Neruda, *The Heights of Macchu Picchu,* J. Cape, 1966, Farrar, Straus, 1967.
Where Babylon Ends (poems), Grossman, 1968.
(Editor and co-translator) *Con Cuba: An Anthology of Cuban Poetry of the Last Sixty Years,* Grossman, 1969.
The Beautiful Contradictions (poems), J. Cape, 1969, Random House, 1970.
October (poems), Trigram Press, 1969.
(Translator) Victor Segalen, *Stelae,* Unicorn Press, 1969.
(Editor) Pablo Neruda, *Selected Poems,* J. Cape, 1970, Delacorte, 1972.
A Nowhere for Vallejo (poems), Random House, 1971.

Lyrics for the Bride of God; Section: The Artemision (poems; also see below), Tree Books, 1973.
The Persephones, Christopher's Books, 1974.
Lyrics for the Bride of God (poems), New Directions, 1975.
Narrative of This Fall, Black Sparrow Press, 1975.
The House of Leaves (poems), Black Sparrow Press, 1976.
The Microcosm, Membrane Press, 1977.
Birdscapes with Seaside, Black Sparrow Press, 1978.
(With Janet Rodney) *The Ground of Our Great Admiration of Nature,* Permanent Press, 1978.
(With Rodney) *The Forest* (poems), Perishable Press, 1978.
(With Rodney) *Atitlan/Alashka,* Brillig, 1979.
The Land Songs (poems), Blue Guitar Books, 1979.
Weekends in Mexico (poems), Oxus Press (London), 1982.
The Desert Mothers (poems), Salt-Works Press, 1984.
At the Western Gates (poems), Tooth of Time Press, 1985.
Palenque: Selected Poems (poems), Oasis Press (London), 1986.
Seeing America First (poems), Coffee House Press, 1989.

Contributor to many anthologies in the United States, including *New Poems 1965: A PEN Anthology of Contemporary Poetry,* edited by Cicely Veronica Wedgwood, *Best Poems of 1971: Borestone Mountain Poetry Awards 1972,* Volume 24, *America: A Prophecy,* edited by Jerome Rothenberg and George Quasha, and *For Neruda, for Chile,* edited by Walter Lowenfels. Contributor to anthologies in France, Italy, and the Netherlands, including *Poeti Inglesi del 900,* edited by Roberto Sanesi, *Anthologie de la Poesie Americaine,* edited by Jacques Roubaud, and *Levenstekens en Doodsinjalen,* edited by Hans Ten Berge. Contributor to periodicals, including *Times Literary Supplement, Observer, New York Times, Credences, Temblor,* and *Sagetrieb.* Contributing editor, *Conjunctions, PO&SIE* (Paris), *Courrier du Centre International de Poesie* (Brussels), and *Modern Poetry in Translation* (London).

WORK IN PROGRESS: Architextures, a book of prose poems; *Auto-Anthropology,* a prose work in three volumes—*Multitude of One: Selected Papers in Poetics and Anthropology; An Abundance of Waters: Text and Textures on Santiago Atitlan, Guatemala,* with Martin Prechtel; third volume to be a thematic study of the object Tarn treated as an anthropological entity.

SIDELIGHTS: Nathaniel Tarn's multi-cultural interests are seen in his early work as an anthropologist and continue in his work as an internationally acclaimed translator, poet, and critic. For his views on "the state of the art of poetry in this complex society," which is, as he told *CA,* "a most complex business," he recommends the essay "Dr. Jekyll, the Anthropologist, Emerges and Marches into the Notebooks of Mr. Hyde, the Poet" in the literary journal *Conjunctions.* His contribution to *American Poetry,* the essay "Child as Father to the Man," he says, also gives insight into his writings.

Important influences on his poetry include Ezra Pound, William Carlos Williams, Hugh MacDiarmid, Charles Olson, Robert Duncan, and Jack Spicer. In addition, poets from many countries—Andre Breton, Guillame Apollinaire, Arthur Rimbaud, Fernando Pessoa, and Rainer Maria Rilke—have shaped his poetic vision. Tarn's characteristic writing style is eclectic, having the inclusiveness and open forms of Walt Whitman. His poems refer to the myths, philosophies, political concerns, plant and animal life, and landscapes known to people from many nations and time periods. In *The Beautiful Contradictions,* Tarn states his personal objective: "It is up to me to call into being everything that is." Like Whitman's style, Tarn's style "is a very original mixture of the high and the low, the deliberately elevated and the humorously familiar," observes a *Times Literary Supplement* reviewer. Writing about *Lyrics for the Bride of God* in *Harper's Bookletter,* Hayden Carruth remarks that "Tarn has attempted . . . a poem in the grand modern matter, after Pound's *Cantos* or Williams' *Paterson* and . . . he has largely succeeded." Of the same book, a *Choice* critic, notes that in this work, too, Tarn sounds "distinctly like Whitman, a Whitman writing about America in the 1970's. But his style is strikingly different and idiosyncratic, and his poems dazzle with a kaleidoscope of bright images."

A number of critics respond negatively to Tarn's long sentences and catalogues. As a *Times Literary Supplement* reviewer puts it in a review of *The Beautiful Contradictions,* "This is the poetry of a man who has come through a tremendous foreign reading list and lived to get it all mixed up for us." Other critics, however, respond more favorably. Of a later book, *The House of Leaves, Times Literary Supplement* contributor D. M. Thomas comments, "There was always a sense of continental ambition in [Tarn's] work, poems that seemed to wish the pages wider. To read his new collection is a little like flying over America: A Whitmanesque grandiloquence . . . , repetition upon repetition, accretion upon accretion. . . . Much of it is beautiful and true."

For a summary of previous stages in Tarn's development as a poet, *American Poetry Review* contributor Rochelle Ratner recommends *Atitlan/Alashka:* "Each previous book that Tarn published has been such a complete vision in itself that we tend to think it is his *only* vision. *Atitlan* not only shows the scope of Tarn's field, it shows the fusion of his various periods." Theodore Enslin remarks in the *American Book Review* that in addition to showing the width of Tarn's range, this collection also shows "how an omnivorous appetite is controlled by a discriminating intelligence, at the same time that the rush of highly colored and charged language fills the landscape with both form and that form's detail." In *At the Western Gates,* published in 1986, Tarn adds new resonance to his images while giving "free play to all the senses," observes a *Voice Literary Supplement* reviewer, who concludes, "with a prophetic sense of sure direction, his new poems move beyond their surface splendor into the depths beneath."

Of the later book *At the Western Gates, Artspace* contributor Gene Frumkin comments, "while these poems are shorter and sing more, on the whole, than Tarn's usual pattern of work, the desert does make its appearance; neither positive nor negative in itself, it brings to the poetry a doubleness, an ambiguity which, as it develops, gives us a sure sign of this poet's mastery. Tarn is thoughtful, religiously, and he is a man whose concern lies with the total culture of any place; the songs of his birds and of his whales are the up and down of a cosmos, his encompassing effort to construct lyricism not only as music but as the music of mind's flow through the mystery of nature." Tarn's next book, *The Desert Mothers,* presents longer poems again, but Frumkin relates that the ideas the poems develop are more significant than their length.

Tarn told *CA* that reviews often overemphasize his style, which he sees "as only one facet of the work as if their were no other facets. This concerns the 'rambling', 'long sentences', 'grandiloquent', 'omnivorous' aspect. I believe that, if one looks at the books, there is an alternation between this aspect and another which is far tighter and more controlled. Also between poems of complexity and simple poems. Also between long lines and short lines, spread and compression. Among controlled, short-lined, simple works, I would place *October;* much of *The House of Leaves;* much of *A Nowhere for Vallejo;* and almost all of *At the Western Gates.* The poems in *Seeing America First* are extremely compressed: seventy poems, each one of which has the exact same number of spaces in each line *when typed* so that the poems are perfectly rectangular, justified on each side, looking *like* prose poems, but *not* prose poems. One cannot be less rambling than that!"

Explaining why he works in both shorter and longer forms, Tarn added, "The complexity/simplicity alternation responds to a belief I have that the fundamental contradiction in the poem's role in society is exasperated today more than at any other time in 'modernist/postmodernist' history. For the craft to progress, the poem has to improve on a long tradition of complexity, difficulty, even obscurity if it is to 'make it new' as Pound prescribed. On the other hand, the whole tradition has of late made it more and more difficult for poetry to find any kind of readership except among other poets. One of the ways of dealing with this is to write (at least) two kinds of poetry so as to give the work as a whole the optimal chance of reaching one or more publics."

BIOGRAPHICAL/CRITICAL SOURCES:

BOOKS

Bartlett, Lee, *Nathaniel Tarn, A Descriptive Bibliography,* McFarland, 1987.
Bartlett, Lee, editor, *Talking Poetry: Conversations in the Workshop with Contemporary Poets,* University of New Mexico Press, 1987.
Bartlett, Lee, *The Sun is but a Morning Star: Essays on Western American Literature,* University of New Mexico Press, 1989.
Fisch, Harold, *The Dual Image,* [London], 1971.
Tarn, Nathaniel, *The Beautiful Contradictions,* J. Cape, 1969, Random House, 1970.

PERIODICALS

American Book Review, Volume 2, number 5, 1980.
American Poetry, Volume 1, number 2, 1984, Volume 1, number 4, 1984, Volume 2, number 1, 1984.
American Poetry Review, Volume 1, number 2, 1984.
Artspace, Volume 5, number 1, 1985-86.
Boundary 2, Volume 4, number 1, 1975.
Choice, November, 1975, April, 1977.
Conjunctions, Number 6, 1984.
Credences, Number 4, 1977.

Harper's Bookletter, October 13, 1975.
Judaism, fall, 1965.
Library Journal, June 15, 1965, April 15, 1971.
New York Times Book Review, September 25, 1966, May 21, 1967, May 7, 1972, September 7, 1975.
Poetry, June, 1968.
Saturday Review, October 9, 1965, December 13, 1968.
Spectator, January 1, 1965.
Sulfur, Number 14, 1985/86.
Times (London), April 6, 1968, June 7, 1969.
Times Literary Supplement, January 7, 1965, October 12, 1967, August 7, 1969, April 9, 1970, August 4, 1972, May 20, 1977.
Voice Literary Supplement, February, 1986.

*   *   *

TATE, Edward
See DRANSFIELD, Michael (John Pender)

*   *   *

TAYLOR, L(aurie) A(ylma)   1939-
(Laurie Taylor)

PERSONAL: Born September 3, 1939, in Tappan, N.Y.; daughter of Edwin (an assistant postmaster) and Lilian (Vanderbilt) Taylor; married Allen H. Sparer, July 17, 1971; children: Eleanor, Catherine. *Education:* Ohio Wesleyan University, B.A. (with honors), 1960.

ADDRESSES: Home—Minneapolis, Minn. *Agent*—Sallie Gouverneur, 10 Bleecker St., No. 4A, New York, N.Y. 10012.

CAREER: Harvard University Medical School, Boston, Mass., medical research technician, 1960-62, 1963-64; Board of Education, Pittsburgh, Pa., educational researcher, 1968-72. Instructor at Southwest Community School, Minneapolis, Minn. Election judge in Minneapolis.

MEMBER: The Loft, Phi Beta Kappa, Pi Mu Epsilon.

AWARDS, HONORS: Award from Minnesota Voices Project, 1981, for *Changing the Past.*

WRITINGS:

(Under name Laurie Taylor) *Changing the Past* (poems), New Rivers Press, 1981.
Footnote to Murder (mystery), Walker & Co., 1983.
Only Half a Hoax (mystery), Walker & Co., 1983.
Deadly Objectives (mystery), Walker & Co., 1984.
Shed Light on Death (mystery), Walker & Co., 1985.
The Blossom of Edna (science fiction), St. Martin's, 1986.
Love of Money (mystery), Walker & Co., 1987.
Poetic Justice (mystery), Walker & Co., 1988.
A Murder Waiting to Happen (mystery), Walker & Co., 1989.

Contributor of fiction, nonfiction, and poetry to periodicals, including *Centennial Review, Carolina Quarterly, Missouri Review, Kansas Quarterly, Poetry Miscellany, Analog, Alfred Hitchcock's Mystery Magazine,* and *Magazine of Fantasy and Science Fiction.*

WORK IN PROGRESS: Reasonable Doubt, a mystery; *The Color of Sanity* and *The Bell Forest,* science fiction; poems; short stories.

SIDELIGHTS: L. A. Taylor told *CA:* "Despite my nifty electronic typewriter, my poems are simple, rather old-fashioned lyrics, often allegorical (though the allegories tend to be well hid-

den). I favor compact images, tightly expressed, and I use them to write about everyday observations and circumstances, accessible to nearly anyone. The poems are full of wordplay, double meanings, slanted meanings, and puns, but few people other than me seem to notice this. In fiction, I like to put ordinary people in extraordinary situations and stand back and see what happens. Mystery novels may seem odd companions to poetry (though I am scarcely the first to write both), but the novels came as part of a natural progression for me, from poetry to experimental and literary short stories, to more traditional stories, and finally to stories in two genres I enjoy reading—science fiction and mysteries. Writing mysteries seemed to be the most natural way to learn to handle novel length, so I started there. If there is a theme or message running through my work, I am not aware of it. I like to tell a good story; I like to sing a good song."

BIOGRAPHICAL/CRITICAL SOURCES:

PERIODICALS

Clues: A Journal of Detection, fall/winter, 1984.
New York Times Book Review, December 18, 1983.

*   *   *

TAYLOR, Laurie
See TAYLOR, L(aurie) A(ylma)

*   *   *

THEOHARIS, Athan G(eorge)   1936-

PERSONAL: Born August 3, 1936, in Milwaukee, Wis.; son of George A. and Adeline (Konop) Theoharis; married Nancy Artinian, August 21, 1966; children: Jeanne Frances, George Thomas, Elizabeth Armen. *Education:* University of Chicago, A.B., 1956, A.B., 1957, A.M., 1959, Ph.D., 1965. *Politics:* Democrat. *Religion:* Greek Orthodox.

ADDRESSES: Home—8527 North Manor La., Fox Point, Wis. *Office*—Department of History, Marquette University, Milwaukee, Wis. 53233.

CAREER: Texas A&M University, College Station, instructor in history, 1962-64; Wayne State University, Detroit, Mich., assistant professor of history, 1964-68; Staten Island Community College of the City University of New York, Staten Island, N.Y., associate professor of history, 1968-69; Marquette University, Milwaukee, Wis., associate professor, 1969-76, professor of American history, 1976—. Thomas B. Lockwood Professor of History at State University of New York at Buffalo, 1982-83.

MEMBER: American Historical Association, Organization of American Historians, Academy of Political Science, American Civil Liberties Union, National Committee for a Sane Nuclear Policy (member of board, 1966), University of Chicago Alumni (member of board, 1968-70).

AWARDS, HONORS: Grants from Truman Institute for National and International Affairs, 1965, 1966, Wayne State University, 1967, Marquette University, 1970, 1979, Institute for Humane Studies, 1971, Field Foundation, 1980, Warsh-Mott Funds, 1980, Fund for Investigative Journalism, 1980, and the C. S. Fund, 1981; American Bar Association Gavel Awards; National Endowment for the Humanities summer fellowship, 1976; Binkley-Stephenson Award, 1979; Albert Beveridge research grant, 1980.

WRITINGS:

Anatomy of Anti-Communism, Hill & Wang, 1969.

The Yalta Myths: An Issue in U.S. Politics, 1945-1955, University of Missouri Press, 1970.

Seeds of Repression: Harry S Truman and the Origins of McCarthyism, Quadrangle, 1971.

(Editor with Robert Griffith) *The Specter: Original Essays on the Cold War and the Origins of McCarthyism,* New Viewpoints, 1974.

(Co-author) *Twentieth-Century United States,* Prentice-Hall, 1978.

Spying on Americans: Political Surveillance from Hoover to the Huston Plan, Temple University Press, 1978.

(Editor) *The Truman Presidency: The Origins of the Imperial Presidency and the National Security State,* Earl M. Coleman, 1979.

(With Melvyn Dubofsky) *Imperial Democracy: The United States since 1945,* Prentice-Hall, 1982.

(Editor) *Beyond the Hiss Case: The FBI, Congress, and the Cold War,* Temple University Press, 1982.

(With John Stuart Cox) *The Boss: J. Edgar Hoover and the Great American Inquisition,* Temple University Press, 1988.

CONTRIBUTOR

B. J. Bernstein, editor, *Politics and Policies of the Truman Administration,* Quadrangle, 1970.

M. Small, editor, *Public Opinion and Historians,* Wayne State University Press, 1970.

Howard H. Quint and Milton Cantor, editors, *Men, Women, and Issues in American History,* Dorsey, 1975.

W. Bier, editor, *Privacy: A Vanishing Value,* Fordham University Press, 1980.

D. Whitnah, *Government Agencies,* Greenwood Press, 1983.

R. Curry, *Freedom at Risk,* Temple University Press, 1988.

OTHER

Contributor to periodicals, including *Nation* and *Journal of American History.* History editor, *U.S.A. Today.*

WORK IN PROGRESS: Research on internal security policy, 1939-53; compiling and editing files of important FBI internal security cases and federal surveillance policy, to be issued on microfilm by University Publications of America.

SIDELIGHTS: Athan G. Theoharis's *The Yalta Myths: An Issue in U.S. Politics, 1945-1955* explores the history of the Cold War policies that developed from the theory that Franklin Delano Roosevelt and Winston Churchill compromised the West in their dealings with Stalin at the Yalta Conference in 1945. "Although the Republicans raised the issue primarily to discredit Truman," Allen Weinstein observes in the *New York Times Book Review,* "Theoharis considers the President almost as culpable as his Congressional opponents in perpetuating 'the Yalta myths.' "

Theoharis examines the domestic effects of Truman's policies in *Seeds of Repression: Harry S Truman and the Origins of McCarthyism.* In that report, according to *New York Review of Books* critic Murray Kempton, "Our desire to have the period's characters rendered in their proper proportions could hardly be better satisfied. McCarthy is relegated in this composition to the place and comparative dimensions of one of Veronese's dwarfs, since it is Mr. Theoharis's judgment that Mr. Truman set the tone of the national possession by fear of the Communist danger and that McCarthyism was only Trumanism carried to its logical conclusion." Kempton concludes that Theoharis's "argument is not without weaknesses; but none of them seriously affects its essential strength. He has successfully, if not always gracefully, closed the question of major blame."

AVOCATIONAL INTERESTS: Sports.

BIOGRAPHICAL/CRITICAL SOURCES:

PERIODICALS

American Political Science Review, spring, 1976.
New York Review of Books, March 11, 1971, September 2, 1971.
New York Times Book Review, March 7, 1971.

*   *   *

THOMAS, David St. John 1929-

PERSONAL: Born August 30, 1929, in Romford, Essex, England; son of Gilbert Oliver (an author) and Dorothy (Kathleen) Thomas; married Pamela Mary Shepherd, February 16, 1954 (divorced); married Georgette Marie Zackey (a psychologist), September 8, 1979; children: (first marriage) Alison Clare, Gareth St. John. *Education:* Attended public schools in Devon, England. *Politics:* Liberal.

ADDRESSES: Home—Hylton 26, Keyberry Park, Newton Abbot, Devon TQ12 1DF, England. *Office*—David & Charles Ltd., Brunel House, Forde Rd., Newton Abbot, Devon TQ12 2DW, England; and David & Charles, Inc., P.O. Box 57, North Pomfret, Vt. 05053.

CAREER: Journalist, broadcaster, and fruit farmer in Devon, England, 1950-70; David & Charles Publishing Group, Newton Abbot and London, England, and North Pomfret, Vt., founder and chairman, 1960.

WRITINGS:

Great Moments With Trains, Roy, 1959.
(Editor) *A Regional History of the Railways of Great Britain,* fifteen volumes, Phoenix House, 1960-80.
The West Country (Volume 1 of *A Regional History of the Railways of Great Britain*), Phoenix House, 1960, 6th revised edition, David & Charles, 1981, published in paperback as *West Country Railway History,* 1974.
The Motor Revolution, Longmans, Green, 1961.
The Rural Transport Problem, Routledge & Kegan Paul, 1963.
(With father, Gilbert O. Thomas) *Double-Headed: Two Generations of Railway Enthusiasm,* David & Charles, 1963.
(With Hubert Bermont) *Nonfiction: A Guide to Writing and Publishing,* David & Charles, 1970, published as *Getting Published,* Fleet Press, 1973.
(With Simon Rocksborough Smith) *Summer Saturdays in the West,* David & Charles, 1973.
(Compiler) *The Great Way West: The History and Romance of the Great Western Railway's Route From Paddington to Penzance,* David & Charles, 1975.
The Country Railway, David & Charles, 1976, Penguin, 1979.
The Breakfast Book, David & Charles, 1981.
(Editor) *Good Books Come From Devon,* David & Charles, 1981.
(With Patrick B. Whitehouse) *The Great Days of the Country Railway,* David & Charles, 1987.
(Editor) *The ABC Alphabetical Railway Guide,* David & Charles, 1987.
(Editor with Whitehouse) *Great Western Railway: 150 Glorious Years,* David & Charles, 1987.

Also contributor of articles to literary and transport magazines.

WORK IN PROGRESS: Additional writings on the social history of railroads, with five books in preparation; also advice on how to write.

SIDELIGHTS: David St. John Thomas told *CA:* "Writing is all about a zest for life and sharing experiences. For me, it began with a love of railways and an enthusiasm to share it through articles, broadcasts, and best-selling books. In 1960 I founded the specialist publishing house of David & Charles, first concentrating on transportation studies, but rapidly widening to cover many hobby and practical subjects with publication of up to two hundred new titles each year. In 1971 the Readers Union Group of Book Clubs was acquired and has been greatly expanded, operating in the same hobby and practical fields.

"Subjects published by David & Charles largely reflect personal interests, including the countryside, natural history, travel, music, and art.

"The unique blend of enthusiasm and commercialism that typifies the company is captured in Good Books Come From Devon, the story of twenty-one years of book publishing. David & Charles has a special attitude toward writers, many of its authors not being full-time writers but those doing a book on a hobby or professional subject. 'Sell the subject' and 'make your words work hard' are two salient points of advice."

In 1988 David & Charles purchased Successful Writers, now renamed David & Charles Writers College, which conducts several mail-tuition courses, and in 1989 launched *Writers News* to help and encourage new writers. As its publisher Mr. Thomas writes his own column of 'gritty advice' about becoming a professional writer.

*   *   *

THOMAS, R(onald) S(tuart) 1913-

PERSONAL: Born March 29, 1913 in Cardiff, Wales; son of T. H. (a sailor); married Mildred E. Eldridge (a painter), 1940; children: Gwydion (son). *Education:* University College of North Wales, B. A., 1935; attended St. Michael's College, Llandaff, 1935-36.

ADDRESSES: Home—Sarn-y-Plas, Y Rhiw, Pwllheli, Gwynedd, Wales.

CAREER: Ordained a deacon of the Anglican Church, 1936, priest, 1937; curate of Chirk, Denbighshire, 1936-40; curate in charge of Tallarn Green, Hanmer, Flintshire, 1940-42; rector of Manafon, Montgomeryshire, 1942-54; vicar of St. Michael's, Eglwysfach, Cardiganshire, 1954-67; vicar of St. Hywyn, Aberdaron, Gwynedd, with St. Mary, Bodferin, 1967-78; rector of Rhiw with Llanfaelrhys, 1972-78.

MEMBER: Campaign for Nuclear Disarmament (committee member and representative of county branch).

AWARDS, HONORS: Heinemann Award, Royal Society of Literature, 1955, for *Song at the Year's Turning: Poems, 1942-1954;* Queen's Gold Medal for Poetry, 1964; Welsh Arts Council award, 1968 and 1976; Cholmondeley Award, 1978.

WRITINGS:

POEMS

The Stones of the Field, Druid Press, 1946.
An Acre of Land, Montgomeryshire Printing Company, 1952.
The Minister (verse play; first produced on Welsh BBC Radio, 1953), Montgomeryshire Printing Company, 1953.
Song at the Year's Turning: Poems, 1942-1954, with introduction by John Betjeman, Hart-Davis, 1955.
Poetry for Supper, Hart-Davis, 1958, Dufour, 1961.
Judgment Day, Poetry Book Society, 1960.
Tares, Dufour, 1961.
(With Lawrence Durrell and Elizabeth Jennings) *Penguin Modern Poets 1,* Penguin (London), 1962.

The Bread of Truth, Dufour, 1963.
Pieta, Hart-Davis, 1966.
Not That He Brought Flowers, Hart-Davis, 1968.
(With Roy Fuller) *Pergamon Poets 1,* edited by Evan Owen, Pergamon, 1968.
Postcard: Song, Fishpaste Postcard Series, 1968.
The Mountains, illustrations by John Piper, Chilmark Press, 1963.
H'm: Poems, St. Martin's, 1972.
Young and Old (children's poems), Chatto & Windus, 1972.
Selected Poems, 1946-1968, Hart-Davis MacGibbon, 1973, St. Martin's, 1974.
What Is a Welshman?, Christopher Davies, 1974.
Laboratories of the Spirit, Macmillan (London), 1975, Godine, 1976.
The Way of It, illustrations by Barry Hirst, Ceolfrith Press, 1977.
Frequencies, Macmillan (London), 1978.
Between Here and Now, Macmillan (London), 1981.
Later Poems, 1972-1982, Macmillan (London), 1983.
A Selection of Poetry, edited by D. J. Hignett, Hignett School Services, 1983.
Poet's Meeting, Celandine, 1984.
Ingrowing Thoughts, Poetry Wales Press, 1985.
Destinations, Celandine, 1985.
Poems of R. S. Thomas, University of Arkansas Press, 1985.
Experimenting with an Amen, Macmillan (London), 1986.
Welsh Airs, Poetry Wales Press, 1987.

EDITOR

The Batsford Book of Country Verse, Batsford, 1961.
The Penguin Book of Religious Verse, Penguin, 1963.
Edward Thomas, *Selected Poems,* Faber, 1964.
A Choice of George Herbert's Verse, Faber, 1967.
A Choice of Wordsworth's Verse, Faber, 1971.

OTHER

Words and the Poet (W. D. Thomas Memorial Lecture), University of Wales Press, 1964.
Selected Prose, edited by Sandra Anstey, Poetry Wales Press, 1983, Dufour, 1984.
Neb: Golygwyd gan Gwenno Hywyn (autobiography in Welsh), Gwasg Gwynedd, 1987.

SIDELIGHTS: Recognized as one of the leading poets of modern Wales, R. S. Thomas writes about the people of his country in a style that some critics have compared to that nation's harsh and rugged terrain. Using few of the common poetic devices, Thomas's work exhibits what Alan Brownjohn of the *New Statesman* calls a "cold, telling purity of language." James F. Knapp of *Twentieth Century Literature* explains that "the poetic world which emerges from the verse of R. S. Thomas is a world of lonely Welsh farms and of the farmers who endure the harshness of their hill country. The vision is realistic and merciless." Despite the often grim nature of his subject matter, Thomas's poems are ultimately life-affirming. "What I'm after," John Mole of *Phoenix* quotes Thomas explaining, "is to demonstrate that man is spiritual." As Louis Sasso remarks in *Library Journal,* "Thomas's poems are sturdy, worldly creations filled with compassion, love, doubt, and irony. They make one feel joy in being part of the human race."

The son of a sailor, Thomas spent much of his childhood in British port towns where he and his mother would live while his father was away at sea. His early education began late and was only sporadically pursued until his father found steady work with a ferry boat company operating between Wales and Ireland,

and the family was able to settle in the Welsh town of Caergybi. After graduating from school Thomas studied for the Anglican priesthood, a career first suggested to him by his mother. As he recounts in his article for the *Contemporary Authors Autobiography Series,* "Shy as I was, I offered no resistance."

In 1936, Thomas was ordained a deacon in the Anglican Church and was assigned to work as a curate in the Welsh mining village of Chirk. In 1937 he became an Anglican priest. The post in Chirk was the first of a series of positions he was to hold in the rural communities of Wales. Between 1936 and 1978, Thomas served in churches located in six different Welsh towns. These appointments gave him a firsthand knowledge of Welsh farming life and provided him with a host of characters and settings for his poetry.

Although he had written poetry in school, it was only after meeting Mildred E. Eldridge, the woman who was to become his wife, that Thomas began to write seriously. At the time they met she had already earned a reputation as a painter, and, as Thomas remarks in his article for the *Contemporary Authors Autobiography Series,* "this made me wish to become recognised as a poet." He began to compose poetry about the Welsh countryside and its people, influenced by the writings of Edward Thomas, Fiona Macleod, and William Butler Yeats.

Perhaps Thomas's best known character is Iago Prytherch, a farm laborer who appears in many of his poems. Thomas describes him in the poem "A Peasant" as "an ordinary man of the bald Welsh hills." Writing in *British Poetry since 1970: A Critical Survey,* Colin Meir explains that Prytherch epitomizes Welsh hill-farming life and "is seen as embodying man's fortitude." A. E. Dyson, in an article for *Critical Quarterly,* finds that Prytherch, being a farmer, is "cut off from culture and poetry, and cut off too . . . from religion. . . . Yet [he] has an elemental reality and power in his life which is in part to be envied."

Prytherch is a kind of archetypal rural Welshman, standing as a symbol for his people. As Knapp remarks, Prytherch "represents the Welsh peasants in all their aspects throughout [Thomas's] poetry." According to Dyson, Prytherch is also used by Thomas as a symbol for humanity itself. His hard labor in an unyielding landscape, though representative of Welsh farmers, also exemplifies the hardships common to all men. "It seems then," Dyson states, "that in finding in the Welsh peasants a 'prototype' of man, Thomas is making a universal statement. . . . This pared-down existence, in a land of ruined beauty belonging to the past, is more human than any educated sophistication. Or perhaps one should say, it is more truly symbolic of the human predicament."

Many of Thomas's poems set his farming characters against the bleak and forbidding landscape of Wales, focusing on the difficulties of rural existence. "Many of his poems offer an unsparingly bleak view of man," Knapp admits, "and . . . even in those cases where hope seems clearly offered, the elements of the drama are still exceedingly grim. . . . The basic postulate is a kind of minimal man, struggling to endure in his little universe. . . . Mostly the visual aspect of the poetry concerns lone figures, working the stony fields, walking along the roads." Comparing Thomas's work with that of Robert Frost, who also wrote of rural life, C. A. Runcie of *Poetry Australia* notes that Thomas's "farmers and labourers and hillmen, unlike Frost's, are not philosophers. Thought has been worked out of them year after year. Only life and a little, obtuse, silent feeling remain."

As a clergyman, Thomas imbues his poetry with a consistently religious theme, often speaking of "the lonely and often barren predicament of the priest, who is as isolated in his parish as Prytherch is on the bare hillside," as Meir writes. "In Christian terms," Dyson explains, "Thomas is not a poet of the transfiguration, of the resurrection, of human holiness. . . . He is a poet of the Cross, the unanswered prayer, the bleak trek through darkness, and his theology of Jesus, in particular, seems strange against any known traditional norm." Anne Stevenson of the *Listener* describes Thomas as "a religious poet" who "sees tragedy, not pathos, in the human condition. . . . He is one of the rare poets writing today who never asks for pity."

Writing in the *Contemporary Authors Autobiography Series,* Thomas asserts that "as long as I was a priest of the Church, I felt an obligation to try to present the Bible message in a more or less orthodox way. I never felt that I was employed by the Church to preach my own beliefs and doubts and questionings. Some people were curious to know whether I did not feel some conflict between my two vocations. But I always replied that Christ was a poet, that the New Testament was poetry, and that I had no difficulty preaching the New Testament in its poetic context."

Although he had already published three books of poetry, Thomas did not gain widespread recognition as a poet until the appearance of *Song at the Year's Turning: Poems, 1942-1954.* This volume, brought out by a major publisher and with an introduction by poet John Betjeman, introduced Thomas to a national audience and "caused quite a stir," according to W. J. Keith in the *Dictionary of Literary Biography.* The collection's poems, marked by a spare and controlled language, earned Thomas widespread critical praise. With each subsequent volume his reputation has increased.

Like the Welsh countryside he writes about, Thomas's poetry is often harsh and austere, written in plain, somber language, with a meditative quality. Runcie describes Thomas's style as consisting of "simple words and short nouns, nouns of such authentic meaning that they rarely need modifiers, moving as beats at a controlled pace in stress accent metre—a constant technique to effect a constant tone, his own inexhaustibly haunting tone that lingers like sounds in a darkness." Writing in *Eight Contemporary Poets,* Calvin Bedient also notes this spare style, claiming that "Thomas puts little between himself and his subject. . . . His poems are ascetic. . . . To seem at once lean and sensuous, transparent and deeply crimsoned, is part of his distinction." Thomas reveals his stylistic intentions in *Words and the Poet:* "A recurring ideal, I find, is that of simplicity. At times there comes the desire to write with great precision and clarity, words so simple and moving that they bring tears to the eyes."

Thomas's interest in such things as his Welsh homeland, his religion, the natural world, and a spare and simple poetic style reflect his disenchantment with the modern world. In *Neb: Golygwyd gan Gwenno Hywyn,* an autobiography, Thomas speaks of his tendency to "look back and see the past as better," according to Gwyneth Lewis in *London Magazine.* On several occasions he has expressed his dismay at this century's industrialization of Wales, arguing that the country's natural beauty has been ruined. In his article for the *Contemporary Authors Autobiography Series,* Thomas lists among his recent concerns "the assault of contemporary lifestyles on the beauty and peace of the natural world." Thomas notes too that religious faith has declined with the emergence of our technological civilization. "We are told with increasing vehemence," he writes in the *Times Literary Supplement,* "that this is a scientific age, that science is transforming the world, but is it not also a mechanized and impersonal age, an analytic and clinical one; an age in which under the hard gloss of affluence there can be detected the murmuring of the starved heart and the uneasy spirit?"

Runcie believes that with Thomas, the poet and the poetry are one. He describes Thomas as "a Welshman and a parson, a tidy, boney man with a thin face rutted by severity. And the poems are the man. Austere and simple and of repressed power." Similarly, William Cole in the *Saturday Review/World* comments that "Thomas is austere, tough-minded, but can bring tears." Looking back on his long career, Thomas writes in the *Contemporary Authors Autobiography Series* that he "moved in unimportant circles, avoiding, or being excluded from the busier and more imposing walks of life." He claims that the critical praise he has received is due to "a small talent for turning my limited thoughts and experience and meditation upon them into verse."

Despite what he sees as a "small talent," Thomas is often ranked among the most important Welsh poets of this century. Writing in the *Anglo-Welsh Review,* R. George Thomas finds him to be "the finest living Welsh poet writing in English." Keith reports that Thomas is "now recognized as a prominent voice in British poetry of the second half of the twentieth century" and "has strong claims to be considered the most important contemporary Anglo-Welsh poet." Meir concludes that Thomas's work expresses a religious conviction uncommon in modern poetry. Thomas, according to Meir, believes that "one of the important functions of poetry is to embody religious truth, and since for him as poet that truth is not easily won, his poems record the struggle with marked honesty and integrity, thereby providing the context for the necessarily infrequent moments of faith and vision which are expressed with a clarity and gravity rarely matched by any of his contemporaries."

BIOGRAPHICAL/CRITICAL SOURCES:

BOOKS

Anstey, Sandra, *Critical Writings on R. S. Thomas,* Poetry Wales Press, 1982.
Bedient, Calvin, *Eight Contemporary Poets,* Oxford University Press, 1974.
Contemporary Authors Autobiography Series, Volume 4, Gale, 1986.
Contemporary Literary Criticism, Gale, Volume 6, 1976, Volume 13, 1980, Volume 48, 1988.
Dictionary of Literary Biography, Volume 27: *Poets of Great Britain and Ireland, 1945-1960,* Gale, 1984.
Dyson, A. E., *Yeats, Eliot, and R. S. Thomas: Riding the Echo,* Macmillan (London), 1981.
Jones, Peter and Michael Schmidt, editors, *British Poetry since 1970: A Critical Survey,* Carcanet Press, 1980.
Keith, W. J., *The Poetry of Nature,* University of Toronto Press, 1980.
Merchant, William Moelwyn, *R. S. Thomas,* Verry, 1979.
New Pelican Guide to English Literature, Pelican, 1983.
Phillips, Dewi, *R. S. Thomas: Poet of the Hidden God,* Macmillan (London), 1986.
Thomas, R. George, *R. S. Thomas,* Longman, 1964.
Thomas, R. S., *Words and the Poet,* University of Wales Press, 1964.
Ward, J. P., *The Poetry of R. S. Thomas,* Poetry Wales Press, 1987.

PERIODICALS

Anglo-Welsh Review, February, 1970, autumn, 1971.
Books and Bookmen, September, 1974.
Critical Quarterly, winter, 1960, summer, 1978, autumn, 1985.
Daily Telegraph Magazine, November 7, 1975.
Hudson Review, spring, 1987.
Library Journal, September 1, 1976.
Listener, April 15, 1976.
London Magazine, December, 1986-January, 1987.
Midwest Quarterly, summer, 1974.
New Statesman, September 29, 1972.
Phoenix, winter, 1972.
Poetry, April, 1974.
Poetry Australia, 1972.
Poetry Wales, spring, 1972.
Review of English Literature, October, 1962.
Saturday Review/World, April 20, 1974.
Spectator, November 8, 1975, April 1, 1978.
Times Literary Supplement, March 3, 1966, June 2, 1978.
Twentieth Century Literature, January, 1971.

—*Sketch by Thomas Wiloch*

*   *   *

THOMPSON, Julian F(rancis) 1927-

PERSONAL: Born November 16, 1927, in New York, N.Y.; son of Julian Francis (a playwright; in business) and Amalita (Stagg) Thompson; married Polly Nichy (an artist), August 11, 1978. *Education:* Princeton University, A.B., 1949; Columbia University, M.A., 1955.

ADDRESSES: Home—P.O. Box 138, West Rupert, Vt. 05776. *Agent*—Curtis Brown Ltd., 10 Astor Place, New York, N.Y. 10003.

CAREER: Lawrenceville School (private school), Lawrenceville, N.J., history teacher, athletic coach, and director of lower school, 1949-61; Changes, Inc. (alternative high school), East Orange, N.J., director, 1971-77; writer, 1979—.

MEMBER: Authors Guild, Authors League of America.

WRITINGS:

YOUNG ADULT NOVELS

The Grounding of Group Six, Avon, 1983.
Facing It, Avon, 1983.
A Question of Survival, Avon, 1984.
Discontinued, Scholastic Inc., 1985.
A Band of Angels, Scholastic Inc., 1986.
Simon Pure, Scholastic Inc., 1987.
The Taking of Mariasburg, Scholastic Inc., 1988.
Goofbang Value Daze, Scholastic Inc., 1989.
Herb Seasoning, Scholastic Inc., in press.

WORK IN PROGRESS: A presently untitled novel scheduled for completion in 1990.

SIDELIGHTS: Julian F. Thompson once told *CA:* "I started to write the young adult novels in 1979. Not long before, I'd resigned after seven years as janitor/teacher/director at a wonderful, exhausting alternative high school that some kids and I had banded together to found, and my wife had gone back to being a full-time student. I'd done my own assignments in a writing workshop at the school all seven years, and I thought I might have taught myself something about writing, and even found a voice that seemed to be my own. It was an old friend, Perry Knowlton, president of Curtis Brown Ltd., the literary agency, who first told me that the book I was writing in 1980 would probably be perceived as a 'young adult' novel. I'd never heard the expression before, so I asked him what one was, and he said it was a book that was (mostly) about kids but wasn't *Lord of the*

Flies or *Catcher in the Rye*. He also [introduced me to] his executive vice president, Marilyn Marlow, which meant I had the finest agent imaginable. To be honest, I didn't care what anybody called my books, as long as somebody published them and other people got to read them, and I still don't. My only strategy is to write down whatever story comes to my mind, as well as I can, and let other people put the labels on. It seems to me that some of my books work at least as well for people beyond their teens— many of whom have told me so—but of course that's a matter of opinion.

"There are a number of reasons for my choosing to write novels that have teenaged protagonists. First of all, I *did* spend over thirty years with people that age, in settings ranging from a state reformatory (on one extreme) to a selective private school (on another). And I really did enjoy the kids I met in all those different places. Naturally, I had a lot of roles and titles through the years, like 'teacher,' 'coach,' 'counselor,' and 'director,' but the one I liked most—corny as this sounds—was 'friend.' I enjoyed hanging out with people that age, not *all* the time (for sure) but some of it. And so it really pleases me to write books that some of them enjoy. I like to think that kids are (somehow) reassured and feel approved of by what they read in my books. I take kids seriously. I want them to know that a lot of the 'answers' that grown-ups give to many questions should not be swallowed whole. I want them to hold onto their hopefulness and wonder, and to their own real selves.

"A librarian has told me that my stuff is 'controversial,' but that's not part of my purpose; it doesn't seem that way to me. I realize, though, that anything a person writes about such things as peer and parent relationships, nuclear and conventional war, or the educational system can be labeled controversial by someone who disagrees with what is written—and I suppose that accounts for her statement. It's possible, too, that some readers take what I write completely literally. That would be a bad mistake; by and large, my novels have (as, thank heaven, reviewers have noticed) a certain amount of surrealistic (and even black) humor in them. I'm pretty sure most kids—and all but the most conservative adults—understand and relax with what I'm up to, sometimes even before they learn what it's called."

*　　*　　*

THOMPSON, Phyllis Hoge 1926-
(Phyllis Hoge, Phyllis Rose)

PERSONAL: Born November 15, 1926, in Elizabeth, N.J.; daughter of Philip Barlow (an engineer) and Dorothy (Anderson) Hoge; married Noel James Thompson (an electrical engineer), June 4, 1964 (divorced); married Bacil F. Kirtley (a folklorist), May 14, 1983; children: (first marriage) Mead Anderson, William Scofield, John C., Jr., Katharine Blair. *Education:* Connecticut College, B.A., 1948; Duke University, M.A., 1949; University of Wisconsin, Ph.D., 1957. *Religion:* Quaker.

ADDRESSES: Home—213 Dartmouth Dr., S.E. Albuquerque, N.M. 87106.

CAREER: University of Wisconsin Extension—Madison, special instructor, 1957-62; Milton College, Milton, Wis., professor of English, 1962-64; University of Hawaii, Honolulu, assistant professor, 1964-69, associate professor, 1969-73, professor of English, 1973-83, professor emeritus, 1983—. Member of board, Hawaii Literary Arts Council, Hawaii Council for Culture and the Arts, Hawaii Committee for the Humanities, and the Poetry Game.

MEMBER: Historic Hawaii Foundation, Phi Beta Kappa.

AWARDS, HONORS: Danforth Associate, 1966—; National Endowment for the Humanities grant, 1968-69; various Hawaii State Foundation grants.

WRITINGS:

(Under name Phyllis Hoge) *Artichoke, and Other Poems,* University of Hawaii Press, 1969.
The Creation Frame, University of Illinois Press, 1973.
The Serpent of the White Rose, Petronuim, 1975.
What the Land Gave, Quarterly Review of Literature Poetry Series, 1981.
Writing of Women: Essays in a Renaissance, Wesleyan University Press, 1985.
The Ghosts of Who We Were, University of Illinois Press, 1986.
(Under name Phyllis Rose) *Jazz Cleopatra—Josephine Baker in Her Time,* Doubleday, 1989.

Contributor to literary journals, poetry magazines, and teaching periodicals, under the name Phyllis Rose until 1968. Editor, *Festival,* 1966, and *Any Direction,* 1977.

WORK IN PROGRESS: Nine Miles Up the Road, nonfiction on the New Mexico ghost town, Mogollon; *There's Justice,* a book of poems; and *New and Selected Poems.*

SIDELIGHTS: Phyllis Hoge Thompson told *CA:* "Poetry is central in my life, despite necessary commitments to teaching, mothering, and wifing. I have a strong sense of place and of how human emotions, human lives, are related to natural surroundings. I love travel, but have rarely been able to go far or long because of family responsibility. I have, however, made a number of visits to Yaddo, which remains the place I work best.

"When I wrote my Ph.D. thesis I chose Yeats. I knew it would take a long time because I was also bearing four children and teaching four nights a week, and I was determined to be sustained, not bored, by my 'real' work. Half a lifetime later, I still return to Yeats, and lately with a vengeance, often choosing his stanza forms and sometimes his themes and subjects as a basis for my own poems. He teaches me not to be afraid of plain truth or bare simplicity or ordinary language. So when my poems 'fail' they may fail by falling to sentimentality through apparent abstraction, but when the risk pays off, they may succeed by clear, simple truth. That's the kind of chance I've chosen to take. I find it even riskier with rhyme, but worth the candle to me. Partly to learn more about the language of poetry, I now have in process a nonfiction book on a New Mexico ghost town based on a weekly column I wrote for *The Silver City Enterprise* in 1987. I've enjoyed doing it. It has given me space to talk about the kinds of things I so far have been unable to put into poems. It also has given me a legitimate way to begin feeling myself a New Mexico writer, in a way I never felt myself to be a Hawaiian one.

"Yeats was crucial to me and Rilke is, and most recently, James Wright. I find the work of William Stafford kin to my way of seeing things. I think long practice in traditional meters yields a flexible, ready music to poetry—even when the form becomes 'free.' My work is centered in my faith, in history, and in love of the land. Since I draw as deeply as I can upon the power I find in nature, I suspect my poems do not appear 'modern,' yet I hope that readers will find them so in my handling of the poetic line."

TITUS, Eve 1922-
(Nancy Lord)

PERSONAL: Born July 16, 1922, in New York, N.Y.; divorced; children: Richard Keen. *Education:* Attended New York University.

ADDRESSES: Agent—McIntosh & Otis, Inc., 475 5th Ave., New York, N.Y. 10017.

CAREER: Free-lance author and lecturer. Director and originator of the annual "Storybook Writing Seminar," Miami, Fla., and Houston, Tex., 1964—.

MEMBER: Authors League of America, Women's National Book Association, Mystery Writers of America.

AWARDS, HONORS: Runner-up for Caldecott Award, 1956, for *Anatole,* 1958, for *Anatole and the Cat.*

WRITINGS:

Anatole, illustrated by Paul Galdone, Whittlesey House, 1956.
Anatole and the Cat, illustrated by Galdone, Whittlesey House, 1957.
Basil of Baker Street, illustrated by Galdone, Whittlesey House, 1958.
(Under pseudonym Nancy Lord) *My Dog and I* (Junior Literary Guild selection), illustrated by Galdone, McGraw, 1958.
Anatole and the Robot, illustrated by Galdone, Whittlesey House, 1960.
Anatole over Paris, illustrated by Galdone, Whittlesey House, 1961.
The Mouse and the Lion, illustrated by Leonard Weisgard, Parents' Magazine Press, 1962.
Basil and the Lost Colony, illustrated by Galdone, Whittlesey House, 1964.
Anatole and the Poodle, illustrated by Galdone, Whittlesey House, 1964.
Anatole and the Piano, illustrated by Galdone, McGraw, 1966.
(Adaptor) *The Two Stonecutters* (from the Japanese), illustrated by Yoko Mitsuhashi, Doubleday, 1967.
Anatole and the Thirty Thieves, illustrated by Galdone, McGraw, 1969.
Mr. Shaw's Shipshape Shoeshop, illustrated by Larry Ross, Parents' Magazine Press, 1970.
Anatole and the Toyshop, illustrated by Galdone, McGraw, 1970.
Basil and the Pygmy Cats, illustrated by Galdone, McGraw, 1971.
Why the Wind God Wept, illustrated by James Barkley, Doubleday, 1972.
Anatole in Italy, illustrated by Galdone, McGraw, 1973.
Basil and the Lost Colony, illustrated by Galdone, Hodder & Stoughton, 1975.
Basil in Mexico, illustrated by Galdone, McGraw, 1976.
Anatole and the Pied Piper, illustrated by Galdone, McGraw, 1979.
Basil in the Wild West, illustrated by Galdone, McGraw, 1981.

Also author, under pseudonym Nancy Lord, of *The Compass Inside Ourselves,* published by Fireweed.

WORK IN PROGRESS: Researching ancient legends of Mexico, particularly those of the Yucatan Peninsula, with Mayan background.

SIDELIGHTS: Eve Titus was originally a professional concert pianist who gave piano recitals in New York, Florida, Arkansas, Texas, Jamaica, and Mexico. She has also cruised the Caribbean on ships as a concert pianist. Titus's original manuscripts are in the Case Collection at Wayne State University, Detroit, Michigan.

MEDIA ADAPTATIONS: Anatole and *Anatole and the Piano* have been made into films.

BIOGRAPHICAL/CRITICAL SOURCES:

BOOKS

Books for Children 1960-1965, American Library Association, 1966.
The Children's Bookshelf, Child Study Association of America/Bantam, 1965.
Huck and Young, *Children's Literature in the Elementary School,* Holt, 1961.
Larrick, Nancy, *A Parent's Guide to Children's Reading,* 3rd edition, Doubleday, 1969.

PERIODICALS

New York Times Book Review, May 9, 1965, September 10, 1967, January 10, 1971, April 29, 1979.
Saturday Review, April 24, 1965, November 8, 1969, August 21, 1971.
Spectator, December 5, 1970.
Times Literary Supplement, April 3, 1969, December 11, 1970, July 2, 1971.
Washington Post Book World, October 15, 1967.*

*   *   *

TODD, Herbert Eatton 1908-1988

PERSONAL: Born February 22, 1908, in London, England; died February 25, 1988; son of Henry Graves (a headmaster) and Minnie Elizabeth Todd; married Bertha Joyce Hughes, 1933 (died, 1969); children: Jonathan (died, 1964), Mark, Stephen. *Education:* Attended Christ's Hospital, Horsham, England, 1919-1925. *Politics:* Conservative. *Religion:* Church of England.

ADDRESSES: Home—St. Nicholas, 2 Brownlow Rd., Berkhamsted, Hertfordshire HP4 1HB, England.

CAREER: Writer. Houlder Brothers Ltd., London, England, shipping clerk, 1925-27; British Foreign and Colonial Corp., London, investment clerk, 1927-29; Bourne & Hollingsworth Ltd., London, hosiery underbuyer, 1929-31; F. G. Wigley & Co. Ltd., London, 1931-69, began as traveler, became director. Broadcaster of "Bobby Brewster" stories and children's musical programs on radio and television; performer in local operatic productions, 1945-62. *Military service:* Royal Air Force, 1940-45; became squadron leader.

MEMBER: Berkhamsted Amateur Operatic and Dramatic Society (choir master, 1948-52; chairman, 1956-60; president, 1961-71).

AWARDS, HONORS: White Rose Award, 1971, for *Bobby Brewster and the Ghost.*

WRITINGS:

JUVENILES; WITH VAL BIRO

The Sick Cow, Brockhampton Press, 1974, 5th edition, 1982.
George and the Fire Engine, Hodder & Stoughton Children's Books, 1976, 2nd edition, 1979.
Changing of the Guard, Hodder & Stoughton Children's Books, 1978.
The Roundabout Horse, Hodder & Stoughton Children's Books, 1978.
The Very Very Very Long Dog, Carousel, 1978, 4th edition, 1981.

The King of Beasts, Hodder & Stoughton Children's Books, 1979.

Here Comes Wordman!, Carousel, 1980.

The Big Sneeze, Hodder & Stoughton Children's Books, 1980, 3rd edition, 1982.

Jungle Silver, Hodder & Stoughton Children's Books, 1981.

The Crawly Crawly Caterpillar, Carousel, 1981.

The Tiny Tiny Tadpole, Carousel, 1982.

The Scruffy Scruffy Dog, Carousel, 1983.

The Tiger Who Couldn't Be Bothered, Hodder & Stoughton Children's Books, 1984.

Clever Clever Cats, Carousel, 1986.

The Sleeping Policeman, Hodder & Stoughton Children's Books, 1988.

Jigsaw-Puzzle, Hodder & Stoughton Children's Books, 1988.

Silly Silly Ghost, Carousel, 1988.

"BOBBY BREWSTER" SERIES

Bobby Brewster and the Winker's Club, Edmund Ward, 1949.

Bobby Brewster, Brockhampton Press, 1954, 8th edition, 1981.

Bobby Brewster, Bus Conductor, Brockhampton Press, 1955, 8th edition, 1981.

Bobby Brewster's Shadow, Brockhampton Press, 1956, 7th edition, 1979.

Bobby Brewster's Bicycle, Brockhampton Press, 1957, 8th edition, 1983.

Bobby Brewster's Camera, Brockhampton Press, 1959, 7th edition, 1982.

Bobby Brewster's Wallpaper, Brockhampton Press, 1961, 6th edition, 1975.

Bobby Brewster's Conker, Brockhampton Press, 1963, 5th edition, 1973.

Bobby Brewster, Detective, Brockhampton Press, 1964, 3rd edition, 1970.

Bobby Brewster's Potato, Brockhampton Press, 1964, 5th edition, 1973.

Bobby Brewster and the Ghost, Brockhampton Press, 1966, 7th edition, 1971.

Bobby Brewster's Kite, Brockhampton Press, 1967, 5th edition, 1981.

Bobby Brewster's Scarecrow, Brockhampton Press, 1967, 5th edition, 1980.

Bobby Brewster's Torch, Brockhampton Press, 1968, 3rd edition, 1971.

Bobby Brewster's Balloon Race, Brockhampton Press, 1970, 5th edition, 1979.

Bobby Brewster's First Magic, Brockhampton Press, 1970.

Bobby Brewster's Typewriter, Brockhampton Press, 1971, 2nd edition, 1972.

Bobby Brewster's Bee, Brockhampton Press, 1972, 3rd edition, 1983.

Bobby Brewster's Wishbone, Brockhampton Press, 1974, 2nd edition, 1977.

Bobby Brewster's First Fun, Brockhampton Press, 1974.

Bobby Brewster's Bookmark, Brockhampton Press, 1975, 3rd edition, 1982.

Bobby Brewster's Tealeaves, Hodder & Stoughton Children's Books, 1979, 3rd edition, 1983.

Bobby Brewster's Lamp Post, Hodder & Stoughton Children's Books, 1982.

Bobby Brewster's Old Van, Hodder & Stoughton Children's Books, 1985.

Bobby Brewster's Hiccups, Hodder & Stoughton Children's Books, 1985.

Bobby Brewster and the Magic Handyman, Hodder & Stoughton Children's Books, 1986.

OTHER

(With Capel Annand) *Blackbird Pie* (juvenile; musical play), Boosey & Hawkes, 1956.

The Dial-a-Story Book, Puffin, 1981.

Also author of five adult musical revues and ten children's musical programs, produced by British Broadcasting Corp. (BBC), 1949-57.

SIDELIGHTS: Herbert Eatton Todd told *CA:* "I write very simple short stories, and insist that each has a plot with a beginning, a middle, and an end. I started as a story*teller,* firstly to my own sons—and from then on I have told stories and talked about writing in over 5000 schools and libraries throughout Britain and in several other English-speaking countries. I have also broadcast and televised my stories on British radio and TV stations and in other countries, many times. I write purely for fun—both for my listeners and readers (I hope) and myself—and only sit down to write a story when I have the urge and when I have formed in my mind the complete plot—most particularly the end."

Several of Todd's books have been translated into foreign languages.*

*   *   *

TOON, Peter 1939-

PERSONAL: Born October 25, 1939, in Yorkshire, England; son of Thomas Arthur (a coal miner) and Hilda (Machel) Toon; married Vita Persram; children: Deborah Anastasia. *Education:* King's College, London, B.D., 1965, M.Th., 1967; University of Liverpool, M.A., 1971; Christ Church, Oxford, M.A., 1973, D.Phil., 1975.

ADDRESSES: Home—Seven Beechside, Staindrop, Darlington, Durham DL2 3PE, England. *Office*—The Vicarage, Staindrop, Durham, DL2 3PE, England.

CAREER: Ordained minister of Church of England; lecturer at Edge Hill College, 1968-73, Latimer House, Oxford, 1973-76, and Oak Hill College, 1976-82; Diocese of St. Edmundsbury and Ipswich, Ipswich, England, director of postordination training, 1982-88; Vicarage of Staindrop, Staindrop, Durham, England, vicar, 1988—.

WRITINGS:

The Emergence of Hyper-Calvinism, Olive Tree, 1967.

Puritans, the Millennium, and the Future of Israel, James Clarke, 1971.

God's Statesman: The Life of John Owen, 1616-1683, Zondervan, 1974.

Evangelical Theology, 1833-1856, Knox Press, 1979.

The Development of Doctrine in the Church, Eerdmans, 1979.

Jesus Christ Is Lord, Judson, 1979.

The Anglican Way, Morehouse, 1983.

Justification and Sanctification, Crossway Books, 1983.

Your Conscience as Your Guide, Morehouse, 1984.

Protestants and Catholics, Servant Publications, 1984.

The Ascension of Our Lord, Thomas Nelson, 1984.

Heaven and Hell, Thomas Nelson, 1985.

From Mind Is Heart: Christian Meditation, Baker Book, 1986.

Born Again: A Biblical/Theological Study, Baker Book, 1987.

Longing for Heaven, Macmillan, 1989.

WORK IN PROGRESS: A book on meditation and western Christians in history and today.

*   *   *

TOPEROFF, Sam 1933-
(Faith Potter)

PERSONAL: Born August 22, 1933, in Brooklyn, N.Y.; son of Morris (owner of a candy store) and Ruth (Reichmann) Toperoff; married Faith Potter (a teacher), October 16, 1966; children: Lily Anna. *Education:* Hofstra University, B.A., 1960; Lehigh University, M.A., 1962. *Politics:* "Monarchist." *Religion:* Society of Friends (Quaker).

ADDRESSES: Agent—Philip G. Spitzer, 788 Ninth Ave., New York, N.Y. 10019.

CAREER: Hofstra University, Hempstead, N.Y., instructor, 1962-69, assistant professor of English, 1969-75, associate professor of art history, beginning 1975, currently professor of English. Volunteer water-meter reader. *Military service:* U.S. Marine Corps, 1954-56.

MEMBER: Yorkshire Terrier Owners of the North Shore.

WRITINGS:

All the Advantages (autobiography), Atlantic Monthly Press, 1967.
Crazy over Horses, Atlantic Monthly Press, 1969.
Pilgrim of the Sun and Stars, Atlantic Monthly Press, 1972.
Porcupine-Man, Saturday Review Press, 1974.
The Democrat (novel), Saturday Review Press, 1976.
(Contributor) Edward Ehre and Irving Marsh, editors, *Best Sports Stories 1978,* Dutton, 1978.
(With James Roosevelt) *A Family Matter* (novel), Simon & Schuster, 1980.
Sugar Ray Leonard and Other Noble Warriors, McGraw, 1987.

Also author, under pseudonym Faith Potter, of a privately printed volume of poetry; contributor to *Best Short Stories 1978,* and to periodicals, including *Sports Illustrated.*

SIDELIGHTS: Sam Toperoff's account of his New York childhood and adolescence, *All the Advantages,* "is a deceptively unsentimental book," notes Jay Neugeboren in the *New York Times Book Review.* "It seems at first to be yet another evocation of a lower-middle-class Jewish family's struggle," the critic explains, yet Toperoff "avoids making his book an exercise in nostalgia. His loving memories are accompanied by a tone of unmistakable and increasing bitterness." The author uses a similarly balanced approach in two accounts of his love for sport, *Sugar Ray Leonard and Other Noble Warriors* and *Crazy over Horses.* In *Sugar Ray Leonard,* for example, "Toperoff mixes in his own autobiography as a boxing fan" with descriptions of the career of welterweight Sugar Ray Leonard, as *Washington Post* contributor Chris Mead observes. "Here there is detail, insight and wry humor," the critic adds, and while Toperoff "wisely concedes that the sport's opponents have the stronger logic on their side," *Sugar Ray Leonard* "shares human riches from boxing—the real choices that makes bravery and passion possible." *New York Times Book Review* contributor Rex Lardner likewise finds that Toperoff does horseracing and betting "a great service in [*Crazy over Horses,*] this immensely funny, sometimes poignant, ever-informative book, a kind of Thinking Man's Guide to the track." In revealing the sport through his personal anecdotes of the track, Toperoff, concludes the critic, "is the class of his field."

BIOGRAPHICAL/CRITICAL SOURCES:

BOOKS

Toperoff, Sam, *All the Advantages,* Atlantic Monthly Press, 1967.

PERIODICALS

New York Times Book Review, September 24, 1967, June 29, 1969.
Time, June 27, 1969.
Washington Post, January 10, 1987.*

*   *   *

TRAIN, John 1928-

PERSONAL: Born May 25, 1928, in New York, N.Y.; son of Arthur Cheney (an author and president of the National Institute of Arts and Letters) and Helen (Coster) Train; married Maria Teresa Cini di Pianzano, 1961 (divorced, 1976); married Frances Cheston, July 23, 1977; children: (first marriage) Helen, Nina, Lisa. *Education:* Harvard University, B.A., 1950, M.A., 1951; graduate study at Sorbonne, University of Paris, 1951-52.

ADDRESSES: Home—Box 157, R.D. 2, Bedford, N.Y. 10506.

CAREER: Paris Review, Paris, France, co-founder, 1952, managing editor, 1952-54; Train, Smith Counsel, New York City, president, 1959—. President, Chateau Malcasse, Lamarque-Margaux, Bordeaux, France, 1970-1980. Trustee of *Harvard Lampoon,* Cambridge, Mass., 1974—. *Military service:* U.S. Army, 1954-56; became first lieutenant.

MEMBER: Order of Colonial Lords of Manors in America, Pilgrims Club, Brooks's Club (London), Travellers Club (Paris), Century Club, Racquet and Tennis Club.

AWARDS, HONORS: Named commendatore of Ordine Della Solidarieta (Italy), 1968, and commendatore of Ordine del Merito Della Republica (Italy), 1977.

WRITINGS:

Dance of the Money Bees: A Professional Speaks Frankly on Investing, Harper, 1973.
The Money Masters: Nine Great Investors—Their Winning Strategies and How You Can Apply Them, Harper, 1981.
Preserving Capital and Making It Grow, Crown, 1982.
Famous Financial Fiascos, C. N. Potter, 1984.
The Midas Touch: The Investment Genius of Warren Buffett—His Career, His Profit Techniques, and How to Use Them, Harper, 1987, reprinted as *The Midas Touch: The Strategies That Have Made Warren Buffett "America's Pre-eminent Investor,"* 1988.
The New Money Masters, Harper, 1989.

"REMARKABLE" SERIES

Remarkable Names of Real People; Or, How to Name Your Baby, illustrations by Pierre Le Tan, introduction by S. J. Perleman, C. N. Potter, 1977.
True Remarkable Occurrences, illustrations by Le Tan, preface by George Plimpton, C. N. Potter, 1978.
Even More Remarkable Names, C. N. Potter, 1979.
Remarkable Words with Astonishing Origins, C. N. Potter, 1980.
Remarkable Relatives, C. N. Potter, 1981.
John Train's Most Remarkable Names, Crown, 1985.

OTHER

Author of regular columns "Financial Strategy" in *Forbes* and "Money Matters" in *Harvard.* Contributor of articles to magazines, including *Reader's Digest, Investor's Digest* (London), *L'Economie* (Paris), and *American Spectator*, and to newspapers, including *New York Times, Wall Street Journal*, and *Washington Post*.

SIDELIGHTS: "History enshrines the deeds and dates of the lofty and mighty, but John Train serves as curator of the bizarre," comments *New York Times* critic Lawrence Van Gelder. An investment counselor by profession, Train is also a zealous collector of curiosa, as indicated by the series of books he began publishing in 1977. *Remarkable Names of Real People; or, How to Name Your Baby*, the first book in the "Remarkable" series, includes entries such as Dr. E. Z. Filler, a dentist, Mrs. Screech, a singing teacher, and Cardinal Sin, the Archbishop of Manila. The second book in the series, *True Remarkable Occurrences*, had its origin in 1952, when Train began collecting accounts of oddities after reading a French newspaper story about a young woman who fell asleep while nursing her baby and awoke to find that she was suckling a snake. After taking the baby's place, the snake, according to the article, waved its tail as a distraction to silence the infant's cries. *Remarkable Words with Astonishing Origins*, the third book in Train's series, is a collection of nearly three hundred word origins, which Mason Buck of the *Los Angeles Times Book Review* called a display of "dedicated etymological sleuthing." It has been followed by *Remarkable Relatives, Even More Remarkable Names*, and *John Train's Most Remarkable Names*.

In addition to the "Remarkable" series, Train has written books in his professional field. The first, *Dance of the Money Bees: A Professional Speaks Frankly on Investing*, is "one of the more entertaining and informative books on the investment game to appear in the last two decades," assesses Christopher Lehmann-Haupt of the *New York Times. The Money Masters: Nine Great Investors—Their Winning Strategies and How You Can Apply Them* receives equally high praise from *New York Times* critic Paul E. Erdman, who calls the book "the best one in the investment field that I have read in years." Critics also use superlatives when recommending *Preserving Capital and Making It Grow* and *The Midas Touch: The Investment Genius of Warren Buffett— His Career, His Profit Techniques, and How to Use Them*. While pointing out that Train's advice will be most useful to those who are already wealthy, Lehmann-Haupt says Train provides "the best advice on matters such as investing in the stock market or putting your money into so-called collectibles that I've ever come across."

BIOGRAPHICAL/CRITICAL SOURCES:

BOOKS

Train, John, *Remarkable Names of Real People; or, How to Name Your Baby*, C. N. Potter, 1977.

PERIODICALS

Chicago Tribune Book World, April 13, 1980.
Los Angeles Times Book Review, December 7, 1980, March 22, 1981, January 12, 1986.
New Statesman, March 31, 1978.
New York Times, December 6, 1978, November 27, 1979, January 8, 1980.
New York Times Book Review, February 3, 1980, March 8, 1981, July 25, 1983, April 28, 1985, May 31, 1987.
Times (London), February 19, 1981.
Times Literary Supplement, November 24, 1978.
Washington Post Book World, February 8, 1981, March 1, 1981.

TRAVERS, P(amela) L(yndon) 1906-

PERSONAL: Born in 1906 in Queensland, Australia. *Education:* Privately educated.

ADDRESSES: Home—Chelsea, London, England. *Office*—c/o William Collins Sons, Ltd., 8 Grafton St., London W1, England.

CAREER: Writer, journalist, dancer, and actress in Australia and England; full-time writer in England, 1930—. Worked for the British Ministry of Information in the United States during World War II. Writer in residence, Radcliffe College, 1965-66, Smith College, 1966-67, and Scripps College, 1970.

AWARDS, HONORS: D.H.L., Chatham College, 1978; *Two Pairs of Shoes* was an American Library Society notable children's book for 1980.

WRITINGS:

Moscow Excursion, Reynal & Hitchcock, 1935.
Mary Poppins (also see below), illustrated by Mary Shepard, Reynal & Hitchcock, 1935, reprinted, Harcourt, 1985.
Mary Poppins Comes Back (also see below), illustrated by Shepard, Reynal & Hitchcock, 1935, reprinted, Harcourt, 1985.
Mary Poppins and Mary Poppins Comes Back, illustrated by Shepard, Reynal & Hitchcock, 1937, reprinted, Harcourt, 1963.
Happy Ever After, illustrated by Shepard, Reynal & Hitchcock, 1940.
I Go by Sea, I Go by Land, illustrated by Gertrude Hermes, Harper, 1941, new edition, Norton, 1964.
Mary Poppins Opens the Door, illustrated by Agnes Sims and Shepard, Reynal & Hitchcock, 1943, reprinted, Harcourt, 1985.
Mary Poppins in the Park, illustrated by Shepard, Harcourt, 1952, reprinted, Peter Smith, 1988.
The Gingerbread Shop (excerpt from *Mary Poppins*), Simon & Schuster, 1952.
Mr. Wiggs Birthday Party (excerpt from *Mary Poppins*), Simon & Schuster, 1952.
Stories from Mary Poppins (excerpt from *Mary Poppins*), Simon & Schuster, 1952.
The Magic Compass (excerpt from *Mary Poppins*), Simon & Schuster, 1953.
The Fox at the Manger, wood engravings by Thomas Bewick, Norton, 1962.
Mary Poppins from A to Z, illustrated by Shepard, Harcourt, 1962.
Friend Monkey, Harcourt, 1971, reprinted, Dell, 1987.
Mary Poppins in the Kitchen, illustrated by Shepard, Harcourt, 1975.
About Sleeping Beauty, illustrated by Charles Keeping, McGraw, 1975.
Two Pairs of Shoes, illustrated by Leo and Diane Dillon, Viking, 1980.
Mary Poppins in Cherry Tree Lane, Delacorte, 1982.

SIDELIGHTS: P. L. Travers grew up listening to old fairy tales told to her by her Scottish and Irish parents. At the age of seven, she began writing her own stories, which sometimes used parts of these old tales, and continued writing until she left home, intending to become a poet. Towards this end, she travelled to Dublin in the 1920s, during the end of the literary renaissance there. She soon became friends with William Butler Yeats, George Russell, and other poets, who were, like her, interested in myths and legends. It was Russell, better known as A. E., who encouraged her to write poems for his paper, the *Irish Statesman*, and who also approved of her early stories involving Travers's now well-known creation, Mary Poppins.

Travers first began to write about Mary Poppins while she was recovering from an illness in the 900-year-old Pound Cottage in Sussex, England. The stories were originally meant only as a way for the author to pass time, but a friend later convinced her to collect them in a book for publication. The result was a success for Travers, and even today her character still appeals to audiences of all ages and has been translated into more than twenty languages. Tributes to Poppins have appeared over the years, including the 1964 movie "Mary Poppins" released by Walt Disney Studios, "Mary Poppins Suite for Orchestra," by Mortimer Browning, and *Mary Poppins,* a dramatization written by Sara Spencer and published by Children's Theater Press around 1940. Horticulturalists have even produced two "Mary Poppins" roses, one of which is called the "Pamela Travers" rose.

The character of Mary Poppins, describes a *Times Literary Supplement* reviewer, "is . . . the embodiment of authority, protection, and cynical common sense; her powers are magical. Basically, she is the Good Fairy, whom we are all seeking, but in priggish human guise." Travers's interest in myths, legends, and fairy tales is also readily apparent in Poppins, being revealed by the magical nanny's remarkable abilities and her friendship with Greek gods and other fantastic characters. But despite their appeal to young audiences, the author is adamant in insisting that the Mary Poppins books are not juvenile books. "I don't know why Mary Poppins is thought of as a children's book," she tells *Washington Post Book World* contributor Frances Maclean. "Indeed, I don't think there are such things. There are simply books and some of them children read."

Neither is Travers interested in recognition for the Poppins books. "I am a writer who likes anonymity," she once told *CA,* "believing that all that concerns the general public is the books themselves which are, in the truest sense, any author's biography." Indeed, she remarks in her *Something about the Author Autobiography Series* entry that the stories she writes find her, rather than the other way around. "I agree with A. E. who said that Mary Poppins came straight out of myth," she writes. "Where else could I have found her or she me?" After she is gone, Travers only wishes that her books will be remembered. In Maclean's article, the author hopes aloud: "Maybe one day no one will know who wrote Mary Poppins."

MEDIA ADAPTATIONS: The movie "Mary Poppins," starring Julie Andrews and Dick Van Dyke, was released in 1964 by Walt Disney Studios.

BIOGRAPHICAL/CRITICAL SOURCES:

BOOKS

Children's Literature Review, Volume 2, Gale, 1976.
Something about the Author Autobiography Series, Volume 2, Gale, 1986.

PERIODICALS

Chicago Tribune Book World, November 9, 1980.
Los Angeles Times Book Review, November 16, 1980.
New York Times, October 4, 1966, October 15, 1966, January 4, 1981, December 19, 1982.
New York Times Book Review, November 7, 1971, September 28, 1975, November 16, 1975.
Publishers Weekly, December 13, 1971.
Times Literary Supplement, November 28, 1952, December 2, 1977, July 23, 1982.
Washington Post Book World, May 13, 1979.*

TRUESDALE, C(alvin) W(illiam) 1929-

PERSONAL: Born March 27, 1929; son of Cavour Langdon (retired president of a plastics company) and Isabel (Hardie) Truesdale; married Joan Wurtele, March 25, 1950; children: Anna, Hardie, Stephanie. *Education:* University of Washington, Seattle, B.A., 1951, Ph.D., 1957.

ADDRESSES: 618 25th Ave. N., Minneapolis, Minn. 55411.

CAREER: University of New Mexico, Albuquerque, instructor in English, 1954-55; Virginia Military Institute, Lexington, assistant professor of English, 1956-62; Macalester College, St. Paul, Minn., assistant professor of English, 1962-67; New Rivers Press, New York City, founder and publisher, 1968—; New School for Social Research, New York City, teacher, 1973—. Former adjunct professor of humanities, Cooper Union, New York City.

WRITINGS:

In the Country of a Deer's Eye [or] *En el pais del ojo de venado* (poetry; bilingual edition), translated into Spanish by Otto-Raul Gonzalez, El Corno Emplumado (Mexico), 1966.
The Loss of Rivers, Azazel Books, 1967.
Moon Shots (poetry; originally published in limited edition as *El Hombre: La Guerra*), lithographs by Lucas Johnson, Mexican Art Annex (New York), 1968.
(Translator with Charles Simic) Ivan V. Lalic, *Fire Gardens: Selected Poems of Ivan V. Lalic,* New Rivers Press, 1970.
The Master of Knives: Poems and Drawings, illustrated by Johnson, Hamman Publishing, 1971.
Plastic Father, Fragments Books, 1971.
Cold Harbors, Latitudes Press, 1973.
(With Robert Bonazzi and Carlos Isla) *Domingo* (poem; bilingual edition), Latitudes Press, 1974.
Doctor Vertigo, Wyrd Press, 1976.
(Editor with D. Clinton and Tom Montag) *An Americas Anthology: A Geopoetics Landmark,* New Rivers Press, 1983.

Contributor of poetry and essays to various magazines. Editor, *Minnesota Review,* 1971—.

WORK IN PROGRESS: Pope John's Motel, a collection of poems.

SIDELIGHTS: In a *Minnesota Review* article on C. W. Truesdale's poetry, Roy Arthur Swanson notes that the poet's personal sense of tragedy has been translated into "a concept of melancholy derived from sense-data" in his poetry. His words "are not cleverly disposed or timed to mechanistic clicks," the critic continues. "They, like those of the best cubistic poetry, lack oily academic ingenuity but not soft, quiet, denotative precision." In addition, Swanson points out that "one of Truesdale's most effective images is geography. . . . He does not mean merely that he needs to *think about* a place's geography; he needs, literally, to think a place's geography. And by sounding out a place's geography," the critic concludes, "he means, again, not merely probing it but also giving it sound: combining earth song with mind music."

BIOGRAPHICAL/CRITICAL SOURCES:

PERIODICALS

Little Magazine, summer, 1971.
Minnesota Review, summer, 1967, Number 3, 1968.*

TRUITT, Gloria A(nn) 1939-

PERSONAL: Born August 26, 1939, in Laurium, Mich.; daughter of Earl Edgar (in industrial sales) and Ellen (Makolin) Smith; married John Truitt (a television chief engineer), June 1, 1963; children: John, Laura. *Education:* Attended Northern Michigan University, 1957-59, 1973. *Religion:* Presbyterian.

ADDRESSES: Home—332 East Ohio St., Marquette, Mich. 49855.

CAREER: South Bend Tribune, South Bend, Ind., promotional writer, 1959; WLUC-TV, Marquette, Mich., promotion manager, 1960-63; writer.

MEMBER: Presbyterian Writers Guild, P.E.O. Sisterhood.

WRITINGS:

FOR CHILDREN

(Contributor) Grace Fox Anderson, editor, *The Peanut Butter Hamster and Other Animal Tails,* Victor Books, 1979.
Nature Riddle Coloring Book: Foods, Standard Publishing, 1982.
Nature Riddle Coloring Book: God's Creatures and Creations, Standard Publishing, 1982.
Nature Riddle Coloring Book: Birds, Standard Publishing, 1982.
Nature Riddle Coloring Book: Animals, Standard Publishing, 1982.
People of the Old Testament, Concordia, 1983.
People of the New Testament, Concordia, 1983.
The Ten Commandments: Learning about God's Law, Concordia, 1983.
Events of the Bible, Concordia, 1984.
Places of the Bible, Concordia, 1984.
Cheerful Chad and Other Children of God, Concordia, 1985.
(Contributor) Ron and Lyn Klug, editors, *The Christian Family Christmas Book,* Augsburg, 1987.
People of the Bible and Their Prayers, Concordia, 1987.
(Contributor) Mervin Marquardt, editor, *52 Stories and Poems for Children,* Concordia, 1987.
(Contributor) Anderson, editor, *Lamb on a Ledge and Other Animal Tails,* Victor Books, 1989.

Also author of *Noah and God's Promise,* Concordia. Contributor to more than a dozen anthologies of stories and verse for children.

OTHER

Author of greeting card verses for Warner Press. Contributor of more than one thousand articles, stories and poems to magazines, including *Christian Living, Discoveries, Moody Monthly, Teen Power, Today's Animal Health,* and *Wee Wisdom.*

SIDELIGHTS: Gloria A Truitt told *CA:* "My first literary effort was completed at the age of eight. The scribbled page remained neglected in a dusty shoe box until twenty-five years later, when I submitted the poem to *Explore.* The reply was, 'Your poem is excellent . . . very lively. Send more!' During the next decade, I wrote more than seven hundred poems and stories while reliving my own childhood fantasies through the experiences of my growing children. My writings reflect my appreciation of life. I see beauty in a lacy spider web and in the violence of a 'nor'wester' blowing in from across Lake Superior. My respect for all living creations is evident in hundreds of factual nature riddles, and much of my work emphasizes my religious faith. After teaching a third grade Sunday school class, I realized many children memorize the Commandments without understanding such words as covet, Sabbath, and adultery. I decided to write a fun-to-read book, using the language and genuine life-situations of a child's world, to give meaning to each of the Ten Commandments. The result was *The Ten Commandments: Learning about God's Law.*

"In addition to my own writings, I share much of my spare time with aspiring young writers. I have been involved with 'young authors' programs and other volunteer work in the public schools. I have also conducted workshops for Northern Michigan University's 'free university' program, and have served as a panelist for Women in the Arts, supported by the Michigan Council of the Arts."

BIOGRAPHICAL/CRITICAL SOURCES:

PERIODICALS

Champaign-Urbana News-Gazette, May 10, 1983.
Green Bay Press Gazette, June 26, 1983.
Houghton Daily Mining Gazette, April 8, 1983.
Marquette Mining Journal, December 2, 1976, February 18, 1978, December 12, 1978, August 7, 1982, March 31, 1983.
Upper Peninsula Sunday Times, March 4, 1979.

*   *   *

TULIS, Jeffrey K. 1950-

PERSONAL: Born October 1, 1950, in Long Branch, N.J.; son of Murray A. (in business) amd Lynn (an artist; maiden name, Hirsch) Tulis; married Sara Jean Ehrenberg (a psychologist), July 16, 1978; children: Elizabeth, Hanna. *Education:* Attended Manchester College, Oxford, 1970-71; Bates College, B.A. (magna cum laude), 1972; Brown University, M.A., 1974; University of Chicago, Ph.D., 1982.

ADDRESSES: Home—7105 Running Rope, Austin, Tex. 78731. *Office*—Department of Government, University of Texas at Austin, Austin, Tex. 78712.

CAREER: U.S. Department of Agriculture, Washington, D.C., aide to Cooporative State Research Service, 1970; *Long Branch Daily Record,* Long Branch, N.J., political correspondent, 1972; University of Virginia, Charlottesville, research associate at White Burkett Miller Center of Public Affairs, 1977-80; University of Notre Dame, Notre Dame, Ind., instructor in government, 1980-81; Princeton University, Princeton, N.J., assistant professor of politics, 1981-87; University of Texas at Austin, associate professor of government, 1988—.

MEMBER: American Political Science Association, Phi Beta Kappa, Chicago Bates Alumni Club (president, 1976-77).

AWARDS, HONORS: American Council of Learned Societies fellowship, 1983-84; Mellon Preceptor, Princeton University, 1985-87; John M. Olin faculty fellow, 1986-87; Harvard Law School fellow in law and politics, 1986-87.

WRITINGS:

(Editor with Joseph M. Bessette) *The Presidency in the Constitutional Order,* Louisiana State University Press, 1981.
(Contributor) Thomas Cronin, editor, *Rethinking the Presidency,* Little, Brown, 1982.
(Contributor) Michael Nelson, editor, *The Presidency and the Political System,* Congressional Quarterly, 1983, 2nd edition, 1988.
(Contributor) Glen E. Thurow and Jeffrey Wallin, editors, *Rhetoric and American Statesmanship,* Carolina Academic, 1983.
The Rhetorical Presidency, Princeton University Press, 1987.

(Contributor) Martin Fansold and Alan Shank, editors, *The Constitution and the Presidency,* University Press of Kansas, 1990.

(Contributor) Sheldin S. Wolin, editor, *Revolution and the Constitution,* University of California Press, 1990.

Editor, Johns Hopkins series in constitutional thought. Contributor to *University of Chicago Law Review, Northwestern University Law Review,* and *Presidential Studies Quarterly.*

WORK IN PROGRESS: Structure and Power in American Politics, 1991.

SIDELIGHTS: The fruit of research in primary documents including presidential papers and hundreds of speech transcripts, *The Rhetorical Presidency* by Jeffrey K. Tulis "is one of the most important statements on the presidency published since the first edition of Richard Neustadt's *Presidential Power* in 1960," relates John J. DiIulio, Jr. in a *Polity* review. The Neustadt classic was due to be replaced, writes Stephen Skowronek in the *Review of Politics,* because of fundamental changes in the function of the presidency. "Simply put, an old presidential politics, framed by formal institutional arrangements and driven by interactions among institutional elites, has given way to a new presidential politics framed by a direct relationship between the president and the people at large and driven by public opinion," Skowronek explains. Tulis maintains that this change is less due to advances in communications technology as to a growing spirit of democracy on the grass-roots level regarding government in America. DiIulio recommends the book above others in the field because it takes into account and surpasses previous scholarship on the presidency in order to demonstrate that "the use of popular or mass rhetoric has become a principal tool of presidential governance."

BIOGRAPHICAL/CRITICAL SOURCES:

PERIODICALS

Polity, winter, 1988.
Review of Politics, spring, 1987.

*   *   *

TURNER, Charles W(ilson)   1916-

PERSONAL: Born November 15, 1916, in Fredericks Hall, Va.; son of Charles Constantine (a merchant) and Edna (Stecher) Turner. *Education:* University of Richmond, B.A., 1937; University of North Carolina, M.A., 1940; University of Minnesota, Ph.D., 1946. *Politics:* Democrat. *Religion:* Baptist.

ADDRESSES: Home—209C Nelson Ct. Apartments, Lexington, Va. 24450. *Office*—Washington and Lee Library, Lexington, Va. 24450.

CAREER: History teacher in high schools in Louisa County, Va., 1937-43; Iowa State College (now Iowa State University), Ames, instructor in history, 1945-46; University of Minnesota, Minneapolis, instructor in history, 1946-47; Washington and Lee University, Lexington, Va., assistant professor, 1946-53, associate professor, 1953-58, professor of history, 1958-82. Member of state selection board for Fulbright scholars.

MEMBER: National Historical Society, Agricultural History Society, Minnesota Historical Society, Rockridge Historical Society (president and member of board of trustees).

WRITINGS:

Chessie's Road, Garrett & Massie, 1956, reprinted, Chesapeake & Ohio Historical Society, 1986.

Mississippi West, Garrett & Massie, 1965.
Mrs. McCulloch's Stories of Old Lexington, McClure Press, 1974.
Medic Fortyniner, McClure Press, 1975.
(Editor) Jeremiah Harris, *An Old Field School Teacher's Diary,* McClure Press, 1975.
(Editor) *Captain Greenlee Davidson's Civil War Letters,* McClure Press, 1975.
(Editor) *Professor George Irwin's War Letters, 1917-18,* McClure Press, 1976.
Stories of Ole Lexington, McClure Press, 1977.
(Editor) *The Prisoner of War Letters of Colonel Thomas Houston, 1863-64,* McClure Press, 1978.
(Editor) *My Dear Emma: War Letters of Colonel James K. Edmundson, 1861-65,* McClure Press, 1978.
(Editor) *The Diary of Henry Boswell Jones of Brownsburg (1842-1871),* McClure Press, 1979.
(Editor) *Jack Campbell's War Diary, 1917-19,* McClure Press, 1980.
(Editor) *Old Zeus: The Letters of Colonel James J. White, 1862-64,* McClure Press, 1983.
Straw in the Wind (autobiography), McClure Press, 1984.
(Editor) *Diary of John Newton Lyle,* McClure Press, 1985.
Civil War Letters of Arabella Speairs and William Beverly Pettit of Fluvana County, Virginia, March 1862-March 1865, Virginia Lithography and Graphics (Roanoke), 1989.

Also editor of *Proceedings,* Rockridge County Historical Society, Volume 4, 1958, and Volume 5, 1963. Contributor of articles on economic and local history to professional journals.

*   *   *

TURNER, Frederick   1943-

PERSONAL: Born November 19, 1943, in England; came to the United States in 1967; son of Victor Witter (an anthropologist) and Edith (a writer; maiden name, Davis) Turner; married Mei Lin Chang, June 25, 1966; children: Daniel, Benjamin. *Education:* Christ Church, Oxford, B.A., 1965, M.A., 1967, B.Litt., 1967.

ADDRESSES: Home—2668 Aster Dr., Richardson, Tex. 75082. *Office*—School of Arts and Humanities, University of Texas at Dallas, Richardson, Tex. 75083.

CAREER: University of California, Santa Barbara, assistant professor of English, 1967-72; Kenyon College, Gambier, Ohio, associate professor of English, 1972—. Founding professor of School of Arts and Humanities, University of Texas at Dallas, Richardson, Tex. Has given poetry readings on various radio shows, including "At the Arabica" (a nationally syndicated program) and has appeared on two Smithsonian World PBS documentaries.

MEMBER: International Society for the Study of Time, Modern Language Association of America.

AWARDS, HONORS: Levinson Poetry Prize.

WRITINGS:

Deep Sea Fish (poetry), Unicorn, 1968.
Birth of a First Son (poetry), Christopher's Books, 1969.
The Water World (poetry), Christopher's Books, 1970.
Shakespeare and the Nature of Time, Oxford University Press, 1971.
Between Two Lives (poetry), Wesleyan University Press, 1972.
(Editor) William Shakespeare, *Romeo and Juliet,* University of London Press, 1974.

(Translator) *Three Poems from the German,* Pothanger Press, 1974.

A Double Shadow (science fiction), Berkley/Putnam, 1978.

Counter-Terra (poetry), Christopher's Books, 1978.

The Return (poetry), Countryman Press, 1981.

Beyond Geography: The Western Spirit against the Wilderness, Rutgers University Press, 1983.

The New World (epic poem), Princeton University Press, 1985.

The Garden (poetry), Ptyx Press, 1985.

Natural Classicism: Essays on Literature and Science, Paragon House, 1986.

Genesis, An Epic Poem, Saybrook, 1988.

Reconstruction Postmodernism (essays), State University of New York Press, 1989.

Eighty Poems by Miklos Radnoti (translations from the Hungarian), Princeton University Press, 1989.

Contributor to *Harpers, Southern Review, Yale Review, Performing Arts Journal, American Theater, Cumberland Poetry Review,* and many other magazines and periodicals. Editor, *Kenyon Review,* 1978-82.

WORK IN PROGRESS: A new collection of poems; various essays.

SIDELIGHTS: Frederick Turner, British writer and philosopher of science, has produced poetry and science fiction that has advanced the appreciation of the common ground on which both verse and narrative stand, says *Dictionary of Literary Biography* contributor Frederick Feirstein. "His poetry integrates his vision as a student of the sciences with his narrative and poetic skills. His book length poem *The Return* . . . has helped to bring both fiction and extended narrative back into poetry, and his . . . book, *The New World* . . . has gone a long way toward reviving the epic form in American and British poetry," Feirstein notes. Turner comments that his commitment is "to the essential unity of nature and history; a belief in creative evolution. I oppose the distinction between science and the humanities; I believe that language is coterminus with the world." He adds that major influences have been William Shakespeare, T. S. Eliot, W. B. Yeats, John Milton, Homer, and Boris Pasternak. His science fiction book *A Double Shadow* has been translated into French and Japanese.

AVOCATIONAL INTERESTS: Natural science, philosophy, anthropology, brain science.

BIOGRAPHICAL/CRITICAL SOURCES:

BOOKS

Dictionary of Literary Biography, Volume 40: *Poets of Great Britain and Ireland since 1960,* Gale, 1985.

PERIODICALS

Missouri Review, winter, 1981-82.
New York Times Book Review, October 27, 1985.

*   *   *

TURNER, Robert F(oster) 1944-

PERSONAL: Born February 14, 1944, in Atlanta, Ga.; son of Edwin W. (a physician) and Martha (Williams) Turner. *Education:* Indiana University, B.A., 1968; graduate study at Stanford University, 1972-73; University of Virginia, J.D., 1981. *Politics:* "Jeffersonian."

ADDRESSES: Home—8222 LaFaye Ct., Alexandria, Va. 22306. *Office*—Center for Law and National Security, School of Law, University of Virginia, Charlottesville, Va. 22901.

CAREER: Stanford University, Hoover Institution on War, Revolution and Peace, Stanford, Calif., research associate and public affairs fellow, 1971-74; U.S. Senate, Washington, D.C., legislative assistant to Senator Robert Griffin, 1974-79; University of Virginia, School of Law, Charlottesville, associate director, Center for Law and National Security, 1981-87; U.S. Department of Defense, Washington, D.C., special assistant to under secretary of defense for policy, 1981-82; counsel, President's Intelligence Oversight Board, White House, 1982-84; U.S. Department of State, Washington, D.C., principal deputy assistant secretary of state for legislative and intergovernmental affairs, 1984-85; U.S. Institute of Peace, Washington, D.C., president, 1986-87; University of Virginia, lecturer in law and in government and foreign affairs, 1987—. *Military service:* U.S. Army, Armor Branch, 1968-71; served in Vietnam; became captain; received Expert Infantryman Badge, Joint Services Commendation medal, and Army Commendation medal with oak leaf cluster.

MEMBER: U.S. Supreme Court Bar, American Bar Association (chairman of committee on congressional-executive relations, 1983-86; member of standing committee on law and national security, 1986—), Virginia State Bar.

WRITINGS:

Myths of the Vietnam War: The Pentagon Papers Reconsidered, American Friends of Vietnam, 1972.

Vietnamese Communism: Its Origins and Development, Hoover Institution, 1975.

The War Powers Resolution: Its Implementation in Theory and Practice, Foreign Policy Research Institute, 1983.

(With John Norton Moore) *The Legal Structure of Defense Organization,* U.S. Government Printing Office, 1986.

(With Moore) *International Law and the Brezhnev Doctrine,* University Press of America, 1987.

Nicaragua v. the United States: A Look at the Facts, Institute for Foreign Policy Analysis, Inc., 1987.

Congress, the Constitution, and Foreign Affairs, University Press of Virginia, 1989.

(Editor with Moore and Frederick S. Tipson) *National Security Law,* Carolina Academic Press, 1989.

Regional editor (for Asia and the Pacific) of *Yearbook on International Communist Affairs,* 1973-74. Senior editor, *Virginia Journal of International Law,* 1979-81.

WORK IN PROGRESS: Restoring the Rule of Law in Foreign Policy, based on the author's testimony before Senate Committee on Foreign Relations and House Committee on Foreign Affairs concerning the 1973 War Powers Resolution, for Pergamon-Brassey; a book on the constitutionality of the use of conditional appropriations by Congress as a means of controlling the President's independent constitutional powers in foreign affairs.

AVOCATIONAL INTERESTS: Tennis, photography.

*   *   *

TUROCK, Betty J(ane)

PERSONAL: Born in Scranton, Pa.; daughter of David, Jr. (a mining engineer) and Ruth (Sweetser) August; married Frank M. Turock (a corporate manager), June 16, 1956; children: David L., B. Drew. *Education:* Syracuse University, A.B. (magna cum laude), 1955; University of Pennsylvania, graduate study, 1955-56; Rutgers University, M.L.S, 1970, Ph.D., 1981. *Religion:* Unitarian Universalist.

ADDRESSES: Home—11 Undercliff Rd., Montclair, N.J. 07042. *Office*—School of Communication, Information, and Library Sciences, Rutgers University, 4 Huntington St., New Brunswick, N.J. 08903.

CAREER: Library coordinator of public schools in Holmdel, N.J., 1963-65; Wheaton Public Library, Wheaton, Ill., storyteller, 1965-67; educational media specialist for public schools in Phoenix, Ariz., 1967-70; Forsyth County Library System, Winston-Salem, N.C., head of branch library, 1970-72, head of east area libraries, 1972-73; Montclair Public Library, Montclair, N.J., assistant director, 1973-75, director, 1975-77; Monroe County Library System, Rochester, N.Y., assistant director, 1978-80; Rutgers University, New Brunswick, N.J., visiting professor, 1980-81, associate professor of library management, networking, and information services, 1981—, full member of doctoral faculty and associate in gerontology at Institute on Aging, 1983. Member of board of directors of Grass Roots, Inc., Montclair; crisis intervention counselor for Contact, Winston-Salem, 1971-73. Advisor for Library Programs, U.S. Department of Education, 1988-89; partner of consulting firm, Rock Associates.

MEMBER: American Library Association (member of coordinating council of task force on women, 1978-80; member of council, 1988-92), Library Administration and Management Association Statistics Section (member of executive board, 1981-83; vice-president, 1981-82; president, 1982-83), Public Library Association (chairperson of publications committee, 1979-82; chairperson of Presidential Task Force on Network Relations, 1982-83), American Association of Information Science, American Association of Library Schools, American Association of University Professors, Rutgers University Graduate School of Library and Information Studies Alumni Association (member of executive board, 1976—; president, 1977-78), Phi Theta Kappa, Psi Chi, Beta Phi Mu.

AWARDS, HONORS: Named woman of the year by Raritan-Holmdel Woman's Club, 1965.

WRITINGS:

Serving the Older Adult: A Guide to Library Programs and Information Sources, Bowker, 1982.
(Editor) *The Public Library in the Bibliographic Network,* Haworth Press, 1987.
Evaluation for Library Managers, Scarecrow, 1988.
Financial Planning for Libraries, Neal-Schuman, 1988.
(Editor) *Libraries and Aging,* McFarland & Co., 1988.
(Contributor) Kathleen Heim, editor, *Adult Services in the 80s,* American Library Association, 1988.

Author of "PDQ: Professional Development Quarterly," a column in *Public Library Quarterly.* Contributor of more than three dozen articles and reviews to library journals. Editor, *The Bottom Line: A Magazine of Financial Management for Libraries,* 1983—.

WORK IN PROGRESS: A study of the role of the federal government in library development.

SIDELIGHTS: Betty J. Turock told *CA:* "Even as a woman in a woman's profession—librarianship—it was hard to move ahead. When I applied for jobs with the potential for advancement, I was told, 'Your credentials were the best of all the candidates, but we had to hire the man. He supports a family.' Or, 'If you were more mobile you'd have more opportunities.' I was a woman educated in the fifties when a career was something to fall back on, and the family was the first priority. I couldn't escape the imposed roles.

"It was only after seventeen years as a corporate-nomad wife—with my work determined by my husband's job locality—that I was able to take a long, upward step professionally in 1973 to become assistant director, then director of the Montclair Public Library. Moving into an apartment away from my family and literally overcoming my fear of flying, I visited them on weekends in Winston-Salem, North Carolina, first from Montclair and later, when I moved on to a larger library system, from Rochester, New York.

"I was on my own for the first time and, because I was viewed from the outside as a runaway wife, my life no longer revolved around couples. I felt isolated until I convinced myself that I had a right to be alone and learned to take strength from other women. Before I could shed my guilt about not always being available to my children, I had to recognize that I had more of a need to arrange their environment than they had a need for me to arrange it. Much of my guilt was based on my wish to be seen as a good parent and not on a denial of parental responsibility.'

"So, as a partner in an early two-career family, a good deal of stress from the changes arose for all of us. But for me the freedom to choose the new lifestyle also brought energy and vitality. The *New York Times* noted that I developed library programs that were nationally recognized for their innovation. That focus on innovation was aimed at democratizing the libraries in which I worked in the belief that a democratic society cannot exist without democratic institutions, institutions responsive to the citizens they serve.

"Thinking of myself first as a woman allowed me to understand the need for freedom and equality in all of us. It made me a risk-taker whether I was working with activists to revitalize a previously segregated library in Winston-Salem or to begin an information and referral service in Montclair. Not all the risks were worth it. Some were errors; some brought pain, but more resulted in personal sustenance.

"Teaching and writing arose from my desire to contribute to my profession to the maximum potential my ability would allow. It was important for me to encourage others to mix the library with the people, to serve the previously ignored, to get involved in community issues, and to be wary of confusing what was expedient and personally rewarding with what was ethical, just, and fair."

BIOGRAPHICAL/CRITICAL SOURCES:

PERIODICALS

New York Times, December 19, 1976.

*   *   *

TUROW, Joseph G(regory)   1950-

PERSONAL: Born April 5, 1950, in New York, N.Y.; son of Abraham (a chemist) and Danuta (Chaikin) Turow; married Judith Forrest (a pediatrician), June 17, 1979. *Education:* University of Pennsylvania, B.A. (with distinction), 1971, M.A., 1973, Ph.D., 1976.

ADDRESSES: Home—321 Bala Ave., Cynwyd, Pa. 19004. *Office*—Annenberg School of Communications, University of Pennsylvania, Philadelphia, Pa. 19104.

CAREER: Drexel University, Philadelphia, Pa., lecturer in communications, summer, 1974, 1975; Purdue University, West Lafayette, Ind., assistant professor, 1976-81, associate professor of communications, 1981-86, faculty fellow at Fowler House,

1976-77; University of Pennsylvania, Philadelphia, associate professor for Annenberg School of Communications, 1986—. University of California, Los Angeles, visiting assistant professor, summer, 1980, visiting associate professor, summer, 1985. Member of advisory panel of Indiana Arts Commission, 1980-83; seminar leader; public speaker; guest on television and radio programs.

MEMBER: International Communication Association, Speech Communication Association of America, Phi Beta Kappa.

AWARDS, HONORS: Award from Speech Communication Association of America, 1977, for article "Another View of Citizen Feedback to the Mass Media"; David Ross fellowship from Purdue University, 1979, 1980-81; awards from International Communication Association, 1981, for article "Unconventional Programs on Commercial Television: An Organizational Perspective," and 1983, for paper "Corporate Planning toward the Coming Information Age: How It Will Affect Mass Media Culture"; Russell B. Nye Award for best article from *Journal of Popular Culture,* 1982; National Endowment for the Humanities grant, 1986.

WRITINGS:

Program Trends in Network Children's Television, 1948-1978 (monograph), Federal Communications Commission, 1979.
Getting Books to Children: An Exploration of Publisher-Market Relations, American Library Association, 1979.
Entertainment, Education, and the Hard Sell: Three Decades of Network Children's Television, Praeger, 1981.
(Editor) *Careers in Mass Media,* Science Research Associates, 1983.
Media Industries: The Production of News and Entertainment, Longman, 1984.
Playing Doctor: Television, Storytelling, and Medical Power, Oxford University Press, 1989.

CONTRIBUTOR

Paul Hirsch, Peter Miller, and F. Gerald Kline, editors, *Strategies for Communication Research,* Sage Publications, 1978.
C. Whitney and James Ettema, editors, *Individuals in Mass Media Organizations,* Sage Publications, 1981.
Robert Bostrom, editor, *Communication Yearbook 7,* Sage Publications, 1983.
W. Rowland and B. Watkins, editors, *Interpreting Television,* Sage Publications, 1985.
Phillip Tompkins and Robert McPhee, editors, *Organizational Communication: Traditional Themes and New Directions,* Sage Publications, 1985.
Clifford Johnson, editor, *The Book of Days,* Pierian, 1987.
Erik Barnouw, editor, *The International Encyclopedia of Communication,* Oxford University Press, 1989.
B. Dervin, L. Grossberg, and E. Wartella, editors, *Paradigm Dialogues,* Sage Publications, 1989.

B. Ruben and L. Lievrow, editors, *Information and Behavior,* Transaction Books, 1989.
The Academic American Encyclopedia, Grollier, 1989.

OTHER

Author of "Outtakes," a column in *EMMY: The Magazine of the Academy of Television Arts and Sciences,* 1980-82. Contributor of articles and reviews to communications and education journals, such as *Communication Research Reports, Journal of Broadcasting,* and *Journal of Communication.* Member of editorial board, *Communication Education,* 1978-82, and *Journal of Broadcasting and Electronic Media,* 1985—; advising and contributing editor, *Journal of Communication,* 1981—; assistant editor, *Central States Speech Communication Journal,* 1983-85; member of founding editorial board, *Critical Studies in Mass Communications,* 1984—.

WORK IN PROGRESS: Research on "new media" and the public relations industry.

SIDELIGHTS: Joseph G. Turow told *CA:* "My primary research and writing revolves around two questions: (1) What forces cause continuity and change in mass media material? and (2) To what extent can publics use those forces to bring about the changes in mass media that they want? The more I learn, the more I realize how complex the answers to these questions are. They are intertwined tightly with the issue of power and control in society. They relate to the broad spectrum of societal resources that define the holders of power and how they use it. And they relate to industrial and organizational processes through which power and control are exercised. Studying this subject is fascinating. Trying to implement changes in the media is more difficult and necessarily frustrating than most people would imagine."

BIOGRAPHICAL/CRITICAL SOURCES:

BOOKS

Benet, James, Arlene Daniels, and Gaye Tuchman, editors, *Hearth and Home,* Oxford University Press, 1978.
Boylan, Robert, Phillip Davison, and T. C. Yu, *Mass Media: Systems and Effects,* Praeger, 1977.
Greenberg, Bradley, *Life on Television,* Ablex Publishing, 1980.

PERIODICALS

AFI Education Newsletter, September-October, 1981.
College and Research Libraries, July, 1979.
Dallas Morning News, October 4, 1981.
Detroit Free Press, January 18, 1981.
HSSE Newsletter, autumn, 1980.
Journal of Communication, spring, 1982.
Journalism Quarterly, August, 1979, spring, 1982.
New York Times, March 25, 1989.
Southern Speech Communication Journal, spring, 1983.
Top of the News, autumn, 1979.
Wilson Library Bulletin, October, 1980.

U

ULENE, Art(hur Lawrence) 1936-

PERSONAL: Born July 13, 1936, in Los Angeles, Calif.; son of John and Fay Ulene; married Priscilla Kalkstein (a television producer), December 18, 1960; children: Douglas, Valerie, Steven. *Education:* University of California, Los Angeles, B.A., 1957, M.D., 1962.

ADDRESSES: Office—2401 West Olive St., Burbank, Calif. 91506.

CAREER: University of California, Los Angeles, Center for Health Science, intern in internal medicine, 1962-63, resident in obstetrics and gynecology, 1963-67; University of Southern California, Los Angeles, assistant clinical professor of obstetrics and gynecology, 1970—. Created "Feeling Fine," on KNBC-TV, 1975—; health commentator for "Today," on NBC-TV, 1976—, and for ABC-TV, 1978. Member of health advisory council of Clearing House for Corporate Social Responsibility; member of interpersonal skills sub-committee of National Board of Medical Examiners. *Military service:* U.S. Army, assistant chief of obstetrics and gynecology at Walter Reed Army Medical Center, 1967-70; became major.

MEMBER: American College of Obstetricians and Gynecologists.

AWARDS, HONORS: National Media Awards from Kidney Foundation, 1977, and Epilepsy Foundation, 1977, Golden Mike Awards from Southern California Radio and Television News Association, 1977 and 1978, and Blakeslee Award from American Heart Association, 1978, all for program "Feeling Fine."

WRITINGS:

Feeling Fine, J. P. Tarcher, 1977.
Help Yourself to Better Health, Perogee, 1980.
Safe Sex in a Dangerous World, Vintage, 1987.
(With Steve Shelove) *Bringing Out the Best in Your Baby: Introducing Discovery Play,* Macmillan, 1987.
Count Down on Cholesterol, Knopf, 1989.

WORK IN PROGRESS: Developing a comprehensive health library for distribution in health care settings.

SIDELIGHTS: Art Ulene's special interest has been the application of modern technology to health education. It was this interest that led him to conceive of the idea for "Feeling Fine," the television feature that promotes better health through viewer participation. His work at the University of Southern California has resulted in the development of self-instructional materials that are in use in medical schools and nursing homes all over the United States. *Feeling Fine* is a best-selling guide to common-sense health care.*

* * *

UNSWORTH, Barry (Forster) 1930-

PERSONAL: Born August 10, 1930, in Durham, England; son of Michael (an insurance salesman) and Elsie (Forster) Unsworth; married Valerie Moor, May 15, 1959; children: Madeleine, Tania, Thomasina. *Education:* University of Manchester, B.A. (with honors in English), 1951.

ADDRESSES: Office—Hamish Hamilton, 22 Wright's Lane, London W8 5TZ, England.

CAREER: Norwood Technical College, London, England, lecturer in English, 1960; University of Athens, Athens, Greece, lecturer in English for British Council, 1960-63; Norwood Technical College, lecturer in English, 1963-65; University of Istanbul, Istanbul, Turkey, lecturer in English for British Council, 1965—. *Military service:* British Army, Royal Corps of Signals, 1951-53, became second lieutenant.

AWARDS, HONORS: Royal Society of Literature-Heinemann Award for Literature, 1974, for *Mooncranker's Gift.*

WRITINGS:

NOVELS

The Partnership, Hutchinson, 1966.
The Greeks Have a Word for It, Hutchinson, 1967.
The Hide, Gollancz, 1970.
Mooncranker's Gift, Allen Lane, 1973, Houghton, 1974.
The Big Day, M. Joseph, 1976, Mason/Charter, 1977.
Pascali's Island, M. Joseph, 1980, published in America as *The Idol Hunter,* Simon & Schuster, 1980.
The Rage of the Vulture, Granada, 1982, Houghton, 1983.
Stone Virgin, Hamish Hamilton, 1985, Houghton, 1986.
Sugar and Rum, Hamish Hamilton, 1988.

OTHER

(With John Lennox Cook and Amorey Gethin) *The Student's Book of English: A Complete Coursebook and Grammar to Advanced Intermediate Level,* Blackwell, 1981.

Also author of television play, "The Stick Insect," 1975.

SIDELIGHTS: Barry Unsworth told *CA:* "My main interest is in writing fiction and in particular the exploration of moral complexities and ambiguities—not philosophical ones. I believe moral curiosity and concern to be the essential equipment for a novelist. Have traveled widely in Greece and Turkey . . . speak the languages of both countries a little but my best language is French, which I speak fluently."

MEDIA ADAPTATIONS: A film adaptation of *Pascali's Island* is being produced by Avenue Entertainment.

BIOGRAPHICAL/CRITICAL SOURCES:

PERIODICALS

Newsweek, January 28, 1983.
New York Times, November 20, 1980, February 7, 1983.
New York Times Book Review, January 11, 1981, March 13, 1983, April 6, 1986.
Spectator, August 24, 1985.
Times (London), June 19, 1980, July 25, 1985.
Times Literary Supplement, August 30, 1985, September 16-22, 1988.
Washington Post, January 24, 1981.
Washington Post Book World, April 3, 1983.

V

Van Der SLIK, Jack R(onald) 1936-

PERSONAL: Born December 14, 1936, in Kalamazoo, Mich.; son of Julius Henry (a tool and die salesman) and Cornelia (Koopsen) Van Der Slik; married Gertrude Jane Bonnema, June 29, 1963; children: Franci Lynn, Gary Jon, Randall Martin. *Education:* Calvin College, A.B., 1958; Western Michigan University, A.M., 1961; Michigan State University, A.M., 1966, Ph.D., 1967. *Religion:* Christian Reformed.

ADDRESSES: *Office*—Department of Political Science, Sangamon State University, Springfield, Ill. 62794-9243.

CAREER: Social science teacher at Bellflower Christian Junior High School, California, 1958-60; Denver Christian High School, Denver, Colorado, teacher, 1961-62; Southern Illinois University, Carbondale, Ill., assistant professor, 1967-71, associate professor of political science, beginning 1971, acting chairperson of department, 1975, associate dean of College of Liberal Arts, beginning 1975; Trinity Christian College, Palos Heights, Ill., academic dean and director of the Illinois legislative studies center, 1978-81; currently faculty member in department of political science, Sangamon State University, Springfield, Ill. Visiting associate professor, Calvin College, 1972-73. Research fellow, Illinois General Assembly Legislative Council, Springfield, 1969-70.

MEMBER: American Political Science Association, Midwest Political Science Association, Southern Political Science Association, Southwestern Social Science Association.

WRITINGS:

(Compiler with George T. Force) *Theory and Research in the Study of Political Leadership: An Annotated Bibliography,* Public Affairs Research Bureau, Southern Illinois University, 1969.

(Editor) *Black Conflict with White America: A Reader in Social and Political Analysis,* C. E. Merrill, 1970.

(Editor with Stephen V. Monsma) *American Politics: Research and Readings,* Holt, 1970.

(With David Kenney and Samuel J. Pernacciaro) *Roll Call!: Patterns of Voting in the Sixth Illinois Constitutional Convention,* University of Illinois Press, 1975.

American Legislative Processes, Crowell, 1977.

(With Norman De Jong) *Separation of Church and State: The Myth Revisited,* Paideia Press, 1985.

(With Kent D. Redfield) *Lawmaking in Illinois: Legislative Politics, People, and Processes,* Office of Public Affairs Communication, Sangamon State University, 1986.

Contributor of articles to *Social Science Quarterly, Business and Government Review, Political Science Quarterly, American Journal of Political Science,* and *Journal of Political Science.*

WORK IN PROGRESS: A study of congressional representation in Illinois.

*   *   *

Van De VALL, Mark 1923-

PERSONAL: Born January 20, 1923, in Heiloo, Netherlands; married Anneke Korthals; children: (previous marriage) Renee, Monique. *Education:* Municipal University of Amsterdam, B.A., 1950, M.A., 1955, Ph.D., 1963.

ADDRESSES: *Office*—Department of Sociology, Erasmus University Rotterdam, Postbox 1738, 3000 DR Rotterdam, Netherlands.

CAREER: State University of New York at Buffalo, professor, 1963-77, adjunct professor of sociology, 1978—; University of Leyden, Netherlands, professor of social research, 1977-88; Erasmus University Rotterdam, Rotterdam, Netherlands, professor of social policy research, 1988—. Director, Leyden Institute for Social Policy Research, 1980-88. Special research fellow, Department of Health, Education and Welfare, Washington, D.C., 1969-71; fellow, Netherlands Institute for Advanced Study in the Humanities and Social Sciences.

MEMBER: International Sociological Association (president, Sociotechnics and Sociological Practice section, 1982—).

WRITINGS:

De Vakbeweging in de Welvaartsstaat, J.A. Boom (Meppel), 1963, translation published as *Labor Organizations: A Macro- and Micro-Sociological Analysis on a Comparative Basis,* Cambridge University Press, 1970.

(With Charles D. King) *Models of Industrial Democracy: Consultation, Co-Determination and Workers' Management,* Mouton, 1978.

Sociaal Beleidsonderzoek, Samsom (Alphen a/d Rijn), 1980.

CONTRIBUTOR

H. Matthes, editor, *Soziologie und Gesellschaft in den Niederlanden,* Luchterhand Verlag (Neuwied/Rhein), 1965.

Milton Albrecht, editor, *Studies in Sociology,* Buffalo Studies, 1965.

Desmond Graves, editor, *Management Research: A Cross-Cultural Perspective,* Jossey Bass, 1973.

Frank Baker and H. C. Schulberg, editors, *Program Evaluation in the Health Fields,* Behavioral Publications, 1977.

D. Horowitz, editor, *Policy Studies Review Annual,* Sage Publications, 1981.

P. J. Taylor and B. Cronin, editors, *Information Management Research in Europe,* ASLIB, 1982.

Frank Heller, editor, *Use and Abuse of Social Research,* Sage Publications, 1987.

OTHER

Also author, with Frans L. Leeuw, of *Sociaal Beleidsonderzoek: Differentiatie en Ontwikkeling,* 1987. Contributor to *Proceedings* of 17th and 22nd annual meetings of Industrial Relations Research Association. Contributor of over fifty articles and reports on sociological and political science subjects, in Dutch, German, French, and English, to periodicals.

WORK IN PROGRESS: With Cheryl Bolas, *Theory and Methods of Social Policy Research.*

*   *   *

van THAL, Herbert (Maurice)   1904-1983

PERSONAL: Born March 30, 1904, in London, England; died December 23, 1983; married Phyllis Mary Bayley. *Education:* Educated at St. Paul's School, London.

ADDRESSES: Home—Flat 5, 31 Clifton Crescent, Folkestone CT20 2EN, England. *Office*—London Management, 235/241 Regent St., London W1A 2JT, England.

CAREER: London Management, London, England, literary agent, beginning 1960. Owner of publishing company, Home & Van Thal.

MEMBER: Society of Odd Volumes, Reform Club.

WRITINGS:

Ernest Augustine, Duke of Cumberland and King of Hanover: A Brief Survey of the Man and His Times, Arthur Barker, 1936.

Recipe for Reading: A Letter to My Godsons, Home & Van Thal, 1945, revised edition published as *Recipe for Reading: A Short Personal Guide,* Panther, 1967.

Fanfare for Ernest Newman, Arthur Barker, 1955.

(Author of introduction) Charles Dickens and Wilkie Collins, *The Wreck of the Golden Mary,* Arthur Barker, 1955.

The Tops of the Mulberry Trees (autobiography), Allen & Unwin, 1971.

Eliza Lynn Linton, The Girl of the Period: A Biography, Allen & Unwin, 1979.

EDITOR

The Royal Letter Book: Being a Collection of Royal Letters from the Reign of William I to George V, Cresset, 1937.

Ernest Newman, *Testament of Music: Essays and Papers,* Putnam, 1962.

Hugh S. Scott, *Young Mistley,* Cassell, 1966.

Rhoda Broughton, *Not Wisely, but Too Well,* Cassell, 1967.

Samuel Langhorne Clemens, *The Gilded Age,* Cassell, 1967.

William Makepeace Thackeray, *Barry Lyndon,* Cassell, 1967.

Herman Melville, *Typee,* Cassell, 1967.

(And author of introduction) George Douglas, *The House with Green Shutters,* Cassell, 1967.

Charles Kingsley, *Alton Locke,* Cassell, 1967.

Robert Louis Stevenson, *New Arabian Nights,* Cassell, 1968.

Robert S. Surtees, *Jorrocks, Jaunts, and Jollities,* Dufour, 1969.

Hilaire Belloc, *Belloc: A Biographical Anthology,* Knopf, 1970.

(With Gervase Hughes) *The Music Lover's Companion,* Eyre & Spottiswoode, 1971.

Michael Kelly, *Solo Recital: Memoirs of Michael Kelly* (abridged edition), Folio Society, 1972.

Walter Savage Landor, *Landor: A Biographical Anthology,* Allen & Unwin, 1973.

Anthony Trollope, *The Domestic Manners of Americans,* Folio Society, 1974.

The Prime Ministers, Stein & Day, 1975.

Edward Lear, *Edward Lear's Journals: A Selection,* reprinted, Arden Library, 1982.

Also editor of book published by Dufour: *Cock and the Anchor,* by Joseph S. Le Fanu.

EDITOR OF ANTHOLOGIES

Victoria's Subjects Travelled: Being an Anthology from the Works of Explorers and Travellers between the Years 1850-1900, Arthur Barker, 1951.

Oriental Splendour: An Anthology of Eastern Tales, Arthur Barker, 1953.

Edgar Allan Poe, *Tales of Mystery and Imagination,* Folio Society, 1957.

Great Ghost Stories, Hill & Wang, 1960.

James E. Agate, *James Agate: An Anthology,* Hart-Davis, 1961.

Master Stories of the Twentieth Century, Pan Books, 1963.

Striking Terror!: A Selection of Great Horror Stories, Arthur Barker, 1963.

(And author of introduction) *Famous Land Battles,* Arthur Barker, 1964.

True Tales of Travel, Adventure, and Discovery, Arthur Barker, 1964.

Famous Tales of the Fantastic, Hill & Wang, 1965.

Tales of Kings and Queens: A Book of Fairy Tales, Hamish Hamilton, 1965.

The Girl on the Bus and Other Love Stories, Pan Books, 1966.

Lie Ten Nights Awake: Ten Tales of Horror, Berkley, 1968.

Collins, *Tales of Terror and the Supernatural,* Dover, 1972.

The Bedside Book of Strange Stories, Arthur Barker, 1974.

Tales of History, Arthur Barker, 1976.

The Second Bedside Book of Strange Stories, Arthur Barker, 1976.

Tales to Make the Flesh Creep: An Anthology of Classic Stories, Constable, 1978.

The Bedside Book of Sea Stories, Arthur Barker, 1979.

The Mammoth Book of Great Detective Stories, Robinson, 1985.

EDITOR OF "THE PAN BOOK OF HORROR STORIES" SERIES

The Pan Book of Horror Stories, Pan Books, 1959, published as *The First Pan Book of Horror Stories,* State Mutual Book, 1982.

The Second . . ., Pan Books, 1960.

The Third . . ., Pan Books, 1962.

The Fourth . . ., Pan Books, 1963.

The Fifth . . ., Pan Books, 1964.

The Sixth . . ., Pan Books, 1965.

The Seventh . . ., Pan Books, 1966.

The Eighth . . ., Pan Books, 1967.

The Tenth . . ., Pan Books, 1969.
The Twelfth . . ., Pan Books, 1971.
The Thirteenth . . ., Pan Books, 1972.
The Fourteenth . . ., Pan Books, 1973.
The Fifteenth . . ., Pan Books, 1974.
The Eighteenth . . ., Pan Books, 1978.
The Nineteenth . . ., Pan Books, 1978.
The Twentieth . . ., Pan Books, 1979.
The Twenty First . . ., Pan Books, 1981.
The Twenty Second . . ., Pan Books, 1982.
The Twenty Third . . ., Pan Books, 1983.

EDITOR OF "THE BEDSIDE BOOK OF GREAT DETECTIVE STORIES" SERIES

The Bedside Book of Great Detective Stories, Arthur Barker, 1976.
The Second . . ., Arthur Barker, 1977.
The Third . . ., Arthur Barker, 1978.
The Fourth . . ., Arthur Barker, 1981.
The Fifth . . ., Arthur Barker, 1981.

BIOGRAPHICAL/CRITICAL SOURCES:

BOOKS

van Thal, Herbert, *The Tops of the Mulberry Trees,* Allen & Unwin, 1971.

OBITUARIES:

PERIODICALS

Times (London), December 28, 1983.*

*   *   *

VINCENT, Claire
    See ALLEN, Charlotte Vale

*   *   *

VOGEL, Ezra F. 1930-

PERSONAL: Born July 11, 1930, in Delaware, Ohio; son of Joseph H. and Edith (Nachman) Vogel; married Suzanne Hall (a psychiatric social worker), July 5, 1953 (divorced); married Charlotte Ikels, November 3, 1979; children: David, Steven, Eva. *Education:* Ohio Wesleyan University, B.A., 1950; Bowling Green State University, M.A., 1951; Harvard University, Ph.D., 1958.

ADDRESSES: Home—14 Sumner Rd., Cambridge, Mass. 02138.

CAREER: Harvard University, Cambridge, Mass., research fellow and lecturer, 1958-60; Yale University, New Haven, Conn., assistant professor, 1960-61; Harvard University, research associate and lecturer, 1961-67; professor of sociology, 1967—, Dillon Professor of International Affairs, 1986—, associate director, 1967-73, and director, 1973-77, of East Asian Research Center, chairman, Council of East Asian Studies, 1977-80, director, U.S.-Japan Program, 1980-87. Trustee, Ohio Wesleyan University, 1970-75, 1980—. Member of various committees on East Asian issues. *Military service:* U.S. Army, 1951-53.

MEMBER: Association for Asian Studies (member of board of directors, 1970-72), American Academy of Arts and Sciences.

AWARDS, HONORS: Harvard Faculty Prize for book of the year, 1970; Guggenheim fellow, 1972; Litt.D., Kwansai Gakuin, 1980, Wittenberg College, 1981, Bowling Green State University, 1982, and University of Maryland, 1983.

WRITINGS:

(Editor with Norman W. Bell) *A Modern Introduction to the Family,* Free Press of Glencoe, 1960, revised edition, Free Press, 1968.
Japan's New Middle Class: The Salary Man and His Family in a Tokyo Suburb, University of California Press, 1963, new enlarged edition, 1971.
Canton under Communism: Programs and Politics in a Provincial Capital, 1949-1968, Harvard University Press, 1969.
(Editor) *Modern Japanese Organization and Decision-Making,* University of California Press, 1975.
Japan as Number One: Lessons for America, Harvard University Press, 1979.
Comeback, Case by Case: Building the Resurgence of American Business, Simon & Schuster, 1985.
(Editor with George C. Lodge) *Ideology and National Competitiveness,* Harvard Business School, Division of Research, 1987.
The Impact of Japan on a Changing World, Coronet Books, 1987.
One Step Ahead in China: Guangdong under Reform, Harvard University Press, 1989.

WORK IN PROGRESS: Researching Japanese industrial policy and U.S.-Japanese relations.

SIDELIGHTS: The increasing U.S. trade deficit with Japan and the growing stature of Japan in the world economy have led to numerous analyses of how Japanese business practices, government, and society have contributed to the country's success, and how these factors differ from U.S. trends. Ezra F. Vogel "has addressed himself to the most important [aspect]," comments *New York Times Book Review* contributor Frank B. Gibney: "what we can learn from the Japanese. His 'Japan as Number One: Lessons for America' is just that, an objective and immensely rewarding appraisal of what the Japanese are good at and how we might emulate them." A long-time scholar of the Far East, Vogel "writes from a deep and subtle grasp—both cognitive and empathetic, mind-grasp and heart-grasp—of Japanese society and culture," notes Ronald Dore in the *Washington Post Book World.* "The Japanese successes he chalks up are first the ingredients and manifestations of the economic miracle," the critic continues; in addition, the book includes "skillful accounts" of the country's systems of education, welfare, and crime control.

Although Vogel presents a thorough portrait of some of the reasons for Japan's rapid economic achievement, Tetsuo Najita faults the author for neglecting the negative aspects of Japanese industrial society, as he writes in the *New York Review of Books:* "Vogel's admiration for these successes blinds him to many of problems in Japan—in large part problems linked to its successful growth. . . . He mentions but dismisses such matters, since for him they are unrelated to the lessons he would teach Americans." *New Republic* contributor Edwin O. Reischauer similarly observes a lack of criticism of Japanese methods, but states that Vogel "does this purposely in order to emphasize the points on which they excel and on which we might try to emulate them." The critic remarks that "we should not complain [about omissions], for Vogel offers us one of the most challenging books of the year," concluding that the author "has something important to tell Americans. The question is whether they will have the patience and openness of mind to listen."

In *Comeback, Case by Case: Building the Resurgence of American Business,* Vogel expands on the measures U.S. government and business could adopt from the Japanese in order to promote economic growth. As Amitai Etzioni describes it in the *Washing-*

ton *Post Book World*, *Comeback* "forcefully argues . . . that the trust Americans put in fiscal and monetary policies is misplaced," and that America needs "a coalition of government, business and labor to foster a national competitiveness strategy." The author then presents several case studies of such coalitions—some Japanese, some American—to advance his idea. "To his credit," asserts *New York Times Book Review* contributor C. Michael Aho, "Mr. Vogel's emphasis is on what the United States can and should do better rather than on whether Japan's [trade] practices are unfair." Nevertheless, Etzioni criticizes Vogel's approach, claiming that his idea does not provide for sufficient political support for such wide-spread cooperation: "Implicit in books such as Vogel's is the notion that the public at large, alarmed by the dire consequences prophesied in them will bring conflicting special interests together under government tutelage. . . . It will take more than a book for Americans to see that we too are a threatened community." In contrast, Aho believes that Vogel's work "reveal[s] numerous insights into the flexibility of Japanese industry and institutions to prepare the way for future growth and commercial success." Despite the lack of a specific scheme for U.S. adoption of Japanese techniques, "Vogel has again written an excellent, thought provoking book that uses Japan as a mirror for America. . . . You will not find [precise strategies] here," the critic concludes. "But that, perhaps, is material for other books. In the meantime, read the case studies to increase your awareness."

BIOGRAPHICAL/CRITICAL SOURCES:

PERIODICALS

Chicago Tribune Book World, January 18, 1981.
New Republic, August 18, 1979.
New York Review of Books, February 21, 1980.
New York Times Book Review, February 25, 1968, June 10, 1979, September 15, 1985.
Washington Post Book World, May 20, 1979, July 7, 1985.

W

WACHS, Saul P(hilip) 1931-

PERSONAL: Born December 24, 1931, in Philadelphia, Pa.; son of Abraham (a Jewish communal servant) and Annette (Schaller) Wachs; married Barbara Ruth Eidelman (a teacher), January 27, 1957; children: Sharona Rachel, Hillel Eliezer, Devora Leah, Aviva Marcia. *Education:* Gratz College, Hebrew Teachers Diploma, 1951; Temple University, B.S., 1953; Jewish Theological Seminary, B.R.E., 1956, B. Sacred Music, 1959; Ohio State University, M.A., 1966, Ph.D., 1970. *Religion:* Jewish.

ADDRESSES: Home—107 Maple Ave., Bala Cynwyd, Pa. 19004. *Office*—Department of Education, Gratz College, Melrose Ave. and Old York Rd., Melrose Park, Pa. 19126.

CAREER: Teacher at Jewish synagogues in Philadelphia, Pa., 1948-53, Mount Vernon, N.Y., 1953-56, Bloomfield, N.J., 1956-60, and Columbus, Ohio, 1960-70, music director in Columbus, 1964-70; educational director at synagogue in New York, N.Y., 1970-72; Brandeis University, Waltham, Mass., assistant professor of Jewish education and director of graduate program at Philip W. Lown Graduate Center for Contemporary Jewish Studies, 1972-75; Gratz College, Philadelphia, assistant professor, 1975-79, associate professor, 1979-84, Rosaline B. Feinstein Associate Professor of Jewish Education, 1984—, chairman of department and dean of college, 1975-80. Trainer at Melton Research Center, 1960-75; visiting assistant professor at Jewish Theological Seminary, 1971-75; visiting associate professor at Boston Hebrew College, 1972-73; visiting professorial lecturer at College of Jewish Studies, American University of Washington, 1983—. Ramah Camps, counselor, 1950-53, division head, 1954-60, education director, 1956-74, music director, 1966. Member of executive council of Akiba Hebrew Academy. Field consultant to Solomon Schechter Day School Association.

MEMBER: International Seminars for Jewish Studies, National Council for Jewish Education (member of executive board), American Association for Jewish Education (member of governing council), Association for Jewish Studies, American Society for Curriculum Development, National Association of Elementary School Principals, Continuing Seminar for Zionist Thought, U.S. Chess Federation (life master), Jewish Community Relations Council of Philadelphia (member of Soviet Jewry committee), Phi Delta Kappa, Mercantile Library Chess Club.

AWARDS, HONORS: Pennsylvania junior chess champion, 1946-47, state speed chess champion, 1949-54; U.S. national ju-

nior speed chess champion and national junior chess champion, both 1951; U.S. national intercollegiate speed chess champion, 1951, 1961; Ohio chess champion, 1961, co-champion, 1968; Aaron Zacks Award from American Association for Jewish Education, 1969; annual award from Philadelphia chapter of American Mizrachi Women, 1980; Louis Pincus Senior Educator Award from Hebrew University of Jerusalem, 1984; faculty award from Gratz College; honorary degree from Ohio State University, 1989.

WRITINGS:

Workshop in Jewish Consciousness Raising, Council of Jewish Federations and Welfare Funds, 1976.
(Contributor) Judith Zimmerman and Barbara Trainin, editors, *Jewish Population,* Federation of Jewish Philanthropies, 1978.
(With Samuel T. Lachs) *Judaism,* Argus Publications, 1979.
(Contributor) Burton I. Cohen and Alexander M. Shapiro, editors, *Essays in Jewish Education and Judaica in Honor of Louis Newman,* Ktav, 1983.
Curriculum for Teaching Mitzvah, United Synagogue of America, 1989.
(Contributor) Steven Katz, editor, *Great Jewish Thought,* B'nai Brith, 1989.
Liturgical Midrashim Conference Proceedings, Rabbinical Assembly of America, 1989.
Curriculum on Prayer for Jewish Day School, United Synagogue of America, 1990.
The Jewish Teacher (monograph), American Jewish Committee, in press.
(Contributor) Murray Friedman, editor, *The History of the Jews of Philadelphia,* American Jewish Committee, in press.

Contributor to education journals and chess magazines.

SIDELIGHTS: Saul P. Wachs told *CA:* "My involvement in Jewish education reflects the strong family tradition of Jewish communal service into which I was socialized. I became interested in prayer and liturgical music due to the influence of cantors Joseph Mann and Max Wohlberg. I sang in synagogue choirs as a child. I was also deeply inspired by Louis Newman and Abraham J. Herschel, two outstanding educators. Summers at Camp Ramah and studies at Gratz College and the Jewish Theological Seminary provided me with models of great educators and teachers. These experiences resulted in my gaining greater insight into the beauty of Jewish tradition.

"During the summer of 1966, I was asked to teach some experimental material in Bible to teenagers at Camp Ramah in Canada. The students reacted very negatively to the material, and I was accused of being a boring teacher. Since I had thought of myself as a good teacher, I was upset. I had some ideas on teaching prayer and liturgy through inquiry, so that students would learn to read critically. Out of desperation, I substituted a lesson on prayer for the scheduled Bible lesson. The students reacted very well. I began to write a 'curriculum,' staying one lesson ahead of the students. By the end of the summer, I knew what I wanted to do with my doctoral study.

"I love to travel," Wachs continued, "and I have lectured in over two hundred communities in North America, Israel, South Africa, and the Soviet Union. Fluency in Hebrew has allowed my wife and me to make contact with Jews in other countries. We especially treasure the memories of these trips and the friendships that we have made during our travels.

"We are proud that our four children continue to study Jewish culture and to work for its preservation and transmission. I believe that a person who is knowledgeable in and proud of his or her heritage can be a force to enrich the larger society. Such a person is more likely to have a sense of self-esteem and to appreciate the ways in which ethnic religious background can contribute distinctive ideas, values, and customs to human culture. My wife and I have been active in interfaith activities to forward this aim. Both of us have been fortunate to have been heirs to a good tradition of family lore, much of which stresses scholarship and community service. My mother was active in social service projects in the Jewish community.

"In Poland, Latvia, Lithuania, and Hungary this tradition was created by our ancestors. From them, my father developed a sense of devotion to family. He came to America as a poor immigrant, and saved his money to help bring brothers here. With his help and that of his brothers and sisters, many came to America who, otherwise, might have been lost in the Holocaust. One of his uncles, Aba (Adolph) Wachs, is credited with bringing more than three hundred people out of Europe and to America. Some day, I hope to help write a history of our family, one of thousands and thousands of families that spanned two worlds at a critical time in Jewish and world history."

Wachs added a final comment: "My wife and I are teachers. We find great joy in the teaching act, seeing in it a paradigm of loving human interaction. Judaism sees in study and teaching, behaviour that is morally significant. We believe that education offers the best hope for humanity in our time and in the future. A recovery of reverence for schools and teachers as primary agents of education is, in our view, vital to the development by society of a good quality of life for all."

*   *   *

WADDINGTON, Miriam 1917-
(E. B. Merritt)

PERSONAL: Born December 23, 1917, in Winnipeg, Manitoba, Canada; daughter of Isidore (a small manufacturer) and Musha (Dobrushin) Dworkin; married Patrick Donald Waddington, July 5, 1939 (divorced, 1965); children: Marcus Frushard, Jonathan John. *Education:* University of Toronto, B.A., 1939, Diploma in Social Work, 1942, M.A., 1968; University of Pennsylvania, M.S.W., 1945.

ADDRESSES: Home—32 Yewfield Crescent, Don Mills, Toronto, Ontario, Canada M3B 2Y6. *Office*—Department of English, York University, Toronto, Ontario, Canada M3J 1P3.

CAREER: Jewish Child Welfare Bureau, Montreal, Quebec, assistant director, 1945-46; McGill University, School of Social Work, Montreal, field instructor, 1946-49; Montreal Children's Hospital, Montreal, staff member, 1952-54; John Howard Society, Montreal, staff member, 1955-57; Jewish Family Bureau, Montreal, caseworker, 1957-60; North York Family Service, Toronto, Ontario, casework supervisor, 1960-62; York University, Toronto, 1964—, began as assistant professor, currently professor of English and Canadian literature. Writer in residence, University of Ottawa, 1974, Windsor Public Library, 1983, and Toronto Metropolitan Library, 1986; Canada Council exchange poet to Wales, 1980; has given poetry readings or lectured at International Poetry Evenings, Struga, Yugoslavia, 1980, Yaddo Artists Colony, and most universities across Canada; annual drama awards judge, Association of Canadian Television and Radio Artists.

MEMBER: International PEN, Modern Language Association of America, Otto Rank Association.

AWARDS, HONORS: Canada Council senior fellowship in creative writing, 1962-63; Canada Council academic grant, 1968-69; Senior Arts fellowship, 1971-72 and 1979-80; J. I. Segal award, 1972, for *Driving Home: Poems New and Selected,* and 1987, for *Collected Poems;* D.Litt., Lakehead University, 1975, and York University, 1985; Association of Quebec and Canadian Literatures Citation, 1979, for her contribution to Canadian literature.

WRITINGS:

Green World, First Statement Press, 1945.
The Second Silence, Ryerson, 1955.
The Season's Lovers, Ryerson, 1958.
The Glass Trumpet, Oxford University Press, 1966.
(Author of poems accompanying photographs) *Call Them Canadians,* edited by Lorraine Monk, Queen's Printer, 1968.
Say Yes (poetry), Oxford University Press, 1969.
A. M. Klein (criticism), Copp, 1970, 2nd edition, 1974.
Driving Home: Poems New and Selected, Oxford University Press, 1972.
The Dream Telescope (poetry), Routledge & Kegan Paul, 1973.
(Editor) *John Sutherland: Essays, Controversies, Poems,* New Canadian Library, 1973.
(Contributor) C. Klinck and R. Walters, editors, *Canadian Anthology,* revised edition, Gage, 1974.
(Editor) *The Collected Poems of A. M. Klein,* McGraw, 1974.
The Price of Gold, Oxford University Press, 1976.
Mister Never, Turnstone (Winnipeg), 1978.
The Visitants, Oxford University Press, 1981.
Summer at Lonely Beach and Other Stories, Mosaic Valley Editions, 1982.
Collected Poems, Oxford University Press, 1986.
Apartment Seven and Other Essays, Oxford University Press, 1989.

CONTRIBUTOR OF TRANSLATIONS

Irving Howe and Eliezer Greenberg, editors, *A Treasury of Yiddish Poetry,* Holt, 1969.
Howe and Greenberg, editors, *Yiddish Stories New and Old,* Horizon Press, 1974.
Howe and R. Wisse, editors, *The Best of Sholom Aleichem,* Simon & Schuster, 1980.
S. Mayne, editor, *Generations,* Mosaic Valley Editions, 1982.

H. Schwartz, editor, *Voices within the Ark: The Modern Jewish Poets,* Avon, 1980.

OTHER

Writer of radio scripts on Chekhov and Poe. Contributor to *Borestone Mountain Best Poems in English,* 1963, 1966, and 1967, and to other anthologies. Contributor of reviews, stories, and articles to magazines and newspapers, including *Canadian Literature, Tamarack Review, Queen's Quarterly, Canadian Forum,* and *Saturday Night.* Poetry editor, *Poetry Toronto,* 1981-82.

WORK IN PROGRESS: Love Poems, 1989.

SIDELIGHTS: Miriam Waddington's poems have been incorporated into a number of works and exhibitions of Canadian artists Helen Duffy, Jo Manning, Tobie Steinhouse, and Sarah Jackson, and about a dozen of her songs have been set to music by various Canadian and American composers. She is fluent in Yiddish and reads French, German, and Hebrew, and has contributed translated poems to many anthologies of Jewish verse. Her work has been translated and published in the Soviet Union, Hungary, Japan, Romania, South America, and China, and her poems have also been broadcast in Canada, New Zealand, and Australia. In 1979, Waddington was honored at the annual meeting of the Association of Quebec and Canadian Literatures for her contributions to Canadian literature.

Waddington is the daughter of Jewish Russian immigrants who were outspoken critics of life in her native Winnipeg, the poet reveals in an essay for *Maclean's* entitled "Exile." As a result, she was conscious that others saw her as significantly different from other Canadians. A concentrated interest in how people relate to each other led her to a career in social work, and later, through her writing, into teaching. Waddington maintains this focus in her writing. Characters in her short fiction collected in *Summer at Lonely Beach and Other Stories* are somewhat outside the Anglo-Saxon middle class social environment, notes *Dictionary of Literary Biography* contributor Laurie Ricou. Her poems are lyrical, expressing personal responses to people and conditions around her.

Waddington once told *CA:* "I began writing poetry when I was ten and never really stopped. I don't know or care what motivates me—maybe it's belief in life itself. To me writing is one aspect of living and being human, of being connected to others. After a lifetime of writing the process is still a mystery to me. I suppose I hope to express the feeling of living in my time and place—not just my own life but in the lives of other people who seem ordinary but never are. It makes me feel less lonesome in the world to believe that I'm part of a huge company of writers—living and dead—who express the continuity of human feeling, making, and learning in a world that is exhausted and violated, but nevertheless inexhaustible.

"The contemporary scene? It is so terrible that it's wonderful that so many authentic writers are still able and willing to write. [George] Gissing's *New Grub Street* was prophetic re the commodification of art and artists in our society. There are too many cookbooks. They tell us how to make and package everything—politics, art, sex, and personality. There is so much individualism in North American art that individuality is (paradoxically) lost. But there are always some authentic artists everywhere at every time, and their work is a refuge, a shelter, and a source of renewal."

BIOGRAPHICAL/CRITICAL SOURCES:

BOOKS

Contemporary Literary Criticism, Volume 28, Gale, 1984.
Dictionary of Literary Biography, Volume 68: *Canadian Writers, 1920-1959,* Gale, 1988.
Heath, Jeffrey M., editor, *Profiles in Canadian Literature 4,* Dundurn Press, 1982.
Pearce, John, *Twelve Voices,* Borealis Press, 1980.

PERIODICALS

Books in Canada, May, 1982.
Canadian Forum, May, 1977.
Canadian Literature, spring, 1973.
Dalhousie Review, summer, 1959.
Essays on Canadian Writing, fall, 1978.
Maclean's, March, 1974.
Poetry, February, 1968.

*   *   *

WARD, E. D.
  See GOREY, Edward (St. John)

*   *   *

WARD, Philip   1938-
  (Darby Greenfield)

PERSONAL: Born February 10, 1938, in Harrow, England; son of Albert Edwin (a company secretary) and Mildred (Elsey) Ward; married Audrey Joan Monk, April 4, 1964; children: Carolyn, Angela. *Education:* Northeastern Polytechnic, London, A.L.A.; studied at universities in Perugia, Italy, in Coimbra, Portugal, and in Lebanon. *Politics:* None. *Religion:* Scientific humanism.

ADDRESSES: Office—Oleander Press, 17 Stansgate Ave., Cambridge CB2 2QZ, England.

CAREER: Chief cataloger at National Central Library, Holborn (now Camden) Public Libraries, Middlesex County Library, and Wimbledon Public Libraries, England, 1962-63; Oasis Oil Co. of Libya, Inc., Tripoli, co-ordinator of library services, 1963-70; UNESCO library consultant in Shibin al-Kum, Egypt, 1973; UNESCO/Indonesia Development of National Library Service Project, Jakarta, Indonesia, project manager, 1973-74; Oxford University Press, Oxford, England, editor of *Oxford Companion to Spanish Literature,* 1974-77; Oleander Press, Cambridge, England, managing director, 1976—.

MEMBER: Private Libraries Association (London; founding secretary), Royal Society of Arts (fellow).

WRITINGS:

(With Roderick Cave) *Simplified Cataloguing Rules for Private Libraries,* Private Libraries Association, 1959.
Periodicals in Libya, Oasis Oil Co. of Libya, 1963.
A Survey of Libyan Bibliographical Resources, [Tripoli], 1964, 2nd edition, 1965.
(Editor) Evenyn Quell, *The Quell-Finger Dialogues,* [North Harrow, England], 1965.
Poems for Participants: A Work-Book, Labris, 1967.
Ambigamus; or, The Logic Box, Wattle Grove Press (Tasmania), 1967.
Loakrime: Idol of the Shattered Pyramid, Openings Press, 1967.
The Theory and Practice of Library Classification, Oasis Oil Co. of Libya, 1968.

A Musical Breakfast (one-act play), Brewhouse Private Press (Wymondham, England), 1968.

Spanish Literary Appreciation (textbook), University of London Press, 1969.

A Lizard and Other Distractions (stories), Magpie Press, 1969.

Okefani: Song of Nij Zitru, Magpie Press, 1969.

The Libyan Research Library Catalog, Oasis Oil Co. of Libya, 1970.

Planning and the Future: A Reading List, Oasis Oil Co. of Libya, 1971.

Planning a National Library Service, Indonesian Library Association, 1973.

Indonesia: The Development of a National Library Service, three volumes, UNESCO (Paris), 1976.

(Editor) *Oxford Companion to Spanish Literature,* Oxford University Press, 1977.

The Keymakers (poems), Interim Press. 1978.

PUBLISHED BY OLEANDER PRESS

Collected Poems, 1960.

(Translator) Lope de Rueda, *Las Aceitunas,* 1962.

(Translator) Miguel Torga, *Jesus,* 1963.

Seldom Rains: Libyan Poems, 1967.

Drama Workshop, 1967.

At the Best of Times: Libyan Poems, 1968.

The Poet and the Microscope, 1968.

Apuleius on Trial at Sabratha (essay), 1968.

Fiction List of Murdoch Lenz, 1969.

Garrity and Other Plays, 1970.

Maps on the Ceiling: Libyan Poems, 1970.

(Editor) *The Libyan Civil Code,* 1970.

(Contributor) Norbert E. Chantz, *Just Pick a Murricane?,* 1971.

The Libyan Revolution, 1971.

(Translator) Angelo Pesce, *Colours of the Arab Fatherland,* 1972.

Pincers (play), 1973.

A House on Fire: Selected Poems, 1973.

(Editor) *Indonesian Traditional Poetry* (anthology), 1975.

Television Plays, 1976.

(Translator) *The Scandalous Life of Cesar Moro in His Own Words: Peruvian Surrealist Poetry,* 1976.

Maltese Boyhood: Stories, 1976.

Impostors and Their Imitators: Poems, 1977.

A Dictionary of Common Fallacies, Volume 1, 1978, Volume 2, 1980.

Cambridge Street Literature, 1978.

(With wife, Audrey J. Ward) *The Small Publisher,* 1979.

(Editor) Richard R. Burton, *The Gold-Mines of Midian,* 1979.

Lost Songs and Other Political Poems, 1981.

A Lifetime's Reading, 1982.

(Translator) Ramon Gomez de la Serna, *Greguerias,* 1982.

TRAVEL GUIDES

Touring Libya: The Western Provinces, Faber, 1967.

Touring Libya: The Southern Provinces, Faber, 1968.

Touring Libya: The Eastern Provinces, Faber, 1969.

Tripoli: Portrait of a City, Oleander Press, 1969.

Touring Iran, Faber, 1970.

(With Pesce) *Motoring to Nalut,* Oleander Press, 1970.

Sabratha: Guide for Visitors, Oleander Press, 1970.

(With Ed van Weerd) *The Way to Wadi al-Khail,* Oleander Press, 1970.

Touring Lebanon, Faber, 1971.

Come with Me to Ireland, Oleander Press, 1972.

Touring Cyprus, Oleander Press, 1972.

The Aeolian Islands, Oleander Press, 1974.

Bangkok: Portrait of a City, Oleander Press, 1974.

(Under pseudonym Darby Greenfield) *Indonesia: A Traveler's Guide,* Oleander Press, Volume 1: *Java and Sumatra,* 1975, Volume 2: *Bali and East Indonesia,* 1976.

Across Arabia, Saudi Arabian Airlines, 1976.

Albania, Oleander Press, 1982.

Ha'il: Oasis City of Saudi Arabia, Oleander Press, 1983.

Japanese Capitals, Oleander Press, 1985.

Finnish Cities, Oleander Press, 1987.

Polish Cities, Oleander Press, 1988.

Rajasthan, Agra, Delhi, Oleander Press, 1989.

Bulgaria, Oleander Press, 1989.

OTHER

Contributor to *Labris* (Belgium), *Libyan Review, Transatlantic Review, Quest, Maelstrom, Private Library,* and numerous other periodicals.

WORK IN PROGRESS: New short stories and radio plays; preparation for new travel guides to Eastern Europe, South India and the Pacific; leading groups of talented mentally-disturbed writers to expand their abilities and discipline.

SIDELIGHTS: "Assembling a private library of world civilisation and living in a close loving family are my twin delights," Philip Ward once wrote *CA.* "I write to fill in gaps in the literature (the first modern English-language guidebook to Albania, for instance, or a corrective reference book on fallacies to expose the superstitious and ignorant theories of cults such as the Bermuda Triangle, Scientology, spoonbending and time regression) and, creatively, to explore tensions such as a poet under totalitarianism (*Lost Songs*) or the conflict between Cortes and Montezuma (*Forgotten Games*).

"As a poet, I pervert the courtly love tradition to encompass eulogy for my own wife. As a playwright, I revert to the tradition before the Greeks invented a third character (and prefer for the same reason plainchant to polyphony). As a novelist, I take the keenest pleasure in persuading the reader to guess which of the words are truths and which fictions. As a travel writer, I erect a scaffolding of images on which the reader may embroider his own canvas—for no country can be perceived alike by two visitors, and a reader is simply a visitor at one remove. As a translator, I seek to restore Spanish literature to the key role it possessed in English at the time of the first Elizabeth. As a reader, I learn languages to take full advantage of publishers' bilingual editions, or to read in the original wherever possible, a model being *The Penguin Book of Russian Verse.* My guide to the greatest world literature, *A Lifetime's Reading* (1982) was published at the age of forty-four, leaving me another lifetime's reading to enjoy.

"I am privileged to be alive at a time of great Renaissance in literature, with Latin American and Eastern European writers dominating the scene, and more important writers creating now than ever before. The task is to struggle free of one's fetters of bias—race, religion, language, class, political indoctrination—and see the world pristine and prelapsarian. A writer should be fresh, alert, but at the same time aware of all the greatest writings—from Tu Fu to Cervantes, from Abu Il-'Ala al-Ma'arri to Chekhov. In other words, a powerful original talent has no right arrogantly to ignore past and present masters. Our lives are too short for ignorance, fear, or hatred."

WATTS, Reginald John 1931-

PERSONAL: Born January 28, 1931, in Essex, England; son of Wilford John Lionel (a marine surveyor) and Julia Doris (Wheeler) Watts; married Susan Roscoe Cushman (a teacher), 1960; children: Charlotte Amelia Roscoe, Marcus Redmayne. *Education:* Attended Bishop's Stortford College, 1944-49. *Politics:* Tory. *Religion:* Church of England.

ADDRESSES: Home—37 Talbot Rd., London W.2, England. *Office*—Reginald Watts Associates Ltd., 1-11 Hay Hill, London W1X 7LF, England.

CAREER: Burson-Marsteller Ltd. (public relations consultants), London, England, vice-president, 1970-77, chairman, 1977-85; Reginald Watts Associates Ltd., London, chairman, 1985—. Past chairman, Bow Group; member, Westminster City Council, 1974-82.

MEMBER: Institute of Journalists, Institute of Public Relations (president, 1989), Institute of Directors (fellow), Carlton Club, Hurlinsham Club.

WRITINGS:

Reaching the Consumer: The Elements of Product Public Relations, Business Books, 1970.
The Businessman's Guide to Marketing, Business Books, 1972.
Public Relations for Top Management, Croner, 1977.
(With Roger Hayes) *Corporate Revolution,* Nichols Publishing, 1986.

Also co-author of *Good Will: The Wasted Asset;* also scriptwriter and consultant for *Reaching European Markets.*

*   *   *

WEARY, Ogdred
See GOREY, Edward (St. John)

*   *   *

WEATHERFORD, J. McIver
See WEATHERFORD, Jack McIver

*   *   *

WEATHERFORD, Jack
See WEATHERFORD, Jack McIver

*   *   *

WEATHERFORD, Jack McIver 1946-
(J. McIver Weatherford, Jack Weatherford)

PERSONAL: Born November 27, 1946, in Darlington County, S.C.; son of Alfred Gregg (an army sergeant) and Anna Ruth (a bus driver; maiden name, Grooms) Weatherford; married Walker Pearce (a filmmaker), June 15, 1972. *Education:* University of South Carolina, B.A., 1967, M.A. (sociology), 1972; University of California, San Diego, M.A. (anthropology), 1973, Ph.D., 1977; attended University of Frankfurt, 1976, Duke University, 1978, Techniche Universitaet, Berlin, and La Universidad Catolica de Ecuador, Quito.

ADDRESSES: Home—834 Summit Ave., St. Paul, Minn. 55105. *Office*—Department of Anthropology, Macalester University, St. Paul, Minn. 55105. *Agent*—Lois Wallace, Wallace Literary Agency, 177 East 70th St., New York, N.Y. 10021.

CAREER: Legislative assistant to U.S. Senator John Glenn, 1978-80; free-lance writer, 1980-82; American University,

Washington, D.C., assistant professor of anthropology, 1982-83; Macalester College, St. Paul, Minn., associate professor of anthropology, 1983—. National Institute of Mental Health trainee in social conflict, 1972-73.

MEMBER: Authors Guild, Authors League of America, American Anthropological Association, American Association for the Advancement of Science, National Writers Union.

AWARDS, HONORS: Grants from Council for European Studies, 1974, and National Science Foundation, 1975-77; fellowships from Deutscher Akademischer Austauschdienst, 1974, National Institute of Mental Health, 1977-79, and American Association for the Advancement of Science, 1978-79; Fulbright-Marshall doctoral fellowship, 1975-76; W. K. Kellogg National Leadership fellowship, 1985-86.

WRITINGS:

(Under name J. McIver Weatherford) *Tribes on the Hill: An Investigation into the Rituals and Realities of an Endangered American Tribe—The Congress of the United States,* Rawson-Wade, 1981, revised edition, Bergin & Garvey, 1985.
Porn Row, Arbor House, 1986.
Narcoticos en Bolivia y los Estados Unidos, Los Amigos del Libro (Bolivia), 1987.
(Under name Jack Weatherford) *Indian Givers: How the Indians of the Americas Transformed the World,* Crown, 1988.

CONTRIBUTOR UNDER NAME J. McIVER WEATHERFORD

H. C. Buch, editor, *Deutschland: Das Kind mit den zwei Koepfen,* Klaus Wagenbach Verlag, 1978.
P. C. Reining and Barbara Lenkerd, editors, *Village Viability in Contemporary Society,* Westview Press, 1980.
George L. Maddox, Illene C. Seigler, and Dan Blazer, editors, *Families and Older Persons,* Duke University, Center for the Study of Aging and Human Development, 1980.
Z. I. Giraldo, editor, *Public Policy and the Family,* Lexington Books, 1980.
Christine L. Fry, editor, *Dimensions of an Anthropology of Aging,* Bergin Publishers, 1981.

Contributor of articles to popular periodicals and scholarly journals, including *Freibeuter, Man, Rocky Mountain News,* and *New York Times.*

WORK IN PROGRESS: A book for Crown on the Indian heritage of America.

SIDELIGHTS: In *Indian Givers: How the Indians of the Americas Transformed World,* Jack McIver Weatherford proposes that "the native cultures of the Americas revolutionized world civilization and would have transformed it even more had American Indian knowledge not been ignored and then destroyed," summarizes Tony Hillerman in the *Los Angeles Times Book Review.* While historians have traditionally studied the effects of colonization on the New World, little has been written about the reverse process; "Weatherford sets out to correct this imbalance," notes Toronto *Globe and Mail* contributor Olive Patricia Dickason, "a task he has undertaken with catchy enthusiasm." In relating the effects of Amerindian agriculture, medicine, mining, architecture, and even political philosophy on European culture, the author displays "none of the musty clumsiness that one expects from academic writing," observes Hillerman. "Weatherford is trying to persuade the public, not to impress historians." As a means of capturing popular interest, Weatherford "[draws] readers into complex subjects by making them personal," Hillerman explains. "It also makes this a lively and interesting book." And while the critics believe the author tries to "prove too much with too little," as Dickason states, nevertheless *Indian Givers* "is a provocative work." As Hillerman comments: "Weatherford is certainly right in his central thesis . . . [as well as] his final argument: that we are losing our opportunity" to learn more of what American Indians have to teach. In *Indian Givers,* the critic concludes, "Weatherford has given us a warning we shouldn't ignore."

Weatherford told *CA:* "After doing research with groups in Africa, Europe, and South America, I still feel that the most exotic and bizarre culture is that of modern-day Americans. Americans are strange, and in my writing I analyze that strangeness and compare it with various tribes around the world. My first book, *Tribes on the Hill,* was an anthropological look at the Congress based on my work there for Senator John Glenn. . . . Then I moved to the other side of Washington to work at night in the red-light district as preparation to write the book *Porn Row,* comparing American sex practices with those of tribal people."

BIOGRAPHICAL/CRITICAL SOURCES:

PERIODICALS

Chicago Tribune, March 30, 1982.
Christian Science Monitor, November 25, 1988.
Globe and Mail (Toronto), February 4, 1989.
Los Angeles Times, December 9, 1981.
Los Angeles Times Book Review, December 11, 1988.
Washington Post Book World, November 13, 1981.

*   *   *

WEEKS, Sheldon G.   1931-

PERSONAL: Born November 18, 1931, in New York, N.Y.; son of Harold Eastman and Virginia (Travell) Weeks; married Sally Shoop, August 18, 1957; married second wife, Margaret Kironde (an artist), January 26, 1964; married third wife, Gudrun Gay; children: (first marriage) Sara Graham, Abigail E.; (second marriage) Harold Mutambuze, Edisa Mirembe; (third marriage) Kristina Elinor Aphra Hayes. *Education:* Swarthmore College, A.B., 1954; Putney Graduate School, A.M., 1960; Harvard University, Ed.D., 1968. *Religion:* Society of Friends.

ADDRESSES: Office—Division of Educational Research, National Research Institute, Waigani, New Guinea.

CAREER: American Friends Service Committee, New York, N.Y., program and youth secretary, 1955-59; Harvard University, Center for Studies in Education and Development, Cambridge, Mass., instructor, 1965-67, assistant professor of education, 1968-69; Makerere Institute of Social Research, Kampala, Uganda, senior research fellow, 1969-72; University of Dar es Salaam, Dar es Salaam, Tanzania, associate professor of sociology, 1972-74; University of Papua New Guinea, Educational Research Unit, Port Moresby, research professor and director, 1975-87; National Research Institute, Waigani, New Guinea, head of educational research division, 1988—. President, Sheffield Projects, Inc. (non-profit organization); trustee, Ghandian Foundation.

MEMBER: African Studies Association, Comparative Education Association, American Sociological Association, Society for Applied Anthropology.

WRITINGS:

Divergence in African Education: The Case of Kenya and Uganda, Teachers College, Columbia University, 1967.

(With C. C. Wallace) *Success or Failure in Rural Uganda: A Story of Young People,* Makerere Institute of Social Research Press, 1975.
National Service and Community Involvement, Educational Research Unit (Papua New Guinea), 1976.
Education and Independence, Educational Research Unit, 1976.
The Story of My Education, Educational Research Unit, 1977.
The Social Background of Tertiary Students, Educational Research Unit, 1977.
Youth in Their Village, Educational Research Unit, 1978.
The "Foster Fallacy" in Educational Planning, Educational Research Unit, 1978.
(With C. Runawery) *Towards an Enga Education Strategy,* Educational Research Unit, 1980.
Oksapmin, Development and Change, Educational Research Unit, 1981.
(With P. Smith) *Teachers and Teaching,* Educational Research Unit, 1981.
(With J. Kelly and J. Moipu) *A West Sepik Education Strategy,* Educational Research Unit, 1982.
(Contributor with G. Guthrie) R. M. Thomas and T. M. Postlewaite, editors, *Schooling in the Pacific Islands,* Pergamon (London), 1984.
(Editor) *Papua New Guinea: A National Inventory of Educational Innovations,* Educational Research Unit, 1985.
(With M. Crossley and J. Sukwianomb) *Pacific Perspectives on Nonformal Education,* University of the South Pacific (Fiji)/University of Papua New Guinea Press (Waigani), 1987.
Education and Change in Pangia, Southern Highlands Province, Educational Research Unit, 1987.
(With D. Knox) *Learning from China: Report of the 1987 Education Research Study Tour,* Educational Research Unit, 1987.
(With J. Waninaca) *A Review of the Education System in East New Britain,* New National Research Institute, 1989.

Has also written under undisclosed pseudonyms; contributor of weekly column on education to the *Times of Papua New Guinea.* Also contributor of numerous articles to professional journals including *African Review, Taamuli, International Social Science Journal, Journal of Developing Areas, Rural Africana,* and *Yagl-Ambu.* Member of editorial board, *Papua New Guinea Journal of Education;* contributing editor, *Africa Today,* and editor of special edition "Education in African Development," February, 1967.

WORK IN PROGRESS: With Margaret Gibson and others, a review of the education system in the Western Province.

SIDELIGHTS: Sheldon G. Weeks told *CA:* "A major challenge writing for an audience in a developing nation is to express ideas in forms free of jargon that make issues available to more people. We have tried to do this through our academic publications at the university. Outreach has been achieved also through popularized articles in the local press and a monthly colour magazine. This has enabled me to merge my concerns for development with my interest in photography. Most recently we have turned to video to try to communicate the results of educational research in a visual form to a wider audience."

*   *   *

WEIGL, Bruce 1949-

PERSONAL: Born January 27, 1949, in Lorain, Ohio; son of Albert Louis and Zora (Grasa) Weigl; married Jean Kondo; children: Andrew. *Education:* Oberlin College, B.A., 1974; University of New Hampshire, M.A., 1975; University of Utah, Ph.D., 1979.

ADDRESSES: Home—State College, Pa. *Office*—Department of English, 117 Burrowes, Pennsylvania State University, University Park, Pa. 16802.

CAREER: Lorain County Community College, Elyria, Ohio, instructor in English, 1975-76; University of Arkansas, Little Rock, assistant professor of English, 1979-81; Old Dominion University, Norfolk, Va., assistant professor of English, 1981-86; Pennsylvania State University, University Park, associate professor of English, 1986—. *Military service:* U.S. Army, 1967-70; served in Vietnam; received Bronze Star.

AWARDS, HONORS: Prize from American Academy of Poets, 1979; Pushcart Prize, Pushcart Press, 1980, for poem "Temple near Quang Tri: Not on the Map"; fellowship in poetry, Bread Loaf Writers' Conference, 1981; grant for creative writing, National Education Association, 1988.

WRITINGS:

Like a Sack Full of Old Quarrels (poems), Cleveland State University Poetry Series, 1976.
Executioner (poems), Ironwood, 1977.
A Romance (poems), University of Pittsburgh Press, 1979.
(Editor) *The Giver of Morning* (essays), Thunder City, 1982.
The Monkey Wars (poems), University of Georgia Press, 1984.
Song of Napalm (poems), Atlantic Monthly Press, 1988.
(Editor with T. R. Hunner) *The Imagination as Glory: Essays on the Poetry of James Dickey,* University of Illinois Press, in press.

WORK IN PROGRESS: The Hand That Takes (poems).

SIDELIGHTS: Bruce Weigl told *CA:* "To be a writer is to accept who you are, your background, the ruckus of your family life, the whole landscape of your past. For me it was steel mills and industrial waste. That's who I was and what I have to go on. If I'm lucky and work hard enough, I can turn the gritty language of an industrial city into poetry."

BIOGRAPHICAL/CRITICAL SOURCES:

BOOKS

Beidler, Philip, *American Literature and the Experience of Vietnam,* University of Georgia Press, 1982.

*   *   *

WEST, James
   See WITHERS, Carl A.

*   *   *

WHIPPLE, Beverly 1941-

PERSONAL: Born June 30, 1941, in Jersey City, N.J.; daughter of Howard and Beatrice (Bodei) Hoehne; married James W. Whipple (an engineer), September 15, 1962; children: Allen, Susan. *Education:* Wagner College, B.S., 1962; Rutgers University, M.Ed., 1967, Ph.D., 1986, M.S.W., 1987. *Religion:* Protestant.

ADDRESSES: Home—31 Northwest Lakeside Dr., Medford, N.J. 08055. *Office*—Jefferson College of Nursing, Rutgers University, Ackerson Hall—006, Newark, N.J. 07102. *Agent*—

Heide Lang, Sanford J. Greenburger Associates, Inc., 55 Fifth Ave., New York, N.Y. 10003.

CAREER: West Jersey Hospital School of Nursing, Camden, N.J., instructor in nursing, 1962-64; Helene Fuld School of Nursing, Camden, instructor in nursing, 1970-75; Gloucester County College, Sewell, N.J., associate professor of nursing, 1975-78; Rutgers University, Jefferson College of Nursing, Newark, N.J., associate professor of nursing, 1988—. Certified sexologist, certified sex educator, and certified sex counselor. Member of faculty at Jefferson Medical College. Vice-president of Burlington County Board of Mental Health, 1976-80. Member of Sex Information and Education Council of the United States; member of United Presbyterian Church task force on women, 1975-77. Guest on "The Phil Donahue Show," and 150 other television shows. Director of Woodstream Residents Association, 1967-71.

MEMBER: American Nurses Association, American Association of Sex Educators and Counselors, American College of Sexologists, Association of Sexologists, Society for Sex Therapy and Research, Society for the Scientific Study of Sex, Zeta Tau Alpha, Kappa Delta Pi, Sigma Theta Tau.

AWARDS, HONORS: Alumnae certificate of merit, Zeta Tau Alpha, 1978; cited as "One of the People to Watch," *Philadelphia Magazine,* 1982, 1983; alumnae achievement award, Wagner College, 1983; authors citation, New Jersey Writers Conference, 1983, 1984; Daniel S. Lehman Fellow, Rutgers University, 1986.

WRITINGS:

(With Alice K. Ladas and John D. Perry) *The G Spot: And Other Recent Discoveries about Human Sexuality,* Holt, 1982.
(Contributor) Benjamin Graber, editor, *Circumvaginal Musculature and Sexual Function,* S. Karger, 1982.
(With Gina Ogden) *Safe Encounters: How Women Can Say Yes to Pleasure and No to Unsafe Sex,* McGraw, 1988.
(Contributor) J. Legur, editor, *Sexual Rehabilitation of the Spinal Cord Injured Patient,* Humana, in press.
(Contributor) *Vasoactive Intesetal Peptide and Related Peptides,* New York Academy of Sciences, in press.

Also contributor, F. Faccenetti and A. Genozzani, editors, *Pain and Reproduction;* also contributor to *Annals* of New York Academy of Sciences, 1986. Contributor to numerous periodicals, including *Journal of Sex Research, Nurse Practitioner, Pain, Topics in Clinical Nursing, Journal of Sex and Marital Therapy,* and *Playboy.*

WORK IN PROGRESS: "My research involves natural methods of pain control, focusing on the analgesic effects of vaginal stimulation"; a book on the stress of sex.

SIDELIGHTS: Beverly Whipple told *CA:* "I feel that *The G Spot* has helped to validate the experiences of many women, and has helped them to feel better about themselves. It has also stimulated more research in the area of female sexual response. *Safe Encounters* offers sex positive suggestions and information for women in the age of AIDS. Much more research needs to be done on female sexuality, and on the sexual needs of individuals with various kinds of illnesses. I am continuing my work in these areas."

The G Spot has been published in fifteen languages.

BIOGRAPHICAL/CRITICAL SOURCES:

PERIODICALS

Glamour, October, 1982.
Playboy, September, 1982.
Self, August, 1982, September, 1982.
Time, September 13, 1982.

*　　*　　*

WHITE, James Boyd 1938-

PERSONAL: Born July 28, 1938, in Boston, Mass.; son of Benjamin Vroom (a doctor) and Charlotte Green (Conover) White; married second wife, Mary Louise Fitch, January 1, 1978; children: (first marriage) Catherine, John; (second marriage) Emma, Henry. *Education:* Amherst College, A.B. (magna cum laude), 1960; Harvard University, A.M., 1961, LL.B (magna cum laude), 1964.

ADDRESSES: Home—1606 Morton, Ann Arbor, Mich. 48104. *Office*—School of Law, University of Michigan, Ann Arbor, Mich. 48109.

CAREER: Foley, Hoag & Eliot, Boston, Mass., attorney, 1965-67; University of Colorado, Boulder, assistant professor, 1967-69, associate professor, 1969-73, professor of law, 1973-75; University of Chicago, Chicago, Ill., professor of law and member of committee for the study of ancient Mediterranean world, 1975-83; University of Michigan, Ann Arbor, professor of law, professor of English, and adjunct professor of classical studies, 1983—. Visiting professor at Stanford University, 1972, University of Chicago, 1973-74, and University of Michigan, 1982; seminar director.

MEMBER: Chicago Council of Lawyers (member of board of governors), Phi Beta Kappa.

AWARDS, HONORS: Sinclair Kennedy travel fellowship, 1964-65; National Endowment for the Humanities fellowship, 1979-80.

WRITINGS:

The Legal Imagination, Little, Brown, 1973.
(With James Scarboro) *Constitutional Criminal Procedure,* Foundation Press, 1976, supplement, 1980.
When Words Lose Their Meaning, University of Chicago Press, 1984.
Heracles' Bow: Essays in the Rhetoric and Poetics of the Law, University of Wisconsin Press, 1985.
Justice as Translation, University of Chicago Press, in press.

Contributor of articles and reviews to law journals.

WORK IN PROGRESS: A book on the origins of constitutional thinking.

SIDELIGHTS: James Boyd White told *CA:* "*The Legal Imagination* examines legal material as if it were literature and asks how the system of discoveries is structured; what its ethical and political implications are; and how a decent person could possibly devote a professional life to speaking and writing in its terms. *When Words Lose Their Meaning* in a sense reverses the process: here I read Homer's *Iliad,* Thucydides's *History,* Plato's *Georgias,* Johnson's *Rambler,* Austen's *Emma,* and Burke's *Reflections* in the intrusive, participatory, reconstructive way in which law students learn to read their cases: as pieces of a larger culture; as contributions to that culture: and as themselves constituting community with their readers, that is, as ethical and polit-

ical works. What influences all my work is a love of the humanities."

BIOGRAPHICAL/CRITICAL SOURCES:

PERIODICALS

Los Angeles Times, December 16, 1986.
New York Times Book Review, September 16, 1984.
Times Literary Supplement, June 12, 1987.

*　　*　　*

WHITE, Steven F(orsythe) 1955-

PERSONAL: Born June 25, 1955, in Abington, Pa.; son of Robert F. and Diane (Forsythe) White; married Nancy Ellen Pierce (a legislative aide), July 21, 1984. *Education:* Williams College, B.A., 1977; University of Oregon, M.A., 1982, Ph.D., 1987.

ADDRESSES: Office—Department of Modern Languages, St. Lawrence University, Canton, N.Y. 13617.

CAREER: Chicano Affairs Center, Eugene, Ore., outreach worker, 1979-80; free-lance interpreter and translator for public defenders of Lane County and Freeman Marine Equipment, Inc., 1981; St. Lawrence University, Canton, N.Y., assistant professor of modern languages, 1987—. Gives poetry readings in the United States, Europe, and Latin America.

AWARDS, HONORS: Academy of American Poets prize, 1975 and 1977; Hubbard Hutchinson fellow, Williams College, in Peru, Chile, Ecuador, and Nicaragua, 1977-79; Fulbright fellow in Chile, 1982-83; National Endowment for the Arts translation fellow, 1988.

WRITINGS:

(Editor and translator) *Poets of Nicaragua,* Unicorn Press, 1982.
Las constelaciones de la historia (poems in Spanish), Editorial America del Sur (Santiago, Chile), 1983.
Burning the Old Year (poems), Unicorn Press, 1984.
(Editor and translator) *Poets of Chile,* Unicorn Press, 1986.
Culture and Politics in Nicaragua: Testimonies of Poets and Writers, Lumen Inc., 1986.
For the Unborn (poems), Unicorn Press, 1986.
(Editor and translator) *The Birth of the Sun: Selected Poems of Pablo Antonio Cuadra, 1935-1985,* Unicorn Press, 1988.
(Translator with Greg Simon) Federico Garcia Lorca, *Poet in New York,* Farrar, Straus, 1988.
From the Country of Thunder (poems), Unicorn Press, 1989.
(Editor) *From Eve's Rib: Selected Poems of Gioconda Belli,* Curbstone Press, 1989.

Work represented in anthologies, including *New Directions Anthology, Aspen Anthology, Anthology of Magazine Verse* and *Yearbook of American Poetry.* Contributor of poems and translations to *Paris Review, Antaeus, Third Rail,* and other magazines.

WORK IN PROGRESS: An edition of the correspondence between Thomas Merton and Pablo Antonio Cuadra; an anthology of contemporary Argentine poetry; a book of essays, *Modern Nicaraguan Poetry's Dialogues with France and the United States.*

SIDELIGHTS: Steven F. White told *CA:* "My poetry undoubtedly has been influenced by my work as a translator of Hispanic American poetry. To avoid misunderstandings and misrepresentations of these poets' works, I felt it was necessary to live in their countries and collaborate with them directly during the translation process. I love the Spanish language and learned it well with a little help from my friends. The task I undertook was not literary, but cultural. Each country is subject to a different historical and geographical context. To reach a provisional understanding of all this, I worked on a sheep farm in Chilean Patagonia, picked coffee in Nicaragua during the 1979 insurrection, and searched for the legendary dolphins in the Amazon River basin of the Ecuadorian jungle. In many poems I've written, there's a sense of timelessness that may in part come from my contact with people inhabiting these intense, isolated landscapes. But my work also bears witness to some important, precise moments in history when entire nations were transformed by the necessity of complete social transformations. I'm committed to a poetry of clear ideas and strong images with an emotional impact; to an art that I feel must be compassionate and humanistic; to a language capable of operating in a highly-charged, persuasive, politicized environment."

*   *   *

WHITMORE, George   1945-1989

PERSONAL: Born September 27, 1945, in Denver, Colo.; died April 19, 1989, in New York, N.Y., from acquired immune deficiency syndrome (AIDS); son of Lowell A. (an airline mechanic) and Irene D. (Davis) Whitmore; companion's name, Michael Canter. *Education:* MacMurray College, B.A., 1967; graduate study at Bennington College, 1967-68.

ADDRESSES: Home—39 Christopher St., No. 2B, New York, N.Y. 10014. *Agent*—Michael Powers, Hutto Management, 110 West 57th St., New York, N.Y. 10019.

CAREER: Planned Population-World Population, New York City, 1968-72, member of editorial staff and coordinator of national abortion referral unit; Citizens Housing and Planning Council, New York City, member of administrative staff, beginning 1972. Member, Gay Men's Health Crisis and Gay Academic Union. *Wartime service:* Conscientious objector; in lieu of military service worked at Planned Parenthood, New York City.

AWARDS, HONORS: Woodrow Wilson fellowship, 1967; Bennington Masters fellowship, 1967; New York State Creative Arts Public Service grant, 1976.

WRITINGS:

Getting Gay in New York (poems), Free Milk Fund Press, 1976.
"The Caseworker" (two-act play), first produced in New York City at Playwrights Horizons, May, 1976.
"A Life of Gertrude Stein: Flight/The Legacy" (two one-act plays), first produced in New York City at Eighteenth Street Playhouse, April, 1979.
The Confessions of Danny Slocum: Gay Life in the Big City (novel), St. Martin's, 1980.
"The Rights" (two-act play), first produced in New York City at The Glines, Network Theatre, January, 1980.
Out Here: Fire Island Tales (stories), Seahorse Press, 1981.
(Contributor) Ian Young, editor, *On the Line: New Gay Fiction,* Crossing Press, 1981.
Nebraska (also see below; novel), Grove, 1987.
Someone Was Here: Profiles in the AIDS Epidemic (nonfiction), New American Library, 1988.

OTHER

Also author of "Secretaries" and "Nebraska," both unproduced plays, and "Beloved Intruders," a radio play. Author of biweekly column, "Literature," *Advocate,* 1975-76. Contributor of stories, articles, poems, and reviews to periodicals, including *Ad-*vocate, Architectural Digest, Boston Gay Review, Drummer, Gentleman's Quarterly, Harper's Bazaar, House and Garden, New York Times, New York Times Magazine, Village Voice, Vogue, Travel & Leisure, and Washington Post. Contributing editor, *Advocate,* 1974-76.

WORK IN PROGRESS: Deep Dish, a serial; *The New York Native.*

SIDELIGHTS: In his 1988 work of nonfiction, *Someone Was Here: Profiles in the AIDS Epidemic,* novelist and playwright George Whitmore offers an "intimate chronicle," according to Stephen S. Hall in the *New York Times Book Review,* which contains "three quiet and true tales of fear and uncertainty in the age of AIDS." Whitmore, who discovered he himself had the fatal disease while writing about it, presents three different accounts of people and AIDS: a gay man from New York and his volunteer counselor at the Gay Men's Health Crisis, a Chicano woman who brings her estranged and dying son home to rural Colorado to care for him, and the AIDS patients and workers at New York City's Lincoln Hospital. "So much attention is devoted to the fear and uncertainty of people who do *not* have AIDS that we should applaud George Whitmore for reanimating our compassion for those who have it," writes Hall, adding Whitmore "has chosen to characterize AIDS as an affliction of the underclass and the disenfranchised, not as a speculative horror for those who are uninfected and at low risk." Although the reviewer finds the writing style at times too restrained, he concludes that "at their best, these snapshots give us crisp, sharp, well-focused glimpses of an almost impossibly large tragedy and help us begin to understand the disease."

Prior to *Someone Was Here,* Whitmore was the author of well-received fiction and plays that openly dealt with gay themes; his 1987 book *Nebraska,* notes Richard Hall in the *New York Times Book Review,* is a "powerful tale" which "combines the coming-out novel with the family novel." "A grimly funny, deadpan American Gothic tale," according to a *Newsweek* reviewer, *Nebraska* chronicles the observations of a young boy (Craig McMullen) who, while adjusting to life after losing his leg in an automobile mishap, discovers that he is gay. Brandon Judell in the *Voice Literary Supplement* describes *Nebraska* as "*Huckleberry Finn* gone awry," adding that "confined to his mattress, much as Huckleberry was to his raft, [Craig] rides through his family's lives with an odd mixture of naivete, rumination, and resourcefulness." In addition to providing vivid accounts of what Judell calls the "twaddle and inadequacies" of the boy's "repetitive lower-class existence," *Nebraska* shows the difficulty of growing up gay in the 1950s. An early incident in Craig's life, which Hall notes "betrays his burgeoning sexuality and [an] uncle's love," eventually "leads to divorce, insanity, even to kidnapping and suicide" in the book. However, "what might sound like a depressing book is really a loving and often amusing one," notes Judell. With his one-legged protagonist, "Whitmore has adroitly created a metaphor for what it is like to grow up gay in America."

Whitmore once commented on his work: "I have been a gay activist since 1972, so it's only natural that my writing interests should center around the subjects of gay liberation and gay life. My first experience in writing was quite academic; but my professional life began with journalism, reporting on progress in gay-rights efforts for national publications. Concurrently, my first book of poetry was the first openly gay volume to be awarded a major grant, in 1976, and my play 'The Caseworker' is among the first 'post-Stonewall' gay dramas. 'The Caseworker' has been called a 'seminal work in gay theater.' With this and other work, I believe I helped developed a basis for modern gay literary criticism. I applied some of these principles to a study of Thoreau and his contemporaries in 'Friendship in New England,' which was well received by Thoreau critics and biographers.

"Recently, I've concentrated on playwriting and fiction. *The Confessions of Danny Slocum* elicited a remarkable reader response. The subject of the book is sex therapy—a fictionalized account of one man's treatment. But this only serves as the spine of the book; it's also an examination (humorous and wry, I should add) of gay life in urban America.

"A career in gay writing (merely being called and thinking of oneself as 'a gay writer' is a new development in the profession, I think) has many rewards. The first among those is the sense of building a minority literature that has in the past been repressed from the outside and often cryptic in its intentions and techniques. It has been very important for me to help to rescue gay works from the past and reassess what has been a fragmented tradition. This undertaking is hardly the kind of thing one can do alone. Gay criticism as such is a highly collaborative effort as many of us across the country (and internationally as well) pool our insights and information. Being a 'post-Stonewall' gay writer has been an exciting undertaking, too. The relationships between politics and journalism, politics and literature, are fascinating, and the influences of progressive movements and/or feminism to what we're doing as gay writers are profound.

"In practice, however, I'd have to say that politics is very distinctly separate from my creative work (though not my daily life) at this point. Unless I set out to write a parable or a broad satire, I've found that political concerns are beside the point in my fiction. Instead, I try to reflect gay life as it really is.

"The accusation always made against gay (or indeed, any minority) literature is that it's too hermetic. I'd say the most hermetic thing about it is how the commercial publishing scene limits it. Aside from the apartheid that exists between the gay world (often loose but sometimes highly ghettoized) and the general culture, gay writers have an uphill battle—first to be understood, then to be published."

Whitmore added: "After a decade or so of gay writing, I think I can say that this particular generation of gay writers will not disappear nor will our works be destroyed. Edmund White, Felice Picano, Armistead Maupin, Paul Monette and many others—not to mention scores of excellent poets—have created a very exciting and durable literature. I'm proud to be part of it."

BIOGRAPHICAL/CRITICAL SOURCES:

PERIODICALS

Newsweek, March 21, 1988.
New York Times Book Review, April 10, 1988, June 19, 1988.
New York Times Magazine, January 31, 1988.
Voice Literary Supplement, December, 1987, June, 1988.

OBITUARIES:

PERIODICALS

New York Times, April 20, 1989.*

*   *   *

WILDAVSKY, Aaron (B.) 1930-

PERSONAL: Born May 31, 1930, in New York, N.Y.; son of Sender and Eva (Brudnow) Wildavsky; married Mary Cadman,

December, 1973; children: (previous marriage) Adam, Sara, Ben, Dan. *Education:* Brooklyn College (now Brooklyn College of the City University of New York), B.A., 1954; Yale University, M.A., 1957, Ph.D., 1959.

ADDRESSES: Home—4400 Sequoyah Rd., Oakland, Calif. 94605. *Office*—Survey Research Center, 2538 Channing Way, University of California, Berkeley, Calif. 94720.

CAREER: Oberlin College, Oberlin, Ohio, instructor, 1958-60, assistant professor of government, 1960-62; research fellow, Resources for the Future, 1962-63; University of California, Berkeley, assistant professor, 1963-65, associate professor, 1965-66, professor of political science, 1966—, chairman of department, 1966-69, dean of Graduate School of Public Policy, 1969-77. Visiting professor at Graduate School and University Center of the City University of New York, 1972, and Columbia University, 1978; adjunct professor, Yale University, 1978. President, Russell Sage Foundation, 1977-78. *Military service:* U.S. Army, 1950-52.

MEMBER: American Political Science Association (president, 1985-86), American Society for Public Administration, Association for Public Policy Analysis and Management.

AWARDS, HONORS: Fulbright grant, 1954-55, for study at the University of Sydney; Guggenheim fellow, 1971; National Academy of Public Administration fellow, 1971—; American Academy of Arts and Sciences fellow, 1973—; Charles A. Merrian Award, American Political Science Association, 1975; LL.D., Brooklyn College of the City University of New York, 1977; Paul Lazarsfeld Award for Research, 1981; Harold Lasswell Award, 1984; John Gaus Award, American Political Science Association, 1989; honorary degree, University of Bologna.

WRITINGS:

Studies in Australian Politics: The 1926 Referendum, Cheshire Publishing, 1958.
Dixon-Yates: A Study in Power Politics, Yale University Press, 1962.
Leadership in a Small Town, Bedminster, 1964.
The Politics of the Budgetary Process, Little, Brown, 1964, 4th edition, 1984.
(With Nelson W. Polsby) *Presidential Elections: Contemporary Strategies of American Electoral Politics,* Scribner, 1964, 7th edition, 1988.
The Revolt against the Masses, and Other Essays in Politics and Public Policy, Basic Books, 1971.
(With Jeanne Nienaber) *The Budgeting and Evaluation of Federal Recreation Programs; or, Money Doesn't Grow on Trees,* Basic Books, 1973.
(With Jeffrey Pressman) *Implementation: How Great Expectations in Washington Are Dashed in Oakland; or, Why It's Amazing That Federal Programs Work at All, This Being a Saga of the Economic Development Administration As Told by Two Sympathetic Observers Who Seek to Build Morals on a Foundation of Ruined Hopes,* University of California Press, 1973, 3rd edition, 1984.
(With Frank Levy and Arnold Meltsner) *Urban Outcomes,* University of California Press, 1973.
(With Naomi Caiden) *Planning and Budgeting in Poor Countries,* Wiley, 1974.
(With David Good) *A Tax by Any Other Name: Budget versus Tax Alternatives for Financing Governmental Support of Charitable Contributions,* Transaction Books, 1974.
(With Hugh Heclo) *The Private Government of Public Money: Community and Policy inside British Political Administra-*

tion, University of California Press, 1974, 2nd edition, Macmillan (London), 1981.

(With Edward Friedland and Paul Seabury) *The Great Detente Disaster: Oil and the Decline of American Foreign Policy,* Basic Books, 1975.

Budgeting: A Comparative Theory of Budgetary Processes, Little, Brown, 1975, 2nd revised edition, Transaction Books, 1986.

Speaking Truth to Power: The Art and Craft of Policy Analysis, Little, Brown, 1979, new edition with a new introduction by Wildavsky, Transaction Books, 1987.

How to Limit Government Spending, University of California Press, 1980.

(With Ellen Tenenbaum) *The Politics of Mistrust: Estimating American Oil and Gas Resources,* Sage Publications, 1981.

(With Mary Douglas) *Risk and Culture: An Essay on the Selection of Technical and Environmental Dangers,* University of California Press, 1982.

The Nursing Father: Moses as a Political Leader, University of Alabama Press, 1984.

(With Carolyn Webber) *A History of Taxation and Expenditure in the Western World,* Simon & Schuster, 1986.

Searching for Safety, Transaction Books, 1988.

The New Politics of Budgetary Process, Scott, Foresman, 1988.

Craftways: On the Organization of Scholarly Work, Transaction Publishers, 1989.

(With Richard Ellis) *Dilemmas of Presidential Leadership: From Washington through Lincoln,* Transaction Publishers, 1989.

EDITOR

American Federalism in Perspective, Little, Brown, 1967.

(With Polsby) *American Governmental Institutions,* Rand McNally, 1968.

(With Seabury, and contributor with Max Singer) *U.S. Foreign Policy: Perspectives and Proposals for the 1970s,* McGraw, 1969.

(And contributor) *The Presidency,* Little, Brown, 1969.

Perspectives on the Presidency, Little, Brown, 1975.

(With Michael Boskin) *The Federal Budget: Economics and Politics,* Institute for Contemporary Studies, 1982.

Beyond Containment: Alternative American Policies toward the Soviet Union, Institute for Contemporary Studies, 1983.

(With Robert T. Golembiewski) *The Costs of Federalism: Essays in Honor of James W. Fesber,* Transaction Books, 1984.

CONTRIBUTOR

Paul Tillett, editor, *Inside Politics: The National Conventions,* Oceana, 1960.

R. Dentler, P. Smith, and Polsby, editors, *Politics and Social Life,* Houghton, 1963.

Congress: The First Branch of Government, American Enterprise Institute for Public Policy Research, 1966.

(With Otto A. Davis and Michael Dempster) Gordon Tullock, editor, *Papers on Non-Market Decision Making,* Thomas Jefferson Center for Political Economy, University of Virginia, 1966.

David L. Sills, editor, *The International Encyclopedia of the Social Sciences,* Volume 2, Macmillan, 1968.

(With Meltsner) John P. Crecine and Louis H. Masotti, editors, *The Role of Public Policy in Urban Economics,* Volume 4, Sage Publications, 1970.

(With Davis and Dempster) R. F. Byrne, Davis, Charles, and Guildford, editors, *Studies in Budgeting,* North-Holland Publishing, 1971.

Evaluation and Reform, Ballinger, 1975.

Accounting, Organizations, and Society, Pergamon, 1976.

Kay Lehman Schlozman, editor, *Elections in America,* Allen & Unwin, 1987.

Gary C. Bryner and Dennis L. Thompson, editors, *The Constitution and the Regulation of Society,* Brigham Young University Press, 1988.

OTHER

Contributor to *Education, Opportunity, and Social Inequality: Changing Prospects in Western Society,* Wiley, and *Urban Analysis,* Gordon & Breach Science Publishers; contributor to numerous professional journals.

BIOGRAPHICAL/CRITICAL SOURCES:

PERIODICALS

Los Angeles Times Book Review, July 4, 1982, July 27, 1986.

New York Times Book Review, October 19, 1980, August 8, 1982, August 3, 1986.

Times Literary Supplement, March 18, 1983.

Wall Street Journal, January 3, 1986.

*   *   *

WILLE, Janet Neipris   1936-
(Janet Neipris)

PERSONAL: Surname is pronounced *Wil*-lee; surname of pen name rhymes with "cypress"; born March 11, 1936, in Boston, Mass.; daughter of Samuel (a salesman) and Dorothy (an administrative assistant; maiden name, Danis) Brown; married Marvin Neipris, September 2, 1957 (divorced, 1979); married Donald J. Wille (an engineer and writer), June 22, 1980; children: Cynthia, Carolyn, Ellen; stepchildren: Christine Wille, Neil Wille. *Education:* Tufts University, B.A. (cum laude), 1957; Simmons College, M.A., 1973; Brandeis University, M.F.A., 1975.

ADDRESSES: Home—100 Bleecker St., New York, N.Y. 10012. *Office*—Dramatic Writing Department, Tisch School of the Arts, New York University, 721 Broadway, New York, N.Y. 10003. *Agent*—Helen Merrill, 377 West 22nd St., New York, N.Y. 10011.

CAREER: University of Montana, Missoula, playwright-in-residence, 1975; Drew University, Madison, N.J., instructor in playwriting, 1975-76; Goddard College, Plainfield, Vt., instructor in playwriting in graduate writing program, 1975-79; WCVB-TV (ABC affiliate), Boston, Mass., staff writer for comedy series "The Baxters," 1977-80; Harvard University, Cambridge, Mass., instructor in playwriting in continuing education department, 1978-80; Tufts University, Medford, Mass., instructor in creative writing, 1978-81; Smith College, Northampton, Mass., playwright-in-residence and instructor, 1980; New York University, Tisch School of the Arts, New York, N.Y., associate professor of dramatic writing, 1980—, chairperson of department. Member of playwrights unit of Circle Repertory Co., 1980—, and American Place Theatre Women's Project, 1980—. Contributing writer for "Women '77," WBZ-TV, Boston, Mass., 1977, and "Impact," WJZ-TV, Baltimore, Md., 1978. Has sat on university and radio media and drama panels.

MEMBER: Dramatists Guild, Writers Guild of America, East, Authors League of America.

AWARDS, HONORS: Sam S. Shubert playwriting fellowship, 1974-75; National Endowment for the Humanities fellowship in playwriting, 1979-80; "The Agreement" was voted into *Best Short Plays,* 1986.

WRITINGS:

PLAYS; UNDER NAME JANET NEIPRIS

"A Time to Remember" (two-act musical), first produced in Boston, Mass., at Statler Hilton, 1967.

"Abe Lincoln" (one-act musical), first produced in Winchester, Mass., at Winchester Public Schools, 1969.

"The Princess and the Dragon" (one-act musical), first produced in Boston at Boston Arts Festival, 1969.

"The Little Bastard" (one-act musical), first produced in Boston at Simmons College, 1971.

"Statues" (one-act), first produced in Waltham, Mass., at Brandeis University, 1974, produced in New York at Manhattan Theatre Club, 1977.

"Exhibition" (one-act), first produced at Brandeis University, 1975, produced Off-Off Broadway at Cubiculo Theatre, 1975.

"The Bridge at Belharbour" (one-act), first produced at Brandeis University, 1975, produced Off-Off Broadway at Cubiculo Theatre, 1975.

"Jeremy and the Thinking Machine" (one-act musical), first produced Off-Off Broadway at Thirteenth Street Theatre, 1977.

"Flying Horses" (two-act), first produced in Missoula, Mont., at University of Montana, 1977.

"Separations" (two-act), first produced in Washington, D.C., at Arena Stage Theatre, 1978.

"The Desert" (two-act), first produced in Milwaukee, Wis., at Milwaukee Repertory Theatre, 1979.

"Out of Order" (two-act), first produced in New York at Harold Clurman Theatre, 1980.

"The Agreement" (one-act), first produced in Westport, Conn., at Town Hall Playwrights Series, 1982.

"Almost in Vegas," first produced in New York at Manhattan Punch Line Theatre, 1985.

"Notes on a Life" (musical), first produced in New York at American Place Theatre by Women's Project, 1985.

OTHER

Also author of three radio dramas, "The Desert," 1979, "The Agreement," 1980, and "The Piano," 1981, for "Earplay" series, PBS; also author of "How Does Your Garden Grow," a drama first broadcast by WCVB-TV, Boston, 1977, and "The President's Assistants," a situation comedy pilot series first broadcast by ABC, 1978. Contributor of articles to periodicals, including *Washington Star, Sidelines,* and *Writer.*

WORK IN PROGRESS: A play, "Southernmost Tip."

BIOGRAPHICAL/CRITICAL SOURCES:

BOOKS

Interviews with Contemporary Women Playwrights, Morrow, 1987.

*   *   *

WILLIAMS, Gurney III   1941-

PERSONAL: Born June 12, 1941, in New York, N.Y.; son of Gurney, Jr. (an editor) and Lois (Jones) Williams; married Linda Payne (a public relations consultant), June 24, 1967; children: Kimberly Payne, Jay. *Education:* Yale University, B.A., 1963; Columbia University, M.S., 1967. *Religion:* Episcopalian.

CAREER: Newsday, Garden City, N.Y., reporter and editor, 1967-70; free-lance writer, 1970—.

MEMBER: American Society of Journalists and Authors.

AWARDS, HONORS: Co-recipient of Pulitzer Prize, 1970, for *Newsday* series of articles on the land dealings of public officials.

WRITINGS:

The Zero People (juvenile), Scholastic Book Services, 1974.
Movie Man (juvenile), Scholastic Book Services, 1975.
Calling Station E-A-R-T-H (juvenile), Scholastic Book Services, 1975.
Writing Careers (juvenile), F. Watts, 1976.
(Editor) *Yachtsman's Choice: The Best of Rudder,* McKay, 1977.
True Escape and Survival Stories, F. Watts, 1977.
(With Joan Glazer) *Introduction to Children's Literature,* McGraw, 1978.
Ghosts and Poltergeists, F. Watts, 1979.
Twins, F. Watts, 1979.
(With Arno F. Wittig) *Psychology: An Introduction,* McGraw-Hill, 1984.

Contributor to magazines, including *TV Guide* and *Reader's Digest.*

SIDELIGHTS: Gurney Williams III once told *CA:* "My father was humor editor of *Collier's* and later *Look* magazine; early exposure to writers and artists he knew sparked my interest. Now, working with my own children, I've become fascinated with children's literature at a time when the literature itself has become more lively and vital than ever before. Writing for children today isn't much different from writing for adults. Children are more resilient than many adults know; they like a good story, and reject sham. I'm trying to meet their need for good writing, avoiding cuteness and condescension."*

*   *   *

WILLIAMS, Kate
   See FLYNN, Donald R(obert)

*   *   *

WILLIAMS, Peter W(illiam)   1944-

PERSONAL: Born August 8, 1944, in Hollywood, Fla.; son of William J. and Harriet E. (Stacey) Williams; married Ruth Ann Alban Schneider, June 1, 1980; stepchildren: Jonathan A. Schneider, Dana A. Schneider. *Education:* Harvard University, A.B. (magna cum laude), 1965; Yale University, M.A., 1967, M.Phil., 1968, Ph.D., 1970. *Religion:* Episcopal.

ADDRESSES: Home—206 Oakhill Dr., Oxford, Ohio 45056. *Office*—Department of Religion, Old Manse, Miami University, Oxford, Ohio 45056.

CAREER: Miami University, Oxford, Ohio, assistant professor, 1970-75, associate professor, 1975-81, professor of religion, 1981—, chair of department, 1984-88, faculty affiliate in American Studies, 1986—. Lecturer in religious studies at Albertus Magnus College, autumn, 1967; adjunct instructor in philosophy and sociology at New Haven College (now University of New Haven), summer, 1970; visiting assistant professor at Stanford University, summer, 1974; visiting associate professor at Bowdoin College, 1974-75.

MEMBER: American Academy of Religion (co-chairman of Consultation on American Popular and Devotional Religions, 1974-80), American Catholic Historical Association, American Society of Church History (council member, class of 1991), American Studies Association, Historical Society of the Episcopal Church, Unitarian-Universalist Historical Society, Cincinnati Historical Society, Phi Beta Kappa (elected to Alpha of Massachusetts chapter, 1965; Iota of Ohio chapter, vice president, 1987-88, president, 1988-89).

AWARDS, HONORS: Woodrow Wilson fellowship, 1965-66; National Endowment for the Humanities fellowships, 1975, 1979-80, and 1984; Miami Faculty Research Committee summer awards, 1979, 1982, and 1989.

WRITINGS:

Popular Religion in America: Symbolic Change and the Modernization Process in Historical Perspective, Prentice-Hall, 1980, published with new introduction, University of Illinois Press, 1989.
(Contributor) Samuel S. Hill, editor, *Encyclopedia of Religion in the South,* Mercer University Press, 1984.
(Contributor) Charles H. Lippy, editor, *Religious Periodicals of the United States,* Greenwood Press, 1986.
(Editor with Lippy, and contributor) *Encyclopedia of Religion in America,* three volumes, Scribner, 1988.
America's Religions: Traditions and Cultures, Macmillan, 1989.
(Contributor) Lippy, editor, *Twentieth Century Shapers of American Popular Religion,* Greenwood Press, 1989.
(Contributor) *Dictionary of Christianity in America,* InterVarsity Press, 1990.
Sacred Spaces, Sacred Places: American Religious Architecture and Landscape, University of Chicago Press, 1990.

Contributor to *World Book Encyclopedia* and *Harper's Dictionary of Religion.* Contributor of nearly ninety articles and reviews to history, American studies, and religious studies journals. Member of editorial boards of *Journal of Religious Studies, Queen City Heritage, Anglican and Episcopal History, Religion,* and *American Culture.*

WORK IN PROGRESS: A bicentennial history of religion in Cincinnati, scheduled for publication by the University of Illinois Press in 1993.

SIDELIGHTS: In his book *Popular Religion in America: Symbolic Change and the Modernization Process in Historical Perspective,* Peter W. Williams explores aspects and forms of popular religion. In particular, the author discusses what he calls "extra-ecclesiastical symbolic activity"—or what David Buchdahl defines in *American Anthropologist* as "the sort of religious behavior that goes on outside of the established churches and seminaries." In doing so, Williams draws upon the historical frameworks of traditional Native American and American Negro religions, folk traditions of Judaism and Catholicism, and movements within Protestantism—all of which he interprets in light of social and cultural changes occurring in two centuries of American history.

"Williams has made good use of classical and current approaches in the social sciences to illuminate particular aspects of religion in the United States," Buchdahl notes. Writing in the *Journal of American Folklore,* Donald E. Byrne summarizes *Popular Religion in America* as representing "a ground-breaking departure from [the approach] usually taken in studies of American religion" as well as "an effort to bridge the interdisciplinary gap between folklore and the study of American religion from the side of American religious scholarship, and to show how diverse folk phenomena can function to elucidate our understanding of American religion."

BIOGRAPHICAL/CRITICAL SOURCES:
PERIODICALS

American Anthropologist, March, 1981.
Journal of American Folklore, October-December, 1982.

*   *   *

WILLIS, Maud
    See LOTTMAN, Eileen

*   *   *

WILLIS, Samuel
    See PARKER, Hershel

*   *   *

WILLOUGHBY, Hugh
    See HARVEY, Nigel

*   *   *

WINKS, Robin William   1930-

PERSONAL: Born December 5, 1930, in West Lafayette, Ind.; son of Evert McKinley and Jewell (Sampson) Winks; married Avril Flockton, 1952; children: Honor Leigh, Eliot Myles. *Education:* University of Colorado, B.A. (magna cum laude), 1952, M.A., 1953; Victoria University, New Zealand, certificate, 1952; Johns Hopkins University, Ph.D. (with distinction), 1957.

ADDRESSES: Home—403A Yale Station, New Haven, Conn. 06520. *Office*—Department of History, Yale University, New Haven, Conn. 06520.

CAREER: University of Colorado, Boulder, instructor, 1953; Connecticut College for Women (now Connecticut College), New London, instructor, 1956-57; Yale University, New Haven, Conn., began as instructor, 1957, associate professor, 1957-67, professor of history, beginning 1967, currently Randolph W. Townsend, Jr., Professor of History, director of Office of Special Projects and Foundations, 1974-76, John B. Madden Master of Berkeley College, 1977-90. Visiting professor, University of Alberta, 1959, University of Malaya, 1962, University of Sydney, 1963, American University, Beirut, Lebanon, 1968, University of Washington, 1977, and University of Stellenbosch, 1983. University of London, visiting fellow at Institute of Commonwealth Studies, 1966-67, and president scholar at School of American Research, 1984. Cultural attache, American Embassy, London, England, 1969-71; adviser to United States Department of State, 1971—. Chairman, National Park Service advisory board, 1981-83; trustee, National Parks and Conservation Association, 1985—; director of Yale conference on the teaching of social studies; member, Council on Foreign Relations.

MEMBER: American Historical Association, Organization of American Historians, Canadian Historical Association, Royal Historical Society (fellow), Asia Society, Athenaeum Reform Club, Royal Commonwealth Society, Yale Club, Explorer's Club (fellow).

AWARDS, HONORS: Fulbright award, 1952; Morse fellow, 1959-60; Social Science Research Council award, 1959-60; Smith-Mundt fellow, 1962-63; senior faculty fellowship, Yale University, 1965-66; Guggenheim fellowship, 1976-77. Honorary M.A., Yale University, 1967; D.Litt., University of Nebraska, 1976, and University of Colorado, 1987.

WRITINGS:

These New Zealanders!, Whitcombe, 1953, 2nd edition, 1966.
New Trends and Recent Literature in Canadian History, American Historical Association, 1959, revised edition, 1966.
Marshall Plan and the American Economy, Holt, 1960.
Canada and the United States: The Civil War Years, Johns Hopkins University Press, 1960, 3rd edition, 1988.
British Imperialism: Gold, God or Glory?, Holt, 1963.
The Cold War, Macmillan, 1964, revised edition (with Dan Yergin), 1978.
(Compiler with John Bastin) *Malaysia: Selected Historical Readings,* Oxford University Press, 1967, revised edition, 1979.
(Author of introduction with others) *Four Fugitive Slave Narratives,* Addison-Wesley, 1969.
Canadian-West Indian Union: A Forty-Year Minuet, Athlone, 1970.
The Blacks in Canada, Yale University Press, 1971.
Slavery: A Comparative Perspective, New York University Press, 1972.
(With others) *The American Experience,* Addison-Wesley, 1972, 3rd edition, 1979.
The Relevance of Canadian History: United States and Imperial Perspectives, Macmillan, 1979, 2nd edition, 1988.
An American's Guide to Britain, Scribner, 1979, 3rd edition, 1987.
Western Civilization: A Brief History, Prentice-Hall, 1979, 2nd edition, Collegiate Press, 1988.
(With daughter, Honor L. Winks) *The St. Lawrence* (juvenile), Silver, 1980.
Modus Operandi: An Excursion into Detective Fiction, Godine, 1981.
(With others) *A History of Civilization: Prehistory to Present,* two volumes, Prentice-Hall, 1984, 7th edition, 1988.
Cloak and Gown: Scholars in the Secret War, Morrow, 1987.

EDITOR

British Empire-Commonwealth: Historiographical Re-Assessments, Duke University Press, 1966.
The Historian as Detective: Essays on Evidence, Harper, 1969.
(With Marcus Culiffe) *Pastmasters: Some Essays on American Historians,* Harper, 1969.
Other Voices, Other Views: An International Collection of Essays from the Bicentennial, Greenwood Press, 1978.
Detective Fiction: A Collection of Critical Essays, Prentice-Hall, 1980, revised edition, Countryman Press, 1988.
Colloquium on Crime: Eleven Renowned Mystery Writers Discuss Their Work, Scribner, 1986.
(With James Rush) *Asia in Western Fiction,* Manchester University Press, 1990.

OTHER

Author of a column on mystery and suspense fiction for *Boston Globe.* Contributor to *American History Review.* General editor, "The Modern Nations in Historical Perspective" series, Prentice-Hall, 1963; editor, "History and Historiography" series, Garland Publishing, 1984-85.

WORK IN PROGRESS: A biography of Frederick Billings; *The Idea of American Imperialism.*

SIDELIGHTS: Robin William Winks, a history professor at Yale University and John B. Madden Master of Berkeley College, has written numerous books concerning his field, several of which discuss such subjects as Canadian history and slavery. More recently, however, he has garnered attention from critics for his writings about detective fiction and real-life espionage.

One of these publications, *Modus Operandi: An Excursion into Detective Fiction,* in which Winks defends the mystery genre as a legitimate form of literature, has been called "one of the most intriguing and satisfying books on the crime field to come along in years" by one *Detroit News* critic. Part of the effectiveness in Winks's writing is due to his approach, say several reviewers. *Washington Post Book World* contributor Michael Dirda, for example, explains that "Winks downplays the puzzle aspect of detective fiction—he has no use for locked-room problems—and emphasizes the social dimension. The mystery illuminates a country, a society, a time, ultimately makes us rethink our values and examine our character."

Winks's interest in detective fiction led him to write his more recent book, *Cloak and Gown: Scholars in the Secret War.* "I wanted to write something factual," he tells Michael Freitag in the *New York Times Book Review,* "something that would help me to see to what extent the fiction had any basis in reality." In *Cloak and Gown* Winks proves that the idea that academics were never involved in espionage is erroneous. "Winks explodes this purer-than-thou theory completely with example after example of how the universities came to the aid of the nation both in public and in secret during time of threat," writes *Washington Post Book World* critic Duncan Spencer. Specifically, the historian focuses on the professors and graduates of Yale University, including such figures of the Office of Strategic Services (the forerunner of the Central Intelligence Agency) as James Angleton, Donald Downes, Joseph Toy Curtiss, and Norman Pearson.

Although *Nation* reviewer Jon Wiener agrees that Winks's book provides "irrefutable evidence that Yale has been entwined in the C.I.A. for decades," he feels that the author fails to thoroughly address his two main questions: "whether there is American imperialism, and whether the C.I.A.'s effort to give historical scholarship a 'social utility' compromised the discipline." Other critics, however, believe that *Cloak and Gown* provides valuable information for the reader who is interested in the history of the C.I.A. "*Cloak and Gown* is not only an entertaining contribution to the secret history of the 1940's and 50's," asserts Godfrey Hodgson in the *New York Times Book Review,* "it is also an important one." Spencer similarly remarks, "This is a book of deep research and fresh views."

Today, the involvement of Yale academics has dropped off considerably. Winks attributes this to two changes in government intelligence since the 1960s. One difference, the historian tells Paul Galloway in a *Washington Post* interview, is that "intelligence today is heavily politicized." Also, Winks continues, spying has become a high-tech operation. "This means you don't need scholars; you need technicians, engineers, computer scientists, mathematicians. . . . That's one of the things that's gone wrong. We depend far too much on electronic intelligence." Because of this fascination with technology, Americans "have forgotten the need to understand other cultures," says Winks. "That's why I feel somewhat pessimistic about the future successes of American intelligence."

AVOCATIONAL INTERESTS: Travel (Winks has been to over 100 countries), national parks, wine, old maps, detective fiction.

BIOGRAPHICAL/CRITICAL SOURCES:

PERIODICALS

Detroit News, January 31, 1982.
Los Angeles Times Book Review, August 23, 1987.
Nation, September 5, 1987.
Newsweek, June 27, 1983.
New York Times, August 11, 1987.

New York Times Book Review, August 16, 1987.
Times Literary Supplement, July 16, 1971, January 9, 1981, March 16, 1984, April 8, 1988.
Washington Post, November 20, 1987.
Washington Post Book World, January 10, 1982, July 10, 1983, September 6, 1987.

*   *   *

WISEMAN, David 1916-
(Jane Julian)

PERSONAL: Born January 13, 1916, in Manchester, England; son of Oscar (a salesman) and Margaret (Hussey) Wiseman; married Cicely Hilda Mary Richards, September 2, 1939; children: Michael, Sally Hilda Wiseman Smith, Patrick, Deborah Margaret Wiseman Lucas. *Education:* Victoria University of Manchester, B.A. (with honors), 1937.

ADDRESSES: Home—21 Treworder Rd., Truro, Cornwall, England. *Agent*—June Hall, 5th Floor, The Chambers, Chelsea Harbour, Lots Rd., London SW10 0XF.

CAREER: Employed by British Institute of Adult Education, London, England, 1946-50; high school teacher in Worcestershire, Yorkshire, and Cornwall, England, 1952-59; high school principal in Doncaster, Yorkshire, England, 1959-63, and Cornwall, 1963-75; Cornwall Education Board, Cornwall, coordinator and adviser on in-service education of teachers, 1975-77; writer, 1977—. Member, Cornwall Education Committee, 1970-75. *Military service:* British Army, 1940-46; became major.

AWARDS, HONORS: Preis der Leseratten, ZDF T-V, West Germany, 1982, and *Horn Book* Honor List citation, both for *Jeremy Visick;* American Library Association Notable Book citation for *Thimbles.*

MEMBER: Society of Authors.

WRITINGS:

JUVENILES

Jeremy Visick, Houghton, 1981 (published in England as *The Fate of Jeremy Visick,* Viking Kestrel, 1982).
Thimbles, Houghton, 1982.
Blodwen and the Guardians, Houghton, 1983.
Adam's Common, Houghton, 1984.
(Under pseudonym Jane Julian) *Ellen Bray,* Morrow, 1985.
Pudding and Pie, Viking Kestrel, 1986.
Jumping Jack, Blackie, 1988.
A Badge of Honour, Blackie, 1989, published as *A Tie to the Past,* Houghton, 1989.
(Under pseudonym Jane Julian) *As Wind to Fire,* Piatkus, 1989.
The Devil's Cauldron (juvenile), Hippo, 1989.

Editor, *Journal of Adult Education,* 1948-51.

WORK IN PROGRESS: Research on period 1870-1914; novels taking up story first begun in *Ellen Bray.*

SIDELIGHTS: Many of David Wiseman's juvenile and young adult novels blend past and present. The author once told *CA* that *Jeremy Visick* "is the story of a tin miner of nineteenth-century Cornwall who dies with his father and two brothers in an underground accident in Wheal Maid mine. Matthew Clemens, a boy of modern times, is drawn across time to meet Jeremy, to share the horror of the mine, and to bring Jeremy's ghost to rest." A *Bulletin of the Center for Children's Books* contributor feels that "Wiseman does a good job of blending the realistic and the fantastic elements of the story, which moves with good pace and suspense."

The author also told *CA* that *Thimbles* "is another story in which a modern child, Catherine Aitken, is caught up in events of the past, events associated with the struggle for universal suffrage in Britain in the early nineteenth century. It tells, through the eyes of two children of the time, the tale of the Peterloo Massacre, when, in August, 1819, a peaceful demonstration was attacked and dispersed by government troops." But "although the historical background of the fantasy sections of this time-slip story is vivid, the fusion of fantasy and reality is less smooth here than it was in the author's Jeremy Visick," writes a contributor in another issue of *Bulletin of the Center for Children's Books.* "The separate parts of the story don't quite blend, and the writing style sags intermittently." However, Susan Ashburner in the *Times Literary Supplement* defends the book as "more demanding than its appearance suggests. Its language is vivid, with a wide-ranging vocabulary." She adds, however, that "the significance of the historical events in the novel might also be difficult [for children] to grasp. . . . Guidance by a sympathetic adult is needed, if the book is to be read at anything other than a superficial level."

Blodwen and the Guardians concerns the "invisible, indefinable, spirits set to guard the tombs of warriors of times long past," the author continues. "A construction company plans to drive a road through the center of the tomb, to the horror of the Guardians and the dismay of Blodwen, a girl who lives in a cottage near the tomb. The story tells how Blodwen and the Guardians combine to frustrate the road-builders and save the ancient ways." Margaret J. Porter in the *Voice of Youth Advocates* considers the beginning of *Blodwen* "a bit slow," but adds that "once you get swept up in the story, it is captivating and well done. There is a good combination of magic and suspense, as well as a twist in a good science fiction plot."

BIOGRAPHICAL/CRITICAL SOURCES:

PERIODICALS

Bulletin of the Center for Children's Books, September, 1981, July/August, 1982.
Times Literary Supplement, November 25, 1983, April 7-13, 1989.
Voice of Youth Advocates, June, 1984.

*   *   *

WITHERS, Carl A. 1900-1970
(Robert North, James West)

PERSONAL: Born March 20, 1900, near Sheldon, Mo.; died January 5, 1970. *Education:* Harvard University, B.A.; graduate study, Columbia University.

CAREER: Writer and researcher in the fields of anthropology and folklore.

MEMBER: American Folklore Society, American Anthropological Society.

WRITINGS:

(Under pseudonym James West) *Plainville, U.S.A.,* Columbia University Press, 1945, reprinted, Greenwood Press, 1970.
(With Alta Jablow) *Rainbow in the Morning,* Abelard-Schuman, 1956.
(Under pseudonym James West, with Abram Kardiner, Ralph Linton, and Cora Du Bois) *The Psychological Frontiers of*

Society, Columbia University Press, 1959, reprinted, Greenwood Press, 1981.

Ready or Not, Here I Come, Grosset, 1964, published as *A Treasury of Games,* 1969.

(Adapter) *The Tale of a Black Cat,* Holt, 1966.

(Adapter) *The Wild Ducks and the Goose,* Holt, 1968.

(Reteller) *Painting the Moon: A Folktale from Estonia,* Dutton, 1970.

(Reteller) *The Grindstone of God: A Fable,* Holt, 1970.

EDITOR

The Penguin Book of Sonnets, Penguin Books, 1943.

Counting Out, Oxford University Press, 1946, published as *Eenie, Meenie, Minie, Mo and Other Counting-Out Rhymes,* Dover, 1970.

(Under pseudonym Robert North) *Town and Country Games,* Crowell, 1947.

A Rocket in My Pocket: The Rhymes and Chants of Young Americans, Henry Holt, 1948, reprinted, 1988.

(Under pseudonym Robert North) *The Treasure Book of Riddles,* Grosset, 1950.

(With Sula Benet) *The American Riddle Book,* Abelard, 1954.

(With Benet) *Riddles of Many Lands,* Abelard, 1956.

(With Ben Botkin) *The Illustrated Book of American Folklore: Stories, Legends, Tall Tales, Riddles, and Rhymes,* Grosset, 1958.

I Saw a Rocket Walk a Mile: Nonsense Tales, Chants, and Songs from Many Lands, Holt, 1965.

A World of Nonsense: Strange and Humorous Tales from Many Lands, Holt, 1968.

(With Jablow) *The Man in the Moon: Sky Tales from Many Lands,* Holt, 1969.*

*   *   *

WODGE, Dreary
  See GOREY, Edward (St. John)

*   *   *

WOLFE, Richard J(ames) 1928-

PERSONAL: Born May 7, 1928, in Pittsburgh, Pa.; son of Francis A. and Helen B. (Miller) Wolf; married Elin Lando, October 30, 1950; children: Gordon V., Roger F., Cecily J. *Education:* University of Pittsburgh, A.B., 1949, graduate study, 1954-55; Carnegie Institute of Technology (now Carnegie-Mellon University), M.L.S., 1954.

ADDRESSES: Home—51 Royce Rd., Newton Centre, Mass. 02159. *Office*—Francis A. Countway Library, Library of Medicine, Harvard University, Cambridge, Mass. 02115.

CAREER: Carnegie Library, Pittsburgh, Pa., supervisor of pages and clerk in department of music, 1947-49; University of Pittsburgh, Pittsburgh, research librarian in reference department and science-technology librarian, 1954-56; New York Public Library, New York, N.Y., assistant in reference department, 1956-64; Indiana University, Bloomington, reference librarian and rare book cataloger at Lilly Library, 1964-65; Harvard University, Cambridge, Mass., rare books librarian at Francis A. Countway Library, 1965-76, curator of rare books and manuscripts at Countway Library and Joseph Garland Librarian of Boston Medical Library, both 1976—. Editor and publisher of Countway Library Associates. Lecturer at Simmons College, 1966-70; A. S. W. Rosenbach Fellow in Bibliography at University of Pennsylvania, 1981; Lewis Wright Memorial Lecturer, American Society of Anesthesiologists, 1986. Member of Bibliographical Society of the University of Virginia. Organizer of symposia. Adviser to Hanna Foundation. *Military service:* U.S. Air Force, intelligence language officer, 1950-53; served in Europe; became first lieutenant.

MEMBER: Bibliographical Society of America, Printing Historical Society, American Antiquarian Society, Sonneck Society, Bibliographical Society (England), Colonial Society of Massachusetts.

AWARDS, HONORS: Grant from American Philosophical Society, 1964; grants from American Council of Learned Societies, 1965 and 1982.

WRITINGS:

(Contributor) *Parthenia In-Violata: A Facsimile of a Seventeenth-Century English Music Book,* New York Public Library, 1961.

(Compiler) *Secular Music in America, 1801-1825: A Bibliography,* three volumes, New York Public Library, 1964.

(Editor) Harold Lancour, *A Bibliography of Ship Passenger Lists, 1538-1825,* revised edition (Wolfe was not associated with previous edition), New York Public Library, 1966.

(Associate editor) *A Concordance to the Writings of William Blake,* two volumes, Cornell University Press, 1967.

(Editor, illustrator, and author of introduction), James Sumner, *The Mysterious Marbler,* Bird & Bull Press, 1976.

(Compiler) *Jacob Bigelow's American Medical Botany, 1817-1821: An Examination of the Origin, Printing, Binding, and Distribution of America's First Color Plate Book, with Special Emphasis on the Manner of Making and Printing Its Color Plates,* Bird & Bull Press, 1979.

(Editor, translator, illustrator, and author of introduction) Franz Weisse, *The Art of Marbling,* Bird & Bull Press, 1980.

(Compiler) *Early American Music Engraving and Printing: A History of Music Publishing in America from 1787 to 1825, with Commentary on Earlier and Later Practices,* University of Illinois Press, 1980.

(Compiler) *The Role of the Mann Family of Dedham, Massachusetts, in the Marbling of Paper in Nineteenth-Century America, and in the Printing of Music, the Making of Cards, and Other Booktrade Activities,* privately printed, 1981.

(Editor) *On Improvements in Marbling the Edges of Books and Paper: A Nineteenth-Century Marbling Account Explained and Illustrated with Fourteen Original Marbled Samples,* Bird & Bull Press, 1983.

(With Benjamin V. White and Eugene Taylor) *Stanley Cobb, a Builder of the Modern Neurosciences,* Francis Countway, 1984.

(Contributor) *Studies on Voltaire,* Voltaire Foundation, 1984.

(With Paul McKenna) *The Contribution of Louis H. Kinder to Fine Bookbinding in America: A Chapter in the History of the Roycroft Press,* Bird & Bull Press, 1985.

(Translator, illustrator, and author of introduction) *Three Early French Essays on Paper Marbling, 1642-1765,* Bird & Bull Press, 1987.

(Illustrator and author of introduction) *The Whole Art of Bookbinding, the Whole Process of Marbling Paper, Reprinted from the Original Editions,* W. Thomas Taylor, 1987.

Marbled Paper, History, Techniques, Patterns: With Special Reference to the Relationship of Marbling to Bookbinding in Europe and the Western World, University of Pennsylvania Press, 1989.

Robert C. Hinckley and the Painting of the First Operation under Ether, Francis Countway, 1989.

Also translator, illustrator, and author of introduction, *The Marbling Art, or Directions for the Making of Combed and Turkish Paper for Bookbinding,* by J. A. F. Schade, 1989.

*   *   *

WOOD, Charles T(uttle) 1933-

PERSONAL: Born October 29, 1933, in St. Paul, Minn.; son of Harold Eaton (an investment banker) and Margaret (Frisbie) Wood; married Susan L. Danielson, July 9, 1955; children: Lucy Eaton, Timothy Walker, Martha Augusta, Mary Frisbie. *Education:* Harvard University, A.B., 1955, A.M., 1957, Ph.D., 1962.

ADDRESSES: Home—7 North Balch St., Hanover, N.H. 03755. *Agent*—Gerald F. McCauley, 141 East 44 St., Apt. 208, New York, N.Y. 10017.

CAREER: Investment trader with Harold E. Wood & Co., St. Paul, Minn., 1955-56, and First Boston Corp., Boston, Mass., 1957; Harvard University, Cambridge, Mass., instructor in history, 1961-64; Dartmouth College, Hanover, N.H., assistant professor, 1964-67, associate professor, 1967-71, professor, 1971-80, Daniel Webster Professor of History, 1980—, chairman of history department, 1976-79, chairman of comparative literature, 1977. Second vice president, New Hampshire School Boards Association, 1974-75.

MEMBER: American Historical Association (chairman, nominating committee, 1977; member, Adams Prize committee, 1976-78), Medieval Academy of America (fellow; member, finance committee, 1979—, council, 1985-87), Conference on British Studies, New England Medieval Conference (president, 1978-79), American Society of Legal History, Society for French Historical Studies, Phi Beta Kappa.

AWARDS, HONORS: Distinguished service award, New Hampshire School Boards Association, 1975; fellowships from American Council of Learned Societies, 1980-81, and American Bar Association, 1981-82; Guggenheim fellow, 1986-87.

WRITINGS:

The French Apanages and the Capetian Monarchy, 1224-1328, Harvard University Press, 1966.
Philip the Fair and Boniface VIII, Holt, 1967, 2nd edition, 1971.
The Age of Chivalry: Manners and Morals, 1000-1450, Weidenfeld & Nicolson, 1970, published as *The Quest for Eternity: Manners and Morals in the Age of Chivalry,* University Press of New England, 1983.
Joan of Arc and Richard III: Sex, Saints, and Government in the Middle Ages, Oxford University Press, 1988.

Contributor to *American Historical Review, Speculum, History and Theory, French Historical Studies, Journal of British Studies,* and *Traditio.*

WORK IN PROGRESS: A monograph on political applications of Arthurian mythology.

SIDELIGHTS: Philip the Fair and Boniface VIII has been translated into Spanish and published in Mexico. Professor Wood is competent in French, Latin and German.

*   *   *

WOOD, Elizabeth A(rmstrong) 1912-

PERSONAL: Born October 19, 1912, in New York, N.Y.; daughter of Herbert Ralph (a dentist) and Winona (Hull) Armstrong; married Ira E. Wood (a retired electrical engineer), May 13, 1947. *Education:* Barnard College, B.A., 1933; Bryn Mawr College, M.A., 1934, Ph.D., 1939.

ADDRESSES: Home—17 Alston Ct., Red Bank, N.J. 07701.

CAREER: Columbia University, Barnard College, New York, N.Y., instructor in geology, 1935-37, 1938-41, research assistant in mineralogy, 1941-42, National Research Council fellow, 1942-43; Bryn Mawr College, Bryn Mawr, Pa., instructor in geology, 1937-38; Bell Telephone Laboratories, Murray Hill, N.J., research physicist (crystallographer), 1943-67. Chair of U.S. National Committee for Crystallography and of U.S. delegation to International Union of Crystallography Assembly, 1957.

MEMBER: American Crystallographic Association (president, 1957), American Physical Society (fellow), American Association of Physics Teachers, Sigma Xi, Phi Beta Kappa, American Iris Society, Appalachian Mountain Club.

AWARDS, HONORS: D.Sc., Wheaton College, Norton, Mass., 1963, Western College for Women, 1965, and Worcester Polytechnic Institute, 1970; distinguished service citation, American Association of Physics Teachers, 1970.

WRITINGS:

Crystal Orientation Manual, Columbia University Press, 1963.
Crystals and Light: An Introduction to Optical Crystallography, Van Nostrand, 1964, 2nd revised edition, Dover, 1977.
Experiments with Crystals and Light, Bell Telephone Laboratories, 1964.
The 80 Diperiodic Groups in Three Dimensions, Bell Telephone Laboratories, 1964.
Science for the Airplane Passenger, Houghton, 1968, 2nd revised edition published as *Science from Your Airplane Window,* Dover, 1975.
(With others) *Pressing Needs in School Science,* American Institute of Physics, 1969.
(With others) *An Approach to Physical Science: Physical Science for Nonscience Students,* Wiley, 1969.
Crystals: A Handbook for School Teachers, Polycrystal Book Service, 1972.
(With others) *Modular Approach to Physical Science,* Houghton, 1974.

AVOCATIONAL INTERESTS: Hybridizing irises, sailing.

*   *   *

WOODHOUSE, Barbara (Blackburn) 1910-1988

PERSONAL: Born May 9, 1910, in Rathfarnham, County Dublin, Ireland; died July 9, 1988, after a second stroke in Buckinghamshire, England; daughter of William (a clergyman headmaster) and Leilah (Masterman) Blackburn; married Michael Woodhouse (a physician), August 7, 1940; children: Pamela, Judith, Patrick. *Education:* Harper Adams Agricultural College, Certificate in Agriculture, 1930. *Politics:* Conservative. *Religion:* Protestant.

ADDRESSES: Home—Campions, Croxley Green, Rickmansworth, Hertfordshire, WD3 3JD England.

CAREER: Dog and horse trainer; television personality; writer. Researcher for Ministry of Agriculture, 1931-33; affiliated with Liebigs Co., Argentina, 1934-37. Director, Barbara Woodhouse & Junia Ltd. (film company), and producer of films, including "Trouble for Juno," "Juno Makes Friends," "Juno the Home Help," "A Star Is Made," "Sinner to Saint," "School for Problem Dogs," "Career with Dogs," "Sing a Song of Sixpence," "Trouble with Junia," "Love Me, Love My Dog," and "Along the Way." Star of British Broadcasting Corp. (BBC) television series, "Training Dogs the Woodhouse Way" and a series on horses and ponies; star of television special programs; guest personality on numerous television and radio programs and at public appearances throughout the world.

AWARDS, HONORS: Numerous awards for work on television, including Pye Colour Television award as the female television "Personality of the Year," 1980, the Multi-Coloured Swap-Shop Star Award, 1980-81, and BBC Children's Television recognition as viewers' "Favourite Lady."

WRITINGS:

Talking to Animals (autobiography), Faber (London), 1954, Norton (New York), 1955, new edition, Faber, 1970, Stein & Day, 1972.
Dog Training My Way, Faber, 1954, new edition, 1970, Stein & Day, 1972.
Chica: The Story of a Very Little Dog, Faber, 1955.
The A-Z of Dogs and Puppies, Parrish, 1956, Stein & Day, 1972.
The Girl Book of Ponies, Parrish, 1956, Stein & Day, 1972.
Difficult Dogs, Faber, 1957.
The Book of Show Dogs, Parrish, 1957.
The Barbara Woodhouse Book of Dogs, Longacre, 1957.
The A-Z of Dogs, Parrish, 1958.
Wendy: The Story of a Horse, Parrish, 1959.
(Author of introduction) *Dogs in Colour,* Batsford, 1960, Viking (New York), 1960.
Know Your Dog: Psychiatry or Sense? (also see below), Parrish, 1961.
The A-Z of Puppies, Parrish, 1962.
Almost Human (autobiography), Woodhouse, 1976, Penguin, 1981.
The World of Dogs, Cartwell Books, 1976.
(Author of foreword) *All about Dogs,* Octopus, 1976.
No Bad Dogs [and] *Know Your Dog* (also see below), Woodhouse, 1978.
Encyclopedia of Dogs and Puppies, Stein & Day, 1978.
Just Barbara: My Story (autobiography), M. Joseph, 1981, Summit Books, 1986.
No Bad Dogs: The Woodhouse Way, edited by J. Silberman and P. Tsubahira, Summit Books, 1982.
Walkies: Dog Care the Woodhouse Way, Benn, 1982, Summit Books, 1983.
The Arco Color Book of Dogs, Arco, 1983.
Barbara's World of Horses and Ponies, Summit Books, 1984.

Also author of *Walkies,* a picture book for children; author of privately printed books, *Talking in Spanish, Talking in German, Talking in French,* and *Talking in Italian,* all published in 1961.

WORK IN PROGRESS: Forward with a Stroke, a book on her recuperation from a stroke, for Summit Books and Weidenfeld & Nicolson.

SIDELIGHTS: Man's best friend reserved worship and adoration for English dog trainer and author Barbara Woodhouse, Gerald Clarke once remarked in *Time.* While Woodhouse's dog training career dates back to early childhood, she first gained worldwide acclaim at age seventy as star of the BBC television series, "Training Dogs the Woodhouse Way." Shouting orders to the human and canine students in her obedience classes, she resembled "a British school mistress or perhaps a well-heeled drill sergeant," punned the *Christian Science Monitor*'s Diane Casselberry Manuel. Viewed throughout the world, the shows

presented Woodhouse's practical, often acerbic advice on how to turn unruly pets into pleasant companions. Comments Clarke: "The dogs appear to be enjoying themselves; the owners, a dozen or so terror-stricken men and women, do not. That, of course, is where all the fun lies for the viewer, in the comic reversal of the customary roles of man and beast."

Maintaining that "there is no such thing as a difficult dog, only an inexperienced owner," Woodhouse claimed it takes most dogs only five or ten minutes to learn basic obedience—to sit, stay, heel and come. Their owners, on the other hand, presented a greater challenge. Week after week, the bumbling humans made mistakes—holding leashes improperly, getting the commands wrong—only to meet with sharp reprimands from their instructor. Accused of tongue-lashing the hapless handlers on the air, Woodhouse explained to Caroline Thompson in the *Los Angeles Times:* "It's a fun scold. My tongue is in my cheek. I couldn't stand it otherwise because, you see, the people do so many stupid things so many times that unless you have a joke about it, you'd be tearing your hair out, wouldn't you? Even if the people look like they're hanging their heads, they're not, really: They know perfectly well it's all a joke. And the dogs love it. There's nothing a dog likes better than a good laugh."

Laughter, some critics claim, forms the basis of Woodhouse's appeal. Labeled "the most original—and unconventionally funny—female personality since Julia Child" by Clarke and according to Manuel, "the first genuine hoot of the eighties" by a London *Daily Mail* writer, Woodhouse presented her subject earnestly while tolerating—even cultivating—an eccentric image that attracted followers wherever she went. During interviews and guest appearances her comments were "a little arrogant, a little batty, eminently practical, unswervingly frank and, at moments, totally absurd," Thompson contends. Always ready with unusual or amusing anecdotes, the animal expert possessed a talent for recognizing and meeting her audience's expectations. She once related in a *People* interview, for instance: "I love spiders. For years we had a pet spider. He had a hole in the fireplace and used to come out at night and sit on my lap and watch the telly." And, disliking the standard obedience command "heel," the trainer promoted an exuberant, sing-song "walkies!" The word has become a Woodhouse trademark, the title of her comic-strip picture book for young readers, and the target of much satire. "But as long as it makes people laugh, I don't mind," Woodhouse told Thompson. "You see, this is the joy of the word 'walkies.' Everybody says it and then shrieks with laughter. I don't have to amuse them, they amuse themselves."

While her approach may have seemed light-hearted, Woodhouse made it clear that her best-selling books, television programs, and personal appearances comprised a serious campaign to make every dog "a decent member of society and a joy to own." At a time when increasing numbers of people charge high fees as dog psychologists, the trainer stated that "a lot of rubbish has been spoken about the psychoanalyzing of dogs in the modern world, and having now trained over 17,000 dogs in twenty years, I feel I am qualified to express an opinion on the subject of dog behavior." In the introduction to *No Bad Dogs: The Woodhouse Way,* she went on to emphasize that "psychoanalysis is impossible . . . since [dogs] cannot answer questions and the concepts of their minds cannot be recalled and probed and changed, cast out or anything else." Instead, the author relied on common sense and ESP to assess difficult dogs. She approached recalcitrant canines by tuning in on their mental wavelength; then, she maintained, it's simply a matter of training with firmness, fairness, and fun. "Telepathy, on the part of dog and owner, plays a vast part in the happy companionship between dog and mankind," she wrote. Woodhouse once summarized for the *Los Angeles Times*'s Ursula Vils: "It doesn't matter what the words are: One day I ran a whole lesson in vegetables; I said 'potatoes' and 'carrots' instead of 'sit' and 'heel.' It's the tone of your voice, your touch. I use three things: touch, tone and telepathy."

Much of the star's reputation as a miracle-worker stems from impromptu demonstrations of "the Woodhouse way." As an awestruck owner stands aside, the trainer commandeers the leash and reforms the four-footed delinquent in less time than it takes to say "*What* a clever dog" (her favorite words of praise). The magic is worked by getting "simpatico," giving a few jerks on a large-link chain choke collar, and using firm commands and hand gestures. Anyone with "a working knowledge of dogs," Woodhouse admitted in *No Bad Dogs,* could do the same: "A human personality can be so powerful that it can make a dog do and think things almost by hypnotism, just as a good actress can carry the audience to the height of happiness or despair with the part she is playing. But when the curtain drops, the atmosphere fades and the audience returns to its mundane affairs. That is why I have refused and shall continue to refuse to take dogs to train without their owners. I know I can make a dog do almost exactly as I wish when alone with it. . . . But will a dog that carries out orders with army-like precision for me, with evident joy on its face, do the same for an owner who may be out of tune with the dog, either from lack of experience or sympathy, or from being just plain stupid, conceited or pigheaded? I know it won't."

In addition to ignorance, selfishness, and stubbornness, Woodhouse identified sentimentality and lack of imagination as the human foibles owners must overcome to succeed in dog training. "Love is one thing; sentimentality is another," she wrote. "Dogs like firm commands and loving praise. . . . Owners fail to realize that if they use firm, confident, kind jerks and a happy tone of voice, most dogs can be cured . . . in a few hours." A good jerk on the large-link chain collar makes a distinct "click" but doesn't hurt the dog, Woodhouse told her students. Disagreeing with many animal behaviorists, she also maintained that the "sky's the limit" when training the household pet. Convinced that dogs can attain the vocabulary of a five-year-old child, she urged people to teach their canine family members as many tasks as possible. Assign a new chore each day, she suggested, pointing out that dogs, like humans, get bored. Left by themselves, they will find their own—often destructive—activities.

Although "the dog lady" (as she was known in Britain) enjoyed an "obscure" history before winning fame at age seventy, according to Roy Fuller in the *Listener,* her youth and early adulthood were not uneventful. "Born . . . into the comfortably-off middle class . . . the death of her father when she was nine made her early life more unconventional than it otherwise would have been (though convention could never have ruled her)," Fuller writes. One of Woodhouse's earliest memories, not surprisingly, is of her first dog. At the age of two she was bitten on the nose by the pup—a mongrel bought from a gypsy. The unpropitious start, she told interviewers, was her own fault. She simply hugged the dog too tightly. Several years later she rescued a pit bull from the Battersea dog pound, smuggled it home on a bus, trained it to be a proper pet, and found it a good home. She's been training animals ever since.

A love of horses likewise began in childhood, when army mounts grazed at the Irish college where her father was headmaster. Woodhouse's interest in training horses eventually took her to Argentina, where she learned the Indians' trick of breathing into a wild pony's nose to tame it. Once you "speak" to a horse in this native language, he'll follow you anywhere, Woodhouse proclaimed. Not content to limit the application of her "God-given gift," as she called it in *People,* Woodhouse also trained a pig on a live television program and a praying mantis during a tour of Africa.

Woodhouse's autobiography *Talking to Animals,* first published in 1954, documents her pre-celebrity days. In addition to relating childhood experiences, it tells behind-the-scenes tales of her career as a motion picture animal trainer. Most famous of her animal proteges were Juno and Junia, Great Danes she owned and trained. The dogs starred in innumerable television and movie productions, including feature films made by the trainer's own cinema company. Commenting on *Talking to Animals,* Fuller notes that "there are a good few useful hints about life . . . besides such general social information as how to . . . in a simple way increase milk-yield in cattle." He concludes: "The force of her narrative is such that one's opinion of Douglas Fairbanks Jr. goes up when one learns that her cow, Snow Queen, fell in love with him, and he is commended for his 'gentle behaviour with her'."

Reviewers of her dog books similarly feel that Woodhouse's personality and the energetic, candid presentation of her ideas offer an interesting experience for readers. Not all critics, however, approve of the training techniques she expounded. Her bestselling *No Bad Dogs,* for example, is "not particularly strong or systematic in describing a specific training program," according to a *Booklist* writer. Commenting in *Library Journal,* Linda Johnson of the Kennels of Wunderland states that Woodhouse tells readers where dogs' problems originate but "never really outlines the steps necessary to correct the problems." Johnson goes on to recommend other authors for "better advice" on training. Even reviewers who find fault with her methods, however, commend Woodhouse for educating the public by encouraging obedience training and pet population control. As they point out, she promotes an attitude beneficial to dogs, their owners, and the community in general by urging dog lovers to make their pets "a joy to own and a nuisance to no one." Woodhouse's unique approach to her subject combines with man's allegiance to his "best friend," observers believe, to insure success. Woodhouse herself attributed much of her popularity to her canine co-stars and the fact that most people are attracted to dogs out of curiosity, love, or both. A London *Times* contributor cites her comment that "dogs do more for people than people do for one another. They don't ask for anything in return. They are not part of today's great 'I want.'" When Julie Rovner in the *Washington Post* asked Woodhouse, "What is it about dogs that so fascinates their owners?" the author summed up: "I think it's the deep adoration you get from a dog that's really trained and looks upon you as the be-all and end-all. There's nothing so flattering. It doesn't matter if your hair needs washing or you've got a sore throat or you're really ghastly to look at. It doesn't matter. The dog loves you. And isn't that nice?"

BIOGRAPHICAL/CRITICAL SOURCES:

BOOKS

Woodhouse, Barbara, *Talking to Animals,* Faber (London), 1954, Norton (New York), 1955, new edition, Faber, 1970, Stein & Day (New York), 1972.

Woodhouse, Barbara, *Almost Human,* Woodhouse, 1976, Penguin, 1981.

Woodhouse, Barbara, *Just Barbara: My Story,* M. Joseph, 1981, Summit Books, 1986.

Woodhouse, Barbara, *No Bad Dogs: The Woodhouse Way,* Summit Books, 1982.

PERIODICALS

Booklist, February 1, 1982.
Chicago Sun Times, October 19, 1983.
Chicago Tribune, January 4, 1987.
Christian Science Monitor, May 13, 1982.
Kirkus Reviews, November 1, 1972, December 15, 1972, February 1, 1974.
Library Journal, March 15, 1973, June 1, 1974, April 15, 1982.
Listener, September 25, 1980.
Los Angeles Times, March 14, 1982, February 9, 1984, June 17, 1984.
Minnesota Daily, January 17, 1983.
New York Times Book Review, January 30, 1983, November 9, 1986.
Observer, December 5, 1982.
People, February 15, 1982.

Publishers Weekly, January 28, 1974, February 19, 1982.
Time, March 12, 1973, December 7, 1981.
Times Educational Supplement, September 4, 1981, October 1, 1982.
Washington Post, February 8, 1982.

OBITUARIES:

PERIODICALS

New York Times, July 11, 1988.
Times (London), July 8, 1988.*

*   *   *

WRYDE, Dogear
   See GOREY, Edward (St. John)

Y

YAGER, Jan 1948-
(J. L. Barkas, Janet Barkas)

PERSONAL: Born December 16, 1948, in Manhattan, N.Y.; daughter of William (a dentist) and Gladys Rose (a teacher; maiden name, Hodes) Barkas; married Fred Yager. *Education:* Hofstra University, B.A., 1970; Goddard College, M.A., 1977; City University of New York Graduate Center, Ph.D., 1983.

ADDRESSES: Office—P.O. Box 20218, Cherokee Station, N.Y. 10028.

CAREER: Macmillan Co., New York City, assistant editor, 1971-73; Grove Press, New York City, editor, 1973-74; Marymount Manhattan College, Manhattan, N.Y., coordinator of Crime Prevention Resource Center, 1978-79; free-lance writer. Lecturer, New School for Social Research, fall, 1973, 1975; visiting professor, Penn State University, spring, 1981; associate professor, New York Institute of Technology, 1983-85. Exhibitor of collages, paintings, and drawings, 1976.

MEMBER: PEN, Authors Guild, Dramatists Guild, Authors League of America, American Society of Journalists and Authors, American Sociological Association, National Organization on Victim Assistance, National Association of Professional Organizers.

WRITINGS:

UNDER NAME J. L. BARKAS

Victims, Scribner, 1978.
The Help Book: A Guide for Your Survival, Scribner, 1979.
Single in America, Atheneum, 1980.
Creative Time Management: Become More Productive and Still Have Time for Fun, Prentice-Hall, 1984.
How to Write Like a Professional, Arco, 1985.
Friendship: A Selected Annotated Bibliography, Garland Publishing, 1985.

OTHER

(Under name Janet Barkas) *The Vegetable Passion: A History of the Vegetarian State of Mind,* Scribner, 1975.
(Under name Janet Barkas) *Meatless Cooking: Celebrity Style,* Grove, 1975.
Making Your Office Work for You, Doubleday, 1989.

Contributor, sometimes under name J. L. Barkas, to *New York Times, Harper's, Family Circle, McCall's, Woman's Day, Modern Bride,* and other periodicals. Drama critic, *Backstage,* 1972-79.

SIDELIGHTS: The mugging of her older brother in 1969 and unsatisfactory reactions from authorities and friends to his death led Jan Yager (the former J. L. Barkas) to devote several years to studying criminology and the effects of violent crime on its victims. "My family and I learned that the violation committed by the criminal is only the first victimization," Yager relates in *Victims,* her analysis of how the casualties of crime are treated. "There are others, just as devastating, perpetrated by society and the criminal justice system. If I spoke about my brother's murder, people recoiled," the author explained. "They didn't empathize, they didn't sympathize, they didn't get angry. They said, 'Well, why was he walking down that street?' 'What time of night was it?' They acted as though Seth had done something wrong, as though I were now doing something wrong to mourn him or to be angry." Yager proposes that most people tend to blame victims in order to feel that crime is something avoidable, rather than a random act. "This may be one of the most shocking, outrageous, and terrifying books you will read this year," asserts *Best Sellers* contributor John L. Stubing. "It is shocking because it shows the true dimensions of a problem we already know to be out of control; it is outrageous because it reveals how poorly we cope with this menace; and it is terrifying because it's about *us.*"

Besides recounting numerous interviews with victims and their families, Yager "records the shocking fact that modern society had virtually no mechanisms for compensating victims until 1964, and shows that there has been a less than overwhelming growth of compassion since then," comments Jay Becker in the *Washington Post.* The author also provides data on the inadequacy of the few victim compensation programs that exist, as well as statistics concerning violent crime. The critic thinks, however, that there is a lack of information about possible solutions. But Stubing believes that *Victims* "is certainly more than an indictment of our system, because [Yager] shows what positive things are being done to alter our sad course. This is no dry scholarly work," the critic continues, for Yager "writes with a restrained passion which smolders throughout." Becker similarly notes that "at her best [the author] recreates the emotions of the victim (and the secondary victim) with a directness and clarity that is impossible to ignore." The critic concludes that "short of working in a crisis center, it is hard to find as poignant and piercing a cry for victims' rights as in [this] book."

Yager recently told *CA* that for her recent book, *Making Your Office Work for You,* "I worked 'undercover' as a temporary in a variety of office settings as well as interviewing and surveying hundreds of office workers and experts in a variety of jobs and occupations. I applied my sociologist's eye and my journalist's skill to seeing the office as a place that should be an extension of who we are, as well as the work we do. One of the key themes to the book is that we all have more control over where we work than we think, whether that is a small workstation in a huge corporation, a corner office with a window in a medium-sized company, or the dining room table in a suburban home. The book covers everything from design, lighting, and organization to health concerns such as indoor air pollution, organizing for safety and less stress.

"In all my books, including my new book on friendship, developed from my dissertation but greatly expanded over the next years, I am committed to helping people take more control over their lives and relationships. I think you can write popular books that are still provocative and solid." Yager added that in addition to writing, "I enjoy giving seminars and workshops related to my various areas of expertise."

AVOCATIONAL INTERESTS: Travel, painting, drawing, cooking, movies, theater.

BIOGRAPHICAL/CRITICAL SOURCES:

BOOKS

Barkas, J. L., *Victims,* Scribner, 1978.

PERIODICALS

Best Sellers, August, 1978.
Chicago Tribune, August 27, 1989.
People, April 30, 1979.
Washington Post, July 17, 1978.

*   *   *

YATES, Frances A(melia)   1899-1981

PERSONAL: Born November 28, 1899, in Portsmouth, England; died September 29, 1981; daughter of James Alfred (a naval architect) and Hannah (Malpas) Yates. *Education:* University of London, B.A., 1924, M.A., 1926, D. Lit., 1967.

ADDRESSES: Office—Warburg Institute, Woburn Square, London WC1H 0AB, England. *Agent*—A. D. Peters & Co., 10 Buckingham St., London WC2N 6BU, England.

CAREER: Private research, writing, and teaching in London, England, 1926-39; University of London, Warburg Institute, London, part-time research assistant, 1941-44, lecturer in Renaissance culture and editor of publications, 1944-56, reader in history of the Renaissance, 1956-67, honorary fellow, 1967-81. Honorary fellow, Lady Margaret Hall, Oxford University, 1970-81; fellow, Society of Humanities of Cornell University. *Wartime service:* Ambulance attendant in London, England, 1939-41.

MEMBER: British Academy (fellow), Royal Society of London (fellow), American Academy of Arts and Sciences (honorary foreign member), Royal Netherlands Academy of Arts and Sciences (foreign member), University Women's Club, V.A.D. Ladies Club.

AWARDS, HONORS: Rose Mary Crawshay Prize, British Academy, 1934, for *John Florio: The Life of an Italian in Shakespeare's England;* Litt.D., University of Edinburgh, 1969, Oxford University, 1970, University of Exeter, 1971, University of East Anglia, 1971, and University of Warwick, 1981; awarded Order of the British Empire, 1972; Wolfson Prize, Wolfson Foundation, 1973, for historical writing; named Dame of the British Empire, 1977.

WRITINGS:

John Florio: The Life of an Italian in Shakespeare's England, Cambridge University Press, 1934, reprinted, Octagon Books, 1968.
A Study of Love's Labour's Lost, Cambridge University Press, 1936, reprinted, Folcroft Press, 1969.
The French Academies of the Sixteenth Century, Warburg Institute, University of London, 1947, reprinted, Kraus Reprinting, 1968.
The Valois Tapestries, Warburg Institute, University of London, 1959.
Giordano Bruno and the Hermetic Tradition, University of Chicago Press, 1964.
The Art of Memory, University of Chicago Press, 1966.
Theatre of the World, University of Chicago Press, 1969.
The Rosicrucian Enlightenment, Routledge & Kegan Paul, 1972.
Astraea: The Imperial Theme, Routledge & Kegan Paul, 1975.
Shakespeare's Last Plays, Routledge & Kegan Paul, 1975.
The Occult Philosophy in the Elizabethan Age, Routledge & Kegan Paul, 1979.
Collected Essays, Routledge & Kegan Paul, Volume 1: *Lull and Bruno,* 1982, Volume 2: *Renaissance and Reform: The Italian Contribution,* 1983, Volume 3: *Ideas and Ideals in the North European Renaissance,* 1984.

Contributor to professional journals. Editor, *Journal of the Warburg and Courtauld Institutes,* 1943-81.

SIDELIGHTS: Through her unique approach to historical study, Frances A. Yates "had a way of altering all one's ideas on her subject, whatever it may be," Rosalie L. Colie wrote in *Comparative Literature,* "and of readjusting all one's ideas on everyone's subject—the Renaissance." Yates focused her historical studies on Renaissance movements involving hermeticism and the Rosicrucians; these movements emphasized the mystical, magical, and psychic aspects of human existence. In illuminating these sixteenth and seventeenth century schools of thought, Yates dealt "with ideas, both in their relatively 'pure' history, and in their social and (especially) their intellectual contexts," noted Colie. In her body of work, the critic added, Yates ranged "over languages and disciplines normally kept separate, to make a cultural recreation of considerable scope." *New York Review of Books* contributor Wylie Sypher offered a similar assessment: "Over the years in a sequence of profoundly researched books [Yates] has been doing nothing less than reinterpreting the nature of Renaissance humanism. Indeed, she has gone far to prove that there were two different Renaissance humanisms: . . . the first academic and stylistic, the other magical and astral."

In *Theatre of the World,* for example, Yates proposed that many of London's theaters, including Shakespeare's Globe, were built with cosmological and mystical requirements in mind. While Vincent Cronin faulted some of the author's arguments, he admitted in *Book World* that Yates "has nevertheless written a penetrating book which throws a spotlight on Renaissance thought, in particular on certain dare-devil dreamers who dabbled in a no man's land between science and magic." Although they may not convince, the critic continued, "her arguments will act as a powerful leaven on the dullish dough of English Renaissance studies." *The Rosicrucian Enlightenment* is another of "a magnificent line of books which are revolutionising our perception of 16th-and 17th-century history," J. H. Elliott claimed in the *New Statesman,* observing that "perhaps the greatest of all Dr. Yates's achievements [was] to bring home to us what genuinely European history entails. . . . Yates has gone farther to uncover a forgotten world of like-minded men who transcended national barriers." The critic also remarked that "the history of the European community will never look quite the same again." *New Statesman* contributor Peter Burke made a similar assessment of *The Occult Philosophy in the Elizabethan Age,* and explained that the book "really scores, thanks to Dr. Yates's amazing learning, . . . in its juxtaposition of unfamiliar with familiar images and texts, juxtapositions which prompt all sorts of reinterpretations."

"[Yates] saw the past in terms of living human beings rather than of impersonal forces, and it was the way people and events were reflected in the minds of contemporaries that she strove to reconstruct through her indefatigable labors," E. H. Gombrich described in his *New York Review of Books* tribute to the historian. "What counted most for her in this work of reconstruction were human contacts and relationships, the network of friendships and hostilities that makes up the living fabric of culture." It was this approach that gave Yates's work its unique, entertaining quality and defied classification; her work, however, was also respected for its scholarly excellence, as Gombrich related: "She was recognized as the pathfinder she was; her books had made her famous, she had vindicated her faith in the historical importance of dreams and dreamers for the course of civilization." "Yates' work is so exceptionally and idiosyncratically original that it cannot really fail to delight, and where one cannot suspend disbelief, one admires all the same," Colie concluded. "Her habit has always been to reach into odd corners, and to pull out plums, peaches, pears, melons—a cornucopia of ideas, all related to fruit. Her cast of mind is unique, her industry is formidable. . . . From any book Miss Yates writes the student learns more than he ever dared bargain for."

AVOCATIONAL INTERESTS: Reading, travel.

BIOGRAPHICAL/CRITICAL SOURCES:

PERIODICALS

Book World, March 1, 1970.
Comparative Literature, spring, 1969.
New Statesman, January 27, 1967, January 26, 1973, January 17, 1975, February 1, 1980.
New York Review of Books, January 29, 1970, October 4, 1973, February 20, 1975, October 16, 1975, March 3, 1983.
Times Literary Supplement, November 10, 1966, September 4, 1969, April 20, 1973.

OBITUARIES:

PERIODICALS

AB Bookman's Weekly, November 2, 1981.
History Today, February, 1982.
Isis, September, 1982.*

*   *   *

YOUNG, Rose
   See HARRIS, Marion Rose (Young)

YOUNGBLOOD, Ronald F. 1931-

PERSONAL: Born August 10, 1931, in Chicago, Ill.; son of William C. (a banker) and Ethel (Arenz) Youngblood; married Carolyn Johnson, August 16, 1952; children: Glenn, Wendy. *Education:* Valparaiso University, B.A., 1952; Fuller Theological Seminary, B.D., 1955; Dropsie College for Hebrew and Cognate Learning, Ph.D., 1961. *Religion:* Baptist.

ADDRESSES: Office—Bethel Theological Seminary West, 6116 Arosa St., San Diego, Calif. 92115.

CAREER: Bethel Theological Seminary, St. Paul, Minn., assistant professor, 1961-65, associate professor, 1965-70, professor of Old Testament, 1970-78; Wheaton Graduate School, Wheaton, Ill., professor, 1978-81, associate dean, 1978-80, dean, 1980-81; Trinity Evangelical Divinity School, Deerfield, Ill., professor, 1981-82; Bethel Theological Seminary West, San Diego, Calif., professor, 1982—. Has spent four summers in Europe as translator-editor of the New International Version of the Old Testament, sponsored by International Bible Society.

MEMBER: International Bible Society (member of board), Society of Biblical Literature, Evangelical Theological Society, Near East Archaeological Society (member of board).

WRITINGS:

Great Themes of the Old Testament, Harvest Publications, 1968, revised edition published as *The Heart of the Old Testament,* Baker Book, 1971.
Special Day Sermons, Baker Book, 1973, revised edition, 1989.
Faith of Our Fathers, Regal Books, 1976.
How It All Began, Regal Books, 1980.
Exodus, Moody, 1983.
(Editor with Morris Inch) *The Living and Active Word of God,* Eisenbrauns, 1983.
Themes from Isaiah, Regal Books, 1983.
(Co-editor with Merrill C. Tenney) *What the Bible Is All About,* revised edition (Youngblood not associated with first edition), Regal Books, 1983.
(Editor) *Evangelicals and Inerrancy,* Thomas Nelson, 1984.
(Co-editor with Walter C. Kaiser, Jr.) *A Tribute to Gleason Archer,* Moody, 1986.
(Editor) *The Genesis Debate: Persistent Questions about Creation and the Flood,* Thomas Nelson, 1986.

Assistant editor, *Baker Encyclopedia of the Bible* (two volumes), 1988; associate editor, *New International Version Study Bible,* Zondervan, 1985; consulting editor, *Nelson's Illustrated Bible Dictionary,* 1986, and Volumes 3 and 4 of *The New International Version Interlinear Hebrew-English Old Testament,* Zondervan, 1982 and 1985; Old Testament editor, *Wycliffe Exegetical Commentary,* Moody. Contributor of numerous articles and book reviews to books and journals, including *Journal of Biblical Literature, Bulletin of American Schools of Oriental Research, Journal of the Evangelical Theological Society, Journal of the Ancient Near East Society of Columbia University,* and *Jewish Quarterly Review.* Editor, *Journal of the Evangelical Theological Society.*

WORK IN PROGRESS: A Survey of the Old Testament, with Herbert Wolf; commentaries on Old Testament books for various publishers.

SIDELIGHTS: Ronald F. Youngblood is fluent in Hebrew and has made eleven trips to the Middle East.

Z

ZEBROWSKI, George (T.) 1945-

PERSONAL: Surname is pronounced Ze-broff-ski; born December 28, 1945, in Villach, Austria; brought to the United States, 1951; naturalized United States citizen; son of Antoni and Anna (Popowicz) Zebrowski. *Education:* Attended State University of New York at Binghamton, 1964-69.

ADDRESSES: Home—P.O. Box 486, Johnson City, N.Y. 13790. *Agent*—Joseph Elder Agency, 150 West 87th St., New York, N.Y. 10024.

CAREER: Science fiction writer and editor. Binghamton *Evening Press,* Binghamton, N.Y., copy editor, 1967; filtration plant operator, New York, 1969-70; State University of New York at Binghamton, lecturer in science fiction, 1971; lecturer for Science Fiction Writers Speakers Bureau; general editor and consultant, Crown Publishers, 1983-85.

MEMBER: Science Fiction Writers of America.

AWARDS, HONORS: Finalist for Nebula Award of Science Fiction Writers of America, 1971, for short story, "Heathen God", and 1984, for short story "The Eichmann Variations"; *Sunspacer* was named outstanding book of the year by *Books for Teens,* 1984, and named a core collection book by *Anatomy of Wonder;* Theodore Sturgeon Award nomination, 1986, for short story "The Idea Trap"; *Library Journal* named *Macrolife* one of the one hundred all time best works of science fiction.

WRITINGS:

The Omega Point (second book in trilogy; also see below), Ace Books, 1972.
(Contributor) Roger Elwood, editor, *Strange Gods,* Pocket Books, 1974.
(Author of introduction) H. G. Wells, *Things to Come,* Gregg, 1975.
The Star Web, Laser Books, 1975.
(Editor) *Planet One: Tomorrow Today* (anthology), Unity Press (Santa Cruz), 1975.
(Editor with Thomas N. Scortia) *Human Machines: An Anthology of Stories about Cyborgs,* Random House, 1975.
(Editor with Jack Dann) *Faster than Light: An Anthology of Stories about Interstellar Travel,* Harper, 1976.
The Monadic Universe and Other Stories, introduction by Scortia, Ace Books, 1977, 2nd edition, introduction by Howard Waldrop, 1985.

Ashes and Stars (first book in trilogy; also see below), Ace Books, 1977.
(Contributor with Patricia Warrick) Warrick, Martin H. Greenberg, and Joseph D. Olander, editors, *Science Fiction: Contemporary Mythology,* Harper, 1978.
Macrolife (novel), Harper, 1979, reissued with an introduction by Ian Watson, Easton Press, 1989.
A Silent Shout (short stories), Educational Development Corporation, 1979.
The Firebird (short stories), Educational Development Corporation, 1979.
(Editor) *The Best of Thomas N. Scortia,* Doubleday, 1981.
(Editor with Isaac Asimov and Greenberg) *Creations: The Quest for Origins in Story and Science* (anthology), Crown, 1983.
The Omega Point Trilogy (includes *Ashes and Stars, The Omega Point,* and *Mirror of Minds*), Ace Books, 1983.
(Contributor) Michael Bishop, editor, *Light Years and Dark* (anthology; includes short story "The Eichmann Variations"), Berkley Publishing, 1984.
Sunspacer (juvenile), Harper, 1984.
The Stars Will Speak (juvenile), Harper, 1985.
(Contributor) Terry Carr, editor, *Universe 16* (anthology; includes short story "The Idea Trap"), Doubleday, 1986.
(Editor) *Nebula Awards 20,* Harcourt, 1986.
(Editor) *Nebula Awards 21,* Harcourt, 1987.
(Editor) *Synergy 1,* Harcourt, 1987.
(Editor) *Nebula Awards 22,* Harcourt, 1988.
(Editor) *Synergy 2,* Harcourt, 1988.
(Editor) *Synergy 3,* Harcourt, 1988.
(Editor) *Synergy 4,* Harcourt, 1989.

Editor of "Modern Classics of Science Fiction" series. Contributor of more than one hundred and fifty stories and articles to anthologies, including *Infinity One, Immortal,* edited by Jack Dann, 1978, and *Science Fiction: Contemporary Mythology,* 1978. Contributor of short stories, reviews, and translations to periodicals, including *Isaac Asimov's Science Fiction Magazine, Fantasy & Science Fiction, Personal Computing, Science Fiction Review,* and *Washington Post Book World.* Editor, *Bulletin of the Science Fiction Writers of America,* 1970-75, 1983—.

SIDELIGHTS: George Zebrowski has won the admiration of science fiction enthusiasts with his stories and novels that "tackle difficult problems of philosophy, technology, and sociobiology . . . to analyze their impact on human beings," notes *Dictionary of Literary Biography* contributor Anthony Manousos. "The Heathen God," a short story nominated for the Nebula Award in 1971, presents characters challenged to consider the importance of religious faith within a culture dominated by advances in science. Also a respected editor in the field, Zebrowski has contributed essays and introductions to collections of prize-winning stories and other science fiction books.

Zebrowski told *CA:* "I have been described as a 'hard SF writer with literary intent'—which makes me sound like a difficult person about to commit a crime of some sort. What 'literary' means in this description, I believe, is that I pay attention to the writerly virtues of style, characterization, and lucid storytelling, as much as I do to what makes a work science fiction—its scientific facts, speculative ideas, and philosophical considerations. Nothing wrong with that; I wouldn't think much of any 'hard SF' writer who would deliberately leave all that out. James Blish, a favorite writer of mine, once said that SF should be hard (thoroughgoing) all the way through—in its ideas and literary virtues, which seems to me to be beyond argument as a prescription. It's the ideal I started with as a writer.

"The knowledge of what one does as an SF writer can be clearly stated, but not easily practiced. One writes fiction which deals with the human impact of possible future changes in science and technology. Even if you remove 'science and technology' you still have 'the human impact of future changes.' You might remove 'future' since many SF works are set in the present or past; but you can still substitute 'imaginary but plausible' here and not violate the spirit of SF. The 'human impact' makes it literature; the 'plausible imaginary changes' make it SF. How well the 'literary' and 'science fictional' conceits come out depends on the ambition and skill of the writer."

Many of Zebrowski's works have been translated into French, Dutch, Portuguese, Japanese, Italian, Spanish, Swedish, and German. His manuscripts, papers, and first editions are being collected by Temple University.

MEDIA ADAPTATIONS: The short story "The Heathen God" was produced as a play by Readers Theater, University of Nebraska, Lincoln, in April, 1983.

AVOCATIONAL INTERESTS: Future studies, chess, classical music, films, tennis, swimming, philosophy of science, and film.

BIOGRAPHICAL/CRITICAL SOURCES:

BOOKS

Dictionary of Literary Biography, Volume 8: *Twentieth-Century American Science Fiction Writers,* Gale, 1981.
Elliot, Jeffrey M., editor, *George Zebrowski: Perfecting Visions, Slaying Cynics,* Borgo Press, in press.
Elliot, Jeffrey M. and R. Reginald, *The Work of George Zebrowski: An Annotated Bibliography and Guide,* Borgo Press, 1986, 2nd edition, 1990.
Gunn, James, editor, *The New Encyclopedia of Science Fiction,* Viking, 1988.
Twentieth Century Science Fiction Writers, St. James Press, 1981, 2nd edition, 1986.

*   *   *

ZIOMEK, Henryk 1922-

PERSONAL: Surname is pronounced *Zyoh*-mek; born January 8, 1922, in Druzbin, Poland; son of Walenty (a manufacturer) and Jozefa (Fijalkowski) Ziomek; married Patricia Ann De Moor (a piano teacher and organist), August 16, 1956; children:

Stanley, John Josef, Paul Henry. *Education:* Attended University of Warsaw, 1939-41; Indiana State University, B.A., 1955; Indiana University, M.A., 1956; University of Minnesota, Ph.D., 1960.

ADDRESSES: Home—370 Rivermont Rd., Athens, Ga. 30606. *Office*—Department of Romance Languages, University of Georgia, Athens, Ga. 30601.

CAREER: Wisconsin State University—Oshkosh (now University of Wisconsin—Oshkosh), 1956-60, began as instructor, became assistant professor of Latin, Spanish, and French; Butler University, Indianapolis, Ind., assistant professor of Spanish and French, 1960-62; Colorado State University, Fort Collins, associate professor of Spanish and French, 1962-64; Ohio University, Athens, professor of Spanish and French, 1964-66; University of Georgia, Athens, professor of Spanish and literature of the Spanish Golden Age, 1966—. Visiting professor of Spanish, University of Warsaw, 1978. Has worked as a commercial artist and as an anthropologist. *Military service:* Polish Underground Army, 1942-44; became second lieutenant. U.S. Army, 1945; served in France.

MEMBER: Asociacion Internacional de Hispanistas, Modern Language Association of America, American Association of Teachers of Spanish and Portuguese, Latin American Studies Association, Polish Institute of Arts and Sciences in America, Comediantes, South Atlantic Modern Language Association, Sigma Delta Pi.

WRITINGS:

Reflexiones del Quijote, Editorial M. Molina, 1971.
(Annotator) Vern G. Williamson, editor, *An Annotated, Analytical Bibliography of Tirso de Molina Studies,* University of Missouri Press, 1979.
Lo grotesco en la literatura espanola del Siglo de Oro, Editorial Alcala, 1983.
A History of Spanish Golden Age Drama, University Press of Kentucky, 1984.
Compendia de la literatura espanola, Panstwowe Wydawnictwo Naukowe (Warsaw), 1986.

EDITOR

(And author of introduction) Lope de Vega, *La nueua victoria de D. Gonzalo de Cordoua* (play), Hispanic Institute, Columbia University, 1962.
Papers of French-Spanish-Spanish American-Luso-Brazilian Relations, University of Georgia Press, 1966.
(And author of introduction) de Vega, *El poder en el discreto* (play; critical edition), Editorial M. Molina, 1971.
(And author of introduction) de Vega, *La batalla del honor* (play), University of Georgia Press, 1972.
Papers on Romance Literature Relations, University of Georgia Press, 1972.
(And author of notes and introduction) de Vega, *La prueba de los amigos,* University of Georgia Press, 1973.
(With Robert W. Linker) Luis Velez de Guevara, *La creacion del mundo* (play; critical edition), University of Georgia Press, 1974.
Velez de Guevara, *El principe vinador* [and] *El amor en vizcaino* (plays), Editorial Ebro, 1975.
Velez de Guevara, *Mas pesa el rey que la sangre, y blason de los Guzmanes* (play), Editorial Ebro, 1976.

WORK IN PROGRESS: Editing, with Ann N. Hughes, a critical edition of Luis Velez de Guevara's *Cerco de Roma por el rey desiderio.*

ZUBIN, Joseph 1900-

PERSONAL: Born October 9, 1900, in Raseiniai, Lithuania; came to United States, 1909; naturalized U.S. citizen, 1929; son of Jacob M. and Hannah (Brody) Zubin; married Winifred Anderson, October 12, 1934; children: Jonathan Arthur, David Anderson, Winifred Anne. *Education:* Attended Baltimore City College, 1917; Johns Hopkins University, A.B., 1921; Columbia University, Ph.D., 1932.

ADDRESSES: Home—190 Highwood Ave., Leonia, N.J. 07605. *Office*—Columbia University, Center for Geriatrics and Gerontology, Tower 3, 29th Floor, 100 Haven Ave., New York, N.Y. 10032; and Veterans Administration Medical Center, 151R Highland Dr., Pittsburgh, Pa. 15206.

CAREER: Columbia University, College of Physicians and Surgeons, New York City, instructor in psychometrics, 1932-34; City College (now of the City University of New York), New York City, instructor in educational psychology, 1934-36; Columbia University, instructor, 1939-47, assistant professor, 1947-50, adjunct professor, 1950-56, professor of psychology, 1956-69, professor emeritus and special lecturer in psychiatry, 1969—; University of Pittsburgh, School of Medicine, Pittsburgh, Pa., Distinguished Research Professor of Psychiatry, 1977—. Diplomate from American Board of Examiners in Psychology, 1950, and New York Professional Licensure in Clinical Psychology; assistant psychologist on mental survey committee, National Committee for Mental Hygiene, 1936-38; New York State Psychiatric Institute and Hospital, New York City, associate research psychologist, 1938-56; New York State Department of Mental Hygiene, New York City, principal research scientist in biometrics, 1956-60, chief of psychiatric research in biometrics, 1956-76, attending biometrician, 1976—; Veterans Administration Medical Center, Pittsburgh, research psychologist, 1976-78, research career scientist and coordinator for research and development, 1978—. Adjunct professor and Gregory Razran Professor of Psychology, Queens College of the City University of New York, 1970; professorial lecturer in research, New York School of Psychiatry, 1971-75; visiting professor at numerous U.S. universities. Consultant to U.S. Veterans Administration, 1956-59, and to National Institute of Mental Health. *Military service:* U.S. Public Health Service, sanitarian with rank of lieutenant commander, War Shipping Administration, 1944-45.

MEMBER: American Psychological Association (fellow), American Psychopathological Association (president, 1951-52), American College of Neuropsychopharmacology (president, 1971-72), American Association on Mental Deficiency (fellow), American Psychiatric Association (honorary fellow), American Genetic Society, Association for Research in Nervous and Mental Disease, American Public Health Association (life member), Psychometric Society, Psychonomic Society, American Statistical Association (fellow), Institute of Mathematical Statistics, American Society of Professional Graphologists (honorary member), Eastern Psychological Association, New York Academy of Medicine (life member), New York Academy of Sciences (honorary life member), Harvey Society, Sigma Xi.

AWARDS, HONORS: Paul H. Hoch Award, American Psychopathological Association, 1968, 1984; M.D., University of Lund, 1972; Stanley R. Dean Award, American College of Psychiatrists, 1974; Sc.D., University of Rochester, 1976; New York Academy of Sciences Award in the Behavioral Sciences, 1981; Society for Research in Psychopathology Award, 1986, for "a lifetime of distinguished contributions"; also recipient of numerous merit and service awards from local, state, and national organizations; recipient of numerous grants.

WRITINGS:

Some Effects of Incentives: A Study of Individual Differences in Rivalry, Teachers College, Columbia University, 1932, reprinted, AMS Press, 1972.

Choosing a Life Work, Union of American Hebrew Congregations, 1937.

(With Grace C. Scholz) *Regional Differences in the Hospitalization and Care of Patients with Mental Diseases,* U.S. Public Health Service, 1940.

(With W. J. Thompson) *Sorting Tests in Relation to Drug Therapy in Schizophrenia,* New York State Psychiatric Institute, 1941.

(With T. S. Lewinson) *Handwriting Analysis: A Series of Scales for Evaluating the Dynamic Aspects of Handwriting,* King's Crown Press, 1942.

Quantitative Techniques and Methods in Abnormal Psychology, Columbia University Bookstore, 1950.

(With others) *Recent Advances in Diagnostic Psychological Testing,* C. C Thomas, 1950.

(With Leonard D. Eron and Florence Shumer) *An Experimental Approach to Projective Techniques,* Wiley, 1965.

(Author of foreword) J. E. Cooper, R. E. Kendall, and others, *Psychiatric Diagnosis in New York and London: A Comparative Study of Mental Hospital Admissions,* Oxford University Press, 1972.

(Author of introduction) S. Fisher and Alfred M. Freedman, editors, *Opiate Addiction: Origins and Treatment,* Halsted, 1973.

(Author of foreword) R. Canro, N. Fox, and L. Shapiro, editors, *Strategic Intervention in Schizophrenia: Current Developments in Treatment,* Behavioral Publications, 1974.

(Author of foreword) B. Gurland and others, *The Mind and Mood of Aging,* Haworth Press, 1983.

EDITOR

Trends of Mental Disease, King's Crown Press, 1945.

Experimental Abnormal Psychology, Columbia University Press, 1957.

(And contributor) *Field Studies in the Mental Disorders,* Grune, 1961.

(With George A. Jervis) *Psychopathology of Mental Development,* Grune, 1967.

(With Howard F. Hunt) *Comparative Psychopathology: Animal and Human,* Grune, 1967.

(With Fritz A. Freyhan) *Social Psychiatry,* Grune, 1968.

(With Charles Shagass, and contributor) *Neurobiological Aspects of Psychopathology,* Grune, 1969.

(With Freedman) *The Psychopathology of Adolescence,* Grune, 1970.

(With Freyhan) *Disorders of Mood,* Johns Hopkins Press, 1972.

(With John Money, and author of foreword) *Contemporary Sexual Behavior: Critical Issues in the 1970's,* Johns Hopkins Press, 1973.

(With Mitchell Kietzman and S. Sutton, and contributor) *Experimental Approaches to Psychopathology,* Academic Press, 1975.

EDITOR WITH PAUL H. HOCH

Psychosexual Development in Health and Disease, Grune, 1949.
Anxiety, Grune, 1950.
(And contributor) *Relation of Psychological Tests to Psychiatry,* Grune, 1952.

(And contributor) *Current Problems in Psychiatric Diagnosis,* Grune, 1953.

(And contributor) *Depression,* Grune, 1954.

Psychiatry and the Law, Grune, 1955.

Psychopathology of Childhood, Grune, 1955.

Experimental Psychopathology, Grune, 1957.

Psychopathology of Communication, Grune, 1958.

Problems of Addiction and Habituation, Grune, 1958.

(And contributor) *Current Approaches to Psychoanalysis,* Grune, 1960.

(And contributor) *Psychopathology of Aging,* Grune, 1961.

(And contributor) *Comparative Epidemiology in the Mental Disorders,* Grune, 1961.

(And contributor) *The Future of Psychiatry,* Grune, 1962.

(And contributor) *The Evaluation of Psychiatric Treatment,* Grune, 1964.

(And contributor) *Psychopathology of Perception,* Grune, 1965.

(And contributor) *Psychopathology of Schizophrenia,* Grune, 1966.

CONTRIBUTOR

B. Glueck, editor, *Current Therapies of Personality Disorders,* Grune, 1946.

T. G. Andrews, editor, *Methods of Psychology,* Wiley, 1948.

F. A. Mettler, editor, *Selective Partial Ablations of the Frontal Cortex,* Hoeber Medical Division, Harper, 1949.

Mettler, editor, *Psychosurgical Problems,* Blakiston Co., 1952.

Nolan Lewis and others, editors, *Studies in Topectomy,* Grune, 1956.

R. A. Patton, editor, *Current Trends in the Description and Analysis of Behavior,* University of Pittsburgh Press, 1958.

B. Pasaminick, editor, *Epidemiology of Mental Disorders,* American Association for the Advancement of Science, 1958.

J. O. Cole, and R. W. Gerard, editors, *Psychopharmacology: Problems in Evaluation,* National Academy of Sciences, National Research Council, 1959.

B. Wigdor, editor, *Recent Advances in the Study of Behavior Change,* McGill University Press, 1963.

A. Welford and J. Birren, editors, *Behavior, Aging and the Nervous System: Biological Determinants of Speed of Behavior and Its Change with Age,* C. C Thomas, 1964.

Symposium: Explorations in Typology with Special Reference to Psychotics, Human Ecology Fund, 1964.

D. Byrne and P. Worchel, editors, *Personality Change,* Wiley, 1964.

O. Klineberg and R. Christie, editors, *Perspectives in Social Psychology,* Holt, 1965.

In Research in Community Mental Health, New Jersey Department of Institutions and Agencies/New Jersey Association of Mental Hygiene, 1965.

Eron, editor, *The Classification of Behavioral Disorders,* Aldine, 1966.

M. Katz, Cole, and W. E. Barton, editors, *The Role and Methodology of Classification in Psychiatry and Psychopathology,* U.S. Department of Health, Education, and Welfare, 1968.

S. B. Sells, editor, *The Definition and Measurement of Mental Health,* U.S. Department of Health, Education, and Welfare, 1968.

L. M. Roberts, N. Greenfield, and M. Miller, editors, *Comprehensive Mental Health: The Challenge of Evaluation,* University of Wisconsin Press, 1968.

W. O. Evans and N. S. Kline, editors, *Psychotropic Drugs in the Year 2000: Use by Normal Humans,* C. C Thomas, 1971.

R. R. Fieve, editor, *Depression in the 1970's: Modern Theory and Research,* Excerpta Medica, 1971.

C. Eisdorfer and M. P. Lawton, editors, *The Psychology of Adult Development and Aging,* American Psychological Association, 1973.

A. Beck, H. Resnik, and D. Lettieri, editors, *The Prediction of Suicide,* Charles Press, 1974.

Gene Usdin, editor, *An Overview of the Psychotherapies,* Bruner/Mazel, 1975.

Freedman, H. I. Kaplan, and B.J. Sadock, editors, *Comprehensive Textbook of Psychiatry,* 2nd edition, Williams & Wilkins, 1975, 4th edition, 1984.

L. J. West and D. E. Flinn, editors, *Treatment of Schizophrenia: Progress and Prospects,* Grune, 1976.

L. L. Adler, editor, *Issues in Cross-Cultural Research,* New York Academy of Sciences, 1977.

G. Albee and J. Joffe, editors, *Primary Prevention in Psychopathology,* University Press of New England, 1977.

R. L. Spitzer and D. Klein, editors, *Critical Issues in Psychiatric Diagnosis,* Raven Press, 1978.

B. B. Wolman, editor, *Clinical Diagnosis of Mental Disorders,* Plenum Press, 1979.

J. E. Barrett, editor, *Stress and Mental Disorder,* Raven Press, 1979.

C. F. Baxter and T. Melnechuk, editors, *Perspectives in Schizophrenia Research,* Raven Press, 1980.

Usdin and I. Hanin, editors, *Biological Markers in Psychiatry and Neurology,* Pergamon, 1982.

V. Sarris and A. Parducci, editors, *Perspectives in Psychological Experimentation: Towards the Year 2000,* Lawrence Erlbaum, 1984.

M. Shepherd, editor, *Handbook of Psychiatry,* Cambridge University Press, 1985.

M. Alpert, editor, *Controversies in Schizophrenia: Changes and Constancies,* Guilford, 1985.

Shagass and R. Josiassen, editors, *Brain Electrical Potentials and Psychopathology,* Elsevier, 1985.

J. S. Strauss, W. Boeker, and H. D. Brenner, editors, *Psychosocial Treatment of Schizophrenia,* Hogrefe, 1987.

D. Magnusson and A. Ohman, editors, *Psychopathology: An Interactional Perspective,* Academic Press, 1987.

M. T. Tsuang, editor, *Handbook of Schizophrenia,* Volume 3, Elsevier, 1987.

Alcohol and Addictive Behavior, University of Nebraska Press, 1987.

S. Wetzler, *Measuring Mental Illness: Psychometric Assessment for Clinicians,* American Psychiatric Press, 1989.

Also contributor to numerous conference proceedings, and to the *Encyclopaedia Britannica.*

OTHER

Author of U.S. Public Health Service and other reports. Contributor to *Annual Review of Psychology,* 1975. Associate editor, *Journal of Applied Psychology,* 1942-48, *Journal of Experimental Psychology,* 1947-50, *Journal of Personality,* 1948-56, *Psychological Monographs,* 1951-58, *Comprehensive Psychiatry,* 1963—, *Journal of General Psychology,* 1964-85, *Journal of Psychology,* 1964-85, *Journal of Abnormal Psychology,* 1964-85, *Biological Psychiatry,* 1970—, *Behavioral and Brain Sciences,* 1981—, *Integrative Psychiatry,* 1984—, and *Journal of Psychopathology and Behavioral Assessment,* 1985—.

*   *   *

ZUCKER, Martin 1937-

PERSONAL: Born December 12, 1937, in New York, N.Y.; son of Harry and Rose (a sign language teacher; maiden name, Weidman) Zucker; married Rosita Gottlieb (an artist), August 6, 1978. *Education:* Occidental College, B.A., 1959. *Religion:* Jewish.

ADDRESSES: Home—12434 Aneta St., Los Angeles, Calif. 90066. *Agent*—Muriel Nellis, 3539 Albemarle St. N.W., Washington, D.C. 20008.

CAREER: Correspondent in Europe and the Middle East for Associated Press (AP), 1965-72; free-lance journalist and founder of Mideast Media, 1972-75; free-lance writer, 1975—. *Military service:* U.S. Army, 1959-61.

WRITINGS:

How to Have a Healthier Dog, Doubleday, 1981.
The Very Healthy Cat Book, McGraw, 1983.
Pet Allergies: Remedies for an Epidemic, Very Healthy Enterprises, 1987.
(Ghostwriter) *Lindsay Wagner's New Beauty,* Prentice-Hall, 1987.

Contributing editor, *Let's Live* and *Men's Fitness.*

SIDELIGHTS: Martin Zucker told *CA:* "The greatest fulfillment I gain from my work is the satisfaction of having written something that hopefully may touch and improve the life of a fellow being."

*   *   *

ZWINGER, Ann (H.) 1925-

PERSONAL: Born March 12, 1925, in Muncie, Ind.; daughter of William Thomas (an attorney) and Helen (Glass) Haymond; married Herman H. Zwinger (retired from U.S. Air Force), June 18, 1952; children: Susan, Jane, Sara. *Education:* Wellesley College, B.A., 1946; Indiana University, M.A., 1950, additional graduate study at Radcliffe College, 1951-52; attended Colorado College, 1963-64, 1978-80.

ADDRESSES: Home—1825 Culebra Place, Colorado Springs, Colo. 80907. *Agent*—Marie Redell-Frances Collin Literary Agency, 110 West 40th St., New York, N.Y. 10018.

CAREER: Smith College, Northampton, Mass., instructor in art history, 1950-51; University of Kansas City, teacher of adult education courses, 1958-60; Benet Hill Academy, Colorado Springs, Colo., instructor in art, 1963-66. Visiting lecturer, Colorado College, 1973-81, 1982—, University of Arizona, 1987. Naturalist-in-residence, Carleton College, 1985. Art work has been exhibited at Carnegie-Mellon University, Pittsburgh, Penn., 1971, Nix Gallery, Colorado Springs, 1978, Tracy Felix ArtSpace, Colorado Springs, 1986, and Fine Arts Center, Colorado Springs. Utility Women's Conference, chairman and member of board of directors, 1984-86, program chairman, 1986-87; director and committee member, American Electric Power Company. Member of board of directors, Friends of the Library, Penrose Public Library, Colorado Springs. Trustee, Colorado Springs School, 1970-74, Palmer Foundation, 1984-90.

MEMBER: John Burroughs Association (director, 1984-87), Authors Guild, Authors League of America, Thoreau Society (president, 1982-84; member of executive board, 1982—), Xerces Society, Guild of Natural Science Illustrators, Nature Conservancy (trustee, Colorado chapter, 1986-89), Thorne Ecological Foundation (director, 1979-81), Colorado Authors' League, Wellesley Club (Colorado Springs; president, 1966-70), Girl Scouts (leader, trainer, trainer of leaders, publications editor, member of various boards of directors).

AWARDS, HONORS: Indiana Authors' Day Award in Nature and Ecology, 1971, for *Beyond the Aspen Grove;* National Book Award nomination, 1972, for *Land above the Trees: A Guide to American Alpine Tundra;* John Burroughs Memorial Association Award and Friends of American Writers Award for nonfiction, both 1976, both for *Run, River, Run: A Naturalist's Journey Down One of the Great Rivers of the West;* D.H.L., Colorado College, 1976, and Carleton College, 1984; Alumnae Achievement Award, Wellesley College, 1977; Sara Chapman Francis Medal, Garden Club of America, 1977; Adult Nonfiction Award, Colorado Author's League, 1984, for *A Desert Country near the Sea;* Adult Article award, Colorado Authors League, 1986, for "The Art of Wandering."

WRITINGS:

(And illustrator) *Beyond the Aspen Grove,* Random House, 1970, University of Arizona Press, 1988.
(With Beatrice E. Willard) *Land above the Trees: A Guide to American Alpine Tundra,* photographs by husband, Herman H. Zwinger, Harper, 1972.
(And illustrator) *Run, River, Run: A Naturalist's Journey Down One of the Great Rivers of the West,* Harper, 1975.
Wind in the Rock: The Canyonlands of Southeastern Utah, Harper, 1978.
(Illustrator) Edward Ricciutii, *Plants in Danger,* Harper, 1979.
(Illustrator) John Burroughs, *Signs and Seasons,* Harper, 1981.
(With Edwin Way Teale) *A Conscious Stillness: Two Naturalists on Thoreau's Rivers,* Harper, 1982.
A Desert Country near the Sea, Harper, 1983.
(Editor) *John Xantus: The Fort Tejon Letters, 1857-1859,* University of Arizona Press, 1986.
Xantus: The Letters of John Xantus to Spencer Fullerton Baird from San Francisco and Cabo San Lucas, 1859-1861, Dawson's Book Shop, 1986.
(Author of foreword) Janice Emily Bowers, *Seasons of the Wind,* Northland Press, 1986.
(Author of foreword) Joseph Wood Krutch, *The Forgotten Peninsula,* University of Arizona Press, 1986.
(Author of foreword) Cynthia Bennett, *Lightfall and Time,* Grand Canyon Natural History Association/Northland Press, 1986.
Colorado II, Graphic Arts Center, 1987.
(Author of foreword) Cathy Johnson, *The Local Wilderness,* Prentice-Hall, 1987.
(Illustrator) Richard Gayton, *Artists Outdoors,* Prentice-Hall, 1988.
The Mysterious Lands: The Four Deserts of the United States, Dutton, 1989.

Contributor to anthologies, including *Of Discovery and Destiny: An Anthology of American Writers and the American Land,* Fulcrum, 1986, *Old Southwest, New Southwest: Essays on a Region and Its Literature,* Tucson Public Library/University of Arizona Press, and *On Nature,* Northpoint Press, both 1987, *Words from the Land,* Gibbs M. Smith, and *Strategies: A Rhetoric and Reader,* Scott, Foresman, both 1988, and *City Places, Open Spaces,* University of Arizona Press, 1989. Also contributor of illustrations to *River Reflections: A Collection of Writings,* East Woods Press. Contributor to *Audubon, Reader's Digest, Orion, Antaeus,* and *Smithsonian.*

WORK IN PROGRESS: A natural history of the Grand Canyon, for University of Arizona Press.

SIDELIGHTS: Ann Zwinger told *CA:* "I began 1989 and a book at the same time with a river trip down the Grand Canyon to count bald eagles in January. The book will concentrate on the natural history of the post-Glen Canyon Dam river. For the next three to four years it will test my endurance, my ability to do research whether dry or wet, my sense of humor, my ability to get off and on a raft without falling in the river, and how many scorpions I can roll up in my air mattress without getting stung. I can hardly wait."